Literature and Society

BY ALBERT GUÉRARD

LITERATURE
AND
SOCIETY

by

Albert Guérard 1880-

*Professor of General and
Comparative Literature
Stanford University*

BOSTON
Lothrop, Lee and Shepard Company
1935

35-272 93

PN
45
G8

To *Emile Legouis*
and *Fernand Baldensperger*
Who Pointed the Way

FOREWORD

This book attempts to state a problem and to define a method. The problem is: to what extent is Literature conditioned by Society? The method is resolutely pragmatic and comparative.

The work may be used as an introduction; it may be considered as a challenge; it is decidedly not a cyclopædia. The author's aim has been to trace the relation between literary facts and other facts of a non-literary nature. It has not been to supply exhaustive information, still less to offer a final solution. The facts themselves are presented only as illustrations; the bibliographical notes are confessedly the merest signposts. Every student of literature must do his own thinking in terms of his own experience.

That experience, even in the case of the average reader, is by no means limited to books of straight Anglo-Saxon origin. Indeed such books would be hard to find: those writers who are almost chemically pure Americans have probably been exposed to such non-American influences as the Bible. The author happens to be, not merely a teacher of General and Comparative Literature, but a believer in it. He borrows his instances from the common fund of our Western civilization, not from a single national hoard. He does so, not because cosmopolitan references sound more erudite, but because they are more accessible. It is safer, in an argument, to adduce Homer, Dante, Goethe or Tolstoy than Charles Brockden Brown or even E. P. Whipple. On the other hand, Walt Whitman and Hermann Melville will serve much better than Palfurius Sura or Julius Tryfonianus. Greatness ignores the accident of political boundaries.

The problems treated in this book do not depend upon the greatness of the writers under discussion. Mediocrity, as a rule, is more "typical" of a civilization than is genius. Quite apart from the question of artistic merit, foreign examples are frequently more telling than their domestic equivalents. We examine them with a mind freer from preconceived ideas. The remoteness, the strangeness of the environment blot out minor issues, and help us focus the main problem more sharply. The purpose of this book remains *the study of literature by Americans and for Americans:* but restricting ourselves to American authors would not be the best way of serving that purpose. "Seeing others," which is comparatively easy, may lead us to that most difficult achievement, "seeing ourselves." There are motes in European eyes, plainly visible across the Atlantic. This is the very essence of the comparative method: some aspects of our own selves — perhaps the most American of all — are best revealed through a German or Italian mirror.

This book, therefore, quotes freely from the most obvious European sources. The author wishes he might have included Asiatic literature as well. But he is no Irving Babbitt: Sanskrit and Chinese are hermetically sealed to him. It happens that a large number of these instances are borrowed from the French. Only a slight effort would have been needed to alter the proportion: Italian, Spanish and German authorities are easily available. The author has preferred to face the accusation of partiality, and preserve the spontaneity and individuality of his work. The terms he uses are those of his own experience, which is mainly Anglo-Franco-American: criticism inevitably contains elements of autobiography.

But he could defend his course on more objective grounds. No supremacy is claimed for French literature: the choice of French examples was not dictated by blind admiration. But it is a fact that the cultural life of England and that of France have been inseparably mingled for eight hundred years. *The Romance of the Rose*, Montaigne's *Essays*, Voltaire's *Candide*, Flaubert's *Madame Bovary*, *Les Misérables*, are in no sense foreign masterpieces. They are less foreign than the home-grown best-seller of yesteryear.

Then it has ever been the ideal of French civilization to *elucidate*. The origins of great movements may be traced to many countries: the neatest formula is usually written down in Paris. Protestantism is by no means France's gift to the world: but it needed a Calvin. The Enlightenment arose in England: but it had to be disseminated through Montesquieu and Voltaire. England muddles through, gloriously, and her achievements are beyond compare, for they can be reduced to no system and to no common measure. It is France's part to evolve the clear-cut Doctrine, the organized School, the definite Institution, through which unconscious trends are at last made manifest.

Although this book is chiefly concerned with the present

ix

and the future of our own literature, all concrete examples had naturally to be sought in the past: who, in the instantaneous present, could tell a lasting trend from a mere eddy? Now our own national past is brief; our literary world has never been fully organized; neither, for that matter, has our "Society." Cincinnati offers no equivalent for the Hôtel de Rambouillet; Chicago has no Academy quite so venerable as the Académie Française; the White House has never filled, in the literary scene, exactly the same place as Versailles under Louis XIV. Our pragmatism compelled us to acknowledge these facts. Our study of the European past implies no superstitious reverence; and, in our last pages, we face the American future without a trace of dismay.

ALBERT GUÉRARD

CONTENTS

CONTENTS

Part III   The Public

Part IV   To-morrow

Part I

The Background of Literature
Race, Environment and Time

Chapter 1

THE PROBLEM

I

ART is the expression of a unique personality; yet there is no literature, not even the wildest Prophetic Books of Blake, that is not, in some measure, the joint production of author and public. He who "voyages through strange seas of thought alone" is not acclaimed as a poet until he returns. How could the critic of literature take cognizance of "the mute inglorious Milton"? As Martial said nineteen centuries ago, "He does not write at all, whose poems are read by none." Shakespeare exists for us because he is acknowledged. Literature may be the reflection of Eternal Beauty: empirically, it is, first of all, the reflection of Public Taste. For the Pragmatist, the corpus, the canon, of literature is determined solely by the fact of recognition. To say: "This man is great" means: "He is accepted by the right people." And who are "the right people"? This is the question that the present book will attempt to answer, concisely, in about a hundred thousand words.

On this pragmatic basis, literature is a social product. It implies language, a means of communication: the One can express himself only in terms accessible to the Many.

3

Language itself is a set of symbols which embody, beyond their plain, literal meaning, all the customs, feelings, beliefs of the group. *King*, for instance, had a different connotation for the seventeenth century absolutist, for the eighteenth century liberal, for the nineteenth century democrat. The throng of images that the word may evoke to-day ranges from the Vicar of God on earth to a comic-opera puppet. A language is not an algebraic code: with the best dictionaries at your command, you literally can not understand an author if you are wholly out of touch with his civilization.

This conception is hoary with age. Implicit in Herder's *Ideen* *, it was already clear in Madame de Staël's work, *On Literature considered in its Relations with Social Institutions,* which appeared in 1800. Its application was codified by Taine, in his *Introduction to the History of English Literature,* with the magic formula *Race, Environment and Time.* Taine himself may be antiquated: his method is still with us. It does not tell the whole truth, nor perhaps the essential truth: but the truth that it tells is far from negligible.

Race, it seems, can not be exorcised from the literary field. Even to-day, reputable critics will speak of "Latins", "Celts" or "Slavs", as if the words had some bearing on the interpretation of masterpieces. Mrs. Gertrude Atherton tells us that human nature is largely a matter of the cephalic index; that *The Scarlet Letter* is incompatible with brachycephaly; and that our dismal naturalism is due to the resurgence of the plebeian Alpine. If a critic

* Herder, J. G.: *Ideen zur Philosophie der Geschichte der Menschheit,* 1784–1791.

4

has never indulged in such racial fantasies, let him cast the first stone.

The concept of *Race* is somewhat enfeebled at present —the nemesis of its own excess; that of *Environment* is as lusty as ever. Environment means more than the physical climate, the geographical habitat: it includes political, social, economic conditions. When Irving Babbitt ascribes to a false conception of democracy the low state of our culture, he is using the method of Taine, just as much as the Critics of the Extreme Left, when they interpret literary history in the light of Karl Marx's Communism.

It might be interesting, therefore, to re-state Taine's famous principles in terms of modern experience; and, as we re-state them, to submit them to the most searching criticism. We have no desire to "explode" Race, Environment and Time: we only want to understand. We all feel that there is "something" to them: but what is that something, and how much of it is there? We have no faith whatever in the holiness of the vague; and we entertain but scant respect for prejudice camouflaging as pseudo-science.

Race, Environment and Time are, roughly speaking, common to author and reader, and affect them very much in the same fashion. They account for folklore, "floating literature", or, in the parlance of to-day, *folkways* and *folksay*. They explain Jack Brown and his favorite pulp magazines even more definitely than they explain Branch Cabell. But literature in the stricter sense, literature as conscious craft, implies a dissociation: the few who are vocal, the many who listen. Authors are, in

5

some very important respects, different from the mass. The laws of civilization, if there be such, do not apply to them with exactly the same incidence. We shall have to consider a series of problems about the Man of Letters as such, the natural gifts which constitute his vocation, the deformations, the aberrations which are his professional risks. Coal miners are exposed to melanosis, white-lead workers to necrosis, writers to various forms of graphitis. A psychological and social study of *Homo Scriptor* may yield curious results.

The dissociation, however, is never complete. The author remains linked with his public—else the Ivory Tower would be his tomb. Every book is a dialogue in which the silent interlocutor, the Reader, can not be ignored. Literature is written for a public, large or small, even when it is written for the express purpose of exasperating that public. It is a reflection, however distorted, of the public mind; and the works that survive for posterity give a fairly accurate definition of the best public taste. But that common word *public* is as elusive as it is convenient. Is there such a thing as a clear, spontaneous *vox populi?* Is not "the public mind" a myth? In literature as in politics, the "public mind" is made up by conscious, vocal, energetic minorities. The masses are offered merely a choice between the rival groups which assume leadership and claim authority.

If we could determine what these centers of influence are, many problems of literature would be elucidated. But we should bear in mind that the "Phantom Public" is evolving: the solutions of yesterday fail to meet present conditions. In the classical age, whose shadow lingers in

Europe, and even, very faint but unmistakable, in the United States, these active minorities were essentially emanations of *Society* in the narrower sense: the Court as the supreme drawing-room, the Salon as a miniature private Court, the Tavern or the Café as an impromptu Bohemian salon, the Academies as the most exclusive of Clubs, the Universities as those places where "gentlemen" were trained. Literature ranked with horsemanship, dancing and table manners among the possessions and distinctive marks of a social élite. This "genteel tradition", as Santayana called it, is no longer "at bay": it is gone. The Neo-Humanists are mourning over a tomb. The disruption of the ancient social hierarchy has destroyed the old scale of literary values. We shall restore "standards" if we restore to their primacy the Monarchy, the Church, the Aristocracy. In spite of such prophets as Charles Maurras and T. S. Eliot, the chances for such a restoration are dim.

In our pluto-democracy, literature may be roughly defined in terms of the book industry. Manuscripts that can not possibly sell are not printed; if printed, they are stillborn. But this affords no key to our problem: the book industry does not know the rules of its own game, and publishers are the first to realize that their trade is a gamble. They do not know enough about our civilization to "give the public what they want." In their own interest, they are eager to know more about the laws of public taste. They would like to possess the infallible recipe for a best-seller; and they dream, not only of the short-lived best-seller, but of the perennial good-seller, i.e. the *classic*. How can classics be told? Forecasting is the test of science as well as the key to successful production. In literature, forecasting is Criticism. The critic should be able to tell: "Such a book will appeal to such a class of readers, in such numbers." He should be: but he is not, to the despair of authors, publishers and public alike. The chaos of our competitive economics is reflected in the chaos of our literary mart.

How can literature transcend such a chaos—the road back to yesterday being irremediably closed? How can it supply the needs of the general public, without the waste, surfeit and spiritual starvation which we are experiencing to-day? *Society* lies in ruins: will our community become a genuine society again, conscious of its organic unity? And can it achieve such a consciousness without becoming a Leviathan, and crushing out of existence all cultural minorities? What chances of life are there under the present dispensation, what chances will there be to-morrow, for the unpopular book, adventurous, subtle, cryptic, or simply unobtrusive and gentle? Now that the élite no longer have a common center and a consolidated prestige, how can the scattered lovers of things rare and delicate be integrated into *a* public without merging altogether with *the* Public?

Literature as one of the elements of a civilization, conditioned if not determined by social life as a whole, reacting upon social life in its turn: such is the problem which we propose to discuss in this book. We do not claim that this is the sole possible approach to literature. As a matter of fact, much of our effort will consist in marking the limits of the sociological method: this work, not committed to materialistic determinism, will never be used as a text book in the schools of Soviet Russia. All aspects of civilization, while they are part of an organic whole, do enjoy a measure of autonomy; and in no case is this autonomy larger than in the case of literature. This other side of the question—the refusal of the artist to bow down, to conform, to serve; the defiant assertion of the Unique against the laws of the herd,—we hope to study in a companion volume on *The Doctrine of Art for Art's Sake.*

II

"What was the largest island in the world before Australia was discovered?"—Why, Australia, of course. Translate this conundrum into literary terms: "Who was the greatest American poet before Jefferson Aloysius Kegelbahn was discovered?" Was it Jefferson Aloysius Kegelbahn?

We are reluctant to admit that, in art any more than in geography, discovery amounts to creation. Discovery is a fortunate incident. The thing is there, even if no human eyes have seen it: remote continent, forgotten civilization, mysterious chemical element, star beyond our ken, *unknown masterpiece.* If Shakespeare's *Hamlet* existed only in a single manuscript, never communicated to living man, buried in some vault at Stratford, would it be any the less *Hamlet?* The question is plain: the answer, be it yes or no, will sound paradoxical or even absurd.

Tradition commits us to the view that there is something intrinsic, essential, eternal, about the masterpiece. Its quality partakes of the supreme *I am that I am.* The

9

masterpiece is such because it reflects some element of absolute truth and beauty. This principle underlies all teaching and all discussion of literature. We take it for granted that there are *standards,* even though we might be embarrassed to define them. By these standards, individual and collective taste should be ruled. You must *learn* to enjoy the Beautiful, just as you must bow to the True and follow the Good. If you do not like what you should like, it argues your own perversity of taste, your unsoundness of mind, your moral depravity. If there be such a thing as essential *Rightness* in literature, it can be taught, and our duty is to submit.

Do not believe that such an attitude is a professor's trick. The average professor is far more sceptical than the most sophisticated sophomore. Pedantry is bred, not by those who crave to teach, but by those who crave to be caught. "Tell us what is *real literature":* and unless you are ready with an orthodoxy, that of Aristotle or the latest Greenwich Village brand, you are despised as spineless or flippant.

This conception may be called *idealistic,* both in the common acceptation of the term and in the more specifically Platonic. Idealism always implies a certain loftiness—the uplifted gaze, the waving *Excelsior!* banner. And it means, more strictly, a belief in a world of permanent values, a world of which our common life is but the broken and distorted shadow. It is a term much abused by its foes, and even more by its friends: we should be glad to find a less ambiguous one. But *absolutism* also has equivocal connotations, and so have *fundamentalism* and *dogmatism*. Whatever the name, we hope the principle is clear.

The notion of permanent values is eminently classical: but it is by no means identical with classicism. In all schools, at all times, the idea of absolute Beauty has been maintained. Certainly the most ardent Romanticists, such as Blake and Shelley, held it more firmly than Pope himself. Romanticism rebelled against conventions, not against verities. It believed that imagination and passion were direct avenues to living truth, while common sense was but the rationalization of prejudice. Before Abraham was, Beauty *is*. The vision of it is *true*. The failure of the average man to see it only proves his infirmity. The Romanticist is a mystic: the individual reaches directly beyond the realm of tame consent. But what he reaches is no less absolute, no less universal, than the dogmas of Classicism.

And the Realist also believes in a world anterior and superior to the individual mind. He also preaches that, when the objective truth is attained, our duty is to submit, or we stand condemned. His method of approach is that of science: observation, experimentation. It differs from the abstract reason of the Classicist, from the passionate imagination of the Romanticist, but his goal is the same: a world of eternal values. Flaubert and Zola are dogmatists: in the name of their orthodoxy, they curse and excommunicate without hesitation.

Dogmatism is almost irresistibly attractive. Away from it, there can be no solid spiritual comfort. We need to be constantly assured that we are right; we are eager to follow the guide who promises the words of eternal life.

Scepticism may bring release and relief for a while: but it offers no resting place. There were positive creeds behind the smile of Montaigne and the grin of Voltaire.

So we should all love to throw ourselves at the feet of the Pontiffs. Unfortunately, there have been, there are still, far too many Pontiffs. We can not worship all the gods: a Pantheon is the temple of the atheist. We must either mutilate our souls in the service of our orthodoxy or recognize that there are many *doxies* with very substantial claims. The Pontiffs keep excommunicating, most impressively, in the name of standards: but the standards remain conveniently vague. And when a standard is so unguarded as to clash with a masterpiece, the standard comes out badly crumpled: Rymer did little damage to Shakespeare. The only safe standard is Catholicity of Taste, the denial of all orthodoxies. The only safe altar in literature is that to the Unknown God.

Thus we are, with deep reluctance and constant hankerings, driven from the dogmatic position. At the other pole of thought, we find *Radical Individualism* ready to welcome us. After striving to conform, to admire the Highest, to enjoy the Best, reproving ourselves for every irrepressible nod or yawn, always fearful lest we be missing just the right thing, and the right shade of the right meaning,—what a pleasure it is to relax, and be frankly, openly, cynically *ourselves!* In homely parlance: "I know what I like when I like it." I am I: why should I be ashamed? I can not add a cubit to my stature, nor think the thoughts of Gertrude Stein. Is this giving up the good fight? No: there is virtue in our apparent capitulation. No literary appreciation can be valid unless it be genuine. We may nod our heads wisely before a "master-piece", and be fooled, like the courtiers in Andersen's Fairy Tale, who went into ecstasies over the King's invisible cloak. If we happen to like *The Shepherd of the Hills* and not *The Faerie Queene,* we should stand heroically, like Luther: "So help me God, I can not otherwise!" Taste is the artistic conscience, and conscience will brook no dictation.

It is difficult to escape from Individualism. It attracts us because it is candid, not because it is easy. Try it for yourself for twenty-four hours: it is the most difficult thing in the world. You will constantly catch yourself using stock judgments, conventional phrases, shibboleths. Do I really like Shakespeare? How can I tell? My conscious mind is a mass of preconceived ideas. I heard his name uttered with bated breath before I could read him; I was taught to admire before I could understand. Is it possible to enjoy any high literature without a corresponding education? Even a virgin mind would have to know Shakespeare's language, and could not understand his English without some familiarity with the civilization he represents. I am blissfully free from bias concerning the Chinese drama: but, as a consequence, an untranslated Chinese play means nothing to me; a translated one, not much more. And what is an education,—culture in Matthew Arnold's sense, the knowledge of the best that has been thought and said—but the transmission of the "right" prejudices?

So we are led to doubt whether *radical individualism* is even a possibility. Every man must follow his own taste in art, his own conscience in moral life. But taste and conscience are never purely his own. They are fashioned by environment, of which education is a part. One man's conscience will tell him that it is wicked to eat steak on Friday. "Superstition!" exclaims his neighbor, whose conscience will tell him it is wrong to doubt the story of Jonah. Taste and conscience are historical and social products.

This is particularly true of literature. With a generous imagination, you may conceive that every human being, under the same circumstances, will be prompted aright by his conscience; you might even admit that every one will respond to the same perfect piece of statuary. But in literature we encounter the boundaries of language, and within these, the further limitation of *availability*. I may have an inborn taste for our mythical Kegelbahn: but, if I never come across his works or even his name, my potential admiration will remain decidedly abstract and tenuous. My taste can exercise itself only within the range of my experience. The books that are not published, not advertised, not recommended by critics, not talked about, not offered in bookstalls, not found on library shelves, do not exist for me. A universal conspiracy forces Shakespeare upon me and withholds Kegelbahn. But for that, I am—partly—free.

Absolute Individualism can not therefore be severed from the social element. What *you* like is an individual choice within a social choice. What is liked by one isolated man, and by that man only, does not take its place in literature. Every poet is great in his own conceit; and at the time of writing at any rate, he feels that what he has to say had never been said before, or never so well.

Self-satisfaction is no sufficient warrant of excellence. A poem is only a candidate to literature: literary rank is conferred from without.

Poets, no doubt, will demur. Yet the history of literature is written in no other terms—including that contemporary history which is called criticism. If Chaucer, Spenser, Milton; if Ezra Pound, Hart Crane, E. E. Cummings exist at all, it is not on their own recognizances, but on the basis of public recognition. By whom? Obviously not by the mob exclusively; still less by the clique exclusively. Neither the best-seller nor the esoteric enigma can be assured of a place in literature. Recognition means the suffrage of a fairly extensive intelligent class.

How large must that class be? That depends upon the period, and the kind of writing. Tolstoy, alone among genuine artists, wanted to include the masses; Stendhal dedicated his work (a master stroke of salesmanship!) *To the Happy Few*. Poetry can do with a very small public; the novel must be of wider appeal; the curse of the talkie is that it must please the million, or fail utterly.

In all cases, the applause of a public, large or small, will not create literary standing, unless the effect be prolonged. Six months hence, the nine-day wonder will not even be a curiosity; and the *cognoscenti* are notoriously more fickle than the crowd. Literature exists *in time,* and the test of time is the most reliable of all. Trifles may endure through the centuries, like the frail flowers of the Greek *Anthology*. Massive epics may crumble, like Bailey's *Festus*. Are the Laureates of the eighteenth century *literature?* No: for they have not survived, except for a scholar like Kemper Broadus. Is Alexander Dumas *literature?* Before you say no, consider that a third and a fourth generation of readers young and old are devouring his romantic tales. Is *Abie's Irish Rose literature?* I am inclined to think, with Professor Baker, that "such popularity must be deserved": but let us wait a while before committing ourselves. Molière's extravaganza, *The Tricks of Scapin,* was frowned upon by Boileau, as unworthy: but it is alive. There is horseplay in *The Taming of the Shrew* and *The Merry Wives of Windsor;* there is a situation both hackneyed and improbable in *The Comedy of Errors;* there is rank melodrama in *Œdipus Tyrannus.* Are they *literature?* Certainly, since they live as literature.

"Time will tell": aye, but will it tell the truth? Few works last long if there is no life in them: but how many potential masterpieces are nipped by unkindly fate?

What we have been discussing is a frankly *pragmatic* conception of literature: literature as the history of reputations. It is hard to put that conception into definite words. "Literature is that which is recognized as such by a sufficient number of people over a sufficient period of time": vagueness in such a case is the beginning of wisdom. I know that such pragmatism is not idealistic: but is there any study of literature that is not based upon it? Every standard textbook includes the names of men whose theories you do not share, whose work you do not enjoy, and yet whom you can not ignore. Why? They had, or still have, a following: *they count.*

Many great ideas, which once were stated in clear-cut terms, require now more elastic definitions. What is

"Religion"? What is "the State"? Do I envy those who can answer with a brief formula, or do I pity them?

Between the pragmatic conception and the individualistic, there is no conflict. Collective opinion is the sum total of private opinions; private opinions are limited and guided by collective factors. Literature is a Club: it has a corporate existence, yet it exists only through its members and for their sakes. You join the group because you find it congenial; but you are ready to sacrifice some of your minor idiosyncrasies. Even if you do not strive to conform, you are unconsciously modeled by your chosen environment; you grow more perfect in the group psychology, which was, to start with, in harmony with your own. Within the group, you have a certain leeway. Once you are fully accepted, you would have to grow frankly obnoxious before you were kicked out. You may influence, perceptibly, the thought of your fellow members. I joined the Homer-Dante-Shakespeare Club because the members I knew, my elders, my teachers, my betters, seemed to me desirable associates. I am free to resign at any time: but I am comfortable in the Club— a trifle lazy perhaps, and maybe a little snobbish. This is the best club in our civilization, so why should I give it up? But do not ask me for the "principles" of the Club: I hold them as Mr. Branch Cabell holds the Thirty Nine Articles of his Church, with my eyes closed. All I know is that it is an association of fine fellows, "ripe and mellow scholars" and thorough gentlemen; and I am proud to belong.

The comparison with the Church may be carried further. For most people, the Church is first of all a congenial Club with a spiritual tinge. As a rule, you do not join the Presbyterian Church because you believe in Presbyterianism: you believe in Presbyterianism because you are a member of the Presbyterian Church. And what is true of the traditional Churches is truer still of the historical parties. But although principles or beliefs are indeed quite secondary, like the colors of a flag, they will be defended with the utmost vigor, even though they may be utterly beyond the grasp of the average member.

In the same way, the Literary Club secretes, as it were, its own orthodoxy. There *must* be a right and a wrong in literature, since there are right and wrong people; and it happens that we are on the right side. The result is a pseudo-dogmatism, a semi-rationalization of our intellectual habits. The supremacy of Shakespeare is obvious in our eyes; we are sane people; therefore all sane people must admit Shakespeare's supremacy. And you have a definite tenet which, if challenged, will be upheld at all cost. This tendency is hard to resist. I remember telling a group of students: *"No man in his senses* would maintain that Art has progressed since the Greeks." As I had been warning them earnestly against all sweeping assertions, they broke into a unanimous smile. I had to correct myself: *"No man in my senses . . ."*

Eternal Verities; spontaneous personal opinions; the custom of the tribe: it is more hopeless to draw boundaries between them than to trace a sensible frontier between Poland and Germany. Impressionism is the basic fact: "I feel, therefore I am." What I do not feel does not count for me. But my impressions have a tendency to organize themselves into a code. What are these abstract ideas? Are they illusions, myths, symbols, or ultimate realities? I know not: at any rate, they are fascinating building blocks for the maturer minds. Radical individualism, dogmatism, may have their sphere of validity. Certain it is that all the literature we can talk about and write about is a social product: the selection and manifestation of a group and of an age, an integral part of our civilization.

III

Etymology, at times a capricious guide, but sensible enough in this case, tells us that *literature* means *writing* (Letters). To be sure, there may be unwritten literature and unliterary writing: but let that pass. Writing remains the standard method of recording, more retentive than memory, and, even to-day, more convenient than the gramophone. When we speak of the "literature" of a subject, we mean everything written about that subject; and I am deluged with "literature" about toothpaste, hosiery, automobiles, free silver and the Shakespeare folios.

Needless to say that this all-embracing acception is of little interest to the *literary* student. Yet, even for him, it is not quite negligible. For one thing, scholarship, his goddess, tends to efface the line between writing that is an art, and writing in general. The classical archeologist, the medieval philologist, will pounce eagerly upon any text that pertains to their period, even though, in subject or form, it has not the slightest claim to literary interest. Nay, they will rather scorn "literary interest" as amateurish and almost frivolous. Our practical, but wholly artificial division of knowledge into *Departments* should not blur the fact that linguistics and some aspects of literary history are historical sciences, and not æsthetic studies at all.

In another respect, the all-inclusive definition of literature is of greater importance. It is a commonplace of criticism that "literature is the mirror of civilization"; and, because it is such a commonplace, we shall not let it pass unchallenged. We expect to show that *artistic* literature is a dangerously distorting mirror: the Coolidgian régime of Louis-Philippe, in France, found its expression in the wildest romanticism. If you want a truer reflection of life, you will have to include the second- and third-raters, and, beyond them, those writers who have no literary standing at all. A critic like Sainte-Beuve, because he was an observer of life,—a passionately cool observer—devoted many of his *Causeries* to people who did not in the least count *as literature*.

If we want to extract from that loose mass of mere writing that which is properly literature, we shall find one delicate criterion after another breaking in our hands. There is no form, there is no theme, there is no mood and no intention that will inevitably stamp a piece of writing as sterling literature. Watch a lake by moonlight: you are persuaded that the long silver ray on the water has an objective existence. Yet the whole lake is illumined, and the shaft of light that reaches to your feet is a delusion. More precisely: it is not the light that is a delusion, but the darkness beyond. All writing is potential literature: the narrow gleaming ribbon moves with the observer.

Our conscious selves are conditioned by the subconscious and the unconscious; and, between the three stages, there are no impassable barriers. A distinct thought, an act of will, may after a time sink below the threshold; an obscure tendency may work its way up to the light. Similarly, the *literature* that emerges as such is not radically different from the *sub-literature* and the *un-literature* which lurk, amorphous, beneath.

Instead of *literature* and *sub-literature,* I have frequently used the terms proposed by Professor Richard G. Moulton: *fixed* and *floating.* Words which have not attained undisputed currency are apt to be misleading: when I asked for an example of *floating* literature, I was answered: "The novels of Joseph Conrad." Again I wish we had at our service more perspicuous expressions; but, in attempting to discriminate between them, we may clear up our own thought.

By *fixed* literature, I mean that kind which is inseparable from a definite authorship and a definite text. An anonymous work may belong to fixed literature: whoever "Junius" may be, we are conscious that there was a man who penned those *Letters.* A corrupt or chaotic text is a text all the same: it is hard for editors to agree on the presentation of Pascal's *Thoughts;* still every page bears Pascal's imperious mark.

If, on the contrary, the actual author and the literal text are matters of indifference, then we have *floating* literature. The first example that will come to mind is that of folklore. We—rather loosely—admit that those popular traditions came to life and grew by a process of spontaneous generation; and although the theme may be definite enough, the details and the wording may vary *ad libitum*. Take a modern form of folklore, the jokes that fill the best page of *The Literary Digest*. Here is a well-known sample: a man was falling from the twentieth story, and, as he passed the tenth, he was asked: "How goes it?"—"All right so far," was the cheerful reply. Now this profound parable was used by Prosper Mérimée, who took it from Voltaire, who had it from Fontenelle. But it does not matter in the least who said it first: our own guess is that it goes back to that ill-fated skyscraper, the Tower of Babel. It matters even less whether the building had six stories or sixty, whether the victim was an Irishman or a Negro, whether he shouted back: "All right so far" or "So far so good." (Under somewhat similar circumstances, Madame Laetitia, Napoleon's mother, used the words: *"Pourvu que cela dure!"*) It is *floating* literature.

Fixed and floating do not correspond to written and unwritten. Not a few Homeric scholars believe that the *Iliad* was fixed before it was put down in writing; and publication in *The Literary Digest* does not moor a "floating" story to an immovable quay wall. The difference is not the same as that between *permanent* and *ephemeral*. Every day sees an enormous batch of new books that are "fixed" enough according to our definition, but will be forgotten to-morrow, while folklore motives are the most enduring element in literature: Aurelio Macedonio Espinosa has traced *The Tar Baby* almost to the Earthly Paradise. Still less does the distinction imply *good* or *bad*. Atrocious foolishness has found its way into print, with the author's name proudly flaunted on the title page, while the homely wisdom and mother-wit of the ages, as well as many tender or tragic stories, may remain "floating" for ever.

We may think that our civilization is too grown-up for folklore. Nothing of the kind. The mind of modern man has not been struck with barrenness. Stories still originate, in smoking compartment, pool room or board meeting, which, if they were found among the Zyrians and the Trobrianders, would be fit subjects for Doctoral Dissertations. Jokes, anecdotes, situations, types, are teeming as much as ever: Senator Sorghum, Farmer Corntossel, Moronia the Office Flapper, Pat and Abie, are authentic products of the popular imagination, no less than the Werewolf, the Ogre, Tom Thumb and Reynard the Fox. Some students of literature and some alert editors are at last making the tremendous discovery that American folks are not wholly dumb. There is in this country a *vox populi* which might be heard, if the professionals did not attempt to drown it. If we followed that line of thought with any consistency, the future of literature would be in the hands of the illiterate.

Language, the warp and woof of literature, affords striking instances of folk creation. Language, and particularly the American language, is constantly renewed through the quaint figures of speech which go by the name of slang. For one picturesque expression deliberately coined by a licensed wisecracker and duly credited to him, there are a hundred that sprang mysteriously from the myriad lips of Demos. No one is accountable for "the cat's meow" and such felicities of speech.

It "springs to the eyes" that floating literature is the store from which fixed literature is constantly drawing. Racine's harmonious lines were written in an idiom derived, however remotely, from the slang of soldiers and traders. Molière confessedly borrowed right and left, not exclusively from the known writers of Greece, ancient Rome, Italy and Spain, but from the inexhaustible fund of Gallic tradition. The most profound of philosophical dramas, *Faust,* was once a puppet show. The rarest flowers of art need a rich popular humus.

With this idea we are in full sympathy: leave literature to the professionals, and it will soon die in their hands, as Latin died when the Humanists vowed to restore Vergilian purity. But it can easily be carried to an absurd extreme. In the eighteenth century, as a reaction against an excessively sophisticated culture, there began a romantic extolling of the primitive, the barbaric, *i.e.* the subconscious and unconscious in literature. Vico, that lonely forerunner, then Herder and all the pioneers of Romanticism, were eagerly listening for "folk's voices." The readers of *Ossian* were enraptured by the "primitiveness" of those poems: the name Macpherson seems linked by fate with sensational hoaxes. In the same line of thought came the theories dissolving Homer into a loose heap of folk tradition. The definite medieval epic, of which the *Song of Roland* is the type, *must* have been preceded by a rich ballad literature, a French *Romancero* of which no trace is to be found. For many scholars, it was a heresy that anything should ever have originated with one definite author: the subconscious held undisputed sway.

Now the wheel has turned again. We are no longer so certain about the poetic power of the collective mind. We believe that the relations between fixed and floating literature are not so one-sided. If conscious individual works constantly arise out of the indeterminate mass, that mass is no less constantly renewed by individual works as they lose their "fixity." The whole process is not a steady ascent, but a *circulus.*

The "just growed" theory is a lazy explanation. It does not stand to reason; neither is it confirmed by experience. It is far more likely that everything that survives in folklore—theme, character, name or phrase—had a beginning, definite although forgotten. Some one invented the Tar Baby; some one was actually the first to mention Paul Bunyan; some one started the joke about the Ford that went to heaven on high. Those creations may have been altered in transmission, contaminated by other creations of the same kind: but they were creations all the same.

We have seen popular slang rising into formal literature: conversely, formal literature unceasingly enriches the vernacular. We use the word *to pander* without remembering the story of *Troilus and Cressida.* We say: *to curry favor,* unconscious that *favor* is really *Favel* or *Fauvel,* the roan horse symbolical of human vanity in a medieval poem. *Renard,* the hero of the satirical folk epic, has entirely displaced the old French word for fox (*goupil*). When we say *quixotic,* we need not be thinking of Cervantes. French working men will refer to a particularly noxious kind of hypocrite as a *tartuffe*, even though they have not read Molière's masterpiece. I was surprised recently to find that many young people, using the word a *babbitt* very freely, did not know Sinclair Lewis.

In the walls of peasants' huts, near Roman ruins, you will find imbedded some half-effaced inscription, some barely recognizable fragment of a classic figure: in like fashion is common speech strewn with blurred and broken literary allusions.

This leads us to wonder whether popular traditions really did spring from the untutored masses, or whether they represent the dim and degraded memories of a vanished formal art. We know that the courtly romances of the later Middle Ages lost caste, and finally reached the villages in debased form: had the process gone a little farther, we might easily have lost sight of their sophisticated origins, and considered *The Four Sons of Aymon* or *Fierabras* as authentic folk tales. There are traces of a Roland Tradition throughout Europe: but, says Professor Hugh Smith, the *Song of Roland* was not the elaboration of preëxisting legends: it was a conscious piece of work, a new departure; it started the vogue for Carolingian epics; and ultimately the story, in vague outline, reached the people.

The *circulus* goes on under our very eyes. Goethe took the Faust motive from floating literature, and turned it, for all time, into one of the major works of fixed literature. For all time? Yes, so far as scholars are concerned. For the average man, Faust is floating again. Almost everybody knows the name, and remembers Gretchen and Mephistopheles: but very little more. The memories evoked by the title *Faust* seldom go deeper than Gounod's opera or Emil Jannings's picture. We have already seen how *Babbitt* has gone floating. Scholars in distant ages will dispute: (a) whether Babbitt was an historical character or a solar myth; (b) whether there was an actual book (an *Ur-Babbitt*) by that name; (c) whether our present text was a late version of the popular Babbitt Saga or Cycle; (d) what on earth it had to do with the mysterious cult known as Humanism.

The problem, it will readily be seen, is a delicate one. Even at present, we are deeply influenced, in history and literature, by the romantic craze for the primitive. The Romanticists loved the past so dearly that they manufactured it to satisfy their desire. Just as they built faked ruins in their gardens, they made up faked "popular traditions" in poetry. In the *Lorelei,* Heine can not drive out of his mind "a legend from most ancient time": but the legend was of recent fabrication, like some of the horrific instruments of torture in the Nürnberg Museum.

A curious aspect of the question is offered by the Napoleonic Legend. It is taken for granted that the Emperor's saga arose from the very hearts of the people; much later, conscious poets, such as Victor Hugo, would take hold of that epic material and shape it into formal narratives. A song of Béranger, *The Memories of the People,* a chapter in Balzac, *The Story of Napoleon told in a Barn,* are accepted as honest transcriptions of Napoleonic folklore. On closer inspection, the evidence dissolves. We know for certain that Napoleon was far from popular during the last years of his reign and immediately after his fall. His *Legend* was started after his death, deliberately; it became one of the great Romantic myths, like Prometheus, Don Juan, Faust, Ahasverus. Neither Béranger nor Balzac was a peasant, nor in close touch with the peasantry. In his *Memories of the People,* Béranger does not even claim to represent actual facts: his song is a prophecy: *"Fifty years hence,* they will be talking of his glory . . ." From 1825 to 1840, Napoleonism was in vogue among the *bourgeoisie* and with some of the Romanticists, for political or æsthetic reasons. King Louis-Philippe himself found it shrewd policy to foster it; the common people came to it but slowly. No doubt, by 1848, when the Emperor's nephew was triumphantly elected President of the Republic, Napoleonism had at last reached the masses: but it did not originate with the masses. Victor Hugo, Béranger, Thiers, Balzac, were the tutors, not the mouthpieces, of the nation. "Artless" memoirs like those of the *grognard* Captain Coignet, were written long after the events, and only because Napoleon-worship had become the fashion. It is interesting to note that those writers who sprang directly from the people, like Michelet and Veuillot, and not from the *bourgeoisie,* were definitely anti-Napoleonic.

We may apply the distinction between *fixed* and *floating* even to evangelical literature. Stories about the Lord, reports of His sayings (*logia*), were at first transmitted orally, without any thought of definite authorship. The gospel "according to" Matthew or Mark, meant a certain line of tradition, not an invariable text. Luke, a conscious author, tells us how he organized these floating elements into a definite whole. John, a supreme poet and philosopher, scorned the task of mere compilation, and gave us a Gospel that bears the marks of his genius. There were many other narratives "afloat": some based on vague hearsay, some tinged with imagination, or slightly twisted so as to serve some particular doctrine, some deliberate although pious frauds. In this mass of edifying literature, the Church operated a selection. Four versions alone were recognized as canonical, and not one jot or tittle of their text could be altered. In theory, no work could be more "fixed" than the Gospel: in fact, the sacred story has returned to the people, has become "floating" again. Only prize pupils in Sunday schools know their gospel narratives in proper sequence, and could give chapter and verse for every quotation. For most of us, it must be confessed that the outlines are blurred and the wording far from certain, as in the case of folklore.

Not only does a theme thus pass from fixed to floating, from floating to fixed, and back again: but, at any moment, it may be fixed or floating according to the experience of the individual reader. *Faust* is not the same to the Goethean scholar and to the man in the street. The Gospel is not the same to the orthodox minister and to the vaguely deistic humanitarian.

Literature may be likened to a saturated solution into which water and chemicals are constantly poured. Crystals are formed, and dissolve again. The crystals are different from the solution in which they are immersed; yet, in essence, they are not different. Thus do masterpieces concentrate the soul of a people, and merge into that soul again.

This opens up a problem which we can only state in naked terms for the present. In former ages, when a literary work was a rare and difficult achievement, when it was polished for many years, transcribed at great expense on the most durable material, accessible only to a few, in constant danger of annihilation, and for all those reasons preserved jealously in the treasure house of mankind, *fixity* in all senses of the word was the ideal. Today, floating literature has innumerable channels of expression: not merely the pulpit, the forum, the gossip of the market place, private correspondence, but the cheap ephemeral book, the magazine, the newspaper, the talkie, the radio. Under these unprecedented circumstances, is fixity possible, is it even desirable? The individual time-defying masterpiece might well be a thing of the past; would its disappearance entail an irremediable loss?

Be this as it may: literature is never a foreign substance erratically imbedded in the body of a civilization: it is part of the general life, it is a function of the general organism. The indifference of the "practical man" to æsthetic values—whether frankly contemptuous or under a veil of frigid reverence — is a needless self-inflicted mutilation. But the aloofness of the mere bookman— author, critic, scholar—in his Ivory Tower is even more deadly to the soul.

Chapter 2

RACE

I

THE criticism which is mere fault-finding went into the discard with our last literary code. The criticism which consists in exclaiming over "beauties" is voted amiably vapid. Impressionism pure and simple has never achieved authority: "Who are you," says the ungentle reader, "that I should bother about your impressions? Have I not impressions of my own?" So, driven from their ancient judgment seats, the critics must find refuge in the temple of the latest idol, Science. They will no longer attempt to condemn or to praise, but only to understand. And, in that vast temple, they seek the very latest altar: young goddesses are most eager to perform miracles, or, in homely parlance, new brooms sweep clean. Hence the favor enjoyed by the New, the Newer, the Newest Criticism, the Sociological kind. A touch of Muscovite red imparts a rich glow to what might easily be a dismal study. And we are offered "the Materialistic Interpretation of Literature" according to the doctrine of Karl Marx.

Perhaps the broom is not quite so new as the sweepers

believe. As early as 1800, the intimate connection between civilization and literature was clearly seen by that
formidable blue-stocking Madame de Staël: the very title
of her book, *On Literature considered in its Relations
with Social Institutions,* is illuminating. It was she, in
particular, who sought to establish that "the North"
was essentially Romantic and Protestant, while "the
South" was Classical and Catholic: one of those dazzling
half-truths far more dangerous than palpable errors. Herder had already expounded similar conceptions, with a
wealth of undigested information and a fine frenzy of
Idealism. Voltaire himself, in his *Century of Louis XIV,*
had given an all-embracing survey of a society, in which
literature took its natural place. So Messrs. V. F. Calverton and Granville Hicks can boast of a distinguished
ancestry.

It was Taine, however, who, with the abstract logic he
professed to despise, hardened a tendency of modern
thought into a doctrine, and expressed the doctrine in
masterful formulæ. Ever since his *Introduction to the
History of English Literature* (1863), the magic words
Race, Environment and Time have been piously repeated. The latest works of the Sociological Critics do not
go far beyond the impressive theories of Taine.

The whole *History of English Literature* was written
as a demonstration of the principles promulgated in the
Introduction, and the whole work might close with Q.
E.D. It belongs exactly to the same generation as Karl
Marx's *Capital,* and, like *Capital,* it shows unmistakable
signs of age. Even in its prime, it never was fully reliable; and few pieces of scholarship retain their author-

ity after threescore and ten. As a demonstration, the *Literary History of the English People,* by the late Ambassador J. J. Jusserand, is far more convincing. Taine's continued appeal is due solely to his vigorous talent: but, as a writer no less than as a scholar, he *dates,* fully as much as his contemporary Matthew Arnold, vastly more than Sainte-Beuve, Renan or Walter Pater. Much of his imperious logic is forced; much of his brilliancy strikes us as glitter. Let us not forget that he was writing under the Second Empire, whose masterpiece was Garnier's gaudy Opera, and that he, the ascetic scholar, collaborated to *La Vie Parisienne.*

Most antiquated of all is the "positivism" of Taine, his naïve worship of facts, facts, facts. It is antiquated because it did not represent the man himself: it was the *Zeitgeist* of Scientific Realism speaking through a sensitive, tormented soul. His phrase: "Vice and virtue are products like vitriol and sugar," is often quoted as an example of crass materialism. Determinism, yes; materialism, no. Taine does not even suggest that vice and virtue are *chemicals;* he only asserts that they are *products,* and this no conservative moralist will deny. If we insist upon the importance of education, a wholesome atmosphere, the avoidance of dangerous associations, it is because we believe, with Taine, that the law of cause and effect is valid even on the ethical plane. On the whole, however, the general impression is not wrong: Taine was committed to the materialistic interpretation of history, including, as a by-product, the history of literature.

We were taught our letters by faithful disciples of Taine. We rebelled against him, because he had been

33

captured by the reactionaries. But these word-battles of the past century are now one with Nineveh and Tyre. Taine is just receding beyond the awkward stage when a writer no longer possesses the liveliness of a contemporary, and has not quite attained the dignity of a classic. We may now come to grips with his thought without awe and without animosity.

His Race, Environment and Time still afford, we believe, a convenient classification. Every one of the three terms is ambiguous, and, in our own study of French Civilization, we adopted in preference the words People, Habitat, Tradition, which seemed to us, at the time, not so cynically question-begging. We must repeat that all such words have no dogmatic value. We shall use them only as points of departure: their full meaning, and the indispensable corrections or qualifications, will appear as the result of the discussion itself.

II

The notion of *Race,* applied to literature, does not belong exclusively to Taine and his followers: it is ubiquitous, and correspondingly loose. Guarded as you may swear to be, you will catch yourself asserting that Yeats's dreaminess, for instance, or Anatole France's clarity, or d'Annunzio's sensuousness, are "racial" traits; and, in so doing, you will be in excellent company, including, among our contemporaries, Mesdames Edith Wharton and Gertrude Atherton. The present writer has been waging his thirty years' war agains the race phantom. This, in itself, is sufficient evidence of his "Latin" blood: no "Anglo-Saxon" would worry so long about a theory.

Taine himself defines Race as "those innate and hereditary dispositions which man brings with him at his birth, and which, as a rule, are linked with marked differences in temperament and bodily structure. They vary with the peoples. Nature offers varieties of men as well as of bulls and horses, some brave and intelligent, others timid and dull. . . ."

A race, therefore, is an example of collective heredity, a strain, a breed, a large family. The qualities it implies are "in the blood": training can work only within the limits of hereditary capacities. Treat a dray horse as though he were a race horse, you will not turn him into a race horse.

Taine does not assert that races are immutable: but he maintains that, if they change at all, it is with infinite slowness. The "primordial characteristics" of a race are the results of "perhaps myriads of centuries." Against such a vast accumulation of forces, the influence of a lifetime is insignificant; even the influence of historical ages —a paltry half dozen of millennia—is barely perceptible. For all practical purposes, the race may be considered as an absolutely fixed element. In other terms, acquired characteristics, including those due to environment, are either not transmitted at all, or are transmitted to an infinitesimal degree. All this is orthodox enough, although Lamarck is raising his head again, and although there is a breed of rats at Stanford University striving hard to establish the transmissibility of acquired characteristics.

Race implies again, although Taine does not say so, that only certain combinations are biologically possible.

35

In many cases, miscegenation means immediate barrenness; in others, the new breed is neither stable nor, *a fortiori*, permanent. Hybrids die out, or revert to the original *true* types. If it were not so, there would be no *races* in the strict sense of the term. Every chance union between different breeds might start a new variety, and the essential notions of distinctness and permanence would be lost. We confess that, however true this may be in the simple world of Mendel's sweet peas, we do not know to what extent it holds good in the case of human varieties.

Another implication is that members of the same group are fundamentally more alike than members of two different groups could possibly be. Here again, we are not fully convinced. Even in the physical sense, we have seen the boundaries between groups waver and practically disappear. We have known white Mediterraneans with dark skins and curly hair, who seemed a great deal closer to the Negro than to the Scandinavian; and other "white" men, in Auvergne, who were curiously akin to some Mongolians and some Red Indians.

Finally—and now we transcend Mendel's realm to pass into the more shadowy world of Gobineau, Chamberlain and Madison Grant—Taine admits that "as a rule", certain physical traits imply corresponding intellectual, moral and spiritual traits. There is a kind of science, of poetry, of virtue, of religion, that goes with a flat nose, and another kind that belongs to aquiline features. We shall see how eagerly Mrs. Atherton swallowed that theory: we may be forgiven if we withhold our assent yet awhile.

So far, we have defined race in the abstract, and contented ourselves with the assertion that there are races among men. If we are challenged to enumerate these races, and to discriminate between them, we shall get ourselves into a very pretty tangle. All the more so because, in literature, the classic and undeniable distinction according to the color of the skin is of little avail. Our field, even though in our conceit we call it *world* literature, is almost exclusively *white* literature. The contribution of the red man is negligible; that of the negro is secondary; and the vast production of the Mongolian is barely beginning to influence ours. The "races" of Taine must be subdivisions of the Indo-European.

Taine evades the difficulty neatly by not defining concrete races at all. In the course of his five volumes, he frequently refers to "the English race" or to "the Anglo-Saxon race." Therein lies a fallacy which is as obvious as it is indestructible.

For, as a rule, when we say *race,* we mean *language group.* We speak of the Latin, the Germanic, the Slavic *races,* while the corresponding realities are the Latin, Germanic, Slavic linguistic families. These terms do not refer to biological kinship: only to affinities in speech. A dusky sergeant, at the time when things were looking gloomy for the Allies, boasted: "Wait till we Anglo-Saxons get into this fight!" He was thoroughly justified. An English-speaking Negro is an Anglo-Saxon in the same sense as Mr. Lloyd George the Welshman. A Zapoteca like Porfirio Diaz becomes a "Latin" just like the Breton, Fleming or Basque who happens to speak French, and like the Bessarabian Jew who has adopted Rumanian. Of two brothers in Upper Silesia, one may turn into a Teuton, the other into a Slav.

We have no desire to minimize the influence of language on thought and literature. In spite of such a miraculous exception as Switzerland, language groups are far more potent realities than are political units. Language is the only true frontier: the one that can not be altered by a stroke of the pen, nor ignored by aëroplane and radio, the one also that levies the heaviest toll on foreign goods. Community of language means even more than ease of communication: it implies a common background of education, common patterns of thought, a common cultural heritage. But, essential as it may be, language is not race; indeed it may have very little to do with race.

France is a "Latin" country: very few genuine Romans settled in Gaul. The soldiers were recruited from all parts of the Empire, and not from Latium alone; the auxiliaries were Barbarians; the traders were mostly Greeks. It was in speech and culture only that the country was "Latinized." Language is most decidedly an acquired characteristic. In this respect, at any rate, we know that our melting pot does melt: the children of immigrants speak the vernacular as purely as Ring Lardner himself. Between 1918 and 1931, the number of French-speaking Alsatians increased threefold; and, in a single generation, our guardianship of the Filipinos has turned a million Malays from "Latins" to "Anglo-Saxons."

We shall have to allude more than once to the Celtic imbroglio. There are definite Celtic languages, all in danger of being shoved over, like Cornish, into the Western sea. A "Celt", small and dark, burly and reddish, melancholy or joyous, is presumably the descendant of people who once spoke a Celtic dialect. But a Protestant from Yorkshire like G. B. Shaw, with very few words of Gaelic at his command, is not seldom referred to as a Celt.

I have often heard, with mild exasperation, that "the French" were congenitally incapable of this or that— fault or virtue, it does not matter. Here, *race* is identified with *nation,* not with language: there are few nations that coincide with a language area. We, for instance, are only a part of the English-speaking world; French spills over several of the political frontiers of France, while Flemings, Alsatians, Bretons, Basques, Catalans, Corsicans, are Frenchmen whose home language is not French.

I am far from denying the existence of national types. You can usually tell a Frenchman from an Englishman, even though both should happen to be tall and blond. To be sure, "Frenchiness" and "Britishness" are to some extent sartorial and tonsorial affairs. A close shave, a Hart, Schaffner and Marx suit, a pair of Harold Lloyd spectacles, will turn Monsieur Gaston Durand into a very acceptable George F. Babbitt. But, even *in naturalibus* or under the same uniform, the difference would persist. Intonation, gestures, glances and smiles, are indelible labels. And to these superficial idiosyncrasies correspond elusive yet unmistakable twists of thought and qualities of feeling. It has been the curse of international life ever since the Great War that France and America, both with the most excellent intentions, could not be brought to think and feel alike.

But again, however potent a force nationality may be, it is not "in the blood", it is not *race*. France and America have marked psychological traits, and act as units, more so perhaps than any other nation: yet neither is a race. There are quite a few prominent Jews and Irishmen, Slavs and Latins, in this country who consider themselves *bona fide* American citizens. France likewise is a melting pot which, at work for twenty centuries at least, has not stopped operations. On the roll of French worthies, we may pick out at random such names as Bonaparte, Brazza, Zola, Gambetta, Galliéni, Antonetti, Giovanninelli; as Kleber, Kellermann, Scherer, Schrader, Zurlinden, Siegfried, Hirschauer; as Clarke, Macdonald, Mac-Mahon, Hennessy, Thompson, Archdeacon, Viele Griffin, Stuart Merrill; as Zyromski, Strowski, José-Maria de Heredia, Zamacois, Psichari and Papadiamantopoulos.

A small isolated country may, in the course of centuries, become literally one great family: it is pretty certain that all Corsicans are cousins. In a much vaguer fashion, this holds true even of England. David Starr Jordan found amusement in the thought that he and a surprising number of noted Americans were all the descendants of Isabelle de Vermandois, who, in her turn, claimed Charlemagne as her ancestor. But, even in the tight little island, the blood relationship between Lady Clara Vere de Vere and Sarah Gamp requires no small amount of faith.

Curiously enough, the most nationalistic element in

all countries is the aristocracy, which is also the most cosmopolitan. A patriotic French Count will marry his daughter to a man with an Austrian or an Italian title, rather than to a plain French *poilu*. The royal "race" of France, symbol of the country's unity, is a hodgepodge of Spanish, Italian, Austrian and German ingredients.

Nationality is not race: it can be acquired. Not through a mere formal document, a treaty or naturalization papers: but through consent, education, environment. Yes, you can tell a Frenchman from an American. But you can likewise tell a French Negro from an American Negro: both bear, beyond cavil, the stamp of their nationality. America and France are usually conceded greater powers of assimilation than most other countries. I have seen on the Boul' Mich' Chinese students who were almost ludicrously French.

The national type is a fact: but it is far more superficial than we are frequently asked to believe. There is more reality in the provinces or sections than in the country as a whole: if an Irishman is not an Englishman, neither is a Catalan a Spaniard, neither is a Breton a Frenchman. Even the *local* type, although more definite, is not the average, but the exception, the extreme, the caricature. We are all aware that the stage Southern Colonel as well as the stage Minnesota Swede have little validity except on the boards. A Frenchman of fair size, who wears no goatee, is not voluble, does not gesticulate, does not kiss ladies' hands, is satisfied with one slice of bread, and is not decorated with the Legion of Honor, is not a *typical* Frenchman at all: only there are millions upon millions like him.

The national type, however real, is less real than the *period* type. Look at old photographs: you can tell at a glance whether they belong to the nineties or the sixties, but closer attention will be needed before you can locate the originals in Scotland, Germany or Pennsylvania. A family portrait strikes you first of all as eighteenth century, before it strikes you as French or English. This is not merely a matter of costume, but also of attitude, expression and even physical traits. There were moments when, throughout Europe, it was fashionable for ladies to have opulent charms; moments (happy moments!) when every one wore the keen and courtly smile so well caught by La Tour; moments when our most solid great-grandmothers were languishing, and our most stodgy great-granduncles looked inspired. The period is a self-determined country of the soul more real than any political area. Fashion is thicker than blood.

We may add that, at least in the old countries, the professional or social type also is more deeply imprinted than the national. Priests, soldiers, business men, professors, mechanics, peasants, sailors, come to look the part of their occupation, even during off-hours. There are therefore many resemblances which imply no blood relationship: they are the result of environment and tradition, not of race.*

Is there a safer criterion of race than either language or nationality? Could it not be found in the "marked differences in bodily structure" mentioned by Taine?

---

*The study of Nationalism and Literature will therefore be reserved for later chapters on Environment and Tradition.

These, at any rate, are plainly hereditary. To be sure, Taine was satisfied with a very general hint: anthropology was still in swaddling clothes at the time. In the last seventy years, these differences have been investigated, measured, classified; and we feel that we are on scientific ground at last.

Anthropology has exercised such a fascination on the literary mind that it might almost be called a branch of literature. The "Nordic Myth", a vague heritage of Romanticism, has been hardened into pseudo-scientific consistency by men of whom Count de Gobineau is the archetype. Diplomat, *littérateur,* philosopher, Orientalist, Gobineau was a near-genius in every line, and has achieved a kind of twilight celebrity in every country but his native France. To the same school of thought belonged Vacher de Lapouge, who punctuated pages of statistical tables with outbursts of somber eloquence, and Houston Stewart Chamberlain, the Anglo-German Wagnerian who won the Iron Cross for his services to German culture. The literature of race philosophy is enormous; it attained genuine and not undeserved popularity in the works of Madison Grant and Lothrop Stoddard, not to mention those of the fantastic Chinese General, Homer Lea. All these books are marked by traits which were already found in Taine: all, in the same trenchant tone, profess the same love for "science", the same contempt for "sentiment", the same stern and virile "realism"; all reveal the same aristocratic haughtiness toward lesser breeds and mongrels; all rejoice in the same Cassandra-like prophecies of doom, for pessimism has always been a source of morose delectation.

As a rule, anthropology is applied to literature, not directly, but through sociology. *The Passing of the Great Race,* the recurrent theme of the authors we have mentioned, will leave a society in which universal dullness or futility must prevail: the "redoubtable Pan-Baeotia" with which Renan threatened us. France, in destroying her Nordic aristocracy, has committed spiritual suicide; the formal graces of her civilization can not veil its fundamental decadence. Undeterred, England, Russia, America, are traveling the same road to the abyss:

Lo! Thy dread Empire, CHAOS!, is restored;
Light dies before thy uncreating word:
Thy hand, great anarch! lets the curtain fall;
And universal darkness buries all.

A few bolder critics have definitely asserted the direct influence of race upon art and literature. A passage from *A Motor Flight through France,* by Mrs. Edith Wharton, offers a notable example of racial determinism in the æsthetic field: Taine would have nodded approval. The author is describing the scene of Salome's dance, as carved in Amiens Cathedral. There is a dog present —an irrelevant element introduced, in the teeth of logic, solely for naturalism and picturesqueness:

"Of composition there is none. . . . And thus one is brought back to the perpetually recurrent fact that all northern art is anecdotic, and has always been so; and that, for instance, all the elaborate theories of dramatic construction worked out to explain why Shakespeare crowded his stage with subordinate figures and unnecessary incidents, and would certainly, in relating the story of Saint John, have included Herod's 'Tray and Sweet-heart' among the dramatis personæ—that such theories are but an unprofitable evasion of the ancient ethnological fact *that the Goth has always told his story in that way.*"

Unfortunately, the argument reposes on an unconscious pun. There is no evidence that Gothic art had anything to do with the Goths. It originated in Northern France half a millennium after the great invasions, at a time when the Pre-Gallic, Gallic, Roman and Teutonic elements in the population had become thoroughly fused. It was known then not as Gothic, but simply as the *new* or the *French* style—*opus francigenum*. Gothic was later applied to it by the Italians as a term of contempt: even in classical French, *Gothique* preserved the meaning of uncouth or barbarous. We may add that in thus insisting on the discursive and episodical character of Gothic, Mrs. Wharton is overlooking the magnificent simplicity and unity of the general plan. Amiens, Rheims, and especially Paris, offer elements of serene logic and even of majestic symmetry which might very well be termed classical. Early Gothic, in particular, is far less fantastic and exuberant than Italian or Spanish Barocco.

Mrs. Wharton herself, by the way, is presumably a Goth, and, in this very involved sentence, tried to write like one. As a rule, however, her art is scrupulously Latin in its economy and neatness; it challenges comparison with Paul Bourget's rather than with Shakespeare's.

Mrs. Gertrude Atherton is more systematic, and more rigorous in her scientific terminology. Her critical essay, "The Alpine School of Fiction" (*Bookman,* March, 1922), a valuable and delightful document, is based on the standard division of European races: the Nordic, the Alpine and the Mediterranean. Nordics are tall, slender, blond, long-headed; Alpines are medium-sized, stocky, varying in coloring but inclined to the darker shades, and round-headed; Mediterraneans are slight, dark and long-headed. The proportion between length and breadth of head is called the *cephalic index*. Stature and coloring may vary to an appreciable extent within the same race and even within the same family: but the cephalic index can be trusted. And with the cephalic index go literary gifts or deficiencies: "Fancy a round head writing *The Scarlet Letter!*" (The Puritans, by the way, were known as Roundheads: but that was only one of those tonsorial facts we mentioned before.) There are breeds of poets, biologically, not metaphorically speaking, as there are breeds of bulls and horses. No man with a cephalic index above 75 can be trusted to write decent lyrics. This is "scientific criticism" with a vengeance.

The literary mind, eager to escape from its own impressionism, ascribes to everything "scientific" a degree of certainty and fixity that true scientists would never claim. Anthropology is a great science: but it is a very young science, still toddling uncertainly. (The older sciences, by the way, are at present just as much "in the making" as their infant sisters.) Its rough and ready classifications are not the law of the Medes and the Persians. If most of the elementary textbooks and secondary authorities adopt without question the division Nordic-Alpine-Mediterranean, many workers at first hand have classifications of their own. Vacher de Lapouge, himself a believer in the Standard Three, recognized that pure types are a minority in Europe. There are tall blonds with round heads that will not fit into the tripartite scheme. That great administrator, Dr. Ray Lyman Wilbur, is too tall for a Mediterranean and too dark for a Nordic. The Cro-Magnons, the curious fossil race still alive in the Dordogne region, have a peculiar head shape.

"You can not get away from the cephalic index," quoth Mrs. Atherton. This called for the obvious retort: "You can not get away with the cephalic index." Jews are supposed to be a race, and certainly have a well marked physical type: yet there are broad-headed Jews and long-headed Jews. A Spanish Basque looks for all the world like a French Basque: but their cephalic indices are different. Franz Boas has cast serious doubts on the cephalic index as a race criterion. It may join the phrenology of Lavater and the facial angle of three generations ago on the great junk pile of science. Hair structure and blood counts are more fashionable criteria to-day.

The tests of comparative racial ability, carried on in some of our large cities, and by Dr. Porteus in Hawaii, are not conclusive, because they start with a loose definition of race. The groups they are comparing have a linguistic, national, social, rather than a biological unity. In Hawaii, for instance, the Portuguese and the Porto-Ricans are listed separately and are indeed different. But there is no Portuguese race and no Porto-Rican race: in both cases, we have to deal with an Iberian-Negroid mixture, in various proportions. All tests, any way, show a wide zone of overlapping. Statistically, the average Greek may be brighter than the average Lapp, or *vice versa:* but you can not tell in advance, from the color of the skin, which child is going to stand higher in the scale. Now literature does not deal with averages, but with individual achievements.

Even if *race* should be entirely a superstition, we know that superstitions are potent factors—tragically so. There are therefore racial themes in literature: works about the Negro and the Jew, works by race-conscious Negroes and Jews. We can not ignore Burghardt Du Bois and Ludwig Lewisohn. The problem, however, is social, cultural, not biological. If you find a "racial" Hebraic tang to some of our smart-set journals, remember that the New York ultra-sophisticate belongs to the same "race" as Spinoza and Jesus. Nordics enjoy Heine, Schnitzler, Wassermann, Bergson, André Maurois, without thinking of their racial origins; and the American students upon whom *L'Abbé Constantin* is so frequently inflicted are apt to entertain the delusion that Ludovic Halévy was a Catholic. Few among the innumerable readers of Alexander Dumas are conscious of the fact that he was a quadroon. René Mayran, the Negro author of *Batouala,* wrote about Central Africa from the point of view of an educated Frenchman. The book belongs to Negro literature exactly in the same sense as *The Magic Isle.*

Need we repeat that we are not denying *heredity?* But heredity is difficult enough to trace, even in the case of a single family: when we come to those vast and loose agglomerations called *races,* the collective heritage

48

carried in the blood becomes extremely elusive. We might admit, for the sake of argument, that Alexander Dumas Fils had inborn capacities for writing, because his father was himself a gifted writer: this is *heredity*. But we have no right to say that he turned into a talented dramatist because his father was a quadroon.

Anthropology is a fascinating science, and may prove a very useful one. But, at the present stage, the "marked differences in bodily structure" suggested by Taine have not been organized into an irrefutable system; still less have the relations between physical and mental traits been satisfactorily established. So far as literature is concerned, cultural elements—language, the political, economic and social régime, a liberal or restrictive tradition, educational opportunities—are vastly more important than race.

Chapter 3

ENVIRONMENT: CLIMATE

"MAN is not alone in the world: nature envelops him, and other men surround him." These external influences which hinder or strengthen man's inborn tendencies constitute his environment (*milieu*). Taine classifies them under three heads: climate, political circumstances, social circumstances.

Climate means more than meteorological conditions: it embraces all geographical factors. Taine had probably borrowed the term from Montesquieu, who had it from Jean Bodin: but no Taine and no Montesquieu were needed to tell us that a gloomy climate spreads gloom, that a harsh climate challenges our energy, that a sunny climate is joyous, a mild climate relaxing, a sultry climate oppressive. It is—or it seems—a fact of common experience. It may be a string of metaphors and a version of the pathetic fallacy.

Montesquieu had said that the mountains breed freedom; Milton before him had spoken of "the Mountain Nymph, sweet Liberty"; whereupon Voltaire remarked that not all the Alpine dwellers were free, while the freest population in Europe, the Dutch, lived below sea-level. An apt lesson in method. General ideas are frequently attractive; but we must not allow ourselves to be seduced. Every one of them is to be treated as a working hypothesis, which requires the support of definite facts.

It would be interesting to collect an Atlas of Literature, devoting one map to the Mystics, another to the Pessimists, another to the great Love Poets, and so on with every important type of genius; and then to confront these maps with others which indicate the standard geographical data—heat, humidity, orography, coast line, rivers. We wonder whether we could scientifically trace the isotherms of melancholy, or the hypsometric contours of wit. We confess that we have not made such a systematic test. A few random attempts, however, may serve as indications of the method.

It seems fairly safe to say that literature thrives best in the temperate zone: the torrid belt and the arctic regions, in comparison, are barren. There have been centers of literary production within the tropics: Cuba, the French West Indies and Réunion, Central America, the northern countries of South America. But, for one thing, they are colonial, not indigenous; and in every case, the effect of latitude is corrected by maritime or mountain influences. The Equator is deadly to the muse. To be sure, India is sweltering in raging heat, and her literature is not to be despised, for all we are so woefully ignorant of it. In our own times, it has given the world Kipling and Tagore. The Ganges holds out a promise to the Niger, the Congo and the Amazon. On the other hand, temperate Australia and New Zealand have not achieved greatness.

The case against the cold countries is not so evident. Northern Germany, Scotland, vast stretches of Russia, the whole Scandinavian world, have decidedly rigorous climates, and stand second to none in literary production. Iceland, within the Arctic circle, has played its very creditable part. In proportion to its population, the frozen North is far more fertile for the spirit than the rank tropics. It must be noted that the North enjoys at least a few weeks of summer heat, whereas the tropics afford no corresponding relief.

The hygrometry of literature is hard to trace. Greece is dry, England is damp, and both have bred great writers. Further still on either side, we find the narrative and poetical wealth of the Arabian desert, and the no less remarkable flowering of song and romance in sodden Ireland.

The influence of sunshine on literature seems to be mostly moonshine. Taine does not fail to contrast the gloomy North and the radiant South, as if the typical product of the Mediterranean world were the Neapolitan tarentella, while the North was constantly keyed up to Young's *Night Thoughts*. Human joy and despair seem to be curiously independent of Nature's alleged mood. The sunny Mediterranean belt gave rise to the Hebrew Scriptures, earnest and terrible rather than light-hearted. Neither *Prometheus* nor *Œdipus* can be called cheerful. Lucretius seems to have closed his eyes to the smiling heavens. In Italy, a strain of deep seriousness and even of despair is no less marked than the joyous acceptance of life. Dante and Michael Angelo are anything but gay; Ugo Foscolo is among the most somber of the Romanticists; Leopardi reaches the nadir of pessimism.

On the other hand, England, in her eternal fog, was justly known as Merrie England, until the Continental Reformation spread its pall of gloom; Shakespeare could write *Hamlet* and *Lear,* but also the *Merry Wives.* Let us go deeper into Cimmerian darkness: in Scotland, when the summer visitor asks the native: "Does it *always* rain here?", he gets the comforting reply: "Oh, no! It sometimes snows." Now medieval and Renaissance Scotland was like England a land of jollity, until a Frenchman, Calvin, cast his spell upon her. Take typical Scots: Robert Burns, Sir Walter, Robert Louis Stevenson, Sir J. M. Barrie: they are not lacking in good cheer. No doubt Carlyle was a Scot, and Carlyle was grumpy: but was the chief cause of his temper geographical? Was it not rather dyspepsia? Or was it Mrs. Carlyle? *

There is no absurdity in this apparent paradox. An unfavorable environment is a challenge: we never feel more keenly alive than when we are going to battle. When we reach home after fighting our way through blustering wind, sleet or snow, the plainest lamplit room will give us a sense of comfort and peace, deeper than a serene sunset over a placid sea. Our reaction against the climate may thus be at least as effective as the expected direct

---

* Statistics of suicide are notoriously unreliable; but figures do not confirm the impression that England has a larger proportion of suicides than France; whereas, in this respect, sunny California tops the list of the States. If a man is unhappy elsewhere, he still has the hope of going to California; if he is unhappy in California, he knows his ills are beyond cure.

action. The net scientific result is that "you never can tell."

Taine alludes also to the physical features of the country—its picturesqueness or its monotony, its rugged or smiling beauty, the graciousness of well-shaped hills, the squalid and sullen look of marshland and mud flats. There again, the literary imagination, with a dash of semi-science, is apt to run amok. The awful majesty of the desert is monotheistic, said Renan (forgetting that monotheism was a late achievement among the Arabs); the epics of ancient India are as overwhelmingly luxuriant as her vegetation; Greek thought is clear-cut like a bare promontory outlined on a limpid sky; English literature has the tang of the sea; France has the reasonableness of her moderate hills and gentle gray heavens; and so on *ad infinitum*. Metaphors again, expressing truths so vague that they cease to be even vaguely true. For, as in the case of heat or cold, we find that literature is surprisingly independent of such circumstances.

Neither the Alps nor the Pyrenees have been the centers of great poetical production. Jean-Jacques Rousseau discovered the beauty of mountains: but that was after he had lived in Paris. On the other hand, Russian literature, a literature of the plains, does not lack massive power; with Dostojewski at any rate, it attains a weird and abrupt intensity which reminds us of stupendous crags rather than of the illimitable steppe. America had Joaquin Miller, the poet of the Sierras: but Chicago, the North West, the whole Mississipi valley, need not despair. Chaucer, Spenser, Shakespeare, Milton, fair representatives of English genius, are only very incidentally poets of the sea. The greatest modern sea writer in English is Joseph Conrad, who came from landlocked Poland. The same is true of France: if Loti came from Rochefort and became a naval officer, Michelet and Victor Hugo, the greatest painters and lovers of the sea, were both landlubbers.

Here again, there is a reason. Literature is not the expression of those daily experiences that we take for granted: intense realization needs the thrill of discovery. The captain who takes his ship once a month through the Panama Canal is not filled with the same awe and wild surmise as "stout Cortez", or was it Balboa? The beauty of Nature is a conquest, not a habit.

Poetical psychology operates in more than one way. Thousands of potential poets of the sea will never sing, because they were born in the heart of a massive continent; whereas every English child has a chance to see the supreme wonder with his own eyes. We may thus distinguish three zones on our literary map. First, the actual mountain, the actual coast line, where familiarity is likely to benumb lyric effusion. Then the areas within easy access of mountain or sea: there opportunities for literature will be abundant, but so abundant that commonplaceness may be the result. Finally, remoter parts, where ocean and peaks are known but dimly, and akin to fairy tales. Supreme poets may appear in any of the three zones: possibly they have their best chance in the third. Our next Laureate of the Atlantic may come from Kansas City as well as from Cape Cod.

Perhaps the most important geographical factor in

literature is *accessibility vs. isolation*. Afghanistan and Abyssinia are seriously handicapped; it would be rash to promise a great cultural future to Kamchatka or the Kerguelen Islands. On the contrary, Honolulu, at the crossroads of the Pacific, is well favored in this respect. There are apparent exceptions: Iceland exists on the map of the epic: but it is as an outpost of a seafaring civilization. R. G. Caldwell told us how romantically remote Santa Fé de Bogotá was in his youth. The stern-wheelers paddled their painful way up the Magdalena river for nearly a fortnight; then followed days on a mule trail; and finally the Athens of South America was reached, renowned for the purity of its language, the graces of its society, its interest in literature. It was a miraculous survival of aristocratic Castilian culture, isolated on the high plateaus of a distant continent.

But with the idea of accessibility, we are introducing another element: the human, the social factor. Physical geography merges imperceptibly into economic and political geography.

Chapter 4

THE ECONOMIC ENVIRONMENT

WE have no lack of critics in America who are offering us an economic (I stand corrected: *the* economic) interpretation of literature. V. F. Calverton is getting to be a veteran in that school; and the latest recruit, Granville Hicks, has managed to attract favorable attention with his *Great Tradition*. A blessing on Karl Marx and all his disciples! Literary knowledge is forever getting cluttered up with the dim and dusty masterpieces of yesterday, with desiccated names of whilom favorites, with toothless theories and outlooks long sightless. Any new method is at any rate a challenge. It goes through our critical lumber room like a devastating housemaid, with powerful Scandinavian arms and a purpose inscrutable to man. When the turmoil is over, things may be a little worse than they were before, but at least they will never be quite the same again.

Saith the prophet, Friedrich Engels: "Marx discovered the simple fact (heretofore hidden beneath ideological overgrowths) that human beings must have food, drink, clothing and shelter first of all, before they can interest themselves in politics, science, art, religion, and the like. This implies that the production of the immediately requisite material means of subsistence, and therewith the existing phase of development of a nation or an epoch, constitute the foundation upon which the state institutions, the legal outlooks, the artistic, and even the religious ideas are built up. It implies that these latter must be explained out of the former, whereas the former have usually been explained as issuing from the latter." *

This passage, involved in style but elementary in thought, shows what a fine, elusive line may at times separate a truism from a fallacy. "One must live": at any rate, no writer can write unless he is alive. *Primo vivere, deinde philosophari:* these words of wisdom were spoken ages before the days of Karl Marx. Engels might have added that man needs a solid earth under his feet, and therefore that geology is the indispensable foundation of all art and all religion. We might further agree that geology is not to be explained in terms of art or religion, although the orthodox have made brave efforts in that line. All this is so obvious that it becomes inane. If we attempt to think with greater precision, then the doctrine propounded by Marx and Engels ceases to be even roughly true.

As man is assured of food and shelter, even of the scantiest, he is free to ponder, to enjoy, and to dream. No doubt his dreaming is to a large extent conditioned by the material world he leaves behind: the literature of conscious protest and wilful escape mirrors the very

---

*Quoted by Max Eastman, Introduction to Modern Library Edition of *Capital and Other Writings*, p. 12.

conditions that it spurns. But, as soon as his bodily wants are satisfied, man is released from immediate necessity. Forgetting for a while appetite and toil, he faces those problems which are beyond any economic régime— the whence and the whither, Nature and the beyond, love and death. He uses symbols, words and illustrations which belong to his age, tribe or class: but they are merely the garments of his thought.

All this may sound like idealistic nonsense: it is literally and pragmatically true. There are moments when I feel at one with Ecclesiastes or Voltaire, although their economic worlds were radically different from mine. There are moments when I am not in perfect harmony with Harold Bell Wright and Gertrude Stein, although both are the "inevitable" products of the civilization which is also responsible for me. When I settle down to enjoy music, I blissfully forget whether Beethoven was the child of capitalism or communism, and whether I myself am a *bourgeois* or a bolshevist. If our critics of the extreme left need sociology before they are able to appreciate Homer, Fielding, or Ogden Nash, it simply proves that they remain on the hither side of literature.

Obviously, physical conditions determine economic development, which, in its turn, influences culture. If the land is too barren to support even a scanty population, no "idealism" will suffice to create the amenities of civilized life. There may be abundant literature *about* the Sahara and the North Pole: we hardly expect literature to take root in arctic ice or desert sand. To this extent, we are as "deterministic" as Taine or Engels.

But, no less obviously, this is true only in extreme cases. In civilization, the human factor is supreme. Many countries, far more richly endowed than Ireland, Scotland or Scandinavia, have contributed far less to culture. Venice and Holland are classical examples of the human will conquering nature. Between material opportunities and human development, the connection is not always inevitable. Between prosperity and cultural achievements, there may be an abyss. Physical geography and economics do not tell the whole tale.

The Economic Interpretation of Literature evokes at once the idea of a debate between Capitalism and Communism. Our pragmatic method prevents us from using these familiar terms. Communism has not "arrived", even in Soviet Russia, and it is far too early to study its influence upon literature. The term Capitalism does not adequately define our composite régime. Speaking with necessary and pardonable roughness, we may recognize, for our purpose, four economic states: the pastoral, the agricultural, the commercial and the industrial.

The first is a great favorite with literary men; the *Pastoral,* the bucolic poem or story, has never been wholly out of fashion for thousands of years. But its greatest vogue is invariably in sophisticated ages: the Alexandrian period, Imperial Rome, the Renaissance, first in Italy, then throughout Europe, the eve of the French Revolution. To the end of the classical era, it was a favorite trick of courtly poets to masquerade as shepherds.

The Hebrew Patriarchs led the pastoral life, and King David, to whom are ascribed some of the greatest lyrics in any language, was himself a shepherd. As we invariably fashion God in our own image, "the Good Shepherd", the One who leadeth us in green pastures, has remained the most permanent picture of the Deity. The Child Jesus was hailed by the Wise Men of the East, but also by humble shepherds. It was felt that tending His flock was not beneath the dignity of God Himself. In every other comparison with some human trade, there would lurk an element of sacrilege: even Mr. Bruce Barton would hardly dare to speak of "the Supreme Realtor."

But Hebrew literature, such as it has come down to us, is essentially the product of the city, Jerusalem, rather than of the tent. The patriarchal age was exalted as a retrospective Utopia: whether it had left authentic traces in narrative and song is far from certain. Even at present, we may find among the Arabs, from Irak to Morocco, dignified and picturesque characters who evoke the memory of Abraham: but their contribution to literature is meager. Genuine Arabic masterpieces are the fruit of the trader's life: they bring the atmosphere of the city mart, the street, the wharf, the court, not the desert.

In European literature, actual shepherds occupy no favored position. He of Ettrick, James Hogg, remains an exception, and not a very significant one. In America, the cowboys have their lyric lore, which was collected by Professor Lomax. It is a minor curiosity, nothing more: the animal stories and the Spirituals of the Negroes rank definitely higher. Samuel Butler was for a while a sheep rancher in New Zealand: but that hardly confers a genuine pastoral character to *Erewhon* or *The Way of All Flesh.*

So we are afraid that the spontaneous literature of the pastoral age is a delusion, although it is a very ancient one. The shepherd's life appeals strangely to the jaded city dweller: it is ample, silent, wind-swept, free. The shepherd moves with the season, like migratory birds and multimillionaires; and he seems to possess the greatest of all luxuries, the one most indispensable to art: *leisure.* The Bucolic is a return to the Golden Age; its attraction is a form of the nostalgic primitivism which has never ceased haunting civilized man. We all dream of Arcady: but Arcady as the best "environment" for literature is a myth.

In the agricultural state, men till the soil and live in permanent homes. Their free wanderings, their spacious leisure, are over; and with them, their noble independence. Peasant democracies are an exception: for untold ages, the serf or even the slave, at best the tenant farmer, formed the majority of the rural element. The full emancipation of the peasantry was achieved in Western Europe only at the end of the eighteenth century or early in the nineteenth; in Russia, two generations later.

As compared with the shepherd, the peasant ceased to be a full man. He was attached to the glebe; the nature of his work made him a perpetual hostage; and his work was never done. Even if he did not sink to the tragic degradation described by La Bruyère, he lacked the variety of experience, the freedom of attitude, the leisure, that would release the poetry in his soul.

The popular literature of the Middle Ages was entirely urban in character, much as it may have lacked in urbanity. In the tales and the farces, the peasant is invariably treated with bitter scorn. *Villein* (villanus, villager) became in French *vilain,* mean and ugly; in English, *villain.* "Thrall, boor, hind, bumpkin, hayseed": the peasant has always been despised as well as maltreated. We hear of literature "springing from the earth": it is doubtful whether the folklore collected among the peasants is purely of peasant origin. Songs or tales came to the village through itinerant minstrels, through an occasional pilgrimage, through a rare visit to some important fair: in all cases, from the town.

Unrelieved by other elements, rural life would be heavily dumb. There is no lack of vivacity among Italian peasants: but the country is so thickly populated, so liberally bestrewn with active townships, so heavily fraught with cultural traditions, that it does not represent the bucolic mind in its awful simplicity. France was until yesterday predominantly an agricultural country, and has brought her full quota to world literature. Predominantly, but never exclusively. French culture has ever been urban, courtly, and, in the last three hundred years, metropolitan: the classical centuries almost forgot Nature altogether. France has no peasant-poet to compare with Burns. Robert Burns was indeed racy of the soil, using village tales as his themes, and the episodes of the ploughed field: yet Robert Burns had received an urban culture. Ireland is a nation of farmers, and has achieved surprising greatness in literature: but would there have been an Irish Renaissance without Dublin—

and London? Our farmers, in these days of universal schooling, the daily press, the automobile, the radio, live under radically different circumstances from those of European peasants a few generations ago. Yet even they, it must be admitted, are almost perfect non-conductors of literature. Poets may arise from the farm, but they have to leave the farm. Vachel Lindsay, with his "ballads exchanged for bread", attempted a back-to-the-land movement: but it was a wilful oddity, and it left no permanent trace.

All this may seem deliberately insulting to the largest and the most indispensable element in society. But it should be remembered that literature is not the whole of life. In essentials,—health, contentment, moral stamina—the derided bumpkin may be far superior to Baudelaire or Oscar Wilde. We do not believe in the congenital and irremediable inferiority of the peasant type: Zola's worst book, *The Soil,* is a tragic and revolting caricature. In his famous poem on Millet's *Man with the Hoe,* Edwin Markham arraigns the oppressors, who have defaced God's image and reduced that living soul to brutishness.* David Starr Jordan, on the contrary, believed that the Man with the Hoe was biologically such. He had not been forced down, or even kept down: his breed was incapable of rising, and race is a more fundamental factor than environment. No one can accuse Jordan of haughtiness, or lack of human sympathy: of farming stock himself, he was at least as generous a democrat as Markham, and at least as good a poet. But

---

* Incidentally, I do not believe that social satire was the intention of Millet himself. His picture was meant to be pure realism, with the touch of sordid ugliness which, at that time, was considered almost indispensable.

64

as a biologist, he was apt to think strictly in biological terms.

Lord Bryce liked to quote the epigram: "Senators are rich; some are Senators because they are rich; some are rich because they are Senators." The debate between Markham and Jordan might be stated in similar terms: "Peasants are dull-witted: are they dull because they are peasants, or peasants because they are dull?" I am not a biologist, and hardly dare to express an opinion. But, for once, I am inclined to side against Dr. Jordan. The case is not clear: it is difficult to distinguish between irremediable stupidity, and atrophy due to unfavorable circumstances. The political personnel of the Third French Republic compares favorably with that of other leading countries; yet, if we look at the picture of a French Cabinet, we realize that some of those men are barely two generations removed from "the man with the hoe." I have had among my American students promising young men who could have posed for that tragic figure. A breed may seem dull, because it is primitive and inarticulate; yet virgin soil is more fruitful than asphalt, and unrefined ore more valuable than tinsel. But we need not take sides in the debate. The purely agricultural state—a village economy such as still prevails in remote parts of Africa, without any higher organization—would be a total blank on our literary map.

The commercial state offers a much more congenial atmosphere. The most perfect masters of art and literature, the ancient Greeks, and, among the Greeks, the Athenians, were essentially traders. The one important city that scorned commerce, Sparta, also turned its back upon art. Even under Roman supremacy, the Greeks retained their leadership in commerce and culture alike. To be sure, the Phœnicians, more thoroughly commercial than even the Greeks, have left us little art and no literature, while we still read, for their beauty as well as for their spiritual significance, the writings of a non-commercial people, the ancient Hebrews. It might seem flippant to retort that, at any rate, the Phœnicians taught us our letters—writing is a by-product of business; and if the Jews were not commercial-minded in Biblical times, they have gloriously made up for it in the last two thousand years.

In the middle ages, we still find commerce and culture going hand in hand. The Court of Champagne, for instance, shone with particular brilliancy in the thirteenth century. It was the means of introducing the Southern lyric into Northern France, and became the center of those great Romances of Chivalry which provided, at the same time, entertainment and a code of refined breeding. Now the wealth and power of the Counts of Champagne rested upon the great fairs, of international importance, which were held in that province. When the fairs were ruined by the Hundred Years' War, the culture of Champagne went down. Medieval England was mainly agricultural: but the England represented by Chaucer was decidedly commercial. No single city since Athens stood so high in culture as Florence: and Florence was above all a commercial community. The political factions were identified with the trades; and, finally, a dynasty of Bankers, the Medici, became Princes, gave a Pope to Rome and Queens to France. The reigns of Francis I and that of Elizabeth were marked by intense economic activity as well as by artistic splendor.

Objections, naturally, flock to our mind. The two communities in which commerce was frankly paramount, Venice and the Netherlands, have produced great art, but no great poetry. Is it impossible for the lyricist to sing, unless he turns his eyes to the hills? Louis XIV apparently scorned trade; he certainly despised the Dutch, who balked and finally defeated him. But the glory of Louis XIV is inseparable from his magnificence, which would have been impossible without Colbert. When the country was ruined by the King's extravagance, French culture suffered an eclipse. Louis XV might be too kingly to "haggle about peace like a merchant", and a nobleman lost caste if he engaged in trade: but French commerce was expanding all the same, and the financiers played an extremely active part in the society of the Enlightenment.

In the eighteenth and nineteenth centuries, England was supreme in commerce even more than in manufacture. Socially, she might be ruled by the rural gentry: intellectually, London's preëminence was beyond challenge. English art, although creditable, did not lead the world; but English thought and English letters undoubtedly did. New York is not America's political center, nor the historical seat of culture, nor the home of the purest aristocracy, nor is it the heart of a manufacturing region. Its literary leadership, which is unquestioned and almost tyrannical, is based on trade, and on the chief instrument, the ultimate refinement of trade, banking.

The individual artist may and probably should spurn riches — *Pecunia tua tecum sit!* — and riches, even unspurned, may pass him by. Yet it is riches that make art as a whole possible. This is not quite so mercenary as it sounds. We bow before the inevitable, we do not worship it: the purest idealist has to recognize the necessity of food without becoming a glutton or even a gourmand. Commerce, creator of riches, is the essence of our civilization. The city, as soon as it is more than a place of refuge perched on a hill, is essentially a market. Commerce means communication, intercourse, exchange: thoughts are bartered as well as wares, and literature is a commerce of the spirit. Commerce means variety of experience; it brings together town and countryside, and cities which are remote and strange. Commerce means the caravan and the ship, which open a trail of longings and dreams. Commerce is a matching of wits: while the immemorial contention with the ground and the seasons makes the ploughman a part of inanimate nature.

Then the commercial community implies a modicum of freedom. Under barbarism or tyranny, commerce is hampered. As Napoleon grew more despotic, he interfered more heavily with trade. The age in which the commercial ideal was most clearly predominant, the eighteenth century, was also the one that evolved a "liberal" economy and an individualistic philosophy. And it is usually conceded—we shall, however, debate the point in its proper place—that liberty is a favorable condition for literature. Civil and economic liberty, at any rate.

Finally, commerce is linked up with prosperity and

peace. Without commerce, even a fertile agricultural country could not rise above mediocrity. And prosperity, although it may become gross, insolent and deadening, is essential to the elaborate arts. The shepherd may play his pipe in the shade: but a symphony, an edifice, a drama, a romance, imply generous leisure, both for creation and for enjoyment, with the plenty and the security that make that leisure possible.

We have heard so much of the Industrial Revolution, which we date back to the days of James Watt, that we unhesitatingly call our culture that of the Industrial Age. This, in our opinion, is at least premature. The world has never yet lived under a pure industrial state: we are barely entering upon it at present.

By the term *business,* we understand as a rule both industry and commerce; but there is a great difference in method and spirit between the two. In the commercial community, distribution operates on a more elaborate scale than production, and brings larger rewards. The merchant is the true prince. He gathers the labor of the agriculturist or small manufacturer, advertises it to the world, and brings it to market. In the industrial community, production is paramount, marketing is secondary: distribution can be effected without commerce. The point of view is different, and the atmosphere will not be equally favorable to literature in both cases.

Industry in the modern sense, *i.e.,* mechanical mass production, was born only yesterday. Until the end of the nineteenth century, America was still overwhelmingly agricultural and commercial; men who are not yet tottering to their grave may remember the days when our industries were referred to as "infants", in great need of protection. Although France, under Louis XVI, had a faint foreshadowing of modern industry, although she made a conscious start under Napoleon III, she is only at present in process of industrialization, and her spiritual leaders are still protesting against the change. The definite industrialization of Germany does not go back beyond the seventies.

England, of course, has a much longer record. But it is surprising how little the Machine Age affected English thought and English institutions for nearly a century and a half. The Industrial Revolution was not clearly focussed in the public mind until it was named by Arnold Toynbee in 1883. For the greater part of the nineteenth century, the landed aristocracy and the squirarchy wrestled for predominance against the merchants rather than against the manufacturers. The working classes voted for the Manchesterian Liberals, a mercantile class, unless, swayed by Jingoism, they turned to the Tories. When foreign observers thought of England's economic supremacy, it was the City, the Bank, the Exchange, Lloyd's, that first came to their minds: the Black Country afforded only a dim fuliginous background. English civilization was extraordinarily complex —nominally feudal and agrarian at the top, essentially colonial, maritime and financial, and all but unconsciously manufacturing. The novel of industrial life was an exception in the nineteenth century, and remains an exception to-day. Walpole, Galsworthy, Priestly, are still Victorian in this respect. H. G. Well's great romance of modern business life, *Tono-Bungay,* depicts the promoter, the advertiser, the merchandiser, not the manufacturer.

Industry was an ugly, ill-kempt infant. It littered the country with incredible squalor. It brought grime and stench, the tenement instead of the cottage, the *pub* instead of the jolly old inn. No wonder poets and prophets united in cursing the new Horror. The craving for storied Yesterday and glamorous Elsewhere, a legacy of Romanticism, intensified the abhorrence of the artistic mind for the hideous present.

The worst of this reaction is over. We are now able to see the elements of power, and therefore of beauty, that industry has to offer. The most disagreeable infantile ailments have been overcome. Dirt, clatter, discomfort, are not necessarily linked with industrialism. They are wasteful and inefficient. Industry is increasingly clean, sanitary, comfortable. As the superficial, temporary objections are disappearing, the lineaments of the full grown industrial state are becoming discernible.

Commerce, so far, has implied liberty, competition, individualism. Industry, even though her "Captains" may do lip service to the gospel of Adam Smith, — industry is profoundly *collectivistic*. It frowns upon competition, which is waste; and upon individualism, which is incompatible with the best use of the machine. Will standardized efficiency provide a favorable atmosphere for literature?

Industrial conditions present such undeniable advantages that it is idle to deplore them: we are not going to smash our machines, like the Erewhonians. On the other hand, these same conditions are the result of human efforts and can be altered by human efforts: there is no cause for meek or craven acquiescence. Certain it is that the Machine Age, when it is in undisputed sway, will change our environment and affect all our values.

Again, we must not forget that we are still in the transition period. English culture, after a hundred and fifty years, has not been fully industrialized. American culture is traveling faster in that direction, but is very far from having reached the goal. France is hesitant, Italy is facing both ways. Russia alone, all adverse traditions swept aside, is rushing headlong into the full Industrial Age. But rushing is not the same thing as living: Russia's crisis does not give even an inkling of what her art might be under normal Industrialism. All images are blurred in the whirlpool. For a *petit bourgeois* Liberal like Georges Duhamel, America offers "scenes of life in the future" from which he recoils. For the average American hybrid, whose mind is partly rural, partly commercial, rather than industrial, Russia is a hideous menace. The industrial community is still in the making: we dare not mix observation and prophecy. For the literature with which we are familiar, the Commercial State is undoubtedly best. Literature under the industrial dispensation may be no less great, but it will be different.

Chapter 5

THE POLITICAL ENVIRONMENT

Man is a political animal, and the organization of the City can not fail to affect his mode of thinking. Among the circumstances that create "environment" and thus influence literature, Taine naturally included political conditions. He contrasted "the two Italian civilizations", that of ancient Rome, and that of the Renaissance. The land was substantially unchanged; the people, in spite of innumerable migrations, had retained their ancient vigor and many of their physical traits—the artist can still find all the "old Romans" he needs in the poorer districts of modern Rome. But the structure of the state and its international position were radically different.

A first glance will convince us that literature has bloomed under all possible régimes: Greek democracy, Roman Cæsarism, the turbulent municipal aristocracy of medieval Italy, feudal France, the national autocracies of Francis I, Elizabeth, Louis XIV, the acephalous bureaucratic government of Louis XV, the landlord and merchant oligarchy of nineteenth century England. Just as climate kills literature only in extreme cases—the absolute

desert of sand or ice—a political régime has decisive
action only when it assumes the most exaggerated form—
absolute anarchy or absolute despotism. But such cases
are exceptional, and can not be permanent.

So, whatever our own preferences may be, it is safe, so
far as literature is concerned, to disregard mere political
forms. In many cases, the differences between them are
merely questions of vocabulary. The French writers of
the seventeenth century, reasonable and upright men,
spoke of the King in terms which, to us, sound fulsome,
absurd and degrading. But, to them, the King was a
living flag, the symbol of unity at home, and national
greatness. Their "royalism" was not abject servility: it
was exactly what we would call to-day good citizenship
and patriotism. In the nineteenth century, a poet like
Victor Hugo could accommodate himself to several successive régimes: he was not a turncoat or a Vicar of
Bray: he served a permanent reality under changing
symbols.

The distinction between Monarchy and Republic is
among the loosest. A constitutional monarchy of the
English or Belgian type is evidently a crowned Republic;
a dictator like Porfirio Diaz is a monarch except in name.
Ancient Poland, with an elective King, was frequently
referred to as a Republic. *Protector,* like Cromwell,
Stadtholder, like William of Orange, *Regent,* like Horthy,
are ambiguous titles. Napoleon was until 1807, on his
coinage, the *Emperor* of the French *Republic,* a confusion
imitated from Augustus himself. Italy offers the uneasy
shadow of an hereditary constitutional monarchy, all but
obliterated by a vigorous dictatorship.

74

The words *democracy* and *aristocracy,* in political parlance, are even vaguer. American Democrats are aristocratic in the South, demagogic in the North. There may be political democracy combined with social aristocracy: such was for a long time the case in certain South American countries. The constitutions gave all power to the people: in reality, it never left the hands of a few privileged families. In Spain, on the contrary, under the forms of a monarchy, absolute or constitutional, and with the most elaborate aristocratic *étiquette,* there prevailed a spirit of genuine democracy: hidalgo and mendigo are brothers. The terms are vague in their political meaning: but, in culture, they stand for two very definite tendencies. There is a "democratic ideal", an art of the people, for the people, and even perhaps by the people, represented by Dickens, Victor Hugo, Tolstoy; and there is an "aristocratic ideal", an art reserved for the élite, the erudite, the sophisticated—Milton *vs.* John Bunyan. The conflict between them is all important in our subject: but it is a social and spiritual problem rather than a political one.

The essential difference, for our purpose, is that between the *autocratic* and the *liberal* states. (*Authoritarian* would be a more accurate term than *autocratic* and *totalitarian* is now in fashion: but both are so ugly that they can appear only under the veil of a parenthesis.) Autocracy, *i.e.,* irresponsible authority, may be exercised by one man—tyrant, despot, absolute monarch, dictator; by a group, lay or clerical—the jealously closed and all-powerful aristocracy of Venice, the Jesuits in eighteenth century Paraguay; by a party—the French Jacobins, the Bolshevists, the Fascists, the Nazis. In all cases, rigid conformity is enforced: in externals, which is easy enough, but also, as searchingly as possible, in the secret of men's thought. The ideal of the Inquisitorial State is to detect and stifle an incipient heresy before it has come to light: prevent the most minute spark, and there will be no conflagration.

A freethinker under Philip II of Spain, a monarchist and Catholic under the French Terror, a determined *bourgeois* in Moscow, a Communist in Los Angeles, are equally under suspicion that they are "about to think criminally." We borrowed three of our four examples from countries supposedly under popular rule: the Liberal State, on the contrary, may exist under a monarchy, even a nominally absolute one, like that of Louis XVI; under an aristocratic or a *bourgeois* régime; and even under a democracy. The *mores* of a country matter far more than its statute book. "I care not who makes our laws, so long as we are free to write our own songs."

We can hardly escape from the hypothesis that the Inquisitorial State creates a spiritual vacuum in which literature languishes and dies. But, according to our rule, we must allow no hypothesis to pass unchecked.

The first objection that comes to mind is the brilliancy of the Augustan Age. Vergil did not simply happen to be the contemporary of Augustus, and his friend: it was the majestic peace of the Empire that made Vergil possible. His gentle silver voice might not have been heard but for the great hush and repose that came upon the Latin world: "A god himself provided this leisure." The case is not decisive. Obviously order, even at the cost of liberty, is more favorable to certain kinds of achievement than the tumult of civil strife. But the autocracy of Augustus was not complete; it was carefully veiled under the traditional forms of the Republic. The spirit of the vigorous old oligarchy had not been fully emasculated; it survived for several generations. Then the writers of the Augustan Age had received their formation under the preceding era: only by its own fruit, that is to say by a second and third generation, can a régime be adequately tested.

The case of Louis XIV, the French Augustus, is strikingly parallel. Here also, we have undoubted autocracy: "What the King wishes is the law"; "For such is the King's pleasure." Louis XIV had no need to say: "I am the State": no one dared to doubt it aloud, very few doubted it even *in petto*. With that formal autocracy came the most perfect flowering of the French genius, the age of Bossuet, Boileau, La Fontaine, Molière, Racine.

On closer inspection, Louis XIV appears somewhat different from the pure autocrat of popular histories. He had no Parliament in the English sense of the term, and the courts of justice that went by that name did not oppose him as they had opposed Mazarin and were to oppose Louis XVI. He had tamed the unruly nobility, and he rode roughshod over any velleity of popular protest. But, a naturally reasonable, moderate, almost timid man, he did not suppress the privileges that limited his own prerogative. Monarchical France was in fact, if not in theory, a complicated system of traditional checks. The Clergy, with its enormous wealth and influence, was to a large extent a self-governing body. The aristocracy, the judiciary, the provinces, the cities, the guilds and crafts, still clung to their ancient rights, which were not to disappear until the Revolution. France had no written constitution, but she had a jungle of "customs" and charters. Modern Royalist historians may choose to exaggerate this aspect: but they are not wholly wrong. The French king appears as the hereditary Protector of innumerable self-governing associations, rather than as the omnipotent despot.

Then, as in the case of Augustus, we must remember that all the great minds that flourished between 1660 and 1685 had reached maturity before absolutism became unquestioned. The Fronde was still a quivering memory: the young King compelled hastily to flee from his capital, the greatest in the land allied with Spain against their lawful sovereign, the royal cause identified with Mazarin, a despised foreign adventurer. The generation which grew up under the first twenty-five years of the autocracy was of far smaller stature: in fact, the period 1685–1715 may be considered as the decadence of pure classicism. Literature bloomed again in the eighteenth century, under a régime which, theoretically autocratic, had the saving grace of being ineffective, and was liberal at least by fits and starts.

The French Revolution had but one poet, André Chénier, and sent him to the guillotine. It is hardly fair, however, to consider a life-and-death crisis as though it were a permanent régime. Even in America, the war years and the post-war hysteria revealed a great deal of the Inquisitorial spirit, which fortunately melted away when "normalcy" was restored. For the same reason, we can hardly judge of the effect that either Bolshevism or Fascism may have on literature.

Napoleon, a third Augustus, restored internal peace, order, prosperity. He desired to foster art and literature; he reorganized the Institute of France, he offered prizes: all in vain. The genuinely great writers under his reign, Madame de Staël, Joseph de Maistre, Chateaubriand, were his determined opponents, one and all. His official poets sank into depths of inanity hitherto unplumbed: it is an era of tenuous ghosts.

French Republican tradition speaks of the Second Empire in the same terms as of the first: while tyranny prevailed, literature, with Victor Hugo, remained in exile. This is a farcical exaggeration. Quite a number of authors did not leave France; many of them—About, Augier, Taine, Renan, Flaubert, Sainte-Beuve, even George Sand, lived on friendly terms, if not with the Tyrant, at least with his cousins, Prince Napoleon and Princess Mathilde. The Tyrant was a gentle Utopian socialist at heart, and France was spiritually so divided that she had never been so free.

Both Alexander I and Nicholas II of Russia had some of the qualities of Napoleon III, although the second Bonaparte, in our own opinion, was immeasurably superior to either. But, during the greater part of the nineteenth century, under Nicholas I, Alexander II, Alexander III, Tsarism was a genuine autocracy. Yet Russian literature, under these despots, took its place among the noblest in the world. Gogol, however, born in 1809, had been influenced by the liberalism with which Alexander I had toyed; he was ultimately an unconscious victim of the increasing vacuum, and never finished his *Dead Souls*. Dostojewski was sentenced to death for plotting against the régime: if he was later converted to "Holy Russia", at any rate his genius was not rooted in conformity. Turgeniev was by temperament and experience an Occidental, a cosmopolite; he was more at home in the Western capitals than in Moscow. Tolstoy's family had preserved the memory of the Dekabrists; the Count himself turned into a Christian anarchist. Not one of the giants was in any sense a product of the autocracy; their presence only registers the failure of the autocracy to suppress dissent.

It is a curious fact that the scientific mind can accommodate itself to tyranny far better than the literary mind. The tyrant is not hostile to the scientist: except when he enters into conflict with religious dogma, the scientist is harmless. His work is frequently esoteric, inaccessible both to the masses and to the governing class: the power of the despot expires at the door of the laboratory. The literary man on the contrary expresses himself in terms that are "understanded of the people"; and express himself he must. Art is individualism, science seeks the subjection of the individual to absolute laws. The philosophers of the Enlightenment, like Voltaire and Diderot, in so far as they were scientifically minded, had for their ideal a beneficent despot rather than a liberal régime. They had been on friendly terms with Frederick II and Catherine II: their successors rallied to Napoleon. Monge, Berthollet, Lacépède, Lagrange, Chaptal, Cuvier, were among the great personages of the Empire (but not Lamarck, too daring in thought to be *persona grata*).

Napoleon himself liked to pose as one of them, a member of the Scientific Section of the Institute. Renan was torn between his literary and his scientific propensities. When the poet in him had the upper hand, he was a liberal; when the scientist prevailed, he dreamed of a dictatorship exercised by the Academy of Sciences, by means of elaborate methods of torture. The very intelligent group that supported Porfirio Diaz called themselves the *Científicos*.

Perhaps the most favorable conditions are found in the Oppressive State that fails to oppress. Complete liberty may degenerate into license and vulgarity: a man has to shout in order to be heard. Ineffective despotism is an ideal environment for culture. It breeds at least a moderate amount of discontent, thus providing an incentive to criticism and therefore to thought. In America, we were until recently so perfectly satisfied with the general principles of our Constitution that our political thought had become atrophied: politics had become a battleground for second-rate personalities and ephemeral issues. We were all so free to think that we did not care to think at all: Abbé Dimnet's charming little book on *The Art of Thinking* came to us with the freshness of a revelation. If we had a "tyrant", he would give us something to think about.

Opposition to despotism creates in us a sense of daring, adventure, heroism. This is particularly welcome to the literary mind, which thrives on exaltation and loves attitudinizing. Victor Hugo never was so well pleased with himself as when he penned the defiant line:

Et s'il n'en reste qu'un, je serai celui-là! *

* And if only one remains (irreconcilable), I shall be that one!

Then "oppression" compels us to use finer tactics and keener weapons, the rapier of allusive irony rather than the bludgeon of blatant assertiveness. This sharpens the wit of author and public alike: the reader watches intently for veiled epigrams, and, in his eagerness, supplies them if they are wanting. Controversy was carried on a very dignified plane under the Second Empire. At the top, there was a very gentle Tyrant; under him, a vast and rather stupid police. Thought was not stifled: but direct insults were barred out. Either the writer had to be satisfied with the discussion of general principles, or he had to use subtler methods than vituperation. France learned a great deal in those days about "Tiberius"; Soulouque, Emperor of Hayti, attracted a disproportionate amount of notice. In the last few months of the régime, the ban was lifted, and vulgarity rushed in like a turbid flood. There were still traces of urbanity in Rochefort's weekly pamphlet, *La Lanterne,* under the Tyranny; there was none in his shrieking *Marseillaise.* Clemenceau, a ruthless censor while he was waging war, had, unconsciously, a refining influence upon journalistic style. I remember a delightful article in a Socialist paper denouncing the oppressive methods of "Lenin": every reader mentally substituted "Clemenceau" and chuckled. Perhaps the Tiger himself grinned. We should thank the Power that compels us to whisper instead of shouting. It is excellent training.

From this somewhat paradoxical point of view, the most favorable age was that of Louis XV. Then ineffectual oppression fostered both true liberty and delicate wit. The great men of the time were alternately petted, admired, feared, imprisoned. When they heard a carriage stop at their door, they never knew whether it was to take them to the Bastille, or to a supper party with the highest in the land. Voltaire, Diderot, Rousseau, knew such exhilarating alternatives. The *Encyclopaedia,* officially confiscated and destroyed, was safely stored against a better day by the very authorities that were supposed to suppress it; it was enjoyed privately by the King in whose name it had been condemned. *Philosophy* had to be supplied through ingenious bootlegging methods, which whetted the natural craving of mankind. In our own country, censorship has repeatedly played the part of the ineffective despot, thus sharpening our taste for literature that is not primitive. But for a providential censor, the general public might never have heard of James Branch Cabell. Now that it can be sold openly, *Ulysses,* an enormous and difficult book, is not likely to have such earnest readers as in the golden days of its outlawry. Boston, in condemning *Candide,* restored freshness to a masterpiece, a task that no professor and very few critics could have achieved.

Inefficient tyranny, better than sheer anarchy, is also far better than a *reasonable* régime: for reasonableness means the dictatorship of the dull. But it must be inefficient, and unfortunately such is not always the case. To say that the spirit invariably triumphs is unwarranted optimism. Even the cautious qualification "in the long run" will not make the assertion quite safe. We know, as a matter of record, that a number of masterpieces have survived persecution: we have no means of knowing how many potential masterpieces have been silently strangled in the

83

dark. The Middle Ages as a whole, Italy after the Renaissance, Spain after the *Siglo de Oro,* Russia and America in the nineteenth century, the English stage from Queen Anne to its very recent revival, all give us a feeling of frustration. The elements of greatness were there in abundance: they should have yielded a richer crop. A blight was at work: spiritual oppression, under various forms, had gone beyond the point where it could be stimulating.

The tyranny of one man, or of a small group, is seldom crushing for any length of time. Except during brief crises, it is rather bracing. The tyranny of the many is far deadlier. You can dodge a sword, if you are nimble enough: you can not escape the invisible, ubiquitous, insidious censorship of Mrs. Grundy. This is a mere restatement of our previous position: *mores* matter more than statute book, social conditions more than political forms.

Chapter 6

THE SOCIAL ENVIRONMENT

I

THE only examples of "social conditions" given by Taine are two religious movements, Christianity and Buddhism: evidently the word "social" covers a multitude of virtues. We shall take it in the more usual sense, which implies the division and relations between classes. But, out of respect for our guide, and not merely on that account, we must devote some attention to religion as a part of the social environment.

In many cases, the religious factor takes precedence over all the rest. When we evoke the Middle Ages, we think of them as Christian first of all, not as feudal. Spain, in our mind, is Catholic, rather than Iberian (whatever that may mean), or peninsular, or semi-African, or imperial. And many interpretations of American culture have been offered, with reverence or derision, in terms of the Puritan spirit.

We have therefore no desire to belittle the religious element. But, as in the case of politics, we find that it does not depend upon any particular form. Just as all kinds of poetry may thrive under King or President, all kinds flourish also under priest or presbyter. Any collection of world classics will contain the works of Pagans, Jews, Catholics, Protestants and Free Thinkers. Prophet and Psalmist, Homer, Plato and Lucretius, the Norse Sagas, Dante and Pascal, Milton and Wordsworth, Blake and Shelley, Rabelais and Rousseau, down to H. L. Mencken and G. K. Chesterton, all have their niche, great or small, in our Pantheon. Nor would it be easy, in many cases, to classify authors according to their religious affiliation.

It is a sobering thought to consider how little our culture has been affected by our nominal faith. The Western world was conquered by a religion which condemned violence and spurned riches: but after nineteen hundred years, it shows little willingness to renounce either. Theoretically, a fatalistic creed should benumb and demoralize those who profess it. But the Calvinism of the Huguenots, the Jansenism of Pascal, the scientific determinism of Taine himself, led to a renewed austerity of life and a more intense vigor of purpose. There seems to be no stronger will than the will which denies its own freedom.

Madame de Staël claimed that Romanticism and Protestantism went together, since both exalted the individual at the expense of established authority; Classicism and Catholicism, on the other hand, were both founded on formal discipline and reverence for the past. There is some truth in that contention. Yet Romanticism was marked by a great revival of Catholic fervor, not only in France, but in Germany. No one could have more of the Romantic quality—the lone venture of an intrepid soul—

than the Catholic mystics, such as Santa Teresa. No one could be more meekly submissive to a traditional orthodoxy and a definite ritual than many conservative Protestants.

So far as culture is concerned, the same difference exists in religion as in politics between the Inquisitorial and the Liberal State. However lofty the faith, if rigidly imposed, it will have a deteriorative influence. It is not Islam that has paralyzed the Arabic world, nor Greek orthodoxy that has hampered Russia, nor Catholicism that has blighted Spain, nor Protestantism that has benumbed large classes in America. It is, in all cases, *l'Infâme,* Intolerance, against which Voltaire waged his lifelong crusade. No religion, not even the weirdest sect in Southern California, can kill art and literature; fanaticism, if unchecked, would do it. Atheistic fanaticism, of course, is no whit better than the rest.

The great centers and the great eras of culture were those in which no single faith wielded exclusive power. In England, the Establishment has never been able to destroy either Catholicism or Dissent; in the eighteenth century came the Deists; in the nineteenth, scientific agnosticism. America started her national life in the free spirit of the Enlightenment. In spite of the clamor of a few fanatics, the Protestant majority shows no desire to disfranchise heretics. France is known as a Catholic country: but, since the Renaissance, four religious traditions have been contending, the Gallican, the Ultramontane, the Protestant, and the free Naturistic faith of Rabelais, Molière, Hugo, Zola—a spiritual family not to be despised. The varieties of religious experience are even more numerous than the sects; and they do not coincide with the sects.

With these words of caution, we are free to admit that the religious atmosphere is of commanding importance for the student of literature. Favorably or adversely, it affects every author who has a soul, even one, like Théophile Gautier, for whom only the external world exists. Every one follows a guidance, wrestles with an angel, or is pursued by the nemesis of a faith. Taine himself was tragically torn. French Rationalism, German Idealism, English Empiricism, the historical spirit that urged the acceptance of Christianity, the experimental method which suggested the agnostic attitude, all strove for his allegiance. He never was able to harmonize Descartes, Hegel, Bacon, Bossuet, Darwin; and, after giving offence to all parties, he sought refuge in the compromise of a Protestant burial.

It is a question whether the religious factor has ever been quite so potent as the national. Every religious war in modern times had a political background. It was not Catholicism that was defeated with the Armada, it was Spain. It was not Popery that was driven from the throne in 1688, but absolutism; it was not Rome and Calvin that fought in sixteenth century France, but aristocratic factions, the Guises, the Colignys, the Bourbons, the Condés. His Most Christian Majesty Francis I allied himself with Turks and Protestants against the leader of European Catholicism, Charles V; Richelieu and Mazarin, princes of the Church, pursued the same policy. If willing martyrdom be the test of faith, then Patriotism in the modern world has millions of martyrs to Christianity's hundreds. When the two rival creeds come to an open clash, as in the question of taking the sword, conscientious objectors (not all of them on Christian grounds) are in a pitiful minority. Mankind is still worshipping tribal gods. And those gods are athirst.

II

As a rule, the words *social conditions* evoke the idea of *classes*. When we speak of a man's social environment, we think of the circles in which he moves familiarly, of the class to which he belongs. The social environment for literature in general means the structure of society, its formal or loose division into classes.

There have been many different social systems in human experience; and there seem to be no fewer in the animal world. At one extreme, we find a régime of rigid classes, with impassable barriers between them. Rigidity can not be complete without hereditary distinctions, and the classes thus hardened from generation to generation are called *castes*. At the other end, we find Shelley's ideal:

> The loathsome mask has fallen, the man remains
> Sceptreless, free, uncircumscribed, but man
> Equal, unclassed, tribeless and nationless,
> Exempt from awe, worship, degree, the king
> Over himself. . .

A beautiful dream, when expressed in Shelley's words; in the eyes of most, a dream; in the eyes of some, not even beautiful. Between these two poles, endless variety prevails. The classes may be so fluid that their very existence may be questioned, as in *White* America; or they may commingle with such difficulty that they almost amount to castes, as in pre-war Prussia. There may be an un-challenged hierarchy of classes, as in nineteenth century England, where every one, thank God, *knew his place;* or there may be open conflict. There may exist a division and balance of power between the classes, or one element may definitely predominate—the aristocracy in old Hun-gary, the middle class in France, the proletariat in Soviet Russia.

Social conditions are easily confused with political conditions. Many of the words in—*cracy,* aristocracy, mesocracy, democracy, offer that ambiguity.* Ideally, the social and the political régimes should be in such close harmony that they might be considered one and the same. Practically, such harmony has hardly ever prevailed. On the eve of the French Revolution, the State was officially an autocracy, with a theocratic foundation and an aristo-cratic coloring; in fact, it was a *bourgeois* bureaucracy, with the nobles as splendid parasites, and the king as an impressive, heavily gilded figurehead. Society, at the same time, was formally dominated by the aristocracy: but its vital power was found in the rich middle class. The most enlightened protectors of the arts, the friends of the *Philosophes,* were financiers. The Marquis de Marigny, whose delicate and generous taste had such an influence on that exquisite period, was a Marquis by the grace of his sister, the Marquise de Pompadour, *née* Poisson, a *bourgeoise.* Madame Geoffrin could not have been pre-sented at Court; but she had her own social realm of the

* However, autocracy, theocracy, technocracy, necrocracy, have no so-cial implications.

Rue Saint-Honoré; artists, poets, philosophers, flocked to her gatherings; foreign princes fondly called her *Maman,* and, returning to their thrones, felt themselves in exile. In a word, the political régime was an absurdity in terms of the social régime; and both were absurd from the point of view of the prevailing doctrines: for the gospel preached by Jean-Jacques Rousseau, and eagerly accepted by the liberal *bourgeoisie,* was undiluted democracy. Confusion could hardly be worse confounded.

It *did* get worse confounded, however, when the word *social* became chiefly connected with the nature of property; when, by the *social* question, men understood the conflict between capitalism and some form of communism. The Social Democrats are not necessarily more socially inclined than other parties; in *The Social Register* and *The Social Revolution,* the word is obviously used in radically different meanings. Until Socialism became the most vital of our problems, class distinctions had very little to do with the various conceptions of property. Although there were survivals of feudalism in France as late as 1789 and in other parts of Europe for several decades longer, all classes accepted individual ownership as a natural and sacred right. The peasant in his field, the artisan in his little workshop, the merchant great or small, the industrialist, the aristocratic landowner, were all of one mind on that point. No difference in wealth, culture, birth or graces, could alter that fundamental unanimity, which, even to-day, is barely shaken in America. Many plebeians, rich or poor, could not be more passionately attached to a régime of private ownership if they belonged to the most ancient aristocracy;

and, among socialist leaders, there are men who came from the upper middle class and even from the nobility. It can hardly be disputed that a proletarian régime would seriously influence our culture. Leon Trotsky has devoted to the problem of *Literature and Revolution* a singularly able and no less singularly inconclusive book. But the new class division, capitalist *versus* proletarian, by no means coincide with the familiar hierarchy, aristocracy, middle class, manual laborers.

Finally, to make confusion absolutely inextricable, class names are frequently used to denote differences in taste. *Aristocratic* stands for *refined; bourgeois,* for *commonplace* and *mediocre; popular,* for *cheap* and *vulgar.* This is not merely insulting: it is woefully inaccurate. The art patronized by the aristocracy may very well be coarse or insipid. As Matthew Arnold noted, the nobles, as long as they retained their separate existence, remained to a large extent Barbarians. There is no proof that the fox-hunting squire, or the Prussian Junker, were particularly urbane and delicate in their æsthetic appreciation. The *popular,* whether springing from the people like the old ballads, or appealing to the people like *Les Misérables,* is not necessarily low. And, throughout the centuries, the middle class has provided the most enlightened element in society.

This triple confusion is best exemplified by the various acceptations of the word *bourgeois.** From its original sense of *city dweller,* the term came to mean *middle class citizen,* as opposed to the non-urban elements, the aristoc-

---

* For a fuller discussion of this term, *cf. Beyond Hatred: Mesocracy in France.*

racy and the peasants. The *bourgeoisie,* not the nobility, was ever since the Middle Ages the mainstay of the French state, and the center of literary activity. But its political supremacy was not officially recognized until 1830, with Louis-Philippe, the Citizen King. With political triumph came spiritual loss of caste: the Romanticists, most of them *bourgeois* themselves, made the word a substitute for Philistine. *Epater le bourgeois*—to flabbergast the Babbitt—was the first duty of every self-respecting artist. The hosier and the grocer were singled out as particularly offensive. Yet William Blake, the perfect incarnation of extreme Romanticism, was the son of a hosier. No one could be more aristocratically disdainful of the Beotian than Ernest Renan: and his mother kept a village grocery store.

Then Marxism made *bourgeois* synonymous with capitalist. For the Marxian, a duke and a wealthy artist are both *bourgeois.* For the artist, King Louis-Philippe and Prince Albert, of the most aristocratic blood in Europe, were hopeless *bourgeois.* I have had a few glimpses of orthodox socialist households, and they were most *bourgeois* of all. There is no case in which it is more indispensable to define our terms.

The classic example of the caste system is furnished by India. Once again, to our shame and regret, we must be satisfied with a question mark. We are not sufficiently familiar, even at second-hand, with the literature of that country to trace any connection between its social structure and its cultural achievements; and we know that our *a priori* sympathies are not to be trusted. A caste system has been repeatedly advocated by men who were great artists: Plato, of course, in his *Republic,* and, a long way behind, Fénelon in his *Telemachus.* Oddly enough, Plato, it will be remembered, banished poets from his orderly state; and there is no promise that the Salentum of Fénelon would produce any great art or great poetry. Aldous Huxley, in his *Brave New World,* gives a Swiftian satire of a scientific commonwealth, biologically divided into castes. Such an environment, in his opinion, would be deadly to all æsthetic values. These literary examples prove very little. On the whole, the sentiment seems to prevail that castes are unfavorable to art; but that sentiment has not hardened into firm belief.

Such an opinion, if it were adopted, could easily be supported by theoretical arguments. A caste-bound world is an immovable world, and therefore likely to be a stupid one: if your chief desire is to prevent change, you must first of all prevent thought. Hard and fast divisions create either sullen resentment or stolid resignation below, inane pride and sloth above: in either case, they are hardly conducive to achievement. The case would be strong, if theories by themselves could carry conviction.

Slavery is one form of the caste system. Antiquity had slaves, and produced art and literature that we still revere. But antiquity preserved a paradoxical kind of cultural democracy: a slave could be a teacher, a philosopher, a poet.

America, both British and Iberian, offered that aggravated form of caste in which social differences are emphasized by race, and indelibly marked by color. Yet culture did not perish among the slave-owners. It is difficult, however, to consider the instance as decisive.

Slavery, as an essential factor in the life of the Southern States, prevailed for barely a hundred years: the attitude of the Revolutionary Fathers on that question was far less bigoted than that of the cotton planters on the eve of Secession. A century is a brief moment in human history.

It can hardly be denied that the effect of slavery on the Negro mind was detrimental: it is highly to the credit of the race that the prolonged ordeal did not wholly destroy its spirit. The subordination, even when it was no longer called slavery, of the Indian element in Mexico and South America, coming after ages of a native caste system, has benumbed the Indian soul: its restoration to normal activity is almost a desperate venture. The whites in both continents are faced with the same problem as Tolstoy's hero in *Resurrection*.

The effect on the dominant caste had certainly not been wholly good. We have repeatedly expressed our affectionate admiration for the Southerners, among whom we spent many happy years; and we have valued friends among South Americans of pure Iberian descent. It always seemed to us that they had not done themselves full justice. They came from the best stock in Europe; they had excellent traditions of culture; they had leisure and wealth; their own contribution, exquisite at times, has been somewhat meager. And we must add that the South remained in close intellectual contact both with England and with the North; Iberian America remained linked both with Spain and with France. Whatever degree of civilization they maintained was not wholly autonomous.

In modern Europe, the caste system has never fully

prevailed. Society in the Middle Ages was stiffly hierarchized: but, just as philosophy in the ancient world
could transcend even the spirit of slavery, Christianity in
our era was able to override or at least to qualify serfdom
and feudalism. The first order in the land was not the
hereditary nobility, but the clergy, recruited from all
classes. If there was a constant tendency to reserve the
highest ecclesiastical dignities to the well-born, that
tendency was never accepted in theory, nor did it entirely
prevail in practice. A commoner could become Abbot or
Bishop; a swineherd, according to popular tradition, was
one of the greatest Popes. The essentially democratic
character of Christianity, Ebionism, the Gospel preached
to the poor, was never wholly forgotten. Bossuet gave
before an aristocratic congregation a sermon on "the
eminent dignity of the poor."

Although no one will insist more than an Englishman
on "good blood" and the hereditary principle, the British
aristocracy never was a closed caste. The younger sons of
younger sons would by slow degrees merge with the
gentry and even relapse into the common people; at all
times, energetic commoners could rise in the social scale,
and ultimately reach the peerage. This process was greatly
accelerated by the economic triumph of the commercial
element in the eighteenth and early nineteenth centuries.
To-day, the descendants of belted earls sit at Westminster
on the same benches as bankers, brewers, and newspaper
barons.

In France, society had a tendency to stiffen on the eve
of the Revolution, and that very stiffening was one of
the direct causes of the great upheaval. Under Louis XVI,

it would have been difficult for Bossuet to receive a bishopric, or Vauban a Field Marshal's baton. But, for hundreds of years previously, much greater fluidity had prevailed. The King's service was the stair by which *bourgeois,* in a few generations, could ascend to the highest nobility. The whole Colbert connection tried to forget the linendraper of Rheims, their forefather, and were granted magnificent titles. Many functions and distinctions carried noble rank with them; aristocratic privileges could actually be bought; and *mésalliances,* although frowned upon, were not unheard of, even in princely families. In the nineteenth century, the exclusive character of the nobility belongs to the realm of polite fiction. All that can be said is that titles still command a premium on the matrimonial market: the aristocratic son-in-law is a stock character in light comedy.

What about the classless world prophesied by Shelley? It has not come to pass even in Russia: else the "class war" would be over, and the "dictatorship of the proletariat" an absurdity. Has it been realized in America? In theory, no doubt: all immigrants are requested to leave their titles behind as they pass through Ellis Island. In practice, the class fluidity which exists in England and in France is even greater in America. But the class ideal, attenuated, half-ashamed of itself, still survives. We need not refer to its most virulent manifestation, color prejudice: we firmly believe that this deplorable feeling is social, not racial, in its origin. But it is found also within the ranks of our White, Nordic and Protestant rulers. There are local centers of resistance to unqualified democracy: many spots in the old South, the First Families of Virginia, the

Daughters of the American Revolution, the Back Bay dynasties of Boston, and, only yesterday, the ghosts of Washington Square, evoked by Mrs. Wharton. Plutocracy is not absolutely irresistible; there are a few strongholds of "Society", beleaguered, indomitable, that can not be forced by any million-dollar artillery.

Until the Post-War Era, when the floodgates that guarded higher education burst open, a degree from a dozen privileged institutions was still vaguely equivalent to a patent of gentlemanliness. Not a few people subject their children to Latin, and, themselves, feign unlimited enthusiasm for golf, because both are examples of conspicuous waste, and appurtenances of the leisure class. During our great Crusade for Democracy, temporary gentlemen by act of Congress were taught to behave offensively to their subordinates: all social intercourse was prohibited between officers and privates, although the example of the French army proved that snobbishness was not essential to discipline. It is openly acknowledged that certain religious denominations enjoy greater social prestige than others. There is profound significance in the folklore saga of Mr. and Mrs. Jiggs: American womanhood is dedicated to the great task of re-creating social distinctions in Lincoln's Republic. The belief that "a man is a man for a' that" is not ingrained in the American mind. We are far less ready to acknowledge social superiorities than are the British or even the French. No true-born American will freely proclaim: "I belong to the lower *bourgeoisie*." But when it comes to asserting our own social superiorities, we challenge the field.

We are intimately persuaded that the spirit of social

distinction is one of the strongest factors in civilization, and, less directly, in culture. In another part of this book, we shall attempt to discuss in some detail the influence of that spirit upon literary production. But we do not believe that spirit to be ineradicable. Certainly the old castes have almost entirely vanished, and the old classes are losing ground. Constant efforts are made to revivify them through an injection of alleged science: but there are serious chances that we shall escape the *Brave New World* with which Aldous Huxley is impishly threatening us.

Even in the interpretation of the past, we are far from claiming that the *class* idea provides a magic key. There are some forms of literature that bear unmistakably the imprint of one class: but even they have been appreciated by the other classes as well. It is most probable that *bourgeois* and common people, in the Middle Ages, enjoyed the fighting epics and the love lyrics that mirrored the life of their *betters*. Conversely, there is every reason to believe that the feudal baron chuckled over the merry tale, or roared at the broad farce of strictly popular origin. Molière made sport of the courtiers while some were sitting, not merely among the spectators, but on the very stage. The aristocracy applauded furiously *Figaro's Wedding,* a brilliant attack against their own privileges. Bunyan has been read in castle halls, and Milton in the backshop. There is a thorough democracy of the nursery tale; even the "sophisticates" are drawn from all ranks; while supreme greatness ignores the barriers of caste.

Chapter 7

THE MOMENT (TIME AND TRADITION)

RACE, according to Taine's conception, is practically independent of time. Elaborated through "myriads of centuries", it remains unaffected by mere historical periods. Climate, by which we mean all the data of physical geography, does alter indeed, but only with geologic slowness. All the other factors in environment change very perceptibly with time. The desert can be made to blossom like the rose, forests can be cleared, marshes drained, lakes created, rivers diverted, in a single generation. Empires melt away, religions lose their hold, social classes are subjected to violent transformations, in the course of a few decades. If we want to define a people's civilization, it is not sufficient to find out what their blood is, and what land they inhabit, but also at what *time* they live. "Truth on the hither side of the Pyrenees," said Pascal, "error beyond." Even more obviously could we assert: "Truth yesterday, error to-day." So the third factor in Taine's formula is *le moment,* which is usually translated by *time.*

But time is an ambiguous word, and does not render

accurately what Taine had in mind. *Time* adds nothing real to *environment:* for environment exists only in time. If you describe the time of Samuel Johnson, you describe his environment, and *vice versa.*

In order to establish a distinction between the two, we might restrict *environment* to the personal circumstances of the writer, and reserve *time* for those more general factors which affect whole groups of contemporaries. Environment would be treated anecdotically, time historically. We may consider the facts of Samuel Johnson's experience, his birth at Lichfield, his education, his life in London, as his environment; eighteenth century England as his time. But the distinction soon breaks down. The central character and the background are part of the same picture.

Boswell was not an unconscious forerunner of Taine: he told us all that he knew about Dr. Johnson simply because he was deeply interested in Dr. Johnson. He did not fail to describe Johnson's earliest environment; and he himself calls our attention upon the fact that the environment depends upon the time:

> His (Johnson's) father is there (on the parish register) styled *Gentleman,* a circumstance of which an ignorant panegyrist has praised him for not being proud; when the truth is, that the appellation of gentleman, though now lost in the indiscriminate assumption of *Esquire,* was commonly taken by those who could not boast of gentility.

At the *time* of Johnson's birth, the word gentleman had a wider meaning than at the *time* when Boswell was writing. Again:

His mother was Sarah Ford, descended of an ancient race of substantial yeomanry in Warwickshire.

What was the connotation of yeomanry in those days? We can not understand the social status of the Johnson family unless we know the social structure of eighteenth century England.

Mr. and Mrs. Thrale, Garrick, Goldsmith, Reynolds, Boswell himself were members of the inner circle; but there were many concentric rings, with no hard and fast division between them. A larger one would take in Chesterfield; George III himself would have to be included. Where does *environment* give place to *time?*

It has been suggested that the economic and social conditions constitute *environment,* the political conditions constitute *time.* Johnson's England was still dominated by the squirarchy but saw the rapid development of the commercial classes and the rise of industry: that is *environment.* Under the nominal rule of the Hanoverian line, it was governed by such men as Walpole, Chatham, North: that is *time.* This distinction seems to us to repose on two antiquated ideas.

The first is that, in history, social and political elements can be separated. Nothing of the kind: not exclusively dynasties, ministries, battles, treaties, belong to history, but economic and intellectual transformations as well. Voltaire was aware of this nearly two hundred years ago, and it were well if the "New Historians" would learn the lesson.

The second delusion is to a large extent the result of the first. Because, for many centuries, political changes were recorded while social changes were not, we are still under the impression that social conditions are quasi-permanent (environment), and political conditions in a constant flux (moment or time). The facts tell a different story. No doubt a nation may scrap its constitution twelve times in three generations, like France between 1789 and 1875, while its economic and social life is not correspondingly modified. But it is perfectly possible also for the social régime to evolve far more rapidly than the political. The forms of English Parliamentary government are substantially the same to-day as in the eighteenth century: but in the meantime, England has gone through a couple of *social* revolutions or rather renovations. The American Constitution is nearly a hundred and fifty years old: our present social-economic régime—the definite subordination of agriculture, mass production in industry, world leadership in finance, the passing of anarchical individualism, the waning of the Puritanical ascendancy, —came to full consciousness only in this generation. This will become increasingly apparent, as we take the habit of considering a masterpiece, a scientific discovery, the invention of a new process, the opening of a market, as no less worthy of a place in history than the Hayes-Tilden or the Harding-Cox contests.

The literal translation *moment* would hardly be more satisfactory. For the usual meaning of *moment* is the instant, the mere flash of time. "A historical moment" would be a snapshot, a still picture, the characters standing immobile on a motionless background. On the contrary, with *time,* Taine wanted to introduce the sense of motion, of change. The same factors, taken statically, form the environment; taken dynamically, they constitute time. We may call this, with the Hegelians, the concept of *becoming;* we may call it *evolution;* more plainly, *history*.

This implies, not merely the fact of change, but change as the result of a force moving in a definite direction. This force Taine calls "acquired velocity": literally *momentum*. If we may use an Einsteinian expression with which the readers of Sunday papers are all familiar, we exist in a space-time continuum. We are not time-less or instantaneous: duration is as indispensable to our existence as dimensions. We can not be thought of without air to breathe or soil upon which to rest our feet: neither can we be thought of without our yesterdays. Shall we add: and without our to-morrows?

It is tempting to assume, as we all do without reflection, that time flows evenly and for all things alike. But this is true only of *conventional time,* as measured by our watches, or by those cosmic chronometers, the revolutions of the heavenly bodies. If we were all carried by the stream of time at the same rate, we would not be conscious of change. Nothing in my room gives me the sense that I am hurled through space at an incredible speed: all the familiar objects remain placidly at their wonted place. It is the unevenness of motion alone that makes motion perceptible. Similarly, time exists for us only because things move at a different tempo. If a whole generation grew old evenly, homogeneously, all keeping the same pace, without contact with a new generation, it would never know it is growing old. If, in a civilization, institutions and beliefs evolved in absolute harmony, preserved exactly the same relation to one another, they would appear to be eternal. But creeds, laws, manners, techniques, wax and wane each in its own fashion. They combine into patterns that are incessantly altering. It is this endless series of dissolving views that we call history, and that gives us the sense of time.

This sense of time is the very essence of *human* culture. Science, in a way, is unhuman. It thinks in light-years, in geological ages, in countless generations. Its time-scale is so enormous, so different from the minute time-scale of human experience, that there is hardly any common measure between them: science seems to be dealing with the eternal. In the eyes of science, two thousand years lend no authority to an error, like the Ptolemaic system: it is but a discarded hypothesis. In art and literature, two thousand years constitute a triumphant "test of time", and amount to immortality.

There is therefore a kind of radicalism inherent in scientific thought. Whatever science believes to be true must be true *in itself,* in terms of to-day as well as of yesterday. Culture is historical: the present exists only in its relation with the past. Science can evolve at any moment a new code of symbols: culture can only alter, but never wholly discard, its inherited modes of expression. Even James Joyce, in his *Work in Progress,* must keep in contact, at least intermittently, with the traditions of the English language.

Tradition!: we have uttered the key-word, perhaps the shibboleth, of all culture: "the best that has been thought and said. . ." always a *has been.* Education consists in preserving and transmitting that heritage; good taste, in conforming to its norm. A *gentleman* is a man with a past: the immediate past of good schooling and favorable home influences; the remoter past of a good ancestry; and the whole past of the race at his command, under the name of culture. The plebeian, the vulgarian, is, as in Rome, *homo novus,* a *new* man.

It would seem like irony if we were to defend the advantages of traditional culture: so plain are they—to every *cultured* mind. It is evidently a benefit to the world that Homer, Plato, Vergil, Dante, have not been allowed to die. The language of every educated man is an unconscious mosaic of allusions; even his random thoughts are laden with the wisdom of the ages. This gives to *literature* worthy of the name a depth of resonance, a richness of harmonics, that plain speech does not possess: imagine Milton or Anatole France without the majestic perspective of their background.

Tradition does not merely preserve masterpieces, isolated and entire, or absorbed into the general thought: it nourishes and enriches the masterpieces themselves. Great works grow after their author's death. Meaning is poured into them; new illustrations are brought forth; their obscurities are elucidated, in ways that the writer may never have dreamed of; every imitation, every quotation from them, every allusion to them, establishes a new contact and brings in new life. The Bible as literature becomes broader and deeper with the centuries: Milton, Blake, Carlyle, Kipling, have created new overtones; even the shrill pipe of Voltaire or Cabell adds an unexpected and subtle note to the magnificence of the concert.

Shakespeare, if he were to take a Shakespeare course in one of our colleges, would be astounded at the profundity of his own *Hamlet;* or rather *Hamlet* is no longer his own: it belongs to innumerable scholars, poets, philosophers, the greatest of whom is Goethe. Similarly, Unamuno's *Don Quijote* shows how much the Knight of the Dismal Countenance has grown in spiritual stature since the days of Cervantes. Molière's *Tartuffe* and his *Misanthrope* have acquired a multitudinous life. The best example of such enrichment is Mona Lisa. Her smile is the symbol of mysteries to which Walter Pater has devoted one of the most elaborate pages in the golden book of English prose. But the mysteries need not have been in Leonardo's mind. They are the sum total of the dreams of ten generations—an increment not entirely earned. In probing the painter's intentions, we have multiplied them a hundredfold. Such is the *momentum* of culture.*

This may become even plainer if we try the counter test, if we examine those books which have failed to grow. A crucial example is offered by the French Bible. In England, the Bible has become a standard for the vernacular; it has generously given of its treasures to all comers, but it has received much in return. When we read the Bible, an innumerable accompaniment of dimly recollected poems, hymns, prayers, sermons, phrases, even homely anecdotes and family happenings, turn the Book into a symphony as rich as life. In France, the Bible has not become rooted in the literary soil; it has remained, for believers, a sacred book; for non-believers, an exotic book.

---

* "On a somewhat lower social plane, she might be a rapacious landlady at the seaside, hopeful of making a favourable impression upon her prospective lodger but quite determined that she shall get decidedly the better of the bargain." Clifford Bax, *Leonardo*, p. 122.

Its grandest imagery appears strange, excessive, Oriental
in character. A few great writers, Bossuet, Racine in his
last two tragedies, Lamennais, Victor Hugo, were steeped
in the Bible. But the inexhaustible lore of Biblical
allusions, reverent or familiar, even frankly humorous at
times, which is part of the English heritage, is sealed to
the French. The French Bible has not *grown*.

Another example from the religious literature of France.
The Huguenots had two great poets, Du Bartas and
Agrippa d'Aubigné. Both wrote on an ambitious scale,
with deep earnestness, and with no lack of spirit. At
present, Du Bartas's epic, *The Week*, is mentioned merely
as an oddity of literature; and, although belated justice
has been done to d'Aubigné's magnificent poem, *The
Tragics*, it has not taken its place among living masterpieces. Every child knows those uninspired rhymesters,
Malherbe and Boileau: only a student looks into
d'Aubigné. Why? Because both the sect to which these
writers belonged, and the literary school they represented,
went down in defeat at the end of the sixteenth century.
The Huguenots, after Henry IV's abjuration, were
doomed to remain a hopeless, isolated, distrusted
minority; the style of the Renaissance, daring, extravagant,
but gorgeously alive, was sacrificed to the clearness, logic
and taste of neo-classicism. Those two poets were debarred from founding a tradition: so with every decade
their language became more antiquated, their obscurities
more obscure, their oddities more shocking. Goethe recognized in Du Bartas a great poet: French critics consider
this judgment as a lapse of taste: "Even a Goethe," they
say, "is no competent judge of a literature not his own."

Both opinions are defensible. Du Bartas was *potentially* a great poet: but circumstances killed those potentialities. His fame did not acquire momentum.

It may be more profitable to insist upon the dangers of tradition than upon its benefits. More profitable, but no whit more original: for the iconoclastic tradition itself is a hoary one. The iconoclastic path, however, is evidently the more perilous, and should be traveled upon with greater care.

If tradition keeps masterpieces alive, it also cumbers the ground with fossils. Not for all time: but for too long a time. Tradition becomes a *necrocracy,* a graveyard government; it makes for a purely retrospective culture, a museum civilization. In its veneration for the antique, it imparts artificial dignity to the antiquated.

In my childhood, I was a constant visitor in the Louvre Museum (I confess I ran through the picture galleries as fast as the slippery floors would allow, in order to reach my real goal, the Naval Collection). Many decades later, back from the Wild West, I was suddenly struck with the dinginess, the pomposity, the commonplaceness of three "old masters" out of four; and I began to see a gleam of sense in Courbet's sally (was it Courbet's?) that the Louvre ought to be burned down. Tradition too sedulously cultivated leads to decadence. We must constantly make an effort to break loose from the necropolis, the library, the museum, and rediscover the world for ourselves.

Momentum, the constant enrichment of the human mind, is a blessed fact in a healthy civilization; but that fact is far wider than what usually goes by the name of tradition. A man who is conscious of momentum is historically minded; he treasures the gifts of the past. But he is likewise a modernist: he believes that the present also is capable of spontaneous activity. The historical spirit is the recognition and acceptance of change. Tradition may be exactly the reverse: the refusal to change. The historical spirit notes facts, but imposes no duty. It is aware that human sacrifices, slavery, tyranny, once existed; that war, certain forms of monarchy and ecclesiasticism, are still with us. But such acknowledgement implies no reverence. These things *were,* or *are:* this does not prove that they *should be.* Tradition, on the contrary, insists that relics of the past must be honored and maintained. The historical spirit is all-inclusive. Everything that exists to-day is the result of yesterday. Radicalism, Bolshevism, Futurism, are historical products just as much as Toryism. Tradition is selective: only certain elements are picked out as deserving to be preserved. Tradition is not only a limited part of life to-day: it is also a limited part of history.

Man would be paralyzed if his memory were too retentive; his mind would be warped, if what he is allowed to remember were too narrowly prescribed. There is only a difference in dignity between *custom* and *tradition;* there is no essential difference between tradition, superstition and prejudice. This seems a hard saying: but tradition is the last defense of the indefensible. A permanent need, manifested afresh every day, is not a custom, a superstition, a prejudice, a tradition. We must have sleep and food, even as our ancestors had them, but not *because* our ancestors had them. We must have religion,

but not because St. Paul said so; and government, even
if Washington had never lived. Neither an experimental
nor a logical truth needs the force of custom: it is not a
"tradition" that water is composed of oxygen and hydrogen. Tradition is dragged in as an argument only to
bolster up absurdity.

Thus "a dull classic" ought to be a contradiction in
terms. If he has become dull, he should no longer be
a classic. Shakespeare is a fact, not a tradition.

The worst feature in tradition-worship is its pharisaism.
We beg leave to quote a characteristic passage from
Aldous Huxley's *Music at Night:*

Culture, as Emmanuel Berl has pointed out in one
of his brilliantly entertaining pamphlets, is like the
sum of special knowledge that accumulates in any large
united family and is the common property of all its
members. "Do you remember Aunt Agatha's ear
trumpet? And how Willie made the parrot drunk with
sops in wine? And that picnic on Loch Etive, when
the boat upset and Uncle Bob was nearly drowned?
Do you remember?" And we all do, and we laugh de-
lightedly; and the unfortunate stranger who happens
to have called feels utterly out of it. Well, that (in its
social aspect) is Culture. When we of the great Culture
Family meet, we exchange reminiscences about Grandfather Homer, and that awful old Dr. Johnson, and
Aunt Sappho, and poor Johnny Keats. "And do you
remember that absolutely priceless thing Uncle Virgil
said? You know: *Timeo Danaos.* . . . Priceless: I shall
never forget it." No, we shall never forget it; and
what's more, we shall take good care that those horrid
people who have had the impertinence to call on us,
those wretched outsiders who never knew dear mellow

Uncle V, shall never forget it either. We'll keep them constantly reminded of their outsideness.*

But those wretched outsiders will strive hard to learn the shibboleth. If the tradition itself is beyond purchase, its external effects may be imitated to perfection. The nemesis of tradition is spurious culture. Sir Edmund Gosse's father believed that God had created the world six thousand years ago, all complete, with its geological strata and their fossils, *as if* it had existed for millions of years. Similarly, the eighteenth century landscape gardener erected ruins in a new park, so as to give it a synthetic flavor of antiquity. Molière's *Would-Be Gentleman* ordered from the best dealers in such wares what the French call "a varnish of culture." *Parvenus* in all countries procure for themselves an ancestral home and ancestral portraits. An American College, Oxford's infant brother, announces: "There is a tradition in this College that Freshmen are not allowed to walk diagonally across the green. This tradition goes into effect next Monday at 8 A. M." Traditional culture which aims at importing fashionable prejudices reminds us of the ingenious processes whereby parchment or ivory may be *aged* with coffee or tobacco-juice; worm holes in furniture faked by firing fine shot; and cobwebs quickly grown to make bottles look venerable. There is nothing finer than the gentleman of the old school—a classical scholar, loyal to his Church and to his King, fond of gentlemanly sports and addicted to gentlemanly tippling. But the institution that turns a modern lad into

* *On the charms of history and the future of the past.*

such a bewigged family portrait is an efficient cobweb factory.

In his eloquent *Prayer for Teachers,* Glenn Frank confesses: "We have been content to be merchants of dead yesterdays, when we should have been guides into unborn to-morrows." Bravely said; but Glenn Frank was challenged to outline a course of literary studies based on his principles, and found it more discreet to refrain: the University President is not strictly accountable for every word of the columnist. There are *yesterdays* that should not die, and *to-morrows* that should never be born—to wit, the next war. The present writer has reached the age when it no longer seems the height of wisdom to kill off the old. But he firmly believes that literary culture need not be identified with tradition worship. The example of science, and of some of the arts, is encouraging in this respect.

We have emphasized the "radicalism" of science; we are aware, however, that the difference between the scientific attitude and the historical is not absolute. The new symbols of science must be integrated with the old; the most revolutionary thought, in order to be intelligible at all, must have some point of contact with traditional thought. And science, not so very long ago, was no less tradition-bound than literature. The *Ipse Dixit* of Aristotle was law in natural philosophy as well as in poetics. The Medical Faculty of Paris fought against Harvey's circulation of the blood, because it had not been taught by "Hippocrates and Galen." The willingness of science to cast aside time-worn hypotheses is a conquest of yesterday.

On the other hand, literature and the arts are attempting to escape from the thraldom of the past. This was one of the ideals of Romanticism: "Who shall deliver us from the Greeks and the Romans?" But the Romantic revolt was neither complete nor consistent. It sought emancipation from certain ancient models: but it was eagerly looking for precedents in other realms: Shakespeare, the Middle Ages, the ballad, the primitive epic. It was a shift from one past to another past—and a more self-conscious one. Perhaps architecture will provide the clearest indication of possible change. Toward the end of the eighteenth century, architecture had become such a slave to classical tradition that "purity of style" was its highest aim; orthodoxy according to Vitruvius led to the most lifeless pastiches. The Romantic nineteenth century widened the field of imitation, but remained scrupulously imitative. When an architect was commissioned to build a railroad station, he had first to consider whether it would be Doric, like the portico to Euston, or Gothic like St. Pancras, or Romanesque, or Renaissance. To-day such antiquarian preoccupations strike us as positively ludicrous. We are creating the art of to-day with the materials of to-day and for the needs of to-day.

This does not imply that we must destroy ancient works of beauty, or relegate them to the position of museum pieces. We still worship in the old Gothic churches; nay, it is legitimate for us to build new Gothic cathedrals like St. John the Divine, if we feel ourselves the spiritual contemporaries of St. Thomas Aquinas rather than of Clarence Darrow and Aimée Semple

McPherson. And if we happen to like Doric columns, we should not scruple at using a few in our skyscraper or railway terminal: provided we express thereby our own delight in the form, and not merely reverence for ancient canons. We must free ourselves from prejudices, including the futuristic prejudice.

The same spirit may prevail some day in literature. To discard tradition does not mean to destroy the past. To know Shakespeare is a privilege, not a duty; to be guided by his standard in our own work would be manifest foolishness.* Shakespeare's aim was frankly to provide entertainment, not to write school texts. The test of a classic is the power to survive. In so far as he is alive, he needs no elaborate explanation. If he is dead, he is no classic. We insult the great writers of the past when we insist that they have to be imposed upon the new generations. So long as we genuinely and fondly remember "Uncle Virgil", he is a delight; if his "priceless things" have to be drilled into us, he becomes an old bore.

Tradition-worship is a survival of the days when human learning was precarious, a small flickering flame to be tended with religious care. We need no altar to the sacred fire, now that any one can buy a box of matches for one penny. Culture is so ubiquitous that one particular book might fall into oblivion without any danger of loss for its essential message. The thought would pass into "floating literature", that is all.

---

* Sir Hall Caine, expressing his æsthetic and scholarly disapproval of spelling reform, said: "Shakespeare's spelling is good enough for me." A "dear old soul", urged to take a trip in an aëroplane, answered: "None of your new-fangled inventions: I prefer to stick to the railroads as God created them." Two perfect examples of the traditionalist fallacy.

Aye, but is there not power in definite knowledge, and charm in conscious allusiveness? You may repeat:

Laugh, and the world laughs with you,
Weep, and you weep alone. . . .

but will you enjoy these words of wisdom quite as much, if you do not remember whether they were written by Martin Tupper or by Ella Wheeler Wilcox? Is it possible to be *cultured* without knowing "the best that has been thought and said"? But, for one thing, is there an infallible canon of the "best", are there "books that every child should know"? From the Chinese point of view, our ripest scholar is a barbarian; from ours, their most learned mandarin is an ignoramus. When H. G. Wells, some quarter of a century ago, visited a girls' college in the Eastern States, he was asked: "Doesn't it remind you of *The Princess?*", and replied ingenuously: "What princess?" They put him down at once as a vulgarian: as though familiarity with a very pretty mid-Victorian poem were a valid test of culture!

No doubt such writers as Milton and Anatole France would lose heavily if we failed to catch all the happy reminiscences of the Culture Family—the trick of phrase borrowed from Uncle Virgil, the naughty twinkle learned from Cousin Voltaire. Apart from the element of snobbishness denounced by Huxley, is the allusive game worth the candle? The phrase must be good, to begin with: if it is not, I care little whether Vergil used it first. True: not quite true. There *is* virtue in allusiveness. It enables us to use condensed formulæ instead of heavy explanations. If, in speaking of the joys of poetry, I mention "Xanadu" or "a peak in Darien", I convey far more than twenty words of mine could express.

But this undeniable advantage is not without drawbacks. The first is that your audience becomes more narrowly circumscribed. To many, your language will appear recondite, or even cryptic. "We accept the risk: we would rather appeal intensely to the qualified few than superficially to the undiscriminating many." A worthy sentiment: but it is by no means certain that the people you include in your magic circle are worth your while and that those whom you leave out are not. In the old days, all forms of superiority were fairly in harmony. Everybody who was anybody was familiar with the vocabulary of the tribe, and with its fund of reminiscences. To-day, this can no longer be taken for granted. The esoteric is no less a danger than the commonplace; most objectionable of all is the commonplace that deems itself esoteric.

The second danger is that conscious allusiveness may detract from a beautiful thought at least as much as it adds. Do we not often wish that we did not remember so much, so that we could come upon simple and great things with the quivering delight of discovery? Why can we not climb our own peaks in Darien? Instead, when we come across:

Our birth is but a sleep and a forgetting . . .

we nod blandly, a little wearily, as to an old acquaintance in whose company we no longer find any zest. O for a course in un-reading, that would blot out all the classics from our minds, and give us a fresh start!

If we abandon, if even we minimize historical culture, shall we not be reduced to the awful simplicity, the functional starkness, the *Sachlichkeit* affected by certain forms of contemporary architecture? It might not be such an unmixed evil. But it need not have any such result at all. The depth and richness of the mind is not measured by historical book learning. If the author be powerful or subtle, scholarliness *may* add to his strength or to his grace; but, if he be commonplace, classical ornaments will be sheer pedantry. Many a don could quote as abundantly as Montaigne or Sir Thomas Browne: but the result would not be literature.

Overtones need not all come from the past. The antique shop is not the only one that is well stored. A *rich* mind is a well-informed, highly organized, sensitive mind. Take, among our contemporaries, those who give us, not the impression of crude power, but that of abundant and varied wealth, easily available, generous without ostentation. At random, we might name André Gide, Stefan Zweig, Aldous Huxley, Ortega y Gasset, Salvador de Madariaga, among these exemplars of modern culture. They allude to the past without hesitation: it is not pedantry in them, but natural familiarity. Yet their outlook is not retrospective: rather circumspective. They live and think in the present. One thought calls for an illustration from politics, another for one from travel. A literary phenomenon evokes a similar scientific phenomenon. Verbal felicities are not limited to classical allusions. Good literature does not feed on literature.

We shall be accused of cultural bolshevism: if this be

treason to humane letters, make the most of it. Our warning against tradition means no irreverence toward the past, no sacrifice of the living past. Hold fast to that which is great and good in terms of the present—the religious truths that are still true, the political doctrines that are still workable, the masterpieces that we still enjoy. For the rest, let the dead bury their dead.

Chapter 8

NATIONALITY AND LITERATURE

IF we follow the convenient groove, we shall take it for granted that, between nationality and literature, there exists an intimate and inevitable connection. Each literature is sharply separated from every other by the high fence of language; each language belongs primarily to some nation.

Exceptions, in their wonted way, will flock to our minds. We are aware that several of them enjoy a paradoxically vigorous life. Few countries have a stronger national feeling than tetraglot Switzerland; and there seems to be no ardent desire, on either side of the water, for the English-speaking world to be reunited. Still, roughly speaking, literature, language, nationality, go together. In the study of an author, the nation is the natural background. Race, environment and time concur in its formation. The perfect nation is one in which men of the same blood and of the same speech dwell close together in the same homeland, cherish the same traditions, are organized under the same laws. In his *History of English Literature,* Taine had constantly in mind the formation of the English nation; his disciple Jusserand made their common ideal plainer when he called his great work *A Literary History of the English People*. The temptation is almost irresistible to turn this approximate truth into a law, and the law into an ideal: literature is, and should be, national. It is the purpose of this work to defy irresistible temptations.

Of the three great factors which we have examined, the one which is most essential in creating and shaping a nation is that of *time*. The most casual observation will convince us that men who live under the same flag are not all of the same breed. America and France, certainly not less nationalistic than other countries, are racially the most heterogeneous of all. It is no less evident that national unity is not the fruit of physical environment. Our four corners, Washington and Florida, California and Maine, differ widely among themselves, and differ at least as much from Iowa or Missouri. In France, the Alps and Brittany, the Pyrenees and Flanders, Alsace and Corsica, are strikingly varied. On the other hand, both sides of a political frontier usually belong to the same physical world: the two banks of the Rio Grande, of the Saint Lawrence, of Lake Leman, of the Rhine, may not be of the same color on our school maps: but nature ignores our conventions. Not even small islands are marked out as forming homogeneous nationalities: there are three definitely conscious peoples in Great Britain, and two in Ireland. The Danube basin, which should form one vast unit, is split up into half a dozen hostile states—hostile even when some of them were living under the same King and

Emperor. All we can affirm of geography is that in certain cases it hinders, in others it favors unity: it never creates it.

A nation is a historical product, a tradition. It is the habit of living together: but it is a habit deepened into consciousness, consent, willingness, *will*. Five centuries of Turkish rule, the immemorial dynasty of the Habsburgs, failed alike to create nations. A nation is a constant act of faith; Poland survived in the hearts of her sons; the United States *is,* because we believe in the United States. A nation is a perpetual plebiscite: but one in which the dead also have a vote. The long-established custom of living together creates a *momentum* which a single generation finds it hard to overcome. Had that faith, obscurely preserved, not been rekindled; had that momentum completely lost its force, Grant's victory would have been in vain, and secession would have been inevitable.

We must cleanse our minds of superstitious awe when we think of the national spirit. Its origin may be obscure, but it is not mysterious; venerable with age, but not sacred. It had to assert its right to existence against the spirit of a larger whole: the countries of Europe are fragments of the Roman, the Carolingian, the Austrian, the Russian Empires; the countries of America had to tear themselves from England or Spain. It had to establish its supremacy over the spirit of smaller units— tribes, provinces, minor states,—themselves struggling for separate life, like Ireland, Catalonia, Porto Rico under our eyes. Neither secession nor annexation is a crime in itself: the stronger will, the longer will, is law.

Had Ireland weakened, Home Rule, and *a fortiori* independence, would have been treason.

Is this desire to form a self-contained unit, this *territorial will,* the very center of human culture? On the face of it, no. Man's basic needs—food, shelter, sex—are no less keenly felt when the boundary line is shifted and the design of the flag altered. The more profound yearnings, the higher achievements, religion, philosophy, science, are independent of frontiers. Neither for the starving man nor for Spinoza does the national state exist. Nationality occupies a middle ground, vast enough, but hard to define, for it is constantly expanding and contracting. And in a similar position, although not absolutely the same, do we find also literature.

The literary tradition and the national tradition merge at many points: but they do not quite coincide. The illiterate may be patriotic, like Joan of Arc; the leaders of literature may be cosmopolitan, like Jean-Jacques Rousseau. Any forcible assimilation between the two traditions would be ludicrous; still worse, any attempt to measure both by the same scale of values. But their close alliance can not be denied. It is often said that European literatures, at the end of the eighteenth century, were renovated through the national spirit. The converse seems to us even truer: the growth of national consciousness is a form of the Romantic revolt. This problem will be examined in its place. But, whichever side we take, we must admit the interaction of the two factors.

The national-political and the national-literary ideals are both *myths:* they are compounded of memories and dreams, far more than of direct experiences. But myths are not delusions or lies; and they have power over the hardest of facts. The national *type,* which plays such a leading part in politics and in literature, has no absolute existence. There is no Platonic "Idea of the English-man", of which all actual Englishmen are but the dis-torted shadows. On the other hand, the English type is no mere fiction, no stock character that can be imperson-ated by any fairly competent actor. England's brilliant success in the last two centuries has spread to the four corners of the earth the Anglomaniac cult, not seldom oddly mingled with Anglophobia. There have been in-numerable "English gentlemen", self-made, in Ham-burg or Bordeaux, in Buenos Aires and Bombay, and even in Kansas City. But the spurious can soon be de-tected from the genuine.

The *type* is not a carnival costume: all its elements are in the man himself. But it is not the whole man: it represents a selection among potentialities. All tenden-cies are latent in all men: the notion of *type* makes it easier, without and within, to capitulate to some incli-nations that we might have resisted, to cultivate others that we might have neglected. I witnessed in the South the tragedy of a fine Negro family gradually giving up the fight, stooping to the standards that were expected of them, almost imposed upon them. Treat a man like a "nigger", make him feel he is a "nigger", and he will act like a "nigger." The *type* incites us both to laziness and to heroism. An Englishman is as proud of his re-fusal to think logically, as of his punctiliousness in wear-ing formal dress for dinner. *Un-English,* it has been said, is a perfect fallacy in one word. But there are few truths as potent as such a fallacy.

We are inclined to think that the *type* idea is a dangerous one. It sanctions weaknesses far more than it fosters strenuous endeavor. The positive virtues are not national. With some slight shift of emphasis, it is right in all countries to be brave, truthful and kind. In essentials, there is no need to remind ourselves: *"Noblesse oblige:* we are from Lichtenstein and must keep up the great Lichtenstein tradition." The notion of type is a tempter at our elbow, encouraging self-indulgence. I may dream of being a great musician: what is the use? I do not belong to a musical race—and I resign myself to slipshod conformities. It is not our strongest points, but our pet failings, that are exalted into national traits, and thus made amiable, lovable, almost admirable. So one country will give prestige to muddleheadedness or snobbishness; another to pedantry or brutality; a third will smile complacently at its loose sexual code; a fourth will take pride in tippling, superstition, race prejudice.

The superficiality of the national type has been proved over and again. We might easily throw out of court any striking exception—a Scottish Sardanapalus, a Neapolitan Calvin, an Alabama Hegel, if such were found. But the commonly accepted national ideal may change in a generation, and even in a few years. No faster, however, than the physical type. Cartoonists still cling to a lanky Uncle Sam and a beefy John Bull, whereas the "typical" American is now heavily built, and the "typical" Britisher is slender. We were so sure that the muzhik worshipped his Little Father the Tsar, and would do so for ever, that some Americans are still shaking their heads incredulously at the Russian Revolution: these people are not playing the game, they are not true to type. Thirty years ago, every hardware salesman in Brummagem was persuaded that he had naval sense in his blood, whereas the Germans were hopeless landlubbers: he may have learned better by this time. Easygoing Italy finds herself suddenly stern and efficient, and seems to like it. Most *types* are as antiquated as the imperial goatee of the stage Parisian.

The type is a Jekyll-Hyde affair. Not merely because we never see ourselves as others see us (*we,* whoever we may be, are invariably good-natured and naïvely trustful, so we are invariably duped by the relentless, scheming, unscrupulous foreigner—whoever *he* may be). But even in our own eyes, we assume widely different aspects. Every nation has its heroic and its cynical moods. Uncle Sam is by turns generous to a fault, the crusader of democracy, pouring his wealth out in the service of "the common cause"; and, almost overnight, he is the suspicious, hard-headed, close-fisted business man, with nothing but scorn for his past generosity. Germany may to-day feel herself Beethoven, to-morrow Frederick II. England is chivalrous and mercantile, proverbially "perfidious" and scrupulously honorable, pitiless and tender. Ireland is lost in a reverie filled with mystic longings and sadness: but a man who attended a New York Police ball reported: "Celtic dreaminess and melancholy have been greatly exaggerated." France, "eternal France", "logical France", perhaps because I know her best, seems to me most bewildering of all—

generous and sordid, mystic and sceptical, invincibly per-
severing and easily discouraged, madly adventurous and
prosaically prudent, Don Quijote and Sancho Panza.
National psychology is not a chaos: but it is a kaleido-
scope, and the pattern may be changed at any moment.
Or again, the national *character* is not Proteus: but it
possesses a richer wardrobe than a Hollywood star, or
William II in all his glory.

All this holds true of the national-literary type. A
tradition is a capricious and weak-minded tyrant. It
hampers you at every turn with its irrational "Thou
shalt" and "Thou shalt not." But it yields flabbily to
determined rebellion: yesterday's bandit receives his
badge as to-morrow's *gendarme*. It is un-French to be
ponderous, un-German to be flippant, un-English to be
analytical . . . until the right man appears.

Let us take as an example the "Gallic" tradition of
irony in French literature. Handed down from the
early Middle Ages, it affected writers who, in other
climes, might have scorned it altogether. Montaigne
was nourished on the mighty classics of Greece and
Rome; he had before his eyes the tragic conflict between
Catholics and Hugenots: but the Gallic tradition made
it possible for him to smile. Pascal is the most profound,
the most ardent, the most tortured of mystics, and a
great mathematician withal: yet he wielded irony with
masterly grace. Voltaire was a philosopher, a scientist,
an historian, a reformer—so earnest that he burnt with
fever at the thought of injustice: yet all we remember
of him is the deadly precision of his wit. Renan was a
strange hybrid of scholarliness and religiosity: had he

lived either at Oxford or Tübingen, he would never have indulged in the voluptuous dilettantism and the urbane raillery of his latter years. Anatole France had the antiquarian tastes of a Benedictine monk, with an Anglo-Saxon propensity to sentiment. *The Crime of Sylvester Bonnard* and *The Book of My Friend* appeal to pure and gentle souls who enjoy a smile half-blurred with tears. Had he been a subject of Queen Victoria, he might have rejected the temptation of writing *The Rôtisserie*. The Gallic smile is found on lips of every shape. In the history of literatures as in the history of nations, a tradition is a very real personage—far more real than most characters of flesh and blood. The Monroe Doctrine counts for much more than President Monroe; the Puritanical Spirit has more substance than Jonathan Edwards.

True: but tradition, as we have seen, is but a small part of the truth, as far as the past is concerned; and it gives no safe indication of any truth to come. Literary tradition has exactly the same value as very incomplete statistics. We agree that there is a "Gallic tradition"; there is a better chance to find it among French theologians than among their German or American colleagues. But some of the greatest French writers—Racine, Montesquieu, Balzac—were affected by it only in their minor works; some others—Corneille, Bossuet, Rousseau, Buffon, Hugo, Zola—show no trace of it at all. At one time, the best representative of Gallic wit was Heinrich Heine, a German Jew; to-day, it might well be Aldous Huxley.

Literary tradition, like political tradition, is as arbitrary in its exclusions as in its inclusions. In three successive centuries, the official leaders of French literature had thought it incumbent upon them to give their country a national epic. They all failed: Ronsard with his *Franciade,* Chapelain with his *Pucelle,* Voltaire with his *Henriade.* Hence the *law: "Les Français n'ont pas la tête épique":* the French have no genius for the epic. It was not realized that the failure was due to the lifeless pastiching of a miraculous *pastiche,* Vergil's *Æneid.* Then the enormous and vigorous body of the French medieval epic was rediscovered; Agrippa d'Aubigné was brought to light; Victor Hugo wrote his uneven but magnificent *Legend of the Centuries;* the epic quality was manifest even in Zola; and the bogus "law" had to slink away.

The unreserved exaltation of Nationalism, both in politics and in literature, is a recent phenomenon. In the Middle Ages, "nations" were but local sections of the Catholic International. In Neo-Classical times, the dynasty, not the nation, was the historical unit: with the Habsburg Empire, this conception survived as late as 1918. Alsace became almost at once a loyal possession of the French crown; only at the time of the Revolution did it grow into an integral part of the French nation. The keenest minds of the eighteenth century owed allegiance to the Enlightenment rather than to the territorial state. Not only did poets and philosophers cheerfully serve a foreign king; but soldiers and financiers felt free to move from land to land. Most influential in French history were the Scot, John Law, the German, Marshal Maurice de Saxe, the Swiss, Necker. When democracy took over the heritage of the dynasties, when Romanticism substituted sentiment for reason, nationalism became supreme.*

Literature offers a parallel evolution. The great themes common to all medieval Europe—the religious works in Latin, the miracles and moralities, the farces and tales, the Carolingian and Arthurian epic cycles, *Reynard the Fox* and the *Romance of the Rose*—give the period a cultural unity far deeper than national differences. Humanism, Neo-Classicism, the Enlightenment, were Pan-European phenomena. A thorough Frenchman like Boileau ignored the purely French writers of the Middle Ages, but had at his finger tips his Greek, Latin and Italian classics. Samuel Johnson was a sturdy, insular Briton: yet he was more familiar with antiquity, with Boileau, Racine, Molière, Rousseau, than with Anglo-Saxon poetry. Goethe was as cosmopolitan as Frederick the Great himself. Even after the Revolution, the French Romanticists were not national: they rebelled against their own classics, and followed with enthusiasm Shakespeare, Ossian, Walter Scott, Byron.

This international spirit did not die a hundred years ago; nor is it, in our own days, limited to a few "men without a country." Cosmopolitanism begins in the nursery, with Æsop, Brer Rabbit, the Grimm Brothers, Andersen, *Pinocchio;* it continues through adolescence, with Jules Verne and Alexander Dumas; it reaches the masses, with the Bible and *Les Misérables;* it tops the best-sellers list, with *All Quiet on the Western Front* or

---

* *Cf.* Albert Guérard: "Herder's Spiritual Heritage: Nationalism, Romanticism, Democracy", in *Annals of the American Academy of Political and Social Science,* July, 1934.

Grand Hotel; it appeals to the educated, with Dostojew-ski, Ibsen, Nietzsche; it is the rule with the sophisticates, with Baudelaire, d'Annunzio, Valle Inclán, André Gide.

Nationalism is a fact: historically, a recent one; according to all indications, transitory; in our opinion, dangerous rather than beneficial, an "aberration" rather than a virtue. But, fortunately, it is not so potent a fact in literature as in politics. All the nationalism of Messrs. W. R. Hearst, William Thompson, and other apostles of American Sinn Fein will not efface *English* literature from our tradition. Even those English writers who have attained greatness after our Declaration of Independence are ours by rights. To this day, we refuse to consider Kipling and Shaw as aliens: their rudeness is of the kind which we allow within the family. No Bismarckian policy could drive Grillparzer or Hebbel out of the German Confederacy; no Italian power can veto the *Anschluss* of Schnitzler, Wassermann, Keyserling, Gottfried Keller, Carl Spitteler, to the spiritual *Reich*. Rousseau never was a true Frenchman in any sense of the term: but the history of French literature can not be written with his name left out.

Some prophets of Nationalism are preaching that the first duty of the American artist is to picture *the American scene.* The Pulitzer prizes were founded to encourage this tendency, although one was awarded to Pearl Buck's epic of Chinese life, *The Good Earth.* If our ideal of literature be phonographic and photographic realism, no doubt we should note those things only which we have actually heard and seen: this condemns equally James Branch Cabell's Poictesme and Thornton

Wilder's Peru. But even this rather partisan conception of art would not make for one hundred per cent Americanism. If an American happens to be better acquainted with the boulevards of Paris than with the superhighways of Detroit, with the beauties of Tahiti than with those of Muncie, Mattoon or Milpitas, by all means let him write *realistically* of that which he knows best. There is no "American scene": there are "American scenes", so varied that no man can master them all or reduce them to a natural unity. And wherever an American artist casts his American eyes upon land or people, he annexes the scene to cultural America. No artist should despise his own folk; none should strive to be exotic and pose as an expatriate in his own country; but no artist either should consider wilful parochialism as his highest duty.

If by "Americanism" those critics mean, not the American scene, but the American ideal, we have a right to ask: "Which?" Whatever may be your criterion, you will find yourself aligned with foreigners against some of your fellow Americans. What is "the American ideal"? Is it Liberty and the Pursuit of Happiness, or is it stern Puritanism? Is it the pioneer's life, the vast open spaces, the ready pistol, the Western romance—or is it high efficiency and mass production, with their inevitable concomitants, intricate organization and mechanical conformity? Is it the Nordic and Protestant tradition, or Jeffersonian free thought? Is it Boston culture, or is it Will Rogers? In all cases, you will banish from your spiritual commonwealth millions of legal voters. Is your horror of the League of Nations to be the supreme test? Then excommunicate the spirit of Woodrow Wilson, Taft, Lowell, Herbert Hoover, Franklin Roosevelt and not a few others. Will you keep your patriotism pure by keeping it undefined? Then you will be most truly international: for "My country, right or wrong!" can be said in all languages, and emotional response to flag waving is very much the same, whatever may be the color of the flag.

Of course it would be pernicious nonsense to believe that Major Henry Bordeaux, because he is a member of the French Academy, stands on a higher level of culture than Sherwood Anderson; but would it be less pernicious to maintain that the Reverend Harold Bell Wright, because he is a true-born American, chock-full of American *mores,* writing an honest-to-God American vernacular, and depicting the wholesome American scene, should mean more to us than Thomas Mann? No, literary nationalism will not do. It is not even an honest prejudice: it is a cult for ultra-sophisticates who, since everybody has discovered Montparnasse, find it smart to rediscover Middletown.

Chapter 9

THE PROPER FIELD OF THE SOCIOLOGICAL METHOD

IT has been a favourite pastime with students of literature to demolish Taine's method; but it pulls itself together again, and bobs up, every decade or so, as "scientific criticism", "sociological criticism", and even—God save the mark!—as "the newer criticism." According to our pragmatic principle, such popularity must be deserved. The foregoing study may have seemed entirely destructive. Our intention, however, was to adjust rather than to disprove. The workman hammering at a block of marble looks as though he were destroying the block: under the sculptor's direction, he is revealing the statue.

The sociological method explains everything *about* literature, but not literature itself. It works as well for the mediocrity as for the man of genius: the worst writer in the language can boast: "I too have Race, Environment and Time!" Its cocksure determinism stumbles at every step upon the unexplainable. Taine provided us with a standard example. He devoted a stimulating and entertaining book to *La Fontaine and His Fables*. Race, environment and time made La Fontaine a "fable-tree", which bore fables as inevitably as a pear tree brings forth pears. But La Fontaine and Racine were both born in Champagne, within a few leagues and within a few years of each other, in exactly the same social stratum. The one wrote mocking and cynical fables, the other tragedies of fatal passion. And of the thousands of Champenois whose "race, environment and time" were the same as theirs, not one can compare with either of them.

We shall not embark upon a sophomoric discussion of determinism. Determinism may be true in the abstract: this is no concern of ours. In the most rigid sciences, such as celestial mechanics, a problem of such complexity may arise, that the human mind has to admit a temporary check. A literary problem is not merely one with three unknown quantities: it is one with an unknown number of unknown quantities. The scientific definiteness of Taine and his successors is a delusion. We felt from the beginning that there was "something" to race, environment and time. After this survey, we still feel that there is "something" to them: how much, we do not know. The terms are loosely defined; the relative value of the three factors is undetermined; and there are other factors in reserve, vaguely called *genius* and *chance,* which may be more powerful still. Taine's *Introduction* is bristling with "laws": but his hard-and-fast critical system reminds us of Alice's croquet party in Wonderland. The arches "Race" walk away; the balls "Environment" uncoil themselves and scurry off; the mallet "Time" stares at you with a puzzled, reproachful expression. The game is all the more delightful for being instinct with life: but the outcome is beyond scientific computation.

Of the three fatidical factors, Environment is at the same time the most obvious and the least certain. Human culture, a product of tradition and will, defies environment with surprising success. At least, this holds good within the brief limits of cultural history—a few hundred years, at most a few thousand. The songs of misty Scotland are enjoyed in arid Australia; the sonnets of the aristocratic Elizabethan Age still serve as patterns in democratic America. There are "world classics" which are treasured in common by all men of European origin, under all climates and all régimes.

Heredity is an undeniable fact: but race, in literature, is a wild hypothesis. We have no right to apply the principles of heredity, with any degree of minuteness and with any hope for accuracy, to the vast, arbitrary groups we call *races*. Even if we had fully established the physical characteristics of the race, we should still be a long way from a scientific connection between the physical and the mental.

There are blonds and brunettes: but blond *vs.* brunette literature is nonsense. Tradition, on the contrary, is a matter of record. We may dislike it, we may fight against it, but it is there. Supposing a mysterious disease should kill off all the blonds: so far as we can foresee, the main course of our civilization would not be altered. There would be plenty of dark-haired scholars to expound Shakespeare, and no lack of dark-haired poets inditing sonnets to their dark-haired ladies. Whether that course would be deflected and its momentum slowed down, is a matter of fanciful surmise. If, on the contrary, all the blonds were taken *at birth* and transported to a continent of their own, without the slightest connection with their history, it is certain that they would not reconstitute, out of their natural gift of blondness, the legacy of our culture, the masterpieces of Homer, Dante, Shakespeare; it is probable that they would not reach an equivalent stage for thousands of years. Culture is tradition, or if you prefer momentum, not race.

When blond Barbarians finally disrupted the decadent Roman world, the result was not a sudden rush of progress, but a relapse into barbarism which lasted for five hundred years. And it would have lasted longer, if so much of the old culture had not survived. So much for the coming upon the scene of a new, and supposedly superior, race.

Let us reverse the terms: in Hayti and Liberia, the accession to power of an "inferior" race has apparently led to a stagnation or regression of culture. But the social aspect of the question is more evident than the racial. If Hayti had been populated with ignorant *white* serfs, and if the mob had killed off or driven away all the elements which had a monopoly of traditional culture, the result would have been a similar set-back. This was not the case with the French Revolution, because, in proportion, the victims were far fewer; and because, among the Revolutionists, a good many were better educated than the aristocracy. The social shift did imply some loss in culture (we have not fully reached again the eighteenth century level), but no catastrophic destruction. There are at present as charming and as cultured people at Port-au-Prince as could be found in a French provincial town of the same size. And it is not proven that a few thousand *white* proletarians, if they had been practically abandoned in the marshes of the West African coast, would have done a much better job than the Liberians. Civilization is not *in the blood:* it is a tradition. And let us hope that its "acquired velocity" is increasing.

This conception is frankly opposed to the fatalism of the Racialists. There is no abyss between man and man. Whatever is *humanly* right can be taught to all men; whatever a nation lacks, it may acquire. There is no French logic and American logic, no English honesty and German honesty, any more than there are Italian triangles and Turkish triangles.

But this view, far from committing us to radicalism, acts as a warning against it. Civilization is a vast collective tradition, far more complex than any mind, far larger than any group; it has momentum; it can not be altered suddenly. An individual child may be easily transplanted; an isolated adult, if he be willing, can be assimilated, although never to perfection; a compact group, even a single family, offers much greater resistance; a whole social class, an entire nationality, can not jump from one civilization to another. Class and nation have a civilization of their own, which permeates their being, and has become second nature. The change of a few words or forms will not alter these deep-rooted facts. It is admitted that the Negroes, at the close of the Civil War, were not ready for wholesale admission to full citizenship. It is now confessed that we can not turn Filipinos into

standard Americans. Japan changed its costume at the
time of the Meiji, but remained the most tradition-loving
of great nations. The Russian Revolution has been surprisingly successful: but only because the discarded civilization was itself a recent importation from the West.

Never and *At Once* are both misleading. But it is possible, through a cautious hybridization of cultures, to
strengthen their common elements and minimize their
differences until they cease to be a cause of strife. We
do not want abruptly to renounce everything American
in favor of a cosmopolitan culture which is still woefully
vague; still less should we throw our whole tradition
overboard, and replace it with some alien nationalism,
after the fashion of certain expatriates. But it would be
no less foolish to deny ourselves enrichment that is ours
for the asking. There is nothing "un-American" about
Homo Sum. Whatsoever is good throughout the world
is ours, and should be incorporated in our tradition. The
only result of Cultural Protectionism would be to stunt
our growth.

The *Racialists* claim that the *Humanists* (in the widest,
Terentian sense of the term) think in lifeless abstractions;
that they know *Man,* an idea, as in the eighteenth century, not the flesh and blood realities, the Englishman,
the Italian, the American. But the Humanist is not
committed to the myth that all men are equal; still less
to the absurdity that all men are identical; he professes,
on the contrary, that all men are different. It is the
Racialist who is creating general types, Platonic ideas,
which have no concrete existence: *the* Negro, *the* Jew,
the Russian, *the* German. In a quarter of a century of

American life, I have met thousands of Americans, but never *the* American, a purely statistical creature, who is five feet nine inches tall, earns $1242.18 a year, owns one sixth of a car, and possesses two and five eighths children.

The application of this discussion to literature is two-fold.

If we are interested in an author, we shall want to know all about him; conversely, knowledge fosters and deepens interest. We are tempted to read the books of the people we have met, and to meet the people whose books we have enjoyed. In that quest for information, "Race, Environment and Time" provide a good general programme. If we go through with it, we shall have no hard-and-fast law, no rule of criticism, no explanation: but we shall have gathered a quantity of facts, conveniently classified, which will enrich our enjoyment. Remove all the scientific claims from Taine's method, and what remains is excellent.

Our second conclusion is that the proper field of literature is *literature,* not nationality, not even language. It is far more important, at every stage of our development, to read good books than to read American books. Washington Irving is a charming minor essayist: but it is better for us to know Goethe than to know Washington Irving. As our opportunities are limited, we should go straight to essentials. In the grammar school as well as in the university, those world masterpieces which have become part and parcel of our own heritage should take precedence of national second-raters. Not only would this bring art into line with religion and science, which are already supra-national; but it would also bring the *study* of literature into line with the actual *facts* of literature. From the kindergarten to the grave, man seeks the best. If the best is grown in our own parish, we must not despise it; but, should it come from the antipodes, it is still the best.

Part II

Homo Scriptor
The Author as a Social Type

Chapter 10

THE LITERARY TYPE

THE reader must be fully persuaded by this time that we have no faith in the objective existence of *types*. Types are abstractions, stiff bloodless creatures of the logical mind. You never can prophesy, with any certainty, whether the member of a given group will act "true to type." Types, however, are not sheer delusion. Their existence is partly statistical, partly mythical. As statistical abstracts, they have some basis in reality; as myths, they have power to inhibit and to encourage.

The "literary type"—the quintessence of innumerable "literary types"—is among the most puzzling of all. None has enjoyed a more prolonged and distinct existence: Plato, Aristotle, Horace, already spoke of poets as a *genus*. None is so self-conscious, and none possesses a stronger formative influence: men strive laboriously to look, dress, talk, drink, love, like poets. On the other hand, the very nature of poetry is individualism. The first article in the code of priest or soldier is: "Thou shalt obey"; in the code of the gentleman: "Thou shalt conform"; in the code of the poet: "Thou shalt be different." As a result, the soldier type is plain, clear-cut, permanent; the poet type is myriad-shaped and elusive.

We are using the word *poet* instead of the more general one *author*. We have no thought of limiting ourselves to the writers of uneven lines; but we do want to limit ourselves to those men in whom the creative, the personal element predominates: and that element is essentially the artistic or poetic.

We shall therefore leave out of our survey, at this stage, all those for whom artistic creation is secondary, even though they may hold an important place in the history of literature. For instance, we shall eliminate from our consideration the *Bookman* in his different varieties—the scholar, the antiquarian, the critic, the professor. He is emphatically a man of letters: on the face of it, far more so than men of fashion like Byron. He may be a master of style. But he is not on the battle line; his activity is in the auxiliary services. This exclusion connotes no lack of respect or affection. We find much more pleasure in good criticism than in poor lyric. The "ripe", "mellow", "fruity" scholar, such as Sir Edmund Gosse or Professor George Saintsbury, is a delightful character indeed: we deeply regret that, west of Boston (or should we say west of Cape Race?) he should be such an exotic. We need scarcely add that the bookman and the artist may blend. There are scholarly poets like Milton, and critics who raise their craft to the creative level like Sainte-Beuve. Walter Pater's thought was too vital, his art was too exquisite, for us to place him among the "mere" bookmen. Creators, on the other hand, may affect the bookish attitude. Anatole France's favorite impersonations, Sylvester Bonnard, Jerome Coignard, Lucien Bergeret, are denizens of Bibliopolis, and smile, not without vanity, at their own pedantry; Cabell added a new involution to his irony through his fanciful and recondite learning.

We love to linger in this twilight zone: but we know that the "typical poet" is not to be found there. The antiquarian might be interested in medals rather than in manuscripts; the collector might be gathering postage stamps or match boxes instead of first editions; the professor might be teaching political history instead of literature, and their psychology, like their mode of life, would remain very much the same.

We must also exclude, under the same rule, those men who use literature only as a vehicle: the statesman, the reformer, the preacher, the philosopher, the historian. Here the distinction is far more delicate. "Pure" poetry, absolutely divorced from thought or purpose, is a will o' the wisp. The most detached artist is preaching; in the name of Art for Art's Sake, he advocates either beauty-worship, or a philosophy of futility. We hope to examine this puzzling problem in a companion volume.

There are, however a number of clear-cut cases. Many leading statesmen in Europe and in America have written books, not invariably poor, and not invariably on political subject. But their most devoted admirers would hardly claim a place in literature for Presidents Hoover and Coolidge, or even for Presidents Wilson and Theodore Roosevelt. In France, Clemenceau the writer was but one of the minor aspects of Clemenceau the man of action. In England, the fairly voluminous *Works* of

Gladstone are a curiosity, and a dusty one at that. The cases of Bryce and Morley would be worth arguing; those of Burke and Macaulay even more so. With Napoleon and Disraeli, we reach genuine artists, poets if you please, that is to say creators: but for them, however, the literary medium was a secondary one. There is no doubt that Rousseau and Carlyle belong to literature, although they preached unceasingly; and that Tolstoy did not lose his literary standing when he wrote *The Kreutzer Sonata, Resurrection,* or even *What is Art?*

We shall not seek the type either among those for whom literature is first of all a gainful occupation: the hackwriter, the author of potboilers, and, in most cases, the journalist. They live by their pen, blunt or sharp; they reap their reward, pitiful or splendid; and they are to be judged by the exacting standard of the commercial world. If they deliver on time the standard article at the standard price, they deserve credit—according to Dun and Bradstreet's. There is nothing more dishonorable about writing readable stories than about manufacturing the chewing gum advertised on the other side of the page.

In this case also, no absolute rule can be laid down. The priest who lives of the altar is not guilty of simony; an author may lose amateur standing without losing his talent. David Starr Jordan defined success as "doing the thing you like and getting paid for it." Shakespeare and Molière were very frankly "in the business." De Foe and Diderot had their years of Grub Street. Alexander Dumas was an *entrepreneur* on a large scale, gathering and marketing the work of Auguste Maquet and a host of others. Balzac's feverish production was a neck-to-neck race with the sheriff. The mighty *Misérables* was deliberately planned and advertised to be a best-seller. Few authors are absolutely free from the mercenary motive—especially if you include social advancement and prestige under material rewards. "No man but a blockhead," said Samuel Johnson, "ever wrote except for money."

I was once taught the useful difference between mushrooms and toadstools; the ones offer a ring which is lacking in the others. But, in many cases, the genuine ring may be so faint as to become invisible; in others, a spurious ring will appear, hard to distinguish from the real one. I decided to leave the matter to experts. In literature, there are works that remain genuine art, although they were frankly made to sell; and commercial articles that closely imitate the artistic. To tell them apart, a delicate touchstone is required.

Finally, we must separate the artistic type from its wilful caricature the Bohemian: "dwellers on the coast of Bohemia" and Philistines at heart, so well depicted by W. D. Howells and Margaret Kennedy; *bona fide* Bohemians also, if they have no claim to art or literature except their bohemianism. Unclipped locks, absinthe and a pack of creditors do not make a poet, if no poems are forthcoming; they only make what Spengler would call a case of *pseudomorphism:* in the vernacular, a faker.

Supposing we had isolated *the typical poet:* what would be the use? A purely negative one perhaps: but negative is not the same as negligible. It will give us no key to the baffling problem of greatness: but it will help us define the problem. If we subtract from both poets the elements common to Campbell and Coleridge, we shall be better prepared to feel the differences.

But this belongs to a criticism of values, with which this book is not concerned. In the study of literature and society, the action of the literary type is of definite importance. Literature, as we have said, is a distorting mirror. Each individual author has his personal equation, his aberration, which must be taken into account. But there are elements common to most writers, and not common to all their contemporaries. These elements define *Homo Scriptor:* it would be a source of error to identify them either with the single writer under study, or with the whole period and nation.

There are, for instance, in certain medieval works as well as in certain grotesque carvings, traces of an irreverent, almost irreligious spirit, which seems incompatible with the "pure" and "ardent" faith of the age. These are found quite early: in the *Pilgrimage of Charlemagne,* which is approximately as old as the *Song of Roland.* The *naïveté* of the time offers a convenient explanation: our ancestors were untaught children, and knew no better. We have our suspicions: the *naïveté* might be found chiefly among the Romanticists, who gave us such a conventional picture of the times "when Knighthood was in flower." The Middle Ages were as frankly anti-clerical as they were superstitious: superstition and anti-clericalism form a loose aggregate, which allows doubt to filter in. The people who made such broad fun of their monks can not have believed every word that the monks told them. Still, we do not want to turn a medieval market or pilgrimage crowd into a Voltairian audience. There was no lack of yokels, and burgesses, and clerics too, who could not tell the difference between an authentic miracle and a miracle of irony: in our own days, they would vote *Thaïs* an edifying tale. Those who knew enough to laugh in their sleeves were, in all likelihood, very few; but, among those few were, first of all, *the poets themselves.*

Their profession attracted men who were clever rather than submissive; who had received the rudiments of an education, but who, like Villon, were ill-adapted to discipline; quite possibly dissolute, and all the more disposed to scoff, as openly as they dared, at all authorities. Ironical freethought, which peers at us so strangely through the veil of naïve orthodoxy, is certainly not representative of the public as a whole, and it is not purely accidental: it is part of one literary type.

We have selected this rather remote and controversial example, because it is not so trite as others. It is plain, for instance, that Romanticism never truly represented the masses or even the classes. It was a fashion among the artists and poets, and is to be explained in terms of artistic or literary psychology. England in the first decades of the nineteenth century, France a few years later, were not in the least romantic, although the vogue prevailing among artists was bound to spread—very thinly—to *bourgeois* drawing rooms and backshop parlors. Under the Second Empire, literature was tinged with pessimism: there is no sign that the French people, from the Imperial Court down to the peasantry, were similarly affected. With all its glitter and corruption, the régime brought solid prosperity, which was honestly enjoyed. The disease known as *Decadence* preyed upon the *literati* in the closing years of the nineteenth century, but spared the nations. This discrepancy was more evident in London than in Paris: the French had some cause for national discouragement; but the England of Victoria's two Jubilees had not deserved Aubrey Beardsley and Oscar Wilde. The sophistication and cynicism that followed the Great War—more accurately, the fruit of America's *gran rifiuto*—betray the state of mind of a very small group. We may have been in the mood for *This Side of Paradise* and *The Sun Also Rises:* but you, and I, and President Coolidge, were not really sophisticated and cynical.

All this simply reasserts the fact that, within the general framework of a society, literature enjoys a large measure of autonomy. In order to understand a writer, it is not sufficient to know the "race, environment and time" factors, which apply equally to author and public. By the fact of becoming an author a man joins a group which, even without any material organization, has an existence, an atmosphere, a code of its own. This group is based first of all on natural selection: few men are forced into successful authorship against their secret inclination. That fundamental element is strengthened by tradition. Obviously, all authors are not alike, any more than all Americans are alike. Obviously also, they are at least ninety-nine per cent human and barely one per cent literary. But that one per cent does influence their literature.

Chapter 11

PHYSIOLOGY OF THE AUTHOR TYPE

Is there a physical type of the author? The reader will remember that, according to Taine, certain "marked differences" in bodily structure corresponded with certain "innate dispositions." Some varieties of men are "capable of superior conceptions and creations, others are limited to rudimentary ideas and inventions, just as there are certain breeds of dogs better fitted for racing, others for fighting, others for hunting, and others still for keeping watch over house or herd." This opens entrancing vistas. If we were able to follow up Taine's suggestions, we might some day pick out our poets and our generals with the same certainty as we get a spaniel or a bulldog.

But we are not even within sight of the goal. I am tolerably familiar with the iconography of authorship, and I find it impossible to visualize the composite picture of "the author." When we can tell, by looking at a portrait, that it represents a poet, it is on account of some artificial detail: the wind-tossed mane and the hygienic loose collar of the Shelleyans, the flowing beard,

like that of a river god, of the ancient philosophers, restored to favor by the poets of the eighteen-sixties, Tennyson, Hugo, Longfellow; the rapt, *Excelsior!* gaze. All
this is pardonable, but histrionic.

Many of our effigies of great writers are thus conven-
tionalized, turned into symbols of the work rather than
likenesses of the man. Rodin gave us a haunting vision
of the Dantesque spirit that conceived the *Human
Comedy:* monstrous, formidable, with unfathomable all-
fathoming eyes, a mouth like a gash tortured into a leer,
the folded arms of defiance, the recoil of fascinated horror. But Monsieur de Balzac in the flesh was short,
podgy, greasy, rubicund, loud and hilarious. Tennyson's
description of Victor Hugo remains strikingly beautiful:

> *Weird Titan,*
> *Cloud-weaver of phantasmal hopes and fears . . .*

But the Weird Titan was small, neat, and rather too
punctilious in his old-fashioned courtesy. Shakespeare's
picture is the only strong argument in favor of the Bacon-
ian hypothesis. It would be ungenerous to dwell on the
regrettable features of certain authoresses, from Madame
de Staël to a modern American poetess. The advent of
photography, and especially of the "candid camera" in
contemporary journalism, has destroyed the myth of the
literary type. We are persuaded that, on their passports,
our most aërial songsters, like the rest of us, resemble
escaped convicts.

Our impressions, although not vague, are, we must
confess, very loose. But, if a conscientious research worker
were to tell us that the average poet is auburn haired,

grayish-blue eyed, and weighs 159 pounds stripped, the natural answer would be: "What of it?" or, for genuine Americans: "Oh, yeah?"

There is one fairly definite notion, however, that bears investigation: poets are sensitive, fragile; their souls wear out their bodies; beloved of the gods, they die young. It is within the reach of any one to work out the vital statistics of the Immortals. Without any effort, innumerable names flow from our fountain pen: Sophocles, Lope de Vega, Calderon, Goethe, Arndt, Paul Heyse, Tolstoy, Metastasio, Goldoni, Carlo Gozzi, Manzoni, Voltaire, Chateaubriand, Lamartine, Mistral, Anatole France, Paul Bourget, Wordsworth, Landor, Samuel Rogers, Carlyle, Tennyson, Browning, Ruskin, Thomas Hardy, Robert Bridges . . . all well beyond the scriptural three score and ten. In terms of life insurance, poets are good risks, and entitled to preferential rates. In only one class do we find greater longevity: among our Southern Negroes. But the imagination of colored folks ranks far higher than their accuracy.

Marlowe, Shelley, Byron, died young; but Marlowe's death, and Shelley's, were due to accidents; Byron's, to very abnormal causes: the three men were vigorous, and even athletic. Chatterton committed suicide. Keats remains the one striking example of a supreme poet cut off in his prime. It is true that we can not take into account all the geniuses that perished before the world had heard their names. It is true also that a long life affords better opportunities for notable performance, and that a very long life will give a good writer rather excessive prominence. The years, as they accumulate, may crush you, or raise you far above the crowd: it depends partly on your skill, and far more on your luck, whether you remain on top of the pile. *Peccavimus:* we made too much of Anatole France, on the strength of his nearing eighty; we accorded him the European primacy once held by Voltaire, Goethe, Hugo and Tolstoy, and made him look absurdly small on the massive pedestal of his fame. We have ranked Thomas Hardy a little too high, simply because he happened to be the last of the Victorians. We are in danger of spoiling G. B. Shaw: the majesty of a living classic does not fit well with his cap and bauble. We may therefore assume that in literature, many writers failed to impress the world simply because time was not granted them; while others rose high partly because they happened to live long. But this is true of all professions. Keats, Poe, Heine, and, in our own days, Katherine Mansfield and D. H. Lawrence, show what can be done in spite of an ailing body; but great achievements, as a rule, are facilitated by physical vigor.

The longevity of the man is not the same as the longevity of the author. Sainte-Beuve claimed that we all carry in our hearts a poet who died young; the writer of verse may not be aware that the poet in him is dead. Many living worthies are statues on their own monuments. Few men have done their best work after sixty. Hardy, whose epic drama *The Dynasts* is held by many to outrank his novels, is one of the exceptions. But, while not supreme, the writings of old men may stand very high. Goethe and Hugo, after seventy, preserved powers that justified their primacy. There are beautiful notes in the swan songs of Landor, Tennyson, Browning. An old writer, quite apart from the inevitable weakening of his faculties, labors under an unjust disadvantage. If he perseveres in the accustomed way, he will be accused of repeating himself. His formula will have lost its freshness; a whole generation of imitators will have made it commonplace. If he wanders into unwonted paths, he is "falling off from his standard", he is "losing himself." When, under Napoleon, the Parisians heard the familiar boom of the cannon of the Invalides heralding some new victory, they shrugged their shoulders with indifference: the public has been less than fair to the latter-day books of Rudyard Kipling. Paul Bourget, well over eighty, is still turning out at least one volume of fiction every year. It sells, it is respectfully and frigidly noticed by the press, but no one pays any serious attention to it. Yet there is no evidence that the new book is noticeably worse than his work half a century ago. This remark, it is true, might cut both ways. Mr. Cabell, at fifty, decided that *James Branch Cabell* was played out; but he at once started a fresh career as *Branch Cabell*. We may live to see *Branch Cabell* exhaust himself by the time he is seventy-five: then *Cabell* will take up the wondrous tale.

Longevity naturally evokes the corresponding term, precocity. When does authorship begin? There are few infant prodigies in literature. The case of Opal Whiteley, which created quite a stir a few years ago, is not authenticated beyond cavil. Her diary was a curiosity rather than a masterpiece: remove the extraneous elements, the age of the authoress, the alleged mystery of her origin, the quaint French names she gave to animals and trees, and very little remains. Her gifts, which can not be denied, have not borne later fruit. We are willing to believe that Daisy Ashford's *The Young Visiters* was not written by J. M. Barrie. Conscious or not, it was a delightful satire: delightful, but extremely slight, and, after all, only a happy accident.

Indeed it seems as though the only art in which children could excel were music. An eight-year-old pianist or violinist, strangely enough, is not a musical box in human shape. He expresses feelings for which he has no words; he may develop, not merely into a great virtuoso, but even into a genuine master. Mozart was such a *Wunderkind*. What is the difference? The actual technique of literature, beyond the elementary knowledge of language, is not so elaborate as that of piano or violin. Does music, in spite of ambitious intellectual *programmes,* express only those rudimentary moods which are common to all ages, and which perhaps reach below the human level as well as above? I have seen *music* looking out of a dog's eyes: but music without words.

The poetic urge comes with adolescence: in this, as in so many other respects, it is strangely akin to love and religion. Poetry marks the early dawn of puberty, the moment when youth falls in love with love. When love dreams assume human form, the poetic impulse loses its perfect clearness.

How is it, then, that masterpieces are written by men in their late twenties, rather than by boys and girls in their teens? But we must distinguish the mental (or better the sentimental) age from the chronological. The true poet is, intermittently at least, the eternal adolescent. Even Goethe at sixty, the glorious head of a great national literature, the dean of European letters, philosopher, scientist, man of the world, Olympian—Goethe could actually fall in love with a child.

Then we must remember that "masterpieces"—the thought will constantly recur throughout this book—are stamped as such by their public; and the influential public, the public that buys books, controls magazines, writes reviews, fills professorships, awards prizes, elects to Academies, is a grown-up public, contemptuous of callow sentiment. Adolescent poets are easily repressed by the irony of their elders, and even more by that of their contemporaries. As a rule, they have not found their proper medium. They can only imitate or rebel: two effective manners of not being themselves. Perhaps the safest hypothesis is that poetry can never be "pure" poetry, sheer music; thought and experience do count, and these deepen with age. All this may explain a certain lag between the poetic impulse, which comes with early puberty, the first poems worthy of notice, which rather belong to the eighteenth or twentieth year, and those revealing full mastery, which have to age in the wood quite a while longer.

If we accept the view that poetry belongs to adolescence, it will be difficult to admit that the poetical gift might manifest itself, *for the first time,* in middle age. Poets are born about sixteen, not about forty. There have been many cases of poets revealing themselves to the public in their late maturity, like Agrippa d'Aubigné, the Huguenot captain, and Thomas Hardy, the realistic novelist. But both of them had written, in privacy if not in secret, for many years. It is not inconceivable that the gift may lie dormant, almost unconscious. Edmund About relates the queer case of Monsieur Guérin, who carried unawares an undeveloped twin in his body; suddenly, the twin began to grow, and had to be obstetrically removed, to the infinite embarrassment of Monsieur Guérin. Such a freak may occur in the literary world. As a rule, whoever did not feel the poetic fire at sixteen will never feel it at all. Potential poets are as numerous as potential lovers or potential Christians; *great* poets, no rarer than great lovers or true Christians. The paucity of genuine poets need not imply that Nature is parsimonious: it may mean that *self-poeticide* is a widely prevalent form of murder.

The author's *temperament,* although it manifestly has a physiological basis, will more naturally be considered under psychology. If we had hundreds of monographs such as the one that Dr. Toulouse devoted to Emile Zola, we *might* discover the physical concomitants that denote literary superiority. So far, there is not even a self-respecting hypothesis in that direction. Phrenology is in disrepute; it may come back—there have been stranger turns of the wheel. The cephalic index, as we have seen, is hardly safer: Mrs. Atherton is an angel who rushed where scientists fear to tread.

There remains one biological factor which might be of capital importance in the study of literature: *heredity*. While *race* is far too hazy a concept to be of serious value, *ancestry* is much more definite. Literary gifts, although they may be revealed and perfected through training, are pretty evidently inborn. The best teaching may enable a man to write correctly, and even to write *well:* it will not turn him into a writer. Ancient experience is in accord with modern science. "Poets are born, not made"; and Boileau, much as he believed in the virtue of Reason, rules, and hard work, opened his *Art Poétique* with the warning: "In vain will a rash author attempt to scale the heights of Parnassus, if he does not feel the secret influence of heaven, if his star, at his birth, has not made him a poet."

As heredity is a patent fact in so many fields, as its laws in simple cases have been defined with remarkable accuracy, we are tempted, with the hasty logic which so often gets the better of scientific caution, to assert that heredity *must* operate in *all* cases. There is no marked ability that is not the sign of an inborn tendency; there is no inborn tendency that could not be traced, if the facts were known, to some ancestor. Sir Francis Galton, in his *Hereditary Genius,* did not fail to include a chapter on *Literary Genius.* As the school of Galton is still lustily alive, as his name is still one to swear by, we urgently recommend the reading of that chapter. In our opinion, it is extraordinarily convincing—in disproof of Galton's thesis.

We start with a fundamental ambiguity. Genius! What is Genius? We shall have to devote a whole chapter to the discussion of that essential term. In common parlance, it denotes a gift so extraordinary that it may well seem mysterious. For Galton and his school, it means simply marked superiority of any kind, established by wide recognition. He includes among his instances many names that no literary critic would ever dream to consider as geniuses. Now this ought to make a marked difference. Mere *superiority* may often be explained in terms of environment: education and opportunities. There are dynasties among professional men, among craftsmen, even among artists, which require no other hypothesis. If a child is decently intelligent, his education in a particular line will begin unconsciously at his father's table, with chance questions answered off-hand by an expert. The child will *play* at his father's craft; later on, his father will be his teacher and his guide, or, at any rate, will be able to pick out for him the best teachers and guides. Tools or books will be available; the boy will have valuable sympathies and connections at the very outset of his career: he is born in the purple. A Huxley, connected on every side, for three or four generations, with science and literature, would be inexcusable if he did not show some brilliancy. In order to catch up with the young aristocrat or plutocrat of culture, the child of the farm or the slum will have to reveal overwhelming powers.

So it is not safe to judge by the men who have done creditable work in their father's line. Their success proves that they were not fools: it does not prove that they were geniuses. With a trifle more luck—greater commanders in the field, an abler assistant at his elbow, a demoralized opponent—the younger Moltke might have been quoted as an outstanding example of military genius running in certain families. He came within an ace of success: and we know that his military gifts were not of the highest order. He was aware of it, and begged the Kaiser not to impose upon him a crushing responsibility. His *apparent* superiority, which fate might have left unchallenged, was entirely due to opportunities. His rise to the supreme position in the German army was not an instance of hereditary genius, but only one of nepotism.

In order to establish Galton's thesis, it would be necessary to discriminate experimentally between inborn gifts and a favorable environment. To that end, we should have to shift the children around—to entrust the heir of the successful man to the petty shopkeeper or the hard-struggling mechanic, and *vice versa*. This would have to be done on a sufficiently large scale; and there is no sign that many families are ready for such a sacrifice in the interests of science. Moreover, the children would have to be unconscious of the change; *and the parents also:* else the essential conditions would not be comparable. We can not sufficiently repeat that it is impossible to experiment with human beings as freely as with rats, guinea pigs, and Mendel's sweet peas.

This quantitative method failing us, we should restrict ourselves to *genius* in its more unquestioned and most striking form, genius such as it appears, in each nation, not more than a dozen times in a hundred years. Within these limits, the theory breaks down altogether. In many cases, we know neither the ancestors of our geniuses nor their progeny; when we do know them, they are not geniuses themselves. There has been no Dante Junior, no Shakespeare the Son, no Voltaire Fils, no Goethe the Younger. The three authentic sons of Napoleon, the Duke of Reichstadt, Count Walewski and Count Léon, revealed no transcendant gifts. Rousseau "experimented" with his children by sending them all to a foundling's hospital: all have disappeared without a trace.

Galton's chapter is so weak that it raises the contrary question: why is it that there is no true "literary peerage", why is there so little transmitted superiority? We must reassure the sons of great writers in the same way as Reverend Clarence Macartney found it necessary to reassure the sons of ministers: favorable instances are numerous enough to prove that there is no inescapable blight. Beyond this it is difficult to go.

Many explanations have been offered for this paradoxical phenomenon. The first is that men of literary genius, when they are parents at all, are not invariably the best of parents. In fact, they are frequently the reverse. The intimate biographies of writers are not always edifying. Irregularities, quarrels, nervousness, despair, often poison the home atmosphere, and would make the growing boy vow that he will get as far away from literature as he can. Unfortunately for this ingenious explanation, it is not confirmed by the facts. Those writers whose lives were unimpeachable, like Tennyson, were not more successful than the others in transmitting their genius. On the other hand, the clearest case of heredity is perhaps that of the two Dumas. The father, with all his absurdities and his commercialism, had indomitable verve and a matchless narrative gift. The son, absurdly depreciated to-day because of his excessive cleverness, perfected the problem play before Ibsen, and the long, brilliant preface on social problems before Bernard Shaw. Now, old Dumas was a flamboyant example of the prodigal father, and took his parental responsibilities with incredible lightheartedness.

Perhaps, in many cases, superiority in the father was the result of a struggle; the son reaches too easily a stage which should be conquered. To win the right of meeting the great on a footing of social equality is in itself a challenge and an education; to take that right for granted, as your father's son, weakens the virtue of the experience. In literature, as in politics or in business, the heir is seldom equal to the founder of the line. Yet his gifts may not be inferior: only they fail to grow, for lack of a sufficient incentive. The romance of success can hardly be repeated generation after generation.

Sonship is therefore a dangerous position in literature. To follow in your father's footsteps condemns you to mere *pastiche;* and so you may well feel discouraged in advance. To depart from his methods and standards carries with it a suspicion of disloyalty. The superficial encouragement of a literary home turns into a very real inhibition.

While the sons of writers are thus hampered from within, they find no predisposition in their favor among the public. Their inferiority is taken for granted. Victor Hugo's sons, Charles and François, had no lack of ability. It is hard to tell how far they would have gone, if in everybody's eyes and in their own, their father's glory had not reduced them to insignificance. His grandson, Georges, was admirably gifted. But the poem of which he and his sister Jeanne were the heroes, or rather the victims, *The Art of Being a Grandfather,* hung like a millstone round his neck. He was The National Infant: France never admitted that he could grow out of his swaddling clothes. He had to be an artist almost surreptitiously. Maurice Rostand wrote the tragedy of his own fate: his father's fame imprisons him as in a "Crystal Tomb."

It is absurd to talk of literary genius as though it could be measured in scientific terms. Ability is inextricably mingled with success, and success with opportunity. Napoleon fifty years earlier or later would not have been the Napoleon we worship. Rousseau's unknown children may have had all their father's *genius:* but that genius was inseparable from a preëxisting movement, of which Rousseau became the symbol even more than the guide.

The history of literature is not that of individual achievements, but that of public taste. This makes the study of hereditary genius practically hopeless: gifts may be transmitted, but not the chance of revealing them. As a concession to Galton, we are willing to admit that great work can hardly be expected from the descendants of unmitigated morons. Even then, we are reluctant to give up the saving clause: "The wind bloweth where it listeth."

Chapter 12

SOCIOLOGY OF THE AUTHOR TYPE

UNDER the wilfully formidable heading *Sociology,* we propose to examine two different problems. The first, and by far the simpler, is: from what class in society do authors principally come? The second, much more puzzling: what is the place of authors *as such* in organized society? Do they naturally aggregate themselves to one of the existing groups, or do they form a group of their own?

I

We note without surprise that, until the nineteenth century, very few writers came directly from the common people. The masses, for one thing, were illiterate; the literature which was fully recognized required a classical education. A young peasant who managed, under such unpromising circumstances, to show some promise, might be steered into the Church and the Universities. If he left those havens of safety, he was seldom heard of again. Villon's posthumous luck was a miracle; he might, however, have preferred a living to a legend. Religious literature, more democratic in certain respects than her profane sister, gave us John Bunyan the tinker; "philosophy" had Diderot, the cutler's son; the lyric offers Bobbie Burns, the Ayrshire peasant.

The nineteenth century gradually removed one disability by offering education more generously, and another by weakening social prejudices. So the sons of working men who made their mark in literature become more numerous as we approach our own times. However, even at present, the proletarians are not represented in the literary field in proportion to their numbers. The parvenu of letters is rarer than the financial parvenu. This does not establish that the poorer classes are, intellectually, the lower classes. It rather indicates that refined, traditional literature is a luxury that the people can not well afford. The first desire of the working man is to turn his son into a *bourgeois,* not into an artist. There is snobbishness no doubt in such a consciousness of the social hierarchy; but there is also a more definite feeling. The poor suffer from insecurity even more than from physical discomfort: what they dream of is an established position. Authorship is a gamble; the fame and emolument that it brings are precarious.

The conditions we have just sketched belong to a passing order. Increasingly, education is placed within the reach of all; increasingly, literature throws off the thrall of certain social conventions. The time may not be far off when a knowledge of literary tradition will be a heavy handicap. The Proletarian State is fostering literature: according to Stuart Chase, an author in Russia may receive the largest income allowed in that country. But the conditions adverse to the literary expression of the working classes had prevailed, almost without a challenge, until a hundred years ago; and, even in America, these conditions have left traces which can not be ignored.

The titled aristocracy, at the other end of the scale, is infinitely more fertile for literature than the masses. If, however, we consider, not their respective numbers, but their respective opportunities, the difference is no longer so striking. In the Middle Ages, the noblemen were fighters, and took pride in their lordly ignorance; but from the dawn of the Renaissance at any rate—earlier in Southern France and Italy—it was no longer ungentle-manly to be literate. The aristocracy had education, leisure, social refinement, prestige: what did they do with all these advantages? No doubt there were great writers among them, and even on the throne: of the two French poets that stand out in the murky welter of the fifteenth century, one was a vagabond, Villon, the other a prince of the royal blood, Charles of Orleans. But the *Debrett's Peerage,* the *Almanach de Gotha* of Literature, remain slim. After all, why should the well-born exert themselves in writing? Their existence, which can be filled with vigorous activity as well as exquisite enjoyment, is their daily masterpiece. Sports, the hunt, the army, diplomacy, court intrigues, court functions, love affairs, are freely open to them. Let others indite: *they* have only to live.

Although we are told that Romanticism and Democracy are both the spawn of Rousseau, Romanticism, at one stage of its development, had an aristocratic tinge (Shelley and Byron were well born), or affected an aristocratic pose. The Baroness de Staël, the Viscount de Chateau-briand, Count Joseph de Maistre, Alphonse de Lamartine,

Alfred de Vigny, Alfred de Musset, Honoré de Balzac, gave French literature—for the unwary—the prestige of a Social Register. And we must not forget that George Sand, although she turned socialist, was Baroness Dudevant and a descendant of Marshal de Saxe, while Victor Hugo was a Spanish Count.

Most of this is an amusing Romantic delusion. The magic *de* is no patent of nobility, even when it is not gratuitiously assumed as it was by Balzac. Chateaubriand, Lamartine, Vigny, belonged to the lesser provincial nobility; but Hugo's title, conferred on his father by King Joseph, had never been recognized either in France or in Spain. As for Mesdames de Staël and Dudevant, the titles belonged to their husbands, who were decidedly husbands *in partibus infidelium*.

In modern English literature, we find great pleasure in some of the work by Lord Dunsany, and, in a semi-literary field, we admire those undoubted aristocrats, Rosebery and Balfour; but no English lord has reached the summit of fame since Byron. Literature has contributed far more to the peerage (Macaulay, Lytton, Disraeli, Tennyson, Morley, Bryce) than the peerage to literature.

It seems as though, in our semi-democratic days, a handle to one's name were a serious handicap. Guarding ourselves against our own unconfessed snobbishness, we refuse to take a literary lord seriously. Alfred de Vigny bragged that he had "stuck on the gilded crest of the nobleman *an iron quill* which was not without beauty." This ludicrous image, ready for the hand of the cartoonist, is perhaps the best symbol of popular opinion on the subject. A belted earl should not be a quill driver: it does not belong to the type.

This leaves us with the middle class as the favored breeding ground of literature. It sounds paradoxical: we are accustomed to consider middle class and Philistinism as equivalent terms, and the *bourgeois* as the very antipodes of the artist. If an artist can not be an aristocrat, he will go straight to the people. The French Romanticists who, about 1824, were all Knights of the Throne and the Altar, by 1830 had cast in their lot with democracy. To-day, a self-respecting poet may be flaming red or lily white, a bolshevist or a royalist: for the middle class, he has the haughtiest scorn.

This attitude, snobbish at times, not seldom generous, must be accepted as a fact. But it does not dispose of the previous fact, that most writers have their origin in the *bourgeoisie*. The two extreme classes are hampered in their cultural development: the lower, by lack of educational facilities, by lack of leisure, by social prejudices that press upon them from without, by an inferiority complex which inhibits them from within; the upper, by the sloth and vanity which come with unearned distinction: like Lord Melbourne, they prize most highly those honors about which "there is no damn'd nonsense of merit." A social curse, a social privilege, are equally benumbing. The *bourgeois* alone has both the incentive and the opportunity.

The middle class reaches indefinitely above and below. In a country like America, it is so freely open to "the people" that the distinction between them is blurred—blurred, but, as we have seen, none the less real. In France, the passage from the one to the other takes at least one generation. On the other hand, there is an upper middle class that mixes freely and actually merges with the gentry. The *bourgeoisie,* in fact, is not a class at all, but the substance of our *bourgeois* world. The aristocracy and the "lower orders" are both survivals. England preserves her Lords as she keeps up the Beefeaters and the Lord Mayor's Show; and I heard, ages ago, Bernard Shaw open a debate at Toynbee Hall on the very sensible proposition "that the working classes are useless, dangerous, and ought to be abolished."

In that enormous middle class, some strata are more favorable than others to the breeding of literary men. The best of all seems to be the professional world: lawyers, doctors, ministers, professors, military and naval officers, civil servants. There we find education, discipline, comfort without display, and a sense that there are obligations superior to material rewards. *"Noblesse oblige"* is far truer of this group than it is of the peerage itself. In classical France, for two centuries, the majority of writers came from that element, especially from minor state officials, and from those legal dynasties which had founded "a nobility of the gown" rivaling, in wealth and influence, the "nobility of the sword."

Most writers, then, are *bourgeois* by birth and education. But they are *bourgeois* out of sympathy with their class. There is a fine indifference to paltry economies and petty conventions among the aristocrats and among the proletarians. The great lord can afford to be careless; the pauper is without care because he is without hope. The *bourgeois,* in between, must scheme, save, keep up all the decencies: admirable virtues, but plodding, lack-luster, almost stodgy, in which there is no romance.

It is natural, therefore, that the artist, on entering upon his career, should leave the *bourgeois* world behind. Not merely the thoroughbred artist: but every young *bourgeois* who has a touch of the poet in him—and there is enough poetry in the very fact of youth to make the experience almost universal. So the son of Respectability has his fling of rebellion; he affects Bohemianism and the latest iconoclastic fad; he flocks to Greenwich Village or Montparnasse. After this generous sowing of wild oats, he returns meekly to his tame *bourgeois* world. Jean Richepin, who posed as a super-tramp and circus athlete—an anticipation of our Jim Tully—ended in the sedate uniform of an Academician, a favorite lecturer to the little white geese and the dowagers of conservative Society. But the Prodigal Son returns with a wistfulness that may find its expression in genuine literature. And, once in a while, he never returns at all.

II

It has been admitted throughout the ages that authors formed among themselves a brotherhood which obliterated social distinction. In the ancient world, the slave as well as the Emperor could be a philosopher and could be a poet. Charles IX, who loved poetry and dabbled in it, was expressing a commonplace of literature when he wrote to Ronsard: "Both of us wear crowns." This principle—at any rate this convention—has been respected in the French Academy ever since its foundation: prince, prelate, poet, meet on equal terms. What place should this Ancient Order of Bards occupy in society?

According to Plato, none whatever: the world is still smiling at this ostracism of poetry by the greatest of metaphysical poets, the father of a noble brood. At the other extreme, possibly no less absurd, we meet the conception of the Poet as prophet, and shepherd of nations. Above our pettifogging parliaments, blind leaders of the blind, we need a House of Seers. In between, we find all possible positions, with two more definite than the rest: the writer as a *parasite*—honored retainer or mere buffoon; the author as *business man*. There are as wide differences among lawyers or among ministers as there are among writers. But we know pretty definitely where the lawyer and the minister, as such, stand in the community. The writer, on the contrary, has not yet found his normal level.

The easiest solution is for the writer to be financially independent. "He inherited a small competence which enabled him to devote himself to literature": such statements abound in biographies. There have always been "gentlemen-writers", and would-be gentlemen as well. Congreve affected to despise his prominence as a playwright; Byron still kept up the pretence that he would receive no payment for his work. (It is true that he allowed his publisher to slip him a check when he was not looking, and grumbled when the check was not handsome enough.) For centuries, English magistrates and members of Parliament went unpaid. Fine disinterestedness on their part, wise economy for the State? As a matter of fact, the practice proved one of the worst fences for the preservation of class monopoly. In the same way, the principle that writers should not be paid would bar out of literature all those who are still under Adam's curse, and have to earn their bread. Besides, if commercialism is a peril to the integrity of literature, so is amateurishness.

There have always been professional authors: in exchanging ballads for bread, Vachel Lindsay was consciously reviving a tradition as old as Homer himself. But the earnings of the profession, until the eighteenth century, were small and precarious. For the solid world, the wandering minstrel is hard to distinguish from the beggar. The famishing poet is a stock character in satire, drama and romance. Victor Hugo made use of Pierre Gringoire as comic relief in the tragic gloom of his *Notre Dame de Paris:* a sketch in light, sure touches, which reveals more humor and delicacy than the Weird Titan is usually given credit for. Rostand followed the same approved line in the second act of his *Cyrano de Bergerac.* At times the smug contempt of the safely established *bourgeois,* like Boileau, for his down-at-heels colleagues, is little short of nauseating.

"Poets must live,"—although the substantial Philistine might very well retort: "I don't see why." So they had to seek the protection of the powerful and the wealthy. The *Patron* is an institution in art and literature. It is one of the painful sides of our study to read the fulsome dedications of great writers to noble lords, and even to obscure plutocrats. Corneille, as proud in his verse as an old Roman or a Spanish hidalgo, discovered extraordinary virtues in a certain M. de Montauron: a recognized manner of holding out his hand. In its most objectionable form, patronage was discarded by Pope, and withered under the scorn of Johnson. But it had survived until Johnson's time. Read again that scathing letter to Lord Chesterfield. It is not a repudiation of patronage: it merely asserts that the noble lord was seeking honor and gratitude for benefits he had not conferred.

Patronage need not always be degrading. Maecenas could be open-hearted as well as free-handed. The most acceptable form of patronage is that which comes from the Sovereign himself. The King's bounty is not an alms, but a national reward. The most independent writers could accept it without a qualm. The list of pensions awarded by Louis XIV honored both the Grand Monarch and the recipients, among whom were found even subjects of enemy countries. Samuel Johnson, with his bristling pride, found no incongruity in being granted a pension: it is true that his rather wicked definition of the term could not be expunged from the mighty *Dictionary*, and caused him some embarrassment. The practice was continued well into the nineteenth century: Victor Hugo, hardly more than a "marvelous boy", was thus rewarded by Charles X, and, as late as 1883, Matthew Arnold was given a pension of two hundred and fifty pounds for his services to literature. Tennyson confessed: "Something in that word 'pension' sticks in my gizzard." That was in 1845. The wound to his gizzard did not prove mortal: he lived forty-seven years longer.

But this frank method is going down with the prestige of monarchy. Writers would feel squeamish at receiving support from politicians; democratic voters, even in the most Athenian of Republics, would grumble at squandering the people's money on loose and idle rhymesters. If the blessings of the party system, log rolling and the pork barrel were introduced into literature, we might have a body of subsidized Pindars that would worthily match the subsidizing Solons: *horresco referens*.

Even in royal days, authors were frequently assisted, not by direct grants, but in the form of sinecures. Racine and Boileau, for instance, were Royal Historiographers who prudently refrained from excessive historiographical zeal. (G. P. R. James, so cruelly burlesqued by Thackeray, was the last Historiographer Royal.) One of the most approved forms of reward was through Church preferment: partly in memory of the days when clerics had a monopoly of learning, partly for the more practical reason that the Church was wealthy, and her wealth at the disposal of the sovereign. There are famous, and indeed glaring, examples of this in English literature. Few men could be less Churchly than Jonathan Swift: insanely proud, savagely partisan, foul in thought and word. But his political services coupled with his literary genius marked him for advancement, which never reached the heights he desired. In Sydney Smith we find, on a much reduced scale, the same combination of politics and wit: the result was a good "living." Even in our own times, Dean Inge's ecclesiastical dignity was the fruit of caustic humor and a fine journalistic sense for effect, no less than of Neo-Platonic scholarship, orthodoxy and saintliness. In Sweden, Tegner, the epic poet, became a bishop, although his private life was far from exemplary. In France, there were, throughout the classical age, "commendatory abbots" whose sacred revenues supported decidedly profane lives. Pierre de Ronsard, some of whose erotic poems are almost Italian in their vivacity, was such a semi-ecclesiastic. Bourdeille, who wrote the spicy private chronicles of the time, has survived under his clerical name of Brantôme. In the eighteenth century, Abbé de Bernis won favor with charming verses on Madame de Pompadour's dimples, and ultimately became a Cardinal: oddly enough, a very good one. Miss Tallentyre will have it—on what authority I know not—that Voltaire himself was offered the red hat. Unfortunately for the gayety of nations, the practice has been discontinued: Mr. James Branch Cabell deserves to be at least a Canon, and Mr. George Jean Nathan an Archdeacon.

As a reward for literary merit, lay sinecures survived longer than ecclesiastical benefices. Until a few years ago, in France, it was the rule to appoint literary characters as heads of the great national libraries and curators of the principal museums. Thus the Arsenal Library, in Paris, was twice a poetical center: with Charles Nodier at the dawn of Romanticism, and, at the close of the nineteenth century, with Jose-Maria de Heredia. Leconte de Lisle, Prince of the Parnassian Poets, was the leonine and saturnine Librarian of the Senate; he had under him a rather fractious sub-librarian by the name of Anatole France. At times, the poet may justify his appointment: Pierre de Nolhac was an excellent curator of Versailles. The Departmental Offices and the City Hall in Paris are swarming with literary men: this is said to increase appreciably the consumption of official paper. It requires an effort to visualize Joris Karl Huysmans, and especially Paul Verlaine, as bureaucrats. The method is not totally unknown in our country: Theodore Roosevelt, so eager for the efficiency of the Civil Service, offered a position in the Customs to Edwin Arlington Robinson. Our rare but sharp encounters with custom officers induce us to believe that they all are poets in disguise: *genus irritabile vatum. . .**

What shall we do with our poets? Alfred de Vigny has devoted to this problem a strange and beautiful book, *Stello*. His survey is not cheering: the aristocratic Ancient Régime allowed Gilbert to starve; the London mercantile plutocracy offered Chatterton a position so menial that he preferred suicide; the democratic French Revolution beheaded André Chénier. It is Vigny's contention that society is *hostile* to poets: it would be more reasonable to say that society does not recognize the poet's right to idleness. Patronage in any form, direct or disguised, from individuals or from communities, offers insuperable difficulties under modern conditions. The Philistine world, *i.e.* the working world, can hardly be expected to take poets at their own valuation, or even at the valuation of a small clique. If writers are recognized by the general public, they need no subsidy.†

There are men of genius who can not sell their wares, or

---

* The United States and the Second Spanish Republic have frequently appointed writers to diplomatic posts.

† A promising way would be for each University to keep a poet, without pedagogical obligation, just as a pet. This, we believe, was tried by Miami University, which, perversely, is not found in Miami, Florida, but in Oxford; and not Oxford, England, but Oxford, Ohio: it seems to play hide-and-seek with the geographer. At least two other cases have reached our notice. The experiment, as far as we know, has not changed the face of the literary world.

who scorn to do so, or who have none to sell: our advice to them would be, not to seek a patron, but to adopt a simple mode of life, work for it, and write in their spare time. We can not recommend Villon's methods of self-support, which included larceny and maybe worse; nor Spinoza's—lens polishing is too close and too sedentary for health and inspiration. An outdoor occupation, not too strenuous, would be ideal. The pastoral tradition might be revived. A forest ranger, a rural mail carrier, have matchless opportunities for poetry. So has a policeman, on a safe beat.

If we reject parasitism, the alternative is to force recognition on your own terms. We have already quoted David Starr Jordan's definition of success: to do the thing you like, and be paid for it. *For it:* not for some make-believe activity. The man of letters *as such* came into his own in the eighteenth century. Alexandre Beljame has shown very convincingly the great difference between the status of Dryden and that of Pope. There was no lack of dignity and sincerity in Dryden: yet, without being mercenary, he was *retained*. De Foe had no standing. Addison and Swift owed theirs partly to political influences. Pope, on the contrary, was The Poet, and nothing else; and Richardson was The Novelist. Henceforth literature could be a wholly independent and respected profession.

Voltaire admired and envied this British sturdiness. He had suffered from the absolute lack of status of the author in France: lionized one day by the most aristocratic society, cudgeled the next without hope of redress. He did more than any one to enhance the prestige of the

Man of Letters: all Europe bowed to King Voltaire in his royal seat at Ferney. But his position was not entirely due to his literary fame. He was a sedulous courtier and a shrewd business man; he would have risen high in any capacity. Rousseau, without such extraneous advantages, achieved even greater success. He raised the power of the Man of Letters in society so high, that he could afford to shun and denounce society. The author as hero or representative man became an acknowledged figure. Goethe conquered a unique place in German life on the sole strength of his writings: at the Court of Weimar, he conferred more honor than he received. Chateaubriand, Lamartine, Hugo, Balzac, Zola, even Anatole France, had the same ambition, which was accepted without a smile: a poet is a Peer of the Realm by right divine, under any régime.

This has never been quite true in America. In the perspective of history, we admit that Villon the outlaw ranks above duke, bishop and king: they are remembered because they were his contemporaries. Shakespeare, in our minds, towers above the aristocracy and the plutocracy of his age. But we are unwilling to recognize, even as a distant possibility, the supremacy of the Man of Letters in our own days. In a list of ten prominent Americans, industrialists, bankers, politicians, movie stars and even gangsters would be far more likely to be included than "mere" writers.

Even with us, the literary profession has risen very high. It has attained prestige: in certain cases, a prestige verging upon absurdity. Its financial rewards are erratic, but occasionally they are great. *Literature* is almost big business:

I remember the announcement that a new book of Mr. Harold Bell Wright (*sic transit!*) was being shipped "by the carload." Yet, with all this prosperity, the standing of the craft remains undefined. For one thing, we all feel that there is no necessary relation between success and merit. We are reasonably certain that a good minister, or a good engineer, or a good lawyer, recognized as such by his peers, will rise in his profession. There can be no such assurance for a good writer. The best critics may praise him, and yet he will fail to catch. Popularity is unaccountable. When it is deliberately sought, it may be purchased too high.

So literature is not a career: it is a gamble. Men excellently endowed for it can not adopt it as a vocation. Much work, and some of the best work, is done on an amateur basis: by men with private means or with other sources of income. Literary men may form national and international associations; if they choose, they may turn themselves into a Union affiliated with the American Federation of Labor. But their organization will only have a loose and superficial relation to the true purpose of literature. Authors do not constitute an "order" in the community, like the medical profession, the bar, or the clergy.

We see no reason to deplore such a situation. "Organization" would make literature the slave of its own past, the tool of a sect, the tool of a particular social system. It would impose upon us "standards", after the desire of the Neo-Humanists. Fortunately, literature remains a living force, never wholly tamed. Official and exclusive possession of the truth makes for legalism, pedantry, pharisaism: whenever that spirit appears in literature, literature turns into a cult, and sickens.

Far from desiring that poets should become a clergy, we would rather see the clergy dissolve into a free company of religious poets. What a magnificent impulse would religion receive, if its ministers were bound by no vows, sworn to no orthodoxy; if they spoke when and where the spirit moved them, and then only; if they were not compelled, in order to earn their stipend, to be "inspired" every Sunday at eleven o'clock! Neither the lyricist nor the mystic can be *retained;* and writing without the lyric note, religion without the mystic flame, are stale and unprofitable.

Chapter 13

PSYCHOLOGY OF THE AUTHOR TYPE

I

In our quest for the *author type,* physiology has been of little avail. A trainer might pick out a likely sprinter or prize fighter; at any rate, he might safely reject the candidates who did not come up to certain specifications. But there is nothing in the physique of a man that marks him out as poetical timber. Sociology leaves our minds in confusion. In the present state of our knowledge, the only definition of *Homo Scriptor* with any claim to validity will have to be a psychological one.

At the outset, we must reiterate the familiar words of caution. Let us not forget that a *type* arbitrarily isolates certain common elements, and gives them what may seem to be excessive prominence. *Homo Scriptor* is first of all *Homo,* presumably *Sapiens.* It must be remembered also that the notion of type takes no account of values. When we seek to define "the author as such", we obtain no clue to the greatness or mediocrity of individual authors. Indeed, the mediocre ones may be "truer to type"; while, in the very greatest, the type becomes a subordinate element. "We were expecting an author," says Pascal, "we find a man": the words apply admirably to Pascal himself. This will explain why our Psychology of the Author may seem disparaging: what we are studying at present is the professional deformation rather than the creative power. The mystery of genius will be reserved for a following chapter.

The fundamental trait in the psychology of authorship is *Conceit*. The word is ugly, and we should like to substitute for it "noble pride", or "consciousness of genius": but remember that we are including in our survey the small as well as the great, and the smaller side of the great. Horace was a man about town, light-hearted, facile, witty: when he remembered he was a poet, he started bragging magnificently, as only poets can: *Exegi monumentum Ære perennius.* . . . This has become an eternally recurrent theme in literature. Poets boast of their immortality, of their power to confer immortality, with unblushing confidence. "Love me," says Ronsard, in all seriousness, to his Helen: "your beauty will pass away, but my words of praise will not pass away." "Marquise," writes Corneille (the provincial Church Elder enmeshed in the toils of a stage coquette), "my gray hair may not appeal to you: but remember I am Corneille; posterity will know of your charms only through my verse."

To all creative writers—poets in the wider sense of the term—might be applied the words of Lanson about Chateaubriand: "He had every form of pride: from the pride which is a virtue, to the pride that is sheer foolishness." Hence the proverbial touchiness of the poet, his enormous appetite for praise, his vanity even in trifling matters. Hence Byron's consciousness of his romantic beauty, hence the dandyism of Bulwer Lytton and Disraeli, the æsthetic refinements of Oscar Wilde. Exceptions? By no means: in the literary quarters of all great capitals, you will meet men who, through some trick of speech or manner, through some oddity of garb, seek to arrest your attention, and proclaim: "Behold! I am a poet."

When the French poets met in Paris, after the death of Léon Dierx, to elect their lawful *Prince,* it is claimed that, on the first ballot, there were three hundred votes and three hundred names proposed; on the second ballot, Paul Fort won with two votes. An unkind legend, in all probability: still it indicates what the world expects of the literary man. Bernard Shaw's colossal conceit is put down by many readers as a rather elementary form of humor. "The greatest dramatist since Shakespeare!—Why *since Shakespeare?*" We rather interpret it as fearless candor. Shaw is in the grand tradition; his defiant self-assertion is far better than the Chinese circumlocutions affected at times by Victor Hugo: "the obscure writer of these insignificant lines."

There is no more outrageous form of conceit than the claim to inspiration; and there is none that is more universal. Literally, it means the assumption of an almost divine character: it is no mere man, but a spirit, a god, who speaks through the poet-prophet, *vates.* In less mystic terms, it implies that the poet's passing fancies possess a value not given to other men's. This is most clearly manifested in the boundless egotism of Rousseau.

He dared to set himself against the world; and ultimately, he forced upon the world a minute account of his own life, omitting no ailment and no turpitude. Evidently, in his opinion, it was of the utmost importance to mankind that these things should be known. Innumerable writers, ever since, have insisted upon "living their private lives in public."

The Ego is hateful was a classical dictum. The Romanticists turned it inside out: The Ego is the very core of literature. And we believe the Romanticists were right. Without some revelation of the author's innermost nature, the finest piece of writing lacks the literary spark. Even Boileau recognized this, with his insistence on "the secret influence of Heaven": it is that gift of the gods, the poet's personality, that makes a poet. Even Zola taught the same doctrine: for him Art was Nature seen through a temperament. Now, any one who, in society, would obtrude his idiosyncrasies upon us would be called insufferably conceited. Imagine a stranger buttonholing you: "Listen to the lovely thoughts that came to me when I was jilted by my sweetheart." That is exactly what the poet does. Why should he not? We like it.

You will demur: you probably have known men who stood high in the literary world and who were unaffected, kind, courteous. I could name two or three myself. Yet I do not believe that this invalidates our diagnosis. First of all, let us remember that all "men of letters" are not "poets", *i.e.,* creators. In the critic, the historian, the philosopher, personality does appear indeed; but, except in rare cases like Carlyle and Nietzsche, it is subdued. Then, men of letters may also be men of the world; they need not be crude. Their conceit will reveal itself in subtler fashion than Shaw's cheerful blatancy, or Victor Hugo's preposterous mock-humility. They may even have the half-apologetic modesty of the highborn: "So sorry I am a Duke; awfully uncomfortable for you, I am sure; but I can't help it." There is also the humility of the *Recessional,* the most boastful of all patriotic songs: "O Lord, we are the mightiest of all nations, and the best: help us bear in mind that we are but men." The poet must have his moments of doubt and despair: but even his self-abasement is only inverted pride, just as John Bunyan, more Luciferian than he knew, claimed to be "the chief of sinners." You may have caught him at a time when he despised, not his own work, but his own glory, because it had spread among fools. More simply: the man of genius usually takes no pride in minor things. He will very sincerely defer to your opinion on some practical matter, with a childlike simplicity that will seem to you touching and delightful: even as Louis XIV, who knew himself to be the Lord's anointed and the absolute master of twenty-four million men, could bow down with charming modesty before Boileau's expert knowledge.*

But, just as Louis XIV never forgot that he was the King, the writer, in his heart of hearts, believes that his Ego is all important; that it is right and proper for him to reveal his secret thoughts, and that the world should receive these confidences in awe and wonder. Without

---

* *Louis XIV:* "Who is the greatest writer under my reign?" *Boileau:* "Sire, Molière"—*Louis XIV:* "I did not think so; but you know better about such things than I do."

such a faith, the lyric flame would die; and it is the lyric glow alone that turns even an inchoate mass of dreary naturalism into a thing of beauty.

The writer *must* be conceited, just as the leader of men must have ambition and self-confidence. "Napoleon," says Common Sense, "was a great man, whose only weakness was his ambition." Common Sense may be responsible for the greatest nonsense. Monsieur Joseph Prudhomme, the symbol of the pompous *bourgeoisie,* put the matter much more tersely: "Had Napoleon remained a modest artillery lieutenant, he would still be on his throne." Napoleon was ambition incarnate: remove ambition, you blot out the career, the man himself. Remove conceit from Bernard Shaw: there will not be enough left to make a Sydney Webb.

Conceit is fostered, in the literary man, by the sense that his achievements are strictly personal, not collective, not fortuitous. In this, he is probably mistaken: the public collaborates with him far more than he knows, and luck is no less essential than desert. But the world, so far, agrees with his view; and, if he compares himself with superior men in other fields, he is justified in his belief. Even a Napoleon must feel that his triumphs are due partly to his lieutenants, to his troops, to his armament, to the morale of the country behind him, to the weakness or the blunders of the enemy. The military leader is a bandmaster, the author is a soloist.

The actor, the musical performer, are in closer touch with the public, breathe their incense in thicker clouds; so their vanity is liable to be, in externals, more flagrant than the author's conceit. But it is not so deep-seated. In so far as they are not fools, the performers are compelled to realize that they are mere interpreters; the applause that goes to them must be shared.

The author's conceit does not depend upon success: it antedates and outlives success. It is a faith, the substance of things hoped for, the evidence of things unseen. It remains unshaken, as a faith should, even though mere "works" should fail. If success comes, the writer is idolized by the outside world, worshipped by an inner circle of devotees. When I had the honor of meeting an illustrious Belgian dramatist, the Lady-in-Waiting whispered to me in religious tones: "The MASTER will now receive you." Even a less mystic head would easily reel in such an atmosphere.

But failure only stiffens pride, makes it more defiant. It increases the sense of difference between the Unique and the Many—"mostly fools," growled Carlyle. (Indeed universal applause should have a sobering effect, but pride receives eagerly with both hands.) To be misunderstood becomes the badge of genius.

It is idle therefore to blame an author for his conceit, any more than a conqueror for his ambition, or a revivalist for his fanaticism. In them, such traits are not faults but the essence of their being. Professor Giese's able arraignment of Victor Hugo could be presented in syllogistic form: Victor Hugo was conceited; conceit is the mark of a mean soul; therefore Victor Hugo had a mean soul. No doubt, if Monsieur Dupont, the corner groceryman, had the conceit of Victor Hugo, he would be a laughable sight. But Victor Hugo was not Monsieur Dupont.

II

The second trait, one upon which everybody seems in agreement, is that the author is, and should be, *temperamental*. He has the right, *ex officio,* to be capricious, unaccountable, irritable: indeed, if he were not, we would begin to question his literary pretensions. As we have seen, the traits that belong to a type, national or social, are artificially exaggerated by the very notion of type. As soon as a man is in military uniform, it becomes more unpardonable for him to be timid, easier to be blunt and even brutal. The would-be man of letters will cherish and over-emphasize whatever modest amount of temperament there is in him, in order to look more perfectly the part. The real man of letters needs no such exertion: but he will indulge more freely in weaknesses which are forgiven in advance, without which, indeed, he would actually disappoint his public.

There is a fancy dress of the Author, therefore, almost as conventional as those of the Italian *commedia dell' arte*. If we disregard the costume and study the man himself, the trait is not so evident. It would seem that the very great writers have exercised wonderful will-power and self-discipline. We limit ourselves to the mightiest: the case is too clear with men like Edward Gibbon or Sir Walter Scott, whose robust talent was evidently assisted by tireless industry. Dante was an excellent scholar, a scientist, a philosopher: all things which require more than temperament. The mere amount of Shakespeare's writings, in addition to his heavy practical responsibilities as an actor-manager, would prove beyond doubt his steadiness as a worker. Voltaire filled nine lives to the brim. One of them was that of a scientist: ahead of the official mathematicians of his country, he understood Newton. Another was that of an historian, and his information was so conscientious, so solid, that for over a hundred years, his *Charles XII,* his *Louis XIV,* were not superseded. In Goethe we find the careful official, the naturalist, the physicist, the scholar, as well as the poet. Victor Hugo wrote down his Apocalyptic visions with the punctuality of a professional scribe. Looseness, irregularity, may not be wholly incompatible with literary gifts; but certainly the *bourgeois* virtues of order and perseverance, far from hindering those gifts, bring about their fullest fruition.

The literary *temperament,* however, is not wholly a fallacy. Undoubtedly there are flashes of unique beauty in the works of the loosest and most irresponsible Bohemians. It is a scandal that Verlaine should be a greater poet than so many unimpeachable professors and ministers addicted to versifying: it is a scandal, but it is a fact. Even in the experience of the greatest, we feel that inspiration is not the evident, inevitable result of hard work. At times, hard work actually seems to hamper it. Fruition comes later, often after giving up in darkest discouragement; it comes without apparent connection with previous effort, as a spontaneous release.

But the preparation, whether they know it or not, was not without avail. The flash may be the delayed reward. Even if it were not, even if it came as a gratuitous gift from above, it makes all the difference whether it be received by a crude, ill-prepared, slothful mind, or by one

ready to respond at once, to follow up with immense resources. In a battle, a commander may have a sudden
intuition of the vital point, the exact minute when a single
effort will be decisive. If he has no reserves, no ammuni-
tion; if his staff is so ill-trained that his command will not
be transmitted, his intuition will be wasted. The violinist
who achieves a miraculous purity of note may be "inspired": but we may be certain he has not been waiting
listlessly for inspiration.

The "release" leaves the author physically, nervously
exhausted. Under the discipline which he must impose
upon himself, he goes through the inevitable cycle: effort-
despair-ecstasy-apathy. This secret rhythm, which he himself can not control, is hard to reconcile with formal
schedules and social obligations. The words that Goethe
applies to the soul in love: *Himmelhoch jauchzend, zum
Tode betrübt,* exulting heaven-high, depressed unto death,
are true also of the mind in literary travail. Writers are,
of necessity, nervous, just as soldiers and sailors have to be
vigorous and brave.

Such an experience is not the privilege of the greatest:
it is inherent in the very nature of the work. A sophomore
feels it, if he takes his English Composition seriously.
Literature requires the *swift* passage from depression to
exaltation, and *vice versa.* That which we feel clearly,
sanely, moderately, equably, does not give us the thrill of
wonder, the response so acute, so exquisite that it is akin
to pain, the sudden rediscovery of life. If we could register
on some instrument the poet's sensitivity, we should
obtain a very jagged line. The *range* may be small, if the
transition be sharp: a drop of a few feet, if abrupt, will

give you more of a shock, and of a thrill, than a gradual descent of a thousand. That is why level sublimity, as in theology or metaphysics, is so frequently uninspiring; that is why a fall may rouse poetry as well as a flight; inspiration comes *de profundis* as well as *de excelsis*.

III

It is commonly accepted that the artistic or poetic temperament does manifest itself in morality also. There is no radical difference between psychology, the key to behavior, and morality, the rule of conduct. The artist or poet does not submit willingly to conventional discipline; or, from a less favorable point of view, he yields without sufficient resistance to all his impulses. When this disposition takes the form of moods and irrepressible gestures, we call it temperament, or simply temper; when it leads to definite action, affecting others, we call it morality, or the breach of it. In both cases, the foundation is the same.

It has long been admitted that the artist is a reprobate, —or a privileged character. Pious provincial communities look askance upon any form of art, because art to them betokens loose living. On the other hand, young people discover for themselves an artistic or poetic vocation, simply as a license to sin magnificently (not unlike the boy who declared himself irresistibly attracted to the sea, and gave as a reason that "a sailor has a wife in every port"). Like most popular opinions, which so easily turn into popular fallacies, this view of the artist's morality is ludicrously distorted—with a basis of truth.

Few writers of note were out and out "bad men." We

have no desire to whitewash Villon, Byron, Poe, Baudelaire, Verlaine, Oscar Wilde. There was perversity in their thought as well as in their lives, and their fame rests, in some small part, on their alleged turpitude. To say that we admire them for their occasional lapses into correctitude would be unconvincing nonsense: it is wicked to tell a lie beyond the limits of credibility. But the fascination of sin is not exclusively due to the reader's diseased curiosity and to his love for scandal: it arises also from the dramatic contrast between aspirations and abjection, the *De Profundis* element so clear in Baudelaire and Wilde, not found in the Marquis de Sade. Paradoxically, these damaged souls bring us closest to the fundamental Christian experience, the conviction of total depravity, the horror and shame of one's self, the desperate appeal to divine mercy. Everything is strangely mingled in these nether poets and in the feelings they stir up in our hearts: mingled, but certainly not wholly base. Whatever interpretation we choose to offer, it must be admitted that this particular circle of Inferno does not fairly represent the literary world. There are enough writers whose lives were blameless to destroy any fancied identity between sin and genius. On the other hand, there have been worse men than Baudelaire among judges, soldiers and priests.

We can not deny that the biographies of many famous authors are not strictly exemplary in the conventional sense. Even Shakespeare—what little we know of him— or surmise—could hardly be held up as a model; nor Lope de Vega, nor Voltaire, nor Goethe, nor Shelley, nor Victor Hugo; least of all Jean-Jacques Rousseau. But does the literary profession stand unique in this respect? The light of publicity always beats more fiercely upon the illustrious than upon the obscure: Frédéric Masson devoted a learned study to every passing affair of Napoleon: no one cares to list the feminine conquests of Colonel So-and-So. But while in other cases, that light is trained from without, in the case of writers it is assisted from within. They glow with indiscretion; they kiss and tell; indeed at times they might be accused of kissing for the sole purpose of telling. That is why alleged literary history so often has the same kind of appeal as the reports of divorce proceedings. We must know for certain with whom Byron misbehaved, and whether there is a suspicion of truth in *Cakes and Ale*. Louis Barthou, a responsible statesman, head of the Reparations Commission, gravely investigated Victor Hugo's good fortunes and misfortunes. Charles Maurras, the profound theorist of a Royalist Restoration, devoted a book to *The Lovers in Venice,* George Sand and Alfred de Musset. No one could swear that stockbrokers are more virtuous than poets: only stockbrokers are not quite so eager to tell of their transgressions; neither are we so eager to know.

It is true that artists are exposed to temptations second only to those of princes and soldiers: the lute, the crown and the sword, far more than the pocket book, act as aphrodisiacs. Mr. Branch Cabell has given us the budget of his average daily mail: it seems mostly made up of violent assaults on his chastity, and of queries about the pronunciation of his patronymic. Mr. George Jean Nathan, in *Monks are Monks,* assures us that the excess of evil brings its own cure, and that every man of literary repute, if the truth were known, deserves to be called Joseph. Mr. Nathan is a shrewd observer, with ample opportunities for gathering reliable information. But he is suspected of a fondness for the paradoxical.*

We may also admit that the artistic temperament is not easily amenable to formal discipline. Especially the Romantic temperament, which may be considered as the most purely artistic of all. The poet must place intensity before conformity: else he is no poet at all. This rejection of rule is frankly immoral, if by morality you mean a conventional code. But such morality we have defined elsewhere as "statistics with a sanctimonious mask." "This thing," says Morality, "is done; that thing is not done." Granted: but why should *I* do the one, and abstain from the other? Heroism and saintliness are not seldom in rebellion against accepted standards. All martyrs were strictly *immoral:* men who defied authority, tradition, convention, majority rule. Socrates was the corrupter of youth. To the present day, we find it difficult to make up our minds about Rousseau. He strove, blundering, to reach the essential moral truth, which is found only in perfect sincerity. He was not a *good* man: yet we must pause before his challenge: "Let any one dare to say: I am better than he!" Shelley did not evolve a workable rule of life, nor did he always act according to the purest light there was in him: yet his morality was infinitely higher than that of the strait-laced and corrupt society that condemned him. There was much looseness,

---

* "The Editors (of the *American Spectator*) are charmed to learn from Federico Vittore Nordelli's 'L'Uomo Segreto' that Luigi Pirandello was faithful to his wife from January 1894 to January 1918."

and pride, and pose, in Byron, with many twisted prejudices, rather worse than the straight kind: yet his rebellion
was fundamentally *righteous*.

In every case, the artist, and particularly the poet, claims
to be an exception: he has unique powers and enjoys
special privileges. Can we safely draw a line between the
exceptional and the *abnormal*? Here we are confronted
with the ancient problem of the kinship between insanity
and genius: the most baffling, the most hotly controverted
aspect of the poet's psychology. Although we have
sedulously attempted to avoid it, we have repeatedly come
across that mysterious term *genius*. With fear and trem-
bling, we shall now attempt to consider it in its bewildering complexity.

Chapter 14

THE ENIGMA OF GENIUS

AFTER the war and the revolution, Berlin took drastic measures to relieve the house shortage. Superfluous rooms were commandeered, and assigned to homeless families. Strangers were thus forcibly brought into unwelcome intimacy. "What did you do then?" we asked some German friends a few years after the crisis. "Oh! we squabbled." There is a house shortage for thoughts; notions that may be of incompatible temper are compelled to dwell together under the roof of a single word. What do we mean by Religion, Love, Socialism, Democracy? Not one single thing in each case; not even varying shades of the same idea; but concepts in sharp conflict. The thoughts that go by the same name are related, no doubt: but they may fight one another with the ferocity inseparable from civil wars and family feuds.

One such divided household is the word *Genius*. We shall attempt to present seven major conceptions of it: seven is a mystic number, and satisfying to the soul. But seven is a strict minimum: a subtler mind could stretch the catalogue to seventy times seven.

I. *Intelligence Quotient 140*

Athirst for precision, we first apply to the expert. Genius is a quality of the human mind, and therefore pertains to the realm of psychology. Psychology has an answer ready, lacking nothing in definiteness. *A Genius is a person whose Intelligence Quotient* (I.Q.) *is 140 or over.* It is the uppermost division in the following scale:

I.Q. below 25   idiot
         25– 50   imbecile

(How advisable it would be, by the way, to substitute in polite conversation the scientific equivalent for the vulgar and offensive term! "The policies of Senator X seem to denote an I.Q. well below 25. . . .")

50– 70	moron
70– 80	borderline
80– 90	dull
90–110	average
110–120	superior
120–140	very superior
above 140	genius or near-genius

If you want further particulars, you will find them in the *Genetic Studies of Genius,* published at Stanford by Professor Lewis Terman and his school. I can particularly recommend Volume II: *The Early Mental Traits of Three Hundred Geniuses,* by Catharine Morris Cox. It is a tome of 842 pages, bulging with statistics, tables and graphs; occasionally, an awe-inspiring algebraic formula fills half a page. The seven main tables in which the chief information is condensed provide fascinating reading. We discover, for one thing, that Ali Wedi Zade, "Albanian robber chief", had I.Q. 155, while Napoleon, a robber chief also (Taine's *condottiere*), measured only 145. Marmont, chiefly known for betraying Napoleon, scores 150; Bernadotte, who managed to found the present Swedish dynasty, 140 only. Evidently Dr. Cox is no Napoleon-worshipper. Marat, the crazy fanatic of the Terror, is credited with I.Q. 170; our Emerson with 155. Victor Cousin, the philosophical mountebank and pontiff of the commonplace, has 180; Diderot, the most dynamic mind of the eighteenth century, 165. Alexander Dumas, the cheerful quadroon, who, by methods akin to Ford's, ran such an efficient romance factory, comes up to 170; Swift to 155: Dr. Cox is free from race prejudice. Wolsey must be the type of a super-genius: 200; Jefferson and Richelieu, 160 only; Rousseau 150 (Professor Irving Babbitt would have guessed 50–70: but he was not trained in the latest psychological methods). Altogether a pretty radical *Umwertung!* We turned eagerly to Shakespeare's line: we found a blank: "No score: insufficient data." This is probably the most scientific statement in the whole book.

Amicus Terman, sed magis amica veritas. We do not believe that, by such methods, even with the most impressive apparatus, any genuine precision could be hoped for. The three hundred worthies who serve as a basis for the study were selected according to some loose "common consent", that is to say haphazard. The facts used in determining their I.Q. were borrowed from biographies of very unequal value, some of them thoroughly uncritical. No "coefficient of credibility" can be much more than the roughest guess. The investigators, however alert and conscientious, were not competent to appraise superiority in domains radically different from their own.

But even if we admitted the validity and accuracy of the method, the use of the term "genius" would remain objectionable. Genius here means a high degree of superiority, the difference between a modest I.Q. 139 and a glorious I.Q. 141. The scheme does not recognize any radical change, any quality that pertains uniquely to genius, and lies beyond mere success or talent. It thus defines genius only by denying it.

The Terman school, which has done such admirable work in the measurement of *gifted children,* would gain if it dropped the unfortunate word *Genius.* Other expressions might be adopted: the American language is never at a loss for ultra-superlatives. Psychologists, who have coined such delightful words as *schizophrenic* and *pyknic,* might easily have enriched our vocabulary with one more Greek monstrosity. At the worst, such a classification as "mental heavyweights" might have done. The class above "a very superior person" immediately brought to our mind the late Lord Curzon and the teasing little rhyme about him. The "Curzon-level" should have been good enough for any one.

Dr. Cox is not to be blamed for the pseudo-scientific use of the word *genius:* neither is Dr. Terman. For Dr. Terman borrowed it from no less an authority than Galton himself, the founder of Eugenics. When we look into

Galton's conception of Genius, we are amazed at its vagueness. Genius, for him, is merely eminence. Hence the extraordinary weakness of his chapter on *Literary Genius*. As we have seen, it opens up a very interesting problem, but exactly the reverse of the one Galton thought he had solved: why is it that so few recognized geniuses are the sons of other recognized geniuses? *Superiority*, evidently, runs in certain families; it is transmitted through the joint influences of heredity and environment, in proportions which have to be finely measured. Superiority, yes: but, if genius is not mere superiority, we are just as much in the dark as before.

II. *The Prodigy*

If we see a man accomplish with extraordinary facility a task which, for the rest of us, would be long and painful, we are tempted to exclaim: "There is a genius!" *Prodigy* would be a safer term. Rapidity, ease, even a high degree of material perfection, matter extremely little: the rarity and value of the result should enter into consideration. A lightning calculator like Jacques Inaudi, a chess player meeting, blindfolded, twenty opponents, a painter who can execute at the same time two pictures with his hands and two with his feet, Charles V dictating at once several dispatches in different languages, all are prodigies, marvelous human instruments, but mere instruments. What is the quality of the mind that uses such a matchless tool? Of what worth is the product? Plain words uttered in the vernacular by Jesus or even by Lincoln outweigh all the polyglot dispatches of Charles V.

The word prodigy is chiefly applied to youthful performers. Those among our readers who may deserve the title need not despair: a few prodigies have turned into geniuses. Mozart is a case in point, and, above all, Pascal —Pascal, a genius by any canon we may choose to apply, and who, in his boyhood, severed from his mathematical books, rediscovered Euclid unaided, using a quaint, childish nomenclature of his own. On the whole, however, the story of prodigies is hardly a cheerful one. Where is Winifred Sackville Stoner, who, a babe in arms, corrected the grammar of her grown-up admirers? Where is William James Sidis, who, at fourteen, "astounded"(?) his Harvard professors by his views on the fourth dimension; who could pick up Russian and Church Slavic in a few weeks; who once sent us a long essay in pellucid Esperanto, proving that the Cro-Magnons were of the same race as the ancient Egyptians; that they spoke the Basque language; that, through Atlantis, they colonized Mexico; who, finally, according to his father, Boris Sidis, formulated the *Law of the Reversibility of Time?* The world is not kind to prodigies; its wonderment is never free from malice; "genius" almost becomes a stigma. The best we can hope for our brilliant young friends, in their maturity, is obscurity and peace. Parenthetically, their parents and educators maintained that neither Winifred Stoner nor William Sidis was a "genius": the merits of their achievements should be ascribed, as in the case of Helen Keller, largely to their teachers.

III. Inspiration

For the plain man, a "prodigy" is merely a two-headed calf. But, in a more religious age, a two-headed calf would have been considered a portent, a miracle. In the conception of genius, there frequently enters the notion of direct intervention from above: the genius is the confidant and the messenger of the gods. The very term genius implies the supernatural, or, if you prefer, the superhuman. It is no mere man who is speaking or working, but, through that man, a *Spirit*. Inspiration explains the apparent ease with which wonders are performed; it also explains the inequality, the unaccountability, of genius. "The wind bloweth where it listeth": the peasant girl, Joan of Arc, the vagabond, Villon, Verlaine, are transfigured for a moment. When inspiration ceases, mere man remains—and how weak, sinful and vain he may be!

This mystic consecration is claimed, not merely for the founders of religions, but for the founders of dynasties as well. Napoleon III elaborated the theory of "Providential Men" as a justification for Bonapartism, imparting to the imperial house a "divine right" more immediate than that of the Bourbons; and it is the sin against the Holy Ghost, in Italy, to doubt the "inspiration" of Mussolini. Poets also boldly assume this prophetic, this Messianic authority: Victor Hugo, in his *William Shakespeare,* drew the portraits of the major geniuses, all stirred by a breath from Beyond, all weird and terrible, all bearing a strange family resemblance to Victor Hugo himself.

All this is poetry—or perhaps mere eloquence. In a sober discussion, this exalted doctrine has no standing. Mysticism and sense have their distinct domains. We do not deny the supernatural claims of genius: we have no means of discussing them. As a rule, when we are using the word genius in a mystic sense, we are merely con-

fessing our own impotence. Whatever we can not understand, whatever we can not explain, even through the
agency of "chance", we ascribe to "genius." It is one of
those residuary and purely negative conceptions, like the
Infinite, or Eternity, which stand for no intelligible reality. Reason in despair seeks refuge in Sublimity. The
word *genius,* in the case of individuals, serves the same
purpose as *Providence* for the world at large. Commynes,
Napoleon, and innumerable others, ascribed their successes to their own foresight and efforts, their failures to
the Inscrutable Will of God. To translate "the will of
God" into terms of puny human experience is nothing but
blasphemous nonsense. A contractor sought release from
an agreement on the plea that the torrential rains which
had hampered the work were "an act of God"; and the
judge in his wisdom decided that "they were not bad
enough for that." Whatever can be apprehended by
human reason is credited neither to Providence nor to
Genius. Such words mark the provisional boundaries of
knowledge.

Although few people nowadays are ready to accept at
its full value the mystic conception of genius, it still imparts to the word a peculiar aura. Genius is a mystery,
and the sacred word must be uttered with bated breath.
For no other reason do we reject and even resent the
Galton-Terman-Cox definition, which fails to recognize
a difference between superiority and genius.

IV. Infinite Pains

For the same reason, the definition of genius as mere
hard work is not likely to prove popular. We take it for

granted that "genius" comes in flashes, and that plodding care is a confession of dullness. Yet the "laborious" theory does not lack support. It was Buffon who wrote: "Genius is but inexhaustible patience." And he lived his law. In a classical age, when men believed that unchangeable truth had been attained and could be taught, application was the sole requisite for success. Even Lessing, although a forerunner of the Romantic revolt, still maintained that any one could write perfect tragedies, if only he would follow closely enough the precepts of Aristotle. In the next century, Carlyle, himself a type of the Prophetic Genius, hurling thunderbolts from his stormy crags, defined Genius as an infinite capacity for taking pains. Edison, a wizard not merely in the eyes of the multitude, but also in those of a literary mystic like Villiers de l'Isle-Adam, originated the homely phrase: "Genius is one per cent inspiration, and ninety-nine per cent perspiration."

We have already seen that, obviously, genius is not incompatible with hard work; in many cases, it would not reveal itself without hard work. Men of the facile and flashy type seldom reach the heights: genius requires either labor or travail, and usually both. A descent into the Nether World was a commonplace of classical epic and medieval poetry: what is most *Divine* in Dante's *Comedy* is not its inspiration, but its faultless art, the indomitable wrestling with a hard material (Gautier's recipe for great poetry), that fearful symmetry, that rigid concatenation of rhyme, which make the hundred Cantos a formidable polished block without a fissure. Du Bartas wrote an epic on Creation, *The Week,* which can boast of more "flashes" than Milton's *Paradise Lost;* Strada elaborated an *Epic of Humanity* in twenty volumes, with more "sublimities" than in Dante's; but their fabrics were loose, and they crumbled. The idea of evolution had been evolving ever since the middle of the eighteenth century; under the name of "the historical spirit", it had become almost a commonplace; as applied to the natural sciences, it was formulated at the same time by Wallace and Spencer as well as by Darwin. Why then does Darwin remain the "genius" whose name is attached to the theory? Because of his inexhaustible patience. Relativity goes back to the Greeks; daring speculations about space and time were vented by H. G. Wells thirty years ago, not only in *The Time Machine,* but in a scientific paper read before a learned society; the "genius" of Einstein is not the intuition of Einstein, but the hard work of Einstein. And, in supporting the "laborious" theory, Edison spoke with good authority. His chosen field was not the free realm of imagination, where a daring adventurer may at any moment stumble upon a discovery: his field was the *laboratory:* he was first of all a worker. The versatile Bohemian Léon Cros invented the gramophone, and Sumner Tainter perfected it; to Moses Gerrish Farmer we owe the incandescent lamp. Yet Edison alone is remembered, and without injustice: for he provided the ninety-nine per cent perspiration.

V. Abnormality, Disease, Insanity

The conception of Genius as balance, health, magnificent sanity, would admirably fit Goethe. George Bernard Shaw, who had a unique opportunity to study the subject by introspection, upheld "the sanity of true genius." Yet he himself flirted with the conception that there was a pathological element in genius. The priest in *John Bull's Other Island,* a figure of matchless appeal among the creations of G.B.S., is a poet with a touch of madness. In *Candida,* the sane, jolly, vigorous parson Morell is contrasted with Marchbanks, a bundle of uncontrolled nerves; and the degenerate poet is preferred to the healthy Philistine.

The idea that genius is connected with mental or physical disease goes back to antiquity. The manifestations of epilepsy and hysteria bear a striking resemblance to those of ecstasy and inspiration. Soothsayers and sybils, St. Paul and Mahomet, could be diagnosed as epileptoids. There were facts enough and to spare in history to supply Lombroso with arguments. Especially as Lombroso considered every harmless eccentricity in the family of a genius as the evidence of a taint, while all men whose sanity could not be impugned were denied the title of genius. Q.E.D.

Both Plato and Aristotle admitted the kinship between genius and insanity. The tradition has been preserved in literature throughout the ages: all great poets claim "rapture", a "fine frenzy", which, by all tests, would indicate abnormality. So well established is this doctrine that the most eminently sane poets are ashamed of their sanity, and fake the ravings that Nature denied them. Boileau, common sense incarnate, when he wrote an *Ode* (and what an Ode!) *on the Siege of Namur,* had to feign "holy intoxication"; but, classical even in his assumed madness, he called it "learned" as well as "holy":

Quelle docte et sainte ivresse . . . .

Longfellow, preaching idealism, chooses a lunatic for his standard-bearer: for no sane person will carry "mid snow and ice a banner with the strange device, *Excelsior!*" Yes, the poets are mad; they know it, they proclaim it, they glory in it. An ancient Greek fallacy here raises its head: if they are truly mad, can we take their word for it?

Lombroso's theory has been refuted times out of number, to the evident satisfaction of the refuters. Still, the association between genius and insanity is of such long standing in the public mind that it can not be dismissed with a shrug. Undoubtedly, we are apt to think of sanity in terms of conservatism, conformity, the average. If such be the case, genius, by common consent, is not sane. So much the worse for sanity, you will say. Granted: but, if we depart from sanity, what will be our guide? Do insanity and genius always diverge from the norm in opposite directions? Or may they not travel at least part of the way together?

The irremediably sane man, the one who, for seven dreary years, "kept cool with Coolidge", sees no vision and dreams no dreams: he is an absolute non-conductor of that mysterious fluid called genius. The sensible man endowed with a higher degree of imagination may toy with visions and dreams. But he never takes them too seriously: his faculty is too weak, or his critical brakes are too efficient. He may be a discriminating reader, a teacher, a cultured dilettante, even a stylist, a skilled rhymester: he will never be a genuine poet. Between his dreams and his practical life, he has established an impassable barrier. The mystic, the prophet, the inventor, the true artist, vaults over the barrier of sense. He believes that his ventures are not without bearing upon practical life; the connection between trance and waking is never completely severed; his visions have a prophetic or symbolical value. He brings them back triumphantly to the world of men: the genius goes "behind the Beyond" with a return ticket. Just one step further: there is the man who sees visions, and is unable to distinguish them from reality: the vision becomes hallucination, genius turns into insanity.

Or, if we want to borrow Coleridge's phraseology: good sense never surrenders "disbelief", *i.e.,* a critical attitude, and thus kills in advance anything beyond its own limits. A half-hearted "suspension of disbelief" may lead to the appreciation, but not to the discovery, of strange, unstandardized values. The "willing suspension of disbelief" is the very atmosphere of poetry and genius. The "total suspension of disbelief" is madness. If Shelley had accepted as literal truth his own *Triumph of Life,* or Coleridge his *Kubla Khan,* the only possible verdict would be "mental derangement."

VI. *Eminence or Recognition*

By what token, then, shall we distinguish between Genius and Insanity? Many eccentrics are geniuses in their own conceit; while Max Nordau, who was no fool, branded as psychopathic, in his *Degeneration,* many works which the world has proudly preserved. Aye: there is the key: *the world* passes judgment. Of genius, intrinsically, we know practically nothing. What we do know is the world's opinion.

The three hundred Geniuses of Catharine Cox represent simply Cattell's list of eminence, with Napoleon, of course, at the head, and Voltaire close upon his heels. That list is about as good as any. Like all other such attempts, it is bound to appear capricious and even absurd in certain cases. For instance, Robespierre, with all the earmarks of mediocrity ranks 28, ahead of Pascal (35), of Leonardo da Vinci (52), of Wagner (188).

Now it is obvious that all eminent men are not counted geniuses; it is hardly less obvious that many geniuses were despised and rejected of men. Indeed, apparent failure seems one of the tests of genius. Some people might entertain favorable doubts as to the "genius" of Edmond Rostand if *Cyrano de Bergerac* had not been performed almost as many times as *Abie's Irish Rose*. Cleon, Balfour and Clemenceau were all credited with the remark, when they were interrupted by unexpected applause: "Did I say something foolish?"

But if immediate success with the crowd is a valid presumption against genius, some kind of response there must be: else genius disappears without a trace. Our Jefferson Aloysius Kegelbahn may be a transcendant poet, and he may know it. But you do not, and there the matter ends for our mute inglorious Milton: mute indeed is he whose words fall on deaf ears. If Alberta Christina's father parades the streets of London as "Sargon, King of Kings", followed by a handful of loafers, we merely smile; let one thousand walk in his steps, we shall take notice; one hundred thousand, he will be a portent, like the founders of certain American sects; one million, and he becomes a major character in history, a genius. Socrates and Jesus had disciples, however few. On a different plane, so had Mallarmé. Without such a chosen band, their names would have perished. If the small company of the faithful had not won larger circles, the founders might have remained oddities in world history rather than geniuses. Paradoxically, genius is a palm conferred by the common man.

VII. *Mutation*

Most men recognize a difference even among the élite of the eminent. There is in genius a touch of strangeness, both sublime and disconcerting; and the admiration it arouses is always tinged with awe. It is hard to do full justice to the perspicuous and sane, like Molière, Voltaire, Gibbon: they have their immediate reward. Genius is the title granted in compensation to those who aspired beyond human power. Washington, in his perfect measure, appeals to us far less than Napoleon the visionary and gambler. Genius is not perfection in achievement, but a groping for something which as yet has no name. The striving for that Something is the first step in revealing and defining it. The "inspiration" theory gives a positive but mythical explanation of that feeling; the "insanity" theory recognizes it negatively. He who does, however supremely, that which has been done before, is not a genius. He who comes with a new gift, were he travel-stained, halting, tongue-tied, has a right to that great name.

A new gift! Is there anything new under the sun? Modern science says yes, in defiance of the old-bachelor philosophy of the Preacher. Not only does everything evolve in nature: but evolution, at times, takes unexpected leaps. The thing of yesterday is not the same as the thing of to-day. It is not even *imperceptibly* different: it may be a radical departure. As H. G. Wells has it, the steamboat did not evolve out of the sailing vessel by a gradual transformation of the galley stove into a boiler. In natural history, there are (or there may be) *mutations* in the sense that De Vries attached to the word. In the history of the human mind, genius is a significant mutation.

At first sight, this does not conflict with the theory that genius is recognized eminence. We have only to reword it: Genius is *recognized innovation*. On second thought, a contradiction appears: the world "recognizes" only that with which it is familiar, and crowns only the paradox which has already become a commonplace. No better example could be found than Jean-Jacques Rousseau. Rousseauism was manifestly floating in the public mind, a doctrine in quest of a Messiah. Jean-Jacques only served as a nucleus of crystallization. The apparent genius worshipped in history is not the true originator: he is the symbol of a thought which, after an obscure struggle, has at last reached public consciousness.

Genius as a creative mutation we do not deny. But the only true geniuses then are the unknown geniuses. Ages before any great revolution in thought, the decisive word was spoken: perhaps half-consciously, perhaps half-jestingly; and that word found no audible echo. It may have been said, apparently in vain, hundreds of times, before the obscure beginnings of growth. The thought now appears as vague misgiving, as idle rebellion, as unname-able aspiration. Thus it spreads until it reaches definite consciousness in some individuals. These individuals may be suppressed or derided; they may be recognized later as true *forerunners*. Finally comes the miracle of luck: the man who speaks the decisive word into ready ears, however few. Then we have messiahs, prophets, poets, inventors, *geniuses*,—the long, anonymous gestation un-recorded and forgotten. The Greeks had an altar to the Unknown God, and every nation has a shrine to the Unknown Soldier. Our Halls of Fame should reserve their finest monuments for the Unknown Geniuses; they are far more vital than those upon whom falls the full light of history.

There is nothing so academic, in popular estimation, as the discussion of a word. What care we for a defini-tion? What we want is the substance. But words are potent. The heap of loose thought covered by the term genius may block the way to useful action. On the whole, we feel that the word genius is useless and dangerous. For one thing, it has a demoralizing effect: genius, be-cause it is beyond convention, is free from any law. The painter in *The Moon and Sixpence* may seduce his bene-factor's wife and abandon her: he is a genius, and skill with the brush (*if ultimately recognized by the dealers*) justifies the infliction of torture and death. A Montpar-nasse lad may drink himself into an insane asylum, and offer chance splashes of paint as a finished picture: in his own eyes, he is a genius, and there may be a few friends for whom the sacred word will be sufficient to silence all criticism.

In history, genius has repeatedly served as an excuse from common sense and decency. It was eminently right that hundreds of thousands should perish in the snows of Russia: Napoleon woefully mismanaged that senseless campaign—but was he not a *genius?* "Do not touch the Concordat!" said J. C. Bodley to his French friends. "Who are you that you should meddle with the work of Genius?" And how would a petty mediocrity in Italy to-day dare to pit himself against the manifest genius of Mussolini? Imagine how much more intelligent the great Russian experiment might be, if the Bolshevists did not have such blind faith in the "genius" of Karl Marx; how much more religious the world would be, were it not for its excessive and oppressive trust in the "genius" of Saint Paul or Mohammed. The idea of genius fosters insane pride in a few chosen souls, servility among the many.

Anything that paralyzes thought is harmful, and such is the effect of that ill-defined term. *Superiority,* in terms of social service, we are ready to accept and reward. Genius as mutation, original, creative, we want to recognize and honor. But every one of us is a potential mutation, a new experiment in the world; this aggregate of atoms which I call myself has never existed before, can not exist elsewhere under exactly the same circumstances of space and time. In so far as he is unique every individual brings a new revelation, has a spark of genius. If only he dared; if only his fellow men were more receptive, less blinded by the worship of past geniuses.

We are not upholding, as in pseudo-democratic doctrine, the commonness of the common man as against the aristocratic gifts of the few: we are pleading for what is uncommon, nay unique, in every common man. Do not bow with superstitious reverence before a few individual geniuses: be ready to recognize *genius* in them, in yourself, in all men. Release the infinitesimal particles of genius in every one of us: heaped up together, they will rise to heights beyond our dreams. Equality is an empty word, and leveling down is a stultifying policy. But no scale of superiority devised so far has any general and final value; a hard-and-fast division between "geniuses" and "non-geniuses" is unscientific as well as deadening. Keep every path open. "Incommensurability" may be an ugly word: but it is a sane doctrine.

Part III

The Public

Chapter 15

THE TACIT INTERLOCUTOR

I

An author speaks the language, wears the costume, follows the customs of a particular civilization: in Taine's terms, he belongs to his "race, environment and time." So does every one of his compatriots and contemporaries. *As an author,* he possesses certain general characteristics which may be said to constitute his vocation; he conforms more or less closely, more or less consciously, to an established professional type; he occupies in that capacity a recognized position in society—recognized even when it is ill defined.

This recognition implies that there is some connection between the author and society as a whole. In so far as the poet is absolutely individual, independent, unique, isolated, he has no standing at all. Society, in its contact with the author, constitutes his *public*.

Our working hypothesis, in this book, is that literature is the joint production of author and public. Writer and reader do not merely belong to the same large cultural group, national or supernational: they collaborate in a very definite manner.

This thesis offers itself under two aspects. The first is what we called, in our introductory chapter, the *pragmatic approach:* literature does not exist *for us* until it has been recognized as such. In the eyes of Apollo, the unknown poet may be the greatest; among mortals, "he whose songs are unread never wrote at all." The specifications for an author are: a soul, an instrument, a public. The third is no less essential than the other two.

This *pragmatic approach* is brutally factual and grossly general; but, on its own field, it can hardly be challenged. The second aspect of the thesis is more controvertible: *the author always writes for a public.* A book is a conversation, urbane or angry, with an unseen but ever-present interlocutor. It is a discussion, a plea, a declaration of love, of hatred, of contempt: never a scroll of undecipherable hieroglyphics tossed indifferently into the void. The author uses the words of his people and of his time; he accepts or combats their prejudices; the public is the mold in which his private thoughts must inevitably be cast.

Now this will very properly be challenged. "The public be damned!" was the motto of poets such as Horace and Ronsard, long before it was adopted by a now vanishing brood of capitalists. (Note that for the capitalist, at any rate, the public he damned so light-heartedly was none the less indispensable.) The true artist, it will be asserted, works for himself alone. We firmly believe this haughty claim to be in a large measure justified. We hope to discuss the point at length in *Art for Art's Sake.* The very essence of art may consist in its absolute independence. At present, we are not concerned with the essence, but with practical facts: the body of works that we actually read, enjoy, criticize. On this purely pragmatic ground, we shall be satisfied with the assertion that the *bulk* of literature is written for a public.

We need not dwell on the enormous amount of writing done confessedly for *profit*—money, social prestige or fame. The thirst for immortality, *Exegi monumentum, Non omnis moriar* . . . , is a desire not merely for a public, but for a perennially renewed public. To write for a public does not imply that you are seeking to please that public: you may elect to tease, to browbeat, to insult your readers. Only you are conscious of their existence and you attempt to secure their attention. In not a few cases, rough methods bring popularity. Aristide Bruant in his famous Cabaret, Miss Texas Guinan in her noted nightclub, G. B. Shaw in his Prefaces, Mr. H. L. Mencken in his *American Mercury,* welcomed their audience with a volley of epithets: *"Bourgeois!*—Sucker!—Pharisee!— Boob!" This seems to establish a delightful footing of intimacy and mutual confidence: "Now that we have been properly introduced, let's have a good time together."

A public, of course, does not mean "the general", notoriously untrained to the subtleties of caviar. It means an audience, if possible an audience of friends, a jury of your peers, as few as you please, sifted by the most rigorous shibboleth you can devise. Even the poems of Emily Dickinson were communicated to a small number of chosen souls. Every piece of writing that is *published,* were it in the most esoteric of "little" reviews, is seeking a public.

223

It may be a public of one: the one whom we are most eager to impress. We are willing to concede that certain famous love poems were originally indited without any thought of their appearing in print. It may be a public so small and so scattered that it has not yet achieved consciousness. It may be a public still unborn and perhaps never to be born: the pathetic "appeal to posterity", a supreme act of faith or a supreme gamble. Thus, in Vigny's poem, the dying navigators entrust their last message to a frail bottle. Such "bottles in the sea" are many posthumous Journals, that of Vigny himself, Amiel's, and, in parts at least, *The Education of Henry Adams.*

Finally, even the works which are written most strictly for one's self alone are written *as if* for a public: else they would hardly be written at all. Suppose a poetical mood comes upon us. What shall we do? There are three possible lines of action, or perhaps three stages. In the first case, we silently enjoy the unformulated ecstasy; no less silently, it disappears; from the literary point of view, it simply does not exist.

Or—second hypothesis—we are tempted to note it down, but we still desire to preserve our secret. Our notation, meant for no other human eyes, would remain a sealed letter to any stranger. So far as the world is concerned, it might as well never have been written: that which remains inviolate in the inner shrine is not "literature."

There are works that hover on the threshold: some incoherent and sublime pages of Pascal, for instance. They reach us because, elliptic, scornful of syntax and logic, they are none the less written almost as if they were meant for a public. They presuppose a common experience, they make use of the accepted signs. Pepys's Diary, obscure in a purely material way, entered literature only because it could be deciphered. It was jotted down in lucid English: the mode of transcription alone was a puzzle. Swift's *Journal to Stella* is literature in so far as its "little language" is a language at all, a code of communication. Its oddities can be mastered, so that the original public of one has been multiplied many thousandfold. The stream of consciousness or interior monologue, a most promising field for revolutionary experiments, offers a variant of the same problem. It attempts to catch thought before it has been fully organized into formal language: but it can not be accepted as literature unless it has some degree of intelligibility.

The cryptic notation, therefore, is merely an intermediate phase which can be resolved into either of the two extremes. If it does keep its secret, it does not count for us. If it can be deciphered, its unconventional form adds to our difficulty, but ultimately it is put into a tongue "understanded of the people"—at least of a few people.

In the majority of cases, a third hypothesis prevails. People who write "for themselves alone" (*you,* reader, I could swear; and myself as well) are using the standard medium; oftentimes, they use it with scrupulous care; and not seldom, they even affect elaborate forms. Why should men adopt an intricate technique, without the remotest hope of being read?

First of all, through the force of imitation and habit. An English engineer, the only white man in a tropical construction camp, will, we are told, don his dress suit for dinner. (For all I know, this English engineer may be a myth: but a myth of such long standing becomes respectable. Anyway, I am using him as an illustration, not as an argument.) He is manifestly a social product; he dresses as though he were bidden to a Duke's, because London, ten thousand miles away, is still his inexorable master. Similar is the case of the man who indites a sonnet and never shows it to a soul. The fact that the engineer is isolated in the jungle, the fact that the sonneteer is not seeking publication, are alike irrelevant. The former does belong to Society, whose remote control he obeys as if by instinct; the latter does belong to the literary world, and follows the canons of that world, which will never know his name.

Why do we put on the formal dress of a conventional poem, or even the semi-formal of correct prose, when we expect no company? Possibly to keep in training against the day when we may get into society. Perhaps because the only way of clearing up our own thoughts is to express them to ourselves as though we were strangers. Perhaps because the future Self for whose benefit we desire to preserve the memory of a golden moment is, we surmise, likely to be more than half a stranger. Chiefly in order to reassure ourselves that we are not dumb, like the beasts in the fields, even though our voice should never be heard. "I, too, am a poet!" we exclaim. We are, in our own eyes, a sovereign *incognito*. When literature is discussed before us, we hug our secret, with an inward smile: "If they only knew!" Too proud to fight—too diffident, too sensitive to face a real public, we revel in the approval of an imaginary one. But the make-believe public for whose praise we are striving has the same effect upon us as an actual public would have.*

II

This part of our book will be mainly devoted to the effect of a special public upon the writer. We shall at present content ourselves with a sketch of the more general influences. It is a delusion to believe that a great man—poet or warrior—would have been great at any time and under any circumstances. Would Napoleon have been the same Napoleon, if he had been a second lieutenant under Louis XVIII? It is hardly less unreasonable to imagine that Shakespeare would have been Shakespeare under Queen Anne or Queen Victoria. Adaptability is not a necessary attribute of genius. On the contrary, we consider the time-server, the opportunist, as more likely to be a clever mediocrity. Scribe, Sardou, Pinero, Benavente, would have been successful, within their limits, in any period and under any régime.

When the man's inner tendencies coincide with those of the times, when author and public are in substantial agreement, the writer is carried by the stream with surprising ease. There were powers in Pope and Johnson that would have manifested themselves even in a Romantic age: but it is more than likely that the full development of their talent and of their fame needed the favor-

---

* Baudelaire has put the matter with his usual savage misanthropy: "I write," he said, "to prove to myself that I am not inferior to those I despise."

able climate in which they lived. This harmony explains the great vogue of men now forgotten, and even the enduring fame of others not intrinsically great. Malherbe was a surly pedant; there were dozens of poets at his time more gifted than he. But literary France, like political France, was craving for discipline, and hailed as a Master this hard-boiled martinet of Parnassus. In like fashion, Calvin Coolidge will remain in history as one of the most successful of our Presidents, because his negative virtues exactly fitted the needs of the hour. Or so we thought.

More profitable is the consideration of times out of joint, of irreconcilable conflict between the author and his public. The most radical effect is to crush the dissenter altogether. From the pragmatic point of view, which must be ours, we are able to consider only those works which have come to light and survived; from the ideal point of view, success is no sure criterion of excellence. In damning the losers in that literary struggle for life, we are adding insult to injury, which is the acme of callous vulgarity. Under given circumstances, a truly great man may be discouraged from even attempting to write. Our familiar "mute inglorious Milton" has no standing in history: yet, have we any right to deny that the germ of genius was in him? How many genuine freethinkers were there in the Middle Ages? How many potential dramatists in eighteenth and nineteenth century England? We shall never know. It is cheap optimism to assert that energy will conquer all obstacles. Disraeli was jeered at when he first addressed the House. He swore: "You shall hear me yet," and he was heard. But his disabilities were superficial in their obviousness; his talent was eminently adaptable. He deliberately sought to win his public, and succeeded. A more genuine soul, a more uncompromising character than Dizzy might have lost the fight—might indeed think that Dizzy's victory was but a capitulation in dazzling disguise.

For it is possible for men to win apparent success, and fail to express their best selves. Their public will not permit it: they are the prisoners of a fame they half despise. If we agreed with Van Wyck Brooks, such would be the ordeal and the tragedy of Mark Twain. Alexander Dumas wanted to be a dramatic poet, and almost succeeded: but he was forced into the position of a romance-manufacturer. I have preserved a queer feeling of sympathy—which, no doubt, would have been extremely unwelcome —for Miss Marie Corelli. Some thirty years ago, she was enormously successful with the sentimental shopgirl we all conceal in our hearts; but, even at the height of their triumph, her lucubrations were held up as the perfect models of the cheap and the tawdry. With this severe judgment I am compelled to concur. Yet I wonder whether the quality of her imagination would not have made her notable at a certain moment of Romanticism. *The Sorrows of Satan* is not a weirder book than *Frankenstein;* and it holds together better than most of the Gothic novels which are now seriously studied by scholars. She came nearly a century too late. If the educated public had not turned down her work in derision, if she could have hoped to please critical judges, she might have been more severe with herself. She wrote at a time when most respectable fiction was realistic or psychological; she was almost compelled not to be respectable—from the artistic point of view.

We have noted so far cases in which this disharmony between author and public had only negative effects: silence, a warped activity, success that does not heal a secret bitterness. It may also lead to the direct expression of melancholy, rebellion, despair. The gentler souls sigh almost inaudibly: Senancour in *Obermann;* Frédéric Amiel in that enormous *Journal* which tells in so many thousand pages why he could not write; *The Education of Henry Adams,* a testament, an indictment, an alibi. There is much of this element in Matthew Arnold's elegiac poetry. With no lack of sympathy for these sensitive writers, we can not but resent the feebly egotistical touch in their lyric frustration; at times, their delicate moaning is hard to distinguish from a whine. Far better is the resolute stoicism of Alfred de Vigny: a hostile world, even when it crushes us, shall not be permitted to gloat over our defeat.

Disharmony may also seek the veil of paradox, cynicism, futility. This is often the key to the Art for Art's Sake attitude, to Gautier's defiant Preface to *Mademoiselle de Maupin,* to much of the career of Oscar Wilde, to Cabell's graceful, all too conscious trifling, a scherzo through which an obstinate lamento is heard. It explains in part certain aspects of post-war literature, the effect of brutal, rasping discords on the too finely strung organism of Aldous Huxley.

Finally, we have open rebellion, the rather histrionic defiance of the Storm and Stress period, revived with even greater dramatic effect by Lord Byron. From Schiller to

Victor Hugo and even Balzac, the outlaw—Karl Moor, Hernani, Vautrin—became the pampered darling of Romantic literature. It would only be fair to discriminate between the purely destructive anarchism of the orthodox Byronians, and the prophetic, the Promethean tinge in Shelley. For Shelley, revolt is not an end in itself, not a cherished pose, but an inevitable phase swiftly to be left behind, the stormy passage to an ideal of serene beauty.

In all these cases, the attitude of the poet is governed by that of the public. Byron might have been a rebel even in a Paradise created according to his own specifications: but it is hard to dispute that Schiller and Goethe were at heart *classicists,* aspiring to a world of order; less obviously, for the curve of his evolution was cut short, this is also true of Shelley. In a Shelleyan universe, much of the Shelley we know would never have been manifested at all: neither his revolts nor his yearnings. He would have had to find other means of self-expression; or, in a paradoxical but inevitable phrase, other modes of *self-unfulfillment.* There is no fulfillment this side the grave.

The luckiest author is the one who comes just at the turn of the tide. The old synthesis is still enthroned, but men are increasingly weary of its lifeless rule. The first who speaks words of release and of promise is hailed as a deliverer. He has at the same time the benefit of the rebellious attitude, which seems heroic; and the benefit of harmony with vast numbers, which brings safety, recognition, power. A few years before, he would have been a sacrificed forerunner; a few years later, a dealer in platitudes. Such was, again, Rousseau's miraculous chance. The "return to Nature" was well under way: it became fully conscious through him. We are appalled at the discrepancy between his sudden rise to fame, his enormous influence (an incubus which tormented Irving Babbitt), and, on the other hand, the rudimentary quality of his thought, the obviousness of his art. It was the public that evolved Rousseauism: Jean-Jacques was only its living symbol.

On a smaller scale, the fate of Rostand is parallel with that of Rousseau. Decadence, esoteric symbolism, naturalistic filth, obscurity and pessimism of all kinds, had palled on the French public. *Cyrano,* gay, brilliantly witty, wonderfully clever in technique, unblushingly sentimental and melodramatic, full of grandiloquent braggadocio, was the perfect antidote both to Mallarmé and to Zola. Readers of to-day can hardly realize what a stir it created in literary Paris: Faguet wept tears of joy, and sang *Nunc dimittis.* The play survives on its own merits, which are great. But it owed its first impetus, the legendary prestige with which it is still surrounded, to the fact that it registered a veering in public opinion. Epoch-making masterpieces are epoch-made. The *Cyrano* we admire is in part a tradition, greater than the mere words of Rostand, greater than Rostand himself. In *L'Aiglon,* the poet, the dramatist, the subject, were all deeper than in *Cyrano:* but the unique chance was gone. Maurice Rostand considers his father's glory as the "crystal tomb" in which the son is imprisoned. But Edmond Rostand himself was such a captive: he could never escape from his own *Cyrano.*

The incentive to create, the author's mood—hopeful, resigned or defiant—, the reception of the work, its later growth, its relapse into oblivion, are all products of the Public: the writer is but a medium.

III. "THE PHANTOM PUBLIC"

We gladly borrow Walter Lippman's phrase. The public is a Phantom which stands constantly at the writer's elbow, dictates to him, stops his pen, even when he is not conscious of its presence. But it is a *Phantom:* it has no shape, no features, no consistency. Clutch it, and your fingers will meet in the void. We speak, at times with superb assurance, of the Public Mind, the People's Voice, which is an echo of God's own. We build political and literary theories on that conception: and lo! it is a phantom.

A phantom, or if you prefer an idea: and how many hard facts have shattered themselves against the un-movable reality of a myth! The public mind exists, since we believe in it; and human intercourse would be im-possible without such a belief. But what are the solid elements in it that can actually be caught in the net of our analysis? Our task is not to deny, not to explain away, but to understand.

Here three hypotheses offer themselves to us. The first is Orthodox Democracy. Every one of us has his opinion, which arises spontaneously in him. In the open forum of public life, these individual opinions are con-fronted; the elements that are purely odd or selfish fail to aggregate, cancel each other, disappear in the mass. The common denominator is automatically arrived at. Groups or men are selected, almost at random, to represent this common factor: in purest democracy, they might be chosen by lot. They have no superiority over the mass, except perhaps the gift of guessing what the public wants. A statesman is one who keeps his ear on the ground *and hears*. The hero is the average man on a gigantic scale: Emerson's conception of Napoleon. The writer of genius is the one who voices the platitude that was on the tip of everybody's tongue: this is a familiar interpretation of Jean-Jacques Rousseau.

The second hypothesis is the Messianic or Prophetic. The mass is inert; there is no spontaneous public opinion. Individuals arise who venture and create: the herd follows. The Tables of the Law were not the fruit of a constitutional Convention: they were brought down from on high.

The third hypothesis we shall call the Aristocratic; or, in order to create that irritation which is sometimes stimulating, the Bolshevistic. It starts neither with the whole mass, nor with the single gifted individual. The unit of action is the small, determined group, the *conscious and organized minority*. The binding force of such a group may be an institution, a class, a clan, a faith; it may even at first be the personality of one man; but that man would be powerless to reach the mass if he were isolated. In all cases, the group is greater than any one of its members. Robespierre, Lenin, Mussolini, exist only through Jacobinism, Bolshevism, Fascism. The 18th Brumaire brought to power a team of "strong, silent men" who, under the chairmanship of Bonaparte, governed France triumphantly for a decade. When Napoleon, drunk with conceit, annihilated their influence, relied solely on his genius, on his prestige, on the devotion of the masses, he destroyed his own Empire. Autocracies and democracies are both delusions.

What is "the American Public Mind", which, according to newspaper reports, is so "grimly determined"? The Government? Congress? famous editors? notabilities with or without definite positions? No: it is mostly in-numerable lobbies, idealistic or selfish, including the Churches, Labor, and the American Legion: in short, any organization run by a few able men for a definite purpose. In those groups which know what they want lies the substance of power. The historical parties wait meekly to have their minds made up by others; the official "leaders" are indicators, not forces. Are these lobbies the natural emanations of the General Public? Are they the followers of inspired prophets? Neither: they are *conscious and organized minorities,* swaying the mass, devour-ing the individual.

One strikingly clear example: in 1870, "France" felt herself insulted, and declared war on Prussia. The Emperor wanted peace; but his fiber was weakened by suffering, and he yielded, his eyes tragically open to the inevitable catastrophe. The Empress wanted war: but she had no decisive voice in a constitutional government. It was therefore "France", and not the sovereigns, that made up "her" mind and carried out "her" will. What was "France"? Thirty-six millions of French peasants, workmen, *bourgeois?* Not at all: France was the Cabinet, Parliament, the Paris Press, the Paris mob: the few thou-sands who had constantly spoken in the name of "France" and who believed that they were "France"; minorities which were conscious and vocal, because of their official position, or simply because of close physical proximity. *They* spoke, or rather they shrieked; they were heard. The thirty-six millions protested in private and silenced their own misgivings: who were they that they should oppose the will of France? The majority can only rally to one of the conscious minorities; and, in 1870, the conscious minorities—Thiers alone dissenting—went mad. The majority, in 1815, wanted neither the Bourbons nor Napoleon, neither reaction, nor military despotism; they allowed the Bourbons to flee, amid jeers, and Napoleon to return, amid the plaudits of a few; passively, sullenly, because they were not steered into a more acceptable alternative.

This theory of the *conscious, organized minority* is not new. It lies back of the good old *conspiracy* of our forefathers. It may be carried to an absurdity. Balzac, in particular, was extraordinarily fond of esoteric history. Beneath the trumpery of high-sounding principles, vast popular movements, resplendent official personages, he wanted to discover the secret deals of the "strong silent men." Hence his admiration for Fouché, who held in his hands the threads of the Empire, so completely that Napoleon, knowing himself betrayed, did not dare to unmask the traitor.

This view, familiar to every reader of the American press, is not seldom called "realistic", with a great affectation of superior wisdom: it is just as likely to be, as with Balzac, a Romantic and melodramatic delusion—pursuing in dark vaults at midnight a mystery that is not there. The fallacy is the assumption that only ruthless men, working in secret for selfish ends, can form a *conscious* *organized minority.** An open conspiracy in the name of an idea may be fully as effective. At the time of the Dreyfus Case, the defenders of the victim were decidedly a small group of energetic men: but they were not, as their adversaries charged, an occult "Syndicate" subsidized by unnameable powers. The Jesuits, the Free Masons, the Jews, the Communists, International Finance, have at various times and in many different countries, not excluding our own, been turned into horrific bogeys. Naïve as this may sound, a certain degree of sincere idealism is essential to prolonged success. A mere gang is soon exposed, or splits into rival gangs. Napoleon III and his followers were not simply a band of greedy ruffians, as Kinglake and Victor Hugo would have us believe. In this negative way, democracy reasserts itself: you can't fool all the people all the time. At least not with the same thing.

In many shapes, ranging from high philosophy to cheap melodrama, the notion of the conscious, organized minorities has become a commonplace of political thought. We do not yet apply it so freely to literary problems. Yet the laws of the formation of public opinion are not radically different in different fields. Neither in literature nor in politics is there an unmistakable, spontaneous *Vox Populi*. No work is ever tossed by an isolated man to the vast, unorganized crowd, and, without preparation, without guidance, eagerly grasped by all and acclaimed as a masterpiece. There must be a nominating committee to anticipate, and to engineer, popular response.

---

* This fallacy, we must confess, has the support of the best dictionaries. *Conspiracy:* a secret combination of men for an evil purpose. Why necessarily evil?

As a matter of fact, the theory of the conscious organized minorities is much more applicable to literature
than to politics. In politics, the ultimate authority of the
mass is officially acknowledged. If Demos is not the
master, he is at least the arbiter between his rival masters.
In literature, there is no universal suffrage. Even in our
days of generous mass education, the most popular works
appeal only to a small minority. The potential reading
public, among 125,000,000 Americans, would be over
60,000,000. A book is sensationally successful when it
reaches half a million readers. Outside of the fiction
field and of the semi-scientific, a *public* is counted, at
best, in tens of thousands. Even for fairly obvious literature, the *public* is barely one in a hundred of the population; for any literature with any taint of subtlety, it is
more likely to be one in a thousand.

Now this scattered, amorphous constituency can not
be reached directly by an individual. Its needs have to
be supplied from a few centers, and through definite
agencies. I may be craving for exactly the kind of verse
that a man ten miles away is writing now: but, in all
likelihood, I shall never hear of him except through New
York.

The *public* therefore is not identical with the *nation*.
But even that smaller community within the community
is not one. The days of "one faith, one law, one king"
are passed, and Pluralism reigns supreme. Not only is
there a pyramid of publics, immense on the Dickens level,
smaller for Robert Browning, until we reach the apex
where James Joyce alone fully understands his *Work in
Progress;* but there are interpenetrating publics, con-

tiguous publics, totally isolated publics. The famous "General" is a myth. If you look up at any time a list of best-sellers, it will give you no intelligible picture of the American mind. Here is one which I noted down a few years ago: it could no doubt be matched to-day. Leaders: Chic Sale, *The Specialist;* Culbertson, *Auction Bridge;* Ernest Dimnet: *The Art of Thinking;* James Branch Cabell. *The Way of Ecben* (this last did not remain long in that proud company). Draw your inferences if you dare.

Is the literary world a chaos then? It certainly is: Mr. Cheney, in his *Survey of the Book Industry,* from the business standpoint, arrived at exactly the same conclusions as the Neo-Humanists. There was some semblance of order in "the old days",—an order which we overemphasize in retrospect—because the leading minorities were indeed conscious and organized: their organization was one with that of society itself. Literature is a gamble now, because we are conducting it on the democratic (or better pluto-democratic) principle, without even the rudimentary consciousness, the rough-and-ready organization, of political democracy.

The way of salvation is not through a return to the ancient cultural hierarchy and its shibboleths which masquerade as standards. The old culture was bound up with a social world which now lies in the dust. Any proposal to organize *literature* (as distinct from the book mart) on the same principles as our economic and political world would probably arouse amused scepticism. For both society and literature, the way out is forward.

Chapter 16

Yesterday: UNIVERSITIES AND ACADEMIES

I

REPEATEDLY in history, minorities had to seize power, to maintain themselves against all comers, and to force recognition. But their ideal is to leave their revolutionary origins behind. Napoleon was not satisfied until he had covered himself with a triple armor of "legitimacy": a democratic investiture, through a series of mock plebiscites; a religious investiture, through the Pope's presence at his coronation; a dynastic investiture, through his marriage with a Habsburg Archduchess. Material authority is precarious; it must receive the consecration of the spirit.

So the tendency of every leading group is to entrench itself in an official position, and seek recognition *de jure* as well *de facto.* Thus social differences become hardened into classes, which would fain turn themselves into castes. Thus a free religious movement becomes a church, with an established clergy. In the literary domain, there is the same tendency to consolidate a situation, to protect vested interests. A literary Church is formed; it has a canon of Holy Scriptures, a formal creed, without which there is no salvation. It has its clergy, with a novitiate and an ordination, with powers to bind and to loosen. That literary clergy is composed of the Professors: a definite example of a small, conscious, organized minority assuming the right to instruct the masses.

The kinship between the Church and the University is not fortuitous. Both had the same origin: the medieval clergy had a monopoly of learning, and theology was the supreme end of their studies. It is with the greatest reluctance that the Churches have given up their paramount influence over education; and they obstinately defend their last crumbling ramparts. Napoleon fashioned his Imperial University after the pattern of a religious order: the staff, although laymen, were to be subjected to quasi-monastic discipline. Oxford and Cambridge were long semi-ecclesiastical in character. Our American Universities show even now unmistakable traces of their churchly origin. Cloisters are still in fashion; Romanesque and Gothic in great favor; the academic gown is a priestly garment. In some of these Abbeys of Learning, the vows of chastity, obedience and poverty are still in honor.

All this may seem, if not fanciful, at any rate irrelevant: harmless survivals or innocent make-believe. But something far more vital endures: the notion of a literary orthodoxy entrusted to the keeping of the literary clergy. There are books that one *must* have read; there are books that one *must* admire. The people come to the Doctors for Doctrine; and they go away much disappointed if the Doctors have no doctrine to offer. At present, dogmatism is still fostered in the grades and in the high schools; and the Universities are compelled to teach and to maintain an orthodoxy in which they no longer believe. A situation not unlike that of the Church at the time of the Renaissance, when Cardinals and Bishops, won over to Pagan art and Pagan learning, were far freer of thought than their flock.

The scholastic attitude, which is that of the Neo-Humanists, is the negation of democracy in literary taste. *Your* opinion is not "as good as any other man's and probably a darn sight better." The few who are trained in the Law have the right to approve and to reject. They substitute their expert judgment for that of the uncultured masses. They prescribe the way in which a young *élite* may become their associates and successors. They preserve the Apostolic Succession from the days of Aristotle; they are in possession of the sacred tradition and its hallowed standards.

Put in these ecclesiastical terms, the doctrine is likely to cause resentment or amusement rather than awe-struck obedience. Yet its influence is almost ineradicable. The teaching of literature is still to an appalling extent the enforcement of conformity. The man who does not know or does not properly admire the *right* thing is ill-educated: either an ignoramus or a heretic.

The direct influence of the Academic Church in contemporary literature is, at first sight, imperceptible. The indirect influence is very real. In preserving the spirit of Tradition, the Pontiffs of Yesterday warp our thought far more than we are aware. Then, although they contribute little to creative literature, they, as a class, are great producers of imitative work, not seldom of high excellence. They write sound and urbane criticism, correct poetry, even cultured fiction. Especially, they compose all the innumerable textbooks of literary history; they control that market at both ends, production and consumption. *Writing* history, if it be done consistently enough, is almost equivalent to *making* history. It takes a great wrench in our minds to realize that possibly *literature* is not identical with what the Professors have been handing down from generation to generation.

There is at least an enormous lag between official teaching and the trend of independent thought. When I was a schoolboy, in the early nineties, I still believed in the unquestionable superiority of the French Classicists, as a body, over Victor Hugo and his barbaric hordes. When I first applied, in a public library, for a volume of Hugo's dramas, I blushed and stammered as though I had been asking for the Marquis de Sade. It took the Scholastic Sacred College half a century to realize that Victor de Laprade, one of themselves, was a nonentity compared with Charles Baudelaire. And, although I am sworn to fearless speaking, I shrink from mentioning American equivalents for that obvious French case. Let the reader be bolder—if he has no academic standing to lose.

The Literary Church, although it deems itself sovereign in its own domain, is, like some of the religious Churches, very much in the hands of the temporal power. This is not mere self-seeking. The Professors are in natural harmony with the conservative class, because it represents, like themselves, authority and tradition. Decorum, good taste, good style, are the qualities which are emphasized in humane letters as well as in polite society. To be thoroughly versed in classical allusions, to know the table of precedence of all literary worthies, are things no less important to the scholar than the mastery of genealogy is to the courtier. The niceties of grammar, the punctilio of diction, correspond to the fine points of etiquette. Not to split an infinitive has exactly the same significance as addressing the second daughter of an Earl in the right form. The University man is part of the conservative scheme: but rather as a dignified retainer, like the Chaplain, than as one of the masters. The professed reverence with which both are surrounded is a courteous fiction: if they cease to "know their place", they lose their standing. They can teach only *ex cathedra,* in which case no one minds what they say.

If a scholar is out of sympathy with the society he should adorn, and expresses his heretical views, he is guilty of a breach of taste, and very properly snubbed or expelled. But even the scholar who, without attacking the existing order, ignores it, refuses to serve it, is first of all and uncompromisingly a scholar, stands condemned. He is the unsocial, boorish *Pedant,* a stock character in comedy from classical times to our own. The perfect scholar is the one who is also a gentleman. The Jesuit Colleges were first of all schools of good manners. Until the war, Oxford and Cambridge were emphatically the seminaries of the aristocracy and gentry. During the same period, American youth sought certain colleges for their social prestige rather than for pure learning. Even at present, "cultural" courses are frequently taken for the *finish* they are supposed to impart. They train you for admission into that desirable and supercilious circle, so well described by Aldous Huxley, in which the "good things" of "Uncle Virgil" are treasured.

It is no pun, but sober etymology, to say that there is *class* in the *classics*. To know the *right* thing admits you among the *right* people. I do not mean for a moment that the classics are wrong, and that the people who enjoy them are wrong. I only mean that the conception of their rightness is apt to be social rather than intrinsic. The man who seeks titled company solely because of its titles proves himself to be no aristocrat but a toady. The one who professes classical orthodoxy because it is "the thing" shows himself impervious to the spirit of the classics.

The social factor has thus been prominent in that culture of which the Professors are the official guardians. I wish Thorstein Veblen had given us a *Literary Theory of the Leisure Class*. His essential notion of *conspicuous waste* would apply admirably to much of our classical education. It is *disinterested*: a splendid claim. But the gentleman alone can afford to be disinterested, because he has no livelihood to earn. Traditional Culture subordinates the paltry questions of the moment, and deals with those problems which are eternal. This also sounds very lofty: but it means a refusal to meet the challenge of the times. To the plain question which rises in every young mind: "Why is there so much injustice in this world?", the answer is offered: "My dear fellow! How dreadfully vulgar! Let us show the fruits of a liberal education, and talk about Petrarch!"

In speaking of "the Professors", we are guilty of an injustice to the present generation. The American Professor of Literature to-day is not a serious danger; first of all because he is not a power, and also because his mind is, in many cases, far more open than New York journalists affect to believe. The Professor, we repeat, is himself a victim of the Professorial tradition. Individually, he frequently seeks to escape; as a member of a group, he is compelled to conform.

Here we have, therefore, the first of our "conscious, organized minorities." In theory, its claims to authority are based upon expert knowledge; in fact, upon the genteel tradition and an alliance with the ruling class. When that alliance is broken, the Professorial Doctrine is rejected as sheer pedantry. When the ruling class abandons the genteel tradition, or loses its own power, the professors' influence sickens and dies.

This influence affects living authors in two ways. Directly, it fosters a scholarly style, and emphasis on correctness, elegance, wealth of allusions. In this form, it was very great during the Classical Age; it has left traces throughout the nineteenth century; it is still felt in England, in Continental Europe, even in America. Much of the charm of Anatole France and Cabell has no other foundation. We taste it and relish it in Huxley, Maurois, Thornton Wilder, Christopher Morley, Willa Cather, not to mention the critics and essayists, and a few smart New Yorkers who might consider it an insult. Oddly enough, it is present in our appreciation of James Joyce: there is in the author of *Ulysses* a Professor, whose recondite allusiveness is enjoyed with conscious pride by all meritorious pupils.

Indirectly, it has fostered, in America particularly, a

deplorable anti-cultural bias: the dread of highbrow stuff, the exaltation of the crude. Because of the scholar's superciliousness, illiteracy has become a virtue, or at least a successful literary trick. Among the innumerable readers of our most popular fiction, a goodly proportion would be perfectly capable of enjoying higher things. But there is on every side—authors, publishers, public—a nervous dread of the professorial taint. This "conscious minority" has become so self-conscious that it is fated to remain an isolated, a hopeless minority. And so it shall remain, until the teaching of literature throws off its traditional shackles.

II

The Professors used to claim authority in the name of a doctrine. This, with the breaking down of the classical synthesis, became more and more of a pretense. The true source of their power, such as it may have been, was their harmony with the tastes of the ruling class. This frankly pragmatic and social ideal is even better represented by the Academies, and particularly by the *Académie Française*.

This illustrious institution is the clearest example of a small group possessing official prestige and influence in the realm of literature. The interest that it presents is therefore not local, anecdotic, antiquarian: the Academy stands for a principle. Whoever is yearning for "order", for definite standards, for a proper hierarchy of values, for an established guardian of sound tradition, for a Supreme Court of correct usage and elegant taste, must consider the French Academy as his Utopia. Matthew

Arnold sighed audibly for such an authority; Professor Irving Babbitt sighed in the secret of his heart. The Academy has been in existence for three hundred years: what has it done for literature?

Its creation is part of the great restoration of order that marked the seventeenth century, and culminated with the maturity of Louis XIV. It is coeval with Descartes's *Discourse on Method:* also a determined effort toward intelligent discipline. It is significant that its founder should have been Richelieu, whose hands of priestly steel wrested France from chaos.

A number of gentlemen were in the habit of meeting informally to discuss questions of literature. Richelieu heard of this little group. He was suspicious of even the most innocent gatherings not under his immediate supervision; he was genuinely interested in letters; so he requested this small knot of friends to form themselves into an official body, under his high protection. They were flattered rather than delighted: but the wishes of His Eminence were law. So the Academy—modestly and sanely called "the French Academy", without any of the extravagant titles then current in Italy—came into being in the folds of the Red Robe. Until the end of the Ancient Régime, it was part of its ritual that on the admission of every new member, some reference should be made to the formidable Founder.

This Academy was, in its prenatal days, a *Club of Gentlemen:* and a club of gentlemen it has remained. Of gentlemen: not of ladies. Madame de Sévigné, Madame de Lafayette, Madame de Staël, George Sand, could never have been admitted. Even in our own days, the

248

French Academy objected to the election of Madame Curie to the Academy of Sciences, for fear her admission might be used as a precedent. No sound reason has ever been offered for this ungallant ostracism. Women were at that time, through the *Salons,* most influential in polite literature. They have never seriously protested against their exclusion: they are satisfied not to be members of the Academy, if only they can make academicians.

Of *gentlemen,* once more: a man who has forfeited the name is debarred from this most exclusive of clubs. Molière was a "mountebank", appearing on the stage in broad farcical rôles: in his lifetime, he could not be thought of as a candidate. After his death, he was admitted in effigy, and his bust bears the handsome apology: "Nothing was lacking to his glory: *he* was lacking to ours." Diderot, the hackwriter and Bohemian, Rousseau the vagabond, in spite of their immense prestige, were not eligible. Neither was Balzac, ever in fear of the sheriff; nor Alexandre Dumas, whose life was a Christmas Pantomime, all glittering tinsel and paste. Zola knocked most insistently at the inexorable door: it became a perennial jest of literary Paris. No jest to him: as the head of the Naturalistic School, he felt it his duty to secure official recognition. He was invariably, almost unanimously, blackballed. His private life was above reproach, and the verbal filth in his works might have been overlooked. But he was accused, not quite fairly, of seeking notoriety and enormous sales through unsavory scandal; and this conduct unbecoming an Academician and a gentleman disqualified him for ever. Jean Richepin, who had posed truculently as a tramp and a rebel, had to repent, recant, atone, in sackcloth and ashes, before his youthful sins were forgiven and his gentlemanly status restored.

So an election to the French Academy is not inevitably the reward of literary excellence. In every generation, there is at least one of the best authors who is pointedly left out, and is said to occupy the forty-first armchair— the number of the immortals being limited to forty. Foreign readers would undoubtedly nominate for that distinction Romain Rolland, one of the first citizens in the coming United States of Europe. But the Academy has not yet forgiven him for standing "above the strife." The argument that his style is "soggy" is not quite ingenuous. Romain Rolland is not great as a word artist. But he writes fully as well as the average run of the Forty; indeed far better than most of them.

While great writers are not seldom left in outer darkness, others are admitted whose literary production is of the slimmest. The first Secretary of the Academy, Conrart, is perhaps the only man who left his name on the honor roll of literature for never writing at all. "Imitate Conrart's prudent silence," was the wise counsel of Boileau. Rostand, in the first act of *Cyrano de Bergerac,* has a *bourgeois* tell his son: "I see many a member . . .; here are Boudu, Boissat, and Cureau de la Chambre, Porchères, Colomby, Bourzeys, Bourdon, Arbaud. . . . All those names, not one of which will die: how beautiful!"—and not even scholars remember a single one of them.

The Academy is an epitome of good French society. It admits writers in so far as they are also gentlemen;

prelates, aristocrats, great lawyers, conservative statesmen, notabilities in every field, provided they are using good French, and have shown some interests in the purity of the language; at times, it elects illustrious Frenchmen, even without such a proviso. It happened that Marshal Foch, as a writer, was well up to the academic average, and Marshal Lyautey distinctly above it; but the one great service of Marshal Joffre to the Republic of Letters was that, as long as he lived, he refrained from publishing his Memoirs.

The French Academy is not therefore a body of technicians. It is not dominated by creative artists: we shall see later how radically different is the private Goncourt Academy. Grammarians, critics, professors and historians of literature are abundantly but not overwhelmingly represented: no pedantry attaches to that august body.

This is not quite in accord with Richelieu's ideal. He meant his Academy to have definite jurisdiction over literary activities. It was at the same time to write the law, and to apply the law. As the collective undying successor of Aristotle, it was to keep the *Rhetoric* and the *Poetics* up to date, by issuing formal treatises on these subjects. And it was to pass judgment on the productions of the day.

In its dogmatic capacity, the Academy has very wisely gone to sleep. The public would be mildly amused if the Forty should ever bring out a Neo-Aristotelian code. Absolutism in literature is dead, although absolutists are very much alive. The publications of the Academy are not commandments, but the register of good usage in vocabulary and grammar. The *Grammar* came out for the first time when the venerable Institution was nearing the close of its third century. This incredibly protracted travail was assisted at the end by Abel Hermant, a licentious and flippant writer who reserves all his purism for matters of diction. The result inevitably evoked Horace's *ridiculus mus:* there is hardly a teacher of Junior French in this country who, single-handed, could not have done better.

The *Dictionary* has at any rate the benefit of a continuous tradition. Every generation or so, a new edition appears. Only those words which are current in polite society are included. Archaisms are dropped out, not without regret; neologisms are admitted, with cautious reluctance. Even slang forces its way into the select company, after a quarantine of a hundred years. *Epatant* has thus acquired citizenship, while the door was firmly closed on the upturned nose of the Midinette. The Academy recognizes only the vocabulary of general conversation: local and technical terms have no standing. This is wisdom, for, in spite of the presence of an occasional scientist, this Club of Elderly Gentlemen is hardly prepared to deal authoritatively with unfamiliar words. France, who loves to tease her Academy with fond familiarity, has not forgotten the definition of a crayfish: "a little red fish that walks backwards."

The Academy, in this respect, is a far better mirror of classical France than the law-giving, law-enforcing body dreamed of by Richelieu. For French classicism was never based solely on abstract logic: it was tradition interpreted by common sense, reasonableness rather than pure reason. The Academy was somewhat similar in character to the old Parliament of Paris, which never had the initiative of laws, but which harmonized the customs and preserved the traditions of legal France, even against the caprices of royal power.

But the Parliament was a court of justice: the Academy attempted to judge—once, and once only. Richelieu referred to his new creation the case of Corneille's *Cid,* which was stirring an unprecedented hubbub in literary Paris. In doing so, the Cardinal showed remarkable moderation. The play was an exaltation of dueling, which he had declared a capital offense; and of Spain, then at war with France. Had Corneille written under Napoleon, Clemenceau or Mr. Mitchell Palmer, he might not have been treated with such ecclesiastical mansuetude.

The problem was the central one of all literary criticism: can we judge according to formal rules, or is pleasure our only law? France had fallen in love with Rodrigue and his Chimène; but the play was "faulty" according to the pseudo-Aristotelian rule of the three unities.

Corneille defended himself with the cunning of a Norman lawyer. The *unity of place* is respected, he claimed, so long as the action remains within the limits of the same city. The *unity of time* allows, not three hours, but a whole day; and *one* day means anything short of *two* days. And he proceeds to show, with his watch in his hand: that two young people could become engaged, their fathers quarrel, the youth kill his prospective father-in-law in a duel, a suit be brought against him in the King's Court, a Moorish invasion be repelled, the victory be reported in full, a second duel fought, and the hero and heroine reconciled, all within thirty-four or thirty-six hours. This, to say the least, strains credibility: yet the law is not formally broken. It shows what can be done with what Irving Babbitt called "an armour of elastic steel."

The judges were torn between their genuine admiration for Corneille and their classical scruples, reinforced by Richelieu's well-known bias. So they returned a halting, non-committal verdict, which pleased neither party, and least of all themselves. This experience discouraged the Academy from ever again acting in a judicial capacity.

But this one equivocal sentence, coupled with Corneille's pettifogging subtlety, burdened France for two hundred years with the rigid formality of the famous "rules." The French public was not clamoring for them: they were imposed from above, by the pedants, the legalists, the Academicians. Had Corneille defied the shades of Aristotle, had the Academy dared to support him in his resistance, much unnecessary stiffness and artificiality could have been spared. But then Corneille would not have been the Corneille we know: the poet of the reasoning disciplined Will; and the Academy would not have been the Academy: the guardian of decency and order on Parnassus.

The French Academy has therefore not done the things it was appointed to do. It has done a few other things, some of them rather unexpected, with respectable but indifferent success. The prizes it awards do not attract much attention: at least not the prizes for literature, for the Academy is also empowered to reward "virtue" (Prix Montyon). It has become the trustee for several fine collections, including the matchless treasures of Chantilly:

a living museum, it might in time become the corporate curator of all antiquarian museums.

Its influence on French literature has been surprisingly small. No great writer has suffered seriously, in fame or profit, from not being an Academician; no academic nonentity has been forced, by virtue of his official immortality, upon a sceptical and unresponsive public. The books which men have refrained from writing for fear of endangering their chances of election were, in all likelihood, better left unwritten. The books composed for the sole purpose of establishing an academic claim could very well have been spared.*

The authority of the French Academy is thus hard to define. But it exists. The Immortals have been the butt of unending pleasantries ever since the days of Richelieu: but in France, ridicule does not kill—it preserves. These very jests are a tribute: no one ever dreams of poking fun at the British or the American Academies. Any Frenchman interested in letters could name offhand half a dozen Academicians: I have met a number of American professors who did not even know we had an Academy.

The first reason for this persistent favor is that the Academy, alone among lay institutions, is connected with the past by a practically unbroken tradition. The French Revolution changed its name for a few years, but could not kill its spirit. France is an intensely conservative country that went through one tremendous up-

---

* General Max Weygand, for instance, wrote a *Turenne* which made him eligible—a *masterpiece* in the sense that the old Guilds gave to the term. This serious, dignified piece of work added nothing to the General's reputation or to the treasures of French Literature.

heaval: the few things that remained unshaken became all the more precious. England has her King, her Lords, her Yeomen of the Guard, her two ancient Universities: France has no such survivals except the Academy.

The Academy is unique in another respect. At all times, it was the meeting point of every form of superiority: birth, station, talent (beauty alone being left out of consideration). The ruling classes in their various degrees find in that literary institution their perfect symbol. Especially at present, when *bourgeois* culture is entrenching itself in France against the onslaught of Russo-American machine-worship, the Academy becomes a new Verdun. In the livid light under the dingy dome, one circular glance will embrace, among the members and in the audience, the leaders of a solid, obstinate, shrewd, hard-working world.* It is not "France" any more than the King was "France": probably less. But it has called itself France for so long, that it never questions its exclusive title to the name.

The power of the Academy is therefore not technical, not artistic, but social. The Academy is not a workshop: it is a Salon, and the emanation of the Salons. Its elections are prepared in the drawing-rooms. Society flocks to its open meetings: a first night at the Opera, a famous race at Longchamp or Chantilly, are plebeian compared with the best academic events. Academicians are great lions. One of them answered congratulations in these candid terms: "Yes, it is a fine position. The uniform is

---

* It was said: "The center of gravity of the Academy is Raymond Poincaré, the center of levity Maurice Donnay." We fully agree with the first part of this epigram.

very becoming. *And one is well fed."* Prominent hostesses have their personal academician as the chief ornament of their gatherings. Anatole France, the most conspicuous example in recent times, thus belonged to the household of Madame Arman de Caillavet: an association singularly profitable from the worldly point of view, but which grew heavily irksome with the years. France would have preferred obscurity and indolence to his success in a society which had lost all its glamor in his eyes.

To sum up: the Professorial Church and the Academy are two "conscious, organized minorities" which claim authority in literature. That authority has never been absolute; it is increasingly ignored, especially in America. But once it was great, and even now it must be taken into account. The study of their influence reveals that literature never is a fully independent realm: it is part of a larger whole, which we call society or civilization. The ideals and the methods of these two Institutions are the same as those of the ruling class—an aristocracy of wealth and intelligence. If the Professors and the Academicians cease to be in harmony with that class, their position becomes unsubstantial, almost shadowy. This has come to pass in our country, where *culture* in the conventional sense is neither frankly democratic nor openly plutocratic. If the ruling class—be it Plutus or Demos—fails to integrate the old culture into its system, and fails likewise to evolve a culture of its own, if superiorities of every kind do not meet and work in harmony, the immediate result is bewilderment, and the next decadence.

Chapter 17

Yesterday: COURTS AND SALONS

IT is an ancient custom to name literary or artistic periods after the ruler of the state. The most widely known example is probably the Augustan Age; the Periclean, the Elizabethan, the Victorian, immediately come to our minds. The Italian Renaissance is often referred to as the era of the Medici; the serene sunlit heights of French Classicism are known as "the century of Louis XIV."

These time-honored appellations are of very unequal value. England had an Augustan Age without an Augustus. We speak of Georgian architecture, although the House of Hanover had little to do with it; in literature, the best that could be said of the Georges is that they were not unworthy of such official poets as Colley Cibber, Whitehead, Warton and Pye. Except perhaps in a few poems of Tennyson, it can hardly be said that the personality of Queen Victoria impressed itself upon Victorian literature. A perfect harmony, through three long generations, grew between her and the dominant class: the Victorian era is one of the most definite in history. But that harmony excluded art, as a discordant note: it is chiefly in a chronological sense that Walter Pater, Algernon Charles Swinburne, Thomas Hardy, can be described as Victorians. Some of these royal names are sheer flattery, others were adopted for the sake of symmetry and convenience. But, under favorable circumstances, which have occurred repeatedly in history, the Sovereigns, through their courts, have wielded a notable influence in the domain of letters.

This is as it should be. Ideally, the Court is, much more than the Academy, the common ground of all superiorities. Historical names, great servants of the state, men of genius in every line: all those who rise, whatever may be their point of departure, must meet near the single summit. When the dynasty is truly the national center, such an ideal is at least partly fulfilled.

Less worthy motives may contribute to the same result. Under the Ancient Régime, authors would gravitate toward the Court for the same reason which induces their successors to seek popularity: the approval of the élite was then the unmistakable sign of success. And the Kings encouraged artists and poets for the same purpose which causes dramatic stars to be nice to journalists. The chief concern of kings is glory: an inglorious king is no king at all. And the trumpets of fame are in the hands of the poets: art is the supreme advertising agent. Imagine the difference if Napoleon III had been wise enough to enlist Victor Hugo as his Vergil; or if Vergil had written the *Chastisements* of Augustus instead of the *Æneid*.

This is true only of the genuine monarchical state, harmoniously hierarchized from the sovereign at the

apex to the masses of the people below. Then the Court
is a unique strategic point: conquer the Court, and the
world is yours. There is no clearer case of a "conscious,
organized minority" acting with the tacit approval of the
passive majority. When that grand national symmetry
is destroyed, the influence of the Court is impaired, and
may vanish altogether. In a tyranny, there is no real
court, only a band of sycophants and executioners. There
is but one thing that it can impose, and that is silence.
Ivan the Terrible could not be the center of a national
culture. Even Napoleon, although he was by no means
an Oriental despot, was too much of an autocrat for the
growth of a literary Court. The élite never fully rallied
to him; between the people and himself, his heterogeneous aristocracy was a screen rather than a link.

When a single element assumes exclusive predominance, whether it be the aristocratic, the military or the
ecclesiastical, the representative character of the Court is
lost, and with it the possibility of wide influence. The
Golden Century of Spanish Literature owes little to the
morose, monastic, bureaucratic inner circle under Philip
II. The moments of full harmony between people, court
and king are rare and fleeting. The first decade of rule
of Francis I offered that character, the best years of Queen
Elizabeth, the young maturity of Louis XIV: hardly
any other in modern history. Frederick II was a man of
letters, and gathered round him wits, philosophers, poets:
but it was a cosmopolitan, French-speaking crowd, alien
to the Germany which was rising in those days. The
King's personal prestige influenced German culture in a
way diametrically opposed to his own Gallicized taste.

Maximilian II in Bavaria, Louis-Philippe in France, Prince Albert in England, Don Pedro II in Brazil, were pathetically worthy men who tried, according to their lights, to play the Augustan rôle; Maximilian of Mexico would have sought a place among them, if his reign had not been so tragic and so brief. They met with indifferent success; indeed, they were frequently called arch-Philistines for their trouble. The Romantic rule of Louis II in Bavaria ended in disaster. The incursions of William II into the domain of culture only roused exasperated irony. One princely Maecenas alone achieved his end: the Grand Duke of Weimar attracted the protaganists of the German spirit to his duodecimo capital, and thus inscribed his name by the side of theirs in the annals of the Fatherland. Here the usual process was reversed: it was not a Court fostering literature, but literature immortalizing a court.

The influence of Elizabeth and that of Louis XIV are subjects so vast, and so generally known, that a mere allusion must suffice. That influence was very real: history, literary no less than political, would be very different without these two proudly conscious figureheads. But it belongs to the past: it would be a miracle if the world were to see again a Gloriana or a Grand Monarch. Even in the countries which have most carefully preserved the trappings of monarchy, its spirit is gone. As Theodore Roosevelt bluntly put it, kingship is equivalent to a lifelong Vice-Presidency. As for our republican courts, their action on literature is microscopic. No less than four Presidents of France were members of the Academy, and not a few of ours had books to their credit. Yet the Elysée and the White House are even farther from the centers of national culture than Buckingham Palace.

But the Court survives at any rate as a shadow: it is to the Court that we owe courtliness and courtesy. And it survives also in solid, ubiquitous, minute fragments: the Salons. With its formal dress and its etiquette, every Salon is a miniature Court, just as every court worthy of the name was a magnified Salon. The quality that made Louis XIV truly regal was not his pride, but his exquisite politeness. He was the perfect host: he enjoyed life, and wanted his friends to enjoy life with him. He was as respectful of their titles and privileges as he expected them to be respectful of his prerogatives. It is not sufficient for a King to be the first gentleman in Europe —witness George IV and Edward VII: but a gentleman he must be, or his court will remain an oppressively tedious show. Napoleon was no gentleman, but a blend of the martinet and the parvenu: hence the failure of the new Augustus to inaugurate a new Augustan Age.

It is a commonplace that literature is the mirror of society; but, until recent times, it was far more accurate to say: "Literature is the mirror of 'Society.'" Pericles was not a stern dictator, but a smiling friend. The atmosphere of Plato's dialogues, particularly the *Symposium,* is that of good company enjoying good talk over good wine. The men who have best rendered the spirit of a perfect week-end party, W. H. Mallock, Aldous Huxley, are the distant but conscious heirs of Plato. Horace, Ovid, Petronius, were "Society" writers in the most sophisticated sense of the term.

262

Yesterday: COURTS AND SALONS

The Barbaric invasions meant darkness and silence for several hundred years. It was in Southern France and Italy that the "social" ideal revived. In the North, the aristocracy lived isolated in their craggy castles, keeping culture away from their moats and portcullis. The urbane tradition had never completely disappeared in the Mediterranean world. Nobles, merchants, poets, could meet on pleasant terms. Among the Troubadours, many were of noble lineage.

Hard work and violent sports are the privileges of men: "Society" is woman's domain. The courtly literature of the South was dominated by the cult of the Lady. The notion that reverence for women is of Northern origin is hardly corroborated either by history or by literature. No one could occupy a more honored position than the Roman matron; and woman, in the early medieval epic, still imbued with the Northern spirit, plays a very subordinate part. In the *Roland,* fair Aude appears but to die: it is a man's world, and roughhewn. In the little courts of Languedoc and Italy, softer influences were at work. Etymologically *chivalry* implies fighting on horseback: the knight is a mere cuirassier. But chivalry came to mean exalted courtesy: uncouth strength bows before gentle grace. *Gallant,* in English, is *valiant; galant,* in French, is *polite,* with a touch of sentimentality.

Southern Princesses carried this new conception to the Northern courts, England, France, Champagne. Chrétien de Troyes transformed the mystic and passionate motives of Celtic legend into codes of *savoir-vivre,* i.e. *savoir-aimer*. In our days, he would conduct a syndicated

263

column of advice to the lovelorn on points of etiquette and sentiment. And his work was followed by the enormous flood of romances which, three centuries later, addled the brains of a worthy country gentleman, Don Quijote by name: Dulcinea was a more indispensable appurtenance of his knightly calling than even Rocinante.

Nothing is more misleading than to dub "Middle Ages" the whole thousand years between the fall of Rome and the Renaissance. We should at least distinguish between the Dark Ages, the Age of Faith, and the Age of Make-Believe, which was that of chivalrous fiction. Joinville, the very human companion of the last Crusader, St. Louis, finds pleasure in the thought that he will retail his prowess in the ladies' drawing rooms. Aucassin prefers to Heaven, the abode of sniveling monks, the other place where he is bound to meet noble knights and fair ladies. Ovid's *Art of Love* was the favorite classic in that age which we call "stern" and "naïve." Boccaccio, whose *Decameron* has a houseparty for its framework, and every kind of love for its theme, started a tradition which, through Chaucer and La Fontaine, has descended to James Branch Cabell and Michael Arlen. The *Romance of the Rose,* in its inception, was an allegory of delicate lovemaking.

Not that "Society" entirely dominated literature: there were poets of the cloister, and poets of the marketplace also. And there were rebellions, coarse but not unwholesome, against the subtleties of aristocratic courtship. Like every over-elaborate ritual, the Society Code engendered formalism, hypocrisy, and ultimately disbelief. The later

Middle Ages were not lacking in works which, like *The Cream of the Jest,* turn abruptly from highflown romance to realism and satire. The most international classic of the period, the *Romance of the Rose,* is Janus-like: William of Lorris all dainty conceits, John of Meung a solid, earthly, freethinking *bourgeois,* who will brook no nonsense.

It was Italy again that served as an inspiration for the greater Renaissance of the sixteenth century. What amazed the Northern men-at-arms, when they swooped upon the land of endless delight, was not the scholarship of a few Byzantine refugees, not even the crumbling remains of Roman grandeur, but the exquisite luxury of social life. The Renaissance influence on thought, style, manners, domestic architecture, is far more Italianate than Greco-Roman. It was Italy that gave the model and formulated the code of courtly behavior. Francis I strove to live up to Italian standards, in surroundings of Italian luxury. Just as Italian gardens spread into Northern climes, every Northern literature in turn had its Italian *Arcadias,* and the love conventions of the sonneteers. We might blot out the *direct* influence of antiquity, and still understand the Elizabethan age; take away the Italian factor, and the whole period is blurred.*

It was again from Italy that France derived the inspiration for her most famous literary salon, the ideal of its kind, the Hôtel de Rambouillet. Henry IV was affable, shrewd, witty in a soldierly way: but years of camp

---

* The Elizabethans themselves would demur: they took pride in following the Ancients, not the Italians, whom they did not respect. Yet their very knowledge of the classics was derived from Italy; and their taste for Latin and Greek was an Italian fashion.

life, at the head of an army which at times was hardly more than a ragged marauding band, had disqualified him for social leadership. And his devouring amorousness was very different from the punctilious deference exacted by the old knightly code. France, after half a century of turmoil, was sighing for order in the state and decorum in society. So young Catherine de Vivonne, Marquise de Rambouillet, familiar with the amenities of Italian life, withdrew as completely as she could from Henry's foul-mouthed and promiscuous circle, and started a little court of her own. Her success was immediate, brilliant and prolonged. Her "Blue Room" became the focus of refined society and polite literature. Even Corneille, who was by no means at his best in a drawing room, appeared at Madame de Rambouillet's; and Bossuet, then a mere boy, gave that aristocratic assembly a foretaste of his sonorous eloquence. We shall see later what excesses of sentimental, psychological and verbal subtlety were encouraged by the Hôtel, and above all by its numberless imitations. *"Précieuses"*, preciosity, became terms of reproach. But we must not forget that the great Salon was at the very heart of dignified literature, and that such admirable women as Madame de Sévigné and Madame de Lafayette were proud to belong to the *Précieux* circle.

With the accession of Louis XIV to personal rule, the literary salon lost its predominant prestige. Louis wanted no prime minister and would tolerate no social rival. No Salon, not even the splendid company of the Great Condé at Chantilly, was allowed to eclipse the Tuileries or Versailles. The highest in the land had but one desire:

to remain at Court, and edge their way to the immediate vicinity of the Presence.

It was this Court, emulated throughout Europe, that gave its tone to so much of European literature. The aristocracy believed that they had to applaud stiff pseudo-classical tragedies for the same reason that the first King of Prussia felt obliged to keep a Royal Mistress: not out of any spontaneous desire, but because Louis XIV had set the example.

With the decline and death of the Grand Monarch, social leadership once more deserted the court and fell into private hands. Louis XV was an absentee king, who watched with imperturbable gravity and a secret chuckle the dissolution of his monarchy: under him, primacy shifted back from Versailles to Paris. The eighteenth century was par excellence the era of Salons. Paris gave the tone, and Europe followed with eagerness. The most unmistakable products of the Salon spirit in English literature are Lord Chesterfield and Horace Walpole. But they were only extreme instances, almost caricatures: a generation later, the Society ideal can be traced, delicate yet definite, in the genteel background of Jane Austen.

Rousseau led the rebellion of the individual against artificial Society: but it must be remembered that his success had its first roots in the very society which he denounced. If he had not been a member of the literary clan in Paris, the frequent guest of financiers and the protégé of aristocrats, his primitivist paradoxes might never have found an audience. It was Society that started the back-to-nature craze: fine ladies, at the Opera, nursed their infants in public; and Marie-Antoinette played the milkmaid in the comic-opera hamlet of Trianon.

The French Revolution and the Empire ruined the influence of the Salon. Madame de Staël, brought up, just before the catastrophe, in the delightful atmosphere of Parisian society, strove heroically for her defeated ideal. Just as she was dreaming that Directoire France might be led back into the vanished Paradise, Bonaparte seized hold of the government. She hoped against hope that he would share his Republican throne with her: all material activities to be his, hers the leadership of public opinion through the social élite. But Bonaparte wanted no public opinion: his own sufficed. So he kept Madame de Staël at arm's length, and his arm was long. Social life was hushed: the police had ears everywhere.

This breaking down of the social ideal is responsible for a sentiment which began with Rousseau and assumed the proportions of a disease: the oppressive feeling of solitude. Man was liberated from the shackles of conventional society, and found himself aching for the familiar chains; individualism brought with it melancholy and despair.

The Salon survived in England and revived in France: but its glory had departed. In France, it suffered particularly from the divorce between the old aristocracy and the modern spirit. From 1830, the fall of the last Bourbon, to the eve of the Great War, the Faubourg Saint-Germain had been sulking. The result was that the highest circles were devitalized—sulking is an uncreative mood—, while Society as a whole was decapitated. In this generation, the attitude of the great noble families is not so hostile: but their half-hearted reconciliation with their own country is the fruit of resignation, not of renewed hope.

Efforts were made throughout the century to stave off this decadence. The Duke of Orleans, eldest son of Louis-Philippe, and his artistic, ambitious German Duchess, attempted to create for themselves an intellectual circle, of which Victor Hugo was the main ornament. The youngest son of the *bourgeois* King, the Duc d'Aumale, sought to revive the alliance between art, literature and Society. He became a member of the French Academy and was universally respected: but the sympathy he inspired was mingled with curiosity, as before the last representative of a fossil race. The cousins of Napoleon III, Prince Napoleon and Princess Mathilde, had personal friends among the best writers of their time, like Sainte-Beuve, Renan and Taine; and even among those who were not supporters of the Imperial régime. Prince Napoleon, a Cæsar estranged from his own class, was hardly the man to set a fashion. As a matter of fact, we think of him rather as a minor member of Sainte-Beuve's group than as a princely patron.

The literary Salon still exists. In a recent study, Madame de Caillavet's was called "the last of the Salons." Who knows? Institutions enjoy at times an interminable evening twilight. There are still barons in France, although their baronies have become impalpable. Marcel Proust's tortuous chronicle of Society in the last fifty years is a record of accelerating decadence. The Academy does not feel complete without a Duke or so: but neither the Faubourg Saint-Germain nor the Faubourg Saint-

Honoré can make or unmake even a third-rate reputation.

In England, the social-literary tradition is not wholly lost. The two historical Universities, as we have seen, were until the war the symbols and the instruments of that alliance. Some aristocrats still deem it an elegance to have a book to their credit. Lord Rosebery's excellent *Napoleon* was a feather in his Scottish cap—but far less brilliant than his winning the Derby. And it is still the right thing for intelligent Society to entertain writers. There is nothing that comes so close to the old ideal as a week-end party in a great country house. There we find, or at least we expect, the blend of superiorities from widely different fields; a blend which must be daring, if it is to have the proper tang, and yet not haphazard, or it will cease to be smooth and palatable.*

The literary chronicle in the best British journals has frequently the tone of a Society column. Just as we want to know the latest fashion in clothes and the latest rumors about engagements, estrangements and flirtations, we like to be informed, a little ahead of our neighbors, that Mayfair is dropping Evelyn Waugh or rediscovering John Galsworthy. Mr. Hugh Walpole, himself a notable product of the social-literary alliance, gives that gossipy flavor to his enjoyable monthly letters. He manages to convey the impression that you are "in the know" without retailing any actual scandal. Others do not show the same restraint. The British aristocracy, we are told, are

* A writer of very humble origin and very unconventional manners like D. H. Lawrence found himself quite naturally hobnobbing and corresponding in familiar terms with titled ladies.

eking out a scanty living by exposing to view each other's washing.

English society is a fact, solid, patent, undeniable: American society baffles, not description merely, but imagination. Its elements are, like our sea power, second to none. But they are not integrated. As we have seen, a reception day at the French Academy reveals a many-sided but closely knit world; and, in spite of gate-crashers, so does a formal affair in London. There are functions in New York where the aristocracies of wealth, wit, beauty, power, may seem to mingle for a moment. But they will soon be dissociated again: they do not belong together. In a very elusive sense, "Society" still controls literature: it is smart to read certain books, to wear certain clothes, to be seen in certain places. But that smartness has no actual, definite center. It is a myth, out of which fabulous sums of very real gold have been coined. So long as wealth, journalistic brilliancy and the book trade have their chief abode in New York, the scholarly and Puritan tradition in New England, the romance of bygone days in Virginia and Louisiana, religion in the Middle West, beauty in Hollywood, and political power in Washington, we can not expect an all-inclusive, and at the same time homogeneous American "Society."

So the very term has become something of a joke: only minds that are primitive are hankering for that un-American ideal. Yet Society in the organic sense, the fusion of all the élites, did exist in Boston, in the almost mythical New York that Mrs. Edith Wharton is attempting to revive for us, in the world of Owen Wister, James Branch

Cabell, Ellen Glasgow. I have seen charming traces of it in a thriving seaport of Texas. The same ideal prevails, we are told, in the Bohemian Club of San Francisco. But not one of these centers ever was national in character; most of them are memories; some may be mere legends.

Whether we like it or not, we Americans must be resigned to democracy. The élites on this side are incommensurable. No common standard of the past will be acceptable to them all—least of all money. And we have almost ceased to pray for a new common standard. Pluralism is here. It does not make for a symmetrical world, like that of Louis XIV. It does not even make for a richly varied one: at first we see nothing but monotonous confusion. We may yet be able to organize, freely, our private universe. But the ideal of *one* great national literature, backed by all the forces of *one* recognized national élite, is evaporating like the ideal of *one* national Church. And hard as England and France may resist, they are bound to follow our course. Society's influence on literature is a thing of the past, because Society itself has dissolved.

We watch its dissolution with mixed feelings. It had many things to its credit that we are reluctant to lose. It had invariably made for elegance of expression without pedantry. To expound vital problems without boring charming ladies requires a difficult technique. Through that exacting school, French has acquired a matchless clarity, which is not inherent in the language itself. Even Descartes the professional scientist, even Pas-

cal the mystic, addressed themselves to the well-bred
rather than to the technicians. Fontenelle was a philosopher for drawing rooms; Montesquieu, a learned magis-
trate, sprinkled his mighty *Spirit of Laws* with neat
epigrams; Voltaire created the "New History" in order
to convince Madame du Châtelet that the study of the
past need not be musty. The tradition is unbroken down
to Renan, Taine, Bergson, Bremond, and the latest doctor's thesis.

No doubt this lucidity may be obtained at the expense
of profundity. Madame de Staël, the very incarnation
of "Society" in literature, appalled sundry German philosophers by requesting "the gist" of their systems in less
than ten minutes. Ten minutes to make clear that which
it had taken them ten years to make obscure! And
Madame de Staël became the laughingstock of the erudite. Yet we wonder whether, of all those dizzy fabrics of thought, much more is actually remembered than
what Voltaire could have expressed in a few pithy para-
graphs. It is all too easy to mistake the turbid for the
profound, and limpidity for shallowness. Certain trans-
lucid passages of Renan have the rich and strange beauty
of submarine gardens. There is a clearness that adds to
the quality of thought, as well as a clearness that de-
tracts from it. Both are, superficially, forms of politeness: the author tries to spare his public unnecessary
pains. But the second is tinged with secret contempt:
"This is all you would understand, anyway." The former is inspired by genuine courtesy: it is rude to offer
the reader an unfinished product.

Such clearness is not an inborn, individual quality: it is part of the social order. The author is conscious of a public which knows the best and is entitled to the best. Such a public wants clearness from a Renan, a Henri Poincaré, a Bergson, not from Walt Mason the Rhyming Optimist or Bruce Barton the Supersalesman of Heaven. England and America desire the same thing, but do not know what to ask for; they were delighted when the French technique was deliberately adopted by Lytton Strachey. It came with the freshness of a discovery: yet Strachey considered himself as a disciple of Fontenelle and Voltaire; and, for nearly half a century, the long series of *French Men of Letters* had been offering, in dainty little volumes, an admirable and truly Stracheyan blend of scholarship and subdued irony.

We are using French literature as an example: we are well aware that France has no monopoly of clear thought and elegant expression. "Whatever is not clear is not French," deserves a place among popular fallacies; the man who coined that phrase had certainly not read Stéphane Mallarmé and Paul Claudel. French "Society" is no more infallible than French dressmakers or French cooks. There are dowds and *gargottes* in Paris; Victor Cousin and Caro were once mistaken for philosophers; and Henry Bordeaux is a member of the French Academy. On the other hand, we have come across no book about France more cogent in thought, more elegantly spare in expression than that of the *German* Ernst Curtius; and none lighter in touch, wittier, more whimsical and yet more searching, than that of the *German*

Sieburg. The best example of Voltairian irony that we know was uttered by the dour old Scot Carlyle; * and we could name half a dozen Londoners now living who beat the Parisians at their own game.

We have praised, unblushingly, the influence of "Society" upon literature. Now for the inexorable law of compensation. The penalty for urbanity is not always shallowness, as Pascal and La Rochefoucauld will testify: but a certain degree of formality. If they do not destroy personality, good manners succeed in veiling it; and conformity in externals obviously leads to sameness or monotony. Professor Babbitt's insistence on standards must bring forth standardized products.

In many fields, the loss is small: only eccentricity is sacrificed. It is disastrous in the lyric. For a "sociable" literature, the Ego is hateful; and lyricism is the exaltation of the Ego. Romanticism, which restored the possibility of lyric poetry, was a revolt against Society. Because France was so eminently sociable, Romanticism in France was only a magnificent accident. Retrospectively, we imagine that Lamartine, Hugo, Vigny, Musset, were the dominant powers during the two great Romantic decades: their classical contemporaries have vanished from sight altogether. But those "dim ultimate Classicists", now so deeply forgotten, were then in almost absolute control of the Academy and of all official positions. The Romanticists were held to be only a noisy band of talented, ill-bred youngsters, who presently would calm down. All later poets in whom the lyric note was unmistakable—Baudelaire, Verlaine, Rim-

---

* Margaret Fuller: "I accept the Universe."—Carlyle: "Gad! she'd better!"

baud, Mallarmé—had little to do with recognized "Society." High-grade French literature often has the faultless elegance and the banal distinction of Beaux-Arts architecture.

"Society" is conscious at times of its own commonplaceness, and seeks to escape from it through excessive refinement. The fear of triteness drives it into Preciosity. The disease goes by many names—Marinism and Concettism in Italy, Gongorism and Cultism in Spain, Euphuism in England. These words denote rare and virulent attacks: but the danger is permanent. The American form of Euphuism is smart wisecracking: some articles in undiluted New-Yorkese are as far-fetched in their allusiveness as the very worst pages that the early seventeenth century had to offer; and they will prove as puzzling to posterity, unless posterity be wise enough to leave them alone.

A "sociable" literature is dominated by woman; and the chief interest of a "society" woman relieved from household duties and family cares, before the days of sports and politics, was Sentiment. Not passion: passion is brutally unsocial; but the pretty game of minute analysis, spending hours before a psychological mirror, splitting hairs into four and then into four again, weighing bubbles in balances of gossamer. Provençal society started the fashions of the Courts of Love, which debated and adjudged fine points of sentimental casuistry, with no less subtlety than the Schoolmen displayed in their theological puzzles. Chrétien de Troyes was a deft dissector. Centuries later (but the line had never been broken), Madeleine de Scudéry mapped in detail "The Land of

Tenderness." The strategy of courtship was as elaborate and slow as that of a Montecuccoli.

The tradition survives: French Academicians are still able to write three hundred pages on the momentous problem: "Will *A* commit adultery with *B* or with *C?*" To the uninitiated, it makes remarkably little difference. America has her Paul Bourget in Mrs. Edith Wharton, and the same kind of appeal, which can not be described as *sexy,* is found in *The Edwardians.*

Society's worst crime is to have fostered cheap society literature, by and for those who have never been there. Such an accusation was leveled against Balzac himself. He was more familiar with business, Bohemia and the underworld than with the noble Faubourg. Still, in his defense be it said, the great realist was conscientious enough to carry on flirtations with a couple of authentic Duchesses, and to marry a Countess. Few of his critics can boast of such a record.

Let us allow the pendulum to swing for the last time. If French Society had not been so familiar with the intricacies of sentimental psychology, would Racine's analysis have been conceivable at all—that probing of the heart as tragically profound as anything in Shakespeare? * Could we have had such a study as *Manon Lescaut,* so level, so gray in coloring, so unerringly human? Or lighter and delightful things, like the comedies of Marivaux and the proverbs of Musset? Or the pitiless autovivisection of Benjamin Constant in *Adolphe?* The crude

* The training begins early. To my knowledge, thirteen-year-old children were assigned this subject: "Analyze the elements of coquetry in Racine's *Andromache.*"

hypotheses, the pseudo-scientific methods, the weird terminology of many psychological sects are poor substitutes for that power of disenchanted, dispassionate observation.

Yet the fact must be faced: "Society" is doomed; and with it a long established standard of literature. We have merely indulged in a few moments of meditation before a tomb. Let others repine: our quest is not ended.

Chapter 18

Yesterday: SCHOOLS, GROUPS AND CLIQUES

"SOCIETY", directly through the Court and Salons, indirectly through the Universities and the Academies, has to a large extent controlled literature. But the writers have also formed autonomous groups of their own. There again, we have "conscious, organized minorities" which determine the action of their members, and assume the leadership of public opinion. An author does not think or feel quite in the same way, nor does he wield the same kind of power when he is isolated as when he is a member of a team.

These groups may affect many forms, from a convivial gathering of friends to a regular Trade Union affiliated with the Federation of Labor. The latter is not in sight: it is well known that writers are not easily amenable to formal discipline. It would be interesting to have H. G. Wells censored for exceeding the Union output, or Bernard Shaw suspended for accepting less than Union wages. But the Union's chief weapon, the strike, would not be effective in literary hands. If professional writers were to strike, the publishers' offices would be besieged with blacklegs; if methods of terrorism kept these away, it would only give the classics a chance; if the classics were destroyed, the readers would simply enjoy a holiday.

Although the literary craft is not capable of rigid organization, and although it is notoriously torn by violent jealousies, there is a point upon which it acts with a single soul: and that is in magnifying the importance of literature. Only once in several generations do we find a traitor to his class like old Malherbe, who averred that "a good poet was of no more value to the state than a good nine-pin player"; but, in his arrogant verses, Malherbe contradicted this cynical sally. The greatest triumph of the advertising industry is to have "sold" the advertising idea to a gullible American public. We spend ten times too much on advertising, but dare not cut out a single cent, any more than we dare cut out competitive armaments. No campaign against advertising would be successful except through advertising methods; and the man who could conduct such a campaign would prefer not to kill the goose which lays the golden eggs. Similarly, we could not call the authors' collective bluff except through a successful book, which would confirm the power of literature. We suspect that the poet's influence often resembles that of Chanticleer, whose song causes the sun to rise—provided it be sung just before dawn.

"Society" with a literary tinge and literary society proper merge by imperceptible degrees. The personnel of two gatherings may be practically the same: in both cases a blend of professional writers and men of the world. The difference would depend upon the geographical location—Chelsea or Mayfair—and upon the quality of the host. But what if the host himself be at the same time an author and a man of affluence? Thus Helvetius and d'Holbach generously entertained the Encyclopedic coterie, and contributed books which would have done credit to starvelings. Thus Samuel Rogers was a poet as well as a banker. We come then to the fine point of distinction: "Which are more memorable, the writings of the host, or his dinners?"

In most cases, however, the difference between the two worlds is definite enough; and, although there is no lack of friendly visiting back and forth, few men are equally at ease in both. As professional authorship is seldom accompanied by great wealth and a smoothly running household, the natural place for writers to gather is the Tavern. So it has been from time immemorial, and we all remember the bouts at the *Mermaid's* or Dr. Johnson's fine eulogy of the *Cheshire Cheese*. A matchless quartet of Classicists, Molière, Racine, La Fontaine, Boileau, used to meet at the *Fir Cone,* or sometimes at Boileau's suburban cottage at Auteuil. Once they went so deep into their potations that they reached the point of absolute pessimism. Only Boileau's unconquerable common sense, still groping and staggering through the fumes, prevented four of France's greatest from jumping into the Seine. Such memories create a bond. It was not purely on theoretical grounds that Boileau defended Racine against discouragement, and told Louis XIV that Molière was the first writer of the age. For every literary group is, and should be, a Mutual Aid Society.

In the eighteenth century, the tavern found a more refined rival in the coffee-house, the Salon and Academy of the true Bohemian. Although the Encyclopedists had friends in many drawing rooms, and could call that of Mademoiselle de Lespinasse their very own, it was in the Cafés that their leader Diderot was seen at his best. In an ultra-conservative country like France, the Café has remained an institution, although hardly a power. It offers a rallying point without infringing on the writer's cherished freedom; and it allows the semi-Bohemian to catch a glimpse of the literary world without any fear of losing caste.

This curiosity, of course, creates a danger. A Café can not be kept a secret. It soon becomes a show place, and visitors from Bucyrus, Bucharest and Buenos Aires flock to see the Lions sip their absinthe. The Lions enjoy their popularity, superficially, and for a very brief time; then despise themselves for it, and move to some unpolluted Helicon, some undesecrated Hippocrene. Chasing the ever shifting center of literature through the cafés, wine-shops, taverns and cabarets of Paris is as exciting as hunting big game in the jungle. Rodolphe Salis made a fortune by frankly commercializing his Montmartre cabaret, the *Black Cat;* and some of the *Black Cat* poets, taught by so able a master, achieved success in solid *bourgeois* terms: Maurice Boukay-Couyba became a Senator and Cabinet Minister; Maurice Donnay a member of the French Academy. Now that jazz bands have displaced poets as Montmartre's chief attraction, a chapter in literary history is closed.

To drink with a man in a public place does not commit you in any way; to eat with him creates a closer relationship. All churches and all trades have had their agapes; indeed, it was seriously prophesied that the new and sorely needed American religion was slowly emerging out of the Rotary Luncheons. The Literary Dinner is a very fine thing, so long at it does not turn into a banquet—a promiscuous gathering where one listens, in weary silence, to a few star performers, wearier than the rest. If the membership is small and stable, and if it implies genuine personal intimacy, the Dinner is a power as well as a delight. It was such a Dinner, at the Magny Restaurant, that knit together the best Parisian minds under the Second Empire: Sainte-Beuve, Renan, Taine, About. Flaubert and George Sand, who had elected to bury themselves in their provinces, attended whenever they happened to be in Paris. Prince Napoleon established a rather precarious contact between that liberal group and the political world. It was the same company, with Sainte-Beuve acting as host, that created an uproar among the Conservatives by eating meat on Good Friday. For the Magny habitués were freethinkers almost to a man, and their scientific Positivism was more threatening for orthodoxy than anti-clericalism of the common kind.

There again we see the tendency of a social gathering among literary men to turn into a school. Boileau and his friends did not meet primarily because they were Classicists: they took their classicism for granted. But they were congenial as boon companions partly because they shared the same views on literature; and their close association brought those views into sharper focus. The

Magny diners were not sworn in advance to support scientific freethought. George Sand, for instance, was a survivor of Romantic Humanitarianism, and she was liked and admired by all of them. But if the group did not rally to a formal doctrine, it created an atmosphere; and an atmosphere was exactly what the doctrine needed for healthy growth.

To pass from the social literary group to the School, one definite element is required: a leader. This quality of leadership is, of course, not literary in itself: it is the same which makes for prominence in business or politics. It is not creative genius, although it is not incompatible with it. Among the poets of the French Pleiad, Joachim du Bellay was at least as gifted as Ronsard, and wrote the able manifesto of the movement: but Ronsard assumed command. Lamartine had won fame when Victor Hugo was still a schoolboy: but Victor Hugo quietly seized the helm. The Goncourts had been *Naturalists* before Zola had reached artistic adolescence: but— much to their chagrin—, they were swept aside.

Leadership is not solely based on self-confidence. There are writers who possess magnificent conceit, yet remain isolated. Rousseau started a revolution, but did not create a school. Chateaubriand was revered as the first writer of his day, yet the actual chief was that young upstart Hugo, who had scribbled on his school books: "I want to be Chateaubriand or nothing." Chateaubriand had to be satisfied with incense: Victor Hugo was followed.

Leadership requires talent, self-confidence, hard work, and above all *a desire for coöperation*. You can not lead a team unless you want a team: a Rousseau, a Chateaubriand, wish to stand alone. Even in death: Chateaubriand is buried on a rock beaten by the waves, and Victor Hugo's bier was followed to the Pantheon by half a million men, *quorum pars parva fui.* Among great writers, some are supreme soloists, some are born conductors.

Both types may be the center of a group. But the admirers of the soloist have no creative element in common; they are not an orchestra, they do not form a school. There is no clearer instance of a *group* than that which gathered round Dr. Johnson. It had congeniality, fixity, loyalty: but it was merely a group. It had very little influence upon literature; and, paradoxical as it may sound, Johnson had very little influence upon his group. They liked him, they admired him, they did not preach his gospel. (But did he have a gospel? His idea of conversation was not to carry conviction, but to unhorse an opponent.) The Doctor's massive strength did not appreciably retard the downfall of classicism. He denounced, shrewdly as well as vehemently, the hoax perpetrated by Macpherson: but "Ossian's" prestige for another thirty years, was immensely greater throughout Europe than Johnson's. Johnson was the triumphant defender of lost causes: an autocrat, not a dictator.

The personal group, worshipping, and not seldom exploiting, a Master, is therefore far less important in literature than the School. It may indeed prevent the formation of a school: the inner circle closes jealously round the god, and wishes to keep exclusive possession of him. Anatole France after 1910 (I dare not mention living

English and American writers) had thus become an idol for the masses, and the prisoner of a self-appointed clergy. He tried to break through that inexorable ring: but the task was beyond an old man's strength, and he had to resign himself to the company of his friends.

The three stages are sometimes found in the career of a single author. First, the voluntary coming together of like-minded men: thus the young French Romanticists met in the drawing rooms of Charles Nodier, at the Arsenal Library; Victor Hugo was a member of that *Cénacle,* as it was called, and barely "first among peers." Then Victor Hugo, with his undoubted genius, his monumental self-confidence, his Napoleonic talent for organization and advertising, forges ahead, issues manifestoes, musters troops, prepares the first night of *Hernani* like the storming of a fortress. The *Cénacle* now meets at his home, and has become the Romantic School. Finally, Victor Hugo, world-famous, surviving his literary epoch by a third of a century, is surrounded by henchmen, the best of whom, Auguste Vacquerie, Paul Meurice, can *pastiche* his more obvious tricks so as to defy detection. It has been wisely said: "To the founder of a school, everything may be forgiven, *except his school."* Here the term *school* is too flattering: the right word is *tail.*

The lassoing of Naturalism by Zola, the locking-up of Symbolism in the dark hermetic cabinet of Mallarmé, the confusion between the Æsthetic Movement and the personal antics of Oscar Wilde, are other examples of the same process. A vague desire leads to a loose association; an inner group turns the association into a machine;

the machine is no sooner perfected than power is cut off; it runs on momentum for a decade or a century, as Pseudo-this or Post-that; until it is properly added to the scrap heap of literary history.

The process is not always complete; there were many abortive schools which remained mere tendencies. These are sometimes vaguely described as "generations." *Art for Art's Sake,* for instance, represents a moment, a mood, a doctrine, not a school. Nothing is more baffling than these creatures of the mist: on that account, historians, retrospectively, and critics, prospectively, are always clamoring for schools, inventing them when they are not forthcoming. With a school, you stand on firm ground.

The founding of a school is of course very flattering to the vanity of the charter members. That is why schools grow with tropical profusion, but not always with tropical exuberance of life. *Classicism* and *Romanticism* on the one hand, *Realism* and *Symbolism* on the other, are four fundamental attitudes, and it was right that they should be organized into schools, in order to reach definite consciousness. But the creation of *Naturalism* was wholly unnecessary: Naturalism is merely the exaggeration of certain aspects in Realism. The name was found, and the man, and the theory: so a new *ism* enriched or cluttered the literary Pantheon. The game is going on as merrily as ever. Jules Romains, when he is not mystifying his fellow doctors with his theories on *extra-retinian vision,* is attempting to start a *Unanimist* school: as if the rudimentary feelings and impulses of masses had not been depicted by Hugo and Zola, among others; as if Stephen Crane had needed Unanimism to render the soul, not of one man, but of a whole regiment in battle. André Thérive—with commendable moderation, it must be said—is pleading for a *Populism* which is at least a hundred years old. We had *Spasmodics,* and *Imagists,* and *Vorticists, Impressionists* and *Expressionists, Pre*-everything, *Post*-everything, *Neo*-everything. The only school that fully appealed to us was *Dada,* a desperate attempt to reach the absolute zero of nonsense. This at least would have given us "the school to end all schools."

The effect of spontaneous groups is stimulating; the effect of schools is deadening. For one thing, schools cause writers to waste in proclamations and controversies much time that might have been devoted to creative art. Then schools compel a consistency which is the negation of life. The loss would be small if only second-raters used the official school stencil: but even great writers, as soon as they are committed to a formula, become, in the name of their principles, slavish imitators of themselves. The very greatest alone escape that paralyzing influence. Homer never knew he was "classical", and that blissful ignorance has made him the classic eternal. Dante thought of himself as a classicist, but fortunately he was mistaken. Shakespeare would have been puzzled by our term Romanticist; Molière was "classical" in *The Misanthropist,* "romantic" in *Don Juan,* "realistic" and even "naturalistic" in *Georges Dandin.* Goethe went through all schools and transcended them all. Balzac died before Realism was named.

The School enforces artificial conformity on men of radically different temperaments; it paralyzes those who

Yesterday: SCHOOLS, GROUPS AND CLIQUES

can not whole-heartedly enlist under its banner. It has all the faults of sect and party, and it seems almost as inescapable. Like all orthodoxies, it creates an elaborate set of false values. The school of yesterday, the rival school of to-day, are swept aside with deadly cocksureness. The school Credo is the letter that killeth.

And by school, sect, party, we mean here the standard, reputable, fully established organization. It is too easy to deride the infinitesimal group of youngsters who fire a few crackers as earnestly as though they were storming the Bastille. They know in the secret of their hearts that it is only boyish play, although they might choose to die rather than confess it aloud. It is the school of the middle aged that counts, and that hurts.

A fully equipped school requires: (a) a tendency; (b) a personnel; (c) a name, even though it be meaningless like Romanticism, question-begging like Classicism, insulting like Decadence; (d) a leader, with staff complete; (e) a doctrine, expressed in critical manifestoes; and (f), certainly not least, a periodical. When two or three young men are gathered together in the name of literature, their first desire is to found a review. The Review is the embodiment of the team spirit. It is an excellent medium for consolidated advertising. The literary field is strewn with those dead leaves, but also enriched. Absurd they may seem to sober eyes; but we believe, and shall later attempt to establish, that the insurgent literary magazine is almost indispensable as a pathfinder.

The reader will immediately think of our *Little Review,* whose story Margaret Anderson has told with such feminine vivacity in *My Thirty Years' War;* of *Transi-*

tion, which, it was suggested, would have been an apter name if spelled backward; in ages already remote, of the *Yellow Book,* with Aubrey Beardsley and Oscar Wilde —a little paper abused and derided in its day, and which has now given its name to a decade. The most complete example is offered by the *Mercure de France* in its earlier period. Under the editorship of Rémi de Gourmont, in the nineties, the *Mercure* was decidedly the organ of the Symbolists and Decadents. It praised them, expounded them, published their work, both in the magazine and in book form. The group was too generously open to be termed a clique: but it formed a team. Those weird unworldly poets worked for their ideals with a persistency, a sense of strategy and discipline, which are lacking in many a plain business man. The group did not exist merely on paper: the writers met in the flesh, in the old-world headquarters of the review, rue de Condé. The editor's receptions gave definite body to a loose mass of protest and yearning. The *Mercure* has become a well-established, and, we hope, a profitable business. But the idealism of its early years has not completely faded away. Perhaps only for auld lang syne, we can not think of the *Mercure* as a mere commercial enterprise.

What is the influence of the schools upon literature? On the authors themselves, we have expressed our opinion that it was wholly bad. On the public at large, the solid mass of readers, it is imperceptible. When hundreds of thousands chose to buy Blasco Ibáñez's *Four Horsemen of the Apocalypse,* or Dreiser's *An American Tragedy,* they could not be deterred by the thought that Naturalism had been dead and buried these many long years—

jam foetet. But, for the steady, enlightened, literary public—perhaps a hundred thousand in each of the leading countries—the Schools still possess some significance.

This, we believe, is a survival of the days when Society felt compelled to take interest in literature; when authors were either members of Society, or had a society of their own. These conditions are passing away: people who never meet can not divide on shibboleths. But they are still casting their shadow behind.

"Schools" start doctrinal controversies: it is their sole *raison d'être.* From the point of view of creative literature, this is sheer waste: controversies are not art, any more than, in the theological field, they are religion. But the debate provides good exercise for thought. The names, the formulae, the organizations, force themselves upon the reader's attention. America would never have listened to the muffled echo of very ancient discussions, if these had not been offered as "the New Humanism", with a first-class staff, resounding manifestoes, symposia for and against. And we must surmise that it is better for a few thousand Americans to talk about Humanism than about the antics of some picturesque Mayor, Governor or Evangelist. It is probably as difficult to bring out a literary idea without a "School" tag, as it would be to market any product without a trade name. Our prophecy is that the "Schools", if they survive at all, will turn more and more into merchandising devices. A shrewd publisher will some day launch *Neo-Post-Vorticism,* with the motto "Floating Power", or "Not a Yawn in a thousand pages!" But this takes us away from Literature as an autonomous realm into our next field of exploration: Literature as Business.

Chapter 19

To-day: LITERATURE AS BUSINESS

So long as "Society" was unshaken, the publishers played a very subordinate part in literature. Few writers relied on book sales for a living. If they had no independent means, they hoped for a sinecure or a pension. Reputations were made *before* works went into print. Publication was the corollary of success, not its prime condition. To work for the booksellers was to avow oneself a hack, and lose caste. Gentlemen merely consented to have a book brought out at the request of their friends.

These conditions, so alien to our methods, have not entirely disappeared. Speeches, sermons, letters, travel notes, occasional verses, a skit for private performance, appear from time to time with the mention that the writer has yielded to the importunities of a too indulgent audience. This blushing reluctance to be dragged on the public stage is not invariably ingenuous: the merest polite hint will serve as an urgent request. But it is more trustworthy in the case of books for private circulation only: Henry Adams's *Mont-Saint Michel and Chartres* was known among a chosen few, before it became a successful business venture.

To-day: LITERATURE AS BUSINESS

This uncommercial tradition has remained stronger (willy-nilly) in poetry than in other branches of literature. In all languages, many books of verse are printed at the author's expense, and chiefly for distribution among his immediate acquaintances. The word *publisher,* in this connection, would be a misnomer, with a touch of cruel irony.

One of the last prominent cases in which fame was achieved before publicity was that of José-Maria de Heredia. His hard, luminous and flawless sonnets, which provide such a favorite exercise for American translators, were known in literary circles through private readings, manuscript copies, and a few samples in the noncommercial reviews. Heredia was already designated for the Academy before the *Trophies* were actually put on sale. Paul Valéry's reputation was for many years purely esoteric. When the general public finally heard his name and was curious to read his books, it was found that a Valéry could not be bought in the open market. It was necessary to use all the "pull" at your command before one of the slim and cryptic volumes could be added to your treasures. This artificial rarefaction, by the way, has turned into an excellent business scheme. As his fame increased, Valéry received more and more for giving less and less. For a few years, he was the author who made most money by refusing to sell. As an Irish critic would put it: "If he had refrained from writing altogether he would be a millionaire."

Another case in which the usual commercial methods do not fully apply is that of the Subscription Book. This is an extension of the "Society" idea. Presumably the author is well known, and samples of his work have been circulated among his friends. It is right that they should manifest their desire by affixing their names to a subscription list. Through this safe and dignified system, which presupposes an organized aristocracy of culture, Pope made himself independent of individual patronage, and likewise of popular favor. Samuel Johnson also used it; but, great as was his integrity, his indolence was at times greater still, and he pocketed advanced subscriptions to books that he forgot to write. The subscription method marked the transition between the gentlemanly era and the commercial. It is still used in special cases, such as expensive scientific works, and handsome limited editions. It strongly appealed to D. H. Lawrence. We shall see that, in a modified form, it might serve again as a transition, this time from the mercantile to the . . . human, for lack of a more definite term.

In all the above cases, the publisher is, like the printer, merely the author's agent. He is supposed to have no initiative and no responsibility. But, with the crumbling down of "Society", all existing criteria lose their validity. There is no orthodoxy that any University or Academy can enforce, no aristocratic group whose word is law, and the authority of the literary cliques does not reach beyond a very narrow circle. We know for certain that the actual reading public is by no means coextensive with the enormous body of potential readers: but we do not know the boundaries of that public, its ramifications, its principles, its tastes. We can only guess and gamble; and the people who are doing the guessing and the gambling for us are the publishers.

And, as they do so, it is they, no longer the professors, Society or the cliques, who are roughly determining what path literature shall take. They are the ineluctable guardians of the gate. In antiquity, even in the Classical Age, an author could read his manuscript to a few friends, and win recognition: in our enormous, multifarious, chaotic world, the individual author is lost. Even if he could afford to have the book printed at his own expense—there are a few reputable firms in that branch of the trade—his chances of success would be slim. The *author's book* starts with a stigma, and is marked out for defeat. Marcel Proust had an enviable reputation in the best Parisian circles, and he was wealthy: yet he knew he would have no chance of attracting attention if he paid out of his own pocket for bringing out his work. No new Walter Scott, no second Dickens could arise unless a publisher gave him leave to try his luck. If you win the publishers to your side, nothing is gained; but, if you fail to win them, everything is lost.

The publishers are therefore the latest and clearest examples of our "conscious, organized minorities." Like the politicians, they claim to represent the public, to give them only what they want. But this is not true even of politicians, who frequently offer us only a choice between two things we equally dislike; and it is less true of the publishers, since there is nothing like organized plebiscites in literature. The desires of the public are known only through the publishers' guesses. Had the publishers in their wisdom decided that the public did not want *All Quiet on the Western Front,* because they were surfeited with war stories, or *The Bridge of San Luis Rey,* because it was too remote, sophisticated and highbrow, there would have been no way of quashing their verdict. There never is any appeal from the publishers to some other authority: the only appeal is from one publisher to another publisher, whose guiding principles are on the whole very much the same. American literature does not reflect the American public mind: it reflects the publishers' opinion of the American mind: and the publishers seem to take a pessimistic view of human nature. Are they right, or do we deserve better? We shall never know to what extent they are misrepresentative men.

We have no intention of presenting publishers as powers of darkness. Young idealists are apt to make that intolerant mistake. Publishers are business men; Art claims (it is one of its minor hypocrisies) to be absolutely disinterested; therefore publishers are the natural enemies of Art. A neatly contrasted Manichean scheme: the authors on the side of the angels, the publishers reducing Beauty and Truth to a question of dollars and cents. Reality is not quite so simple. Even in the theological domain, we are beginning to suspect that the Devil has been maligned, and should be given his due.

An author whose fancy lightly turns to thoughts of pelf is no rarity in the literary world. If it be sordid to be paid for one's efforts, not a few writers are guilty of that crime. The publishers are in business: but, as in the case of many other business men, their trade also happens to be their hobby. They deal in books because they like them, and not exclusively because they think books a more profitable "line" than paint or glue. They too are *book-men:* the literary atmosphere is congenial to them; their minds like to dwell on literary themes. For over a century, the heads of the great firms in Europe and in America have been men of liberal culture. Up to the present at any rate, the publisher, cynically indifferent to the quality of his wares, provided they bring quick returns, the dealer in scandal and filth, the expert in bally-hoo, the practitioner of cut-rate and cut-throat methods, has never stayed in the business long enough to affect literature.* On the contrary, there are innumerable examples of publishers bringing out the work of an unknown author, not even as a gamble, but as a service; or, if the word sounds too sanctimonious, as a satisfaction to their personal pride. Serious books that can at best break even over a period of years are brought out for the honor of the firm. Not to mention Anglo-Saxon examples, Victor Bérard's thought-provoking and erudite studies on the *Odyssey* were a family sacrifice of the Armand Colin house on the altar of humane letters. Honesty is the best policy in the long run. Many of us do not run quite long enough to discover it: but publishing concerns are among the very oldest in the business world, and a decent regard for the opinion of mankind is one of their assets.

Even the man new to the trade prefers good books to poor ones: not entirely as a matter of good taste and individual prestige, but as a plain business proposition. A steady good-seller (this, as we suggested, might be ac-

---

* Questionable methods, unfortunately, are not always spurned by publishers who ought to know better. The scandal caused by Paul Margueritte's *La Garçonne*—a mistaken book, but an honest one—was due to the fact that the publishers had called attention to the most *risqué* passages. The advertisements of Aldous Huxley's *Brave New World* overemphasized the spiciest episode. Both authors belonged to literature, and should have been treated with greater respect.

cepted as a pragmatic definition of a *classic,* but it applies
also to a standard cook book) is obviously safer than a
meteoric best-seller. Any publisher would prefer to build
up the honest, solid reputation of a Galsworthy rather
than stun the public with *The Cradle of the Deep.*

In all countries, but particularly in England and in
France, good publishers have become social centers. The
head of the firm has a Salon as well as an office. Successes
are celebrated like family affairs. Many books have been
written bearing on the influence of publishers as the
nucleus of a literary group. These, and the correspondence
of noted writers, give an impression of mutual trust and
cordiality. The unworldly genius chained to a rock and
fighting off the vultures is sheer nightmare. It is true
that many publishers are decently well off, and that
not a few geniuses go hungry. Yet it may be said
that publishers have suffered more from the unreli-
ability of geniuses than geniuses from the greed of publishers.

We are frankly giving an idealized picture, knowing
full well that there are bad publishers as there are bad
ministers, bad grocers and worse authors. We should like
to believe that this ideal will remain permanently with
us; but we are afraid that it belongs to a period that is
disappearing. In the hierarchized society of the ancient
régime, which lingered through the nineteenth century,
there were dynasties, not only on the throne, but in the
professions, in the trades, in the crafts. They had solid
family traditions and a sense of *Noblesse Oblige.* One was
destined from the cradle to be a judge, a carpenter, a
bookseller. Making money was not the uppermost pre-

occupation: it was not negligible by any means, but, with decent care and industry, an adequate return could be taken for granted. Making a name for one's self was almost plebeian: the name was made, and had only to be maintained. This quasi-feudal conception is waning: the miracle is that it should not have disappeared altogether. Increasingly, business will be strictly business. We felt, poignantly, the difference when a friendly London publisher of the old school sold out, at eighty, to a large and aggressive firm. Shall we see again the days when a publisher's office was in verity his den, lined with favorite old books, family portraits, and mementoes of famous associates? When his private apartments were actually over the shop, and were pervaded with the same atmosphere?

It would be hard for the book industry, in a capitalistic civilization, not to become frankly capitalistic. We may expect to see it dominated by huge impersonal concerns which, instead of keeping in their files chatty letters from their author-friends, will think in scientific graphs, and feel not at all. Into this world of soulless giants, personality will break forth once in a while, in the form of a young Napoleon of trade, ruthless, efficient, self-centered. Increasingly, "mere" literature will be looked upon with an indulgent smile.

Good or bad, the publishers control literature as they never have before. What are they going to do with it? We have no experience whatever of the book trade, and prudence compels us to let the publishers speak for themselves. We have picked out two works bearing directly on the subject, because they are as sharply contrasted as possible. They present the opposition of two spirits, two methods, perhaps two civilizations and two ages.

Bernard Grasset * is already a publisher of mature experience, although still a youngish man. He selected publishing as a profession because of his sincere love for letters. He placed at the service of his enthusiasm certain aggressive qualities which would have made him a success in any country and in any trade. He was not merely a competent merchant—the dreary *Homo Economicus* buying in the cheapest market, selling in the dearest: he was able to realize that conditions were changing, and to take advantage of the change. Convinced that the modern publisher does represent the "conscious minority" occupying a strategic position, he believes that the publisher should frankly assume leadership.

We have seen that in the old days, social values created literary values. The discovery of a new talent came from the self-styled élite: the publisher merely registered their selection. Now, in a society in turmoil, no one is able to take the initiative, *unless it be the publisher himself*. It is his part to pick out a likely winner in the literary race, to groom him and train him, and give him a start. Just to print a book, place it for sale, send a hundred copies to reviewers, insert paid advertisements in the proper magazines, is mere routine work: it requires no imagination, no mental energy. A book cast into the literary sea in that mechanical manner will sink like lead, and no praise from the experts will make it float. The great business of the publisher is not so much to choose a book as to *launch* it.

* Bernard Grasset: *La Chose Littéraire*, Paris, Gallimard, 1929.

To-day: LITERATURE AS BUSINESS

In Paris, Bernard Grasset is working in a transitional world, where social and literary elements are still interwoven. The disintegrating aristocracy of birth and intellect cling to the belief that they are dictating literary taste; the parvenu aristocracy of wealth, the Post-War *Nouveaux Riches,* would like to share that privilege; but, old or new, rich or poor, they are in no condition to formulate that taste for themselves. They are arbiters who need expert prompting. In steps our publisher: through social contacts and press influences, he "makes up the mind" of the would-be dictators. When he has induced one small group to "discover" his author, he uses that group to win the larger circle of those who want to be "in the know." It is not a campaign of crude ballyhoo, but one of whispered suggestions. Then the pump is properly primed: we are ready for the general public. And, as often as not, the general public remains placidly indifferent.*

In other words, the publisher attempts to do in a few weeks what Madame Arman de Caillavet did for Anatole France in fifteen years. Naturally, Time fails to respect that which is done without his collaboration. But who cares for Time nowadays? It may be the next fallacy to be exploded by the mathematical hyperphysicists. The method, therefore, is not new: it is the good old "puffing" (shall we say "puffing and blowing"?) of our ancestors. What is new is its commercial application by efficiency experts.

* Frank Swinnerton agrees with Grasset: advertising and favorable reviews don't sell books. What sells books is *talk*—among the right people. Swinnerton's *Authors and the Book Trade* (A. Knopf, 1932) is a very pleasing, easy and adequate survey of the problem.

This subtle game, in which genuine art, snobbishness and business sense are so cunningly blended, is exactly similar to that of the great dressmakers. In the old days again, the initiative of fashion actually belonged to the society ladies themselves. They chose their styles, with the assistance of their *couturières,* who were not yet *couturiers.* Their success was a personal one: a dazzling young Countess was herself the artist and the work of art, and not a mere titled *mannequin.* Then, in the very measure in which the prestige of old Society was waning, the collaboration of the *couturiers* became more exacting. Under the Second Empire, the old aristocracy kept away from the Court, and there were adventurers and parvenus among the personal friends of Their Majesties. Paris no longer admired Madame Untel, but Worth's creation for Madame Untel. The initiative had passed to the *couturier:* but he still had to work through high society. At present, the models are created rue de la Paix, and are displayed by the *mannequins* in the salons of the firm, or at the races: Society takes notice and follows. Success still depends on Society's approval, but the styles no longer originate with Society. Bernard Grasset and his rivals are the Worths, the Paquins, the Patous of literature. If they decide that novels shall be worn shorter this season, that Lesbianism or the interior monologue are *passés,* that a touch of Communistic Red or Royalist White is all the rage, then we shall repeat, with imperturbable assurance: "Oh! no one reads a full-size novel any more!—Proust? The passing of the Marcel wave!—Moscow is the new Athens."

Bernard Grasset is not fooling his public: he is trying

to secure recognition for the things he genuinely likes.
But he is not such a humbug as to claim that he is giving
the Public what they want. The public do not know what
they want, and probably should not have it if they knew.
He tells the public what they ought to want, which is
exactly the service expected of a conscious, organized
minority.

Only his system is based on the insecure survival of the
Society ideal. When that is gone, other means will
have to be devised. But we need not be concerned about
such a contingency. Barring a Bolshevist revolution, the
twilight of *bourgeois* society in France may be intermi-
nably prolonged. At least, it is likely to outlive M.
Bernard Grasset.

La Chose Littéraire is hardly more than a pamphlet:
only thick paper, large type and generous margins give
it the bulk and dignity of a standard French yellowback.
Its method of treatment is, like its physical presentation,
very elegant and very slight. When we pass from this
brief and pleasant causerie to Mr. Cheney's formidable
volume,* we realize that there is an ocean between Paris
and New York. Mr. O. H. Cheney does not deal with
such a frivolous thing as "literature", but with the solid
reality of the Book Industry; and in order to give the
Association for which the Survey was made a full dollar-
for-dollar value, he embodies in his text pages of tabulated
or graphic statistics. We have had no glimpse of either
man's inner sanctum; we imagine M. Grasset in a study
with touches of the Bohemian studio; and Mr. Cheney

---

* O. H. Cheney: *Economic Survey of the Book Industry*, 1930–31. National
Association of Book Publishers.

in the impressive office of the competent executive. Yet there is more epigrammatic wit in the American product than in the French; and also a franker confession of bewilderment. M. Grasset still believes that publishers can lead; Mr. Cheney does not know whither publishers are driven—a piece of wisdom which must be accounted a bargain at ten dollars net.

Why are books selected for publication? Why do they sell? Why do they cease to sell? A triple mystery. The one thing that Mr. Cheney's statistics clearly bring out is the haphazard conditions of the industry. It caters to no definite public, and it does not market an indispensable commodity. As it is without guide, the trade seems bent on imitating the magnificent wastefulness of Nature. Infant mortality among books is appalling. And there is another aspect of the question which is not within the scope of Mr. Cheney's survey. From the business point of view, a perfect score for a firm would be an uninterrupted series of large sales. From the artistic point of view, the enormous success of certain books is even more to be deplored than the undeserved neglect of others.

A firm which has some notable triumphs to its credit, some of them not of an obvious kind, had the splendid idea of asking the public pointblank why they bought and read certain books, and what they were interested in. This document, which must have reached nearly every American home, is well worth reproducing:

Dear Reader: To aid in an important survey, please check in the squares below the reasons prompting the purchase of (fill in title of book in which you find this card):

To-day: LITERATURE AS BUSINESS

Review in	Appearance of Book . . . .
Advertisement in	Listed as best-seller . . . .
Recommended by	Widespread Discussion . . . .
Circular or Catalogue from	Bookstore display . . . .
Suggested by bookstore	Published by So-and-So . . . .
Author's previous book	Attractiveness of title . . . .
Author's reputation	Interest in subject . . . .
Gift	Other Reasons . . . .

I am interested in (here follow 21 kinds, from Religion to Cross-Word puzzles.)

Certain items in this questionnaire ought to be of much practical value to Messrs. So and So. It is well to know whether the good word of such or such a critic actually carries weight; and whether *The Consolidated Western Clay Products Journal* is a proper advertising medium for treatises on Auction Bridge. But even if such a tabulation gave us a clearer view of what has happened, it could hardly provide a rule for the future. I am willing to check on Messrs. So and So's list that I am interested in Detective Fiction: *with the proviso that it be good,* and Messrs. So and So have no way of knowing what *I* mean by good. I am not sure that I know myself. I have never been addicted to Westerns so far, but I am ready to be converted by a masterpiece. A success in one subject may favor a new success of the same kind, or it may hinder it: Wells's *History* seems to have helped Van Loon's: it might just as well have killed it. If everybody is reading debunking biographies, or works about Russia, or flamboyant praises of Mexico, we may be on the point of declaring ourselves utterly weary of the stuff, and the next book, which may be the best of all, will be voted commonplace and tedious. This is also true of a man's reputation. Too sensational a vogue is rather a danger than a promise. We are apt to deal harshly with our fads of yesteryear. We visit upon them our own sins of gullibility and gregariousness. We want to assure the world and ourselves that we were not actually taken in by Monsieur Coué.

Perversely enough, the economic trend of book producing is uneconomic. From a business point of view, the ideal would be steady sales steadily expanding. Instead of that even flow, the trade tends to develop seasonal floods. The Christmas rush, which should be checked, is encouraged. It is quite true that a book is always a fairly safe gift. It is flattering for the recipient to be credited with literary taste; and a well-selected volume does not look so futile or so stingy as the average two- or three-dollar knickknack. Still, there are quite a few Americans who buy books for themselves and read all the year round. And every new morn is somebody's birthday.

More dangerous than the seasonal peak is the brevity of success, followed by total neglect. Books hailed as "epics", "devastating", "epoch-making" (the blurb writers are overworking a few words which need eternal repose) will be dimly remembered in a few months; another little flare of semi-popularity with the cheap reprint, and they are gone for ever. If we resign ourselves to this jerky tempo, the quiet, unobtrusive book will have absolutely no chance. Stendhal prophesied in the eighteen thirties: "I shall be understood about 1880." And it came to pass, because French literature at that time offered the possibility of slow, barely perceptible growth. If a new Stendhal failed to catch within three months, his career would be at an end.

This American craving for the very latest model, this

306

necessity for sudden success, favor waves, crazes, sensationalism. Worst of all perhaps, they almost compel the good writer to overdo. The public, having no corporate existence, has no memory; it is more and more difficult for fame to acquire momentum. So a self-respecting author, if he does not want to be forgotten, is forced to bring out his works in quick succession; or, if he allows too long an interval to elapse, he has to stake his reputation again on each new battle. After a few years of silence, he must "stage a comeback", a notoriously difficult thing to do.

The other uneconomic tendency in the trade is its gambling character. Too many books are published, with a wild alternation of a few "best-sellers" and a majority of "flops." Obviously it would be better if we had fewer books, none of them sensationally successful, all selling decently well. That could be the case, if it were possible to anticipate the desires and measure the appetite of the indefinite monster whom we are all trying to serve. Catching the public's fancy is frankly a matter of luck: so it becomes good business to have as many tickets as possible in the lottery, and hope for the one big prize that will recoup many losses. It is not wisdom, but a counsel of despair. But again, if the publishers keep their eyes fixed on the 100,000 mark within six months, the fine, quiet, exceptional book will gradually be ruled out.

The leaders of the industry themselves deplore these conditions. In other respects, however, the book trade conforms more closely to sound economic principles, but with results that are scarcely less disastrous for literature. If the gambling element could be eliminated—the unpredictable windfall, the wastefulness of innumerable failures—the industry would strive for orderly, standardized mass production, which is the key to efficiency. This point has already been reached by the great popular magazines. These wonders of the Western World are quite frankly a branch of the advertising trade, with art and literature offered only as a bait. They need enormous sales to make their advertising space valuable; so they can not afford to employ writers who are not themselves nationally advertised products. They know, and most of their readers know, that the work of their most highly paid contributors is, to put it courteously, not strikingly good. But you can trust the label: from coast to coast, you know what you are buying, which is true neither of the pulp magazines nor of the highbrow reviews. And the few big packers of serial fiction overshadow the book market as well. In a capitalistic Utopia, literary production could be consolidated into four or five Syndicates, which would provide at the same time the efficiency of concentration and the blessings of competition.

This danger would be enormously increased, if the movement for cheaper books were to succeed. A shrewd citizenry, in which the Scottish strain has remained potent, loves a bargain, as a compensation and an excuse for its intermittent recklessness. Not seldom it loves a bargain *dearly*. When the corner drug store offers you a neatly bound volume, with a flamboyant jacket, an alluring title, a well-known author's name, the whole for 99 cents, with a tube of dental paste thrown in, you would feel yourself a simpleton if you walked away to the book shop, and bought exactly the same kind of work for $2.50. But cheap editions can be justified only by enormous sales; and the cult of sudden, massive success is a threat to all the more delicate values.*

Book production, if these tendencies were unchecked, would soon find itself in the same plight as its great rival, the talking pictures. There also, the experimental, the subtle, the rare, that secret power which reveals itself by slow degrees, are accounted damning sin. It would not do for a picture to be understood "about 1980": it is a big investment, it must take at once, or be a dead loss. The vast American public must be pleased; and, as that public is very dimly known, only the most approved gags and tricks can be used. When a film is declared "daring", it is because it exaggerates, not because it explores. Unless foreign countries follow the lead of Germany in repelling the American invasion, Hollywood will be the unquestioned world capital, and will spread a dead level of vulgarity for the greatest happiness of the greatest number.

This is gloomy prophesying: but we are nearer of kin to Mark Tapley than to Dean Inge or Mr. Joseph Wood Krutch. Let the worst come to the worst! We shall later attempt to sketch a literary Utopia: let us now conjure up a literary nightmare. Five or six publishers only, each with a staff of a dozen authors, are publishing a limited number of titles which sell by the million. The industry is consolidated, organized, made efficient, beyond

---

* This objection applies only to new books. The cheap *reprint*, on the contrary, has many admirable points. In my youth, I read some of the finest English books in sixpenny editions, which sold then for 4d½ (9¢). France has series of excellent modern fiction, with wood cuts, for 15¢; and certain American *Libraries* are a boon and a blessing.

the rosiest dreams of Mr. O. H. Cheney. In such an atmosphere, would literature perish?

Who knows? We might have an age after the heart of the Neo-Humanists—if Neo-Humanists have anything so romantic as a heart. It would be a world of standards, with very definite rules. The few masters of the craft would reach an extraordinary degree of technical skill, or, if you prefer, of efficiency. And, as in such an age, politics, religion, art, would all be integrated under the general formula of BUSINESS, it would bring our present chaos to an end, it would be a discipline of life, a new classicism.

Such an ideal would not only satisfy Irving Babbitt (who, if he had survived into that millennium, might have been the Will Hayes of Humane Letters), but it would also rejoice the soul of Tolstoy. For it would be a thoroughly democratic art, purged from all sophistications and morbidities, intelligible at once to every man. To the supercilious, it might seem primitive and crude. But this is merely a matter of comparison. The *common* level need not be low; and nothing prevents it from rising steadily. The cheapest cars to-day are marvels of refinement compared with the luxury cars of twenty-five years ago.

Under this Dictatorship of the Intellectual Proletariat, it is not inevitable that all the élites should be guillotined, or reduced to sullen silence. But the élites would have to dissolve as distinct bodies; and, if they wanted to be heard, they would be compelled to use a tongue understood of the people. An artist to-day is tempted to address exclusively his peers, and to use their cryptic jargon. When all literature has become one gigantic *Saturday Evening*

Post, he will have no choice but to place his power at the service of popular art. The patriotic tragedy of Æschylus, the thumping melodrama of Shakespeare, the edifying, sentimental, detective romance in *Les Misérables,* show that it is not impossible to live in close touch with the masses, yet soar to the heights.

You will say that the very essence of the poet is to be *different.* Granted: but great art could be different *within* the common medium, not *aside* from it. Even to-day, a page may be of the rarest quality, without such artificial signs of distinction as Mallarmé's syntax or Joyce's vocabulary. The poet will write for the masses, and also for himself. A few notes may be lost by his enormous public without spoiling their enjoyment of the whole. And, through these few notes, he has saved his soul.

Nor will those few notes die unheard. They will reach, within the vast throng, the few who are no longer allowed to isolate themselves. They will create a mysterious communion rarer in quality than the fussy little circles of Greenwich Village. To be aggressively, boastfully esoteric is a childish prank. To conceal, with apparent artlessness, the Secret within the Obvious, is a searching delight. Even to-day, a book which will be read by a few thousands is perhaps meant for less than a score. Pascal, in his Vision, exacted from Christ the assurance: "I have shed such and such a drop of blood *for thee.*" I, the isolated reader, feel that my own poets have written such or such a word for me, for me alone, and for none besides.

Big Business,—or its extreme limit, the Biggest Business of all, Bolshevism,—can kill only external differences. The hierarchy of literature would reappear within the apparently homogeneous mass. All men would read the same words: there would be as many different resonances as there are individual souls.

Mr. Cheney, who is a very stimulating writer, has thus enticed us into the land of his dreams, a thoroughly organized and efficient book industry; and we have found that his Utopia might be habitable after all. Somehow, all ideals converge. It is a pity that their meeting point should be just beyond Nowhere.

For there is little hope or danger of our ever reaching such a degree of organization. People can standardize their plain, basic necessaries, and even their material luxuries: not their æsthetic satisfactions. Our needs might very well be served by a single railroad system; one big firm could supply bread, or even automobiles, for us all; but no syndicate could long preserve a monopoly of literature. There are two tendencies at work in the world: opposite, not antagonistic. The one is toward more unity on the material plane (standardization); the other toward more diversity on the spiritual plane (pluralism).

All that we need retain of Mr. Cheney's survey is a confession of despair: the industry is in a state of chaos, and no simple measures could create order.

Why balk at chaos? Liberty means chaos, compared with the orderliness of death. But our chaos is excessive. This, in our opinion, is due to the faint-heartedness of the publishers, who dare to gamble, but not to lead. If *they* refuse to be our "conscious organized minority", to whom shall we turn?

Chapter 20

To-day: GROPING TOWARD A RATIONAL ORGANIZATION

I

WE have seen that the publishers were "leaders" blindly guessing whither the flock wanted to be led. Neither they, nor the public, and the authors least of all, are satisfied with the situation. The thought that religion, politics and business are all in the same plight brings rather wan comfort. "Confusionism", as Irving Babbitt named the spirit of our age, is the most cheerless of religions.

Is there any way out of this morass? Must we wait until our civilization be "integrated" again? But, if every branch of human activity were to wait for every other, movement of any kind would become unthinkable. *Planning* is a fine, energetic motto; but planning means the coördination of efforts, and first must come the effort.

We have attempted to show that the old literary order depended upon a social structure which is now a memory. Pure commercialism has evolved no new order of its own: in theory and in practice, commercialism is anarchy. We shall now examine a few efforts toward a more rational organization of literature. We have no faith in any one panacea. What is of interest in any proposed reform is the recognition of an evil, the affirmation of a spirit, and a call to renewed activity. And this is the sign and promise of returning grace.

The times, being hard, are not unfavorable. Grievous as the sins of Capitalism may be, self-complacency is no longer one of them. Our world is in a penitent mood: world war, political futility, economic chaos, have shaken its confidence. This is all to the good. We have more faith in chastened Capitalism than in arrogant Communism. The Arch-Tempter's name is cocksureness.

If commercialism be the enemy of literature, the most obvious solution would be to take business out of publishing. Books should be published because they are good, and not exclusively because they bring money. There is nothing revolutionary about such an attitude. The most orthodox capitalist admits that business should not be the rule in matters of the spirit. We resent the intrusion of commercialism into science or religion. We do not—confessedly—give positions of national trust to the highest bidder, although we sometimes seek our representatives in the cheapest market. Books are not purely a "commodity": they fulfill at present many of the functions which, in the Middle Ages, were reserved to the Church and the Universities. It would not be absurd if literature also were excepted from the field of competitive economics.

Several agencies could take the place of the commercial publishers. The first is the State. In addition to official documents (which, in war times particularly, often rise to the dignity of fiction), it may bring out, as in Russia and Mexico, cheap editions of the classics and of popular textbooks. Vasconcelos believed that the Enneads of Plotinus were indispensable to the regeneration of the Indian *peon*. Washington, less idealistic, distributes tons of informative "literature", not all of which is wasted.

The second is the University Press. It usually limits itself to scientific and scholarly books. When it ventures, in a half-hearted way, to bid for the favor of the general public, it is not strikingly successful. It might be desirable if the Universities were to assume full control of learned editions, research publications, highly technical treatises. Books of reference, dictionaries and Encyclopædiæ should come under some *Inter-University Bureau of Intellectual Standards*. When the venerable *Britannica* or a prominent seat of higher learning adopt methods of high-pressure salesmanship, we have in both cases the same sense of incongruity. The Professor in print should be as dignified as the Professor in the lecture room. And yet . . . is *salesmanship* so radically different from *education*? The same definition: "Inducing a man to get what he does not want", might frequently apply to both.*

The third is the privately endowed Press. The institution I dream of would have to be wealthy enough to make some impression on the gigantic American market. It would restrict its activity exclusively to literature as an art, leaving to the trade practical works and books for mere entertainment, to the Universities all scientific publications. It would never seek popular success; but it is

---

* The religious Presses, circulating books at cost or giving them away, are even better examples of non-commercial publishing. A 500-page volume of Swedenborg may be had for a nickel.

not inconceivable, if the Press acquired any kind of prestige, that substantial success would follow. It would pay each accepted manuscript a minimum representing the time spent upon it under decent conditions of comfort; if the sales justified additional compensation, it would give the author royalties on the usual basis. Manuscripts would be submitted anonymously. A veteran of literature would have no better chance than the sophomore who deftly imitates his style; less of a chance than the freshman who, for a wonder, should bring something actually *fresh*. If the established author wants to capitalize on his past successes, let him make his terms with the commercial publishers. The Press would have two autonomous departments, called respectively *Tradition* and *Experiment*.

Our millionaires are a breed of men of whom we are justly proud. But they are far too imitative, that is to say oddly self-diffident. Their benefactions follow a few well-worn grooves. As a result, we have an actual plethora of Universities, and certain Peace Societies spend much of their income on activities rather remotely connected with peace. A *Memorial Press for Fine Literature,* on a sufficiently large scale, has not yet been tried, and should prove tempting. The suggestion is freely offered to any millionaire friendly to the Muses. If I were a millionaire myself, there are seven or eight better uses I could think of for my orphaned pelf.

These solutions are attractive. But they repose on the assumption that a non-commercial body would know how to pick the *good* books. On what authority? In virtue of what principles? One thing is certain: we do not want to entrust the fate of literature to the State, if the

State is to be represented either by the politicians or by
the bureaucrats. Shall we be guided by the professors of
literature and the academicians in the name of tradition?
Or by "Society" in the name of "good taste"? But, if we
still believed in these conservative authorities, our difficulty would not exist.

We might have the editorial board elected by the writing profession. The constituency might be hard to define:
yet it would not be so vague as either "Society" or the
"general public." The board would acquire thereby no
pontifical infallibility: but a fair degree of competence
might thus be secured. Creative artists are not necessarily
poor judges of their own craft; some of the shrewdest
criticism has been written by the best poets. When our
Foundation had been under way for a few years, the
electoral college might be limited to the authors whose
work it had accepted.

Commercial or philanthropic, official or private, any
publishing concern can not be worth more than its body
of advisers. In this respect, the best firms have maintained a highly creditable level. When books are passed
upon—to mention a few names at random, by Anatole
France, by George Meredith, Edward Garnett, E. V.
Lucas, Frank Swinnerton, or, in this country, by W. C.
Brownell or Willa Cather, there is little cause for com-
plaint. Indeed, *business* is not seldom better equipped, at
that crucial point, than the University presses.

Other things being equal, however, our Foundation
would have a decided advantage over the commercial
publishers. When a reader reports favorably upon a fine
piece of work, he also has to answer the question: "Will it

sell?" And he may have, sorrowfully, to answer: "It will not." In the trade, this means, in the majority of cases: Thumbs down. The endowed Press would be serenely indifferent to probable sales.

Another way of escape from unmitigated commercialism is the *subscription series*. This method has long been a familiar one in music and the drama. The national repertory theatres of France have three sources of income: State subsidies, yearly subscriptions, and box office receipts. When a young gas fitter with a passion for the stage, Antoine, started his *Théâtre Libre,* he organized it on the advanced subscription principle. With a modest and fairly steady backing—never fully adequate, alas!— he was able to produce daring plays, experimental plays, translations from unfamiliar literatures. Many a battle was lost: but no disaster was irretrievable. For the *Théâtre Libre* had a certain momentum; and when finally it went down, it had renovated the French drama.

The same system can be applied to literature. Charles Péguy had a curious publication, called the *Notebooks of the Fortnight.* It was not a magazine: each number was an independent volume by a single author. The editor's own works appeared in that fashion; and, in addition, he revealed his personality in prefaces, postfaces and interfaces, through many a page of perversely repetitious and ponderously insistent prose, shot through with passages of strange poetical power. Péguy's circulation, we believe, was about three thousand: modest enough, yet far greater than might have been hoped for by some of his collaborators, had they used the ordinary channels. The Péguy group was not rich, not powerful in political and academic circles, not drilled to repeat a shibboleth; but it had a common ideal of intellectual honesty, which had been its bond during the Dreyfus Affair. That small but solid group counted among the shock troops of the literary world. Romain Rolland's interminable *Jean-Christophe* first appeared in the form of *Notebooks*. It is doubtful whether this mighty work would have been accepted by any commercial publisher. A trade-wise business man would have guessed that in France, a country notoriously indifferent to music, and worse than indifferent to Germany, no public could be found for the slow biography of a child musician in a small Rhenish court. The Péguy phalanx broke the ring of prejudice. *Jean-Christophe* was reprinted in a trade edition, and won world-wide acclaim.*

Between the subscription series and the Review of the usual type, there is only a technical difference in the distribution of the installments. The *uncommercial literary magazine* is one of our strongest hopes of salvation. By this means, poets can still hail each other, and play between the enormous iron feet of the Book Trade Robots. In so far as it embodies the prejudices and vanities of a clique, the "little" Review is futile and even dangerous. In so far as it represents the flame of youthful faith and indignation, the refusal to serve either Mammon or the Law of the Pharisees, it is holy even when it is ludicrous.

With a pitiful circulation, it is not negligible. Its contributors and readers (usually they are one and the same, a small devoted company) will not altogether forget its

---

*More recently, Louis Hémon's *Marie Chapdelaine* had been published twice (as a serial and in Canada) without attracting any attention. It was included in the *Green Notebooks,* a series inspired by Péguy's, and, through that select public, was revealed to the general reader. The trade edition went into the hundreds of thousands.

message, even when they sober down into right-thinking (*i.e.* unthinking) *bourgeois*. Between the experimental vanguard, which at times seems *perdu,* and the main body, there are *liaison* agents. Shrewd editors like to do literature a good turn, and at the same time give their magazine a name for moderate daring and safe liberalism. So an author not infrequently passes from the esoteric little Review to the periodicals run on a sound business basis.

This transfer from the uncommercial to the commercial, however, is not without peril. We are astonished and delighted at times to find the names of genuine artists on the announcements of frankly industrial publications. But in many cases, it is their name only, not their integrity, that they carry over into the mighty organs of Philistia. The million readers of these triumphant magazines want to be flattered by the thought that they too are patrons of "real art"; but they do not want to face the humiliating experience of not understanding a word. So a tactful compromise is reached, and we have stories signed—shall we call it, for the sake of safety, George Meredith?—which might have been concocted by—let us say Marie Corelli. The voice is Jacob's, but the hands are Esau's.

The uncommercial series or review is bound to be an ephemeral affair. It is identified with its editor, and uncommercial editors die young. They are killed in three ways: by the mere accident of disease, murder or war; by failure—here we have an illimitable field of little white crosses—; * and, no less inexorably, by success. An editor whose originality has become an asset is compelled to

* "The little magazines which die to make verse free." (Alice B. Toklas).

standardize that originality, that is to say to embalm it. Péguy had just reached that point when the war broke out. Had his *Notebooks* continued, they would no longer have been a living force, but a historical document. Henry Holt could not have kept the *Unpopular Review* alive, without achieving a measure of popularity. And it must have been galling for the most Swiftian of our critics to find himself with such a handsome following of "Yahoos" and "Boobs", to use his favorite terms. Naturally, the independent review must seek a public. But the test comes inevitably when the expansion of that public has to be purchased by a compromise. As soon as an editor asks himself: "This is fine stuff: but how will it affect my circulation?"—may his mess of pottage agree with him! He has bartered away his birthright.

All this does not mean that we consider the "little" review futile, or the successful review stupid. Both fulfill their function. But the review of insurgency can not lead for long, and the review of conformity can not lead at all. It is vain to hope for an institution that will combine steady moderation and daring originality. Just as Protestantism has long ceased to protest (except against religious free thought), so the various *Mercuries* have become as respectable as the *Atlantic Monthly* and the *Revue des Deux Mondes*.

But, on the whole, the periodicals hold out a much fairer promise to literature than the book trade. This for two reasons: they permit of freer experiments, and they have a fairly consistent public. No firm can expect one of its books to be bought simply because it bears the firm's imprint. But a magazine has a subscription list, and a large or small following of regular purchasers. A magazine is actually an organized unit of the reading public, a diffused Salon, the best substitute we have for defunct "Society." It is a pluralistic organization: there are innumerable periodicals, and every intelligent reader is supposed to glance at quite a few. But it is not pure chaos, like the book mart. Mourn who will for departed unity: we must find our bearings in a complex of interpenetrating universes.*

II

We have so far considered *organization* from the point of view of the producer—publisher or editor. We have seen that the noncommercial leader must, like his commercial brother, soon abdicate leadership. When he has defined and won his public, he becomes that public's prisoner. Wriggle as we may, we can not elude the fact that literature is brought out *for the sake of the consumer.* If not, why produce or publish at all? Sing to yourself and for yourself, and be satisfied. In the words of popular wisdom: "He who pays the pipers calls the tune." In the modern vernacular: "The customer is boss." So literary organization might come in the form of a Consumers' League.

One such League is almost ready to our hands: some kind of an *entente* among the Public Libraries. The Libraries are strategic points: but the Librarians are a

---

* We firmly believe that the periodical should be the main channel of publication, the book the exception. It were better if innumerable works of an ephemeral nature, well worth reading, never came out in book form at all. And, by ephemeral, we do not mean simply light fiction, but many serious contributions to political or scientific controversies. Books are too lumbering to keep up with the development of modern physics, for instance; and the Soviets, we are told, are wisely introducing the magazine textbook.

"minority" that has not yet achieved "consciousness." They too are paralyzed by that false conception of democracy which would leave all initiative to the masses. The masses are incapable of initiative; their one desire is to be, if not driven by a Mussolinian whip, at any rate firmly and wisely guided.

The "public demand" which Librarians heed with the same subserviency as politicians, is not spontaneous and divine: it is engineered by some aggressive advertiser, or is the result of some unaccountable craze. Public servants are supposed to serve the interests, not the whims, of the public. It seems a criminal waste of public monies for a City Library to purchase one hundred copies of some cheap thriller which no one will touch in less than a year. It is a capitulation to vulgarity, on the part of those who are paid to know better. It might be a safe rule for libraries not to buy any novel less than five years old. Current fiction could be made entirely self-supporting on a "cent-a-day" basis.

We are aware of two dangers. The first is excessive centralization. Just as the Napoleonic minister could pull out his watch and say: "At this moment, the same Latin text is dictated for translation in every school of the Empire," a Federal Director of Libraries could boast: "Ten thousand cities are receiving from our office their identical weekly pabulum. One hundred and twenty-five million minds with but a single thought! What a glorious achievement!" But, with the present resources of America, a standardized list would not necessarily involve standardized thought. It would be impossible to draw up a list of two or three hundred self-respecting books without having to include works of many kinds, and on opposite sides.

The second objection is that the body of Librarians is not prepared to assume such a responsibility. The days when a person of a literary turn of mind drifted naturally into a librarianship have been ended by our cult of material efficiency. Trained librarians are administrators, accountants, office workers, but not critics. After all, a great library is a complex machine, not a field wherein to roam and browse at will. We still believe that every library should provide a living and friendly guide for its readers; it might be well, in many cases, if the teachers of literature were also part-time librarians. This genuine influence can be felt in small places where personal contact is maintained; and the modest lot of such a librarian ought to be an enviable one. But that ideal is not unthinkable even in the largest cities. In mammoth department stores, the salesman is supposed to inform, suggest, advise: our libraries are too often conducted on the cheaper and quicker "Help yourself" or "Grocerteria" system.

But we have to note as a fact that the Librarians, at present, refuse to lead: false democracy, soulless efficiency, wise agnosticism, we know not. Perhaps they are justified in their self-effacement. Certain it is that with a bolder library system, no promising manuscript need be rejected for lack of a sufficient public: the library market alone would justify the printing of a small edition. The Directors of Art Museums are not so modest. They do not wait for a clear command from the crowd. They buy what they think is best, and then open their gates wide.

Another Purchasers' Organization is the Book Club. It is radically different from the old circulating library, which occasionally used the name, but exercised no control on your choice. It rather resembles the subscription series or the periodical: you commit your literary welfare, for a year, into the hands of an editorial board. Péguy was really the dictator of a book club which chose for you one volume every fortnight. Whether the Editor selects the works in manuscript, or already printed; whether he brings them out each under separate covers, or all jumbled in twelve monthly installments: these are details of organization, which do not affect the principle.

An excellent bookseller and super-*bouquiniste,* M. Edouard Champion,* the Paris agent for many scholars throughout the world, offered his foreign customers to pick out for them the best French books of the month. In this special case, the Book Club is particularly justified. Even a professional student finds it difficult, across the Atlantic, to follow the whirligigs of Parisian taste. Without believing in M. Champion's infallibility, one could trust him to know what books literary Paris was talking about. It is an extension of the "Society" idea.

The problem is not quite so simple when the Book Clubs operate in our own country. Then the two usual objections are raised: the fear of standardization, the surreptitious reintroduction of the business spirit. The first objection, as in the case of the Libraries, does not seriously frighten us. No single book club is within astronomic distance of securing a strangle hold of the

---

* His father was, in the book business, the successor of Anatole France's father.

market; not all the rival Book Clubs combined could do it; no appeal to the Sherman Act is needed. And the material advantages of the Book Clubs are many. They bring literature to the doorsteps of people remote from any decent book shop. They create a habit. They make book buying easy: to sign a check once a year is simplicity itself. People eat more on the "American plan" than when they have to order every item of every meal *à la carte;* and they spend sums on their own cars that they would grudge in the form of taxi fares. The Book Clubs' selection has such an advertising value that it increases the sales through the regular trade channels. All this, however, merely affects the *volume* of business, in which we confess that we are but tepidly interested. What about the *quality?* The Book Clubs claim that they have repeatedly secured the rewards of a best seller for serious works which otherwise would never have reached that heaven of American literature. They represent definite, enlightened, responsible leadership. The members of the board are few, well known, and trusted.

All this is excellent: but the second objection is more formidable. The curse of big business swiftly overtakes every American success. Péguy organized a healthy little market among three thousand friends; so he could publish—not every fortnight by any means—works of *rare* value, which otherwise would have been totally ignored. A board with a hundred thousand customers to please will attempt to give you the best—provided the best be acceptable to the hundred thousand. If not, sorrowfully but firmly, like their colleagues in the regular trade, they must declare: "We can't touch it." Once in a while, the

Book Clubs have made an unpopular book popular; but, on rare occasions also, the commercial firms have the same feat to their credit. The Book Club is absolutely one with the Book Trade in pursuing the great modern fallacy, the bane of literature: *sudden and massive success.*

III

The valuable element in the Book Club, as we have seen, is responsible, enlightened leadership. The curse is compromise with the business spirit. Can not the two be divorced? They can be, and are, in the *Literary Prize.* When the decision of a Book Club committee helps the sales outside its membership, its effects are exactly those of a Prize.

The prize goes back to antiquity, and flourished in the Middle Ages: Victor Hugo, in his boyhood, received one in the *Floral Games* of Toulouse, instituted in the fourteenth century. The Newdigate, at Oxford, has a splendid roll of winners, with such names as Matthew Arnold and Julian Huxley. As a rule, however, the *prize competition,* in which the subject is set, remains formal and barren: imagine bursting into lyric flame about *Timbuctoo!* Edwin Markham, we believe, has won more such tournaments than any man in his generation: but it is not as a prize winner that he deserves to be remembered.

There is one exception, however: one which justifies, for once, the horrible epithet *tremendous.* It is to such a competition that we owe Jean-Jacques Rousseau. An obscure middle aged bohemian, part musician, part botanist, hopelessly mediocre in both capacities, he read the announcement of the Academy of Dijon, hesitated,

picked out the paradoxical side, and became famous overnight. He was pinned down to his paradox by his success:
happier he, and the rest of mankind, if the unconscious
revolutionists of placid Dijon had not stirred up his
easily addled brain!

The prize, in modern literature, has multiplied like a
weed. Every University, every Academy, every firm, every
periodical, must take its hand in the game. We are nearing the time when the law will have to intervene and protect us against prizes no less than against lotteries. Else
every American youth or maiden, every matron craving
for pin money, every professor and minister, every retired
business man, every unwilling inmate of a State or Federal
Institution, will be scribbling away on the elusive
chance.

We need not insist upon the American prizes: they are
familiar to every reader. The Harper Novel Prize has an
excellent record; an Atlantic Monthly competition discovered Mazo de la Roche, a creditable if not a sensational
service to American letters; the Dial award went to Van
Wyck Brooks, whose delicate work had been consistently
indifferent to the cheaper forms of success. The Pulitzer
Prize is well worth having, although Sinclair Lewis found
it profitable to spurn it. We do not sympathize with
Sinclair Lewis's haughty refusal: but it is indicative of
current opinion in American literary circles. There is
no fault to find with our prizes: they simply fail to rouse
enthusiasm, or even interest.

France is prize-ridden even worse than we are; and
the prize steeple-chase is sometimes conducted with an
unscrupulous energy that would do credit to Wall Street

or Tammany Hall. But there is one prize which has attained unique prestige and power: the one awarded by the Goncourt Academy.

In opposition to Richelieu's forty Immortals, the ten Goncourt Academicians are all professional writers. At first, they were the personal friends of the founders, and represented the principles of Naturalism: but their interests are steadily widening. A self-recruiting body, they are all veterans with a firmly established reputation. But popular success counts for very little with them: Elémir Bourges, for instance, never reached the general public at all. Here we have a perfect example of the "conscious, organized minority": this small group, tightly knit, has acquired a prestige greater than that of its members taken separately; and its award confers fame. Literary France takes little interest in the elections to the Goncourt Academy, but waits with breathless suspense for the Goncourt Prize. Exactly the reverse is true of the Académie Française.

The one great service of the Goncourt Academy was to reveal Marcel Proust, who otherwise might have remained an illustrious unknown. There was courage also in endorsing Barbusse's *Under Fire,* when the war spirit was still raging. Some of the selections were indifferent, one at least, in our opinion, a glaring mistake.* Still, the Goncourt Prize holds its own, against innumerable imitative rivals. It does not truckle to business: it dictates to business. Its award almost automatically ensures sales that reach into the hundred thousands.

---

* *Batouala:* René Mayran, a very civilized colored Frenchman, has done far better work than this pseudo-primitive African tale.

In this case, the prestige of the Prize is due entirely to that of the jury. This is not so evidently true of the Nobel Foundation. The Swedish Committee fills no one with awe. It has performed its task honorably, not brilliantly. It has been slightly handicapped by the unfortunate word "idealistic" literature, attached to his bequest by the Dynamite King. This term introduces a non-artistic, possibly an anti-artistic element. The Committee has perhaps been guided by the desire of keeping a fairly even balance between the Latin and the Teutonic language groups; it certainly has failed to pick out the best representatives of Spain; it has been rather niggardly to us, and over-generous to the Scandinavian countries. But on the whole its decisions have been accepted with little grumbling. The prestige of the Nobel Prize is not due to the quality of the jury, but, on the one hand, to the munificence of the reward, on the other to its international character. Its standing with the best authors is shown by the fact that Shaw, who scoffs at all official honors, gladly accepted the Nobel palm without keeping the money; and that Sinclair Lewis, who scorned the Pulitzer, was proud of the Nobel. Its influence with the public can be measured in terms of increased sales. It had been difficult to interest a French publisher in *The Peasants,* by Ladislas Reymont: as soon as the Nobel award was known, the translation became marketable.

These two prizes illustrate very clearly the two different purposes of such institutions. The Goncourt Prize is a *discovery:* it reveals and imposes a struggling author; therefore it needs the backing of a jury with strong professional authority.* The Nobel Prize means the *confirmation* of established fame: therefore the prestige of the jury is of minor importance. The Committee merely registers a well-known fact; it is the prizeman who confers dignity upon the prize, not the reverse.

Strictly, the Confirmation Prize carries coal to Newcastle. It matters little, to the recipients or to the world at large, that Anatole France or G. B. Shaw should get additional honors or profits. They were tolerably conspicuous and comfortably well off without any further distinction. Within the limits of a national literature, therefore, the confirmation prize is useless, and its funds might be used to far better purpose. But the Nobel Prize is saved from futility by its international character. Mere *confirmation* in the author's own country, it is *discovery* for the rest of the world. *Babbitt,* for instance, was barely known in France before the Swedish spotlight fell on Sinclair Lewis.†

IV

Whichever road we take, there is a point where we encounter the same sign. The publishers—commercial, State, University, endowed—can help literature if they or their responsible assistants are good judges; a subscription series, a periodical, a book club, each is worth what its editorial board is worth; a prize counts or not, according

---

* It was questioned whether the Goncourt Prize could legitimately be given to Marcel Proust, who was middle-aged and wealthy, and had already published with some acceptance; it was wise, in our opinion, to rule that Proust was "young and struggling" within the meaning of the act.

† There is a third kind, which has its justification: the *consolation prize,* given to a man whose career has been long, distinguished, yet not dazzlingly successful. The French Academy awards not a few of those—naturally without confessing their true nature; and they are not absolutely unknown in America.

to the authority of the jury. Ultimately, we are always thrown back upon a small body of men, who are trusted to *know*. If knowledge and power are divorced, chaos must prevail, as confessedly, it does at present. The expert has, not the first word, but the last, in medicine, law, engineering: why not in literature? The man who knows, or claims to know, about literature is the critic. Give me a good critical police, and I shall give you a thriving literary state.

Proposed with such bluntness, the autocracy of the critic sounds preposterous. The familiar phrase arises invincibly again: "Not even a beautiful dream." For, in other domains, the charlatan can be told from the genuine expert by means of objective tests. "Laws" take their place in scientific thought only if they can be submitted to experimental verification. A bridge which stands a given load is an adequate bridge. But to what reagents, to what strain, can we submit a book? In what scales can it be weighed? Our sole objective criteria are crudely pragmatic: "the court of public opinion", "the test of time." Neither is applicable to the manuscript which comes to you fresh from the author's mind, with the secret of a new day between its leaves, if you had eyes to see.

We must renounce, and we gladly renounce, the idea of a definite, monopolistic body of critics, passing formal sentences. In the absence of critical law, we have to be satisfied with a vaguer entity, the *critical spirit*. All men have it, just as all men have the creative power; but some men have it in a higher degree. Only, while public opinion gladly recognizes creative superiority, it is far more reluctant to admit critical superiority. Every man wants to judge for himself, to be his own critic. Ultimately and in theory, he is right: and he should be his own poet too. In practice, he judges only of the things which have been picked out for him by the publishers, the editors, the Book Clubs, the prize juries, *i.e. by critics*. Since the intervention of critics is indispensable, the public should strive to have the best, the most sensitive, the most highly trained, the most disinterested; and the only way of securing their services is to grant them proper recognition. Authors and public too often unite in deriding critics, all the while unconsciously guided by vague, anonymous, irresponsible criticism. This is a suicidal policy. The key to better literature is better criticism, and the key to better criticism is better critics: a platitude which involves a revolution.

This revolution is under way. Within the last twenty-five years, the change in American criticism has been startling. There had always been distinguished critics in America; but, for a long time, their tone had been decidedly academic, and they were devoid of any vital influence. To-day, pedantry and superciliousness are on the wane; "culture", by a natural reaction, has become almost a term of reproach. The critic walks cheerfully among men of the present. The progress in the number, quality and circulation of the critical reviews must needs carry with it an increase in power.

What would the critics do with that power? Reveal it by cutting down the profits of popular writers, as Thackeray, with his burlesques, killed the vogue of G. P. R. James, as Jules Lemaître extinguished poor Georges

Ohnet? It may have to be done at times: some reputations are a national blight. This would apply only to the exposure of pseudo-artists: as a rule, the entertainers are doing a good job in a non-literary field, and should be left undisturbed. Will the critics on the contrary boost the sales of deserving writers—a Midas-like gift credited to Octave Mirbeau and to William Lyon Phelps? As an incidental result, this is not to be despised. But why think in terms of sales? Sales are indispensable to professionals: the fewer professional authors we have, the better perhaps for literature. Genuine writers, as distinguished from educators, propagandists and entertainers, would as a rule be all the greater if they limited themselves to one book every five or six years—half a dozen works in a lifetime. In any decent civilization, this should be easily achieved by any man who feels the urge within him; and it would not interfere with a gainful occupation.

What can the critics do then? In a country of 125,000,000 people, all with some kind of an education, it is a scandal that there should be no market for a book which competent judges *know* to be worth while. The first service of the critics, therefore, must be to organize small, definite, enlightened *publics,* which will make the circulation of the unusual work a practical possibility. But the greatest service is not commercial. It is to provide a *critical* audience, one that knows the difference, one that understands and appreciates the effort, even when it can not fully accept the result. This mutual recognition of a few congenial souls, without any official ties, without any formal creed, is at the same time a stimulus and a reward. Without it, official honors and wealth, to the genuine artist, are a derision, and his conscience can never be at peace. It alone can relieve the gnawing self-doubt and the bitterness of the isolated worker. To turn the critics into a conscious and organized minority is the first requisite for a healthy literature.

Chapter 21

INFLUENCE OF LITERATURE UPON LIFE

I

THERE is no influence that is not reciprocal. This, a truism in physics, less obvious in sociology, may seem a paradox in literature. If the earth "attracts" the moon, so does the moon attract the earth. The jailer, on duty, is the prisoner of the convict; the victorious nation imposes upon itself a heavy tribute in order to protect the fruit of victory. An imitator of Ibsen does not react upon the man Ibsen, who is dead, but upon the fame of Ibsen, which is alive. He may enhance his master's glory, by swelling the train of worthy Ibsenians; he may detract from it, by making Ibsenism commonplace or ludicrous. If the forces of civilization have a definite action upon literature, we may be certain that literature is not without influence upon the course of civilization.

Some forms of this influence have already been indicated in the study of the *Literary Type*. A man's life is shaped by his conscious desires: if he wants to be an artist, he will be tempted to indulge in the temperamental oddities or excesses by which artists are supposed to be characterized. This, as we have seen, is particularly marked along the literary fringe, among "the coast dwellers of Bohemia": but genuine artists are not free from this tendency. Literature may set the fashion of fatal pallor: and Lord Byron, first victim of Byronism, is compelled to drink vinegar. Goethe's *Werther* and Vigny's *Chatterton* were responsible for the suicide of several young poets. Musset and George Sand conscientiously assayed a grand passion which was not in their nature: but they were writers, and literature in their day was romantic: so romantic they had to be. Nero, at least in the picture drawn by Renan, is a striking example of the spurious artistic ideal carried into real life.

This *literaritis* (the hybrid name is hardly worse than the disease) spreads easily from writers and would-be writers to mere readers, and to whole circles in society. It is noted that children want to play-act the stories they hear. The *Golden Legend* inspired young Anatole France with the desire of becoming a "hermit and saint in the calendar." Little boys of a less holy disposition prefer to be pirates, explorers, soldiers, or even gangsters. Nor is this limited to childhood. Don Quijote is the perfect instance of a reader so enthusiastic, so convinced, that he must live the life of his book heroes. While Honoré d'Urfé's pastoral romance *L'Astrée* was an idealized picture of *Précieuse* society, it also served as a model. More than two centuries later, exactly the same phenomenon occurred with Balzac's *Human Comedy:* in both cases, groups of people adopted the names of their favorite characters, and patterned their speech and their actions upon theirs. André Maurois, in an episode of *Mape,* analyzes such an example of conscious Balzacianism. *Madame Bovary* shows the intrusion of literary romanticism into a dull provincial life: poor Emma is the victim of her reading, almost as clearly as Don Quijote. *Hedda Gabler,* as interpreted by Jules Lemaître, is a satire on pseudo-Ibsenism by Ibsen himself. The heroine tries her best to live her life in beauty, and makes such a sorry mess of it that even death fails to achieve tragic dignity. Marie Bashkirtscheff was preparing herself to be a Hedda Gabler in real life. It is said that the braggadocio of *Cyrano de Bergerac,* the waving of the arrogant plume in the face of danger, led young French officers, in 1914, to useless and therefore criminal sacrifice. H. G. Wells has an amusing picture of the soldier who, chiefly through the use of gory expletives, consciously strives to be Kiplingesque. Examples are legion. Perhaps they are not quite fair to literature. For we note only the excess, the pose, the craze, the disease, and call them *literary:* it stands to reason that literature has an edifying influence also. But the word edifying is a stench in the nostrils of "pure" artists, and they hasten to disclaim any power for good.

In more diffused fashion, literature, as we have seen, tends to the fixation of the national type. *The* Frenchman, *the* German, are mostly book products. There probably are some French people who, like M. Lacarelle in Anatole France, feel it a duty to court every woman, in obedience to the Gallic tradition. *Noblesse oblige* and its obligations may be far from pleasant. By 1914, the Germans had forged for themselves a barbaric ideal, out of the *Nibelungen* and Nietzsche, which at times oddly superimposed a formidable frown upon rosy, chubby, bespectacled countenances. It was they who invented the

Hun myth—and waxed exceeding wroth when the rest of the world accepted it. Indeed we have already expressed our opinion that Nationalism was to a large extent a creation, and is to-day a survival, of the Romantic movement. The degree in which nations are swayed by literary and artistic ideals is seldom fully realized by historians. History is a pageant, a drama, and its æsthetic interpretation is more reliable than the economic. The economic is too sensible to be adequate.

We do not propose to discuss this idea at length in the present volume. Let a few familiar examples suffice, not as a demonstration, but as an indication. Among the direct causes of the French Revolution, the activities of the *Philosophes* are seldom omitted: "It is all Voltaire's fault, and Rousseau's," became the monotonous refrain of the conservatives; and those *Philosophes* were men whose prestige rested, first of all, on their literary fame. Beaumarchais's sparkling and daring comedy *Figaro's Wedding,* is cited among the signs of the impending catastrophe. The political and religious Restoration which prevailed in Europe after 1815 reflected the love of the Romanticists for historical pageantry: the coronation of King Charles X at Rheims was a triumph of the Walter Scott spirit. Sympathy with the cause of Greek independence was enhanced by the enormous fame of Lord Byron. The Napoleon of legend, far more vivid in our minds than the Napoleon of plain fact, was likewise a Romantic creation. It was literature that made the Second Empire possible, although Béranger, Victor Hugo and Thiers turned away in disgust from the work of their own hands.

Nor is this special to France. The Hohenzollern régime, from 1871 to 1918, represented neither the tradition of Frederick II, nor the aspirations of German democracy, and still less the necessities of a modern, scientific and industrial state: it was a scene from a second-rate pseudo-Wagnerian opera, a belated piece of literary Romanticism, introduced on the political stage by the supreme "realist" Bismarck.

This influence of literature may be focussed in the conception of *the Poet as Prophet:* were not the prophets of Israel great poets first of all? France is the least Biblical of modern nations: but in this respect, she is the true heir of ancient Judea. The power, greater than any king's, wielded by Voltaire and Rousseau, served as a precedent. Chateaubriand was persuaded that it was he who had restored in France Catholicism and the Bourbons; he constantly compared himself with Napoleon, and felt himself a national hero of the same magnitude. Lamartine, in the *bourgeois* Parliament of Louis-Philippe, represented "the constituency of the ideal"; and the Romantic revolution of 1848 chose him as its inevitable leader. Victor Hugo became the spiritual head of continental democracy and free thought, the irreconcilable enemy of Napoleon III, the ghostly father of the Third Republic. Zola, as the chief of the Naturalistic school, felt that he was *ex officio* the public defender of truth and justice. In Anatole France, the sense that the man of letters is called to leadership wrestled oddly, and at times victoriously, with his inborn indolence and his ingrained scepticism.

In Germany, the literary revival preceded and guided the political: Goethe was forced into the position of a national symbol, while his spirit remained cosmopolitan. The Young German movement was a blend of literature and politics. Wagner, Nietzsche, Treitschke, without holding political office, had their rôle in German history. In Italy, Dante was a national standard at a time when the country had become a mere geographical expression. Young Italy, like Young Germany, was first of all an open conspiracy of poets. Mazzini's eloquence was part of his power. Gabriele d'Annunzio was persuaded that artistic primacy even when it is tinged with decadence, is a call to action and a claim to command. The downfall of the Spanish throne was heralded by two authors as radically different as could be imagined, Blasco Ibáñez and Miguel de Unamuno; the new Spanish Republic was able to send as ambassadors great writers instead of mere grandees. After the aspirations of Ireland were shattered by the Parnell scandal and the fiasco of the Liberal Party, the national soul was placed in the keeping of the poets, and it was the literary Renaissance that prepared the political resurrection.

In England, Byron and especially Shelley had the souls of prophets. Carlyle formally draped himself in the prophet's mantle, blessing under his breath, cursing thunderingly, for fifty years. Ruskin was a gentler Carlyle; William Morris united in himself socialism, art and literature. Even Matthew Arnold condescended to point the way. Dickens made popular fiction a denunciation of abuses; Charles Reade also worked for reform through romances; an amiable minor novelist, Walter Besant, had his share in the People's Palace idea. Imperialism, whose father was a literary statesman, Disraeli, was sharply focussed by a poet, Kipling. It is worth noting that British Imperialism, a great force at the end of the nineteenth century, remained a sentiment which never found either its political or its economic expression. Among the elder writers of our own times, not a few have a robust faith in their right to guide, and, if need be, to drive: Shaw and Wells urging us forward, Chesterton and Belloc prodding us back.

America is the country where literary fame is most completely divorced from political authority. Emerson's following was large, but loose: it lost itself in the infinite shadowy pastures of Transcendantalism. *Uncle Tom's Cabin,* of course, was a portent; James Russell Lowell and not a few others placed their talent at the service of a great cause; Walt Whitman alone strove consciously to be our prophet: but he never attained the position of a Victor Hugo or even of a Carlyle. There is an ambiguous zone between literature and social action, where Winston Churchill meets William Allen White, where Frank Norris and Jack London are not very far from Upton Sinclair. Burghardt du Bois and Ludwig Lewisohn are prophets indeed, but for their own people only. Sinclair Lewis reminds us at times of H. G. Wells: but he is a reporter with a gift for caricature, rather than a constructive propagandist. Theodore Dreiser and Sherwood Anderson seem tempted by the rôle of an American Zola. And it can not be denied that H. L. Mencken has some kind of influence on American life. Indeed, he has many kinds of influence: but, after canceling their contradictions, it is not easy to measure the net result. To the average American, the idea of the poet as guide is grotesque beyond words. The poet, as we are taught in the kindergarten, is a demented person who goes flaunting the strange device *Excelsior!* and gets very properly killed for refusing to heed the practical man.

II

We have no mystic faith in the vision of rhymester or fictionist. A man is not necessarily God-inspired because he tells things that are not so. But the action of literature upon life may be justified without any appeal to supernatural powers. We all know the paradox propounded by Oscar Wilde and James Branch Cabell: *Nature imitates Art*. In less defiant terms, *literature is not mere experience, but experiment.** If this be so, literature occupies an essential place in the life of the community.

It was Zola, we believe, who first gave prominence to the term *experimental* in literary theory. By "the experimental novel", he meant something far deeper than the trying out of a new technique. His "Naturalism" was modeled and named after the natural sciences; his master was the physiologist Claude Bernard, whose *Introduction to Experimental Medicine* was one of the decisive books of the age. Zola's vast cycle *The Rougon-Macquart,* was "the natural and social history of a family under the Second Empire." And so, with a wealth of clinical documents, Zola proceeded to "demonstrate" and "prove" heredity. In this arrogant form, Zola's pretension is palpably absurd. A novel with heredity as its central

* The same idea was ably expressed by that stimulating teacher, Richard Moulton.

motive "proves" heredity exactly as a ghost story proves the existence of ghosts.

It is not within art's domain to prove anything. We translate the French expression *pièce à thèse* by *problem play*. But our phrase is a platitude: every play, even the broadest farce, is a problem. The French term is a fallacy: no play can establish a thesis. Art, to be valid as art, must be human, personal, individualized; and no single instance is an argument—it is at best an illustration. Victor Hugo wanted to show that the *Coup d'Etat* of Louis-Napoleon in December 1851 was a crime. He picked out one episode: a child had been killed by a stray bullet, and the corpse was brought to his grandmother, whose despair was heart-rending. The story is told with matchless restraint and power. It is great art; it would be highly effective with an emotional jury; but it *proves* nothing at all. The affair was an accident; the murderous bullet might just as well have come from a Republican rifle. In the Holy Revolutions of which Victor Hugo had made himself the high priest, innocent blood was also shed—far more than in the brief and vigorous police operation of December 1851. Similarly, *Madame Bovary* proves nothing against the reading of romantic fiction by provincial *bourgeoises*. Not all country doctors' wives were perverted by George Sand; and adultery probably existed before literature. But if art does not *prove,* with the rigor of science, it *explains*. Every poem, novel or drama is a working hypothesis. The subject itself provides the data: a character, a situation, a sequence of events. The writer's task is to present these data in such a fashion that they carry conviction. If the reader does not exclaim: "It must have been so!" then the author has failed. As Gertrude Stein put it with unwonted lucidity: "Composition is explanation." Explanation is not identical with formal logic or with the Q.E.D. of Euclid. The state that the author wants to explain may be one of confusion, of bewilderment, of mystery, of madness. *To explain* means: *to make convincing*.

Shakespeare, for instance, will take jealousy, Molière or Balzac avarice, Meredith egotism, and see how these forces work out under definite circumstances. Or we may start from a situation: social conflict in *Germinal* or *The Weavers,* miscegenation in *The Quaint Companions,* war in *Under Fire* or *All Quiet on the Western Front,* and draw out its consequences. Or again, we may be given the facts, authentic or fictitious: a scandal, a murder case, an estrangement, an idyl. Every event implies a mystery story: the problem is to provide the motives that will make the facts intelligible. It is not necessary that these motives be analyzed with the minuteness of a Henry James or a Marcel Proust. They may be implied, without comment, in the order of presentation: a method which the plainest art and the most subtle have in common: Harold Bell Wright meets Katherine Mansfield.

This applies not only to biography, not only to those novels and dramas which borrow their subjects directly from life, but also to the most fanciful, the most whimsical fiction. For a satire, a fairy tale, a hallucination always are the refraction or the transposition of some real experience, and have a logic of their own.

And this applies no less to the lyric. The lyric, intensely personal, immediate, spontaneous, spurns the very idea of "explanation", which seems to involve argument. "Why should I stoop to explain? Here is what I feel: take it or leave it." Yet every lyric is a fragment of an autobiographical narrative, and offers a problem. The lyric is a mood: I am glad or depressed. The poem itself is the hypothesis that accounts for the mood. I may choose to ascribe my elation to love, to the shy caresses of the spring, to the thought of God; if I am "perturbed unto death", I may blame disease, doubt, a faithless one, bad weather, democracy, the machine age, religion. Music alone conveys mood in absolute purity: literature must *explain*.

All this simply deepens the meaning of the word *convincing*. Convincingness is the one test of art. Whether it be a lyric cry, a realistic tale, a fantasy, it must be intelligible if it is to be human. And this inner necessity reduces almost to the vanishing point the share of absolute caprice. We fully agree with Lloyd Morris: "The responsibilities of a novelist towards his material are all but inexorable; the attempt to escape from them, all but disastrous." This is nothing but a re-phrasing of Horace's familiar warning against the *Deus ex machina*. If you juggle with your experiment, if you introduce, surreptitiously or brazenly, a new element out of keeping with the conditions defined by yourself, the result is inartistic. If you solve a psychological tangle by means of an automobile accident, or, as in *The Constant Nymph*, with an irrelevant disease, the reader feels cheated. Several of Molière's endings fall under that condemnation. They do not detract from the value of his plays solely because

346

they are so ingenuously artificial. The great artist tells us: "Here I rest my case: so far as I am concerned, the comedy is over." The actor-manager adds with good-humored contempt: "But as you would not know when to go home, I am going to give you the traditional last scene." It is a notice to put on your wraps and avoid the rush.

A work of fiction is not a proof as mathematicians understand proof, not a document that historians or sociologists can quote as an authority, not a piece of evidence in the eyes of the law: it has nothing to do with the facts that are accomplished, with *dead truth*. But it is an element in deciding upon a future course, *in creating living truth*. Inevitably, that which carries artistic conviction also carries moral conviction.

Fiction serves as experiment, *i.e.* as a substitute for actual experience, as directed experience within a definite field. If a novel presents, cogently, searchingly, the difficulties, the ultimate success or failure of some unequal mating—patrician and plebeian, white and black, Jew and Gentile, youth and eld—we can not help being biassed thereby. Subconsciously perhaps, we shall be urged one way or the other if ever we have to face the same problem in actual life. Every written romance breeds romance, every book filled with the fascination of war brings war a little nearer. I have been deterred from tormenting even the most repulsive animals by Victor Hugo's poem, *The Toad*. The supreme Master taught through parables.

Shall we be told that, in a scientific age, we should be guided, not by hypotheses, but by established facts?

Every decision is a choice between rival hypotheses: the future, hypothetical itself, can be dealt with in no other way. To build or not to build a bridge across the Golden Gate was a very practical problem. But, when we had amassed all available data, the two alternatives were still two pieces of Utopian fiction, two Wellsian *Anticipations,* the one optimistic, the other pessimistic. "Supposing the bridge is built: traffic will be immensely quickened, a splendid area will be opened to the city's overflow, a monument of startling majesty will be added to our treasures."—"Supposing the bridge is built: earthquakes will make it unsafe, ferries will remain cheaper and prevent adequate returns, an enemy could wreck the structure and bottle up our fleet, a unique marvel of nature will be marred for all time." Within the ascertained data, the hypothesis which is the more *convincing* deserves to win. Engineers and realtors have stolen the word *vision* from the poets, just as they have stolen the word *service* from the priests.

III

Fiction, if it moves us at all, is invariably an incentive or a deterrent. We are all Don Quijote and Emma Bovary. He was mad, and she was weak, because they had poor standards of art. They accepted as convincing works that should have been rejected. But even the flimsiest tale weaves itself into our lives.

This is why civilization—the consciousness of collective life—must take cognizance of literature. As a power, therefore as a danger. Censorship is as indispensable to the state as any other form of police; which does not mean that it should be entrusted to the usual police and exercised by the same methods.

When authors claim irresponsibility, and therefore complete freedom, they advance either of two pleas: the scientific or the imaginative. According to the first, their books offer nothing which does not exist in nature: they are not adding to the sum total of evil. The Praying Mantis devours her mate in the very act of union: to know this fact is no crime, not to know it is sheer ignorance.

But literature is not science: it does not present the dead facts, dispassionate, dehumanized: it arranges the facts into a living, convincing sequence. Any psychiatrist could tell us far worse facts than Baudelaire: but Baudelaire offers us the "flowers of evil", the fascination of sin, the apology of perversity.

The second plea is that art leaves actual truth behind, exists in a free world of its own, unhampered by contact with practical responsibility. Titania and Ariel laugh at statute books. This was Charles Lamb's apology for the licentiousness of Restoration comedy, and James Branch Cabell's defense *pro domo sua*. But if art does go beyond life, it opens the path for life to follow. The charming aërial puppets that mince and strut in Poictesme evoke in us definite attitudes of mind, which we carry back into the gross world of Lichfield. And Cabell himself tells us, with amusement that has long lost its edge, of all the fair readers who claim to follow the Cabellian gospel, and urge the author to do likewise.

I believe that literature does matter, and therefore I believe in censorship. I most heartily disbelieve in the present methods of censorship. It is entrusted to the wrong men: bureaucrats acting at the behest of bigots. It is chaotic, clumsy and therefore ineffective: its blunders and contradictions form an amusing tale. But for such ineffectiveness let us be duly thankful! A thorough inquisition backed by public opinion could stifle thought for centuries.

Censorship, as we have said, not seldom advertises that which it would suppress. We have seen that to the prosecution of *Jurgen* we owe Cabell as a national figure; and that our college students can not be bribed to read *Ulysses*—tougher than any assignment in the most dismal of sciences—now that it does not have to be bootlegged. It might be wise, sigh the ministers, to place the Old Testament on the *Index Expurgatorius.*

The maladministration of censorship is its only redeeming grace. The real danger is that censorship is invariably reactionary. It defends that morality which, left stranded by the stream of life, has ceased to be moral at all. Censorship is the bulwark of the past: vested interests, abuses, prejudices, superstitions. It was a board of censors that dealt with Socrates and Jesus. As long as censorship means *the right to suppress,* it must remain an incubus.

We need a far more active and potent censorship, an intellectual police with more accurate weapons. And its name is *competent criticism.* If you think a book is urging the wrong thing, do not suppress the book: it would circulate underground, or start a whole crop of books on the same subject. You can not cure a disease by concealing its symptoms. Instead of suppressing, *discuss.* If the book carries false conviction, which makes it spurious art as well as dangerous teaching, expose the fallacy. If you are disgusted with *What Is Wrong With Everything,* try to show *What Is Right With Everything.* If you are tired of everlasting sex books, laugh them off with *Is Sex Necessary?*

Literature is not independent: but it should be autonomous. Just as a scientific fact is amenable only to the laws of science, a literary danger should be met only by literary weapons. To bring Galileo, Darwin or Einstein before a Tennessee jury pushes back the limits of the absurd. To raid a bookstore and burn an edition, even by the authority of the law, is not a civilized method. It is stopping your opponent's mouth with your fist: the argument of the bully. Only a book can censor a book. Whatever is attacked by human thought, and can not be defended by human thought, deserves to fall.

Part IV

To-morrow

Chapter 22

GRAPHOPOLIS: A UTOPIA FOR LITERATURE

PLATO, greatest of poets, banished poets from his Republic. On the other hand, the knights-errant of the Ideal would scorn the ideal State, and the land of dreams is not fit for dreamers. Denounce the ugliness and vulgarity of our age as savagely as you please, and the poets are with you; but any definite scheme of reform will make the artistic temperament shudder. The poetic mind is invincibly attached to the picturesque past, and averse to the logical, purposive future. Victor Hugo abominated the metric system as much as Anatole France despised Esperanto; and Sir Hall Caine, worthily expressing the prejudices of his fellow-craftsmen, declared that "Shakespeare's spelling was good enough for him." In our own days, George Moore may be considered as the *beau idéal* of consistent art worshippers, and to his mind, social progress, including universal education, is "not even a beautiful dream." When genuine artists stoop to practical schemes of improvement, they immediately lose caste: Anatole France's *On the White Stone* is dismally Philistine. Utopia is the paradise of the common-place.*

This opposition between two kinds of prophets—poets and reformers—is a paradox and a problem. The problem is not so fanciful for our own time and our own country as it may appear at first. Are we Americans losing poetic power because we are drawing dangerously near the dismal coast of Utopia? For in comparison with nineteenth-century Europe and its marvelous flowering of artistic genius, twentieth-century America is Utopia indeed. Our cataclysmic industrial progress, our boundless democracy, our universities wide open to the masses, have outstripped the imaginings of such prophets as Saint-Simon and Cabet. Prosperity may be in eclipse for a season as a result of excessive riches, but surely such an absurd evil is not beyond cure. Rabelais's *Thélème* is literally fulfilled in a great coeducational institution on the Pacific Coast. I heard Pastor Russell tell us that the millennium had begun in 1897; we had merely failed to realize the fullness of our beatitude. We are already treading the pavements of the New Jerusalem. It is hard to conceive a material Utopia as far ahead of our present civilization as we ourselves are ahead of "the Man with the Hoe." We may travel much faster to-morrow; we may add a telephote to our telephone, and shake hands with distant friends through a teledactyl; we may even skyrocket to Mars or Venus over the week-end; in other words, we can make the world infinitely

* Cf. also Aldous Huxley: "The Boundaries of Utopia" (*Virginia Quarterly*, Jan. 1931; and "The Boundaries of the Promised Land" (*Fortnightly*, Dec. 1930. J. W. Krutch: "Literature and Utopia" (in *Was Europe a Success?*, 1934).

smaller and destroy the last vestiges of solitude and privacy. But the actual limits of a material Utopia are within the range of our conception, if not of our attainment. Just as victory over matter is almost within our grasp, we lose all conceit with it. The miracle of radio, as Aldous Huxley remarked, has chiefly served the broadcasting of twaddle. Interstellar communication might very well bring us no nearer spiritual perfection. The conditions vaunted as ideal by the Boosters' Clubs and other disciples of Macaulay seem to produce no Shakespeare; and there are many who wonder whether the same soil and the same climate can be equally favorable to poets and plumbers.

Mr. Stuart Chase has touched upon the problem in his suggestive book *Men and Machines*. But the difficulty does not lie chiefly with mechanical appliances: it lies rather with the mechanical spirit, the spirit of standardization; and that spirit seems inseparable from a normal, harmonious, classical, static, or Utopian world. We might smash all the machines, as they did in Erewhon, and spiritually find ourselves none the richer. Arcadian simplicity may be as tedious and stifling as the zippy atmosphere of Zenith; indeed, Sheila Kaye-Smith has found unplumbed stupidity in unplumbered villages. Here is our dilemma: we do not want brutal and wasteful anarchy, but perfect organization turns society into a soulless machine. Poetry is the eternal protest against the mechanizing trend towards Utopia.

In presence of such a problem three attitudes are possible. The first is, candidly and heartily, to damn art and literature. If they are in any way incompatible with

357

sanity and sanitation, decency, comfort, orderliness, let them go!—a good riddance. Spiritual values which can not be translated into terms of good citizenship have no validity at all. But this opinion is seldom frankly voiced: the rankest utilitarian does lip-service to anti-utilitarianism. He has his pew in church, and allows his wife to lionize long-haired virtuosi. Unfortunately perhaps, the thorough-going Benthamite of to-day is dumb, in the original meaning of the term.

This leaves us with two solutions, in both of which the claims of art and those of the social order will be recognized. Strange yoke-fellows, which may shy at each other! We must on no account start with the heretical assumption that art may have a social message: let us be faithful (provisionally) to the sacred doctrine of art for art's sake. But no artist will object if we admit that art is worth while, and that conditions inimical to art are therefore undesirable. Let us, then, ask the artists themselves to write the specifications of their own Utopia. They like neither our present world, nor the world that reformers are attempting to create: what kind of a world do they want? In other terms, what civilization would be most favorable to the creation of art?

The last method of approach would be to admit the feasibility, nay the inevitability, of a materialistic and social Utopia of the standard type. But, instead of taking it for granted, as George Moore does, that all art will of necessity perish in such an atmosphere, we may attempt to forecast what forms of art could possibly survive, and even what new kinds might be evolved. Are we sure that art depends entirely upon ignorance, injustice and chaos? Are irregular verbs alone fit to be used in poetry and love? Let us assume the perfect state so dreaded by poets: could a niche be found for them?

The nearest approximation to an artistic Utopia remains William Morris's *News from Nowhere:* a paradise for house decorators and Roycrofters, a magnified Carmel-by-the-Sea before they put in the drains. The book is still a delight: but it is pretty thoroughly unconvincing. For it is ambiguous in its ideal and in its methods. Purely archaic in spirit, it brushes aside all the conquests of the machine age; yet it admits the services of a mysterious "Power" which is the ultimate triumph of science and industry. Then Morris was a professed Socialist as well as an artist: the pure note of the poet comes perilously near the propagandist's falsetto.

André Maurois offers a strictly literary Utopia in his fantastic trifle, *Voyage to the Island of the Articoles.* But the intention is too evidently satirical, not constructive. And the target of his satire is neither art nor society— only the well-known foibles of professional men of letters. For our purpose, this charming pamphlet is of no avail. A Utopia for Writers is by no means the same thing as a Utopia for Literature; just as a Utopia for Lawyers would not be a Utopia for Law; just as a clerical Utopia would be very different from a religious one. Utopia, for the special class, means privilege: a Utopia for singers is a state in which singers are rare, precious and treasured. Utopia for an ideal means on the contrary its universal diffusion.

All Utopias are retrospective as well as prospective;

their Golden Age is made up of elements borrowed from the past. We shall follow the same method in describing, without irony, the civilization of *our* Articoles. We shall take into account the lessons of history as well as the desires of men. We shall apply our familiar instrument, the theory of Taine: art is determined by race, environment and time. If this rule be true, it ought to be reversible: in order to secure the kind of art we want, what social conditions are necessary? This question resolves itself into the historical problem: under what conditions has the art we admire been produced in the past?

It is evident that in such a complex product, no single factor is absolutely indispensable. An unfavorable climate for instance, may be offset by an abundance of natural resources. It is evident also that, if our prescriptions were taken too literally, they would sound like a satire of Taine's ideas and of the whole sociological method in artistic criticism. With these words of warning, we may embark for Graphopolis, in the Land of the Articoles.

Graphopolis lies in the temperate zone. The tropics have failed so far to produce a literature that would rank supreme: yet they have natural wealth, beauty, a teeming population. The arctic regions can boast of Iceland, which, in proportion to its numbers, took a high place among centers of poetry; but we are safe in assuming that the mean temperature of Graphopolis is decidely higher than that of Rejkjavik. There are sharply contrasted seasons—an almost torrid summer, a mellow golden autumn, a glorious winter of hard frost and snow, followed by the yearly miracle of the spring: how much poorer would poetry be in a land without April! Scotland is not barred out as the possible seat of our Utopia: a surly clime drives you to the fireplace and books—or to the radiator and poker. Too ideal a climate might be a handicap: I would not endorse the claims of San Diego, where they play the organ outdoors every day in the year, or those of Yuma, Arizona, where they offer you a free lunch every day the sun does not shine.

The country round Graphopolis is a varied land of mountains and vales, with a rugged, deeply indented coast. Mountains alone will not necessarily evolve great art: watches, cheese and hotels, not the poems of Carl Spitteler, are the chief products of Switzerland. At sea level or below, the Dutch and the Venetians have created great schools of painting: they are less prominent as writers—perhaps for the lack of Parnassian heights to scale. Moderate cliffs and crags will do, as in England, Scotland or Attic Greece; even the molehills of Rome, Florence and Paris may suffice. But the devastating platitude of Russia and of our Middle West is an obstacle to be overcome: Russia had no great literature until the nineteenth century. We once tried to induce a millionaire to give Houston, Texas, an artificial hill, in the hope of making that friendly city the Athens of the southwest. Cathedral Heights and the Palisades will serve the purpose for New York, and Twin Peaks for San Francisco; but for Chicago there is little hope.

Graphopolis is watered by a noble river, which in olden times was worshipped as a god. Poets find inspiration in the thundering falls above the city; in the swift-flowing stream, which they liken to human destiny, and which grows sluggish before it merges with the measureless sea; in the somber fury of the turbid floods in early winter or spring. It is also convenient for a watery grave: romantic Paris needs the Morgue. The banks of the Chicago drainage canal rather discourage lyrical effusion. The Los Angeles river, so far as we know, has not yet become famous in song; yet it is not much worse than the classic Ilissos. Although the land is well watered, it would be advisable to have a small desert at hand: here Los Angeles scores a definite point. But Los Angeles, wasteful of artistic possibilities, is reclaiming its desert—as shortsighted as the fabled Auvergnats, who, blessed with the possession of a volcano, carelessly allowed it to become extinct.

Graphopolis is not a vast empire. A huge country is slow-witted. Whether it lives under a tyranny, or enjoys the alleged benefits of democracy, it is inclined to think in masses, crudely. How much more favorable is the city-state, Athens or Florence, or the tiny principality, like Weimar! A ruler has a ruler's psychology, whether he rule a thousand men or a hundred million; Dante was as truly an ambassador as Paul Claudel; a court is a court, even though it be that of the Hawaiian Islands or that of Emperor Soulouque. And patriotism, in the city-state, is concentrated, vivid, all-pervading, not a dull thing of hearsay and statistics. Party politics assume the dramatic intensity of family feuds. The city wall is infinitely more real than the arbitrary frontier. The artists in Montmartre once proclaimed the secession of the sacred mound from the deplorably *bourgeois* French Republic; and they were well advised. In Chesterton's fantasy, the Napoleon of Notting Hill reconstitutes a colorful world on a purely local basis. The original Napoleon owed his greatness to his Corsican cradle. Culturally, vast entities are barren. The formula of the future is communalism as in 1871—a world federation of independent cities.

What kind of community is Graphopolis—pastoral, agricultural, commercial, industrial? Pastoral life has given life to a huge body of literature. In so far as herding is a lazy life, it favors dreaming, the prerequisite of all artistic expression; but it favors even more the vague musing which is so characteristic of contented cows. Pastoral poetry is mostly the work of city dwellers, and remains exceedingly conventional: Theocritus and Vergil are not much more convincing than eighteenth-century shepherdesses. Pasture land, like the desert, should be kept as a minor background; as the very center of the literary scene, it would prove disappointing.

Agriculture is far less favorable to artistic expression than cattle or sheep ranching; it is too busy a life, a life of constant, absorbing, benumbing care. So, in our modern folklore, the cowboy is the hero, the hayseed the butt of ridicule. Yes, Burns did sing in his furrow, and cast a word of Franciscan sympathy to the "wee, sleekit, tim'rous, cowerin' beastie", whose housie he had laid in ruins. But how many Burnses are there on the roll of fame? France was long a land of peasants, but only the city birds were vocal. The fields are needed for material sustenance and spiritual refreshment, but the artistic power of Graphopolis, like the political, is concentrated in the city. "Urbanity", "civilization", imply the *urbs* and the *civitas*.

Graphopolis is therefore a mart and a workshop, a place wherein the wits of men are sharpened by constant fencing. But Graphopolis is no mere country town, the all-sufficient center of its own rural district. Such a condition would lead to parochialism and intellectural atrophy. Graphopolis is a commercial power, sending caravans and argosies to the farthest ends of the world. Preferably, it is a *thalassocracy,* like Athens, Venice, the Hanseatic League, Holland, Scandinavia, or Portugal at the time of her literary glory. Overseas trade is of commanding cultural importance, for it brings wealth, leisure and luxury, broadens the horizons, fosters the spirit of adventure. So to the wharves of Graphopolis cluster ships of all nations, spice-laden, freighted with dreams, even when they carry nitrates, hides or guano. To Anatole France, who accused her of lacking imagery, the philosophical poetess Madame Ackermann triumphantly replied: "No imagery? Have I not THE SHIP?" A complete bard is as inconceivable without the ship as without the spring.

Many arts and crafts are plied in Graphopolis: for artisans are creators of beauty, and may sing at their work. But the country is not predominantly industrial. It is somewhat premature to condemn industry as artistically barren. Industry is a very young giantess, barely out of an ailing infancy and of a sprawling, brawling, sulky, quarrelsome childhood. So far it has made for ugliness, hardly mitigated with evidences of power. We are told that a new beauty can already be descried under the grime; but it takes very optimistic eyes to see it. Industry, as distinct from the crafts, means mass production. The maker loses his individuality: freshness, creative power, spontaneity, are ruled out of his life; and all originality is likewise eliminated from the product. Witness the short stories turned out to-day by our most approved literary factories.

It is commercial England, seafaring England, with the sturdy background of rural England, that has made England's name glorious in art and letters. It was in its commercial, not in its industrial, days, that New England was a power of the spirit. New York's intellectual supremacy has a mercantile rather than a manufacturing basis. Let us admit, then, that Graphopolis is poor in coal and iron, so that she will not be tempted to turn into Pittsburgh or Birmingham.

The crowds of Graphopolis are at home in the streets of their city; they do not rush feverishly, but they can afford to saunter and loiter. They stop for a friendly chat, they gaze at the evanescent and delightful art of window display, they have time to admire a marble statue in a public square; and, no less frankly, they feast their eyes on those living statues for whom the country is famous. They listen to some orator, poet or musician at the crossroads; they sip the ambrosia of the land at little tables set on the very sidewalks, under the trees.

There is great variety among the types you meet in Graphopolis. A few dashes of color are noticeable—ebony black, brown, red and yellow, with many shades which demonstrate that no race prejudice prevails. But these picturesque notes are the exception: the enormous majority of the inhabitants belong, broadly, to the same race; and that race, needless to say, is our own. Asia and Africa each have their Graphopolis, friendly and independent.

The coexistence in any large number of widely different breeds creates such harrowing problems that no Utopia could settle them or survive them. Almost inevitably, pride, oppression, jealousy, resentment would spring up. One race, in all probability, would isolate itself in splendid conceit and quasi-mystic snobbishness, thus stunting its own intellectual growth and mutilating its human sympathies: a superior caste is never more than the pitiful fragment of what it might have been. Yet we might conceive of conditions similar to those which prevail in Hawaii, where stocks from all parts of the world mingle with almost complete freedom. The literary results of miscegenation in Alexander Dumas and Burghardt Du Bois are decidedly encouraging. Perhaps in Graphopolis eugenics will have reached such a point that various bloods can be exactly dosed for the procreation of a great dramatist, a lyric poet, a sculptor, or an inspired cook; while race mixture would be sternly prohibited when the result is likely to be a synthetic-syndicated humorist.

Graphopolitans, as we visualize them, are white. But they are not all blonds. Complexions may be olive, amber, magnolia, ruddy and even pinkish; only the chalky pallor induced by artificial means will be under the ban. Hairs may range from Venetian red to raven black, through all the tints of bronze and gold: sonneteers would not be happy without dark ladies as well as ladies fair. Stature may be *petite* or impressively tall; figures slender or majestically rotund: we could not think of banishing G. K. Chesterton. On the whole, there may be a slight predominance of the Mediterranean type; but Nordics will not feel out of their element. Alpines specialize in plodding research and dismal realism: we have Mrs. Gertrude Atherton's word for it, and she has it on the authority of Madison Grant, who had it from Houston Stewart Chamberlain, who had it from Gobineau, who had it from God himself: so the chain of evidence is perfect. Alpines will have their modest place in the general scheme; but no book of poems will be allowed to appear if the author's cephalic index is above eighty. This simple rule will avert many literary calamities.

These people speak a sonorous, highly inflected, strongly accented language, full of idioms, allusive phrases, veiled metaphors, quaint survivals and delightful absurdities. They love it so that they revel in playing with it: they are great punsters, and they are constantly coining new words, logical or fanciful, pregnant with thought or merely musical. They rejoice in the possession of many dialects and forms of slang, closely related enough to remain mutually intelligible, but different enough to give a racier tang to any man's speech. Purism and standardization are frowned upon as inartistic: teachers in elementary schools strive to release the latent originality of their students in matters of spelling and syntax. The Graphopolitans, like the Greeks and like Shakespeare, are not vitally interested in the speech of other nations: they have too rich a fund of their own. They realize, further, that polyglottism is not conducive to literary excellence: neither university professors, nor *concierges* in cosmopolitan hotels rank very high as creative artists. A simple, practical, artificial language is used for business, for scientific purposes, for international relations, and even for those branches of literature in which logical thought is of more importance than form. The literary tongue is held too sacred for such commonplace or utilitarian services.

In politics as well as in religion, Graphopolis is pluralistic, or, in simpler parlance, tolerant. A goodly proportion of the population owe allegiance (including a very light contribution towards the upkeep of the court) to King Wenceslaus XI, who is known as a good sport, and represents the gorgeous tradition of a thousand years. His annual procession through the streets of the city on the fifth of November is a magnificent pageant. Others pay tribute to Emperor Tamburlaine XXIII, a mild little scholar who, by immemorial custom, never moves without an escort of wild horsemen. Still others do homage to Queen Cleopatra XLV, the winner of a beauty contest; and not a few join the strict, austere organization known as the Anarchistic Brotherhood. It makes little difference, as the mere business of the State is transacted by managers, mostly Alpines, independent of king, queen, emperor, or grand Anarch.

The managerial State lives at peace with all its neighbors; but the king and the emperor occasionally wage war against each other or against foreign foes. The populace looks forward to these contests with the keenest delight. The ringing challenges, the Pindaric poems and battle hymns, the enthusiastic meetings or rallies on the eve of the strife, the departure of the gaily-clad heroes for the Field of Glory, add enormously to the enjoyment of life. Pacifists who would suppress that supreme form of entertainment are summarily condemned, by such authorities as Elie Faure, as the enemies of art and poetry. The Field of Glory is a large and wild tract reserved for that purpose within convenient distance of Graphopolis; from neighboring hills, and from specially built towers, the whole population can follow the magnificent spectacle. The return of the conquering host, laurel-wreathed, with a golden nimbus in the sunset fire, is a sight never to be forgotten; but connoisseurs aver that a defeated army, slinking in, ghost-like, in the dead of the night, produces a subtler and more profound effect.

In religion, all creeds are welcome, except scientific determinism, which spells artistic death. Graphopolitans are good pragmatists: all faiths are valid if they *work*—that is to say if they enhance the enjoyment of beauty. Hellenism, Hebraism and Christianity alternate in popular favor, and at times blend rather prettily. Some artists claim that without Paganism there can be no salvation, and they are seen devoutly prostrate in the fanes of Aphrodite. But it is usually conceded that Christianity offers a more dramatic setting for human destiny, and casts a richer glow round the mysteries of birth and death. The notion of sin, in particular, is considered as a marvelous, an inexhaustible artistic device. Frankly acknowledging the services of æsthetes to the true faith, the Graphopolitan Church has beatified Baudelaire and James Branch Cabell. We need hardly say that a notable number of Graphopolitans are orthodox devil-wor-shippers.

There are classes, although there are no castes, in Graphopolis: several aristocracies, several clergies, a vast *bourgeoisie* with many subdivisions, and tiers upon tiers of "masses." These classes are definite enough: a man knows without a doubt whether he belongs to the upper middle class or the lower nobility; but interpenetration is not absolutely barred. The classes are in constant rivalry, and even in conflict, but not at war. A system of airtight compartments between the social ranks would be detrimental to culture; but the total abolition of class distinction, if it were possible, would be even more deadly. For art as such thrives only on a class basis: whatever is universally enjoyed ceases to exist for the genuine æsthete, and "popular" literature is a fallacy. The creation and appreciation of art are essentially methods of securing admission among an élite.

The Graphopolitan social scale is established on the basis of literary taste—from the highest aristocracy who, in the nursery, read James Joyce's latest, to the lower middle class, who can barely rise to the level of *The Little Minister*. The chief interest in Graphopolitan life is the breathless attempt of each class to catch up with the one immediately above. As soon as an élite is over-taken, it ceases to be an élite, and its proud place is assumed by another group, which, in its turn, will strain every nerve to keep ahead in the chase. It is the national game. Fads, cults, shibboleths may be resorted to in order to baffle pursuers. But it is considered poor sports-manship to take refuge in total incomprehensibility: it is as bad as shooting the fox, which, to the British, is the sin against the Holy Ghost.

Artists enjoy the picturesqueness and dramatic possibilities of the social ladder, with clusters of men fighting for a precarious foothold at every rung. Poets move up and down at will: they associate with kings or beggars, and consciously relish the paradox of both situations. Each class has a traditional costume, a code of ethics, a manner of speech of its own, which are carefully preserved *in fiction*. In real life every one is aiming to imitate the oddities of some other class, above or even below, and the result is delightfully confusing.

There are marriage laws in Utopia, and they are extremely strict. Without them, half of the world's tragedies, and four fifths of its comedies, would cease to exist. These laws are part of the indispensable conventions of dramatic or narrative art. Judging by the precedent of the most purely *artistic* civilization that ever bloomed, that of the Troubadours, we may surmise that in Graphopolis poets will love with special ardor every wife not their own. The honor of the Graphopolitan husband will be satisfied if the verses inspired by his wife are of sufficient merit: G. B. Shaw gave us an adumbration of such a state in his skit *How he lied to her Husband*. For worthless poetry the only redress is an exchange of visiting cards, seconds, and bullets. For a woman to be sung by three bad poets in succession gives the husband sufficient ground for divorce without alimony. A chivalrous custom provides that the woman should have the first chance of using a love affair for literary purposes: the man's version can appear only six months later. A quaint statute, honored mostly in the breach, prohibits addressing the same intimate poems to more than five lovers.

What think you of such a world: Cabell, Valle Inclán, d'Annunzio, exquisite company of exiled prophetic Graphopolitans? Would you find in it enough color, chivalry, adventure, and that tang of sorrow which makes life doubly sweet? Or will you spurn a world visibly made to your order, because it would rob you of the divine discontent and the transcendental scorn which mark you as poets?

Chapter 23

LITERATURE IN UTOPIA

FOR literature such as we now enjoy it, Utopia would be a lethal chamber. Our art needs inequalities, contrasts, catastrophes, reactionary yearnings, millennial hopes, abysmal despairs, the subtly pungent odor of decay, and mystic premonitions of a far-off spring: a gloriously imperfect, capricious, almost chaotic world. With peace, with order, with justice, there would spread over the earth the pall of uniformity, mother of *taedium* and herald of spiritual death.

Needless to say that such a contingency is infinitely remote, like the cooling off of the sun. At any rate, it lies farther beyond the range of practical consideration than the exhaustion of our coal supply. Be not dismayed: for untold generations there will be enough misery and madness among men to keep poetical fires burning. When the more obvious ills are cured, more refined ones will come to light: there is ever a new peak of discontent to be climbed. So long as there is maladjustment, dissatisfaction, desire, we have not fully entered upon our Utopian heritage, and poets will have their say.

Still, we should not entertain too blind a faith in the perpetuity of human wrongs. They might fail us at any moment. The acceleration of human progress is such that the millennium might burst upon us with catastrophic suddenness. The extinction of desire might come in lieu of satisfaction, and produce the same benumbing effect. In the happy Coolidgian Age, "kickers" and "knockers" were sternly discouraged: in a world further advanced towards Utopia, discontent of any kind might be considered as the most heinous social sin. The apostles thereof would be eliminated as undesirable. Euthanasia would weed them out; eugenics would see to it that the breed remain extinct. In Utopia only those loyal and law-abiding citizens will be allowed to live whose social instincts are in perfect harmony with the organization of the State. In the Conformist's paradise, life will become purely automatic, hope disappearing along with fear.

It may be objected that literature is not merely the mirror of contemporary life. True: a Utopian world might enjoy vicariously, through art, the wickedness and distress of our age, just as the epic grandeur of the Napoleonic era was enjoyed by the peace-loving subjects of Louis-Philippe, the aristocratic calm of the Augustans by a busy plebeian public, the naïve faith of the Middle Ages by the sophisticates of the Post-Voltairian era. But if literature thus became purely retrospective, it would inevitably lose its vitality. Great art can not subsist on ghosts and make-believe. A hundred years ago, our ancestors enjoyed, romantically, knights, bandits and pirates: to-day these charming characters belong chiefly

374

to very juvenile fiction; grown-ups greet them with a smile which is wistful, but also half contemptuous.

Literature in historical setting has not completely lost its appeal, because the problems of the past are still essentially our problems. On a different scale, with different weapons, with different battle cries, the world of ten centuries ago was a world of struggle, very much like our own. In less picturesque garb, bandits, pirates and knights are still with us. But Utopian society will be vexed by none of our cares, and therefore will be thrilled by none of our interests.

When told that the people had no bread, Marie Antoinette (so runs the legend) ingenuously exclaimed: "Why don't they eat *brioches?*" She was living in an artificial Utopia, had no experience of actual suffering, and her imagination could not stretch across the chasm. Our descendants will evince the unwitting callousness of Marie Antoinette. We can not actually re-create a vanished world: we can only deck ourselves in the trappings of the past, as for a masquerade, or project our living sentiments on a picturesque antiquarian background. A literature based on the problems of a bygone age will first become superficially romantic, then purely conventional, and ultimately meaningless. This process is taking place under our eyes. The theme of the long-lost child, which delighted antiquity, the Middle Ages, and even classical Europe, has sunk to the level of cheapest melodrama. Military prowess, exploration, even the conquest of wealth and power, will go the same way: all such subjects will seem absurd when men are assigned their function in the commonwealth as the result of blood tests and skull measurements. Many of our students to-day can not understand why the Victorians made such a fuss over the loss of their orthodoxy; a book like Froude's *Nemesis of Faith* now belongs to history, not to living literature, and even the irony of Rose Macaulay in *Told by an Idiot* is too retrospective to be fully enjoyed. The problems of to-day will cast their shadows for centuries to come, just as we are still vexing our souls in this twentieth century over issues which properly belong to the Middle Ages; but the shadow will ultimately melt away altogether. The literature of Utopia will have to be founded on the problems of Utopia. If there be no problems, there will be no literature.

Utopian conditions, however, do not spell the death of *literature,* but only of a literature based upon physical adventures, contrast, surprise. In other words, they might imply simply the downfall of a superficially dramatic, or melodramatic, conception of art. In a world thoroughly conscious, organized and stabilized, the romance of accident, sudden rise, violent collapse, will cease to be significant, and therefore will cease to be interesting. Even *Œdipus Rex* might be discarded on that score. But the result would be refinement rather than barrenness: the trim garden would take the place of the wilderness. A great loss! I do not know: there is beauty in Versailles. The fear of sudden death, no doubt, gives great zest to life; at every moment you rejoice that you have been spared yet a little while; perfect security would destroy that thrill, which makes the mere fact of existence a boon. But the man who has no pestilence and no murderer to dread need not perish of boredom. He will have time to live, instead of merely begging for life. His ordered life will confess the beauty of the world's peace.

We might anticipate that, in this quieter and more spacious existence, our Utopian would have leisure for art as an exquisite luxury. Even though art should lose all deeper significance, it might retain its price as gratuitous activity, as play pure and simple. Only in Utopia is it possible for art to exist solely for art's sake. Under the present dispensation some purpose will almost inevitably be injected: even George Moore was proud that a home for unwed mothers was named after his *Esther Waters*. There is no artist who does not denounce or extoll, no artist who does not preach: the most disinterested can not refrain from denouncing the Philistines and preaching the cult of Beauty. The art that will disappear with the sordid or tragic chaos of our society is only an art of propaganda; and surely George Moore, H. L. Mencken or James Branch Cabell should be the last to plead for its retention. O bliss! In Utopia there will be no causes to serve.

No doubt literature would tend to be static in a static world. Will the thought be quite so appalling if we substitute "permanent" for "static"? What do the Classicists, and the Neo-Classicists, and most of all our Neo-Neo-Classicists, stand for except enduring values and unchangeable laws? Writers in Utopia will not be worse off than La Bruyère, who opened his book with the words: "All has been said, and there remains nothing to be said, after six thousand years of human thought." Originality of theme has absolutely nothing to do with literary merit. As Pascal remarked, although two players are using the same tennis ball, one of them places it better. Merely as a game, the combinations of words are infinitely more inexhaustible than those of chessmen.

Such a formal conception of art would lead to the worship of technique and total indifference as to subject matter. In Utopia a poet might be a prince among his peers for having brought together two unexpected epithets applied to a saucepan. In the past such conditions have invariably denoted decadence. The last poets of the Middle Ages rejoiced in metrical acrobatics, just as the last schoolmen were noted for tight rope walking over a logical abyss. The last defenders of Classicism at the end of the eighteenth century could describe the most commonplace object or happening in smoothest and most elegant verse, and managed to be perfectly definite without ever calling a thing by its rude proper name. Banville, beloved and revered by Swinburne, was the star juggler and tumbler of late Romanticism; and Jean Giraudoux among the living can give the tritest thought such unexpected piquancy that he almost deserves to live in Utopia. If all "purpose" could be banished, and form alone be sovereign, then the kingdom of Pure Poetry desired by George Moore and Henri Bremond would be at hand.

As nothing happens in Utopia, literature, after a transition period, will cease to deal with deeds, and will become entirely introspective. Long after the physical universe has been reduced to order, the heart will remain unruly and the mind mysterious. So "landscapes of the soul" and "climates of feeling" will take the place of our coarse and obvious material descriptions. Violent passions, being anti-social, will long have been trained out of human nature: shades of likes and dislikes, the ghost of jealousy, the gleam of a scruple, a flicker of remorse, will be examined under a high-power microscope. Not a murder case, but the faint velleity toward the use of an expletive, may be a fair subject for a novelist of the year 3000. The psychological fiction of the French may give us an adumbration of what we have a right to expect in Utopia. Racine's tragedy *Bérénice* is a sigh in sixteen hundred lines; Marivaux "weighed airy trifles in scales made of gossamer"; Proust rediscovered his whole sensitive childhood in a bite of *madeleine* dipped in a cup of tea; and the analyst of to-morrow will out-Proust Marcel Proust as decisively as Proust himself went beyond Marie Corelli.

To our untutored taste Utopian literature would probably seem morbidly sentimental and absurdly finicky: every feeling would be isolated, magnified, placed under various lights, submitted to endless reagents, so as to be studied and enjoyed with absolute fullness. Similarly, a Texas rancher, used to guessing at a glance the weight of a live steer, would scorn the meticulous methods of the physicist, who measures a fraction of a milligramme under truly scientific conditions. The cowboy may have more native genius; but modern civilization pins its faith to the methods of the laboratory.

The possibilities of psychological romance in Utopia are unfathomable. We may take it for granted that the more obvious sentiments will have ceased to exist as fit subjects for literature: perhaps they will have ceased to exist altogether. But then we shall reach from the conscious, too clearly mapped out, into the subconscious and the unconscious. A psychological drama will take place on many planes; each new depth explored will reveal another depth still unplumbed. We could conceive of a stirring piece dealing with the obscure struggle between two embryonic thoughts, in the inmost recesses of a man's soul. The climax would be reached when the victorious idea rises to the threshold of consciousness. It might be that in the process the rivals should get inextricably entangled: the emergent thought, bearing the name of the one, would borrow most of its substance from the other: for Fate will not cease to be ironical in Utopia. The subconscious preparation of a Fundamentalist sermon implies a whole epic of spiritual warfare, more fascinating than Napoleon's titanic blundering in his Russian campaign. Our descendants will not starve for lack of fun.

If psychological training should progress in such a way as to make mind reading a common achievement and telepathy a possibility, then new problems and new techniques will open before the fictionist. Man evolved speech so as to conceal his thought: what is going to happen when that coarse mask is torn aside? The difficulty will be to *think* in such a way as to preserve inviolate the privacy of one's ultimate self. Certain thoughts will be used as smoke screens or camouflage for other thoughts. O'Neill and Pirandello are already attempting such dramas of the dark within; but their method of symbolical presentation is still crudely primitive. In order fully to fathom a novel or play of the thirtieth century, the reader will have to combine the acumen of Bergson,

Einstein and Paul Valéry. We may imagine the smile of
the Utopians if they were to unearth the sophomoric
subtleties of Henry James or Marcel Proust.

As Utopia reaches its perfection, even psychology may
cease to offer entrancing mysteries. Not that there will
ever be a lack of inner worlds to conquer: but the urge
to discovery might become atrophied through premature
self-satisfaction. When psychology has thus attained the
definiteness and rigidity of a mechanism, it will be dead—
that is to say, it will have become a full-fledged science
at last. And the artists of the thirty-second or thirty-
fourth centuries will feel anxious again about the future
of their craft.

Idle fears once more! Long before we are seriously
concerned about the exhaustion of certain sources of
power, such as coal, other sources are discovered or rediscovered, such as waterfalls, the winds, the waves, the
tides, the sun's rays: to-morrow we may release and
harness atomic energy. Literature may face the future
with like confidence. If the human mind should ever
become scientifically known in its inner workings, in
its relations with other minds and with the physical universe, there would still remain the boundless field of
Metaphysics.

Metaphysics is to be found, evanescent or in solid
nuclei, through many poetical masterpieces of the past;
but it was blended with melodrama and psychology,
with mere adventure and with human personalities.
Now such a mixture denotes a primitive state of culture.
A chemist to-day would laugh at the idea of translating
the formula H_2O into a poetical masque, the courtship

of the nymph Hydrogen by the swain Oxygen: science is direct and stark. Philosophy also may be stripped of ornaments which are little better than puerile. The *Divine Comedy* and *Faust* are grand metaphysical epics: in an adult world, the puppet show element in Goethe's masterpiece, the lurid popular imagery in Dante's, would disappear altogether, like dross under an acid. The metaphysical would survive unalloyed. Could it be enjoyed in such a form? Yes, by readers with proper gifts and training. It is hard for a layman to realize that certain musicians can *read* a symphony silently and derive profound enjoyment from it; that a great mathematician can *read* pages of formulæ with perfect understanding and intense delight. In the Utopian world, Spinoza and Hegel will be considered, as they ought to have been from the first, as poets, "cloud-weavers of phantasmal hopes and fears." The destiny of the *thing-in-itself* will thrill our great-grandchildren as keenly as the matrimonial tangles of Arthur and Evelina thrill us to-day.

The Utopian mind, after reaching the ultimate confines of its domain, might, however, refuse to venture into metaphysics at all. What if Metaphysics were, not the Unknown, but simply the Impalpable Inane? To plunge into its void would be sheer suicide. "The Science of the Unknowable" is little better than an absurdity, and Herbert Spencer knew it well. This condemnation of metaphysics, if it were accepted, would leave Mysticism unscathed. For, at all stages of human development, there will be a feeling that cosmic life is greater than organized science; and intuition, in the thirtieth century, will take its flight no less boldly than in the twentieth. Its expression will not be so crudely anthropomorphic: but it can never be fully scientific either. A surmise, a revelation, can only be indicated in symbolical terms. There always will be a touch of wildness in the affirmations of the mystics; for any adventure beyond the norm of experience is by definition *un-safe* and *in-sane*. The marginal ground, the debatable borderland between accepted reality and reality still in the making, will ever be the realm of dreams and fancies, intuitions and visions, and will never cease bearing poetical fruit. This as long as we see only as through a glass darkly, as long as we do not know even as we are known.

This leads us to the Supreme Utopia, when all veils are removed, and we contemplate the splendor of truth face to face: what are the possibilities of literature in heaven? According to the most approved authorities on the subject, the sole poetical *genre* to survive will be an eternal hymn of praise. Without challenging these authorities, we have a right to wonder whether their lyrical paradise be the very last stage. For the separation between Creator and creatures, implied in such a ritual, means limitation, incompleteness, and therefore longing, and therefore sorrow. Perfect bliss is inconceivable until the lost are all redeemed, and all individuals are absorbed again into the One. Then the song of praise itself will be stilled, and the absolute silence of Nirvana will prevail throughout eternity. At this extreme limit Utopia does indeed necessitate the complete extinction of all literature.

But not until then.

Let us wake up. What is the sense of all this nonsense? Believe it or not, O practical Anglo-Saxon reader, there is some sense to it; and since you challenge me to draw explicitly the moral lessons of my apologue, here they are, duly tabulated:

I. The hostility of the alleged artistic soul to industrial and social progress is based on a fallacy. Chaos, injustice, greed and suffering are not essential to poetry. The opposition of æsthetes to such causes as pacificism, simplified spelling, a reformed calendar, an international language, world organization, a planned economy, is founded on a crude conception of art. Art under Utopia will simply be more disinterested and more refined than it is at present. Material standardization need not hurt the soul. It simply enables us to waste less time and thought on worldly goods, thus releasing the spirit. What if we should all wear the same brand of clothes and drive the same kind of automobiles? Our remote ancestors had "standardized" on nakedness and pedestrian transportation.

II. It is not so idle as it may seem to follow as we have done, in free yet logical fancy, certain tendencies of the present. Some aspects of psychological literature, for instance, might easily be considered as sheer eccentricities. O'Neill, Pirandello, Proust, Joyce, "got away with it", at least for a season. But, for their own good and ours, should they not remain unique? Is their art a picturesque blind alley? Or is it destined to broaden into a main avenue? It has been our purpose to show that, as the gates of physical adventure were closing, our best chance lay in the direction of an ever more searching psychology.

There are posers and morons among the cryptic writers of to-day; but there are men also who are pathfinders, blazers of trails, and not mere oddities.

III. The great danger which menaces all Utopias is not achievement, but stagnation. This danger is with us to-day: for stagnation is the price we have to pay for complacency. If we persuade ourselves that our Constitution, our economic régime, our religious creeds, our morals, are fundamentally and unchangeably right, then we shall have reached at a single bound Utopia in all its horror—a Utopia of conformity and dullness, worse than any cycle of Cathay. Tennyson's mid-Victorian wisdom remains true three generations later:

> And God fulfills Himself in many ways,
> Lest one good custom should corrupt the world.

It is for poets to discover new ways in which God may fulfill Himself. The Utopia just ahead, the dream born of Protest, will save us from the slough of self-satisfaction. So long as we are made to realize that this is not God's own country, there will be some hope of salvation.

Chapter 24

THE PROSPECT FOR AMERICAN LITERATURE

I

WHILE protesting as vigorously as we could against the literary jingo, we protested no less vigorously against the literary expatriate. Literature and civilization can not be divorced: the American background affects us at every turn. It is normal that we should be most interested in the life of our own country; and the natural conclusion of our survey is: "What is the bearing of all this upon American literature?"

There is another reason why we should attempt to translate our theories into strictly American terms: it is the severest test to which they could be submitted. No general idea should shrink from the plain question: "For instance?" And the more immediate our knowledge, the more definite our challenge. Rousseau started his sketch of human evolution with the liberating words: "First of all, let us brush aside the facts!" And if Taine chose English literature for the demonstration of his doctrine, it was partly because he and his readers knew it far less thoroughly than French literature. This should be a warning; we have little use for a truth which can not thrive in our home atmosphere.

"We Anglo-Saxons" (if I may quote the colored sergeant again) are not so fond of finespun theories as
Taine was. But there is one case in which we appeal to
"race, environment and time" very freely: as an alibi
for our alleged inferiority in literature. An adopted son,
I might hesitate to mention the subject. But there is no
secret about it: it has become part of the American tradition.

Self-depreciation is not strictly an American fault:
we have fully discovered the tonic effect of self-confidence
and the educative value of boosting. We take legitimate
pride in our natural resources, our enterprise, our athletic records, our wealth and health, our power of organization, our general smartness. There are only two
points about which we are positively humble: diplomacy
and literature. We take it for granted that we can not
deal with other governments without being invariably
duped—a delusion which would be amusing if it were
not so dangerous: it has retarded the recovery of the
world by at least a decade. And we are also persuaded
that we can not beat the foreigners at the literary game.
Even the apostles of American literature suffer from
the same inferiority complex. The Great American Masterpiece which they herald is, like Prosperity, always
lurking just round the corner. It has not come yet, because. . . . In both cases, our humble mindedness is an
inverted form of pride. We are too frank and open to
have our Metternichs and our Talleyrands. And we are
too sensible, too practical, too manly, to take literature
very seriously, like those effete Europeans.

The rest of the world, pardonably, accepts our own

verdict. If we, the most indomitable of optimists and the most efficient of advertisers, acknowledge and blazon forth our own defeat, Europe will be too courteous to contradict us. There is no inborn dislike abroad for American things: our films and our cocktails are still in great favor. But there are far fewer American books successful in Europe than European books popular on this side. While we gather Olympic palms by the armful, we lag behind minor countries among the contenders for the Nobel Prize in Literature. And our single successful champion won with a vigorous caricature of Americanism: we are still wondering whether the honor was a compliment.

Naturally, when Europeans take us at our word, we bristle up and curse their insolence. We are like Cyrano: we may freely indulge in pitiless quips about our noses, but we do not permit an outsider even to raise his eyebrow. Forty years ago, the French were loudly proclaiming—to themselves—their own decadence: but they were chagrined and indignant when the rest of the world echoed their self-criticism. It was William II himself who compared German "frightfulness" with the scourge of the Huns: but no one outside Germany was allowed to take him seriously. We alone have the right to call our brother: "Thou boob." Non-Americans are therefore requested to skip this chapter altogether.

"What is the matter with us?" There is no fault to find with our *race,* since we have not any; nor with our *climate,* since we have all kinds, mostly exceptional. The first alibi is our youth, which Oscar Wilde aptly called our oldest tradition. We are the direct heirs of

European civilization, and the Declaration of Independence did not break the chain. The Bible and Shakespeare are ours as much as they are England's. As a matter of fact, we seldom realize that we are to-day *the oldest nation in the world*. The American mind came to consciousness in the second half of the eighteenth century, and, theoretically at least, it has not altered. Materially, we have ploughed virgin soil; but our thinking is scrupulously that of the Fathers. In the last hundred and fifty years, England has been recast a couple of times; so have Italy, France, Germany. Russia, Turkey, India, China are lusty infants, rather unruly and untidy as infants are apt to be. America, in contrast, has the bland composure, the serene self-satisfaction, of a Gilbert ancestral portrait.

Our second handicap is the lack of a national language. Until we have a vernacular, we shall obscurely feel ourselves mere "colonials" and satellites. The desire for a speech of one's own is universal among nations. Sensible and progressive Norway wants to break away from Danish and make its local dialect official. Ireland is striving desperately to unlearn English, which it uses so forcibly, and revive Celtic, a wraith. A master of incisive *English* prose is advocating "an American language." The sign *English Spoken, American Understood,* which tourists claim to have seen on European shops, would point in the right direction: unfortunately, we believe that sign to be a senescent myth. The fact that the London edition of *Babbitt* required a glossary is more definitely encouraging. It is usually admitted, although not with the proper degree of pride, that many of our political leaders have discarded the use of English.

Is it a fact that no great literature can be produced in a borrowed language? Neither Alexandria nor Syracuse could compare with Athens: but their culture was more brilliant than that of any other Greek city. Few Latin writers of the first rank came from beyond the confines of Italy: but, by the time Latin civilization had spread to the outlying provinces, it already was decadent in Rome herself. Spanish and Portuguese America is no better off than we are. The French colonies offer a creditable roll of fame: but their literary sons made their careers in Paris, and did not start an autonomous colonial culture. Australian literature, like the continent itself, is semi-desertic. All this, in our opinion, only proves that precedents are of no avail when we have to deal with the unprecedented. There has never been, so far as we know, a "colony" that could compare with the United States to-day. In William Bennett Munro's neat phrase: "We can teach History, but History can not teach us." If English were an alien tongue, artificially superimposed upon native dialects, as it is in India and in the Philippines, it would probably have a paralyzing effect upon literature. But English is now healthily rooted in our soil, and has no local competitor.

If we did need "an American language" before we could produce genuine literature, our chances would be slim indeed. All the forces of modern civilization are against the formation of new local dialects: the old ones are disappearing so fast, that scholars find it difficult to register them. In the Middle Ages, two English valleys,

less than a hundred miles apart, were more deeply separated than Chicago and London are to-day. Each of
these cities can read every morning the latest scandal from
the other; each can call the other on the 'phone; both
listen to the same lecturers, the same discs, the same
talkies, the same radio broadcast. Even in my youth,
while I found it difficult to understand a Yorkshireman,
I had no trouble with a New Zealander or a Californian.

Will America's ever fresh fountain of speech, slang,
help create a new dialect? Only in a very fleeting and
superficial fashion. Most of those spontaneous creations
live but for a moment, and do not contribute to the permanent vocabulary. Those which survive infallibly reach
London. And it is easy to prophesy that the process will
be further accelerated. It used to take decades for an
American joke to be understood in England; now, it is
merely a matter of years.

The next two hypotheses can be neatly paired off. Our
inferiority, says Irving Babbitt, is due to our neglect
of standards. We have lost our sense of values, because
Democracy refuses to accept enlightened Leadership.
"What must one think of a country," asks one of our
foremost critics, "whose most popular orator is W. J.
Bryan, whose favorite actor is Charlie Chaplin, whose
most widely read novelist is Harold Bell Wright, whose
best known evangelist is Billy Sunday, and whose representative journalist is William Randolph Hearst?" *
Salvation is to be found only in the good old ways. If
we were consistent, we should all proclaim ourselves,
with T. S. Eliot, Royalists, Catholics and Classicists. But

* *Democracy and Leadership*, p. 240.

this is only a counsel of perfection: we might get by with sound Republicanism, sturdy individualism, the Puritan tradition and compulsory Latin. A cultural heaven for Harvard professors.

But to this *fundamentalist* thesis may be opposed the *modernistic*. America has no literature commensurate with her other achievements, because she is still hampered by standards which do not belong to her own civilization. We reject feudal titles, but we piously preserve medieval reputations. We are now doing great things in architecture because we are worrying a little less about Tudor and Queen Anne, Palladian Renaissance or Louis Seize: but our literary education is still antiquarian. Our closest bids to literary greatness were not Bryant and Longfellow, but Walt Whitman and Mark Twain. Unfortunately both labored under the delusion that the literature of a vast new continent should be loose and sprawling. We might just as well assert that the literature of a small country like Scotland must be "tight", and that of Chile "elongated": all variants of the geographical fallacy.

The Neo-Humanists, we believe, are not a majority even among American professors; but they have behind them the force of a united tradition, whereas the Modernists can only express, often with absurd emphasis, vague and conflicting hopes. The result is that the sane, educated *bourgeoisie,* still the backbone of the literary public, is almost solidly fundamentalist.

The same conflict occurs in all countries. It is particularly ardent in France, where the Classics are a party issue. But nowhere, to our knowledge, is the conservative élite so contemptuous of the masses as with us, nor the masses so perfectly oblivious of the élite. There is no communication between them, no cross-fertilization. Irving Babbitt preached only to his own parishioners.

The fifth obstacle in the path of American literature is, or rather was, the heavy cost of Americanization. On account of the diversity of our origins, an enormous effort was expended in bringing us all into line. This was the first aim of our education; and, beyond our school years, it absorbed much collective and individual energy. The community striving so hard to turn all its members into Americans, the man whose chief desire was to remake himself into an American, had little spiritual power left for anything else. Our one great masterpiece was the creation of "the American type." We need not blush at the result: it is fully as good as such things can be. But it is not an artistic achievement, just because it is standardized. Good citizenship has been identified with conformity, mass thinking, mass sentiment: under such conditions, conventionality and superficiality are almost inevitable. Only a country and a man who take themselves for granted can express their souls.

We have greater faith in America than the rabid Americanizers. We should have liked America to impose only the strictest minimum of uniformity, for practical purposes; and to respect, nay to welcome, the varied traditions that the immigrants brought with them. In the slums, we strive to root out the memory of the old lands; but in the colleges, we try our best to teach the history of European civilizations. It does not pay to turn all newcomers into spiritual paupers. Had we preserved,

instead of tossing aside, our multifarious European heritage, the result would have been, not a nation superficially
homogeneous (far more homogeneous now, in externals,
than any in Europe), but an Americanism at the same
time richer in pattern and deeper in spirit. For there
were sufficient foundations for a genuine, uncoerced
Americanism. We all came to America because we felt
in us something of the American soul; and the opportunities of the new life, without any compulsion, would have
welded us all together. We have been too modest; we
have sought to make America a nation just like those of
the old world, while this might have been a new venture,
the first conscious unit of a world commonwealth.

All this is purely retrospective, and our regrets are
futile. Forcible Americanization may have been an incubus; but it is losing force. Not because we no longer
have faith in it, but because its work is done. For half
a generation already, immigration has been reduced to
a negligible point. Assimilation is no longer a pressing
problem. Henceforth, an American may dare to be himself, to think for himself, without being afraid of seem-
ing un-American. The obsession that everybody had to
be exactly like everybody else, is lifted from our minds.
If we do not choose, we shall not have to be "individual-
ists" according to the prescribed pattern, or "Protestants"
who fail to protest. This may release, for the benefit of
literature, marvelous reserves of frozen power.

That "American type" which we sought to impose
upon all dwellers in the land was created by two sets
of factors: a natural selection from the various elements
in Europe, and the physical task of subduing a continent.
The first is the more important: had the most listless of

Europeans been dumped on our Eastern coast instead of the most eager, they would have vegetated, "gone native", or disappeared altogether. But we shall take up first the material aspect, because of its comparative simplicity.

Nations, like Tennyson's God, fulfill themselves in many ways. Our way, for two centuries, was to tame the wilderness. Such a formidable challenge could not fail to absorb a great part of our national energy. When the work was practically completed, the momentum carried us into another field, which the English and the Germans had already mapped out for us: industrial expansion. Technique became the new frontier, with the same adventurous glamour as the old. Men went higher and faster, instead of plunging farther towards the setting sun.

It can hardly be denied that this led to the subordination of disinterested culture. In popular estimation, the poets are not such red-blooded he-men as the Typical American; they are constantly under suspicion of not being in fullest sympathy with their time and with their nation. Even when they are thoroughly American, they must realize that, as mere *singers,* they can not compare with the *doers.* The American epic writer is the pioneer, the discoverer of new lands, new resources, new processes.

This phenomenon is by no means unique. A similar explanation may be offered for the acknowledged inferiority, in literature, of the Romans to the Greeks:

Tu regere imperio populos, Romane, memento
(*haec tibi erunt artes*)

During the French Revolution and Napoleon's Empire, political and military activities drained all the vigor of the land. The only writers who were not feeble ghosts were in opposition. The case of Balzac clearly illustrates our point. Balzac could be summed up in one word: ambition. He had on his table a statuette of Napoleon, the god of Successful Ambition. Had he lived twenty-five years earlier, Balzac would have sought to be an administrator or a Marshal of the Empire; had he been born twenty-five years later, so as to be in the fullness of his young manhood when the Second Empire opened an era of industrial expansion, he would have tried to be a financial magnate. His ideal was Power through Wealth: the central character in the *Human Comedy* is Money. But in the cautious *bourgeois* world of Louis-Philippe, his grandiose commercial imagination was out of place. He failed in business, and his literary career was to a large extent a magnificent substitute for a vanished dream, just as Madame de Staël's career was a compensation for disappointed love. Had Balzac lived in America, he would have been Astor, Gould, Vanderbilt, Morgan, Hill, Harriman, Carnegie, Rockefeller, rather than, as he modestly styled himself, a Field Marshal of Letters.

We do not mean that all European Shelleys, had they been Americans, would have turned into Fords, and all American Chryslers, in Europe, might have been Tennysons. But many of our successful business men—I am thinking at present of a great railroad executive—might have chosen to be writers instead, *if it had been the thing,* if it had offered commensurate rewards. All gifts are not interchangeable: but the greatest of all is energy, and it can assume many shapes.

Here again, we are in all probability standing at the

end of a period: André Maurois was right in calling the Puritan, the Pioneer and the Robber Baron "the three American ghosts." The last geographical frontier is gone; and, although the frontier of technique is capable of indefinite extension, its conquest is no longer a rough-and-tumble adventure. The discoverers, in the new age, will be scientists rather than fighters; and their work will be closely coöperative, almost anonymous, instead of brilliantly individualistic. If the heroic period of material expansion be past, heroic souls will seek other forms of self-expression, and art will come into its own.

Art, for one thing, requires leisure, and hitherto we have despised leisure. The man of leisure, in our eyes, is an idler, a parasite. If it be the sign of a gentleman to scorn toil, the only American equivalent for the gentleman is the tramp. We have not yet learned the virtue of leisure: but leisure has been brutally forced upon us, in huge chaotic blocks, under the name of unemployment. We are compelled to admit that a saner distribution of leisure is needed; and, as leisure becomes a normal fact, we shall have to fill it intelligently. The exclusive predominance of the material producer is nearing its end.

We said that the American type was the result of a natural selection. This, of course, is not wholly true. Some of us were transported; some left the old country for its own good; and, just before the Great War, the shipping companies were coralling hordes of emigrants, not infallibly the most promising material: no alien was undesirable in their eyes, provided his fare be paid. But, as a rule, it took decision, energy, stamina, to break loose and try again. So we are a people of adventurers: there is nothing in our heritage that belongs so legitimately to all of us, whatever our speech or creed may have been; and nothing from which we may derive juster pride.

All this—self-confidence, optimism, vigor—is what the Pioneers brought with them; but, as Mrs. Edith Wharton says, think of what they left behind. They left behind squalor, inequality, oppression: but, at the same time, historical culture. The people who abandoned Europe for America were those who placed *something*—freedom of worship, political liberty, economic opportunity—immeasurably above the enjoyment of the storied past. They would rather be free citizens in the monotonous Prairie, nay in the desert or the swamp, than subjects in the shadow of the noblest cathedral. They may have been idealists, or materialists, or a combination of both: but, in all cases, they were not predominantly artistic.

I know many people in Europe, no less energetic than the majority of us, who would shudder at the thought of settling in America. Sheer prejudice? No: I have also known many Europeans on this side, who, in spite of brilliant success, felt themselves in exile, and returned at the first opportunity: there is something lacking in the American atmosphere without which they can not live. *We* accepted the sacrifice; we, and our ancestors before us, did not place cultural opportunities first and foremost. If there is any reality to that vague entity, the American Type, it must include a healthy dose of Philistinism along with its splendid element of energy.

Culture is not a mere accumulation of material objects: it is the sum of memories and desires. We started our national life with a very scant cultural equipment: we had left most of it behind. Scant, but not negligible: in the first half of the nineteenth century, our hoard was increasing on the Atlantic seaboard. But the two centers in which that capital of culture was accumulating both lost their predominant influence: the Old South through the Civil War, New England through the flood of immigration and the Westward movement. Typical America to-day is Middle Western: and the Middle West is now to New England what New England once was to Europe: the aggregation of those for whom cultural interests are not paramount. For a certain type, it is better to live impoverished in Boston than prosperous in Iowa.

There are forms of self-fulfillment, nobler than riches, which are more freely open in America than in Europe, and thus successfully compete with art and literature: I mean the supreme poetry of this life, love; and of the life to come, religion. The European "marriage of convenience" is a frustration which calls for a compensation in the form of literature. In a country like France, where the Roman Catholic tradition prevails; or in one where the sects are fully stabilized, as in England, certain forms of creative mysticism express themselves in lyric, drama, romance. In America, the great longing may be satisfied by creating or joining a new cult. The founders of the Latter Day Saints or of Christian Science had in them (no less than the promoters of transcontinental railways) a genius which, with different opportunities and under a different discipline, might have given us a new *Divine Comedy*, a new *Paradise Lost*. The Four-Square Evangelist of Southern California might have been our Marie Corelli: the same luxuriant imagination is found in both. The Wesleyan movement, although its followers seldom boast of the fact, was part of Pre-Romanticism. There was enough spiritual energy in England for both a religious revival and a literary awakening: in America, the religious side has taken the upper hand. We have fewer supreme poets, but we have a far greater number of strange sects. When "men of culture" affect to despise old-fashioned religion and new-fangled cults, they do not realize that millions are obtaining, through such means, the gorgeous vision, the mystic tremor, the ultimate catharsis, that the learned receive only at second-hand, and frequently not at all. The common man converted by the crude eloquence of a Salvationist may stand closer to the spirit of Dante and Milton than the grammarian and the allusion chaser.

We have enumerated no less than seven reasons for our self-confessed inferiority in literature, to wit:

1: the brevity of our national existence;
2: the lack of a national language;
3: our "democratic" departure from time-honored standards (Irving Babbitt);
4: our superstitious reverence for standards, mostly alien and outworn;
5: the heavy spiritual toll of wholesale Americanization;
6: the overwhelming task of mastering a new continent; and, consequently, the exaltation of the *doer,* the scorn of leisure;

7: the natural selection, in the formation of our people, of men who did not place culture foremost; and, as a special instance, the successful competition of romantic love and religion with art and literature.

Our conclusions, in practically every case, were far from discouraging. All these factors may have hampered America's cultural development: but not one of them operates with full force to-day. Our "youth" is far behind; Americanization and the material conquest of the land are practically complete; leisure is ours—far more of it than we want; the artistic temperament is resurgent. All our alibis are fast losing their validity. We shall have to produce masterpieces, or know the reason why.

II

"In 1593," reports Fontenelle, "a tooth of gold was discovered in the mouth of a seven-year-old boy, in Silesia . . . Horstius, Rullandus, Ingolsteterus, Libavius, wrote learned treatises on that miraculous portent, sent by God himself to comfort the Christians afflicted by the Turks. . . . A goldsmith, examining the tooth, discovered that it had been very cunningly covered with gold leaf. People first wrote books, and then consulted the expert." *

Critic, *de te fabula*. We had our sport endeavoring to explain a fact which is generally taken for granted. Why not vary our amusements by challenging the fact itself?

We shall not try to disprove American inferiority by measuring ours, point by point, with other national literatures. Dear old Saintsbury, at the close of his *French*

* Fontenelle: *Histoire des Oracles.*

401

Literature, awards France first place in a few "events", second in many others, as if he were the judge of an Anglo-French track meet. Such comparisons escape being offensive only when they are frankly ridiculous.

Neither shall we dispute the point by comparison with the past. The parallel of age with age is as delusive as that between country and country. If we were to believe the blurbs, every season would bring forth a fresh crop of "epoch-making" masterpieces: only they totally fail to make an epoch. Mass production is no argument in our favor: but it creates an unfair basis of judgment. From the past, only the best stands out: the rest is forgotten, or definitely subordinated. *Our* best is so closely enmeshed with the very good, the not so good, the mediocre, the worthless, that the boldest critics dare not attempt to disentangle the bewildering mass. And, as we have seen, old masterpieces have not merely mellowed with age, they have grown. What a century will do to *Death comes to the Archbishop,* I do not know.

No critic knows, and every critic likes to play safe. It takes an erratic and sensation-loving freelance like Papini to question the literal inspiration and inerrancy of Shakespeare. Self-respecting scholars, with a reputation to lose, will not admit in so many words that *The Faerie Queene* is intolerably inflated, and *The Vicar of Wakefield* the merest trifle. We may join in a collective revolution of taste, but we do not like to travel alone: the same cause which makes us superstitious about the past makes us over-diffident about the present. Sainte-Beuve himself was practically blind to the greatness of his contemporaries. We shall not start a new Quarrel of the Ancients and the Moderns: the old one has proved insoluble.

Our defense of the present is based, not on comparison, but on the refusal to compare. Between the modes of expression of our ancestors and those of to-day, there is no common measure. Was Alexander of Macedon a greater general than Foch? How can we tell? What would Alexander's special gifts have done under the conditions of modern technique? The conditions of literature to-day are radically different from those of a mere hundred years ago.

The change which has come upon them is twofold. On the one hand, the literary public is now boundless. In theory, it is co-extensive with the mass of the nation; in practice, it reaches—fitfully—to the very depths, and no limits can be safely assigned to it: for there is no recognized "Society" which can dictate our taste. On the other hand, the ideal of fixity is disappearing from all realms of thought. We have not abandoned the notion of permanence: but it is a living, growing permanence, which manifests itself under a ceaseless variety of appearances.

A hundred years ago, Victor Hugo had prophesied something of the kind: *"Ceci tuera cela,"* *this* will kill *that,* said Claude Frollo, the somber archdeacon of Notre Dame; the printed press will kill the cathedral. At a time when the book was too fragile, too rare, too difficult of access, to be relied upon as the universal vehicle, it was the cathedral that served as the permanent repository of a people's culture. But the printing press makes the book more imperishable in its ubiquity than the cathedral in its mountainous massiveness. The unchangeable Bible

403

of stone becomes too costly, too cumbrous, too inadaptable. Spiritual life deserts it, and rushes eagerly, through a thousand springs, into an irresistible stream. Innumerable copies may be destroyed; many books may perish altogether; others come pouring in, and the stream sweeps on, changing at every moment, eternally the same.

Exactly what the book, according to Victor Hugo, did to the cathedral, other modes of expression, more ubiquitous still, are doing to the book. The *Classic,* the work of a lifetime, destined to endure for centuries, is a monument: the magazine, the newspaper, the radio, the talkie, are innumerable living voices. We are seeking the truth of to-day, striving to reach the men of to-day, content that the ephemeral in us be forgotten altogether. If we have added an infinitesimal particle of enduring truth, it will be true to-morrow in the words of to-morrow.

The change has already come with full force in the sciences. The great scientific classic, an authority for ever, has been left far behind. "The rate of progress in science nowadays is much too great for such works as Newton's *Principia,* or Darwin's *Origin of Species.* Before such a book could be completed, it would be out of date. In many ways, this is regrettable, for the great books of the past possessed a certain beauty and magnificence, which is absent from the fugitive papers of our time, but it is an inevitable consequence of the rapid increase of knowledge, and must therefore be accepted philosophically." *

Scientists may be resigned to the undeniable loss: but what about artists? Renan, an exquisite stylist and a worshipper of beauty, agreed in advance with Bertrand Rus-

* Bertrand Russell, *The Scientific Outlook,* p. 55.

THE PROSPECT FOR AMERICAN LITERATURE

sell: *"Immortality* does not consist in being read by posterity. We must give up such an illusion. The future shall not read us. This we know, and rejoice. So much the better for the future! We shall have led posterity beyond the need of reading us."

Beyond!

Art is the eternal frontier, and the artistic impulse is that of the pioneer. This spirit is desperately needed in American culture. We had it geographically, we still have it industrially; in things of the spirit, we cling to the good old ways, the slowly desiccating wisdom of our ancestors. Not only in Russia, in China, in Italy, do we have the sense of a venture, desperate but exhilarating, an old continent left behind, the unplumbed, uncharted sea ahead: but even in England, in Germany, in France, mankind is consciously in the re-making. America, in comparison, is a sedate country, in which everything of importance has been settled for ages, and is supposed to be settled for ever.

The task of American literature is not to sing the pioneer of the material world, the conqueror of the Western plains, the Argonaut, the builder of skyscrapers and aëroplanes. Let him be honored: but his deeds suffice to his praise. Literature is not a belated and faded imitation of life, but life itself in the experiment. Organized experience is no longer alive: mechanical laws force out and supplant the will of man. From this materialization, art offers an escape; perhaps the sole escape. Art is a flight, not from life, but from death.

BIBLIOGRAPHY

Acknowledgments

*The preparation of these Bibliographical Notes was a
family enterprise; my wife and son must be ready to accept their full share of blame for all errors and omissions.*

*For abundant aid cheerfully given, my heartiest thanks
are due to:*

Mrs. Eleanor Clement Jones, of the Harvard Psychologi-
    cal Clinic
Miss Edith Ronald Mirrilees, of Stanford University
Mrs. Isabel Paterson, of the New York Herald-Tribune

*I would also add that several passages in this book ap-
peared in* The American Mercury, Books Abroad, The
Nineteenth Century and After, *and* Scribner's Magazine.
*Our thanks are hereby tendered to the editors of these
periodicals, for past hospitalities, and for the exhumation
permit.*

A. G.

Bibliographical Notes

The study of Literature as a social phenomenon is not so much a *subject* as a *method*. It has therefore no special bibliography: every piece of creative literature is a valid document, and many works of criticism or literary history have important contributions to offer. The purpose of this inquiry is merely to define a point of view: every reader must organize the field of his own experience. In the following notes, I have listed a few books which afford good illustrations of the various points discussed in this volume. Many of them contain extensive bibliographies. Unless otherwise indicated, the place of publication is New York, and the date that of the edition I have used. No indication is given in the case of easily accessible classics.

GENERAL INTRODUCTIONS

Moulton, Richard Green: *The Modern Study of Literature: an Introduction to Literary Theory and Interpretation,* University of Chicago Press, 1915. (A practical and stimulating guide.)

Baldensperger, Fernand: *La Littérature, Création, Succès, Durée,* Paris, E. Flammarion, 1913.

Ermatinger, Emil (editor): *Philosophie der Literaturwissenschaft,* Berlin, Junker und Dünnhaupt, 1930.

SOCIETY SURVEYED BY LITERARY MINDS

Books of this kind offer an excellent preparation for the reverse process: literature viewed by the social scientist.

Many of the Essays of Carlyle and Matthew Arnold belong to this category. Among recent works, the following will serve as specimens:

Brooks, Van Wyck: *Letters and Leadership,* The Viking Press, 1918.

Babbitt, Irving: *Rousseau and Romanticism,* Boston, Houghton Mifflin Company, 1919.

Babbitt, Irving: *Democracy and Leadership,* Boston, Houghton Mifflin Company, 1924.

Krutch, Joseph Wood: *The Modern Temper,* Harcourt, Brace and Company, 1929.

Krutch, Joseph Wood: *Was Europe a Success?* Farrar & Rinehart, Incorporated, 1934.

Lippmann, Walter A: *A Preface to Morals,* The Macmillan Company, 1929. (I wonder if Mr. Lippmann would resent being called a literary mind?)

Russell, Bertrand: *The Scientific Outlook,* W. W. Norton & Company, Inc., 1931. (Curiously prophetic of Huxley's *Brave New World.*)

Huxley, Aldous: *A Brave New World,* Doubleday, Doran & Company, Inc., 1932.

Ortega y Gasset, José: *The Revolt of the Masses,* W. W. Norton & Company, Inc., 1932.

Mumford, Lewis: *Technics and Civilization,* Harcourt, Brace and Company, 1934.

Part I The Background of Literature: Race, Environment and Time

It is impossible to give a separate bibliography for each chapter, as the topics inevitably overlap. This overlapping is in some cases due to confusion of thought. (How difficult it is to keep distinctly apart Race, Language, Nationality!) But it may also result from natural connections: economic, social, political conditions react upon one another.

WORKS ON THE SOCIOLOGICAL INTERPRETATION OF LITERATURE

The classic on the subject is:

Taine, Hippolyte: *Introduction to the History of English Literature,* Paris, Hachette et Cie, 1863. (Many editions and translations; separate edition of the Introduction, with notes by Irving Babbitt, D. C. Heath and Company.)

Taine, Hippolyte: *La Fontaine et ses Fables,* Paris, Hachette et Cie, 1861. (A good illustration of the method.)

The social point of view is implied in the title of:

Francke, Kuno: *A History of German Literature as Determined by Social Forces,* (earlier: *Social Forces in German Literature*), Henry Holt and Company, Inc., 1901.

Thorndike, Ashley H.: *Literature in a Changing Age,* The Macmillan Company, 1920.

Thorndike, Ashley H.: *Outlook for Literature,* The Macmillan Company, 1931.

Calverton, Victor F.: *The Newer Spirit: A Sociological Criticism of Literature,* Boni & Liveright, 1925. (*Newer* is amusing: but the book is not humorous.)

Ichowicz, Marc: *La Littérature à la Lumière du Matérialisme Historique,* Paris, M. Rivière, 1929. (A formidable title. "If the light that is in thee be darkness, how great is that darkness!")

Berl, Emmanuel: *Mort de la Pensée Bourgeoise: la Littérature,* Paris, Grasset et Cie, 1929.

THE SOCIOLOGICAL APPROACH TO AMERICAN LITERATURE

Parrington, Vernon Louis: *Main Currents in American Thought: an Interpretation of American Literature from the Beginnings to 1920.* Harcourt, Brace and Company, 3 vols., 1927-1930. (Title and to some extent method inspired by Georg Brandes's *Main Currents in Nineteenth Century Literature.* A standard work.)

Perry, Bliss: *The American Mind: American Traits in American Literature,* Boston, Houghton Mifflin Company, 1912.

Perry, Bliss: *The American Spirit in Literature: a Chronicle of Great Interpreters,* New Haven, Yale University Press, 1918.

Mumford, Lewis: *The Golden Day: a Study in American Experience and Culture,* Boni and Liveright, 1926.

Calverton, Victor F.: *The Liberation of American Literature,* Charles Scribner's Sons, 1931.

DeVoto, Bernard: *Mark Twain's America,* Boston, Little, Brown & Company, 1932.

Lewisohn, Ludwig: *Expression in America,* Harper & Brothers, 1932.

Hicks, Granville: *The Great Tradition,* The Macmillan Company, 1933.

RACE

Until the eighteenth century, the Race idea had been applied (very sporadically) to political theory, but hardly to literature. *Cf.:*

Barzun, Jacques: *The French Race: Theories of its Origins and their Social and Political Implications,* Columbia University Press, 1932.

Herder was chiefly responsible for the inextricable confusion between Race, Language, Nationality. *Cf.* his *magnum opus:*

Herder, Johann Gottfried: *Ideen zur Philosophie der Geschichte der Menschheit,* 4 vols., 1784-1791.

Ergang, Robert R.: *Herder and the Foundations of German Nationalism,* Columbia University Press, 1931.

For a very brief discussion:

Guérard, Albert: "Herder's Spiritual Heritage", *Annals of American Academy of Political and Social Science,* July 1934.

In the same line:

Fichte, Johann Gottlieb: Addresses to the German Nation (Purity and Primitiveness of the German Race. *Cf.* particularly Address VIII: *The Definition of a Nation in the Higher Sense of the Word, and of Patriotism*), 1807-1808.

The modern master of the Nordic Mythicists is:

Gobineau, Comte Arthur de: *Essai sur l'Inégalité des Races Humaines,* Paris, Didot, 4 vols., 1853-1855.

In the same line of passionate fuliginous thought:

Chamberlain, Houston Stewart: *The Foundations of the Nineteenth Century,* 2 vols., Dodd, Mead & Company, 1912.

Discussed by:

Hertz, Friedrich: *Race and Civilization,* The Macmillan Company, 1928.

Grant, Madison: *The Passing of the Great Race,* Charles Scribner's Sons, 1916.

Stoddard, T. Lothrop: *Racial Realities in Europe,* Charles Scribner's Sons, 1924.

Stoddard, T. Lothrop: *The Rising Tide of Color Against White World Supremacy,* Charles Scribner's Sons, 1920.

McDougall, William: *Is America Safe for Democracy?* Charles Scribner's Sons, 1921. (A great psychologist in strangely . . . entertaining company.)

For a less inspired but more reliable approach:

Ripley, William Z.: *The Races of Europe,* D. Appleton & Company, 1899 (many later editions). (Still a very convenient compilation of facts and a capital presentation of problems.)

Pittard, Eugène: *Race and History: an Ethnological Introduction to History,* Alfred A. Knopf, 1926.

Boas, Franz: *The Cephalic Index,* American Anthropologist, New York, Vol. I, 1899.

Boas, Franz: *Anthropology and Modern Life,* W. W. Norton & Company, Inc., 1928.

Anthropology leads to the still more dangerous field of:

RACE PSYCHOLOGY AND ETHNOPSYCHOLOGY

Garth, Thomas Russell: *Race Psychology: a Study of Racial Mental Differences,* McGraw-Hill Book Company, Inc., 1931.

Porteus, Stanley David: *Temperament and Race,* Boston, R. G. Badger, 1926.

Porteus, Stanley David: *Race and Social Differences,* Clark University Press, 1930.

Fouillée, Alfred: *Psychologie du Peuple Français,* Paris, Félix Alcan, 1898.

Fouillée, Alfred: *Esquisse Psychologique des Peuples Européens,* Paris, Félix Alcan, 1902.

Le Bon, Dr. Gustave: *The Psychology of Peoples, its Influence on their Evolution,* London, 1899.

Lacombe, Paul: *La Psychologie des Individus et des Sociétés chez Taine, Historien des Littératures,* Paris, Félix Alcan, 1906.

Brownell, William Cary: *French Traits,* Charles Scribner's Sons, 1908.

Cf. supra: Perry, Bliss: *The American Mind;* and *The American Spirit.*

Huntington, Ellsworth: *The Character of Races As influenced by Physical Environment, Natural Selection and Historical Development,* Charles Scribner's Sons, 1925.

Madariaga, Salvador de: *Englishmen, Frenchmen, Spaniards: an Essay in Comparative Psychology,* Oxford University Press, 1931.

PHYSICAL ENVIRONMENT

The ancestor (in modern times) of the "Doctrine of Climates" is:

Bodin, Jean: *Les Six Livres de la République,* Genève, Cartier, 1599. (First edition: 1576.)

And the most famous early exponent is:

Montesquieu, Charles Louis de Secondat: *L'Esprit des Lois,* 1748.

Huntington, Ellsworth: *Civilization and Climate,* New Haven, Yale University Press, 1915.

Cf. supra his: *Character of Races,* Charles Scribner's Sons, 1925.

Febvre, Lucien: *A Geographical Introduction to History,*
Alfred A. Knopf, 1925. (Good working bibliography.)

THE COMMUNITY: POLITICAL, SOCIAL, ECONOMIC ENVIRONMENT

(a) *Literature and Democracy*

The general surveys of Society listed at the beginning of
these Notes have much to contribute to this question;
usually in a very pessimistic spirit.

Cf. also McDougall, William: *Is America Safe for Democracy?* Charles Scribner's Sons, 1921.

Gummere, Francis Barton: *Democracy and Poetry,* Boston, Houghton Mifflin Company, 1911.

(b) *Literature and Social Classes*

will be studied in greater detail in Parts II and III.

(c) *Literature and Economics*

Morris, William: *Lectures on Socialism:* "Art under
Plutocracy", 1883; "Art and Socialism", 1884. *Collected
Works,* XXIII, Longmans Green and Co., 1915.

Matthews, Brander: "The Economic Interpretation of
Literary History", in: *Gateways to Literature,* Charles
Scribner's Sons, 1912.

Sinclair, Upton: *Our Bourgeois Literature, the Reason
and the Remedy,* 31 pp. Chicago, Kerr. No date.

Sinclair, Upton: *The Cry for Justice: an Anthology of the
Literature of Social Protest,* Philadelphia, The John C.
Winston Co., 1915.

Sinclair, Upton: *Mammonart, an Essay in Economic Interpretation,* Pasadena, the Author, 1925.

Cf. Calverton, Victor F.: *The Liberation of American Literature,* and Hicks, Granville: *The Great Tradition.*

(d) *Literature and (Russian) Marxism*

Strachey, John: *Literature and Dialectical Materialism,* Covici Friede, 1934. (In bulk, a pamphlet; in purport, a treatise. Strachey has little to say; but, for that little, he has an audience—favorable or antagonistic.)

Trotsky, Leon: *Literature and Revolution,* International Publishers, 1925. (A difficult, unconvincing book, but full of hints and glimpses.)

T. S. Eliot gave an interesting commentary on the above and on Calverton's "Liberation of American Literature" in his *Criterion,* January, 1933.

Freeman, Joseph, *et al.: Voices of October: Art and Literature in Soviet Russia,* The Vanguard Press, 1930.

Reavey, George, and Slonim, Marc: *Soviet Literature: An Anthology,* Covici Friede Books, 1934.

Eastman, Max: *Artists in Uniform: a Study in Literature and Bureaucratism,* Alfred A. Knopf, 1934. The former editor of *The Masses* brings a scathing indictment, not of the Socialistic, but of the Totalitarian State. In the same spirit, *cf.:*

Fabbri, Luce: *Camisas Negras,* Buenos Aires, Nervio, 1934. (Chapter V: "Las Dictaduras y la Cultura"; a fine, although partisan, contribution from an unexpected source.)

(e) *Literature and Utopia*

The problem of Literature and Society from a different time-angle:

Huxley, Aldous: "The Boundaries of the Promised Land",
London, *Fortnightly Review,* December 1930: "The
Boundaries of Utopia", *Virginia Quarterly Review,*
January 1931.

Krutch, Joseph Wood: "Literature and Utopia", in: *Was
Europe a Success?* Farrar & Rinehart, Incorporated,
1934.

This, of course, barely touches upon The Literature of
Utopia, which is boundless. *Cf.:*

Mumford, Lewis: *The Story of Utopias,* Boni and Liveright, 1922.

Russell, Mrs. Frances Theresa: *Touring Utopia; the Realm
of Constructive Humanism,* Dial Press, Lincoln Mc-
Veagh, 1932.

TRADITION

(a) *Tradition,* in the meaning of *that which survives,*
is obviously the basis of all literary history, and needs no
special illustration. However, we may mention as typical:

Wendell, Barrett: *The Traditions of European Literature.
From Homer to Dante,* Charles Scribner's Sons, 1920.

Engel, Eduard: *Was bleibt? Die Welt-Literatur,* Leipzig,
Koehler & Amelang, 1928. (Contains also a statement
and brief treatment of general problems.)

Buck, Philo Melvin: *The Golden Thread,* The Macmillan Company, 1931.

(b) The spirit of *Tradition* as *the Wisdom of Prejudice,*
a reaction against the rationalism of the eighteenth century, is best expounded in:

Burke, Edmund: *Reflections on the French Revolution,*
1790. This attitude, which was *not* traditional in Eng-

land at the time, dominated the nineteenth century. It merged with the Nationalism of Herder (q.v.) and— *longo intervallo*—with that of Maurice Barrès. On Barrès, *cf.*:

Curtius, Robert Ernst: *Maurice Barrès und die geistigen Grundlagen des Französischen Nationalismus,* F. Cohen, Bonn, 1921.

Guérard, Albert: *Five Masters of French Romance,* Charles Scribner's Sons, 1916.

(c) *Tradition* as *the Key to Order:* a very different conception from the above, although not irreconcilable with it. Already clear in:

Arnold, Matthew: *Culture and Anarchy,* 1869. Best exemplified in the Neo-Classicists, Neo-Humanists and Neo-Thomists.

Brownell, William Cary: *Criticism,* Charles Scribner's Sons, 1914.

Brownell, William Cary: *Standards,* Charles Scribner's Sons, 1917.

More, Paul Elmer: *Shelburne Essays,* Boston, G. P. Putnam's Sons, 1904 *seq.: The Greek Tradition,* 5 vols., 1917–1927. (Philosophical.)

Foerster, Norman: *The American Scholar; a Study in Litterae Inhumaniores,* University of North Carolina Press, 1929.

Foerster, Norman (editor): *Humanism and America,* Farrar & Rinehart, Incorporated, 1930. A collective declaration of principles, which called for the counterblast:

Grattan, Clinton Hartley: *The Critique of Humanism; a Symposium,* Harcourt, Brace and Company, 1930.

Foerster, Norman: *Toward Standards,* Farrar and Rinehart, Incorporated, 1930. Appropriately dedicated to Willa Cather and Robert Frost.

Probably the most authoritative of the Traditionalists is:

Eliot, Thomas Stearns: *The Sacred Wood,* London, Messrs. Methuen, 1920. Particularly the essay: "Tradition and the Individual Talent."

Eliot, Thomas Stearns: *Selected Essays,* 1917–1932, London, Faber & Faber, Limited, 1932.

Eliot, Thomas Stearns: *After Strange Gods,* Harcourt Brace and Company, 1934. Also the Collection of his quarterly *The Criterion;* and *The American Review.*

Many of these critics were manifestly influenced by French thought. The French leaders of the movement are Ferdinand Brunetière, Charles Maurras and Jacques Maritain. As channel of this influence *cf.:*

Babbitt, Irving: *The Masters of Modern French Criticism,* Boston, Houghton Mifflin Company, 1912. Particularly Chapter X: "Brunetière", and Chapter XI: "Conclusion", (94 pp.).

(d) *Miscellaneous Connotations of Tradition* will be found in:

Santayana, George: *The Genteel Tradition at Bay,* Charles Scribner's Sons, 1931.

Various Authors: *Tradition and Experiment in Present-Day Literature;* addresses delivered at the City Library Institute, London, Oxford University Press, 1929.

Huxley, Aldous: *Music at Night,* Doubleday, Doran & Company, Inc., 1931.

Hicks, Granville: *The Great Tradition,* The Macmillan Company, 1933.

Part II *Homo Scriptor:* The Author as a Social Type

I. OBJECTIVE STUDIES

Can *Homo Scriptor* be studied from without? Hardly. The purely scientific mind dealing with pure literature is like a blind man discoursing on colors. *Cf.* however a few notable attempts:

Nordau, Max: *Degeneration,* D. Appleton & Company, 1895. (An Epigone of the scientific-realistic age fights a rear guard action against resurgent Romanticism.)
Attempted refutation of the above by:

Shaw, George Bernard: *The Sanity of Art: an Exposure of the Current Nonsense about Artists being Degenerate,* London, Constable & Company, Ltd., 1911. (*Vide infra* under "Genius and Insanity.")

Eastman, Max: *The Literary Mind; its Place in an Age of Science,* Charles Scribner's Son, 1931. (Janus-like, and eloquent with both mouths. Really a defense of true literature against cults and cliques, from Neo-Humanism to Unintelligibility. The unfortunate hero in Huxley's *Brave New World* is a perfect example of "the literary mind and its place in an age of science.")

The experimental approach:

Toulouse, Dr. Edouard: *Emile Zola: Enquête Médico-Psychologique sur les Rapports de la Supériorité Intellectuelle avec la Névropathie. Introduction Générale,* Paris, Société d'Editions Scientifiques, 1896. (Not merely thorough, but absolutely exhaustive.)

Binet, A., and Passy, J.: "Études de Psychologie sur les

421

Auteurs Dramatiques", *Année Psychologique*, I, 1894, pp. 60–175.

Binet, A.: "La Création Littéraire: Portrait Psychologique de Paul Hervieu", *Année Psychologique*, X, p. 162.

Clark, Edwin L.: "American Men of Letters; their Nature and Nurture." *Studies in History, Economics and Public Law*, Vol. 72, Columbia University Press, 1916.

HEREDITY

Galton, Sir Francis: *Hereditary Genius*, D. Appleton & Company, 1891. (First published 1869.)

II. LITERARY DOCUMENTS

The best authority on *Homo Scriptor* is *Homo Scriptor* himself: confessions, memoirs, diaries, letters. The next best is the sympathetic study of literary men by critics who themselves belong to literature. The prototype of self-revealing documents is, of course:

Rousseau, Jean-Jacques: *Confessions* (published 1781–1788).

The literary type par excellence, the Poet, is found in its purity among the major English Romanticists. Blake, however, can not serve as a norm even of the abnormal. Both Coleridge and Wordsworth are partly obscured by a smoke screen of doctrines. The obvious Byronic pose makes it difficult to reach the true Byron. Shelley and Keats are probably the most valuable specimens; Keats at present seems the favorite.

Carpenter, Edward, and Barnefield, George: *Psychology of the Poet Shelley*, E. P. Dutton & Co., Inc., 1925.

Lowell, Amy: *John Keats,* 2 vols., Boston, Houghton Mifflin Company, 1925.

Murry, John Middleton: *Keats and Shakespeare,* Oxford University Press, 1925.

Weller, Earle V.: *The Autobiography of John Keats.* Compiled from his Letters and Essays. Stanford University Press, 1933.

Krutch, Joseph Wood: *Edgar Allen Poe: a Study in Genius,* Alfred A. Knopf, 1926.

Baudelaire, Charles: *Lettres,* 1841–1866, Paris, 1907. (If an antidote were needed against *Les Fleurs du Mal,* none better could be devised than Baudelaire's correspondence. The study of Oscar Wilde is less profitable, because the problem is befogged with irrelevant elements.)

Mumford, Lewis: *Herman Melville,* Harcourt, Brace and Company, 1929.

(After several attempts, the psychological biography of Ambrose Bierce remains to be written. Van Wyck Brooks's *Ordeal of Mark Twain* hovers between the psycho-analytical and the sociological interpretations.)

Moore, George: *Confessions of a Young Man,* Modern Library, 1917.

Moore, George: *Hail and Farewell (Ave, Salve, Vale),* 3 vols., London, William Heinemann, Ltd., 1914–1926. (Almost chemically pure as a literary type. Such purity is not an element of greatness.)

In recent literature, D. H. Lawrence has already become the center of a Golden Legend. None of the books about him compares with:

Huxley, Aldous: *The Letters of D. H. Lawrence, edited*

and with an Introduction by Aldous Huxley, The Viking Press, 1932.

As a fascinating oddity, note:

Symons, Alphonse J. A.: *Frederick Baron Corvo (Frederick Rolfe)*, The Macmillan Company, 1926.

For a better understanding of the pure literary type (the disinterested creative artist), a comparison with the semi-literary may be useful:

Charteris, Sir Evan Edward: *Life and Letters of Sir Edmund Gosse,* Harper & Brothers, 1931. (The perfect "man of letters.")

Bradford, Gamaliel: *The Journal of Gamaliel Bradford,* 1883–1932, edited by Van Wyck Brooks, Boston, Houghton Mifflin Company, 1933. (The tragedy of a "man of letters" whose dream it was to be a creative artist, and who knew the difference.)

Bennett, Arnold: *The Journal of Arnold Bennett,* 1896–1928, The Viking Press, 1933. (A shrewd business man who kept account of every word and every penny.)

Rinehart, Mary Roberts: *My Story,* Farrar & Rinehart, Incorporated, 1931. (Shows how wholesome, good and clever both personality and writing can be, without any claims to "literature.")

WRITING AS A PROFESSION. SOCIAL STANDING OF AUTHORS

Putnam, George Haven: *Authors and their Public in Ancient Times.*

Putnam, George Haven: *Books and their Makers during the Middle Ages,* Vol. I: 476–1600. Vol. II: 1500–1709, G. P. Putnam's Sons, 1896–1897.

Holzknecht, Karl J.: *Literary Patronage in the Middle Ages,* University of Pennsylvania Press, 1923.

Sheavyn, Phoebe: *The Literary Profession in the Elizabethan Age,* Manchester, University Press, 1909.

Beljame, Alexandre: *Le Public et les Hommes de Lettres en Angleterre au XVIIIème Siècle: Dryden, Addison et Pope,* Paris, Hachette et Cie, 1883.

Collins, A. S.: *Authorship in the Days of Johnson,* (Routledge), E. P. Dutton & Co., Inc., 1927.

Collins, A. S.: *The Profession of Letters,* (Routledge), E. P. Dutton & Co., Inc., 1928. (Continues the account of the relationship of authors to their patrons and to publishers from 1780 to 1832.)

Vigny, Alfred de: *Stello, ou les Diables Bleus: Première Consultation du Docteur Noir,* 1832. (A romantic and profound treatment of the theme. Deserves to be better known.)

Cf. also: Part III: "The Public; Society; Groups and Cliques; Publishers."

THE ENIGMA OF GENIUS

Lombroso, Cesare: *The Man of Genius,* London, Walter Scott, 1895 and 1901. (Marked differences between the two editions.) (The vigorous restatement of a very ancient paradox.)

Türck, Hermann: *The Man of Genius,* London, A. & C. Black, Ltd., 1914. (Contains a discussion and refutation of Lombroso.)

Guilbert, Dr. Charles: *L'Envers du Génie: Gérard de*

Cf. also Nordau, Shaw, Toulouse, *supra.*

Nerval, Baudelaire, Alfred de Musset, Rollinat, Paris, Albin Michel, 1927.

Cox, Catharine Morris: *Genetic Studies of Genius:* Vol. II: "The Early Mental Traits of Three Hundred Geniuses", Stanford University Press, 1926.

Marks, Jeannette: *Genius and Disaster,* Adelphi Co., 1925.

Lange-Eichbaum, Wilhelm: *Das Genie-Problem: eine Einführung,* München, Ernst Reinhardt, 1931. *id: The Problem of Genius,* translated by Eden and Cedar Paul, London, Kegan Paul, French, Trubner and Co., Ltd., 1931.

Lange-Eichbaum, Wilhelm: *Genie, Irrsinn und Ruhm,* München, Ernst Reinhardt, 1929. (Perhaps most original and most valuable in its treatment of Fame; but the discussion of Genius and Insanity is remarkably sane.)

Part III The Public

GENERAL

The study of Literature as a branch of social psychology is not yet fully organized; the close kinship in method and spirit between evangelization, education, criticism, propaganda and advertising is hardly ever confessed. It may be advisable therefore, to approach the problem of Public Opinion through political books, and test the results in the literary field.

One of the pioneers in Collective Psychology was the ever-ebullient polygraph:

Le Bon, Dr. Gustave: *The Crowd,* London, T. Fisher Unwin, 1896.

BIBLIOGRAPHY

McDougall, William: *Introduction to Social Psychology*, London, Messrs. Methuen, 1908.

McDougall, William: *Group Mind*, G. P. Putnam's Sons, 1920.

Lippmann, Walter: *Public Opinion*, Harcourt, Brace and Company, 1922.

Lippmann, Walter: *The Phantom Public*, Harcourt Brace and Company, 1925.

Dewey, John: *The Public and its Problems*, Henry Holt and Company, Incorporated, 1927.

Convenient Instruments:

Young, Kimball, and Lawrence, R. B.: "Bibliography on Censorship and Propaganda", *University of Oregon Publication, Journalism Series, I.* No. 1, March 1928.

Young, Kimball: *Social Psychology*, F. S. Crofts & Co., 1930.

Graves, W. Brooke: *Readings in Public Opinion; its Formation and Control*, D. Appleton & Company, 1928.

Childs, H. L.: *A Reference Guide to the Study of Public Opinion*, Princeton, Princeton University Press, 1934.

With special application to Literature:

General:

Schücking, Lewin Ludwig: *Die Soziologie der literarischen Geschmacksbildung*, München, Rosl, 1923.

Cf. Baldensperger, Fernand: *La Littérature, Création, Succès, Durée*, Paris, E. Flammarion, 1913.

Cf. Lange-Eichbaum, Wilhelm: *Genie, Irrsinn und Ruhm*, München, Ernst Reinhardt, 1929.

Blankenship, Russell: *American Literature as Expression of the National Mind* (suggested readings), Henry Holt and Company, Incorporated, 1931.

As special examples of the study of Fame:

Chew, Samuel C.: *Byron in England, his Fame and After-Fame,* Charles Scribner's Sons, 1924.

Blanchard, Frederick: *Fielding the Novelist, a Study in Historical Criticism.* (Vogue, recognition, fame.) New Haven, Yale University Press, 1926.

This method is far more general in Comparative Literature than in the purely national field; *cf.:*

Baldensperger, Fernand: *Goethe en France,* Paris, Hachette et Cie, 1920.

Carré, Jean-Marie: *Goethe en Angleterre,* Paris, E. Plon, Nourrit et Cie, 1920.

"SOCIETY": COURTS AND SALONS

General:

Traill, Henry Duff (editor): *Social England: a Record of the Progress of the People,* etc. 6 vols., G. P. Putnam's Sons, 1894–1902.

Turberville, Arthur Stanley (editor): *Johnson's England: an Account of the Life and Manners of his Age,* 2 vols., Oxford University Press, 1933.

And, of course, Pepys, Evelyn, Boswell, Madame d'Arblay, Chesterfield.

Beljame, Alexandre: *Le Public et les Hommes de Lettres en Angleterre au XVIIIème Siècle: Dryden, Addison et Pope,* Paris, Hachette et Cie, 1883.

Tinker, Chauncey Brewster: *The Salon and English Letters:* Chapters on the "Interrelations of Literature and Society in the age of Johnson", The Macmillan Company, 1915.

Gleichen-Russwurm, Alexander von: *Geselligkeit: Sitten*

und Gebräuche der Europäischen Welt, 1789–1900, Stuttgart, Julius Hoffmann, 1910. (A very agreeable bird's-eye view.)

Recent documents in American literature:

Atherton, Gertrude: *Adventures of a Novelist*, The Liveright Corporation, 1932.

Wharton, Edith: *A Backward Glance*, D. Appleton-Century Company, Inc., 1934. (Reveals perfect indifference of New York "Society" to literature half a century ago.)

Luhan, Mabel Dodge: *Intimate Memories*. Vol. I: "Background", Harcourt Brace and Company, 1933. (Buffalo Society was even more impervious to literature than New York Society.)

The French Salon is an inexhaustible subject. *Cf.* any standard bibliography of French Literature, Lanson, Thieme, Nitze and Dargan, etc. Classic Comedies: *Les Précieuses Ridicules, Les Femmes Savantes*. Edouard Pailleron: *Le Monde ou l'on s'ennuie*, 1881; *cf.* two recent examples:

Pouquet, Jeanne Maurice: *The Last Salon: Anatole France and his Muse*, Harcourt, Brace and Company, 1927. (Why "the last?")

Daudet, Léon: "Salons et Journaux" in: *Souvenirs des Milieux Littéraires, Politiques, Artistiques et Médicaux*, 2 vols., Paris, Nouvelle Librairie Nationale, 1920–1926.

And many indications in Marcel Proust: *À la Recherche du Temps Perdu*.

LITERARY SOCIETY: GROUPS, CLUBS, BOHEMIANISM

Allen, Robert J.: *The Clubs of Augustan London*, Harvard University Press, 1933.

Shelley, Henry Charles: *Inns and Taverns of Old London*, London, Sir Isaac Pitman & Sons, Ltd., 1909. ("Setting forth the historical and literary associations of those ancient hostelries, together with an account of the most notable coffee-houses, clubs and pleasure gardens of the British Metropolis.")

The most extensive document on the social aspects of literary life:

Goncourt, Edmond de: *Journal des Goncourt, Mémoires de la Vie Littéraire*, Paris, Charpentier, 1891 *seq.* (Several volumes still unpublished.)

Parry, Albert: *Garrets and Pretenders: a History of Bohemianism in America*, (extensive bibliography), Covici Friede, 1933.

Howells, William Dean: *Literary Friends and Acquaintances; a Personal Retrospect of American Authorship*, Harper & Brothers, 1901.

Garland, Hamlin: *Roadside Meetings*, 1930.

——— *Companions of the Trail*, 1931.

——— *My Friendly Contemporaries; a Literary Log*, 1932. All three, The Macmillan Company.

Emerson, Edward Waldo: *The Early Years of the Saturday Club*, 1855–1870, Boston, Houghton Mifflin Company, 1918.

Howe, M. A. DeWolfe: *Later Years of the Saturday Club*, 1870–1920, Boston, Houghton Mifflin Company, 1927.

Van Vechten, Carl: *Peter Whiffle, his Life and Work*, Alfred A. Knopf, 1927. (An amusing and innocuous satire of certain American cliques at home and abroad.)

Anderson, Margaret: *My Thirty Years' War,* Covici Friede, 1930. (Strenuous liveliness.)

Stein, Gertrude: *The Autobiography of Alice B. Toklas,* Harcourt Brace and Company, 1933.

Burdett, Osbert: *The Beardsley Period, an Essay in Perspective,* Boni & Liveright, 1925.

Cf. Smith, Cedric Ellsworth: *The Yellow Book; a Selection,* Hartford, Edwin Valentine Mitchell, 1928.

Cf. Beer, Thomas: *The Mauve Decade,* Alfred A. Knopf, 1926.

Rascoe, Burton: *"Smart Set" History: Introduction to "Smart Set" Anthology,* Reynal and Hitchcock, 1934.

Nathan, George Jean: *Intimate Notebooks,* Alfred A. Knopf, 1932.

Clark, Emily: *Innocence Abroad,* Alfred A. Knopf, 1931. (Little magazine *The Reviewer,* Richmond.)

THE BOOK TRADE AND ITS INFLUENCE UPON LITERATURE

Cheney, O. H.: *Economic Survey of the Book Industry,* 1930–1931, National Association of Book Publishers, 1932.

Grasset, Bernard: *La Chose Littéraire,* Paris, N.R.F. (Gallimard), 1929.

Duffus, Robert L.: *Books, their place in a Democracy,* Boston, Houghton Mifflin Company, 1930.

Swinnerton, Frank: *Authors and the Book Trade,* Alfred A. Knopf, 1932.

Page, Walter Hines: *A Publisher's Confession,* Doubleday, Page & Co., 1905.

(*Cf.* Hendrick, Burton Jesse: *The Life and Letters of*

Walter H. Page, 3 vols., Doubleday, Page & Co., 1922–25.)

Unwin, Stanley: *The Truth about Publishing,* London, George Allen & Unwin, Ltd.

McClure, Samuel Sidney: *My Autobiography,* F. A. Stokes Company, 1914.

Holt, Henry: *Garrulities of an Octogenarian Editor. With Other Essays Somewhat Biographical and Autobiographical,* Houghton Mifflin Company, 1923.

Tooker, Frank L.: *Joys and Tribulations of an Editor,* The Century Company, 1924.

Whyte, Frederick: *William Heinemann,* London, Jonathan Cape, Ltd., 1928.

Doran, George H.: *Chronicles of Barabbas,* Harcourt, Brace and Company, 1935.

INDEX *

* CAPITALS: topics. *Italics:* titles of books. Small Roman: proper names.

433

447

449

INDEX

Rudolf Aschenauer

KRIEG OHNE GRENZEN

Der Partisanenkampf gegen Deutschland 1939–1945

RUDOLF ASCHENAUER

Krieg ohne Grenzen

Der Partisanenkampf gegen Deutschland 1939–1945

DRUFFEL-VERLAG
LEONI AM STARNBERGER SEE

Schutzumschlag H. O. Pollähne, Braunschweig

D
802
A2
A8
1982
Dec.1991

Internationale Standard Buchnummer
ISBN 3 8061 1017 4

Inhaltsverzeichnis

Einleitung

Louis de Jong hielt am 24. Mai 1956 anläßlich einer Tagung des Instituts für Zeitgeschichte in München über das Thema ,,Zwischen Kollaboration und Résistance" einen Vortrag. In ihm bedauert er, daß nicht genügend Unterlagen über den Widerstand vorhanden sind.

De Jong bringt zum Ausdruck: ,,Die lückenlosesten dokumentarischen Unterlagen über den europäischen Widerstand hätten wir bei den Akten des Reichssicherheits-Hauptamtes, der Abwehr und der Geheimen Feldpolizei finden können, soweit sie Hitlers Werkzeuge in seinem Kampf gegen den Widerstand waren. Wie glücklich würden wir uns schätzen, wenn wir die wöchentlichen Meldungen vollständig besitzen würden, die aufgrund aller vom Staatssicherheitsdienst gesammelten Nachrichten zusammengestellt wurden. Das sich hieraus ergebende Bild würde zwar nicht in allem der Wirklichkeit entsprechen, aber es würde sich schon lohnen, es näher zu betrachten. Und welch ein Segen wäre es, wenigstens für uns, wenn die Archive aller Büros und Organisationen zugänglich würden, die auf seiten der Alliierten und der Russen während des Krieges die Aufgabe hatten, die Flammen des Aufruhrs zu entfachen. Es ist unmöglich, eine ernsthafte Geschichte der Partisanenbewegung in den von den Deutschen besetzten Teilen Rußlands zu schreiben, ohne daß man Kenntnis von den Dokumenten des Moskauer Büros hat, das in ständigem Kontakt mit Teilen dieser Bewegung stand. Unsere Kenntnis des westeuropäischen Widerstandes wird lückenhaft bleiben, solange die Akten von Organisationen wie des American Office of Strategic Service, der British Political Warfare Executive und der Special Operations Executive geheim bleiben."

Das größte Interesse an den Unterlagen des europäischen Widerstandes gegen Hitler müßten die Deutschen selbst haben. In den deutschen Landen werden Prozesse mit dem Hintergrund der Jahre 1939–1945 geführt, ohne daß die Gerichte im Besitz ausreichender Unterlagen sind. Ohne Gesamtzusammenhänge zu überblicken, kann man sich kein sicheres Urteil erlauben.

Louis de Jong nennt eine Reihe von Fundstätten. Ich könnte noch mehr aufzählen. Zur Einsicht wären aber auch die Dokumente der jüdischen Institute erforderlich. Das Londoner Foreign Office müßte die gesperrten Dokumente zum Fall Rudolf Heß freigeben.

Solange viele Quellen verschlossen sind, ist nur ein Versuch möglich, eine Arbeit über den ,,Krieg ohne Grenzen" zu schreiben, in welcher die Themen der modernen Kriegführung, des Partisanen- und Untergrundkrieges behandelt und Aktionen der Nachrichtendienste nicht ausgeklammert werden.

Thesen der Sowjetzone

Die Ostberliner Regierung behauptet, daß sie durch ihre Politik, Gesetzgebung und Rechtsprechung ständig ihre Verpflichtungen aus der internationalen Rechtslage erfüllt. Sie kommt auf die Grundsätze zurück, die im Potsdamer Abkommen vom 2. August 1945, im Londoner Vier-Mächte-Abkommen vom 8. Aug. 1945 und dessen Bestandteil, dem Statut für den Internationalen Militärgerichtshof, zum Ausdruck kommen. Weiter bezieht sie sich auf die Konvention über die Nichtanwendbarkeit von Verjährungsbestimmungen auf ,,Kriegsverbrechen und auf Verbrechen gegen die Menschlichkeit" vom 26. Nov. 1968, die von der XXIII. Tagung der Vollversammlung der Vereinten Nationen beschlossen wurde und am 11. Okt. 1970 in Kraft getreten ist.

Als These wird dabei herausgestellt: ,,Der deutsche Imperialismus und Militarismus hatte am 1. Sept. 1939 mit dem Überfall faschistischer Truppen auf Polen den Zweiten Weltkrieg entfesselt. Einen bestehenden Nichtangriffspakt zerreißend, erfolgte dann am 22. Juni 1941 entsprechend Hitlers Weisung Nr. 21 (Fall Barbarossa) vom 18. Dez. 1940 der überraschende Überfall auf die Sowjetunion, das Haupthindernis für die Eroberung und Weltherrschaftspläne des deutschen Imperialismus, die zugleich den Klassenzielen der reaktionären Kräfte des Weltimperialismus entsprachen und einen Versuch darstellten, über den Erdball wieder die ungeteilte Herrschaft des Kapitalismus herzustellen. Der faschistische deutsche Imperialismus wollte die durch den Ersten Weltkrieg verlorene Machtposition zurückgewinnen, diesmal mit ,tauglicheren' Mitteln große Teile der Welt erobern, dabei ganze Völker ausrotten und den ersten sozialistischen Staat vernichten. Obwohl diese Ziele mit verschiedensten ökonomischen, politischen und ideologischen Mitteln angestrebt wurden, war der bewaffnete Kampf ein Hauptelement der faschistischen deutschen Weltherrschaftspläne, die zusammen mit uferlosen Kriegszielen, abenteuerlichem militärischem Denken, Antikommunismus und Rassismus auf das engste von vornherein mit der Bereitschaft verbunden waren, sich bei diesem bewaffneten Kampf über alle Normen des Völker- und Kriegsrechts und der Kriegführung hinwegzusetzen. Hauptbestandteile der Militärdoktrin des faschistischen deutschen Imperialismus waren die Lehren vom totalen Krieg und die sogenannte Blitzkriegstheorie, was nichts anderes als die rücksichtsloseste Kriegführung und Einsatz aller Mittel bedeutet, wobei die Wehrmacht von Anfang an ein Instrument der barbarischen Kriegführung des deutschen Imperialismus und Militarismus war. Die beabsichtigte Liquidierung der UdSSR war der Kern der geplanten faschistischen ,Neuordnung' im europäischen und asiatischen Raum. Als Teil dieser ‚Neuordnung‘ sah der am 12. Juni 1942 verabschiedete Generalplan Ost die Ausrottung von Millionen Polen, Ukrainern u. a. slawischen Völkern sowie die Kolonialisierung Osteuropas vor. Sie bedeutete militärisch und politisch, daß andere Staaten oder Staatsgebiete in das faschistische Deutsche Reich einverleibt bzw. – wie der europäische Teil der Sowjetunion – in deutsche Kolonialgebiete verwandelt werden sollten; ökonomisch, um die Wirtschaft der okkupierten Gebiete dem deutschen Finanzkapital unterzuordnen und die schonungsloseste Ausbeutung und völlige Entrechtung der Werktätigen zum Zwecke der Erzielung von Höchstprofiten zu betreiben . . .

Die faschistische Okkupationspolitik, die durch die Wehrmacht gemeinsam mit den verschiedensten Monopol- und Staatsorganen verwirklicht wurde, hatte die Versklavung, Ausplünderung und Ausrottung ganzer Nationen und Bevölkerungsgruppen zum Ziel.

Der deutsche faschistische Imperialismus bereitete den Krieg gegen die Sowjetunion als Vernichtungskrieg gegen dieses Land und seine Völker vor und führte ihn entsprechend dieser Zielsetzung. Der Krieg gegen die Sowjetunion war inhaltlich primär ein Klassenkrieg des Imperialismus gegen den Sozialismus . . .

Als ein ungerechter Krieg zweier imperialistischer Koalitionen um die Neuaufteilung der Welt begonnen, verwandelte sich der Zweite Weltkrieg durch die aktive Teilnahme der Völker und schließlich 1941 durch den Kriegseintritt der Sowjetunion endgültig in einen gerechten antifaschistischen Befreiungskampf. In diesem Kampf entwickelten sich, auch im Hinterland der faschistischen Armeen, starke, ständig anwachsende, nationale Befreiungs- und Partisanenbewegungen, die, auf das Volk gestützt, um die Befreiung des Heimatlandes rangen.“

[Zitate aus der Urteilsbegründung eines Gerichtes der „DDR“]

Vom Krieg und seinen Methoden

Seit Jahrhunderten leben die Menschen in Zeiten der Spannungen und Wandlungen. Hinter uns liegen Jahrhunderte unerhörter technischer Entwicklung. In der Renaissancezeit wurden die Menschen sehend. Von hier spannt sich ein weiter Bogen des Fortschrittes, der für die Zukunft sehr gefährlich werden kann. Dieser Fortschritt wurde in der Literatur schon als ,,Todesengel" bezeichnet.

Weltreiche entstanden; Weltreiche gingen unter. Neue Ideologien traten hervor aus dem Dunkel, um bald wieder in die Nacht zu verschwinden und durch neue ersetzt zu werden. Auch die Kriegführung war dem Wandel unterworfen. Die kriegerischen Auseinandersetzungen wurden umfassender, grausamer. Die Technik gab ihnen immer größere zerstörerische Kraft.

Das Buch ,,Der Krieg ohne Grenzen" behandelt nicht das Thema des gerechten Krieges mit seinen Problemen. Es soll auch nicht Angriffs- oder Verteidigungskrieg in den Vordergrund gestellt werden. Beschrieben wird die Entwicklung zum totalen und globalen Krieg, das Zusammenwirken der verschiedensten Elemente in ihm und die Wirkung in der Umwelt. Wenn wir die neueste Zeit mit dem Mittelalter vergleichen, so zeigt sich eine bemerkenswerte Parallele. Kriegsregeln- und gebräuche werden je nach dem Gegner und dessen Weltanschauung verschieden angewandt.

Vor Beginn des deutsch-sowjetischen Krieges hielt Adolf Hitler vor der Generalität in der Reichskanzlei eine Rede. Generalstabschef Halder notierte im Zusammenhang mit den Ausführungen des Staatschefs am 30. März 1941:

,,Kampf zweier Weltanschauungen gegeneinander. Vernichtendes Urteil über Bolschewismus, ist gleich asoziales Verbrechertum, Kommunismus ungeheuere Gefahr für die Zukunft. Wir müssen von dem Standpunkt des soldatischen Kameradentums abrücken. Der Kommunist ist vorher kein Kamerad und nachher kein Kamerad. Es handelt sich um einen Vernichtungskampf. Wenn wir es nicht so auffassen, werden wir zwar den Feind schlagen, aber in 30 Jahren wird uns wieder der kommunistische Feind gegenüberstehen ... Es muß verhindert werden, daß eine neue Intelligenz sich bildet. Hier genügt eine primitive sozialistische Intelligenz ...

Im Osten ist Härte mild für die Zukunft." Generaloberst Halder unterzeichnete am 3. April 1941 einen Befehl, in welchem ausgeführt wird: ,,Aktiver oder passiver Widerstand der Zivilbevölkerung ist mit scharfen Strafmaßnahmen im Keime zu ersticken. Selbstbewußtes und rücksichtsloses Auftreten gegenüber den deutschfeindlichen Elementen wird ein wirksames Vorbeugungsmittel sein."

Am 6. Juni 1941 übersandte General Warlimont an das Oberkommando des Heeres und das Oberkommando der Luftwaffe zur Weiterleitung einen Befehl, in welchem ausgeführt wird: ,,Im Kampf gegen den Bolschewismus ist mit dem Verhalten des Feindes nach den Grundsätzen der Menschlichkeit oder des Völkerrechts nicht zu rechnen. Insbesondere ist von den politischen Kommissaren aller Art als den eigentlichen Trägern des Widerstandes eine haßerfüllte, grausame und unmenschliche Behandlung unserer Gefangenen zu erwarten . . .

Die Urheber barbarisch-asiatischer Kampfmethoden sind die politischen Kommissare. Gegen diese muß daher sofort und ohne weiteres mit aller Schärfe vorgegangen werden. Sie sind daher, wenn im Kampf oder Widerstand ergriffen, grundsätzlich sofort mit der Waffe zu erledigen.''

Generalfeldmarschall Erich von Manstein, Oberbefehlshaber der 11. Armee, führte in einem Befehl aus:

,,Seit dem 22. Juni steht das deutsche Volk in einem Kampf auf Leben und Tod gegen das bolschewistische System. Dieser Kampf wird nicht in hergebrachter Form gegen die sowjetische Wehrmacht allein nach europäischen Kriegsregeln geführt. Auch hinter der Front wird weitergekämpft . . . Das Judentum bildet den Mittelsmann zwischen dem Feind im Rücken und den noch kämpfenden Resten der Roten Armee und der Roten Führung. Es hält stärker als in Europa alle Schlüsselpunkte der politischen Führung und Verwaltung, des Handels und des Handwerks besetzt und bildet weiter die Zelle für alle Unruhen und möglichen Erhebungen. Das jüdisch-bolschewistische System muß ein für allemal ausgerottet werden. Nie wieder darf es in unseren europäischen Lebensraum eingreifen . . .

Für die Notwendigkeit der harten Sühne am Judentum, dem geistigen Träger des bolschewistischen Terrors, muß der Soldat Verständnis aufbringen. Sie ist auch notwendig, um alle Erhebungen, die meist von Juden angezettelt werden, im Keime zu ersticken.''

Zu dem gleichen Zeitpunkt entwickelte der Oberbefehlshaber der 17. Armee, Generaloberst Hermann Hoth, folgende Gedankengänge in einem Befehl:

,,Es ist uns in diesem Sommer immer klarer geworden, daß hier im Osten innerlich unüberbrückbare Anschauungen gegeneinander kämpfen; deutsches Ehr- und Rassegefühl, jahrhundertealtes Soldatentum und asiatische Denkungsart . . .

Klar erkennen wir unsere Sendung, die europäische Kultur zu retten vor dem Vordringen asiatischer Barbarei. Wir wissen jetzt, daß wir gegen einen erbitterten und zähen Gegner zu kämpfen haben. Dieser Kampf kann nur mit der Vernichtung des einen oder des anderen enden; einen Ausgleich gibt es nicht.''

Bemerkenswert ist, daß der Armeeoberbefehlshaber, General Heinrich von Stülpnagel, am 30. Juli 1941 einen Befehl unterschrieb, der verlangte, wenn im Falle von Sabotage oder Angriffen auf Armeeangehörige die Täter nicht festgestellt werden könnten, sollten zur Vergeltung Juden oder Kommunisten, besonders jüdische Komsomolzen erschossen werden.

Wenn wir die Neuzeit mit dem Mittelalter vergleichen, so gibt es eine Übereinstimmung darin:

Mit welchen Gegnern Krieg geführt wird.

Den Krieg mit den Sowjets betrachtete Hitler als Weltanschauungskrieg.

Im christlichen Mittelalter gibt es Versuche der Kirche, die Kriegsgebräuche zu mildern.

Gregor IX. sprach sich gegen den ,,Gebrauch von Maschinen geschleuderter Geschosse" aus.

Der Ehrencodex des Rittertums schrieb Ritterlichkeit gegen den Gegner vor, der desselben Glaubens und des gleichen Standes war.

Der Völkerrechtler Nys weist darauf hin, daß im Mittelalter der Krieg den Charakter unerhörter Grausamkeit hatte. Gefangene wurden verstümmelt, Ländereien verwüstet, Städte zerstört und sonstige unerhörte Greuel begangen. Dies war insbesondere in den Kreuzzügen und auch gegen politische Gegner der Päpste der Fall. Unrichtig ist die Auffassung, daß in den Urzeiten die souveränen Großfamilien den größten Teil ihrer Geschichte mit Krieg ausfüllten. Ein Eroberungskrieg war fast ausgeschlossen. Die Beziehungen waren meistens friedlicher Natur.

In der Antike gab es Beschränkungen der Kriegführung durch Sitte und Moral. Grausam waren die Assyrer, milde die Inder. In seinem Werk ,,Die politische Philosophie des Altertums" schreibt Stanka, daß sich der assyrische König Assurnasipal rühmte: ,,Die Stadt eroberte ich, warf 800 ihrer Kämpfer mit den Waffen nieder, ihre Köpfe schnitt ich ab, viele lebende Männer nahm ich gefangen, die übrigen verbrannte ich im Feuer. Ihre reiche Beute führte ich fort. Einen Pfeiler von Lebenden und Köpfen errichtete ich beim Stadttor, 700 Männer spießte ich bei ihrem Stadttore auf Pfähle, zerstörte die Stadt, machte sie zu Schutt und Brachfeld. Ihre Knaben und Mädchen verbrannte ich zu Asche."

In seiner Geschichte des Völkerrechtes hebt Nußbaum hervor: ,,Doch so etwas wie den Codex der Manu oder die Sanftmut der Inder gab es in Griechenland nicht."

Auch die römische Kriegsführung war grausam.

Der arabische Islam kannte Schranken.

Verboten war die Tötung von Frauen und Kindern, die Vergiftung des Trinkwassers und die unnötige Verlängerung des Krieges bis zum Frieden. Hagenbach beschreibt im Band II ,,Kirchengeschichte" das Verhalten Saladins, nachdem er im Jahre 1187 in Jerusalem eingezogen war: „Mit Milde wurden die christlichen Einwohner der Stadt behandelt – dies im beschämenden Gegensatz gegen die Greuel, welche die ersten Kreuzfahrer an den Mohammedanern und Juden ihrer Zeit geübt hatten."

Es ist im Zeitalter der Menschenrechte unverständlich, wenn bei dem militärischen Vorgehen gegen sogenannte „wilde Völkerschaften" die Meinung vertreten wurde, daß die Normen des völkerrechtlichen Kriegsrechtes nicht zu beachten seien. Erst seit den Genfer Konventionen von 1949 gilt der Satz eines humanitären Minimums. Vorher gebrauchte man den Begriff „Expedition" oder „Kolonialkrieg" bei Unterdrückung von „Aufständen". Man sprach von „polizeilichen Erfordernissen in gewissen entfernten Gegenden".

Es sei der Bericht des englischen Luftmarschalls Sir Ellington vom 11. Nov. 1925 über britische Bombenangriffe unter Verwendung von Zeitzündern im Wazistan beachtet. Die englische Luftwaffe griff größere Dörfer, reine Höhlenwohnungen, zerstreute Hütten und Einfriedungen ohne jegliche Bedeutung an.

In dem Werk „A Digest of International Law" (Band VII) gibt Moore den Befehl Washingtons an General Sullivan wieder:

„But you will not by any means listen to overture of peace before the total ruin of their settlement is effected . . .

Our future security will be in their inability to injure us, the distance to which they are driven, and in the terror with which the severity of the chastisessement they service will inspire them."

*

Heute unterscheiden wir zwischen einem Krieg mit konventionellen Waffen und einem Atomkrieg. Während bei einer konventionellen Kriegführung rechtliche Beschränkungen noch möglich erscheinen, ist dies bei einer nuklearen kaum zu erwarten. Der Versuch einer kriegsvölkerrechtlichen Regelung erscheint bei einer massenweisen Herstellung und Bereitschaft zur Verwendung der Atom- und Wasserstoffbombe sinnlos. Es gibt in einem solchen absoluten Krieg noch weniger als im Zweiten Weltkrieg die Unterscheidung zwischen Kombattanten und Nichtkombattanten. Bedauerlich ist, daß die Rechtsverletzungen der Siegermächte im Zweiten Weltkrieg, die auf dem Gebiet des See- und Luftkriegsrechtes liegen, nicht im erforderlichen Ausmaß gewürdigt wurden. Dies gilt auch für das Thema Untergrund- und Partisanenkrieg.

Man könnte den Schluß ziehen, daß das gesamte Kriegsrecht eine Illusion darstellt.

Damit soll die Bedeutung des großen Holländers Hugo Grotius nicht herabgesetzt werden, der versuchte, für die Neuordnung der Gesellschaft allgemeine Grundsätze rechtlich-politischer Art zu entwickeln.

Sven Hedin erwähnt in seinem Buch „Jerusalem", das 1928 erschienen ist, daß Napoleon 1799 bei Jaffa die Erschießung von 3000 türkischen Kriegsgefangenen anordnete, weil er nicht in der Lage war, sie zu verpflegen. Er wollte sie nicht freilassen. Deshalb befahl er, daß kein einziger mit dem Leben davonkommen dürfe. Diese Handlung ist charakteristisch für einen Mann, der am 26. Juni 1813 in Dresden zu Fürst Metternich sagte: „Die Heerfahrt nach Moskau hat mich 300 000 Mann gekostet, aber es waren keine 30 000 Franzosen dabei" (Quelle: Helfert „Marie Luise", Wien 1873, Seite 386).

In der Zeit Napoleons war auch von Clausewitz, dessen Denkungsart über das militärische Fachgebiet hinaus wirksam wurde, tätig. Von Bedeutung wurden seine Gedanken über die Volksbewaffnung, den „Bandenkrieg", den Widerstand und den möglichen Erfolg bei Mißverhältnissen. Der russische Widerstand im Jahre 1812 gegen Napoleon wurde die Grundlage seines Denkens. Hätte der große Korse von seiner Militärmacht von 600 000 Mann – so argumentiert von Clausewitz – noch 250 000 zurückgebracht, so hätte er nicht den Mißerfolg erlitten, der tatsächlich eintrat.

Mit Recht führte ein deutscher Offizier 1944 in einer alten deutschen Hansestadt aus: „Der Krieg ist nach Clausewitz kein losgelöstes Fachgebiet, sondern er ist nur ein Mittel der Politik, und er ist von ihr abhängig. Nicht nur kriegerische Mittel wirken sich im Kriege aus und führen zu kriegerischen Erkenntnissen innerhalb der kriegerischen Handlung; von Clausewitz erlebt schöpferisch, daß die Politik den Krieg entscheidend bestimmt. Die politische Elementarkraft der Französischen Revolution bricht durch die alte Welt des veralteten Kriegswesens der dynastischen Zeit . . . Eine ganz neue, durch die Politik bedingte Kriegskraft tritt auf . . ."

Für Clausewitz ist eine Verteidigung an sich, losgelöst von der „Lebensganzheit", nur Erstarrung und ein leerer Begriff, starr wie der Tod. Gegenüber der Erstarrung ist der äußerste Grad der Verteidigung der Rückzug in das Innere des Landes mit dem hiermit verbundenen Zeitgewinn. Durch Zeitgewinn und Rückzug bestimmt der Verteidiger für die Gesamthandlung den besten Zeitpunkt und den günstigsten Raum, von dem er zur Offensive antreten kann. Dieses Mittel wandten die Russen 1812 gegen Napoleon an. Auch gegen Hitler wurde es ein wirksames Mittel der sowjetischen Kriegführung zur Herbeiführung seiner Niederlage.

Die strategische und die taktische Verteidigung verlangt nach Clausewitz nicht nur vom Soldaten die höchsten seelischen Kräfte, sondern auch vom Volke. In klarer Erkenntnis formuliert der von mir erwähnte Verfasser die Arbeit über Clausewitz: „Ein gesunder und kräftiger Widerstandswille gehört nach Clausewitz dazu, wenn die Bewohner des Landes den Feind nicht mit Angst erwarten, sondern mit Selbstvertrauen, mit ruhiger Besonnenheit und mit der Notwendigkeit ihres Lebenskampfes." Clausewitz ist der Anschauung, daß der Krieg durch Napoleon dem Wesen des absoluten Krieges nahegekommen ist. Nach ihm muß der kriegerische Akt in einer „Welt der Totalerscheinung" gesehen werden. Der Krieg ist ein Teil eines Ganzen, das man Politik nennt. Clausewitz schreibt: „Es ist überhaupt nichts so wichtig im Leben, als genau den Standpunkt auszumitteln, von welchem die Dinge aufgefaßt und beurteilt werden müssen, und an diesem festzuhalten. Denn nur von einem Standpunkt aus können wir die Erscheinungen mit Einheit auffassen, und nur die Einheit des Standpunktes kann uns vor Widersprüchen sichern!"

Der Zweite Weltkrieg schuf neue Dimensionen in der Kriegführung: Die sozialrevolutionäre Methode des Partisanenkrieges und der Einsatz aus dem Luftraum. Professor Carl Schmitt machte über diese Entwicklung in seinen Arbeiten „Das Raumbild des nach Land und Meer getrennten Kriegsschauplatzes", „Wandel der Kriegsschauplätze" und in „Der Nomos der Erde" (Verlag Duncker und Humblot) grundlegende Ausführungen.

Im Ersten Weltkrieg traten auf dem Meere die U-Boote auf, im Zweiten Weltkrieg entstand der Krieg aus der Luft mit der Atom-Bombe auf Hiroshima und Nagasaki und den Raketen V 1 und V 2. Wir wissen zwar, daß der Partisan, an ein Nachrichtennetz angeschlossen, mit Maschinenpistolen, Handgranaten und Plastikbomben arbeitete. Doch aus der Luft wurde er mit Waffen und Nahrungsmitteln versorgt. Besteht die Möglichkeit, daß er in Zukunft mit taktischen Atomwaffen arbeiten kann? Dies würde ihn zur Schlüsselfigur der Weltgeschichte machen.

In Vorträgen am 15. März in Pamplona und am 17. März 1962 in der Universität Saragossa entwickelte Schmitt bemerkenswerte Gedankengänge. Diese sind so wertvoll, daß sie nachstehend wiedergegeben werden: „Lenin hat den begrifflichen Schwerpunkt vom Krieg auf die Politik, d. h. auf die Unterscheidung von Freund und Feind verlagert. Das war sinnvoll und nach Clausewitz eine folgerichtige Weiterführung des Gedankens vom Krieg als einer Fortsetzung der Politik. Nur ging Lenin als Berufsrevolutionär des Weltbürgerkrieges noch weiter und machte aus dem wirklichen Feind den absoluten Feind.

Clausewitz hat vom absoluten Krieg gesprochen, aber immer noch die Regularität einer bestehenden Staatlichkeit vorausgesetzt. Er konnte sich den Staat als Instrument einer Partei und eine Partei, die dem Staat befiehlt, überhaupt noch nicht vorstellen. Mit der Absolutsetzung der Partei war auch der Partisan absolut geworden und zum Träger einer absoluten Feindschaft erhoben. Es ist heute nicht schwer, den gedanklichen Kunstgriff zu

18

durchschauen, der diese Veränderung des Feindbegriffes bewirkte. Dagegen ist heute eine andere Art der Absolutsetzung des Feindes weitaus schwieriger zu widerlegen, weil sie der vorhandenen Wirklichkeit des nuklearen Zeitalters immanent zu sein scheint. Die technisch-industrielle Entwicklung hat nämlich die Waffen des Menschen zu reinen Vernichtungsmitteln gesteigert. Dadurch wird ein aufreizendes Mißverhältnis von Schutz und Gehorsam geschaffen: die eine Hälfte der Menschen wird zu Geiseln für den mit atomaren Vernichtungsmitteln ausgerüsteten Machthaber der anderen Hälfte. Solche absoluten Vernichtungsmittel erfordern den absoluten Feind, wenn sie nicht absolut unmenschlich sein sollen. Es sind ja nicht die Vernichtungsmittel, die vernichten, sondern Menschen vernichten mit diesen Mitteln andere Menschen.

Der englische Philosoph Thomas Hobbes hat den Kern des Vorgangs schon im 17. Jahrhundert (de homine IX, 3) erfaßt und mit aller Exaktheit formuliert, obwohl damals (1659) die Waffen noch vergleichsweise harmlos waren. Hobbes sagt: der Mensch ist anderen Menschen, von denen er sich gefährdet glaubt, um ebensoviel gefährlicher als jedes Tier, wie die Waffen des Menschen gefährlicher sind als die sogenannten natürlichen Waffen des Tieres, z. B. Zähne, Pranken, Hörner oder Gift. Und der deutsche Philosoph Hegel fügt hinzu: die Waffen sind das Wesen der Kämpfer selbst.

Konkret gesprochen bedeutet das: die suprakonventionelle Waffe supponiert den suprakonventionellen Menschen. Sie setzt ihn nicht etwa nur als ein Postulat einer ferneren Zukunft voraus; sie unterstellt ihn vielmehr als eine bereits vorhandene Wirklichkeit. Die letzte Gefahr liegt also nicht einmal in dem Vorhandensein der Vernichtungsmittel und einer gegebenen Bosheit der Menschen. Sie besteht in der Unentrinnbarkeit eines moralischen Zwanges. Die Menschen, die jene Mittel gegen andere Menschen anwenden, sehen sich gezwungen, diese anderen Menschen, d. h. ihre Opfer und Objekte, auch moralisch zu vernichten. Sie müssen die Gegenseite als Ganzes für verbrecherisch und unmenschlich erklären, für einen totalen Unwert. Sonst sind sie eben selber Verbrecher und Unmenschen. Die Logik von Wert und Unwert entfaltet ihre ganze vernichtende Konsequenz und erzwingt immer neue, immer tiefere Diskriminierung, Kriminalisierungen und Abwertungen bis zur Vernichtung alles lebensunwerten Lebens.

In einer Welt, in der sich die Partner auf solche Weise gegenseitig in den Abgrund der totalen Entwertung hineinstoßen, bevor sie sich physisch vernichten, müssen neue Arten der absoluten Feindschaft entstehen. Die Feindschaft wird so fruchtbar werden, daß man vielleicht nicht einmal mehr von Feind oder Feindschaft sprechen darf und beides sogar in aller Form vorher geächtet und verdammt wird, bevor das Vernichtungswerk beginnen kann. Die Vernichtung wird dann ganz abstrakt und ganz absolut."

Die klassischen Kriegführungsregeln und die Interessen der Mächtigen

In den Jahren von 1879 bis 1907 entwickelten sich in lückenhafter Art kriegsrechtliche und humanitäre Kodifikationen.

Die I. Haager Friedenskonferenz nahm am 20. Juni 1899 eine Resolution nachstehenden Inhalts an: „In der Erwartung, daß später ein durchaus vollständiger Kodex der Kriegsgesetze gegeben werden kann, hält es die Konferenz für zweckmäßig festzustellen, daß in den nicht in dieser Konvention vorgesehenen Fällen die Bevölkerungen und die Kriegführenden unter dem Schutz und der Herrschaft des Völkerrechtes bleiben, wie sie sich aus den unter zivilisierten Nationen festgestellten Gebräuchen, aus den Gesetzen der Humanität und aus den Forderungen des öffentlichen Gewissens ergeben." (Martens, Nouveau Recueil Géneral de Traités, Leipzig 1901, 2. Serie, Band XXVI, Seite 592.) Professor Friedrich von Martens, kaiserlich russischer Rat, hatte diese grundsätzliche Stellungnahme bereits 1874 in der Brüsseler Landkriegsdeklaration entwickelt. Diese trat aber nie in Kraft. Mit fast gleichem Wortlaut findet sie sich als Absatz 9 in der Präambel des IV. Haager Abkommens vom 18. Okt. 1907.

Der Hauptgrund der Kriegshumanität ist, die Zielsetzung durch unerlaubte Kampfmethoden zu verhindern, was mit erlaubten Mitteln nicht oder nur schwer erreicht werden kann. Von Martens wendet sich weniger an den Soldaten als vielmehr an die Staatsmänner und Politiker.

Den Anlaß zu dieser Formel gaben die Meinungsverschiedenheiten über den Freischärlerkampf. Es konnte keine Einigung über den Begriff „Kriegführende" erzielt werden. Die kleineren Staaten wollten das Merkmal der „Belligérants" sehr weit fassen. Wortführer war der belgische Delegierte Auguste Bernart. Seinem Streben, den Ausschluß der Bevölkerung von jeder Kampfbeteiligung zu verhindern, schlossen sich der Schweizer Delegierte, Oberst Künzli, der Niederländische Vertreter, General den Beer-Poortugael sowie General Sir John Ardagh an. Im Gegensatz zu den Ländern mit größeren Streitkräften waren sie der Auffassung, auf den Guerillakrieg nicht verzichten zu können.

Es kam zu einem Kompromiß: Durch Artikel 9 (später 1) wurden die Kombattanten-Eigenschaften unter bestimmten Voraussetzungen auf Nichtsoldaten-Milizen und Freikorps ausgedehnt. Gefordert wurde dabei die Bestimmung eines verantwortlichen Führers, ein bestimmtes, aus der Ferne erkennbares Abzeichen, offene Führung der Waffen, Beachtung der Gesetze und Bräuche des Krieges.

20

Artikel 4 des revidierten Kriegsgefangenenabkommens von 1949 erklärt die Legalisierung der organisierten Widerstandsbewegung.

Der Petersburger Völkerrechtslehrer strebte nach Humanität, das Ziel erreichte er nicht. Mehr Erfolg hatte der Schweizer Henry Dunand, der bei der Gründung des Internationalen Roten Kreuzes mit dem Friedenspreis ausgezeichnet wurde.

Nicht Humanität, sondern machtpolitische Interessen und das Streben nach Erfolg bestimmen die Kriegführung. Der Grundsatz, keine unnötigen Leiden zu verursachen (Artikel 23 e der Haager Landgerichtsordnung), wurde nicht selten durchbrochen. Infanteriegeschosse mit leicht deformierter Spitze, benannt nach einer ehemaligen Munitionsfabrik bei Kalkutta – Dumdum-Geschosse –, wurden verwandt. 1899 stimmten der englische und USA-Delegierte gegen das Verbot ,,Ersticken durch Gase". Sie standen auf dem Standpunkt, daß man sich nicht durch unüberlegte Beschlüsse der Mittel berauben dürfe, deren man sich vielleicht einmal mit Erfolg bedienen könne. Nicht das Giftgasverbot des Genfer Protokolls von 1925, sondern die Angst der Gegner verhinderte die Anwendung der Kampfgase.

Es wird häufig übersehen, daß die militärischen Interessen für die Kriegführung und damit für das Kriegsrecht eine überragende Bedeutung haben. Nicht so sehr humanitäre Gesichtspunkte bilden für das Kriegsvölkerrecht eine Grundlage, sondern der Gesichtspunkt, daß der Gegner über das militärisch Notwendige hinausgeht. Wenn Lauterpacht in ,,The Problem of the Revision of the Law of War" erklärt, daß das Kriegsrecht angesichts der ungeheuren technischen Umwälzung und der Erfahrungen zweier Weltkriege lückenhaft und revisionsbedürftig ist, so ist diese Formulierung ungenügend.

Das Kriegsrecht befindet sich in einem chaotischen Zustand. Es wird durch den totalen und absoluten Krieg in seiner Existenz bedroht, zumal die brutalste Form der modernen Kriegführung, der Luftkrieg, kaum einer wirksamen Kontrolle unterworfen werden kann. Im Krieg zeigt sich der anti-ethische Charakter der staatlichen Machtpolitik. Bemerkenswert ist, daß der Grundsatz der Ritterlichkeit und der Christlichkeit, die im Mittelalter nur für Angehörige des eigenen Glaubens galten, seit der Renaissance und der Reformation insbesondere im Zeitalter der Aufklärung und des Liberalismus auf alle Menschen ausgedehnt, doch insbesondere von den Angelsachsen nie ganz akzeptiert wurde. Es wurde nie vollständig anerkannt, daß der Krieg eine Beziehung von Staat zu Staat, nicht von Mensch zu Menschen ist. Es ist auffallend, daß die Seekriegsdeklaration von 1909 durch Großbritannien nicht ratifiziert wurde, so daß die englische Admiralität den Seekrieg weitgehend unter Mißachtung des strittigen Völkergewohnheitsrechtes führen konnte.

Nach dem Ersten Weltkrieg wurde das Kriegsgefangenenrecht und die Anwendung des Giftgases nicht geregelt. Nach dem Zweiten Weltkrieg unterblieb eine umfassende Kodifizierung des Seekriegs- und Luftkriegsrechtes. Man prangerte nur Verstöße der unterlegenen Seite an.

Im Zweiten Weltkrieg spielen die Widerstandsbewegungen eine große Rolle. Wie Professor Dr. Friedrich Berber im ,,Lehrbuch des Völkerrechtes" – zweiter Band – richtig bemerkt, überläßt das Völkerrecht die Organisation der Streitkräfte im Frieden und im Krieg dem Gutdünken der einzelnen Staaten. Rechtlich ohne Bedeutung ist die Aufstellung eines Berufsheeres, eines Milizheeres, eines Heeres auf Grund der allgemeinen Wehrpflicht oder einer Mischung der genannten Formen.

Die Widerstandsbewegungen brauchen keine eigene Regierung zu haben, notwendig ist aber, daß sie aus einer militärischen auf Befehl und Gehorsam gegründeten Organisation bestehen. Sie müssen ein bleibendes, aus der Ferne erkennbares Kennzeichen wie die Uniform haben. Eine Armbinde muß so befestigt sein, daß sie nicht beliebig abgestreift werden kann. Die Waffen sind offen zu tragen. Deren Verbergen ist verboten, um plötzliche heimtückische Angriffe unmöglich zu machen. Die Widerstandsbewegungen haben diese Gesetze und Gebräuche zu achten. Daran hat sich auch durch die III. Genfer Konvention nichts geändert (vgl. Art. 4 A [2]).

Im Zweiten Weltkrieg wurde durch den sowjetischen Generalstab und England – Sir Gubbins – ein Sabotage- und Widerstandsnetz organisiert, das völkerrechtswidrig war. Die Anforderungen der Landkriegsordnung wurden nicht erfüllt. Die Besatzungsmacht eines Gebietes erhält keine Souveränitätsrechte, sondern hat gemäß Art. 43 LKO alle von ihr abhängigen Maßnahmen zu treffen, ,,um nach Möglichkeit die öffentliche Ordnung und das öffentliche Leben wiederherzustellen und aufrechtzuerhalten".

Annexion und Staatenneubildungen stellen ein Völkerrechtsdelikt dar. Auch die Absetzung der Regierung des Feindstaates, wie sie in der deutschen Proklamation vom 25. Sept. 40 verkündet wurde, durch die der König von Norwegen vorübergehend den Thron verlor, ist ein Verstoß gegen das Völkerrecht. Das gleiche gilt von der Annexion Finnlands durch Rußland während des russisch-schwedischen Krieges 1808/1809, die Errichtung des Königreiches Polen durch die Mittelmächte 1916, die Annexion von polnischen Gebietsteilen 1939, von Eupen und Malmedy 1940 durch Deutschland, die Herauslösung von Gebietsteilen aus Jugoslawien und die Errichtung neuer Staaten auf dem Boden dieses Landes durch die Achsenmächte 1941, die Angliederung von Königsberg und von Teilen von Ostpreußen sowie Südsachalins und der Kurilen durch die Sowjetunion 1945, die Einverleibung Ostdeutschlands in Polen durch Gesetz vom 11. Jan. 49. Dagegen kann die Besatzungsmacht Militärgerichte mit Jurisdiktionsgewalt gegenüber den Bewohnern des besetzten Gebietes einsetzen, um die Einhaltung ihrer Rechtsnormen zu erzwingen.

Die Zivilbevölkerung schuldet der Besatzungsmacht Gehorsam, aber keine Treue. Die IV. Genfer Kommission von 1949 regelt das Verhältnis der Bevölkerung des besetzten Gebietes zur Zivilverwaltung. Im Gegensatz zur Zeit vor 1949 dürfen bei einem Anschlag auf die Besatzungsmacht nur die Schuldigen zur Rechenschaft gezogen werden, nicht die Bewohner eines Dorfes, in dem der Anschlag stattgefunden hat.

Nach Artikel 34 der IV. Genfer Konvention dürfen keine Geiseln genommen werden. Deportationen und Zwangsevakuierungen sind nur aus Gründen der Sicherheit und der militärischen Notwendigkeit erlaubt. Die Besatzungsmacht kann auch heute noch die Todesstrafe für Spionage, schwere Sabotage an militärischen Einrichtungen und vorsätzliche Tötungsdelikte verhängen. Eine Schranke für die Todesstrafe stellt der Umstand dar, daß die Verfassung des besetzten Staates keine Todesstrafe kannte.

Immer noch werden in einseitiger Weise Verstöße der Deutschen gegen die klassischen Regeln der Kriegführung in das Feld geführt. Verschwiegen wird, daß z. B. trotz des Bestehens der Haager Landkriegsordnung am 23. Aug. 1955 durch französische Truppen bei Philippeville (heute: Skikdz) laut Meldung der Pariser Zeitung „Le Monde" Frauen und Kinder niedergemacht wurden. Ähnliches geschah im Oktober 1956 laut DPA/Reuter-Meldung vom 16. Okt. 1958, die über eine Gerichtsverhandlung berichtete, bei Kafer Kassim durch israelische Truppen.

Es sei gestattet, die Methoden der angloamerikanischen Kriegführung näher zu betrachten. Sie sind sehr hart: Nicht gedeckt ist der Feuerüberfall britischer Kriegsschiffe auf die Hauptstadt des neutralen Dänemark (1807), der Hunderte von Einwohnern das Leben kostete.

Es ist im Zeitalter der Menschenrechte unverständlich, wenn bei dem militärischen Vorgehen gegen sog. „wilde Völkerschaften" die Meinung vertreten wurde, daß die Normen des völkerrechtlichen Kriegsrechtes nicht zu beachten seien. Erst seit der Genfer Konvention von 1949 gilt der Satz eines humanitären Minimums. Vorher gebrauchte man den Begriff „Expedition" oder „Kolonialkrieg" bei Unterdrückung von Aufständen. Man sprach von „polizeilichen Erfordernissen in gewissen entfernten Gegenden". Den Bericht des englischen Luftmarschalls Sir Ellington vom 11. Nov. 1925 über britische Bombenangriffe unter Verwendung von Zeitzündern in Wasistan habe ich im gleichen Zusammenhang schon genannt.

Wir kennen den häufig angegriffenen Satz von Kaiser Wilhelm II. über die Kriegführung, als deutsche Expeditionstruppen im Jahre 1900 nach China entsandt wurden. Als in den Jahren 1899/1900 europäische Mächte besondere Interessensphären verlangten und sich dies von der chinesischen

Regierung bestätigen ließen, brach eine starke fremdenfeindliche Bewegung aus, hinter der ein Geheimbund (Boxer) mit ursprünglich religiösen Zielen stand. Dieser politisierte sich und erlangte als „Liga für Recht und Eintracht" 1900 große Bedeutung, vor allem in Tschi-li, Schantung und Schan-si. Ausländerfeindliche Ausschreitungen, besonders das Christenmassaker von Pau-tingfu im Mai 1900, veranlaßte das Eingreifen ausländischer Mächte (England, Frankreich, Rußland, Deutschland). Dies ist der Hintergrund der spontanen Äußerung, die deutschen Expeditionstruppen „sollten keinen Pardon geben und keine Gefangenen machen". Diese sogenannte „Anregung", die der Impulsivität des Hohenzollernfürsten entsprach, wurde nie befolgt. Mehr entsprachen sie den Worten des Ersten Seelords Admiral John Fisher und der harten, ausdauernden englischen Art der Kriegführung: „Man muß es denen zu Hause und im Ausland genügend einhämmern, daß man beabsichtigt, seinen Feind mit Füßen zu treten, wenn er am Boden liegt, daß man seine Gefangenen in Öl sieden und seine Frauen und Kinder foltern wird." So äußerte sich der englische Admiral gegenüber dem englischen Publizisten William Thomas Stead, der beim Untergang der Titanic am 15. April 1912 um das Leben kam. Stead wurde u. a. durch die Wochenschrift „War against War" bekannt. Er verfaßte die Werke „The United States of Europe" (1899) und „Le parlement de l'humanité" (Haag 1907). John Fisher bestätigte seine Einstellung zur Kriegführung in einem Brief an Lord Esher: „Es ist eine Dummheit, den Krieg für die gesamte feindliche Zivilbevölkerung nicht so abscheulich wie möglich zu machen." Einen Rat Churchills hatte angeblich Lord Kitchener in die Tat umgesetzt, als er die gesamte wehrfähige Bevölkerung des Sudan ausrotten ließ, um neue Unruhen zu unterbinden. Dies gestand er dem großen Forscher und Deutschenfreund Sven Hedin (vgl. Sven Hedin: „Bagdad, Babylon, Ninive", Leipzig 1918).

Von Churchill stammt, wie behauptet wird, aus dem Jahre 1901 die spontane Äußerung, alle alten Buren müßten erschossen werden, damit ihre Kinder Respekt vor der britischen Macht bekämen. Lord Kitchener, der 1870/71 auf französischer Seite als Freiwilliger kämpfte und mit dem Panzerkreuzer „Hampshire" im Sommer 1916 bei den Orkney-Inseln unterging, als er zur Organisierung der russischen Armee von Scapa Flow aus seine Reise angetreten hatte, ist der Verfechter härtester Methoden. Der Sieger von Omdurman, der in Faschoda dem französischen Major Marchand entgegentrat, zeigte im Burenkrieg dieselbe brutale Rücksichtslosigkeit wie bei der Niederwerfung des Mahdi-Aufstandes. Er führte die Konzentration von Frauen und Kindern durch, um die Burenkrieger mürbe zu machen. 26 000 KZ-Insassen kamen infolge mangelhafter Ernährung und sanitärer Betreuung ums Leben. Die „Daily News" behauptete in der Ausgabe vom 9. Febr. 1901, daß von 92 000 internierten Frauen und Kindern „ein Drittel" verstorben sei. Nähere Berichte über die Verhältnisse in den Lagern befinden sich in „The Brunt of the War", ein Buch, das Miss Emily Hobhouse, die Nichte des Oberhausmitgliedes Lord Hobhouse, 1902 herausbrachte.

Smuts, später britischer Feldmarschall, schrieb 1901 an Martinus Steyn, den Präsidenten des Oranje-Freistaates: „Wüßte die Welt nur ein Hundertstel dessen, was die Engländer hier in den Freistaaten anrichten, würde sich die ganze Christenheit die Kleider zerreißen und zum Himmel schreien wegen dieser unbeschreiblichen Barbarei." Der Gerechtigkeit halber sei festgestellt, daß die zerstörten Farmen mit englischen Mitteln wiederaufgebaut wurden. Tote dagegen werden – wie bekannt – nicht wieder lebendig.

Das Kriegsvölkerrecht –
eine Illusion?

In der heutigen Zeit könnte man den Schluß ziehen, daß das gesamte Kriegsrecht eine Illusion darstellt. Damit soll die Bedeutung des großen Holländers Hugo Grotius nicht herabgesetzt werden, der im Namen des Rechts verfolgt wurde. Der niederländische Jurist Hugo Grotius, eigentlich Huig de Groot, geboren am 10. Apr. 1583, gestorben am 28. Aug. 1645 in Rostock, studierte in Leiden, wurde 1607 Generalfiskal und 1613 Ratspensionär in Rotterdam. Nach der Niederlage der Remonstranten, deren Lehre er durch Schriften verteidigt hatte, wurde er verhaftet und 1619 zu lebenslänglichem Gefängnis verurteilt. 1621 glückte seine Flucht nach Paris. 1631 kam er für kurze Zeit nach Rotterdam. Er mußte wieder fliehen, und über Hamburg erreichte er Schweden, dessen Gesandter er von 1634–1644 am französischen Hof wurde.

1609 veröffentlichte er seine Schrift ,,Mare liberum". Dort stellte er den Grundsatz der Freiheit der Meere auf. In seinem Hauptwerk ,,De iure belli ac pacis" (Paris 1625), legte er, vom Naturrecht ausgehend, die Grundlagen für ein Völkerrecht. Grotius fordert Toleranz gegen alle Religionen, Intoleranz aber gegen die Leugner von Gott und Unsterblichkeit.

Grotius versuchte, für die Neuordnung der Gesellschaft allgemeine Grundsätze rechtlich-politischer Art zu entwickeln. Wenn Lauterpacht in ,,The Problem of the Revision of the Law of War" erklärt, daß das Kriegsrecht angesichts der ungeheuren technischen Umwälzung und der Erfahrungen zweier Weltkriege lückenhaft und revisionsbedürftig ist, so ist diese Formulierung ungenügend. Das Kriegsrecht befindet sich in einem chaotischen Zustand. Es wird durch den totalen und absoluten Krieg in seiner Existenz bedroht, zumal die brutalste Form der modernen Kriegführung, der Luftkrieg, kaum einer wirksamen Kontrolle unterworfen werden kann.

Es ist bedauerlich, daß die Rechtsverletzungen der Siegermächte im Zweiten Weltkrieg nicht im erforderlichen Ausmaß gewürdigt wurden. Dies gilt nicht nur für den Partisanen- und Untergrundkrieg, sondern auch für den Luftkrieg.

Es ist zu unterscheiden zwischen einem Krieg mit konventionellen Waffen und einem Atomkrieg. Während bei einer konventionellen Kriegführung rechtliche Beschränkungen noch möglich sind, ist dies bei einer nuklearen kaum zu erwarten. Der Versuch einer kriegsvölkerrechtlichen Regelung dürfte bei einer massenweisen Herstellung und Bereitschaft zur Verwendung der Atom- und Wasserstoffbombe sinnlos sein. Es gibt bei einem

26

solchen absoluten Krieg noch weniger eine Differenzierung zwischen Kombattanten und Nichtkombattanten als im Zweiten Weltkrieg.

Im Jahre 1923 erschienen im AJIL auf Seite 245 ff. die Haager Luftkriegsregeln, die keine unmittelbare Gültigkeit hatten. Trotzdem glaubte man an eine Übereinstimmung im Sinne des Artikels 24 Abs. 1, in dem es heißt: ,,Das Luftbombardement ist nur zulässig, wenn es gegen ein militärisches Ziel gerichtet ist, d. h. ein Ziel, dessen völlige oder teilweise Zerstörung für den Kriegführenden einen klaren militärischen Vorteil darstellen würde." Nach Artikel 24 Abs. II wird die Bombardierung von militärischen Streitkräften, militärischen Werken, militärischen Anlagen oder Depots, von Fabriken, die bedeutende oder wohlbekannte Zentren darstellen und zur Herstellung von Waffen, Munition und typisch militärischen Bedarfsgegenständen dienen, von Verkehrs- und Transportlinien, die für militärische Zwecke benutzt werden, als erlaubt erklärt.

Artikel 22 spricht das Verbot des Luftbombardements zur Terrorisierung der Zivilbevölkerung und Zerstörung oder Beschädigung von Privateigentum nichtmilitärischen Charakters oder zur Verletzung von ,,Nichtkombattanten" aus. Seitens der Weimarer Republik wurden der Abrüstungskonferenz in Genf am 18. Febr. 1932 u. a. nachstehende Vorschläge vorgelegt:

,,Die Unterhaltung jeglicher Luftstreitkräfte wird verboten . . ."

,,Das Abwerfen von Kampfmitteln jeder Art aus Luftfahrzeugen sowie die Vorbereitung hierfür ist ohne jede Einschränkung zu untersagen."

Am 31. Mrz. 1936 schlug die nationalsozialistische Regierung des Deutschen Reiches vor, den Abwurf von Bomben jeglicher Art auf offene Ortschaften zu verbieten, die sich außerhalb der Reichweite der mittleren, schweren Artillerie der kämpfenden Fronten befinden.

Spaight bringt in seinem Werk ,,Air power and war rights", Seite 248, zum Ausdruck, daß dieser Vorschlag ehrlich gemeint war. Dagegen vertrat Großbritannien lange vor 1939 in dem ,,Masterplan" den Gedanken des Luftkrieges gegen das deutsche Hinterland. Der schwere Langstreckenbomber wurde entwickelt. Spaight erklärt ausdrücklich, es sei ,,doch recht wahrscheinlich . . ., daß unsere Hauptstadt und unsere Industriezentren nicht angegriffen worden wären, wenn wir weiterhin Angriffe gegen entsprechende Ziele in Deutschland unterlassen hätten."

Der Zweite Weltkrieg brachte jedoch Flächenangriffe, Gebietsbombardierungen und Terrorangriffe auf die deutsche Zivilbevölkerung mit sich. Aufschlußreich sind die Zahlen: auf England gingen 56 000 Fliegerbomben nieder; auf deutsches Territorium und mit dem Deutschen Reich verbündete Länder und besetzte Gebiete hingegen 955 044 Tonnen britischer und 1 000 000 amerikanischer Bomben.

Eine Verhöhnung des Völkerrechtes muß in dem Vergleich gesehen werden, den Stowel in „American Journal of International Law" zieht, indem er sagt, die Atombombe sei der „göttliche Wind" gewesen, „der Japan vor dem nationalen Harakiri gerettet habe" (AJIL 1945, Seite 786). Auch die Worte des amerikanischen Präsidenten Truman vom 9. Aug. 1945 sind nicht überzeugend: „Wir haben sie gegen diejenigen eingesetzt, die uns ohne Warnung in Pearl Harbor angegriffen haben, gegen diejenigen, die amerikanische Gefangene ausgehungert, geschlagen und hingerichtet haben ... Wir haben sie eingesetzt, um die Agonie des Krieges abzukürzen, um das Leben von Tausenden und Abertausenden von jungen Amerikanern zu retten" (E. Menzel, Wörterbuch des Völkerrechtes I, S. 104).

Militärische Kriegsmaßnahmen, die in ihren Auswirkungen auch die Zivilbevölkerung einbeziehen, sind außerhalb des Operationsgebietes verboten. Zu erwähnen sind in diesem Zusammenhang Flächenbombardements von Wohngebieten und der Abwurf von Atombomben über Städten sowie die Anwendung von Kampfmitteln gegen das Hinterland, „die ihrem Wesen nach nicht auf ein bestimmtes und begrenztes Ziel gerichtet werden können, sondern deren Ziel infolge ihrer großen Streuung ein ganzer Landstrich, ein Teil des Feindgebietes schlechthin ist." Ausnahmen sind zugelassen bei vom Gegner vorher begangenen Völkerrechtsverletzungen, die Anlaß zu Repressalmaßnahmen gaben.

Atomvergeltung ist nur gegen erfolgten Atomangriff möglich.

Nach Anlage II Nr. 1 des Protokolls Nr. III über die Rüstungskontrolle vom 3. Oktober 1954 (BGBl 1955 II, S. 269) wird die Atomwaffe als Kampfmittel bezeichnet, „das Kernbrennstoff oder radioaktive Isotope enthält oder eigens dazu bestimmt ist, solche aufzunehmen oder zu verwenden oder das durch Explosion oder andere unkontrollierte Kernumwandlung des Kernbrennstoffes Massenzerstörungen, Massenschäden oder Massenvergiftungen hervorrufen kann". Es kann kein Zweifel daran bestehen, daß ein unmittelbarer Angriff gegen die Zivilbevölkerung einen Verstoß gegen das Völkermordabkommen vom 9. Dez. 1948 darstellt.

Die Anwendung der Atomwaffe kann weder durch die „militärische Notwendigkeit" noch das „Recht der Selbsterhaltung" gerechtfertigt werden. Oppenheim irrt, wenn er zur Rechtfertigung der Anwendung der Atomwaffe ausführt: „Against an enemy who violates rules of the law of war on a scale to vast as to put himself all together outside the orbit of consideration of humanity and compassion."

Vor der Herrschaft des Faschismus in Italien entwickelte ein italienischer Militärtheoretiker, General Giulio Douhet (1869–1930), um das Jahr 1920 in seinem Buch „Il dominio dell' aria (Die Luftherrschaft)" die umstrittene Lehre, man solle den Gegner so gut wie ausschließlich durch massive Bombenoffensiven in die Knie zwingen. Er stellt heraus, nach der Erringung der

Luftherrschaft könne kein Volk den Angriffen auf Städte und Industriezentren widerstehen. Er hatte diese revolutionäre Theorie bereits zur Zeit des Ersten Weltkrieges vertreten.

Der britische General Hugh Trenchard, später Marschall of the Royal Air Force, erhielt im Mai 1918 den Befehl, ,,unabhängige Luftstreitkräfte aufzustellen, um Deutschland mit Bomben anzugreifen''. In einer Denkschrift schreibt Trenchard: ,,Hauptbestand einer jeden Luftstrategie ist der unabhängige strategische Einsatz von Kampfflugzeugen. Operationen zur Unterstützung der Armee und der Marine sind von zweitrangiger Bedeutung, falls sie einmal notwendig sein sollten. Sie lenken nur von der Hauptaufgabe ab.'' Mit einer Luftflotte von 100 Flugzeugen führte Trenchard Mitte Mai 1918 die erste Luftwaffenoperation gegen das kaiserliche Deutschland aus.

Ab 1920 wird die These vertreten: ,,Der Krieg ist unterschiedslos gegen das gesamte Feindgebiet zu führen, ohne Beschränkung der erlaubten Ziele, also auch mit Flächen-, Gas-Großangriffen ... Als entscheidender Wehrmachtsteil ist die Luftwaffe einzusetzen, die in selbständigem, zusammengefaßtem und rollendem Einsatz das Kriegspotential und den Kampfwillen seiner Bewohner zerschmettert.''

Nach Douhet ist der Krieg ein ,,totaler Krieg gegen den gesamten Lebensraum des Feindes, ohne natürliche Unterscheidung von Front und Heimat oder Streitkräften und Zivilbevölkerung ... Der Krieg ist stets unmenschlich. Die Mittel, die in ihm Verwendung finden, werden ausschließlich nach ihren Wirkungen unterschieden. Wer auf Leben und Tod kämpft – und anders kann man heutzutage nicht mehr kämpfen –, der hat das heilige Recht, alle vorhandenen Mittel einzusetzen, um nicht selber zugrunde zu gehen. Sich in den Untergang des eigenen Volkes zu schicken, um nicht gegen irgendwelche papierene Konventionen zu verstoßen, wäre Wahnsinn.''

Kalt bemerkt der britische Luftwaffengeneral J. M. Spaight: ,,Die Zivilpersonen schmieden die Waffen zum Hinschlachten unserer Freunde und Verwandten. Sie haben kein Recht auf Unverletzlichkeit und verdienen keine Träne des Mitleids.''

Im Deutschen Reich ist General Walter Wewer, nach 1933 der erste Generalstabschef der Luftwaffe, ein überzeugter Anhänger der Douhetschen Theorie. Er ist aber Realist und erkennt, daß sich sein Land kaum die strategische Bombenflotte einer Weltmacht leisten kann. Oberst Wewer, später Generalmajor, vertrat die Ansicht, daß ein Luftangriff im geschlossenen Verband als Hochangriff geführt werden müsse, nur in Ausnahmefällen seien Tiefangriffe nötig. Die wirtschaftlichen Zentren des Gegners seien zu vernichten. Verfüge dieser über stärkere Luftwaffenverbände, so müßten diese ausgeschaltet werden, bevor die wirtschaftlichen Zentren angegriffen werden könnten. Wewer propagierte den Präventivschlag, d. h. den überraschenden Luftangriff auf alle feindlichen Flugplätze mit ihren Flugzeugen. Dann sollte die Zerstörung der gegnerischen Kriegs- und Versorgungsindustrie erfolgen. 1936 verunglückte Wewer. Für seinen Nachfolger war die taktische Zusammenarbeit der Luftwaffe mit dem Heer das wichtigste. Die von Wewer angebahnten Beschaffungspläne für schwere Bomberverbände wurden aufgegeben. Deutschland baute zweimotorige taktische Mittelstreckenbomber.

England ging von dem Gedanken aus, die Moral der Bevölkerung müsse gebrochen werden. Dazu seien die Großstädte geeignet. Diese seien in Trümmer zu legen.

Im Zweiten Weltkrieg beliefen sich die Verluste der britischen Zivilbevölkerung auf 60 585 Tote, die deutschen Verluste auf 635 000. Churchill griff auf die Methoden Lord Kitcheners zurück. Liddell Hart hatte auch vorgeschlagen, zwecks Kriegsverkürzung gegen die Zivilbevölkerung Giftgas und Bomben zu verwenden, obwohl das Pariser Traktat von 1856 Feindseligkeiten gegen Nichtkombattanten verbot, und die Petersburger Erklärung von 1868 nur die Schwächung der militärischen Feindkräfte erlaubte.

Dresden ist ein Musterbeispiel der illegalen Kriegführung. Dieses Massenbombardement auf die sächsische Stadt war weder notwendig noch irgendwie kriegsentscheidend. Im Grundsatz glich diese Art des Krieges dem Vorgehen gegen die Buren und der Hungerblockade von 1914–1918, durch die nach einer Schätzung 400 000 Deutsche ihr Leben verloren. Diese Blockade verstieß auch gegen die Londoner Seerechtsdeklaration vom 20. Febr. 1904.

Im Zweiten Weltkrieg zeigte sich, daß die Angloamerikaner im strategischen und taktischen Einsatz der Luftwaffe den Deutschen überlegen waren. Hervorgehoben werden muß, daß der britische Physiker Sir Robert Wattson 1935 seinem Land durch eine Arbeit über die Entdeckung und Ortung eines Flugzeuges durch Radiomethoden einen Vorsprung verschaffte. In demselben Jahr wurde im englischen Kriegsministerium das sogenannte ,,Tizard-Komitee für die wissenschaftliche Überwachung der Luftverteidigung" gegründet. Jäger sollten mit Hilfe des Funksprechverkehrs vom Boden aus an die georteten Bomber geführt werden. Den Vorsprung Englands in der Hochfrequenztechnik konnte Deutschland nicht aufholen.

Bis zum Feldzug gegen die Sowjetunion, der als ,,Weltanschauungskrieg" bezeichnet wurde, legte Hitler Wert auf eine gegenseitige rücksichtsvolle Kriegführung. Die Bombardements von Warschau und Rotterdam fallen unter den Gesichtspunkt der militärisch zulässigen Belagerungsbeschießung. Die Luftoperationen in Polen und Holland dauerten nur wenige Wochen. Die späteren deutschen Bombenflüge gegen englische Städte und Industriezentren – London, Coventry, Birmingham, Southampton sollten die englische Regierung zur Aufgabe völkerrechtswidriger Bombardierung zwingen.

Die Kriegführungsmethode, insbesondere im Luftkrieg, glich der, die verschiedene Generäle in den Vereinigten Staaten von Nordamerika im Bürgerkrieg anwandten. General Sheridan erklärte gegenüber dem Fürsten von Bismarck im Jahre 1870, die richtige Strategie sei, den Bewohnern soviel Leiden zuzufügen, daß sie sich nach dem Frieden sehnen. Es dürfe den Leuten nichts bleiben als die Augen, um den Krieg zu beweinen. US-Brigadegeneral Jacob S. Smith befahl im 2. Philippinenkrieg, alle männlichen Einwohner, denen man habhaft werden könne, ab dem 10. Lebensjahr umzubringen (vgl. Feststellung des Kriegsgerichtes von Manila vom 17. Febr. 1902). Im Befehl von Smith hieß es: ,,I want no prisoners. I wish to kill and burn; the more you kill and burn, you will please me . . . The interior of Samar must be made a howling wildernis . . .'' Die ,,New York Evening Post'' schrieb: ,,Unsere Truppen auf der Insel Samar befolgen eine Politik des Massenmordes, und in den Augen der Welt stehen wir entehrt da.'' General Smith wurde mit einem Verweis bestraft.

Guerillas und Partisanen

Das Wort „Guerillas" wurde zum ersten Mal in den Jahren 1808–1813 gebraucht, als das spanische Volk gegen die regulären Truppen Napoleons kämpfte. Für den Korsen war es nicht schwierig, in Spanien die schwachen Truppen der spanischen Streitkräfte zu zerschlagen. Seinen Besatzungstruppen gelang es jedoch nicht, das Land zu beherrschen. Die Pyrenäenhalbinsel ist gebirgig. Dichte Wälder wachsen auf ihr. Wenige, schlechte Straßen verbanden die Ortschaften. Ungefähr 200 regionale Kleinkriege breiteten sich in Asturien, Aragonien, Katalonien, Navarra, Kastilien usw. aus. Die irregulären Verbände bereiteten den Franzosen furchtbare Verluste. Man kann die Toten und die Verletzten bis zu 100 Mann täglich schätzen. Selbst größere Truppenkontingente wurden angegriffen. Die Zusammenarbeit mit „Banden" anderer Provinzen entstand. Juan Martin Diaz, der sagenumwobene „Empezinado", wurde zum Schrecken der Franzosen, der die Straßen von Madrid nach Saragossa unsicher machte. Damals zeigte sich bereits, daß der Guerillakrieg nicht eine Kriegsart, sondern eine Form der Kriegführung darstellt.

Die strategisch schwächere Seite wählt Zeit und Ort sowie Form ihrer Unternehmungen. Dazu kam, daß auf der iberischen Halbinsel die Guerillas mit den englischen Streitkräften in Portugal und Spanien zusammenarbeiteten. Mit Recht kann man zweifeln, ob Wellington dort gesiegt hätte, wenn die spanischen Freiheitskämpfer nicht gewesen wären.

Nach Clausewitz wurde oft die Hälfte der französischen Streitmacht, nämlich 250 000–260 000 Mann, durch 50 000 irreguläre Kämpfer gebunden. Es fragt sich, ob Napoleon die Völkerschlacht von Leipzig im Jahre 1814 verloren hätte, wenn die schwere kriegerische Belastung im Westen Europas nicht gewesen wäre. Die Geschichte zeigt, daß ein besetztes Land durch Taten beherzter Männer, die in Gebirgen und Wäldern operierten, den Anstoß zur Befreiung des Landes erhalten konnte.

Im Hundertjährigen Krieg verloren die Engländer den größten Teil Frankreichs durch die Taktik des damaligen Marschalls von Frankreich, Du Guescelin, die darin bestand, daß er englische Truppen in der Nacht angriff, ihre Nachschubkolonnen vernichtete und die Garnisonen überfiel. Du Guescelin vermied den offenen Kampf. Die Engländer verloren, ohne daß ihnen die Gelegenheit zur Schlacht gegeben war, das Land, das sie in offenem Kampf erobert hatten.

Zahlreich sind die Guerillakriege zwischen 1814 und 1914. Im Ersten Weltkrieg zeigte T. E. Lawrence, der exakt Clausewitz studiert hatte, in Vorderasien, was durch Guerillakriegführung erreicht werden konnte. Als erster erkannte er, daß die Guerillakriegführung nicht immer mit Kampf verbunden ist. In „Seven Pillars of Wisdom" – die sieben Säulen der Weisheit – zeigt Lawrence die Planung auf, die die Niederlage der Türkei in Arabien herbeiführte. Ich zitiere: „In der türkischen Armee war das Material knapp und kostbar. Es gab weit mehr Soldaten als Gerät . . . Nicht die Zerstörung der Armee, sondern die Vernichtung des Materials mußte daher das Ziel sein." Offene Kämpfe verbot Lawrence. Dafür ließ er die Araber Eisenbahnbrücken, Tunnels und Schienenstränge sprengen. Gegen befestigte Bahnstationen, Stützpunkte und Garnisonen wurden Störangriffe geführt oder sie wurden bedroht. Nicht Medina – Mekka war bereits gefallen – wurde Angriffsziel, sondern die zu dieser Stadt führende Eisenbahnlinie.

Durch Lawrence zerfiel die türkische Schlagkraft in Arabien. Er war ein Wegbereiter der Kleinkriegführung und faßte deren Taktik in fast wissenschaftlicher Form zusammen. Gewagt, aber nicht ohne Bedeutung ist seine Behauptung, daß es keinem Feind möglich sei, ein Land zu besetzen, das Guerillakrieg führt, es sei denn, daß jedes Fleckchen Boden durch Truppen besetzt gehalten werden kann.

Lawrence, von Geheimnissen umwittert, war eine bedeutende Persönlichkeit. Er hat das Schicksal Vorderasiens mitgestaltet, mag auch der Stern des englischen Feldmarschalls Allenby, dem Tel Aviv eine Straße geweiht hat, heller leuchten. Es wurde über Lawrence eine Anzahl Bücher geschrieben.

T. E. Lawrence selbst publizierte außer den „Sieben Säulen der Weisheit", „Revolt in the Desert" (Der Aufstand in der Wüste), „Secret Dispatches from Arabia" (Geheime Telegramme von Arabien). Lawrence's Leistungen fanden in Rußland und China große Anerkennung. Sir Gubbins, der große englische Mann des Untergrundkrieges während des Zweiten Weltkrieges, geboren auf den Hebriden, Sohn eines englischen Diplomaten, dürfte in gewisser Hinsicht zu den Schülern von Colonel Lawrence, der im übrigen keine militärische Schulung erhalten hatte, gehören.

Marxismus – Leninismus
und der Partisanenkrieg

Von Karl Marx stammt der Satz: ,,Der Erfolg rechtfertigt die Mittel." Über die Partisanenkriegführung sagt er: ,,Wenn eine Nation um ihre Freiheit kämpft, braucht sie sich nicht an die anerkannten Regeln der Kriegführung zu halten. Massenaufstände, revolutionäre Methoden, Guerillabanden überall – das sind die einzigen Mittel, durch die eine kleine Nation hoffen kann, sich selbst gegen einen zahlenmäßig stärkeren und besser ausgerüsteten Gegner zu behaupten. Wenn diese Methoden angewendet werden, dann können schwächere Kräfte selbst einen stärkeren und besser organisierten Gegner überwinden."

Karl Marx' Gedankenwelt, die überwiegend von nichtproletarischem Denken getragen wurde, gewann eine ungeheure geschichtliche Bedeutung. Ein wesentlicher Teil der Arbeiterbewegung erhob sie zum Glaubensbekenntnis.

Karl Marx studierte 1835–1841 in Bonn und Berlin Staatswissenschaft, Geschichte und Philosophie. Er schloß sich der Junghegelschen Lehre an. Nach der Doktorpromotion wollte er sich der akademischen Laufbahn widmen. Er wurde aber Journalist.

Nach seiner Heirat mit Jenny von Westphalen, Halbschwester des preußischen Ministers Ferdinand Otto Wilhelm von Westphalen, ging er 1843 nach Paris. Von Westphalen selbst gehörte im Kabinett von Manteuffel in Berlin zu den schärfsten Reaktionären.

Wenig bekannt ist, daß Marx auch Militärschriftsteller war. So befaßte er sich in der ,,Neuen Rheinischen Zeitung" anläßlich der italienisch-österreichischen Auseinandersetzung im oberitalienischen Raum mit dem Thema Kleinkrieg.

Lenin (Uljanow Wladimir Iljitsch), geboren in Simbirsk am 22. Apr. 1870, gestorben in Gorkij bei Moskau am 21. Jan. 1924, Gründer der Russischen Sowjetrepublik, war der Sohn eines geadelten Schulinspektors. Er studierte Rechtswissenschaft in Kasan und beteiligte sich an der revolutionären Bewegung. 1887 war sein Bruder Alexander nach einem Attentat auf den Zaren hingerichtet worden. Daraufhin wurde er selbst in ein Dorf des Gouvernements Kasan verbannt, wo er sich auf das Staatsexamen vorbereitete, das er 1891 in Petersburg bestand. Er ließ sich zunächst als Rechtsanwalt in Samara, sodann 1894 in Petersburg nieder. In der Verbannungszeit in Sibirien lernte er 1897 seine Lebensgefährtin kennen, die Sozialistin Nadeschda Konstantinowna Krupskaja. Sie wurde als Tochter eines adligen Beamten 1869 zu Rassanowa in Polen geboren. 1908 heiratete Lenin sie. Im November 1917 stürzte Lenin seinen Vorgänger Kerenskij und leitete bis zu seinem Tod 1924 die bolschewistische Regierung, wenn er auch seit 1922 krank war.

Die „Gesammelten Werke" des großen Strategen des Klassenkrieges, wie ihn Losowsky nennt, brachte das Marx-Engels-Institut in Moskau heraus. Im Jahre 1906 schrieb er seinen berühmten Artikel über die Partisanenkriegführung.

Als er seine Arbeit zu Papier brachte, erreichte die terroristische Phase der ersten Revolution ihren Höhepunkt. Boris Suvarin berichtet in seiner Schrift „Lenine, Aperçu historique du Bolchevisme", Paris 1935, S. 92, daß im Oktober 1906 121 Terrorakte verübt, 47 Zusammenstöße zwischen Revolutionären und der Polizei stattgefunden und 362 Enteignungen vorgenommen worden seien. Festzustellen ist, daß zur Zeit, als Lenin seinen Aufsatz niederschrieb, der unter dem Titel „Parisanskaja woina" in allen fünf russischen Ausgaben der „Gesammelten Werke" („Sotschinenija") nachgedruckt wurde, daß Partisanenkrieg nicht die Umschreibung eines Guerillakrieges im modernen Sinne ist, sondern Terror, Überfälle und Räubereien bedeutet.

Enteignung war gleichzusetzen mit Raub von Geld aus Banken, Steuereinzugsstellen, Postbüros. Zollämtern, Bahnhöfen usw. Kleine Firmen, Bäckereien und Dorfläden wurden häufig des Geldes ledig. Beteiligt waren auch gewerbsmäßige Langfinger und berufsmäßige Räuber. Für Stadtoperationen gab es kleine Kampfgruppen. Auf dem Lande waren nicht selten große bewaffnete Banden in Ausübung des Terrors tätig.

Zunächst lehnten die russischen Sozialdemokraten den Terror ab, den im wesentlichen die Sozialrevolutionäre betrieben. In den Jahren 1905 und 1906 unterstützte ihn jedoch die bolschewistische Fraktion der russischen sozialdemokratischen Partei. Bomben wurden in geheimen bolschewistischen Laboratorien hergestellt.

Lenin arbeitete später – im Jahre 1915 – das Buch von Clausewitz „Vom Kriege" auf das genaueste durch. Dies zeigen die von ihm gemachten deutschen Auszüge und die Randbemerkungen in russischer Sprache. Durch die Eintragungen in seinem Notizheft (Tetradka) schuf er eines der großartigsten Dokumente der Geistesgeschichte. Das „Institut für Marxismus-Leninismus" beim Zentralkomitee der SED hat eine deutsche Ausgabe von Lenins Tetradka veröffentlicht. Werner Hahlweg, der 1954 im Archiv für Kulturgeschichte, 36. Band, S. 30–39 und 357–387, einen Aufsatz „Lenin und Clausewitz" schrieb, stellt fest, Lenins Bedeutung liege darin, daß er Clausewitz aus dem Stadium der bürgerlichen Revolution von 1789 in die „Proletarische Revolution" von 1917 weitergeführt habe.

Hahlweg hebt hervor: Mit der Formel „der Krieg ist die Fortsetzung der Politik" klärt Lenin „nahezu die gesamten Kernfragen der Revolution in ihrem Kampf: Wesenserkenntnis (Klassenanalyse) des Weltkrieges und damit zusammenhängende Probleme wie Opportunismus, Vaterlandsverteidigung, nationaler Befreiungskampf, Unterschied zwischen gerechten und ungerechten Kriegen, Verhältnis von Krieg und Frieden, Revolution und Krieg, Beendigung des imperialistischen Krieges durch Umsturz im Inneren seitens der Arbeiterklasse, Revision des bolschewistischen Parteiprogramms."

Eine Randbemerkung zu einer Stelle des 23. Kapitels von Buch II (Schlüssel des Landes) ist aufschlußreich für Lenins Denkungsart. Er unterscheidet zwischen Woina (Krieg) und Igrá (Spiel). Der große kommunistische Theoretiker betrachtete den Staatenkrieg des kontinentalen europäischen Völkerrechts als bloßes Spiel, mehr und minder als Duell zwischen sanktionsfähigen Gegnern, während die von ihm vertretene Idee, „der Krieg der absoluten Feindschaft", keine Regeln kennt.

Der Partisan, Träger der absoluten Feindschaft zwischen dem Leninismus/Marxismus und dem Klassenfeind, dem Bourgeois mit seiner Gesellschaftsordnung, ist der Vollstrecker der absoluten Feindschaft. Lenins Philosophie in Verbindung mit der sozial-revolutionären Partisanen- und Untergrundbewegung zerstörte die europäische Welt, um die Napoleon und der Wiener Kongreß rangen.

Joseph Marie, Comte de Maistre, geboren am 1. April 1753 in Chandery, gestorben am 26. Febr. 1821, 1802 sardinischer Gesandter in Petersburg, 1817 Staatsminister, Verfechter des Ancien Regime, befürchtete in einem Brief vom August 1811 an Graf Pellegrino Rossi, der am 15. Nov. 1848 in Rom ermordet wurde, einen akademischen Pugatschow. Er erinnert damit an den Führer des russischen Volksaufstandes im September des Jahres 1773, der von den leibeigenen Bauern und den fremdvölkischen Wolgavölkern unterstützt wurde. General Panin schlug Pugatschow bei Sarepta im August 1774 vernichtend. Dieser wurde am 21. Jan. 1775 in Moskau hingerichtet.

Nach de Maistre ist ein akademischer Pugatschow ein Russe, der „eine Revolution auf eine europäische Weise begänne". Der in südlichen Landen geborene Aristokrat denkt an entsetzliche Kriege. Wenn diese kommen, dann würde ihm die „Sprache fehlen, um zu sagen, was man dann zu befürchten hätte". Aber mehr oder weniger bleibt es bei einer klugen Kritik, ähnlich wie bei Graf Antoine Riverol. Die Thesen Lenins sind:

1. Der Marxismus verwirft alles abstrakte Denken und alle doktrinären Vorschriften über Kampfarten. Er ruft zu einem sorgfältigen Studium des Massenkampfes auf, der sich zur Zeit abspielt.

2. Der Marxismus verneint niemals „irgendeine bestimmte Kampfmethode", geschweige denn will er sie für immer verwerfen. Der Marxismus beschränkt sich nicht auf diejenigen Kampfarten, die zu einem gegebenen Zeitpunkt sowohl praktisch wie auch traditionell sind. Er vertritt die Ansicht, daß als Folge von Änderungen in den sozialen Bedingungen unvermeidlich neue Kampfformen entstehen werden ...

3. Lenin fordert, daß die verschiedenen Kampfarten innerhalb ihres historischen Rahmenwerkes analysiert werden. Konflikte außerhalb ihrer historischen und konkreten Umgebungsbedingungen zu diskutieren, heißt, den elementaren dialektischen Materialismus falsch verstehen. An verschiedenen Punkten der wirtschaftlichen Entwicklung und je nach den sich ändernden politischen, nationalen, kulturellen, sozialen und anderen Bedingungen können verschiedene Kampfarten an Bedeutung gewinnen und sogar vorherrschend werden ...

4. Lenin führt aus: „Lassen Sie uns die historische Entwicklung der verschiedenen Aktionsarten betrachten, die die Revolution aufkommen ließ. Zunächst gab es Streiks der Arbeiter aus sozialen Gründen (1896 bis 1900), dann politische Demonstrationen durch Arbeiter und Studenten (1901–1902), Bauernunruhen (1902), anschließend die Anfänge politischer Massenstreiks, verschiedentlich in Verbindung mit Demonstrationen (Rostow 1902, Streiks im Sommer 1903, die Affäre vom 22. Januar 1905), politischen Generalstreik mit örtlichen Barrikadenkämpfen (Oktober 1905), Barrikadenschlachten, geführt von einer großen Menge [von Revolutionären], sowie einen bewaffneten Aufstand (Dezember 1905), friedliche Parlamentskämpfe (April–Juli 1906), örtliche Militäraufstände (Juni 1905 bis Juni 1906) und örtliche Bauernaufstände (Herbst 1905 bis Herbst 1906)."

5. Der große Theoretiker stellt fest: „Bewaffneter Kampf wird von kleinen Gruppen und von Einzelpersonen geführt, von denen einige Mitglieder revolutionärer Parteien sind. Der bewaffnete Kampf richtet sich auf zwei verschiedene Ziele, die man scharf voneinander unterscheiden muß. Das erste Ziel besteht darin, Einzelpersonen wie hohe Beamte und Angehörige niederen Ranges in der Polizei und in der Armee zu töten. Das zweite Ziel ist, von der Regierung wie auch von Privatpersonen Geld einzutreiben. Ein Teil des erbeuteten Geldes wird für Parteizwecke verwendet, ein anderer Teil für Waffen und für die Vorbereitung des Aufstandes und der Rest für den Unterhalt von Personen, die sich an dem von uns beschriebenen Kampf beteiligen."

Mao Tse-tung ist der größte Theoretiker und Praktiker der revolutionären Kriegführung. Genau wie Lenin, Trotzki und Stalin hat er Clausewitz gelesen. Seine wichtigsten Schriften über diese Kriegführung verfaßte er in den Jahren 1936–1938. In diesen stellt Mao politische Erziehung und die Notwendigkeit einer disziplinierten Armee in den Vordergrund. Er formuliert: ,,Das Volk ist wie das Wasser und die Armee ist wie der Fisch darin." Seine Lehren finden sich in den Schriften: ,,Strategische Probleme des chinesischen Revolutionskrieges" (1936), ,,Strategische Probleme im Guerilla-Krieg gegen die Japaner" (1938) und ,,Über den hinhaltenden Krieg" (1939).

Drei Phasen stellt er in der Kriegführung heraus. Der Offensive des Feindes stellt er die strategische Defensive gegenüber; in dieser findet die Vorbereitung zur eigenen strategischen Offensive statt. Der Feind wird in die Defensive gedrängt und unterliegt. In der Zeitschrift ,,Peoples China" vom 1. Juli 1951, Seite 29, findet sich ein Artikel unter der Überschrift: ,,How the Chinese People defended the Land against the Japanese Fascist Aggressors": Es heißt: ,,Besondere Aufmerksamkeit verdient, daß ein so umfassender wie hinhaltender Guerillakrieg in der gesamten Militärgeschichte der Menschheit etwas Neuartiges darstellt. Dieser Zustand ist untrennbar von der Tatsache, daß wir im 20. Jahrhundert inzwischen aus den ‚dreißiger' in die ‚vierziger' Jahre hinübergewechselt sind."

Große Beachtung finden Maos Gedankengänge: ,,Ohne politisches Ziel muß Guerillakriegführung zum Mißerfolg führen; wird von ihr jedoch ein politisches Ziel verfolgt, das mit den politischen Zielen des Volkes unvereinbar ist, so daß dessen Unterstützung ausbleibt, so muß auch dies zu einem Mißerfolg führen. Dies ist der Hauptgrund, weshalb die Guerillakriegführung nur eine Form des Revolutionskrieges sein und warum sie nicht im Rahmen irgendeiner Gegenrevolution angewendet werden kann. Dies kommt daher, weil der Guerillakrieg in erster Linie durch die Massen organisiert und weitergeführt wird und er, sobald diese Massen nicht mehr hinter ihm stehen oder Teilnahme und Mitarbeit ausbleiben, weder überdauern noch sich entwickeln kann."

Walter D. Jacobs faßte in der Arbeit ,,Mao Tse-tung als Guerillakämpfer näher betrachtet", die grundliegenden Prinzipien zusammen:

1. Der Feind geht vor, wir gehen zurück.
2. Der Feind macht halt, wir stören ihn.
3. Der Feind ermüdet, wir greifen an.
4. Der Feind zieht sich zurück, wir verfolgen ihn.

Mit Recht führt Jacobs aus: ,,Die Bildung von Stützpunktgebieten scheint auf den ersten Blick mit der Idee des Guerillakrieges (oder, um genauer zu sein, des ju tschi tschan) unvereinbar. Mao vertritt die Ansicht, Guerillas ohne Stützpunkte seien herumstreunende Insurgenten und könnten keine Beziehung zu den politischen Bestrebungen der einheimischen Bevölkerung haben. Der durch und durch politische Charakter der Lehre von Mao schließt eine solche Auffassung völlig aus. Das Stützpunktgebiet dient außer politischen auch absolut militärischen Zwecken. Aus einleuchtenden militärischen Gründen lag es gewöhnlich in den Bergen, obschon Mao flaches Gelände nicht ausschloß. Tschu Teh hat in seinen Bemerkungen über das Gebiet der Wutai-Berge eine Beschreibung der militärischen Rolle der Stützpunktgebiete gegeben. Er sagte: ,,Unsere regulären Truppen können zu diesen Stützpunkten zurückkehren, um sich auszuruhen, ihre Bestände aufzufüllen und die Ausbildung zu verbessern. Guerillatruppen und die Massen können dort geschult, kleine Arsenale, Schulen, Lazarette, genossenschaftliche und regionale Verwaltungsorgane zentral angelegt werden. Aus diesen befestigten Stützpunkten heraus können wir zum Angriff auf japanische Garnisonen, Forts, Munitionslager, Kommunikationslinien und Eisenbahnen antreten. Sobald sie diese Ziele zerstört haben, können unsere Truppen verschwinden und anderswo zuschlagen."

Wenn Mao den Guerillas rät, strategisch defensiv und strategisch offensiv zu sein, will er nur sagen, daß es abwechselnd Zeiten geben wird, in denen die Guerillas einmal in der Verteidigung, einmal im Angriff sein werden. Die Einschärfung, zum Bewegungskrieg überzugehen, ist das Kernstück der Gedanken Maos. Für ihn ist Guerillakriegführung ein Vorspiel für die reguläre Kriegführung. Aus Guerillas werden reguläre Soldaten. Im besten marxistischen Sinne meint Mao, daß die Guerilla mit zunehmender Zahl und Qualität sich von selbst in eine reguläre Armee verwandelt, die einen Bewegungskrieg führen kann.

Mao Tse-tung wäre beinahe als Politiker und Militär in der Zeit vom Oktober 1933 bis 23. Oktober 1934 gescheitert.

Tschiang-Kai-schek setzte vom Dezember 1933 bis Oktober 1934 fünf größere Vernichtungsvorstöße gegen die Kommunisten an, von denen vier abgewiesen wurden. Die fünfte Einschließung begann im Oktober 1934. Marschall Tschiang-Kai-schek umschloß die Verbände Mao Tse-tungs mit einem eisernen Ring, während eine Feuerwalze ihre Beweglichkeit hemmte. Auch die örtliche Landbevölkerung wurde daran gehindert, mit Mao zusammenzuarbeiten. Dadurch wurde die Versorgung gestört, die das Verhalten der Bevölkerung ermöglicht hatte.

Der chinesische kommunistische Parteiführer, der Marschall Tschiang-Kai-schek zur Aufgabe des Festlandes zwang, stellt nach Dinegar fünf Kriterien für die Partisanenkriegführung heraus:

1. Wenn der Feind seine Verteidigungslinien übermäßig ausgedehnt hat und nicht ausreichende Kräfte gegen ihn konzentriert werden können, dann müssen die Guerillas ihn zerstreuen, belästigen und demoralisieren.

2. Wenn Guerillas vom Feind umzingelt sind, zerstreuen sie sich, um sich zurückzuziehen.

3. Zerstreuen, wenn die Beschaffenheit des Geländes das Handeln begrenzt.

4. Zerstreuen, wenn das Vorhandensein von Nachschub das Handeln begrenzt.

5. Zerstreuen, um Bewegung über ein weites Gebiet hin zu erleichtern.

Ich habe wiederholt behauptet, daß der deutsche Generalstab vor 1939 Kenntnis von der kommunistischen Partisanenkriegführung hatte. Dies ergibt sich u. a. daraus, daß die Taktik der „5. Einschließung" weniger auf Tschiang-Kai-schek, sondern auf seine deutschen Berater zurückgeht. Auch Snow ist in seinem Buch „Red Star over China" (Roter Stern über China) der gleichen Auffassung. Er führt die von Tschiang-Kai-schek eingeschlagene Taktik auf Generaloberst Hans von Seeckt zurück.

Bereits im März 1932 schrieb General Wetzel an Seeckt, man suche in China einen Mann, der mehr innenpolitische Kenntnisse haben müsse. Wetzel schreibt: „Ich darf dabei hinzufügen, daß nicht ich selbst, sondern ein chinesischer Minister auf den Gedanken kam, sich in dieser Angelegenheit an Herrn Generaloberst zu wenden."

Wetzel schrieb im Mai 1932 als Berater Tschiang-Kai-scheks weiter: „. . . was den Fall der Einladung E. E. anbelangt, so hängt dies mit der Wertschätzung deutschen Wesens, vor allem militärischen Könnens und Schaffens . . . zusammen . . . Öfters hat der Marschall mich nach der Aufbauarbeit E. E. an der Reichswehr gefragt . . ." Mitte Mai 1933 trifft von Seeckt in Shanghai ein.

Die Zeitungen empfangen ihn mit Begrüßungsartikeln. Man nennt ihn den Great Soldier und fragt: „Mystery Visit to Far East. What is his mission here?" Tschiang empfing ihn zu einem regen Gedankenaustausch in Kuling. Sven Hedin berichtet, daß von Seeckt in China sei, um den chinesischen Marschall bei der Organisation des chinesischen Heeres zu beraten.

Am 10. September 1933 ist der deutsche General wieder in Berlin. Dort erreichten ihn Briefe, wieder nach China zu kommen.

Vor Ende des Jahres berichtet von Seeckt dem Reichspräsidenten von Hindenburg und dem Reichskriegsminister von Blomberg über seine Chinareise. Am 2. Nov. 1933 schreibt er seiner Frau, die Enkelin Ernst Moritz Arndts war, daß er während eines kurzen Aufenthaltes lange Unterhaltungen in den Bergen mit dem militärischen Haupt Chinas, dem Marschall Tschiang-Kai-schek gehabt habe. Am 7. Dez. 1934 verließ von Seeckt als offizieller Berater des chinesischen Marschalls Berlin. Er weilte aber nur kurze Zeit in China.

Stalins These im Zweiten Weltkrieg lautete: Im Rücken Partisanen, an der Front sog. Verbrüderung.

Sowjetische Partisanen fesselten über 20 deutsche Divisionen, wodurch sie im großen Ausmaß den Ausgang des Zweiten Weltkriegs beeinflußten. – General Helmut Staedtke formulierte am 17. Oktober 1956 in Anlehnung an Mao Tse-tung: Partisan ist der Kämpfer der genannten %₁₀ einer Kriegführung, die nur das letzte Zehntel den regulären Kräften überläßt. – Stalin verband in dem ,,Großen Vaterländischen Krieg" 1941/45, wie er von den Sowjets genannt wird, ,,patriotische Selbstverteidigung" mit der kommunistischen Weltrevolution, wobei er auch rücksichtslos polnische Partisanen, denen er seine Kampfesweise aufzwang, grausam opferte (Warschau 1944!).

Stalin führte den Begriff der absoluten Feindschaft nach dem Krieg weiter. Nicht mit Unrecht wurde darauf verwiesen, daß die reguläre Rote Armee erst dann erscheint, wenn die Voraussetzungen für die kommunistische Machtübernahme gegeben sind. Dies bedeutet – es mag für manche europäische Regierung nicht angenehm sein, dies zu hören: einen Friedensschluß im Sinne des klassischen Völkerrechts wird es zwischen dem sowjetischen Block und Staaten, die auf einer anderen weltanschaulichen Basis aufgebaut sind, nie geben können. Am 8. Mai 1945 kapitulierte die Deutsche Wehrmacht bedingungslos. Nur die Fortsetzung des Krieges in umgekehrter Frontstellung hätte den Frieden und ein Deutschland mit den Weimarer Grenzlinien bringen und das Elend der Deutschen in Osteuropa verhindern können. Bis jetzt laufen die Grenzen ohne Friedensvertrag zwischen ,,West- und Ostdeutschland" genauso, wie sie damals zwischen den angloamerikanischen und den sowjetischen Truppen vereinbart wurden.

Die Sowjetunion und das Völkerrecht

William C. Bullitt, ein enger Berater Roosevelts und denkbar scharfer Gegner des nationalsozialistischen Deutschlands, schrieb 1946 über die Sowjetunion ein aufsehenerregendes Werk: „Approach to the Sowjetunion." In ihm stellt er fest, daß die UdSSR, ungeachtet ihres Bündnisses mit den angelsächsischen Staaten und den Teheranern, Ialtaer, Moskauer und Potsdamer Vereinbarungen, die Politik der Unterwühlung fortsetze. Die einzige Möglichkeit zur Vermeidung eines Krieges werde es sein, die Sowjetunion durch überlegene militärische Kräfte dauernd in Schach zu halten. Er vertrat die Auffassung, daß vertragliche Bindungen nichts bedeuten würden.

Die Sowjetunion ist bereit, höchstens für eine Übergangszeit – in der Hauptsache zu ihrem Vorteil – die Notwendigkeit der widerwilligen und widerruflichen Anerkennung gewisser Konventionsregeln des Völkerrechtsverkehrs zu akzeptieren.

Der sowjetrussische Völkerrechtler Korowin veröffentlichte 1929 in Moskau unter dem Titel „Völkerrecht der Übergangszeit" eine Arbeit. In ihr heißt es: „Es ist zu beachten, daß die alte Maxime ‚Wo Gemeinschaft, dort Recht' nicht nur ein Produkt juristischer Dialektik, sondern auch eine soziologische Tatsache ist. Soweit die Sowjetrepubliken durch die Gewalt der Tatsachen dazu gezwungen sind, eine gewisse geschichtliche Periode im Kreis der ‚kapitalistischen Einkreisung' zu durchleben, und neben Sowjetrußland auch noch sonstige Staatsbildungen existieren, müssen die Beziehungen Sowjetrußlands zu ihnen unvermeidlich auf dieser oder jener rechtlichen Basis der ‚Übergangszeit' beruhen. Fraglich ist nur ihre Art."

Die Sowjetunion kann also auf die Dauer kein loyaler Teilnehmer der Völkerrechtsgemeinschaft sein. Unverrückbare Ziele der Weltrevolution stehen dagegen.

Die Sowjetunion ist grundsätzlich Vertreter des Souveränitätsgedankens in unbeschränkter Form. Diese Auffassung vertritt Professor Korowin, der völkerrechtliche Interpret des Kremls, auch nach 1945. Angeblich „aus Selbsterhaltungsgründen" dürfe sich die Sowjetunion keine Konventionsregeln anlegen. Daher ist die Sowjetunion für das Vetorecht im Sicherheitsrat der UNO.

Die Klausel „rebus sic stantibus" findet in der Sowjetdoktrin die größtmögliche Ausdehnung. Klarheit muß darüber bestehen: wenn der am Völkerrechtsverkehr teilnehmende Staat grundsätzlich die Rechtssubjektivität der anderen Staaten, wie der Professor des osteuropäischen Rechts, Dr. Reinhard Maurach, sagt, mißachtet, so kann sich in den Beziehungen eines solchen Staates zu seiner Umwelt nur ein waffenstillstandsähnliches Verhältnis, ein gewisser taktisch bedingter und zeitlich beschränkter Modus vivendi ergeben.

Die sowjetischen Völkerrechtler vertreten den Standpunkt, daß die Sowjetunion auf die Beseitigung der anderen kapitalistischen Völkerrechtssubjekte hinarbeiten muß. Ein System dauerhafter und von gegenseitiger Achtung getragener Rechtsregeln zwischen der Sowjetunion und den Staaten westlicher Kulturauffassung ist bei dieser Lage unmöglich. Dies könnten eigentlich die Staatsmänner erkennen, die auf den KSZE-Nachfolgekonferenzen agieren lassen. Das Völkerrecht mit seinen Regeln ist nach sowjetischer Auffassung je nach Interessen der Weltrevolution anzuwenden.

Korowin lehrt: ,,Einerseits wissen wir besser als irgend jemand, daß nicht durch die Unterschrift einer bürgerlichen Regierung und nicht durch Motive formeller Scholastik die Treue den übernommenen Verpflichtungen im allgemeinen und gegenüber sozialistischen Staaten im besonderen gewahrt wird . . . der relative Wert (solcher Kriegskonventionen) ist auch für Sowjetrußland anzuerkennen, aber mit der ,unvermeidlichen Verbesserung' im Bezug auf die soziale Revolution in Form der Clausula rebus stic stantibus."

Gleichgültig ist, wie der Krieg eröffnet wird. Ein Krieg, den die Sowjetunion führt, ist ipso jure ein Verteidigungskrieg, weil er unter dem Begriff der ,,Klassenselbstverteidigung" geführt wird. Offen ließ Korowin die Frage, ob die UdSSR die Regeln des Gefangenenrechtes anerkennen würde. Bemerkenswert ist der Satz, daß die Sowjetunion im Falle eines Krieges mit den kapitalistischen Staaten erhebliche Unterschiede machen würde, je nachdem es sich um ,,Klassenfeinde" oder ,,Proletarier" handle.

Im besetzten Gebiet wird Inhaftierung und Verbannung der Kriegsgefangenen für zulässig erklärt, sofern diese Gruppen eine Gefahr für die Sowjet-Armee darstellen. Dabei ist die Vermutung ausreichend (potentieller Gegner). Wenn einerseits auch das Geiselsystem eine grundsätzliche Ablehnung erfährt, so wird andererseits betont, daß bei besonderen Verhältnissen dieses Prinzip in besonderen Lagen durch den Gesichtspunkt der Zweckmäßigkeit gerechtfertigt ist. Für die Geiselnahme kämen besondere Personengruppen wie Bürgermeister, Notare, Lehrer und Pfarrer in Frage. Offen läßt Korowin die Frage, ob die Sowjetunion sich im besetzten feindlichen Gebiet an die Haager Landgerichtsordnung halten würde.

Er schreibt: ,, . . . entsteht die Frage, ob man die Tatsache als unrechtmäßig bewerten kann, daß auch die Sowjetmacht sich nicht im mindesten verpflichtet fühlt, die Unverletzlichkeit der Ausbeutung und die Unerschütterlichkeit der kapitalistischen Ordnung in den Grenzen des okkupierten Territoriums zu beschirmen, sondern daß sie im Gegenteil für ihr sozialistisches Sein jede mögliche Hilfe (Finnland, Polen, Estland, Lettland) dem

Streben der örtlichen werktätigen Massen zur Organisierung der Gesellschaft auf sozialistischer Grundlage angedeihen läßt. Die revolutionären Komitees, die Unterstützung des Entstehens nationaler Sowjetrepubliken und die sonstigen Elemente der Sowjetisierung sind die Folge davon."
Professor Dr. Reinhard Maurach, den ich in einem Prozeß vor dem amerikanischen Militärgerichtshof als Gutachter einführte, folgerte aus den vorhandenen sowjetischen Unterlagen: „. . . als der Krieg mit Deutschland begann und als nicht nur aufgrund der sowjetischen Theorien gewonnene Präsumptionen, sondern auch schon Erfahrungen über die Einstellung der Sowjetunion zum Kriegsrecht vorlagen . . . In ihrem Zusammenwirken haben diese Schlußfolgerungen und Erfahrungen die bolschewistische Grundthese im wesentlichen erhärtet, die Auffassung nämlich, daß die Sowjetregierung nur bereit ist, in der ‚Übergangszeit' die Regeln des Völkerrechtes in gewissen Sinne anzuerkennen, daß sie aber im Falle des entscheidenden Zusammenstoßes zwischen ihr und den kapitalistischen Staaten sich grundsätzlich freie Hand zu wahren gewillt ist."
Für die UdSSR ist das Völkerrecht eine diplomatische Waffe zur Verwirklichung ihrer revolutionären Ziele. Moskau gibt Rechtsbestimmungen preis, wenn dies den Interessen der unabwendbaren kommenden Revolution entspricht.
Die Interventionspolitik seit 1917 zeigt, daß die Außenpolitik Moskaus nur unter diesem Gesichtspunkt zu verstehen ist.
In der sowjetischen Deklaration über die Völker Rußlands vom 2. Nov. 1917 wurde den Nationalitäten des Zarenreiches die Freiheit der Selbstbestimmung einschließlich der Loslösung versprochen. Die sowjetische Regierung ließ sich jedoch von den sozialistischen Parteien der selbständigen Staaten um Hilfe gegen die Unterdrückung anrufen. So wurden Georgien, Armenien und Aserbeidschan 1920 sowjetisch. In Tannu-Tuwa und in der äußeren Mongolei wurden Vasallenstaaten errichtet.
Moskau förderte Unruheherde an den europäischen Grenzen. Als Beispiel kann die finnisch-karelische ASSR an der finnischen Grenze genannt werden, aus der nach Abschluß des ersten Finnlandkrieges die finnisch-karelische Bundesrepublik entstand. Auch die moldauische ASSR an der rumänischen Grenze gehört in diesen Zusammenhang. Die Eingliederung Estlands, Lettlands und Litauens wurde mit Hilfe eines Paktes zur gegenseitigen Hilfeleistung vollzogen. Die Sowjetunion erhielt durch die Verträge das Recht, Truppenlager, Flottenstützpunkte und Flugplätze in den drei Staaten zu errichten. Am 14./16. Juni 1940 behauptete der Kreml grundlos, die Beistandspakte seien verletzt worden. Die Umbildung der Regierungen im Baltikum und der Einmarsch weiterer sowjetischer Truppen wurde gefordert. Nach Annahme der Ultimaten fanden unter inoffizieller Aufsicht

und Kontrolle der sowjetischen diplomatischen Behörden unter einem ad hoc geschaffenen Wahlsystem, das die Sowjetverfassung von 1936 zum Vorbild hatte, Parlamentswahlen statt. Allein der „Verband des arbeitenden Volkes" war in der Lage, Wahlkandidaten aufzustellen. Versuche der übrigen Parteien scheiterten. Es gab einen Begriff, der ausschlaggebend wurde: „Feinde des werktätigen Volkes."

Mit Finnland wurden bis zum 29. Nov. 1939 Verhandlungen über Gebietsabtretungen mit der legalen finnischen Regierung geführt. Am 29. Nov. 1939 erklärte der Kreml, er sei an die Bestimmungen des 1932 geschlossenen und bis 1945 laufenden Nichtangriffspaktes nicht mehr gebunden. Am 30. Nov. 1939 begannen die Angriffsoperationen. Die führende sowjetische Zeitung, die „Prawda" (Nr. 277/1939), berichtete, daß die finnische kommunistische Partei eine Regierung gebildet habe, die die sowjetischen Territorialwünsche akzeptieren werde. Im Grenzort Terioki agierte eine kommunistisch geführte, „demokratische" finnische Regierung unter dem Vorsitz des Kommintern-Mitgliedes Kuusinen.

Am gleichen Tag gab letzterer eine Regierungserklärung ab. Die „diplomatischen Beziehungen" mit der UdSSR wurden aufgenommen. Der Oberste Rat der Sowjets erkannte sofort die Regierung zu. Am 2. Dez. 1939 wurde mit ihr ein gegenseitiger Beistandspakt abgeschlossen. Die sowjetischen Gebietsforderungen wurden anerkannt. Der sowjetische Außenminister Molotow konnte am 5. Dez. 1939 an den Völkerbund telegrafieren: „URSS ne se trouve pas en état de guerre avec la Finlande . . . Elle se trouve en relations pacifiques avec la République démocratique de Finlande."

Der Bolschewismus
in nationalsozialistischer Sicht
und Propaganda

Der Begriff „Judo-Marxismus" geht auf die Anfänge des Nationalsozialismus zurück. Nach Ende des Ersten Weltkrieges findet sich in Polen der Begriff „Jewish-Bolschewiki". – Im Herbst 1936 wurde dem Bolschewismus nach dem Reichsparteitag die schärfste Kampfansage erteilt. Eine rege publizistische und pseudowissenschaftliche Tätigkeit setzte ein. Die „Antikomintern" wurde gegründet. Parteiamtlich geförderte Personen wie Fehst, Poehl-Agthe, Bockhoff und Ehrt schrieben über die „Vereinigungstheorie des jüdischen Marxismus". Der „Eckart-Kampf-Verlag" und der „Nibelungen-Verlag" wurden bekannt. Die vertretenen Theorien finden sich als Grundsätze in den Schulungsbriefen der Partei, in den Schulungslagern, in der Presse und in den offiziellen oder offiziösen Kundgebungen, Reden und Ansprachen der größeren und kleineren Parteiführer.

Es ist nicht meine Aufgabe, die vertretenen Thesen in den genannten Veröffentlichungen, aus denen sich eine völlige Unkenntnis der wechselnden Schicksale des jüdischen Volkes in der Sowjetunion ergibt, zu behandeln. Herauszustellen sind einzig und allein die psychologischen Auswirkungen einer Doktrin.

1981 erschien im Piper-Verlag in München eine Biographie von „Karl Marx, Sein Leben und seine Zeit". Der Verfasser, Friedenthal, der 1979 in London verstarb, konnte seine Arbeit nicht ganz vollenden. Das Buch zeigt auf, wie einseitig die Publizisten in der ganzen nationalsozialistischen Herrschaft Karl Marx darstellten. Heinz Aposch schreibt in der „Neuen Zürcher Zeitung" vom 5. Nov. 1981 eine glänzend formulierte Kritik: „Wir lernen den Sohn des liberalen Rechtsanwalts in Trier kennen, der zum Protestantismus konvertierte, aus beruflichen Gründen, aber auch, wie Heine sagte, um das ‚Entréebillet zur europäischen Kultur zu erwerben' . . . Sein Vater nennt ihn ein ‚Glückskind', er bedarf beachtlicher Geldmittel und erwartet, daß sie stets vorhanden sind.

In der Zeit des Nationalsozialismus wurde argumentiert: Marx sei Jude gewesen, die jüdische Lehre enthalte ausschließlich jüdische Logik. Sie sei der Versuch der Tarnung einer angestrebten jüdischen Weltherrschaft. Die praktische Verwirklichung dieses getarnten jüdischen Traumes nach der Weltherrschaft sei der Bolschewismus. Beweis dafür biete der unverhältnismäßig große Anteil jüdischer Führer im bolschewistischen Staatsinstrument.

Auf Seite 157 seines Buches „Bolschewismus und Judentum" (1934), erschienen im Dietrich-Eckart-Kampf-Verlag in Berlin, hebt Fehst hervor: „So steht heute das russische Volk wieder vor der historischen Aufgabe, sein Land von der Fremdherrschaft zu befreien, die vom Judo-Marxismus gegen das russische Volk ausgeübt wird. Der nationale Freiheitskampf des russischen Volkes ist zugleich ein Kampf gegen den Todfeind aller Nationen – die kommunistische Internationale, in deren Gestalt der völkervernichtende Marxismus und das internationale Judentum ein Bündnis gegen Frieden und Freiheit der Welt geschlossen haben."

Fehsts Argumentation ist primitiv, doch darauf kommt es nicht an, sondern einzig und allein – wie ich bereits hervorhob – auf die psychologische Auswirkung. Eine staatliche Propaganda in einem totalitären Staat hat ihr Ziel nicht erst dann erreicht, wenn tatsächlich alles als wahr geglaubt wird, was sie verkündet, sondern schon dann, wenn sie eine Atmosphäre geschaffen hat, in welcher Kritik oder Ablehnung undenkbar wären.

Und Moskau befiehlt

Generaloberst Jodl erklärte in seiner Vernehmung vor dem Internationalen Militärgerichtshof in Nürnberg zum Vorgehen der Sowjets am 5. Juni 1946: ,,Wenn Sie das nicht glauben wollen, was ich Ihnen hier sage, dann lesen Sie mal die Meldungen der Abwehr nach, die wir über das Verhalten der Kommissare in den besetzten baltischen Staaten bekommen haben; dann werden Sie ein Bild bekommen, was von diesen Kommissaren zu erwarten ist.''

Daher lege ich Teile des Weißbuches ,,Das Jahr des Grauens – Lettland unter der Herrschaft des Bolschewismus 1940/41'' vor – auch stellvertretend für von der bolschewistischen Partei anderswo verursachte Vorkommnisse.

Hinzufügen möchte ich, daß auch dieses ,,Weißbuch'' die Verantwortung jüdischer Kommissare in Lettland behandelt.

Das Weißbuch wurde von lettischer Seite unter dem Motto zusammengestellt: ,,Der Bolschewismus hat die Ehre und die Menschenrechte des Volkes in Schmutz getreten, den Menschen erniedrigt und ihn seiner persönlichen Freiheit beraubt, das gesamte Wirtschaftsleben zerstört und die Kultur vernichtet.''

In dem Einleitungskapitel heißt es: ,,Das lettische Volk, das unbeschützt in den Wirbel der weltweiten Umwälzungen und Ereignisse hineingerissen wurde, hat ein Jahr unter dem Joch des Bolschewismus hinter sich. In dieser Zeit verlor es seine Selbständigkeit und war schließlich gezwungen, dem Bolschewismus unzählige Menschenleben und große materielle Werte zu opfern. Das vorliegende Werk soll nicht nur eine engere Auswahl für den Bolschewismus besonders charakteristischer Zeugnisse darstellen, sondern in der Hauptsache diese als anschaulichen Bericht über die überstandene Schreckenszeit der Nachwelt und denen, die sie nicht miterlebt haben, übermitteln. Es soll auch eine ernste Mahnung für die sein, die den Bolschewismus nicht kennen oder ihn nicht richtig beurteilen . . .

Auch die Roten Truppen der Bolschewisten, die 1919 ins Land einbrachen, hatten das gleiche Bestreben: den baltischen Raum dem europäischen Kulturkreis zu entziehen und ihn endgültig dem Osten einzuverleiben . . .

Wenn die Meinung besteht, daß es leichter ist zu zerstören als aufzubauen, so unterliegt es keinem Zweifel, daß es kaum eine geübtere und unbarmherzigere Kraft gibt als den Bolschewismus. Im Laufe dieses einen Jahres haben die Bolschewisten nicht nur das, was das lettische Volk in mühevoller Arbeit errungen hat, vernichtet, ihre Vernichtungswut wandte sich auch gegen alles, was die ganze Menschheit in vielen Jahren der Arbeit und des Kampfes erreicht hat. Es sei hier nur hingewiesen auf die Abschaffung des Privatbesitzes, die Bolschewisierung der Immobilien, Enteignung der Ersparnisse, Aufteilung der Bauernwirtschaften, ganz zu schweigen davon, daß dem Menschen die private Initiative genommen, seine Menschenrechte eingeschränkt oder gar abgeschafft und jede persönliche Sicherheit verwehrt war, wobei die einzelnen Gesellschaftsschichten im Namen der ‚Diktatur des Proletariats‘ gegeneinander aufgehetzt wurden . . .

Unter hartem Zwang und gegen seinen Willen mußte das lettische Volk eine Sacima (Parlament) wählen, deren Abgeordnete den ‚Willen des Volkes‘ dadurch zum Ausdruck brachten, daß sie für die Gründung Sowjet-Lettlands und den Anschluß an die Sowjetunion eintraten.‘‘

Wie ein roter Faden lassen sich durch das Jahr des Grauens zwei Richtungen verfolgen, deren Endziel ohne Zweifel die Vernichtung des gesamten lettischen Volkes war:

1. ‚‚die Zerstörung der wirtschaftlichen Kräfte und des materiellen Wohlstandes,

2. die Bestrebung, den guten Geist, die moralische Kraft des Volkes zu vernichten und seine Ehre in den Schmutz zu ziehen. Es ist bezeichnend, daß keinerlei politische, wirtschaftliche und physische Verluste das lettische Volk während der Bolschewistenzeit so bedrückten wie gerade diese moralische Erniedrigung: das Gefühl des Ausgeliefertseins an die Willkür, die seelischen Leiden beim Anblick der Vernichtung alles dessen, was der gesunde Menschenverstand bisher als positiv angesehen hatte, und schließlich das Fehlen jeder Zukunftsaussicht. Das Volk wurde dem geistigen Stumpfsinn zugeführt, der jetzt auf den Gesichtern der bolschewistischen Generation zu lesen ist. Der Mensch wurde zu einem Mechanismus gestempelt, der nach bolschewistischem ‚Plan und Grafik‘ arbeitet, die gesamte Führung aber lag in den Händen der Kommunistischen Partei der Moskauer Zentrale . . .‘‘

Die Einleitung weist noch auf die Tschekakeller und die Leichen der zu Tode gemarterten Opfer hin.

So fing es an

Am 15. Juni 1940 hatten sich lettische Frauen und Männer zum Sängerfest in Dünaburg versammelt. Niemand ahnte, daß es das letzte freudige Volksfest sein sollte. In der Nacht vom 14. zum 15. Juni fiel eine Gruppe bewaffneter Bolschewisten in Lettland ein und verübte ihre erste Schandtat. Ein Grenzwächterhaus wurde in Brand gesteckt, mehrere Grenzwächter ermordet, 43 friedliche Bewohner der Umgebung wurden festgenommen und über die Grenze geschleppt, nur weil sie versucht hatten, das Feuer zu löschen. Mit dieser Bluttat begann das Jahr des Grauens. Von diesem grausamen Übergriff wurde die Öffentlichkeit einige Tage darauf durch die Presse in Kenntnis gesetzt, und zwar erschien eine kurze Notiz der Lettländischen Telegrafenagentur vom 15. Juni, die lediglich die sachliche Feststellung enthielt, daß ein Grenzwächterhaus in der Ortschaft Maslenki an der lettisch-sowjetischen Grenze im Morgengrauen des 15. Juni in Brand gesteckt wurde, zwei Grenzwächter und eine Frau ermordet, eine andere Frau und ein vierzehnjähriger Junge schwer verwundet in der Nähe des abgebrannten Hauses gefunden wurden. Elf Grenzwächter und mehrere Einwohner des Ortes wurden verletzt. Eine Untersuchungskommission unter Leitung des Kommandeurs der Grenzwächterbrigade, General Bolstein, habe sich an den Tatort begeben, um die näheren Umstände zu klären.

Am frühen Morgen des 17. Juni 1940

überschritten zahlreiche motorisierte Einheiten und Panzer der Sowjet-Armee die Ostgrenze Lettlands und machten sich auf den Weg zur Hauptstadt, die sie am Mittag erreichten. Die überraschten Einwohner Rigas hatten für die ungebetenen Gäste, die in langen Kolonnen durch die Straßen der Stadt marschierten, nur ein finsteres Schweigen und feindselige Blicke.

Die Fälschung des Volkswillens

Um der Welt Sand in die Augen zu streuen und sie von den brutalen Gewaltmethoden abzulenken, griffen die Bolschewisten zu dem für sie charakteristischen und zynischen Mittel der Fälschung des Volkswillens mit Hilfe des Wahlterrors. Die Bevölkerung wurde gezwungen, am 15. und 16. Juli an den Wahlen zur Sacima (Parlament) teilzunehmen. Man ließ einfach die Arbeiter und Angestellten der Werke und Behörden, ebenso auch Einheiten der Armee in Reih und Glied zu den Wahlen marschieren. Wer keinen Vermerk im Paß vorweisen konnte, mußte befürchten, eines Tages als Feind der Sowjetmacht festgenommen zu werden. Schon am 21. Juli wurde die erste große Fälschung des Volkswillens als Beschluß der neugewählten Sacima bekanntgegeben: Die Gründung der Sowjetischen Sozialistischen Republik.

Am 5. August war das Schicksal Lettlands besiegelt – an diesem Tage hörte der lettländische Staat auf zu existieren. Blutiger Hohn klingt aus den

Zeilen der „Iswestija" vom 6. August: „Gestern beschloß der oberste Rat der UdSSR in getrennter Abstimmung der Kammer einstimmig, die Forderungen der lettländischen Sacima anzunehmen und die Sowjetlettische Sozialistische Republik in die Union der Sowjetischen Sozialistischen Republiken aufzunehmen. Es lebe Sowjet-Lettland, die gleichberechtigte Republik im brüderlichen Bund der Sowjetunion!"

„Für die Idee Marx – Engels – Lenin – Stalin"

Unter dieser Devise stand eigentlich das ganze bolschewistische öffentliche Leben. Alle Gebiete des menschlichen Daseins mußten vom Standpunkt der Prinzipien der kommunistischen Lehre betrachtet werden, wobei die Bolschewisten sich verpflichtet fühlten, die breitesten Volksmassen mit der Behauptung zu behelligen, daß der Marxismus kein politisches System, sondern eine Wissenschaft sei. An der Universität wurde diese „Wissenschaft" als neues Lehrfach eingeführt, und zwar als wichtigstes Fach mit einem Lehrstuhl des „Marxismus-Leninismus". Lehrkräfte waren „Kapazitäten" aus der Sowjetunion, deren Bildung sich meist auf den Besuch verschiedener Agitations- und Spionageschulen oder des „Instituts der Roten Professur" der Moskauer Professoren-Schnellpresse beschränkte. Ihre „wissenschaftlichen Verdienste" hatten nichts mit der Wissenschaft im landläufigen Sinn zu tun. Meist waren es Erfolge im Aufbau der Kommunistischen Partei oder jahrelange Gefängnishaft im zaristischen Rußland. Die theologische und philosophische Fakultät wurde geschlossen und – wie bezeichnend – die Logik als Lehrfach abgeschafft. An die Stelle der erfahrenen alten Lehrkräfte traten sofort die schon erwähnten Moskauer Genossen.

Die Kriegshetze beginnt . . .

Da Lettland nun „gleichberechtigtes" Mitglied der UdSSR geworden war, mußte es selbstverständlich auch alle Verpflichtungen, die diese „Ehre" mit sich brachte, in Kauf nehmen.

Es begann die Einberufung der Wehrfähigen . . .

Wer das Jahr des Grauens miterlebt hat, weiß nur zu gut, mit welcher Offenheit die Soldaten der Sowjetarmee, die Parteiagitatoren und oft auch Juden vom kommenden Krieg sprachen und die Überzeugung laut werden ließen, daß die Rote Fahne auch in Berlin wehen müsse, damit auch das deutsche Volk endlich „befreit" werde. Die Öffentlichkeit wurde allmählich mit dem Gedanken vertraut gemacht, daß ein Krieg gegen Deutschland unvermeidlich sei, wobei besonderer Nachdruck auf die „kapitalistische Einkreisung" gelegt wurde, durch die die UdSSR ständig bedroht werde.

Das nannte man Religionsfreiheit

. . . bezeichnenderweise richtete sich die ganze Gottlosenpropaganda, selbstverständlich groß aufgezogen, nur gegen die christlichen Konfessionen . . . Der Besuch der Gottlosen-Ausstellungen war für Soldaten, Schuljugend, Betriebsangehörige, praktisch für alle obligatorisch. Im übrigen blieben die Bolschewisten bei dieser Gottlosen-Propaganda nicht stehen, sondern leiteten später auch praktische Maßnahmen gegen die Kirche ein; so wurden als Auftakt zu einer zweifellos beabsichtigten Liquidierung der Konfessionen zwei evangelisch-lutherische Kirchen in Lagerhäuser verwandelt, und in vier katholischen Kirchen in Lettgallen wurden Tanzsäle eingerichtet. Eine Neuerscheinung im „Gesellschaftlichen Leben" waren die Clubhäuser und Clubräume der Roten Garde und der GPU. In sehr vielen Fällen wurden die Gebethäuser der Religionsgemeinschaft als zweckmäßig betrachtet und enteignet. Einsprüche der Religionsgemeinschaften waren natürlich zwecklos.

Stummer Protest!

Es bedarf keiner besonderen Beweisführung, daß sich das lettische Volk in seiner Gesamtheit von diesem System der Willkür und Sinnlosigkeit abschloß. Durchaus verständlich ist es, daß der Druck Gegendruck erzeugte und die Spannung zwischen dem lettischen Volk und den Roten Machthabern von Monat zu Monat wuchs. Die offene Ablehnung brachte neue verschärfte Verfolgungen. Jeder, der die Internationale nicht mitsang, an den Umzügen und Wahlen nicht teilnahm oder sich eine kritische Bemerkung erlaubt hatte, wurde als Feind des bolschewistischen Systems verfolgt.

Die Nacht zum 14. Juni

In der Nacht zum 14. Juni 1941 begannen Massenverhaftungen und Verschleppungen. Da die Vorbereitungen für diese Gewaltaktion, die schon lange Zeit im Gange waren, auf das sorgfältigste geheimgehalten wurden, ist es verständlich, daß dieser Überfall des Untermenschentums die Unglücklichen völlig unerwartet traf und nur die wenigsten Zeit fanden, sich durch die Flucht dem grausamen Schicksal zu entziehen . . . Man konnte die Transporte nicht grausamer durchführen. Wie Vieh wurden die Unglücklichen in den Waggons zusammengepfercht, ohne Rücksicht auf Alter und Geschlecht, ohne Nahrung und ohne Wasser, ja ohne die primitivsten Einrichtungen. Kinder und Greise wurden durch die Unmenschlichkeit des Verfahrens ohne weiteres dem Tod preisgegeben, da allenfalls körperlich kräftige Menschen diese Tortur aushielten.

Nach Sibiriens Tundren

Die von den Bolschewisten hinterlassenen Unterlagen geben Hinweise, wo die Verschleppten in Zukunft zur Zwangsarbeit eingesetzt werden sollten.

GPU

Jeder, den die Bolschewisten verfolgten, kam – wenn er sich nicht durch die Flucht der Verfolgung entzogen hatte oder verschleppt wurde – in die Folterkammern der GPU. Das Grauen, die Schmerzen und Leiden, die die unglücklichen Gefangenen dort auszustehen hatten, lassen sich nicht beschreiben . . .

Die ,,demokratischste Konstitution der Welt", die Konstitution Stalins, die den Völkern der Sowjetunion, zu denen nun auch das lettische Volk gehörte, eine glückliche, sonnige Zukunft verhieß, brachte unfaßbares Grauen . . .

Die Henker des lettischen Volkes

Als Henker werden beschuldigt: ,,Schustin, Volkskommissar des Inneren (GPU), später Volkskommissar für staatliche Sicherheit. Novik, Volkskommissar des Inneren, würdiger Nachfolger Schustins. Moses Citrons, Arzt des Dünaburger GPU-Gefängnisses . . ." Alle drei sind Sowjetbürger jüdischer Herkunft.

Schustin

wird beschuldigt, ein Sammelurteil über 78 Angeklagte gefällt zu haben. Es heißt: ,,Darunter mit roter Tinte die ,Urteilsbegründungen des Kommissars für innere Sicherheit . . .': ,In Anbetracht der sozialen Gerechtigkeit sind alle zu erschießen.'

Hier die ‚Verbrechen‘, die mit dem Tod bestraft werden mußten;
‚sang lettische Volkslieder‘,
‚hat am 1. Mai die Internationale nicht mitgesungen‘,
‚stammt von Großgrundbesitzern ab‘,
‚hielt sich während des Fliegeralarms auf dem Friedhof auf‘,
‚war Mitglied einer Korporation‘,
‚war Mitglied der ehemaligen Schutzwehr‘,
‚war Polizeibeamter‘,
‚war antibolschewistisch gesinnt‘,
‚verhielt sich verächtlich gegen Sowjetsoldaten‘,
‚äußerte sich verächtlich gegen die kommunistische Partei‘,
‚ehemaliger Adjutant des lettischen Staatspräsidenten‘,
‚stiftete Haß gegen andere Völker‘ . . .“

So endete das Jahr des Grauens – Jahresbilanz der Bolschewistenzeit:

Die Macht, die im Namen der Freiheit, Gleichheit und Brüderlichkeit mit Versprechungen eines glücklichen Lebens und einer sonnigen Zukunft kam, hat über das lettische Volk tiefstes Elend, Mord und Grauen gebracht . . . 34 250 Menschen sind verhaftet, verschleppt, ermordet oder verschollen . . . Das alles geschah im Zeichen des Sowjetsterns und der ‚‚freiesten Verfassung aller Völker‘‘, der Konstitution Stalins. Während die roten Machthaber von Freiheit und Glück redeten, zertraten sie Freiheit und Glück der Menschen, stießen sie in Trostlosigkeit, Verzweiflung und Elend.

(Der Autor des Buches ist sich bewußt, daß das Weißbuch ein propagandistisches Mittel darstellt, aber darüber gibt es keinen Zweifel, daß wesentliche Grundlagen behandelt werden.)

Der Partisanenkrieg als Kampfmittel der Weltrevolution

Die Abteilung Wissenschaft beim Zentralkomitee der Sozialistischen Einheitspartei stellte am 17. Dezember 1958 die Bedeutung des Partisanenkampfes für die Niederlage des nationalsozialistischen Reiches heraus, während in der Bundesrepublik das Hauptinteresse der Entwicklung der Judenfrage galt.

Zweifellos rechnete die nationalsozialistische Führung mit einem Partisanen- und Untergrundkrieg: sie erkannte jedoch nicht die Intensität dessen, was bevorstand. Daher traf sie falsche Maßnahmen.

Hitler war sich nicht darüber im klaren, daß mit dem Partisanenkrieg eine neue Kampfform, eine neue Qualität in der Strategie und Taktik des modernen Krieges, eine ,,Veränderung der herkömmlichen oder konventionellen Kampfesweise entstanden war".

Daß mit dieser neuen Kampfesführung eine Abkehr von dem klassischen Kriegsvölkerrecht verbunden ist, wird heute noch von hohen Justizstellen nicht gesehen.

Himmler bezeichnet nach dem Bulletin Glówenej Komisji Badania Zbrodni Hitlerowskich Polsce, Warschau 1960, Heft XI, S. 202, ,,die Partisanen neben der Infanterie, Artillerie und anderen als eine ,neue Waffengattung'."

Einen Schlüssel zu Himmlers Einstellung gibt der Satz aus einem Vortrag, den der damalige Reichsführer SS im Jahre 1937 (vgl. ,,Neuer Vorwärts", Prag, 26. Sept. 1937 (Beilage) hielt:

,,Wir werden in einem künftigen Krieg nicht nur die Front der Armee auf dem Lande, die Front der Marine zu Wasser, die Front der Luftwaffe in der Luftglocke über Deutschland haben, wie ich es nennen möchte, sondern wir werden einen Kriegsschauplatz haben: Innerdeutschland."

Wenn auch Himmler nur die innerdeutschen Widerstandsbewegungen im Auge hatte und dabei zwischen den von Moskau geleiteten Widerstandsbewegungen und anderen Gruppierungen zu unterscheiden ist, so muß gesagt werden, daß die ersteren unter dem Gesichtspunkt der bolschewistischen Weltrevolution zu sehen sind. Mit Recht führt Generaloberst Rendulic, den ich vor dem Clemency-Board vertrat, aus: ,,In keinem Krieg der bisherigen Geschichte hatte der Partisanenkampf eine solche Bedeutung wie im letzten Weltkrieg."

Er stellt damit in seinem Ausmaß ein Novum der Kriegsgeschichte dar. Sein Aufflackern und seine mit den Jahren sich ständig steigernde Intensität in der UdSSR, Polen, auf dem Balkan, aber auch in Frankreich und Italien hat das Gesicht des Zweiten Weltkrieges mitbestimmt."

Bereits 1870 schrieb Friedrich Engels über den Partisanenkampf: „Dieses stetige Nagen des Volksaufstandes unterhöhlt auf die Dauer die stärkste Armee und läßt Stück für Stück von ihr abbröckeln, und zwar, was die Hauptsache ist, ohne mindesten Ausgleich auf der Gegenseite." – Als Element der kommunistischen Weltrevolution ist er heute aktuell, er bringt den bewaffneten Aufstand mit sich und mündet in den regulären Krieg.

Nach Ernesto Che Guevara ist der Partisanenkampf ein Kampf der Massen. Er wird diktiert von den Bedingungen des Kräfteverhältnisses.

Nach kommunistischer Auffassung war der Partisanenkrieg die einzige Möglichkeit über die Wiederherstellung der nationalen Unabhängigkeit hinaus, Ziele im Sinne der bolschewistischen Weltrevolution zu verfolgen und zu erreichen. Er begann mit dem passiven Widerstand – auch unter der Parole „Arbeite langsam, Kamerad" – mit Befehlsverweigerung, Verbreitung illegalen Propagandamaterials, Sabotage der Produktion und des Verkehrs.

Kühnrich führt als Beispiel des irregulären Kampfes an:

a) „Vernichtung von Soldaten und Offizieren der Okkupanten sowie von Landesverrätern und Quislingen,

b) Vernichtung der Militärtechnik der Okkupanten (Liquidierung von Militärbasen und -lagern, Überfälle auf kleinere Einheiten und Garnisonen, auf Flugplätze und Züge),

c) Störung und Vernichtung der Verbindungslinien, Nachschubstrecken und Transportmittel (Sprengung von Bücken, Zugentgleisungen, Überfälle auf Militärzüge und Kraftwagen, Abfangen von Kurieren, Unterbrechung der Gleisanlagen sowie der Telefon- und Telegraphenverbindungen),

d) Bindung von gegnerischen Truppen und Zermürbung ihrer Kampfmoral,

e) Aufklärungs- und Nachrichtentätigkeit (zum Schutz der Partisanen, der Vorbereitung ihrer Aktionen und zur Übermittlung an die regulären Streitkräfte der Anti-Hitler-Koalition),

f) Störung der Kriegsproduktion (Vernichtung von Rohstoffen, Produktionsanlagen, Energiequellen, Kraftwerken, Sabotage, Arbeite-langsam-Methode),

g) Desorganisierung der Verwaltungsstellen und Okkupationsbehörden des Gegners (Überfälle auf Ämter und Behörden sowie auf führende Personen, Vernichtung von Akten, Lahmlegung des Nachrichtenapparates),

h) Schutz der Zivilbevölkerung,

i) politische Arbeit unter der Bevölkerung und den Okkupanten (Agitation und Propaganda ...)"

Die Partisanen- und Widerstandsbewegung war bereits vor 1939 tätig. Sie zeigt sich auch nach 1945 im Sinne der Weltrevolution. Im Programm und Statut der KPdSU heißt es:

„Die sozialistischen Revolutionen, die antiimperialistischen nationalen Befreiungsrevolutionen, die demokratischen Volksrevolutionen, die großen Bauernbewegungen, der Kampf der Volksmassen für den Sturz faschistischer und sonstiger Tyranneien wie auch die allgemeindemokratischen Bewegungen gegen die nationale Unterdrückung – all das verschmilzt zu einem einheitlichen, weltumspannenden revolutionären Prozeß, der den Kapitalismus untergräbt und zerstört." Propagiert wird, daß die kommunistische Widerstandsbewegung im Zweiten Weltkrieg ein Teil des jahrhundertealten Ringens sog. fortschrittlicher und demokratischer Kräfte gegen Unterdrückung und Reaktion ist.

Zwischen den Kriegen in Ost und West

Im Jahre 1940 erhielt der Schweizer Oberbefehlshaber, General Guisan, ein Schreiben. Darin wird über den Kreis um Hauptmann Hausamann, der mit dem in Kaufbeuren geborenen und nach Luzern ausgewanderten Meisteragenten Rösler in Verbindung stand, berichtet. In dem Schreiben heißt es:

„Zur ‚Aktion Nationaler Widerstand‘ haben sich u. a. bekannt Männer wie Nationalrat Aeri, Basel, Nationalrat Gafner (Oberst im Generalstab), Bern, Nationalrat Feldmann, Bern, Nationalrat Oprecht, Zürich, Professor Rappard, Genf, Pfarrer Dr. Gutzwiller, Zürich, Oberst Oskar Frey, Schaffhausen, Hauptmann im Generalstab Frick, Ständerät Klöti, Generaldirektor Mussard von den General-Motor-Werken.

Nach unseren Feststellungen stimmen die Angaben im beiliegenden Spezialbericht, wonach Männer verschiedener politischer Lager, Parlamentarier aller Parteien, Vertreter beider Landeskirchen usw. der ‚Aktion Nationaler Widerstand‘ angehören. Es ist angesichts dieser Tatsache verfehlt, von einer einseitig orientierten oder gar camouflierten Organisation der Linken zu sprechen. Wir konstatieren im Gegenteil, daß die Vertreter der Sozialdemokratie in der Minderzahl sind. Andererseits verstehen wir, daß eine Aktion wie die ‚Aktion Nationaler Widerstand‘ etwas Halbes wäre, würden nicht auch die Vertrauensträger der Arbeiterschaft in dieser vertreten sein.

Hauptmann Hausamann erklärt uns, daß er die ‚Aktion Nationaler Widerstand' nach der Rede von Bundesrat Pielt ins Leben gerufen habe und daß er sich auch heute noch ohne Vorbehalt zu dieser bekenne. Dagegen sei er, nachdem die ‚Aktion' stark geworden und durchorganisiert war, wieder in den Hintergrund getreten . . .

Es könne ihn, so erklärt Hauptmann Hausamann weiter, nichts davon abhalten, das zu tun, was er im Interesse des Landes als notwendig erachte. Dabei sei er sich selbstverständlich bewußt, daß er im Militärdienst stehe . . .

Gegen den Anwurf an die Adresse von Hauptmann Hausamann, er sei ‚bekannt einseitig eingestellt', müssen wir uns verwahren. Wir wissen aus jahrelangen Beobachtungen (Hauptmann Hausamann wirkt seit 20 Jahren publizistisch und in anderen Formen für unsere Landesverteidigung, seit zehn Jahren arbeitet er für unsere Sektion . . .), daß Hauptmann Hausamann stets seinen geraden Weg ging . . . Abschließend gestatten wir uns den Hinweis, daß die ‚Aktion Nationaler Widerstand', deren Ziel nach dem beiliegenden Spezialbericht es ist, die ‚günstigsten politischen und geistigen Bedingungen für den Einsatz der Armee zu schaffen bzw. zu erhalten', das Wohlwollen und die Unterstützung des Herrn Oberbefehlshabers verdient.‟

Im Jahre 1982 gab die Allgemeine Schweizerische Militärzeitschrift im Verlag Huber & Co., AG – 8500 Frauenfeld, eine Arbeit von Dr. Hans Rudolf Fuhrer unter dem Titel ,,Spionage gegen die Schweiz – Die geheimen deutschen Nachrichtendienste gegen die Schweiz im Zweiten Weltkrieg 1939–1945‟ heraus. Es wäre wünschenswert, wenn von demselben Herausgeber eine Arbeit erscheinen würde, die die Tätigkeit der alliierten Nachrichtendienste behandelt. Aus dieser Arbeit sind die engen Verbindungen des Hauptmann Hausamann ersichtlich, die – man möchte sagen – seit 1942 amtlichen Charakter haben. Die große Zeit Hausamanns liegt nicht vor diesem Zeitpunkt, sondern später.

Trotzdem müssen die Berichte eingebaut werden, obwohl sie im Gegensatz zu deutschen Darstellungen liegen.

Bemerkenswert ist ein Brief des Schweizer Abwehrchefs Roger Masson an den Oberbefehlshaber der Schweizer Armee vom 1. 12. 1943, in welchem darauf hingewiesen wird, daß Allen W. Dulles in einem kleinen Kreis dem Hauptmann Hausamann mitgeteilt habe, daß sich der General und Oberstbrigadier Masson mit den SS-Offizieren Schellenberg/Eggen getroffen habe. Daraus ersehe man, daß die alliierten Kreise in der Schweiz über alles genau im Bilde seien. Schellenberg habe in Berlin berichtet, daß General Guisan erklärt habe, die Schweiz würde gegen die Alliierten ebenso wie gegen die Achse kämpfen. Dieser Bericht sei an das Auswärtige Amt weitergeleitet worden. Der alliierte Diplomat habe sich sehr gewundert, warum die Schweiz mit Leuten Himmlers, der persönlich der Schweiz sehr schlecht gesinnt sei, mehr Kontakt pflegen würden als mit Köcher... In seiner Arbeit „Zwischen allen Fronten – Der Zweite Weltkrieg aus der Sicht des Büros Hausamann" von Matt, erschienen auch in Frauenfeld, wird die Sache etwas anders dargestellt. Der Verfasser schildert, daß Hausamann während eines Mittagessens mit dem General Guisan gefragt worden sei, ob er Allen W. Dulles kenne. Hausamann habe die Frage genügt, um zu wissen, daß er Masson vor der Verbindung zu Schellenburg zu warnen habe.

Es handelt sich also bei Hausamann um eine nachrichtendienstliche Schlüsselfigur.

Die Darstellung, die Hausamann gibt, steht im Widerspruch zu deutschen Dokumenten. Der Entschluß, gegen die Sowjetunion vorzugehen, fiel nach diesen spätestens mit der Jugoslawienkrise, also im März 1941. Die Mobilmachung der Roten Armee bestand seit dem finnischen Krieg. Sie wurde durch Timoschenko intensiviert.

Auf den Gebieten des Heeresaufbaues, der Rüstung und der wirtschaftlichen Verlagerung von Betrieben in das Innere Rußlands wurden Vorbereitungen getroffen. Der Aufmarsch der sowjetischen Verbände im Westen ging ab Mai 1940 vor sich. Von der deutschen Abwehr war er klar erkannt. Ab September 1940 wurde die deutsche Wehrmacht wesentlich verstärkt. Letzeres ergibt sich auch aus den Hausamann-Berichten.

Man wundert sich allerdings darüber, mit welcher Genauigkeit Herr Hausamann über die Truppenbewegung vom Westen nach dem Osten unterrichtet war.

Transporte liefen nach Finnland seit dem Sommer 1940 und waren stärker als 10 000 Mann. Der Aufmarsch der deutschen Armee war Anfang Juni bis auf die Balkanverbände beendet. Reste der 12. Armee blieben in Griechenland und Jugoslawien, die Masse der 11. Armee in Rumänien und die schnellen Verbände der Panzergruppe 4 (Heeresgruppe Nord) und der Panzergruppe 1 (Heeresgruppe Süd) wurden zugeführt. Sicher ist, daß Stalin mit den Lieferungen im Frühjahr 1941 Zeit gewinnen wollte.

Nach deutscher Darstellung sind Meinungsverschiedenheiten im Führer-Hauptquartier in jedem Fall im Juni 1941 nicht nachweisbar.

Herrn Hausamann dürften die Berichte aus dem Reich teilweise von einer französischen oder einer Emigrantenquelle übermittelt worden sein.

Der sowjetische Aufmarsch wurde ab Mai 1941 zweifellos als bedrohlich angesehen. Den Russen war aber nach deutscher Ansicht der Historiker bekannt, daß der deutsche Aufmarsch bereits vollendet war.

Die Verlegung der Luftwaffe geschah frühzeitig und stützte sich auf die Erkundungsergebnisse seit Oktober 1940.

Am 19. Juni war alles entschieden. Dies stimmt mit den Memoiren des

Generalfeldmarschalls Fedor von Bock, die in diesem Buche herangezogen sind, überein. Das Stichwort für den Operationsbeginn, ,,Dortmund", war gegeben.

Warnungen vor einem russischen Präventivangriff kamen im Mai von Hitler.

Es ist fast unglaublich, daß man den Feldzug gegen die Sowjetunion auf 12 Wochen veranschlagte.

Zusammen mit den Mitteilungen des Schweizer Hauptmanns Hausamann ist ein Artikel aus den ,,News Chronicle" vom 10. Mai 1941 interessant.

Der Gewährsmann ist unbekannt.

In dem Zeitungsbeitrag heißt es:

,,Hitler plant in den nächsten Wochen eine Zusammenkunft mit Stalin. Schulenburg ist beauftragt, hierfür in Moskau Fühler auszustrecken und Treffen der beiden Diktatoren zu arrangieren. Hitler wird weitreichende Vorschläge zur Regelung der deutsch-russischen Beziehungen auf weite Sicht unterbreiten. Es ist folgendes vorgesehen:

Rußland in ganz Asien einschließlich Indien und Japan freie Hand zu lassen, mit einem Ausgang zum persischen Golf durch den Iran.

Wirtschaftlich soll Rußland in großen Mengen Rohmaterial liefern, besonders ukrainischen Weizen und kaukasisches Öl für deutsche Maschinen und schwerindustrielle Produkte.

Angesichts des zu erwartenden nahen Kriegseintritts der USA möchte Hitler England und den USA mit einem völlig von ihm beherrschten Europa gegenübertreten sowie mit dem freien Zugang zu den russischen Rohmaterialien. Dieses würde ihm die Aussicht auf einen endlos in die Länge gezogenen Krieg und die Vorteile eines Kompromiß-Friedens eröffnen.

Stalin seinerseits ist nicht geneigt, unter dem Druck der ständigen Bedrohung durch einen deutschen Angriff große Konzessionen zu machen. Daher werde Hitler ihm grandiose Vorschläge und Sicherheitsgarantien unterbreiten.

Weil Stalin dem Führer ebenbürtig und gestützt auf die volle Autorität seiner Stellung im russischen politischen System gegenübertreten will, nimmt man an, daß er die ganze Vollmacht und das formelle Prestige der Ministerpräsidentschaft, ähnlich der Stellung des Führers im Reich, in seiner Person vereinigt hat. Es würde ihn bei den kommenden Verhandlungen in eine günstigere Situation bringen.

Stalin ist darüber völlig im Bilde, daß die deutschen Vorbereitungen für einen Angriff auf Rußland abgeschlossen sind. Ob Stalin Hitlers Vorschläge ablehnt oder annimmt, wird davon abhängig sein, ob sie genügende Zusicherungen für Sicherheit und Gebietserweiterungen für Rußland enthalten.

Bejahendenfalls wird er akzeptieren. Wenn nicht, gibt es keine andere Alternative als den Krieg.

In jedem Falle muß Stalin in der Lage sein, sofortige und weitreichende Entscheidungen zu treffen und ihre Durchführung zu sichern, ein weiterer Grund für seine Übernahme der Ministerpräsidentschaft."

Unentschlossenheit?

Im Jahre 1940 stand Hitler auf dem Höhepunkt seiner Macht. Frankreich unterzeichnete am 22. 6. 1940 in Compiègne den Waffenstillstandsvertrag. In einem kleinen Walddorf an der belgisch-französischen Grenze, 9 km nordwestlich von Rocroi, glaubte Hitler, Großbritannien werde nach dem Zusammenbruch seines Bundesgenossen zu einer Verständigung bereit sein. Er gab Anordnung zu einer teilweisen Demobilisierung des Heeres. Auf dem 1000 m hohen Kniebis westlich von Freudenstadt, wohin am 25. Juni das Führerhauptquartier verlegt wurde, entwarf er die Rede, die er im Berliner Reichstag zu halten gedachte. Hitler hoffte mit England zu einem Frieden zu kommen.

Am 19. Juli 1941 erklärte er: ,,In dieser Stunde fühle ich mich verpflichtet vor meinem Gewissen, noch einmal einen Appell an die Vernunft auch in England zu richten. Ich glaube dies tun zu können, weil ich ja nicht als Besiegter um etwas bitte, sondern als Sieger nur für die Vernunft spreche. Ich sehe keinen Grund, der zur Fortsetzung dieses Kampfes zwingen könnte. Ich bedaure die Opfer, die er fordern wird. Auch meinem eigenen Volk möchte ich sie ersparen . . . Herr Churchill mag nun diese meine Erklärung wieder abtun mit dem Geschrei, daß dies nur die Ausgeburt meiner Angst sei und meines Zweifels am Endsieg. Ich habe dann ebenfalls mein Gewissen erleichtert gegenüber den kommenden Dingen." Der Appell blieb völlig wirkungslos. In England zeigten sich keine Anzeichen einer Friedensbereitschaft. Im Osten stiegen dunkle Wolken auf.

Am 16. Juli 1940 erließ Hitler die Weisung Nr. 16 über die Vorbereitungen einer Landungsoperation gegen England. Als Kernsatz stellte er heraus: ,,Da England trotz seiner militärisch aussichtslosen Lage noch keine Anzeichen einer Verständigungsbereitschaft zu erkennen gibt, habe ich mich entschlossen, eine Landungsoperation gegen England vorzubereiten und, wenn nötig, durchzuführen. Zweck dieser Operation ist es, das englische Mutterland als Basis für die Fortführung des Krieges gegen Deutschland auszuschalten und, wenn es erforderlich sein sollte, im vollen Umfang zu besetzen."

Am 1. August 1940 erfolgte die Weisung Nr. 17 für die Fortführung des Luft- und Seekrieges gegen England. Hierzu befahl Hitler: ,,Die deutsche Fliegertruppe hat mit allen zur Verfügung stehenden Kräften die englische Luftwaffe möglichst bald niederzukämpfen. Die Angriffe haben sich in erster Linie gegen die fliegenden Einheiten, ihre Bodenorganisation und Nachschubeinrichtungen, ferner die Luftrüstungsindustrie einschließlich der Industrie zur Herstellung von Flakgerät zu richten.

Zweitens, nach Erringung einer zeitlichen oder örtlichen Luftüberlegenheit ist der Luftkrieg gegen die Häfen, hierbei insbesondere gegen Einrichtungen der Lebensmittelbevorratung, und ferner gegen die Einrichtungen der Lebensmittelbevorratung im Inneren des Landes weiterzuführen. Angriffe gegen die Häfen der Südküste sind mit Rücksicht auf eigene beabsichtigte Operationen im möglichst geringen Maße anzusetzen."

Terrorangriffe als Vergeltung behielt Hitler sich vor.

Die Vorbereitungen für die Landung in England (,,Seelöwe") waren auf den 15. Sept. 1940 abgestellt.

Hitler war sich über die Schwierigkeiten des Unternehmens ,,Seelöwe" völlig im klaren. Großadmiral Raeder wies in einer Denkschrift vom 19. Juli darauf hin, daß die erste Welle der Landungstruppen an der offenen Küste ausgeschifft werden müsse. Dies sei aber infolge der Gezeiten, der Strömungen und der Dünung sehr schwierig. Er erklärte weiter, daß England bei Landungsoperationen die ganze Kampfkraft seiner Flotte einsetzen werde. Er stellte auch die Frage, inwieweit es möglich sei, daß die englische Führung eine Sperre zwischen den gelandeten Truppen der ersten Welle und den folgenden Transporten bilden könne. Als großes Problem stellte er die Frage vor Augen, ob die Verteidigungskräfte an der Küste von der deutschen Luftwaffe so vernichtend getroffen werden können, daß die Landung ohne nachdrückliche Artillerieunterstützung von See her gelinge. Die Gewinnung der Luftherrschaft sei entscheidend.

Bisher wurde ein Gesichtspunkt nicht behandelt. Admiral Canaris trug vor, daß die Landstreitkräfte im englischen Mutterland Ende August 35 Divisionen betragen würden, von denen etwa die Hälfte einsatzbereit sei. Canaris hatte am 21. Juli 1940 zur Vorbereitung der Invasion von Generalfeldmarschall Keitel den Auftrag, in England eine große Aufklärungsoperation vorzunehmen (Aktion ,,Hummer"). Der Chef des deutschen Geheimdienstes gab diesen Auftrag an Hauptmann Wichmann weiter. Anthony Cave Brown, der im Zuge der Materialsammlung für sein Buch ,,Bodyguard of Lies" den Oberst Ulrich Ließ interviewte, der während des Zweiten Weltkrieges in der Abteilung West tätig war, brachte sein Gespräch mit dem deutschen Offizier zu Papier: Ließ erklärte: ,,Während des Falles Gelb" kam ich zu dem Schluß, daß seine (des Admiral Canaris) offensiven geheimdienstlichen Operationen gegen Frankreich, Norwegen, Belgien und die Niederlande vorbildlich waren.

Von dem, was er in Zusammenhang mit ,,Seelöwe" tat, konnte man das nicht behaupten. Damals glaubte ich, daß er zwar nach außen hin so tat, als gebe er sich alle Mühe, daß er aber nicht mit voller Überzeugung gegen England vorginge. Wir bekamen nie die Nachrichten aus England, die wir brauchten, um Stärke der Briten und Aufmarsch richtig einzuschätzen."

Am 2. September 1940 meldete Canaris an Hitler . . ., die Briten würden über 37 voll ausgebildete kampfbereite Divisionen verfügen. In Wirklichkeit waren es stärkemäßig 29 Divisionen.

Zu dieser Frage schreibt Helmut Greiner, der im Wehrmachtsstab tätig war, in seinem Buch ,,Die oberste Wehrmachtführung" 1939–1943 auf Seite 137: ,,Die britischen Landstreitkräfte im Mutterland schätzte die Abteilung Fremde Heere West des Generalstabes des Heeres Ende August auf 35 Divisionen, von denen sie aber nur etwa die Hälfte als verwendungsbereit ansah. Nach den vorliegenden Nachrichten waren hiervon 16 Divisionen an der Küste eingesetzt, die übrigen 19 als operative Reserve zurückgehalten. Die Gesamtstärke der auf der britischen Insel verfügbaren Erdtruppen wurde von Agenten mit 1 640 00 Mann angegeben, von denen 320 000 Mann ausgebildet, 100 000 Mann Reservisten, 900 000 Rekruten und 320 000 Homeguards sein sollten." In Wirklichkeit verfügte das britische Heimatheer Mitte August über 26 Felddivisionen. Nach den Memoiren Winston Churchills standen davon 8½ Divisionen an der Ostküste bis zur Washbucht, 7 anschließend bis Dover, 3 als Reserve um London, 5 an der Süd- und 2 ½ an der Westküste.

In seinem Buch ,,Operation Sea Lion" (New York 1957) behauptet Peter Fleming schließlich, der Chef der deutschen Abwehr habe darauf hingewiesen, die Kombattanten von ,,Dünkirchen" seien nicht in der Stimmung, Frieden zu schließen.

Man kann heute sagen, daß der deutsche Nachrichtendienst in England nicht gut war.

Eine gewisse Bedeutung erlangte Alfred George Owens unter dem Decknamen Snow.

Die Engländner konnten ihn schon am 4. Sept. 1939 festnehmen. Es gelang ihnen, ihn umzudrehen. Snow versorgte die Abwehrstelle Hamburg mit falschen meteorologischen Daten.

Hitler wurde unschlüssig, zudem er im Osten bereits eine Gefahr erblickte. Er verschob die Operation ,,Seelöwe" auf unbestimmte Zeit.

Im August 1940 brachte Generaloberst Jodl eine Alternative zu der Operation ,,Seelöwe" in Vorschlag. Vorgesehen war:
1. Den Luftkrieg bis zur wehrwirtschaftlichen Vernichtung Südenglands fortzuführen,
2. den U-Boot-Krieg unter völliger Ausnutzung der französischen Basis zu steigern,
3. die Wegnahme Ägyptens mittels einer, falls erforderlich, mit deutscher Unterstützung von Libyen aus von der italienischen Wehrmacht zu führenden Offensive durchzuführen und
4. Gibraltar im Zusammenwirken mit Italien und Spanien zu erobern.

Am 4. Nov. 1940 beauftragte Jodl General Warlimont, den Entwurf einer Weisung zur Vorbereitung von Operationen gegen Gibraltar, Ägypten und Griechenland vorzubereiten. So heißt es in den Weisungen Nr. 18 bis 19 a wie folgt:

Weisung Nr. 18:

Ziffer 1: Das Ziel meiner Politik gegenüber Frankreich ist, mit diesem Land in einer für die zukünftige Kriegführung gegen England möglichst wirkungsvollen Weise zusammenzuarbeiten. Frankreich wird dabei vorläufig die Rolle einer ‚nichtkriegführenden Macht' zufallen, die in ihrem Hoheitsgebiet, besonders in den afrikanischen Kolonien Maßnahmen der deutschen Kriegführung zu dulden und, soweit erforderlich, auch durch Einsatz eigener Verteidigungsmittel zu unterstützen hat . . .

Ziffer 2: Politische Maßnahmen, um den baldigen Kriegseintritt Spaniens herbeizuführen, sind eingeleitet. Das Ziel des deutschen Eingreifens auf der Iberischen Halbinsel (Deckname Felix) wird sein, die Engländer aus dem Mittelmeer zu vertreiben. Hierbei soll

a) Gibraltar genommen und die Meerenge abgeschlossen werden,
b) verhindert werden, daß sich die Engländer an einer anderen Stelle der Iberischen Halbinsel oder der Atlantischen Inseln festsetzen.

Ziffer 3: Hier nicht von Bedeutung

Ziffer 4: Oberbefehlshaber des Heeres trifft Vorbereitungen, um im Bedarfsfall aus Bulgarien heraus das griechische Festland nördlich des Ägäischen Meeres in Besitz zu nehmen und damit die Voraussetzung für den Einsatz deutscher Fliegerverbände gegen Ziele im ostwärtigen Mittelmeer zu schaffen, insbesondere gegen diejenigen englischen Luftstützpunkte, die das rumänische Ölgebiet bedrohen.

Um allen möglichen Aufgaben gewachsen zu sein und die Türkei in Schach zu halten, ist den Überlegungen und Aufmarschberechnungen der Einsatz einer Armeegruppe in Stärke von etwa 10 Divisionen zugrundezulegen. Auf eine Benutzung der durch Jugoslawien führenden Eisenbahn wird für den Aufmarsch dieser Kräfte nicht zu rechnen sein. Um den Zeitbedarf für den Aufmarsch abzukürzen, ist eine baldige Verstärkung der deutschen Heeresmission in Rumänien in einem mir vorzuschlagenden Ausmaß vorzubereiten. Oberbefehlshaber der Luftwaffe bereitet im Einklang mit den beabsichtigten Heeresoperationen Einsatz deutscher Luftwaffenverbände auf dem südostwärtigen Balkan und den Einsatz eines Flugmeldedienstes an der Südgrenze Bulgariens vor. Die deutsche Luftwaffenmission in Rumänien wird in dem mir vorgeschlagenen Umfang verstärkt.

Wünsche der Bulgaren für Aufrüstung des Heeres (Waffen- und Munitionslieferungen) sind entgegenkommend zu behandeln.

Ziffer 5: Politische Besprechungen mit dem Ziel, die Haltung Rußlands für die nächste Zeit zu klären, sind eingeleitet. Gleichgültig, welches Ergebnis diese Besprechungen haben werden, sind alle schon mündlich befohlenen Vorbereitungen für den Osten fortzuführen. Weisungen darüber werden folgen, sobald die Grundzüge des Operationsplanes des Heeres mir vorgetragen und von mir gebilligt sind." (12. Nov. 1940)

Weisung Nr. 19 (Unternehmen Attila):
Ziffer 1: ,,Für den Fall, daß sich in den jetzt von General Weygand beherrschten Teilen des französischen Kolonialreiches eine Abfallbewegung abzeichnen sollte, ist die schnelle Besetzung des heute noch unbesetzten Gebiets des französischen Mutterlandes vorzubereiten (Unternehmen Attila). Gleichzeitig kommt es dann darauf an, die französische Heimatflotte und die auf heimischen Flugplätzen befindlichen Teile der französischen Luftwaffe sicherzustellen, zumindest aber ihr Übergehen zur Feindseite zu verhindern. Die Vorbereitungen sind zu tarnen, um Alarmierung der Franzosen im militärischen wie politischen Interesse zu vermeiden.
Ziffer 2: Der Einmarsch hat gegebenenfalls so zu erfolgen, daß
a) starke motorisierte Gruppen, deren ausreichender Luftschutz sicherzustellen ist, im Zuge der Garonne bzw. der Rhône schnell bis zum Mittelmeer durchstoßen, möglichst frühzeitig die Hafenplätze (vor allem den wichtigen Kriegshafen Toulon) in Besitz nehmen und Frankreich vom Meer abriegeln,
b) die an der Demarkationslinie stehenden Verbände auf der ganzen Front einrücken." (10. Dez. 1940)

Weisung Nr. 20: (Unternehmen Marita):
Ziffer 1: ,,Der Ausgang der Kämpfe in Albanien läßt sich noch nicht übersehen. Angesichts der bedrohlichen Lage in Albanien ist es doppelt wichtig, daß englische Bestrebungen, unter dem Schutz einer Balkanfront eine vor allem für Italien, daneben für das rumänische Ölgebiet gefährliche Luftbasis zu schaffen, vereitelt werden.
Ziffer 2: Meine Absicht ist daher:
a) In den nächsten Monaten in Südrumänien eine sich allmählich verstärkende Kräftegruppe zu bilden,
b) nach Eintreten günstiger Witterung – voraussichtlich im März – diese Kräftegruppe über Bulgarien hinweg zur Besitznahme der ägäischen Nordküste und – sollte dies erforderlich sein – des ganzen griechischen Festlandes anzusetzen (Unternehmen Marita). Mit der Unterstützung durch Bulgarien ist zu rechnen.
Ziffer 3: hier nicht von Bedeutung

Ziffer 4: Das Unternehmen Marita selbst ist auf folgender Grundlage vorzubereiten:
a) Erstes Ziel der Operation ist die Besitznahme der ägäischen Küste und des Beckens von Saloniki. Fortsetzung des Angriffs über Larissa und die Enge von Korinth kann notwendig werden.
b) Der Flankenschutz gegen die Türkei wird der bulgarischen Armee zufallen, ist jedoch darüber hinaus durch Bereitstellung deutscher Verbände zu stärken und zu sichern.
c) Ob sich bulgarische Verbände außerdem am Angriff beteiligen, ist ungewiß. Ebenso ist die jugoslawische Haltung jetzt noch nicht klar zu übersehen."(13. Dez. 1940)

Seit Ende Juli 1940 warnte Canaris einerseits Hitler, Gibraltar anzugreifen. Andererseits aber rät der deutsche Abwehrchef dem General Franco, er solle an einem Unternehmen „Felix" nicht teilnehmen. Begründen könne dies der spanische Generalissimus damit, daß er von Deutschland für ein solches Unternehmen 38-cm-Geschütze brauche. Diese könne das Großdeutsche Reich jedoch nicht liefern.

Am 23. Oktober 1940 kam Hitler mit Franco in Hendaye am Fuße der Pyrenäen zusammen.

Die Begegnung wurde für Hitler zu einem Fehlschlag.

Der spanische Außenminister, Serrano Suñer, hatte Franco vorher, wie Jan Colvin in „Masterspy" berichtet, davon unterrichtet „er habe in Berlin den Eindruck gehabt, daß alles, was mit Spaniens Belangen zu tun hat, völlig durcheinander geraten sei". Es wird hinzugefügt: „Einer der Gründe für diese Verwirrung ist die eigenartige Rolle, die Admiral Canaris spielt." Wir wissen, daß in Spanien ein Freund des deutschen Abwehrchefs saß, Don Juan March, der auch Beziehungen zu dem englischen Kollegen von Canaris, Sir Menzies, unterhielt. Don Juan March spielte in Spanien keine geringe Rolle, er war auch in den Geldadel erhoben worden. Jan Colvin, der im Einvernehmen mit Canaris gute Beziehungen zu den Engländern unterhalten hatte, schreibt:

„In Spanien hatte er (Canaris) auf weite Sicht etwas erreicht. Er hatte dieses geheimnisvolle Land vor unendlichen Qualen bewahrt."

Bei dieser Sachlage erhebt sich die Frage, inwieweit die Pläne Hitlers im Ausland bekannt waren. Aus dem Archiv Hausamann entnehme ich: Militärischer Bericht vom 16. Okt. 1940: „Die planmäßig vorgesehene Bewegung deutscher Heeresverbände nach Rumänien geht weiter über das in der Presse berichtete oder vermutete Ausmaß hinaus . . . Das Gesamtbild ist zur Zeit folgendes:
1. Die auf Heeresgruppenstärke gebrachten und größtenteils schon seit langem auf Südost eingeteilten, bisher hauptsächlich in Niederösterreich,

Mähren und in der Slowakei befindlich gewesenen Heereseinheiten werden je ungefähr zur Hälfte nach der Walachei und nach Siebenbürgen vorgeschoben . . .

2. In kurzem, voraussichtlich Mitte der nächsten Woche wird auf diese Weise eine deutsche Armee in der Walachei und an der Sereth-Puna-Linie und eine zweite Armee in Siebenbürgen (Gebiet Klausenburg-Hermannstadt-Kronstadt-Schäßburg-Mediasch) stehen . . .

3. Gleichzeitig hat das Wehrmachtoberkommando eine außerordentlich weitgehende Verstärkung und Ostbewegung der schon bisher in Oberschlesien, Westgalizien und im südöstlichen Teil des Gereralgouvernements Polen überhaupt gesammelten Heereseinheiten in Gang gebracht. Die Verstärkung erfolgt auch hier aus der ostfranzösischen Heeresreserve und durch Abberufung von Reservedivisionen aus Ostdeutschland. Die Absicht in diesem südpolnischen Aufmarschsektor ist die, so rasch als möglich eine sehr starke Armeegruppe mit wenigstens 16 Divisionen in einer Weise zu sammeln, daß diese Gruppe jederzeit mit Stoßrichtung Lemberg eingesetzt werden und als drastisches Druckmittel gegen Rußland wie als Flankenschutz der südlich auf dem Balkan vorgehenden deutschen Armeen verwendet werden kann. Die Sammelplätze dieser Armeegruppe werden ostwärts bis zur Linie Lublin-Przemysl vorgeschoben."

Am 22. Okt. 1940 wird unterstellt, daß ein noch so starker Einsatz russischer Kräfte in der Moldau nichts an der politischen Situation auf dem Balkan ändern könne. Rußland könne im Krieg gegen das Deutsche Reich zwar 100 deutsche Divisionen in Atem halten, aber es könne nicht den Balkan erobern und den Engländern, Türken und Griechen die Kriegführung auf dem Balkan und an einer Südfront, die nur einen kleinen Teil der deutsch-russischen ausmacht und den britisch-türkischen Kontakt mit Rußland strategisch sicherstellt, abnehmen. Militärisch und politisch sei überdies Moskau an einer Kriegführung auf dem Balkan nur dann interessiert, wenn durch sie außer Bulgarien auch Jugoslawien der deutsch-italienischen Herrschaft entzogen bzw. wenigstens Jugoslawien zur Widerstandsleistung befähigt wird.

Außenpolitische Fragen

Die sowjetische Außenpolitik zielt und zielte einerseits darauf ab: Durchbruch durch den Sund, über das Nordkap und Spitzbergen zum Atlantik und die Gewinnung der Herrschaft über die Dardanellen. Andererseits wird sie getragen von einer expansiv-missionarischen Ideologie und den Gedanken der Revolutionierung der Welt zu einem von Moskau geführten kommunistischen Weltsystem.

Nach wie vor gilt als Lehrsatz kommunistischer Taktik, ,,daß man die Gegensätze und Widersprüche zwischen Kapitalismen, zwischen zwei Systemen kapitalistischer Staaten ausnutzen und sie gegeneinander hetzen muß." (W. Lenin, Rede in der Versammlung der Zellensekretäre der Moskauer Organisation in der KPR am 26. Nov. 1920)

In den ,,Ausgewählten Werken W.I. Lenins, Band X, S. 105 findet sich der Satz: ,,Lavieren, Verständigung und Kompromisse mit möglichen (wenn auch zeitweiligen, unbeständigen, bedingten) Verbündeten, eine Taktik, die notwendig sei wie bei einem schwierigen Aufstieg auf einen noch unerforschten und bis dahin unzugänglichen Berg: manchmal umzukehren, die einmal gewählte Richtung aufzugeben und verschiedene Richtungen zu versuchen."

Auf der Neujahrstagung des ZK der KP im Jahre 1925 erklärte J.W. Stalin: ,,So werden wir als letzte auftreten, und wir werden auftreten, um das entscheidende Gewicht auf die Waagschale zu werfen, ein Gewicht, das ausschlaggebend sein dürfte." So begründete Stalin seine Absicht vor dem Politbüro am 19. Aug. 1939, den Vertrag mit dem Reich zu schließen, wie er am 25./26. Aug. 1939 zustande kam.

Darüber berichten die Havas-Agentur; der Pester LLoyd, und auch der ,,Dernier Rapport, Politique Polonaise 1926–1939" (Neuchâtel à Paris, Seite 332), der von dem ehemaligen polnischen Außenminister Beck niedergeschrieben wurde, bestätigt dies. Stalins Ansicht war: Mit dem Nichtangriffspakt mit Rußland würde Deutschland gegen Polen militärisch vorgehen; die Westmächte würden aufgrund ihrer Verpflichtungen eingreifen. An einem Krieg habe die Sowjetunion Interesse. Dieser müsse bis zur Erschöpfung der Kriegführenden dauern; die Sowjetunion müsse sich gut vorbereiten für den Augenblick der Beendigung des Konfliktes und auf ihre Stunde warten.

Das Oberkommando des Heeres sah seit dem 21. Juli 1940 die große Gefahr aus dem russischen Raum. Unter deutschem diplomatischem Druck fand vom 12.–14. Nov. 1940 die bedeutungsvolle Konferenz zwischen Hitler und Molotow statt. Der sowjetische Außenminister traf mit dem neuen

Botschafter Dekanosow, einem Georgier, am 12. Nov. 1940 in Berlin ein. Hitler vertrat die Auffassung, daß Deutschland durch den Erwerb von Gebieten in Mittel- und Westafrika seine Rohstoffbedürfnisse sicherstellen müsse. Für das japanische Reich könne sich nur südlich der Inseln Raum für den Überschuß der Bevölkerung bieten. Italien schaffe sich ein großes Kolonialreich. Durch die Ausdehnung der Sowjetunion nach dem Süden könne für diese viel gewonnen werden, darunter ein eisfreier Hafen.

Molotow ging bei seinen Ausführungen sofort auf die finnische Frage ein. Er hob hervor, daß die Verhandlungen mit Finnland hinsichtlich Petsamo sich versteift hätten. Als möglichen Grund sah er an, daß das Deutsche Reich weitgehende wirtschaftliche Abmachungen mit der finnischen Regierung getroffen habe und auch Waffen liefere.

Hitler begründete seine Haltung: im schweren Kampf mit den Angelsachsen müsse verhindert werden, daß Gefahren für sein Land durch die Nichtlieferung von Rohstoffen entstehen. Diese seien jedoch nur in den neutralen nordischen Staaten vorhanden. Jede Störung bedeute eine Schwächung des deutschen Kriegspotentials.

Wenn zwischen der Sowjetunion und Finnland ein Krieg ausbrechen würde, könnte der englische Gegner unter dem Vorwand, Finnland zu helfen, sich in Nordeuropa festsetzen.

Molotow wies den Gedanken von sich, daß der von ihm vertretene Staat die Absicht habe, gegen Finnland Krieg zu führen. Er müsse seinerseits fragen, ob die deutsche Reichsregierung anerkenne, daß der finnische Staat als Nachbarland zur sowjetischen Interessenssphäre gehöre.

Hitler erwiderte, er habe diese Frage bereits beantwortet, und stellte heraus, daß ein kriegerisches Vorgehen der Sowjetunion gegen Finnland im gegenwärtigen Zeitpunkt zu einer schweren Belastung der deutsch-sowjetischen Beziehungen führen würde.

In der zweifellos einseitigen Darstellung ,,Die Außenpolitik des Dritten Reiches – Versuch einer Darstellung" (,,Wahn und Wirklichkeit") schreibt Kordt, der im diplomatischen Dienst des Deutschen Reiches stand und zum Widerstandskreis des 20. Juli gehört: ,,Was für den Norden gelte, treffe auch für den Balkan zu. Jeder Krieg störe Deutschlands Versorgung und gebe den Angelsachsen, wie deren Hilfe für Griechenland beweise, Gelegenheit zur Einmischung. Nun habe die Sowjetunion Ende Juni plötzlich ein Ultimatum an Rumänien gestellt und außer der Abtretung Bessarabiens auch noch die Nordbukowina gefordert, von der im deutsch-sowjetischen Vertrag keine Rede gewesen sei. Es habe Deutschland einige Mühe gekostet, König Carol zur Annahme der ultimativen sowjetischen Forderungen zu bewegen. Hiernach sei auch durch andere Revisionsforderungen der rumänische Staat in seinen Grundfesten erschüttert worden. Um die Ordnung dort aufrechtzuerhalten – Deutschland sei vor allem am rumänischen Öl interessiert –, habe er für die Rumänien angeratenen Zugeständnisse eine Gegenleistung machen müssen. Die rumänische Regierung habe eine Garantie der Achse gefordert, ohne die ihre Autorität nicht aufrechterhalten werden könne. Zu einer Befassung mit der Sowjetunion, durch deren plötzliches Vorgehen der Stein ins Rollen gekommen sei, habe die Zeit gefehlt." Dies erklärte Hitler dem sowjetischen Außenminister.

Molotow erwiderte, diese deutsche Erklärung veranlasse ihn, zu einem weiteren wichtigen Punkt überzugehen und folgenden Vorschlag zu machen. Die Sowjetunion wünsche, mit Bulgarien ein Vertragsverhältnis einzugehen, ähnlich dem, das zwischen Deutschland und Rumänien bestehe. Die Sowjetunion beabsichtige nicht, die soziale Ordnung dort zu ändern oder das Königshaus zu beseitigen. Sie wolle jedoch ein Verteidigungsbündnis mit Bulgarien abschließen und dort gewisse Garnisonen unterhalten. Ein sowjetisch-bulgarischer Vertrag solle den Zugang zum Mittelmeer schützen. Von dort aus seien schon häufig in der Geschichte Angriffe gegen Rußland geführt worden. Um endlich Sicherheit gegen solche Angriffe zu haben, wünsche die Sowjetunion eine unbedingte Festlegung ihrer Stellung an den Meerengen. Die Erfahrungen mit der türkischen Politik würden seine Regierung hierin bestärken. Die Sowjetunion wolle Land- und Seestützpunkte an den Meerengen errichten und diese gemeinsam mit der Türkei verteidigen.

Hitler fragte darauf, ob Bulgarien die Sowjetunion ebenso wie Rumänien Deutschland um eine solche Garantie gebeten habe.

Molotow erklärte, er wolle die deutsche Stellungnahme erfahren. Erst dann könne man über weitere Fragen sprechen. Hitler erwiderte, die Lage in Rumänien sei von der in Bulgarien grundverschieden. Hinsichtlich der Meerengen könne er ohne Einholung seines Bundesgenossen Mussolini keine Antwort geben. Der sowjetische Außenminister erwiderte, dieser Fragenkomplex sei äußerst wichtig, er wäre für eine baldige Prüfung dankbar.

Nach der Rückkehr nach Moskau übergab Molotow dem deutschen Botschafter von Schulenburg am 25. Nov. 1940 eine zusammenfassende Darlegung des sowjetischen Standpunktes. Moskau würde die grundsätzlichen deutschen Verträge unter nachstehenden Bedingungen annehmen:

a) Rückzug der deutschen Truppen aus Finnland. Die Sowjetunion werde für friedliche Beziehungen zu Finnland sorgen. Die deutschen Wirtschaftsinteressen in Finnland (Ausfuhr von Holz und Nickel) würden geschützt werden.

b) Innerhalb der nächsten wenigen Monate solle die Sicherheit der Sowjetunion an den Meerengen durch einen gegenseitigen Beistandspakt zwischen der Sowjetunion und Bulgarien sowie durch die Errichtung einer Basis für Land- und Seestreitkräfte der Sowjetunion im Gebiet des Bosporus und der Dardanellen aufgrund eines langdauernden Paktvertrages gewährleistet werden.

c Das Gebiet von Batum und Baku in allgemeiner Richtung zum Persischen Golf solle als Einflußsphäre der Sowjetunion anerkannt werden.

d) Japan verzichte auf seine Kohlen- und Ölkonzessionen in Nordsachalin.

Der Leser mag entschuldigen, wenn hier politische und militärische Planungen und Ereignisse trotz aller Leiden und Menschenverluste, die auf Zehntausenden von Familien lasten, unter dem Gesichtspunkt eines gigantischen Schachspiels betrachtet werden. Für das deutsche Volk mögen die Ereignisse von 1939 bis 1945 ein Menetekel sein. Man überschätzte die eigene Kraft und unterschätzte die gegnerische.

Nach dem Frankreich-Feldzug gab es vier Kraftfelder: Rußland, Südosteuropa, Mittelmeer und Vorderasien. Unverständlich ist es, daß deutscherseits die militärische Bedeutung von Malta nicht erkannt wurde. Ohne die vollständige Ausschaltung dieser Insel hätte, wie Generalfeldmarschall Kesselring mir sagte, die Offensive Rommels in Nordafrika nicht beginnen dürfen. Die Kraftfelder will ich in getrennten Abschnitten behandeln.

Sowjetunion:

Hausamann berichtet unter dem 15. Okt. 1940, daß die Überführung der meisten Verbände aus Ostfrankreich nach dem Osten vom deutschen Wehrmachts-Oberkommando beschlossen und bereits in Durchführung begriffen sei. Wortwörtlich heißt es: ,,Beigetragen zur Zurückstellung von Bedenken gegenüber russischer politisch-militärischer Empfindlichkeit und etwaiger dem Reich gefährlich werdender Reaktion ist die Tatsache, daß das Oberkommando der Roten Armee neuerdings durch große Manöver im Gebiet von Berditschew Eindruck auf die deutschen Entschließungen zu machen sucht und damit selbst die ausschließlich militärisch bestimmte Natur der deutsch-russischen Beziehungen zur Geltung bringt.''

Die militärische Druckverschärfung gegenüber Rußland wurde vom Wehrmachts-Oberkommando für nötig erachtet, weil eine russische Nichteinmischung in die Balkanoperation nur dann wahrscheinlich ist, wenn Moskau die deutsche Offensivkraft nicht auf die Stoßrichtung Südost beschränkt sieht, sondern mit der Verteidigung von Ostgalizien rechnen muß.

Zum Ausdruck wird gebracht, daß gleichzeitig das Wehrmacht-Oberkommando eine außerordentlich weitgehende Verstärkung und Ostbewegung der schon bisher in Oberschlesien, Westgalizien und im südöstlichen Teil des Generalgouvernements Polen gesammelten Heereseinheiten in Gang gebracht hat. Die Verstärkung werde auch hier aus der Heeresreserve in Ostfrankreich und durch Abberufung von Reservedivisionen aus Ostdeutschland erfolgen. Ihr Umfang lasse sich noch nicht übersehen, mache aber 6 Divisionen aus und werde voraussichtlich noch beträchtlich erweitert werden. Die Absicht in diesem südpolnischen Aufmarschsektor sei, so rasch als möglich eine sehr starke Armeegruppe mit wenigstens 16 Divisionen in einer Weise zu sammeln, daß diese Gruppe jederzeit mit Stoßrichtung Lemberg eingesetzt werden und als drastisches Druckmittel gegen Rußland wie als Flankenschutz der südlich auf dem Balkan stehenden deutschen Armeen verwendet werden könne. Die Sammelplätze würden ostwärts bis zur Linie Lublin-Przemysl vorgeschoben.

Am 22. Okt. 1940 wird in einem Bericht zum Ausdruck gebracht: ,,Zu den Vorbereitungen und Maßnahmen, durch welche die Reichsführung jetzt die Sowjetregierung zur endgültigen Aufgabe ihrer zweideutigen Haltung und zur Entscheidung für oder gegen die großdeutsche Europaordnung und deren Ausdehnung auch auf den Balkan zwingen will, gehört unter anderem die sehr weitgehende Neueinschaltung von Finnland in das deutsche militärische Kräftefeld . . . Seit dem 24. September sind vom deutschen Wehrmacht-Oberkommando alle Maßnahmen getroffen worden, um nötigenfalls eine überraschend schnelle Besetzung von ganz Nordfinnland bis einschließlich Uleåborg im Süden durchführen zu können und jede russische Gegenaktion unter Benutzung der Murmansk-Bahn von vornherein unmöglich zu machen." Festzustellen ist in dem Zusammenhang, daß eine heerestaugliche Verkehrsverbindung zwischen Petsamo und Kivajärvi fertiggestellt wurde.

Die Schweizer Quelle bringt am 24. Okt. 1940 klar zum Ausdruck, daß maßgebend für die Entschlüsse der Führungsspitze des Deutschen Reiches die endgültige Ausschaltung der latenten Gefahr militärischer Rückendrohung durch Rußland noch vor der amerikanischen Präsidentenwahl war.

Mit dem versuchten militärischen Druck waren Maßnahmen gegen jede Art von russenfreundlicher oder kommunistischer Tätigkeit im deutschen Machtbereich gegeben. Bemerkenswert ist, wie die Schweizer Quelle berichtet, daß während der Ausübung des militärischen Druckes der deutsche Botschafter von der Schulenburg eine Formel für das russische Nachgeben, die mit den Prestigebedürfnissen des Kreml in Einklang zu bringen war, übermitteln sollte. Diese Formel sollte an die russische Verständigung mit dem Reich auf der Basis appellieren, daß sich Moskau an der Ausschaltung des türkisch-britischen Gefahrenherdes durch Gleichschaltung mit der deutschen Politik aktiv beteilige.

Die Wahl, vor welche Berlin Moskau stellte, sei, entweder mit Deutschland zusammen die Türkei aus dem britischen Sicherheitssystem herauszulösen oder zuzusehen, wie sich das Reich allein oder im deutsch-italienischen Interesse weiterhin auf dem Balkan einrichtet und die Lösung der sogenannten türkischen Frage in die Hand nimmt.

Europa sollte für die Russen wie für die Amerikaner zum „hoffnungslosen Fall" werden. Als Mittel dazu sollte der Umstand in den Vordergrund gestellt werden, daß gegen die Bolschewisten der europäische Kontinent unter Führung Hitlers einiger ist als der alte Kontinent gegen den zaristischen Herrscher im Jahre 1812. Durch die Konferenz Hitler-Laval und Hitler-Franco sollte unter anderem dieser Gedanke gefördert werden.

Am 18. Okt. 1940 wurde gemeldet, daß russische Truppenverbände aus den an türkisches Gebiet anschließenden russischen Grenzbezirken zurückgezogen wurden. Das Oberkommando der Roten Armee hob damit die im September 1939 und im April 1940 veranlaßte Verstärkung der georgischen Armeebereitschaft auf der ganzen Linie auf.

Dem geplanten Schritt des deutschen Botschafters von der Schulenburg kam das russische Außenkommissariat dadurch zuvor, daß es am 27. Oktober 1940 durch Notenüberreichung um Aufschluß über die Stellungnahme der Reichsregierung gegenüber den von Mitgliedern der bulgarischen Regierung öffentlich geäußerten Ansprüchen auf nichtbulgarisches Gebiet ersuchte. Die Äußerung der Reichsregierung ist unter Hinweis auf die deutsch-russischen Vereinbarungen gegenseitiger Konsultation in den die unmittelbaren Interessen beider Mächte berührenden Fragen und ferner unter Hinweis darauf erbeten worden, daß die erwähnten bulgarischen Ansprüche voraussichtlich nicht ohne Krieg verwirklicht werden und aus diesem Grund die Sowjetunion nicht gleichgültig lassen könnten.

Zum Besuch des sowjetischen Außenministers in Berlin bringt Hausamann zum Ausdruck, daß der sehr erwünschte Gegenbesuch Molotows „unter Druck der im Oktober durchgeführten neuen Konzentration stärkerer deutscher Wehrmachtsteile im Osten und Südosten zustande gekommen ist."

Unter dem 18. Nov. 1940 wird zum Ausdruck gebracht, daß kurz vor der Entsendung Molotows nach Berlin sowohl sich die russische Regierung im Fall der bulgarischen Gebietsansprüche als auch die Reichsregierung in der sog. türkischen Frage an die bestehende Vereinbarung des rechtzeitigen Meinungsaustausches halten werde.

Nicht erfüllt wurde u. a. die Erwartung des deutschen Außenministers, im Abschlußkommuniqué die Feststellung des definitiven Charakters der seit September 1939 gegebenen deutsch-russischen Grenzziehung zu erklären.

Der russische Außenminister habe vielmehr die Notwendigkeit einer ins einzelne gehenden deutsch-russischen Verständigung vor allem über die wirtschaftliche Gleichberechtigung und Bewegungsfreiheit in den Nord- und Südost-Staaten, besonders in Rumänien und Bulgarien, in den Vordergrund gestellt.

Am 23. Nov. 1940 berichtet Hausamann über die Weiterführung der Verhandlungen in Moskau, daß das russische Außenkommissariat den Abschluß eines umfassenden russisch-rumänischen Wirtschafts- und Güteraustauschvertrages forderte, der u. a. auf der Weiterversorgung von Bessarabien mit rumänischen Rohstoffen und bedeutenden Mengen Erdöl, Mineralien, Holz basiert. Ihn mache Rußland zur Bedingung einer Bereinigung der Südostfragen, welcher die Sowjetregierung zustimmen könne. Der deutsche Botschafter von der Schulenburg sei neuerdings darauf aufmerksam gemacht worden, daß die Sowjetregierung Vorschläge der Reichsregierung erwarte, welche gemäß dem deutsch-russischen Konsultativ-Abkommen eine Verschiebung des Gleichgewichtes in den Angrenzerstaaten durch einseitige militärische Maßnahmen ohne vorherige gegenseitige Fühlungnahme für die Zukunft ausschließt. Klar mußte der deutschen Reichsregierung vor Augen treten, daß die Erfüllung des russischen Wunsches auf Sicherstellung des bessarabischen Erdölbedarfs aus rumänischen Quellen darauf abzielt, auf Kosten des Ölexports nach dem Reich auch den großen Erdöl- und Benzinbedarf der jetzt in Bessarabien konzentrierten Teile der Roten Armee zu decken.

Am 5. Dez. 1940 hebt Hausamann hervor, daß Ende November in Rumänien rund 55 000 Mann motorisierte deutsche Einsatzdivisionen gelegen hätten, dazu starke Kontingente Flak und Flieger, die hauptsächlich im Erdölgebiet stationiert seien. Eine vorgesehene Erhöhung der Bestände an Luftlandetruppen sei auf russischen Einwand hin unterblieben, ebenso die in Durchführung begriffene Verstärkung der deutschen Erdtruppen.

Die Zuspitzung der Lage zeigt die umfangreiche Neuorganisation Ende des Jahres 1940 im Westen der Halbinsel Kola auf militärischem Gebiet. Im Mittelpunkt stand die Aufstellung einer zweiten, für den Polarkrieg auszubildenden russischen Division, deren Einheiten in den Lagern und neuen Kasernen der Orte an der Kandalakschabucht stationiert wurden.

Im russisch-finnischen Krieg verfügte die Sowjetarmee in diesem Raum nur über eine Division mit dem Kommandositz in Murmansk. Auf deutscher Seite ist zu vermelden, daß der Weg Rovaniemi-Rovanen-Polmak zum deutschen Etappenweg ausgebaut wurde. Zwischen Polmak und Hammerfest wurde die Verbindung über Lakselven unter großem technischem und Kostenaufwand hergestellt. In Finnisch-Lappland und im Gebiet von Finnisch Karungi-Torneå-Rovaniemi veranlaßte das deutsche Wehrmacht-Oberkommando die Planung von militärischen Anlagen größeren Umfangs sowie die Bildung von Luftstützpunkten und Fliegerhorsten.

Besonders erfolgreich waren die von der Delegation Schnurre geführten Verhandlungen zur Neuformulierung des deutsch-russischen Wirtschafts- und Handelsabkommens nicht. Es wurde ein vorläufiger Abschluß erzielt, jedoch nicht auf der Basis der deutschen Vorschläge. Die Wiederaufnahme des Güteraustausches zwischen dem Reich und den ehemaligen Ländern Estland, Lettland und Litauen wurde von der Sowjetregierung abgelehnt. Sie wurde an die Bedingung der restlosen Befriedigung der russischen Ansprüche im Wirtschaftsverkehr mit Rumänien geknüpft. Die gewünschte Mehrlieferung von Manganerzen, Chrom, Häuten und Futtergetreide wurde teils als unmöglich, teils infolge russischen Eigenbedarfs als undurchführbar abgelehnt. Abhängig war die Erfüllung des deutschen Wunsches auch von der Lieferung deutscher Maschinen und solcher deutscher Industrieprodukte, mit deren fristgerechtem Export im Kompensationsverkehr das Reich Rußland gegenüber im Rückstand war. Eine Verständigung auf der Grundlage der deutschen Vorschläge konnte nur in nebensächlichen Fragen, z. B. in der Wiederaufnahme des Exportes von landwirtschaftlichen Produkten zweiter Qualität aus Litauen gegen erweiterte Lieferungen der deutschen chemischen und elektrotechnischen Industrie erzielt werden. Völlig negativ blieb der deutsche Versuch, einen Wiederverkauf von Buntmetallen, die Rußland einführt, durchzusetzen.

Abschließend darf berichtet werden, daß die Sowjetregierung am 21. Dezember 1940 schärfste Verwahrung gegen die von der rumänischen Regierung verfügte Donauverkehrskontrolle und einseitige Reservierung der rumänischen Donauhäfen und Donautransportmittel zugunsten einer Macht (Deutschland) eingelegt hat. Auf Veranlassung der deutschen Regierung begründete die rumänische Regierung die vorläufige Unterlassung einer abschließenden Stellungnahme zu dem russischen Protest mit dem erst bevorstehenden Amtsantritt des neuen rumänischen Außenministers.

Das deutsche Auswärtige Amt sah sich veranlaßt, dies der rumänischen Regierung Moskau gegenüber zu raten, da deutsche wirtschaftliche Begehren durch Moskau abgelehnt worden waren.

Der deutsche Delegationsführer Schnurre hatte darüber berichtet.

Die Ablehnung vermehrter Wirtschaftshilfe durch Moskau überzeugte das deutsche Reichsaußenministerium davon, daß die Sowjetregierung auf der ganzen Linie – nicht nur in den Japan und Bulgarien betreffenden Fragen – eine dem Reich und Italien „schädliche" Politik zu verfolgen suche. Diese Entwicklung suchte Berlin durch verschärften Druck auf Moskau aufzuhalten. Die Verstärkung der deutschen Heeresverbände in Altrumänien diente nicht nur dem Schutz deutscher Interessen, sondern auch dem obengenannten Zweck.

Schließlich ist zu erwähnen: es lagen dem deutschen Oberkommando Nachrichten vor, daß in den Vereinigten Staaten von Nordamerika eine große Zahl von Bestellungen amerikanischer Jagd- und Kampfmaschinen durch Großbritannien in Kriegsflugzeuge mit weitem Aktionsradius und in

Fernbomber umgewandelt wurden. Der größte Teil der Bestellungen mit Lieferterminen nach dem 1. Oktober 1941 ist von diesen Umdispositionen in der britischen Luftrüstung erfaßt.

Das deutsche Oberkommando rechnete mit dem Kriegseintritt der Vereinigten Staaten auf seiten des englischen Weltreiches.

Weisungen

Wie Walther Hubatsch in seinem Buch „Hitlers Weisungen für die Kriegführung 1939–1945" unter Bezugnahme auf Grimms Wörterbuch (Band XIV, 1. Jan. 1955) schreibt, ist unter „Weisung" zu verstehen: „Befehl, Auftrag, Anweisung, daß man etwas tun soll, häufig mit abhängigem Infinitiv . . ." Die Weisungen Hitlers bezeichnen vorausschauende Operationsabsichten. Sie stehen in einem politischen Zusammenhang.

Weisung Nr. 21 – Fall „Barbarossa".

„Die deutsche Wehrmacht muß darauf vorbereitet sein, auch vor Beendigung des Krieges gegen England Sowjetrußland in einem schnellen Feldzug niederzuwerfen (Fall Barbarossa).

Das Heer wird hierzu alle verfügbaren Verbände einzusetzen haben mit der Einschränkung, daß die besetzten Gebiete gegen Überraschungen gesichert sein müssen . . .

Der Schwerpunkt des Einsatzes der Kriegsmarine bleibt auch während eines Ostfeldzuges eindeutig gegen England gerichtet.

Den Aufmarsch gegen Sowjetrußland werde ich gegebenenfalls acht Wochen vor dem beabsichtigten Operationsbeginn befehlen. Vorbereitungen, die eine längere Anlaufzeit benötigen, sind – soweit noch nicht geschehen – schon jetzt in Angriff zu nehmen und bis zum 15. Mai 1941 abzuschließen."
(18. Dez. 1940)

Weisung Nr. 20 – Unternehmen „Marita" v. 13. Dez. 1940
Der Ausgang der Kämpfe in Albanien läßt sich noch nicht übersehen. Angesichts der bedrohlichen Lage in Albanien ist es doppelt wichtig, daß englische Bestrebungen, unter dem Schutz einer Balkanfront eine vor allem für Italien, daneben für das rumänische Ölgebiet gefährliche Luftbasis zu schaffen, vereitelt werden.
Meine Absicht ist daher: a) in den nächsten Monaten in Südrumänien eine sich allmählich verstärkende Kräftegruppe zu bilden, b) nach Eintreten günstiger Witterung – voraussichtlich im März – diese Kräftegruppe über Bulgarien hinweg zur Besitznahme der ägäischen Nordküste und – sollte dies erforderlich sein – des ganzen griechischen Festlandes anzusetzen (Unternehmen „Marita"). Mit der Unterstützung durch Bulgarien ist zu rechnen . . ."(13. Dez. 1940)

Weisung Nr. 22:
Mithilfe deutscher Kräfte bei den Kämpfen im Mittelmeerraum.
,,Die Lage im Mittelmeerraum, in dem England überlegene Kräfte gegen unsere Verbündeten einsetzt, erfordert aus strategischen, politischen und psychologischen Gründen deutsche Hilfeleistung. Tripolitanien muß behauptet, die Gefahr eines Zusammenbruchs der albanischen Front beseitigt werden. Darüber hinaus soll die Heeresgruppe Cavallero befähigt werden, im Zusammenhang mit den späteren Operationen der 12. Armee auch von Albanien aus zum Angriff überzugehen." (11. Jan. 1941)

Weisung Nr. 25:
1. ,,Der Militärputsch in Jugoslawien hat die politische Lage auf dem Balkan geändert. Jugoslawien muß auch dann, wenn es zunächst Loyalitätserklärungen abgibt, als Feind betrachtet und daher so rasch als möglich zerschlagen werden.
2. Meine Absicht ist, durch eine konzentrische Operation aus dem Raum Fiume-Graz einerseits und dem Raum um Sofia andererseits in allgemeiner Richtung Belgrad und südlich in Jugoslawien einzubrechen und die jugoslawische Wehrmacht vernichtend zu schlagen, außerdem den äußersten Südteil Jugoslawiens vom übrigen Land abzutrennen und als Basis für die Fortführung der deutsch-italienischen Offensive gegen Griechenland in die Hand zu nehmen. Die baldige Öffnung des Donau-Verkehrs und die Besitznahme der Kupfergruben von Bor sind aus wehrwirtschaftlichen Gründen wichtig. Durch die Aussicht auf Zurückgewinnung des Banats und von Mazedonien wird versucht, Ungarn und Bulgarien für die Teilnahme an den Operationen zu gewinnen. Die innerpolitische Spannung in Jugoslawien wird durch politische Zusicherungen verschärft werden." (27. März 1941)

Weisung Nr. 27:
,,Die jugoslawische Wehrmacht befindet sich in der Auflösung. Damit sind im Verein mit der Ausschaltung der griechischen Thrazien-Armee und der Inbesitznahme des Beckens von Saloniki sowie des Raumes um Florina die Voraussetzungen geschaffen, um nach Heranführen ausreichender Kräfte zum Angriff gegen Griechenland anzutreten mit dem Ziel, die dort stehende griechisch-englische Kräftegruppe zu vernichten, Griechenland zu besetzen und damit den Engländer endgültig vom Balkan zu vertreiben." (25. Apr. 1941)

Weisung Nr. 28 – Unternehmen ,,Merkur":
1. ,,Als Stützpunkt für die Luftkriegführung gegen England im Ost-Mittelmeer ist die Besetzung der Insel Kreta vorzubereiten (Unternehmen Mer-

kur). Hierbei ist davon auszugehen, daß das gesamte griechische Festland einschließlich des Peloponnes in der Hand der Achsenmächte ist." (25. Apr. 1941)

Weisung Nr. 30 – Mittlerer Orient:
„Die arabische Freiheitsbewegung ist im Mittleren Orient unser natürlicher Bundesgenosse gegen England. In diesem Zusammenhang kommt der Erhebung des Irak besondere Bedeutung zu. Sie stärkt über die irakischen Grenzen hinaus die englandfeindlichen Kräfte im Mittelorient, stört die englischen Verbindungen und bindet englische Truppen sowie englischen Schiffsraum auf Kosten anderer Kriegsschauplätze. Ich habe mich daher entschlossen, die Entwicklung im Mittleren Orient durch Unterstützung des Irak vorwärtszutreiben.

Ob und wie die englische Stellung zwischen Mittelmeer und Persischem Golf – im Zusammenhang mit einer Offensive gegen den Suezkanal – später endgültig zu Fall zu bringen ist, steht erst nach ‚Barbarossa‘ zur Entscheidung." (23. Mai 1941)

Südosteuropa

Hermann Göring, der Oberbefehlshaber der deutschen Luftwaffe, hielt es für notwendig, eine Horchstelle im Kaukasus einzurichten. Daher machte er einen solchen Vorschlag Adolf Hitler. Göring ging davon aus, daß die Westmächte planen würden, eine Orientarmee unter dem französischen General Weygand aufzustellen, um gegen die Ölfelder des Kaukasus und von Baku zu operieren.

Dadurch sollte die Ölzufuhr nach Deutschland abgeschnürt werden.

Der französische Botschafter in Ankara, Massigli, berichtete am 1. Apr. 1940: ,,Der britische Botschafter ist am 26. März vom Foreign Office gebeten worden, seinen Eindruck von der wahrscheinlichen Haltung der türkischen Regierung im Falle eines interalliierten Angriffs auf Baku mitzuteilen."

Am 28. Mrz. 1940 hatte Massigli festgestellt: ,,. . . Ein Luftangriff auf Baku bringt eine Überfliegung türkischen Gebietes von nicht einmal 200 km mit sich . . . Die Flugzeuge können aber sehr gut unbemerkt passieren." Belegt werden kann diese Behauptung, die auch die Planung eines Angriffskrieges von Churchill und Reynaud gegen die Sowjetunion enthält, durch die in der französischen Stadt La Charitè aufgefundenen Akten des französischen Generalstabes. Unter den Dokumenten befinden sich auch Unterlagen, die Jugoslawien belasten. Daher stellte der frühere jugoslawische Ministerpräsident Zwetkowić fest: ,,Unsere Situation in Berlin war nach dem Niedergang Frankreichs erschüttert. Die in La Charitè von den Deutschen im Juni 1940 beschlagnahmten Akten enthüllten unsere Aktion mit Frankreich und kompromittieren uns in den Augen Hitlers. Hitler hatte nachher kein Vertrauen zu uns."

In seinen ,,Memoiren", Band 3, 1. Buch, S. 159 gibt Churchill zu, die Errichtung einer Balkanfront gegen Deutschland angestrebt zu haben. Er schreibt: ,,Den Deutschen war es damals sehr darum zu tun, alle Störungen in Osteuropa zu vermeiden. Sie fürchteten, das werde ein englisches Vorgehen auf dem Balkan zur Folge haben und könne die Russen zu einem weiteren aktiven Eingreifen veranlassen."

Aus einem Bericht von Léon Wenger vom 1. Okt. 1939 an die französische Regierung geht die Zielsetzung hervor, den Deutschen das rumänische Öl zu sperren. Der französische Generalissimus Gamelin schrieb am 6. Mrz. 1940 nieder, daß ,,Frankreich es für wünschenswert und möglich hält,

a) den Zugang zu den Meerengen und zum Ägäischen Meer über den Balkan für Deutschland und die Sowjetunion zu sperren,

b) im Inneren des Balkan auf einer ungeheuren Abnutzungsfront die

Armeen der Balkanländer und sowjetrussischen Streitkräfte entgegenzustellen."

Anfang Oktober 1940 griff Mussolini gegen den Willen Hitlers Griechenland an, was ernste Verstimmungen zwischen den beiden Diktatoren hervorrief.

Nach dem Zusammenbruch Frankreichs trat im Zusammenspiel mit England die Sowjetunion an die Stelle unseres französischen Nachbarn. Nicht mit Unrecht stellt Johann Wuescht in ,,Jugoslawien und das Dritte Reich – Eine Dokumentationsgeschichte der deutsch-jugoslawischen Beziehungen von 1933–1945" fest:

,,Während Hitler sich krampfhaft bemühte, seine Militärmacht intakt zu halten . . ., versuchte Churchill diese furchtbare Kraft durch Erhöhung immer neuer Fronten zu schwächen und zu verzetteln, ohne Rücksicht auf den jeweiligen örtlichen militärischen Ausgang . . . Man darf es heute bereits als eine geschichtliche Tatsache hinnehmen, daß Hitler den Krieg im europäischen Südosten nicht wollte. Hitler wollte Frieden auf dem Balkan, der ihm den ungestörten Bezug von Mineralöl, Rohstoffen und Lebensmitteln aus Südosteuropa ermöglichte und Deutschland gegebenenfalls einen sicheren Flankenschutz gegen England und die Sowjetunion gewährleistete."

Die Einstellung Hitlers zu Jugoslawien wird durch die Tatsache klar, daß trotz aller italienischen Intrigen Deutschland Jugoslawien einen Rüstungskredit in Höhe von 200 Millionen RM gewährte und Waffen, Flugzeuge, Flakgeschütze und anderes Waffenmaterial nicht gegen Devisen, sondern auf Clearingskonto lieferte. Die Anleihe wurde ohne politische Bedingungen gewährt.

Am 25. März 1941 trat Jugoslawien dem Drei-Mächte-Pakt bei. Die Reichsregierung hatte versichert, sie werde während des Krieges nicht den Durchmarsch oder den Durchtransport von Truppen durch das jugoslawische Staatsgebiet verlangen. Von geschichtlichem Interesse ist es, daß die Putschisten in Belgrad überlegten, vor oder nach dem Paktbeitritt Jugoslawiens loszuschlagen. General Greifenberg erklärte, daß die Jugoslawen gegen die 12. Armee an den Grenzen Bulgariens, das seit 1. März 1941 dem Dreierpakt angehörte, ihre Truppen aufmarschieren ließen.

In Griechenland befanden sich Anfang März 1941 180 britische Flugzeuge. Bis 16. März 1941 standen dort 20 000 Mann, die bis zum 25. März einschließlich der RAF auf 50 000 Mann verstärkt wurden.

Lord Halifax äußerte sich im Frühjahr 1941 zu den Ereignissen auf dem Balkan: ,,Hitler muß diesen Feldzug gegen seinen Willen führen . . ." In der ,,Chicago Tribune" wird festgestellt: ,,Hitler ist gegen seinen Wunsch in einen kostspieligen Balkankrieg verwickelt worden . . ." Churchill drückte sich ähnlich aus.

Heute ist unbestritten, daß auf Veranlassung des führenden Mannes im britischen Geheimdienst, Sir Steward Graham Menzies, britische Agenten den General Bora Mirkowić, der die jugoslawische Luftwaffe kommandierte, zu einer Revolte in Belgrad anstifteten. Als der Morgen des 27. März 1941 graute, hatten sich probritische Revolutionäre in den Besitz aller taktisch wichtigen Punkte in der jugoslawischen Hauptstadt gebracht. Sie besetzten auch das königliche Schloß. Die Regierung wurde gestürzt, Prinzregent Paul festgenommen und nach Griechenland in das Exil geschickt.

Bei Einbruch der Nacht war der Staatsstreich zu Ende. General Dušan Simović hatte die Macht übernommen.

Von der sowjetischen Regierung in Moskau erhielt Jugoslawien umfangreiche Waffenlieferungen unter der Bedingung der Geheimhaltung gegenüber Deutschland.

Am 5. Apr. 1941 wurde in Moskau der jugoslawisch-sowjetrussische Freundschafts- und Nichtangriffsvertrag unterzeichnet.

Generalfeldmarschall List, der verantwortlich für die Operationen in Südosteuropa war, erklärte am 4. Juli 1946: ,,Mir gegenüber wurden etwa 15 jugoslawische Divisionen gemeldet, denen ich nur sehr unterlegene Kräfte entgegenzustellen hatte."

Verwirrendes Spiel

Dem Schweizer Hauptmann Hausamann war bekannt, daß zwischen den Generalstäben des deutschen Heeres und des Luftwaffen-Oberkommandos einerseits und dem Bevollmächtigten des bulgarischen Generalstabes seit 10. Oktober 1940 in Sofia und seit 12. Okt. 1940 gleichzeitig in Plewna Besprechungen stattfanden und nach der Landung britischer Truppen auf Kreta auf dem westlichen Peloponnes (Katakolon) und im Hafen von Zente britische Einheiten ausgeschifft wurden.

Am 11. Nov. 1940 meldet er: ,,Britische Spezialtruppen sind bisher mit Sicherheit auf griechischem Territorium im Raum von Athen, auf der Insel Salamis, am Kanal von Korinth, im nordwestlichen Peloponnes, dem Gebiet von Pyrgos, auf den Inseln Zante, Kythara und Kreta festgestellt."

Aufschlußreich ist die Stelle in einem Bericht vom 12. Nov. 1940: ,,Bei den Berichten über die deutsche Bereitschaft handelt es sich um Nachrichten von einem mir sehr bekannten hohen Offizier der ehemaligen österreichischen Armee, der bei Kriegsausbruch im deutschen Generalstab der Abteilung Südost in leitender Stellung zugeteilt wurde und der uns laufend über die geplanten wie über die durchgeführten Verschiebungen im Südosten unterrichtet, falls er diese Unterrichtung im Interesse der Schweiz gelegen ansieht."

Gestützt auf die Schweizer Quelle kann gesagt werden: Rußland war zu keinem Zeitpunkt bereit zu dulden, daß Streitkräfte der Achsenmächte die Dardanellen schützten. Die Sowjetunion konnte einerseits nicht zulassen, daß dieser Ausgang in die Weltmeere von den Achsenmächten kontrolliert werden würde. Andererseits war der Augenblick für die Sowjetunion noch nicht gekommen, sich in die deutsch-englische Auseinandersetzung einzuschalten. Rußlands Diplomatie begnügte sich vorläufig darauf, alle Bestrebungen zu unterstützen, welche geeignet waren, dem Deutschen Reich das Festsetzen im Raum des Schwarzen Meeres unmöglich zu machen. In diesem Zusammenhang zog der Kreml seine Truppen aus Georgien zurück, um es der Türkei zu ermöglichen, seine an der türkisch-russischen Grenze gebundenen beträchtlichen Heeresteile an die bulgarisch-türkische Grenze zu verlegen. In der Erkenntnis, keine Entscheidung in Bulgarien erzwingen zu können, strebte die Sowjetregierung eine Gleichschaltung der türkischen und der bulgarischen Politik an. Vertreter Sowjetrußlands wurden in Sofia und in Ankara vorstellig, um beide Regierungen auf die Nichtduldung der Anwesenheit militärischer, diplomatisch nicht legitimierter Sonderkommandos der Kriegführenden auf ihrem Hoheitsgebiet festzulegen. Bei der rumänischen Regierung wurde in scharfer Form auf schwerwiegende Folgen einer Mißachtung der russischen Interessen hingewiesen.

Ende Dezember 1940 überflogen demonstrativ mehrfach russische Kampfflugzeuge die befestigten Gegenden der Norddobrudscha, wo schwere Geschütze seitens der rumänischen Wehrmacht aufgestellt worden waren.

Die bulgarische Regierung sah sich veranlaßt, um sich vor einem jugoslawisch-türkischen, von England über Griechenland unterstützten militärischen Zusammenspiel zu sichern, bei der jugoslawischen Regierung in Belgrad vorstellig zu werden. Deutscherseits wurde von Jugoslawien verlangt, daß es jede weitere militärische Maßnahme unterläßt, die als Bedrohung der bulgarischen Westgrenze oder als Vorbereitung des Zusammenschlusses jugoslawischer Streitkräfte mit griechischen oder türkischen verstanden werden müßte.

Gegen Mitte Februar 1941 gab Belgrad der Reichsregierung die Antwort, sie werde sich jeder weiteren Maßnahme zur Erhöhung des Effektivbestandes der jugoslawischen Streitkräfte enthalten.

Am 19. Febr. 1941 empfing der deutsche Außenminister von Ribbentrop den sowjetrussischen Botschafter Dekanosow zu einer Aussprache und übergab ihm ein Memorandum zum italienisch-griechischen Konflikt, in welchem sinngemäß ausgeführt wird: Der Wunsch der deutschen Reichsregierung gehe dahin, den deutsch-griechischen Krieg zu lokalisieren. Sie gehe darin mit der Sowjetregierung einig. Die Gleichartigkeit dieser Wünsche und Interessen legten indessen auch die politische Übereinstimmung der beiden Mächte in der Beurteilung derjenigen kriegführenden Macht nahe, die sich in den italienisch-griechischen Konflikt bereits eingemischt habe, auf griechischem Boden bereits bewaffnete Kräfte unterhalte und Anstalten treffe, um von Griechenland aus weitere Teile Südosteuropas in den Krieg zu ziehen. Trotz dieser britischen Vorbereitungen, die sich nicht nur gegen Italien, sondern auch unmittelbar gegen das Reich richteten, habe die Reichsregierung bisher in der Hoffnung auf eine Bereitschaft der griechischen Regierung, den Krieg zu beenden, von militärischen Maßnahmen zur Unterbindung einer britischen Balkankriegführung abgesehen. Die Geduld der Reichsregierung könne aber nicht unbegrenzte Zeit in Anspruch genommen werden. Solange die griechische Regierung, bestärkt durch die türkische, ihre militärische Bindung an Großbritannien nicht gelöst habe, könne das Reich einerseits nicht auf militärische Maßnahmen verzichten, die jeder denkbaren Entwicklung wirksam begegnen würden. Aber auch dann, wenn das Reich zum Handeln gezwungen würde, werde es sich auf solche Maßnahmen beschränken, die dem Bedürfnis der an einer friedlichen Entwicklung interessierten Staaten Südosteuropas gerecht werden und dem Versuch einer Kriegführung auf dem Balkan ein schnelles Ende bereiten. Es sei an der griechischen und – in zweiter Linie – an der türkischen Regierung, ihre Haltung einwandfrei im Sinn der Unterstützung oder Nichtunterstützung der britischen Kriegführung in Südosteuropa klarzustellen und damit selbst über ihre Verwicklung oder Nichtverwicklung in die britisch-deutsche Auseinandersetzung zu entscheiden, die das Reich bisher von Südosteuropa ferngehalten habe.

Der deutsche Reichsaußenminister gab der Erwartung Ausdruck, daß die Sowjetregierung sich nach Prüfung des Memorandums dem von der Reichsführung eingenommenen und nach Lage der Dinge unveränderlich festgelegten Standpunkt nicht verschließen werde. Der Reichsaußenminister erklärte, daß Eingriffe in die Souveränität der südosteuropäischen Staaten oder Veränderungen territorialer Art in Südosteuropa von der Reichsführung nicht beabsichtigt seien und daß demgemäß auch ein Anlaß zu einem deutsch-russischen Meinungsaustausch gemäß Konsultativ-Abkommen nicht gegeben sei. Die Reichsregierung habe die Hoffnung, daß die Sowjetregierung in Würdigung des deutschen Standpunktes und der deutschen Absichten ihren Einfluß besonders auf die Entschließungen der türkischen Regierung dahin geltend mache, daß diese ihre militärischen Maßnahmen dem Verhalten einer neutralen Macht anpasse.

Im März 1941 wechseln die Szenen atemberaubend. Großen Anteil daran hat außer dem Engländer Sir Menzies der USA-Oberst Donovan. Hitler empfing den jugoslawischen Ministerpräsidenten Zwetković in Berchtesgaden. Deutsche Truppen marschieren in Bulgarien ein. Daraufhin legt die Sowjetregierung politisch ihre Position gegen Bulgarien und das Reich fest, falls die Türkei kämpft und England sie nicht im Stich läßt. Diese Stellungnahme wird von Berlin als Versuch aufgefaßt, die Türken gegen Deutschland in Front zu bringen. Durch eine Sonderbotschaft an den türkischen Staatspräsidenten sollte die türkische Regierung vor die Wahl zwischen unbedingter Neutralität (erklärtem Desinteressement an der britisch-griechischen Front) und einer Situation gestellt werden, in der nicht Griechenland, sondern die Türkei es sei, der sich ein deutscher Angriff zuwenden würde.

Es wurde erwartet, daß diese Aussicht den türkischen Generalstab bewegte, die türkische Regierung zu veranlassen, dringend an die Russen zu appellieren, sich militärisch nicht festzulegen. Papen wurde zur Zusage ermächtigt, daß die Deutsche Wehrmacht von jeder Festsetzung im Gesamtgebiet Südost-Bulgariens einschließlich der von Griechenland annektierten Gebiete absieht, sofern die türkische Regierung eine bulgarisch-türkische Nichtangriffsverpflichtung bekräftigt.

Hausamann bemerkt dazu: ,,Kriegspolitisch ist das Ziel der deutschen Reichsführung nicht auf die Eroberung, sondern auf die Gleichschaltung der Türkei gerichtet. Der Gedanke einer gewaltsamen Erzwingung des Durchmarsches durch Kleinasien oder einer gewaltsamen Besetzung türkischen Territoriums zwecks Errichtung von Stützpunkten der Luft- oder Landkriegführung am östlichen Mittelmeer liegt aus strategischen und organisatorischen Gründen dem deutschen Generalstab fern . . . Das Ziel der deutschen bzw. der deutsch-italienischen Kriegführung unter Benutzung der Balkanbasen sind für das erste nur die Besetzung von Nordgriechenland und die dadurch ermöglichte luftstrategische Überlegenheit im gesamten Nordteil des östlichen Mittelmeeres unter Einschluß des Dodekanes. Sind diese Ziele erreicht, so sind nach Auffassung der deutschen Wehrmachtführung auch die britisch-türkischen Seeverbindungen, auf denen die britisch-türkische Allianz beruht, unterbunden."

Der deutsche Botschafter in Belgrad erhielt nach dem 8. Mrz. 1941, an dem die Einberufung einer größeren Anzahl von Reservisten in den meisten jugoslawischen Militärbezirken erfolgte, die Anweisung, dies in scharfer Form zu beanstanden.

Seit dem 9. März 1941 trafen in Piräus britische Truppentransporte ein. Die Truppen wurden sofort mit der Bahn nach dem Norden weitertransportiert. Die britischen Ausschiffungen wurden in den Nächten vom 9./10., vom 10./11. und 11./12. Mrz. 1941 fortgesetzt. Der Effektivbestand der jugoslawischen Armee erhöhte sich seit dem 8. März 1941 um 80 000 Mann. 24 kriegsstarke Divisionen und 200 000 Mann für Infanterieverbände zweiten und dritten Ranges standen im Kriegsfalle zur Verfügung.

Das Oberkommando der Roten Armee baute nach der Stationierung der deutschen Truppen in Bulgarien östlich vom rumänischen-Rusi bis an und unter den Dnjestr im Raum von Kižinew und Balta militärische Positionen aus und zog Panzertruppen, Artillerie und Elite-Infanterie im südlichen Bessarabien teilweise am Pruth und an der Donau zusammen. Grenzschutztruppen wurden an die Pruthgrenze an der nördlichen Moldau geschickt.

Diese Umgruppierungsmaßnahmen der beiden in Bessarabien liegenden russischen Armeen stellten eine starke, massive Bedrohung der Dobrudscha und der nordöstlichen Walachei dar. Das russische Oberkommando ging davon aus, daß es dadurch möglich sei, das nördliche und mittlere Bessarabien so lange zu halten, bis die militärische Zusammenarbeit Moskaus mit den deutschen Balkangegnern im Schwarzmeergebiet hergestellt sein würde. Auf jeden Fall bedeutete die Umgruppierung in Bessarabien die Formierung einer stoßkräftigen Armee gegen die Dobrudscha und Galatz-Foesani.

Die 2. Armee sollte sich zur Norddeckung der 1. westlich und östlich von Kižinew in Bereitschaft halten. In Verbindung damit standen die russischen Transporte, die seit März in die seit Frühling 1940 neu errichteten Garnisonen und Lager auf dem westlichen und südwestlichen Teil der Halbinsel Kola liefen. Dazu kommt, daß in diesem Nordraum gleichzeitig große Übungen sowjetischer Fliegerverbände stattfanden.

Prinzregent Paul stand vor der schweren Entscheidung zwischen Deutschland und England. Der jugoslawische Ministerpräsident teilte zunächst im Auftrag des Prinzregenten der deutschen Reichsregierung mit, daß die abschließende Beratung und Beschlußfassung über die Neugestaltung der deutsch-jugoslawischen Beziehungen erst nach der Behebung der im Kabinett aufgetretenen Meinungsverschiedenheiten, möglicherweise erst nach einer Neubildung der Regierung möglich sei. Der deutsche Gesandte von Heeren erklärte in Belgrad, daß für die Entscheidung die Regentschaft verfassungsmäßig allein zuständig sei und die deutsche Regierung eine endgültige Stellungnahme erwarte.

Die Lage war aber auch für die Achsenmächte infolge der innenpolitischen Verhältnisse in Italien kompliziert. Am 17. Mrz. 1941 gibt Hausamann einen Bericht aus erstklassiger italienischer Quelle (königliches Kabinett) wieder, der von einer Ausschaltung Mussolinis und einer Regierungsübernahme durch Grandi spricht. ,,Kurz vor Beginn des Einmarsches deutscher Truppen in Italien waren dort im vollen Einverständnis mit dem König alle Vorbereitungen getroffen, eine neue Regierung an das Ruder zu bringen mit Grandi als Ministerpräsident, Farinacci als Minister ohne Portefeuille usw. Diese Regierung war gedacht als Übergangskabinett unter Ausschaltung von Mussolini. Ihr hätte nach kurzer Zeit ein weiteres Kabinett mit Badoglio als Ministerpräsident folgen sollen.

In Verwirklichung dieses Planes hätte der König darauf rechnen können, daß der gesamte italienische Adel hinter ihn getreten wäre. Die Ausführung verzögerte sich, weil Sondierungen in England ergeben hatten, daß die britische Regierung Verhandlungen über einen Sonderfrieden nur unter der Bedingung aufnehmen wollte, daß Italien den Engländern auf italienischem Territorium Stützpunkte für die englische Luftwaffe und Marine einräume.

Als Mussolini von diesen Verhandlungen Kenntnis erhielt, erfolgte seine Reise nach Berchtesgaden mit dem Ergebnis, daß rasch nachher deutsche Truppen in Italien einrückten. Damit durchkreuzte Mussolini die Absichten des Königshauses.

Inzwischen aber hatte in Libyen der englische Vormarsch begonnen.

Im Vertrauen darauf, daß das italienische Königshaus in seinen Bemühungen erfolgreich sei, hatte Graziani im Einverständnis mit Badoglio davon abgesehen, nachhaltigen Widerstand durch die italienischen Armeen zu erzwingen.

Das Ergebnis ist bekannt: Die Bemühungen des Königshauses scheiterten, die englischen Divisionen ließen die italienischen Truppen in Libyen nicht mehr zur Ruhe kommen. Badoglio mußte mit zahlreichen Offizieren des italienischen Hochadels gehen. Graziani wollte zurücktreten, wurde aber nicht entlassen, um das Gesicht zu wahren. Die Deutschen brachten eine Kolonialdivision nach Libyen, um den Italienern den Rücken zu stärken. Im Einverständnis mit Mussolini übernahm die deutsche Wehrmacht das Oberkommando über die vereinigten italienisch-deutschen Heere in Italien usw.

Im Augenblick stand der gesamte italienische Adel im schärfsten Gegensatz zu Mussolini. Man sprach bei Hof wie in der Armee nur von der deutschen Okkupation. Weil der Adel mit seiner Auffassung nicht hinter dem Berge hielt, machte sich auch im Volk ein defaitistischer Geist breit, der (so sagte der Gewährsmann, selbst Mitleid des italienischen Hochadels, wörtlich) zum Zusammenbruch führen muß. Mag diese Mitteilung auch übertrieben sein! Wenn man rückblickend die Ereignisse betrachtet, muß dennoch gesagt werden, daß hinter diesen Informationen viel Wahres steht.

Doch zurück nach Jugoslawien. Prinzregent Paul entschied: Jugoslawien tritt dem Dreierpakt Deutschland–Italien–Japan bei.

Der Regierungssturz in Belgrad und seine Folgen

Maček, eine einflußreiche Persönlichkeit im kroatischen Raum, wurde bei seinen Bemühungen, eine enge Verbindung zwischen Jugoslawien und Deutschland zu schaffen, von maßgebenden Kreisen des nichtserbischen Handels und der Industrie gestützt. Er erklärte dem Prinzregenten Paul offen, daß sich Kroatien lieber autonom erkläre, als an der Seite Serbiens in einen aussichtslosen Krieg zu ziehen. Der Prinzregent erteilte daraufhin der Regierung Zwetković–Maček am 23. März 1941 alle Vollmachten, um mit Berlin zu verhandeln. Den Beitrag Jugoslawiens zum Drei-Mächte-Pakt betrachtete das Auswärtige Amt als einen großen Erfolg der deutschen Diplomatie.

Hausamann schreibt am 27. Mrz. 1941: ,,Das jugoslawische Sich-Besinnen auf das, was man unter nationaler Ehre und Würde versteht, kann kriegspolitische Folgen von allergrößter Tragweite haben." Er stellt fest, daß die deutsche Heeresleitung sich infolge des Umsturzes in Jugoslawien vor eine wenig beneidenswerte Situation gestellt sah. Wörtlich sagte er: ,,Greift sie (die Heeresgruppe List) jetzt an (und sie wird angreifen müssen), dann ist sie ständig in beiden Flanken bedroht. Greift sie (entgegen Erwarten) nicht an und wartet sie die Verstärkungen ab, dann gelingt es den Griechen möglicherweise, in Albanien Erfolge zu erzielen . . . Die Entscheidung im Südosten hat aber noch ganz andere Auswirkungen. Das wird die Verhandlungen mit Matsuoka in Berlin in einer für Deutschland ungünstigen Richtung beeinflussen, wird Frankreich widerspenstig machen, wird Spanien zum Abwarten veranlassen, wird den in Nordafrika befehlenden Franzosen den Rücken stärken, wird die in Abessinien kämpfenden Italiener entmutigen, wird die Russen zur Erwägung veranlassen, ob nicht der Moment gekommen sei, die Schwenkung gegen Deutschland auszuführen und vorerst einmal die Zufuhr von Rohstoffen zu bremsen."

Am 31. Mrz. 1941 bringt Hausamann folgende Meldung: ,,Der politisch-strategische Zusammenhang der berichteten sowjetrussischen Armeekonzentration in Bessarabien und an der ungarischen Grenze in Ostgalizien mit dem Regierungssturz in Jugoslawien wird immer deutlicher . . . Es kann nicht mehr bezweifelt werden, daß der jugoslawische Generalstab gerade im Hinblick auf die strategische Ausschaltung Ungarns über den russischen Gesandten bzw. Militärattaché ermunternde Zusagen erhalten hat. Diese Zusagen dürften auf den Entschluß der serbischen Generäle, Zwetković zu stürzen, von erheblichem Einfluß gewesen sein."

Die jugoslawische Wehrmacht hatte am 26. März etwa 550 000 Mann mobilisiert, von denen etwa 500 000 Angehörige des Heeres und 50 000 Angehörige der Marine, der Marine-Küstenverteidigung und der Luftwaffe waren. Am 27. Mrz. 1941 wurden von der neuen Regierung weitere 300 000 Mann einberufen. Damit waren 65 % aller Militärdienstpflichtigen mobil gemacht. Nach Ausscheiden der unzuverlässigen oder nur bedingt zuverlässigen Truppenteile aus kroatischen, slowenischen oder slawonischen Garnisonen verfügte das jugoslawische Heer nach der am 27. Mrz. 1941 erweiterten Mobilmachung über 36 Divisionen und über ungefähr 10 Divisionen Infanteriereserve. Die jugoslawische Luftwaffe hatte einen Bestand von etwa 20 000 ausgebildeten Fliegertruppen mit 1500 Flugzeugführern, Kampffliegern, Schützen usw. und ungefähr 600 Maschinen, meist Jagdflugzeugen und leichten Bombern. Es wird gesagt, daß die jugoslawische Luftwaffe doppelt so stark war wie die griechische Luftwaffe im November 1940.

Meldungen lagen vor, daß die englische Luftwaffe in ganz Südosteuropa und Nordafrika außerordentlich verstärkt wurde. Mit dem Einsatz von 2500 bis 3000 Maschinen der RAF in Afrika und am östlichen Mittelmeer war zu rechnen.

Am 3. Apr. 1941 setzte die Belgrader Regierung die Mobilmachung durch Einberufung der Wehrpflichtigen von weiteren Jahrgängen, u. a. 1899 und 1900, fort. Ausgenommen von den Aufgeboten wurden einzig und allein die kroatischen Militärbezirke. Der größte Teil der Heeresverbände wurde in Bosnien, Montenegro und Mittelserbien gesammelt. Die auffallendsten Truppenkonzentrationen vollzogen sich im Viereck Krusevac–Zajecar–Nisch–Pirot.

Als Einzelheiten des Putsches wurden aus englischer Quelle bekannt: ,,Offiziere der jugoslawischen Luftwaffe waren die ursprünglichen Initianten der Bewegung . . . Sie wurden durch Offiziere der königlichen Garde unterstützt. Die zum Handeln entschlossene Armeeleitung versammelte sich in der Nacht des Umsturzes um Mitternacht im Kriegsministerium, wo sie die telefonischen Meldungen ihrer Untergebenen abwartete . . .''

Als alle Regierungs- und öffentlichen Gebäude besetzt worden waren, begab sich General Simović zum königlichen Palast und verlangte, daß der König geweckt würde. Der junge König erschien im Morgenrock mit schlaftrunkenen Augen. Er wurde von General Simović mit folgenden Worten angesprochen: ,,Majestät, von jetzt an sind Sie König Jugoslawiens und üben selbst die Herrschaftsrechte aus.'' Herr Zwetković wurde nach Mitternacht gefangengenommen. Bei seiner Ankunft im Kriegsministerium drang er auf eine Besprechung mit General Simović. ,,In wessen Namen haben Sie die Macht ergriffen?'' waren seine ersten Worte an seinen Nachfolger. „Im Namen derjenigen, die Sie nie vertreten haben, im Namen des Volkes", war die kurze Antwort des Generals.

Die neugebildete jugoslawische Regierung bestand aus Vertretern aller politischen Parteien: von der äußersten Rechten (welche in den verflossenen Jahren diktatorisch regierte: Jevtić) über die Altradikalen (Ninčić und Tifunović) bis zu den Jungradikalen, Demokraten und linksorientierten Agrariern.

Der Entschluß, dem Drei-Mächte-Pakt beizutreten, wurde dem gestürzten Minister Antić, der entscheidenden Einfluß auf Prinzregent Paul hatte, angelastet.

Am 4. Apr. 1941 wurde der gesamte Donauverkehr durch die jugoslawischen Militärbehörden gesperrt. Er legte außer 50% des gesamten, zwischen Deutschland einerseits und Rumänien und Bulgarien andererseits abzuwickelnden Wirtschafts- und Güteraustauschverkehrs auch die mit ungarischen und rumänischen Schleppern betriebenen Kriegsmaterialtransporte lahm.

In Berlin wurde diese Maßnahme als bewußte Eröffnung feindseliger Handlungen gewertet. Sie wurde auf die Initiative des britischen Reichsgeneralstabes zurückgeführt. Mit fast 60% wurde der vom Reich nach Bulgarien sowie etwa 25% der vom Reich nach Rumänien geleitete Transportverkehr unterbunden. Die Zufuhr russischer Güter nach dem Reich auf der Donau war von der Sowjetregierung schon vor Wochen gesperrt worden.

Folgende für das Reich bestimmte Tagesmengen rumänischer und bulgarischer Exportgüter fielen aus: 1800 t Rohöl und Erdölprodukte, 800 t Getreide und Futtermittel, 1500 t andere Nahrungsmittel, hauptsächlich Gemüse, Vieh, Eier und tierische Fette, 160 t Holz, etwa 300 t andere Güter, u. a. Mineralien, Metalle, Häute, Leder, Tabak usw. Zu dieser Tagesmenge von rund 3200 t rumänischer und bulgarischer Exportgüter kamen noch etwa 1000 t für Italien bestimmte rumänische und bulgarische Güterlieferungen im Tagesdurchschnitt hinzu, die auf den Donautransport unbedingt angewiesen waren. Von der Sperre des Gütertransitverkehrs auf den jugoslawischen Bahnen wurden noch weitere rund 300 Rohstoffe und Produkte betroffen, die Italien täglich aus Rumänien und Bulgarien bezog.

Der Krieg in Südosteuropa brach aus. Der Feldzug, der zugunsten des Deutschen Reiches endete, dauerte nicht lange. Die ägäischen Inseln wurden besetzt. Andros, Tinos, Syros und Mykonos waren seit 1. Mai 1941 in deutscher Hand. Marine- und Luftlandetruppen landeten auf Ikaria und Samos. Auf Rhodos, das damals zu Italien gehörte, wurde ein Stützpunkt errichtet. Es ergab sich eine hervorragende Ausgangsposition für den Einsatz schwerer deutscher Bomber zum Angriff auf Kreta, Zypern und Alexandria sowie für die Überführung von Truppen und Material auf dem Luftweg nach Syrien und dem Irak.

Der deutsche Botschafter von Papen hatte der türkischen Regierung Anfang Mai 1941 zur Kenntnis zu bringen, daß sie der Ansammlung einer britischen Armee an den Grenzen der Türkei und im Osten Syriens nicht untätig zusehen könne.

Im Irak war im April 1941 ein Staatsstreich von Raschid Ali, der gegen England gerichtet war, gelungen. Berlin nahm außerdem an, daß die Stellung des französischen Generals Deutz, der als Anwalt der deutsch-französischen Zusammenarbeit galt, gegenüber seinen Offizieren, Beamten und Soldaten gefestigt war. Man spielte mit dem Gedanken, Syrien und das Königreich Hedschas in den Krieg einzubeziehen und die antibritischen Elemente im Irak, Iran und in Syrien zu stärken.

Nach Hausamann wurde die Boden-, Material- und Transportorganisation für die deutsche Luftwaffe im Irak und in Syrien eingeleitet. Bis Ende des Monats Mai sollte die Überführung von zwei starken Fliegerverbänden auf syrische und irakische Flugplätze möglich sein, so berichtet Hausamann am 19. Mai 1941.

Ende Mai 1941 fiel Kreta. Bedenken traten im Kreise der deutschen Wehrmacht im Juni auf. Es wurde befürchtet, daß das verfrühte Losschlagen von Raschid Ali im Irak auf die militärische Lage im Osten unangenehme Folgen haben könne.

Englische Truppen könnten aus Palästina nach Syrien vorstoßen. In Nordafrika liefen die Operationen nicht nach Plan. Gesagt wurde, daß General Rommel enorme Ausfälle an Kampffahrzeugen habe. Dazu kam, daß Feldmarschall von Brauchitsch die Entwicklung im Fernen Osten sehr skeptisch beurteilte. Er befürchtete, daß die Sowjetunion ein Doppelspiel betreibe und darauf warte, Deutschland in einem günstigen Augenblick in den Rücken zu fallen. Derselben Auffassung war auch Rundstedt.

Am 2. Juni 1941 liegt dem Schweizer Nachrichtendienst die Meldung vor: ,,Alle der irakischen Armee zugeteilten Sonderkommandos der deutschen Wehrmacht mit Ausnahme der im Mosulgebiet und bei den Kerkuker Ölfeldern stationierten Flieger und Luftwaffenbeobachter sind nach Syrien zurückgenommen worden." Dies gelte auch für alle Heeresangehörigen einschließlich Waffen und Material. Die für die irakische Armee bestimmten Waffen und Munitionsvorräte aus deutschen und französischen Beständen wurden aufgrund eines Befehls vom 27. Mai 1941 ebenfalls zurückgefordert. Seit Mitte Mai 1941 hatte die Sowjet-Diplomatie in Ankara und Teheran ihren Einfluß dahingehend geltend gemacht, sich dem Transport von Truppen und Kriegsmaterial in die arabischen Länder zu widersetzen. Das Verhältnis Deutschlands zur Türkei verschlechterte sich immer mehr.

Hausamann berichtete unter dem 13. Juni 1941, daß der nochmalige Versuch, die türkische Regierung in der syrischen Frage prodeutsch festzulegen, gescheitert sei.

Am 11. Juni 1941 wurde der Befehl gegeben, die Hälfte der Wehrmachtsangehörigen aus Syrien zurückzuziehen.

Wehrmachtskommandos verblieben in Aleppo, Ladikije, Kattime und Baalbek.

Weitere Verhandlungen mit der Sowjetunion bleiben ohne Erfolg

Am 18. Febr. 1941 wies die Sowjetregierung die deutsche Reichsregierung darauf hin, daß sie gemäß dem deutsch-sowjetischen Konsultativabkommen bisher jede einseitige Einmischung in die kriegerische Verwicklung zwischen Italien und Griechenland unterlassen habe und ein gleiches Verhalten auch von der deutschen Regierung erwarte.

Sie deutete unübersehbare Folgen an.

Sowjetische Lieferungen nach dem Reich wurden seit Februar 1941 mit der Begründung gestoppt, daß die verschiedenen Schienenstränge, vor allem die für das Rollmaterial, für umfangreiche Wehrmachtstransporte in den Schwarzmeerraum benötigt würden.

Der deutsche Sicherheitsdienst stellte fest, daß die UdSSR den Übertritt von polnischen Parteigängern der KP über die Grenze organisierte. Verhöre ergaben, daß die Sowjetunion systematisch Propagandisten in das Generalgouvernement schicke, um gegen das nationalsozialistische Regime Stimmung zu machen. In Radom und Lublin mußte aus diesem Anlaß je ein Dezernat eingerichtet werden.

Am 4. Mrz. zitiert Hausamann aus einem Brief eines auf bürgerlichem Boden stehenden Rußlandkenners, auf dessen Urteil man etwas geben könne: ,,Das Problem Rußland ist vollkommen klar. Es hat nur einen Wunsch, nur ein Ziel jetzt, . . . den Krieg möglichst in die Länge zu ziehen. Diesem Wunsche ordnet es alles unter. Es wird neutral sein, solange es kann, dann wird es, wenn es sein muß, sich auf die Seite schlagen, die ihm diejenige scheint, welche zu einem Separatfrieden geneigt sein könnte oder überhaupt zu einem Frieden.

Man weiß heute, daß Moskau fieberhaft rüstet, daß es sich gegen Osten sichern will, indem es mit Japan zu irgendeinem vorläufigen Kompromiß kommen will, bis es in Europa sieht, was vor sich geht. Am russischen Radio sagt man dem russischen Volke jeden Tag: ,Seid auf alles gefaßt! Der Krieg kann jeden Tag ausbrechen. Habt keine Angst, Eure Regierung verrät die Weltrevolution nicht, sie wird keine Interessen der Sowjetunion opfern, sei es, für wen es wolle!' Man genierte sich auch gar nicht, Deutschland ziemlich unfreundlich zu behandeln. In Vorträgen über den Nationalsozialismus kann man recht pikante Sachen erfahren. Die Militärspezialisten bewerten die Chancen eines deutschen Sieges gegenwärtig nicht hoch. Sie glauben weder an das Unterseeboot noch die Luftwaffe als entscheidendes Mittel, den Krieg zu gewinnen. Man hat manchmal auch das Gefühl, Rußland vermittle an England unter der Hand recht wertvolle Nachrichten. Ganz eigenartig ist es, was in Griechenland und in der Türkei vor sich geht. Ich habe ein merkwürdiges Gefühl, daß dort die Engländer einen Schachzug vorhaben."

Ende Mai traf die Nachricht ein, daß in Ostgalizien und im südöstlich angrenzendem Gebiet (Czernowitz, Kamenez-Podolsk) eine Umgruppierung der dort seit Frühling 1940 organisierten russischen Armeen im Gang oder vielleicht schon durchgeführt ist. Die Umgruppierung lief parallel zu den sowjetischen Maßnahmen in Bessarabien, über die seinerzeit berichtet worden war, und stellte einen Armeeverband in Richtung auf die rumänische Bukowina und ungarische Karpato–Ukraine in Offensiv-, die zweite Armee hinter der Linie Chyrow–Sokol (Bug) in Defensiv-Front. Ebenso wie in Bessarabien war ein weit rückwärts reichender Einsatz von Truppen und Arbeitern im Schanz- und Straßenbaudienst festgestellt worden.

In Berlin häuften sich die alarmierenden Informationen über drohende sowjetische Teilnahme am antideutschen Kesseltreiben auf dem Balkan. In Helsinki forderte die Sowjetregierung von der finnischen Regierung in scharfer Form Auskunft über die neuesten militärischen Maßnahmen, die die finnische Regierung im Gebiet von Petsamo getroffen hatte. In Zusammenhang damit wurden neue Militärtransporte der Roten Armee nach Murmansk und Kola gebracht, die aus Petsamo gemeldet und von der deutschen Luftaufklärung in Nordnorwegen bestätigt wurden. Bei den beanstandeten finnischen Maßnahmen handelte es sich um Ausbau und Verstärkung der Luftabwehr und der Befestigungen im Petsamogebiet, ferner um Straßenbau und andere Arbeiten, welche der finnische Kriegsminister in Verbindung mit dem deutsch-finnischen militärischen Zusammenwirken anordnete.

Es ist bekannt, daß die Sowjetunion auf die finnische Nickelproduktion im Petsamogebiet Anspruch erhob. Berlin hielt an seiner Weigerung, die Finnen von der Pflicht der Nickellieferung nach Deutschland zu entbinden, fest und verlangte von Helsinki die Einleitung von Schutzmaßnahmen gegen die Drohung der Sowjets.

Zwischen dem Reich und der UdSSR verschlechterte sich das Verhältnis immer mehr. Seit Mitte April 1941 wurden die sowjetischen Lieferungen von Rohstoffen und Lebensmitteln vollkommen abgestoppt. Alle deutscherseits vorgebrachten Vorstellungen blieben ergebnislos. Die sowjetischen Öllieferungen, welche Deutschland zugeteilt waren, wurden seit Unterbrechung der Rohstofftransporte an das Reich auf dem Seewege durch Schiffe der roten Flotte an Jugoslawien gegeben.

Mit sofortiger Wirkung berief am 6. April 1941 Moskau seinen Gesandten in Helsinki ohne Bestellung eines Nachfolgers zurück. Die Sowjet-

Regierung ließ durchblicken, daß sie die finnische Regierung nicht mehr als selbständig betrachte.

Am 18. Apr. 1941 legt Hausamann nieder: ,,Im gesamten polnisch-westgalizischen und nordungarischen, nach Osten bzw. nach Nordosten verlaufenden Straßengebiet wird seit ca. 10 Tagen die technische Organisation für Aufmarsch und Materialnachschub einer Heeresgruppe von 3 Armeen mit größter Beschleunigung vervollständigt. Die Organisation erfolgt rückwärts bis Brünn, Wien und Budapest. Sie erstreckt sich im Norden bis ins Lubliner Gebiet und im Süden bis zum Borgopaß (Verbindung Bistritz–Kimpolung) . . .

Alle mit diesen Vorbereitungen verbundenen Maßnahmen des deutschen Wehrmachts-Oberkommandos einschließlich der verfügten Truppenkonzentrationen in der östlichen Walachei und in Ungarn dienen zunächst nur der militärischen Konkretisierung des politischen Druckes, den das Reich auf die Russen ausübt, um diese vor jeder Art weiterer Einmischung in die deutsche Südost- und Orientkriegführung abzuschrecken . . .''

Am 19. Apr. 1941 wird die Meldung bestätigt, daß die gesamten bisher über die Donau und über Konstanza geführten Rohstofflieferungen der Sowjets an Deutschland von der UdSSR eingestellt wurden. Hervorgehoben wird, daß diese auch nicht auf Bahntransporte übernommen wurden.

Hausamann rechnet mit militärischen Operationen gegen die Sowjetunion ab Ende Mai 1941. Er bemerkt: ,,Sofern solche überhaupt nötig sind. Ebensogut wäre denkbar, daß Rußland unter dem deutschen militärischen Druck ,freiwillig' gibt, was Deutschland fordert.'' Unter demselben Datum berichtet er, daß alle in Deutschland weilenden Handelsdelegationen, Vertretungen und Missionen der Sowjetunion, welche nicht den diplomatischen Schutz genießen, nach der UdSSR zurückgerufen werden.

Bedeutsam ist die Meldung, daß für die deutsche Reichsregierung die Notwendigkeit sehr bald, auf jeden Fall noch im Mai, gegeben sei, die Sowjetunion vor die Wahl eines neuen Freundschaftspaktes oder des Kriegszustandes zu stellen. Grund dafür seien in erster Linie wehrwirtschaftliche und ernährungspolitische Gründe. Seit 6. April 1941 habe das Reich Importausfälle aus dem Südosten und aus der Sowjetunion in solchem Ausmaß zu verzeichnen, daß der notwendige Ausgleich nur durch eine mehr oder weniger zweckmäßig ausgeübte deutsche Organisation der Sowjet-Ausfuhr und durch eine mehr oder weniger verhüllte deutsche Zwangswirtschaft bei der russischen Produktion oder der bisher noch teilweise von Rußland erfaßten Produktion anderer Länder (z. B. Rumänien, Türkei) herbeigeführt werden könne.

Die Sowjetunion erließ eine Verordnung, welche den Güter-Transitverkehr durch ihr Gebiet der Regierungskontrolle unterstellte und von Einzelbewilligungen abhängig machte. Dadurch wurde der gesamte kriegswirtschaftliche Güteraustausch zwischen Deutschland und Japan betroffen.

Am 6. Mai 1941 kündigte Berlin der Sowjetregierung die Wiederaufnahme der Donauschiffahrt im uneingeschränkten Umfang bis spätestens 15. Mai 1941 an. Berlin machte Vorschläge bezüglich der Wiederaufnahme des unterbrochenen deutsch-sowjetischen Güteraustausches im gesamten Nordwestverkehr, ferner hinsichtlich der Bereitstellung von Donautransportmitteln. Hausamann sagt dazu: ,,Die Vorschläge der Reichsregierung sind äußerst präzis, dringlich und so gehalten, daß nur eine Annahme oder Ablehnung in Frage kommt." Die Antwort der Sowjets wurde bis spätestens 12. Mai 1941 erbeten.

Am 13. Mai 1941 wird gemeldet, daß die an der Sowjet-Grenze vom Nordkap bis zum Schwarzen Meer stehenden deutschen Verbände vorerst in ihren Unterkünften bleiben, in erster Linie als Druckmittel zur Durchsetzung politischer Ziele, im übrigen bereit, jederzeit den Vormarsch anzutreten, wenn die UdSSR den deutsch-japanischen Wünschen nicht Gehör schenken sollte. Hausamann sagt dazu: ,,Der deutsche Aufmarsch in Nord und Ost hat überdies den Zweck, die Russen davon abzuhalten, militärisch aus ihrer Passivität herauszutreten. Gestützt auf hier vorliegende Nachrichten und in Beachtung der allgemeinen Lage, wie sie sich darbietet, erwarte ich noch diesen, spätestens Anfang kommenden Monats ein deutsch-japanisch-russisches Abkommen, welches Deutschland den Rücken für den Kampf im Nahen Osten und im Südwesten freimacht – sofern nicht noch vor dem Abschluß desselben Amerika in den Krieg eintritt."

Eine Meldung vom 14. Mai 1941: ,,Die für 15. Mai 1941 verfügte Einsatzbereitschaft aller Heeresverbände in der Wehrmachtgruppe Ost ist durch Sonderanordnung des Oberkommandos der Wehrmacht aufgehoben worden. Die Verbände der Heeresgruppe, die im südlichen Generalgouvernement und auf slowakischem und ungarischem Gebiet gesammelt sind, beziehen die größtenteils rückwärtigen Quartiere vom 1. April oder verbleiben, wenn noch nicht vorgerückt, in den Sammel- und Reservelagern. Die fälligen Bewegungen der motorisierten und Panzerverbände in Richtung Grenze unterbleiben. Ausgenommen von der Verfügung ist die Luftwaffe. Die neue Verfügung ist völlig unerwartet; über die Gründe, die sie veranlaßt haben, ist noch nichts zu erfahren."

Am 14. Mai 1941 meldet Hausamann weiter: ,,Die Sowjetregierung hat der Wiederaufnahme des über Konstanza und Galatz laufenden Donau-Transitverkehrs grundsätzlich zugestimmt und die Wiederaufnahme der unterbrochenen Lieferungen russischer Güter nach Regelung der Transportmittelfrage in Aussicht gestellt. Die russischen Lieferungen auf dem Donauweg dürften indessen günstigenfalls infolge der entstandenen Transport- und Transportmittelschwierigkeiten mit ⅔ des früheren Umfanges erst ab Juni wieder einsetzen können.

Noch nicht geregelt ist der Transit deutscher, für den japanischen Rüstungsbedarf bestimmter Lieferungen, die auf der Transsibirischen Bahn zu befördern sind ..."

Unter dem 16. Mai 1941 hebt Hausamann hervor, daß prominente Männer der Wehrmacht das Ablassen von Rußland sehr ungern sehen. Sie sind der Meinung, daß es richtiger gewesen wäre, jetzt zuzuschlagen, statt den Sowjets die Zeit zu weiterer militärischer Vorbereitung zu geben. Einmal komme der Kampf mit dieser Macht doch, dann jedoch unter entsprechend ungünstigeren Bedingungen.

In der zweiten Hälfte Mai setzten dann die Lieferungen von Lebensmitteln und Rohstoffen aus der UdSSR nach Deutschland wieder ein, und zwar im nicht geringem Umfange. Dagegen brachte die Sowjetunion die aus dem Fernen Osten, von Japan und Mandschukuo, erwarteten Transporte von dringend notwendigen Rohstoffen nicht in Gang. Im Stabe des General Thomas bewertete man das sowjetische Verhalten als erneuten Beweis, daß der kommunistischen Staatsführung nur insoweit zu trauen sei, als man sie kontrollieren könne. Auf ihre Vertragstreue zu bauen, wäre verfehlt. Es bedürfe des ständigen Druckes, ja der Bedrohung, wenn Deutschland nicht riskieren wolle, daß die UdSSR bei jeder passenden und unpassenden Gelegenheit – meist dann, wenn Deutschland an einer Front stark engagiert sei – aus der Reihe tanze.

Die Taktik der Sowjets störte im übrigen die von Berlin gewünschte Entwicklung im Orient. Die türkische Ablehnung des deutschen Wunsches nach politischer Unterstützung der irakischen Forderungen bezüglich des Rückzuges der britischen Truppen wäre ohne Billigung durch Moskau nicht möglich gewesen.

Am 12. Juni 1941 fanden gemäß Weisung der zuständigen deutschen militärischen Befehlsstellen großangelegte Übungen der Flieger, Fliegerabwehrverbände und der örtlichen Luftschutzorganisationen statt.

Hausamann meldet unter dem 12. Juni 1941, daß zwischen Deutschland und Rußland noch immer Verhandlungen im Gange seien mit dem Ziel, die russische Wirtschaft den derzeitigen und künftigen Bedürfnissen der Achsenkriegsführung im weitgehendsten Maß dienstbar zu machen. Da Rußland nur sehr widerstrebend nachgebe, sehe sich Deutschland gezwungen, den Druck auf Rußland laufend zu verstärken. Die deutschen Verhandlungsbeauftragten seien ermächtigt, der russischen Delegation mit militärischen Maßnahmen zu drohen, wenn Rußland die deutschen Forderungen nicht vorbehaltlos akzeptiere. Die Instruktion der Russen hinwiederum laute dahin, nur Schritt um Schritt zurückzuweichen, jede Position zäh zu diskutieren, die Verhandlungen nach bester Möglichkeit hinauszuschleppen, es aber gegebenenfalls nicht zum Bruch kommen zu lassen.

In Böhmen und Mähren ereigneten sich Ausschreitungen, Sabotageakte und passiver Widerstand. Frhr. von Oelhafen wurde als Bevollmächtigter der Reichsregierung mit sofortiger Wirkung nach Prag entsandt . . .

Am 14. Juni 1941 befahl das Oberkommando der Wehrmacht die Wiedereinnahme der vorgeschobenen Quartiere und Lager nahe der Grenze. Dieser Maßnahme kommt, wie Hausamann sagt, demonstrative Bedeutung zu. Ihr Zweck sei die Ausübung politischen Druckes auf Moskau, um eine sowjetische Stellungnahme gegenüber England und Amerika, eine sowjetische Begünstigung der deutschen Bestrebungen zur Eingliederung der Türkei in das deutsche Kräftespiel und die angestrebten wirtschaftlichen Zugeständnisse der Sowjets zu erreichen.

Eine Meldung vom 19. Juni 1941 besagt: ,,Die laufenden Verhandlungen zwischen Berlin und Moskau über technische und wirtschaftliche Fragen, von welchen die Agentur TASS berichtet und die sich aus dem Vollzug bestehender Abkommen und Vereinbarungen ergeben, gehen weiter . . .

Die große Forderung, die das Reich unabhängig von den laufenden Verhandlungen zu gegebener Zeit der Sowjetunion gegenüber erhebt, kann nicht bloß auf politisch-diplomatische Weise geltend gemacht werden. Sie wird zur Zeit durch die militärische Machtdemonstration im gesamten Ostraum unter Vorspannung der Hilfsvölker des Reiches der Regierung in Moskau zur Kenntnis gebracht . . .

Der konkrete Inhalt des ,großen' deutschen Begehrens ist der Sowjetregierung selbstverständlich bekannt. Diese weiß, daß von ihr – noch bevor die amerikanische Kriegsentscheidung gefallen ist – die politisch-militärische Selbstabdeckung auf Kriegsdauer, und zwar entweder in der Form der Einordnung in die Drei-Mächte-Ordnung oder in der Form der Mitwirkung an der Selbsteinkreisung und an der Abschließung vom britisch-amerikanischen Machtbereich verlangt wird.''

Hausamann schreibt noch am 20. Juni 1941: ,,Die Sowjetregierung hat Vorschläge der Reichsregierung über einen Vertragsabschluß überreicht bekommen, der die politisch-wirtschaftlichen Beziehungen zwischen den europäischen Drei-Mächte-Pakt-Staaten einerseits und der Sowjetunion andererseits zum Gegenstand hat. Die Vorschläge sind am 16. Juni der Sowjetregierung überreicht worden. Es besteht kein Zweifel, daß die Reichsregierung jetzt entschlossen ist, noch in diesem Monat eine endgültige russische Entscheidung, die militärische Überraschungen des Reiches an dessen Ostfront für Kriegsdauer ausschließt, zu erzwingen (siehe unsere diversen Berichte, welche besagen, daß Deutschland von Rußland eine massive Demobilmachung usw. verlangen wird).''

Entscheidende Tage

In „Bodyguards of Lies" führt Anthony Cave Brown aus: „Canaris hatte sich wie auch andere höhere Offiziere der Wehrmacht gegen das Unternehmen Barbarossa, den Feldzug gegen Rußland, geäußert. General Ulrich Liss sagt, Hitler habe diesen Feldzug mit strategischem Geschick vorbereitet, beharrlich und unverzichtlich." Brown übersieht einige Ereignisse, die seit dem Besuch Molotows in Berlin im November 1940 bis zum 18. Juni 41 die politische Landschaft verändert hatten.

Der Balkan war durch Aktionen Stalins und Mussolinis in Bewegung geraten. Durch den von General Sir Steward Menzies, dem Chef des britischen geheimen Nachrichtendienstes (MIG), auf Befehl Churchills initiierten Putsch in Belgrad am 27. März 1941, bei dem die Generäle Boro Mirković und Dušan Simović eine führende Rolle spielten, scheiterte der Beitritt Jugoslawiens zu dem am 27. Sept. 40 geschlossenen Dreimächtepakt zwischen Deutschland, Italien und Japan.

Das Ziel Moskaus waren in Rumänien die Erdölfelder von Ploesti. Im äußersten Norden richtete Stalin seine Politik auf die Nickelfelder im Raum von Petsamo aus. Die Bemühungen der deutschen Diplomatie in Ankara blieben ohne Erfolg.

Umsonst schienen die Opfer bei der Eroberung Kretas gebracht worden zu sein. Die Insel wurde nie eine Basis für deutsche Operationen einer geplanten Zangenbewegung im östlichen Mittelmeer.

Das Planspiel „Otto" steht nicht in Verbindung mit der Planung „Barbarossa", sondern sollte der Abwehr eines drohenden Vormarsches der Roten Armee in den Südostraum dienen.

In wirtschaftlicher Hinsicht hatte die Sowjetunion begonnen, Lieferungen zu verschleppen oder einzuschränken.

Hausamann meldet am 21. Juni 41, die deutsche Reichsregierung habe Moskau vorgehalten, daß durch die Sowjet-Annexionen in Finnland und in Rumänien sowie durch die Sammlung gewaltiger Truppenmassen der Roten Armee an den Grenzen der Staaten ostwärts von Deutschland die Wirtschaft dieser Länder schwer zerrüttet, die Volksernährung in Frage gestellt und eine große Masse von Einwohnern der betreffenden Länder im Militärdienst beansprucht werde, also der produktiven Arbeit entzogen sei. Dieser Zustand sei nicht haltbar. Eine umfassende Neuregelung in dem Sinne, daß die Sowjetunion die europäischen Dreimächtepaktstaaten als wirtschaftliche, insbesondere als wehrwirtschaftliche Einheit anerkenne und den wirtschaftlichen Bedürfnissen dieses Blockes Rechnung trage, müsse als notwendig erachtet werden.

Inoffiziell wurde der Moskauer Regierung mitgeteilt, daß Berlin das deutsch-kontinentale Versorgungsproblem entweder im Osten oder im Südosten und im britischen Orient lösen müsse. Deutschland würde eine mit Moskau einvernehmliche Lösung vorziehen.

Weiter wird gemeldet, daß Moskau umfassende Vorbereitungen zu Zerstörungen in der Wirtschafts- und Verkehrsorganisation des eigenen Landes befohlen habe, vor allem in Bessarabien und im Baltikum. Die Quelle hebt hervor, zahlreiche Aussagen von gefangenen Sowjet-Offizieren stellten klar, daß in der UdSSR rasch nach dem Flug von Rudolf Heß mit der Erstellung der Kampfbereitschaft begonnen worden sei.

Rösler, der genaue Informationen aus Berlin erhielt, vertrat die Auffassung, daß die Entscheidung zum Einmarsch in den sowjetischen Raum erst kurz vor dem 22. Juni 41 gefällt wurde. Die Tatsache, daß die Sowjetunion als Antwort auf das deutsche Begehren die Reserve I einberief, hat zur Folge, daß Moskau den deutschen Wünschen nicht nachkommen werde. Die Meldung aus Moskau habe in Berlin bestürzend gewirkt.

Der Einmarschentschluß wurde, wie die Schweizer Quelle meldet, sehr ungern gefaßt. Aber es sei notwendig gewesen, der Organisierung der Reserve I zuvorzukommen. Zu dieser Reserve gehörten alle voll ausgebildeten Mannschaften der Jahrgänge bis 1905: „Die Elite der Roten Armee." Wortwörtlich heißt es in dem Schweizer Bericht: „Dieser in der Mobilmachung zuvorzukommen, kann für den Kampfverlauf von großer Bedeutung sein."

In einer Vorbemerkung zu einem Bericht vom 1. Okt. 41, der einen Putschplan gegen die Regierung Pétain (späterer Zeitpunkt desselben: 15. Nov. 1941), die Annullierung des Waffenstillstandsvertrages mit Deutschland und Italien und die Ausrufung einer neuen französischen Regierung zum Gegenstand hat, wird darauf hingewiesen, daß er aus erstklassiger Quelle stammt.

Auch zu einem Kreis bei der deutschen Luftwaffe (Harro Schulze-Boysen von der Roten Kapelle) bestand Verbindung. Unter dem 4. Aug. 41 wird darauf verwiesen, daß es sich bei den berichteten Ausführungen um Erklärungen eines höheren deutschen Offiziers, eines engen Mitarbeiters der Generäle Moor und Udet handelt.

In einem anderen Bericht wird als Quelle eine Persönlichkeit genannt, die in heiklen ausländischen Problemen zu tun gehabt habe. Unter diesen Umständen verdienen die „Hausamann-Berichte" zur Frage der Auslösung des deutsch-sowjetischen Krieges Beachtung. Aus den Berichten dürfen nachstehende Einzelheiten entnommen werden: 23. Juni 41: „Der Entschluß, gegen die Sowjet-Union den Krieg zu eröffnen, ist erst am 20. Juni, d. h. erst in der Nacht vom 20. auf den 21. Juni gefaßt worden. Die Wen-

101

dung ist ausschließlich auf die russische Generalmobilmachung zurückzuführen. Diese war nicht erwartet worden.

Die Wehrmachtbereitschaft ist weder im nördlichen Teil des Generalgouvernements noch in Ostpreußen und in Finnland perfekt. Sie muß, namentlich in der Luft, erst noch vervollständigt werden.

Die Eröffnung der Kriegshandlungen bezweckt zunächst die Störung und
Erschwerung der russischen Mobilmachung. Das Interesse an der Störung
und Lähmung des russischen Aufmarsches ist schließlich vom Oberkommando der Wehrmacht als vordringlich jeder anderen Erwägung überge-
ordnet worden.

Der Entschluß zum Losschlagen ist unter ungemein komplizierten Umständen gegen die Meinung des Reichsaußenministers und der maßgebenden Instanzen der Wirtschaftsführung zustande gekommen . . .

Nach Finnland sind größere deutsche Truppentransporte erst am 19. Juni
abgegangen. Die Transporte zwischen 14. und 19. Juni waren äußerst begrenzt. Überführt wurden in dieser Zeit etwa 10 000 Mann, davon mindestens die Hälfte Flak.

Noch nicht einsatzbereit sind die deutschen Heeresverbände in Rumänien. Mehrere Divisionen sind von Griechenland her über Bulgarien noch
unterwegs . . .“

„. . . Im Wehrmachtsgeneralstab wurde im Gegensatz zu Ribbentrop die
von der Sowjet-Regierung in den letzten Tagen verfügte Generalmobilmachung als eine russische Antwort bewertet, die jeglicher Aussicht auf Erfolg
der eingeschlagenen Druck- und Drohpolitik den Boden entzogen hat. Die
Rechnung mit russischer Kapitulationsbereitschaft, die im Maß der militärischen Kraftdemonstration an den russischen Westgrenzen zunehme, wurde
als Fehlrechnung bezeichnet, nachdem die Sowjet-Regierung die Mobilmachung in Gang gesetzt und die systematische Zerstörung in exponierten
Gebieten des russischen Westens bereits begonnen hatte.

Die russischen Mobilmachungsmaßnahmen waren tatsächlich wider Erwarten so umfangreich und entschlossen, daß eine militärische Kräftever-
schiebung zugunsten der Russen zu fürchten gewesen wäre, wenn man etwa
noch eine oder zwei Wochen lang auf der Rippentropschen Methode be-
harrt und eine Lösung ohne Gewaltanwendung versucht hätte.

Obwohl auch der Wehrmachtgeneralstab die Waffenentscheidung im
deutsch-russischen Verhältnis davon abhängig gemacht wissen wollte, daß
sie dem Reich aufgezwungen werde, war seit 19. Juni der Standpunkt der
Wehrmachtführer dem des Reichsaußenministers entgegengesetzt.

Die Informationen, die Ribbentrop gegeben hat, wurden u. a. von Göring
aufs schärfste kritisiert. Der Reichsaußenminister wird von dieser Seite
dafür verantwortlich gemacht, daß mit dem russischen Entschluß zur Gene-

ralmobilmachung nicht gerechnet worden sei und daß Maßnahmen zur Organisation eines ausreichenden, schlagartigen Einsatzes der Luftwaffe gegen die russischen Aufmarschplätze und -strecken erst jetzt getroffen werden müssen.

Der Reichsaußenminister hält daran fest, daß auch nach Durchführung der weitgehenden russischen Mobilmachung die Politik planmäßiger Druckausübung jeder anderen Lösung vorzuziehen gewesen wäre. Er stützt sich auf die Ansicht der Mehrzahl der Wehrwirtschaftsführer, ferner aber mit Nachdruck auch darauf, daß die russische Wehrmacht zur Offensive in jedem Falle unfähig, also auch im voll mobilisierten Zustand kein Hindernis für eine spätere ultimative Behandlung der Moskauer Regierung hätte sein können. Im Gegenteil hätte man erwarten können, daß die Mobilmachung dem Regime nur organisatorische Schwierigkeiten bereiten und sich als stumpfe Waffe erweisen werde, wenn gleichzeitig auch die deutsche Ostwallbereitschaft progressiv verstärkt worden wäre . . ."

Die durch die russische Generalmobilmachung geschaffene Lage hat das deutsche Wehrmacht-Oberkommando noch am 19. Juni 1941 zu einer Reihe neuer Maßnahmen veranlaßt. Die wichtigste dieser Maßnahmen, auf die man bis 19. Juni 41 in Erwartung maßvoller militärischer Reaktion der Sowjet-Regierung glaubte verzichten zu können, ist die volle Besetzung der ostpreußischen und Ostsee-Basen durch die Reichsluftwaffe. Diese erfolgt auf Kosten der Luftbereitschaft über der Nordsee und des Luftwaffeneinsatzes gegen englisches Gebiet von holländischen und belgischen Plätzen aus. Die Seefliegergruppe III mit Kommandositz Dagebüll in Nordfriesland bezieht jetzt die Einsatzbasen der Flottenstationen Danzig und Pillau . . .

Außer der Seefliegergruppe III wird mindestens noch ein starker Verband der Reichsluftwaffe aus dem Bereich der Wehrmachtgruppe West nach Ostpreußen abberufen. Möglicherweise erfolgen noch weitere Abberufungen, wenn der britische Einsatz über der Nordsee und über dem Kanal nicht noch bemerkenswert zunimmt . . ."

24. Juni 41: „Am 20. Juni eröffnete die Wehrmachtführung dem deutschen Oberkommando, daß nach den eingegangenen Nachrichten eine weitere Duldung der russischen Aufmarschvorbereitungen verhängnisvolle Folgen haben könne. Befürworter sofortigen Handelns waren die meisten Wehrmachtführer. Es wurde von ihnen geltend gemacht, daß sich die russische Mobilmachung mit der Tendenz vollziehe, große Heeresmassen im Norden nördlich der Düna und im Süden zwischen Dnjestr und Dnjepr zu sammeln, um durch Druckkonzentration auf die deutschen Heeresflügel die relative Schwäche der nichtzentralen rückwärtigen Verbindungen des deutschen Heeres auszunützen. Die Vereitelung dieser Absicht wurde als äußerst dringlich betont, zumal nach eingegangenen Nachrichten mit großen

Zerstörungen im ostgalizischen, bessarabischen und litauischen Verkehrsnetz durch die russischen Truppen zu rechnen sei.

Der gesamte Eisenbahnverkehr Rußland–Generalgouvernement und Rußland–Ostpreußen war am 20. Juni 1941 abends eingestellt worden.

Alle deutschen Ostseetransporte nach Finnland stehen seit 20. Juni abends unter Geleitschutz der Kriegsmarine und der Luftwaffe der Flottenstationen.

Am 20. Juni 41 begann die russische Ostseeflotte den finnischen Meerbusen zwischen Hangö und Dagö, ferner die Rigaer Bucht zwischen Svalferort (Oesel) und Lyserort (kurländische Küste) durch Minen zu sperren."

25. Juni 41: ,,Zu den wenigen Wehrmachtführern, die den Entschluß zum Einmarsch in Rußland aufzuhalten versucht haben, hat Generalfeldmarschall von Reichenau gehört. Die Einwände, die Reichenau im einzelnen gemacht hat, sind nicht bekannt. Bekannt ist aber, daß sich Reichenau bereits im Frühling 1939 bei Festlegung der Aufmarschpläne für den Krieg mit Polen gegen jedes Verfahren ausgesprochen hat, das die Möglichkeit einer gleichzeitigen militärischen Beanspruchung Deutschlands durch Frankreich und Rußland nicht von vornherein ausschließt. Es ist auch bekannt, daß Reichenau zu den hohen Offizieren gehört hat, welche die Weltkriegserfahrungen 1914/18 in dem Sinn verstanden wissen wollten, daß die kriegswirtschaftliche Versorgung des Reiches in einem mehrjährigen Krieg nur zu Wasser, aber nicht zu Land, besonders nicht durch Landgewinn im Osten erkämpft werden kann.

Unabhängig von Reichenaus Stellungnahme verlautet, daß vom Reichsaußenminister und von ihm nahestehenden Personen vor der Gefahr einer russisch-britisch-amerikanischen Kräftezusammenballung mit dem Ziel einer Ausschaltung Japans und eines unübersehbaren Landkrieges in russischen Reichsgebieten gewarnt worden ist, die zu besetzen oder zu sichern Deutschland weder willens noch fähig sei. Von diesen Seiten wird gefragt, wie einem etwaigen Zusammenschluß von China, Indien und Russisch-Asien, wenn er nicht durch japanische Intervention verhindert wird, durch Einsatz des deutschen Heeres und der deutschen Luftwaffe militärisch begegnet werden soll, und zwar vor allem dann, wenn England mit amerikanischer Flotten- und Luftwaffenhilfe im Westen oder im Mittelmeer (z. B. durch eine Aktion in Französisch-Nordafrika) größere Teile der Deutschen Wehrmacht zum Kampf an der ,,Westfront" zwingen sollte.

Daß es nach Eintritt Amerikas in den Krieg in der Macht einer entschlossenen britisch-amerikanischen Kriegführung gestanden hätte, eine Zweiteilung des deutschen Wehrmachteinsatzes in einem quantitativ empfindlichen Ausmaß zu erzwingen, ist im deutschen Wehrmachtgeneralstab nicht bestritten worden. Daß ein solcher britisch-amerikanischer Entschluß jetzt noch, und zwar noch vor Niederbekämpfung des russischen Widerstandes, gefaßt und wirksam zur Ausführung gebracht werden kann, ist indessen als unwahrscheinlich und – was den tatsächlichen militärischen Einsatz und Erfolg betrifft – als ausgeschlossen erachtet worden. Die Rüstungsversäumnisse der amerikanischen Regierung, die z. B. bis zum Augenblick noch nicht einmal die Bewaffnung der Handelsschiffe in Angriff genommen hat, lassen dem Wehrmacht-Oberkommando den raschen Kriegsentschluß der amerikanischen Regierung als möglich, eine etwaige tatsächliche amerikanische Kriegführung aber noch mindestens auf die Dauer des Sommers für das Reich als ungefährlich erscheinen. Dies um so mehr, als die allgemein im öffentlichen Bewußtsein verankerte britisch-amerikanische Kriegsrechnung immer noch auf Zeitgewinn und die damit verbundene Vorstellung einer militärischen Kräfteverlagerung zugunsten von Großbritannien hinausläuft.

Ernster genommen wurde bis zuletzt, also bis zur Eröffnung des Krieges gegen die UdSSR, die Gefahr einer sowjetischen Kriegführung, die durch die Sammlung großer Heeresmassen im östlichen und südöstlichen Teil von Europäisch-Rußland eine zweite, zeitraubende und ungemein schwierige Aufmarschorganisation der deutschen Wehrmacht nötig machen mußte, selbst wenn der jetzt eröffnete Angriff auf der Hauptfront vollen Erfolg gebracht und die Besetzung von Westrußland ermöglicht hat. Für die Annahme einer solchen sowjetischen Kampfstrategie sind jedoch, obwohl diese naheliegt, konkrete Anhaltspunkte bisher nicht gegeben. Es scheint vielmehr, daß die kriegsstarken Heeresverbände der Roten Armee, insbesondere die motorisierten und die Panzer-Verbände, fast ausnahmslos den Frontarmeen und einigen Reserve-Armeen, z. B. denen im Kiewer und im Moskauer Raum, zugeteilt worden sind. Trifft diese Annahme zu, die sich auf den Nachrichtendienst des Wehrmacht-Oberkommandos stützt, so kann die Entscheidung im Kampf gegen die Widerstandsorganisation der Sowjets voraussichtlich noch im Juli mit endgültigem Ergebnis erzwungen werden. Die volle Heeres- und Luftstärke soll und wird nach Eintreffen der noch über Bulgarien unterwegs befindlichen Divisionen der Heeresgruppe v. List bis 29. oder 30. Juni erreicht sein.

Der Befehl zum Einmarsch in die Sowjetunion wurde äußerst kurzfristig gegeben; dies zeigt die Tatsache, daß in der Garnisonsstadt Königsberg bei der Truppe normaler Betrieb herrschte. Keine Alarmzeichen waren erkennbar. Erst in der Nacht zum Sonntag wurde der Telefon- und Telegrammverkehr gesperrt und ein Fahrverbot erlassen.

Mit zwei Auszügen aus Berichten vom 27. Juni 41 sei das Kapitel „Entscheidende Tage" abgeschlossen:

. . . „Informationen aus Berlin besagen, daß im Führerkreis wie unter den obersten militärischen Führern bis in die Stunden der Entschlußfassung große Meinungsverschiedenheit herrschte, ob der Angriff auf Rußland im gegenwärtigen Zeitpunkt wünschbar sei oder nicht. Für sofortiges Losschlagen setzten sich ein u. a. Brauchitsch, List, Rundstedt, Fromm, Göring. Gegen den Feldzug im jetzigen Zeitpunkt waren u. a. Reichenau, fast die gesamten Führer des Wehrwirtschaftsstabes im Oberkommando der Wehrmacht, dann aber auch Goebbels und vor allem Himmler. Insbesondere Himmler warnte eindringlich und mit der Begründung, daß dieser Feldzug, jetzt ausgelöst, höchst unpopulär sei und selbst in breiten Kreisen der Partei nicht verstanden werde. Denn (so argumentiert Himmler) gerade in Parteikreisen habe die Parole „Kampf den Plutokratien" besonders verfangen. Daß jetzt auch das kommunistische Rußland wieder „Erzfeind" sein soll, mache die breite Masse des Volkes irre. Was man im Volke dem Reichskanzler immer als Großtat diplomatischer Geschicklichkeit anrechnete, sei gewesen, daß er es verstanden habe, sich mit dem deutsch-russischen Pakt im Osten den Rücken für den Kampf im Westen frei zu machen. Kein Pakt sei so populär gewesen wie jener mit Rußland. Die breite Masse werde sich zweifellos der Zeit von 1914–18 entsinnen, wenn jetzt der Kampf auch im Osten entbrenne, und sie werde entsprechend reagieren. Denn die Wendung sei zu plötzlich erfolgt. Himmler sieht, so besagen die Informationen, schwarz.

Er äußert, daß es schwer sein werde, die Disziplin aufrechtzuerhalten, wenn im Osten Rückschläge erfolgen sollten . . ."

Begegnung mit Adolf Hitler

Generalfeldmarschall von Bock berichtet:

Am 27. Sept. 1940 mußte sich Feldmarschall von Bock wegen einer Magenkrankheit „ins Bett legen", wie er sich in seinem Tagebuch ausdrückt. Von dort aus leitete er seine Heeresgruppe zunächst selbst. Da sich seine Krankheit verschlimmerte, wurde er dann durch Generalfeldmarschall List vertreten.

Am 11. Nov. 1940 besucht ihn Hitler. Der Feldmarschall berichtet in seinem Tagebuch: „. . . ist sehr freundlich und besorgt. Er ist außer sich über die italienische Eskapade nach Griechenland, die Italien uns nicht nur verheimlicht, die es auf Befragen abgestritten habe. Des Führers Versuch, durch seine Reise nach Florenz das Unheil zu verhindern oder die Dinge wenigstens so lange hinauszuschieben, bis wir helfend eingreifen konnten, sei vergeblich gewesen: Mussolini habe erklärt, die im Gange befindliche Aktion nicht mehr aufhalten zu können. Die nächste, recht unangenehme Folge sei die Bedrohung der rumänischen Ölfelder durch die englische Luftwaffe von Saloniki her. Diese Gefahr sei so groß, daß sie uns zu Gegenmaßnahmen zwingen könnte . . . Was im Osten werden soll, ist eine noch offene Frage; die Verhältnisse können uns dort zum Eingreifen zwingen, um einer gefährlicheren Entwicklung zuvorzukommen." Das Gespräch, das eine halbe Stunde dauerte, fand am Krankenbett des Feldmarschalls statt.

Am 1. Dez. 1940 besuchte Hitler ihn anläßlich seines 60. Geburtstages. Von Bock schrieb nieder, der deutsche Staatschef habe „die Licht- und Schattenseiten der großen Lage ruhig und klar" gesehen. Einem Eingreifen auf dem Balkan stehe „mancherlei hemmend" entgegen.

Bei diesem Besuch kam Hitler auch auf Rußland zu sprechen. Er erklärte nach Bock: „Die Ostfrage wird akut. Zwischen Rußland und Amerika sollen Fäden laufen; damit ist auch eine Verbindung Rußland – England wahrscheinlich. Das Ende einer derartigen Entwicklung abzuwarten, sei gefährlich. Werden aber die Russen ausgeschaltet, so hat England keine Hoffnung mehr, uns auf dem Kontinent niederzuringen, zumal ein wirksames Eingreifen Amerikas dann durch Japan, das nun den Rücken frei hat, erschwert wird."

Am 31. Jan. 1941 tritt Generalfeldmarschall von Bock nach vier Monaten Krankheit wieder den Dienst an und nimmt an einer Besprechung des Oberbefehlshaber des Heeres mit den Oberbefehlshabern der Heeresgruppen teil. In ihr bestätigt von Brauchitsch, daß Italien die deutsche Führung mit dem Angriff auf Griechenland überrascht habe und daß der Befehl zur „Vorbereitung des Kampfes mit Rußland" gegeben wurde.

Am 1. Febr. 1941 meldet sich von Bock bei Hitler ab. In der entsprechenden Tagebucheintragung heißt es: „Wieder spricht er (= Hitler) sich über die Gesamtlage aus. Die Auswirkungen der italienischen Mißerfolge seien noch zuwenig zu übersehen, daß es im Augenblick schwer sei, auf dieser schwankenden Basis zu großen Entschlüssen zu kommen... Die Notwendigkeit der Vorbereitung des Kampfes gegen Rußland begründet der Führer damit, daß dies große Ereignis die Welt sehr schnell von den afrikanischen Gegebenheiten ablenken und vor eine neue Lage stellen werde. ‚Die Herren in England sind ja nicht dumm, sie tun nur so!‘, und sie werden einsehen, daß die Fortsetzung des Krieges für sie zwecklos wird, wenn nun auch Rußland geschlagen und ausgeschaltet ist." Hitler war bei der gegebenen Situation zum Kampf entschlossen.

In einer weiteren Eintragung heißt es: „... Militärputsch in Jugoslawien! Die Regierung und der Regent, (zu dessen Begleitung ich seinerzeit in Berlin kommandiert war) sind beseitigt; in Belgrad finden deutschfeindliche Demonstrationen statt. Die Engländer haben anscheinend viel gezahlt." – Generalfeldmarschall von Bock spricht die Hoffnung aus, daß die „große Operation durch die notwendige Bereinigung des Balkans" sich nicht verzögert.

Eintragung 30. Mrz. 1941: „Der Führer spricht in der Reichskanzlei vor den für die Ostfront vorgesehenen Heeresgruppen und Armeeführern... Von Jugoslawien und vom bevorstehenden Angriff auf Griechenland spricht der Führer nicht, wohl aber von der ‚Quelle allen Übels‘, dem verfehlten italienischen Angriff in Albanien. Auch die anderen Schlappen Italiens, die nicht zum geringen Teil eine Folge des albanischen Unternehmens sind, werden gewürdigt... – Eingehend entwickelt der Führer die Notwendigkeit, Rußland niederzuwerfen. Ständige Bedrohung in unserem Rücken, ständige kommunistische Gefahr, Möglichkeit für England und Frankreich, in Rußland eine neue Front gegen uns aufzubauen." – Hitler ging von dem Gesichtspunkt aus, Rußland „mit eigenem freiem Raum" zu schlagen. Ausdrücklich erklärt er, er wäre ein Verbrecher an der Zukunft des deutschen Volkes, wenn er nicht zufassen würde. 1939 wäre Stalin bereitwillig auf den im August geschlossenen Vertrag eingegangen in der Hoffnung, Deutschland in den Krieg zu locken.

Im Tagebuch wird unter dem 14. Juni die Rußlandoperation mit den Heeresgruppen und Armeeführern erwähnt. Unter diesem Datum führt Generalfeldmarschall von Bock aus:

„Nach Tisch spricht der Führer über die Lage: Je mehr er im Laufe der Monate über den Entschluß zum Angriff auf Rußland nachgedacht habe, um so fester sei er geworden. Rußland sei eine schwere Rückenbedrohung für Deutschland, und wir müssen jetzt den Rücken freihaben; sei es erst einmal zu Boden geworfen, so habe England auf dem Kontinent keinen Bundesgenossen mehr zu gewinnen, und nur auf dem Kontinent sei Deutschland zu schlagen. Gelingt es nach dem Siege über Rußland wenigstens, die dort stehenbleibenden Teile der Wehrmacht – im ganzen rund 65–75 Divisionen – aus dem Lande zu versorgen, so seien Ernährung und Rohstoffversorgung Deutschlands auf absehbare Zeit gesichert. Eine große Zahl von Divisionen könne ferner nach Abschluß der Operationen im Osten aufgelöst und der Wirtschaft wieder zugeführt werden, die dann ihre Rüstungsarbeiten vermindern und sich wieder vermehrt anderen Aufgaben zuwenden könne. Dies alles wird England sehen, und es ist anzunehmen, daß es dann den hoffnungslosen weiteren Kampf aufgibt. Der Führer hofft, daß dies schon in den ersten Monaten nach Beendigung der Ostoperation zutage treten wird – er hat Rußland vor einiger Zeit die Frage vorgelegt, ob es bereit sei, mit Deutschland zusammenzugehen. Rußland hat mit ausweichenden Gegenfragen geantwortet, die deutlich zeigten, daß es nur darauf ausgeht, seine Macht zu stärken. Die Erfahrung habe zudem gelehrt, daß Rußland frech wird, sobald es Deutschland anderwärts gebunden weiß, wie z. B. im Herbst 1939, als es Litauen entgegen jeder Verabredung für sich in Anspruch nahm. Ob und welche Gebiete Deutschland nach errungenem Siege übernehmen solle, werde überlegt; klar sei, daß der russische Einfluß aus der Ostsee verdrängt werden und daß Deutschland sich bestimmten Einfluß im Schwarzen Meer sichern würde, denn dort lägen jetzt lebenswichtige Interessen für uns wie z. B. das Öl . . .‟

Mit einer Eintragung am 20. Juni 1941 darf ich schließen. Diese beweist, daß die Sowjetführung nicht überrascht war, als es zum Krieg mit Deutschland kam. Ich will die dies beleuchtenden Sätze aus dem Tagebuch niederlegen. Von Bock schreibt:

,,Ein Herr von H., der eben aus Moskau zurückkommt, besucht mich und schildert die Verhältnisse jenseits der Grenze. Danach haben die führenden Leute in Rußland keinen Zweifel, daß der Krieg kommt . . .‟ Endlich: Hitler sah die Untergrund- und Partisanengefahr.

Am 4. Juni schreibt von Bock: ,,Eine Verfügung des Oberkommandos der Wehrmacht regelt das Verhalten der Truppe gegenüber der russischen Zivilbevölkerung. Sie ist so gehalten, daß sie praktisch jedem Soldaten das Recht gibt, auf jeden Russen, den er für einen Freischärler hält – oder zu halten vorgibt – von vorne oder von hinten zu schießen. Jeden Zwang zur Ahndung in dieser Richtung liegender Vergehen lehnt die Verfügung ab, auch dann, ,wenn ein militärisches Verbrechen oder Vergehen vorliegt.‘

Brauchitsch hat eine Ergänzung zu dieser Verfügung gegeben, die sie wohl abschwächen soll, was aber nur unvollkommen gelingt. Gleichzeitig kommt ein Telegramm mit der Weisung, die Ausgabe der bereits in der

Hand der Armee befindlichen Verfügung anzuhalten, bis andere Bestimmungen eingehen. Greiffenberg, der gerade beim O.K.H. ist, gebe ich den Auftrag, bei Halder festzustellen, ob die angekündigten Bestimmungen wesentliche Änderungen der Verfügung bringen. Ist dies nicht der Fall, so soll Greiffenberg dem Oberbefehlshaber des Heeres melden, daß nach meiner Auffassung die Verfügung in dieser Form untragbar und mit der Manneszucht nicht vereinbar sei . . ."

Wenn wir die Berichte Hausamanns mit den Unterlagen aus dem Archiv des Auswärtigen Amtes, die Dr. Carrol und Theodor Eppstein unter dem Titel ,,Das Nationalsozialistische Deutschland und die Sowjetunion 1939–1941" herausbrachten, vergleichen, so können wir heranziehen:

a) Telegramm des Deutschen Botschafters an den Reichsaußenminister (Moskau 4. April 1941, Ankunft 0.55; Citissime! Geheim) über Stellungnahme Molotows zum Abschluß eines Freundschafts- und Nichtangriffsvertrages mit der neuen Jugoslawischen Regierung: ,,Molotow bezeichnet ihn als positiven Beitrag zu dem auch von Deutschland gewünschten Frieden."

b) Aufzeichnung über den augenblicklichen Stand sowjetischer Rohstofflieferungen nach Deutschland von Dr. Schnurre vom 5. April 1941 (Ha Pol 1975/41 g):
,,Zusammenfassend kann gesagt werden, daß nach anfänglichen Stockungen die augenblicklichen Lieferungen der Russen recht beträchtlich sind und der abgeschlossene Wirtschaftsvertrag vom 10. Januar d. J. von russischer Seite erfüllt wird."

c) Telegramm: Der Reichsaußenminister an den Deutschen Botschafter in Moskau (Ab Berlin, am 6. 4. um 4.30 Uhr, an Moskau am 6. 4. um 9.35 Uhr – Diplogerma Moskau Citissime):
,,Ich bitte Sie, Herrn Molotow in den frühen Morgenstunden des Sonntags, 6. April, aufzusuchen und ihm mitzuteilen, daß die Reichsregierung sich genötigt gesehen habe, zu einer Aktion in Griechenland und Jugoslawien zu schreiten . . . Reichsregierung habe seit einigen Tagen präzise Nachrichten, daß der jugoslawische Generalstab mit dem Oberkommando der in Griechenland gelandeten englischen Expeditionsarmee gemeinsame Operation gegen Deutschland und Italien vorbereitet habe, die dicht vor ihrer Durchführung stehe . . ."

d) Telegramm des deutschen Geschäftsträgers in Moskau an das Auswärtige Amt vom 22. April 1941, 0.005 – Ankunft: 22. April 1941, 3.30:
,,Beschwerde über fortlaufende Verletzung der Grenze der UdSSR durch deutsche Flugzeuge."

e) Mitteilung des Oberkommando der Wehrmacht WFSt/Abt. L (1 Op) Nr.

00731 a/41 g Kdos vom 23. April 1941 über sowjetrussische Grenzverletzungen durch sowjetische Flugzeuge.

f) Telegramm des Militärattaché bei der Deutschen Botschaft in Moskau an das Oberkommando der Kriegsmarine vom 24. 4. 1941:
,,Nach Angabe des italienischen Botschaftsrates, L. Mascia, sagt englischer Botschafter, Sir Stafford Crips, 22. Juni als Tag des Kriegsbeginns voraus."

g) Telegramm des Deutschen Botschafters in Moskau an das Auswärtige Amt (offen) vom 13. 6. 41:
,,Tass erklärt, daß Deutschland an die Sowjetunion keinerlei Forderungen territorialen und wirtschaftlichen Charakters gestellt hat und die gegenwärtigen stattfindenden Einberufungen der Reservisten der Roten Armee und die bevorstehenden Manöver nichts anderes bezwecken als die Schulung der Reservisten und die Kontrolle der Arbeit des Eisenbahnapparates."

h) Telegramm des Reichsaußenministers an den Deutschen Gesandten in Budapest aus Venedig vom 15. Juni 1941, Ankunft 15. Juni 1941, 22.15 Uhr:
,,Ich bitte Sie, dem ungarischen Ministerpräsidenten folgendes mitzuteilen: Im Hinblick auf die starke Anhäufung russischer Truppen an der deutschen Ostgrenze werde der Führer voraussichtlich bis spätestens Anfang Juli gezwungen sein, das deutsch-russische Verhältnis eindeutig zu klären und hierbei gewisse Forderungen stellen."

i) Brief Hitlers an Mussolini vom 21. Juni 1941:
,,Ich habe mich . . . entschlossen dem heuchlerischen Theater des Kreml ein Ende zu bereiten . . . Wenn ich Ihnen, Duce, erst in diesem Augenblick diese Mitteilung zugehen lasse, dann geschieht dies, weil die endgültige Entscheidung selbst erst heute um 7.00 Uhr abends fällt . . ."

k) Die letzte Unterredung zwischen dem Reichsaußenminister und dem sowjetrussischen Botschafter in Berlin, Dekanosow, fand am 22. 6. 41 um 4.00 Uhr morgens im Auswärtigen Amt statt.

Stalin und der deutsche Einmarsch in die Sowjetunion

Stalin dürfte über den Ausbruch des Krieges zwischen dem Deutschen Reich und der Sowjetunion nicht überrascht gewesen sein. Furchtbar traf ihn nur die Katastrophe der sowjetischen Truppen im Mittelabschnitt.

Stalin verfuhr, wie gesagt, im Zweiten Weltkrieg nach den Methoden eines Lenin und Mao. Der Generalsekretär der Kommunistischen Partei der Sowjetunion baute nach der Unterzeichnung des deutsch-sowjetischen Paktes vom August 1939 Sibirien in einem unerhörten Ausmaß aus. Seit 1940 verlegte er Truppen nach dem Westen.

Aus der Truppenverlegung kann auf die Vorbereitung eines Krieges gegen den Westen geschlossen werden. Diese Auffassung läßt sich auch durch die Eintragungen in den Memoiren des französischen Ministerpräsidenten Daladier und des englischen Botschafters Sir Henderson stützen.

Nach meiner Ansicht fiel Adolf Hitler in drei von dem undurchsichtigen genialen Stalin gestellte Fallen herein:

1. 1939 Abschluß des deutsch-sowjetischen Nichtangriffspaktes mit geheimen Zusatzabkommen.

2. Aufmarsch der Roten Armee an der Grenze zwischen dem deutschen Einflußgebiet und der Sowjetunion.

3. Vormarsch auf Stalingrad im Zuge der Operation ,,Blau".

Den Machtkampf mit der Tuchatschewski-Gruppe, in dem Heydrich mit Hilfe des ehemaligen zaristischen Generals Skobin eine bedeutende Rolle spielte, hatte der georgische Diktator 1937 gewonnen. Stalin verfügte in General Jan K. Bersin, einem alten Bolschewisten, der 1938 erschossen wurde, über einen hervorragenden Geheimdienstchef.

Die Komintern hatte in jedem Land einen eigenen Informationsdienst aufgebaut, der politische und wirtschaftliche Nachrichten für Moskau sammelte.

Der NKWD, der ursprünglich für die innere Sicherheit der Sowjetunion verantwortlich war, erhielt Nachrichtenaufträge im Ausland. Zwischen General Bersin und Richard Sorge bestand eine enge Freundschaft. Im Jahre 1933 wurde letzterer – seit 1918/1919 Mitglied der Kommunistischen Partei Deutschlands – von Bersin aufgefordert, zu einem Treffen mit Leopold Trepper, geboren in Nowitorg (Neumarkt) in Polen, nach Moskau zu kommen. Dr. Sorge erhielt dort den Auftrag, in Japan eine Nachrichtengruppe aufzubauen. Er wurde Japankorrespondent der ,,Frankfurter Zeitung".

General Bersin rechnete vom Ende des Spanischen Bürgerkrieges bis zum Kriegsausbruch in Europa mit zwei Jahren. Im Herbst 1937 beauftragte er Leopold Trepper, eine Nachrichtenorganisation zu gründen, die unter dem Namen „Rote Kapelle" bekannt wurde. Es ist nicht nötig, die Geschichte der „Roten Kapelle" zu erzählen. Bemerkenswert sein dürfte, daß in der von Großvogel, dessen Familie aus Straßburg stammte, und Trepper gegründeten Firma Jules Jaspar, dessen Bruder einmal in Belgien das Amt des Ministerpräsidenten bekleidete, Direktor war. Von Brüssel aus wurden Zweigniederlassungen in Dänemark, Schweden und Norwegen gegründet. Trepper gab Richard Sorge die ersten Geldmittel. Am 13. Januar 1941 wurden in der belgischen Hauptstadt die Firma „Simexco" und in Paris das Unternehmen „Sinnex" aufgebaut. Doch bekleidete Trepper dort kein Amt. Generaldirektor bei der Pariser Firma wurde Alfred Corbin.

Von Mai 1940 bis November 1942 gingen 1500 Funksprüche nach Moskau. Sendestation war Lafitte bei Paris. Auch die illegale französische kommunistische Partei übermittelte Nachrichten, und zwar an die kommunistische Zentrale in Moskau. Die Berliner Gruppe funkte über Schweden, Holland, die Schweiz und Frankreich.

Trepper meldete 1940, daß die 4., 12. und 18. deutsche Division aus dem Unternehmen „Seelöwe" (geplante Landung in England) abgezogen seien. Dr. Sorge verständigte die Moskauer Zentrale unmittelbar nach Erlaß der Weisung 21 (Unternehmen „Barbarossa"), die Hitler am 21. Dezember 1940 erließ, von dieser wichtigen Maßnahme. Anfang 1941 erhielt Moskau Kenntnis über deutsche Bombenplanungen auf Leningrad, Kiew und Wiborg sowie die Zahlen der gegen die Sowjetunion bereitstehenden Divisionen. Am 12. Mai 1941 wußte Moskau, daß 150 Divisionen auf der Seite des Gegners bereitstanden. Am 15. Mai 1941 läßt Trepper über General Susloparow, den sowjetischen Militärattaché in Vichy, Angriffsplan und ursprüngliches Angriffsdatum – 15. Mai 1941 – übermitteln. Er gab auch die Änderung des geplanten Einmarschtages und dessen endgültiges Datum bekannt. Schulze-Boysen bestätigte das Datum. Am 11. März 1941 erhielt der sowjetische Botschafter in Washington die Pläne „Barbarossa". Am 10. Juni 1941 ist der englische Unterstaatssekretär Cadogan in der Lage, ähnliches Moskau zukommen zu lassen. Nach Marschall I. Filip Golikow, der von Juni 1940 bis Juli 1941 den Nachrichtendienst der Roten Armee leitete, war Moskau rechtzeitig über die Termine und die Daten des geplanten deutschen Einmarsches gegen die UdSSR unterrichtet. Bekannt war Moskau auch das militärische Potential und die Lage auf dem Gebiet der Rüstung im Deutschen Reich.

In dem großen Spiel tritt auch Dimitrij Manuilski, dessen Frau Lebede die Sektion Frankreich in der Komintern leitete, in Erscheinung. Von Manuilski stammen die Sätze, daß die Nationalsozialistische Deutsche Arbeiterpartei in den Städten von 10 %, auf dem Lande von 4 % Kommunisten unterwandert sei. 1939 gab Manuilski die Parole aus, der Krieg zwischen dem nationalsozialistischen Deutschland und den französisch-englischen Verbündeten sei ein Krieg zwischen Imperialisten.

Im Gegensatz zu Hitler, der Nachrichten des Geheimdienstes häufig mißachtete und sich stets bemühte, seine eigene Konzeption durchzudrücken, ist von dem mißtrauischen Stalin nicht anzunehmen, daß er eine Flut von Warnungen ignoriert hat. Der große politische und militärische Schachspieler in Moskau, der im August 1939 grünes Licht zum Ausbruch des Zweiten Weltkrieges gab, befolgte die Grundsätze Mao Tse-tungs: Den Gegner kommen lassen, sich zurückziehen und dabei die Gegenoffensive vorbereiten sowie gleichzeitig den Aufstand in den vom Feind besetzten Gebieten entfesseln. Dann sollte die Gegenoffensive beginnen.

Diese Rechnung ging zunächst bei den Sowjets nicht auf. Im Mittelabschnitt der Front kam es bei den sowjetischen Truppen zu einer Katastrophe. Stalins Niederlage stand vor seinen Augen. Dr. Sorge verhinderte sie. Der Zweite Vaterländische Krieg konnte beginnen.

Über die Stärke der Roten Armee hatte Berlin schon Ende Dezember 1939 Nachrichten erhalten. Die Abteilung Oberquartiermeister IV – Fremde Heere Ost II – gab am 19. Dezember 1939 unter Nummer 1995/39 g ein Werturteil über die Rote Armee nach den Berichten über den Einmarsch in Polen, im Baltikum und in Finnland ab. In diesem Bericht wird hingewiesen, daß die Rote Armee zahlenmäßig ein riesiges Kriegsinstrument darstellt.

Aus dem von den Sowjets besetzten Polen wurden zwei Heeresgruppen mit 6 Armeen gemeldet. Diese hatten 24–36 Schützendivisionen sowie 5 Kavalleriekorps mit etwa 15 Kavalleridivisionen und 3 motorisierte Korps mit etwa 9 Tankbrigaden. Im allgemeinen stammten die Kräfte nur aus den an Polen angrenzenden Militärbezirken. Aus anderen Militärbezirken wurden 1939 außerdem zuverlässige Regimenter und Abteilungen herausgesucht und in Polen eingesetzt. An der finnländischen Grenze waren 7 Schützenkorps mit über 20 Schützendivisionen und 8–10 Tankbrigaden bekannt. In jedem der drei baltischen Staaten stand eine mit Kampfwagen verstärkte Schützendivision. Die deutsche Heeresleitung zog den Schluß, daß 150 Schützendivisionen, 38 Kavalleriedivisionen und 32 Tankbrigaden (über 3000 Kampfwagen) mobil gemacht worden waren. Die sowjetischen Kampfmittel galten, im großen gesehen, als neuzeitlich.

Der Bericht zieht folgenden Schluß: ,,Die Rote Armee wurde von der Abteilung Ost immer für befähigt gehalten, einen Verteidigungskrieg zu führen. Es hat sich aber auch als richtig erwiesen, daß es nicht ausgeschlossen sei, daß die Führer der Sowjetunion unter gewissen Voraussetzungen bei ihrem gegenwärtigen Zustande auch einen Angriffskrieg führen würden. Die Entscheidung hierzu lag aber anscheinend nicht in Händen der militärischen Führer, sondern allein bei der politischen Leitung. Bestätigt wird, daß durch Nachrichten, die über den Angriff auf Finnland vorliegen und die besagen, daß der Angriff seine Hauptbilligung durch Ždanow, den politischen Leiter des Verwaltungsbezirks Leningrad, gefunden habe. Ždanow ist Mitglied der Regierung und des Obersten Rates sowie des Hauptvollzugsausschusses der Kommunistischen Partei und damit engster Mitarbeiter Stalins."

Wiederholte Abwehrnachrichten deuten darauf hin, daß seit Februar 1940 aus der Westukraine systematisch Aussiedlungen stattfinden. Ausgesiedelt werden Polen, aber auch Juden und Ukrainer. Die Transporte gehen angeblich nach Innerrußland. Der Befehl trifft die Auszusiedelnden überraschend, das Gepäck, welches mitgeführt werden darf, ist sehr gering.

Das Gebiet, in dem die Aussiedlungen stattfinden, erstreckt sich entlang der neuen rumänisch-russischen Grenze und entlang der deutsch-russischen Interessengrenze. Die Tiefe der Zone soll etwa 6 km betragen, weiter sollen angeblich alle am San gelegenen Häuser geräumt werden. Ähnliche vereinzelte Nachrichten liegen auch aus der Gegend von Augustowo vor.

Angesiedelt werden Russen aus dem Innern Rußlands, z. T. auch Ukrainer (Kommunisten).

Ein systematischer Beamtenwechsel (Austausch von Polen gegen Russen) findet bei allen Verwaltungen und bei der Eisenbahn statt.

Die Grenzsperrung wird energisch vorwärtsgetrieben. Gegenüber Rumänien ist die Grenze schon jetzt fast hermetisch geschlossen. Ein Flüchten über die Grenze ist außerordentlich gefährlich, da die Posten sofort das Feuer eröffnen. Die Zahl der Flüchtlinge wird immer geringer. Die Grenzüberwachung ist sehr streng und wird durch Stacheldrahtzäune bis zu 2 m Höhe, Grenzwachen zu Pferde und zu Fuß und MG-Posten unterstützt.

Meldung Fremde Heere Ost OQU IV – Nr. 2400/40 Lagebericht über die vermutlichen derzeitigen Heeresstärken zum Zeitpunkt des 29. Apr. 1940 weist aus:

„Militärbezirk Kiew etwa 550 000 Mann
Militärbezirk Charkow etwa 60 000 Mann
Militärbezirk Odessa etwa 100 000 Mann
Militärbezirk Nordkaukasus etwa 80 000 Mann
Militärbezirk Transkaukasus etwa 100 000 Mann –
insgesamt etwa 900 000 Mann."

Die Gesamtstärke der Roten Armee wird zur Zeit auf 3–3,5 Millionen Mann geschätzt. „Einschränkend darf darauf hingewiesen werden, daß der Militärbezirk Kiew im Frieden schon sehr stark belegt gewesen ist."

Im Frühjahr setzte dann regelmäßig die Ausbildungstätigkeit der Truppe im Gelände ein. Jede russische Division verfügte über ihr eigenes Zeltlager, das im Sommer 3–4 Monate lang bewohnt wird. Im Jahre 1940 mußten aber die Manöverübungen im Gelände und Märsche zu den Truppenlagern besonders auffallen, da die Truppe zum größten Teil mobile Stärke hat. In diesem Jahre kamen die aufgestellten Reservedivisionen hinzu, deren Zahl im Militärbezirk Kiew auf mindestens acht Schützendivisionen geschätzt wurde. Erwähnenswert ist auch, daß Meldungen vorliegen, die besagen, daß im Frühjahr 1941 starke Partisanenübungen stattfanden.

Daher ist kaum anzunehmen, daß die gemeldeten Truppenansammlungen und Truppentransporte mit Aufmarschgedanken an der Grenze nichts zu tun hatten. Die Gesamtlage in Europa in militärpolitischer Hinsicht zeigt, daß der Südostraum und der Nahe Orient Spannungsgebiet geworden waren und daß deshalb Rußland für seinen Teil die militärischen Maßnahmen traf, die die Durchführung seiner Politik in Südosteuropa und im Nahen Orient unterstützen sollten.

Die Belegungsstärken zeigten, daß Rußland jederzeit genügend starke Kräfte an der rumänischen Grenze stehen hatte, um überraschend eine Angriffsoperation zu beginnen. Eisenbahntransporte waren nicht notwendig, da in wenigen Nachtmärschen durch die russischen Truppen der südlichen Militärbezirke die einzunehmenden Aufmarschräume erreicht werden konnten. Mit Hilfe der günstig verlaufenden Bahnen konnten in kurzer Zeit aus dem Inneren Rußlands die Truppen im Westen wesentlich verstärkt werden.

Eine Angriffsoperation gegen Rumänien hing lediglich von den politischen Verhältnissen ab. Zu einer solchen Aktion war Rußland jederzeit in der Lage. Gelände- und Witterungsverhältnisse hielten grundsätzlich Rußland, wie die Angriffsoperation gegen Finnland zeigt, von einem einmal gefaßten Entschluß nicht ab.

Die Vortragsnotiz über Sowjetrußland des Oberkommandos des Heeres – Generalstab des Heeres OQU IV Abt. Fremde Heere Ost (II) – Nr. 4032/40 geh. vom 12.12.1940 schildert:

,,Als Folge des Gebietszuwachses 1940 ist in der territorialen Einteilung der Militärbezirk Archangelsk (Befehlshaber Generallt. Katschalow) neu gebildet worden. Die genauen Grenzen sind nicht bekannt. Er umfaßt anscheinend einen Teil des bisherigen Mil.Komm. Nordrußland sowie das Gebiet um Murmansk und die Grenzgebiete des nördlichen Karelien . . .

Die Einberufung zur Ausbildung des ersten Arbeitsdienstpflichtkontingents (vgl. Vortragsnotiz Fremde Heere Ost (II) Nr. 3642/40 geh. v. 18.10.40) ist am 25.11. abgeschlossen worden. Der Unterricht hat am 21.12. begonnen. Insgesamt wurden einberufen:

600 000 Jugendliche, d a v o n rd. 300 000 in Gewerbeschulen,
　　　　　　　36 000 in die Eisenbahnschulen,
　　　　　　250 000 in die Fabrikschulen . . ."
Aus den Unterlagen des Arbeitsstabes S (März 1941) ist zu entnehmen:
1. 2. 41: Lubomel stark belegt mit Truppen aller Waffengattungen
22. 1. 41: Kowel – technischer Eisenbahnzug, Ausrüstung unbekannt;
Truppen folgender Waffengattungen: Infanterie, Artillerie, Flak, Pioniere,
Kavallerie und Nachrichtentruppen.
Bezeichnend ist, daß vermerkt wird, „General Rosenfeld" (Jude).
Anfang Februar 1941: Rozyszoze (20 km norwestlich Luck) Infanterieeinheit in Stärke eines Bataillons
26. 2. 41: 25 leichte Panzerwagen am Nordrand des Ortes in einem Holzschuppen
Anfang Februar 1941: Nowe Siolo (2 km südlich Cieszanow) „4 Langrohrgeschütze wurden vom Bahnhof Oleszycze nach Vorwerk Nowe Siolo gebracht, (dazu) 1 Kavallerieschwadron Nr. unbekannt".
Ende Februar 1941: Oleszycze (30 km nordostwärts Jaroslau) Teile Infanterie Nr. unbekannt, Teile Artillerie Nr. unbekannt.
15. 2. 41: Olchawa (10 km nordostwärts Jaroslau, Vorwerk) im Walde
nordostwärts Olchawa Panzerkampfwagen, Anzahl unbekannt.

Vermerkt wird, daß die Orte Dubno, Luck, Rozyszoze und Kowel viel
schwächer mit Truppen belegt sind als im Sommer und Herbst 1940.
Februar 1941: Torczyn (20 km westlich von Luck) Pionierbataillon 108
(insgesamt etwa 150 Mann je Kompanie), Bataillonskommandeur „Kapitän Hajworonzow, anscheinend Jude".

„Die von Anfang März bis jetzt gemeldeten Truppenbewegungen in Bessarabien und den baltischen und westlichen Militärbezirken zeigen ein Aufschließen der russ. Truppen auf die deutsche Grenze von Osten nach Westen.

Aus Bessarabien liegen nur Meldungen über Eintreffen neuer Einheiten
vor. Kischinew und Umgebung mit Truppen stark belegt. In Kischinew
wahrscheinlich 2. mot./mech. Brigaden (bisher noch nicht bekannt).

Im westlichen Militärbezirk rückten die Truppen in Richtung auf die
Linie: Bargelow-Osowiec–Zambrow auf. Ob die Truppen die Linie überschritten haben, geht aus den Meldungen nicht hervor.

Im baltischen Militärbezirk sind die Russen bis an die deutsche Grenze
aufgeschlossen. Der Suwalki-Zipfel scheint von Süden und Norden her von
stärkeren Kräften als bisher eingeschlossen zu sein. Die Feldbefestigungen
in Gegend Virbalis (65 km ostw. Insterburg) sind besetzt worden. Außerdem wurden dauernde Eisenbahntransporte von Leningrad nach Litauen
gemeldet.

Truppenbewegungen von Westen nach Osten sind bisher noch nicht gemeldet worden."

Abwehrstelle in K.W. I, Zusammenfassung Nr. 2405/41 I Hg. vom 24. 3. 1941 stellt hinsichtlich Truppenteil, Standort und Beobachtungsdatum folgendes fest:

Truppenteil:	Standort:	Standort:	Beob. Datum:
	Lettland:		
V. Sch. Korps (lett.):	*Riga*	Riga	14. 2. 41
1. Sch. Div. m. Teilen:	*Riga*	Wilna	10. 3. 41
402. Haub. Art. Rgt. RGK	*Riga*	(Mörser-Rgt. 402)	Ende Febr.
		Belderaa b/Riga	
7. 1. TankRgt. m. Teilen	*Riga*	–	
Inf. Kriegsschule	*Riga*	–	
2. Rgt. P U D (?)	*RYA?*	–	
338. Funk-Lausch-Abt.	*RYA?*	–	
25. abk. Ingenieure?	*RYA?*	–	
27. Kav. 6. Kp.?	*RYA?*	–	
28. Kav. 6. Kp.?	*RYA?*	–	
1. Sch. Div.	*Tukkum*	Tuckuma	5. 3. 41
18. Artl. Rgt.	*Limbazi*, 36 km	Batiatycze	1. 9. 40
	w. Wolmar		
Sch. Korps (Führungsstab)	*Dünaburg*	Dünaburg (Wilna? 10. 3.)	Ende Febr.
1. mot. Sch. Div. mit Teilen	*Dünaburg*-Lager	Finnland	10. 1. 40
		8. Arm. zughg. Funk	
23. Sch. Div. m. Teilen	*Dünaburg*	Balt. Mil. Bez.	8. 2. 41
302. Haub. Art. Rgt. RGK	Dünaburg	–	
20. Kav. Korps Rgt. RGK	*Mitau*	Mitau	20. 2. 41
550. Sch. Rgt.	*Mitau*	–	
17. Verbindungs-Rgt.	*Mitau*	–	
450. Telegr. Bau-Kp.	*Mitau*	–	
186. Sch. Rgt.	*Saldus*, 75 km	Goldingen	10. 2.
	w. Mitau	Frauenburg (Saldus)	
		Ast XX	Anf. März
366. Sch. Rgt.	*Friedrichstadt*	–	
	Jaunjelgava		
Stab d. stoikl.? Bez.	*Libau*/Liepaja	–	
67. Sch. Div. (Stab)	*Libau*	Libau (OKH-Lagek.	
		15. 2., Fr. H. Ost)	
56. Sch. Rgt.	*Libau*	Lemberg (Ast Krak.)	7. 12. 40
94. 1. Art. Rgt.	*Libau*	–	
242. Haub. Art. Rgt.	*Libau*	–	
195. Sch. Rgt.	*Kuldiga*, 130 km	Frauenburg (Saldus)	5. 3. 41
	w. Riga		
114. Sch. Rgt.	*Priekule*, 5 km	Slonim (Ast Krakau)	3. 2.
	ostw. Cesis	Pruzana	4. 2.
128. Sch. Div. (Stab)	*Gulbene*	Raum Gulbene-Jakob-	23. 1.
		stadt als mot. (OKH Fr.	(5. 3.)
		H. Ost LgKrte 15. 2. 41.)	

Truppenteil:	Standort:	Standort:	Beob. Datum:
126. Sch. Div. m. Teilen	*Jekabpils* Jakobstadt	Jekabpils (OKH Lagek.)	15. 2. 41
8. mot. Rgt.	*Madona*, 75 km ostw. Riga	–	
385. 1. Art. Rgt.	*Krustpils* Kreuzberg	–	
501. Haub. Art. Rgt.	*Krustpils* Kreuzberg	–	
690. Sch. Rgt.	*Plavinas* Stockmannshof	–	
18. Tank Div. (Stab) = mot. mech-Brig.?	*Cesis* Wenden	–	
138. (Schreibf. 183.?) Sch. Div. (Stab)	*Cesis* Wenden	183. Sch. Div. Wenden	5. 3.
35. Tank Rgt.	*Cesis* Wenden	–	
285. Sch. Rgt.	*Cesis* Wenden	Wenden	18. 2. 41
295. Sch. Rgt.	*Valmiera* Wolmar	Wolmar	18. 2. 41
36. Tank Rgt.	*Valmiera* Wolmar	–	
243. Sch. Rgt.	*Talsi/Talsen*	Talsen	5. 3. 41
	Litauen:		
X. Sch. Korps-Stab	*Telsiai/Telsche*	Wilejka (OKH Lagek.)	15. 2. 41
115. Sch. Div. Stab	*Telsiai/Telsche*	(Grodno 15. 6. 40)	
708. Sch. Rgt.	*Telsiai/Telsche*	*(Grodno 15. 6. 40)*	
371. Haub. Rgt.	*Telsiai/Telsche*	–	
133. bes. Flak Art. Abt.	*Telsiai/Telsche*	–	
III. (mot.) mech. Korps (Stab)	*Vilnius/Wilna*	Wilna	10. 3. 41
179. Sch. Div.	*Vilnius/Wilna*	Wilna	1. 3. 41
84. mot. Div.	*Vilnius/Wilna*	(Finnland 24. 2.)	
41. mot. Sch. Rgt.	*Vilnius/Wilna*	–	
46. Tank Rgt.	*Vilnius/Wilna*	–	
Koluft 110. Flugbasis	*Vilnius/Wilna*		
26. Korps-Kav. Rgt.	*Vilnius/Wilna*	Kowno (abmarschiert?)	1. 3.
110. Haub. Art. Rgt. RGK	*Vilnius/Wilna*	Balt. Mil. Bez.	8. 2.
Stab d. 11. Armee	*Kowno/Kaunas*	Kowno	15. 3.
IV. (?) Sch. Korps	*Kowno/Kaunas*	–	
I. Sch. Korps (Stab)	*Kowno/Kaunas*	Kowno	7. 2.
5. Sch. Div.	*Kowno/Kaunas*	Kowno	12. 12.
22. 1. Tankbrig. m. Teilen	*Kowno/Kaunas*	*Balt. Mil. Bez.*	8. 2.
429. Haub. Art. Rgt.	*Kowno/Kaunas*	–	
21. topograf. rinktine?	*Kowno/Kaunas*	–	
7. b-nas VNDS	*Kowno/Kaunas*	–	
8. Ponton-Btl.	*Kowno/Kaunas*	–	
Inf. Kriegsschule	*Kowno/Kaunas*	–	
Stab d. Bes. Bez.	*Kowno/Kaunas*	–	
33. Sch. Div. (Stab)	*Mariampole*	Balt. Mil. Bez.	8. 2.
82. Sch. Rgt.	*Mariampole*	Lomza	28. 11.
92. Haub. Art. Rgt.	*Mariampole*	–	

Truppenteil:	Standort:	Standort:	Beob. Datum:
10. Sch. Div. Stab	*Plunge*	Telsche	Ende Febr.
5. Tank Div. m. Teilen	*Alytus/Olita*	Olita	10. 3.
164. Schw. Rgt.	*Vilkaviskis*	Wilkowischken	Anf. Dez.
	Wilkowischken		
73. Sch. Rgt.	*Kalvaria*	Kalvaria	18. 8. 40
98. Sch. Rgt.	*Rietavas*, 35 km	Lomza	23. 10. 40
	sw. Telsche		
62. Sch. Rgt.	*Kretinga*	(Krottingen 8. 11.)	
	Krottingen	Grodno	Ende Jan.
30. 1. Art. Rgt.	*Sateikiai*, 29 km	Raum Ponjewisch	18. 7. 40
	no. Krottingen	FeHoSte.	
140. Haub. Art. Rgt.	*Skuodas*, 54 km	Litauen FeHoSte	19. 7. 40
	nw. Telsche		
571. Sch. Rgt.	*Varniai*, 29 km	–	
	Telsche		
638. Sch. Rgt.	Plinksiai	Litauen FeHoSte	6. 6. 40
313. 1. Art. Rgt.	*Tryskiai*, 21 km	Litauen FeHoSte	26. 6. 40
	ono. Telsche		
Stab d. stont. (?) Bez.	*Schaulen/Siauliai*	–	
219. bes. Sappeur Btl.	*Renova*, 31 km	–	
	ostw. Telsche		
452. Haub. Art. Rgt.	*Panevezye*	Gut bei Ponjewisch	3. 3. 41
	Ponjewisch		
Koluft 13. Flugbasis	*Panevezys/*	–	
	Ponjewisch		
607. Sch. Rgt.	*Panevezys/*	(Radviliskis Anf. 40)	
	Ponjewisch		
185. Sch. Div. Stab	*Radviliskis*	Radviliskis	Anf. Sept. 40
		(HOIII Kowno)	
660. Sch. Rgt.	*Radviliskis*		
I. Sch. Korps (Stab)	*Siauliai/Schaulen*	Wilna	15. 2. 41
		O.K.H. Lagek.	
415. Sch. Rgt.	*Siauliai/Schaulen*	–	
466. Sch. Rgt.	*Taurage/*	–	
	Tauroggen		
414. 1. Art. Rgt.	*Taurage/*	–	
	Tauroggen		
125. Sch. Div. (Stab)	*Raseiniai*	Balt. Mil. Bez.	8. 2. 41
657. Sch. Rgt.	*Raseiniai*		
749. Sch. Rgt.	*Seredzius*, 36 km	–	
	nw. Kowno		
459. Haub. Art. Rgt.	*Seredzius*, 36 km	–	
	nw. Kowno		
470. 1. Art. Rgt.	*Dv. Cervanai?*	–	
201. mot. Rgt.	*N. Wilna*	201. Sch. Rgt. Wilna	10. 3.
	(N. Wilna)	(Czerwony-Bor 17. 3.)	
184. Sch. Div. (Stab)	*Utena?* 96 km	(Gaizunai Febr. 41)	15. 3.
	n. Wilna	Wilna	
297. Sch. Rgt.	*Utena?* 96 km	(Gaizunai Febr. 41)	Jan. 1941
	n. Wilna	Wilna	
262. Sch. Rgt.	*Pasvalys?* 36 km	Trakai (22 km	
	n. Ponjewiach	w. Wilna)	
294. Sch. Rgt.	*Zarasai?* 24 km	Wilna	2. 2.
	sw. Dünaburg		

Truppenteil:	Standort:	Standort:	Beob. Datum:
Tank Div. (Stab)	*Ukmerge/* *Wilkomierz*	Gaizunai	10. 3.
2. mot. Rgt.	*Ukmerge/* *Wilkomierz*	–	
3. Tank Rgt.	*Gaizunai,* 35 km no. Kowno	–	
4. Tank Rgt.	*Gaizunai,* 35 km no. Kowno	–	
2. Art. Rgt.	*Kedainiai,* 40 km n. Kowno		
	Estland:		
Stab d. 8. Armee	*Tallinn/Reval*	Mitau (u. Ruhnental)	25. 8. 15. 2.?
XII. Sch. Korps-Stab	*Tallinn/Reval*	Estland	26. 2.
180. Sch. Div. (Stab)	*Tallinn/Reval*	Estland OKH Lagek.	15. 2. 41
16. Sch. Div.	*Tallinn/Reval*	Balt. Mil. Bez. (Olita ?März 41)	8. 2.
18. Tank Brig. m. Teilen	*Tallinn/Reval*	Balt. Mil. Bez.	8. 2.
Inf. Kriegsschule	*Tallinn/Reval*	–	
22. Sch. Rgt.	*Tallinn/Reval*	–	
167. Sch. Rgt.	*Tallinn/Reval*	(Nowogrod-Stawiski Krak.	1. 11. 40)
155. Sch. Rgt.	*Kopli* (Vorstadt Reval)	Zambrow	28. 11. 40
42. Sch. Rgt.	*Türi u. Paide* Weißenstein, 9 km so. Tallinn	Bialystok	12. 2. 41
85. Sch. Rgt.	*Tamsala/Tamsal* 83 km oso. Reval	–	
219. Sch. Rgt.	*Rakvere,* 93 km o. Tallinn	Finnl. (z. 8. Armee gehör.) FeHoSte	5. 2. 40
539. Haub. Art. Rgt.	*Rakvere,* 93 km o. Tallinn	–	
Sch. Korps (Stab)	*Tartu/Dorpat*	Estland	10. 3.
182. Sch. Div. (Stab)	*Petseri,* 0 km so. Tartu	Tartu OKH Lagek.	15. 2. 41
232. Sch. Rgt.	*Petseri,* 0 km so. Tartu		
171. Sch. Rgt.	*Petseri,* 0 km so. Tartu		
140. Sch. Rgt.	*Viri,* 60 km s. Tartu	Raum Lomza	8./10. 3. 41
227. Sch. Rgt.	*Valga* (Walk)	Walk	18. 2.
286. Sch. Rgt.	*Valga* (Walk)	Walk (Kohorch Ost)	25. 2.
96. 1. Art. Rgt.	*Valga* (Walk)	Walk (Kohorch Ost) (EstlandFeHoSte 19. 2.)	30. 1.
11. Sch. Div. (Stab)	*Marva,* 192 km o. Tallinn	Schaulen (Verwechslg. m. Korps XI?)	Ende Febr.
320. Sch. Rgt.	*Marva,* 192 km o. Tallinn	–	
72. 1. Art. Rgt.	*Marva,* 192 km o. Tallinn	–	

Truppenteil:	Standort:	Standort:	Beob. Datum:
113. Sch. Rgt.	*Jichva*, 153 km o. Tallinn	Finnl. (z. 16. Armee geh. 9. 2.) Lemberg (Krak).	17. 8. 40
10. Sch. Div.	*Viliandi* (Fellin)	Fellin	21. 2.
173. Sch. Rgt.	*Priarny* (Pernau)	Pernau (90. I. D. Ko- horch Ost 12. 2. Bielsk?)	23. 1. 41
149. Haub. Art. Rgt.	*Viliandi*/Fellin	Pernau (Kohorch Ost)	3. 11. 40
249. Sch. Rgt.	*Haapsalu/Habsal* 85 km sw. Tallinn	–	
224. 1. Art. Rgt.	*Haapsalu/Habsal* 85 km sw. Tallinn	–	
233. Haub. Art. Rgt.	*Haapsalu/Habsal* 85 km sw. Tallinn	(60 km o. Lemberg Krak.)	21. 2. 40
19. Sch. Rgt.	*Ezelie sala?*	Dorpat (Kohorch Ost)	23. 1. 41

Fernschreiben vom 26. Mrz. 41 besagt:
„In der Nacht vom 15. zum 16. 3. 41 trafen aus Richtung Kowno 2 russ. Militärtransporte mit Infanterie und schw.mot.Art. ein. Die Truppen rückten sogleich in Richtung Liudwinawas (8 km südlich Mariampol) weiter. Die Russen treffen eilige Vorbereitung zur Einberufung der Wehrpflichtigen vom 18. bis 45. Lebensjahr. Die Einberufungsbefehle sind bereits ausgestellt (Nachricht vom Meldeamt Lazdijai). Flüchtling meldet: Am 21. Mrz. 41 trafen in Kartenai 70 mittlere und schwere Tanks ein. In Kartenai liegen außerdem 2 schw. Batl., die vor etwa 2 Monaten von Krottingen dorthin verlegt. wurden . . .“

Die Anlage zu Ast Krakau, Tagebuch Nr. 1278/41 I H geh. vom 29. 3. 1941 besagt:

1. *L o m z a*
   13. Sch.Div.
   (A.O. Lt.Ast.I Nr 1627/41 I H geh. v. 6. 3. in Zambrow gemeldet.)
   Der Div. unterstehen folgende Sch.Regter:
   Sch.Rgt. 119 – Standort A n d r z e j o w o
                (südl. Zambrow)
                (A.O. am 22. 10. 40 in Zambrow gemeldet. Bezug Ast. Krakau Nr. 3546/40 I H geh. v. 15. 11. 40).
   Sch.Rgt. 172 – Standort C z e r w o n y B o r
                (südl. Lomza)
                (A.O. am 28. 12. 40 in Tarnopol gemeldet. Bezug: Ast. Krakau Nr. 631/41 I H geh. v. 19. 2. 41).
   Sch.Rgt. 213 – Standort unbekannt.
   Quelle: Deserteur.
   Zeit: 19. 3. 41.

2. *P i s z c z a* (54 km südl. Brest Lit.)
   Eine mot. Kolonne, Truppenzugehörigkeit unbekannt.
   Ausrüstung: 60 dreiachsige, gl. Lkw.
   Quelle: V-Mann des Zoll, eigene Feststellung.
   Zeit: 3.2.41.
3. *S z a c k* (60 km nordwestl. Kowel)
   Eine Schützen-Einheit Nr. und Stärke unbekannt
   Eine Art.-Einheit Nr. u. Stärke unbekannt.
   Quelle: V-Mann des Zoll, eigene Feststellung.
   Zeit: 3.2.41.
4. *R o z y s z c z e* (52 km südostw. Kowel)
   Stab einer Sch.Div. Nr. unbekannt
   Untergebracht im Magistratsgebäude.
   Eine Panzer-Einheit Nr. unbekannt
   (A.O. Bestätigung. Bezug Ast. Krakau Tgb. Nr. 1112/41 I H geh. v.
   19.3.41).
   Eine Art.-Einheit Nr. unbekannt
   Ist am Südrand der Stadt untergebracht.
   Einheit ist Mitte Februar 41 in Rozyszcze eingetroffen.
   Quelle: V-Mann a. Probe von II, eigene Feststellung.
   Zeit: 2.3.41.
5. *L u c k*
   Eine Sch.Div. (mot.) Nr. unbekannt
   Untergebracht im Vorort Krasne. Div. ist Januar 41 aus Leningrad
   gekommen.
   Quelle: V-Mann a. Probe von II, eigene Feststellung.
   Zeit: 2.3.41.
6. *R o w n e*
   Ein Korps-Stab (Nr. unbekannt)
   (A.O. mit Funklagemeldung 2/3 v. 6.3.41 ist das XXVII Sch.Korps in
   Rowne gemeldet.)
   Ein Sch.Rgt. Nr. unbekannt
   Ein Kav.Rgt. Nr. unbekannt
   Ein Art.Rgt. Nr. unbekannt
   Ein Feld-Art.Rgt. (mot.) Nr. unbekannt
   Eine Panzereinheit Nr. unbekannt
   Untergebracht in ehem. Zwiebackfabrik.
   Kasernen sind mit Truppen überfüllt. Regimenter sind Dezember 40
   aus dem Inneren Rußlands eingetroffen. Die bis dahin dort liegenden
   Einheiten sind in Richtung Lemberg abgerückt.
   Quelle: V-Mann a. Probe, eigene Feststellung.

Zeit: 2.3.41.
7. *B r o d y*
   Ein Sch.Rgt. Nr. unbekannt
   Ein Kav.Rgt. Nr. unbekannt
   Quelle: Flüchtling, eigene Feststellung.
Zeit: 14.3.41.
8. *Z l o c z o w*
   Ein Sch.Rgt. Nr. unbekannt
   (A.O. am 18.11.40 ein Sch.Rgt. in Zloczow mit unbekannter Nummer gemeldet. Bezug: Ast. Krakau Nr. 129/41 I H geh. v. 15.1.41).
9. *L e m b e r g*
   Stab 4.Sch.Div.
   (A.O. am 11.1.41 in Grodno gemeldet. Bezug: Ast. Krakau Tgb. Nr. 374/41 I H geh. v. 4.2.41. Nachprüfung eingeleitet.)
   Stab ist im Hotel Brakowski auf dem Bernardynskiplatz untergebracht.
   Quelle: Flüchtling.
Zeit: 10.3.41.
   Stab 55. *Sch.Div.* in der Nacht 18./19.2.41 aus L e m b e r g in unbekannter Richtung abgerückt. (A.O. wahrscheinlich Merkfehler, gemeint wird die 50. Sch.Div. sein.)
10. *U s t r z y k i   D o l n e*
    Stab 5. Sch.Div.
    (A.O. 1.1.41 in Kowno gemeldet. Bezug Ast. Krakau Nr. 374/41 I H geh. v. 4.2.41).
    Kommandeur: General S e m e n o w, der in C h y r o w auf einem Landgut wohnt.
    Quelle: UV-Mann des RV 712, der in Ustrzyki Dolne als Postbote tätig ist und das Stabsgebäude oft aufsucht.
Zeit: 18.3.41.
    Lt. Meldung eines Flüchtlings hat sich die 5. *Sch.Div.* im Januar 1941 in H o r y n (b. Luniniec) befunden.

1. *L o m z a*
   Zwei Kav.Rgter. Nr. unbekannt
   (A.O. Bestätigung, 2.1.41 ein Kav.Rgt. ohne Nr. gemeldet. Bezug: Ast. Krakau Nr. 374/41 I H geh. v. 4.2.41.)
   Kav. Rgter. liegen in den Kasernen des ehem. poln. Sch.Rgts. 33. Vermutlich handelt es sich um Kosaken-Rgter., von denen das eine breite rote und das andere blaue Biesen trägt.
   Quelle: RV-2007 – eigene Feststellung.

Zeit: 8. 3. 1941.
2. *Zambrow*
Stab 13. Sch. Div.
(A.O. Bestätigung, 10. 2. 41 in Zambrow gemeldet. Bezug: Ast. Krakau
Nr. 1628/41 I H geh. v. 6. 3. 41.)
Sch.Rgt. 148
(A.O. Bestätigung, 28. 11. 40 in Zambrow gemeldet. Bezug: Ast. Krakau
Nr. 4198/40 I H geh. v. 21. 12. 40.)
Quelle: UV-Mann des V-Kosenko, eigene Feststellung.
Zeit: 28. 2. 41.
3. *Pinsk*
Sch.Rgt. 205
 Kommandeur: Oberst S z a k o w
 Rgt. liegt in den sog. ,,roten Kasernen".
Quelle: RV 2007, eigene Feststellung.
Zeit: 5. 3. 1941.
4. *Zolkiew*
Parkplatz von Panzertruppen
 An der Str. Lemberg–Rawa Ruska (2 km nordwestl. Zolkiew) Panzer-
kampf- und Panzerspähwagen. Genaue Zahl unbekannt.
Quelle: Flüchtling, eigene Feststellung.
Zeit: 12. 3. 41.
5. *Lemberg*
Stab 4. Sch. Div. Durch FS voraus
 Untergebracht im Hotel Krakowski, Platz Bernardynski.
Quelle: Flüchtling, von Bekannten in Lemberg gehört.
Zeit: 10. 3. 41.
Kav.Rgt. 16
(A.O. 28. 11. 40 in Zolkiew ohne Nr. gemeldet. Bezug: Ast. Krakau Nr.
294/41 I H geh. v. 29. 1. 41.)
 Rgts.Stab in der Krasnoarmejskaja Str. (Haus-Nr.?)
Quelle: Flüchtling, von Bekannten gehört.
Zeit: 1. 3. 41.
Panzerwagenschule für Uffz.
 Untergebracht in der Kleparowska Str. (Haus-Nr.?)
Quelle: Flüchtling, von Soldaten gehört.
Zeit: 2. 3. 41.
6. *Machnow* (12 km südostw. Tomaczow-Lub.)
Ein Sch.Rgt. Nr. unbekannt
Quelle: Flüchtling, eigene Feststellung.
Zeit: 2. 3. 41.

7. *Vierzhica* (21 km südostw. Tomaszow-Lub.)
Ein Artl.Rgt. Nr. unbekannt.
   Rgt. ist Anfang März ins Dorf eingerückt. Geschütze etwa 5 m Rohr-
   länge, bespannt mit 6 Pferden. Einzelne Geschütze Gummibereifung,
   bespannt mit 4 Pferden. Kal. unbekannt.
   Quelle: Flüchtling, eigene Feststellung.
   Zeit: 11. 3. 41.
8. *Vorwerk Potocki* (17 km süd-südostw. Tomaszow-Lub.)
   Eine Panzereinheit Nr. unbekannt
   Bestehend aus etwa 80 Panzerkampfwagen und 50 Panzerspähwägen.
   Panzerkampfwagen mit einem Turm und 2 MG, fahren auf Wegen auf 6
   Rädern, im Gelände auf Raupenketten (T 26?). Panzerspähwagen 2
   MG, auf 2 Achsen, bewegen sich beinahe geräuschlos. (Bronjeford?)
   Quelle: Flüchtling, eigene Feststellung.
   Zeit: 6. 3. 41.
9. *Vorwerk Lubycza-Krolewska* (14 km süd-südostw. Tomaszow-
   Lub.)
   Kav.Schw. Rgts. Nr. unbekannt
   Quelle: Flüchtling, eigene Feststellung
   Zeit: 2. 3. 41.
10. *Rasdolnaja* (nördl. v. Wladiwostok)
    Sch.Rgt. 17
    (A.O. Bestätigung. Bezug: Fula v. 6/2. 11. 2. 41 in Rasdolnaja erstmalig
    gemeldet.)
    Quelle: Briefe von Soldatenangehörigen.
    Zeit: 26. 3. 41.

Heute wird gesagt, daß Stalin durch den deutschen Einmarsch in die
Sowjetunion überrascht worden ist. Man weist auf die ungeheueren Verluste der Sowjets hin, die kaum eine andere Macht der Erde hätte überwinden
können. Die Stärke der Russen hat bereits im Jahre 1556 ein Abgesandter
der britischen Krone namens Chancellor erkannt. Er stellt fest: Wenn die
Russen eines Tages ihre Macht kennen, werden sie eine Gefahr für ganz
Europa sein, und von ihren Nachbarn wird bald nur ein schäbiger Rest
übrigbleiben.
   Die Stärke der Roten Armee hat sich gezeigt. Das Deutsche Staatsoberhaupt hat sie unterschätzt. Man sagt, daß die Rote Armee in der Umrüstung
begriffen war. Vergessen aber wird, in welch gigantischer Weise die Sowjetunion Sibirien rüstungsmäßig, wirtschaftlich und militärisch vor und nach
Abschluß des Paktes mit Deutschland vom 26. Aug. 1939 ausgebaut hatte.
   In einer gewissen Überheblichkeit wurde vor Beginn des Rußlandfeldzu-

ges auf die sowjetische Kriegführung verwiesen. Man nahm als Maßstab den finnischen Krieg und übersah dabei, daß an dieser Auseinandersetzung nur der Leningrader Militärbezirk beteiligt war. Nicht gesehen wurde, mit welcher Umsicht die Sowjetunion im Fernen Osten kämpfte. Der damalige deutsche Militärattaché in Moskau, Kästring, war ein Warner auf einsamer Flur. Die Weisung Adolf Hitlers, nicht über die Linie Archangelsk-Astrachan Erkundigungsflüge durchzuführen, hatte äußerst nachteilige Folgen. Deutschland verspielte viel in den ersten Monaten des Krieges. Die Bevölkerung Westrußlands wurde durch den Einmarsch überrascht. Teile der Einwohner des besetzten Gebietes empfingen die deutschen Truppen mit Blumen und Beifall, in der Ukraine mit Brot und Salz. Aber die deutsche Führung versäumte, ein klares Kriegsziel zu geben. Dadurch, daß nichts gesagt wurde über die Zukunft dieses Raumes, verlor Deutschland eine einmalige Chance. Die kommunistische Partei konnte auf dem besetzten Gebiet Widerstandszellen bilden. Zuverlässige und für den Untergrund fähige Funktionäre blieben planmäßig zurück oder gingen bald in ihren früheren Tätigkeitsraum. Sie hatten die Widerstandsbewegung zu aktivieren und im rückwärtigen deutschen Heeresgebiet die notwendigen Verbindungen herzustellen. Arbeiter- und Jugendgruppen wurden für den illegalen Kampf organisiert. Der Krieg sollte ein Volkskrieg werden. Aus dem Gegnerbegriff entstand der Feindbegriff.

Bewußt wurden von der auf dem Rückzug befindlichen Roten Armee Greuel an verschiedenen Orten an lebenden und toten deutschen Soldaten begangen, um die Führung eines klassischen Krieges zu erschweren.

Die deutsche militärische Führung sollte sich veranlaßt sehen, abscheuerregende Maßnahmen zu befehlen. Ich glaube nicht an die Richtigkeit der Sätze, die Chruschtchow auf dem XX. Parteitag der KPdSU 1956 hinsichtlich des Verhaltens Stalins in den ersten Kriegswochen aussprach:

,,Man darf auch nicht vergessen, daß Stalin nach den ersten schweren Niederlagen an der Front glaubte, daß dies das Ende sei. In einer seiner ersten Reden sagte er damals: ,Alles, was Lenin geschaffen hat, haben wir für immer verloren . . .' Stalin mischte sich gleichzeitig in Operationen ein und erteilte Befehle, die die wirkliche Situation an den einzelnen Frontabschnitten außer acht ließen und die deshalb zwangsläufig zu schweren Verlusten führen mußten." (Krasnaja Swezda, Nr. 8 vom 14. Febr. 1956.)

Chruschtchow hielt eine Rede in der Entstalinisierungsepoche. Sie diente auch der Tarnung des wirklichen Geschehens.

Die deutschen Maßnahmen schufen für den kommunistischen Agitator einen fruchtbaren Boden. Aus dem kommunistischen Funktionär wurde der ,,vaterländisch" gesinnte Patriot, der dem russischen Menschen die Vernichtung seines Lebens vor Augen stellen konnte. Gleichzeitig benutzte er alle Möglichkeiten, um den „Sowjetmenschen" aufzuzeigen, wie der Feind geschlagen werden kann. Das Ansehen der Deutschen wurde systematisch gemindert, indem die Nichtbefolgung der Anordnungen der Besatzungsmacht erzwungen wurde. Kollektivmaßnahmen wurden provoziert, die zum größten Teil Schuldlose treffen mußten. Dadurch vergrößerte sich der Kreis des Widerstandes.

In seiner klaren Konzeption rief Stalin zum nationalen Freiheitskampf auf. Seinen Völkern versicherte er die Sympathie aller Völker, die mit Einschluß der besten Menschen Deutschlands auf der Seite der Sowjetunion stünden und ihren heroischen Kampf und die von ihr ergriffenen Maßnahmen billigten. Stalin rief aus, daß der Krieg gegen das faschistische Deutschland ein Kampf auf Leben und Tod sei. Er sei kein gewöhnlicher Krieg zwischen militärischen Kräften, sondern ein Kampf des gesamten Sowjetvolkes gegen die faschistische Unterdrückung, ein „vaterländischer Krieg", der auch allen Völkern Europas helfen werde, die unter dem Joch des deutschen Faschismus litten. Stalin erklärte: „Der Feind ist grausam und unerbittlich. Er setzt sich das Ziel, unseren Boden, der mit unserem Schweiß getränkt ist, zu okkupieren, unser Getreide, unser Erdöl, die Früchte unserer Arbeit an sich zu reißen."

Partisanenkrieg in der Sowjetunion

Erwähnenswert ist, daß der Schwede Arvid Fredborg bereits 1944 in seinem Buch „Behind the steel wall" schrieb: „Die Russen hatten ihn (den Partisanenkrieg) seit Jahren vorbereitet, hatten Vorräte an Munition, Waffen und Nahrungsmitteln gehäuft, Radiostationen errichtet und ihre Soldaten systematisch in der Partisanentaktik ausgebildet. Sobald die reguläre Armee den Rückzug antrat, gingen die Partisanen sofort ans Werk . . ., offenbar nach den Gesetzen hoher Strategie arbeitend. Sie konzentrierten sich an wichtigen Punkten und hatten ihre Basen auf Gebieten, welche sie in Frieden ließen. Es waren die Partisanen und nichtregulären Soldaten, welche den Krieg in Rußland, Jugoslawien und anderswo so grausam machten. Da Zivilpersonen hereingezogen wurden, wurden Grausamkeiten auf beiden Seiten verübt."

Verständlich ist, daß Entsetzen und Zorn die deutschen Truppenführer ergriffen, als sie von den durch die Sowjets angerichteten Greueln Kenntnis erhielten.

Ungefähr zwei Jahrzehnte ist es her, daß ich in einer Arbeit, die ich mit Hilfe eines von schwerem Schicksal betroffenen Mitarbeiters fertigte, Geschehnisse aus dem Ostraum behandelte. In der Einführung schrieb ich: „Die Zusammenstellung soll aufzeigen, daß die Gesichtspunkte der Sicherheit bei Führung eines ‚Krieges neuen Typus' von überragender Bedeutung waren und der Ausgangspunkt der Befehle und Weisungen nicht in der rassistischen Grundlage, z. B. in der Zielsetzung der ‚Endlösung der Judenfrage' zu erblicken ist.

Die deutsche Staatsführung und mit ihr das Oberkommando der Wehrmacht und die sicherheitspolitischen Organe hatten seitens der Sowjetunion eine Kriegführung zu erwarten, die außerhalb des geltenden Völkerrechts lag. Auf der deutschen Seite wurde der Standpunkt vertreten, daß dieser Kriegführung hauptsächlich unter dem Gesichtspunkt der vorbeugenden Gefahrenabwehr begegnet werden könne, die offensiv und defensiv zu gestalten sei.

In diesem Rahmen gesehen, war der ‚Barbarossa-Befehl' nicht ein Befehl in Dienstsachen. Er proklamierte vielmehr den Kriegsausnahmezustand im ‚Barbarossa-Raum', in welchem die marxistische Lehre von der psychischen und physischen Vernichtung einer ganzen Klasse in die Praxis umgesetzt war.

Sinowjew führte am 10. Aug. 1918 und am 18. Sept. 1918 in diesem Zusammenhang aus: ‚Die Bourgeoisie tötet einzelne Individuen, wir aber bringen ganze Klassen um.' ‚Von den Millionen Einwohnern Rußlands müssen wir 90 Millionen für uns gewinnen, der Rest muß ausgerottet werden.'" In der Hoffnung, daß sich Kriege vermeiden lassen und sich die geschilderten und zu schildernden Vorkommnisse nicht wiederholen, hätte ich es vorgezogen zu schweigen. Aber der Weg zu einer Auseinandersetzung, der auf beiden Seiten keine Gnade kennt, muß geschildert werden. Im übrigen stellen Afghanistan und Polen ein Menetekel dar.

Man muß auch wissen, daß Stalin am 3. Juli 1941 einen Befehl erließ, in welchem es heißt: ,,. . . In den vom Feind besetzten Gebieten müssen Partisanenabteilungen zu Fuß und zu Pferd gebildet und Diversionsgruppen geschaffen werden zum Kampf gegen die Truppenteile des feindlichen Heeres, zur Entfachung des Partisanenkrieges und überall und allerorts zur Sprengung von Brücken und Straßen, zur Zerstörung von Telefon- und Telegrafenverbindungen, zum Niederbrennen der Wälder, der Versorgungslager und der Trains. In den okkupierten Gebieten müssen für den Feind und alle seine Helfershelfer unerträgliche Bedingungen geschaffen werden; sie müssen auf Schritt und Tritt verfolgt und vernichtet und alle ihre Maßnahmen müssen vereitelt werden. Den Krieg gegen das faschistische Deutschland darf man nicht als einen gewöhnlichen Krieg betrachten. Es ist zugleich der große Krieg des Sowjetvolkes gegen die deutschen Faschisten."

Stalins Befehl wurde – wie auch ein unmittelbar nach Beginn des Ostkriegs ergangener Aufruf Molotows – über die sowjetischen Rundfunksender und in Flugblättern verbreitet.

Am 1. Mai 1942 erließ Stalin einen Tagesbefehl, in dem er ausführt: ,,Unsere Kämpfer sind böser und erbarmungsloser geworden. In allen vom Feind besetzten Gebieten ist die Sabotage in der Kriegswirtschaft, die Sprengung deutscher Depots, die Vernichtung deutscher Transportzüge und die Tötung deutscher Soldaten und Offiziere zur täglichen Erscheinung geworden.

Ich befehle den männlichen und weiblichen Partisanen, unter dem siegreichen Banner des großen Lenin den Kampf im Rücken der Eindringlinge noch zu verstärken, die Nachrichten- und Transportmittel des Feindes zu zerstören und die Stäbe und technischen Mittel des Feindes zu vernichten."

Es ist nicht zu bestreiten, daß entsprechend den Aufrufen Partisaneneinheiten entstanden, die aus den sogenannten Zerstörungs-(Istrebitelnyj-)-Kommandos gebildet wurden. Diese zerstörten von Anfang an systematisch öffentliche Betriebe, Elektrizitäts- und Wasserwerke, Fabriken, Eisenbahnanlagen, Wohnhäuser, Bürogebäude, Kirchen, Brücken und Nachrichtenanlagen. Mit Benzinkanistern ausgerüstete Brandkommandos zerstörten Städte und Stadtteile. Umfangreiche Sprengungen, teils durch Minen, teils durch die lange vorher in Minenkammern eingebauten Sprengladungen, verursachten schwere Verluste unter den deutschen Truppen und der Zivilbevölkerung.

Die kommunistischen Zerstörungskommandos führten beim Herannahen der deutschen Truppen ferner Massenerschießungen von Gefängnis- und Lagerinsassen und von mißliebigen Landeseinwohnern durch und waren an Verschleppungszügen beteiligt, die in der Regel auf Fußmärschen „liquidiert" wurden. Die in den Gefängnissen in Litauen, Lettland, Estland, Ostpolen, Weißrußland und der Westukraine inhaftierten politischen Häftlinge, deren Zahl in die Zehntausende ging, wurden noch in den Gefängnissen oder Lagern „liquidiert".

Josef Mackiewicz berichtet in „Katyn – Ungesühntes Verbrechen" von „ganzen Haufen von Leichen, die in den Gefängnissen entlang der Grenze gefunden wurden" und von dem „scheußlichen Gemetzel" der Sowjets an den Gefängnisinsassen.

Oberstleutnant Prawdzic-Slaki gibt einen Bericht über die Liquidierung der etwa 20 000 Insassen der Gefängnisse und Lager in Minsk und anderen Orten Weißrußlands, die am 24. Juni 1941 erfolgt ist.

Während des Vormarsches der deutschen Truppen und in Durchführung des Stalin-Befehls vom 3. Juli 1941 und auch nach bereits erfolgter deutscher Besetzung wurden z. B. in Rowno, Kiew, Charkow, Dnjepropetrowsk, Saporože, Kriwoj-Rog, Stalino, Maikop, Artemovsk, Ordžonikidzegrad, Kowno, Dünaburg, Riga, Witebsk, Smolensk, Orel u. a. vielen Orten riesige Zerstörungen durch Brandstiftungen und Sprengungen angerichtet. Erwähnenswert ist auch, daß in der Nacht zum 14. Juni 1941 auch 10 000 Esten und 35 000 Litauer verhaftet und nach dem Norden und Osten der UdSSR deportiert wurden.

Abschließend darf ich unter dem Titel „Lemberger Erlebnisse" aus dem Buche von Hermann Teske „Die silbernen Spiegel" nachstehende Beschreibung bringen: „Nach Eintreffen des neuernannten Ia der Division konnte sein Stellvertreter sich wieder seinen Transportaufgaben widmen. Seine günstige Vorwärtsstaffelung benutzte er dazu, weit vor der Truppe in Lemberg mit der dortigen Eisenbahndirektion wertvollste Unterlagen und Dokumente sicherzustellen.

Zuvor aber hatte er noch ein anderes, grausames Erlebnis, das durch seine Parallelität einen leider unbekannten, aber wesentlichen Beitrag zur Aufhellung der Morde von Katyn gibt. Als er am 30. Juni 1941 morgens in die im großen ganzen zerstörte Stadt hineinfuhr, befanden sich in ihr lediglich das national-ukrainische Freikorps ‚Nachtigall', das die wichtigsten Gebäude besetzt hatte, und auf der Zitadelle die Vorausabteilung der 1. Gebirgsdivision. SS-Einheiten oder -Kommandos – wie später behauptet worden ist – wurden nicht festgestellt. Bei der Verbindungsaufnahme mit ukrainischen Eisenbahnbeamten wurde der erste in der Stadt auftauchende rotbehoste Generalstabsoffizier aufgefordert, die in den Gefängnissen der Stadt liegenden, Tausende zählenden Leichen zu besichtigen. Auf Grund vorhandener Tagebuchaufzeichnungen können folgende Feststellungen gemacht werden: In der sogenannten ‚Alten Gendarmeriekaserne' an der spitzen Ecke der Ul. Kopernika und der Ul. Lecna Scapnieny am Fuße der Zitadelle lagen sämtliche Zellen des mehrstöckigen Gefängnisses, das zuletzt der GPU gehört hatte, voll mit mehreren aufeinandergeworfenen Schichten Leichen. Trotz des starken Verwesungsgeruches – es war ein sehr heißer Tag – konnte die Tötung, durchweg Schußwunden, noch nicht allzu lange her sein, da das Blut noch frisch war. Die Sowjettruppen hatten erst am Morgen Lemberg verlassen. Die Toten, Männer und Frauen, oft verstümmelt, waren Zivilisten. An einer Mauer im Hof lagen noch etwa zehn Leichen in großen Blutlachen. Den Gerüchten nach handelte es sich um 300–400 Personen. Ein ähnliches Bild bot sich dem widerwilligen Betrachter dieses menschlichen Unglücks in der Remiza M.K.E. in der Ul. Grodekka, nur daß dort die Leichen – gerüchteweise 1300 – in den Kellern und auf dem Hof lagen, mit Benzin übergossen waren und langsam verkohlten. Die Ausdünstung war so stark, daß die Straße gesperrt werden mußte. Nach zuverlässigen Zeugenaussagen sollen ferner in der Kantine einer Kaserne 200 Kinderleichen gelegen haben, eine davon in Kreuzesform an die Wand genagelt.

Befragungen in der Bevölkerung ergaben, daß die Ermordeten sämtlich der polnisch-ukrainischen Intelligenz Lembergs und der Umgebung angehörten, die der NKWD vor Abzug der Sowjettruppen aus der Stadt beseitigt hatte." Das Präsidium des Obersten Rates der Sowjetunion hat im September 1940 die Gründung eines Unionsvolkskommissariats angeordnet. Dieses führte die Bezeichnung „Volkskommissariat für Staatskontrolle". Zum Volkskommissar wurde durch Erlaß vom 6. Sept. 1940 der bisherige erste Stellvertreter des Volkskommissars für Verteidigung, L. S. Mechlis, ernannt. Gleichzeitig wurde Mechlis, wie es in der Vortragsnotiz des Oberkommandos des Heeres Qu IV, Generalstab des Heeres, Abteilung Fremde Heere Ost (II c) – Nr. 3472/40 geh – vom 19. September 1940 heißt, stellvertretender Vorsitzender des Rates der Volkskommissare. Eine Entbindung vom bisherigen Posten fand nicht statt.

Die Aufgabe des neuen Volkskommissariats, das große Vollmachten besaß, war eine strenge Kontrolle über die Verrechnung und Ausgabe von Staatsgeldern und von materiellen Werten sowie eine Überwachung der Durchführung von Regierungsbeschlüssen, auch in der Roten Armee und Roten Flotte. Weiter wurde dem Volkskommissariat das Recht zugestanden, allen in den Bereich der Staatskontrolle fallenden Volkskommissaria-

ten, Hauptverwaltungen, Komitees und den diesen unterstellten Unternehmungen verbindliche Anweisungen zu geben, Abrechnungen, Erklärungen
und Aufklärungen zu fordern und nötigenfalls Bestrafungen und Amtsent-
hebungen durchzuführen.

Eine rumänische Meldung stellt fest, daß 80 % der ihm unterstehenden
Kommissare Juden waren. In NS-Prozessen erwähnte ich dies, nicht zur
Verteidigung des Kommissarbefehls, sondern vielmehr als Erklärung. Zum
Ausdruck brachte ich häufig, daß ich den Kommissarbefehl und die Mas-
senerschießungen durch die Einsatzgruppen für nicht vertretbar und völ-
kerrechtswidrig halte.

Keinen Zweifel aber kann es darüber geben, daß die Partisanenbewegung eine unerhörte Rolle spielte und in Gesamteuropa ihre Zusammenhänge zu sehen sind. Kampfanweisungen förderten Partisanenkrieg. Ich
darf auf die Richtlinien für die Organisation und die Tätigkeit der Partisaneneinheiten und Diversionsgruppen vom 20. Juli 1941 in OKH/Gene-
ralstab des Heeres/O. Qu IV – Abt. Fremde Heere (II) Nr. 1600/41 vom
31. Aug. 1941 hinweisen. Zu erwähnen ist auch der Bericht der Verwaltung
politische Propaganda der Nordwestfront in Anlage zum KTB 1 Heeresgebiet Nord, 31. März–19. Okt. 1941.

Kleinste Verschwörergruppen sowie im verstärkten Umfang Partisaneneinheiten wurden aufgestellt. Bei ersteren finden wir ein Vorbild in den
Petraschewzen aus der Frühzeit der Anarchistenbewegung. Dostojewskj
gibt in seinem Roman ,,Dämonen" (besser: Die Teufel) einen Einblick in
die Arbeits- und Wirkungsmethode der Petraschewzen.

Wir übersehen heute die Belastungen, denen die Truppe ausgesetzt war.
Im Hintergrund stand das Bild des Bolschewismus, wie es die deutsche
Propaganda gezeichnet hatte. Bereits zu Beginn des Krieges gegen die Sowjetunion wurden Vorfälle gemeldet, in denen verwundete deutsche Soldaten hinter den eigenen Linien verstümmelt aufgefunden wurden. So kam es,
daß in diesem Krieg gegen einen Gegner, der aus dem Dunkeln operierte,
auch aus Unsicherheit und Nervosität härteste Maßnahmen durchgeführt
wurden. Ein Beispiel: Als eine Fahrzeugkolonne der 1. Infanteriedivision
im Waldgebiet bei Ljadi von Partisanen im Juli 1941 zusammengeschossen
worden war und wenig später der Divisionskommandeur und Stabsangehö-
rige erschossen waren, hatten sich alle über 14 Jahre alten männlichen
Personen von 20.00 Uhr bis 6.00 Uhr morgens an einem bestimmten Platz
aufzuhalten. Bei Fehlen eines der Männer war ein Familienmitglied als
Geisel festzunehmen.

Bei Vorfällen, die die Sicherheit der Truppe gefährdeten, wurde Geiselnahme befohlen. Zur Auswahl stand die russische und jüdische Bevölkerung, insbesondere aber die kommunistische zur Verfügung. Jedes uner-

laubte Umherziehen der Landeseinwohner von Ort zu Ort wurde untersagt. Bei Nichteinhaltung des Verbots wurde Erschießung anbefohlen. Diesem Befehl lag ein erbeuteter Armeebefehl des Sowjetmarschalls Timoschenko zugrunde. Der Marschall verlangte, die nachlässige deutsche Straßensicherung auszunutzen. Der Oberbefehlshaber der 6. Armee weist in seinem Befehl vom 10. Okt. 1941 darauf hin, daß die gefangenen russischen Offiziere hohnlächelnd erzählten, die Agenten der Sowjets bewegten sich unbehelligt auf den Straßen und äßen häufig in den deutschen Feldküchen mit.

Es kam so weit, daß Heufuhren und geschlossene Särge nach Waffen untersucht werden mußten. Wie ich weiß, wurde in Rußland im allgemeinen der Tote im offenen Sarg zu Grabe getragen. Die Partisanen, die im verschlossenen Sarg Waffen von Ort zu Ort transportierten, erklärten als Grund dafür, daß der Sarg geschlossen sei, in ihm befinde sich ein an einer Seuchenerkrankung Verstorbener. Der Heerespolizeichef schreibt:

,,Eine große Gefahr für die Befriedung der Gebiete bildet das Auftreten von Zigeunerbanden, deren Angehörige sich bettelnd im Lande herumtreiben und den Partisanen weitgehend Zubringerdienste leisten. Würde nur ein Teil der Verdächtigen und der Partisanenbegünstigung überführten Zigeuner bestraft, so würde der verbleibende Teil der deutschen Wehrmacht nur noch feindlicher gegenüberstehen und sich noch mehr als bisher den Partisanen zur Verfügung stellen. Es ist deshalb notwendig, derartige Banden rücksichtslos auszurotten.''

Bereits am 12. Mai 1942 hatte die Bezirkskommandantur 822 im Bereich der 281. Sicherungsdivisionen den Ortskommandanturen befohlen, Zigeuner stets wie Partisanen zu behandeln. Aufgrund dieses Befehls wurden von der Ortskommandantur Noworschew Zigeuner erschossen. Die Exekution führte die Geheime Volkspolizei 714 aus. Der zuständige kommandierende General befahl die Einschränkung des Grundsatzbefehls. Er erlaubte die Exekution, wenn eine Hilfstätigkeit zugunsten der Partisanen festgestellt wurde.

Der weite Raum im Osten bereitete der deutschen Führung große Schwierigkeiten. Das rückwärtige Heeresgebiet Mitte hatte im Oktober 1941 eine Ausdehnung von 200 000 qkm. Zur Sicherung dieses Raumes standen 3 Sicherungsdivisionen zur Verfügung. Es handelt sich um die neu aufgestellten, aus älterem Personal bestehenden Infanteriedivisionen 707 und 339 mit je zwei Infanterieregimentern und einer SS-Brigade. Allein die Infanteridivision 707 mit ihren Regimentern und einer Nachschubkompanie hatte ein Gebiet von fast 50 000 qkm zu sichern. Die gleiche Schwierigkeit hatte die 9. Armee, deren Hinterland rund 10 000 qkm mit ungefähr

1500 Dörfern und Kolchosen umfaßte. Abgesehen von dem Personal der rückwärtigen Stäbe standen der Armee nur 16 Kompanien mit je 80–90 Soldaten für die Überwachungsaufgaben zur Verfügung. Die Sowjetregierung leitete am 19. Juli 1941 der Reichsregierung eine Note zu, in der sie erklärte, die Bestimmungen der Haager Landgerichtsordnung, das Genfer Protokoll, das Verbot des Gaskrieges und die Genfer Konvention über die Behandlung der Kriegsgefangenen zu beachten, soweit sich die deutsche Seite an diese Bestimmungen halte. Festzustellen ist jedoch, daß die Anlage der sowjetischen Kriegführung gegen die Haager Landkriegsordnung verstieß.

Am 13. September 1941 klärte ein Erlaß des Oberbefehlshabers des Heeres die Rechtslage: ,,Russische Truppen und Gruppen, die nach Erlöschen der eigentlichen Kämpfe aus Verstecken hervorkommen, sich erneut zusammenschließen, zu den Waffen greifen und gegen unsere rückwärtigen Verbindungen zusammenhanglos auf eigene Faust kämpfen, sind als Freischärler anzusehen. Es ist Sache der Truppenkommandeure bzw. Befehlshaber, im Einzelfall nach der taktischen Lage die Entscheidung zu treffen." (OKH General zur besonderen Verwendung bei Oberbefehlshaber des Heeres, Az: 454 Gruppe RWES. Nr. 1678/41, geh. vom 13. Sept. 1941). Diese Weisung war nicht glücklich. Die sowjetischen Soldaten konnten von Furcht bewogen sein, daß sie nach Gefangennahne nach und nach erschossen würden. Darauf wies die sowjetische Propaganda hin. Zu berücksichtigen ist das offensichtliche Hungersterben der Kriegsgefangenen in den Dulags (Durchgangslager).

Es ist daher verständlich, daß viele russische Soldaten versuchten, unbemerkt unterzutauchen und den Weg in die Geborgenheit der Wälder zu beschreiten. Ich glaube, daß die kaum glaubliche schlechte Behandlung der Kriegsgefangenen durch das deutsche Heer im Osten noch bedeutsamer ist als das völkerrechtswidrige Vorgehen gegen die Juden.

Der Leser wird überrascht sein, wenn er erfährt, daß bereits 1942 von den Sowjetbotschaften in den Hauptstädten der mit dem Sowjetstaat verbündeten Länder Berichte über das Wirken der Partisanen herausgegeben wurden.

Im Herbst 1941 erkannten deutsche Truppenführer die steigende Partisanengefahr. An der Eisenbahnstrecke Fastow – Smela – Aleksandria – Krementschug – Dnjepropetrowsk fanden zahlreiche Gleissprengungen statt. Der Befehlshaber des rückwärtigen Heeresgebietes Süd befahl daher in den an der Strecke gelegenen Ortschaften die Stellung von Geiseln und die Festnahme aller nichtortsansässigen Personen. Ein bis 2 km breiter Streifen beiderseits der Eisenbahnstrecke war zu räumen. Die gestellten Geiseln sollten bei Fortdauer der Sprengungen aufgehängt werden.

Im Militärarchiv in Freiburg befinden sich Berichte der 444. Sicherungs-division, die im Sumpfgebiet des unteren Dnjepr bei Nikopol eingesetzt war. Am 8. Oktober 1941 erhielt die Division vom Armeeoberkommando 11 den Befehl, das Gebiet von Partisanen zu säubern. 2500 deutsche Solda-ten umstellten die Sumpfinsel. Ein Junge von 13 Jahren schlich sich durch die deutschen Posten und berichtete von dem bevorstehenden deutschen Angriff. Ein Funkspruch der Roten Armee wies die Partisanengruppe an, in kleineren Gruppen den Durchbruch zu wagen. Eine solche Gruppe war mit Maschinengewehren, 2000 Handgranaten, Handfeuerwaffen und großen Mengen von Tol-Sprengstoff ausgerüstet. Kommandeur war Major Sacha-row. Dieser vereinigte sich dann später mit anderen Partisanengruppen aus Nikopol und Kriwoj Rog. Der Stabschef der Südarmee leitete sie weiträu-mig. Er schuf immer neue Schwerpunkte. Nikopol ist Mittelpunkt des Mangan-Erzgebietes.

Der Leitende Feldpolizeidirektor bei der Sicherungsdivision 444 gibt in seiner Meldung vom 5. Nov. 1941 (Tagebuch Nr. 623/41 g) den Einsatzbe-richt der Geheimen Feldpolizei vom 9.–21. Okt. 1941 weiter, aus dem hervorgeht, daß im rückwärtigen Heeresgebiet 1025 Partisanen getötet wurden. Aus seinem Bericht vom 20. Juni–16. Sept. 1941 geht hervor, daß vom Beginn des Barbarossa-Feldzuges bis zu dem eben genannten Zeit-punkt 467 Eisenbahnbrücken zerstört und an 250 Stellen die Schienen unterbrochen wurden.

Als Gesamtbild für das Jahr 1941 ist festzuhalten: Die Partisanenbatail-lone hatten eine Stärke von 80–150 Mann. Sie waren im Besitz von Maschi-nengewehren, Gewehren und Handgranaten. Ihre Aufgabe bestand in der Durchführung von bewaffneten Überfällen und der Zerstörung von militä-rischen Objekten. Bei bodenständigen Partisanengruppen, deren Stärke ei-ner Kolchose entsprach, bildeten meistens die Jungkommunisten den Kern. Sie verfügten über Handfeuerwaffen. Bekannt ist das Partisanengewehr, das infolge des verkürzten Laufes leicht unter der Jacke verborgen werden konnte. Partisanengruppen hatten auch Spezialaufträge auszuführen. Für Einzelgänger kam auch die Organisierung von Partisanengruppen oder die Ausführung von Sabotageakten in Frage.

Den planmäßigen Aufbau beweist die Tatsache, daß im September 1941 in fast allen Städten des frontnahen sowjetischen Hinterlandes Partisanen-schulen bestanden. Sowjetische Angaben besagen, daß während der Mona-te August und September 1298 Personen für den Partisanenkampf ausge-bildet und in die besetzten Gebiete eingeschleust wurden.

Als wichtigster Grundsatz wurde bei den Partisanen gelehrt: Zerstreuung nach der Aktion und Zusammentreffen in einer Entfernung von einigen Kilometern. Grausam klingen die Worte, daß alle Zeugen des

Überfalls, gleichgültig ob Mann, Frau oder Kinder, getötet werden sollten. Daß der Partisanenkrieg einer Planung und nicht einer Notlösung entsprach, zeigt ein Bericht der 32. Infanteriedivision, Abt. I c/Ia, Nr. 282/41 g vom 13. Nov. 1941. Es handelt sich um einen Vernehmungsbericht, in dem ausgeführt wird, daß im Juli 1941 bereits eine Kontoristin als Kontaktperson ausgebildet wurde. Sinja Tjeljez – so ihr Name – wurde einer Gruppe zugeführt, die die Aufgabe hatte, Passierscheine zu organisieren. Auch die Frauen und Kinder hatten ihre Aufgabe.

Während der Zeit vom 27. Juni bis 5. August 1941 wurden 624 Jugendliche zur Organisierung von Konsomolzellen in das von den Deutschen besetzte Gebiet gesandt. Die Konsomols handelten kühn. Aus einem Bericht ist zu entnehmen: ,,Drei begannen zu singen und zu tanzen. Die Soldaten (Italiener) blieben stehen, um zuzuschauen. Als eine große Gruppe von Soldaten zusammengekommen war, schossen die Jungen plötzlich . . . und schleuderten mehrere Handgranaten. 9 Soldaten und 1 Offizier wurden getötet." Über die Zusammenarbeit von Kindern mit Einheiten der Roten Armee berichtet Hesse in seiner Arbeit über den Partisanenkrieg in zutreffender Weise. Er schreibt auf Seite 112: ,,Von besonderer Hilfe sind die Kinder als Kundschafter. Eine Gruppe Jungen und Mädchen, die von einem Jungen mit Namen Wladimir Mironow geführt wurden, halfen bei mehreren Gelegenheiten den Einheiten der regulären Armee, feindliche Kräftekonzentrationen zu zerschlagen. Bei einer Gelegenheit entdeckten der 13jährige Eugen Zelinskij und sein Freund Paul Tropko den Aufenthalt deutscher Truppen und belieferten den Kommandeur eines sowjetischen Panzerzuges mit den notwendigen Informationen. Der Panzerzug verlor keine Zeit, griff an und zerschlug die feindliche Konzentration."

Wie den Einsatz der Kinder rühmen sowjetische Kriegsberichte auch die von patriotischem Geist getragene Einsatzbereitschaft von Frauen. Sie standen als Kämpferinnen in den Reihen der Partisanengruppen, waren als Kundschafterinnen tätig, besorgten Nahrungsmittel für die Partisanen und betreuten die Verwundeten. Nach sowjetrussischen Meldungen existierten während des Krieges Partisanengruppen, die ganz aus Frauen bestanden. Nicht selten bewiesen diese Frauen während der Kampfaktionen außergewöhnliche Tapferkeit und Kaltblütigkeit. Ein sowjetischer Bericht aus der Entstehungszeit der Partisanenbewegung weiß von diesen Einsätzen unter Führung oder unter Beteiligung von Frauen zu berichten: ,,Manchmal sind in diesem Kriege die Frauen die Führer von Männern. Eine Partisanengruppe wird von Maria D. geführt, die Vorstandsmitglied der Kolchose ,,Krasnij Pahar" ist. Diese Gruppe füllte viele Brunnen mit Erde, zerstörte wichtige Brücken und zerschnitt Telephondrähte. Einmal gelang es ihnen, vier deutsche Kraftradmelder zu fangen. Von ihnen erfuhren sie, daß eine Fahrzeugkolonne mit Ersatzteilen für Panzer in der Nacht vorbeikommen sollte. Die Gruppe legte sich in den Hinterhalt. Am frühen Morgen wurde die Fahrzeugkolonne auf einer engen Waldstraße überfallen. Acht Fahrzeuge wurden zerstört, die Ersatzteile wurden in den Sumpf geworfen.“

Mehrere Frauen erhielten für die während der Partisanenunternehmungen bewiesene Tapferkeit von höchster sowjetrussischer Regierungsstelle Auszeichnungen und Belobigung.

Hesse weist auf I. Krawtschenko hin, der für Weißrußland bei einer Partisanenzahl von 370 000 Kämpfern einen Anteil von 16 % Frauen annimmt. Krawtschenko schreibt: ,,Unter denen, die vom Präsidium des Obersten Sowjet für hervorragende Verdienste im Partisanenkampf ausgezeichnet wurden, ist ein Mädchen (Mitglied des Konsomol) mit Namen Abramowa . . .“ Aus der Schrift ,,We are Guerillas“ bringt Hesse den Hinweis: ,,Ein Fernspähtrupp der Roten Armee traf im Rücken der Deutschen kürzlich auf eine Partisaneneinheit, die ganz aus Frauen bestand, mit der einzigen Ausnahme des Kommandeurs, eines 60 Jahre alten Kolchos-Sattlers.

Deutscherseits setzte man nichts anderes als Repressalien dagegen. Die 6. Armee stellt im Dezember 1941 fest: ,,Im Armeegebiet ist das Partisanenwesen so gut wie beseitigt. Die Armee schreibt es den rigorosen Maßnahmen zu, die angewandt wurden: die Drohung, der Bevölkerung alle Lebensmittel wegzunehmen und die Dörfer zu verbrennen, wenn sie Partisanenaufenthaltsorte nicht rechtzeitig anzeigte, hatte vollen Erfolg . . . so wurden im Armeegebiet mehrere tausend öffentlich gehängt oder erschossen. Mehrere hundert in Charkow . . . Seither haben die Sabotageakte aufgehört . . .“ Nach Ansicht der Führung der 6. Armee mußte die Bevölkerung vor deutschen Maßnahmen mehr Furcht haben als vor dem Terror der Partisanen.

Das Armeeoberkommando 6, Abt. I a meldet am 7. Dez. 1941 an die Heeresgruppe Süd: ,,Als Erfahrung ist festzustellen: nur solche Maßnahmen führen zum Ziel, vor denen die Bevölkerung noch mehr Furcht hat als vor dem Terror der Partisanen.“

Die große Bedeutung der Partisanen zeigen Vorkommnisse im Raum zwischen dem Fluß Lowat und der von Dno nach Loknja führenden Eisenbahnstrecke auf. Ende November 1941 war dieser Teil des Hinterlandes der 16. Armee völlig von Partisanen beherrscht. Es entstand die Gefährdung der Strecke von Leningrad nach Newel und von Pleskau nach Staraja Russa.

Die Halbinsel Krim wurde während der Nürnberger Prozesse durch die Auseinandersetzung zwischen dem genialen Feldmarschall von Manstein und dem Chef der Einsatzgruppe D unter Führung des scharfsinnigen späteren SS-Gruppenführers Otto Ohlendorf durch die von deutscher Seite durchgeführten breiten Erschießungsmaßnahmen bekannt. Ich glaube nicht, daß damals die Ereignisse in ihrem ganzen Zusammenhang richtig gewürdigt wurden. In einem späteren Prozeß in München gegen X. und andere wurde ebenfalls die Partisanenfrage ungenügend geprüft.

Die Krim war für die Bolschewisten historischer Boden. Das Jaila-Gebirge im Süden und die Nordküste am „Faulen Meer" waren für den Partisanenkampf sehr geeignet. Die 11. Armee hatte bereits zu Beginn der Offensive gegen die Krim ihre Schwierigkeiten. Am unteren Dnjepr und der Meerenge von Perekop kam es zur Berührung mit starken Partisanengruppen. Der Raum von Tschelbasy und Aleschki mußte mehrmals durchgekämmt werden. Die Partisanen standen unter Leitung sowjetischer Beamter und Parteifunktionäre.

Im Tätigkeits- und Lagebericht der Einsatzgruppen Nr. 7 (1. bis 30. Nov. 1941) werden als Organisatoren der K.P.-Sekretär und Bürgermeister von Cherson und der Wirtschaftsdirektor dieser Stadt genannt. Frühzeitig waren auf der Krim Depots mit Munition, Lebensmitteln, lebendem Vieh und anderen Versorgungsgütern für den Partisanen-Einsatz angelegt worden. Versprengte, gut bewaffnete Soldaten der Sowjettruppen einschließlich von Partisanen und Offizieren waren in die illegalen Verbände aufgenommen worden.

AOK 11 I c/AO, Nr. 2392/41 geh. vom 26. Nov. 1941 berichtet, daß 33 Vernichtungsbataillone mit je 200–220 Mann gut ausgerüstet bereitstanden. Kommandeur der Partisaneneinheiten der Krim war Oberstleutnant Makrouson. Aus den Tätigkeitsberichten der Einsatzgruppe Nr. 10 vom 1.– 28. Febr. 1942 und Nr. 8 vom 1.–31. Dez. 1941 geht hervor, daß die Straße von Jalta über Aluschka nach Simferopol von Partisanen bedroht wurde. Es kam so weit, daß der Verkehr nur im Geleitsystem durchgeführt werden konnte. Die im Jailagebirge liegenden Partisanengruppen wurden auf 10 000 Mann geschätzt.

Von Manstein bildete einen Stab für die Partisanenbekämpfung. In diesem Zusammenhang sind zu nennen: der I a der Armee, Oberst Stephanus, der I c, Major Riesen, und der Oberquartiermeister, Oberst Hauck. Die 11. Armee ging von dem Grundsatz aus: „Die Bevölkerung muß mehr Angst vor unseren Vergeltungsmaßnahmen haben." Unterstützung der Partisanen wie auch das Nachgeben gegenüber gewaltsamen Forderungen wurden mit Geiselerschießungen und dem Niederbrennen von Ortschaften bestraft.

Am geglückten Landungsmanöver zwischen Eupatoria und Šarki wirkten Partisanengruppen mit einer Gesamtstärke von 900 Mann mit. Die Landungstruppen wurden mit 3 U-Boot-Jägern und 200 Fischkuttern an Land gesetzt. Eupatoria fiel in 30 Minuten. Angriffspläne wiesen auf die Mitwirkung der Zivilbevölkerung hin, die die Wiedereroberung der Stadt durch die Rote Armee in einem Freudentaumel feierte. Acht Tage später war Eupatoria wieder in deutscher Hand. Das Armeeoberkommando hielt eine Sühnemaßnahme für erforderlich. Ich stand in Eupatoria vor der Mahntafel. Die Zahl der russischen Opfer wurde ungefähr verzehnfacht. Erschossen wurden über 1300 Personen. Eine Tragödie spielte sich ab. Der Einspruch gegen die Sühnemaßnahme kam zu spät.

(vgl. Ortskommandatur I (V) 227, Dienststelle Feldpostnummer 45876, an Korrück 553 vom 11. Dez. 1941 – Nachtrag)

1942 waren dann die Krimtataren im Jailagebirge südlich Simferopol und in der Nähe der Straße Simferopol – Bachtschisarai konzentriert. Einen Einblick über die Vorkommnisse dürfte ein Bericht über die Erschießungen im Bereich der 11. Armee vom 22. Juni 1941 bis August 1942 im Auszug gewähren, den ich vor Jahren Stellen der Justiz und der Kirche vorlegte.

Noch härterer Partisanenkrieg

Der Winter 1941/42 brachte der deutschen Ostfront eine unerhörte Krise. Widerstand und Kampfgeist der deutschen Soldaten werden in der Geschichte des deutschen Heeres nie vergessen werden. Furchtbar waren die Verluste. Im Kriegstagebuch Halders werden diese am 25. März 42 auf 1 073 000 Mann geschätzt. Aber auch die Partisanengruppen litten in den Wäldern unter Kälte, Schnee, Nahrungsmittelmangel und ertrugen unsagbare Entbehrungen. Sie hielten durch. In dieser Zeit gelang es der Moskauer Zentrale, Führungskräfte und Tausende von Partisanen in die befohlenen Konzentrationsgebiete zu senden. Die Partisanengruppen gewannen an Durchschlagskraft.

Es rächte sich, daß deutsche Abschreckungsmaßnahmen russische Menschen zu den Partisanen in die Wälder trieben. Die Landeseinwohner halfen durch Nahrungsmittelbeschaffung. Überfälle auf Kolchosen, die diesem Zweck dienten, wurden mit ihrer Hilfe ausgeführt. Aber bei solchen Aktionen blieb es nicht. Kriegsgefangenenlager wurden angegriffen. Wenn Streit in seinem Buch die totalen Maßnahmen kritisiert, so muß gesagt werden, daß in dem weiten Raum des Ostens Ausbrüche von Kriegsgefangenen für das Hinterland eine ungeheure Gefahr bedeuteten. Die kritische Frontlage brachte eine weitgehende Entblößung des Landes von Sicherheitskräften. Dies bot den Partisanen Gelegenheit zu Angriffen, durch die deutsche Garnisonen und Gendarmerieposten in dauernder Spannung gehalten wurden. Der deutsche Soldat fühlte sich immer verlorener in dem weiten, fremden Land.

Im Oktober/November 1941 waren mit Hilfe der 31. russischen Armee 29 Partisanenabteilungen in einer Stärke von 1700 Mann aufgestellt. Sie wurden in die Nahtstellen der Heeresgruppen Nord und Mitte eingeschleust. Ihr Wirken während der sowjetischen Winteroffensive war nicht unbedeutend. Sie trugen dazu bei, daß der Rückzug der 9. deutschen Armee und der 3. Panzerarmee sich nach dem Scheitern der deutschen Offensive auf Moskau außerordentlich verlustreich gestaltete.

Partisanengebiete, auch Partisanenrepubliken entstanden. Es sind drei im Raum von Smolensk und vier von Orel-Kursk zu nennen. Der Rajon Kritschew Rudolbelka wurde zu einem Zentralpunkt. Das Partisanengebiet in den Brjansker Wäldern hatte mit seinen 500 Ortschaften eine Länge von 260 und eine Breite von 50 Kilometer. Nach der Ereignismeldung Nr. 180 des Chefs der Sicherheitspolizei und des SD IV A 1 – 1 B/41 g RS vom 13. Mrz. 42 wurde ein Wehrmacht-LKW auf der Straße Roslawl-Brjansk am hellen Nachmittag überfallen und alle Soldaten erschossen. Ein OD-

Mann, der sich frei bewegen konnte, wurde als Agent der Partisanen festgestellt. Das Partisanenregiment „24. Jahrestag der Roten Arbeiter- und Bauernarmee" befand sich südlich von Wjasma und übte die Herrschaft in 16 Ortschaften aus. Minsk war ein weiterer Mittelpunkt der Partisanen, ebenso im Hinterland der 16. Armee das Gebiet von Dedawitschi.

Im Frühjahr 1942 standen auf weißrussischem Gebiet 227 Partisanenabteilungen und 19 Partisanenbrigaden.

In den Bjansker Wäldern standen 48 Partisanenabteilungen mit 9776 Partisanen, während im Leningrader Gebiet 2 Brigaden mit 2000 Mann operierten.

Nicht unterschätzt werden darf die Bedeutung der Partisanenbewegung auf das Ablieferungssoll des landwirtschaftlichen Sektors.

Der Partisanen- und Untergrundkrieg war bei Beginn des Rußlandfeldzuges bereits vorbereitet

Generaloberst Halder schrieb am 11. Aug. 1941: ,,Die allgemeine Lage zeigt immer deutlicher und klarer, daß der Koloß Rußland, dessen Vorbereitung auf den Krieg mit all den Schwierigkeiten verbunden war, die Vielvölkerstaaten eigen sind, von uns unterschätzt worden ist. Diese Feststellung erstreckt sich auf alle wirtschaftlichen und organisatorischen Gebiete, auf die Verkehrsmittel und besonders auf rein militärische Momente. Zu Beginn des Krieges standen uns etwa 200 Divisionen des Gegners gegenüber. Heute zählen wir bereits 360 gegnerische Divisionen.''

Der skeptische deutsche Generalstaabschef weist darauf hin, daß die deutschen Truppen an allen Frontabschnitten erschöpft sind. Er schreibt: ,,Das, was wir jetzt unternehmen, ist der letzte und zugleich zweifelhafte Versuch, den Übergang zum Stellungskrieg zu verhindern. Das Oberkommando verfügt nur über äußerst beschränkte Mittel. Die Heeresgruppen sind durch natürliche Grenzen (Sümpfe) voneinander getrennt. Wir haben unsere letzten Kräfte in den Kampf geworfen.''

Bereits vier Wochen vorher berichtete die Heeresgruppe Mitte dem Oberkommando über die Probleme, die dadurch gegeben waren, daß Teile der Truppen für die Bekämpfung von Partisanen freigestellt werden mußten. – Am 29. Juni 1941 stellt die Heeresgruppe Mitte fest: ,,Die Vollendung der Vernichtungskämpfe im Osten wird sich wesentlich von den Kämpfen im Westen unterscheiden. Wenn im Westen die eingeschlossenen Kräfte des Gegners mit Beendigung der Kämpfe im großen und ganzen fast freiwillig hundertprozentig in die Gefangenschaft gingen, so wird das hier vollkommen anders vor sich gehen. Ein großer Prozentsatz der Russen verbirgt sich in großen, teilweise nicht durchkämmten Gebieten, in Wäldern, auf Feldern, in Sümpfen usw. Dabei werden Bataillone mit voller Bewaffnung noch einige Zeit in solchen Gebieten durch Partisanenabteilungen gefährdet sein.''

Am 25. Juli 1941 wies das Oberkommando der Wehrmacht darauf hin, daß die Partisanen eine ernste Gefahr für die deutschen Verbindungslinien bilden würden. – Am 2. Aug. 1941 befahl General von Salmuth, der Kommandierende General des XXX. AK., auf das härteste gegen die Partisanen vorzugehen. In seinem Bereich ereigneten sich die Erschießungen von Kodyma, die vor einem deutschen Gericht Prozeßgegenstand waren. In dieses Verfahren wurde ein Protokoll eingeführt, aus dem sich ergibt, daß jüdische Sowjetbürger in einer kritischen Situation des obengenannten AK einen Aufstand planten.

Die Heeresgruppe Süd mußte am 1. Okt. 1941 die Evakuierung des Gebietes von 1–2 km Breite entlang der Bahnstrecke Kasatin–Fastow–Smela–Krementschug–Alexandrowka–Dnepropetrowsk anordnen. Bereits am 29. Juni 1941 konnte Stalin zum Partisanenkrieg auffordern. Am 18. Juli 1941 war es dem Politbüro des Zentralkomitees der Sowjetunion möglich, eine klare Richtlinie ,,Über die Organisierung des Kampfes im Rücken der deutschen Truppen" herauszubringen. Der Übergang in die illegale Tätigkeit der Kommunistischen Partei wurde geregelt. In der Nacht des 25. Juni 1941 berieten die Funktionäre der Gebietskomitees der Kommunistischen Partei der Ukraine über die Koordinierung des Partisanenkampfes. Bis Mitte Juli standen 133 Organisationsgruppen, Lehrgänge fanden statt, Sonderschulen wurden eingerichtet.

Vom Juli bis September 1941 konnten in der Ukraine 122 Partisanenabteilungen mit 5809 Personen- und Diversionsgruppen eingesetzt werden. Dabei zählten die letztgenannten Gruppen 743 Personen. Im Jahre 1941 waren 23 illegale Gebietskomitees, 63 Stadtkomitees und 564 Rayonskomitees tätig geworden.

Die Konsomols stellten 11 Partisanenabteilungen mit einer Gesamtstärke von 1500 Kämpfern auf. 7000 Mitglieder des Konsomol wurden in andere Partisaneneinheiten überführt. – Mitte August verfügte die karelische Autonome Sozialistische Republik über 15 Partisaneneinheiten mit insgesamt 1771 ,,Kampfgenossen". – Bevor die deutschen Truppen den Raum von Gomel betraten, waren dort 70 Partisanenabteilungen und 37 illegale Organisationen gebildet worden. Das Gebietskomitee bereitete sich auf die Illegalität vor. Verbindungen zwischen den Stützpunkten, Lebensmittel- und Munitionslagern bestanden. – In Mogilew waren im Juni 1941 vom Zentralkomitee der Kommunistischen Partei Weißrußlands 28 Partisanenabteilungen aufgestellt worden, die in das rückwärtige deutsche Heeresgebiet gebracht wurden. Aus Liosno wurden 29, aus Roslawl 8, aus Gomel 23 Abteilungen im Juli 1941 in den Einsatz gebracht.

Ein ähnliches Bild zeigt sich im Gebiet von Kalinin. Als die deutschen Truppen dort einrückten, konnten die Sowjets auf Partisanenabteilungen mit 1630 Bewaffneten zurückgreifen. Außerdem gab es 22 illegale Rayon- und Stadtkomitees der Partei und 24 illegale Rayonkomitees des Konsomol.

Im Jahre 1941 operierten in den Räumen von Minsk, Witebsk, Mogilew, Gomel, Polozk, Pinsk, Brest, Wilna und Baranowitschi 437 Abteilungen mit mehr als 7200 Kämpfern.

Im Smolensker Gebiet waren 2000 Kommunisten und 5000 Konsomolzen im Untergrund. Auch im Oreler Gebiet war der Untergrund- und Partisanenkrieg vorbereitet worden. Als die deutschen Truppen den Raum besetzten, gingen 46 Abteilungen mit 2300 „Genossen" in die Wälder. Kühnrich bemerkt zu Recht: „Das Brjansker Gebiet, später eines der größten Partisanenzentren, war von Anfang an Operationszentrum der Partisanen. Dort existierten bereits im September 1941 20 Partisanenabteilungen mit 2500 Kämpfern. Das Gebietskomitee der KPdSU von Kursk organisierte mehr als 30 Abteilungen. Wie sich trotz des Terrors die Partisanenbewegung ständig ausbreitete, geht aus der zahlenmäßigen Entwicklung der Partisanenbewegung im Gebiet von Smolensk hervor. – In den Gebieten von Mogilew, Gomel, Polozk und Witebsk wurden 187 Parteizellen mit etwa 1000 Kommunisten noch vor der Okkupation vorbereitet. Sie waren die Keimzellen und die leitenden Zentren für die Organisierung und Durchführung der Partisanenaktionen. – Auch auf der Krim bildete sich trotz ungünstiger Bedingungen von Kriegsbeginn an eine starke Partisanenarmee, die am 20. Nov. 1941 – nur wenige Tage nach der Okkupation dieses Gebietes – bereits 27 Abteilungen mit einer Stärke von 3 734 Mann umfaßte. Dazu kamen 200 Kommunisten und Konsomolzen, die in Ortschaften für andere Aufgaben zurückgeblieben waren."

Feldmarschall von Manstein erklärte: „Es kann keinem Zweifel unterliegen, daß auf der Krim eine weitverzweigte Partisanenorganisation bestand, die seit längerer Zeit vorbereitet worden war. Die 30 Zerstörerbataillone waren nur ein Teil dieser Organisation. Die Masse der Partisanen lag im Jailagebirge. Es muß dort gleich zu Beginn viele Tausende gegeben haben."

Im Raum von Tschernigow kamen 1941 von Juli bis Oktober 368 deutsche Soldaten und 103 Polizisten durch Untergrundkämpfer um. Drei Eisenbahnbrücken flogen in die Luft, fünf Munitionslager wurden gesprengt.

An der Nordwestfront töteten Partisanen 1941 im Juli und August 736 deutsche Soldaten; gleichzeitig vernichteten sie sechs Panzer. 16 Brücken wurden in die Luft gesprengt. Im Oktober betrugen dort die deutschen Verluste durch die illegale Kampfführung der Sowjets bereits 977 Soldaten. Zwei Lager mit Munition und Heeresgut wurden zerstört. 31 Brücken, ein Eisenbahnzug und ein Militärzug wurden vernichtet.

Im Leningrader Raum bildete sich in den ersten Tagen des Juli 1941 unter dem Sekretär des Gebietskomitees, Bumagin, eine Operationsgruppe. Bis zur Besetzung des Gebietes durch die deutschen Truppen wurden 125 illegale Partei- und 85 Konsomol-Einheiten von 5, 7 und 10 Mann aufgestellt. Im Juli/August 1941 waren 191 Partisanengruppen vorhanden, von denen jede eine Stärke von 30–50 Personen hatte.

Zwei Beratungen am 11. und 13. Juli 1941 regelten den Übergang der

145

KPdSU in die Illegalität. In den westlichen und südwestlichen Rayons waren vor Besetzung durch die deutschen Streitkräfte Partisanenstützpunkte mit Waffen, Lebensmittel- und Munitionsvorräten entstanden.

Bis September 1941 wuchs die Zahl der Partisanen auf 18 000 Mann an. Seit 27. Sept. 1941 bestand ein Leningrader Gebietsstab, der die Operationen mit den regulären sowjetischen Truppen abstimmte. Bis Ende des Jahres 1941 fielen 3610 deutsche Soldaten ihnen zum Opfer. 26 Lager und Wehrmachtsgut wurden zerstört, 43 Militärzüge zum Entgleisen gebracht, 72 Brücken gesprengt.

Erfolgreich operierten die Untergrundkämpfer auch auf dem Gebiet von Charkow und Smolensk. Bis Oktober 1941 vernichteten sie 72 LKW's, zehn Treibstoff- und Munitionslager sowie 30 Brücken.

Die Partisanen schleusten außerdem auch 30 000 russische Soldaten aus den eingekesselten sowjetischen Armeen hinter die Front der Sowjets. Als Bilanz im Belorussischen Gebiet wird vom 22. Juni 1941 bis 1. Nov. 1941 seitens der sowjetischen Seite herausgestellt: Tötung von über 87 000 deutschen Soldaten und 3800 Polizisten, Entgleisung von 830 Militärzügen, Zerstörung von 5 Panzerzügen, 4773 Kraftwagen, 178 Flugzeugen, 358 Panzern, 154 Eisenbahn- und anderen Brücken sowie 248 verschiedenen Lagern.

Mag diese Statistik auch übertrieben sein. Beträchtliche Erfolge können nicht bestritten werden.

In der sowjetischen Partisanenliteratur treten Namen wie S. A. Kowpak, A. F. Fjodorow, S. W. Rudnew, K. S. Saslonow, W. I. Koslow, A. M. Saburow, P. K. Ponomarenko in Erscheinung.

Die Etappe wurde zum Kampffeld. Die sowjetischen Militärhistoriker sehen als größte Leistung der Partisanenbewegung im Jahre 1941 die Verhinderung des Blitzkrieges Adolf Hitlers gegen die Sowjetunion an. Ihre Tätigkeit in Verbindung mit der Schlacht von Moskau wird gerühmt.

General von Stülpnagel, damals Oberbefehlshaber der 17. Armee, später bekannt geworden als Militärbefehlshaber Frankreich und Angehöriger des Kreises des 20. Juli, kam nach einer Dienstfahrt im Jahre 1941 zur Überzeugung, daß keine klare Auffassung über die deutschen Aufgaben in den besetzten Gebieten und die erforderliche Einstellung der deutschen Soldaten bestehe. Er wies darauf hin, daß der Krieg gegen die Sowjetunion eine andere Kampfesführung erfordere als die vorhergegangenen Feldzüge. Damals ließ er sich zu einem Befehl verleiten, dessen Formulierungen in der heutigen Zeit nicht vorstellbar sind. Von Stülpnagel führt aus:

„. . . Es ist uns in diesem Sommer immer klarer geworden, daß hier im Osten zwei innerlich unüberbrückbare Anschauungen gegeneinander kämpfen: deutsches Ehr- und Rassegefühl, jahrhundertealtes Soldatentum und asiatische Denkungsart und ihre, durch eine kleine Anzahl meist jüdischer Intellektueller aufgepeitschten primitiven Instinkte: Angst vor der Knute, Mißachtung sittlicher Werte, Nivellierung nach unten, Wegwerfen des eigenen wertlosen Lebens. Stärker denn je tragen wir in uns den Gedanken an eine Zeitwende, in der dem deutschen Volk kraft der Überlegenheit seiner Rasse und seiner Leistungen die Führung Europas übertragen ist. Klar erkennen wir unsere Sendung, die europäische Kultur zu retten vor dem Vordringen asiatischer Barbarei. Wir wissen jetzt, daß wir gegen einen erbitterten und zähen Gegner zu kämpfen haben. Dieser Kampf kann nur mit der Vernichtung des einen oder des anderen enden: einen Ausgleich gibt es nicht." Der Armeebefehl schließt mit den Worten: ,,. . .Rußland ist nicht ein europäischer, sondern ein asiatischer Staat. Jeder Schritt weiter in dieses freudlose, geknechtete Land lehrt diesen Unterschied. Von diesem Druck und den zerstörenden Kräften des Bolschewismus müssen Europa und insbesondere Deutschland für alle Zeit freigemacht werden."

Die deutsche Heeresleitung glaubte dem Untergrund- und Partisanenkrieg nur mit Gewalt begegnen zu können. Deshalb wandte sie falsche, zu brutale und zu breit angelegte Vernichtungsaktionen an. Diese Kampfführung mußte ohne Erfolg sein. Ebenso versagte die deutsche Propaganda, weil ihr die notwendige Vorstellung eines politischen Zukunftsbildes fehlte.

Mit Worten, die der Sender ,,Donau" am 31. Juli 1941 ausstrahlte, war es nicht getan: ,,Von der Ostfront wird berichtet, daß zahlreiche Gruppen von Sowjetsoldaten sich in den Wäldern verbergen, Raubzüge in die Nachbarschaft unternehmen und gelegentlich versuchen, die deutschen Verbindungslinien zu unterbrechen. Wenn sie bei solchen Unternehmen Waffengewalt anwenden, werden sie sofort von den deutschen Truppen gestellt und vernichtet. Wenn sie sich jedoch lediglich verstecken und die deutschen Soldaten Wichtigeres zu tun haben, wird ihnen auf andere Weise begegnet. Dann tritt der deutsche Propagandist in Aktion, und ein Russisch sprechender Offizier ruft über einen Lautsprecher: ,Eure Truppen sind geschlagen, wir werden Euch gut behandeln und Euch zu essen und zu trinken geben.' Nach einiger Zeit sind dann entfernter Balalaikaklang und die weichen Klänge russischer Volkslieder zu hören. Die brutalisierte Seele der russischen Soldaten beginnt sich zu lösen. Dann beginnt der deutsche Offizier von neuem und spricht ihnen von ihren Frauen, ihren Kindern und ihrer Ernte. Bald danach beginnen sich die ersten Schatten aus ihren Verstecken zu lösen, in denen sie bis dahin nur durch Furcht und Lügenmeldungen über die Deutschen gehalten wurden."

Plakate mit einem Inhalt wie folgt hatten wenig Erfolg: ,,Partisanen sind Deine Feinde! Sie rauben Dein Vieh und Deine Nahrung! Partisanen bedrohen Dein Leben!" ,,Wer Partisanen beherbergt, unterstützt oder ihren

Aufenthalt kennt, ohne ihn anzugeben, wird mit dem Tode bestraft." „Das Dorf, in dem Partisanen Unterstützung finden, wird abgebrannt, die Einwohner enteignet, der Starost erschossen." „Es ist Dein eigener Vorteil, wenn Du meldest! Du sicherst Dein Leben und erhältst außerdem eine hohe Belohnung an Geld und Land." „Nieder mit den Partisanen! Helft den Weg für ein freies, glückliches Leben ohne die Henkershand der Kommissare ebnen!" – All das war wirkungslos oder erreichte sogar das Gegenteil.

Die Ernährungslage und die deutschen wirtschaftlichen Maßnahmen brachten eine Stärkung der Partisanenfront. Wie wenig der Feldzug gegen die Sowjetunion wirtschaftlich vorbereitet war, zeigt folgendes Beispiel: In der im November 1941 genommenen Stadt Charkow empfahl die deutsche Besatzungsbehörde den Einwohnern, die Stadt nach Ost oder West zu verlassen, da die Nahrungsmittel fehlten. Dabei war es gleichgültig, ob sich diese in den sowjetischen Herrschaftsbereich begaben.

Den russischen Städten, die erobert wurden, fehlten überhaupt nach den planmäßigen Zerstörungen durch die Sowjetbehörden die Versorgungseinrichtungen. Der eiskalte, menschenverachtende Diktator Stalin nahm auf den Hungertod seiner Bevölkerung keinerlei Rücksicht. – Der Chef der Sicherheitspolizei und des SD meldet unter IV A–I B Nr. 1 B/41, gRs. am 16. Jan. 1942: „Die Bevölkerung ist durch die Zerstörungen der Roten Armee ohne Licht, Wasser und Gas, ein Drittel der Bevölkerung hungert." Die deutsche Besatzungsmacht schuf aber keine Abhilfe. So kamen Stalins Worte und Propagandamaßnahmen gut an. Am 24. Jahrestag der Oktoberrevolution appellierte er in der Moskauer U-Bahn-Station „Majakowski" an die große Vergangenheit des Russischen Reiches. Den Krieg Hitlers verglich er mit dem gegen Napoleon. Puschkin, Tolstoj, Gorki, Tschechow, Pawlow, Suworow und Kutosow wurden herausgestellt.

Stalin proklamierte: „Die deutschen Eindringlinge wollen den Vernichtungskrieg gegen die Völker der Sowjetunion. Nun gut! Wenn sie einen Vernichtungskrieg wollen, werden sie ihn haben. Unsere Aufgabe wird es jetzt sein, bis zum letzten Mann alle Deutschen zu vernichten, die gekommen sind, unser Land zu besetzen. Kein Erbarmen mit den deutschen Eindringlingen! Tod den deutschen Eindringlingen!"

Der Anteil der Partisanen an den sowjetischen Erfolgen

Schlacht vor Moskau

Bereits in der Schlacht vor Moskau im Jahre 1941 zeigte sich das Zusammenwirken zwischen Partisanenverbänden und der Roten Armee. Am 4. Nov. 1941 wurde eine Gruppe von Partisanen des Snamensker Rajons beauftragt, die Eisenbahnbrücke an der Station Ugra zu zerstören, die an der für den deutschen Nachschub wichtigen Strecke Wjasma-Brjansk lag. Die Aktion war von Erfolg gekrönt.

An den Ausweichstellen Godunowka-Ugra sprengte eine andere Snamensker Partisanentruppe einen deutschen Militärtransport in die Luft. 300 deutsche Soldaten wurden getötet. – Aus der Partisanengruppe ,,Tod dem Faschismus" zerstörten Einheitsangehörige an 15. Dez. 1941 an der Strecke Ugra-Wjasma zwei Militärzüge, wobei 20 Waggons vernichtet und ungefähr 200 Deutsche getötet wurden. Eine andere Partisanengruppe hatte am 13. Dezember einen ähnlichen Erfolg.

Hinter der deutschen Linie des Moskauer Frontgebietes operierten 41 Partisanenabteilungen und 337 andere Gruppen mit 10 000–15 000 Kämpfern. Von ihnen wurden nach N. I. Schagatin/I. P. Prussanow ,,Die Sowjetarmee – Armee neuen Typs" (Berlin 1959) 18 000 deutsche Soldaten getötet, sechs Flugzeuge, 222 Panzer und Panzerspähwagen, 102 Geschütze außer Gefecht gesetzt, rund 1000 LKW's, 742 Eisenbahnwaggons und 29 Verpflegungs- und Munitionslager zerstört.

Das Fehlschlagen der Operationen vor Moskau, für die insbesondere die Nachrichten Dr. Sorges aus Tokio an die kommunistische Zentrale von Bedeutung waren, hatte zur Folge, daß Hitlers nächste Offensive sich auf den Südabschnitt der Ostfront beschränken mußte.

Die Stalingrad-Operationen der Partisanenbewegung konnten 1942 mit den Bewegungen der Roten Armee auf das genaueste abgestimmt werden. In der Verordnung über die Funktion und die Tätigkeit des zentralen Stabes wurde festgelegt, daß er im Einklang mit den Anordnungen des staatlichen Verteidigungskomitees zu Fragen der Partisanenbewegung den Befehlen des Volkskommissars für Verteidigung und den Beschlüssen des Zentralkomitees der KPdSU im engsten Einvernehmen mit der Partei, den Stellen von Armee und Staat zu arbeiten habe.

Im August/September 1942 fand in Moskau eine wichtige Konferenz mit den Kommandeuren der großen Partisanenverbände statt. Die Bildung von

149

Partisaneneinheiten in Ortschaften, Maßnahmen gegen die feindlichen Verbindungslinien und den feindlichen Nachschub wurden festgelegt. Eigentliche Agitationsgesichtspunkte wurden geprüft und herausgestellt. Im September/November 1942 schickte das Zentralkomitee der Kommunistischen Partei in der Ukraine 23 Organisationsgruppen in den Raum von Saporože, Kirowgrad, Odessa, Nikolajew, Lemberg usw.

Der Deckname für die Offensive Stalingrad–Kaukasus hieß ,,Operation Blau". Über deren Planung und Durchführung wurde Moskau von deutscher Seite von Anfang an auf dem laufenden gehalten.

Die ursprüngliche Konzeption sah den Einsatz von Verbänden der Heeresgruppe A unter Feldmarschall List mit der 17. und der 1. Panzerarmee sowie der 4. Armee und der 6. Armee unter Feldmarschall von Bock vor. Die Heeresgruppe B sollte in breiter Front nach Osten zur Wolga vorstoßen. Nach Ausschaltung der Rüstungsindustrie im Raum von Stalingrad durch Luftwaffe und Artillerie sowie der Unterbrechung der wichtigsten Transportmöglichkeiten über die Wolga hatten die beiden Heeresgruppen nach Süden zu schwenken und das Erdölgebiet im Kaukasus zu erobern.

Beim deutschen Oberkommando gingen Berichte ein, daß angeblich wenig verläßliche Sowjet-Divisionen gegenüberständen. Auch der Schiffsverkehr auf der Wolga steigerte sich nicht. Überdies wurde dem OKW berichtet, daß die Verteidigungsstellungen nur provisorisch ausgebaut seien und in der Steppe Arbeitsbataillone in Eile Panzersperren errichteten. Daraus zog Hitler den Schluß, daß die Rote Armee in Stalingrad kaum ernstlichen Widerstand leisten könnte. Er änderte die Planung und befahl die möglichst rasche Einnahme der nach Stalin benannten Stadt. Den Rückzug der Roten Armee sah Hitler unter dem Gesichtspunkt der Desorganisierung an, während es sich um einen befohlenen, geordneten, planmäßigen Rückzug handelte.

Hitler befahl den Heeresgruppen das Vorgehen in zwei verschiedenen Richtungen: Heeresgruppe B durch die Steppe nach Stalingrad, Heeresgruppe A in Richtung Kaukasus.

Verzögerungen traten ein, die die russische Verteidigungskraft stärkten. Meldungen wurden mißachtet, nach denen die Russen über eine Million frischer Soldaten hinter der Wolga versammelten.

Am 13. Juli hatte Stalin befohlen, die sowjetischen Truppen bis zur Wolga zurückzunehmen.

Stalingrad, eine Stadt, die große historische Bedeutung hat, war in Verteidigungsbereitschaft zu setzen. Von hier hatten 1237 die Mongolen ihren Eroberungszug nach Westen begonnen, der sie bis vor Krakau und nach Schlesien führte. Dieser Ort – jetzt Wolgograd – war von der Natur her ein Zentralpunkt für den Handel und ein Einfallstor nach Asien.

1670 herrschte in der Stadt des gelben Wassers, „Sarisu", der berühmte Kosakenführer Stenka Rasin. In der Zeit des Aufstandes gegen die Zarin Katharina die Große erstürmte Jemeljan Pugatschew die Stadt.

Im Raum von Zarizyn und südlich davon vor dem Kaukasus erfüllte sich auch das Schicksal weißrussischer Truppen, die von zwei Generälen geführt waren und gegen den Bolschewismus kämpften.

Am 23. August 1942 gegen Mitternacht erreichten deutsche Truppen (16. Panzerdivision) die Vororte von Stalingrad.

Sie hatten die 3. Infanteridivision mot) und die 20. Infanteridivision (mot) weit hinter sich gelassen. Die Falle beginnt sich zu schließen.

Craig berichtet: „Nördlich des Don setzten die Russen ihren Aufmarsch fort. Die Truppenbewegungen gingen nachts vor sich. Aus Moskau und dem Ural trafen in langen Eisenbahnzügen über 200 000 Soldaten ein. Schwere Artillerie, Hunderte von Panzern, fast 10 000 Kavalleripferde wurden mit Plattformwagen auf der eingleisigen Bahnstrecke transportiert, die zu den Sammelpunkten Serafimowitsch und Kletskaja 160 bis 200 km nordwestlich von Stalingrad führte. Die Politoffiziere der Sowjets waren unermüdlich an der Arbeit, um bei den Truppen den richtigen Kampfgeist zu wekken. Jeder neue Soldat erhielt im Rahmen einer Feier seine Waffe vor der Fahne seines Regiments überreicht. Es wurden Kriegslieder gesungen; Parteifunktionäre hielten Ansprachen, in denen von der Erfüllung der Vaterlandspflicht durch jeden einzelnen die Rede war.

Die meisten Soldaten waren so beeindruckt von diesen Feierstunden, daß sie tatsächlich ‚moralisch bis an die Zähne bewaffnet‘ zu ihren Einheiten zurückkehrten. Bei einem derart massiven Aufmarsch konnte es nicht ausbleiben, daß die Deutschen Wind von diesen Vorgängen bekamen. Russische Überläufer berichteten zum Erstaunen der Offiziere, die sie verhörten, daß nicht nur am Don Divisionen und Armeen einträfen, sondern auch südlich von Stalingrad vor der 4. Panzer-Armee im Raum Beketowka und Zaza-See. Nachrichtenoffiziere wie Karl Ostarhild stellten diese Angaben zusammen, untermauerten sie durch eigene Beobachtungen und abgehörte Funksprüche und kamen zu dem eindeutigen Schluß, daß ein Angriff des Feindes auf beide Flanken bevorstehe." In seinem Buch „Der Partisanenkrieg von 1941–1945" schreibt Kühnrich auf Seite 140/41: „Auf der Konferenz der Kommandeure der Partisaneneinheiten im September 1942 erhielten Saburow und Kowpak die Aufgabe, mit ihren Einheiten einen Streifzug über den Dnepr zu unternehmen. Sie sollten die hinter dem Dnepr gelegenen Gruppierungen des Gegners, seine Verbindungs- und Nachschubwege, Flugplätze, Depots, Befestigungsanlagen und die Lage der faschistischen Dienststellen und Behörden sowie den Grad der Ausplünderung des Landes erkunden. Diese Ermittlungen waren für die Vorbereitung der sowjetischen Offensiven notwendig. Die konkrete Aufgabe für den Streifzug war am 5. September 1942 vom Oberkommando der Roten Armee gegeben und vom Zentralen Stab der Partisanenbewegung am 16. September 1942 befohlen worden.

In diesem Befehl hieß es:

1. Die vereinigte Partisanenabteilung Sabanin (Pseudonym für Saburow – H. K.) geht im Zusammenwirken mit den Abteilungen Kowaljas (Pseudonym für Kolpak) in die Rayons Kasimirowska, Weledniki und Owrutsch mit der Aufgabe der Diversion gegen die Eisenbahnlinien
a) Korosten – Berditschew,
b) Korosten – Kiew,
c) Owrutsch – Tschernigow und gegen die Straßen
d) Owrutsch – Žitomir,
e) Korosten – Kiew,
f) Owrutsch – Tschernigow.

2. Vorbereitung von Landeplätzen für Flugzeuge in den Rayons Owrutsch, Slowetschno oder an anderen für die Abteilung günstigen Punkten.

3. Herstellung der Verbindung zu den Abteilungen, die in den während des Marsches zu überquerenden Gegenden operieren, besonders zur Abteilung Fjodorows.

Außerdem waren Stützpunkte und Reserven in den Dörfern zu schaffen, neue Partisanen zu gewinnen, ein Nachrichtensystem und ein Kundschafternetz in den Dörfern bis hinein nach Kiew aufzubauen, aber weiterhin auch solche Aufgaben zu lösen, wie die Vernichtung von Kraftwerken, Lagern, Flugplätzen, Reparaturwerkstätten, der Militärtechnik und lebenden Kraft des Feindes sowie seiner Verbindungs- und Nachschubmittel.

Kolpak schrieb in seinen Aufzeichnungen über das Ziel dieses Streifzuges: ‚Wir hatten Anweisung erhalten, auf Žitomir und Kiew vorzustoßen; das rechtsseitige Dneprgebiet mit seinem verzweigten Eisenbahn- und Straßennetz und seinen zahlreichen Flußübergängen war im Augenblick von erstrangiger strategischer Bedeutung. Unsere Aufgabe bestand in der Diversionstätigkeit auf den wichtigen Nachschubstraßen zur Wolga und zum Kaukasus, wo gerade entscheidende Kämpfe stattfanden. Gleichzeitig sollten wir feststellen, welche Befestigungen von den Okkupanten auf dem rechten Dnepr-Ufer angelegt worden waren. Man rechnete damit, daß dieses Ufer sehr bald der Schauplatz erbitterter Kämpfe werden würde.‘‘

Auf Seite 142/143 schreibt er: ,,Der Verband Saburows hatte einen 500-Kilometer-Marsch durch Wälder und waldlose Gebiete der Ukraine vor sich. Der Marsch, der am 26. Oktober 1942 mit 1620 Partisanen begann, wurde gründlich vorbereitet. Am 11. September hatten die Kommandeure, Kommissare und Sekretäre der Parteiorganisationen des Verbandes die vor ihnen stehenden Aufgaben beraten. Vier Tage später befahl Woroschilow die Rückziehung des Saburow-Verbandes aus dem Kampf und den Übergang des Verbandes zum Streifzug. Es blieben nur wenige Wochen, um alle sich aus der Veränderung der Kampfbedingungen ergebenden Fragen der Umorganisierung des Verbandes, der Ausbildung für die besonderen Bedingungen eines langen Marsches, der Sicherung, Geheimhaltung und nicht zuletzt der Bewaffnung zu lösen. Flugzeuge brachten Waffen und Ausrüstungen, darunter auch Geschütze.

Der Weg des Verbandes war hart und mußte unter ständigen Gefechten zurückgelegt werden. Auf dem Marsch wurden Garnisonen und Stützpunkte des Gegners vernichtet, Transporte überfallen, Brücken zerstört, Eisenbahnlinien unterbrochen. Am 26. November war der vorgesehene Raum nach 30 Tagen Marsch unter Überquerung von acht Eisenbahnlinien und acht Hauptstraßen sowie solcher Flüsse wie des Dnepr, der Desna, des Snow und des Pripjet erreicht. 67 Kampfhandlungen wurden dabei durchgeführt, wobei sechs Rayonzentren eingenommen und die dortigen Garnisonen des Gegners zerschlagen wurden . . . Die gegnerische Etappe kam durch diese Streifzüge der Partisanen völlig durcheinander, was sich auf die gesamte Kriegführung auswirken mußte. In den folgenden Jahren wurden noch größere Streifzüge unternommen. Es war augenscheinlich, daß die Partisanenbewegung zu einem festen Bestandteil des Plans zur Zerschlagung der faschistischen Truppen, zu einem strategischen Faktor des sowjetischen Oberkommandos und zur ‚zweiten Front‘ in der UdSSR geworden war."

Zutreffend sind die Bemerkungen Kühnrichs an anderer Stelle seines Buches: „Für die Ergänzung der Hitlerarmeen mit Menschen und Material sowie für ihre ständige Versorgung waren die Nachschublinien die Achillesferse der faschistischen Operation geworden. Pausenlos fuhren Züge und Transportkolonnen mit Soldaten, Waffen, Munition, Verpflegung und Treibstoff an die Front. Es war deshalb keinesfalls Zufall, daß sich im Sommer und Herbst 1942 die Schläge der Partisanenabteilungen hauptsächlich gegen die Verbindungslinien des Gegners richteten. ‚Ihr Kampf zwang die deutsche Führung, etwa 350 000 Mann zum Schutz der Verbindungslinien und zur Bekämpfung der Partisanenabteilungen einzusetzen.‘ Wenn wir in Betracht ziehen, daß die zur Einnahme von Stalingrad eingesetzten Truppen etwa die gleiche Stärke hatten, wird klar, in welchem Ausmaß die Partisanenaktionen die Hitlersche Kriegführung störten und welche Unterstützung des Verteidigungskampfes der Roten Armee sie bedeuten . . . Die Erhöhung der Schlagkraft und Aktivität der sowjetischen Partisanen in dieser Zeit war eine nicht unwesentliche Unterstützung für die Kämpfe an der Wolga. Es läßt sich nur schwer schätzen, welche unmittelbaren Auswirkungen es hatte, wenn beispielsweise die belorussischen Partisanen ihre Aktivität so steigerten, daß sie gegenüber dem 1. Halbjahr 1942 mit monatlich 20 in die Luft gesprengten Militärzügen der Faschisten im zweiten Halbjahr bereits 150 bis 160 Züge monatlich vernichteten. Die für die Schlacht an der Wolga so entscheidende Nachschubstrecke Brest–Gomel wurde in der Nacht zum 3. November 1942 dadurch lahmgelegt, daß die 137 Meter lange Eisenbahnbrücke über den Ptitsch gesprengt und dadurch für 18 Tage der Verkehr gestoppt wurde."

Kursk

Über die „Operation Zitadelle", den Angriff auf den Frontbogen bei Kursk, ist schon viel geschrieben worden. Am 5. Juli 1943 traten deutsche Divisionen – nach mehrfachem Verschieben des Angriffszeitpunktes – zur letzten großen Angriffsoperation im Osten an. Hitler wollte einerseits eine starke Ausgangsposition für Operationen nach dem Osten wie auch eine starke Position gegen sowjetische Vorstöße nach Westen und Südwesten schaffen. Er befürchtete auch eine Landung in Griechenland.

Um den deutschen Aufmarsch für die Operation „Zitadelle" zu stören, erfolgten am 21. März 1943 nahe der zweispurigen Eisenbahnbrücke bei Wygonitschi über die Desna auf der Strecke Bojansk–Gomel, die stark bewacht wurde, Sprengungen größeren Ausmaßes. Weitere Sprengungen fanden auf der Strecke Smolensk–Brjansk und bei Kritschew statt. Am 1. Mai 1943 wurde die Südbrücke bei Kiew gesprengt. Für den deutschen Aufmarsch zur Offensive waren besonders die Zerstörungen der Bahnhöfe und Nachrichtenverbindungen von Bedeutung.

In seinen Ausführungen zur Partisanenlage schreibt Dr. Ernst Klink in Verbindung mit der Schlacht von Kursk, durch die Hitler die Initiative in der Sowjetunion zurückzugewinnen versuchte.

„. . . wurde den Heeresgruppen befohlen, bis zum 5. Mai ihre Absichten auf dem Gebiete der Bandenbekämpfung für die nächsten Wochen unter Angabe der von ihnen getroffenen besonderen Maßnahmen (Alarmeinheiten, Eingreifgruppen) zu melden. Dies war die befehlsmäßige Grundlage der nunmehr im Operationsgebiet der Heeresgruppe Mitte eingesetzten Maßnahmen gegen die Partisanen, insoweit sie sich in zeitlichem und räumlichem Zusammenhang mit der Vorbereitung der Operation „Zitadelle" auswirkten.

Der Kommandierende General der Sicherungstruppen und Befehlshaber im Heeresgebiet Mitte meldete am 9. Mai 1943 dem Oberkommando der Heeresgruppe Mitte ausführlich über die Entwicklung der Bandenlage im

Heeresgebiet. Es waren wichtige Eisenbahnstrecken in einer Länge von rund 2200 Kilometer und wichtige Straßen in einer Länge von rund 1000 Kilometer zu sichern. Darüber hinaus waren Versorgungseinrichtungen, Stützpunkte, wirtschaftliche Objekte und die landwirtschaftliche Nutzung des Landes zu schützen. Hierfür standen 59 Bataillone zur Verfügung, davon 15 ungarische, ein französisches, 13 landeseigene und vier Polizeibataillone. Zum Eisenbahnstreckenschutz waren 37 Bataillone eingesetzt, zur Straßensicherung acht, zur Vorfeldsicherung an Straßen und Eisenbahn sowie zum Schutz wirtschaftlicher Objekte zwölf. Für den beweglichen Einsatz standen noch zwei Bataillone zur Verfügung.

Aus der unzureichenden Stärke der eigenen Kräfte ergab sich die Forderung nach aktiver Bekämpfung der Partisanen in ihren Zentren. Die hierzu dem Oberbefehlshaber im Heeresgebiet Mitte zur Verfügung stehenden Kräfte waren jedoch für eine solche Aufgabe nicht geeignet; deshalb wurde gefordert, die Truppen zur Verfügung zu stellen."

Die sowjetische Führung massierte im Raum von Kursk stärkste Kräfte und baute ein tiefgestaffeltes Verteidigungssystem auf. Das sowjetische Oberkommando teilte den Partisanenverbänden zunächst die Aufgabe zu, während des Aufmarsches der deutschen Truppenverbände die Angriffstruppen genau festzustellen. Die eingleisige Strecke Smolensk – Roslawl – Brjansk – Orel und die zweigleisige Linie Minsk über Gomel nach Brjansk waren zu überwachen und zu bedrohen.

Deutsche Sicherungskräfte versuchten die Gefahrenlage zu beseitigen. Ständig patrouillierten Einheiten an den genannten Strecken. Blockhäuser wurden beiderseits der Eisenbahnlinie aufgestellt. Die Bäume in der Waldgegend wurden bis zu 30 km beiderseits der lebenswichtigen Verkehrsadern beseitigt. Nahe der Eisenbahn gelegene Ortschaften wurden evakuiert und zerstört.

Im Mai 1943 verzögerten Angriffe der Partisanen den Bahnverkehr. Nach Teske (,,Partisanen gegen die Eisenbahn") wurden in diesem Monat auf der Strecke Żlobin–Gomel 35 Lokomotiven und 106 Waggons beschädigt oder vernichtet. Im Juni 1943 wurden 298 Lokomotiven und 1222 Waggons beschädigt und 44 Brücken gesprengt. Man hatte täglich mit 24 Unterbrechungen des Bahnnetzes der Heeresgruppe Mitte zu rechnen.

Infolge der Verschiebung der deutschen Angriffsoperationen konnten Frontverbände zur Säuberung des Operationsraumes eingesetzt werden, insbesondere zwischen dem Fluß Desna und der Bahnlinie Brjansk–Lokat.

Am 13. Mai 1943 erging der Operationsbefehl für Unternehmen ,,Nachbarhilfe I". Am 27. Mai 1943 wurde die Aktion ,,Nachbarhilfe II" befohlen. (Vgl. Komück 559/I a 34 E/43 geh. Befehl für die Säuberung des Kletnja-Waldes vom 27. Mai 43, AOK 4, I a, Beilage 1 zum KTB Nr. 16/

34558/17). Ein weiteres Unternehmen lief unter dem Namen ,,Freischütz'' unter Leitung der 2. Panzerarmee. (Vgl. Fernschriftlicher Befehl an AOK 4 v. 8. Mai 1943, in AOK 4, I a, Beilage 1 zum KTB Nr. 16 – 34558/17 –) Hierzu waren von der 4. Armee die 6. Infanteriedivision und ein verstärktes Infanterieregiment der 31. Infanteriedivision zuzuführen. Mit der Durchführung von ,,Freischütz'' wurde das Generalkommando LV. Armeekorps beauftragt. Das Korps hatte durch konzentrischen Angriff die Feindkräfte im Armeebereich zwischen der Bolwa und der Bahn Brjansk–Žukovka sowie in dem Waldgelände nordwestlich von Brjansk und dem offenen Gelände um Wettnja zu vernichten, das Gelände zu säubern und zu befrieden. Die Kräfte der Partisanen waren wie folgt erkannt:

die 3. Partisanendivision,

die Brigade Orloff,

die Brigade Solotuchin,

kleinere Gruppen.

Bei Beginn des Unternehmens wurden diese Gruppen auf insgesamt 4000 bis 6000 Mann geschätzt; nach Überläufer- und Gefangenenaussagen ergab sich im Verlauf des Unternehmens jedoch, daß höchstens 3000 Mann in dem Operationsraum waren. Das LV. Armeekorps zog eine Kampfgruppe der 5. Panzerdivision, die 6. Infanteriedivision, Kräfte des Kommandanten des rückwärtigen Gebietes und den Oststab z. b. V. 455 zusammen. Es war beabsichtigt, noch die 10. Infanteriedivision (mot.) und ein verstärktes Grenadierregiment der 31. Infanteridivision heranzuziehen. Der Angriff begann am 21. Mai nach einem sorgfältig getarnten Aufmarsch. Die Luftwaffe griff mit 65 Einheiten die befestigten Stellungen und Lager an, auch in den folgenden Tagen wurden zahlreiche Einsätze zur Unterstützung der infanteristischen Kräfte geflogen. Dabei stellte sich heraus, daß die Partisaneneinheiten außer Maschinengewehren auch noch über 2-cm-Flak verfügten. Erst am 24. Mai kam es zu größeren Zusammenstößten mit geschlossenen Partisaneneinheiten. Die größten Schwierigkeiten für die deutschen Truppen bereitete der andauernde Regen, der das ohnehin schwer zugängliche Gelände noch schwieriger machte. Erhebliche Verluste ergaben sich durch die zahlreichen Minen, oft nur mit behelfsmäßigen Mitteln hergestellt und auf den wenigen gangbaren Wegen verlegt.

Vorausgegangen waren vom 24. Apr. 1943 bis 1. Mai 1943: Die Aktion der 293. Infanteriedivision zur Unterbindung von Anschlägen auf die Eisenbahnlinie Brjansk–Dudorowski, vom 4. bis 7. Mai 1943 die Aktion ,,Finkenfang''.

Die deutsche Offensive aus dem Raum Kursk-Orel scheiterte.

Sowjetische Sommeroffensive 1943

Am 3. August 1943 begann die sowjetische Sommeroffensive mit dem Angriff von fünf Armeen der Woronesch-Front beiderseits der Stadt Bjelgorod.

Die deutschen Bekämpfungsmaßnahmen hatten in der ersten Julihälfte die Partisanenaktionen verringert. In starkem Maße lebten sie in der zweiten Monatshälfte auf. Die wichtige Eisenbahnstrecke von Chuttow über Michailowski nach Brjansk auf dem Höhepunkt der deutschen militärischen Krise wurde durch 430 Sprengungen für zwei Tage ausgeschaltet. 1114 Sprenganschläge im Juli standen 841 im Juni gegenüber. Auch rollendes Material konnten die Partisanen vernichten. Ein Treibstoffzug, zwei Munitionszüge und ein mit ,,Tigerpanzern" beladener Zug flogen zwischen Minsk und Gomel in die Luft.

358 Lokomotiven und 1295 Waggons fielen aus.

Im deutschen Bahnhilfspersonal waren eingeschleuste Partisanen, die die Transporte meldeten. Im Heizmaterial der Lokomotiven waren im übrigen auch Sprengstoffpakete.

In der Nacht vom 2. auf 3. August detonierten während des Rückzugs der deutschen Truppen der Heeresgruppe Mitte auf die Dnjepr-Linie 8422 Minen. Fast alle für militärische Bewegungen notwendigen Verbindungen wurden für längere Zeit unterbrochen. Die doppelgleisige Strecke Minsk–Orscha–Smolensk, von Bedeutung für den Nachschub von drei Armeen, konnte nur zeitweise befahren werden. Monate später wurde sie durch die neuerbaute Strecke von Parafjanow nach Lepel ersetzt, die durch das gefährliche Partisanengebiet führte. Die Streckenlänge des unbrauchbar gemachten Schienenmaterials hatte ein Ausmaß von 250 km. Im Bereich der Heeresgruppe Mitte wurden 20 505 Sprengstellen festgestellt.

Die Sowjets hatten in hervorragender Weise den ,,Schienenkrieg" entwickelt, der von der Masse der Zivilbevölkerung unterstützt wurde. An diesem, der sich auch gegen die Brücken richtete, nahmen von Ende September bis November 1943 120 000 Partisanen teil. An ihm waren nicht nur die Großverbände Linkows, Grižins, Kagustaws und Koslows, sondern auch kleinere ortsfeste Verbände beteiligt. Dazu kam, daß zum Streckenschutz eingesetzte Osteinheiten zu den Partisanen überliefen.

In Bd. III, S. 552 sagt die ,,Geschichte des Großen Vaterländischen Krieges": ,,Im August 1943 brachten ukrainische Partisanen 665 Züge zum Entgleisen, doppelt soviel wie in den vergangenen zwei Kriegsjahren. Im zweiten Halbjahr 1943 verursachten sie 3200 Zugentgleisungen und sprengten oder verbrannten 260 Brücken. Die Partisanen des Gebietes Kamenez-Podolsk zerstörten in den Monaten Juli bis August 158 deutsche

Transportzüge und setzten den Streckenabschnitt Schepetowka–Tarnopol außer Betrieb. Die Abteilung ‚Za Rodinu' brachte in den Monaten Juli und August 40 Züge zum Entgleisen und lähmte den Knotenpunkt Sarny. Mehrere Abteilungen des einheimischen Sicherungsdienstes, die geschlossen zu den Partisanen übergelaufen waren, griffen am 17. August 1943 den Bahnhof Krolewszczyzna mit Maschinengewehren, Granatwerfern und Panzerabwehr-Geschützen an und verursachten großen Schaden." (s. H. Teske, Die silbernen Speigel, S. 194)

In der Offensive der Sowjets 1944

Im Monat Januar 1944 wurden 840 Anschläge gegen die Bahnlinien im Mittelabschnitt geführt. 158 wurden verhindert. Hauptangriffsziel war die Strecke Brest–Kowel. Nun begannen die Partisanen die Lokomotiven mit leichten Geschützen und Panzerbüchsen zu beschießen.

Hesse stellt in seiner Arbeit über den ,,Partisanenkrieg in der Sowjetunion von 1941 bis 1944" fest: ,,Die Lage an der Front führte in den Monaten April und Mai 1944 zu erneuter Verlagerung der Angriffsschwerpunkte nach Westen. Die Tätigkeit der Partisanen dehnte sich auf neue Gebiete, wie das Generalgouvernement und das Gebiet um Bialystok, aus. In dem nach Westen verschobenen Transportbereich Mitte wurden für den Monat April 1013 Partisanenanschläge mit 1575 Sprengungen gemeldet; in räumlicher Aufstellung entfielen dabei auf das Operationsgebiet 100 Anschläge, 652 auf den Raum Minsk, 116 auf den Raum Witebsk, 128 auf das Generalgouvernement und 17 auf den Raum Bialystok. Erkennbare Angriffsschwerpunkte bildeten sich an den Flügelstrecken der Heeresgruppe und an der Strecke Brest–Orscha. Im Monat Mai betrug die Gesamtzahl der Anschläge 1052 bei 1584 Sprengungen; 1249 Minen konnten in diesem Zeitraum vor der Explosion aufgenommen werden. Während der ganzen Aktionsphase unterstützte die Rote Armee die Partisanen durch Versorgungsflüge. Allein im Monat April 1944 wurden 1359 Einflüge in das Heeresgruppengebiet Mitte gemeldet."

Tatsache ist, daß durch den ,,Schienenkrieg" andere Aufgaben der Partisanen nicht vernachlässigt wurden.

Hesse sagt: ,,Besonders die Partisanen-Brigaden und -Abteilungen in den Brjansker Wäldern trugen zum Erfolg der Angriffsoperationen der Sowjetarmee bei. So unterstützten 13 Partisanen-Brigaden Anfang September 1943 den Angriff der 11. Gardearmee. Einige Abteilungen der Partisanen-Brigade ,,Smert Nemezkimokkupantam" (Tod den deutschen Okkupanten) unter P. A. Ponurowski und I. G. Chorochawin griffen den

Bahnhof von Sineserki an der Bahnlinie Brjansk–Lgow an und schnitten nordwestlich Nawlja mehrere deutsche Einheiten bis zum Eintreffen der Roten Armee von allen Verbindungen ab. Die Brigade ,,Za Rodinu" (Für die Heimat) griff 30 Kilometer südwestlich Nawlja den Bahnhof von Kokorewka und zurückrollende Truppentransporte an; sie zerstörte die Bahnlinie Nawlja-Susemka und hielt die Bahnstationen bis zum Eintreffen der Sowjettruppen besetzt. Diese Unterstützung durch die Partisanenverbände ermöglichte es den sowjetischen Angriffstruppen, die Brjansker Wälder fast kampflos zu durchschreiten und in zwei Tagen die Desna zu erreichen. In ähnlicher Weise unterstützte die 1. Partisanen-Brigade von Kletnja den Angriff der 50. sowjetischen Armee. Als die Armee am 20. September 20 Kilometer südlich Roslawl ihren Angriff auf Grund des erbitterten deutschen Widerstandes einstellen mußte, erhielten die Partisanen den Auftrag, den Gegner von hinten anzugreifen. Am 23. September griffen die Truppen der 50. Armee und die Partisanen die deutschen Truppen frontal und im Rücken an und zwangen sie, hinter den Fluß Iput auszuweichen."

Herausgestellt werden muß, daß die irregulären sowjetischen Verbände die von den Deutschen auf dem Rückzug gesprengten Brücken mit Hilfe der einheimischen Bevölkerung schnellstens reparierten, so daß die Übergänge beim Eintreffen der Roten Armee sofort benützt werden konnten.

Diesem Umstand ist es zuzuschreiben, daß es nicht möglich war, die Dnjepr-Linie als Verteidigungsstellung zu stabilisieren. Der Partisanenverband aus Tschernigow ,,Za Rodinu" bereitete bei den Dörfern Terenzy und Donanotowo am Dnjepr für die 60. sowjetische Armee 3 Übersetzstellen vor. Für das 13. sowjetische Schützenkorps schuf der Partisanenverband ,,M. M. Kozjubinski" sechs Übergangsstellen über den Dnjepr und schlug Wege durch Wälder und Sümpfe.

Im Nordabschnitt beherrschten Ende des Jahres 1943 die Partisanen zwei Rayons des Hinterlandes der 16. Armee. Im rückwärtigen Gebiet der Heeresgruppe standen 27000 Partisanen. Sie warteten die Anfangserfolge der sowjetischen Offensive zwischen dem Finnischen Meerbusen und dem Ilmensee ab. Dann gingen sie gegen die West-Ost-Verbindung Narwa–Gatschina vor. Nachdem die Richtung der sowjetischen Stoßarmeen klar zu erkennen war, richteten sie ihre Angriffe gegen Straße und Eisenbahn Pleskau – Luga – Leningrad. Gleichzeitig wurden durch Aktionen die Bahnlinien Dno–Leningrad und Dno–Nowgorod gestört. An der Eisenbahnlinie Pleskau–Leningrad gab es an 157 Unterbrechungen, an der Linie Dno nach Leningrad über 300. Den Verstärkungen, die am 19. Jan. 1944 an die Ilmenseefront marschierten, wurden Feuergefechte geliefert. Es kam so weit, daß die örtlichen Reserven der Fronttruppe den Schutz der Eisenbahnlinie übernehmen mußten.

Durch Gleissprengungen an der Strecke zwischen Dno – Šzolzy – Utorgosch wurde die 8. Jägerdivision aufgehalten. Sie konnte die um Nowgorod kämpfenden Truppen nicht mehr verstärken. Das alte ,,Naugard" mußte geräumt werden. Die 12. Panzerdivision, die von der Heeresgruppe Mitte zur Heeresgruppe Nord verlegt wurde, hielt vor Luga die Sprengungen der Eisenbahnlinie auf. Luga mußte vor Eintreffen der Division geräumt werden. Die Truppe wurde dann in die Nahtstelle zwischen 16. und 18. Armee geleitet, die ursprünglich durch die 58. Infanteriedivision gesichert werden sollte. Das Verschieben der Division durch die Eisenbahn scheiterte an der Unpassierbarkeit der Strecke. Der dadurch notwendige Fußmarsch durch die gefrorenen Sümpfe östlich des Peipus-Sees wurde durch Gefechte mit Partisanen behindert.

Im baltischen Raum selbst konnte keine Partisanenbewegung ins Leben gerufen werden, die mit der Stärke der im russischen Großraum operierenden Partisanen vergleichbar war.

Dagegen wurde die Entwicklung im Mittelabschnitt katastrophal. Dort befanden sich am 1. Jan. 1944 Partisanenverbände mit einer Stärke von 140 000 Mann; sie wurden durch solche aus dem Norden, die über die Linie Polozk–Witebsk in den Raum von Lepel eindrangen, verstärkt. Die Sicherungstruppen konnten nur den Versuch unternehmen, die Hauptverkehrslinien zu sichern. Die Herrschaft im weiten Lande mußten sie den Partisanen überlassen.

Zur Vorbereitung der sowjetischen Sommeroffensive befahl der zentrale Partisanenstab, bestimmte Landesteile im Gebiet der Heeresgruppe Mitte bis zum Eintreffen der Angriffstruppen zu befestigen. Landkorridore wurden gebildet, durch die sich die deutschen Truppen zurückziehen sollten und die durch schnelle Sowjetverbände leicht verschlossen werden konnten. Im Frühsommer 1944 wurden die Sperrgebiete mit den ,,Kanälen" errichtet.

Vor dem nördlich und südlich der Bahnlinie Witebsk–Polozk–Dünaburg gelegenen Gebiet wurden die irregulären Verbände konzentriert, die auch durch die Luft versorgt wurden.

Die Heeresgruppe Mitte versuchte, von März bis 22. Juni, dem Tage des Beginns der sowjetrussischen Sommeroffensive, die Partisanengefahr zu beseitigen. Teile der 3. Panzerarmee und der 6. Armee sowie der Polizeitrupp ,,von Gottberg" wurden eingesetzt.

Das Unternehmen ,,Regenschauer", das am 11. Apr. 1944 begann, hatte Erfolg. Die im Gebiet von Uschaschi konzentrierten Partisanenverbände mit einer Stärke von 17 500 Mann mußten sich in die Wälder westlich und südwestlich der Stadt zurückziehen.

Im Anschluß an die Operation der Kampftruppen der 3. Armee traten die 201. Sicherungsdivision und die Infanteriedivision 95 als Kampfgruppe „Krehan" von Südosten und die Polizeiverbände unter SS-Gruppenführer von Gottberg von Westen und Südwesten (Unternehmen „Frühlingsfest") an. Am 5. und 6. Mai wurden die Reste der Partisanenverbände, die sich in einer hoffnungslosen Lage befanden, im Raum von Bartarowo, Borowyje und Karawaino-See gefangengenommen. 4000 Partisanen gelang es, der Einkesselung zu entgehen. 7011 Partisanen wurden während der Kämpfe getötet.

Das Vorspiel zur sowjetischen Offensive des Jahres 1944 im Mittelabschnitt gaben die Partisanenverbände.

In der Nacht vom 19. zum 20. Juni 1944 griffen sie sämtliche Verbindungslinien der deutschen Heeresgruppe an.

Über zwei Drittel der Sprengungen des Monats Mai – fast 11 000 – wurden in dieser Nacht durchgeführt. Dadurch entstanden Unterbrechungen der Verbindungswege auf längere Zeit.

An der ganzen Front schoß die sowjetische Artillerie in einem ungeheuren Ausmaß. Im Raum Witebsk standen 380 Rohre je Frontkilometer.

Konzentriert setzten zugleich mit dem Artilleriebeschuß massierte Luftangriffe ein. Dann erst griff die Sowjetarmee mit Teilen der 1. Baltischen und der 3. Baltischen Front die 3. deutsche Panzerarmee an. Weiterer Angriffspunkt war im Raum der 9. Armee das XXXVI. Panzerkorps südlich der Beresina.

Nördlich von Rogatschew im Bereich der 4. Armee waren Schwerpunkte das XXXIX. Panzerkorps beiderseits der Straße Wjasma–Mogilew und das XXVII. Armeekorps an der Autostraße Minsk–Smolensk.

Die Führung der Heeresgruppe hatte zudem den sehr starken sowjetischen Angriffspunkt nordwestlich von Witebsk in ihrem Ausmaß nicht richtig erkannt. Vor der beabsichtigten Offensive täuschten die Sowjets auch durch einen Aufmarsch von Leerzügen in ihrem nach Westen vorspringenden, auf Brest–Litowsk weisenden Frontbogen vor Kowel einen beabsichtigten Angriff in dieser Richtung vor.

Das deutsche Oberkommando zog die verfügbaren Reserven vom Norden zum Südflügel der Heeresgruppe Mitte ab, während die Sowjets mit stärksten Kräften im Norden bei Witebsk angriffen.

Die Reserven konnten infolge der von den Partisanen durchgeführten Gleissprengungen nicht mehr nach dem Norden verlegt werden. Der deutsche Generalstab der Heeresgruppe Mitte hatte keine Folgerungen aus dem Umstand gezogen, daß der vor einigen Wochen erfolgte Abtransport der Truppenteile vom Nordflügel der Heeresgruppe durch Partisanenaktionen nicht gestört wurde. Die Lufterkundung war überdies unmöglich. 40 einsatzbereiten Jagdflugzeugen standen 4500 sowjetische Flugzeuge gegenüber. Der Großteil der Luftflotte 6 war nach dem Westen gezogen worden. So kam es, daß südostwärts von Witebsk tiefe Einbrüche in die Hauptkampflinien des VI. Armeekorps erfolgten und die Front des IX. Armeekorps beiderseits des Obdol-Flusses aufgerissen wurde.

Am 23. Juni griffen die Sowjets die 4. deutsche Armee an. Südostwärts von Witebsk gelang den Sowjets der operative Durchbruch durch die Stellungen dieser Armee. Witebsk wurde eingeschlossen. Die Sowjets verfügten über eine starke Übermacht. 126 Schützendivisionen, sechs Kavallerie-Divisionen, 16 motorisierte Brigaden und 45 Panzerbrigaden standen ihnen zur Verfügung. An der Straße Wjasma–Mogilew waren allerdings die erzielten Erfolge bescheiden.

Am 24. Juni erfolgten südlich an der Front der 9. Armee Angriffe im Bereich des XXXI. Panzerkorps in Richtung auf Bobruisk. Das VI. Armeekorps erlitt bei Boguschewskoje am 25. Juni einen vollständigen Zusammenbruch. Die sowjetischen Panzerverbände erlangten unbehinderte Bewegungsfreiheit nach Westen und Süden.

Der 4. und 9. Armee drohte die Einschließung. Die Lage der in Witebsk eingeschlossenen Truppen wurde hoffnungslos. Ein Ausbruchsversuch scheiterte. Schnelle Verbände der Sowjets stießen über Senno in die Flanke der 4. Armee.

Eine der größten Niederlagen deutscher Truppen in ihrer Geschichte zeichnete sich ab. Die doppelseitige Einkesselung der Heeresgruppe drohte. Orscha ging verloren. Entlang der Straße Bobruisk–Mogilew wurden die Verbindungen zwischen der 9. und 4. Armee getrennt. Die Sowjets drangen mit ihren Angriffsflügeln im Süden auf Sluzk und im Norden auf Molodetschno vor.

Die Durchbrüche der Sowjets konnten nicht durch die in den Kampf geworfenen Regimenter der 5. Panzerdivision und der aus Sicherungstruppen gebildeten ,,Gruppe von Saucken" abgeriegelt werden. Der 4. Armee unter dem Armeeführer Vinzenz Müller verblieb nur die Rückzugsstraße zur Beresina. Am 2. Juli erreichten Verbände der Sowjets die Bahnlinie Baranowitschi–Minsk und Molodetschno–Wilna.

Die 4. Armee konnte Minsk nicht mehr erreichen.

Am 8. Juli 1944 kapitulierte die 4. Armee.

Die sowjetischen Angriffstruppen überrollten die Partisanengebiete. Dort nahmen sie geeignete Partisanenverbände auf. Andere Partisanengruppen machten auf Tausende versprengter deutscher Soldaten Treibjagd. Am 3. Juli 1944 erreichten die Sowjets bereits den Nordrand der Pripjet-Sümpfe.

Mitte Juli zog sich die Front von Pinsk–Pruzana–Wolkowysk–Grodno über Dünaburg nach Pleskau. Anfang August 1944 stand die Sowjetarmee vor Warschau.

Das Überschreiten der sowjetischen Grenze bedeutete nicht das Ende der Partisanentätigkeit. In Rumänien verbanden sich die Partisanen mit der prokommunistischen „Vaterländischen Front".

Teile von Fjedrows Kampfverband wurden in die Slowakei befohlen. Die Partisanenbrigaden „Satanowski", „Chruschtschow" und weitere Verbände westlich des San und der Weichsel wurden in den polnischen Raum befohlen. Bilgoraj wurde ein Zentralpunkt.

Polen

In der deutschen und polnischen Geschichte gibt es eine große Parallele: Teilung des Staates, bei Polen freilich nach und vor jahrhundertelanger Beherrschung fremden Volksbodens. Polen vor 1939 wurde von Angehörigen verschiedener Nationalitäten bewohnt. Neben den Polen bildeten die Deutschen, die Juden, die Ukrainer, die Weiß- und Großrussen, die Litauer, die Tschechen und Tataren einen nicht unerheblichen Bestandteil.

Im Jahre 1921 gab es nach einer amtlichen polnischen Statistik im damaligen polnischen Staat

18 820 163 Polen

3 899 323 Ukrainer,

2 111 304 Juden,

1 060 041 Weißrussen,

1 058 824 Deutsche

235 281 andere.

Die polnische Statistik dürfte die Zahlen der nichtpolnischen Bevölkerung, insbesondere der Deutschen und Juden, zu niedrig angesetzt haben.

Aus dem Jahre 1933 liegen andere Zahlen vor. Dies gilt vor allem für die deutsche Minderheit und die jüdische Gruppe. Die Deutschen waren vor allem in den früheren preußischen Gebieten vertreten. Der Deutsche kam nicht als Eroberer nach Polen, er wurde von polnischen Königen, pommerellischen Herzögen, geistlichen Fürsten und Korporationen und dem polnischen Adel als Landmann und Städtebauer in das Land gerufen.

Nach Wiedergründung des polnischen Staates nach dem Ersten Weltkrieg sind aus den ehemaligen preußischen Provinzen infolge der rücksichtslosen Entdeutschungspolitik 800 000 Deutsche abgewandert.

Die Juden stammten zum Teil aus Westeuropa, besonders aus Deutschland, wo sie wegen der Judenverfolgungen im 12.–14. Jahrhundert auswanderten. In Polen lebten sie fast ausschießlich in Städten, wo sie neben Handel auch alle Handwerke und das Fuhrwesen betrieben. Die große Masse war arm und wohnte in engen Judenvierteln. Einige Städte wiesen bis 80 % Juden auf. Polen hatte prozentual das stärkste Judentum der Welt. An zweiter Stelle stand das benachbarte Litauen. Hinsichtlich der absoluten Zahl der Juden wurde Polen neben den USA nur vom europäischen Rußland überflügelt, das zahlenmäßig die meisten Juden der Welt innerhalb seiner Grenzen beherbergte.

Von 2 849 020 Juden entfielen 1933 in Polen allein 1 500 489 oder 55 % auf das kongreßpolnische Gebiet mit den Wojewodschaften Warschau, Lodz, Kielce, Lublin und Bialystok, auf Galizien 740 323 oder 26 % und auf den räumlich größten Teil Polens, nämlich die ostpolnischen Wojewodschaften Wilna, Nowogrodek, Polesie und Wolhynien 441 630 oder 15,5 %. Die Ursache für die gegebene Zusammenballung der Juden ist größtenteils in den zaristischen Regierungsmaßnahmen zu suchen, die die Aussiedlung der Juden aus den baltischen und russischen Gebieten und deren Ansetzung in Kongreßpolen zum Ziele hatten.

Die damalige Konzentrierung der Juden in den Städten findet ihre teilweise Erklärung in den zaristischen Ausnahmegesetzen, die u. a. den Juden den Erwerb ländlichen Grundbesitzes und damit die Niederlassung auf dem Lande erschwerten oder unmöglich machten, ferner in der steigenden Intensivierung und Rationalisierung der Betriebe auf dem Lande, die auch bestrebt waren, durch Schaffung von Ein- und Verkaufsgenossenschaften und Gründung von Konsumvereinen den Juden aus seiner früheren Monopolstellung als unumgänglichen Vermittler zwischen Großhandel und Landbevölkerung und umgekehrt immer mehr zu verdrängen. Es war also nicht der Land- und Erwerbshunger der Landbevölkerung, sondern die steigende wirtschaftliche Konkurrenz auf dem Lande, die den Juden in die Stadt zwang. Dadurch entstand sehr oft eine gewisse Proletarisierung der jüdischen Bevölkerung.

In dem Verfahren gegen B. in Darmstadt führte ich zur Beleuchtung und Erklärung der Lage, nicht zur Rechtfertigung der Maßnahmen gegen die Juden aus:

Professor Burkhardt, vor 1939 Hoher Kommissar des Völkerbundes für Danzig und später Präsident des Internationalen Roten Kreuzes in Genf, nimmt in seinem Buch ,,Meine Danziger Mission 1937–1939'', erschienen München 1960, auf eine Unterredung mit dem polnischen Ministerpräsidenten Slawoj-Skladkowskij Bezug, der ihm erklärte, daß 90 % aller Kommunisten in Polen Juden und 60 % aller Juden Kommunisten seien. Das Polen bis zum Jahre 1939 war antisowjetisch ausgerichtet. In diesem Zusammenhang sind die Äußerungen von Interesse, die der jüdische Schriftsteller Tennenbaum in seinem Buch ,,Underground'', erschienen im Jahre 1952 in New York, aufzeichnet: ,,Gazeta Warszawska'' vom 23. Nov. 1933: ,,Wenn wir die Aufgaben erfüllen wollen, die vor uns stehen, dann müssen wir die Juden aus Polen wegschaffen.'' (Tennenbaum, S. 54). Im Jahre 1936 erklärte der Vizemarschall des polnischen Sejm, Miedzinski, einer der engsten Mitarbeiter von Marschall Pilsudski, in einer Rede im Reichstag: Polen habe Platz nur für 50 000 Juden (Tennenbaum, S. 54). Bevor der Zweite Weltkrieg begann, sagte der polnische Außenminister zur Zeit der EvianKonferenz im Jahre 1938, daß in Polen für die Polen ,,eine Million Juden überzählig'' sei. Tennenbaum selbst schreibt auf Seite 47 seines Buches: ,,Die Geschichte des neuen Polen begann mit neuen Pogromen. Es gab

Massaker in Lemberg, Warschau, Krakau, Wilna, Minsk und Pinsk, von den „kleineren Pogromen" in Städten und Dörfern gar nicht zu reden."

„Im Jahre 1920 wurde Polen in den Krieg mit den Sowjets verwickelt, und selbstverständlich wurden die „jüdischen Bolschewiken" während des Rückzuges gezüchtigt und während des Vormarsches bestraft."

Nicht das Jahr 1936 ist die Geburtsstunde des Begriffes „Judo-Marxismus", sondern das Jahr 1920.

Der 6. deutschen Armee fielen nach dem Einmarsch in das sowjetische Gebiet Unterlagen in die Hand, die im Mai 1941 erstellt worden waren. In der Ausarbeitung „Plan für die politische Sicherung der Armee-Operation" sowjetischer Streitkräfte gegen Polen wird ausgesprochen: „Es ist notwendig, dem Feind einen sehr starken, blitzartigen Schlag zu versetzen, um die moralische Widerstandskraft der Soldaten zu erschüttern . . . Ein blitzartiger Schlag durch die Rote Armee wird zweifellos ein Anwachsen und Vertiefen der bereits sich bemerkbar machenden Zersetzungserscheinungen im feindlichen Heer zur Folge haben . . . Im allgemeinen werden die Kampfhandlungen sich auf dem Gebiet des Feindes abwickeln, besonders dort, wo die ukrainische und jüdische Bevölkerung vorherrscht (Bezirk Cholm und nördlich davon).

Die Polen sind gegenüber der UdSSR loyal gesinnt.

Die Wegnahme und Ausfuhr von landwirtschaftlichen Produkten, Vieh, Herden, der Abschub von Jugendlichen zur Arbeit nach Deutschland, die Bestimmungen über die Verteilung der Arbeitskräfte, die besondere Unterdrückung der Juden, der große Mangel an Industriewaren, die Einführung der Arbeitskarten, die politische Unterdrückung und der politische Zwang – das alles ruft ein Wachsen der feindseligen Stimmung gegen die Deutschen hervor."

In einer Ausarbeitung „Stimmung Bevölkerung im Generalgouvernement – Stand am 1. Mai 1941" der 8. sowjetischen Armee heißt es: „Die Bevölkerung ist mit dem politischen Regierungssystem aus folgenden Gründen sehr unzufrieden:

1 a) Umsiedlung der Juden ins Ghetto, wo sie von deutschen Behörden tierisch behandelt werden . . .

3 b) Die Stimmung der polnischen Bevölkerung neigt mehr nach der Sowjetseite als nach der deutschen.

3 c) Es ist damit zu rechnen, daß seitens der jüdischen Bevölkerung die Rote Armee aktive Unterstützung erhalten wird mit Ausnahme der großen Kaufleute . . .

Die Beurteilung der jüdischen Bevölkerung im Osten seitens der sowjetischen Führung könnte als richtig eingeschätzt werden, schreibt Josef Tennenbaum in seinem „Underground, the story of a people", erschienen in

New York 1952. Wörtlich sagt er: „Im Jahre 1941 erleuchtete die von Stalin befohlene Politik der „verbrannten Erde" die Straße der Nazi-Invasion mit brennenden Dörfern und rauchenden Gehöften ... Die Juden waren die ersten, die zur Partisanenbewegung aufriefen. Sie übernahmen die Führung im organisierten Guerillakampf zu einer Zeit, als noch umherirrende Banden ohne klar bestimmte Aufgaben in den Wäldern streiften."

In der polnischen Geschichte dominiert Jahrhunderte hindurch der Kampf mit den Deutschen um die Herrschaft über den Raum zwischen Elbe und Oder, in welchem einst Slawenstämme mit starken ostgermanischen Elementen wohnten, und das immer wiederkehrende Bestreben der Polen, an die Ostsee vorzudringen. Dies trotz der Tatsache, daß es sich fast überall um Slawen, doch nicht um Polen handelte. Die Gleichsetzung Slawe = Pole ist eine bekannte falsche historische Behauptung der Polen. Das Reich Mieszkos wird in der Hauptsache den Raum der ehemaligen Provinz Posen, östlich davon bis zur Pilica, nordöstlich bis zur Weichsel, nördlich bis zur Netze, westlich bis zur Netze, westlich bis zur Oder und teilweise (Land Lebus) darüber hinaus umfaßt haben. Erst gegen Ende der Regierungszeit der großen Piasten wurde den Böhmen Schlesien entrissen. Polen erlebte unter den Jagiellonen (1382–1572) seine Blüte, in der Zeit der Wahlmonarchie (1572–1772) den Niedergang.

In den Verträgen zwischen Preußen, Rußland und Österreich vom 15. Jan. und 15. Aug. 1772 wurde die erste polnische Teilung vereinbart. Österreich erhielt die Zips, den südlich der Weichsel gelegenen Teil Kleinpolens, Rotrußlands mit Lemberg und den westlichen Teil Podoliens (Ostgalizien), insgesamt 81 900 qkm;

Preußen bekam Westpreußen außer Danzig und Thorn und den Netzedistrikt mit Bromberg (insgesamt 36 300 qkm);

Rußland eignete sich das Gebiet östlich der Düna und des Dnjepr mit den Städten Dünaburg, Polozk, Witebsk und Mogilew (insgesamt 92 000 qkm) an. In den an Rußland wie an Österreich und Preußen abgetretenen Räumen gab es nur polnische Minderheiten. Das Preußen zufallende Gebiet war altpreußisch. Es hatte zum Ordensstaat gehört.

In der Konvention von Petersburg vom 23. Jan. 1793 einigten sich Preußen und Rußland über das noch bestehende selbständige Polen. Nun erst erhielt Preußen die Städte Danzig und Thorn mit ihrer deutschen Bevölkerung, aber auch ganz Großpolen mit den Städten Posen und Kalisch, Kujawien und einen Teil von Masowien mit Plock. – An Rußland fiel der Rest der Ukraine, der östliche Teil Podoliens und Wolhyniens und Weißrußland mit Minsk (insgesamt 250 200 qkm), lauter von Ostslawen besiedeltes Gebiet.

Kościuszko versuchte, die Freiheit und Selbständigkeit Polens 1793/

1794 zu retten. Am 10. Okt. 1794 wurde er von den Heeren der Russen und Preußen bei Maciejowice geschlagen. Suwarow nahm am 1. Nov. Praga bei Warschau ein. Durch die dritte polnische Teilung am 3. Jan. 1795 erhielt Österreich Kleinpolen bis zum Bug mit den Städten Krakau, Radom und Lublin. Preußen bekam den Rest von Masowien mit Warschau sowie die Gebiete von Bialystok und Suwalki, außerdem ein kleines Gebiet in der Provinz Neuschlesien. Preußen wie Österreich begegneten der Westausdehnung Rußlands so weit östlich wie möglich. Rußland erhielt Kurland, das eigentliche Litauen mit Wilna und Grodno, das Land um Brest–Litowsk und den Rest Wolhyniens (120 000 qkm). Polen war somit als selbständigen Staat von der Landkarte Europas verschwunden.

1797 fochten im französischen Revolutionsheer die Legionen des polnischen Generals Dombrowski. Im Tilsiter Frieden, nach dem Sieg über Preußen, errichtete Napoleon I. das Herzogtum Warschau, dessen Herrscher dem Namen nach Friedrich August I. von Sachsen wurde. Es umfaßte die in den polnischen Teilungen erfaßten Gebiete außer Westpreußen und Danzig. Als Napoleon über Österreich gesiegt hatte, kam 1809 Westgalizien hinzu. Napoleon verfolgte das Ziel, durch diese Lösung Rußland und Preußen gebietlich zu trennen, einen eigenen Verbündeten zwischen sie zu schieben und Frankreichs Gegner somit in Schach zu halten. Die polnische Armee unter Fürst Poniatowski sollte für die Interessen Frankreichs kämpfen. Es ist die gleiche Vorstellungswelt wie die von Versailles bis Mitterrand.

Durch den Wiener Kongreß (1815) erhielt Preußen von seinen Erwerbungen außer Westpreußen noch Danzig, die Gebiete von Thorn und Bromberg und einen Teil Südpreußens als neue Provinz Posen zurück. Österreich behielt seine gewonnenen Gebiete aus der ersten Teilung. Krakau wurde eine ,,freie Stadt". Das um Posen verkleinerte Gebiet des bisherigen Herzogtums Warschau wurde als Königreich Polen (sog. Kongreßpolen) in Personalunion mit dem russischen Kaiserreich verbunden.

Am Ende des Ersten Weltkrieges wurde der polnische Staat wieder errichtet. Der Versailler Vertrag vom 28. Juni 1919, den Dmowski und Paderewski als Vertreter Polens unterzeichneten, sprach der neuen polnischen Republik den größten Teil der Provinz Posen zu. Danzig wurde unter Völkerbundsaufsicht gestellt und als Freie Stadt vom Reich getrennt. Nur ein kleiner Teil Westpreußens, ein Teil des südlichen Ostpreußen und der größte Teil Oberschlesiens durften über ihre Staatsangehörigkeit abstimmen. Dies war allein dem Eingreifen des englischen Ministerpräsidenten Lloyd George zuzuschreiben.

Eine schwere Belastung für Polen wurde das Verhältnis zu seinen Minderheiten, die fast zwei Fünftel der Bevölkerung des Staates ausmachten. Gewalt schuf nach dem Ende des Ersten Weltkrieges unter Verletzung des

Selbstbestimmungsrechtes einen „Gürtel der gemischten Bevölkerung" an den Ostgrenzen des Deutschen Reiches und Österreichs.

Die Nationalitätenfrage trat in das Zentrum der europäischen Politik. Hier war jeder gegen jeden: die Slowaken gegen die Tschechen, die Kroaten gegen die Serben, die Ungarn gegen die Juden, die Polen gegen die Deutschen usw. in einer unendlichen Variation. Die Friedensverträge von Versailles, St. Germain und Trianon, welche die Nationalitäten in Staatsvölker und Minderheiten aufteilten, hatten in dieses Chaos keine Ordnung bringen können. Die Zustände im „Gürtel der gemischten Bevölkerung" waren vergiftet. Gewalt hielt die Staaten in diesem Gürtel mühsam zusammen. Gewalt kam, um zu vernichten. Und doch bestanden vor allem zwischen Polen und der Tschechoslowakei ebenfalls territoriale Unstimmigkeiten.

Gewalt gegen Gewalt

Im Archiv des jetzigen polnischen Innenministeriums in der Warschauer Pulawskistraße befinden sich die Berichte der Einsatzgruppen der deutschen Sicherheitspolizei von September und Oktober des Jahres 1939. Auf den Umschlägen ist die Aufschrift zu lesen: „Hauptamt Sicherheitspolizei Berlin, Sonderreferat Unternehmen Tannenberg." Es sind die Meldungen für die Tage vom 6. Sept. – 5. Okt. 1939.

Täglich wurden zwei Meldungen erstattet. Sie werden auszugsweise ohne Kommentar wiedergegeben. Der Leser wird selbst erkennen, was davon mit dem Kriegsvölkerrecht zu vereinbaren ist. Gewalt steht gegen Gewalt.

Die Einsatzgruppenberichte zeigen einerseits Massenverhaftungen und Erschießungen unter Anwendung eines kollektiven Systems durch die deutsche Polizei auf, die in Verbindung mit der deutschen Wehrmacht tätig war. Auch Grundzüge einer der katholischen Kirche und den Juden feindlich gegenüberstehenden Politik werden sichtbar. Auf der anderen Seite dürfen die Bedrohungen und Gewalttaten auf polnischer Seite nicht übersehen werden. Eindeutig geht aus den Meldungen hervor, daß das Hinterland der deutschen Armeen durch „Banden" gefährdet war.

Die Bromberger Blutnacht tritt in Erscheinung.

Auszug aus:
„Die Berichte der Einsatzgruppen der Sicherheitspolizei im Polenfeldzug 1939"

6. 9. 1939 – Einsatzgruppe III

In Kempen sind Franktireure nicht tätig gewesen, wohl aber in den nördlichen Gebieten des Landkreises. Die Stadt Ostrowo, die bis auf etwa 1000 Einwohner entvölkert ist, war stark gegen die polnische Regierung eingestellt, weil auch dort sämtliche Beamten und wohlhabenden Personen die Stadt verlassen hatten. Die Gefängnisse wurden von den Polen geöffnet und die zurückgebliebene Bevölkerung den Plünderungen und Räubereien der etwa 100 Verbrecher ausgeliefert. Von den über 200 in Kempen ansässigen Juden sind drei Viertel geflüchtet. Für die Verbliebenen wurde durch das Einsatzkommando ein jüdischer Kommissar ernannt.

Die katholische Kirche in Kempen bildet nach der Besetzung eine Anlaufstelle für die polnische Bevölkerung. Am Sonntag, den 3. Sept. 1939, waren die Kirchen in Kempen überfüllt, so daß sich vor den Kirchentüren Ansammlungen bildeten. Der Geistliche ermahnte zur Ruhe und Würde und riet, Auslassungen über die Lage in der Öffentlichkeit zu unterlassen und in den Wohnungen vorzunehmen. Der als übler Deutschenhetzer bekannte Probst von Kempen ist festgesetzt worden.

Die evangelische Kirche setzt sich im wesentlichen aus Deutschstämmigen zusammen. Der Kempener Pfarrer Lic. S c h i l d b e r g wird als Führer der Volksdeutschen in der Umgebung betrachtet. Er ist in der Zwischenzeit zum kommissarischen Bürgermeister von Kempen ernannt worden. Mit weiteren 15 Volksdeutschen hat er schon früher nachrichtendienstlich gearbeitet.

Einsatzgruppe IV:

In Konitz und Umgebung wimmelt es noch von polnischen versprengten Truppen und Freischärlern. Die Einsatzgruppe hat Verstärkung und Einsatz von Ordnungspolizei beantragt, um den geplanten Vormarsch in Richtung Bromberg vorzubereiten.

In der Tucheler Heide befinden sich 800 freigelassene Zuchthäusler, die zusammen mit Freischärlern und polnischen Aufständischen eine große Gefahr bilden. In der Nähe von Tuchel sind Arbeitsdienstmänner, lediglich mit Spaten bewaffnet, zur Bewachung von Munitionslagern eingesetzt worden. In der Nacht vom 4. auf den 5. Sept. 39 soll eine Anzahl von diesen durch Aufständische und Zuchthäusler erstochen worden sein.

Einsatzgruppe V:

Hinter der Front machen sich ziemlich viel Franktireure bemerkbar, die nicht gefaßt werden können, da Truppen hierfür nicht zur Verfügung stehen und Ordnungspolizei gänzlich fehlt.

Es ist festgestellt worden, daß die Dienststellen der polnischen Grenzwacht der 1. und 2. Linie nicht, wie bisher angenommen wurde, ihre Dienstgebäude und Privatwohnungen planmäßig geräumt haben, sondern zum großen Teil überstürzt unter Zurücklassung des gesamten Materials geflüchtet sind.

Bei der Besetzung von Bromberg ist unmittelbar mit den deutschen Truppen ein Trupp der Einsatzgruppe IV eingerückt. Auch die Männer dieses Einsatztrupps mußten dabei von der Waffe Gebrauch machen. – Die sicherheitspolitischen Arbeiten wurden sofort aufgenommen. Es konnte erreicht werden, daß ein Aufruf zur Abgabe der Waffen vom Bürgermeister und dem Probst des Bischofs mitunterzeichnet wurde. – In Bromberg haben Straßenkämpfe Verluste gefordert. 18 Volksdeutsche waren am Eingang der Stadt von den Polen niedergeschossen worden. Plünderungen wurden versucht. Es wird jedoch scharf durchgegriffen. Das Erforderliche ist durch den Chef der Einsatzgruppe IV veranlaßt. – Bromberg wird in einigen Tagen Sitz des Einsatzkommandos 1 der Einsatzgruppe IV werden. – In Nakel herrscht jetzt Ruhe.

In Graudenz wurden neben sonstigen Festnahmen auf Ersuchen der Ortskommandatur 25 Personen als Geiseln festgesetzt. Zwei Polen wurden beim Plündern im polnischen Grenzkommissariat betroffen. In Graudenz, Löbau, Soldau und anderen Orten werden die Dienstgebäude sämtlicher Behörden der Grenzwachtposten, der Grenzkommissariate, der Staatspolizei, des Postamtes, der Starostei durchsucht. Es wurden Geheimakten, Schriftmaterial, Karteien und Lichtbildmaterial vorgefunden. Ebenso wurden die Räume der jüdischen Synagogen und Gemeinden durchsucht. In Graudenz wurden für die 600 Köpfe starke jüdische Gemeinde zwei Bevollmächtigte eingesetzt. Diese haben innerhalb 14 Stunden ein namentliches Personenverzeichnis und Vermögensaufstellung vorzulegen. Sämtliche männlichen führenden Juden in Graudenz sind geflohen. Die Abwanderung der übrigen Juden wird vorbereitet. Dem katholischen Klerus in Graudenz wurde die Auflage gemacht, Predigten bis zur endgültigen Regelung weder in polnischer noch in deutscher Sprache zu halten. Gestattet wurde die Liturgie, Andachten und die rein religiös-konfessionelle Betätigung in polnischer Sprache.

Bis zum 8. Sept. 1939

Einsatzgruppe II

Durch das energische, rücksichtslose Einschreiten von Wehrmacht und Einsatzkommando ist in Tschenstochau völlige Ruhe eingekehrt. Den ganzen Tag über dauerten Durchsuchungen mit motorisierten Streifen insbesondere durch die Arbeiterviertel an. Spitzel wurden in den einzelnen Organisationen angesetzt. In Lublinitz wurde die gesamte Kartei der Aufständischen erfaßt. Im übrigen sind die Akten in der Hauptsache von den Polen vernichtet worden.

Einsatzgruppe IV:

Durch die Terrormaßnahmen der polnischen Truppen in Bromberg sind die Volksdeutschen noch sehr eingeschüchtert. Sie glauben teilweise immer noch, daß die Polen wieder zurückkommen könnten. Der größte Teil der bei der Einsatzgruppe bekannten Volksdeutschen ist nicht mehr aufzufinden. Es besteht nur geringe Wahrscheinlichkeit, daß sie sich verborgen halten. Es ist vielmehr anzunehmen, daß der größte Teil von ihnen ermordet worden ist. Da die Truppe weiter im Vormarsch begriffen ist, besteht ein Schutz der noch verbliebenen Volksdeutschen im wesentlichen nur im Rahmen der sicherheitspolizeilichen Einsatzgruppe.

Einsatzgruppe IV:

Die Wehrmacht stieß beim Einmarsch in die Stadt Bromberg auf Widerstand, der durch die vom polnischen Stadtkommandanten eingesetzte Bürgerwehr geleistet wurde. Hierbei wurde ein Leutnant erschossen und ein Major gefangengenommen. Reguläre polnische Truppen befanden sich nicht mehr in der Stadt. Durch Verhandlungen des Generals von G a b l e n z wurde erreicht, daß der Bürgerwehr die Rechte einer regulären Truppe eingeräumt werden; das heißt, sie wurde nicht als Freischärler behandelt.

Wie den Aussagen von angelaufenen Vertrauenspersonen zu entnehmen ist, herrscht unter den Volksdeutschen allgemein eine große Furcht vor Terrorakten durch die polnische Bevölkerung. Diese Befürchtungen werden noch dadurch verstärkt, daß in polnischen Kreisen das Gerücht umgeht, Bromberg werde bald wieder von den Polen zurückerobert werden. Dieser Zustand wird dadurch verschlimmert, daß sämtliche führenden Köpfe der Volksdeutschen ermordet oder verschleppt sind und der polnischen Flüsterpropaganda deutscherseits keine wirksame Gegenpropaganda entgegengesetzt wird. Bis jetzt fehlt der Einsatz der Propagandaabteilung der Wehrmacht. Das Fehlen genügender Feld- und Ordnungspolizeikräfte ermöglichte das Plündern zahlreicher deutscher Geschäfte durch den polnischen Mob, wobei sich auch deutsche Truppen beteiligten. Die nachrichtendienstliche Arbeit ist dadurch erschwert, daß etwa 90% der in Aussicht genommenen V-Männer ermordet oder verschleppt sind.

Bis 10. Sept. 1939:

Einsatzgruppe V:

140 Personen mußten festgenommen werden. Es fanden Durchsuchungen in allen öffentlichen Ämtern und bei allen Körperschaften in Löbau, Mlawa, Ciechanów und Przasznitz statt. Außerdem wurde der größte Teil der etwa 50 jüdischen Geschäfte in Graudenz durchsucht.

Die Stimmung in der deutschen Bevölkerung ist gut. Sie wird jedoch getrübt durch die immer wieder vorkommenden Überfälle durch polnische Banden.

In den Städten leidet die Stimmung auch durch die mangelhafte Versorgung mit Lebensmitteln. Das gilt besonders für Mlawa. Die polnische Bevölkerung kehrt in großer Zahl zurück, da sie merkt, daß sie von deutschem Militär nichts zu fürchten hat. Ihre Haltung ist jedoch deutlich ablehnend.

Besondere Vorkommnisse: Abwanderung der Graudenzer Juden dadurch vorbereitet, daß der jüdischen Gemeinde aufgegeben wurde, binnen drei Tagen 20 000 Zloty zwecks Schaffung eines Auswanderungsfonds aufzubringen. Von 350 Juden in Mlawa wurden 66 Männer im Alter von 15 bis 60 Jahren und drei Frauen festgenommen und südostwärts Chorzele im Einvernehmen mit dem dortigen Truppenführer in das noch nicht besetzte polnische Gebiet abgeschoben. 70 Juden aus Przasnitz wurden in der Nähe von Friedrichshof nach Polen abgeschoben. Den übrigen besonders in den Kreisstädten noch anwesenden zahlreichen Juden werden im Einvernehmen mit den Ortskommandaturen strenge Auflagen unter schwerer Strafdrohung bei Verstoß auferlegt.

Zahlreiche Volksdeutsche sind von den Polen verschleppt worden. Schon vor etwa drei Wochen erhielten z. B. in Przyskysz[1] die Volksdeutschen den Befehl, sich in das Innere Polens zu begeben.

Meldungen bis zum 11. Sept. 1939

Einsatzgruppe IV:

Die auf Grund der immer noch andauernden Überfälle auf Deutsche angekündigte durchgreifende Säuberungsaktion in Bromberg hat am 10. Sept. 1939 vormittags 6.30 Uhr begonnen und wird erfolgreich fortgesetzt. Der Reichsführer-SS hat auf Grund der Meldung über die zahlreichen Feuerüberfälle auf deutsche Truppentransporte, Dienststellen und Militärstreifen in Bromberg befohlen, vornehmlich aus den Kreisen der polnischen Intelligenz in Bromberg und zusätzlich von den Kommunisten 500 Geiseln festzunehmen und bei den geringsten Aufstands- und Widerstandsversuchen rücksichtslos durch Erschießung von Geiseln durchzugreifen.

Bis zum 12. Sept. 1939

Einsatzgruppe IV:

Am 10. Sept. 39 um 16.45 Uhr auf Wehrmachtsbefehl zur Vergeltung für neue nächtliche Schüsse auf deutsche Soldaten 20 Polen durch Feldgendarmerie erschossen. Zur Säuberungsaktion vom 10. Sept. 39: Häuser sehr oft leer, da Flüchtlinge noch nicht zurückgekehrt und nächtliche Schießer wahrscheinlich noch in Wäldern verborgen. Diese Säuberung daher ungenügend. – Reinigung der umliegenden Wälder am 11. Sept. 39 früh durch Ordnungspolizei. – Beteiligung polnischen Militärs am Greuelmord steht fest. – Polnischer Fähnrich hat drei Deutsche erschossen. Vernehmungen laufen.

In Hohensalza Greuelfunde sichergestellt (Kinder mit abgehackten Händen), Diplomaten und Ausländer zur Besichtigung zugesagt.

Sonstige Meldungen:

Die Staatspolizeistelle Danzig teilt mit, daß besonders führend und hetzerisch tätig gewesene Polen nach Gdingen geflüchtet sind. Der polnische Widerstand um Gdingen war am 12. Sept. 1939 besonders nachhaltig. Polnische Artillerie belegte die deutschen Bereitstellungsräume mit Streufeuer. Zahlreiche polnische Siedler kehren auf ihre Siedlerstellen zurück.

Bis zum 13. Sept. 1939:

Einsatzgruppe I:

Der deutsche Generalkonsul in Krakau, August Schillinger, wurde in der Nacht vom 2. auf 3. Sept. 1939 von der polnischen Polizei verschleppt mit weiteren fünf Konsulatsangestellten. Der holländische Konsul hatte den Schutz des Konsulats übernommen und dieses dem Leiter der Einsatzgruppe nach seinem Eintreffen übergeben. Vier weitere Konsulatsangehörige hatten sich versteckt und befinden sich wohlbehalten in Krakau. Über das Schicksal des Generalkonsuls ist nichts bekannt.

Am 12. Sept. 1939 wurden ● (im Original unleserlich) Juden erschossen, weil in der Nacht vom 11. auf 12. Sept. 1939 aus deren Häusern auf vorbeiziehende Posten der Luftwaffen geschossen wurde. Es wurden ferner fünf Mörder erschossen, die aus dem Zuchthaus entsprungen waren und wieder eingefangen wurden.

Einsatzgruppe II:

Zur Untersuchung der Ermordung des Generalmajors der Ordnungspolizei R ö t t i g wurde eine Mordkommission zusammengestellt mit der Aufgabe, den Tatort zu untersuchen und festzustellen, ob unter Umständen nicht doch Einwohner aus der Ortschaft Konskie als Täter in Frage kommen. Ferner wurde die Erschießung von 20 Geiseln angeordnet.

Einsatzgruppe IV:

Ein Sondergericht unter dem Landgerichtspräsidenten von Schneidemühl wollte in Auftrag von Staatssekretär Freisler in Bromberg tätig werden und die Täter des Bromberger Blutsonntags aburteilen. Da keine abzuurteilenden Täter mehr vorhanden waren, konnte das Gericht seine Tätigkeit nicht aufnehmen.

Einsatzgruppe V:

505 Personen festgenommen. Sämtliche öffentlichen Gebäude der Standorte wurden durchsucht. Wichtiges Aktenmaterial wurde nicht gefunden; dieses ist entweder verschleppt oder verbrannt worden. Die Kreisstadt Pultusk zählte bei dem Einmarsch etwa 18 000 Einwohner, darunter 9000 Juden; etwa 4000 Einwohner sind geflüchtet. Die Zahl der z. Z. in Pultusk wohnenden Juden beträgt etwa 7000. Registrierung ist in die Wege geleitet. Junge Juden betätigten sich für die illegale KPP und sind geflüchtet. In der Kreisstadt Makow waren von 6800 Einwohnern 50 Juden.

Einsatzgruppe II:

Die zur Untersuchung der Ermordung des Generalmajors der Ordnungspolizei R ö t t i g eingesetzte Mordkommission hat folgende Feststellungen getroffen:
Generalmajor Röttig ist nach Mitteilung des AOK im Kampf mit regulären polnischen Truppen auf der Straße Opoczno–Tomaszów gefallen. Seine Leiche ist noch nicht gefunden. Durch Befehl des AOK sind Erschießungen als Vergeltungsmaßnahmen anläßlich des Todes des Generalmajors Röttig strengstens untersagt. Das AOK hat auf diesen Vorfall hin alle männlichen Zivilpersonen im Alter von 18 Jahren in Konskie und der weiteren Umgebung, insgesamt etwa 5000 Personen, festgenommen und in ein Lager bei Konskie bringen lassen. Im Einverständnis mit Orts- und Lagerkommandant wurden die Gefangenen durchgekämmt. Dann wurden 120 Personen, Juden, Polen und Soldaten in Zivil, die, obwohl sie nicht verletzt waren,

blutige Wäsche trugen und im Besitz von deutschem Sold waren und daher als Urheber an der Niedermetzelung deutscher Soldaten betrachtet wurden, erschossen.

Bis zum 14. Sept. 1939

Einsatzgruppe II

Zur Vorbereitung der in Aussicht genommenen Abschiebung der Juden sind sechs maßgebliche Juden aus der jüdischen Gemeinde Tschenstochau beauftragt, bis zum kommenden Sonntag eine vollständige Liste der in der Stadtgemeinde Tschenstochau ansässigen Juden zu erstellen. Bei dieser Anweisung ist die Durchführung einer jüdischen Hilfsaktion zum Vorwand genommen worden.

Im Zusammenhang mit der Erfassung aller Volksdeutschen im Raume von Tschenstochau konte die Feststellung gemacht werden, daß diese Volksdeutschen, die sich besonders im letzten Jahr unter einem ungeheuren nationalen Terror befunden haben, noch außerordentlich verschüchtert sind und, da sie von großem Verkehr und von allen Nachrichtenmitteln abgeschnitten sind, noch immer eine Rückkehr der Polen und die damit für sie verbundenen grausamen Folgen befürchten. Es würde zweckmäßig sein, in diesen volksdeutschen Siedlungen möglichst schnell junge deutsche Volksschullehrerkräfte aus dem Reich einzusetzen, deren Aufgabe es sein müßte, nicht nur die Kinder zu unterrichten, sondern auch die geistige Führung in einem solchen Dorf zu übernehmen und die Bevölkerung zu politisieren. Seitens der Einsatzgruppe II wird zunächst beabsichtigt, jedem dieser Dörfer ein Gemeinschaftsempfangsgerät zur Verfügung zu stellen.

Mit dem AOK. 10 ist vereinbart worden, daß von den weiter vorrückenden Einheiten der Technischen Nothilfe und des Arbeitsdienstes je eine Gruppe zur Sicherung der Betriebe in Tschenstochau zurückbleibt. Mit den Vorarbeiten für die Sicherung der Eisenerzgruben und -hütten im Südteil des Kreises Tschenstochau ist begonnen worden.

Bis zum 15. Sept. 1939

Einsatzgruppe V:

350 Personen wurden festgenommen, darunter fünf entflohene Zuchthäusler, die der Strafanstalt Graudenz wieder zugeführt wurden.

Im Bereich des Einsatzkommandos 1 wurden Amtsgebäude und Wohnung des geflüchteten Bischofs in Lomza durchsucht. Vorgefundenes Schriftmaterial und sonstiges Inventar des Bischofs von Lomza wurde sichergestellt. Bei der Fortsetzung der Durchsuchungsaktionen der in jüdischen Händen befindlichen Speicher in Makow konnten 748 Sack Getreide sichergestellt werden. Außerdem wurden große Bestände an Zucker und Reis, die versteckt gehalten wurden, beschlagnahmt.

In der Synagoge in Pultusk wurde eine Kiste mit Silber- und Goldsachen gefunden und beschlagnahmt.

Das Schloß des Fürsten Radziwill in Serock, das vor der Stellung der deutschen Artillerie und unmittelbar hinter der deutschen Infanteriestellung liegt, wurde beschlagnahmt. Bestandsaufnahme der vorgefundenen Werte ist eingeleitet. Während der Durchführung der Bestandsaufnahme wurde das Schloß von polnischer Artillerie beschossen. Zwei Geschosse trafen die Terrasse und ein Geschoß das Dach. Außer Sachschaden sind Verluste nicht zu verzeichnen.

In Graudenz ist die Sicherstellung der größeren jüdischen Geschäfte als beendigt anzusehen. Diese Geschäfte wurden deutschstämmigen Vertrauensleuten übergeben, die mit dem Verkauf der vorgefundenen Ware begonnen haben und für ordnungsmäßige Geschäftsführung dem Treuhänder gegenüber verantwortlich sind. Die täglichen Geschäftseinnahmen werden dem Treuhänder zugeführt, der die Einnahmen nach Abzug der Geschäftsunkosten auf das errichtete Sonderkonto des jüdischen Auswanderungsfonds einzahlt.

Der Hirtenbrief des Weihbischofs Dominik aus Pelplin wurde durch Plakatanschlag der Bevölkerung in Graudenz bekanntgegeben und trägt zweifelsohne zur Befriedung der kirchlichen Lage bei.

Bis zum 16. Sept. 1939

Einsatzkommando 16 (Danzig):

Die Zahl der in Gdingen festgenommenen Personen beträgt 6000–7000. Der größte Teil wurde bereits überprüft, etwa 3000 konnten als „staatspolizeilich unbedenklich" entlassen werden. 2800 sind bis zur einwandfreien Personenfeststellung zurückbehalten worden, darunter 300–400 im Hinblick auf ihre Stellung als Geiseln. Etwa 50–60 Personen, die bereits in Danzig verhaftet werden sollten oder nach denen von deutschen Staatspolizeistellen gefahndet wird, sind besonders verwahrt worden. Die Wehrmacht hat ebenfalls etwa 4000 Personen festgenommen, die in den nächsten Tagen noch überprüft werden müssen.

178

Die Marinestation Oxhoeft nördlich Gdingen verteidigt sich nach wie vor nachhaltig trotz heftigen Artillerie-Beschusses.

Einsatzgruppe II: (bezieht sich auf Tschenstochau)

Die Zeitung ,,Goniec Częstochowskie", ein früheres nationales polnisches Hetzblatt, wird nunmehr von einem Beauftragten des Reichspropagandaamtes herausgegeben. Sie erscheint zweisprachig. Die erste Auflage erschien am 14. Sept. 1939 mit 10 000 Stück.

Die Sichtung des vorliegenden Materials hat eine Liste ergeben, in der alle leitenden Persönlichkeiten sowie der Vorstand des Aufständischen-Verbandes erfaßt sind. Das Erforderliche wird veranlaßt.

Bei von der Front zurückkehrenden Truppenabteilungen ist große Erbitterung darüber zu bemerken, daß es ihnen seitens der höheren Stäbe ausdrücklich verboten ist, bei Angriffen oder Übergriffen von Zivilisten energisch von sich aus anzugreifen.

Träger der chauvinistischen Haltung ist vor allem die heranwachsende Jugend. Sie wurde vor allem in den Schulen intensivst in polnisch-chauvinistischem Sinne erzogen und hat nur von der Verherrlichung Polens und der Herabwürdigung Deutschlands gehört. Auf die Jugend wird das größte Augenmerk zu richten sein.

In der Provinz haben die Polen zum Teil nach dem Weiterrücken der Wehrmacht wieder eine offen antideutsche Haltung eingenommen. Da besonders Waldgegenden von der Wehrmacht noch nicht gesäubert sind, besteht für die Bevölkerung große Gefahr für Leben und Eigentum. Die Evangelische Kirche betont, daß sie wesentlichster Stützpunkt des Deutschtums in Polen gewesen sei.

Bis zum 17. Sept. 1939

Einsatzgruppe I:

Im Laufe des 15. Sept. 1939 mußten insgesamt 23 Personen erschossen werden. Es handelt sich dabei zum Teil um solche Personen, die eine Nachrichtenorganisation für die polnische Armee aufgezogen hatten, z. T. um Juden, aus deren Häusern auf deutsche Soldaten geschossen worden war, ferner um noch in den Gefängnissen einsitzende Schwerverbrecher.

Ein von der Einsatzgruppe I erstatteter zusammenfassender Bericht über die Lage innerhalb ihres Bereiches liegt als Anlage bei.

Einsatzgruppe II:

Am 14. und 15. Sept. wurde das Verbrecherviertel Stradom in Tschenstochau überholt. Die Zahl der Festnahmen beläuft sich auf rd. 200. Von der Nebenstelle Tarnowitz wurde ein Insurgent erschossen. Die Bewaffnung der Einsatzgruppen konnte um drei schwere Maschinengewehre und 10 000 Schuß Munition vermehrt werden.

Lagebericht der Einsatzgruppe I vom 15. Sept. 1939

1. *Die allgemeine Lage:* Die Entwicklung im Raum der Einsatzgruppe I (Wojewodschaften Schlesien und Krakau mit Teilen von Lemberg) war dadurch gekennzeichnet, daß die polnische Bevölkerung von der raschen Entscheidung völlig überrascht wurde und zunächst wie vor den Kopf geschlagen war. Die große Masse der Landbevölkerung steht auch jetzt noch unter dem Eindruck der Greuelhetze der letzten Monate, die sich in einer panischen Furcht vor einer anbrechenden deutschen Schreckensherrschaft äußerte. Die nationalbewußte Stadtbevölkerung verhielt sich resigniert und in Krakau passiv, nicht zuletzt deshalb, weil die gesamte politische, geistige und wirtschaftliche Führungsschicht geflüchtet oder unter den polnischen Waffen ist. In den ersten Tagen war insbesondere bei der ärmeren Bevölkerung ein Stimmungsumschwung festzustellen der Art, daß die Regierungsclique das Volk irregeführt und ein völlig falsches Bild über die eigene militärische Stärke und die Verfassung der deutschen Wehrmacht verbreitet hatte. Hoffnungen auf eine neue soziale Ordnung und antisemitische Tendenzen, die vorwiegend religiösen und wirtschaftlichen Ursprungs sind, spielen mit.

Inzwischen beginnt sich das verbliebene polnische Bürgertum wieder innerlich zu fangen. Die Kräfte, die sich unter der Leitung des Erzbischofs Sapieha im Krakauer Bürger-Komité sammeln, wirken unter der Parole einer loyalen Zusammenarbeit mit den deutschen Stellen für die Normalisierung des gesamten Lebens und die Wiederherstellung von Ruhe und Ordnung. Sie zielen aber gleichzeitig auf einen engen Zusammenschluß der Bevölkerung ab, wie er bisher in der polnischen Bevölkerung nicht möglich gewesen ist. Ansätze einer Sammlung des ganzen Volkes und einer breiten, gegen die deutsche Besatzung gerichteten Arbeit treten in den nach dem Verschwinden der gesamten Krakauer Presse neugegründeten „Dziennik Krakowski" zutage. Es wird angedeutet, daß die Besetzung der Stadt noch keineswegs einen Endzustand zu bedeuten braucht, das letzte Wort über die Unabhängigkeit des Staates vielmehr an anderer Stelle und nach dem Kriegsende gesprochen werde. Allmählich fällt die ausländische Rundfunk-propaganda wieder auf fruchtbareren Boden und wirkt sich in einer erheblichen politischen Gerüchtebildung aus.

Ist von einem organisierten, aktiven Widerstand in der Wojewodschaft Krakau wenig zu spüren, so liegen die Verhältnisse in Schlesien als dem Kerngebiet der polnischen Aufständischenorganisationen wesentlich anders. Da der alte Stamm dieser Organisationen und Wehrverbände nach den bisherigen Beobachtungen keine Verstärkung aus der Bevölkerung verzeichnen kann, ist anzunehmen, daß eine rücksichtslose Ausmerze der Banden, Dachschützen und Saboteure zur Beseitigung dieser Unruhefaktoren führt. Der Rückkehr zu allem entschlossener polnischer Elemente nach Kriegsschluß wird durch eine Auswertung des inzwischen staatspolizeilich erfaßten Materials vorgebeugt.

Bis zum 19. 9. 1939

Einsatzgruppe V

In der Kreisstadt Lomza mit 25 000 Einwohnern befanden sich 10 000 Juden. Täglich kehrten Flüchtlinge nach Lomza zurück. Sie wurden überprüft. Verwertbares Material in der Starostei im bischöflichen Adressenmaterial der katholischen Aktion war sichergestellt.

Die Intelligenzschicht und der größere Teil der Juden – darunter auch der Synagogenvorstand und Rabbiner – sind geflüchtet. Mitglieder der jüdischen Gemeindevertreter wurden mit der Aufstellung eines namentlichen Personenverzeichnisses beauftragt. Eine Vermögensbestandsaufnahme ist eingeleitet. Die Führer polnischer Vereine sind geflohen. Die Überprüfung der rückkehrenden Flüchtlinge wurde gemäß Anweisung A.O.K. III aufgenommen. Ebenso erfolgt die Überprüfung der von der Feldgendarmerie festgenommenen wehrfähigen Polen.

Der Verdacht, daß Juden Eisenbahnattentate bei Chorzele ausgeführt haben, hat sich nicht bestätigt. Von den vorläufig festgenommenen Juden sind sechs Wehrfähige dem Zivilgefangenenlager in Hohenstein überstellt worden.

Bis zum 20. Sept. 1939

Einsatzgruppe II z. b. V.

Am 16. und 17. Sept. 1939 wurden Insurgenten, Plünderer usw. erschossen. Die Zahl der Füsilierten erhöht sich somit auf 72.

In der Stadt Posen selbst wird bei den Volksdeutschen in den Vorstädten die Unsicherheit genährt durch das herausfordernde Benehmen vorwiegend halbwüchsiger polnischer Elemente. Klagen der Volksdeutschen darüber, daß die Polen trotz der starken in Posen konzentrierten deutschen Macht sich mit Belästigungen hervorwagen, halten an. Im wesentlichen beschränkt sich jedoch der polnische Widerstandswille auf passive Resistenz, die sich aber den Volksdeutschen gegenüber vornehmlich im Geschäftsleben in betonten Rücksichtslosigkeiten und Benachteiligungen äußert.

Nachdem die materielle Not die polnischen Volkskreise in immer weiterem Umfange erfaßt, beginnt der Haß der Polen sich mehr und mehr auf die eigene Führerschicht zu konzentrieren. Daneben wird jedoch immer noch versucht, die Meldungen der deutschen Erfolge durch Verbreitung der entgegengesetzten englischen Nachrichten als falsch darzustellen.

Bis zum 21. Sept. 1939

Einsatzgruppe VI

Festnahmen: 104 Personen, darunter vorwiegend entwichene Fürsorgezöglinge, Strafgefangene sowie Polen, die wegen Mißhandlung von Volksdeutschen, Hetzpropaganda und Bandendiebstahls angezeigt waren. Durchsuchungen: 26.

Im Zuge einer Aktion gegen aufrührerische Banden in Schrimm wurde eine größere Anzahl, darunter Schwerverbrecher, die noch einige Jahre Zuchthaus abzusitzen hatten, festgenommen. Da die Verbrecher Widerstand leisteten, mußte von der Schußwaffe Gebrauch gemacht werden. Es wurden 20 Polen getötet.

Aus der Provinz wird gemeldet, daß die polnische Bevölkerung nach dem Abzug deutscher Truppen oder bei schwachen deutschen Schutzkontingenten in einzelnen Ortschaften nach wie vor Gewalttaten gegen Volksdeutsche verübte. Ebenso sind noch Diebstähle und Plünderungen an der Tagesordnung.

In Posen ist u. a. aufgefallen, daß junge Polen sich die Häuser derjenigen Volksdeutschen aufschreiben, die Hakenkreuzflaggen zeigen.

Einsatzgruppe VI

Festnahmen: 31 Polen wegen verschiedener Straftaten. Weitere 31 Personen wurden bei der planmäßigen Durchsuchung eines Stadtviertels nach Waffen wegen verbotenen Waffenbesitzes vorgeführt. Abgesehen von vornehmlich im Süden der Provinz Posen durchgeführten Durchsuchungen wurden insbesondere in Posen-Stadt und Schroda Waffen, Geldbeträge, Goldsachen und Radiogeräte beschlagnahmt.

Hauptsächlich aus Posen-Stadt wird berichtet, daß sich Jugendliche auf Anstiftung von Erwachsenen planmäßig störend insbesondere durch Abreißen von Plakaten und Vernichtung von Hakenkreuzfahnen betätigen. Eine besondere Aktivität wurde unter den Studenten festgestellt, die insbesondere aus englischen Rundfunksendungen stammende Gerüchte verbreiten. Verschiedene Anzeichen deuten darauf hin, daß sie Geldmittel von fremden Agenten zur Verfügung gestellt bekommen haben. Von Polen wurde geäußert, daß die Teilnehmer an der geplanten Kundgebung der Volksdeutschen für eine spätere Vergeltungsaktion vorgemerkt werden sollen. Insbesondere sind Träger eines wachsenden Widerstandes auch einzelne polnische Geistliche. Die Landbevölkerung ist wegen der neuen Aussaat beunruhigt. Die Organisation der Herbstbestellung ist bisher nicht in ausreichendem Maße durchgeführt worden. Es wird damit gerechnet, daß der größte Teil einer Jahresernte an Getreide als verloren gelten muß. Besondere Preissteigerungen wurden bei Manufakturwaren festgestellt, für die bereits doppelt und dreifach so hohe Preise wie früher verlangt wurden.

Wegen der teilweise unzulänglichen Ernährung und wegen Mangel an Ärzten wird ernstlich mit der Gefahr von Seuchen gerechnet. In den Kreisen Konin und Wreschen ist die Ruhr aufgetreten.

Bis 24. Sept. 1939

Einsatzgruppe II

Unter deutschen Kolonisten im Kreise Ostrow hat eine Erregung Platz ergriffen, weil man befürchtet, daß dieses Gebiet durch die Russen besetzt wird.

An der Narew-Brücke in Ostrolenka wurden Juden gestellt, die sich wegen angeblicher Zerstörung ihrer Wohnungen im sowjetisch besetzten Gebiet ansiedeln wollten. Sie wurden zurückgeschickt.

In Seben wurden drei Personen festgenommen, die sich eidlich verpflichtet hatten, im Falle eines Krieges mit Deutschland im Rücken der deutschen

Truppen Eisenbahn- und Straßensprengungen sowie Brandlegungen vorzunehmen. Außerdem sollten sie Autofallennägel streuen. Sie haben in den Monaten Juni bis August 1939 an drei- bis fünftägigen Sprengkursen in Seradowo (50 km hinter Warschau) und in einem Wald bei Modlin teilgenommen. Diese Kurse wurden von einem polnischen Offizier in Zivil geleitet. An ihnen nahmen etwa 25 bis 30 Personen im Alter von 23 bis 50 Jahren teil. Den Teilnehmern war streng verboten, sich einander nach Namen und Herkunft zu befragen. Verrat wurde mit dem Tode bedroht. Den auf diese Weise Ausgebildeten wurde durch Unbekannte mit Kraftwagen Sprengstoff übermittelt. Von diesen wurde er sodann zunächst vergraben. Zur Ausführung von Sabotageakten ist es jedoch nicht gekommen, weil die Festgenommenen vor dem Einmarsch der deutschen Truppen in das Innere Polens flüchteten. Sie sind nunmehr nach ihrer Rückkehr festgenommen worden. Sie sind geständig, gewußt zu haben, daß sie die Sprengstoffe und Waffen gemäß den Aufforderungen der deutschen Zivilverwaltung unmittelbar nach ihrer Rückkehr hätten abliefern müssen. Sie wollten jedoch angeblich ihren Schwur nicht brechen. Das Sabotagematerial, das den drei Festgenommenen ausgeliefert war, ist sichergestellt. Ein weiterer Pole, der an einem solchen Sprengkursus teilgenommen hat, ist flüchtig. Das ihm ausgelieferte Material konnte noch nicht sichergestellt werden.

Einsatzgruppe VI

Die Deutsche Evangelische Kirche hat die Verbindung zum Reiche inzwischen aufgenommen. Da unter den Rückkehrern sich sämtliche verschleppten Geistlichen befinden, dürfte in den nächsten Tagen die Arbeit in vollem Umfang aufgenommen werden.

Das Judentum bemüht sich, aus gesammelten Geldern den notleidenden Gemeindemitgliedern Lebensmittel-Zuschüsse zu geben. Einzelne jüdische Flüchtlinge sind inzwischen ebenfalls zurückgekehrt.

Bis zum 26. Sept. 1939

Einsatzgruppe VI

Zwei Personen, bei denen bei der Suchaktion am 20. Sept. 1939 Waffen vorgefunden wurden, sind dem Kriegsgericht vorgeführt und zum Tode verurteilt worden. Diese Urteile bedürfen allerdings noch der Bestätigung des Militärbefehlshabers, die für einen Fall voraussichtlich gegeben wird.

Die Lage in den Kreisen Konin und Turek ist noch sehr unruhig. In den Wäldern sind noch kleinere polnische Banden versteckt, die in den Nachtstunden in deutsche Gehöfte einfallen. Die Bevölkerung verhält sich zwar nach außen hin ruhig, scheint aber heimlich den Banden Hilfe zu leisten. Die deutschen Einwohner fühlen sich verständlicherweise erheblich bedroht. Es soll vorgekommen sein, daß nach der militärischen Durchdringung des Gebietes polnische Bauern über zurückgekehrte Deutsche Gericht abgehalten und einzelne Rückkehrer ermordet hatten.

Bis zum 27. Sept. 1939

Einsatzgruppe II

Vier berüchtigte Insurgenten in Lublinitz leisteten bei der Festnahme erheblichen Widerstand und versuchten zu entkommen. Es mußte deshalb von der Schußwaffe Gebrauch gemacht werden. Dabei wurden alle vier erschossen.

In Konskie ist die Synagoge abgebrannt. Es liegt offensichtlich Brandstiftung vor. Täter unbekannt, vermutlich Polen, da Spannung zwischen Polen und Juden in Konskie außerordentlich stark.

Eine große Gefahr auch für die Zukunft bilden die durch die Polen vorgenommenen Entlassungen sämtlicher Strafgefangenen, wie z. B. Räuber, Mörder und sonstige Zuchthäusler. Hier wird anhand der Gefängnisbücher eine Sonderfahndungsliste zusammengestellt.

Einsatzgruppe III

Die Aktion gegen die Juden wird planmäßig fortgeführt. Da Listen und Kartotheken nach dem augenblicklichen Stande der jüdischen Bevölkerung nicht vorhanden sind bzw. nur in Lodz gewisse Anhaltspunkte anhand der vorhandenen Kartotheken der jüdischen Vereinigungen zu gewinnen sind, wird zunächst die Erfassung der Juden und hier insbesondere die der ländlichen jüdischen Bevölkerung betrieben.

Einsatzgruppe VI

Festgenommen wurden insgesamt 44 Personen, darunter:
9 Polen wegen Mordverdachts,
7 Polen wegen Mißhandlung von Volksdeutschen,
4 Polen wegen Verdachts staatsfeindlicher Betätigung.

Die Volksdeutschen in Stadt und Provinz Posen fühlen sich immer noch in unmittelbarer Gefahr. Im Stadtteil Wilda hat das sich dort noch in großer Zahl herumtreibende Gesindel deutsche Straßenbenennungen abgerissen. Es wurde festgestellt, daß nach 20 Uhr in Hauseingängen sich Horden polnischer Burschen zusammenfinden. Belästigungen Volksdeutscher halten auch in anderen Stadtteilen an. Im Bezirk Schroda ist die Lage nach wie vor sehr unsicher. Es soll sich dort die Zentrale für die Verschleppungen und Ermordungen Volksdeutscher befunden haben. Die Rädelsführer sollen sich noch heute in Schroda versteckt aufhalten.

Bis zum 29. Sept. 1939

Einsatzgruppe V

Unter den 14 im Kreise Soldau festgenommenen Personen befinden sich Boleslaw Suchomski und Kasimir Depczyski, beide aus Soldau, die in Diensten eines aus Soldau geflüchteten polnischen Geheimpolizisten Newiro und der polnischen Staatspolizei standen. Beide sollen an der Aufstellung der Geiselliste mitgearbeitet haben. Depczynski war ferner Redner der Polnischen Nationalen Partei.

Die Erfassung der polnischen Intelligenz, Geistlichkeit usw. wird fortgesetzt. Juden werden in größeren Kolonnen über die Demarkationslinie abgeschoben.

Bis zum 30. Sept. 1939

Einsatzgruppe III

Die Tatsache, daß die in Warschau eingeschlossenen Truppen kapituliert haben, ging wie ein Lauffeuer durch die Bevölkerung. Während in Kreisen der Volksdeutschen über diesen neuen Erfolg der deutschen Truppen große Freude herrschte, beginnt nunmehr die polnische Bevölkerung sich dessen bewußt zu werden, daß die polnische Armee und damit auch der polnische Staat völlig vernichtet sind. Die Niedergeschlagenheit unter den Polen ist um so größer, als sie noch immer auf die ihnen früher so oft versprochene englische und französische Hilfe gehofft hatten. Die Mißstimmung gegen die frühere polnische Regierung nimmt immer größeren Umfang an. Es wird unter den Polen offen darüber gesprochen, daß die Bevölkerung weitgehend getäuscht und durch ständige Lügenmeldungen über Deutschland hinters Licht geführt worden sei.

Bei der Erfassung des politischen Aktenmaterials, das in der Hauptsache durch die 5. Polizeibrigade in Lodz bearbeitet wurde, ist reichhaltiges Material über die Arbeit der kommunistischen Partei in der Wojewodschaft Lodz und über kommunistische Funktionäre gefunden worden. Die Auswertung und Sichtung dieses Materials wird z. Z. durchgeführt und die Fahndung nach kommunistischen Funktionären, die fast sämtlich flüchtig sind, fortgesetzt.

Die Einzelaktionen gegen jüdische Verbände, Vereinigungen usw. wurden fortgesetzt. So wurde u. a. die Allgemeine Zionistische Organisation in Lodz, Srodmiejska 29, aufgelöst und sachdienliches Material beschlagnahmt. Der Vorsitzende dieser Organisation, ein gewisser Jerzy Rosenblatt, hält sich mit seiner Familie angeblich in der Schweiz auf. Dagegen konnten die beiden anderen Vorstandsmitglieder Markus Marchew und Oszer Szapiro festgenommen werden. Ferner wurde die jüdische Organisation Kibbutz Gordona in Lodz, Klinskiego 86, überholt. Auch hier wurde Schriftenmaterial beschlagnahmt. Die Vorstandsmitglieder dieser Organisation sind geflohen. Nach vertraulichen Mitteilungen beginnen die Juden damit, ihre Wertgegenstände bei arischen Personen zu verstecken. Im Zuge der Ermittlungen wurden bei dem volksdeutschen portugiesischen Vizekonsul Paul Schulz, Srodmiejska 36, die von einer Jüdin verborgenen Wertsachen beschlagnahmt, und zwar u. a. 15 Goldstücke zu 20 Golddollar, acht Goldstücke zu zehn Goldrubel, verschiedene andere ausländische Goldmünzen und ein Koffer mit Silbergegenständen.

Besonders zahlreiche Fälle von Verschleppungen Volksdeutscher haben sich in Wloclawek ereignet. Im Einvernehmen zwischen Wehrmacht und Kommandos der Sicherheitspolizei werden Ausgrabungsaktionen in der Umgegend von Wloclawek durchgeführt, da mit Sicherheit angenommen wird, daß ein großer Teil der Verschleppten von den Polen ermordet und verscharrt worden ist.

Einsatzgruppe VI

Der Fürst-Primas Dr. Hlond und die mit ihm geflüchteten Domherren haben nach Aussage eines deutschen katholischen Geistlichen die wesentlichsten Akten mitgenommen, vermutlich jedoch einen Teil im Diözesan-Archiv untergebracht.

Einsatzkommando 16

Das Einsatzkommando 16 hat nunmehr seine Tätigkeit im gesamten Bereich des Militärbefehlshabers Danzig-Westpreußen aufgenommen. Die Überprüfungen in Gotenhafen sowie im Seekreis sind im wesentlichen abgeschlossen. Zur Zeit sind in Gotenhafen rund 120 Personen als Geiseln festgenommen. Die Zahl der auf Grund reichsdeutscher oder Danziger Fahndungsmaßnahmen Festgenommenen beträgt 130 und die Zahl der aus vorbeugenden Gründen Festgenommenen insgesamt 2250.

Im Kreise Strasburg sind Anfang September ebenfalls fast sämtliche Verbrecher aus den Gerichtsgefängnissen herausgelassen worden. Die eingeleiteten Fahndungsmaßnahmen haben bereits zur Wiederaufnahme einiger Verbrecher geführt.

Bis zum 1. Oktober 1939

Einsatzgruppe III

Aus Kreisen der Lehrerschaft, die sich in der Hauptsache an der deutschfeindlichen Propaganda und Verhetzung des polnischen Volkes gegen die Deutschen beteiligt hat, wird unter der polnischen Bevölkerung das Gerücht verbreitet, daß die durch deutsche Rundfunkstationen übermittelte Nachricht vom Falle Warschaus nicht den Tatsachen entspreche, daß vielmehr die russische Armee weiter im Anmarsch sei und bis zur ehemaligen deutsch-russischen Grenze z. Z. des zaristischen Rußlands vorrücken würde.

Die Aktionen gegen die jüdischen Organisationen und ihre Führer wurden planmäßig fortgesetzt. So wurden die Geschäftsräume der jüdischen ,,Kulturliga" überholt und das vorgefundene Material sichergestellt und ausgewertet. Verschiedenen Meldungen, daß sich in Händen der Juden noch zahlreiche Waffen befinden, wurde nachgegangen. Die vorgenommenen Durchsuchungen verliefen jedoch zunächst ergebnislos. Es ist beabsichtigt, im Rahmen einer Großaktion gegen die jüdischen Stadtviertel erneute Feststellungen in dieser Richtung zu treffen. – Auf Grund der Anordnung, daß Juden nur Geldbeträge bis zur Höhe von 200 Zl. im Hause halten dürfen, haben die Einzahlungen bei den Banken in den letzten Tagen einen beträchtlichen Umfang angenommen.

Neben der Erfassung der katholischen Geistlichen und den Feststellungen über ihre deutschfeindliche Tätigkeit werden die einzelnen religiösen Organisationen hinsichtlich ihres Aufbaus und ihrer Aufgaben im Rahmen ihrer kirchlichen und politischen Tätigkeit überprüft.

Eingehende Ermittlungen wurden gegen die in Lodz bestehenden Unterorganisationen des bekannten Westmarkenverbandes durchgeführt. – Eine besonders fanatische Gruppe stand in enger Beziehung zu der französischen Firma Allart, Rousseau u. Comp. Ein Teil der Führer dieser Gruppe wurde festgenommen. Die jugendlichen nationalpolnischen Kreise insbesondere der polnischen Intelligenz sind größtenteils organisiert in dem Verband ,,Junger Polen". In den Geschäftsräumen der in Lodz und in den Kreisen Lodz, Kutno, Leczycza und Brzeziny bestehenden Unterorganisationen wurden Durchsuchungen vorgenommen und die Führer festgenommen. Die Erfassung der Mitglieder dieser außerordentlich gefährlichen Organisation wird weiter betrieben.

Einsatzgruppe IV

Festnahmen: 21 Personen, darunter Lehrer, Lehrerinnen und Gutsbesitzer, acht Personen wegen politischer oder krimineller Delikte bzw. auf Grund von Fahndungsersuchen, vier Personen wegen Spionage, vier Personen wegen deutschfeindlichen Verhaltens.

Nach Aussagen von weißrussischen Flüchtlingen herrscht in den von den Russen besetzten Orten ein wüstes Durcheinander. Die Bevölkerung zeigt schon jetzt deutlich einen kommunistischen Einschlag. An erster Stelle seien es die Juden gewesen, die ihre Häuser mit roten Fahnen geschmückt hätten. Im Brest sei nach dem Einmarsch der russischen Truppen ein großer Freudenumzug von den Juden veranstaltet worden.

Bis zum 2. Okt. 1939

Einsatzgruppe III

In den letzten Tagen konnte festgestellt werden, daß sich die Polen verschiedentlich zu Rundfunkabhörgemeinschaften zusammenschließen, um vor allem die französischen Sender Paris, Toulouse, Straßburg und Lyon zu hören, deren Sendungen nicht zuletzt auf die Aufrichtung der gedrückten Stimmung unter den Polen abgestellt sind.

Im Zuge der Aktionen gegen die politischen polnischen Verbände und Vereinigungen wurden die Räume der ,,Liga Morska Kolonialna" (Meeres- und Kolonial-Liga) überholt und Mitgliederlisten und Karteien beschlagnahmt. Das vorgefundene Material wird im Einvernehmen mit dem SD ausgewertet.

Bis zum 4. Okt. 1939

Einsatzgruppe VI

Festgenommen wurden insgesamt 27 Personen. Darunter wegen Mißhandlung und Beraubung notgelandeter
deutscher Flieger 7 Personen,
wegen Plünderns 4 Personen,
wegen Diebstahls 4 Personen,
wegen Notzucht 2 Personen,
wegen Mißhandlung Volksdeutscher 1 Person,
wegen Widerstands und Bedrohung je 1 Person,
zur Verbüßung längerer Freiheitsstrafen 4 Personen.

Bis zum 5. Okt. 1939

Einsatzgruppe III

Bei den Ermittlungen gegen die jüdischen Organisationen ist es gelungen, eine Organisation zu ermitteln, die als die Zentrale der jüdischen
Emigranten angesehen werden kann.

In polnischen Kreisen wird erbittert gegen die Einsetzung deutscher
Treuhänder für polnische Geschäfte Sturm gelaufen. Die Maßnahmen werden, verbunden mit Beschimpfungen gegenüber den deutschen Stellen, als
unhaltbares Unrecht bezeichnet. Es wird auch davon gesprochen, die
Volksdeutschen hätten von sich aus Zwischenfälle in Szene gesetzt und
seien für Erschlagungen Volksdeutscher selbst verantwortlich. Dies sei vorgenommen worden, um einen Grund zu einem Vorgehen gegenüber den
Polen zu haben.

In volksdeutschen Kreisen wird unvermindert stark das Problem der polnischen Rückkehrer (Militär und Zivil) und die Handhabung der Charakte-
risierung als Volksdeutsche beanstandet. Am 6. und 10. Oktober hat die in das eroberte Warschau eingerückte
Einsatzgruppe VI zwei Berichte an die in Warschau befindliche ,,Außen-
stelle" des Chefs der Zivilverwaltung bei der 8. Armee (Sitz Lodz) erstattet.

Sicherheitspolizei
Einsatzgruppe IV   Warschau, den 6. 10. 1939

Tätigkeitsbericht

Ungeheure Notlage, Verschüchterung der Bevölkerung. Das bei den Polen in 25 Polizeikommissariate eingeteilte Warschau schildert die Kommissariate II, III, IV als ausgesprochene Ghetto-Gegenden. Nach einer Aufstellung sollen 31. Dez. 1938 374 000 Juden gezählt worden sein (bei 1 196 000 Einw. und 17 772 Häusern). Die polnische Kriminalpolizei unter Führung eines Oberstleutnants Wasilewski zählt heute noch ca. 360 Beamte, die unter Aufsicht der Einsatzgruppe zu entsprechenden Arbeiten untergeordneter Bedeutung herangezogen werden. Die Judenerfassung erfolgt nach den vom RFSS und Chef der Dtsch. Polizei herausgegebenen Richtlinien dadurch, daß ein aus 24 prominenten Juden bestehender Ältestenrat von der Einsatzgruppe bestimmt wird, der voll verantwortlich für die Durchführung aller Anweisungen der Einsatzgruppe ist, eine Judenzählung nach Altersklassen und Geschlecht durchzuführen und eigene Vorschläge für die Judenerfassung in Ghettos zu machen hat. Einsatzgruppe wird sich hierbei mit militärischen Dienststellen und CdZ (Chef der Zivilverwaltung) in Verbindung setzen. Die jüdische Kultusgemeinde mitsamt Präsident und Schriftführer wurde ebenso wie das jüdische Museum sichergestellt. Der Großmeister der polnischen Nationalgroßloge, Prof. Wolfke, wird eingehend vernommen und zur Berichterstattung darüber ebenso über ein ihm geläufiges Gebiet (Stand der augenblicklichen Hygiene in Warschau) aufgefordert. Gleichzeitig werden alle mit polnischen Kranken belegten Lazarette auf den Gesundheitszustand überprüft. Nach noch nicht bestätigten Angaben soll unter der polnischen Jugend eine Flüsterpropaganda betrieben werden, die Waffen nicht abzugeben, sondern sie in Gärten zu vergraben. Weiter nach ungeprüften Angaben, daß nachts von Schwarzsendern in Warschau durchgegeben wird, daß die Bevölkerung ausharrt, da bereits eine neue polnische Regierung in Paris gebildet sei.

Sicherheitspolizei
Einsatzgruppe IV   Warschau, den 10. 10. 1939

Tätigkeitsbereicht

Katastrophale Ernährungslage, weniger Mangel an Lebensmitteln als Fehlen von Transportmitteln sowie einer geregelten und sachgemäßen Verteilung. Folge der Katastrophe ist Preiswucher, Säuglinge sehr stark durch Milchmangel bedroht. Mangel ist, daß Groß- und Kleinhandel keine Erlaubnisscheine zum Einkauf außerhalb Warschaus erhält.

Ein polnisches Propagandaamt wurde in der Nowy Swiat 23 sichergestellt, geschlossen und ausgewertet. In diesem Amt wurden alle denkbaren

Schikanen der Hetze gegen Deutschland vorgefunden. Beigegebenes Hetz-material zur Kenntnis.

Am 8. Okt. 1939 wurden insgesamt 354 Priester und Lehrer festgenom-men, die durch ihre für den polnischen Chauvinismus erwiesene Haltung eine nicht zu unterschätzende Gefahr für die Sicherheit der deutschen Trup-pen, der deutschen Beamten wie der deutschen Zivilbevölkerung dar-stellen.

Polen im Untergrund

Nationalpolnischer Widerstand

Polen ist ein Beispiel dafür, daß nicht jede Untergrund- und Wider-standsbewegung bolschewistisch ist.

Der polnische Staat wurde durch Versailles anno 1919 geschaffen. Mit dem 17. September 1939 hörte er praktisch auf zu existieren. An diesem Tage verließ die polnische Heeresleitung und die polnische Regierung mit ihren führenden Behörden das Land, um nach Rumänien zu fliehen.

Die Angehörigen der polnischen Armee wurden entweder Kriegsgefan-gene der deutschen Wehrmacht oder Gefangene der Sowjetunion. Ein Teil konnte sich der Gefangennahme entziehen. Im polnischen Untergrund der Jahre 1939/40 gab es ein aus den verschiedensten Parteien zusammenge-setztes Parlament, das nach Bedarf einberufen wurde.

General Karaszewicz-Tokarzewski, der zu den Verteidigern von War-schau im September 1939 gehörte und im März 1949 bei seinem Versuch, illegal in den von der Sowjetunion besetzten Teil Polens zu gelangen, von der NKWD verhaftet wurde, gründete am 27. Sept. 1939 mit Offizieren und Politikern mehrerer Parteien einen ,,Dienst am Siege Polens" (Sluzba Zwyciestwu Polski) = SZP mit Vollmacht des polnischen Oberkommandie-renden Rydz-Smigly, der früher dem vertrauten Kreis um Marschall Pil-sudski angehörte. Edward Rydz-Smigly war 1921 Inspekteur, 1935 Gene-ralinspekteur und 1936 Marschall der polnischen Armee geworden. Ihm wird heute die militärische Niederlage Polens angelastet. Die Vollmacht zur Gründung der Organisation überbrachte Divisionsgeneral Juliusz Rómmel. Die offizielle Gründungsversammlung der SZP fand jedoch erst nach der Kapitulation Warschaus im Keller des Warschauer Sparkassengebäudes an der Swieto-Krzyska-Straße statt. An dieser Versammlung nahmen teil: Oberst Rowecki (seit 1935 Kommandeur einer Panzerbrigade), der Sejm-marschall (Reichstagspräsident) Maciej-Rataj als Vertreter der Volkspartei (SL), Professor Roman Rybarski als Vertreter der Nationalpartei (SN), der

Abgeordnete Mieczyslaw Niedzialkowski als Vertreter der Sozialdemokratie (PPS) und der Stadtpräsident von Warschau, Stanski.

Zuzugestehen ist, daß sich Entschlossenheit und Härte, Improvisationskunst und Erfindergeist im Kampf der Widerstandsbewegung gegen die deutsche Besatzungsmacht im außerordentlichen Maße zeigten. Im Untergrund Polens gab es Gerichte, die sowohl über Kollaborateure und Angehörige der deutschen Besatzungsmacht, deren Beseitigung dem polnischen Untergrundstaat als notwendig erschien, Urteile fällten. Geheime Exkutionskommandos vollstreckten sie.

Die Nationalpolnische Bewegung stützte sich auf die national- und antikommunistisch eingestellten bürgerlichen und bäuerlichen Kreise. Sie betrachtete Deutschland als Hauptgegner, lehnte aber auch den Kommunismus scharf ab. Sie verfolgte folgende Ziele: Im Osten Grenze vom Sept. 1939 (Grenze des Rigaer Vertrages von 1921), im Norden und Westen Gebietserweiterung auf Kosten Deutschlands, enge Zusammenarbeit mit Ungarn. Die britische Regierung bemühte sich, die sogenannte Londoner Polnische Exilregierung zur Anerkennung der von der Sowjetunion als Grenzlinie geforderten ,,Curzon-Linie" zu veranlassen. Bis 1944 verliefen die Verhandlungen ergebnislos.

Die nationalpolnische Widerstandsbewegung wurde von der polnischen Regierung in London geleitet. Als Staatspräsident fungierte Wladyslaw Raczkiewicz. Die herausragende Persönlichkeit war Wladislaw Sikorski, der bei einem Flugzeugabsturz bei Gibraltar 1943 umkam. Er war Berufssoldat. Dieser Gegner Pilsudskis hatte als kommandierender General in Lemberg seinen Abschied genommen. In London wurde er Ministerpräsident der polnischen Exilregierung. Gleichzeitig übte er das Amt des Oberbefehlshabers der polnischen Streitkräfte aus.

Nach dem Tod Sikorskis gehörten der polnischen Exilregierung seit dem 14. Juli 1943 an: Stanislaw Mikolajczyk, Ministerpräsident; Jan Kwapinski, stellv. Ministerpräsident und Minister für Industrie, Handel und Schiffahrt; Tadeusz Romer, Außenminister; General Marian Kukiel, Verteidigungsminister; Wladyslaw Banaczyk, Innenminister; Prof. Stanislaw Kot, Informationsminister; Dr. Ludwig Grosfeld, Finanzminister; Jan Stanczyk, Arbeits- und Wohlfahrtsminister; Prof. Waclaw Komarnicki, Justizminister; Marian Seyda, Staatsminister zur Vertretung auf der Friedenskonferenz; Karol Popiel, Staatsminister für die Planung der zukünftigen Verwaltung; Zygmunt Kaczynski, Staatsminister für Erziehung; Henryk Straßburger, Staatsminister für polnische Angelegenheiten im Mittleren Osten.

Die in Warschau gegründete SZP unterstellte sich der Exilregierung. Die SZP, die von dem ,,Politischen Rat" der am 3. Okt. 1939 gegründet wurde, stellte zwei Hauptaufgaben heraus. Kampf gegen die deutsche Besatzungsmacht innerhalb der Vorkriegsgrenzen einschließlich der Sammlung der Reste der ehemaligen polnischen Armee und Zusammenarbeit mit den Zentralstellen der provisorischen nationalen Regierung im Rahmen eines abgestimmten Aktionsplanes. Die SZP war sozusagen als Bindeglied zwischen der alten polnischen Armee und der späteren Heimatarmee gedacht, die aus dem ZWZ hervorging.

Aus einem Gehlen-Bericht vom 1. Juli 1944 ist zu entnehmen: ,,In Polen ist die Regierung durch einen ,stellvertretenden Ministerpräsidenten' als Delegierten der polnischen Regierung und Leiter der illegalen Staatsverwaltung vertreten. Als ,Delegat' wird der ,Landesminister' Jan Kowsky genannt. Ausführendes Organ dieses Regierungsvertreters ist die ,illegale Landesregierung', die sich auf die vier größten Vorkriegsparteien Nationalpartei (SN), Nationale Arbeiterpartei (SP), Volkspartei = Bauernpartei (SL) und Sozialistische Partei (WRN) sowie den von ihnen gebildeten ,Rat der Nationalen Einigkeit' (RJN) stützt. Träger der aktiven Widerstandsbewegung ist der ,polnische Aufstandsverband' (PZP), auch als PZW oder POW bezeichnet. Er ist die Dachorganisation der illegalen ,Landesarmee' (AK). Die ,Landesarmee' (Armija Krajowa) untersteht dem Londoner ,Oberbefehlshaber der polnischen Wehrmacht', General Sosnkowski, der in Polen durch den ,Landeskommandanten', Generalmajor Tadeusz Graf Komorowski (Deckname ,Bor'), vertreten wird." General Kazimierz Sosnkowski war seit 1910 enger militärischer Mitarbeiter Pilsudskis, zuletzt von 1929–1939 Armeeinspekteur. Nach dem Tod Sikorskis wurde er von 1943–1944 Oberbefehlshaber der polnischen Streitkräfte. Infolge der Differenzen zwischen der Sowjetunion und Polen mußte er zurücktreten. Formell wurde ihm die mangelhafte Unterstützung des Warschauer Aufstandes vorgeworfen.

Im Gehlen-Bericht heißt es weiter: ,,Die territoriale Gliederung der ,AK' (Armija Krajowa) lehnt sich vermutlich an die Gliederung der polnischen Wehrmacht der Vorkriegszeit an. Die Stärke der ,AK' soll am 1. Febr. 1944 angeblich 90 000 Mann betragen haben, von denen weniger als ein Drittel ausreichend, der Rest nur unzureichend oder gar nicht bewaffnet gewesen sein soll. Im Mob-Fall war angeblich mit einer Stärke von 100 000 bis 200 000 zu rechnen, von denen jedoch nur ein Teil über Waffen verfügen würde.

Aufgabe der ,AK' ist die Vorbereitung und Durchführung eines Aufstandes, der für den Augenblick eines Zusammenbruchs der deutschen Ostfront geplant ist. Im Zusammenhang mit dem Aufstand sollen die Aktionen ,Bariera' (Sperrgürtel) und ,Ostona' (Abschirmung) durchgeführt werden, die vermutlich die Versammlung neu herangeführter deutscher Kräfte im Generalgouvernement verhindern und das Aufstandsgebiet gegen einen von Osten kommenden Gegner abschirmen soll. Der Aufstand soll durch die in Großbritannien aufgestellte polnische Luftwaffe sowie durch polnische Luftlandetruppen und Fallschirmjäger unterstützt werden. Die ‚AK' hat besondere ‚Luftabteilungen' gebildet, die gut geschult sind und angeblich unter der Leitung aus England gekommener Offiziere stehen; sie sollen vermutlich im Lufttransport an besonders wichtige Einsatzstellen gebracht werden.

Die ‚AK' verfügt über ein ausgedehntes Nachrichtennetz, das eng mit dem britischen Nachrichtendienst zusammenarbeitet. Neben der ‚AK' bestehen zwei der inneren Sicherheit dienende Organisationen: die ‚Leitung des unterirdischen Kampfes' (KWP), welche eine mit einer Sondergerichtsbarkeit verbundene Überwachungstätigkeit gegenüber der ‚AK' ausübt, und das ‚Korps der öffentlichen Sicherheit' (KPP), welches Polizeiaufgaben erfüllt."

Dem Hauptkommando der „AK" unterstanden ein Gebietskommando Westgebiet, ein Gebietskommando Generalgouvernement sowie ein Gebietskommando Ostgebiet. Das Gebietskommando Westgebiet gliederte sich in die drei Wehrkreise Pomerellen, Posen und Lodz, das Gebietskommando Generalgouvernement setzte sich aus den Wehrkreisen Warschau, Radom, Lublin, Siedlce, Krakau und Lemberg zusammen. Ein weiteres Wehrkreiskommando ist fraglich. Das Gebietskommando Ostgebiet hatte vier Wehrkreise: Wilna, Bialystok, Weißruthenien und Wolhynien.

Erwähnt muß werden, daß auch außerhalb Polens militärische Einheiten und politische Organisationen wirkten.

Die polnische Regierung in London war nach England orientiert. Am 17. Sept. 1939 hat der damalige polnische Staatspräsident Mascicki sein Amt auf Racknewicz übertragen. Dieser nahm die Dismesion des letzten polnischen Ministerpräsidenten, General Slawoj-Sladkowski, entgegen und übertrug Sikorski das Amt des polnischen Regierungschefs.

Nach Ausbruch des deutsch-sowjetischen Krieges kam am 30. Juli 1941 ein Vertrag zwischen der Sowjetunion und der polnischen Regierung zustande. Die Beziehungen verschlechterten sich aber ständig. Nach der Aufdeckung der Morde von Katyn am 25. Aug. 1943 wurden die diplomatischen Beziehungen zwischen der Exilregierung und Moskau abgebrochen.

Nach dem Zusammenbruch des polnischen Staates im September 1939 war es Teilen der polnischen Wehrmacht gelungen, über das neutrale Ausland zum Teil nach Frankreich, zum Teil nach Syrien zu entkommen. Aus diesen wurde, wie Gehlen berichtet, die neue polnische Wehrmacht gebildet. Die 1942 aus der Sowjetunion und dem Iran kommenden polnischen Verbände kamen hinzu. 1944 umfaßten die neuen polnischen Streitkräfte mit etwa 40 000 in Großbritannien und zwei Korps mit etwa 80 000 Mann im Mittelmeerraum eine nicht unbeachtliche Streitmacht von rund 150 000 Soldaten. Zur polnischen Wehrmacht stießen später die neu nach England und Palästina übergetretenen Truppenteile.

Gehlen argumentierte zu diesem Thema: „Die in Großbritannien stehenden Verbände, zu denen auch Luftstreitkräfte gehörten, sollen angeblich bei einem Aufstand in Polen gegebenenfalls als Luftlandetruppen oder Fallschirmjäger eingesetzt werden. Die im Mittelmeerraum befindlichen Kräfte sollten seinerzeit nach polnischen Plänen an einem Stoß von Italien oder aus dem Balkan durch Ungarn auf Polen beteiligt werden." Den bewaffneten Kampf führten die einerseits vom Osten, andererseits vom Westen geleiteten Partisanengruppen. Teilweise sprachen sich die Führer ab, teilweise handelten sie getrennt.

1940/41 wurden bereits Liquidierungen von Kollaborateuren durchgeführt. Diversionsakte fanden statt. Sogenannte Todesstrafen an Zuträgern der Sicherheitspolizei und an Polizeibeamten, so drückt man sich in Polen aus, wurden vollstreckt. Unmittelbar nach dem Einmarsch der deutschen Truppen in die Sowjetunion bildeten sich aus linken Widerstandskämpfern und aus sowjetischen Soldaten, die aus Kriegsgefangenenlagern geflüchtet waren, Partisanengruppen, die sich fast ausschließlich auf den Raum Lublin konzentrierten.

Im Frühjahr 1942 ging die von der Polnischen Arbeiterpartei organisierte Volksgarde zur planmäßigen Partisanentätigkeit über. Bis Ende 1942 operierten 52 Partisanenabteilungen im Generalgouvernement. 1943 wurden mehr größere Abteilungen organisiert. Sie traten insbesondere in den Räumen Lublin, Kielce, Krakau, Rzeszow, Śląsk und in Masowien auf. In Warschau wird heute betont, daß die Landesarmee Anfang 1943 den bewaffneten Kampf aktivierte.

Am 13. Dez. 1939 erließ General Sikorski nachstehende Verordnung: „Entsprechend dem Beschluß des Ministerrats vom 8. November 1939 berufe ich einen Ministerausschuß für die Angelegenheiten der Heimat ein. Seine Aufgaben bestehen in der Wahrnehmung sämtlicher Angelegenheiten, die die Heimat und die geheimen Anstrengungen des Volkes betreffen, die darauf gerichtet sind, Polen von der Herrschaft des Feindes zu befreien. Die Vorbereitungen zum aktiven Kampf gegen die Besatzungsmacht werden dem ‚Zwiazek Walki Zbrojnej‘ (ZWZ = ‚Verband zum bewaffneten Kampf‘), einer streng geheimen militärischen Organisation, übertragen." – Zum Vorsitzenden dieses Ministerausschusses und Oberkommandierenden des ZWZ wurde General Sosnkowski ernannt, der sich ebenfalls in Paris befand. Als solcher war er Stellvertreter des Obersten Befehlshabers und diesem unmittelbar unterstellt.

Wesen und Zweck des ZWZ waren in seinen Satzungen folgendermaßen

umrissen: „Der ZWZ ist als militärische Zentralstelle eine Organisation, die im Heimatgebiet tätig ist; sie darf als solche in keinem Fall als Vereinigung mehrerer ähnlicher Organisationen aktiv werden. Der ZWZ ist eine nationale und überparteiliche, alle sozialen Schichten der Bevölkerung umfassende Organisation; sie nimmt in ihren Reihen alle aufrechten Polen ohne Rücksicht auf ihre politische Überzeugung auf, die die Besatzungsmacht aktiv bekämpfen wollen und die den hohen moralischen Anforderungen, welche eine solche Aufgabe an jeden einzelnen stellt, entsprechen. Der ZWZ ist eine streng geheime, auf den Grundsätzen bedingungsloser Zucht und Disziplin sowie bedingungslosen Gehorsams aufgebaute militärische Organisation. Der Freiwillige legt vor seiner endgültigen Aufnahme in die Reihen des ZWZ folgenden Eid ab: ‚Vor Gott dem Allmächtigen und vor der heiligen Jungfrau Maria, Königin der Krone Polens, lege ich meine Hand auf dieses heilige Kreuz, das Zeichen des Leidens und der Erlösung, und schwöre, daß ich die Ehre Polens mit aller mir zu Gebote stehenden Kraft verteidigen und daß ich mit der Waffe in der Hand kämpfen werde, um mein Vaterland von der Sklaverei unter Einsatz meines Lebens zu befreien. Ich schwöre, daß ich meinen Vorgesetzten gegenüber bedingungslos gehorsam sein und jederzeit strengste Verschwiegenheit wahren werde.‘ – Nach Ablegung dieses Eides wurde der Freiwillige vom Einheitsführer mit folgenden Worten aufgenommen: „Ich nehme Dich in die Reihen der Soldaten der Freiheit auf. Der Sieg wird Dein Lohn sein. Verrat wird mit dem Tode bestraft." Die rechtliche Stellung der ZWZ wurde durch einen Erlaß vom Januar 1940 wie folgt festgelegt:
„1. Der ZWZ ist ein Teil der Streitkräfte der Republik Polen. Der Oberkommandierende des ZWZ untersteht unmittelbar dem Obersten Befehlshaber der polnischen Armee.
2. Jeder Offizier und Soldat der polnischen Armee, der dem ZWZ beitritt und am Kampf des ZWZ teilnimmt, gilt auch weiterhin als Soldat der polnischen Armee, der an der Front steht; als solchem stehen ihm sämtliche Rechte eines Soldaten des aktiven Dienstes zu.
3. Alle Mitglieder des ZWZ, die vorher nicht den Streitkräften der Republik Polens angehörten, können auf Antrag des Oberkommandierenden des ZWZ in die polnische Armee aufgenommen werden."
Durch den gleichen Erlaß wurde Oberst Rowecki zum Kommandeur der ZWZ in den von deutschen Truppen besetzten Teilen Polens ernannt, während General Tokarzewski mit der Führung dieser Organisation im sowjetisch besetzten Teilgebiet Polens ernannt wurde. Rowecki wurde im Juni 1943 von der deutschen Polizei verhaftet; an seine Stelle trat Oberst Graf Komorowski. Der bisherige Stabschef, General Belczynski, wurde Stellvertreter. Komorowskis Deckname war Bor (Wald).

Auf die Aktivität der polnischen Widerstandsbewegung wirkte die allgemeine politische Lage und die Entwicklung an den übrigen Fronten ein. Als es den deutschen Truppen 1940 gelang, Dänemark, Norwegen, Holland, Belgien und Frankreich zu besetzen, mußte sich ihre Tätigkeit auf die Stabilisierung der polnischen Verbände, auf Spionage innerhalb der deutschen Besatzungsmacht und auf innerpolitische Propaganda, die sehr intensiv betrieben wurde, beschränken.

1939 und 1940 haben Deutschland und die Sowjetunion im Kampfe gegen die polnische Widerstandsbewegung zusammengearbeitet. Der Beginn des deutsch-sowjetischen Krieges brachte eine Änderung. Die polnische Exilregierung befahl mit der Wiederaufnahme der diplomatischen Beziehungen zu Moskau – die polnische Botschaft in der Sowjetunion wurde in Kuibyschew errichtet – die Einstellung des Kampfes gegen die Sowjets; statt dessen wurden deutsche Truppentransporte und Transporte von Kriegsmaterial Zielpunkte des polnischen Widerstandes. Die ununterbrochen durch Polen rollenden Truppen erlitten empfindliche Verluste an Menschen und Material. Auch mit den Vorbereitungen eines allgemeinen Aufstandes konnte begonnen werden.

Vom 15. Februar 1941 bis zu dem Tage, als die deutschen Truppen Polen verließen, fanden von England nach Polen 488 Versorgungsflüge statt; 64 Flugzeuge, darunter 24 mit polnischer Besatzung, wurden abgeschossen. Auf dem Luftwege gelangten auch 353 Spezialisten und Instrukteure nach Polen.

General Sikorski befahl am 30. Oktober 1941 durch Anweisung Nr. 52: ,,Gleichzeitig erkläre ich, daß die zuständigen Behörden keine Demobilisierung angeordnet haben. Demgegenüber sind alle diejenigen, die in der letzten Zeit im aktiven Militärdienst gestanden haben, als weiterhin in diesem Dienst stehend zu betrachten. Wer sich meinem Befehl widersetzt, wird gemäß Artikel 45, 59, 62, 64 oder 66 des Militärstrafgesetzbuches bestraft.''

1942 gelang es der von London aus geleiteten polnischen Widerstandsbewegung, ihre Untergrundorganisationen im polnischen Raum auszubauen. Am 14. Febr. 1942 befahl der polnische Oberbefehlshaber von London aus die Umbenennung des ,,Bundes des bewaffneten Kampfes'' in ,,Landesarmee'' (Armija Krajowa).

Am 3. Sept. 1941 hatte Sikorski bereits depeschiert: ,,1. In der jetzigen Lage ist die militärische Organisation in der Heimat, die ich als Hauptteil der von mir befehligten Streitkräfte betrachte, im zukünftigen Kampf um die Wiedergewinnung der Unabhängigkeit Polens die wichtigste bestimmende Kraft.

3. Die Erfolge, die auf diesem Gebiet der Hauptkommandant des ,Bundes

des Bewaffneten Kampfes' erzielt hat, sind groß. Trotzdem gibt es in der Heimat noch militärische Gruppierungen, die separat oder in Opposition stehen, und es müssen gegen diese Organisationen alle Mittel angewandt werden, um sie dem Hauptkommandanten des ‚Bundes des Bewaffneten Kampfes' unterzuordnen.

4. Mit der Herausgabe obiger Anordnung muß ich die Gewähr haben, daß in den Reihen des ‚Bundes des Bewaffneten Kampfes' keinerlei Arbeit politischen Charakters ausgeführt wird. Die Berichte des Vertreters der Regierung sowie des Hauptkommandanten des ‚Bundes des Bewaffneten Kampfes', die ich erhalten habe, zeugen davon, daß der Hauptkommandant des Bundes diesen Grundsatz einer jeden Armee gut versteht und einhält. Ich erwarte, daß der Hauptkommandant mit der ihm eigenen Energie die Befolgung seiner Befehle hinsichtlich der Trennung des ‚Bundes des Bewaffneten Kampfes' von der Politik überwacht, wobei ich hinzufügen möchte, daß ich diese Befehle kenne. Diejenigen, die sich nicht an diese strikte Weisung halten, sind aus der militärischen Arbeit auszuschließen.''

1944 gliederte sich die Landesarmee territorial in die Gebiete Warschau, Bialystok, Lemberg, West mit den Bezirken Posen und Pomerellen sowie in die selbständigen Bezirke Warschau-Stadt, Kielce, Lodz, Krakau, Śląsk (Schlesien), Lublin und Wilna. Mitte 1944 war die Landesarmee rund 300 000 Mann stark. Geführt wurde sie von ehemaligen Berufsoffizieren und Unteroffizieren sowie Reserveoffizieren. Die Masse der Soldaten kam aus den verschiedensten gesellschaftlichen Gruppierungen und eingegliederten Organisationen. Durch Waffenabwürfe wurde sie vom Westen versorgt, der auch für die Finanzierung aufkam. Bor-Komorowskis Nachfolger war General Leopold Obulizki (,,Niedzwialdek'').

Die Historiker der Warschauer Paktstaaten behaupten, das Ziel sei die Vorbereitung eines allgemeinen Aufstandes zum Zeitpunkt des Abzuges der deutschen Truppen und die Ermöglichung der Regierungsübernahme durch die Delegatur der Londoner Exilregierung gewesen, die ein Polen mit den Grenzen vom 1. Sept. 1939 im Osten beanspruchte.

Ab Herbst 1942 waren die Kräfte der Kedyn (Kierownictwo Dywersje) tätig. Sie setzten die Angriffe des ,,Vergeltungsbundes'' (Zwiaziek Odweru) und des ,,Fächer'' (Wachlan) fort, die zum großen Teil gegen die Kräfte der deutschen Besatzungsmacht gerichtet waren. Auch wurden im verstärkten Maße Partisanenabteilungen gebildet.

Im September 1942 begann der Zusammenschluß mit der ,,Nationalen Militärorganisation'' (Narodowa Organizacja Wojskowa), die eine Stärke von ungefähr 80 000 Mann hatte. Ein Teil unterstellte sich Rowecki. Ab Frühjahr 1941 war eine Organisation unter Franciszek Kaminski tätig gewesen (Bataliony Chopskie – BCH). Mitte 1942 wurden ,,Spezialabteilungen" (Oddzaly Specjalne – OS) gebildet, die die Aufgaben hatten, die Zwangseintreibungen durch die deutschen Besatzungskräfte zu verhindern. Dabei waren Gemeindeämter, Lebensmittellager, Sägewerke, Molkereien und auch landwirtschaftliche Verteilungsstellen zu vernichten.

Die Bauernbataillone erreichten Ende 1942 eine Stärke von 72 000, im Dezember 1943 135 000 und im Juni 1944 157 000 Mann. Es waren vier Offiziersschulen vorhanden, in denen 300 Offiziere ausgebildet wurden. Ebenfalls gab es eine größere Anzahl von Schulen für Unteroffiziere. Auch Lehrgänge für diese Dienstgrade wurden durchgeführt. Ebenfalls wurde für die Diversionsausbildung gesorgt. Diversion ist ein strategisches Unternehmen, das den Feind von der Richtung der geplanten Hauptaktion ablenken soll. Die Bauernverbände verfügten über eigene Sanitätsdienste, die 6000 Frauen umfaßten. Ihnen gehörten die Krankenschwestern des ,,Grünen Kreuzes" an, das zur illegalen Frauenorganisation ,,Frauenbund" (Ludowy Zwiazek Kopiet – LZK) zu rechnen ist. Die Führung der SL-Roch und das Hauptkommando der Bauernbataillone erklärten sich bereit, ihre Kräfte am Vorabend des allgemeinen Aufstandes dem Oberkommando der Widerstandsarmee in Polen zu unterstellen, das von der Exilregierung zu ernennen war. Der Oberbefehlshaber der Landesarmee telegrafierte am 23. 7. 1943 an die Londoner Exilregierung:

,,Aktives antideutsches Auftreten ist notwendig, weil:

a) wenn wir dieses nicht weiter organisieren und leiten, dadurch eine völlige Übernahme der Initiative auf diesem Gebiet durch die Polnische Arbeiterpartei erfolgen kann, was die Übernahme der geistigen Führung des gesamten dynamischen Teils der Gesellschaft durch sie zur Folge hätte;

b) die Repressalien und der deutsche Terror den Geist in der Gesellschaft immer mehr lähmen. Unsere Kampftätigkeit macht deutlich, daß wir nicht nur Schläge hinnehmen, sondern auch verteilen, wodurch die Gesellschaft ihre Niedergeschlagenheit überwinden und den Terror besser ertragen kann;

c) unsere bewaffneten Aktionen auf die Deutschen in Polen höchst deprimierend wirken, die Verwaltung zerrütten, die Ausbeutung des Landes erschweren sowie bedeutende deutsche Militär- und Polizeikräfte binden;

d) die Kampftätigkeit zur Vorbereitung unserer jungen Abteilungskommandeure notwendig ist . . ."

Es wurde am 30. Mai 1943 ein entsprechender Vertrag abgeschlossen. Gleichzeitig faßte die Führung der SL-Roth den Entschluß, den Sicherheitsapparat bei der Widerstandsbewegung, der bei der Delegatur gebildet worden war, zu überwachen. Im Sommer 1943 erging die vertrauliche Empfehlung, in das Sicherheitskorps (Panstwony Korpus Bezieczenstwo) und in den Selbstverwaltungsschutzdienst (Stracz Samor Zydowa) einzutreten. Es wurde auch eine „Volkssicherheitswacht" (Ludowa Stracz Bezpieczenstwa) geschaffen. In sie gliederten sich die seit Mitte 1942 entstandenen Spezialabteilungen ein. Als Ergebnis kann festgestellt werden, daß etwa 40 000 Angehörige der taktischen Einheiten der Bauernbataillone der Landesarmee unterstellt wurden. Dies bedeutet, daß die Mehrzahl selbständig blieb. Ein Teil der Bauernbataillone schloß sich der Armija Ludowa (Volksarmee) an.

Endlich gab es seit 1941 die „Nationale Militärorganisation" (Narodowa Organizacja Wojskowa). Es bestanden 14 Bezirkskommandos: Krakau, Warschau Hauptstadt, Warschau Land (Wojewodschaft Warschau), Radom-Kielce, Tschenstochau, Lublin, Südost (Wojewodschaften Lemberg, Tarnopol und Stanislau), zentrales Industriegebiet, Wojewodschaft Rzeszów-Podlasie, Bialystok, Nowogrodek, Posen, Pommerellen und Śląsk (Schlesien). Die „Nationale Militärorganisation" in der Stärke von 80 000 Mann setzte sich aus der Polnischen Pfadfinderjugend (Hanrcerstwo Polskie) und der „Jugend Großpolens" zusammen. Hinter ihr standen das Kleinbürgertum, die Großgrundbesitzer und in einer Reihe von Orten die Bauernjugend in den national-katholischen Vereinen. Zuzurechnen zur „Nationalen Militärorganisation" ist die „Nationale Militärische Frauenorganisation" (Narodowa Organizacja Wojskowa Kopier). Ihre 10 000 Mitglieder arbeiteten als Sanitäter, Melder, Verteiler und Kuriere.

Die polnisch-kommunistische Widerstandsbewegung

Bekannt dürfte sein, daß die Kommunistische Partei Polens durch die Kommunistische Internationale 1938 aufgelöst wurde. Dadurch gingen alle organisatorischen Verbindungen verloren. Um die erwachsenen Nachteile zu beseitigen, versuchten einzelne, politische illegale Gruppen zu bilden. In Warschau entwickelten sich die ersten Keime der kommunistischen Widerstandsbewegung. Im Frühjahr 1941 bildete sich „der Verband der Freunde der UdSSR" (Stowarzyszenie Brcyjaciol USRR), die in sich seit Ende 1939 in verschiedenen Stadtbezirken von Warschau arbeitende kommunistische Gruppen vereinigte. Ihr gehörten an: Josef Balcerzak, Serafin Bruzdzinski, Bronislaw Gajewski, Pjotr Grusczynski, Kasimierz Grodecki und Bronislaw Piotrowski. Nach dem 22. Juni 1941 wurde eine „Arbeitergarde" gebildet. Sie hatte Sabotage- und Diversionsaufgaben. U. a. befreite sie sowjetische Kriegsgefangene. Der Verband entfaltete ebenfalls im Warschauer Ghetto seine Tätigkeit. Er hatte dort mehr als 400 Mitglieder.

Auf Initiative von Mitgliedern der Transportarbeiter-Gewerkschaft bildete sich bereits Mitte Mai 1940 in der polnischen Hauptstadt der „Bund der Arbeiter- und Bauernräte" (Zwiazek Rad Robotniczo – Chlopskich „Mlot i Sierb"). Im Herbst 1940 schloß sich diesem Bund eine Gruppe von Anhängern der Volkspartei aus Nordmasowien und linke Sozialisten an. Anfang 1941 verbreitete er seinen Einfluß auf die Wojewodschaften Warschau, Kielce, Lublin, Rzeszów und Śląsk (Schlesien) aus.

Vor Gründung der Polnischen Arbeiterpartei arbeitete der „Bund des Befreiungskampfes" (Zwiazek Walki Wyzwolenczej – ZWW), der im August 1941 durch den Zusammenschluß verschiedener bereits seit Frühjahr 1940 wirkender kommunistischer und linker sozialistischer Gruppen entstanden war. Er wurde geführt von Jerzy Albrecht, Josef Balcerzak, Marian Spychalski, Franciszek Leczycki und Jerzy Walter. Er schuf auch ein militärisches Kommando und sammelte Waffen. In seine Tätigkeit fielen Überfälle auf Industriebetriebe und Verkehrsunternehmen.

U. a. wirkten in Warschau zwei weitere kommunistische Organisationen: die „Proletarier" und die „Spartakisten". Letztere wurde bereits im November 1939 auf Initiative der Sozialisten und der Kommunistischen Jugend gebildet. Sie forderte ein Bündnis mit der Sowjetunion.

In Lodz entstand die Organisation „Kampffront für Unsere und Euere Freiheit" (Front Walki za Nasza i Wasza Wolnosc). In Posen arbeitete die Organisation „KPP", im Gebiet von Lublin „die Kampforganisation des

Volkes" (Bojowa Organizacja Ludowa – BOL), in und um Kielce die ,,Arbeiter- und Bauernvereinigung" (Zjednoczenie Robotniczo – Chlopskie), in und um Rzeszów die ,,Bauern- und Arbeitertat" (Czyn Chlopsko – Robotniczy) und der ,,Bund der Patrioten des Karpatenvorlandes" (Zwiazek Patriotow Podkarpackich), im Gebiet Krakau die Organisation ,,Volkspolen" (Polska Ludowa). Im Dąbrowna-Becken und in Schlesien finden wir den ,,Verband der Freunde der UdSSR" und die Organisation ,,Hammer und Sichel" (Mlot i Sierp). Die Organisationen befahlen das Nichtbefolgen der Anordnungen der deutschen Besatzungsmacht. Sie sammelten in Verstecken die Waffen, übten in Industriebetrieben Sabotage, störten den Eisenbahnverkehr und vertrieben illegale Zeitungen und Flugblätter.

Es begannen auch die Überfälle auf motorisierte Transportkolonnen und deutsche Militäreinheiten aus dem Hinterhalt. Aus dieser Zeit ist Major Henryk Dobrzanski (,,Hubal") bekannt. Ende September 1939 bildete er aus einem Teil des 110. Ulanenregimentes und einer kleinen Gruppe des 102. Ulanenregimentes eine illegale Kampfeinheit. ,,Hubal" erreichte den Raum von Warschau nach der Kapitulation der Stadt. Von dort aus wollte er sich mit einer Gruppe von Freiwilligen nach Ungarn durchschlagen. Er bestand auf dem Marsch dorthin einige Gefechte. In den Wäldern der Puszcza Kozienicka vernichtete er eine deutsche Autokolonne. Er erreichte mit seiner Gruppe die Gory Swietokrzyskie. Dort entschloß sich der Major, den Partisanenkampf aufzunehmen. Die Mehrheit der Gruppe ging mit ,,Hubal" in die Wälder von Suchedniow, später in die von Konskie. Im Winter 1941/42 hielt er sich mit seinen Kampfgenossen in den Wäldern von Spala und von Przysucha auf. Es gelang ihm, eine Partisanenabteilung mit der Stärke von 300 Mann zu schaffen. So konnte er einen Kavalleriezug, einen Artilleriezug und eine Gruppe für schwere Maschinenwaffen bilden. Er führte ständig kleinere Überfälle durch. Den deutschen Einheiten gelang es nicht mehr, die waldreichen Gegenden der Gory Swietokrzyskie zu beherrschen.

Der ,,Bund des bewaffneten Kampfes" befahl Major Hubal die Auflösung der Organisation, da sie den Zeitpunkt einer militärischen Auseinandersetzung noch nicht gekommen sah. Auf diese Art und Weise verkleinerte sich die Einheit ,,Hubal" auf 100 Mann. Dazu ist die von ihm gebildete illegale Organisation zu rechnen, die Einfluß bis hinter die Pilica im Norden und nach Staszow im Süden hatte. Am 30. März kam es nahe Huciska zum Kampf mit deutschen Einheiten. Hubal wurde zum Rückzug in die Wälder von Suchedniow gezwungen, wo er wieder angegriffen wurde.

Am 30. Apr. 1940 fiel ,,Hubal" in den Wäldern von Spalor. Im Zusammenhang mit der Partisanentätigkeit ,,Hubal" wurden in einigen Dörfern des Kampfgebietes Polen hingerichtet, und Dörfer wurden zerstört.

Gehlen berichtet

,,Nach der Inbesitznahme ostpolnischen Gebietes durch die SU im September 1939 wurden sofort 200 000 polnische Offiziere und Soldaten in sowjetrussische Kriegsgefangenschaft überführt, anschließend die politisch verdächtigen Bevölkerungsschichten in NKWD-Lager eingeliefert und schließlich auch große Teile der übrigen Bevölkerung zwangsweise in das Innere der SU umgesiedelt. Insgesamt wurden gegen 2 000 000 polnische Staatsangehörige in die SU verschleppt. Durch den Vertrag vom 30. Juli 1941 gelang es der Londoner ‚Polnischen Regierung‘, unter Ausnützung der Notlage der SU die Entlassung zahlreicher Polen aus den Arbeits- und Umsiedlungslagern, ihre Anerkennung als polnische Staatsangehörige und die Einrichtung von zahlreichen polnischen Vertretungen in der SU zur Betreuung dieser polnischen Staatsangehörigen durchzusetzen. Darüber hinaus konnte General Anders im Auftrage der Londoner ‚Regierung‘ die sog. ‚Sikorski-Armee‘ in der SU aufstellen, die angeblich eine Stärke von 12–16 Divisionen erreichte. Im Herbst 1942 wurde ein Teil dieser Verbände (insgesamt etwa 130 000 Soldaten und Zivilpersonen) nach dem Iran überführt, wo General Anders aus ihnen und den schon zuvor in Palästina stehenden Truppenteilen die jetzt im Mittelmeerraum befindlichen beiden Korps aufstellte.

Mit zunehmender Verschlechterung des Verhältnisses zur ‚Polnischen Regierung‘ begann die Sowjetregierung den Polen gegenüber eine neue Haltung einzunehmen. Anfang 1943 wurden alle noch auf sowjetrussischem Gebiet befindlichen Polen zu Staatsangehörigen der SU erklärt und damit die ‚Polnische Regierung‘ von jeder Betätigungsmöglichkeit in der SU ausgeschaltet.

Etwa gleichzeitig mit dem Abbruch der diplomatischen Beziehungen rief die Sowjetregierung im Frühjahr 1943 den ‚Bund polnischer Patrioten‘ (ZPP) ins Leben, an dessen Spitze die kommunistische Schriftstellerin und frühere polnische Lehrerin Wanda Wassilewska trat. Der ‚Bund polnischer Patrioten‘ tritt unter sowjetischer Unterstützung für die Schaffung eines ‚demokratischen‘, d. h. bolschewistischen Polen ein, das im Osten durch die ‚Curzon-Linie‘ begrenzt und im Westen und Norden durch deutsches Gebiet erweitert werden soll." Der Bund ,,Polnischer Patrioten" (Zwiazek Patriotow Polskich, ZSSR), der seinen Sitz in Moskau hatte, setzte sich zusammen aus: Wanda Wassilewska, Vorsitzende; Andrzej W. Witos. stellv. Vorsitzender. Sonstige Mitglieder u. a.: Generalleutnant Berling, Pfarrer Franciszek Kupsz, Leutnant Klos, Brandes, Dr. B. R. Drobner, J. O. Parnas, L. B. Chwistek, S. K. Ednrychowski, J. K. Stachelski, S. O. Skrzecuewski.

Nahziel der kommunistischen Widerstandsbewegung war die Volkserhebung gegen die Deutschen. Mit Recht sagt Gehlen in seinem Bericht, daß durch Provokation deutscher Sühnemaßnahmen der Deutschenhaß der Bevölkerung aufgestachelt werden soll. Als Fernziel nennt er die Beseitigung aller ,,reaktionären" Elemente, die Schaffung eines freien Polen und die als ,,Demokratisierung" bezeichnete Bolschewisierung . . .

Träger der kommunistischen Widerstandsbewegung war die ,,Polnische Arbeiterpartei" (PPR). Ihre Tätigkeit vollzog sich besonders in Mittel- und Westpolen sowie Ostoberschlesien, während die kommunistische Bewegung in Ostpolen und Galizien vom Zentralkomitee der Allrussischen Kommunistischen Partei geleitet wurde. Bezeichnend ist, daß die Lemberger Zweigorganisation der PPR im Jahre 1943 in die ,,Partisanenabteilung der Westukrainer" umgebildet wurde. Sie nahm selbständig Verbindung mit der Sowjetukraine auf.

Die PPR hatte 3 Zentralabteilungen für Siedlce, Warschau und Tschenstochau. Diesen drei Zentralabteilungen unterstanden die Bezirkabteilungen Ostrow, Siedlce, Lukow, Warschau, Petrikau, Żyrardów und Grojec. Der ,,Bund polnischer Patrioten" übertrug dem wegen kommunistischer Betätigung aus der früheren polnischen Wehrmacht entlassenen damaligen Oberstleutnant Berling im Mai 1943 den Aufbau polnischer Verbände auf sowjetrussischem Gebiet. Im August 1943 wurde die Aufstellung der 1. Division ,,Tadeusz Kosciuszko", im September 1943 der 2. Division ,,Henryk Dombrowski" und im März 1944 der 3. Division ,,Romuald Traugutt" durchgeführt. Im März 1944 wurden die genannten Verbände zur polnischen Armee unter Generalleutnant Berling zusammengefaßt. Die 1. Division unterstand Generalmajor Kiniewicz, die 2. dem Generalmajor Siwicki und die 3. dem Generalmajor Halicki.

*

In der kommunistischen Literatur wird die These vertreten, daß der Kampf um die nationale Unabhängigkeit Polens mit dem Ringen um die soziale Befreiung und um eine revolutionär-demokratische Umgestaltung Polens, die nur mit Hilfe aller sog. fortschrittlichen Kräfte des Volkes und mit Unterstützung der Sowjetunion verwirklicht werden konnte, verbunden werden mußte. Daher war eine einheitliche Partei der Arbeiterklasse, die in der Lage war, ein entsprechendes militärisches, soziales und politisches Programm zu formulieren, aufzubauen.

Mitte 1941 erging die Empfehlung des Exekutivkomitees der Komintern, die Partei wieder herzustellen. Es wurde eine Planungsgruppe mit Marceli Nowotko und Pawel Finder gebildet. Ende Dezember 1941 flog diese nach Moskau. Am 28. Dez. 1941 sprangen Marceli Nowotko, Pawel Finder,

Pinkus Kartin, Czeslaw Skoniecki, Maria Rutkiewicz und Boleslaw Molojec in der Gegend von Wiazowna bei Warschau mit Fallschirmen von Moskau kommend ab. Im Laufe der Zeit gelangten auf demselben Weg die übrigen Mitglieder der Initiativgruppe in die verschiedenen Gebiete Polens. Am 28. Mai 42 fand in der Wohnung von Juliusz Rydygier im Stadtviertel Zoliborz, Krasinskistraße 18, die Gründungsversammlung der Polnischen Arbeiterpartei statt. Vertreten waren der ,,Bund des Befreiungskampfes" aus der Gruppe ,,Proletarier", der ,,Verband der Freunde der UdSSR" und der ,,Bund der Arbeiter- und Bauernräte". Pawel Finder legte den Plan zum Aufbau der Partei sowie den Entwurf der ersten programmatischen Erklärung vor, der akzeptiert wurde. Die Teilnehmer der Versammlung einigten sich auf den Namen ,,Polnische Arbeiterpartei" (Polska Partia Robotnicza, PPR). Es wurde beschlossen, die einzelnen kommunistischen Widerstandsbewegungen aufzulösen. Ihre Mitglieder sollten in die Reihen der ,,Polnischen Arbeiterpartei" eintreten.

Es wurde ein ,,Dreiergremium" als Führungsspitze gebildet. Diesem Gremium gehörten Marceli Nowotko als Sekretär sowie Pawel Finder und Boleslaw Molojec an. Letzterer wurde Ende 1942 als schuldig am Tode von Nowotko betrachtet und hingerichtet. Der neugegründeten Partei traten in kurzem alle linken Widerstandsgruppen bei. Zu dem Vorgang schrieb der ,,Bund des Befreiungskampfes in seinem Blatt ,,Wir siegen" u. a.: ,,Die Entstehung der Polnischen Arbeiterpartei entspricht unseren Wünschen. Als Ausdruck unserer restlosen Solidarität mit der politischen Erklärung der Polnischen Arbeiterpartei gibt die Zentralexekutive des ,,Bundes des Befreiungskampfes" den Willen der Mitglieder der gesamten Organisation, den ,,Bund des Befreiungskampfes" aufzulösen, bekannt. Gleichzeitig fordert sie alle Mitglieder und Sympathisierenden des ehemaligen ,,Bundes des Befreiungskampfes", alle ehrlichen Polen, denen die Sache der Freiheit teuer ist, auf, in die Reihen der Polnischen Arbeiterpartei einzutreten. In diesen Reihen müssen wir unsere Kampfanstrengungen verdoppeln, die Polnische Arbeiterpartei wird uns auf den Weg des unbeugsamen und siegreichen Kampfes zu einem unabhängigen und freien Polen führen."

Die Polnische Arbeiterpartei stellte auch eine bewaffnete Organisation, die ,,Volksgarde" (Gwardia Ludowa – GL) auf, die im Frühjahr 1942 den Partisanenkampf in den polnischen Gebieten aufnahm. In den NS-Verfahren wird häufig das Wort ,,Mai-Aktion" für Erschießungen der Juden gebracht. Im Juli 1942 beginnt die furchtbare Vernichtungsaktion im Warschauer Ghetto, in welchem sich einige hundert kommunistische Zellen befanden. Daher darf gefragt werden: Besteht zwischen der Entwicklung im Jahre 1942 sowie den furchtbaren Ereignissen und den völkerrechtswidrigen Befehlen der Besatzungsmacht irgendeine Verbindung?

Die Ursache zur Bildung der Bauernbataillone liegt in der deutschen Planung der Aussiedlung der polnischen Bauern aus dem Gebiet von Zamość. Sie gingen zum großen Teil aus den „Spezialabteilungen" (Uddziały Specjalne) hervor. Wir finden sie auch in den Räumen Hrubieszów, Sandomierz und Olkusz.

Besondere Bedeutung wird in Warschau dem Einsatz der „Polnischen Volksarmee", des „Sicherheitskorps", der „Volksarmee der Arbeiter der polnischen Sozialisten" und den militärischen Abteilungen der „Polnischen sozialistischen Partei" zugemessen. Genannt werden auch die Widerstandsorganisation „Greif von Pomorze", die „Bewaffnete Konföderation" u. a. Organisationen. Die Tätigkeit der Jugend wird gerühmt.

Von Interesse sind die Sätze „Die Partisanenabteilungen und die in den Städten wirkenden Kampftrupps rekrutierten sich im bedeutenden Maße aus Jugendlichen. Auch die berühmten Warschauer Bataillone – das Bataillon der Volksgarde ‚czwartacy' und die Bataillone der Landesarmee ‚Żoska' und ‚Parasal' bestanden aus Mitgliedern illegaler Jugendorganisationen des ‚linken Kampfbundes der Jugend' und der Pfadfinderorganisation ‚Graue Reihen'." Tüszyński schildert auch das Zusammenwirken der von Ost und West geleiteten Widerstandsorganisationen und stellt fest:

„Da zwischen den zentralen Führungsorganen der wichtigsten Widerstandsorganisationen Meinungsverschiedenheiten bestanden oder sie sogar politische Feindschaft trennte, war es für die Entwicklung des bewaffneten Kampfes von größter Bedeutung, wie sich das Zusammenwirken zwischen den Abteilungen unterschiedlicher Richtungen auf dem Schlachtfeld gestaltete. In diesem Zusammenhang muß hier festgestellt werden, daß es zwischen Abteilungen der Volksgarde, der Bauernbataillone, der Landesarmee und anderen in vielen Kämpfen und bewaffneten Aktionen zum Zusammenwirken kam. Manchmal tauschten sie Losungen untereinander aus, oder sie unterzeichneten spezielle Vereinbarungen über die Zusammenarbeit. Diese Zusammenarbeit zwischen Abteilungen unterschiedlicher Organisationen wirkte sich günstig auf die Entwicklung des Partisanenkampfes in den jeweiligen Gebieten aus. Dort, wo es zum Zusammenwirken gekommen war, konnten die Partisanen ihre Kampfpläne leichter erfüllen. Dort hingegen, wo man die Zusammenarbeit ablehnte, profitierten nur die Okkupanten daraus, was manchmal tragische Folgen nach sich zog."

Der genannte polnische Autor stellt fest, daß die „Front des bewaffneten Kampfes" seit Mitte 1942 immer mehr neue Gebiete Polens erfaßte: Pomorze (Pommerellen, Beskid, Śląsk (Ostoberschlesien), Bialystok und den nördlichen Teil von Mazowsze (Masowien). Ausdrücklich hebt er hervor: „die meisten Partisanenabteilungen bildeten sich . . . vor allem in den Räumen Lublin, Kielce und teilweise Krakau."

Am 21. Juli 1943 erklärte Heinrich Himmler das Generalgouvernement und den Bezirk Bialystok für Bandenkampfgebiete, wie es auch für Kroatien und die Untersteiermark, Oberkärnten (Oberkrain), das ,,Reichskommissariat Ukraine" und für einen Teil des ,,Reichskommissariats Ostland" geschah.

Vorgetragen werden muß, daß nach polnischer Darstellung in den Reihen der polnischen Partisanenbewegung Angehörige anderer Nationalitäten kämpften: Russen, Ukrainer, Grusinier, Belorussen, Aserbaidschaner, Deutsche, Juden, Slowaken, Magyaren, Tschechen, Franzosen, Italiener, Serben, Slowenen, Kroaten und Engländer.

Das Zentralkomitee der Polnischen Arbeiterpartei brachte auch drei Zeitschriften mit den Namen ,,Trybuna Wolnosci", ,,Trybuna Chropska", ,,Gwardzista" sowie mehrere lokale Zeitungen heraus. Mitte 1942 gelang es der PPR, die Mehrheit der polnischen Gebiete zu erfassen. Die Polnische Arbeiterpartei, die auf marxistisch-leninistischer Grundlage gebildet wurde, griff auf eine langjährige Erfahrung der polnischen revolutionären Bewegung zurück. Als Hauptaufgabe sah die Partei den Kampf gegen die deutsche Besatzungsmacht an. Das Programm der PPR war identisch mit der Strategie und Taktik der Internationalen Kommunistischen Bewegung.

Die Volksgarde hatte die Aufgabe, den Partisanenkampf zu führen. In der ersten Nummer der Zeitung ,,Gwardzista" heißt es: ,,Die Aufgabe der Volksgarde ist es, in den vordersten Reihen dieses Kampfes zu stehen. Ihr Bestreben ist es, den Kampf der bewaffneten Avantgarde der Befreiungsbewegung ehrenvoll zu erfüllen. Ihre Aufgabe ist es, Kämpfer für die Sache der Befreiung der polnischen werktätigen Massen auszubilden und im Kampf zu stählen."

Der Ausbau der Gwardia wurde begünstigt durch die Erfahrungen einiger von Kommunisten geleiteter Organisationen, die bereits in den Jahren 1940/41 gewirkt hatten. Es sind der ,,Bund des Befreiungskampfes", der ,,Verband der Freunde der UdSSR", die ,,Arbeiter- und Bauernkampforganisation" und die ,,Kampffront für unsere und euere Freiheit". Jedes Parteimitglied sollte ein Kämpfer der Volksgarde sein.

An der Spitze der Volksgarde stand bis August 1942 Marian Spychalski (,,Marek"); ihm folgte dann Franciszek Jozwiak (,,Franek" oder ,,Wit").

Im Jahre 1942 bestanden 12 territoriale Bezirke der Organisation:

1. Warschau
2. Warschau-Vororte am linken Weichselufer
3. Warschau-Vororte am rechten Weichselufer
4. Lublin
5. Radom
6. Kielce

7. Tschenstochau
8. Krakau
9. Sląsker Kohlenbecken (Ostoberschlesien u. östl. angrenzende Gebiete Russisch-Polens)
10. Lodz
11. Posen
12. Plock

Mitte 1942 wurden Gebietskommandos als höchste territoriale Organe der Volksgarde geschaffen: I (Warschau), II (Lublin), III (Kielce/Radom), IV (Krakau), V (Lodz). Außerdem entstand das Gebietskommando Lemberg, dessen Organisatoren polnische und ukrainische Kommunisten waren. Warschau wurde unmittelbar dem Hauptstab der Volksgarde unterstellt. Mitte 1943 wurde das Gebietskommando Śląsk gebildet, während das Gebiet Lemberg in der Ukraine westlich des Dnjepr aus dem Organisationsnetz der Volksgarde ausgegliedert und der Führung der sowjetischen Partisanenbewegung in der Ukraine unterstellt wurde.

Warschau behauptet, daß die Abteilung der Volksgarde „S. Czarniecki" unter Franciszek Zubrzycki („Maly Franek") als erste Mitte Mai 1942 in den Partisanenkampf eingriff. Die Partisanenabteilung war mit Hilfe der Führung der Polnischen Arbeiterpartei und der Volksgarde organisiert worden. Der „Gwardzista" veröffentlichte dazu einen Befehl des Hauptstabes der Volksgarde. Gleichzeitig hebt Warschau hervor, daß bereits im Herbst und Winter 1939 in verschiedenen Gegenden Polens Partisanen und Abteilungen tätig gewesen seien. Bemängelt wird aber, daß bis Frühjahr/Sommer 1942 die Partisanengruppen ohne Pläne und ohne einheitliche Führung gekämpft hätten. Hervorgehoben wird ihre Konzentrierung in den Wäldern von Lublin und Bialystok.

Vorwürfe werden von kommunistischer Seite gegen von der Londoner Exilregierung geführte Einheiten gemacht, die zur Vernichtung kommunistischer Verbände beigetragen hätten. In den Partisanenabteilungen kämpften auch Hunderte von sowjetischen Soldaten, die aus Kriegsgefangenenlagern geflüchtet waren. Sowjetrussische Führer waren zum Beispiel W. Wojtschenko („Saschka"), F. Kowalow („Fjodor") und J. Salnikow („Jascha").

Gruppen des „Kampfbundes der Jugend" (Zwiazek Walki Mlodyzh–ZWM") verstärkten im Frühjahr 1943 die Volksgarde. Diese waren besonders tätig in Warschau.

Im Hinterland hatte die Volksgarde Stützpunkte.

Die enge Verbindung mit den Sowjets war gegeben. Bereits in der Nacht vom 16. zum 17. August 1941 wurde die Gruppe „Michael" (Hauptmann

Nikolay Arciszerwski) in Polen abgesetzt. Der Kommandeur dieser Gruppe baute ein umfangreiches Kundschafternetz auf, das insbesondere auf die deutsche Luftwaffe, das Eisenbahntransportwesen und auf die Häfen an der Ostsee gerichtet war. Die Gruppe Michael informierte den Generalstab der sowjetischen Streitmacht über die Zahl der transportierten technischen Waffen der mechanisierten Truppen. Auch die Verschiebungen der deutschen Truppen durch Polen wurden gemeldet. Der Informationsdienst der Volksgarde selbst konzentrierte sich auf das Eisenbahntransportwesen und die Rüstungsindustrie. Bedeutsam ist die Tatsache, daß gleichzeitig mit der Landesarmee, aber unabhängig von ihr der Nachrichtendienst der Volksgarde Informationen über das Forschungszentrum für Raketenwaffen in Peenemünde gewann.

In der zweiten Hälfte des Jahres 1944 wurden im Hinterland der deutschen Truppen mehrere dutzend polnische und polnisch-sowjetische Gruppen in verstärktem Maß abgesetzt, die Informationen über Stärke, Truppenverschiebungen und Befestigungsanlagen der deutschen Wehrmacht sammelten.

Dem SD-Führer Dr. Strickner ist nur sehr teilweise zuzustimmen, wenn er in seinem Bericht über eine Neuordnung der Politik im polnischen Raum (RSHA III P 2 v-Dr. Str.-So) vom 18. Oktober 1944 schreibt: ,,Die seit 1939 vertretene Polenpolitik ging von folgenden vier Voraussetzungen aus:

1. dem tausendjährigen Kampf zwischen dem deutschen und dem polnischen Volk, der polnischen Kriegsschuld und der Ermordung zehntausender Volksdeutscher im September 1939.
2. Der biologischen Unterwertigkeit des größten Teiles des polnischen Volkes und der aus einer Vermischung erwachsenden Gefahr für den deutschen Volkskörper.
3. Der Tatsache, daß große Teile des Gebietes, das Polen 1939 bewohnten, dem Reich wieder eingegliedert (eingegliederte Ostgebiete) bzw. der übrige Teil als künftiger deutscher Siedlungs- und Volksboden (GG) angesehen wurde.
4. Einem baldigen Kriegsende.

Folge war eine dogmatisch-rassistische Polenpolitik für den Augenblick, die eine Endlösung der Verdrängung des Polentums aus dem das Reich interessierenden Raum in den Osten als Fernziel voraussah. Es war die Politik, die das polnische Volk auf den Raum des GG zusammendrängte (Evakuierungen aus den eingegliederten Ostgebieten), es politisch zu neutralisieren suchte und den Polen dort, wo er mit deutschen Menschen zusammenlebte oder leben mußte, unwürdig behandelte, um alle politischen und biologischen Gefahren für das deutsche Volk nach Möglichkeit auszuschließen. Eine letzte und offizielle Entscheidung über das endgültige

Schicksal des Polentums fiel nicht. Wenn auch das GG gelegentlich als „Heimstätte des polnischen Volkes" bezeichnet wurde, so war die deutsche Führung bemüht, dem Polentum dieses Gefühl einer Heimat nicht zu geben, sondern es über die deutschen Absichten, über sein Schicksal nach dem Kriege im unklaren zu lassen. Die Aussiedlung (anstatt Vernichtung) der polnischen Intelligenz aus den eingegliederten Ostgebieten in das GG führte dort zu einer Konzentration des politischen Polentums überhaupt, die um so gefährlicher wurde, als keine Sicherheitsventile für eine politische Tätigkeit offengelassen waren oder genehmigt werden konnten. Bis in das Jahr 1942 hinein konnte von einer durchaus vorhandenen Bereitwilligkeit und Mitarbeit insbesondere der polnischen Bauern und Arbeiter gesprochen werden, wenn auch bereits damals die Verhältnisse auf wirtschaftlichem Gebiet (mangelhafte Erfassung und infolgedessen Schleichhandel) zum Teil unerfreulich waren und den Fähigkeiten der deutschen Verwaltung kein besonderes Zeugnis ausstellten. Gefördert durch die Feindpropaganda und im wesentlichen verursacht durch die militärischen Rückschläge des Reiches sowie durch die hin- und her schwankende Polenpolitik des GG, die insbesondere den Polen immer wieder den Eindruck deutscher Schwäche vermittelte, hat sich bis zum Warschauer Aufstand die innenpolitische Lage des Generalgouvernements wesentlich verschlechtert und zu einem solchen Anwachsen der Tätigkeit und Macht der Widerstandsbewegung geführt, daß praktisch von ihr als Staat im Staate gesprochen werden kann. Die infolge Menschenmangel unzureichenden deutschen Bekämpfungsmaßnahmen und der häufige Kurswechsel in der Polenpolitik sowie Verfallserscheinungen innerhalb des deutschen Sektors im Generalgouvernement (Warschau nächst Paris umfangreichster Etappen- und Fleischhandelsplatz) unterstützten die Widerstandsbewegung besonders stark.

Politisch falsche Maßnahmen (Polenaussiedlung in Zamość, Arbeiterfang-Aktionen usw.) verstärkten den politischen Widerstandswillen . . . Allgemein fehlte die einheitliche Linie in der Polenpropagandapolitik des GG. Zu all dem kommt einerseits der ausgesprochene Freiheitswille des Polentums, andererseits seine konspirative Veranlagung. Daneben spielte die P-Kennzeichnung der Polen im Reich, die als diffamierend empfunden wurde, eine Rolle, ebenso wie alle durchgeführten Beschränkungen des kulturellen Eigenlebens, besonders auch auf dem Gebiete der Volksbildung und Erziehung sowie die geringe Beteiligung an der Verwaltung.

Das polnische Volk fühlte sich z. T. durch alle diese Maßnahmen von deutscher Seite und besonders durch fehlende deutsche Äußerungen über sein Schicksal im neuen Europa aus der europäischen Völkergemeinschaft ausgestoßen und fürchtete, daß es ähnlich wie das jüdische Volk in seiner völkischen Substanz vernichtet werden sollte.

Die fast tausendjährige Sehnsucht der Polen nach einem Großpolen ist heute mehr denn je in jedem Polen lebendig. Er ist dafür imstande, jedes Opfer zu bringen. Die Behandlung eines Volkes mit Methoden, die England für außereuropäische Völker (Blechlöffel und Kattun) anwandte, ist daher von vornherein auf das polnische Volk nicht anwendbar."

Sabotage, illegale Waffenproduktion, Kampf gegen Schiene und Straße

Im Kampf gegen die deutsche Besatzungsmacht spielen Sabotage, illegale Produktion von Waffen und Kampfmitteln eine große Rolle. Bedeutend ist die Herstellung von Handgranaten. Allein in Warschau wurden mehr als 100 000 gefertigt. Auch die Menge hergestellter Minen, Maschinenpistolen („Sten" und „Blyskawica") ist groß. Die illegale Produktion von Waffen – auch in Ghettos – fand unter primitiven Bedingungen statt. Noch heute wird von kommunistischer Seite hervorgehoben, daß die Widerstandsbewegung nur 440 Tonnen Waffen und techn. Geräte von den Westalliierten erhielt, während an Frankreich 10 000 Tonnen und an Jugoslawien 20 000 Tonnen aus der Luft und 75 000 Tonnen auf dem Seeweg ausgeliefert wurden. Albanien, Griechenland und Italien haben angeblich mehr als Polen erhalten. Die illegale landeseigene Produktion fand gleichsam vor deutschen Augen statt. Eine Gruppe von Physikern, Chemikern und Ingenieuren arbeitete ohne Unterbrechung am geeigneten Material. Für die deutsche Wehrmacht gab es im Generalgouvernement 37 Werke, die Kriegsmaterial produzierten. Polnische Geheimgruppen versorgten daraus die Widerstandsbewegung mit Rohmaterial und Fertigprodukten. Auch Überfälle auf Lager und Transportzüge dienten dem Zwecke der Waffenbeschaffung für einen geplanten Aufstand.

In den Jahren 1943–44 erreichte die illegale Kampfmittelproduktion ihren Höhepunkt.

Die Untergrundbewegung verfügte über

5 mechanische Werkstätten mit 44 Werkzeugmaschinen,

2 Werkstätten mit Drehbänken für Maschinenpistolenläufe,

2 Werkstätten für serienmäßige Zusammensetzung von Maschinenpistolen,

4 Werkstätten für die Produktion von Handgranaten,

3 Schießstände,

3 Produktionsstätten für Sprengstoffe,

1 Pyrotechnisches und Chemisches Labor,

2 Forschungs- u. Prüfungslabors,

1 Werkstätte für serienmäßige Zusammensetzung von Flammenwerfern,

2 Prüfstände für Flammenwerfer,

1 Konstruktions-, Zeichen- und Lichtpausbüro.

Die amtliche polnische Statistik gibt vom 1. Januar bis 30. Juni 1944 folgende Erfolgsbilanz:

1.	Lokomotiven beschädigt	8 930 St.
2.	Eisenbahnzüge zur Entgleisung gebracht	732 St.
3.	Eisenbahnzüge in Brand gesetzt	448 St.
4.	Eisenbahnwaggons beschädigt	10 058 St.
5.	Eisenbahnbrücken gesprengt	38 St.
6.	Kraftfahrzeuge zerstört	4 326 St.
7.	Flugzeuge zerstört	28 St.
8.	Kesselwagen zerstört	1 167 St.
9.	Brennstoff vernichtet	4 674 t
10.	Brennstofftanks beschädigt	3 t
11.	Wehrmachtsdepots in Brand gesetzt	122 t
12.	Teilzerstörungen im Warschauer Stromversorgungsnetz	638 t
13.	Armeehauptdepots in Brand gesetzt	8 St.
14.	Fabriken zerstört	7 St.
15.	Maschinen der Rüstungsproduktion zerstört	2 827 t
18.	Überfälle auf Deutsche mit tödlichem Ausgang (einschließlich 769 Überfälle auf prominente Angehörige der SS und Polizei, die in der ersten Hälfte des Jahres 1944 ermordet wurden).	5 733.

Die Statistik zählt außerdem 92 Fälle von Sabotage bei der Fabrikation von Artilleriegeschossen und Geschützen, 4800 Fälle von Sabotage bei der Fabrikation von Sendern für Flugzeuge und Flugzeugmotoren und schließlich 25 000 Sabotageakte verschiedener Art auf.

Die Sabotage war außerordentlich wirkungsvoll.

In der Landwirtschaft wurde die Ablieferung von Agrarerzeugnissen, Fleisch- und Molkereiprodukten be- und verhindert. Abgelieferte Produkte wurden vernichtet.

Berichte des „Bundes des Bewaffneten Kampfes" zeigen auf, daß bis März 1941 1700 Werkzeugmaschinen und 107 Bordfunkgeräte mit Mängeln oder mit Verspätung produziert wurden.

95 % der 600 000 hergestellten Kondensatoren hatten technische Fehler. In Schlesien wurden in der zweiten Hälfte 20 000 unbrauchbare Geschosse produziert, 656 Kraftwagen und 22 Flugzeuge beschädigt. Allein im Oktober und November 1941 wird von 35 Tonnen verseuchtem Öl berichtet. Aufgezählt wird die Beschädigung von 374 Kraftwagen. Darüber hinaus setzten Sabotagetrupps vier Fabriken in Brand.

Im dritten Viertel 1941 sank die Produktion infolge langsameren Arbeitstempos und der Sabotage um 30 %. In den folgenden Jahren nahm die Sabotagetätigkeit bedeutend zu.

Welche Bedeutung die Sabotage in Polen hatte, ergibt sich aus den Äußerungen des Inspektors der Rüstungsindustrie im „Generalgouvernement", General Schindler, auf einer Tagung des Kriegswirtschaftsstabes am 22. Sept. 1943 in Krakau: Das „Generalgouvernement" produziere ein Viertel bis ein Drittel der ganzen Infanteriemunition, Tausende von Granaten, Hunderte von Geschützen und eine große Zahl von Panzerwagen. Größere und größte Schwierigkeiten ergaben sich aus der Tätigkeit der „Banden" in den Rüstungsbetrieben. Beispiele: In den Zellgarn-AG-Werken in Litzmannstadt wurden im August 1942 die Maschinen außer Betrieb gesetzt. Die Fabrik arbeitete fünf Tage nicht mehr. In Ostrowies konnte ein Hochofen für 14 Tage infolge eines Sabotageaktes außer Betrieb gesetzt werden. Im Sommer 1943 sank die Produktion Hasag-Fabrik in Skarrzysko-Kamienna wesentlich, die Rohstahlproduktion der Eisenhütte von Tschenstochau um 18 %. Die Lieferung von Panzerteilen in Stalowa Wóla erreichte einen Rückstand von zwei Monaten. Eine große Anzahl von Sabotageakten in Erdölgruben, in kleineren Industriebetrieben wurde nicht nur im Inneren der Betriebe, sondern auch von außen durchgeführt. Es gibt keinen Zweifel, daß die Partisanen die deutschen Eisenbahntransporte außerordentlich nachhaltig trafen. Die 8 bis 9 wichtigsten Eisenbahnlinien, die das Reich mit der Ostfront verbanden, führten durch Polen, auch neun von 12 Hauptverkehrsstraßen in den sowjetischen Raum liefen durch polnisches Gebiet. Die „Gwardzirta" betonte am 1. Juli 1942: „Die Hauptaufgabe der Volksgarde muß jetzt der Kampf gegen den Kriegstransport sein, und die Hauptlosung der Partisanen muß lauten:

„Kein einziger Militärzug darf im Osten ankommen. Kein einziges Bahngleis darf brauchbar sein." Derartige Weisungen wurden auch in Zukunft ständig wiederholt. Von Mai bis Dez. 1942 wurden 30 Züge zum Entgleisen gebracht. Am 14. September 1942 zerstörte die Volksgarde-Abteilung „Tadeusz Kościuszko" die Eisenbahnanlagen auf der Station Szastarka im Gebiet von Lublin. In der Nacht vom 7. zum 8. Oktober 1942 wurden Gleise auf sechs Strecken rund um Warschau gesprengt. In der Nacht vom 16. zum 17. November 1942 zerstörten Partisanengruppen Anlagen auf der Strecke Radom – Deblin – Luków – Terespol. Eine Brücke wurde gesprengt, andere zerstört. Fünf Transportzüge wurden zum Entgleisen gebracht.

Im Jahre 1943 vermehrten sich die Anschläge auf den deutschen Eisenbahntransport außerordentlich. In der Nacht vom 31. Dez. 1942 und 1. Januar 1943 wurden südlich Lublin vier Brücken zerstört und sechs Stationen der Bahnanlagen beschädigt.

Zwei Züge entgleisten. – Der 25. Febr. 1943 brachte in 24 Stunden durch Anschläge im Raum von Krakau ein Verkehrschaos. Zwischen Mydlniki und Zabiersów ließen Kampftrupps einen Schnellzug entgleisen. Die Folge war, daß ein Militärtransportzug auf ihn auffuhr. Zwischen Skavina und Borek Szlachecki gelang es polnischen Partisanen ebenfalls, einen Militärzug zum Entgleisen zu bringen. Ähnlichen Erfolg hatten sie zwischen Podleźe und Staniatki. Zwischen Bochnia und Rzezawa gelang es ihnen, einen Zusammenstoß zweier Züge herbeizuführen. Zwischen Borek Falecki und Skawina glückte eine Gleissprengung. – Im Raum der Lysa Góra wurde der Verkehr auf der Schmalspurstrecke lahmgelegt. Damit wurde Abfuhr und Abbau von Eisenkies im Bergwerk „Staszic" unterbrochen, was sich auf die industrielle Erzeugung auch für Stahlproduktion auswirkte.

Schwer getroffen wurde zwischen dem 26. und 28. September 1943 der Warschauer Verkehrsknotenpunkt. Die Brücke über den Fluß Okrzejka wurde zerstört. An einigen Stellen in Warschau wurden die Gleise gesprengt. Innerhalb von drei Tagen entgleisten zwischen Wawer und Olszynka, bei Legionowo, Elsnerowo, Zyszin und Żyrardów Züge. Gemeldet wird von kommunistischer Seite:

„1943 führte die Volksgarde 169 Aktionen und die Landesarmee 99 Aktionen durch, bei denen sie Züge angriffen, zum Entgleisen brachten oder zerstörten. Die Volksgarde konnte in 113 Aktionen Bahnstationen, Blockstellen, Brücken und Gleise zerstören oder beschädigen, während die Landesarmee in 15 Aktionen Stationen und Brücken zerstörte oder beschädigte. Die Volksgarde rief durch ihre Aktionen 55 Unterbrechungen im Eisenbahnnachrichtennetz hervor, die Landesarmee insgesamt 216.

Die Bilanz der Jahre 1942/43 enthielt mehr als 800 Eisenbahnaktionen, darunter mehr als 300 im Eisenbahnnachrichtennetz, und Tausende von Sabotageakten im gesamten Eisenbahnwesen. Das war schon ein sehr spürbarer Schlag gegen eines der verwundbarsten Glieder der faschistischen Kriegsmaschinerie."

Der Aufstand in Warschau im Jahre 1944

Tatsache ist, daß die Sowjets Unterdrückungsmaßnahmen gegen die nationalen Kräfte und die Intelligenz nach ihrem Einmarsch in Ostpolen durchführten – Vernichtungsmaßnahmen an den Polen gab es auch in der Sowjetunion. Katyn ist ein Beispiel. Im sogenannten Generalgouvernement wuchs der Widerstand der Polen gegen die deutsche Besatzung. Ein Großteil der Landesarmee unter Graf Tadeusz Komorowski erhob sich im Aug. 1944.

Trotz mancher kritischen Situation behielten die Deutschen die Oberhand. Das Oberkommando der Heeresgruppe Mitte gibt für die Lage im September 1944 nachstehendes Bild:

„Die im Stadtgebiet Warschau kämpfenden Aufständischen wurden nach dem Vordringen der Front bis an das östliche Weichselufer zunächst vom Westufer der Weichsel abgedrängt; sodann wurden die einzelnen Aufstandsherde niedergekämpft bzw. zur Kapitulation gezwungen. Als erste kapitulierten die Vorstädte Mokotow und Zoliborz, schließlich auch die beiden in der Stadtmitte in der Hand der Aufständischen verbliebenen Stadtteile. Dabei stellte sich heraus, daß an dem Kampf in Warschau neben der AK auch zahlenmäßig schwächere, aber gut bewaffnete Teile der AL – zum Teil unter Führung russischer Offiziere – teilgenommen hatten. Auch kleine Teile der sowjet-polnischen Armee Berling waren über die Weichsel zu den Aufständischen gestoßen. Laufenden Zuzug hatten die Aufständischen von der Bandenansammlung in den Kampinos-Wäldern über Zoliborz erhalten. Die dort verbliebenen Bandenkräfte wurden durch Angriff von Osten abgedrängt und wichen nach Westen, Südwesten, teilweise auch in südlicher Richtung aus. Über ihren Verbleib sind noch keine sicheren Feststellungen getroffen. Es ist jedoch anzunehmen, daß sie Verbindung mit den im Raum Skierniewice, Tomaszów, Opoczno stehenden Bandenkräften suchen werden. Ihre Stärke kann mit 4000–5000 Mann angenommen werden.

Unterstützt wurde der Zusammenbruch des Aufstandes in Warschau durch starken Mangel an Lebensmitteln, Wasser, Sanitätsmaterial sowie durch scharfe Streitigkeiten zwischen den Abteilungen der AK und AL, die schließlich zur offenen Sabotage der beiderseits gegebenen Befehle und zu bewaffneten Auseinandersetzungen führten.

An Gefangenen wurden 17 000 Mann eingebracht; die Zahl der blutigen Verluste wird von polnischer Seite auf 10 000 geschätzt. Die Verluste der Zivilbevölkerung sollen ein Vielfaches davon betragen. Die Zahl der abgelieferten Waffen bleibt auffallend hinter der Gefangenenzahl zurück. Es ist damit zu rechnen, daß Waffen in größerem Umfang in geheimen Waffenlagern zurückblieben.

Im Generalgouvernement, insbesondere im Raum Tomaszów – Petrikau – Opoczno sowie südlich der Heeresgruppengrenze im Raum Radom – Konskie – Kielce wurden wiederholt starke Bandenkräfte bestätigt, von denen namentlich eine Gruppe von etwa 2000 Mann im Przysucha-Wald (W Radom) für den Bereich der Heeresgruppe von Bedeutung werden könnte. Bei dieser Gruppe wurde durch V-Männer wiederholt die Anwesenheit englischer Offiziere gemeldet. Auch im Raum Sochatschew (W Warschau) soll ein englischer Offizier Lytley die Widerstandsbewegung leiten.

Die im Bereich der 2. und 4. Armee vereinzelt aufgetretenen AK-Abteilungen haben keine besondere Bedeutung gewonnen. Die Bereitschaft der

AK für eine großangelegte Operation in der Provinz wird nach Beutepapieren von polnischer Seite nicht allzuhoch bewertet. Mit Ausnahme der Inspektorate Litzmannstadt und Schlerarz wird in allen anderen Inspektoraten mangelnde Organisation, schlechte Feindaufklärung, unzureichende Bewaffnung, schlechte Waffenpflege, Mangel an Nachrichtenmaterial festgestellt.

Zahlreiche sowjetische Kundschaftergruppen der Roten Armee waren auch im Berichtsmonat im gesamten ostpreußischen Raum eingesetzt. Besondere Schwerpunkte scheinen die Räume N Scharfenwiese, Augustow, Grajewc und Insterburg – Königsberg zu bilden. Dabei wurde mehrfach die Zusammenlegung mehrerer Gruppen in gemeinsame Lager beobachtet.

Die in Warschau eingeschlossenen Aufständischen leisteten während des Berichtsmonats bis zur Kapitulation zähen und erbitterten Widerstand, obwohl das Ausbleiben der erhofften englisch-amerikanischen und der russischen Unterstützung sowie der Mißerfolg des Aufstandes eine weitgehende Entmutigung zur Folge hatte. Es erfolgte über Tag eine starke Luftversorgung durch ein englisch-amerikanisches Geschwader von etwa 120 Maschinen mit Waffen, Munition und Verpflegung. Die aus großer Höhe über Warschau und den Kampinos-Wäldern abgeworfenen Versorgungsbehälter fielen zum größten Teil in eigene Hand . . .

Nach Abwehrmeldungen benützt die AL die infolge der Mißerfolge der AK eingetretene Enttäuschung zur Zersetzung der AK-Abteilungen. Sie versucht, AK-Ausweise zu erhalten und mit ihrer Hilfe in der AK Fuß zu fassen, um hier und unter der evakuierten Bevölkerung kommunistische Zellen zu bilden. Die Londoner Regierung hat nach Gefangenenaussage der AK befohlen, sich geschlossen den Sowjets zur Verfügung zu stellen. Eine weitere Konspiration sei zwecklos, da den Russen während des Aufstandes alle AK-Funktionäre durch die AL gemeldet worden seien.

Andererseits wird von der AK-Führung über das Absinken der Moral in den AK-Abteilungen geklagt. Es sollen Plünderungen von AK-Abteilungen vorgekommen sein, die sich als AL-Abteilungen tarnten, um straflos Gewalttätigkeiten gegen die Bevölkerung unternehmen zu können. Unter diesen Umständen gewinnen die rechtsradikalen NSZ-Abteilungen, die zum großen Teil auf Befehl der Londoner Regierung in der AK aufgegangen waren, aber ihren Zusammenhang gewahrt haben, erneuten Einfluß auf die national eingestellten Teile der AK.

Sowjetische Kundschaftergruppen wurden im Berichtsmonat durch mehrere zusammengefaßte Unternehmen gegen die Gruppen Lossj, Jasen, Kasbek und ZOA zum Kampf gestellt und versprengt.

Die Auswirkungen des Zusammenbruches des Warschauer Aufstandes auf die polnische Widerstandsbewegung lassen sich noch nicht übersehen.

Sicher ist, daß die AK in Warschau nicht nur die besten, aktivsten Kräfte, sondern wahrscheinlich den Großteil der ihr zur Verfügung stehenden Waffen verloren hat, selbst wenn erhebliche Teile davon in geheimen Lagern der Stadt zurückgeblieben sein sollten. Allein diese Tatsachen dürften die Aktionsfähigkeiten der AK-Abteilungen in der polnischen Provinz angesichts des von jeher bestehenden empfindlichen Waffenmangels entscheidend beeinträchtigen.

Es kommt hinzu, daß der Aufstand erneut die Unfähigkeit der Polen zur Bildung einer geschlossenen nationalen Front erwiesen hat. Die AK ist infolgedessen nicht imstande, ihre an sich umfassende, sorgfältig durchgebildete Organisationsgrundlage auszunutzen. Sie hat ferner erkennen müssen, daß sie die Stärke der deutschen Abwehr, ebenso aber auch die Macht der RA und den schonungslosen Vernichtungswillen der russischen Führung unterschätzt hat. Nach dieser Klärung der Kampflage ist es nicht sehr wahrscheinlich, daß die AK-Führung den Versuch wiederholen wird, bei einem etwaigen weiteren russischen Vormarsch wichtige Teile des Landes vor den Russen in Besitz zu nehmen und ihnen gegenüber die nationalen Ansprüche der legalen polnischen Regierung zu vertreten.

Es dürfte möglich sein, zumindest die nationalpolnischen Kreise für eine neutrale Haltung, wenn nicht gar für eine aktive Unterstützung des deutschen Abwehrkampfes gegen den Bolschewismus zu gewinnen. Eine Bereitschaft dazu wird nach Gefangenenaussagen sowohl unter Angehörigen der AK wie unter der Zivilbevölkerung mehrfach geäußert. Man beginnt in Polen den Russen als das größte Übel anzusehen, während man angesichts der Kriegslage von Deutschland ein größeres Entgegenkommen als bisher erwartet.

Zwangsläufig würde eine solche Umstellung der nationalen Kreise allerdings alle linksgerichteten Polen den sowjetischen Elementen in die Arme treiben, von denen nach Scheidung der Geister eine wesentlich hemmungslosere Fortsetzung des Bandenkrieges zu erwarten sein dürfte, als er bisher von der AK geführt wurde."

(Oberkommando der Heeresgruppe Mitte-Abt. I c/AO Abw.) Nr. 5880/ 44 geh)

Es ist schwierig zu schätzen, wie viele Menschen durch den Warschauer Aufstand umgekommen sind. Die Führung der 9. Armee geht am 1. Aug. 1944 für Warschau von einer Einwohnerzahl von 1–1,5 Millionen Menschen aus. Das ,,Biuletyn Informacyiny" nimmt für das Jahr 1943 974 765 polnische und 24 222 deutsche Einwohner an. Vor der Eroberung durch die Sowjets flüchteten Polen und Deutsche aus Warschau. 1944 dürfte die Stadt 950 000 Einwohner gehabt haben. Die Ráda Glowna Opie Kuricza gibt an, daß bis Oktober 1944 150 000 Menschen durch Luftangriffe, Artilleriebeschuß, Seuchensterblichkeit und Massenexekutionen umkamen, davon 10 % um den 5. Okt. 1944. Vor der Eroberung der Stadt durch die Sowjets flüchtete eine große Anzahl von Deutschen und Polen.

Die Verluste der Landesarmee bei dem Aufstand im Jahre 1944 dürften mit 9700 Gefallenen, 6000 Verwundeten und 6000 Vermißten nicht zu hoch gegriffen sein.

Das exilpolniche Generalstabswerk nimmt 15 200 Tote und Verwundete und 7000 Schwerverwundete an.

Die deutsche Lage in der Zeit des Aufstandes war schwer.

Ein Blick auf die Karte genügt, um das Gesamtbild in Erscheinung treten zu lassen. Beachtet müssen ebenfalls die in Ostpreußen, in Rumänien und in der Slowakei bestehenden Gefahrenherde werden.

Zusammenbruch der Heeresgruppe Mitte als Ausgangspunkt für den Warschauer Aufstand

Am 28. Juli 1944 erhielt die Armjja Krajowa nachstehende Weisung: ,,Der Ministerrat hat am 28. Juli 1944 beschlossen, den Regierungsdelegierten (Jańkowski = Sobol in Warschau) zu bevollmächtigen, alle sich aus dem Tempo der sowjetischen Offensive ergebenden Entscheidungen, wenn nötig, ohne vorherige Vereinbarung mit der Regierung (London) zu treffen."

Ministerpräsident Mikolajczyk teilte dem Residenten Jańkowski mit: ,,In der Kabinettssitzung fiel einstimmig der Beschluß, Sie mit der Ausrufung des Aufstandes zu dem von Ihnen gewählten Zeitpunkt zu betrauen. Wenn möglich, benachrichtigen Sie uns vorher! Abschrift über Armee an Kommandanten der AK. Stem." (Deckname für Mikolajczyk.)

Bor-Komorowski berichtet: ,,Nach den mir gegebenen Berichten waren die deutschen Verteidigungslinien am 28. Juli durchbrochen worden, und die sowjetischen Kräfte hatten Otwock, Falenica und Józefów in den Warschauer Außenbezirken erreicht. Wir hörten auch, daß Panzereinheiten, die im Südabschnitt des deutschen Brückenkopfs durchgebrochen waren, bis Anin und Wolomin vorgedrungen waren. Sowjetische Spähtrupps näherten sich, nachdem sie die Weichsel überschritten hatten, Mszczonów (30 Meilen südwestlich Warschau) und operierten tief im Rücken der deutschen Linien des Warschauer Gebiets. Am 30. Juli traf einer unserer Nachrichtenoffiziere bei Radość 10 Meilen von Warschau auf eine sowjetische Panzerkolonne, die wahrscheinlich einen starken Spähtrupp bildete. Er sprach mit einigen Männern der Kolonne, und alle äußerten durchaus optimistisch, daß die Russen in den allernächsten Tagen Warschau nehmen würden. Später zogen sich die Panzer ungehindert nach Osten zurück. Unsere Informationsstellen auf der anderen, der östlichen Weichselseite, die am östlichen Stadtrand an den Außenbezirken der Vorstadt Praga verteilt waren, schickten ununterbrochen Berichte vom Auftreten sowjetischer Spähtrupps in der Nachbarschaft oder sogar innerhalb der Außenbezirke von Praga. Einem dieser Trupps in Stärke von dreißig Mann, der deutsche Mäntel (greatcoats) über sowjetischen Uniformen trug, gelang es am 30. Juli, das Zentrum der Vorstadt Zeran zu ereichen. Die Verteidigung des Brückenkopfes lag in den Händen der 73. deutschen Infanteriedivision, die von kleinen, eilig zusammengerafften Infanterieeinheiten, SS, Polizei und Luftwaffe unterstützt wurde. Am 30. Juli aber begann die von Italien abgezogene Division Hermann Göring von Westen her durch die Stadt zu marschieren."

,,Am 31. Juli erhielten wir die Nachricht vom weiteren Vorgehen des sowjetischen Keils, der tief innerhalb der feindlichen Linien operierte. Die Anwesenheit sowjetischer Einheiten in Raość, Wiazowna, Wolomin und Radzymin wurde berichtet, die alle 8–10 Meilen von Warschau entfernt liegen. Unter den deutschen Einheiten in Legionowo brach eine Panik aus, und die Garnison verließ unter der Führung des Kommandeurs die Kasernen. Bei hellem Tag marschierte eine ziemlich bedeutende Gruppe Soldaten der AK zu den verlassenen Gebäuden und bewaffnete sich mit den vom Feind zurückgelassenen Waffen. In Warschau verminten deutsche Pioniere die Brücken über die Weichsel. Das deutsche OKW meldete am frühen Nachmittag: ,,Heute begannen die Russen einen Generalangriff auf Warschau von Südosten". Ein Sowjetkommuniqué meldete die Gefangennahme des Kommandeurs der 73. deutschen Inf.-Div. Das bewies, daß die Russen sich nicht nur in der Nähe, sondern bereits innerhalb des deutschen Warschau-Brückenkopfes befanden. Am gleichen Tag hörten wir über Funk, daß Premierminister Mikolajczyk nach Moskau abgereist war. Am 31. Juli sollte Monter B. C. Chruściel, unser Kommandant für den Bereich Warschau, um 6 Uhr zum Hauptquartier kommen. Er kam unerwarteterweise um 5 Uhr mit der Nachricht, daß sowjetische Panzereinheiten, die in den Brückenkopf eingebrochen waren, die (deutsche) Verteidigung desorganisiert hätten und daß sich Radość, Milosna, Okuniew, Wolomin und Radzymin bereits in sowjetischer Hand befänden.

Nach einer kurzen Besprechung entschied sich, daß der Augenblick, für die Befreiung Warschaus zu kämpfen, gekommen sei. Ich erwartete den Beginn des sowjetischen Angriffs stündlich. Obwohl jede Entscheidung über den Kampf innerhalb des ,Burza'-Planes gänzlich bei mir lag, wollte ich in diesem Ausnahmefall, in dem das Schicksal der Hauptstadt auf dem Spiel stand, meinen Entschluß dem Regierungsvertreter zur Zustimmung unterbreiten. Ich schickte sofort meinen Adjutanten zu ihm und bat, er möge mich aufsuchen. Er war in einer halben Stunde bei mir. Ich legte ihm kurz die Situation dar. Meiner Meinung nach war es der richtige Zeitpunkt, den Kampf zu beginnen.

Er hörte mich bis zum Ende an und stellte dann den verschiedenen Stabsmitgliedern einige Fragen. Nachdem er seine Lagevorstellung vervollständigt hatte, drehte er sich zu mir mit den Worten um: ,,Also schön, dann los."

Ich wandte mich an Monter als den Kommandeur des Warschauer Stadtbezirks, der ebenso mit den ,Burza'-Vorbereitungen wie mit der Führung des Kampfes betraut war: ,,Morgen um Punkt 17 Uhr haben Sie mit den Operationen in Warschau zu beginnen".

Davor warnte der polnische Oberbefehlshaber, General Sosnkowski, durch Funkspruch vom 29. Juli 1944, der in London am 2. Aug. 1944 eintraf und am 6. Aug. 1944 in Warschau weitergegeben wurde. ,,Der Kampf gegen die Deutschen muß in der ,Burza'-Form fortgesetzt werden. Dagegen bin ich unter den gegenwärtigen Umständen absolut gegen einen allgemeinen Aufstand, dessen historischer Sinn sich mit Notwendigkeit darin ausdrücken muß, daß man die eine Besatzung gegen die andere eintauscht. Ihre Beurteilung der Lage bei den Deutschen muß sehr nüchtern und real sein. Irrtümer in dieser Hinsicht wären sehr kostspielig."

Bis Mitte des Jahres 1944 funkten die Nationalpolen genaue Nachrichten über die Verteidigung der deutschen Verbände im ,,Generalgouvernement" nach London. Sie verschätzten sich aber über die Zielsetzung der sowjetischen Truppen. Rokossowskis Verbände marschierten gegen die Mittelweichsel und nicht gegen Warschau. Die Operationsabsichten waren der Londoner Exilregierung unbekannt. Eine Abstimmung zwischen Moskau und London war nicht getroffen. Es hätte wie in Jugoslawien operiert werden müssen, wo ein englischer Verbindungsoffizier mit seinen Funkern saß.

Aus den Unterlagen der 9. Armee – KT/9 Anlage IV/1 und VII/3 (V c Meldung), KT/9, Anlage III/2, KT/9, Anlage V/I und KT/9 vom 26. u. 29. 7. sowie 1. Aug. – geht hervor, daß deutscherseits der Aufstand erwartet wurde. Aber die Wehrmachtsführung hatte mit einem sowjetischen Entsatz Warschaus und einer Abstimmung zwischen Heimatarmee und Sowjetunion gerechnet, ja sogar mit der Ausweitung des Aufstandes auf ganz Polen. Das OKH warnte für den 9. Aug. 1944, 16.30 Uhr, vor dem Ausbruch eines allgemeinen Aufstandes, zu dem es jedoch nicht kam. (KT/9 Anlageband X). Am 9./10. Sept. 1944 verstärkte sich der Eindruck eines gemeinsamen polnisch-russischen Vorgehens.

Das Kriegstagebuch der 9. Armee berichtet am 16. Sept. 1944 weiter: ,,Mit dem heutigen Tag beginnt eine neue Phase im Kampf um den Großraum Warschau/Modlin. Nach den Aufklärungsergebnissen und dem Ablauf der Kämpfe muß damit gerechnet werden, daß der Feind mit einer aus den polnischen Divisionen gebildeten neuen Südgruppe (1. polnische Armee?) über die Weichsel setzen wird, um in und nördlich Warschau unter Ausnützung des Aufstandes einen Brückenkopf zu bilden und mit einer nördlichen Gruppe (47. Armee) den Südflügel des IV SS.-Panzerkorps zu zerschlagen und über die Weichsel nach Westen vorzustoßen. Die 47. Armee wird dabei ihr erstes Ziel auf die Kampinoswälder westlich der Straße Warschau–Modlin richten, in denen sich Banden in einer Stärke bis zu 8000 Mann befinden sollen, die gut organisiert, mit Funkstellen, Flug- und Abwurfplätzen ausgestattet sind und durch die feindliche Luftwaffe laufend unterstützt werden. Gelänge diese Absicht, so kann der Feind durch dieses von uns nicht beherrschte umfangreiche Gebiet, ohne Widerstand zu finden, bis tief in den Rücken der 9. Armee vorstoßen und die gesamte Warschaustellung, insbesondere aber zunächst die Front im Weichsel-Narew-Dreieck zum Einsturz bringen. Darüber hinaus würden schwerste Gefahren für Ostpreußen heraufbeschworen, da der Weg nach Danzig dem Gegner offenliegen müßte. So zeichnen sich große operative Gefahren ab. Die Kämpfe dieses Tages werden bereits mit starken Panzerkräften und großem artl. Aufwand geführt, doch lassen sie den eigentlichen Höhepunkt noch erwarten. Wiederum liegt die gesamte Kampftätigkeit der Armee auf ihrem Nordflügel und in Warschau . . ."

18. 9. 1944: ,,Zum ersten Mal setzen nämlich an diesem Tag die Aufständischen in den Kampinoswäldern zu offensiver Tätigkeit an. Sie tun dies in taktischer Übereinstimmung mit dem Angriff der Russen von jenseits der Weichsel, so daß das Zusammenspiel und das Vorliegen einer gemeinsamen Planung einwandfrei angenommen werden dürfen. Kurz nach 11 Uhr wird aus dem Südostteil der Kampinoswälder ein Angriff der Aufständischen gemeldet, und ebenfalls 11 Uhr setzt das Trommelfeuer des Russen auf dem Südflügel des IV. SS-Pz.-Korps ein, über den der kürzeste Weg in die Kampinoswälder führt."

Um 12 Uhr desselben Tages wird von der Luftflotte 6 der Anflug von 250 USAF-Bombern mit Fallschirmjägern für ungefähr 13.15 Uhr über Warschau gemeldet. In Wirklichkeit handelte es sich um 110 Boeing-Bomber mit Versorgungsbomben. Skeptisch berichtet das deutsche Kriegstagebuch:

,, . . . so hat doch dieser Einflug, der ebenfalls in bemerkenswerter Übereinstimmung mit den Angriffen der Russen und der Aufständischen steht, die Gefahren gezeigt, mit denen die Armeeführung zu rechnen hat, zumal die amerikanischen Bomber offensichtlich nicht ihre ganzen Frachten entladen haben – vielleicht weil die Angriffe der Russen und der Aufständischen nicht durchschlugen und das große Spiel nicht zum Tragen kam."

Nicht übersehen darf werden, daß die Sowjets angebliche russische Artillerie-Offiziere mit Funkgerät für B-Stellen in Zoliborz, in der Innenstadt und im Südkessel abspringen ließen. Sie waren jedoch keine Verbindungsoffiziere zur Heimatarmee. In diesem Zusammenhang wird von polnischer Seite von einer ,,phantasievollen" Gestalt, dem Hauptmann Konstantin Kalugin, berichtet. Heute sehen nationale Exilpolen in dem Vorgang ein Täuschungsmanöver der Sowjets.

Am 3. August 1944 wurde Kalugin als Abwehroffizier der Roten Armee zu General Chruściel gebracht. Der angeblich in Stalingrad geborene Offizier der Roten Armee behauptete, im Raum Lublin am 15. Juli abgesprungen zu sein. In Warschau setzte er eine Botschaft an Stalin auf, die von Chruściel autorisiert wurde. Der Funkspruch ging nach Moskau, ohne von dort beantwortet zu werden. Kalugin machte daraufhin den vielsagenden Vorschlag, die in Warschau vertretenen Links-Parteien möchten sich mit einem Hilfsersuchen direkt an Stalin wenden. Dies geschah nicht, dagegen wandte sich Chruściel brieflich an den sowjetischen Kommandeur von Obwock. Es erfolgte keine Reaktion. Am 11. Sept. 1944 erwähnt Graf Bor-Komorowski den Kalugin-Funkspruch in einem Hilfsappell an Rokossowski, der polnischer Volkszugehörigkeit war.

Angeblich ließ Marschall Rossokowski Kalugin erschießen. Wahrscheinlich gehörte er einerseits zu den Personen, die die kommunistische Machtübernahme in Warschau vorbereiten sollten, andererseits dürfte der Kreml mit dem sowjetischen Hauptmann und den abgesprungenen Artillerie-Offizieren den Zweck verfolgt haben, die Illusion auf sowjetische Hilfe zu erwecken und zu stärken. Die national-polnische Führung vertraute ihm fast ausnahmslos. Der Widerstand solle möglichst große Verluste bei den national-polnischen Widerstandskämpfern mit sich bringen. Im Endergebnis dürfte ein Vergleich mit Katyn berechtigt sein.

Die Beziehungen zwischen der polnischen Exilregierung und Moskau waren 1944 schlecht. Der Präsident der Vereinigten Staaten von Amerika, Roosevelt, regte bei St. Mikolajczyk an, durch einen Besuch bei Stalin die Anerkennung eines nicht-kommunistischen Polen zu erreichen. Die Aktion Burza sollte dabei zeigen, daß von der Londoner Exilregierung geführte Kräfte in Polen wirksam auftreten könnten. Stalin negierte den Schritt. Er vernichtete die Burza-Aktion im Raum von Wilna. Er täuschte Schwierigkeiten vor Praga vor. Das Tass-Kommuniqué vom 13. Aug. 1944 distanzierte sich vom Warschauer Aufstand. Unterstützt wird diese Feststellung durch die Eintragung im deutschen Kriegstagebuch der 9. Armee: ,,Erster Abwurf von Versorgungsbomben anscheinend britischer Herkunft zu diesem Zeitpunkt." Mc. Narney und Slessor wiesen darauf hin, daß die Luftunterstützung leicht von den Russen geleistet werden könne.

Von sowjetischer Seite kam jedoch keine Hilfe.

Die polnischen Kommunisten in Moskau bildeten das Lubliner Komitee.

Es ging ihnen um ein kommunistisches Polen. Klar ist feststellbar, daß Rola-Zymierski und Bierut anfangs von dem Aufstand keine Kenntnis nahmen. Wanda Wasilewska behauptete sogar, daß er nicht existiere. Osobka-Morawski leugnete noch am 9. Aug. 44 die Anwesenheit Bor-Komorowskis in Warschau. Die Verantwortung für den Warschauer Aufstand 1944 wird den Londoner Emigrationskreisen zugeschoben.

Ich bin Deutscher. Dies hindert mich aber nicht, von einer polnischen Tragödie zu sprechen. Bereits damals zeichnet sich ab, daß der Verlierer des Zweiten Weltkrieges nicht allein Hitler, sondern der gesamte Westen sein würde.

Der zeitgeschichtliche Betrachter kann nicht den Telegrammwechsel zwischen Stalin und Churchill übersehen. Der englische Premierminister wendet sich am 4. Aug. 1944 an Stalin: ,,Auf dringende Anforderung der polnischen Untergrundarmee werden wir – je nach Wetter – etwa 60 t Ausrüstung und Munition über dem Südwestteil von Warschau abwerfen, wo sich ein polnischer Aufstand im heftigen Kampf gegen die Deutschen befinden soll. Es heißt auch, daß sie um russische Hilfe bitten, die sehr nahe zu sein scheint. Sie werden von 1½ deutschen Divisionen angegriffen. Dies könnte für Ihre Operation von Nutzen sein." Der sowjetische Diktator antwortete: ,,Ich glaube, daß die Ihnen von den Polen übermittelten Nachrichten weitgehend übertrieben sind und kein Zutrauen verdienen. Dies konnte man schon aus der Tatsache entnehmen, daß die polnischen Emigranten bereits für sich in Anspruch genommen haben, sie hätten mit ein paar vereinzelten Einheiten Wilna eingenommen; sie meldeten das sogar im Rundfunk. Aber natürlich entspricht das keineswegs den Tatsachen. Die Heimatarmee der Polen besteht aus wenigen Einheiten, die sich fälschlich als Divisionen bezeichnen. Sie haben weder Artillerie noch Luftwaffe noch Panzer. Ich kann mir nicht vorstellen, wie diese Einheiten Warschau erobern sollen, für dessen Verteidigung die Deutschen vier Panzerdivisionen eingesetzt haben, darunter die Division Hermann Göring."

In den Nächten vom 13. und 14. August sowie vom 14. und 15. Aug. 1944 wurde versucht, 30 Flugzeuge, dann 26 Flugzeuge aus Italien nach Polen einzufliegen. Der Erfolg war äußerst klein. Die RAF hatte sich von der 8. und 9. Amerikanischen Luftflotte Flugzeuge ausgeliehen. Einige gerieten auf sowjetisch besetztes Gebiet.

Daher bestellte in der Nacht zum 16. Aug. Wyśinski im Auftrag der sowjetischen Regierung den amerikanischen Botschafter zu sich und übergab ihm zur Vermeidung von Mißverständnissen nachstehende Feststellung: ,,Die Sowjetregierung kann sich natürlich nicht der Tatsache widersetzen, daß englische oder amerikanische Flugzeuge im Gebiet von Warschau Waffen abwerfen, weil dies eine amerikanische und britische Angelegenheit ist. Aber sie ist entschieden dagegen, wenn amerikanische oder britische Flugzeuge nach dem Waffenabwurf im Gebiet von Warschau auf sowjetischem Gebiet landen, denn die Sowjetregierung will sich weder direkt noch indirekt mit dem Abenteuer in Warschau identifiziert wissen."

Zum gleichen Zeitpunkt telegraphierte Stalin an Churchill: ,,Nach den Verhandlungen mit Herrn Mikolajczyk habe ich befohlen, daß das Kommando der Roten Armee kräftig (intensiv) Waffen im Sektor Warschau abwirft. Es ist auch ein Fallschirmverbindungsoffizier abgesprungen, der nach dem Bericht des Kommandos sein Ziel nicht erreicht hat, weil er von den Deutschen getötet wurde. Ich habe mich weiterhin mit der Warschau-Affäre etwas näher vertraut gemacht und bin überzeugt, daß die Warschau-Aktion ein leichtsinniges und schreckliches Abenteuer darstellt, das der Bevölkerung schwere Verluste verursacht. Das wäre nicht eingetreten, wenn das sowjetische Kommando vor dem Beginn der Warschau-Aktion unterrichtet worden wäre und die Polen mit ihm Verbindung gehalten hätten. In der nun entstandenen Lage ist das sowjetische Kommando zu der Überzeugung gekommen, daß es sich von dem Warschauer Abenteuer distanzieren muß, weil es weder direkt noch indirekt die Verantwortung für die Warschau-Aktion übernehmen kann."

Daher wendet sich am 18. Aug. 1944 Churchill an den amerikanischen Präsidenten:

1. ,,Durch die russische Weigerung, der amerikanischen Luftwaffe Hilfe für die heroischen Aufständischen in Warschau zu gestatten, ist eine Episode von tiefer und weitreichender Ernsthaftigkeit geschaffen. Diese wird noch durch das eigene (russische) vollkommene Versäumnis verschärft, auf dem Luftweg Hilfe zu bringen, obwohl sie nur wenige Meter entfernt sind. Wenn, was so gut wie sicher ist, dem deutschen Triumph in dieser Hauptstadt ein Massaker folgt, sind die daraus entstehenden Konsequenzen überhaupt nicht abzusehen.

2. Wenn Sie es für richtig halten, bin ich bereit, eine persönliche Botschaft an Stalin zu senden, wenn Sie selbst eine entsprechende getrennte Botschaft schicken. Noch besser als zwei getrennte Botschaften wäre eine gemeinsame, von uns beiden gezeichnete.

3. Die glorreichen und gigantischen Siege, die von den Streitkräften der Vereinigten Staaten und Englands in Frankreich errungen wurden, haben die Lage in Europa weitgehend verändert, und es kann sehr gut sein, daß der von unseren Armeen errungene Sieg in der Normandie an Größe alles übertrifft, was die Russen bei allen besonderen Gelegenheiten erreicht haben. Ich glaube deshalb, daß sie vor dem, was wir bisher gesagt haben, einigen Respekt haben, wenn es einfach und offen dargelegt wird. Wir sind Nationen, die einer hohen Sache dienen, und müssen zum Welt-

frieden ein echtes Bekenntnis ablegen, selbst auf die Gefahr hin, daß Stalin das übelnimmt. Es ist gut möglich, daß er das nicht tut."

Am 20. August 1944 erfolgt die gemeinsame anglo-amerikanische Botschaft an Generalissimus Stalin: „Wenn die Anti-Nazis in Warschau wirklich sich selbst überlassen werden, denken wir an die Meinung der Welt. Wir glauben, daß wir alle drei das Äußerste tun sollten, um dort so viele Patrioten wie irgend möglich zu retten. Wir hoffen, daß Sie sofort Vorräte und Munition bei den Patrioten in Warschau abwerfen. Oder sind Sie damit einverstanden, unseren Flugzeugen zu helfen, dies sehr schnell zu tun? Wir hoffen, Sie stimmen zu. Die Zeitfrage ist hierbei sehr wichtig."

Stalin antwortet am 22. August 1944:

1. „Die Botschaft von Ihnen und Herrn Roosevelt über Warschau habe ich erhalten. Ich habe dazu folgendes zu sagen: – Früher oder später wird sich jedem die Wahrheit über die Verbrechergruppe herausstellen, die sich in das Warschau-Abenteuer eingelassen hat, um die Macht zu ergreifen. Diese Leute haben den guten Glauben der Einwohner Warschaus ausgenutzt, um viele nahezu unbewaffnete Leute den deutschen Kanonen, Panzern und Flugzeugen entgegenzuwerfen. Es ist eine Situation entstanden, in der jeder neue Tag nicht den Polen zur Befreiung von Warschau, sondern den Hitleristen zum Zusammenschießen der Einwohner Warschaus verhilft.

2. Hier nicht von Bedeutung.

3. Vom militärischen Gesichtspunkt ist die entstandene Lage, die zunehmend das Interesse der Deutschen auf Warschau zieht, in gleicher Weise ungünstig für die Rote Armee wie für die Polen. Die sowjetischen Truppen, die erst kürzlich neuen und bemerkenswerten Anstrengungen der Deutschen, zum Gegenangriff überzugehen, Widerstand entgegensetzten, unternehmen inzwischen alles nur Mögliche, um diesen Angriff der Hitleristen zu zerschlagen und zu einem Großangriff im Gebiet von Warschau überzugehen. Es kann kein Zweifel bestehen, daß die Rote Armee keine Anstrengungen scheut, die Deutschen um Warschau zu schlagen und Warschau für die Polen zu befreien. Das wird die beste und wirksamste Hilfe für jeden Polen sein, der Antinazi ist."

Nachdem Churchill nach dem 24. Aug. 1944 bei Roosevelt Unterstützung für Warschau zu erhalten suchte, antwortete der amerikanische Präsident: „Der Nachschub für die Warschau-Polen durch uns ist, wie mir gesagt wird, so lange unmöglich, ehe wir nicht die Erlaubnis erhalten, auf sowjetischen Flugplätzen zu landen und zu starten. Ihre Benutzung für den Einsatz zur Unterstützung Warschaus wird gegenwärtig durch die russischen Stellen verhindert. Ich sehe nicht, welche weiteren erfolgversprechenden Schritte wir gegenwärtig unternehmen können."

Die Vereinigten Staaten zogen ihre Hand von Warschau zurück

Churchill bereitete nachstehende Antwort an Stalin vor. ,,Wir wollen dringend US-Flugzeuge von England schicken. Gibt es irgendeinen Grund, warum die uns hinter der russischen Front zugewiesenen Auftankplätze nicht benutzt werden sollten, ohne daß danach gefragt wird, was sie unterwegs unternommen haben? Auf diese Weise könnte Ihre Regierung den Grundsatz, sich von dieser besonderen Episode distanziert zu haben, aufrechterhalten. Wir sind davon überzeugt, daß kampfunfähige britische oder amerikanische Flugzeuge, die hinter der Front Ihrer Armee landen, entsprechend Ihrer sonstigen Verfahrensweise Hilfe zugesichert erhalten.

Unsere Sympathien sind bei diesen ,,fast unbewaffneten Menschen'', die aus besonderem Glauben die deutschen Panzer, Kanonen und Flugzeuge angegriffen haben, aber es ist nicht unsere Sache, ein Urteil über jene zu fällen, die den Aufstand angestiftet haben, zu dem Radio Moskau bestimmt wiederholt aufgerufen hat. Wir können nicht glauben, daß die Grausamkeiten der Hitlerleute aufhören, wenn der Widerstand zu Ende geht, sondern dies wird der Augenblick sein, in dem sie wahrscheinlich voller Wildheit damit beginnen. Das Massaker von Warschau wird für uns bestimmt ein konfliktgeladenes Ereignis sein, wenn wir uns alle bei Kriegsende wiedersehen. Deshalb schlagen wir vor, die Flugzeuge zu schicken, es sei denn, Sie verbieten es ausdrücklich.''

Churchill fügte hinzu: ,,Falls er hierauf nicht antworten sollte, glaube ich, sollten wir die Flugzeuge schicken und dann zusehen, was weiter geschieht. Ich kann mir nicht vorstellen, daß man sie mißhandelt oder festhält. Nachdem dies unterschrieben wurde, habe ich erfahren, daß die Russen sogar bestrebt sind, Ihnen ihre Flugplätze wegzunehmen, die in Poltava und sonstwo hinter ihrer Front liegen.''

Volle 26 Tage nach Beginn des Aufstandes vom 26. Aug. 1944 antwortete Roosevelt: ,,Ich glaube, daß es im Hinblick auf die Kriegführung auf lange Sicht sich für mich nicht als vorteilhaft herausstellen würde, mich mit Ihnen an der vorgeschlagenen Botschaft an Stalin zu beteiligen, aber ich habe nichts dagegen, daß Sie Ihrerseits eine solche Botschaft schicken, wenn Sie es für richtig halten. Um zu dieser Schlußfolgerung zu kommen, habe ich Onkel Joes gegenwärtige Haltung zu der Hilfe für die Untergrundkräfte in Warschau, wie sie in seiner Botschaft an Sie und mich zum Ausdruck kommt, seine ausdrückliche Weigerung, uns die russischen Flugplätze für diesen Zweck benutzen zu lassen, und die gegenwärtig laufenden amerikanischen Besprechungen über eine zukünftige Benutzung anderer russischer Stützpunkte in Rechnung gestellt.''

Am 1. September 1944 sah sich der polnische Oberbefehlshaber General Sosnowski gezwungen, den Tagesbefehl Nr. 9 an die polnische Heimatarmee zu erlassen: ,,Fünf Jahre sind seit dem Tag vergangen, seit Polen angesichts der Aufmunterung durch die englische Regierung und im Besitz ihrer Garantie zum einsamen Kampf mit der deutschen Macht antrat ... Der Herbst-(Polen)-feldzug verschaffte den Verbündeten acht Monate wertvollster Zeit und erlaubte Großbritannien, seine Rüstungslücken so weit aufzufüllen, daß die Luftschlacht über London und den britischen Inseln, die einen Wendepunkt in der Geschichte darstellte, gewonnen werden konnte ... Seit einem Monat verbluten sich die Helden der Heimatarmee zusammen mit dem Volk von Warschau allein ... Das Volk von Warschau ... verlassen an der Front des gemeinsamen Kampfes mit den Deutschen, das ist das tragische und ungeheuerliche Rätsel angesichts der technischen Stärke der Verbündeten, ein Rätsel, das wir Polen zu lösen nicht imstande sind, denn wir haben noch nicht den Glauben daran verloren, daß das moralische Recht die Welt regiert, daß wir nicht zu glauben imstande sind, der Opportunismus der Menschen werde sich angesichts der physischen Stärke soweit durchsetzen, daß man dem Todeskampf der Hauptstadt jenes Landes gleichgültig zusieht, dessen Soldaten so viele andere (europäische) Hauptstädte mit eigener Hand schützen ... Die Sachverständigen möchten uns das Ausbleiben einer Hilfe für Warschau mit technischen Gründen erklären. Es werden die Argumente Verlust und Erfolg vorgeschoben. Der Verlust von 27 Maschinen über Warschau während eines Monats bedeutet nichts für die Luftwaffe der Verbündeten, die augenblicklich Zehntausende von Flugzeugen jeder Art und jeden Typs besitzen. Und wenn man abrechnen will, dann müssen wir daran erinnern, daß die polnische Luftwaffe in der Schlacht um London im Jahre 1940 40% ihres Bestandes als Verlust einbüßte, während bei der Hilfsaktion für Warschau nur 15% der Besatzung fielen. Seit fünf Jahren kämpft die Heimatarmee gegen die Deutschen unter fürchterlichen Bedingungen, von denen die Welt des Westens gar keine Vorstellung haben kann ... Warschau wartet nicht auf leere Lobesworte, nicht auf Ausdrücke der Anerkennung, nicht Mit- und Beileids-Versicherungen. Es wartet. Es wartet auf Waffen und Munition ...''

Churchill richtete am 4. Sept. 1944 zwei weitere Telegramme an Roosevelt:

1. ,,Das (englische) Kriegskabinett ist zutiefst über die Lage in Warschau und die weitreichenden Auswirkungen auf unsere zukünftigen Beziehungen zu Rußland angesichts der Stalinschen Verweigerung von Flugplatzhilfe bestürzt.

2. Darüber hinaus hat, wie Sie wissen, Mikolajczyk an das polnische Befreiungskomitee seine Vorschläge für ein politisches Übereinkommen ge-

macht. Ich fürchte, daß der Fall Warschau nicht nur jede Hoffnung auf einen Fortschritt zerstören, sondern auch die Stellung von Mikolajczyk selbst fatal untergraben wird.

3. Mein nachstehendes Telegramm enthält den Text eines Funkspruches, den das Kriegskabinett als solches an unseren Botschafter in Moskau gesandt hat, und auch einen Appell, den die Frauen Waschaus an den Papst gerichtet haben und der vom Vatikan unserem Botschafter übergeben wurde.

4. Der einzige Weg, um den in Warschau kämpfenden Polen rasche Hilfe zu bringen, würde für die US-Luftwaffe darin bestehen, Nachschub abzuwerfen und dabei russische Flugplätze zu benutzen. Angesichts dessen, was auf dem Spiele steht, bitten wir, daß Sie erneut den hohen Einsatz wagen. Könnten Sie nicht Ihre Luftwaffe ermächtigen, diese Operation auszuführen, und, wenn erforderlich, auf russischen Flugplätzen auch ohne deren formelle Zustimmung landen? Angesichts Ihres großen Erfolges im Westen kann ich mir nicht denken, daß die Russen dieses fait accompli zurückweisen. Sie könnten es sogar begrüßen, weil es sie aus einer scheußlichen Situation befreit. Wir würden natürlich mit Ihnen die volle Verantwortlichkeit für jede Aktion, die von Ihrer Luftwaffe unternommen wird, mittragen."

Der englische Botschafter erhielt den Funkspruch des britischen Kriegskabinettes vom 4. Sept. 1944: ,,Das Kriegskabinett hat auf seiner heutigen Sitzung die letzten Berichte über die Lage in Warschau geprüft. Sie erweisen, daß die dort gegen die Deutschen kämpfenden Polen in einer verzweifelten Klemme stecken.

Das Kriegskabinett möchte die Sowjetregierung wissen lassen, daß die öffentliche Meinung in diesem Land über die Vorgänge in Warschau und die furchtbaren Leiden der Polen dort tief beunruhigt ist. Wie auch Recht oder Unrecht über die Auslösung des Warschauer Aufstandes verteilt sein mögen, das Volk von Warschau kann nicht für die getroffenen Entscheidungen verantwortlich gemacht werden. Unsere Bevölkerung kann es nicht verstehen, warum den Polen in Warschau nicht von außen materielle Hilfe zugekommen ist. Daß diese Hilfe deshalb nicht geschickt werden konnte, weil sich die Moskauer Regierung geweigert hat, der Luftwaffe der Vereinigten Staaten die Landung auf in russischer Hand befindlichen Flugplätzen zu gestatten, ist jetzt öffentlich bekanntgeworden.

Wenn jetzt obendrein die Polen in Warschau von den Deutschen besiegt werden sollten – und das wird, wie wir unterrichtet werden, in zwei oder drei Tagen der Fall sein –, wird der Schock auf die öffentliche Meinung hier unberechenbar sein. Es ist dem Kriegskabinett schwer verständlich, ob die Weigerung der Moskauer Regierung die Verpflichtung der britischen und amerikanischen Regierung in Rechnung gestellt hat, den Polen in Warschau zu helfen. Die Handlungsweise der Moskauer Regierung, die das Absenden einer solchen Hilfe verhindert, scheint uns im Widerspruch zu dem Geist der alliierten Zusammenarbeit zu stehen, auf den Sie und wir sowohl in der Gegenwart und in Zukunft soviel Wert legen.

Angesichts der Wertschätzung für Marschall Stalin und die Völker der Sowjetunion, mit denen in Zukunft zusammenzuarbeiten unser aufrichtigster Wunsch ist, hat mich das Kriegskabinett ermächtigt, diesen Appell an die Sowjetregierung zu richten, jedwede in ihrer Macht liegende Hilfe zu leisten und vor allem Vorsorge zu treffen, daß US-Flugzeuge zu diesem Zweck auf Ihren Flugplätzen landen können."

Präsident Roosevelt richtete am 5. Spetember 1944 an Ministerpräsident Churchill nachstehendes Telegramm: ,,In Beantwortung Ihrer Telegramme werde ich von meinem Office of Military Intelligence unterrichtet, daß die kämpfenden Polen sich von Warschau zurückgezogen haben und daß die Deutschen jetzt die alleinige Herrschaft ausüben.

Das Problem einer Hilfe für die Polen in Warschau ist deshalb unglückseligerweise durch den Aufschub und das deutsche Vorgehen gelöst worden, und es scheint jetzt nichts von uns für sie getan werden zu können.

Ich bin lange Zeit sehr bekümmert gewesen, weil wir den heroischen Verteidigern Warschaus keine ausreichende Hilfe zu leisten imstande waren, und ich hoffe, wir werden zusammen noch imstande sein, es Polen zu ermöglichen, in diesem Krieg mit zu den Siegern zu gehören."

Es gibt heute keinen Zweifel, daß zu dem Mißlingen des Warschauer Aufstandes die sowjetische und amerikanische Haltung beitrugen.

Es erfolgten als letzter Einsatz nach Art von Werbeflugunternehmen durchgeführte Tagesflüge von 110 Boeing-Flugzeugen am 18. Sept. 44, wie er auf der Strecke England – Zielgebiet, Poltava – Zielgebiet – England schon erprobt war.

Wie von Krauhals richtig schreibt, wurden zu insgesamt 18 Angriffen die sowjetischen Flugplätze Poltava, Mirgorod und Pyratin als Hilfsbasen der Sowjetunion benutzt.

Churchill und Roosevelt kamen in Quebec überein, die letzten wenig erfolgreichen Flugunternehmen zu wiederholen. – Am 5. Oktober 1944 aber kapitulierte Warschau.

Burza

Ein Mittel zur Vernichtung rechtskonservativer Polen

Im Herbst 1943 wurde die Aktion Burza (Gewittersturm) entwickelt, die verstärkte Aktionen in den Gebieten vorsah, denen sich die Front näherte. Sie ging auf einen Vorschlag von Rowecki zurück. Der Vorschlag stammt aus dem Februar 1943. Rowecki schreibt:

„Wenn die Russen bei der Verfolgung der Deutschen einmarschieren, ergibt sich die Notwendigkeit, den Aufstand nicht gleichzeitig im ganzen Lande auszulösen, sondern nacheinander, abschnittsweise und im Osten beginnend.

So würde der erste Abschnitt die Gebiete ostwärts (einer Linie) von Wilna im Norden bis Lemberg im Süden erfassen.

Der zweite Abschnitt würde in der Gegend von Brest am Bug, Bialystok und weiter südlich an der Bug/San-Linie enden.

Ein weiterer Abschnitt umfaßt das übrige Land. Es ergibt sich die Notwendigkeit, daß Sie, Herr General (Sikorski), mich ermächtigen, den Aufstand wenigstens in den ersten beiden Abschnitten auszulösen, denn der Augenblick des (Aufstands-)Ausbruchs steht mit dem Einmarsch der Russen und nicht mit dem Grad der Auflösung bei den Deutschen in Zusammenhang."

Sikorski rechnete mit einer bereits im März 1943 vorausgesagten Verschlechterung des polnisch-russischen Verhältnisses. Für diesen Fall befahl er eine modifizierte Aktion „Burza". So sollten sich die zivilen Teile des polnischen Untergrundes im Augenblick des sowjetischen Einmarschs zu erkennen geben, die Soldaten sich aber nicht enttarnen, sondern sich nach Westen zurückziehen, „um sie vor der Vernichtung durch die Russen zu schützen."(!)

Am 27. Oktober 1943 gab die polnische Exilregierung in London an die AK-Führung in Warschau, die inzwischen Komorowski übernommen hatte, die Instruktion Nr. 5989, in der es unter anderem heißt: (Art. A/II) „Wenn sich ergibt, daß kein Einverständnis der Alliierten zu dem vorstehenden Plan (des allgemeinen Aufstandes) zu erzielen ist, weil deren Strategie die Möglichkeit (eines tief in den Kontinent geführten Stoßes) nicht vorsieht und die deutsche Front noch ohne Zersetzungserscheinungen zurückweicht, fordert die Regierung das Land zu versteckten Sabotage-Diversions-Aktionen gegen die Deutschen auf. Diese Aktionen haben dann nur politisch-demonstrativen Charakter. Die Regierung wird sich alle Mühe geben, daß auch in diesem Fall die Alliierten die Heimatarmee und die Zivilbevölkerung mit den zur Selbstverteidigung und Diversion erforderlichen Mitteln versorgen."

Weiter heißt es in der gleichen Instruktion über die polnisch/sowjetischen Beziehungen (Art. B/II): „Polnisch/sowjetische Beziehungen sind nicht aufgenommen worden. Dem Einmarsch sowjetischer Truppen geht ein bewaffnetes Auftreten gegen die Deutschen im Sinne von Art. A/II voraus."

Die Planung der Aktion „Burza" war schon in ihrem Entstehen politisch gegen die Sowjetunion und militärisch gegen die Deutschen gerichtet. Die Befehle der Aktion um den 1. Dez. 1943 sahen vor, daß kein allgemeiner Aufstand das ganze Land erfassen sollte, sondern daß durch Angriffe gegen die Deutschen in der zurückweichenden deutschen Front Verwirrung gestiftet werden sollte. Die Aktionen sollten vor allem auf dem flachen Land, in Waldgebieten, Einzelsiedlungen und in Dörfern stattfinden. Ebenfalls kamen kleine Städte in Betracht.

Die Aktion „Burza" sollte in dem Augenblick anlaufen, in dem sowjetische Truppen zum ersten Mal die Grenzen des polnischen Staates von 1939 überschritten. Dies geschah in den ersten Januartagen 1944 ostwärts Sarny (am 3./4. Januar 1944 an der Bahnstrecke Olewsk-Rokitno).

Die polnische Landesarmee in Wolhynien konnte die Aufgabe, die Deutschen zu stören und gegenüber der sowjetischen Streitmacht als „Territorialherrscher" aufzutreten, nicht erfüllen. In dieser Landschaft standen ihr die ukrainische Unabhängigkeitsbewegung, die Deutschen und die von der NKWD geführten Sowjetpartisanen gegenüber. So zogen sich die nationalen Kräfte auf den Raum um Kowel zurück, das bereits 180 km westlich der alten polnisch-sowjetischen Grenze lag. Richtig ist, daß sie der deutschen Besatzungsmacht von Januar bis April 1944 stark zu schaffen machten. Der politische Endzweck aber wurde nicht erreicht.

Als die Sowjets die deutsche Heeresgruppe Mitte schwer bedrängten, war das Abrollen der Aktion „Burza" im Gebiet von Wilna fällig. Sie griff Ende Juli auf die Gebiete Bialystok, Lublin und Kleinpolen über und erreichte das Gebiet um Reschew und erfaßte mit dem 1. August 1944 Warschau. Während des Warschauer Aufstandes erfolgten auf dem flachen Lande keine Operationen, die AK-Führer gingen daran, Warschau zu unterstützen. Die Entsatzversuche von Warschau wurden durch die Rote Armee und die deutsche Besatzungsmacht vereitelt. Die Armja Krajowa führte daher während des Warschauer Aufstands die örtlichen „Burza-Aktionen" weiter. Die deutsche Funkabwehr erhielt Kenntnis von diesen neuen Befehlen. Daher warnte das Oberkommando des Heeres: „Am 2. August 1944, 16.30 Uhr ist mit dem Aufstand im Generalgouvernement zu rechnen."

Im Raum von Bialystok und Lublin operierte im Rahmen der „Burza"-Aktion die Armja Krajowa im Juli erfolgreich. Dadurch wurde der deutsche Rückzug beschleunigt. Nach Beendigung der Kampfhandlungen beschuldigten die Sowjets die AK-Offiziere, mit den Deutschen zusammengearbeitet zu haben. Sie verhafteten dieselben. Ganze Abteilungen wurden entwaffnet und zum Unterschreiben einer Beitrittserklärung in die „Berling-Abteilung" gezwungen. Die sowjetischen Maßnahmen fanden zwischen dem 26. und 30. Juli 1944 statt.

Im August 1944 wurden in dem genannten Raum massenweise AK-Angehörige verhaftet, die von der NKWD in das von der SS geräumte Majdanek eingeliefert wurden.

Diese Geschehnisse waren der AK-Führung in Warschau bekannt, ehe sie den Befehl zum Warschauer Aufstand gab.

Als im Zuge der „Burza"-Aktion die polnische nationale Führung die Eroberung Wilnas befahl, kam es zur Verbindungsaufnahme mit Offizieren der sowjetischen Fronttruppen. Gemeinsam gingen Abteilungen der Armja Krajowa und die Rote Armee gegen die deutschen Truppen vor, die nach dem Westen auswichen. Im Raume von Wilna, wo die Kräfte der polnischen Landesarmee südwestlich der Stadt in der Puczsza Rudnica zusammengezogen wurden, verschlechterte sich das Verhältnis zu den Sowjets sehr schnell. Ein Einmarsch in die Stadt Wilna, wo Pilsudski geboren war, wurde verboten. In einer Fühlungnahme zwischen dem AK-Führer Krzyzanowski (Wilk) und dem Befehlshaber der 3. Weißrussischen Front, Černichovski, wurde erster am 14. Juli 1944 getäuscht. Die Sowjets versprachen Waffen und die Zulassung einer von der Berling-Armee unabhängigen polnischen Brigade, die aus AK-Angehörigen bestehen sollte.

Am 16. Juli 1944 wurde der AK-Führer und sein Stab zu einer Besprechung nach Wilna befohlen. Sie wurden verhaftet und in die NKWD-Gefängnisse der Stadt gebracht. Die AK-Offiziere wurden von ihren Truppen getrennt, die AK-Angehörigen von einer sowjetischen Panzerdivision umstellt. 30 sowjetische Schlachtflieger schossen auf die zum Ausbruch ansetzenden Polen mit Bordwaffen. Am 27. August 1944 brachten die Sowjets den letzten AK-Führer im Raum Wilna mit 35 Angehörigen seines Stabes um.

Im Raum von Lemberg begann die sowjetische Offensive Mitte Juli. Die „Burza"-Aktion setzte im März 1944 ein. Als die Kämpfe in Lemberg am 26. Juli 1944 beendet wurden, erklärten die Sowjets, daß die polnischen „Abteilungen" nicht länger zum Kampf benötigt wurden. Am 31. Juli 1944 wurden die Offiziere der Teile der Armja Krajowa, die im Gebiet von Lemberg operiert hatten, zu einer Besprechung bestellt. Wie ihr Führer kehrten sie von dieser nicht mehr zurück.

Polen zwischen Ost und West

Der polnischen Exilregierung in London wird von sowjetrussischer Seite zum Vorwurf gemacht, daß sie keine echte Zusammenarbeit mit der revolutionären polnischen Bewegung anstrebte. Sie und ihre Gesinnungsfreunde hätten ständig ihre antikommunistische Vorstellung hervorgehoben. Es hätte die Konzeption des bewaffneten Aufstandes durchgesetzt werden müssen.

Die Regierung unter Sikorski und dessen Nachfolger seien von zwei Feinden ausgegangen – von Deutschland und der Sowjetunion. In nicht zu verantwortender Weise habe die Regierung ihre Strategie mit den Zielsetzungen der Westalliierten verbunden. Erst unter dem Druck der kommunistischen Widerstandsbewegung sei die ,,Armja Krajowa" zum planmäßigen Partisanenkampf übergegangen. ,,Verbohrte Einstellung zur Sowjetunion sowie der Mangel an Realismus zur Sowjetunion" und der von ihr geführten Landesarmee hätten sich verhängnisvoll auf die Lage in Polen ausgewirkt, wie der polnische Autor Tuszynski betont. Die falsche ideologische Konzeption der westlich orientierten Widerstandskräfte habe den Verlust vieler Menschen und Mittel zur Folge gehabt. Der ,,Bund des bewaffneten Kampfes" war nach offizieller polnischer Darstellung keine politische Organisation. In ihr hätten sich die rechtsgerichteten Militärorganisationen der sog. ,,halbfaschistischen nationalen Streitkräfte" befunden, die die alte Gesellschaftsordnung verteidigten und eine neue nicht wollten. Rechtsgerichtete Kräfte hätten sich bereits damals für die Wiederherstellung der alten gesellschaftlich-politischen Ordnung ausgesprochen und eine aggressive antikommunistische und antisowjetische Propaganda entfaltet. Sikorski fürchtete deutsche Vergeltungsmaßnahmen. Am 28. November 1942 umriß er seinen Standpunkt gegenüber der Sowjetunion in einer Instruktion an Rowecki: ,,Die von Ihnen so richtig gestellte Frage, wie sich die Untergrundarmee in der letzten Kriegsphase gegenüber der Sowjetunion verhalten soll, beunruhigt mich ständig ... Während man an meiner Idee, die gegenwärtig von Deutschland besetzten Gebiete bis an die Ostgrenzen Polens durch amerikanisch-englisch-polnische Truppen zu besetzen, grundsätzlich festhält, hat man jegliche Entscheidung darüber auf die Zukunft verschoben. Es hängt das auch von Rußland ab, dessen Stellung immer stärker wird ... Die Frage der Grenzen zwischen Polen und Rußland konnte nicht bestimmter als durch die Annullierung der zwischen Deutschland und Rußland geschlossenen Teilungsverträge formuliert werden ... Es hängt alles von dem im gegebenen Augenblick gerade herrschenden Kräfteverhältnis ab ... Vielleicht wird die polnische Regierung mit amerikanischer und britischer

Unterstützung die Sowjetregierung veranlassen können, unsere Rechte im Osten anzuerkennen und gleichzeitig unsere Ansprüche im Westen zu unterstützen, die Ostpreußen, Danzig und eine Berichtigung unserer Grenzen umfassen, wie sie für die Sicherheit unserer Ostseehäfen erforderlich sind; das Oppelner Schlesien sollte an Polen zurückkehren . . . Ich habe aber auch mit einer Entwicklung zu rechnen, die dazu führt, daß die Rote Armee bei der Verfolgung des Feindes die Grenzen der Republik Polen überschreitet. Eine bewaffnete Auseinandersetzung der Untergrundarmee mit den einmarschierenden Sowjettruppen wäre reiner Wahnsinn . . . In diesem Falle würde ich deshalb befehlen, daß sich die Untergrundarmee darauf einrichtet, sich zu enttarnen und mobil zu machen. Sie sollte so stark wie möglich sein und ihren Souveränitätsstatus und ihre positive Haltung gegenüber der Sowjetunion betonen. Ich werde dieser Haltung der Armee und der Heimat international den Weg bereiten; denn dort wird die politische Entscheidung über die Festlegung unserer Grenzen getroffen werden. Es ist auch notwendig, daß die Heimat und vor allem die militärischen Organisationen eine vollkommen einheitliche Front bilden und der kommunistische Einfluß keinen Vorrang hat . . . Verräter von der Art des Oberst Berling und der Wanda Wasilewska werden in die Fußstapfen der in Polen einmarschierenden Sowjettruppen treten, und sie werden alles nur Mögliche tun, eine Spaltung der polnischen Nation und eine Unterwühlung des polnischen Staates herbeizuführen. Nach meiner Rückkehr nach London (von Washington) wird die Regierung ihrem Vertreter in der Heimat die entsprechenden Instruktionen geben. Eines der Ziele meiner Reise wird es sein, Unterstützung für einen Kampf gegen Anarchie und Kommunismus in Europa dadurch zu gewinnen, daß der Kontinent mit großen Mengen an Lebensmitteln, Medikamenten und Kleidung versorgt wird . . ."

Im Jahre 1943 trat eine zweifellos von den Sowjets angestrebte Verschlechterung der polnisch-sowjetischen Beziehungen ein. Die Sowjets erklärten alle in der Sowjetunion befindlichen Personen polnischen Volkstums, die vorwiegend aus den ostpolnischen Gebieten stammten oder dort 1939 von ihr angetroffen wurden, zu sowjetischen Staatsbürgern. Sie beschlagnahmten etwa 600 polnische, in der Sowjetunion seit 1941 aufgebaute Einrichtungen, wie Lebensmittelverteiler, Altersheime, Verwaltungsstellen. All dies geschah vor der Entdeckung der Massengräber bei Katyn.

Die Beziehungen zwischen der Londoner Exilregierung und Moskau wurden abgebrochen. Dadurch war es Moskau möglich, das mit der Londoner Exilregierung bestehende Bündnis, das am 30. Juli 1941 geschlossen war, aufzukündigen.

Die Polnische Landesarmee fürchtete 1944 ständig die Möglichkeit, daß die ausgezeichnet organisierten Kommunisten in Polen das Gesetz des Handelns an sich reißen. Am 22. Juli 1944 wurde in Cholm von der Sowjetunion das „Polnische Komitee der nationalen Befreiung" ausgerufen. Drei Tage später wurde dieses nach Lublin verlegt. Es erhielt den Namen „Lubliner Komitee". Dieses Komitee, das als Gegenregierung zur polnischen Exilregierung in London und zu der in Warschau befindlichen Untergrundregierung angesehen werden muß, besaß in der Roten Armee den größten Bundesgenossen.

Von großem Interesse ist, daß Mitte März 1944 in kleinen wolhynischen Städten Führer der polnischen Landesarmee von den Sowjets kurzerhand erschossen wurden. Eine größere Abteilung der Armja Krajowa im Raume von Kowel, die mit sowjetischen Kavallerieverbänden zusammenarbeitete, hatte auf Weisung der Sowjets Mitte April bis zum letzten Mann zu kämpfen. Im entscheidenden Augenblick wurde sie allein gelassen. – Im Wilna-Gebiet (Wilna und Nowogrodek) kämpften im Januar 1944 ungefähr 12 500 Mann der Armja Krajowa gegen die deutschen Truppen. Dort waren die sowjetischen Partisanenabteilungen sehr stark. Die Sowjets verhinderten eine Zusammenarbeit mit der Führung der Kräfte der polnischen Landesarmee. Diese erhielt durch Zufall Kenntnis von einem Befehl der Sowjets, der die Vernichtung der AK-Einheiten vorsah.

Die bürgerlichen Gruppierungen hätten die Vereinigung der Westukraine und Weißrußlands mit einem neuen Polen und somit die Gebiete angestrebt, die vor dem Zweiten Weltkrieg zum polnischen Staatsgebiet gehörten. Auch hier habe die Bourgeosie eine großangelegte antisowjetische und antikommunistische Propaganda betrieben. Der Vorwurf wurde auch erhoben, daß linksorientierte Partisanenkräfte durch Überfälle nationalistischer Gruppen zerschlagen wurden.

Die „Rzeczpospolita Polka", das Organ der Delegatur, veröffentlichte im März 1942 unter dem Titel „Angesichts des Versuches der kommunistischen Wühlereien" einen Aufsatz, in welchem darauf hingewiesen wurde, daß die „Ungeniertheit der kommunistischen Elemente" so weit gehe, daß sie die polnische Bevölkerung zu bewegen suche, jetzt schon Diversionsaktionen und die Partisanentätigkeit gegen die Deutschen aufzunehmen. In ähnlicher oder noch viel schärferer Form wurden die Polnische Arbeiterpartei und die „Volksgarde" von anderen nationalpolnischen Zeitungen angegriffen.

Für den historischen Betrachter ergibt sich nachstehendes Bild: Die polnische Widerstandsbewegung wurde nach der Errichtung des Generalgouvernements von der NKWD und der deutschen Sicherheitspolizei bekämpft. Die NKWD unterhielt Verbindungsoffiziere zum deutschen Generalgouverneur in Krakau. Von September 1939 bis zum 21. Juni 1941 zogen die Sowjets im ostpolnischen Raum ein hervorragendes Agentennetz auf. Die Tätigkeit der sowjetischen Agenten wurde durch die geographische Beschaffenheit des Grenzraumes und die Umsiedlungsaktionen der Deutschen erleichtert.

Marian Spychalski, der nach 1945 zeitweise polnischer Kriegsminister war, gründete in der polnischen Hauptstadt mit deutscher Zustimmung einen „Verband für polnisch-sowjetische Freundschaft".

Die Sowjets waren über die Tätigkeit der deutschen Besatzung in Polen wie auch über die Stärke der polnischen Widerstandsgruppen laufend sehr gut unterrichtet. Dies gilt auch für den deutschen Aufmarsch gegen die Sowjetunion.

Vom 18. September 1939 bis zum 21. Juni 1941 hatten die polnische Bevölkerung in Ostpolen und die polnischen Widerstandsbewegungen sehr unter den sowjetischen Machthabern zu leiden. Die Art des Vorgehens der Roten Armee gegenüber der polnischen Zivilbevölkerung unterschied sich nicht von dem Verhalten, das die deutsche Bevölkerung 1945 in Mittel- und Ostdeutschland erleben mußte. 1939/40 fanden die ersten Massenverhaftungen und -verschickungen nach Innerrußland statt. Auf diese Art und Weise dürften ungefähr 1,2 Millionen ostpolnischer Bevölkerung dorthin gekommen sein. In erster Linie ging man gegen die Personen vor, die widerstandsverdächtig erschienen. Die Bildung einer Untergrundarmee wurde auf diese Art und Weise im Keime erstickt.

Bekannt wurde auch, daß die NKWD über besondere Verbindungsleute unter jenen polnischen Offizieren verfügte, die das besondere Vertrauen des Untergrundes hatten. Der Landesarmee wurde nach dem 21. Juni 1941 die Umstände bekannt, unter denen sich die Aufstellung polnischer Einheiten in der Sowjetunion vollzog.

Die Londoner Exilregierung hoffte, daß durch den Abschluß des sowjetpolnischen Militärabkommens vom 30. Juli 1941 und den Erlaß einer sog. Generalamnestie für alle Polen in der Sowjetunion (12. August 1941) eine Verbesserung der Lage der Polen in der Sowjetunion eintreten würde. Aber je mehr der deutsche Vorstoß gegen Moskau sich verlangsamte und scheiterte, desto mehr wurde Versorgung und Ernährung der Bevölkerung östlich von Kujbyschew beschränkt.

Im März 1942 stimmte Stalin der Bitte zu, die General Sikorski im Sommer 1941 ausgesprochen hatte, die polnischen Truppen aus der Sowjetunion herauszunehmen. Im Sommer 1942 wurden auf englisch-amerikanischen Druck drei weitere polnische Divisionen nach dem Iran abtransportiert.

Die Sowjets widersetzten sich jedoch einem weiteren Zustrom von Polen zu Sammelpunkten in der Sowjetunion. Es konnten dadurch keine weiteren Kräfte außerhalb der Sowjetunion tätig werden. Richtig ist, daß General

Sikorski den Sowjets mißtraute. Er schränkte den sowjetischen Einfluß auf technische Hilfen ein. Aber bereits am 27. Dezember 1941 scheiterte die Zusammenarbeit. Eine Abgrenzung der beiderseitigen Arbeitsräume entlang der Grenze von 1939 konnte nicht vorgenommen werden.

Im Frühjahr 1942 wurde sich die Londoner Exilregierung darüber klar, daß sowjetische Rundfunksender in polnischer Sprache zum sofortigen Aufstand gegen die Deutschen in Polen aufforderten. Die Rote Armee wurde als Befreier Polens bezeichnet. Bekannt ist der Aufruf, in welchem es heißt: ,,Polnische Brüder, die Zeit, eine entscheidende Aktion gegen die Hitleristen zu beginnen, ist da. Die Rote Armee rückt heran, und ihre Siege bringen Euch die Stunde der Befreiung und die Wiederherstellung eines freien und unabhängigen Polen."

Die Sowjetunion nützte in hervorragender Weise die verzweifelte Stimmung zur Bildung einer eigenen kommunistischen Widerstandsbewegung in dem von den Deutschen besetzten Polen aus. Bemerkenswert ist, daß am 6. Oktober 1941 Sikorski und am 16. Mai 1942 die Londoner Exilregierung gegen das Absetzen von sowjetischen Fallschirmspringern in der Gegend von Cholm, Lublin und der Lysa Góra protestierten.

Polnischer Widerstand außerhalb Polens

Im Zweiten Weltkrieg kämpften Bürger polnischer Nationalität in Widerstandsorganisationen und Partisanenbewegungen in Gesamteuropa. In Frankreich lebten damals ungefähr 500 000 Polen. Sie setzten sich aus Arbeitsuchenden der Vorkriegszeit und aus Polen zusammen, die sich nach dem September 1939 dorthin durchgeschlagen hatten. In der Hauptsache hielten sie sich in Nordfrankreich auf. Etwa 35 000 Mitglieder zählten die mit der kommunistischen Partei verbundenen Organisationen, die im Rahmen der Nationalen Front unter der Führung der ,,Organisation der eingewanderten Arbeiter" kämpften.

Zunächst war sie an der Verteilung von Flugblättern, Herstellung von illegalen Presseartikeln und Organisierung von Streiks beteiligt. Zu erinnern ist dabei an die Zeit vom Sommer 1940 bis Mitte Mai 1941; eine große Rolle spielten sie bei den Arbeitsniederlegungen im Nordbecken.

Die ,,Polska Organizacja Niepodleglost – Monika" unterstand als zivilmilitärische Organisation der polnischen Exilregierung in London. Sie wartete die Zeit der Landung ab und bildete ein Netz in den Departements Nord und Pas-de-Calais. Der Hauptaktionsraum war Südfrankreich.

Die polnischen-französischen Kundschafter- und Diversionsnetze (,,Resaux") waren mit der britischen Organisation für Sonderaktionen (Special Operations Executive) und mit dem französischen zentralen Nachrichten- und Aktionsbüro (Bureau Central de Renseignement et d'Action) verbunden.

Leutnant der Reserve Andrzej Wysogota-Zakrzewski, der nach seinem Tod den Rang eines Oberstleutnants erhielt, gründete unter dem Namen ,,Visigoths-Lorraine" oder ,,Szarzy Ludzie" (Graue Leute) ein Netz, das die Flucht aus Frankreich organisierte. 4800 kamen auf diesem Wege aus dem französischen Besatzungsgebiet, darunter zahlreiche alliierte Flieger. Die Organisation arbeitete mit sowjetischen Kundschafter- und Diversionsgruppen in Frankreich zusammen, u. a. mit der Gruppe ,,Waterfront" unter Oberleutnant Leonid Teretschenko.

Zu nennen ist auch die Kooperation mit den französischen Widerstandsorganisationen wie ,,Combat", ,,Libération" und ,,Francs-Tireurs" sowie der Ora (Organisation de Résistance de première Armée). Aus offiziöser kommunistischer Beschreibung darf entnommen werden:

,,Im Frühjahr 1944 wurden die Partisanenformationen beider polnischer Strömungen der Widerstandsbewegung den Französischen Streitkräften des

Inneren (Forces Françaises de l'Interieur–FFI) eingegliedert, die von dem Französischen Nationalen Befreiungskomitee ins Leben gerufen worden waren. Die FFI vereinigten alle französischen Widerstandsorganisationen einschließlich der Geheimarmee, der ,,Widerstandsorganisation der Armee", der linksstehenden Organisation FTP (FTP MOI) und der zu dieser Zeit gegründeten Patriotischen Miliz. Die linken polnischen Widerstandsorganisationen und Partisaneneinheiten bewahrten ihren nationalen Charakter, ihre organisatorische Struktur und Selbständigkeit sowie ihre Namen. Die Partisaneneinheiten und -gruppen operierten als Einheiten der FTP – FFI. Ihre Tätigkeit wurde von dem im April 1944 gegründeten Polnischen Komitee der Nationalen Befreiung in Frankreich (Polski Komitee Wyzwolenia Narodowego we Francij) und von einem Netz von örtlichen Komitees koordiniert. Die unter dem Einfluß der Exilregierung stehende Strömung wirkte unter der Bezeichnung ,,Polnische Organisation zum Kampf um die Unabhängigkeit – FFI."

Im Sommer 1944 beteiligten sich polnische Widerstandskämpfer am gesamtnationalen Aufstand in Frankreich und an den Befreiungskämpfen der französischen Städte Alés, Albi, Marseille, Nizza, Grenoble, Lyon, Clermond-Ferrand, Toulouse, Dijon, Lille, Carmaux, Cognac, Autun und Paris. Insgesamt nahmen etwa 50000 Polen an der Widerstandsbewegung in Frankreich teil. Davon kämpften mehr als 20000 mit der Waffe in der Hand in den Reihen der FTP – FFI (FTP MOI) und der Polnischen Patriotischen Miliz (Polska Milicja Patriotyczna). Etwa 7000 gehörten den Partisaneneinheiten der ,,Polnischen Organisation zum Kampf um die Unabhängigkeit – FFI" an."

Allgemein wird seitens des Ostblocks behauptet: ,,Im Oktober 1940 traten Polen den ersten bewaffneten Organisationen, den ,,Spezialorganisationen" (Organisations Spéciales de Combat – OS) und den ,,Jugendbataillonen" (Battaillons de la Jeunesse – BJ) bei, die auf Initiative der Französischen Kommunistischen Partei in den Arbeiterzentren des okkupierten Nordfrankreich gegründet worden waren und sich im Mai 1941 zur Widerstandsorganisation ,,Franc-Tireurs et Partisans" (FTP) vereinigten. Diese Organisation hatte eine besondere internationale Gliederung: die FTP MOI. In ihrem Rahmen entstanden insgesamt 23 polnische Abteilungen der FTP MOI. Außerdem kämpften viele Polen in französischen oder internationalen Abteilungen der FTP.

Zu den führenden Funktionären der linken Strömung der französischen Widerstandsbewegung und des Partisanenkampfes gehörten u. a. die Polen Boleslaw Maslankiewicz, Jan Rutkowski (,,Szymon"), Rudolf Larysz, Stanislaw Kubacki, Józef Spiro, Wladyslaw Kudla (,,Wacek"), Jan Blache (,,Gregorz"), Roman Kornecki, Stanislaw Kuc, Franciszek Mogilany, Boleslaw Jelen, Wladyslaw Tylec, Jan Gerhard („Jean"), Jan Skowron, Roman Piotrowski („Maurice"), Józef Szynczak, Antoni Chrost („Pepé"), Franciszek Papież, Józef Epsztein, der populäre „Colonel Gilles" und Zygmunt Czaika.

Im Herbst 1943 entstand der in beiden Zonen Frankreichs wirkende „Bund der Polnischen Jugend GRUNWALD" (Zwiazek Mlodziezý Polskiej „Grunwald") mit Stanislaw Steplewski, Michalina Malek und Józef Zakrzewski an der Spitze. Zu den aktiven Funktionären des „Bundes der Polnischen Jugend GRUNWALD" gehörten u. a.: Franciszek Milczek, Stanislaw Szumilas, Mieczyslaw Bargiel, Zdzislaw Grundzień, Mieczyslaw Grudzień, Edmund Czekala und Jan Pieczonka. Im Dezember 1943 bildeten polnische Frauen eine illegale Organisation, die sich später „Bund der Frauen MARIA KONOPNICKA" (Zwiazek Kobiet im. Marii Konopnickiej) nannte und eine Mitgliederzahl von 12 000 erreichte. An der Spitze dieser Organisation standen Aniela Makuch, Barbara Malek und Stefania Czarnecka.

Von den linken Organisationen ist auch noch die „Hilfsorganisation für das Vaterland" (Organizacja Pomocy Ojczyznie) zu erwähnen, die im Sommer 1942 in Südfrankreich gegründet wurde. Ihre Begründer waren u. a. Henryk Jabloński (Redakteur der Zeitschrift „Womit kehren wir zurück?"), Jan Gladysz, Michal Rusinek, Franciszek Kawecki und Wladyslaw Badura.

Im Winter 1943/44 stellte die linke polnische Strömung in der französischen Widerstandsbewegung eine bedeutende politische und bewaffnete Kraft dar. Polen beteiligten sich an den Partisanenkämpfen in Nordfrankreich, in den östlichen Departements, im Zentralmassiv, am Fuße der Alpen, in den Pyrenäen, im Raum zwischen Narbonne und Marseille, in Paris, Lyon, Saint-Etienne, Toulouse und Lille.

Im Herbst 1944 entstanden aus den linken polnischen Partisanengruppen reguläre militärische Einheiten, die in die 1. Französische Armee eingegliedert wurden. Sie stießen mit den Franzosen in das Gebiet der oberen Donau vor.

In den belgischen Widerstandsorganisationen kämpften 2000 Polen, die teils von der Kommunistischen Partei Belgiens, teils von der Exilregierung in London oder von anderen Zentren geleitet wurden.

Die meisten polnischen Widerstandskämpfer gehörten der „Unabhängigkeitsfront" und deren Militärorganisation an, der „Armée Belge de Partisans", die kommunistisch ausgerichtet war. Daneben gab es Polen in der national-polnischen „Geheimarmee" (Armée Secrète), die der belgischen Exilregierung unterstand. Auch in der Armée Blanche sowie in der „Front der Wallonen" fanden wir Polen.

In Verbindung mit der „Front der Wallonen" wurde im Sommer 1942 das „Polnische Komitee der Befreiung T. Kościuszko" (Polski Komitee Wyzwolenia imienia T. Kościuszki) gegründet, die die linken polnischen Widerstandsgruppen in Belgien leitete. In den Ardennen bauten sie mit belgischen Maquis eine Partisanenbasis auf.

Als Organisatoren der linken polnischen Widerstandsbewegung werden u. a. aufgezählt: Ludwik Warmuz, Maksymilian Bartz, Czeslaw Gutowski, Kazimierz Adamczyk, Marian Szymek, Wojciech Gramatyka, Michal Kiryczuk, Jan Olszański sowie Edward Gierek, Bergmann in der Grube „Zwartberg" bei Genk und Spitzenfunktionär der Kommunistischen Partei Belgiens in Limburg. Edward Gierek war Redakteur einer illegalen polnischen Zeitung und Initiator zahlreicher antifaschistischer Aktionen. Außerdem trug er im Raum Limburg zur Zusammenarbeit der Belgischen Partisanenarmee mit der Organisation „Witte Brigade" bei.

Auf Initiative der polnischen Linken in Belgien (u. a. Ludwik Warmuz, Maksymilian Bartz, Edward Gierek) entstand der „Verband polnischer Patrioten in Belgien" (Zwiazek Patriotów Polskich w Belgii), der auf seiner zweiten Tagung im April 1945 Edward Gierek zum Sekretär der Hauptverwaltung des Verbands wählte.

Es braucht nicht erwähnt werden, daß Polen in der sowjetischen Partisanenbewegung kämpften. Ihre Zahl dürfte über 10000 Mann liegen. Genannt werden als Organisateure und Kommandeure: Oberst A. Brinski, General W. A. Begma, General A. F. Fjodorow, Oberst D. N. Medwedew, Hauptmann I. Schitow, in den belorussischen Gruppierungen unter General W. S. Korsh („Komarow"), General W. Tschernyschow, General F. Kapusta, Oberst S. Sikorski, General W. I. Koslow, Oberst G. M. Linkow sowie Männer in den litauischen Gruppierungen unter M. Sumauskas und G. Zimanas.

Weiter gehörten den sowjetischen Partisaneneinheiten an: In Wolynien Józef Sobiesiak („Maks"), Jan Burzyński, Zofia Satanowska, Robert Satanowski, Wincenty Rozkowski, Kazimierz Turewicz, Stanislaw Wroński, Mikolaj Kunicki, Stanislaw Szelest, Mikolaj Kozubowski; im „Distrikt Galizien" Jakub Sliwka, Stanislaw Ziaja, Aleksander Leszczyński, Leon Smoleński, Józef Matwiszyn, Tadeusz Gajewski; in Westbelorußland Czeslaw Klim, Czeslaw Warchocki, Czeslaw Szelachowski, Zdzislaw Frankowski, Wojciech Zbilut, Leon Onichimowski, Aleks Zylewicz, Benedykt Szymanski, Józef Marchwiński, Adam Swietorzecki; im Gebiet von Wilna Jan Przewalski, Witold Sienkiewicz.

In der Tschechoslowakei kam es im Herbst 1939 bereits zu Kontakten zwischen Polen, Tschechen und Slowaken. In der Slowakei halfen Einwohner polnischen Offizieren und Soldaten bei der Flucht nach Ungarn.

Polnische Berg- u. Hüttenarbeiter schlossen sich im Gebiet um Karwin und um Mährisch-Ostrau sowie in dem Hüttenzentrum von Trinec in den Jahren 1939 bis 1941 mit den dortigen Einwohnern zu Widerstandsgruppen zusammen.

Einige hundert Polen nahmen am Slowakischen Aufstand von August bis Oktober 1944 teil.

Nachstehende slowakische und sowjetische Partisaneneinheiten seien genannt, in denen sie kämpften: ,,K. Gottwald", ,,L. Svoboda", ,,J. Zizka", in der Einheit unter P. Welitschko, in der Einheit ,,J. Nalepka" und in der Einheit unter W. Karassjow, in den Einheiten ,,Tschapajew", ,,Za Svobodu Slowanu" (Für die Freiheit der Slawen), ,,Jánošik" und ,,Za Rodinu". Im Kampf im Raum Baňská Bystřica (Neusohl), Staré Hory, Nemecká, Jasenie ließen viele ihr Leben. Auch in Widerstandsgruppen Böhmens und Mährens befanden sich Polen. In den Sudeten und im Raum Mährisch-Ostrau wurden polnische Fallschirmspringer abgesetzt.

In Jugoslawien:

In Bosnien unterstützen Polen die jugoslawischen Widerstandskämpfer. Gegen Ende des 19. Jahrhunderts und Anfang des 20. Jahrhunderts hatten sich ungefähr 20000 Polen aus den Gebieten, die Österreich zugefallen waren, im bosnischen Kreis Prnjavor angesiedelt.

Von den Nachkommen der Polen kämpften zunächst einzelne Gruppen vereinzelt in verschiedenen jugoslawischen Einheiten. Im Frühjahr 1944 wurden sie zu einem Bataillon in der Stärke von 500 Mann zusammengefaßt. Dieses kämpfte am Fluß Vrbas, um die Städte Banja Luka und Kotor-Varoš sowie auf den Höhen von Vucjak.

Nach dem Kriege siedelte sich die Mehrheit der polnischen Partisanen in den polnisch annektierten Gebieten an. Sie ließ sich in der Umgebung von Bunzlau in Niederschlesien nieder.

In Serbien organisierte 1943 der polnische Hauptmann J. Maciag (,,Nesz") im Auftrag der Londoner Exilregierung eine Partisanenabteilung in Stärke von 300 Mann. Anfang 1944 nach dem Tod von ,,Nesz" führte Z. Katuszewski die Einheit.

Auch Slowenien wurde im Jahre 1945 ein Betätigungsgebiet der polnischen Partisanen. Sie wurden von Marceli Nowotko unter dem Decknamen ,,Stary" (= ,,Der Alte") geführt. Dieser war früher Sekretär der polnischen Arbeiterpartei.

Ihr gehörten die einstigen Gefangenen eines am Loiblpaß errichteten Nebenlagers des Konzentrationslagers Mauthausen an, vorwiegend Mitglieder der Polnischen Arbeiterpartei, die 1943 in Litzmannstadt verhaftet worden waren. Geführt wurden sie von J. Rzetelski.

Polnische Partisanen waren auch an den Kämpfen um Triest und Rijeka (Fiume) beteiligt. Eine besondere Rolle in Slowenien spielte Tadeusz Sadowski („Tomo"), der Ende 1943 an der Sprengung eines Quecksilberbergwerks in Jdrija sowie eines Benzinlagers in den Podstajmski-Höhlen mitwirkte.

In Griechenland:

Polen wirkten auch in der Griechischen Volksbefreiungsarmee (Elas), die von der griechischen Nationalen Befreiungsfront (EAM) auf Initiative der Kommunistischen Partei Griechenlands gegründet worden war. In der Gegend von Trkkala stand die Gruppe „Bard" (J. Walerko); sie operierte in Zusammenarbeit mit dem Oberbefehlshaber der Elas, General Sarafis. Polnische Zwangsarbeiter aus Agrinion, Gravià bei Lamia an den Thermopylen und aus Arta bildete eine antideutsche Widerstandsgruppe, die mit örtlichen Zellen der Elas zusammenarbeitete. Polnische Kräfte wirkten im griechischen Mazedonien sowie in Thessalien. Der Pole Jerzy Jwanow-Szajnowicz leitete die Untergrundgruppe „Jwanow" und andere Diversionsgruppen, darunter die „Organisation zum Schutz der Arbeit".

Seine Einheiten zerstörten und beschädigten eine große Anzahl deutscher und italienischer Flugzeuge in der Fabrik Malzinolti im Stadtteil Neu-Phaleron von Athen. Die Versenkung von U–113, des Zerstörers „Hermes" und des Transportes „San Isidore" ist Jerzy Jwanow-Szajnowicz zuzuschreiben. In den Einheiten des Griechischen Nationaldemokratischen Vereins (EDES), die englisch orientiert waren, befanden sich ebenfalls polnische Widerstandskämpfer.

In Italien:

Polen bestätigten sich im Untergrund in Ligurien, Piemont, in der Lombardei und in der Toskana. Größere Gruppen wirkten auch in den Garibaldibrigaden, u. a. in den Brigaden „Giustizia e Libertá" und „Matteotti". Major Feliks Bykonacki kommendierte die Partisanenbrigade „Bevilacqua" in Ligurien.

In Norwegen:

Hier war die kommunistische Widerstandsbewegung schwach. Eine polnische Gruppe aus dem Ermland und Masuren bildete die Organisation „Rodlo". Der Name stellt eine Symbolbezeichnung der Polen in Deutschland (Zwiazek Polaków w Niemczech) dar. „Rodlo" führte eine Reihe von Sabotage- und Diversionsaktionen durch. Anfang 1945 versenkten sie ein deutsches Transportschiff.

In Dänemark

war im Untergrund der Leutnant zur See, L. Maslocha in Kopenhagen tätig, dem sich eine Gruppe Vorkriegsemigranten und Dänen anschlossen. Auch in Bornholm arbeitete eine Zeitlang eine Gruppe polnischer Widerstandskämpfer.

Spionage:

Dazu ein kurzes Wort. Die polnische Spionage konzentrierte sich in der Hauptsache auf das Eisenbahnwesen. Sie gewann auch wichtige Informationen über das Forschungszentrum für Raketenwaffen in Peenemünde. Dringende Erkenntnisse wurden einerseits direkt nach Moskau gefunkt, andererseits bediente sich der polnische Nachrichtendienst auch illegaler sowjetischer Sender auf polnischem Gebiet.

In der zweiten Hälfte des Jahres 1944 wurden im deutschen Hinterland polnische und polnisch-sowjetische Fallschirmgruppen abgesetzt, die die Sowjets über Stärke, Truppenverschiebungen und Verteidigungsanlagen informierten. Sie trugen auch zum Erfolg der sowjetischen Winteroffensive 1944/1945 bei.

Die Gruppe „Michal" (Kommandeur: Hauptmann Mikolaj Arciszewski), die am 16./17. Aug. 1941 abgesetzt wurde, hatte rasch im gesamten polnischen Bereich ein Spionagenetz aufgebaut; in ihm wurden die Verschiebungen der deutschen Truppen auf das genaueste angegeben. Von Bedeutung waren insbesondere die Meldungen über die transportierten technischen Waffen der mechanischen Truppen.

Juden im Widerstand

Zur Frage der Liquidierung der Ghettos

Von polnischer und kommunistischer Seite wird die Bedeutung der Juden im Widerstand gebührend herausgestellt. Ich selbst bin auf die Frage der Endlösung in dem historischen Zeugenbericht Adolf Eichmanns genügend eingegangen. Im Deutschlandfunk brachten in einem Dialog Dr. Schoeps und Dr. Krausnick eine Kommentierung. In dieser sagte Dr. Schoeps: ,,Ich möchte . . . fragen, ob das Erscheinen dieses Buches für die Bundesrepublik von Wichtigkeit ist, oder ist das eine Belanglosigkeit, auf die man verzichten kann?" Dr. Krausnick erwiderte: ,,Nein, es ist zweifellos eine Enthüllung besonderer Art, die das Buch bringt."

Dr. Schoeps erklärte: ,,Es ist zu hoffen, daß natürlich auch die wissenschaftliche Forschung sich dieses Buches bedient, dieses Buch heranzieht für weitere Erforschung der Thematik."

Mir geht es nur um die Wahrheit, daher meine große Bitte an die Wissenschaftler, sie mögen zur Forschung und zur Aufhellung der Vergangenheit sich auch des Buches ,,Der Krieg ohne Grenzen" bedienen. Dabei möchte ich sie insbesondere bitten, Augenmerk auf Zusammenhänge im Raum Lublin zu richten.

Nichts habe ich in Verbindung mit dem Partisanenkampf meinen damaligen Ausführungen in meiner Kommentierung Adolf Eichmanns hinzuzufügen oder hinwegzunehmen.

Ich schrieb in meiner Kommentierung zu ,,Adolf Eichmann":

,,Tatjana Berenstein, Artur Eisenbach, Bernard Mark und Adam Rutkowski gaben eine Dokumentation unter dem Titel ,,*Ausrottung und Widerstand der Juden in Polen während des II. Weltkrieges* – Faschismus, Ghetto- und Massenmord" heraus. Träger der Arbeit ist das Jüdisch-Historische Institut in Warschau. Über den Kampf gegen die Okkupationsmacht finden sich bemerkenswerte Sätze sowie Unterlagen. Im Einleitungskapitel heißt es: ,,Während der Hitler-Okkupation *kämpften Juden in Polen an allen Fronten des antifaschistischen Widerstandes.* Sie kämpften Schulter an Schulter mit den polnischen Soldaten während der heldenhaften Verteidigung Warschaus. Viele von ihnen gehörten verschiedenen Organisationen und Kampfgruppen des illegalen Polen an und nahmen an den Aktionen und Kämpfen der Swardia Ludowa (SL), der Volksgarde, einer linken polnischen Militärformation, und der Armja Krajowa (AK), der Heimatarmee, teil. Außerdem gab es auch Partisanengruppen, die ausschließlich aus Juden bestanden.

Schon in den ersten Okkupationsmonaten beginnt unter der jüdischen Bevölkerung eine *geheime Bewegung,* die sich immer mehr verbreitet. Ihre *Hauptbasis* wird das *Warschauer Ghetto,* wo viele illegale Zeitungen herausgegeben werden. Die Widerstandsbewegung in Warschau beeinflußt die jüdischen Gruppen in anderen Gebieten Polens . . ."

Hervorgehoben wird, daß im März 1942 im Warschauer Ghetto ein Antifaschistischer Block geschaffen wurde, dem die kommunistische PPR, die polnische Arbeiterpartei und links-zionistische Organisationen (Haschomer Hazair, Poale Zion, Hechaluz) angehörten. Im Oktober 1942 wurde diese antifaschistische Front, deren Ziel der Kampf gegen die Okkupanten gewesen sei, erweitert, und eine *jüdische Kampforganisation* (Żydowska Organizacja Bojowa, ZOB) *sei geschaffen worden,* der die erwähnten Organisationen des Antifaschistischen Blocks, die sozialistische Partei ,,Bund" und einige kleinere Jugendgruppen angehört hätten. Die *Hauptaufgabe* der jüdischen Kampforganisation sei *der bewaffnete Kampf* gegen den Okkupanten, die Verteidigung der jüdischen Bevölkerung gewesen.

Es heißt wörtlich weiter: ,,Unter der Leitung der Jüdischen Kampforganisation bereitet sich der Rest der Ghettobevölkerung zum aktiven Widerstand vor; die Jüdische Kampforganisation sammelt Waffen und verbirgt sie und organisiert eine militärische Ausbildung; die Bevölkerung baut unterirdische Bunker, um sich vor den Razzien zu verstecken, mit denen die Nazis die Juden zur Deportation zusammentreiben . . ."

Vom Zeitpunkt an, als sich in den Ghettos ein Widerstand entwickelte, erwogen die jüdischen Kämpfer die Möglichkeit von zwei Kampffronten: In den Ghettos und *in den Reihen der Partisanen.* Schon im Juli 1942 verband sich die erste Gruppe aus dem Warschauer Ghetto mit der Partisanenbewegung. Vom Herbst 1942 an flüchteten die Juden aus den Ghettos in den Distrikten Lublin, Radom, Bialystok und aus dem östlichen Teil des Distrikts Warschau massenweise in die Wälder, wo sie sich entweder den Partisanengruppen der Volksgarde oder besonderen jüdischen Partisanentrupps anschlossen.

Die polnische Widerstandsbewegung hatte eine hervorragende Bedeutung. Die Kämpfe in den Ghettos, in den KZ-Lagern und die Widerstandsbewegung haben verhältnismäßig große Kräfte der Okkupanten gebunden.

Von Reuben Ainztein wurde ein Werk unter dem Titel ,,Jewish Resistance in Nazi-Occupied Eastern Europe" (London, Paul Elek) herausgebracht. Der Verfasser weist darauf hin, daß z. B. die Bildung einer jüdischen Widerstandsbewegung und zweier militärischer Organisationen mit der alleinigen Absicht, eine bewaffnete Revolte durchzuführen, überwiegend auf Teenager und Leute um 20 herum zurückgeht, die vier politischen Gruppen angehörten: Dem Bund der zionistischen Jugendorganisation, umfassend den rechten Flügel von Revolutionären bis zum extrem linken Flügel von Hashomer Hazair und die Kommunisten.

Auf Seite 572 heißt es: ,,. . . im Herbst 1941 die polnischen Sozialisten ihre eigene Organisation schufen, formierte der Bund eine gleichwertige Organisation im Ghetto . . .'' ,,. . . Die Gründungsmitglieder der Kommunistischen Partei Polens begannen sie wieder aufzubauen im Jahre 1940. Die wichtigsten Teile waren ,,Sichel und Hammer'', die Gesellschaft der Freunde der UdSSR . . .'' Im letzten Satz des zweiten Absatzes wurde darauf hingewiesen, daß alle diese Organisationen ihresgleichen im Warschauer Ghetto hatten. Seite 573, letzter Satz: ,,Im März 1942 begannen die ,leftwing'-Zionistenführer ihre Arbeit, eine geeinte jüdische Kampforganisation zu schaffen, zusammen mit den Kommunisten . . .'' Seite 574, Kapitel 5 hebt hervor, daß im März 1942 die left-wing-Zionisten sich zum ersten Mal im Warschauer Ghetto trafen. Auf Seite 598 wird darauf hingewiesen, daß der Aufstand in Warschau von abgesprungenen jüdischen Offizieren der Roten Armee geführt wurde.

Einzelmeldungen, Verlautbarungen, Aufrufe bestätigen den von jüdischer Seite geleisteten Widerstand. Auf Aktionen folgten automatisch Gegenaktionen. Im Warschauer Ghetto wurde im März 1942 der antifaschistische Block geschaffen. Es gehörten ihm folgende Geheimorganisationen an: Die polnische Arbeiterpartei (PPR) und die linken zionistischen Organisationen Haschomer, Hazaer, Hechaluz und Poale Zion. Uns sind auch die Führer der Organisationen bekannt: Josef Lewartowski, Mitglied des ZK der kommunistischen Partei Polens, der langjährige Leiter der linken Poale Zion, Szachno Sagan, Josef Kaplan, Leiter der Haschomer, Hazaer, Izhak Cukierman, Funktionär des Hechaluz.

Der antifaschistische Block gab in jiddischer Sprache die illegale Zeitschrift ,,Der Ruf'' heraus. Von ihm wurden die ersten Kampfgruppen im Ghetto organisiert, die unter der Führung des ehemaligen Kapitäns der internationlaen Brigaden in Spanien, des Kommunisten Andrzej Szmidt, und des Funktionärs der Haschomer, Hazaer, Mordechja Anielewicz, standen.

Der 6. deutschen Armee fielen nach dem Einmarsch in den sowjetischen Raum Unterlagen in die Hand, in denen es heißt: ,,Es ist notwendig, dem Feind einen sehr starken, blitzartigen Schlag zu versetzen, um die Widerstandskraft der Soldaten zu erschüttern . . . Im allgemeinen werden die Kampfhandlungen sich auf dem Gebiet des Feindes abwickeln, besonders dort, wo die ukrainische und jüdische Bevölkerung vorherrscht . . .''

Anfang November 1942 wurde die jüdische Kampforganisation (Żydowska Organizacja Bojowa, ŻOB) gegründet. Auf diese wurde bereits hingewiesen. Außer den am antifaschistischen Block beteiligten Gruppen gehörten auch die Jüdische Sozialistische Partei „Bund" und jüdisch-zionistische Jugendvereine wie Gordonia und Hanor Hazioni an.

Die jüdische Kampforganisation wurde in Warschau geführt von Mordechai Anielez (Haschomet Hazair). Mitglieder des Stabes waren: Michal Rosenfeld (Kommunist), Hersz Berlinski (linke Paole Zion), Izhak Cukierman (Hechaluz) und Marek Edelman (Bund). Diese Organisation führte auch die Bestrafung von sogenannten Verrätern durch. So wurde Jakub Lejkin, der stellvertretende Chef des jüdischen Sicherheitsdienstes, am 29. Okt. 1942 nach einem Feme-Urteil getötet.

Auch über den Kampf polnischer, jüdischer, weißrussischer, russischer und deutscher „Antifaschisten" in Bialystok im März 1943 kam ein Bericht heraus. Es wird ausgeführt:

Die antifaschistische Organisation beauftragte eine Gruppe von Widerstandskämpfern, den Beauftragten der jüdischen Selbstverteidigung, die Waffen zu beschaffen und sie ins Ghetto zu schmuggeln hatten, behilflich zu sein. Eine russische Gruppe, die in der Bialystoker Konspiration tätig war, kam der jüdischen Selbstverteidigung aktiv zu Hilfe. Dieser Gruppe gehörten meistens sowjetische Staatsangehörige und Offiziere der Roten Armee an, die vom Feind abgeschnitten worden waren und sich in Bialystok unter falschem Namen verbargen. An der Spitze dieser Gruppe standen die sowjetischen Staatsangehörigen: Sachar (Pseudonym „General Sacharow"), Michail Barburin („Mischa"), Iwan Orlow („Wanja") und Wolkow. Sie brachten den Juden wichtige Nachrichten und Waffen; sie halfen dem Ghetto, Fühlung mit der Partisanenbewegung aufzunehmen. Michail Barburin war Chauffeur von Frank, dem Ortsgruppenleiter der NSDAP, und stellte stets, sein Leben aufs Spiel setzend, das Auto seines Chefs der Ghetto-Selbstverteidigung zur Verfügung. Jüdische und weißrussische Mädchen transportierten in Franks Auto illegale Schriften und Waffen."

Den 1. Mai 1943 im Bunker einer jüdischen Kampforganisation schildert ein Insasse namens B. Berg mit folgendem Wortlaut: „Der 1. Mai ist gekommen. Wir stellen den Rundfunkempfänger auf den Sender Moskau ein. Wir hören den 1.-Mai-Befehl Stalins, des Befreiers der Völker, auf den die Augen nicht nur des Restes der jüdischen Ghettokämpfer, sondern der ganzen fortschrittlichen Menschheit gerichtet sind. Wir hören von der ungeheuren, zerschmetternden Niederlage der deutschen Armee bei Stalingrad, von den über 300 000 Gefallenen, von Hunderten von Städten und Tausenden von Dörfern, die von der Hitler-Okkupation befreit worden sind. Es ist klar, daß Stalingrad als Anfang vom Ende der Hitlerherrschaft anzusehen ist. Für 10 Uhr haben wir unsere 1.-Mai-Versammlung festgesetzt . . .

‚Kampfgenossen' – beginnt seine Rede Genosse Szachne bei tödlicher Stille und tiefstem Ernst aller im Bunker Versammelten. In seinen großen, tiefen Augen ist abgründiger Schmerz, jedoch weder Niedergeschlagenheit noch Resignation zu lesen. Mit außergewöhnlicher Ruhe erklärt er die Bedeutung des 1. Mai. Beurteilt unsere Lage und sagt: ‚Unser Kampf wird unzweifelhaft von einer großen historischen Bedeutung nicht nur für das jüdische Volk, sondern auch für die ganze europäische Widerstandsbewegung sein, die gegen den Nazismus kämpft' . . . Die bewaffneten Kämpfer stimmen still, aber entschlossen die Internationale an . . . Indem wir die Internationale sangen, fühlten wir alle, daß unser letzter Kampf nahte."

Am 16. Aug. 1943 erließ die Vereinigte Antifaschistische Organisation einen Aufruf zum bewaffneten Widerstand. Er schließt mit den Worten: „Jüdische Jugend! Möge Dir das Beispiel und die Tradition vieler Generationen von jüdischen Kämpfern und Märtyrern, Denkern und Baumeistern, Pionieren und Schöpfern als Vorbild dienen! Geh auf die Straße hinaus und kämpfe! Hitler wird den Krieg verlieren; die Achse der Sklaverei und Menschenfresserei wird von der Erdoberfläche weggewischt werden. Die Welt wird gesäubert werden. Angesichts der sonnigen Zukunft der Menschheit darfst du nicht wie ein Hund sterben! In den Wald, zu den Partisanen! Flüchte nicht aus dem Ghetto – ohne Waffen wirst du getötet; wenn du deine nationale Pflicht erfüllt hast, – geh in den Wald! Waffen kannst du von jedem Deutschen im Ghetto erbeuten. Sei stark!"

Nicht übersehen werden darf die Wirkung des Aufrufes der jüdischen Konferenz, die am 24. Aug. 1941 in Moskau stattfand, durch die die Juden auf der ganzen Welt zum Kampf gegen Hitler aufgerufen wurden. Groß war der Widerhall der Sätze: „Nehmt an der edlen Selbstaufopferung der unbezwingbaren Guerillakämpfer teil! Entfaltet überall eine umfassende Propaganda für die Solidarität und die aktive Hilfe für die Sowjetunion . . . Die Menschheit wird von der braunen Pest befreit werden. Eure Pflicht ist es, bei ihrer Ausrottung zu helfen. Tut Eure Pflicht in diesem heiligen Krieg!"

In der Schrift „Martyrium, Kampf und Vernichtung der jüdischen Bevölkerung im Radomer Distrikt während der Hitler-Okkupation" von Rutkowski wird ausgeführt: „Die erste derartige Aktion wurde im Radomer Ghetto am 19. Februar 1942 (Donnerstag) durchgeführt, als deren Ergebnis die Hitlerleute an Ort und Stelle über vierzig Menschen getötet und ungefähr 40 Personen nach Auschwitz deportiert haben. Unter den Erschossenen war eine bedeutende Anzahl kommunistischer Agitatoren. Im Laufe des Februar, März und April 1942 erfolgten weitere Serien von Verhaftungen und Deportationen im bzw. aus dem Radomer Ghetto, deren Opfer meist Schmuggler von Lebensmitteln und Fleischer sind. Im April steigen die Stärke und die Anspannung der terroristischen Aktionen besonders. In der Nacht vom 27. auf den 28. April führte man gleichzeitig in beiden Radomer Ghettos (Gliniza und an der Walowa) eine Aktion gegen Arbeiter-Agitatoren, antifaschistische Aktivisten und besonders gegen Kommunisten durch. Sie betraf u. a. Leute, die aus der Sowjetunion zurückgekehrt waren. Die Hitlerleute erschossen damals an Ort und Stelle ungefähr 70 Juden und deportierten einige Hunderte in die Konzentrationslager.

Analoge Aktionen wurden bei Anwendung identischer Methoden auch in Kielce, Tschenstochau, Ostrowjez, Opoczno, Tomaszów/Masowjetzki, Radomsko usw. durchgeführt. Der April-Aktion in Kielce ist eine Aktion vorangegangen, die Ende des Jahres 1941 gegen linksgerichtete politische Agitatoren, gegen diejenigen, die aus der Sowjetunion zurückgekehrt waren (nach Juni 1941 – A. R.), sowie gegen Reserveoffiziere durchgeführt wurde.

An demselben Tage wie in Radom erfolgte eine blutige Aktion in Tomaszów/Masowjezki (27. April), die Arbeiter-Agitatoren sowie Schmuggler in einer Gesamtzahl von einigen zehn Personen umfaßte.

Am 6. Mai erfaßte eine der Reihenfolge nach vorgenommene Aktion einige zehn Personen aus der Intelligenz und jüdischen Reserveoffizieren des polnischen Heeres, und am 7. Mai räumten die SS-Leute ihre Gehilfen aus dem Kreise des örtlichen Judenrates hinweg.

Emanuel Ringelblum bringt beim Analysieren in jener Zeit der Quellen und der Ursachen dieser Welle der Morde und Verhaftungen im Frühjahr 1942 die Annahme vor, daß diese blutige Aktion mit „dem Aufenthalt Himmlers im Generalgouvernement, wo er wahrscheinlich seinen Untergebenen Befehl gab, unter der jüdischen Bevölkerung mit Hilfe einer ‚Dosis Terror und des Blutbades' Angst zu verbreiten, damit sie den Kopf nicht zu hoch hält", zusammenhängt.

Von polnischer und kommunistischer Seite wird die Bedeutung der Juden für die militärische Auseinandersetzung herausgestellt

Auffallend ist, daß der Vernichtungsaktion des Warschauer Ghettos eine Großaktion des Befehlshabers der Sicherheitspolizei und des SD gegen die entstehende neue Kommunistische Partei Polens und ihre Untergrundorganisationen in der Nacht zum 28. Apr. 1942 in den Räumen Warschau, Krakau, Radom und Lublin vorherging. Insgesamt 931 Personen, darunter 400 Juden, wurden festgenommen. Über die Zusammenhänge des Frühjahrs 1942 in der Judenpolitik dürften ebenfalls Unterlagen im Jüdischen Historischen Institut in Warschau vorhanden sein, aus denen sich ergibt, daß Himmler die Befehle persönlich gab, daß die Sicherung des Hinterlan-

251

des der Ostfront eine Rolle spielte und die zentralgesteuerte Aktion in Polen die Zielsetzung hatte, die potentiellen Anführer und Organisatoren der „Antifaschistischen Bewegung des Widerstandes" die Möglichkeiten der Führung zu nehmen und die Bevölkerung vom Widerstand und Kampf gegen die Okkupationsmacht abzuhalten.

Nicht umsonst sieht sich der Chef der Sicherheitspolizei und des SD ab 1. Aug. 1941 veranlaßt, vierzehntägige Berichte über die Lage im Generalbouvernement zu vergleichen (vgl. Schnellbrief vom 24. Juli 1941 – IV D 2 – 260/41). Nicht ohne Grund heißt es bereits in einer Anlage zu einem Bericht des RSHA nach der Besetzung von Dänemark und Norwegen: „Die Stimmung der Juden hat sich gleichfalls verschlechtert, da die Proletarisierung dieser Elemente fortschreitet ... Darüber hinaus steht fest, daß die Juden Hauptträger der Gerüchteverbreitung sind."

Nach dem Frankreich-Feldzug wird in einer weiteren Anlage hervorgehoben: „Diese Schichten erhoffen vom Sieg des Bolschewismus die Weltrevolution und eine grundlegende Wendung ihres Lebensstandards."

Es entstand für das Reichssicherheits-Hauptamt das Bild: Die Distrikte Lublin und Warschau sind außerordentlich gefährdet. Die Neigung der polnischen Bevölkerung, sich nach der bolschewistischen Seite zu orientieren, wächst.

Bereits im Verfahren gegen B. in Darmstadt führte ich die Meldung Nr. 9 vom 26. Juni 1942 an, die der Chef der Sicherheitspolizei herausgab. In ihr heißt es: „Nachrichtendienstlich wurde seit Beginn 1942 immer mehr festgestellt, daß die sowjetrussischen Widerstandsbewegungen sich mit Gliedern der polnischen Widerstandsbewegung nicht nur ideologisch immer mehr trafen, sondern es auch zwischen ihnen zu organisatorischen Ansätzen eines gemeinsamen Kampfes kam, zum Teil mit Hilfe des Judentums als Nachrichtenträger, Waffenschmuggler und Stimmungsmacher. Auch den Partisanengruppen selbst liefen immer mehr Juden zu. Bis zum Spätherbst 1941 war in den ehemaligen ostpolnischen Gebieten das Auftauchen von Heckenschützen partisanenmäßiger Natur eine Einzelerscheinung, während seit März 1942 aus diesen Gebieten ebenso viele Meldungen über Werbung, Aktionen und Erfolge der Partisanen einlaufen wie aus den altsowjetischen Gebieten."

Die Situation, von der die Wehrmacht ausging, umschreiben Lageberichte der Oberfeldkommandanturen und Feldkommandanturen im Generalgouvernement.

Der Stadtkommandant Minsk des Wehrmachtsbefehlshabers Ostland stellte in seinem Monatsbericht vom 1.–10. Nov. 1941, Ziffer 3, fest: „Die gegen die Juden als Träger der bolschewistischen Idee und Führer der Partisanenbewegung eingeleiteten Maßnahmen sind von fühlbarem Erfolg."

Bereits in dem Bericht der Kommandatur Warschau Qu. Nr. 219/41 geh. vom 20. Apr. 1941 (Akte 75022/4 – Militärhistorisches Forschungsamt Freiburg), einem Monatsbericht für die Zeit vom 15. März bis 15. Apr. 1941 unter der Überschrift ,,Beobachtungen und Feststellungen außerhalb der Truppe", heißt es: ,,Die Stimmung im Judenviertel ist ganz prorussisch ...".

Der Monatsbericht (für die Zeit vom 16. Aug.–15. Sept. 1941) der Kommandantur Warschau vom 20. Sept. 1941 – Nr. 553/41 geh. – (Akte 75022/6 – Militärhistorisches Forschungsamt Freiburg) bringt unter 7. ,,Beobachtungen und Feststellungen außerhalb der Truppe" zum Ausdruck: ,,Anders ist die Auffassung in den niederen, d. h. kommunistischen Schichten der Bevölkerung und den Juden. Hier wird in jeder Weise mit Rußland sympathisiert, wie es auch in der Anbiederung mit Kriegsgefangenen, Hilfeleistung für entflohene russische Kriegsgefangene etc., zum Ausdruck kommt.

Mit dem Winter 1941/42 bahnt sich im Osten eine deutsche Katastrophe an. Unter dem 28. Mai 1942 stellt das OKH/Gen. Qu. II 3631/42 geh. fest: ,,War die Entwicklung der Dinge bislang so, daß sich zunächst, wie schon früher berichtet, Banden aus versprengten Rotarmisten, aus den von den deutschen Truppen besetzten Orten geflüchteten Kommunisten ohne einheitliche Führung und Ausrichtung bildeten . . . , so zeigt sich jetzt mehr und mehr, daß diese zunächst unabhängig voneinander operierenden Einheiten unter einheitlicher Führung zusammengefaßt und damit zu einer immer größer werdenden Gefahr für die Sicherheit werden."

Unter dem 15. Juni 1942 berichtet im Auftrag des Reichskommissars Lohse – Tgb. Nr. 785/42 geh.: ,,Es ist festgestellt worden, daß die Bürgermeister polnischer Nationalität mit den kommunistischen Umtrieben sympathisieren." Die Entwicklung, die ihren ersten Höhepunkt im Frühjahr 1942 erreicht hatte, nimmt im Laufe des Jahres 1942 immer mehr zu, so daß in einem Fernschreiben vom 17. Mai 1943 – FS Nr. 1786 – an den Beauftragten für den Vierjahresplan die Regierung des Generalgouvernements meldet: ,,Banden-Unwesen im Generalgouvernement nimmt von Tag zu Tag in erschreckendem Umfang zu. System und Anlage der Überfälle lassen schließen, daß Produktionsvernichtung zum Hauptprogramm der Banden gehört."

Die Oberfeldkommandantur Lemberg (365) hebt im Bericht für die Zeit vom 16. Juni–15. Juli 1941 (Ia Nr. 347 geh.) vom 18. Juli 1941 hervor: ,,VIII Sonstiges: 1. Zivilbevölkerung: Sympathien mit Sowjetrußland sind zweifellos in größerem Maße in jüdischen Kreisen vorhanden gewesen, in denen man in den ersten Tagen große Hoffnungen auf Befreiung von der deutschen Herrschaft durch die Bolschewisten hegte." Lakonisch kurz ist die Feststellung der Kommandantur Warschau vom 19. Juli 1941 in dem

Monatsbericht für die Zeit vom 16. Juni–15. Juli 1941 (Ia Nr. 5866/41) in Punkt 7.: „Beobachtungen und Feststellungen außerhalb der Gruppe (Seite 19): ‚Die Juden: Ihr heißer Wunsch ist Deutschlands Vernichtung.'" In dem Lagebericht vom 1.–15. Febr. 1942, den unter dem 20. Febr. 1942 die Kommandantur des Sicherungsgebietes Weißruthenien, d. h. das Kommando der 707. Infanteriedivision herausgab, wird festgestellt: „Über Juden und Polen ist dem in den vorausgegangenen Lageberichten Gesagten hinzuzufügen, daß sie dem Kommunismus und der Organisation des Partisanentums in jeder nur denkbaren Weise in die Hände arbeiten und Vorschub leisten. Die Juden sind deshalb ohne jede Ausnahme mit dem Begriff Partisan identisch."

Das Schicksal des jüdischen Ghettos in Warschau

Am 22. Juli 1942 begann die Warschauer Ghettoaktion. Staatssekretär Ganzenmüller erhielt über das menschenunwürdige Unternehmen, das Unzähligen großes Leid brachte, von Karl Wolff, dem nachmaligen höchsten SS- und Polizeiführer in Italien, den „berühmten Brief" vom 13. Aug. 1942 aus Winniza: „Mit besonderer Freude habe ich von Ihrer Mitteilung Kenntnis genommen, daß nun seit 14 Tagen täglich ein Zug mit je 5000 Angehörigen des auserwählten Volkes nach Treblinka fuhr . . ." Bis zur Absendung des Briefes war fast die Hälfte der Bevölkerung aus dem Ghetto „ausgesiedelt". Dessen Fläche konnte verringert werden. Am 16. August wurden für 30 000 jüdische Arbeiter aus dem Ghetto neue Arbeitsbescheinigungen ausgestellt.

Am 20. Okt. 1942 starb Lejkin, der Kommandeur des jüdischen Ordnungsdienstes. An dem gleichen Tage erkannten alle politischen Gruppen die Befehlsgewalt des jüdischen Widerstandskomitees an. Es ist nicht verwunderlich, daß zwischen den Juden und der linksgerichteten Widerstandsbewegung sich eine immer stärker werdende Verbindung entwickelte. Zwischen den sowjetischen Kriegsgefangenen und Organisationen wie der „Arbeiter- und Bauern-Kampforganisation" südlich von Lublin, der „Kampforganisation des Volkes" (Bojowa Organizacja Ludowa) nördlich von Lublin, der „Arbeiter- und Bauern-Vereinigung" (Zjednoczenie Robotnico-Chopskie) im Bezirk Kielce und des „Verbandes der Freunde der UdSSR" in Warschau hatte sich ein „Schutz- und Trutzbündnis" herausgebildet.

Der Sekretär der Polnischen Arbeiterpartei, Marceli Nowotko, telegraphierte am 24. Juni 1942 an den Generalsekretär der Kommunistischen Internationale, Georgi Dimitroff: „Unsere Arbeiter und Bauern gewähren Tausenden von Soldaten und Kommandeuren der Roten Armee, die aus den deutschen Kriegsgefangenenlagern geflüchtet sind, Unterschlupf. Überall stehen wir mit ihnen in Kontakt und helfen nach besten Kräften. Wir haben beschlossen, sie in unsere Partisanenabteilung aufzunehmen." Polen beherbergte aus den Ghettos geflüchtete Juden. Sie beschafften Ausweise, Kleidung, Medikamente und Nahrungsmittel. Allein in Warschau erhielten 20 000 Juden Unterkunft. Auch die Londoner Exilregierung half. Der ,,Rat zur Hilfeleistung für Juden" (Zegota), dessen Vorsitzender Julian Grobelny, Mitglied der Polnischen Sozialistischen Partei (PPS-WRN), nach dessen Verhaftung Roman Jablonowski war, wurde gegründet. Dem ,,Rat" gehörten u. a. an: Tadeusz Reck (Volkspartei – St. Roch), Ferdinand Arczynski (Demokratische Partei) und Piotr Gajewski von der Arbeiterpartei, ferner Polnische Sozialisten und Leon Fajner, Mitglied des jüdischen Bundes. Die ,,Zegota" rettete vor allem in Krakau, Lemberg und anderen Städten Zehntausende von Juden. In Warschau wurde das ,,Komitee zur Hilfeleistung für Bewohner des Warschauer Ghettos" unter Franciszek Loczycki in das Leben gerufen.

Auf militärischem Gebiet wurden jüdische Kampfgruppen aufgebaut. Waffen wurden in die Ghettos geliefert. Geflüchtete Juden führten – insbesondere in Warschau und Lublin – Partisanenabteilungen. Vor allem in den Wäldern von Parczew und in der Puszcza Solska bei Lublin bauten Gruppen Waldlager auf. Die polnische Arbeiterpartei, die Volksgarde und die Polnischen Sozialisten hatten eigene Kampfgruppen im Warschauer Ghetto. Als der Aufstand in Warschau im Jahre 1943 ausbrach, unternahmen Kampfabteilungen der Landesarmee, der Volksgarde und des ,,Sicherheitskorps" mehrere große Aktionen gegen die Absperrungsmannschaften der Deutschen.

Das amtliche Warschau vertritt den Standpunkt, daß der jüdische Widerstand trotz aller Aufrufe durch rechtsgerichtete, zionistische und orthodoxe Kreise gegen die Maßnahmen der deutschen Besatzungsmacht zu schwach war. Es wird bedauert, daß die Warnungen der illegalen Presse nicht befolgt wurden.

So schrieb die ,,Trybuna Wolności" der Polnischen Arbeiterpartei: ,,Nur ein kompromißloser Widerstand in jeder Situation, nur eine aktive Haltung und nicht das passive Warten auf das Blutbad kann Tausende, Zehntausende von Menschen retten, auch wenn es Opfer fordern wird . . . Man muß der Polizei Widerstand leisten. Jedes Haus soll zu einer Festung werden."

Hervorgehoben wird als beinah einzige Widerstandsorganisation die Ende 1942 auf Drängen der Polnischen Arbeiterpartei gegründete Antifaschistische Partei. Die ihr angehörenden Vereinigungen schlossen sich im Oktober 1942 zum ,,Jüdischen Nationalkomitee" (Żydowski Komitet Narodowy) zusammen. Um dieselbe Zeit entstand die ,,Jüdische Kampforganisation" (Żydowska Organizacja Bojowa – ŻOB) unter der Führung von Mordechay Anielewicz. Daneben bestand im Ghetto der jüdische Militärbund (Żydowski Zwiazek Wojskowi – ŻZW). Letztgenannte Organisation arbeitete mit illegalen polnischen Verbänden zusammen. Von ihnen erhielt sie auch Waffen und Sprengmittel. Es wurde ihnen möglich, die Produktion von Handgranaten und Brandflaschen aufzunehmen. Zusätzlich wurden Maschinengewehre und Granaten geliefert. Den jüdischen Aufständen kamen auch sowjetische Fliegerkräfte zu Hilfe. Sowjetische Kampfflugzeuge flogen in der Nacht vom 13. und 14. Mai 1943 einen Bombenangriff.

Die Haltung der Juden im Warschauer Ghetto war bedeutsam, da Verbindungsmänner in andere ,,Judenlager", z. B. nach Bialystok und Tschenstochau, geschickt wurden. In Bialystok kam es am 19. Februar 1943 sowie zwischen dem 16. und 20. Aug. zu Kämpfen, in Tschenstochau am 25. Juni 1943. Auch in Treblinka und Sobibor ging man zum Angriff über. In Treblinka organisierte der Hauptmann der ehemaligen polnischen Armee, Leichert, den Aufstand. In Sobibor bereiteten ihn Offiziere der Sowjetarmee, A. Perschinski und L. Fendler. vor.

Illusionistische Vorstellungen der nationalsozialistischen Führung des Deutschen Reiches über die Aufteilung des Ostraumes

Es liegt ein Dokument vor: Eine Aufzeichnung der Besprechung Hitlers mit Göring, Rosenberg, Lammers, Keitel und Bormann vom 16. Juli 1941, die fünf Stunden dauerte. Diese Niederschrift ist allerdings sehr umstritten, da Bormann in solche Aufzeichnungen seine eigenen Gedankengänge einbrachte. In der Besprechung wurden neue Grenzen erörtert und Kriegführungsmethoden besprochen. Die Teilnehmer der Besprechung gingen von unrealistischen und fehlerhaften Gesichtspunkten aus. Hitler bezeichnet es als wesentlich, daß die Zielsetzung seiner Ostraumpolitik nicht vor der ganzen Welt bekanntgegeben wird. Nach ihm handelte es sich darum, „nichts für die endgültige Regelung zu verbauen" und es darauf abzustellen, „daß wir die Bringer der Freiheit" seien.

Hitler betonte nach Bormann weiter: „Die Krim muß von allem Fremden geräumt und deutsch besiedelt werden." Man müsse bedenken, daß die sowjetische Regierung Deutsche und Tataren ausgesiedelt habe. Er führte weiter aus, daß das altösterreichische Galizien Reichsgebiet werden müsse. Hitler erklärte: „Jetzt ist unser Verhältnis zu Rumänien gut, aber man weiß nicht, wie künftig zu jeder Zeit unser Verhältnis sein wird. Auch wenn wir einzelne Gebietsteile jetzt schon aufteilen, immer müssen wir als Schützer des Rechts und der Bevölkerung vorgehen." Demgemäß seien die jetzt notwendigen Formulierungen zu wählen. „Wir sprechen nicht", so fährt der damalige ‚Führer und Reichskanzler' fort, „von einem neuen Reichsgebiet, sondern von einer durch den Krieg notwendigen Aufgabe." Das Baltikum müsse jetzt bis zur Düna in Verwaltung genommen werden.

Reichsleiter Rosenberg betonte: „Nach seiner Auffassung sei in jedem Kommissariat eine andere Behandlung der Bevölkerung notwendig. In der Ukraine müßten wir mit einer kulturellen Betreuung einsetzen, wir hätten dort das Geschichtsbewußtsein der Ukrainer zu wecken und eine Universität in Kiew zu gründen; gewisse Selbständigkeitsbestrebungen müßten gefördert werden." Göring stellt sich demgegenüber auf den Standpunkt, daß zunächst die Ernährung gesichert werden müsse. Alles andere könne doch erst viel später geschehen.

Der Reichsmarschall bat Adolf Hitler um Mitteilung, welche Gebiete anderen Staaten zugesagt seien.

Hitler erwiderte, Antonescu wolle Bessarabien und Odessa nebst einem Streifen, der von Odessa in Richtung West-Nordwest führe. Die neuen von Antonescu gewünschten Grenzen seien wenig außerhalb der alten rumänischen Grenzen gelegen.

Das Baltenland müsse Reichsgebiet werden.

Nördlich der Krim müsse ein erhebliches reichsdeutsches Hinterland entstehen, die Wolgakolonie und das Gebiet um Baku sei als Reichsgebiet vorgesehen. Die Finnen würden Ostkarelien wollen, doch solle wegen der großen Nickelvorkommen die Halbinsel Kola zu Deutschland geschlagen werden. Mit aller Vorsicht müsse die Angliederung Finnlands als Bundesland vorbereitet werden. Das Gebiet um Leningrad werde von den Finnen beansprucht werden. Hitler erklärte, er wolle diese Stadt den Finnen geben, nachdem sie dem Erdboden gleichgemacht worden sei.

Militärisch vertrat Hitler nach Bormann den Standpunkt, daß die Bildung einer militärischen Macht im Osten nie mehr in Frage komme, auch wenn der Krieg lange geführt werden müsse. Alle seine Nachfolger sollten wissen, daß die Sicherheit nur dann gegeben sei, wenn westlich des Urals kein fremdes Militär existiere. Den Schutz dieses Raumes vor allen möglichen Gefahren übernehme Deutschland. Eiserner Grundsatz sei, daß niemand außer den Deutschen Waffen trage. Dieser Gesichtspunkt sei außerordentlich bedeutsam. Selbst wenn es möglich sei, irgendwelche unterworfenen Völker zur Waffenhilfe heranzuziehen, so sei dies falsch. Unbedingt und unweigerlich würde dies eines Tages gegen Deutschland ausschlagen. Jeder, der nur schief schaue, müsse totgeschossen werden.

Feldmarschall Keitel betonte, für Ruhe und Sicherheit seien die Einwohner selbst verantwortlich zu machen. Es sei natürlich nicht möglich, für jeden Schuppen und für jeden Bahnhof eine Wache zu stellen.

Die Einwohner müßten wissen, daß jeder erschossen wird, der nicht funktioniert, und daß sie für jedes Vergehen zur Verantwortung gezogen wurden.

Diese Gedankengänge bildeten die Grundlage der verhängnisvollen Besatzungspolitik auf sowjetischem Gebiet.

Auch zur Partisanenfrage wird Stellung genommen.

In brutaler Weise wird der Sicherungsgedanke des Raumes in den Vordergrund gestellt. ,,Dieser Partisanenkrieg hat auch wieder einen Vorteil; er gibt uns die Möglichkeit auszurotten, was sich gegen uns stellt." In dieselbe Richtung gehen zwei Passagen auf Seite 9 des Dokumentes: ,,Der Führer sagt dem Reichsmarschall und dem Feldmarschall, er habe immer darauf gedrängt, daß die Polizei-Regimenter Panzerwagen bekommen; für den Einsatz der Polizei in den neuen Ostgebieten sei dies höchst notwendig, denn mit einer entsprechenden Anzahl von Panzerwagen könne ein Polizei-

Regiment natürlich eine Vielfaches leisten. Im übrigen, betont der Führer, sei aber die Sicherung derzeit sehr dünn."

Der Reichsmarschall werde aber alle seine Übungsplätze in die neuen Gebiete verlegen, und wenn es notwendig sei, dann könnten selbst Ju 52 bei Aufruhr Bomben werfen. Der Riesenraum müsse so rasch wie möglich befriedet werden...

Selbstüberschätzung
und Fehleinschätzung

Übereinstimmung dürfte darüber gegeben sein, daß ein großes Problem für die deutsche Kriegführung der Riesenraum der Sowjetunion darstellte. Ebenfalls wird richtig sein, daß die Stärke der sowjetischen Untergrund- und Partisanenkriegführung unterschätzt wurde.

Über die Behandlung der russischen Kriegsgefangenen ist schon viel geschrieben worden. Sie war inhuman.

Die Führung der Wehrmacht sah mit Sicherheit ein, daß der Kommissarbefehl juristisch und politisch sehr problematisch sei.

Ich glaube, daß es keinen Einwand gibt, wenn gesagt wird, daß er gegen die klassischen Kriegsregeln verstieß und den Widerstand gegen die deutschen Streitkräfte stärkte.

Der September 1941 brachte einen Höhepunkt in dieser Befehlsgebung. Am 12. Sept. 1941 erklärt das Oberkommando der Wehrmacht (WFSt/ Abt. L (IV/qu) Nr. 02041/41 geh.): ,,Der Kampf gegen den Bolschewismus verlangt ein rücksichtsloses und energisches Durchgreifen, vor allem gegen die Juden, die Hauptträger des Bolschewismus.''

Der Chef des Oberkommandos der Wehrmacht befiehlt am 16. Sept. 1941 (WFSt/Abt. L (IV/qu) – Nr. 002060/41 gKdos.): ,,. . . Seit Beginn des Feldzuges gegen Sowjetrußland sind in dem von Deutschland besetzten Gebiet allenthalben kommunistische Aufstandsbewegungen ausgebrochen. Die Formen des Vorgehens steigern sich von propagandistischen Maßnahmen und Anschlägen gegen einzelne Wehrmachtsangehörige bis zu offenem Aufruhr und verbreitetem Bandenkrieg. Es ist festzustellen, daß es sich hierbei um eine von Moskau einheitlich geleitete Massenbewegung handelt, der auch die geringfügig erscheinenden Einzelfälle in bisher sonst ruhigen Gebieten zur Last zu legen sind . . . Die bisherigen Maßnahmen, um dieser allgemein kommunistischen Aufstandsbewegung zu begegnen, haben sich als unzureichend erwiesen. Der Führer hat nunmehr angeordnet, daß überall mit den schärfsten Mitteln einzugreifen ist, um die Bewegung in kürzester Zeit niederzuschlagen. Nur auf diese Weise, die in der Geschichte der Machtergreifung großer Völker immer mit Erfolg angewandt worden ist, kann die Ruhe wiederhergestellt werden.''

Repressalerschießungen bei einem Verwundeten 1 : 50, bei einem Toten 1 : 100, bei völkerrechtswidrigen Überfällen würden angeordnet.

Unangemessen sind auch die Bestimmungen in der Verordnung gegen die Unterstützung von Saboteuren und entwichenen Kriegsgefangenen vom 10.

Juni 1942, wenn es heißt: ,,Wer einem Bandenmitglied, einem Saboteur, einem gemeingefährlichen Verbrecher oder einem entwichenen Kriegsgefangenen durch Gewährung von Unterkunft oder Kost, durch Verschaffung von Kleidungsstücken oder auf andere Weise Hilfe leistet, wird mit dem Tode bestraft. In minder schweren Fällen kann auf Zuchthausstrafe erkannt werden. Gleiche Strafe trifft den, der die Anzeige bei der nächsten Dienststelle oder dem nächsten Militärkommando unterläßt, wenn er von dem Auftreten eines Bandenmitglieds, eines Saboteurs, eines gemeingefährlichen Verbrechers oder eines entwichenen Kriegsgefangenen Kenntnis hat.''

Deutsche Fehler in der Besatzungspolitik unterstützen Partisanen- und Untergrundkriegführung

Im April 1943 sprach General Haseloff, Chef des Stabes der deutschen Besatzungsmacht in Polen, davon, daß wachsende Not, zunehmende Einengung der Freiheit, psychologisch falsche Behandlung, seelische Bedrückung, falsche Härte bis zu krasser Ungerechtigkeit, völlige Mißachtung – verbunden mit mangelnder Fürsorge – den Polen den letzten Rest von Glauben an einen guten Willen der Deutschen nahmen.

Es war eine Politik, die das polnische Volk auf das Gebiet des Generalgouvernements zusammendrängte, es zu neutralisieren suchte und die Polen dort, wo sie mit deutschen Menschen zusammenlebten oder leben mußten, differenziert behandelte, um alle angeblichen politischen und biologischen Gefahren für das deutsche Volk nach Möglichkeit auszuschließen.

Von 1939 bis 1942 oder besser bis zur Mitte des Jahres 1943 versuchte die deutsche Verwaltung im Generalgouvernement wie eine Kolonialmacht zu regieren. Aus dem Band ,,Schutzbereich des Reichsverteidigungsausschusses für Polen" (Az: 12593/box 124/17c – Militärarchiv in Freiburg –), in dem sich die Teilniederschrift für die Sitzung des Reichsverteidigungsausschusses und die Niederschrift des Reichsverteidigungsausschusses für Polen vom 2. Mrz. 1940 in Warschau befindet, ergibt sich folgender Standpunkt: Die Polen behalten eine Heimstätte im Generalgouvernement. Die Bezeichnung ,,Polenreservation" wird gebraucht. Es wird nicht germanisiert. Den Polen ist jedoch vollends das Rückgrat zu brechen, so daß sie nie wieder den geringsten Widerstand leisten könnten. In eine ähnliche Richtung geht der Vorschlag des Generalgouverneurs für die besetzten polnischen Gebiete zur Änderung der vorläufigen Zoll- und Verwaltungsgrenzen zwischen dem Reich und dem Generalgouvernement.

Propagiert wird, daß Deutschland vor dem Schritt zum Weltreich steht und im zunehmenden Maß Völker, die nicht deutsch sprechen, in seine Machtsphäre genommen werden. Für die Polen gebe es nur die Möglichkeit, sich hundertprozentig zu fügen oder zu revoltieren.

Zuzugestehen ist aber, daß der Generalgouverneur bereits am 4. März 1940 gegen die Verantwortlichen illegaler Juden- und Flüchtlingstransporte, denen viele Menschen zum Opfer fielen, ein Verfahren wegen Mord androhte. 1943 wurde unter dem polnischen Grafen Ronigier ein ,,polnischer Hilfsausschuß" eingesetzt, der den Kriegszustand zwischen Polen und Deutschen abbauen sollte mit der Zielsetzung, den Polen eine eigene Verwaltung zu geben. Auszüge aus dem Diensttagebuch des Generalgouverneurs, die sinngemäß wiedergegeben werden, beweisen dies. Am 23. Juli 1943 heißt es dort: Der Kriegszustand zwischen Deutschen und Polen müsse abgebaut werden. Dies sei furchtbar schwer, denn im Reich herrsche die Meinung vor, daß die Polen die Todfeinde Deutschlands seien. Man berufe sich dort auf die Erfahrung, die die deutsche Volksgruppe im früheren Polen habe machen müssen. Die deutsche Verwaltung des Generalgouvernements habe nun das polnische Volk eingehend studiert und kennengelernt. Sie wolle nun, so erklärte Frank dem Grafen Ronigier, einen neuen Versuch machen. Es sei eine deutsche Pflicht, die Kultur der Polen zu schützen. Bekanntlich gebe es militante Menschen. Als solcher habe sich im Distrikt Lublin der SS- und Polizeiführer Globocnik erwiesen. Er sei abberufen worden. Im Laufe der Jahre müsse man zu einem vernünftigen gegenseitigen Verhältnis gelangen. Schritt um Schritt werde man den Polen entgegenkommen.

Aus der Eintragung vom 24. Juli 1943 ergibt sich, daß Dr. Frank versuchte, bei Himmler ein grundsätzliches Verbot weiterer Polenaussiedlungen zu erreichen. Eintragung vom 2. Aug. 1943: Es sei klar, daß die reinen Terrormethoden sowie die Kollektivjustiz falsch sei. Eintragung vom 2. Aug. 1943: Vor allem die Vorstellung sei zu bekämpfen, daß das Generalgouvernement Kolonie ist. Eintragung vom 5. Aug. 1943: Sie stellt fest, daß die Aus- und Umsiedlung im allgemeinen beendet sei. – Eintragung vom 26. Okt. 1943: Keine Wiederherstellung des polnischen Staates. Die Polen hätten allerdings die Chance, unter deutscher Führung zu ihrem eigenen Wohl ihre wohlbehütete Lebens- und Kulturarbeit in den Dienst Europas zu stellen. –

Die Eintragung vom 17. Febr. 1944 enthält die Planung einer antisowjetischen Liga. Dr. Frank führt aus: ,,Ihre Gründung bedeutet . . . die Heranziehung des polnischen Volkstums zu einer politischen Willensbildung und Willensänderung.'' Bis jetzt seien die Polen politisch ohnmächtig. Nach der Bildung der antisowjetischen Liga seien sie von der deutschen Führung jedoch als Angehörige des neuen Europa anerkannt.

Die Eintragung vom 5. Apr. 1944 faßt die Besprechung mit dem Fürsterzbischof Sapia-Lemberg zusammen. Dr. Frank verweist hier als Beispiel des Aufbaues auf die bis 1918 bestehende österreichisch-ungarische Donaumonarchie. Hitler sei mit dieser Idee einverstanden. Weiter erklärt der Generalgouverneur, daß die Vorbereitungen für höhere Schulen im Gange seien. Man habe die Hochschulkurse in Lemberg bereits für Polen geöffnet. Im September 1944 werde die Mittelschulbildung möglich sein.

Eintragung vom 5. Aug. 1944: Botschaftsrat Schumburg übermittelt dem Generalgouverneur eine vertrauliche Nachricht, nach welcher Möglichkeiten bestünden, zwischen der deutschen Regierung und der polnischen Exil-regierung Verbindungen über einen vertraulichen Verbindungsmann in Budapest aufzunehmen. Dr. Frank bittet festzustellen, welche Stellungnahme Ribbentrop einnehme, und erklärt sich bereit, mit Ribbentrop zu sprechen. Die Eintragung enthält die Erklärung Dr. Franks, daß die Bereinigung des deutsch-polnischen Verhältnisses überfällig sei. Er lehnt die Methode schärfster Gewalt gegenüber dem Polentum ab. Eintragung vom 4. Sept. 1944: Der Generalgouverneur ist gewillt, wie sich die Lage auch entwickle, an dem von ihm eingeschlagenen Kurs festzuhalten. Es werde davon abhängen, wie sich die Dinge entwickelten. Im positiven Sinne werde er im gegenwärtigen Augenblick jeden Schritt begrüßen, der geeignet sei, mit den Polen zu einer grundsätzlichen Klärung der Gesamtsituation zu kommen.

Die Zerstörung Warschaus liege in deutscher Hand, und niemand könne sie verhindern. Er sei entschlossen, diesen Kaufpreis hinzunehmen. Die Lage Deutschlands erfordere eine gewisse Bereitwilligkeit zu Konzessionen. Er würde einverstanden sein, die Wojds zu einer wirklichen Verwaltungsinstanz zu erheben, denen von den Kreishauptmännern gewisse Funktionen übertragen werden können. Dr. Frank fordert Vermenschlichung und eine gerechte Behandlung des Polentums.

Bemerkenswert ist die Haltung des Staatssekretärs Dr. Stuckart. Am 18. Okt. 1944 schreibt er: ,,So fruchtbar die Verwirklichung des an sich wohl schon in früherer Zeit erwogenen Gedankens auch wäre, die einheimische Bevölkerung durch Beschaffung von Beratungsorganen zu einer fruchtbaren Mitarbeit bei der Verwaltung des Landes heranzuziehen, so erscheint es mir doch zweifelhaft, ob der gegenwärtige Zeitpunkt geeignet ist, im Generalgouvernement eine Verordnung der beabsichtigten Art hinzunehmen." Gedacht war an die Bildung eines Beratungsorganes der einheimischen Bevölkerung zur Erhaltung des polnischen Volkstums und zur Sicherung ihrer Lebensgrundlagen auf Landesebene.

Dr. Stuckart schreibt weiter: ,,Gegebenenfalls lasse die verschiedene Lage in Teilen des Generalgouvernements eine differenzierte Behandlung des Problems als angezeigt erscheinen." Am 18. auf 19. Mai 1944 hatte auch eine Besprechung Dr. Franks mit Heinrich Himmler stattgefunden. Die darüber vorhandene Eintragung sagt, daß allein die Methoden, wie sie der Generalgouverneur herausgearbeitet habe, im gegenwärtigen Augenblick die richtigen seien, wenn es auch notwendig erscheint, den Widerstandsbewegunngen und Aufstandsversuchen mit schärfster sofortiger Gewaltkonzentration zu begegnen.

Der Wandel der Besatzungspolitik – dies muß festgehalten werden – beginnt vor der Stalingrad-Katastrophe, denn eine Eintragung vom 1. Juli 1942 besagt, daß das Recht garantiert werden müsse, auch im Rahmen der europäischen Neuordnung die kleinen Völker gegenüber den großen zu schützen. Zusammengefaßt darf festgestellt werden, daß sich 1942/1943 die Einstellung in der Frage zum Polentum änderte. Die Periode der Erschießung von Angehörigen der polnischen Intelligenz war längst vorbei. Die Erschießungen gebildeter Polen, wie sie in Lemberg und in Krakau stattgefunden hatten, ereigneten sich nicht wieder. Aber die Wandlung der Polenpolitik kam zu spät.

Sowjetunion, Es war nicht glücklich, kein Kriegsziel in der Rußlandpolitik herausgestellt zu haben. Von einer einheitlichen Koordinierung war nicht zu sprechen.

Konzeptionell standen sich gegenüber: Adolf Hitler, in seinen Anschauungen beeinflußt durch die Verhältnisse in der Habsburger Donaumonarchie, Martin Bormann mit seinen Dienststellen, Alfred Rosenberg, Reichsminister für die besetzten Ostgebiete, und sein mächtiger Gegenspieler Erich Koch, Gauleiter von Ostpreußen und Reichskommissar für die Ukraine, Heinrich Himmler mit seinem Apparat und Hermann Göring mit seiner Machtfülle.

In meinen Gesprächen mit Otto Ohlendorf und Walter Schellenberg – in der Zeit der Nürnberger Prozesse und meines Auftretens vor dem Clemency Board – weiß ich, daß Bormann und Heinrich Müller von den Leitern der Abteilung III und des RSHA des Zusammenspiels mit Moskau verdächtigt wurden. Erich Koch, der ehemalige kleine Eisenbahnbeamte aus Nordrhein-Westfalen, sagt von sich selbst, daß er Angehöriger der Kommunistischen Partei geworden wäre, wenn er nicht zur NSDAP gestoßen wäre. Koch, der noch in polnischer Haft auf ostpreußischem Gebiet lebt, war Nationalbolschewist. Rosenberg wird heute kritisiert, daß er an einen Cordon sanitaire im Osten dachte – an Staaten, die von Deutschland abhängig waren.

Die Gegenfrage sei erlaubt: Gibt es nicht Parallelen in der Politik Washingtons und Moskaus? Die Furcht vor dem ,,russischen Koloß" besteht auch heute. Immerhin darf gesagt werden, daß der hingerichtete deutsche Reichsminister für die besetzten Ostgebiete im Gegensatz zu Himmler und Bormann Verständnis für die Nationalitätenfrage hatte.

In seiner Arbeit ,,Der Zukunftsweg einer deutschen Außenpolitik" (München, Eher-Verlag, 1927) schreibt er: ,,An eine Wiedererstehung eines nationalen Großrußland im alten Sinn ist nicht zu denken." Rosenberg sah Unterschiede unter den Völkern des Ostens. Er ging von einer Staatsbildung der Ukraine, Weißrußlands, der baltischen Staaten, des Kaukasus und Zentralasiens aus.

Im Gegensatz zu einem antikommunistischen verkleinerten Einheitsstaat mit Selbstverwaltung stellte er in seiner Denkschrift Nr. 1 vom 2. April

1941 (ND 1017–Ps XXVI) heraus: Die politische Aufgabe in diesem Gebiet (= Ukraine) ist die Förderung des nationalen Eigenlebens bis zur eventuellen Errichtung einer Eigenstaatlichkeit mit dem Ziel, allein oder in Verbindung mit dem Don-Gebiet und dem Kaukasus als Schwarzmeerbund Moskau stets in Schach zu halten und den großdeutschen Lebensraum von Osten her zu sichern.

Nach Rosenberg müsse gesprochen werden ,,vom ukrainischen Volk und seiner Freiheit", von der ,,Befreiung der Völker des Kaukasus" und der ,,Errettung der estnischen, lettischen und litauischen Nationen."

Zweifellos vertrat Rosenberg im Einklang mit Paul Rohrbach den Standpunkt, daß ein Krieg mit dem Ziel, ein ungeteiltes Rußland zu errichten, auszuscheiden habe. Die Freiheitsbestrebungen der Völker im russischen Raum müßten in ganz bestimmte staatliche Formen gebracht werden. Der Reichsminister dachte daran, aus dem Territorium der Sowjetunion Staatsgebilde organisch herauszuschneiden und gegen Moskau aufzubauen. Klar – aber zu schwach – vertrat er den Standpunkt, daß das eroberte Territorium nicht als Ausbeutungsobjekt behandelt werden dürfe.

Rosenberg ist vollständig zuzustimmen, wenn er in den ,,Allgemeinen Richtlinien für die politische und wirtschaftliche Verwaltung der besetzten Ostgebiete " vom 25. Juni 1941 ausführt: ,,Das Schlimmste, was vom politischen Standpunkt aus eintreten könnte, wäre, daß das Volk angesichts unserer wirtschaftlichen Ausbeutungsmaßnahmen zu dem Ergebnis kommt, daß das jetzige (= deutsche Regime) ihm größere Not bereitet als der Bolschewismus."

Hitler selbst vertrat noch in den Führerbesprechungen vom 9. und 11. August 1943 den Standpunkt, daß ,,kleine souveräne Staaten keine Daseinsberechtigung" mehr hätten. Dem deutschen Staatsoberhaupt schien es allein erforderlich zu sein, Verwaltungsbestimmungen zu erlassen. Ein einheitlicher, grundsätzlicher Entwurf zur politischen Lenkung im sowjetrussischen Raum fehlte. Oberflächlich und nichtssagend waren die Pläne, die Völker Rußlands zu gewinnen. Gesichtspunkte einer extremen militärischen Notwendigkeit, zweifellos durch den Riesenraum bedingt, aus denen völkerrechtswidrige Handlungen erwuchsen, beherrschten das Denken der deutschen Führung.

Himmler, der 1939 das Amt des ,,Reichskommissars für die Festigung des deutschen Volkstums" erhielt, war nicht allein für die Umsiedlung der Volksdeutschen, sondern auch für die politische Sicherung der Ostgebiete zuständig, wobei auch betont werden muß, daß er und seine Dienststellen, Einsatzgruppen und Einsatzkommandos auf das engste mit der Wehrmacht zusammenarbeiteten. Himmler betrachtete die Bevölkerung im Osten, von Ausnahmen abgesehen, als ,,führerloses Arbeitsvolk".

Auf einer Rede in Bad Schachen im Oktober 1943 betonte er: ,,Ich weiß auch, daß es bei den Russen sehr fähige Ingenieure gibt, daß es sehr fähige Fachleute gibt . . . ich persönlich glaube, daß slawische Völker auf die Dauer eine Weiterentwicklung der Kultur nicht zustande bringen . . .'' Er hob hervor, daß man bei der Behandlung dieser Menschen nicht von anständigen deutschen Gesichtspunkten ausgehen kann. Andere Maßstäbe seien anzulegen. ,,Sie mögen es grausam nennen, aber die Natur ist grausam.'' Im Umgang mit dieser ,,osteuropäisch-mittelasiatischen Menschenhorde'' – so ist unter dem 14. Oktober 1943 an anderer Stelle zu lesen (ND 070–L, XXXVII) – ,,müssen wir eine Absage erteilen der falschen Kameradschaft, der falsch verstandenen Barmherzigkeit, der falschen Weichheit und einer falschen Entschuldigung vor uns selbst. Wir müssen in diesen Dingen den Mut zu brutaler Wahrheit und Offenheit finden. Dann und nur dann wird das Dritte Reich eine Aussicht haben, den Krieg zu gewinnen.''

Martin Bormann, der nach dem Flug von Rudolf Hess nach England zum mächtigsten Mann des Großdeutschen Reiches nach Hitler wurde, galt als ,,Mephisto'' im deutschen politischen Leben. Seine Einstellung zeigt sich in seinen Bemerkungen im Jahr 1942 nach einer Fahrt in der Umgebung von Winniza (vgl. Dallin, Deutsche Herrschaft in Rußland, S. 469): ,,Dieser Kinderreichtum kann uns eines Tages zu schaffen machen . . . Es liegt nicht im deutschen Interesse, daß sie sich stärker als bisher vermehren. Der volkliche Druck dieser Russen oder sogenannten Ukrainer wird den Deutschen in gar nicht allzu ferner Zeit wieder gefährlich werden . . .''

Es ist verständlich, daß Bormann kurz darauf an NSDAP-Stellen schrieb: ,,Auf Wunsch des Führers gebe ich Ihnen Anweisung, in den besetzten Ostgebieten die folgenden Grundsätze zu beachten. Die Gefahr, daß sich die nichtdeutsche Bevölkerung in den besetzten Ostgebieten stärker als bisher vermehrt, ist sehr groß, denn die ganzen Lebensumstände werden für die nichtdeutsche Bevölkerung selbstverständlich viel besser und gesicherter. Gerade deshalb müssen wir die notwendigen Vorkehrungsmaßnahmen gegen die Vermehrung der nichtdeutschen Bevölkerung treffen. Deshalb soll auch keinesfalls eine deutsche Gesundheitsfürsorge für die nichtdeutsche Bevölkerung in den besetzten Ostgebieten einsetzen. Ein Impfen z. B. der nichtdeutschen Bevölkerung und ähnliche vorbeugende Gesundheitsmaßnahmen sollen keinesfalls in Frage kommen . . .'' (Bormann an Rosenberg, 23. Juli 1942, ND NO – 1878 – auch 1648 PS).

Zu bemerken ist, daß Erich Koch zu gleicher Zeit zum Ausdruck brachte: ,,Denn eines Tages wollten wir ja doch dieses gesamte Land deutsch besiedelt haben.'' Diese Bemerkung steht im Gegensatz zu Rosenbergs Rede vom 18. Dez. 1941 in Berlin.

Erich Koch, der auch nach seiner Ernennung zum Reichskommissar der

Ukraine Gauleiter von Ostpreußen blieb und somit über eine unerhörte Machtfülle verfügte, scheint als ,,Herrscher in der Ukraine" den Wunsch gehabt zu haben, seine ehemalige Liebe zur Sowjetunion vergessen zu lassen. Er spielte sich als Repräsentant des Herrenvolk-Gedankens auf und war der Auffassung, die Ostvölker hätten die Pflicht, den Deutschen zu dienen. Deutschland habe ein Recht, die eroberten Gebiete auszubeuten. Gleich seinem Herrn und Meister, dem Reichsleiter Bormann, vertrat er den Standpunkt, daß die einheimische Intelligenz und alle Gruppen, die der deutschen Besatzungsmacht nach seiner Auffassung hätten gefährlich werden können – gleichgültig, ob Russen, Ukrainer oder Juden –, zu vernichten seien. Charakteristisch für Koch sind die Sätze: ,,Die Bevölkerung muß arbeiten, arbeiten und nochmals arbeiten." ,,Daß der geringste deutsche Arbeiter rassisch und biologisch tausendmal wertvoller ist als die hiesige Bevölkerung."

Am 29. Oktober 1943 (ND 290 PS XXV) schrieb Koch an das Ostministerium: ,,Im Falle von Widerstand sind die Gehöfte von Arbeitsverweigerern niederzubrennen, Verwandte als Geiseln festzunehmen und in Zwangsarbeitslager zu bringen." Als Rosenberg Anfang Juni 1943 die Bekanntmachung über die Einführung bäuerlichen Grundeigentums verfügte, sabotierte Erich Koch diese. Bis September 1943 ging das Tauziehen. Die Durchführung des Erlasses fand nicht statt.

Wirtschaftsstab Ost, Ostministerium und Himmler kamen überein, die Angelegenheit zu vertagen. Resigniert mußte der Wirtschaftsstab feststellen: ,,Der letzte und äußerste Trumpf der Agrarpolitik, das Geschenk des Grundeigentums an landhungrige Bauern, war nutzlos ausgespielt, ja das spätere Totschweigen der zunächst im Zusammenhang mit einer Ministerreise groß herausgebrachten Deklaration mußte geradezu den Eindruck der Unehrlichkeit machen."

Rosenberg war der dynamischen Persönlichkeit von Koch nicht gewachsen. Rosenbergs Ukrainekonzept zerfiel. Im Krieg sollte die Ukraine das Reich mit Nahrungsmitteln und Rohstoffen versorgen. Nach Kriegsende sollte ,,die Errichtung eines freien ukrainischen Staates im engsten Bündnis mit dem Großdeutschen Reich" den deutschen Einfluß im Osten sichern. Beeinflußt von Dr. Leibbrandts ukrainischen Beratern schrieb Rosenberg nieder: ,,müssen möglichst bald alle Fragen in Angriff genommen werden, die eine psychologische Wirkung auszustrahlen imstande sind, d. h. es müssen ukrainische Schriftsteller, Gelehrte und Politiker für die Belebung des ukrainischen Geschichtsbewußtseins eingesetzt werden, um zu überwinden, was der bolschewistisch-jüdische Druck in diesen Jahren an ukrainischem Volkstum vernichtet hat." Er dachte auch an die Errichtung einer ukrainischen Universität.

Wie Generaloberst Franz Halder berichtet, hat der Stab Oldenburg Richtlinien ausgearbeitet, die am 2. Mai 1941 genehmigt wurden. In ihnen wird hervorgehoben, daß der Krieg nur weiterzuführen sei, wenn die gesamte Wehrmacht im dritten Kriegsjahr aus Rußland ernährt werde. Es wird nicht in Frage gestellt, daß . . .zig Millionen Menschen verhungern, wenn das Notwendige aus dem Land herausgeholt wird. Amtschef des Stabes Oldenburg war General Thomas, übrigens ein entschiedener Gegner Hitlers. Aus diesem Stab wurde der Wirtschaftsstab Ost.

Verhängisvoller als diese Richtlinien wirkte sich die Behandlung der sowjetischen Kriegsgefangenen aus. Es sei an das Wort gedacht: ,,Wer unter den Kriegsgefangenen nicht arbeiten will, muß verhungern." In den Augen der russischen Zivilbevölkerung war das Schicksal der russischen Kriegsgefangenen von größerer Bedeutung als das der Juden. Bis Mitte Dezember 1941 betrug die Zahl der russischen Kriegsgefangenen 3 800 000. Warnungen über die getroffenen deutschen Maßnahmen gab es eine Anzahl. Dr. Joseph Goebbels selbst stellte im September 1941 fest: ,,Wir haben gewaltige militärische Erfolge errungen, aber wir haben noch immer keinen konstruktiven Plan für Rußland. Wo wir als Befreier erscheinen sollten, kommen wir als Eroberer." Walter von Conradi, tätig im deutschen Rundfunk, schrieb in einer Aufzeichnung vom 17. Nov. 1941: ,,Auf die Dauer ist es unmöglich, die Bevölkerung der besetzten Ostgebiete im dunkeln über die Zielrichtung der neuen politischen Ordnung zu lassen." Er stellte sich ein Rußland in einem Vereinigten Europa vor. Der Bevölkerung sollte gesagt werden, daß die Deutschen weder Gebiet beanspruchen noch die Wiedereinsetzung der Gutsbesitzer planen würden.

Ich will an Professor Dr. Oberländer, den Dr. Adenauer als Bundesminister für Vertriebenenfragen in sein zweites Kabinett berief, und an Karl Georg Pfleiderer, den späteren Botschafter der Bundesrepublik in Belgrad, erinnern. Von Oberländer stammen die Sätze: ,,Die Stimmung der Bevölkerung hat sich meist schon wenige Wochen nach dem Einrücken der deutschen Truppen wesentlich verschlechtert. Woran liegt das? Wir zeigen . . . eine innere Abneigung, ja einen Haß gegen dieses Land und eine Überheblichkeit gegen dieses Volk, die jede positive Zusammenarbeit von selbst ausschließen . . . Die Bevölkerung auf dem Lande ist über ihre Zukunft völlig im ungewissen . . . Die Requisition des letzten Huhnes ist psychologisch genauso unklug wie das Abschlachten tragender Säue und der letzten Kälber . . . Jede Unterdrückungspolitik muß in diesem Land mit einem ungeheueren Beamtenapparat . . . und mit geringsten wirtschaftlichen Leistungen enden . . ."

In einer Denkschrift vom Herbst 1942 betonte Dr. Oberländer, daß viele deutsche Bemühungen nicht an dem, was gefordert werde, sondern an dem, wie es gefordert werde, scheitern würden. Im Juni 1943 stellte er fest, ein neues Europa sei ohne slawische Völker nicht denkbar, die Agrarreform zu beschleunigen, eine tolerante Kulturpolitik sei am Platze und eine politische Erklärung für die Zukunft erforderlich. Erfolge dies nicht, so würden die Losungen „Zweiter vaterländischer Krieg", „Sowjetnationalstaat", „Jeder Sowjetbürger ein Partisane", „Slawen, vereinigt Euch" ihre bittere Wirkung zeigen.

Auch der spätere Botschafter der Bundesrepublik, von Herwarth, damals einer der Verbindungsoffiziere des AA zur Wehrmacht, war sich über die falsche Politik im Ostraum im klaren. Er prägte den Satz: „Russen sind nur durch Russen zu besiegen."

Es muß festgestellt werden, daß ab Sommer 1942 der Widerstand der Wehrmacht gegen eine Ostpolitik wuchs, deren maßgebende Träger wir herausgestellt haben. Am 18. Dezember 1942 fand eine Konferenz zwischen hohen Wehrmachtsoffizieren und Beamten des Ostministeriums im früheren Gebäude der Sowjetbotschaft statt, auf der Rosenberg betonte, es sei an keine größere deutsche Siedlung im eroberten Raum gedacht.

Als Vertreter der Abteilung Kriegsverwaltung des OKH erklärte Oberst Schmidt von Altenstadt, der vor Beginn des „Barbarossafeldzuges" in der Panzerschule Wustrow den Ic's der Armeen und Armeekorps die Sicherungs- und Abwehraufgaben der Sondereinheiten Heinrich Himmlers aufgezeigt hatte: „Der augenblickliche Tiefstand in der Haltung der Bevölkerung ist weiterhin nicht tragbar. Ein Umbruch der deutschen Politik im russischen Raum ist erforderlich. Der Ernst der Lage und die notwendige Verstärkung der Truppen verlangen eindeutig die positive Mitarbeit der Bevölkerung."

Im Protokoll vom 18. Dezember 1942 heißt es weiter: „Es gilt nun, vor allen anderen Aufgaben die Bevölkerung zur Beteiligung am Kampf gegen die Sowjets zu gewinnen. Hierfür müssen politische Voraussetzungen geschaffen werden, die der Bevölkerung den Kampf sinnvoll machen. An ihrer Bereitschaft, gegen die Sowjets im Bandenkrieg, an der Front oder hinter der Front zu kämpfen, besteht kein Zweifel, wenn es gelingt, eine völlige Abkehr von den bisherigen Methoden ihnen sichtbar vor Augen zu führen ... Die Parole für diesen Raum kann angesichts der Bedeutung des Augenblicks nur lauten: Aufnahme der Bevölkerung als Verbündete im Kampf gegen die Sowjets unter verständnisvoller Zulassung eines Eigenlebens mit den erforderlichen politischen und wirtschaftlichen Konsequenzen."

General Reinhard Gehlen, im Zweiten Weltkrieg Chef der Abteilung Fremde Heere Ost, drückte sich mitten in der Stalingrad-Krise nüchtern aus: „Dem Anwachsen der Partisanenbewegung kann nur begegnet werden mit einer radikalen Änderung der deutschen Taktik, wozu u. a. eine programmatische Erklärung der deutschen Führung mit der Zusicherung gehört, daß Rußland nicht einen Kolonialstatus, sondern Selbstregierung erhalten werde. Es ist naiv anzunehmen, den russischen Nationalismus dadurch auszumerzen, daß man ihn totschweigt. (Die Russen) wollen nicht als Landsknechte dastehen, die ihr Vaterland für ein Stück Brot verraten . . . Der bessere Russe hat mehr Selbstachtung, als man ihm zuschreibt . . . 25. Nov. 1942, H 3/191, CRS.

Mit der Lage im sowjetischen Raum befaßten sich auch nichtdeutsche Persönlichkeiten. Der italienische General Giovanni Messe, dessen faschistisches Regime gegen fremdes Volkstum eingestellt war und Expansionspolitik trieb, sieht eine ,,platonische" Einsicht maßgebender Stellen, beklagt aber das Fehlen von Mut und Initiative (vgl. Giovanni Messe, ,,Der Krieg im Osten", Zürich, Thomas-Verlag, 1948). In einer Denkschrift, die er im Osten verfaßte, schreibt er: ,,Deutschland strebt nicht danach, das bolschewistische Regime durch irgendein anderes zu ersetzen, sondern will sich ganz Osteuropa als wirtschaftliche Einflußzone unmittelbar sichern. Die Behandlung der Bevölkerung und der Gefangenen sowie die Ausbeutung der örtlichen Bodenschätze verraten oft Mangel an Voraussicht, Widersprüche in den Richtlinien, Zusammenhanglosigkeit und Unstabilität bei den höheren militärischen, politischen und wirtschaftlichen Organen, die mit der Verwaltung der besetzten Gebiete beauftragt sind. Deutschland hat es nicht verstanden, bei der Bevölkerung der besetzten Gebiete Sympathie und die Bereitschaft zur Zusammenarbeit zu erwecken . . ."
Zweifellos waren die Fragen im Ostraum kompliziert. In der ukrainischen nationalen Bewegung standen sich die Melnik- und Bandera-Gruppe gegenüber. Stefan Bandera war nach dem deutsch-polnischen Krieg aus der polnischen Haft entlassen worden, in der er im Zusammenhang mit der Ermordung des polnischen Innenministers Bronislaw Pieracki seit 1934 einsaß. Er war der Verfechter einer vergrößerten selbständigen Ukraine. Bandera wurde, da er seine politischen Ziele nicht aufgab, in das Konzentrationslager Auschwitz eingewiesen. 1959 wurde er in der Katzmeierstraße in München von dem sowjetischen Agenten Stachynsky ermordet, der von dem Bundesgerichtshof – 3. Strafsenat – in Karlsruhe zu sieben Jahren Freiheitsentzug verurteilt wurde.

Die Bandera-Bewegung organisierte gegen die deutsche Besatzungsmacht gerichtete Untergrundarbeit. Die Melnikgruppe erklärte sich zehn Tage vor Ausbruch des deutsch-sowjetischen Krieges als einzige legitime Regierung der Ukraine.

Kurze Zeit nach Ausbruch des Krieges zwischen Deutschland und Rußland brach in Lemberg ein Aufstand aus, der vor allem von den ukrainischen Nationalisten angestiftet wurde. Die Rote Armee schlug ihn nieder. 4000 Ukrainer fanden durch den NKWD den Tod.

Ein 80 m tiefer Salzbergwerkschacht bei Dobromil wurde mit Leichen überfüllt gefunden. Am 30. Juni 1941 proklamierte OUNB (Bandera-Gruppe) einen selbständigen ukrainischen Staat. Seit dem 2. Juli 1941 begannen die Verhaftungen unter den Bandera-Anhängern. Das Ukrainische Nationalkomitee unter Stetsko wurde aufgelöst, Bandera nach Berlin gebracht. Galizien wurde am 1. Aug. 1941 ein Teil des sogenannten Generalgouvernements. Transistrien wurde Rumänien übergeben. Beide Maßnahmen führten zu einem gegnerischen Verhältnis der Bevölkerung zu Deutschland. Die Melnikgruppe wurde kurze Zeit toleriert.

Am 17. Febr. 41 wurde Melniks ,,National-Rada" aufgelöst. Aus Freunden wurden Gegner.

Der Lagebericht der Einsatzgruppe Nr. 8 vom 1.–31. Dez. 41 meldet, daß die Bandera-Gruppe auch auf der Krim tätig sei. U. a. war die Einsetzung von Bürgermeistern und die Aufstellung von Miliztruppen geplant. Im März 1942 wurden in Žitomir führende Persönlichkeiten der Bandera-Bewegung verhaftet, Roman Harček starb durch Erschießung. Im Mai bildete sich das ukrainische Freikorps ,,Poliska Sitsch" und die Freikorps-Gruppe ,,Freie Kosaken". Ihr Ziel war die Bildung eines Staates Ukraine.

Als Zentrale wurde der Raum zwischen Pinsk und Sarm angesehen. Am 2. Febr. 1942 meldete die Ereignismeldung UdSSR Nr. 164: Früher festgestellte Bindungen zwischen NKWD und OUN erwiesen sich als eng und kompliziert. Eine in Czernowitz erscheinende Untergrundzeitung ,,Metschen" (,,Durch das Schwert") forderte die Ukrainer auf, sich gegen die Deutschen zu erheben. Am 17. Juli 1942 berichtete der Chef der Sicherheitspolizei und der SD von einem Aufruf: ,,Den Deutschen soll man, wo man kann, einen Dolch in den Rücken stoßen."

In Litauen wurde eine selbständige litauische Regierung unter Kasimir Seipra, dem früheren litauischen Gesandten in Berlin, verhindert. Die frühere Regierungspartei Smetanas wurde favorisiert. Der frühere Ministerpräsident Voldemaras wurde als Stütze der Besatzungsmacht angesehen. Die Stadt Wilna, aus der Pilsudski stammte, entwickelte sich zu einem politischen Problem. Die polnischen Geheimbünde Polska Organizacja Wojskowa und Zwiazek Wolnych Polakow bildeten eine starke politische Gruppe in Litauen.

In einem litauischen Flugblatt aus Kowno heißt es: ,,Aufruf an die Einwohner. Die Deutschen kämpfen für die Freiheit der Nationen, sie sterben für die Rechte des neuen Europa. Wir Litauer haben schon voll empfunden, was die versprochene Freiheit bedeutet. Der deutsche Kreuzritter hat das litauische Volk betrogen. Der Litauer ist heute rechtlos und Sklave. Der

Litauer hat schon begriffen. Wache auch Du, Partisan, auf und geh mit der ganzen litauischen Nation zusammen! Der Deutsche begann durch Deine Hand die jüdischen Volksangehörigen zu morden. Sie haben das jüdische Gut geraubt. Sei gewiß, Partisan, Du wirst denselben Weg gehen. Du bist das Werkzeug der deutschen Kreuzritter, um unschuldige litauische Einwohner zu morden. Einmal müssen wir alle sagen: Es ist genug, Ströme unschuldigen Menschenblutes zu vergießen. Den Kreuzrittern müssen wir alle den Kampf ansagen. Wir wissen, daß die Deutschen jedem anderen Volksangehörigen dasselbe wünschen wie den Juden. Höre auf zu morden, oder Du wirst von der Hand Deiner Brüder fallen. Wir wollen nicht, daß durch Deine Hände das litauische Volk ausgerottet wird.

Wisse, daß unser Auge Dich überall beobachtet, sogar unter Deinen Freunden. Tod den Kreuzrittern!"

In Lettland stützte sich die deutsche Verwaltung auf die ursprünglich antideutsch, aber antisemitisch eingestellte Partei Perkon Krust (,,Donnerkeil"). Die politischen Kräfte des früheren Ministerpräsidenten Ulmanis wurden beiseite geschoben, der Verwaltungsapparat aus der vorsowjetischen Zeit nicht herangezogen. Dadurch sank die deutschfreundliche Stimmung außerordentlich. Im Lagebericht Nr. 10 für die Zeit vom 1.–28. Febr. 1942, herausgegeben am 11. März 1942, heißt es: . . . ,,hinausschieben klarer Entscheidungen über die künftige staatsrechtliche Stellung trug zur Versteifung des nationalen Widerstandes bei." Die Auszahlung von Löhnen, die unter denen der sowjetischen Herrschaftszeit lagen, trugen zum Aufkommen einer deutschfeindlichen Stimmung bei. Durch Aufstellung eines unglücklichen Arbeitsbeschaffungsprogramms wurde der Erfolg der im Frühjahr 1942 eingeleiteten Lettisierung der Kleinindustrie und der Handwerksunternehmen vergeben.

Im Gegensatz zu Lettland und Litauen war das Verhältnis in Estland zwischen Besatzungsmacht und Bevölkerung entspannt. Die Bereitschaft zur Aufstellung einheimischer Selbstschutzorganisationen war vorhanden. Mit Hilfe der Esten konnten kommunistische Widerstandsorganisationen aufgedeckt werden.

Der Wille zur Wiederherstellung der politischen Selbständigkeit bestand ohne Zweifel. Es zeigte sich jedoch auch das Bestreben, eine finnisch-estnische Union zu bilden.

Sie wurde von dem Dorpater Universitätsprofessor Dr. Makk propagiert, der die ,,Gesellschaft finnischer Stammesverwandter" bildete.

Einen Höhepunkt in der Auseinandersetzung stellt ein Vortrag dar, den Professor Soschalslasky unter dem Motto ,,Wahrheit ist auf die Dauer die beste Politik" über das Verhalten der deutschen Verwaltungsstellen im besetzten sowjetischen Territorium und zur sog. russischen Befreiungsbewegung hielt. Im Frühjahr 1943 sprach Soschalslasky vor deutschen Propagandaangehörigen in Weißrußland. Über die Rede wurde der Oberbefehlshaber der Heeresgruppe Mitte unterrichtet. Die schriftliche Ausfertigung trägt auf der ersten Seite rechts oben die Paraphe Gehlens. Soschalslasky führte u. a. aus: In der großen Masse der loyal gebliebenen Bevölkerung ist das einstige feste Vertrauen auf den deutschen Sieg verschwunden. Noch mehr ist sogar das Prestige der kulturellen Überlegenheit Deuschlands durch den Mangel an psychologischem Verständnis und die Fehler der deutschen Politik und Propaganda unterwühlt. Das ungeheuere geistige Kapital, das in Gestalt der Gefühle und Meinungen der Russen in der Zeitspanne von 1914 bis 1941 gesammelt worden war, über das Deutschland verfügte, ist unvorsichtigerweise verschwendet. An seine Stelle tritt immer mehr der Skeptizismus und sogar die Ironie, die durch ihre Verschmähung der geistigen Faktoren, die ihnen in die Hände fielen, durch ihr übersteigertes Selbstvertrauen, ihren Hochmut und die Überschätzung eigener Kräfte hervorgerufen worden sind. All das wird durch jene oft ungeschickten Maßnahmen, durch die sie ihre Fehler zu verbessern suchen, nur gesteigert.

Praktische Folgen daraus sind: Anwachsen des Partisanentums, Wiederhinwendung der russischen Jugend zum Bolschewismus, nachdem sie zuerst unter dem Eindruck der deutschen Erfolge abwartend geworden war, und immer wachsende Niedergeschlagenheit der loyalen und deutschfreundlichen Teile der Bevölkerung.

Alles das sind unleugbare Tatsachen. Und doch besitzt Deutschland auch jetzt noch eine große Gelegenheit, die zu unterschätzen ein letzter, diesmal verhängnisvoller Fehler wäre. Deutschland und die überwiegende Mehrzahl der loyal bleibenden Russen verbindet noch immer ein gemeinsamer Feind. Dieser Feind ist der Bolschewismus. Der größte Teil der Bevölkerung, besonders die von dem Kolchosentum befreite Bauernschaft will nicht die Rückkehr der Bolschewisten, denn sie bringt ihr zum mindesten den wirtschaftlichen, in vielen Fällen aber auch den physischen Untergang.

Professor Soschalslosky hebt endlich hervor: ,,Nein, man braucht nicht das, man braucht etwas anderes. Von Deutschland erwarten die Russen ein fair play, eine gerade, aufrichtige und offene Handlungsweise. Es ist nötig, nicht nur die Politik dem russischen Volke gegenüber von Grund auf zu ändern, sondern es einfach zum Kampfe gegen den Bolschewismus aufzurufen und die Lösung seines Schicksals in seine eigenen Hände zu legen. Die Formen dieses Überganges zu einer neuen Politik sind Frage und Taktik. Durch ein Übereinkommen mit Männern, die Deutschlands Vertrauen genießen und von Deutschland für die Ausführung dieses Unternehmens berufen werden müssen, kann diese Frage gelöst werden. Meinerseits schlage ich in folgendem diese Formen vor.

Ich spreche das unumwunden und offen aus: Auf der Grundlage der Gleichberechtigung, denn es ist unmöglich, die Wahrheit zu verschweigen. Auf Grund der gegenwärtigen allgemeinen militärischen Lage ist das Ziel, Europa zu beherrschen und die Zukunft Deutschlands auf Kosten Rußlands für 1000 Jahre zu sichern, unerreichbar. Deutschland ist zwar ein großes und mächtiges Land, aber wie die Geschichte des Weltkrieges 1914–18 und die Entwicklung des gegenwärtigen Krieges zeigt, ist bei dem augenblicklichen Zustand der Zivilisation einem einzigen Lande, so stark es auch sein mag, keine Möglichkeit gegeben, die Verhältnisse auf dem europäischen Kontinent nach seiner eigenen Willkür zu organisieren. Vor dieser unabänderlichen Wirklichkeit muß nun auch Deutschland sich beugen.

Für jeden, der die gegenwärtige Lage vorurteilslos betrachtet, ist völlig klar, daß es sich jetzt nicht mehr um die Hegemonie Deutschlands in Europa, sondern um seine Existenz, um seine und Europas Rettung vor den Greueln des Bolschewismus handelt. Die Stunde schlägt. Noch eine Weile, und es wird zu spät sein. Der Verlust von Tunis gibt den Angloamerikanern das Sprungbrett nach Italien, wo ihre Landung von unabsehbaren Folgen begleitet sein kann. Die immer wachsende Überlegenheit der Westmächte in der Luft droht die Industrie und sogar das Leben innerhalb Deutschlands stillzulegen. Die heranrückenden Gefahren kann man nur durch volle Ausnutzung der Hilfsquelle, von der oben gesprochen wurde, abwehren. Man muß eine freie russische Bewegung in Gang setzen, die Deutschland zu Hilfe kommen wird."

Balkan

Nicht glücklich war die Entwicklung in Südosteuropa. Feldmarschall von Weichs schreibt: ,,Unseren Einsatz auf dem Balkan verdanken wir der Politik und militärischen Schwäche Italiens. Die Eroberungen, die wir machten, sollten sich als Danaergeschenk im wahrsten Sinne des Wortes erweisen. Als ich am 17. Mai 1941 den Balkan verließ, ahnte ich nicht, unter welchen veränderten Verhältnissen ich ihn 1943 wiedersehen sollte."

Über die Gründung des Kroatischen Staates berichtet der Generalfeldmarschall: ,,. . . Die Geburt dieses Staates machte zuerst einen etwas operettenhaften Eindruck. Als ich in Agram am 13. April eintraf, begrüßte mich der kroatische General Kvaternik, der zunächst das ,freie Kroatien' konstituierte. Er war alter k. u. k. Oberst, der Typ des ehemaligen österreichischen Offiziers, von guter militärischer Erscheinung, mit festem, soldatischem Auftreten und großer Redegewandtheit. Politisch hatte er wohl etwas wirre Ideen. Er versicherte mir, daß Kroatien baldigst eine Armee aufstellen werde, die Schulter an Schulter mit den Deutschen auf jedem beliebigen Kriegsschauplatz kämpfen werde.

Etwas ermüdet von verschiedenen Truppenbesuchen, hoffte ich etwas ruhen zu können. Doch das wurde mir nicht gegönnt. Man eröffnete mir, daß anläßlich der Neugründung im Staatstheater eine Festvorstellung, und zwar ,Parzifal', stattfinden werde, daß als äußeres Zeichen der Verbundenheit von Deutschland und Kroatien auch ich daran teilnehmen müsse und Kvaternik mich in meinem Hotel abholen werde.

Aber fast zwei Stunden wartete ich in meinem Hotel, ebenso das Publikum geduldig im Theater. Kvaternik kam nicht. Er war angeblich auf einer Fahrt nach auswärts in deutsche Marschkolonnen geraten und dadurch aufgehalten worden. Schließlich entschloß man sich, ohne den General zu beginnen, und ich fuhr allein ins Theater, dort begrüßt von einer Gruppe von Herren, nach unseren Begriffen merkwürdig gekleidet, teils mit einem kapuzinerbraunen Touristenanzug, der kroatischen Parteiuniform, teils mit Smoking, zu dem nach dortiger Mode Schlipse mit langen Goldfransen getragen wurden. Das war die neue Regierung und der Theater-Intendant. Die Vorstellung begann.

In der Pause nach dem ersten Akt erschien endlich Kvaternik, ebenfalls bekleidet mit der Parteiuniform, begrüßte mich mit großem Redeschwall und erklärte, nachdem er sich an dem aufgebauten guten Buffet gestärkt hatte, daß er nunmehr zum Staatsakt schreiten werde. Er nötigte mich, neben ihn an die Brüstung der Proszeniumsloge zu treten, und schmetterte eine zündende Rede in das Publikum. Da die Rede kroatisch gehalten war, verstand ich sie nicht, wußte auch nicht, warum er mir unter dem Jubel des Publikums wiederholt die Hand drückte. Die Rede endete mit fünf Nationalhymnen: zwei deutschen, zwei italienischen und einer kroatischen. Für uns Deutsche wirkte die Veranstaltung eher komisch als feierlich. Dann wurde die Vorstellung fortgesetzt. Ich ging nach Hause.

Am nächsten Tage erschien Dr. Ante Pavelić. Er kam aus der Emigration in Italien und trat mit der Bezeichnung Poglavnik die Stelle des Staatsoberhauptes an. Unter dem Einfluß des deutschen Auswärtigen Amtes war diese Auswahl getroffen worden. Ob sie glücklich war, sollte sich erst später zeigen.

Pavelić, eine schlaue, gewandte, aber undurchsichtige Persönlichkeit mit etwas dunkler Vergangenheit, betonte zunächst seine Deutschfreundlichkeit. Er hob mir gegenüber hervor, daß die Kroaten keine Slawen, sondern Ostgoten seien, die sich durch Zufall eine slawische Sprache zugelegt hätten. Äußerlich freilich hatte der Poglavik nichts Gotisches. Er beförderte – als erste Amthandlung – seinen bisherigen Platzhalter Kvaternik zum Feldmarschall. Als Glaise, der sich als alter k. u. k. Kamerad ein offenes Wort erlauben konnte, meinte, ein Marschall ohne Armee sei doch etwas Lächerliches, sah Kvaternik das zwar ein. Doch es war zu spät, die Beförderung stand bereits in der Presse . . ."

Die Kapitulation Jugoslawiens im Jahre 1941 bedeutete nicht das Ende des Krieges. Dies war für die deutschen Soldaten, die die Geschichte Südosteuropas nicht kannten, eine große Überraschung. Oberst Dragoljub Mihailović, der letzte Stabschef der Četniks vor Ausbruch des Krieges, anerkannte die Kapitulation nicht.

König Peter II. beförderte ihn von London aus zum General. Die West-Alliierten und auch zunächst der Kreml betrachteten ihn als Oberbefehlshaber der jugoslawischen Heimatarmee. Ihm standen als Hauptgegner die Ustaschas gegenüber, deren Ziel die Errichtung eines kroatischen Nationalstaates war. Die Auseinandersetzungen zwischen Kroaten und Serben kosteten letztere 700 000 Menschenleben.

Das grausame Verhalten der Ustaschas wirkte sich auch gegen deutsche Soldaten aus, die angesichts der kroatischen Selbständigkeit nur beschränkt handlungsfähig waren.

Die Verhältnisse zwangen auch eine integere Persönlichkeit, ihr Amt als bevollmächtigter Deutscher General aufzugeben, Edmund Glaise von Horstenau.

In der Herzogewina wurden durch Ustascha-Einheiten, Četniks, Tito-Partisanen, private Banden sowie deutsche und italienische Sicherheitstruppen 183 000 Menschenleben getötet. Von den Tito-Partisanen wurden nach der ,,Befreiung" 210 000 Menschen umgebracht.

In der Herzogewina wie in Bosnien verloren viele Angehörige der Muselmanischen Legion mit ihren Frauen und Kindern das Leben. Die Intelligenz- und Führungsschicht wurde fast gänzlich ausgerottet. In Montenegro konnte Tito erst Mitte 1943 Fuß fassen. 70 000 Muslims wurden getötet.

Besonders tragisch ist das Schicksal der Volksdeutschen. Einst kamen aus allen Teilen des Reiches, insbesondere aus Süddeutschland, Deutsche, die die sumpfigen Flußniederungen von Donau, Drau und Save kultivierten. Die deutschen Einwanderer siedelten in Syrmien, einer Gegend westlich von Belgrad zwischen der Donau im Norden und der Save und der Drau im Süden mit dem Mittelpunkt Ruma. Nördlich der Donau liegt die Batschka mit einem Ring deutscher Siedler, der sich bis Ungarn hinein erstreckte. Deutsche Sprachgruppen (z. B. die Gottschee) hielten sich auch in Slowenien. In Dalmatien und Bosnien gab es nur wenige deutsche Siedlungen. Insgesamt lebten in Jugoslawien 600 000 Deutsche.

Der Rückzug der deutschen Wehrmacht brachte über die deutsche Volksgruppe in Jugoslawien eine Katastrophe. Die Bewohner der Streusiedlungen in Bosnien und Dalmatien konnten rechtzeitig nach Süddeutschland und Österreich zurückgenommen werden. Die Batschka, das Land nördlich der Donau, konnte als an Ungarn gefallenes Territorium nicht geräumt werden. Dasselbe gilt für Syrmien, da Ungarn und Rumänien die Front wechselten und die Rote Armee überraschend schnell nach Westen vordrang.

Als die sowjetischen Truppen südlich von Belgrad das Morawa-Tal erreichten, gab Heinrich Himmler, im Vertrauen darauf, daß die Donaustellung gehalten werden könne, den Befehl, die Evakuierung der Syrmien-Deutschen zu verschieben. Tausende von Deutschen blieben in den Dörfern. Ein „blutiges Strafgericht" brach über sie herein.

In der „Dokumentation der Vertreibung der Deutschen aus Mitteleuropa", Band V, Jugoslawien, sind Teile der grauenvollen Vorgänge festgehalten: Volksdeutsche Dörfer wurden als Konzentrationslager eingerichtet und die darin inhaftierten Deutschen ohne Unterschied des Alters und Geschlechts getötet. Soldaten der Waffen-SS-Division „Prinz Eugen" wurden summarisch zu Tode gefoltert. In einem Ort bei Ruma wurden ganze Familien lebendig begraben. Offiziell wird die Zahl der in Jugoslawien getöteten Volksdeutschen mit 140 000 angegeben. Nach anderen Quellen sind es mit den in Zwangsarbeitslagern Verstorbenen 260 000.

Nach dem Zusammenbruch Jugoslawiens entwickelte sich zwischen Kroaten und Serben ein Vernichtungskrieg, der dazu führte, daß Josip Broz-Tito auf kroatischem Gebiet sein Führungszentrum aufbaute. In ihm gingen auch Tausende von deutschen Soldaten unter.

Josip Broz-Tito, der in dem jugoslawischen Königreich bereits im Untergrund gearbeitet hatte – 1920 wurde die jugoslawische Kommunistische Partei infolge eines geglückten Attentats auf den Innenminister des Landes verboten –, verfügte ebenfalls über große Sympathien in der Oberschicht und vor allem bei deren Jugend.

Kroaten operierten bereits 1919 gegen den jugoslawischen Staat. Einer der Träger der Bewegung gegen einen Vielvölkerstaat war Ante Pavelić, der am 14. Juli 1889 in Bradina/Herzogewina geboren wurde. Als 21jähriger machte er sein Abitur. Während seiner Studentenzeit trat er der Studentenorganisation ,,Junges Kroatien" bei. Im Jahre 1915 promovierte er zum Dr. jur. Er wurde bald Parteisekretär des rechten Flügels der ,,Staatsrechtspartei". 1927 wurde er als Abgeordneter der Stadt Zagreb (Agram) Mitglied der Skuptschina, wo er sofort die Autonomie Kroatiens forderte. Nach einer bewaffneten Auseinandersetzung im Belgrader Parlament, die neben zwei Verwundeten drei Kroaten das Leben kostete, gründete Ante Pavelić eine bewaffnete Verschwörungsgruppe unter dem Namen ,,Hrvatski Domobran" (bewaffnete Heimwehr), deren Führer Eugen Kvaternik wurde, ein Sohn des ehemaligen k. u. k. Obersten Slavko Kvaternik und Nachkomme des 1871 erschossenen Aufstandsführers Eugen Kvaternik.

Nach parlamentarischen Krisenjahren übernahm am 6. Jan. 1929 König Alexander selbst die Macht. Am 7. Jan 1929 gründete Pavelić die ,,Ustascha Hrvatska Refoluciorna Organizacija" (UHRO). Nach der geheimen Gründung dieser Organisation gingen Pavelić und die wichtigsten Führer in das Ausland. Der Redakteur der Ustascha-Zeitung ,,Hrvat", Gustav Percec, wählte Ungarn, wo er in Janka Puszta an der jugoslawischen Grenze ein Schulungslager schuf, in dem die Methoden des Terrors und der Subversion gelehrt wurden.

Dr. Pavelić selbst begab sich zunächst nach Wien, dann nach Sofia. Dort kam er mit Ivan Mihailow, dem Chef der mazedonischen Geheimorganisation ,,Imro", zusammen. Am 20. April 1929 veröffentlichten sie ein geheimes Manifest, in dem zum Sturz des Belgrader Regimes aufgefordert wurde. Dafür wurde Ante Pavelić in Abwesenheit zum Tode verurteilt. Seine nächste Station war Italien. Mussolini wies ihm, seiner Frau und seinen drei Kindern Bologna als Wohnsitz zu. In Fontechio bei Arezzo und in San Demetrio baute er je zwei Lager auf, in denen Kader für eine Aufstandsbewegung herangebildet wurden. Er redigierte in Italien auch eine Zeitung, die an alle Auslandskroaten verschickt und nach Kroatien eingeschmuggelt wurde. In Wien und Berlin erschienen die kroatischen Korrespondenzen ,,Gric" und der ,,Kroatische Informationsdienst", später umgetauft in ,,Kroatiapress". Außerdem kam die Wochenzeitung ,,Nezavisna Država Hrvatska" (,,Der unabhängige Staat Kroatien") heraus. Dr. Branamirz, bisher in Wien tätig, übernahm in Berlin die Redaktion der Ustascha-Presse.

Im April 1930 fand in Baden bei Wien eine jugoslawische Emigranten-Konferenz statt. Auf ihr ergriffen Mihailow und Pavelić das Wort. Nicht nur mit publizistischen Mitteln, sondern auch durch Sabotageakte sollte auf die Probleme in Jugoslawien hingewiesen werden. Im Sommer 1932 „übte" Dr. Pavelić im Velebitgebirge einen Aufstand, der schnell niedergeschlagen wurde. Auf den jugoslawischen König selbst wurde im Herbst 1934 anläßlich seines Besuches in Agram ein Attentat geplant. Die Vorbereitungen leitete der Kommandant des Ustascha-Lagers in Janka Puszta, Gustav Percec, dessen Geliebte Jelka Pogorelec in Diensten der serbischen Polizei stand. Das Attentat mißglückte.

Aber am 9. Oktober 1934 kamen in Marseille König Alexander I. und der französische Außenminister Barthou durch ein Attentat um. Die französische Polizei nahm eine Anzahl Ustascha-Männer fest, die an der Vorbereitung der Aktion beteiligt waren. Sie wurden von einem französischen Gericht in Aix en Provence zu Gefängnis verurteilt. Der von der Menge gelynchte Mörder gehörte der „Imro" an. Aufgrund der blutigen Ereignisse von Marseille forderte die französische Regierung die Auslieferung von Pavelić, Eugen Kvaternik und Oberstleutnant Percević. Der Auslieferungsantrag wurde abgelehnt.

Pavelić wurde in Abwesenheit zum zweiten Mal zum Tode verurteilt. Italien mußte aber internationale Verwicklungen befürchten. Daher wurde der spätere Poglawnik in Turin für kurze Zeit in eine Art Ehrenhaft genommen. Später brachte ihn die italienische Regierung nach Siena, wo er eine Villa bezog. Er erhielt eine monatliche Staatspension von 5000 Lire. Die Ustascha-Lager löste Mussolini auf. Die Ustascha-Angehörigen wurden auf die Liparischen Inseln verbannt.

Hermann Göring, der als Vertreter des Reiches an den Beerdigungsfeierlichkeiten des Königs in Belgrad teilnahm, versprach eine Überprüfung der Ustascha-Bewegung in Deutschland. Zahlreiche kroatische Presseorgane mußten auf Weisung von Berlin ihr Erscheinen einstellen.

Der Zweite Weltkrieg kam

Am 28. März 1941 wurde Dr. Ante Pavelić in der Villa Torlonia empfangen und ihm das Versprechen gegeben, ihn in Agram an die Macht zu bringen. So überschritt Pavelić am 13. April 1941 bei Fiume (heute „Rijeka") die Grenze. Am Abend erreichte er Karlovac. Am 15. April 1941 traf er in Agram ein und übernahm sofort die Regierung, die umgehend von der

Reichsregierung anerkannt wurde. Zum Entsetzen des Poglavnik annektierte Mussolini kroatische Gebiete, z. B. Dalmatien, was zu einer inneren Krise des Landes führte.

Der am 17. April 1941 gebildeten kroatischen Regierung gehörten an:

Dr. Ante Pavelić als Ministerpräsident und Außenminister,

Slavko Kvaternik als stellvertretender Ministerpräsident, Marschall und Heimwehrminister,

Eugen Kvaternik als Staatssekretär im Innenministerium und Leiter des Sicherheitsdienstes,

Dvafer Kulonević als Vizepräsident,

Dr. Andrija Arkuvić als Innenminister,

Dr. Mile Budak als Kultusminister,

Dr. Jurko Puk als Justizminister,

Dr. Lovro Sulić als Wirtschaftsminister.

Während Broz-Tito und Pavelić revolutionäre Figuren sind, ist General Nedic die tragische Figur in der jugoslawischen Geschichte. Der General sah es nur als seine Aufgabe an, seinem Land zu dienen. 1941 war er in deutsche Kriegsgefangenschaft geraten. Auch als Ministerpräsident blieb der royalistische Serbe ,,ein von der Kriegsgefangenschaft beurlaubter Regierungschef", im Gegensatz zu Mihailović, den die Engländer schließlich fallenließen. Nedić gelang es, sein Gebiet im Laufe der Zeit zu konsolidieren, während Pavelić's Machtbereich oft nicht weiter als bis zum ,,Ende der Agramer Straßenbahn" reichte.

Der Balkan war bereits 1941 Brennpunkt des Partisanenkrieges. Aus dem Mai 1941 ist ein Aufruf der Kommunistischen Partei bekannt, in dem es hieß: ,,Wie wir gesehen haben, ist das Land zerstückelt und zwischen einigen imperialistischen Eroberern aufgeteilt. Das kann jedoch kein Hindernis für ein weiteres geeintes Wirken der Kommunistischen Partei Jugoslawiens darstellen, kein Hindernis für den gemeinsamen Kampf der Völker Jugoslawiens für ihre Unabhängigkeit und Freiheit bedeuten. Das kann den gemeinsamen Kampf der Völker aller Gebietsteile gegen den Okkupanten und seine Agenten im Lande nicht aufhalten. Die Völker werden sich unter der Leitung der Kommunistischen Partei Jugoslawiens die Freiheit, Unabhängigkeit und eine bessere Zukunft selbst erringen, denn das stellt die Lebensaufgabe und das Ziel der Vorhut des Proletariats, der Kommunistischen Partei Jugoslawiens, dar."

Vom Mai bis Juni 1941 traf die Kommunistische Partei Jugoslawiens die Vorbereitungen für den bewaffneten Aufstand. Am Tage des Ausbruches des deutsch-sowjetischen Krieges forderte das Zentralkomitee der Kommunistischen Partei Jugoslawiens zur Unterstützung der Sowjetunion auf.

In dem Aufruf hieß es: ,,Dieses neue unerhörte Verbrechen der faschisti-

schen Mörder erfüllte nicht nur die Herzen dieses Zweihundertmillionen-
volkes mit maßloser Erbitterung, sondern auch die Herzen der Werktätigen
in der ganzen Welt. Doch die blutdürstigen faschistischen Verbrecher und
ihre Satrapen in den übrigen kapitalistischen Ländern haben sich diesmal
stark verrechnet. Sie haben jetzt keine schwachen europäischen, von verrä-
terischen kapitalistischen Cliquen geführten Staaten vor sich, Länder, die
innen faul, uneinig und durch die verräterische Arbeit der fünften Kolonne
geschwächt sind, sondern das einheitliche Zweihundertmillionenvolk der
großen Sowjetunion, das sich um die heroische Partei der Bolschewiki
schart . . . Proletarier aller Länder Jugoslawiens, nehmt euren Platz in der
ersten Kampfreihe ein . . . Schließt eure Reihen um eure Vorhut, die Kommunistische Partei Jugoslawiens! Jeder auf seinem Platz! Erfüllt unerschüt-
terlich und diszipliniert eure proletarische Pflicht! bereitet euch schnell für
die letzte und entscheidende Schlacht vor! Laßt nicht zu, daß das teure Blut
des heroischen Sowjetvolkes ohne eure Teilnahme vergossen wird! Eure
Losungen müssen sein: Kein Arbeiter und keine Arbeiterin darf nach dem
faschistischen Deutschland gehen, um mit ihrer Arbeit die Kräfte der faschistischen Banditen zu stärken! Keine Kanone, kein Gewehr, keine Ku-
gel, kein Getreidekorn darf mit eurer Hilfe in die Hände der faschistischen
Verbrecher gelangen! Mobilisiert eure Kräfte, damit unser Land nicht zur
Versorgungsbasis der faschistischen Horden wird, die wie tollwütige Hunde
die Sowjetunion überfallen haben, unsere teure sozialistische Heimat, unsere Hoffnung und unseren Leuchtturm, auf den die Augen der gequälten
werktätigen Menschheit mit Hoffnung gerichtet sind" . . .

Am 27. Juni 1941 wurde der Oberste Stab der Volksbefreiungsabteilun-
gen der Partisanen gebildet. Kommandeur war der Generalsekretär der
Kommunistischen Partei, Josip Broz-Tito. Am 4. Juli 1941 befahl er: ,,Auf
in den Kampf! In den Kampf gegen die faschistische Okkupantenbande,
deren Ziel nicht nur die Vernichtung der besten Volkskämpfer, sondern die
aller Slawen auf dem Balkan ist, deren Ziel die Versklavung der ganzen
Welt und die schrecklichste Herrschaft über die Völker ist, die die Geschichte kennt. Auf in den Kampf, denn die Stunde hat geschlagen, um das
Joch der faschistischen Okkupanten abzuwerfen. In den Kampf, denn das
schulden wir den Sowjetvölkern, die auch für unsere Freiheit kämpfen. In
den Kampf, in den letzten Kampf zur Vernichtung der faschistischen Pest!"

Am 7. Juli 1941 brach in Serbien der bewaffnete Aufstand aus, am 15.
Juli in Montenegro, am 22. Juli in Slowenien, am 27. Juli 1941 in Kroatien,
Bosnien und in der Herzogewina.

Der Befehlshaber der Sicherheitspolizei und des SD in Belgrad, Dr. Weimann, sagte nach seiner Gefangennahme aus: ,,Schlagartig setzten im ganzen Lande Sabotage und Terrorakte ein, die sich von Tag zu Tag mehrten.

Eine wirksame Bekämpfung durch eigene Kräfte war nicht möglich. Die wenigen Landesschützenbataillone wurden als Sicherung für eigene Objekte voll benötigt... die Lage der deutschen Wehrmacht wurde immer bedrohlicher. Die bald täglich erlassenen Aufrufe und Drohungen hatten eher gegenteiligen Erfolg. Täglich wurden Offiziere und Soldaten aus dem Hinterhalt oder auf den Hauptstraßen der Städte ermordet. Auf den Sender Belgrad wurde ein Sprengstoffanschlag verübt, aus einem Gefängnis und zwei Krankenhäusern festgenommene Personen befreit, wobei die serbischen und deutschen Wachposten getötet, mehrere Wehrmachtsgaragen überfallen und die darin parkenden Fahrzeuge zerstört wurden. Der ehemalige Militärbefehlshaber, General Schröder, ließ daraufhin 13 Personen erschießen und die Vollstreckung veröffentlichen. Da die Terrorakte jedoch noch weiter zunahmen, ließ der Nachfolger General Schröders, General Dankelmann, fünf der festgenommenen Täter auf der Terazia in Belgrad durch den Strang hinrichten, wobei die serbische Polizei ihrerseits auch noch zwei Exekutionen durchführte."

In seiner weiteren Aussage weist Weimann darauf hin, daß von der Ostfront Truppen abgezogen werden mußten.

In Montenegro, Serbien und der Herzegowina, in Lika, Kordun und Banija kam es zum Volksaufstand. Entlang der Verbindungslinien wurden Garnisonen der Besatzungstruppen überfallen. Besetzt von den Partisanen wurden die Städte Užice, Kruponj, Cačak, Uzička, Pozega, Invajicu, Kolusin, Damilovgrad, Zabljak, Sarnik, Drvar, Mrkonjećrad, Donki Lapać.

Erbitterte Kämpfe entwickelten sich in Kragujevać, Kraljevo, Valjero, Niksić, Bosanski, Petrovać, Bilece, Bihać und Gospić. Pero Moraca schreibt in seinem Buch ,,Die Völker Jugoslawiens im Zweiten Weltkrieg":

,,Die Partisanenaktionen sind in vielen okkupierten Städten mit Erfolg durchgeführt worden. Allein in Belgrad wurden im Juli 1941 50 Aktionen ausgeführt. Es wurden u. a. acht große Automobilgaragen, drei Benzin- und Munitionslager, zwei Kasernen usw. in Brand gesetzt. In Split wurde eine Gruppe von Besatzungsoffizieren mit Handgranaten überfallen; in Niš geschah dasselbe. Auf dem Flughafen in Jagodina wurden einige Flugzeuge verbrannt. In Agram wurden auf der Hauptpost und in einigen Fabriken Diversionen durchgeführt; eine Ustascha-Abteilung wurde mit Handgranaten überfallen, und es erfolgte eine Reihe von Überfällen auf deutsche Offiziere und Polizeiagenten. In Ljubljana war die illegale Bewegung sehr gut organisiert: Stoßtrupps überfielen höhere Okkupations- und Quislingfunktionäre; in der Stadt arbeitete eine illegale Radiostation usw. Erfolgreiche Aktionen wurden in Mostar, Kragujevać, Sarajevo, Šibenik, Karlovać und in vielen anderen größeren Städten ausgeführt."

Im Herbst 1941 waren große Teile Jugoslawiens befreit oder standen unter der Kontrolle der Partisanen, deren Reihen ständig anwuchsen und zu einer immer größeren Gefahr für die Aufrechterhaltung der Okkupation wurden. Ende 1941 umfaßte die Volksbefreiungsbewegung in Jugoslawien bereits 80 000 Kämpfer, die in 44 Partisanenabteilungen, 14 Bataillonen und einer proletarischen Brigade organisiert werden. Sie unterstanden dem Obersten Stab der Volksbefreiungs-Partisanenabteilung, der wiederum örtliche Stäbe in Kroatien, Slowenien, Serbien, Mazedonien, der Herzogewina und anderen Gebieten hatte.

Das Oberkommando der Wehrmacht sah sich veranlaßt, die Besatzungstruppen in Jugoslawien zu verstärken. Die 342. Division kam aus Frankreich, ein Regiment aus Griechenland, die 113. Division wurde von der deutsch-sowjetischen Front herausgezogen.

Nicht unerwähnt sei, daß auch Albanien von dem Aufstand erfaßt wurde. Am 8. Nov. 1941 wurde die Albanische Kommunistische Partei gegründet.

Für Albanien gilt der Satz: ,,Wer Albanien beherrscht, beherrscht das Mittelmeer."

Der Schriftsteller, der diesen Satz prägte, führt dazu aus: ,,. . . Albanien besitzt eine hervorragende strategische Lage, eine Schlüsselstellung sowohl für Land- wie für weltwichtige Seeverbindungen: Durch Albaniens bis zu 2600 Mehter hoch aufragende Kalkgebirge gruben die Flüsse Drin, Semeni und Vijose gewaltige Schluchten; sie bilden die einzigen günstigen Wege des westlichen Balkans nach dem Innern der südosteuropäischen Halbinsel. Albanien beherrscht die Wege von der Adria zum Schwarzen Meer, schon die Via Egnatia, die Straße, die Rom mit Byzanz verband, führte über Albanien . . . Über Albanien führen die klassischen Einfallswege nach Griechenland: Der von Argyrokastron nach Janina, der Hauptstadt des Epirus, der von Klisura nach Koritsa und zum Metsovon-Paß, der den Weg nach Thessalien öffnet, dazu die Straße von Koritza nach Kastoria oder Florina, von wo aus Mazedonien und Saloniki zu erreichen sind. Und wie im Altertum erwiesen sich diese natürlichen Routen zur Zeit der kommunistischen Revolte in Griechenland in den Jahren von 1944 bis 1945 als Verbindung von entscheidender Bedeutung . . ."

In meinem Plädoyer im Prozeß gegen Legationsrat Dr. Franz Rademacher in Bamberg führte ich aus: ,,Bereits unter dem 13. 9. 1941 forderte Major iG Jais, Verbindungsoffizier des Wehrmachtsbefehlshabers Südost vom höheren Kommando LXV: ,Um die Möglichkeit eines rücksichtslosen Vorgehens, Niederbrennen aller Siedlungen, aus denen oder in deren Nähe auf die Truppen geschossen wird, zu schaffen, erscheinen entsprechende Bekanntmachungen durch Rundfunk, Presse, Anschläge und Flugblätter wichtig.' Dieser Satz, entnommen aus dem Exposé des genannten Majors, ,Beurteilung der militärischen Lage in Serbien Nr. 2', verlangt die Durchführung von kollektiven Gewaltmaßnahmen, wie sie auf dem sowjetrussischen Kriegsschauplatz durchgeführt wurden.

Der Befehl vom 25. 9. 1941 bildet drei Geiselgruppen: nationalistische, bürgerlich-demokratische und kommunistische.

Da das Schwergewicht des Aufstandes auf der kommunistischen Seite lag, waren zu Sühnemaßnahmen vorwiegend der Kreis – ich bediene mich der damaligen Ausdrucksweise – der Kommunisten und ihrer Helfershelfer heranzuziehen.

Im OKW-Befehl vom 12. 9. 1941 werden die Juden – in der Formulierung der damaligen Zeit – als Hauptträger des Bolschewismus bezeichnet.

Überblicken wir das Thema der Geiselerschießungen in der Gesamtschau und im großen Zusammenhang, dann ist es bei den grundlegenden Richtlinien und Weisungen, die zur Sicherheit der Truppen gegeben wurden, nicht verwunderlich, daß General Böhme nach den Ereignissen von Topola das Schwergewicht der Erschießungen auf den jüdischen Bevölkerungsteil verlegte. Es nimmt nicht wunder, daß der Bevollmächtigte Kommandierende General für Serbien die Verhaftung aller Juden befiehlt . . .

Der Befehl vom 25. 10. 1941 betrachtet – wie der Befehl vom 10. 10. 1941 – Juden und Zigeuner ganz allgemein als ein Element der Unsicherheit und damit der Gefährdung der öffentlichen Ordnung und Sicherheit. Deshalb waren in Durchführung des Befehls vom 10. 10. 1941 alle jüdischen Männer und alle männlichen Zigeuner als Geiseln der Truppe zur Verfügung zu stellen.

Ich wies auf die Meldung des Chefs der Sicherheitspolizei in Belgrad hin, in der es heißt:

‚Als Vergeltungsmaßnahmen für 21 gefallene deutsche Soldaten der Wehrmacht sind 2.100 Juden . . . zur Verfügung gestellt. Exekution wird durch Wehrmacht durchgeführt. Erfassung aller männlichen Juden in Belgrad durchgeführt. Vorarbeiten für Judenghetto in Belgrad beendet. Nach bereits durch Befehlshaber Serbien befohlenen Liquidierung der restlichen männlichen Juden wird das Ghetto etwa 10000 Judenweiber und Kinder umfassen.‘

Dies sind fürchterliche Sätze. Die Handlungsweise rächte sich auch. Schwierigkeiten bereitete auch die Frage der Deportation. Dazu nahm ich, wie folgt Stellung:

‚Der damalige Oberst Pensel hatte durchaus recht, wenn er bemerkte, er wüßte nicht, daß General Böhme die Juden nach Rumänien, nach Rußland oder in das Generalgouvernement deportieren wollte. Er könne es jedoch nicht ausschließen.‘

Ich fügte hinzu: ‚Im alten Serbien, aus der Zeit vor dem Balkankrieg lebten ca. 12000 Juden, davon 8500 in Belgrad, dazu kommen die Juden aus den Gebietsteilen von Bosnien und Herzogewina, die nicht Bestandteile des neugeschaffenen Staates Kroatien wurden. Eine bedeutende Rolle in dem jüdischen Drama spielt aber die Tatsache, daß die Juden mit jugoslawischer Staatsangehörigkeit aus der an Ungarn gefallenen Batschka von General Dankelmann und dem Beauftragten des Auswärtigen Amtes übernommen wurden. Die Regierung Laszlo Bardossy schaffte sie einfach nach Beschlagnahme ihrer Habe über die Donau.

Serbien brannte. Und so wollte der Beauftragte des Auswärtigen Amtes, Benzler, das wieder loswerden, was er übernommen hatte. Durch seine Telegramme nach Berlin, seine Hinweise auf die gefährliche Lage, die Beteiligung von Juden bei zahlreichen Sabotage- und Aufruhrakten begründet er seinen Wunsch nach Deportierung. Daher sein Verlangen, 8000 männliche Juden so rasch wie möglich außer Landes zu bringen. Benzlers Fernschreiben liegen im September 1941, das letzte vom 28. 9. 1941 unterstützten die Generäle Böhme und Dankelmann.‘‘‘

Es ist selbstverständlich, daß die deutsche Niederlage in der Winterschlacht vor Moskau den Widerstand der Partisanen in Jugoslawien stärkte. Nicht umsonst schreibt der Oberbefehlshaber der 12. deutschen Armee am 19. März 1942: ,,Es muß damit gerechnet werden, daß im Frühjahr in Serbien und dem von deutschen Truppen besetzten Teil Kroatiens wieder Aufstände im größten Umfang beginnen.‘‘

Auf Europa übertragen bedeutet dies, daß starke Nebenkriegsschauplätze mit ihren Widerstandsgruppen die deutschen Truppen fesselten, daß deutsche Streitkräfte gegen die Sowjetunion fehlten. Die Bedeutung der jugoslawischen Widerstandsbewegung ergibt sich aus dem Bericht des Generals der Artillerie, Bader, der angibt, daß vom 1. September 1941 bis 12. Februar 1942 7756 Personen gefallen sind oder erschossen wurden und 20 149 durch ,,Sühnemaßnahmen‘‘ umkamen. Verständlich ist seine Feststellung: Angesichts der außerordentlich schwierigen Geländeverhältnisse – mindestens die Hälfte des Landes besteht aus mehr oder weniger weglosem Waldgebirge von 500–800 m Höhe – erscheint eine völlige Niederwerfung der Aufstandsbewegung mit den zur Zeit verfügbaren Kräften undurchführbar.‘‘

Im Winter und Frühjahr 1942 hatten die deutschen Truppen Erfolge zu verzeichnen. Von Juni 1942 bis Januar 1943 operierten die Partisanenverbände von Montenegro gegen Westbosnien und Kroatien. Ein geschlossenes Territorium von 50 000 qkm wurde von Partisanen beherrscht, die auch in Slawonien und Slowenien ihre Herrschaft ausdehnten. In Serbien und Mazedonien wurde ihre Macht immer größer. Ende 1942 umfaßte die ,,Volksbefreiungsarmee‘‘ 150 000 Mann.

Am 26. und 27. November 1942 wurde in Bihać der ,,Antifaschistische

Rat der Volksbefreiung Jugoslawiens" (AVNOJ) gebildet, der sich nach Pero Moraca die „Grundaufgabe" stellte, „als höchster Vertreter der Volksbefreiungsbewegung auf die weitere Vereinigung aller Kräfte des Volkes zum Kampf gegen die Okkupanten und die einheimische verräterische Reaktion einzuwirken."

Im Sommer 1944 nahm die Gesamtlage an der Ostfront eine katastrophale Entwicklung an. In der „Geschichte des Großen Vaterländischen Krieges der Sowjetunion" (Bd. IV) wird festgestellt: „Um weiter in Richtung Warschau–Berlin vorstoßen zu können, mußte man die starken Gruppierungen in Rumänien und in den baltischen Republiken zerschlagen."

Für die zu verteidigende Front, die 850 km lang war, standen 650 000 Deutsche, Rumänen und Slowaken zur Verfügung. Bei ihrem Angriff suchten die Sowjets den schwächsten Punkt aus, nämlich die Nahtstelle zwischen der 6. deutschen und der 3. rumänischen Armee.

Das Standardwerk „Geschichte des Vaterländischen Krieges" berichtet: „Die Oberbefehlshaber der Fronten massierten an den nur 16–18 Kilometer breiten Durchbruchsabschnitten starke Kräfte; sie setzten dort je Kilometer 240 bis 243 Geschütze und Granatwerfer mit einem Kaliber von 76 Millimetern und stärker ein. Eine solche Artilleriedichte war selbst für Operationen des Jahres 1944 ungewöhnlich. Aber der erste Stoß mußte mit solcher Wucht geführt werden, um die Verteidigung innerhalb kurzer Zeit zu durchbrechen und einen schnellen Vormarsch in das Innere Rumäniens zu sichern. Das sowjetische Oberkommando hatte die Oberbefehlshaber der Fronten angewiesen, eine entsprechende Artilleriedichte zu schaffen. Die Anzahl der Geschütze und Granatwerfer an den Durchbruchsabschnitten beider Fronten war bei allgemein doppelter Überlegenheit ungefähr sechsmal größer als die des Gegners . . ."

Immer mehr verschlechterte sich die Lage auf dem Balkan. Im Herbst 1943 entsandte Hitler Hermann Neubacher nach Belgrad, Tirana und Agram. Über seine Aufgabe berichtet er: „Es war ein Trümmerhaufen, in den ich gestellt wurde. Mein neuer Sonderauftrag war eine Folge der Vereinheitlichung der militärischen Befehlsgebung auf dem Balkan. Die Heeresgruppe E – Saloniki – (Generaloberst Löhr) wurde im Sommer 1943 der Heeresgruppe F – Belgrad – (Generalfeldmarschall Freiherr von Weichs) unterstellt. Es lag nahe, auch die diplomatischen Dienststellen im Raume der Heeresgruppe F zu koordinieren, um zu vermeiden, daß Vertreter des Auswärtigen Amtes der Wehrmacht gegenüber verschiedene oder gar gegensätzliche Standpunkte vertreten . . .

Wenn je in einem Raume die Koordination der Außenpolitik notwendig war, dann war es der Balkanraum während des Krieges. Die neuen Grenzziehungen hatten die Verzahnung der nationalen Siedlungsgebiete nicht verbessert. Die alten Gegnerschaften erhielten eine neue blutige Nahrung, und zu den alten Verwicklungen trat die ganze Problematik der Besetzung durch auswärtige Mächte. Somit hatte mein Auftrag eine vernünftige Grundlage. Aber dieser Auftrag war nicht so umfassend, wie der Titel ‚für den Südosten‘ besagte; Kroatien und Bulgarien gehörten nicht dazu. Ich hatte also keinen direkten Einfluß auf die Vorgänge in Kroatien, welche meine Politik in Serbien schwer belasteten. Es war mir ebensowenig möglich, die Okkupationsmethoden der Bulgaren auf serbischem Boden in Sofia direkt zu beeinflussen. Die indirekte Einflußnahme führte aber in beiden Fällen über deutsche Gesandte, die sich ‚solidarisiert‘ hatten. Dieselbe Solidarisierung machten mir aber die Ustascha-Kreise in Agram und die großbulgarischen Kreise in Sofia zum Vorwurf. Ich galt dort als ausgemachter Serbenfreund. Die Gefahr der Solidarisierung war in meinem Falle gering, denn ich hatte gleichzeitig mit Ungarn, Rumänien, Serbien, Montenegro, Albanien und Griechenland zu tun. Wahr ist, daß ich im Hauptquartier hartnäckig für eine Änderung der deutschen Politik den Serben gegenüber gekämpft habe. Die Serben waren ein Freiwild für alle geworden. Das wäre an sich noch kein politisches Argument gewesen, ich sah aber in einem vernünftig behandelten Serbien eine der stärksten Positionen gegen die Bolschewisierung des Balkan. Der Druck der kroatischen und bulgarischen Nachbarschaft lastete von Anfang an bis zum Ende auf meiner Mission in Serbien . . .“

Die Erfolge der Sowjets führten zum Sturz von Marschall Antonescu, zur Kapitulation und zum Frontwechsel Rumäniens. Als die Angriffsrichtung des sowjetischen Staates bekannt wurde, führten die Heeresgruppen F und E die Unternehmen ,,Kreuzotter‘‘ und ,,Rübezahl‘‘ durch, die gegen die griechischen und jugoslawischen Partisanen gerichtet waren. Der Raum zwischen Karpaten und Ägäis war eine Gefahrenzone erster Ordnung geworden.

Am 27. Aug. 1944 kündigte der bulgarische Ministerpräsident durch eine Regierungserklärung im Sobranje das deutsch-bulgarische Bündnis auf. Am 5. September 1944 erklärten die Sowjets den Bulgaren den Krieg. Am 6. September 1944 erreichte die Rote Armee die rumänisch-bulgarische Grenze.

Der weitere Verlauf der Operationen wurde von dem bewaffneten Aufstand der bulgarischen Partisanen abhängig gemacht. Mit Hilfe heimlicher Anhänger überrumpelten sie am 9. September 1944 die bisherige Regierung und kämpften unter sowjetischem Oberkommando in Jugoslawien, Ungarn und Österreich.

Am 9. und 10. September 1944 hatte die Abteilung ,,Fremde Heere Ost‘‘ zu berichten: ,,Nach Rundfunkmeldung hat die Rote Armee auf Grund der bulgarischen Kriegserklärung an Deutschland die Kampfhandlungen gegen bulgarische Truppen eingestellt, so daß mit raschem Fortschreiten der Besetzung des bulgarischen Raumes gerechnet werden muß. Der Einmarsch der 3. Ukrainischen Front mit 37., 46. und 57. Armee, IV. Garde (mech.) Korps und VII. (mech.) Korps nach Bulgarien hat sich bestätigt. Anfänge sollen Plovdiv (130 km südostwärts Sofia) und Burgas erreicht haben."

10. 9. 1944: „. . . In Bulgarien wird der Gegner mit den Kräften der 3. Ukrainischen Front das gesamte Staatsgebiet schnell unter scharfe militärische Kontrolle nehmen, um dadurch die politische Umbildung im sowjetischen Sinne noch zu beschleunigen . . ."

Anfang September 1944 setzten sich Partisanenkorps aus dem Süden und Südwesten Serbiens in allgemein nördlicher Richtung in Bewegung. Die von Ostserbien nach Norden operierenden II. und III. Partisanenkorps stießen in den Raum von Negotin vor, um mit der Roten Armee Verbindung aufzunehmen. Die in Westserbien stehenden Kräfte des I. und XII. Korps erreichten bis Mitte September das Gebiet von Valjevo, das eingeschlossen wurde. Nach der Einnahme der Stadt stießen die Partisanenkräfte gegen die Save, mit der Hauptmasse aber gegen Richtung Topola-Avantjevolać, wo sie die Hauptdurchgangsstraße Belgrad-Niš bedrohten. Starke Tito-Verbände besetzten das Timok-Tal und nahmen Zajicar. Weitere Partisanenverbände drangen in den Rücken der deutschen Stützpunkte im Donaubogen vor, um mit den Sowjets zusammenzuwirken.

Die Räumung Albaniens wurde am 3. Okt. 1944 befohlen. Tito-Kräfte konnten im Narenta-Tal festen Fuß fassen. Die Rückführung des XXI. Gebirgs-Korps wurde erheblich gefährdet. Tirana konnte erst am 17. Nov. 1944 verlassen werden. Das XXI. Gebirgs-Korps vermochte sich schließlich von Podgorica (heute: Titograd) nach Prijepolje zurückzuziehen, wo es Anschluß an die aus Mazedonien kommenden Verbände der Heeresgruppe E fand.

Die 22. Infanterie-Division, die schwerste Kämpfe bei Kumnovo-Pristina durchgestanden hatte und dann bei eisiger Kälte in Tropenuniform die 1200–1300 m hohen Pässe Duga Poljana, Sjenica und Karanla überschritten hatte und ohne Unterkünfte im hohen Schnee biwakieren mußte, hatte das Gebirgskorps freizukämpfen.

Die Soldaten der 22. Infanterie-Division erfüllten den Befehl des Oberbefehlshabers der Heeresgruppe E: „Seitdem die 22. I. D. nach langer Wacht auf Kreta an der Ostfront der Heeresgruppe eingesetzt wurde, habt Ihr überall an Brennpunkten der Abwehrkämpfe gestanden und Euch hervorragend bewährt. Ihr habt im Strumica-Raum in beispielhaftem Angriffsgeist eine bulgarische Armee vernichtend zurückgeschlagen, bei Carevo Selo dem Feind einen unüberwindlichen Riegel vorgeschoben und ostwärts

Kumanovo seine hartnäckigen Durchbruchsversuche auf Skoplje (Skopje) abgewiesen. Ihr habt bei Bujanovce standgehalten und bei Podujevo in vorbildlicher Weise gekämpft. Nach langen Kämpfen und Märschen kann der Div. keine Kampfpause gewährt werden, sondern sie muß unverzüglich von Prijepolje aus zum Stoß nach Südwesten antreten, um sich dem in harten Durchbruchskämpfen in Montenegro stehenden XXI. Geb. A. K. entgegenzukämpfen. Damit erhält sie einen für die weitere Kampfführung der Heeresgruppe ausschlaggebenden und zugleich kameradschaftlichen Auftrag . . ."

Am Ende des Rückzuges in Südosteuropa stehen die fürchterlichen Greueltaten der Titopartisanen an den deutschen Soldaten, die in jugoslawische Kriegsgefangenschaft geraten waren.

Über die Lage in Jugoslawien berichtet der von Hausamann herausgegebene Informationsdienst.

6. 10. 41. Politischer Bericht (–1–):

Die Lage erfordert auch in Kroatien den immer umfangreicher werdenden Einsatz deutscher Wehrmachtteile, Polizeiformationen und Polizeispezialisten. Die kroatische Ustascha erweist sich als nicht in der Lage, die öffentliche Ordnung allein herzustellen und aufrechtzuerhalten. Seitens der verantwortl. deutschen Stellen wird die Ustascha nachgerade als ,,Horde von Henkern" überall da eingesetzt, wo man deutschen Truppen das Gemetzel ersparen will bzw. wo deutsche Truppen nicht mit der erwünschten Grausamkeit vorgehen würden.

Auch die in Kroatien eingesetzten italienischen Funktionäre einschließlich der italienischen Truppen vermochten nicht, die verantwortl. deutschen Instanzen zu überzeugen, daß sie die Situation zu meistern in der Lage seien.

6. 10. 41. Militärischer Bericht (–1–):

Von den serbischen Truppen und Freischärlern im Zlatibor- und Pobjenik-Gebiet (zwischen Nova-Varoš und Višegrad) ist nach der Zerstörung der Stadt Užice mit der vergeltungsweisen Erschießung deutscher gefangener Offiziere und Soldaten im Fall jeder weiteren Tötung von Geiseln durch den Militärbefehlshaber in Belgrad oder dessen Untergebene gedroht worden. Die Drohung ist durch Ausstreuung von Flugblättern bekanntgemacht worden, welche die Freischärler in Nowa-Varoš gedruckt haben.

Gleiche Drohung mit gleichen Repressalien haben auch die im serbisch-kroatischen Grenzgebiet kämpfenden serbischen Truppenführer auf dem Javor-Plateau bekanntgemacht. Kampfgruppen dieses großen serbischen Freischlärlerverbandes haben nacheinander in Zvornik, bei Losnica, in Sabac und in Mitrovica durch Überfall und im Gefecht weit über 500 deutsche Wehrmachtsangehörige gefangengenommen und entführt. Auch in Užice sind durch Überfall an die hundert deutsche Offiziere und Soldaten in serbische Gefangenschaft geraten. Die Vorstellung eines Bandenkrieges wird der Wirklichkeit schon seit ca. sechs Wochen nicht mehr gerecht. Es kämpfen ganze Bataillone serbischer Truppen geschlossen unter Führung der Offiziere, die sie im April gehabt haben. Die rücksichtslose Jagd auf Serben mit guter nationaler Haltung, die vom Militärbefehlshaber in Belgrad und von der Ustascha-Miliz in Kroatien organisiert worden ist, hat nur die Folge gehabt, daß sich viele Tausende von ehemaligen Offizieren und Soldaten der serbischen Regimenter schleunigst aus exponierten Wohnorten entfernt und ins Gebirge zu ihren Waffenlagern begeben haben. Dieser Prozeß dauert fort. Jede Expedition deutscher und italienischer Truppen, die irgendwo talaufwärts unternommen wird, hat die sofortige Zusammenballung von neuen Kampfgruppen zur Folge.

16. 11. 41. Militärischer Bericht (–1–):

Informationen aus guter Quelle besagen, daß die deutschen Besetzungstruppen in Serbien immer mehr an Boden verlieren. In Praxis sei die Lage derzeit so, daß sich nur mehr Belgrad, Niš und die Eisenbahnverbindung Belgrad–Niš–Sofia mit den Orten entlang dieser Strecke zuverlässig in deutscher Hand befinden. Alle andern Gebietsteile Serbiens seien teils wieder im festen Besitz der serbischen Freiheitskämpfer, teils von diesen ständig gefährdet.

6. 8. 42. Militärischer und politischer Bericht (–1–):

Der achsenseitige Bahnverkehr Ljubljana (Laibach)–Zagreb (Agram) ist in der Gegend von Steinbrück seit der Nacht zum 1. August stillgelegt; in der Nacht zuvor (Nacht zum 31. Juli) war die Eisenbahnverbindung zwischen Triest und Laibach unterbrochen worden. Die Unterbrechung des Bahnverkehrs ist durch Sprengungen und Zerstörungen in der Gegend von Steinbrück und bei der Station Unterloitsch (auf italienischem Staatsgebiet) erfolgt. Die Sprengungen wurden von größeren Freischärlergruppen ausgeführt. Die Sprengung in der Gegend von Steinbrück hat großen Umfang; der Verkehr Laibach–Agram lag auch am 2. August noch still.

Zur Kontrolle und zur Säuberung in den Karawanken sind von Cilli und Klagenfurt sofort deutsche Gebirgstruppen abgegangen.

Zwischen Fiume und Banjaluka sind die Verbindungen über Bihać–Krupa schon seit dem 24. Juli unterbrochen. Größere Gruppen gut bewaffneter Kroaten, zu denen serbisch-bosnische Truppen unter Führung von Offizieren gestoßen sind, haben sich in den Bergen und Hochtälern der Kleinen Kapela und im ganzen Gebiet westlich der Una festgesetzt. Eine ganze Reihe von italienischen Militär- und kroatischen Ustascha- und Gendarmerieposten sind hier zwischen 20. und 28. Juli niedergemacht worden, u. a. bei Krupa und in Petrovac. Praktisch ist der größere Teil des Gebietes zwischen dem Grimic-Gebirge und der Küste am Velebitgebirge (Korlacca-Kanal) im Aufstand. Die Herrschaft haben die Italiener bloß im Lica-Tal und an den größeren Plätzen an der Küste.

Die sog. kroatische Regierung übt jetzt praktisch die Verwaltung und Polizeiaufsicht im größeren Teil des Landes nicht mehr aus. Nach Bericht, den v. Kasche erstattet hat, sind von den 19 000 Offizieren, Unteroffizieren und Mannschaften der ehemaligen jugoslavischen Armee und Sicherheitspolizei, die der kroatische Staatschef Pawelić seit seiner Machtergreifung bewaffnet hat, jetzt glücklich 6000 zu den Freischärlern übergelaufen.

11. 8. 42. Militärischer Bericht (–1–):
Kampfhandlungen im ehemaligen Jugoslavien:
Die Einschließung der serbisch-bosnischen Truppen des Generals Mihailović im Gebiet zwischen dem Lim- und dem Tara-Tal (zwischen Durmitor und Zlatar) und das geplante konzentrische Vorgehen gegen sie ist den achsenseitigen Verbänden noch nicht möglich gewesen. Die deutscherseits eingesetzten Verbände der Waffen-SS haben sich trotz Anwendung neuer Methoden (u. a. Abführung der Gesamtbevölkerung aus dem nach Kampf gesicherten Vormarschgebiet) bis jetzt weder im Limtal noch im Taratal vereinigen können. Im Limtal stehen die deutschen Verbände erst bei Uvać, die italienischen bei Berane. Östlich von Uvać und östlich von Višegrad ist noch das ganze Berggebiet, das das Nova Varoš deckt, von einer bedeutenden Menge von sehr gut ausgerüsteten serbischen Truppen, Spezialisten im Gebirgskampf, besetzt. Gegen sie müßte achsenseits ein größerer Verband von Gebirgstruppen mit reichlicher Artillerie eingesetzt werden, welcher fehlt.

20. 8. 42. Militärischer Bericht (–1–):
Die berichtete Expansion der serbisch-bosnischen Truppen in N o r d - w e s t - B o s n i e n hat Fortschritte gemacht, nachdem kroatische Ustascha-Mannschaften und Bauern in Garnisonen und Orten des oberen Unatales und der westlich und östlich anschließenden Gebirgsgegenden zu den eingebrochenen Abteilungen des Generals Mihailović übergelaufen sind.

Die von der Agramer Regierung in Nordwest-Bosnien aufgestellte kroatische Sicherungstruppe, geführt von Major Jelcek, ist in Auflösung. Sie stand in einem italienischen Divisionsverband. Die meisten Mannschaften waren auf Posten und voneinander weit entfernte Plätze verteilt. Der größere Teil der Truppen ist mit den Unteroffizieren unter Zurücklassung der Offiziere in der Zeit nach dem 13. August zu Mihailović übergelaufen.

Die wichtige Verbindungsstraße Zermanje-Vrelo–Bihać, die westlich vom Unatal über die Orte Doljane und Nebljuje führt, ist mit Ausnahme eines kleinen südlichen Stückes fast ganz von den Serben und Bosniaken in Besitz genommen.

Bulgarien

In Bulgarien fand, wie wir wissen, lange vor dem 22. Juni 1941 ein Tauziehen um den politischen Kurs der Regierung statt. Die Bulgarische Arbeiterpartei leistete den prodeutschen Bestrebungen starken Widerstand. In Plovdiv erfaßte am 19. Juni 1940 alle Tabakverarbeitungsbetriebe der Streik. Dieser griff auf andere Städte und Industriezweige über. 20 000 Tabakarbeiter, 5000 Textilarbeiter und 5000 Arbeiter anderer Berufe traten insgesamt in den Ausstand.

Im Oktober 1940 forderte die Bulgarische Arbeiterpartei die Annäherung an die Sowjetunion. Als Bulgarien am 1. März 1941 dem Drei-Mächte-Pakt beitrat, verurteilte dies das Zentralkomitee der Bulgarischen Arbeiterpartei und trat für den Abschluß eines Beistandpaktes mit der Sowjetunion ein. An Mauern und Zäunen war zu lesen: ,,Nieder mit den deutschen Agenten in der Regierung! Nieder mit dem faschistischen Deutschland! Nieder mit Hitler! Schluß mit der Teuerung und dem Elend! Gebt die Internierten frei! Raus mit den Hitlerbanden! Es lebe das freie Bulgarien!"

Am 22. Juni 1941 erklärte das Zentralkomitee der Bulgarischen Arbeiterpartei: ,,In dem neuen Krieg, der Europa von Grund auf erschüttern wird, sind die Sympathien des bulgarischen Volkes ganz auf der Seite der Brudervölker der UdSSR." Zum Ausdruck wird gebracht, daß es der Kraft des Sozialismus gelingen wird, ,,ihr Gewicht in die Waagschale des Endsieges zu werfen, der nur ein Sieg der Sowjetunion und des Sozialismus sein kann".

Bereits am 24. Juni 1941 wurde durch Bildung einer Militärorganisation der bewaffnete Kampf vorbereitet. Kampfgruppen wurden im Transportwesen und in der Industrie aufgestellt, Überfälle auf Militärverbände, SS und Polizei geplant. Aufrufe wie ,,kein einziger Soldat an die Ostfront" wurden bei der bulgarischen Armee verteilt.

Die bulgarischen Verbände in Jugoslawien wurden aufgefordert, sich der jugoslawischen Partisanenbewegung anzuschließen. Am 23. Juli 1941 begann der Sender ,,Christo Botev" mit seinen Sendungen. Am 27. Juli 1941 brachte er einen neuen Aufruf des Zentralkomitees der Bulgarischen Arbeiterpartei: „Mit den anderen Völkern gegen den Faschismus kämpfen und zu seiner Niederlage beitragen bedeutet Kampf für unsere eigene Freiheit und Unabhängigkeit, für eine wahre und völlig nationale Einheit, für brüderliche Verständigung mit den übrigen Balkanvölkern . . . Laßt uns unverzüglich handeln, mit allen Mitteln handeln, laßt uns das Hinterland der faschistischen Bande zerstören! Wir wollen den deutschen Faschisten kein Getreide und keine Produkte geben, und das, was sie und ihre bulgarischen Helfershelfer uns mit Zwang nehmen, wollen wir mit allen möglichen Mitteln vernichten! Für die Faschisten soll ‚eine unerträgliche Atmosphäre‘ geschaffen werden."

Sabotagegruppen entstanden in Städten und Dörfern. Im Gebiet von Plovdiv operierten die großen Partisaneneinheiten „Christo Botev" und „Anton Ivanow". Ebenfalls entstanden dort feste Stützpunkte des bewaffneten Kampfes.

Am 17. Juli 1942 wurde das Programm der Vaterländischen Front verkündet, das vom Auslandsbüro des Zentralkomitees der Bulgarischen Arbeiterpartei unter der Leitung von Georgi Dimitroff ausgearbeitet worden war. Als Hauptaufgabe wurde herausgestellt: Verhinderung der Beteiligung Bulgariens am Krieg, Abzug der bulgarischen Truppen aus Jugoslawien und Griechenland, Beseitigung der sogenannten deutschen Okkupanten im eigenen Land, die Einstellung der Unterstützung Deutschlands mit Lebensmitteln und Rohstoffen, die Herstellung der Freundschaft und der Zusammenarbeit mit der Sowjetunion und den Balkanvölkern. Die Umstellung des damals in Bulgarien herrschenden Systems wurde gefordert. Die „antifaschistischen" Kämpfer sollten aus der Haft entlassen, die sogenannten demokratischen Rechte des Volkes wiederhergestellt werden. Weiter wurde gefordert, die „faschistischen" Organisationen aufzulösen und die Armee von dem „Monarcho-faschistischen" Einfluß zu befreien. Schließlich wurde die soziale Verbesserung für das bulgarische Volk als weiterer Programmpunkt herausgestellt.

Hundert Komitees der Vaterländischen Front entstanden im Laufe der Zeit. Von Januar bis Juni 1942 fanden 31 Sabotage- und Diversionsakte sowie bewaffnete Überfälle usw. statt. Bis Oktober 1942 zählen wir eine Steigerung der Aktionen auf 242.

Griechenland

Auch in Griechenland darf die Bedeutung des von Moskau gesteuerten Widerstandes nicht übersehen werden. Das Zentralkomitee der Kommunistischen Partei Griechenlands forderte am 1. Juni 1941 zur Befreiung des Landes von der deutschen und italienischen Besatzungsmacht sowie zur

Unterstützung der Sowjetunion auf. Eine provisorische Regierung sollte gebildet und eine konstituierende Versammlung einberufen werden. Im September 1941 wurde zum Zusammenschluß aller nationalen Kräfte und zum Kampf mit allen Mitteln des Streiks, der Sabotage und des bewaffneten Kampfes aufgerufen.

Die Kommunistische Partei, die Bauernpartei, die Sozialistische Partei, die Volksdemokratische Union und die Sozialdemokratische Partei schlossen sich zur Nationalen Befreiungsfront (EAM) zusammen. Diese sollte zum Träger des Partisanenkampfes in Griechenland werden.

Anfang 1942 entstand die ELAS als Befreiungsarmee, d. h. als bewaffnete Organisation der EAM.

Rumänien

Von der Regierung Ceausescu wird herausgestellt, daß die Kommunistische Partei führend gegen das Antonescu-Regime und die im Lande befindlichen deutschen Truppen war. Am 27. Juni 1941 forderte die Kommunistische Partei zum Sturz der ,,Militärfaschistischen Diktatur" und zur Beendigung des Kampfes gegen die Sowjetunion auf. Am 8. Juni 1941 stellte sie heraus: ,,Die historische Aufgabe und die Verantwortung der Kommunistischen Partei Rumäniens gegenüber dem rumänischen Volk gebieten, Seite an Seite mit dem großen Sowjetvolk und mit den anderen vergewaltigten Völkern in Rumänien den Kampf für den Sturz des deutschen blutigen Faschismus und seiner Helfershelfer aus allen Ländern zu organisieren, für die Verjagung der deutschen Besatzung aus Rumänien, für die Vernichtung der Verräterbande, die sich, mit Antonescu an der Spitze, des Staatsruders bemächtigt hat, für die Befreiung des Landes vom blutigen deutschen Joch, für den Sieg der Sowjetunion und für ein freies und unabhängiges Rumänien."

Zur Organisierung des Partisanenkampfes wurde am 6. September 1941 aufgerufen. Proklamiert wurde, ,,es sei Pflicht eines jeden rumänischen Patrioten, der die Freiheit und Unabhängigkeit des rumänischen Volkes liebt, die Kriegsproduktion, den Transport von Munition, Waffen und Armeen für den blutigen Unterdrücker des rumänischen Volkes, für den Krieg Hitlers zu verhindern. Seine Pflicht ist es", so heißt es in dem Aufruf weiter, ,,mit der Waffe in der Hand gegen die Hitlerarmee zu kämpfen".

Hingewiesen wurde auf diesen Aufruf in einem Referat auf der Internationalen Konferenz der Geschichte der Widerstandsbewegung vom 15.–19. April 1962.

Zunächst trat der Widerstand durch die Tätigkeit kleiner Gruppen hervor. Partisanenabteilungen bildeten sich später heraus, so daß am Anfang

Sabotageakte die Störung der Produktion und die Aufklärungsarbeit zur Sammlung der Antonescu-feindlichen Kräfte im Vordergrund stand.

Am 11. Juli 1942 wurde das Munitionslager am Rande der Stadt Bacau und ein deutsches Treibstofflager in Brand gesetzt. Dadurch wurde eine große Anzahl von Waggons von Munition und Flugzeugbenzin vernichtet. Das Arsenal in Tirgoviste wurde im Sommer des Jahres 1942 zerstört. Ende 1942 flog die Waffenfabrik in Avrik in die Luft. Anfang 1943 wurde eine nicht unbeträchtliche Menge Artilleriemunition in den Werken von Mirsa zerstört. In den Lemaitrewerken machten Arbeiter wichtige, für die Armee bestimmte Teile unbenutzbar und verursachten zahlreiche Fertigungsfehler. Die Arbeiter in den Reschitzawerken sabotierten die Arbeit tagelang. Kanonen und Kampfwagen wurden unbrauchbar gemacht. Eisenbahnarbeiter aus Bukarest, Temeschburg, Arad, Simeria, Ploesti und Kronstadt verhinderten Truppen- und Waffentransporte an der Front. Sie erreichten dies, indem sie das Heißlaufen der Wagenachsen verursachten. Die Waffenfabrik in Avrik flog Ende 1942 in die Luft. Vernichtet wurde auch das Waffenlager in Tirgoviste. Auf der Strecke Bukarest–Konstanza ließen Eisenbahner Züge mit deutschen Truppen und Waffen entgleisen.

Über den Anfang der Widerstandsbewegung berichtete Gh. Matei in seiner Arbeit ,,Die Hitlerpolitik in Rumänien und der Kampf des rumänischen Volkes für den Sturz der faschistischen Regierung und gegen das Hitlerregime": ,,Bereits in den ersten Kriegstagen ist in Constanza eine Reihe von Sabotageaktionen organisiert worden; als erste die Zerstörung der Kabel, die die deutschen Luftabwehranlagen mit elektrischem Strom zu speisen hatten. Einen Monat später waren die Deutschen über den Umstand besorgt, daß im Prahova-Tal die ,Lage' wegen der zahlreichen Sabotageakte ,unerträglich' ist."

Tschechoslowakei

Dieselbe strategische Bedeutung wie Albanien im Hinblick auf das Mittelmeer nimmt die Tschechoslowakei zu den Ländern Südosteuropas ein. In der Auseinandersetzung mit der Entwicklung der Tschechoslowakei im Zweiten Weltkrieg findet sich wie für die südosteuropäischen Länder die These:

,,Der Schutz und die Verteidigung des ersten sozialistischen Staates der Welt, dessen Existenz den proletarischen Klassenkampf in den kapitalistischen Staaten beflügelte und erleichterte, war eine Voraussetzung für den Sieg des Sozialismus in anderen Ländern. Es war deshalb auch nicht zufällig, daß die imperialistischen Großmächte Hitlerdeutschland bis 1939 und sogar in der ersten Periode des Zweiten Weltkrieges freie Hand im Osten gegeben hatten. Das haben die kommunistischen Parteien, das hat die Arbeiterklasse in den verschiedenen Ländern begriffen, und das haben letztlich auch andere Schichten des Volkes erkannt, die in der Widerstands- und Partisanenbewegung wirksam wurden. Von den Aktionen ,,Hände weg von Sowjetrußland!" in den Jahren der ausländischen Intervention nach 1917 bis zum mächtigen Aufschwung der Widerstandsbewegung nach dem 22. Juni 1941 zur Unterstützung der Sowjetunion und der Roten Armee führt ein direkter Weg des proletarischen Internationalismus.

Deshalb versuchten die Nazis, dem beim Überfall auf die Sowjetunion am 22. Juni 1941 zu erwartenden Aufschwung der antifaschistischen Widerstandsbewegung zuvorzukommen, und leiteten eine große Verfolgungsaktion gegen die Mitglieder der kommunistischen Parteien in allen europäischen Ländern ein."

Am 15. März 1939 veröffentlichte bereits die Kommunistische Partei der Tschechoslowakei einen Aufruf, in welchem es heißt: ,,Die Arbeiterklasse, die schon so oft in den ersten Reihen der nationalen Verteidigung stand, wird jetzt wieder zur festen Stütze der nationalen Widerstandsbewegung. Die Kommunisten . . . erklären vor dem ganzen Volk, daß sie aufopferungsvoll und tapfer in der Vorhut des nationalen Widerstandes um die Wiederherstellung der Freiheit und Unabhängigkeit der tschechoslowakischen Nation kämpfen werden."

Am 28. Oktober 1939 kam es anläßlich des Jahrestages der Gründung der ersten Tschechoslowakischen Republik zu Kundgebungen und Zusammenstößen in Prag, Ostrau, Kladno und anderen Städten. Im Herbst 1939 begannen Sabotageakte in der Rüstungsproduktion. Die Arbeitsproduktivität wurde gesenkt.

Vorgeworfen wird der Geheimen Staatspolizei, daß sie von Anfang 1940 bis Frühjahr 1941 in Böhmen ungefähr 1800 und in Mähren etwa 2500 kommunistische Funktionäre inhaftierte. Hervorgehoben wird, daß es den Sicherheitsorganen gelang, das erste illegale Zentralkomitee im Lande zu verhaften. Die Exekution seiner Mitglieder wird angeprangert.

Im Jahre 1942 begann der Partisanenkrieg. In einem Aufruf wurden die Tschechen aufgefordert, sich daran zu beteiligen. Wortwörtlich heißt es in ihm, daß der große, grandioseste Schicksalskampf der ganzen Geschichte, den die Rote Armee mit den Horden faschistischer Bestien im Osten führe, auch der Kampf für die Zukunft, für das Schicksal, für die Freiheit sei.

Die ersten Partisanenabteilungen bildeten sich aus Arbeitern, Bauern, deportierten Soldaten der slowakischen Armee und entflohenen Häftlingen aus Konzentrationslagern.

Berichtet wird, daß Heinrich Fanfera und Hans Schwarz zur Unterstützung des Untergrundkampfes in die Tschechoslowakei gesandt wurden.

In der Slowakei wurde Ende 1941 von dem illegalen Zentralkomitee der Kommunistischen Partei der Slowakei Richtlinien zur Gründung von Partisanengruppen gegeben. Die ersten bezeichneten sich als Janosik-Kampfgruppen nach der slowakischen legendären Gestalt Janosik.

Der Verlag Orbis in Prag brachte eine Dokumentensammlung ,,Die kämpfende Tschechoslowakei", bearbeitet von Jiři Dolezal und Jan Krčn heraus, die aus Prager Sicht einen Überblick über die Ereignisse von 1938–1945 gibt. Die Abtretung der Gebiete, die durch das Münchner Abkommen zu Deutschland kamen und zum größten Teil von Deutschen bewohnt wurden, wird als Raub bezeichnet.

Im Dezemberaufruf der Illegalen Partei der Tschechoslowakei an das gesamte tschechische Volk wird geschrieben: ,,Die barbarische Handlungsweise der Hitlerfaschisten und Okkupanten ist in den letzten Tagen gegen das ganze tschechische Volk gerichtet... Der Kampf geht weiter – die faschistischen Horden haben den Trauerzug unserer heldenhaften Studenten, die ihrem in der Aktion des 28. Oktobers bestialisch ermordeten Kameraden die letzte Ehre erweisen wollten, in roher Weise überfallen. Die Studenten leisteten dem nazistischen Feind Widerstand. Die Hitlerknechte rächen sich grausam. Nach dem Muster der amerikanischen Gangster überfielen sie ein Studentenheim und die angrenzenden Gebäude; sie marterten und verschleppten alle seine Bewohner in ihre Gefängnisse."

Der Chef der Sicherheitspolizei und des SD in Prag berichtete am 16. September 1940: ,,Die Kommunistische Partei der Tschechoslowakei (KPČ) bildet eine besondere Sektion der Komintern und ist nicht der deutschen Sektion angeschlossen. Durch die langjährige Zersetzungstätigkeit der Kommunisten in der alten ČSR hatten sie die Möglichkeit, sich auf den illegalen Kampf vorzubereiten. Im Protektorat finden wir daher eine kommunistische Bewegung, die sich auf breite Widerstandskräfte der tschechischen Bevölkerung stützt. Wenn z. B. im Bereich der Staatspolizeileitstelle Brünn seit Beginn dieses Jahres 2500 kommunistische Funktionäre festgenommen wurden, so deutet dies auf eine fest fundierte Organisation hin, die einen breiten Boden in der Bevölkerung besitzt. Demzufolge bestand und besteht auch heute noch trotz häufiger Zerschlagung eine geschlossene kommunistische Partei der ČSR. Böhmen allein besteht aus acht, Mähren aus fünf Kreisen der illegalen KPČ. Die Kreise sind wieder in Bezirke, Stadtleitungen, Ortsgruppen und Fünfergruppen untergeteilt. Neben dieser regional gegliederten Organisation bestehen innerhalb der KPČ ein organisatorischer, ein politischer und ein technischer Apparat, die getrennt voneinander arbeiten. Wie im Altreich nach der Machtübernahme gelingt es den Staatspolizeistellen des Protektorats immer wieder, der KPČ heftige Schläge zu versetzen und ihre Organisation zu zerschlagen. Als Folge zeigt sich auch hier, wie aus der Statistik in Abschnitt V ersichtlich, eine abnehmende Tätigkeit. Die alten geschulten Funktionäre lassen sich eben, sobald sie festgenommen sind, nicht so leicht ersetzen. Es fehlt der KPČ an Nachwuchs. Wenn andere Umstände nicht hinzutreten, kann man den Schluß ziehen, daß die Tätigkeit der KPČ für die Zukunft im Abnehmen begriffen ist."

Über den Besuch Dr. Hachas in Berlin im Jahre 1939 haben Historiker schon viel geschrieben. Nicht erwähnt wird aber, daß der in London lebende, damalige Expräsident Dr. Benesch in den ersten Kriegsjahren durch Vermittlung illegaler tschechischer Organisationen mit dem Präsidenten Dr. Hacha und einigen Mitgliedern der Protektoratsregierung Verbindungen unterhielt. Der Deckname für Hacha ist Havel, für Ingenieur Elias, der von 1939 bis 1941 Vorsitzender der Protektoratsregierung war, Porok. Letzteren verhaftete die deutsche Behörde noch 1941. Elias wurde später hingerichtet.

Dr. Benesch führte am 24. Juni 1941 aus: ,,Übergeben Sie bitte diese Botschaft sofort an Havel und Porok und verlangen Sie von ihnen Antwort für mich. – Der Krieg tritt jetzt in eine neue entscheidende Phase. Das, was geschieht, wird schon großen innenpolitischen Einfluß haben und über unsere weitere Entwicklung entscheiden. Die Teilnahme der Slowaken an dem Krieg gegen Rußland wird bei ihnen alles desorganisieren und wird für die Slowakei katastrophale Folgen haben. Die tschechischen Länder müssen das unter allen Umständen vermeiden.

Im Interesse der Ehre des Volkes, im Interesse seiner Einheit in der Nachkriegszeit und um gleich nach dem Krieg einen heftigen Streit zu vermeiden und besonders um dem Kommunismus keinen Vorwand und keine Ursache zu geben, auf Grund von berechtigten Vorwürfen, wir hätten Hitler geholfen, die Macht zu erobern, müssen Sie Ihre Politik überprüfen und definitive Maßnahmen treffen. Von heute an dürfen unsere führenden Leute, darf die Regierung und selbstverständlich auch der Präsident in keiner Form nachgeben. Es ist gefährlich, dadurch, daß Sie die Interessen der Nation irgendwie wahren wollen, den Eindruck zu erwecken, daß Sie den Nationalsozialismus unterstützen oder ihm im Kriege gegen Rußland helfen. England und Amerika gehen heute mit Rußland, wir sind dort, wo wir im Jahre 1938 hätten sein sollen. München ist diplomatisch und politisch wiedergutgemacht, und es ist notwendig, aus dieser neuen Situation die Konsequenzen zu ziehen.

Im Januar 1941 richtete Klement Gottwald aus Moskau an das illegale Zentralkomitee der Kommunistischen Partei der Tschechoslowakei eine Funkdepesche. Aus ihr darf entnommen werden: „Die gegenwärtige Kriegslage ist durch verstärkte Tendenzen zur Ausbreitung des Krieges und Einbeziehung aller imperialistischen Großmächte in den Kampf um die Neuaufteilung der Welt gekennzeichnet. Die Propaganda über einen bereits sicheren Sieg Englands oder Deutschlands ist ein Bluff. Auch die sog. europäische Ordnung unter deutscher Führung ist nur ein Wunschtraum der Nazis.

Alles hängt von der weiteren Entwicklung des Krieges ab. Die Kräfte der imperialistischen Gegner werden erschöpft, während die revolutionären Kräfte wachsen. Der Standpunkt der Sowjetunion bleibt auch weiterhin selbständig und wachsam.

Innenpolitisch muß nach allen Richtungen mit einer verschärften Germanisierung der tschechischen Länder gerechnet werden. Massenaussiedlungen der tschechischen Bevölkerung einschließlich der Bauern, so wie es die Okkupanten in Polen und Lothringen praktizieren, sind nicht ausgeschlossen. Die Germanisierungsbestrebungen gehen mit den an die tschechische Bourgeoisie gerichteten schmeichelhaftesten Verlockungen Hand in Hand. Die von Goebbels geleitete Kampagne um die sog. Reichsgesinnung der Tschechen ist als Beispiel anzusehen.

Die bisherigen Siege Deutschlands und dessen vermeintlich feste Herrschaft über das kapitalistische Europa verursachen im tschechischen Lager einen Zwiespalt über den weiteren unvermeidlichen Weg des Volkes. Der Hauptteil der Bourgeoisie, die nicht emigrierte, empfiehlt aus gewinnsüchtigen und Klassengründen die Ergebenheit an Berlin und schildert sie als den einzigen Weg zur Erhaltung der Nation. Als Beispiel dient die Loyalitätskampagne des Národní souručenství.

Unsere Linie im Kampfe für die nationale Befreiung der tschechischen Nation bleibt unverändert. Dabei tritt immer klarer der Zusammenhang zwischen der nationalen und der sozialen Befreiung, zwischen nationaler

Befreiung und Sozialismus hervor. Die Arbeiterklasse an der Spitze mit der Kommunistischen Partei der Tschechoslowakei hat jetzt große Möglichkeiten, die Führung der nationalen Befreiungsbewegung zu gewinnen.

1941 erließ das illegale Zentralkomitee der Kommunistischen Partei der Slowakei das sogenannte Organisationsstatut der Jánošík-Kampfgemeinschaften, in dem festgestellt wird:

„...Die deutschen Imperialisten wollen in diesem Kriege alle kleinen Völker Europas vernichten, vor allem jedoch die slawischen Völker. – Dieser teuflische Plan wird jedoch den blutigen germanischen Kannibalen nicht gelingen. In allen von den Deutschen okkupierten Ländern wächst von Tag zu Tag eine Massenwiderstandsbewegung gegen die verhaßten Eindringlinge. Es naht die entscheidende Stunde, in der die breiten Massen nicht mehr die faschistische Unterdrückung werden ertragen können und es ihnen gleichgültig sein wird, ob sie unter den Füßen der fremden Schinder Hungers sterben oder lieber im Partisanenkampf gegen sie als Helden fallen. Die kommunistische Partei ist jedoch davon überzeugt, daß kein Patriot und tapferer Slowake den Deutschen zuliebe als demütiges Lamm Hungers sterben wird, er wird auch nicht für ihre barbarischen Interessen an der Ostfront verbluten, sondern lieber in die Jánošík-Partisanengemeinschaften eintreten, wo er zusammen mit den tschechischen, polnischen und ungarischen Partisanen entschlossen und mannhaft gegen die deutschen Okkupanten, gegen Unrecht und Gewalt, für nationale und soziale Freiheit, für Brüderlichkeit unter den Völkern und für ein neues, glückliches Leben und einen ewigen Frieden kämpfen wird!"

Die Sicherheitspolizei

beurteilte die Tätigkeit der illegalen Kommunistischen Partei im Protektorat im Jahre 1941 wie folgt:

„War die Errichtung des Protektorats in den Augen des tschechischen Intrigantentums eine Okkupation, die es bei Gelegenheit abzuschütteln galt, so sah das Tschechentum beim Eintritt der Sowjetunion in den Krieg das Zeichen zum aktiven Kampf gegen den Nationalsozialismus. Insbesondere die illegale Kommunistische Partei (K.P.Č.) arbeitete unter Einsatz aller zur Verfügung stehenden Mittel an der Revolutionierung des tschechischen Volkes und an der intensiven Vorbereitung zum bewaffneten Aufstand. Dabei gingen die Kommunisten mit unverschämter Offenheit vor. So wurden in zwei Fällen illegale kommunistische Druckschriften sogar auf offener Straße verteilt.

Allein aus der Beobachtung der Propaganda war deutlich die Entwicklung der politischen Lage zu erkennen. Ende Juni 1941 wurde in Aufrufen des Zentralorgans der illegalen K.P.Č., „Rudé právo", die Arbeiterschaft zum einheitlichen Kampf aufgerufen und dabei erstmalig die Waffe des Generalstreiks erwähnt.

Ende Juli erschienen bereits Flugblätter, die die von Stalin in seiner Rede vom 3. Juli 1941 aufgezeigte nationale Linie enthalten und in denen in klarer Form zu Sabotageakten aufgefordert wurde. Die illegale Arbeit in den Betrieben wurde mehr und mehr intensiviert. Allein im Bereich der Staatspolizeileitstelle Prag wurden über 20 kommunistische Betriebszellenorganisationen, vorwiegend in Rüstungsbetrieben, festgestellt, wovon die stärksten im Industriegebiet Kladno als Schacht- und Hüttenorganisationen und in den Škoda-Werken in Pilsen aufgezogen worden waren.

Mitte August 1941 wurde die Flugblattpropaganda weiterhin intensiviert, wobei vorwiegend die Arbeiter zu Streiks und Sabotagehandlungen aufgefordert wurden. Im Rahmen dieser Propagandaaktion wurden Zufahrtsstraßen zu größeren Industriewerken regelmäßig mit Streuzetteln belegt, in denen zum Generalstreik aufgefordert wurde. Die Folge dieser systematischen Streikhetze waren verschiedene Arbeitsniederlegungen in Betrieben, vorwiegend Rüstungsbetrieben, darunter die geschlossene Arbeitsniederlegung von 2000 Arbeitern der „Walter-Flugzeugmotorenwerke". Nur durch scharfen, rücksichtslosen Zugriff war es möglich, diese Arbeitsniederlegungen, als deren Ursache in fast allen Fällen geringe Lebensmittelzuteilung und niedrige Löhne von den Arbeitern vorgeschoben worden waren, in Grenzen zu halten.

Im Laufe des Septembers ging die kommunistische Propaganda dazu über, in Anlehnung an die ausländischen Funksendungen konkrete Einzelanweisungen zur Sabotage zu erteilen. Die Verhältnisse hatten sich bis dahin soweit zugespitzt, daß im Protektorat in Kürze mit einem bewaffneten Aufstand zu rechnen war. Von der illegalen K.P.Č. waren bereits Anweisungen zur Beschaffung von Waffen und Sprengstoffen ergangen.

Die Verhängung des Ausnahmezustandes und die Einführung der Standgerichte Ende September 1941 wirkten geradezu schockartig auf die kommunistische Tätigkeit, die zunächst vollkommen verschwand und erst in den letzten Oktobertagen wieder langsam auflebte. Doch machte sich die systematische Zerschlagung der kommunistischen Funktionärkörper deutlich bemerkbar. Der vorhergehenden Aufrollung der Zentralleitung der illegalen KPČ einschließlich der ihr unterstellten Apparate, wie funktechnischer Apparat, Paßfälscherapparat, Finanzapparat und Zentralverbindungsapparat, war im September die Aushebung eines technischen Apparates der KPČ in Prag gefolgt, wobei u. a. über 100 kg Drucktypen und mehrere Klischees für den Druck von Führerkarikaturen sichergestellt werden konnten.

Unter dem Druck der Ereignisse beschritt die illegale kommunistische Bewegung hinsichtlich ihrer illegalen Massenarbeit völlig neue Wege. Hatte sie vor Beginn des deutsch-sowjetrussischen Krieges eine Zusammenarbeit mit der tschechischen Widerstandsbewegung schärfstens abgelehnt, so versuchte sie nunmehr, mit dieser zur Erhöhung ihrer Schlagkraft eine gemeinsame Basis zu erhalten. Diese immer mehr sich herauskristallisierende Linie zeigte sich am deutlichsten in einem Ende Oktober erschienenen Aufruf der Zentralleitung der illegalen KPČ, in dem die Gründung eines nationalrevolutionären Ausschusses veröffentlicht wurde. Gemäß dieser neuen Haltung verschwanden die kommunistischen Parolen vollkommen aus der Propaganda, die sich national tarnte. In gemeinsamen Aufrufen der Zentralausschüsse der KPČ und des tschechoslowakischen nationalen Widerstandes wurde die Bildung nationalrevolutionärer Ausschüsse unterzeichnet, die das gesamte tschechische Volk ohne Rücksicht auf die soziale, politische und religiöse Zugehörigkeit zusammenfassen sollten. Die vereinheitlichte Kampfführung wirkte sich im Auslande insofern aus, als vom ehemaligen Staatspräsidenten der ČSR, Beneš, auch frühere kommunistische Abgeordnete in den Staatsrat der tschechischen Emigrantenregierung aufgenommen wurden.

Es ist verständlich, daß nach Beginn des deutsch-sowjetrussischen Krieges mit der zunehmenden illegalen kommunistischen Propagandatätigkeit auch die Sabotagetätigkeit im Protektorat anstieg und im Vergleich zum Reichsgebiet wesentlich stärker bemerkbar wurde. Das Vorwiegen von Bremsschlauchdurchschneidungen ist auf die verhältnismäßig starken roten Eisenbahnorganisationen zurückzuführen.

Ende Oktober 1941 gelang es, einen kommunistischen Terrorapparat auszuheben, der unter der Leitung eines Juden mit der fabrikationsmäßigen Herstellung von Brandsätzen und Sprengkörpern begonnen hatte. Die Herstellung hatte der tschechische Besitzer eines Rüstungsbetriebes übernommen. Bei der Aktion wurden 106 größtenteils fertiggestellte Brandsätze erfaßt. Sechs waren Ende September bei der Ausführung von Sabotageakten bereits verwendet worden. Die Terrorgruppe hatte schon zu tschechischen Kommunisten in der Ostmark Verbindung aufgenommen."

Vielsagend ist ein Bericht des Befehlshabers der Sicherheitspolizei und des SD über die Tätigkeit der Kommunistischen Partei der Tschechoslowakei in Böhmen und Mähren und im slowakischen Staat über das Jahr 1943:

„Die Kommunistische Partei der Tschechoslowakei, die als Sektion der Komintern in ihrer legalen Zeit die ihr von Moskau zugesprochene Aufgabe, die Tschechoslowakei als Basis des Kommunismus im Herzen Europas auszubauen, mit allen politischen und konspirativen Methoden zu verwirklichen suchte, bildete vor der Schaffung des Protektorats den Hauptrückhalt für die deutsche kommunistische Emigration und für die illegale Arbeit der Kommunistischen Partei Deutschlands von außen. Sie verfügte stets über eine gute legale Organisation, die sich in Geheimapparaten der Partei bis zu einer gewissen Vollendung verfeinerte.

Vom Gegner aus betrachtet, war es für die KPČ eine Selbstverständlichkeit, die illegale Arbeit nach der Schaffung des Protektorats mit erhöhten Anstrengungen fortzusetzen. Es erübrigt sich, die verschiedenen Phasen der Zerschlagung der illegalen KPČ seit 1938, bei der Tausende von Funktionären erfaßt wurden, zurückblickend darzulegen. In den Vordergrund rückt die Betrachtung des Kommunismus im Protektorat seit dem Beginn des Krieges.

Die Zielsetzung der Kommunistischen Partei der Tschechoslowakei erstreckte sich – 1942 beginnend –

a) auf die Gewinnung aller Tschechen und –

b) auf den korporativen Zusammenschluß sämtlicher illegal tätiger Gegnergruppen,

um gemeinsam die ,,Nationale Revolution" und den ,,Freiheitskampf" des tschechischen Volkes durchzuführen. Unter diesen weitgefaßten Plänen vollzogen sich auch die in sich abgeschlossenen, wiederholten Aufbauversuche des kommunistischen Parteiapparates.

Auf illegaler Basis wurde der überparteiliche ,,Zentrale nationalrevolutionäre Ausschuß der Tschechoslowakei" gebildet, dem der ,,Zentralausschuß der Kommunistischen Partei der Tschechoslowakei" und andere Verbände des ,,heimatlichen Abwehrkampfes" angeschlossen wurden. Der Führungsanspruch der Kommunisten war, ohne nach außen hin festgelegt zu sein, praktisch durch die Stärke und durch die Aggressivität der KPČ gegeben.

Diese Vereinheitlichung der Gegner mit der Schaffung einer Dachorganisation paßte einerseits in die von der Komintern gegebene nationalrevolutionäre Ausrichtung des Kommunismus und bildete andererseits die Grundlage für die national ausgerichtete kommunistische Parteipropaganda.

Das Jahr 1943 brachte in Böhmen und Mähren die ständig fortlaufende Zerschlagung des illegalen kommunistischen Parteiapparates, bei der das Hauptgewicht

a) auf das Erkennen der Struktur der illegalen KPČ und

b) auf die Ergreifung des Funktionärkörpers gelegt wurde.

Der regional erkannte Aufbau der Partei führte zur Festnahme der zentralen Landesleitung und der Leitungen für Böhmen und Mähren. Diesen Festnahmen schlossen sich in laufenden umfassenden Zugriffen die Festnahmen der illegalen Gebiets- und Kreisleitungen an. Diese erstreckten sich über das gesamte Land. Sie wurden bis zum Ende des Jahres 1943 mit anhaltender Stärke, nunmehr auch auf kleinere Parteieinheiten übergehend, in planvoller Arbeit fortgesetzt.

Außer den Erkenntnissen, die über die Verbindungen zum „Zentralen nationalrevolutionären Ausschuß" Aufschluß gaben, waren folgende bedeutend:

a) die Zusammenarbeit mit aus Moskau eingesetzten Agenten,

b) das Erkennen der Sabotage- und Terrororganisationen der KPČ im Rahmen der Partei,

c) die Aufdeckung der Verbindung der KPČ mit den Kommunisten in der Slowakei,

d) die Zusammenarbeit der Kommunisten mit geflüchteten russischen Kriegsgefangenen.

Diese vier Erkenntnisse bildeten jeweils die Grundlage für wiederum umfassende exekutive Zugriffe.

Die KPČ verfügte bei dem Zugriff über Spezialabteilungen, „Apparate", die, teils errichtet, teils in den Anfängen stehend, bis zu den Untergliederungen durchorganisiert waren.

Von diesen Spezialapparaten interessieren neben den Einrichtungen, die eine kommunistische Partei auch während ihres legalen Bestehens illegal führt, Stoßtrupps für die Waffen- und Sprengstoffbeschaffung, teils unter dem Begriff „Partisanen" zusammengefaßt, Erkundungs- und Spionagetrupps und die kommunistischen Kader in der Protektoratspolizei und in sämtlichen sonstigen Zweigen der Protektoratsverwaltung.

Sicherstellung von Waffen und Sprengstoffen aller Art und von Kurzwellentelefonsendern ergaben wiederholt Aufschluß über die technisch gute Ausrüstung der KPČ.

In Böhmen und Mähren hatten sich nach den polizeilichen Maßnahmen nach dem Attentat auf den stellvertretenden Reichsprotektor und weiter bedingt durch den scharfen Zugriff der Polizei bei der Aufrollung illegaler Organisationen Interessengemeinschaften illegal aufhältlicher Funktionäre aus verschiedenen politischen Gruppen gebildet. Diese schlossen sich unter dem in der Tschechoslowakei seit dem Weltkrieg 1914–1918 zum Begriff gewordenen Namen „Grüner Kader" zusammen. Der Zusammenschluß erfolgte teils der Not gehorchend, teils war er die Auswirkung der Aufrufe des sowjetischen Rundfunks an das tschechische Volk, die Arbeitsplätze zu verlassen und in den Wäldern „Partisanenarbeit" zu leisten.

Wiederholte Aktionen führten zur Aushebung verschiedener Bunker und Höhlen, zur Erfassung der Insassen und erheblichen Materials von Waffen und Sprengstoff.

Die illegalen, ausgebauten Waldlager sollten die Ausgangspunkte der

305

Sabotage- und Terrortätigkeit und damit die Anfänge einer Bandentätigkeit bilden. Auch hier haben die frühzeitigen Zugriffe die Pläne des Gegners zunichte gemacht.

Die Tätigkeit der Kommunistischen Partei der Tschechoslowakei hat sich in der gleichen Ausrichtung im Sudetengau gezeigt. Die ständige Ergänzung der Exekutivarbeit der Dienststellen der Sicherheitspolizei im Protektorat mit denen im Sudetengau war auch hier erfolgreich.

Im Protektorat haben das ständige Schritthalten und die wiederholt präventiv dem Gegner vorgreifenden Exekutivmaßnahmen der Sicherheitspolizei den in sich stark und straff organisierten Kommunismus als direkte Gefahr stets ausschalten können."

Nach der Erhebung der Slowakei zum selbständigen Staat versuchten die slowakischen Funktionäre der Kommunistischen Partei der Tschechoslowakei, die illegale Arbeit als selbständige „Kommunistische Partei der Slowakei" fortzusetzen. Eine im Januar 1940 gebildete Landesleitung der kommunistischen Partei für die Slowakei setzte die kommunistische Arbeit in der Art der tschechischen kommunistischen Partei fort. Die regionale Einteilung der Partei hielt sich an das bis dahin bestehende Muster.

Eine Anerkennung der Kommunistischen Partei der Slowakei durch die Komintern als selbständige Sektion erfolgte nicht.

In den von dem früheren Parteiführer und Vertreter der Kommunistischen Partei der Tschechoslowakei bei der Komintern gefaßten Beschluß über die Aktivierung der kommunistischen Arbeit in der ehemaligen Tschechoslowakei wurde die Slowakei einbezogen. Im April 1941 wurden entsprechende Funktionäre von Moskau aus eingesetzt. Sie waren mit Richtlinien versehen, die für die Parteipolitik maßgebend waren. Die bisherige Propaganda für die Eingliederung der Slowakei in den Sowjetstaat wurde zurückgestellt; dafür wurde die Errichtung eines „Nationalen Sowjetstaates der Slowakei" zur Aktionslosung.

Durch die aufgedeckten Verbindungen der Kommunisten im Protektorat zur Slowakei wurde die Struktur des illegalen Parteiapparates der Slowakei erkannt. In gemeinsamer Arbeit der deutschen und slowakischen Polizei wurden die illegalen kommunistischen Gruppen in der Slowakei nachhaltig zerstört. Die große Zahl jüdischer Funktionäre und die Mitarbeiter der Intelligenz in den kommunistischen Organisationen fiel besonders auf. Die bereits abgeschlossen gewesenen Versuche der Schaffung direkter Funktionärverbindungen über die damalige russische Grenze bei Lemberg nach Moskau wurden verhindert.

In der Slowakei gelangten die Einheitsbestrebungen der Kommunisten später zu einem Erfolg, der die Bedeutung und die Gefahr des Kommunismus auch hier herausstellte.

Die bis zum Ende des Jahres 1943 fortgesetzten Exekutivmaßnahmen gegen die kommunistischen Gruppen in der Slowakei haben bewiesen, daß die illegale Tätigkeit den organisatorischen Umfang des im Jahre 1941 zerschlagenen kommunistischen Parteiapparates nicht mehr erreichen konnte."

Aus den Maitagen des Jahres 1943 (4. Mai 1943) liegt ein Brief des späteren Generalsekretärs N. S. Chruschtschow und N. Watutin an Oberst Svoboda vor. Das Schreiben lautet:

,,Herr Oberst!

Am 29. April 1943 haben wir Ihre Einheit besucht, um denjenigen Soldaten und Offizieren staatliche Auszeichnungen zu übergeben, die sich in den Kämpfen gegen unseren gemeinsamen Feind, gegen die deutschen faschistischen Okkupanten, ausgezeichnet haben.

Während des Aufenthaltes bei Ihrer Einheit haben wir uns mit der Organisation der Ausbildung und der Vorbereitung für die neuen Kämpfe gegen den Hitler-Faschismus vertraut gemacht.

Sie waren zu dieser Zeit dienstlich zur Verhandlung über Dienstsachen und zur Übernahme einer hohen staatlichen Auszeichnung, des Lenin-Ordens, nach Moskau berufen worden. Über Ersuchen Ihrer Offiziere haben wir die Dekorierung der Offiziere und Soldaten, die sich in den Kämpfen ausgezeichnet haben, bis zu Ihrer Rückkehr verschoben.

Ihre Einheit hat den Befehl zum sofortigen Übergang auf einen anderen Abschnitt erhalten. Wir bedauern daher sehr, daß wir keine Möglichkeit haben, die Soldaten und Offiziere, unsere Freunde, zu dekorieren, die an unserer Front gemeinsam mit der Roten Armee in harten Kämpfen gegen die deutschen Okkupanten im Raume Charkow kühn, tapfer und opfermütig gekämpft haben.

Wir halten es daher für besser, den kühnen Offizieren und Soldaten, die sich in den Kämpfen ausgezeichnet haben, die staatlichen Orden in Ihrer Anwesenheit zu übergeben. Wir haben das Einverständnis unseres Kommandos erhalten, Ihrer Einheit die Auszeichnungen erst auf dem neuen Standort zu übergeben. Die Übergabe wird in kürzester Zeit durch die Regierung aus Moskau erfolgen. Wir werden auch weiterhin bemüht sein, daß die Übergabe der Orden organisatorisch beschleunigt wird.

Wir danken Ihnen, Ihren Soldaten und Offizieren herzlich für die gemeinsamen Kampfaktionen und wünschen Ihnen weitere Erfolge bei der Formierung Ihrer Einheiten und bei deren Vorbereitung auf neue, harte Kämpfe bis zur endgültigen Vernichtung der Hitler-Usurpatoren, die auf den Boden unserer Länder eingebrochen sind.

Für die künftigen Kämpfe wünschen wir Ihnen persönlich und Ihrer Einheit hervorragende Erfolge bei der Vernichtung unseres gemeinsamen

Feindes. Wir wünschen Ihrer Einheit, daß sie zur Garde-Einheit ernannt wird.

Und deshalb: für den Endsieg über den gemeinsamen Feind!

Der Befehlshaber der Truppen	Das Mitglied des Militärrates
der Woronescher Front	der Woronescher Front
Armeegeneral	Generalleutnant
N. Watutin	N. Chruschtschow"

Der slowakische Nationalrat übernimmt am 1. September 1944 die gesetzgebende und vollziehende Gewalt sowie die Verteidigung der Slowakei: „Alle demokratischen und fortschrittlichen Organisationen und Richtungen in der slowakischen Nation, die einen ständigen Kampf gegen das bisherige faschistische Regime in der Slowakei und gegen seine deutschen faschistischen Verbündeten führten, haben am heutigen Tage den Slowakischen Nationalrat als höchstes Organ des slowakischen Widerstandskampfes im Lande gebildet.

Aus diesem Grunde übernimmt der Slowakische Nationalrat, der allein berechtigt ist, im Namen der slowakischen Nation zu sprechen, am heutigen Tage in der ganzen Slowakei die gesetzgebende und vollziehende Gewalt sowie die Verteidigung der Slowakei. Er wird diese Gewalt so lange ausüben, bis das slowakische Volk auf demokratische Weise seine gesetzlichen Vertreter bestimmt.

Unser Widerstandskampf im Lande, wie er bisher im vollen Einvernehmen mit dem tschechoslowakischen Widerstandskampf im Ausland geführt wurde, will auch weiterhin in Einheit und Zusammenarbeit unseren Kampf zum Siege führen.

Wir sind für ein brüderliches Zusammenleben mit der tschechischen Nation in einer neuen Tschechoslowakischen Republik. Die verfassungsrechtlichen, sozialen, wirtschaftlichen und kulturellen Fragen der Republik werden in gegenseitigem Einvernehmen durch die gewählten Vertreter des slowakischen und tschechischen Volkes im Sinne der demokratischen Grundsätze, des Fortschritts und der sozialen Gerechtigkeit definitiv geregelt werden.

Neben der politischen Befreiung ist unser Ziel, den sozial schwachen Schichten des Volkes, insbesondere dem slowakischen Arbeiter und Bauern ein besseres und glückliches Leben zu sichern. Im Interesse einer Erhöhung der Lebenshaltung des Volkes sind wir für eine gerechte Aufteilung des Nationaleinkommens und für eine Neuregelung des Bodenbesitzes und Bodeneigentums zugunsten der Kleinbauern. Der Arbeiter soll einen dem höheren Lebensstandard entsprechenden Lohn sowie einen Anteil am Ertrag seiner Arbeit erhalten ...

Banská Bystrica, am 1. September 1944. Der Slowakische Nationalrat"

Der tschechische Nationalrat erließ am 7. Mai 1945 eine Proklamation, aus der im Auszug wiedergegeben wird:

„Soldaten der revolutionären Armee! Heldenhafte Bevölkerung Prags! Genossen, Arbeiter! Brüder und Schwestern!

Mehr als sechs Jahre lang haben uns die Hitler-Banditen mit Füßen getreten und gedemütigt. Heute erleben wir die Stunde, in der die Macht dieser Henkersknechte zu Ende geht. Gerade heute kapitulierte Hitler-Deutschland vor den Verbündeten. Uns Tschechen war es bestimmt, die erste Nation zu sein, die von den Stiefeln der deutschen Imperialisten niedergetreten wurde. Es ist uns Tschechen bestimmt, auch das letzte Volk zu sein, das dieses Joch zerschmettert. Auf uns, nach Prag sind die Blicke des ganzen tschechischen und slowakischen Volkes, die Blicke der ganzen Welt gerichtet. Wir, die Bürger der Stadt Prag, der Stadt einer großen ruhmreichen Geschichte, werden den Ruhm des tschechischen Volkes bis zu jenen Höhen emporheben, zu denen ihn in der Vergangenheit der große Žižka und sein Tábor emporhob.

Auf in den Kampf, auf zum Barrikadenbau, auf die Barrikaden! Es lebe der Kampf! Es lebe die Revolution! Hoch die Prager Revolutionäre! Hoch die verbündeten Armeen! Hoch die Rote Armee! Es lebe Präsident Beneš! Es lebe der Große Stalin, Tod den deutschen Okkupanten!

Der Tschechische Nationalrat"

Lidice

England hinter dem Attentat auf Heydrich

Aus den noch vorhandenen Unterlagen des RSHA darf aus einem Bericht über das Attentat auf den stellvertretenden Reichsprotektor von Böhmen, SS-Obergruppenführer Reinhard Heydrich, dieses entnommen werden. Der Weg nach England:

„Nach der Errichtung des Protektorates begannen Tschechen aus Böhmen und Mähren einzeln oder gruppenweise illegal nach Polen zu der dort im Aufbau befindlichen tschechischen Legion überzutreten, deren Großteil dann über Gdingen nach Frankreich gelangen konnte.

Nach dem Zusammenbruch Polens stießen Tschechen auf dem Wege über die Balkanstaaten, Istanbul, Kairo, Marseille zur tschechischen Legion in Frankreich, die mit den Resten britischer Truppen nach England gebracht wurde.

Bei diesen Legionären handelte es sich um Tschechen, die, haßerfüllt gegen das Deutschtum, bereit waren, mit der Waffe auf seiten der Feindmächte für den Zusammenbruch Deutschlands zu kämpfen, um die Errichtung einer neuen tschecho-slowakischen Republik durchzusetzen.

Aus den Reihen dieser tschechischen Legionäre, die fast durchwegs in ehemaligen tschechoslow. Infanterie-, Train- oder Pionier-Formationen längere Zeit gedient haben, wurden in England aufgrund freiwilliger Meldung die zuverlässigsten ausgesucht, um als Fallschirmagenten ausgebildet zu werden . . .

Einsatz der tschechischen Fallschirmagenten

Der Einsatz des ersten Fallschirmagenten über dem Protektorat erfolgte am 4. Okt. 1941. Er wurde vor seinem Abflug von dem sogenannten tschecho-slowakischen Kriegsminister in London, General I n g o , persönlich verabschiedet und sollte Funkgerät und Chiffrierschlüssel einer Spezialgruppe der tschechischen Widerstandsbewegung im Protektorat überbringen. Er wurde am 25. Okt. 1941 von der Staatspolizeileitstelle Prag festgenommen.

In der Folgezeit wurden die Fallschirmagenten gewöhnlich in Dreiergruppen angesetzt, die jeweils unter dem Befehl eines tschechischen Offiziers standen.

Die zur Spionage vorgesehenen N a c h r i c h t e n t r u p p s sind mit Sende- und Empfangsgeräten, mit reichlichem Ersatzmaterial, einige mit einem Spezialkurzwellenpeilgerät (Tarnbezeichnung: Rebekka) ausgestattet.

Dieses Gerät peilt selbständig auf einer bestimmten Wellenlänge britische Flugzeuge in einem Umkreis von 100–150 km an und dient somit als Richtungsweiser.

Die Sabotagetrupps sind mit modernsten Sprengmaterialien verschiedenster Art versehen.

Nur in Ausnahmefällen werden Einzelagenten als Kuriere abgesetzt. Sie haben Geld, Ersatzteile, Chiffrierschlüssel, Gift usw. zu überbringen.

In zwei Fällen kam es zum Einsatz von Fünfergruppen, die aus Nachrichten- und Sabotageagenten kombiniert waren.

Die Aufgaben der Agentengruppen waren unterschiedlicher Art und sahen Sabotageakte, vor allem Sprengungen verkehrswichtiger Eisenbahnbrücken und lebenswichtiger Betriebe, z. B. der Eisenbahnbrücke bei Prerau, des Generators des Fernheizwerkes Brünn, der Eisenbahnbrücke Pisek–Tabor, des Aufbaus eines Nachrichtennetzes im Protektorat in Verbindung mit tschechischen Widerstandskreisen vor . . .

Bisher erfaßte und ausgehobene Anlaufstellen

Die ersten zum Einsatz gelangten Fallschirmagenten erhielten in England Anlaufstellen genannt und hatten den Auftrag, über diese weitere Anlaufstellen zu schaffen.

Es wurden bisher 49 Anlaufstellen, davon

12 in Pardubitz
10 in Prag
 9 in Bernatitz
 6 in Liditz
 5 in Königgrätz
 3 in Pilsen
 2 in Lecaky
 1 in Bad Behlograd
 1 in Nemce

ausgehoben und 120 Tschechen festgenommen. Diese Zahl erhöht sich laufend, da z. B. bei Vernehmungen in der Nacht zum 13. 7. 42 allein 10 weitere tschechische Familien angefallen sind, die noch ermittelt und festgenommen werden müssen.

Aufklärung des Anschlags auf SS-Obergruppenführer Reinhard Heydrich

Als erste Maßnahme nach dem Mordanschlag (27. 5. 42) wurde die Kontrolle der aus Prag herausführenden Straßen und Bahnhöfe veranlaßt, um das Verlassen der Stadt durch verdächtige Personen zu erschweren.

Ergebnis der allgemeinen Maßnahmen

Die in der Nacht zum 28. Mai 1942 durchgeführte Fahndung in Prag hatte in erster Linie politischen und demonstrativen Charakter.

Ein Fahndungserfolg konnte nach aller Voraussicht nicht erwartet werden und wurde auch, abgesehen von der Ergreifung mehrerer außerhalb des Attentatsfalles liegender krimineller und politisch-illegaler Elemente, nicht erzielt.

Ein Teil der im Zuge der Großfahndungsaktion festgenommenen Personen wurde Standgerichten überwiesen. Die Standgerichte Prag und Brünn haben in der Zeit vom 28. Mai 1942 bis 3. Juli 1942 insgesamt 1 3 3 1 P e r s o n e n , darunter 2 0 1 F r a u e n , zum Tode verurteilt.

Nach dem 3. Juli 1942 (Aufhebung des Ausnahmezustandes) sind Todesurteile nicht mehr ausgesprochen worden. Alle Urteile wurden sofort durch die Ordnungspolizei vollstreckt.

Gegen die Orte L i d i t z bei Kladno und L e ž a k y bei Louka Bez. Chrudin wurden besondere Vergeltungsmaßnahmen durchgeführt. Die Einwohner beider Ortschaften hatten im vollen Bewußtsein ihrer Handlungsweise tschechischen Fallschirmagenten Unterschlupf und Unterstützung gewährt. In der Ortschaft L o ž a k y (8 Häuser mit 33 Männern und Frauen) lag die Leitstelle der Fallschirmagenten und die Funkverbindung nach London.

Die ersten positiven Hinweise auf die Täter

Ausschlaggebend waren die Angaben des Protektoratsangehörigen Karl C u r d a , der sich am 16. Juni 1942 bei der Staatspolizeileitstelle Prag freiwillig meldete und schließlich zugab, Fallschirmagent zu sein.

C u r d a hatte eine der am Tatort zurückgelassenen Aktentaschen mit besonderen Merkmalen wiedererkannt. Er hatte vor dem Attentat die Tasche in der Wohnung der Eheleute S v a t o s , Prag, im Besitze eines Fallschirmagenten – wie sich später herausstellte, war es der Attentäter G a b - ć i k – gesehen. C u r d a wußte auch, daß dieser Agent einen engen Freund hatte – später ermittelt als Jan K u b i š –, der ebenfalls Fallschirmagent war.

Damit waren die ersten positiven Hinweise auf die Attentäter gegeben. Die weiteren Ermittlungen ermöglichten eine schlagartige Aushebung mehrerer Anlaufstellen in Prag und Umgebung, darunter auch die Anlaufstellen S v a t o s und M o r a v e c .

Die Aushebung in der Karl-Borromäus-Kirche

Im Laufe des 17. Juni 1942 und in der Nacht zum 18. Juni 1942 ergaben sich schließlich zwei voneinander unabhängige Hinweise auf die Karl-Borromäus-Kirche in Prag, wo sich die beiden Attentäter verborgen halten sollten.

Da einerseits durch die Aushebung der Anlaufstellen Gefahr bestand, daß die Täter gewarnt wurden, andererseits der Verdacht geäußert wurde, daß in die Kellerräume der Kirche geheime Kanäle münden – die sofort herbeigeschafften Grundrißpläne gaben keine Auskunft –, wurde die Aushebungsaktion am 18. Juni 1942 früh 4.15 Uhr mit besonderer Sorgfalt und unter Anlegung eines weiteren und eines engeren Sicherungsgürtels, insbesondere unter Beachtung aller Kanalausgänge an der Moldau, begonnen.

Bereits wenige Minuten nach dem Eindringen des Durchsuchungskommandos der Staatspolizeileitstelle Prag in das Schiff der Kirche erhielt es gleichzeitig von den Emporen und dem Chor der Kirche Feuer.

Mehrstündige Versuche, die Agenten, die sich auf den Emporen hinter den Säulen und in den in den Kellerräumen gelegenen Katakomben ausgezeichnet verschanzt hatten, lebend zu überwältigen, mißlangen, obwohl alle zur Verfügung stehenden Mittel (darunter auch Wasser und Gas) ausgeschöpft wurden.

Da die Möglichkeit eines Entweichens durch einen Geheimgang in Betracht gezogen werden mußte, ging schließlich ein Stoßtrupp der Waffen-SS vor.

Fünf Agenten wurden tot aufgefunden, zwei weitere lebten zwar noch, starben aber unmittelbar nach ihrer Bergung, ohne das Bewußtsein wiedererlangt zu haben.

Die in der Kirche aufgefundenen Munitionsvorräte, Matratzen, Decken, Kleidung, Wäsche, Lebensmittel und sonstige Bedarfsgegenstände bewiesen, daß ein großer Helferkreis um die Attentäter und Agenten besorgt war.

Die Identifizierung der getöteten Agenten

Zehn Personen, welche die beiden Attentäter vor, bei und nach der Tat gekannt, gesehen oder kennengelernt hatten, bezeichneten unter den Toten übereinstimmend und einwandfrei die Attentäter.

Unter den elf in der Kirche vorgefundenen Pistolen wurden auch die beiden Colt-Pistolen Nummer 539 370 und 540 416 ausgemittelt, aus denen, durch die kriminaltechnische Untersuchung festgestellt, am Tatort und auf der Flucht die Kynoch-Munition verschossen wurde.

Die Rekonstruktion der Ausführung des Anschlags

Nachdem die beiden Attentäter in der Nacht zum 2. Dez. 1941 abgesetzt worden waren, hielten sie sich in der Folgezeit abwechselnd bei S v a t o s , Prag 1, Melantrichgasse 15,

Moravec, Prag, Biskupecstraße,
Bauc, Prag, Lumirgasse 1,
Patok, Prag XII, Kolinerstr. 11, auf. Sie hatten ursprünglich die Absicht,
den Anschlag in Jungfern-Breschen auszuführen, ließen aber im Hinblick
auf die starke Bewachung diesen Plan wieder fallen. Anfang Mai funkte
Bartos nach London, daß das in Vorbereitung befindliche Attentat keinen
Nutzen bringen würde.

„. . . Dieses Attentat würde in nichts den Verbündeten Nutzen bringen,
und für unser Volk würde es unabsehbare Folgen haben. Es würde nicht nur
unsere Geiseln und politischen Häftlinge gefährden, es würde auch tausende andere Leben fordern, es würde die Nation in eine unerhörte Unterdrückung werfen, gleichzeitig würde es auch die letzten Reste jeglicher
Organisation wegfegen. Damit würde es unmöglich gemacht, daß hier noch
etwas Nützliches für die Verbündeten getan werden könnte . . .“

Der Funkspruch schloß mit der Bitte um Weisung, daß der Anschlag
nicht durchgeführt werden solle, räumte aber ein: „. . . Sollte es aus ausländischen Gründen dennoch erforderlich sein, so möge es auf den hiesigen
Quisling, in erster Reihe auf E.M. (Anmerkung Propagandaminister des
Protektorats Emanuel Moravec) unternommen werden . . .“

Ein Widerruf ist nicht erfolgt.

Zwölf Tage lang beobachteten die Attentäter auf der Strecke Jungfern-
Breschan die Fahrten des SS-Obergruppenführers Heydrich, wobei sie,
wie sie erzählten, den Stellvertretenden Reichsprotektor bei den Vorbei-
fahrten in unterwürfiger Haltung durch Abnehmen des Hutes und durch
Verbeugung grüßten.

Nachdem sie den geeignetsten Ort für den Anschlag ausgekundschaftet
hatten, erwarteten sie am 27. Mai 1942 die Vorbeifahrt.

Gabćiks Versuch, mit der Maschinenpistole zu feuern, mißglückte. Da
warf Kubiś die durch den Spezialzünder äußerst empfindliche Bombe.

Bereits vorher hat er gelegentlich des Vorzeigens der Bombe erklärt, daß
er sie mit einer rollenden Bewegung aus der Hand gleiten lassen müsse,
damit er nicht selbst zu Schaden komme.

Nach der Tat begaben sich die beiden Attentäter getrennt zu verschiedenen Anlaufstellen. Der Bombenwerfer Kubiś fand zuerst Unterschlupf in
der Wohnung des Protektoratsangehörigen Novak. Das Fahrrad, das er
zur Flucht benutzt und vor einer Prager Bata-Filiale abgestellt hatte, wurde
kurz nach seinem Eintreffen bei Novak von dessen 14jähriger Tochter ab-
geholt. Novak war früher Ortsgruppenleiter des Sokol in Bodenbach und
in dieser Eigenschaft dem Gauobmann des Sokol, dem Lehrer Zelenka
(Deckname Hajski) unterstellt, mit dem er in Prag wieder Verbindung
aufgenommen hatte.

Nachdem sich K u b i š in der Wohnung des N o v a k sein blutendes Gesicht abgewaschen hatte, begab er sich in die Wohnung des Z e l e n k a in Prag-Veitsberg, von wo er aufgrund einer Weisung des B a r t o s an alle in Prag befindlichen Agenten in die Karl-Borromäus-Kirche weitergeleitet wurde.

Am 3. Juni 1942 ging von London bei der Funkstelle des B a r t o s in Pardubitz der nachstehende Funkspruch aus England ein, der den letzten Beweis über die Anstifter und Hintermänner des Attentats liefert: ,,Vom Präsident: Es freut mich, daß ihr die Verbindung aufrechterhieltet, und danke Ihnen wärmstens. Ich sehe, daß ihr und alle Eure Freunde voll Entschlossenheit seid. Es ist mir ein großer Beweis dafür, daß der Standpunkt des ganzen Volkes felsenfest ist, ich versichere Sie, daß es einen Erfolg bringt. Die Begebenheiten von zu Hause wirken sehr stark und rufen große Anerkennung für die Resistenz des tschechischen Volkes aus.''

Die furchtbare Vergeltung

Es wird weiter berichtet:

,,Vergeltungsmaßnahmen gegen die Ortschaft Liditz

Gegen die Ortschaft L i d i t z in Böhmen wurden Vergeltungsmaßnahmen durchgeführt, weil flüchtige tschechische Fallschirmagenten nach ihrem Absprung aus englischen Flugzeugen in dieser Ortschaft angelaufen sind und sowohl von den Verwandten von ebenfalls bei der tschechischen Legion in England stehenden Dorfeinwohnern sowie von einem großen Teil der Ortsbewohner unterstützt wurden. Der Ort Liditz war schon immer als stark kommunistisch verseucht bekannt.

Die Ortschaft, die aus 95 Häusern besteht, wurde vollständig niedergebrannt, 199 männliche Einwohner über 15 Jahre wurden an Ort und Stelle erschossen, 184 Frauen in das Konzentrationslager Ravensbrück, 7 Frauen in das Polizeigefängnis Theresienstadt, 4 schwangere Frauen in das Krankenhaus in Prag, 88 Kinder nach Litzmannstadt überführt, während 7 Kinder unter einem Jahr in ein Heim nach Prag gebracht wurden. 3 Kinder werden zur Eindeutschung in das Altreichsgebiet gebracht. Eine schwerkranke Frau liegt noch im Krankenhaus in Kladno.

Standgerichte Prag und Brünn

A. Das Standgericht P r a g hat in der Zeit vom 28. 5. 1942 bis 3. 7. 1942

zum Tode verurteilt	936 Personen,
hiervon Männer	804,
Frauen	132

Die Verurteilung erfolgte wegen:
1. Gutheißung   389 Personen,
2. unbefugten Waffenbesitzes   70 Personen
3. Verbindungen aufrechterhalten und Unterschlupf
   gewährt   405 Personen
4. polizeilich nicht gemeldet   67 Personen
5. falscher Anschuldigungen   5 Personen

B. Das Standgericht B r ü n n hat in der Zeit vom 28. 5. 1942 bis 3. 7. 1942
   zum Tode verurteilt   395 Personen,
   hiervon Männer   326,
        Frauen   69
   Die Verurteilung erfolgte wegen:
1. Gutheißung   88 Personen,
2. unbefugten Waffenbesitzes   19 Personen,
3. Verbindungen aufrechterhalten und Unterschlupf
   gewährt   247 Personen,
4. polizeilich nicht gemeldet   38 Personen,
5. falsche Anschuldigungen   3 Personen.

Nach Bekanntwerden der deutschen Strafaktion gegen das Dorf Liditz
steht diese völlig im Mittelpunkt der Londoner Hetzpropaganda. Einerseits
wird die Strafaktion gegen Liditz als Gipfel der ,,sinnlosen Wut" der Deutschen wegen der vierzehntägigen ergebnislosen Fahndung nach den Atten-
tätern hingestellt, auf der anderen Seite als Beweis, daß tatsächlich ein
Widerstand der gesamten tschechischen Bevölkerung bestehe, der nun
deutscherseits bereits mit solchen Maßnahmen gebrochen werden müsse.
Es folgen nun tagelang die wüstesten Beschimpfungen der deutschen Nation und des Führers, der mit dem Hunnenkönig Attila verglichen wird,
sowie immer wiederholte Rachedrohungen . . .''

Italien

Die Kommunistische Partei Italiens brachte im Juni-Aufruf 1940 und in einem Aufruf vom Mai 1941 ihre Stellung zum Krieg zum Ausdruck. Sie forderte den Sturz des Faschismus, den Bruch des Abkommens zwischen Italien und Deutschland und trat für einen gemeinsamen Kampf aller Parteien, Organisationen und politischen Gruppen auf der Grundlage eines konkreten Programms ein.

Als Mussolini gestürzt und Marschall Pietro Badoglio zum Ministerpräsidenten und Oberbefehlshaber ernannt worden war, wurde die Tätigkeit der Widerstandsgruppen immer stärker und wirksamer. Partisanengruppen, Brigaden und Divisionen operierten im gesamten von den Deutschen besetzten Raum.

Ende September 1943 (29. Sept. 1943) wurden westlich Terano Bandenlager genommen und dabei 800 Gewehre, 12 Geschütze und 30 Kfz erbeutet. Im Raum von Calice, Imperia und Savona operierten im Januar 1944 Partisanengruppen. Auch der Raum von La Spezia wird unsicher gemacht. Zu großen Befürchtungen gaben die Aktionen der Partisanen um Görz, Udine, Triest, Fiume sowie Tolmein Anlaß. Die 13. Partisanendivision mit der Brigade Bardicik und Gregercio im Bereich des Karfreit, die 20. Partisanendivision mit den Brigaden Lamana, Proletarka ostwärts Görz bis Villa del Nevero sowie der XVIII. Sipca-Brigade in Drenkia – 8 km von Tolmein – steigerten die Sorgen, zumal Verbindungen zwischen slowenischen und italienischen Partisanen offenkundig wurden. Nicht zu übersehen ist zudem, daß die gesamte jugoslawische Adriaküste durch Titopartisanen beherrscht wurde.

Neben Sabotagen und Überfällen der außerhalb des regulären Kriegsrechtes kämpfenden Truppen und Verbände wurden in der für Deutschland arbeitenden italienischen Industrie Streiks durchgeführt.

Am 26. Februar 1944 gab die Armeegruppe von Zangen einen Bericht heraus, in dem die Genehmigung einer Aktion gegen Banden ersucht wird. Es wird ausgeführt: ,,Armeegruppe beabsichtigt, unter Leitung des Befehlshabers in der Op.-Zone Adriat. Küstenland zur unumgänglich notwendigen Festigung der deutschen Stellungen in Istrien ein großzügiges Säuberungsunternehmen gegen das Bandenunwesen durchzuführen. Hierzu ist die Beteiligung der 16. SS-Pz.Gr.Div. mit allen Teilen für die Dauer von etwa 10 Tagen erforderlich. Vorgesehene Aufgabe für die 16. SS.Gr.Div. Durchkämmen der ganzen Halbinsel von Nord nach Süd bei Absperrung durch 162. (Turk) Div. und Teile der 188. Res.-Geb.Div. 16. SS-Pz.Gr.Div. ist nach jetzigem Aufstellungsstand zu dieser Aufgabe befähigt. Für die Ausbildung wird das Unternehmen sehr förderlich sein. Die noch fehlende Kfz.-Ausstattung ist dazu nicht erforderlich. Armeegruppe bittet, das Einverständnis des Reichsführers SS und entsprechende Befehle an 16. SS-Pz.Gr.Div. herbeizuführen."

Als die Alliierten am 22. Jan. 1944 bei Anzio und Nettuno landeten, funkte das alliierte Oberkommando am 22. Jan. 1944 an die Widerstandsgruppen nachstehende Botschaft: ,,Vom alliierten Oberkommando für Rom und ganz Italien ist die Stunde des bedingungslosen Kampfes mit allen verfügbaren Mitteln gekommen . . . Sabotiert den Feind . . . Blockiert seine Rückzugsstraßen und zerstört seine Telefon- und Telegrafenverbindungen bis auf den letzten Draht . . . Schlagt überall zu und kämpft unermüdlich und ohne politische Vorbehalte weiter, bis unsere Truppen da sind . . . Benachrichtigt alle Gruppen und Parteien."

Generalfeldmarschall Albert Kesselring stellt in einer Erklärung vom 10. April 1953 hinsichtlich Rom fest: ,,In welcher einige tausend Kommunisten straff organisiert und gut bewaffnet sowie – unabhängig davon – cirka 8000 Mann starke Kader unter Führung der besten italienischen Offiziere im Untergrund Roms bereitstanden, die lediglich auf den Einsatzbefehl aus dem alliierten Hauptquartier von Caserta warteten."

Die Heeresgruppe C meldete an das Oberkommando der deutschen Wehrmacht in der ersten Hälfte Februar 1944: ,,Stimmung und Haltung der italienischen Bevölkerung waren bisher gekennzeichnet durch Abwarten und Teilnahmslosigkeit."

In Rom fanden im März 1944 vor dem Attentat in der Via Rasella eine Reihe von Überfällen und Sabotagehandlungen statt:

Es ist nicht von ungefähr, daß der Chef des Stabes des Oberbefehlshabers Südwest in einem Telefongespräch am 23. Mrz. 1944 nach dem Attentat in der Via Rasella mit dem Chef des Stabes der 10. Armee darauf hinweist, daß in Zukunft im Verhältnis 1:10 bei Geiselerschießungen zu verfahren sei.

Am 27. Mrz. 1944 bringt der Oberbefehlshaber der 10. Armee gegenüber Feldmarschall Kesselring seine Sorge in Zusammenhang mit der Partisanengefahr zum Ausdruck. Besonders liege ihm die Gegend Rieti am Herzen, weil sie der zentrale Knotenpunkt der Nachschubstraße sei. Nicht umsonst hebt der Ia der 10. Armee am 28. März 1944, wie bereits erwähnt, hervor, daß die Armee nach dem Abzug des I./SS-Pol.Rgt.20 und der II./Rgt.3 Brandenburg nicht mehr in der Lage sei, in dem Gebiet des rückwärtigen Armeegebiets und der nördlichen taktischen Armeegrenze die Küstensicherung und Bandenbekämpfung zu übernehmen.

Im März ist die Lage so, daß ständig mittlere und kleinere Gruppen der Partisanen, die über einen gut funktionierenden und engmaschigen Nach-

318

richtendienst verfügen und ständig den Aufenthalt wechseln, zur Aktion übergegangen sind und – meist bei Nacht – häufige Überfälle auf Einzelfahrzeuge, Posten und Wachen verüben.

In Anbetracht der gegebenen Lage werden im Bereich des Oberbefehlshabers Südwest Stäbe für Bandenbekämpfung, z. B. unter Oberst Schanze und Major Hermann, aufgestellt. Eine klare Zuständigkeitsabgrenzung gegenüber dem Bevollmächtigten General der Deutschen Wehrmacht findet statt.

Bandenabschnitte werden gebildet. Im Raum der 10. Armee werden zu bandengefährdeten Straßen erklärt: Ascoli-Accumoli, Porto S. Giorgio-Formo-Amandola-Accumoli, Acerata-Amandola-Accumoli, Macerata-Foligno, Chiaravalle-Jossi-Visso, Macerata-S. Severino-Castel Raimondo, Avezzano-Rieti, Aquila-Accumoli, Antrodoco-Accumoli, Aquila-Terano.

Unter dem 8. Apr. 1944 stellt der Oberbefehlshaber Südwest – Ic fest: ,,Terroristenanschläge und Bandenunwesen im italienischen Raum haben weiter zugenommen."

Bezeichnend ist: Aus den vorliegenden Meldungen der 10. Armee im Zeitraum vom 1. – 15. Mrz. 1944 ergibt sich, daß sich unter den Partisanen eine große Anzahl von Slawen befindet. Aus dem Raum Ostra – Montecarotto – Genga – Cingoli – Filottrano wird gemeldet, daß sich dort 600–700 Widerstandskämpfer befinden, unter diesen auch Slawen und Briten.

Die Anwesenheit einer aus 400–500 Köpfen bestehenden Partisanengruppe ergibt sich aus Meldungen über den Raum Fossato – Cancelli – Fabriano – Metélica – Esanatoglia. Unter den Partisanen befinden sich ebenfalls Slawen. Die Existenz von 1200–1500 italienischen und slawischen Partisanen wird aus dem Raum Montatto – Monastero – Sarnono – Piobbico gemeldet.

Nach vorhandenen Meldungen befanden sich weiter im Raum Penna – S. Giovanni – Monte S. Martino 300 Briten und Slawen. Die Intensität des Partisanenkampfes zeigen die Ic.-Tagesmeldungen des Oberbefehlshabers Südwest vom 1. Mrz. 1944 – 20. Apr. 1944 über die Verluste der Partisanen:

1.–10. Mrz. 1944: 131 Tote, 121 Gefangene sowie 97 festgenommene verdächtige Zivilisten. 11. Mrz. – 20. Mrz. 1944: 797 Tote, 312 Gefangene und 244 festgenommene verdächtige Zivilisten. 21. - 31. Mrz. 1944: 841 Tote, 259 Gefangene und 226 verdächtige Zivilisten. 1.–10. Apr. 1944: 630 Tote, 347 Gefangene und 305 festgenommene verdächtige Zivilisten. 11.–20. Apr. 1944: 1093 Tote, 273 Gefangene sowie 413 festgenommene verdächtige Zivilisten.

Das italienische Volk in seiner Masse stand jedoch weder hinter der Badoglio-Regierung noch hinter Mussolini und seinen Bundesgenossen.

319

Die Heeresgruppe C konnte an das Oberkommando der Deutschen Wehrmacht in der ersten Hälfte Februar 1944 melden: „Stimmung und Haltung der italienischen Bevölkerung waren bisher gekennzeichnet durch Abwarten und Teilnahmslosigkeit. Diese Haltung hat sich auch durch die Landung bei Nettuno mit ihrer unmittelbaren Bedrohung Roms nicht geändert." Die Lage änderte sich jedoch im Monat März, in welchem das Attentat in der Via Rasella die Flamme des Aufstandes im italienischen Volk entfachen sollte.

In Rom fanden im März 1944 vor dem Attentat in der Via Rasella nachstehende Überfälle und Sabotagehandlungen statt:

2. März 1944: Viale Giulio Cesare,
5. März 1944: Piazza dei Mirti,
8. März 1944: Via Savolino,
9. März 1944: Via Claudia,
10. März 1944: Via Tomacelli.

Auch außerhalb Roms nahm die Partisanentätigkeit zu.

In dem Bericht der Armeegruppe von Zangen vom 29. März 1944 an das Oberkommando Heeresgruppe C/1 c über die Bandenlage für die zweite Hälfte März 1944 wird hervorgehoben, daß sich die Banden wie folgt räumlich gliedern:

1. Räume NW Vercelli-Novara-NW Turin, S-SW Turin, N-SO Cunio, S Asti;
2. SW Modena-S Forli-W Macerata;
3. Provinzen Laibach, Fiume, Pola, Triest, Görz, Udine.

Nachstehende Gruppenbildungen ließen sich erkennen: Banden kommunistischen Charakters, zusammengesetzt aus arbeitsunwilligen Fabrikarbeitern der Großstädte, ehemaligen Soldaten, entlaufenen Kriegsgefangenen verschiedener Nationalitäten und unzufriedenen Elementen aller Volksklassen, Badoglio-Anhänger, Banden, die sich aus flüchtigen Verbrechern, Versprengten usw. zusammensetzen.

Hervorgehoben wird, daß in der gedanklichen Ausrichtung teils offene, teils getarnte kommunistische Tendenzen überwiegen und der militärischen Führung zur Durchsetzung des politischen (kommunistischen) Führungsanspruches Kommissare gegenüberstehen. Ausdrücklich wird gesagt, daß die Banden zum größeren Teil nicht uniformiert seien.

Wörtlich wird hinsichtlich der Operationszone Adriatisches Küstenland darauf hingewiesen: „Der kommunistische Führungsanspruch hat sich uneingeschränkt durchgesetzt. Die weit fortgeschrittene straffe truppenmäßige Gliederung der Partisanenkräfte ... steht in klarer organisatorischer Verbindung zu der eindeutig kommunistisch ausgerichteten groß-jugoslawischen, auf die Eingliederung in die Sowjet-Union hinarbeitenden Tito-Bewegung in Gestalt des sogenannten antifaschistischen Volksbefreiungsrates Jugoslawiens . . . Geschätzte Bandenstärke aufgrund von Abwehrmeldungen nach dem Strand von Mitte März: insgesamt etwa 25 000 Mann . . . Die seit kurzem laufende Austauschbewegung zwischen Kräften des istrisch-slowenischen und des kroatischen Raumes ist von erheblichem Einfluß auf Istrien-Slowenien.

Das Attentat in der Via Rasella

Festzustellen ist, daß der Führer der Italienischen Kommunistischen Partei, Togliatti, es befohlen hat. Es sollte als Fanal des Aufstandes in die Geschichte der Kommunistischen Partei Italiens eingehen. Die für die Ausführung benötigten Kräfte wurden von weither nach Rom geholt. Der Explosion fielen 44 Menschenleben zum Opfer. 32 Angehörige einer deutschen Polizeitruppe, die aus Südtirolern bestand, und zwei italienische Zivilpersonen wurden sofort getötet. Zehn weitere Angehörige der Truppe erlagen in der Folge ihrer Verletzungen. Andere verloren das Augenlicht, auch Amputationen mußten vorgenommen werden.

Die Planung Togliatis ging, psychologisch gesehen, voll auf. Die deutsche Führung tat das, was die Organisatoren des Attentats als Reaktion der Besatzungsmacht erwarteten: Sie verfügte eine im Rahmen der von der Reichsführung gegebenen Befehle liegende, furchtbare Vergeltungsmaßnahme, der 335 Personen zum Opfer fielen. Zu erwähnen ist, daß nach dem Tod des 33. deutschen Soldaten im Rahmen der Repressalie 1:10 die Zahl der in den Ardeatinischen Höhlen zu Erschießenden von 320 auf 330 erhöht wurde, 5 Personen wurden zuviel erschossen. Diese letztere Exekution geht auf einen Zählfehler zurück, für den der damalige Kommandeur der Sicherheitspolizei in Rom, Herbert Kappler, nichts konnte.

Konsul Moellhausen berichtet in seinem Buch ,,Die gebrochene Achse'', daß der Stadtkommandant von Rom, Generalleutnant Mälzer, ohne Überlegung und Berücksichtigung der Folgen den Stadtteil, in welchem das Attentat stattgefunden hatte, sprengen wollte. Zur Durchführung dieser Gewaltmaßnahme waren bereits die notwendigen Vorbereitungen getroffen. Zum Teil war der Sprengstoff schon abgeladen worden. Des weiteren drohte der deutsche Stadtkommandant von Rom die Erschießung von 1000 Geiseln an. Daß dies alles nicht erfolgte, ist mit ein Verdienst von Herbert Kappler.

Über die Hintergründe des Attentats veröffentlichte der italienische Journalist G. Blasi in der Tageszeitung ,,Il Secondo d'Italia'' einen Bericht, in welchem er ausführte, daß der Befehl Togliatis zum Attentat erging, um die deutsche Führung zu Repressalien herauszufordern, wie sie von ihr angekündigt worden waren.

Blasi, der bis zum 10. Mai 1944 einer kommunistischen Aktionsgruppe angehörte, die er verließ, als er hinter die Absicht der kommunistischen Planer kam, hebt hervor, daß die Attentäter auf Vorstellungen ihrer Kampfgefährten, sich zur Verhütung der Repressalien zu stellen, erklärten: ,,Unser Blut ist wichtig für die Welteroberungspläne der kommunistischen Idee, dagegen fällt das Leben einiger Italiener nicht in das Gewicht.``

Über die Ereignisse am 23. und 24. März 1944 in Rom nimmt Robert Katz in seinem Buch ,,The Death in Rome``, dessen Originalausgabe im Verlag Collier – Mac Millan – London – New York und in Übersetzung unter dem Titel ,,Mord in Rom`` im Desch-Verlag in München erschienen ist, Stellung. Darin heißt es: ,,Feldmarschall Albert Kesselring kehrte um 19.00 Uhr von der Frontbesichtigung zurück. An diesem 23. März hatte er die Truppen von Mackensens 14. Armee inspiziert. An diesem Tage hatte Kesselring bei Anzio die Kampfkraft seiner 65 000 Mann starken Streitmacht begutachtet. Jetzt bei Rückkehr ins Hauptquartier auf dem Monte Sorrate beschloß Kesselring die Verschiebung des für den 29. März angesetzten Gegenangriffs gegen die Briten und Amerikaner.`` (113/114). ,,Sein Stabschef General Westphal erstattete ihm nun über das Attentat in der Via Rasella Bericht.`` (114) ,,Kesselring unternahm gar nichts. Er enthüllte auch kaum seine Gedanken. Nach einigem Überlegen rief er das OKW an und ließ sich direkt mit Jodl verbinden . . . Die Unterredung zog sich in die Länge. Das OKW überließ die Einzelheiten schließlich den Männern an der Front. Kesselring glaubte sich soeben ,,ehrlich um eine humane Haltung bemüht zu haben.`` Er erteilte nunmehr dem Kommandeur der 14. Armee folgenden Befehl: ,,Töten Sie für jeden Deutschen zehn Italiener. Der Befehl ist sofort auszuführen.``

Diese Darstellung stützt sich hauptsächlich, wie Robert Katz angibt, auf die Verhandlung gegen Feldmarschall Albert Kesselring in Venedig, wie sie in den United Nations War Crimes Comission, Law Reports of Trials of War Criminal`` wiedergegeben ist. Sie stimmt mit dem tatsächlichen Ablauf der Ereignisse nicht überein.

Der Oberbefehlshaber der Heeresgruppe C, Feldmarschall Kesselring, besichtigte die Abschnitte des I. Fallschirm-Korps, des LXXVI. Panzer-Korps und die Dienststelle des Höheren Arko 317, die zur 14. Armee gehörten, am 29. März 1944. – Feldmarschall Albert Kesselring war vom 22.–25. März 1944 nicht auf seinem Gefechtsstand auf dem Monte Sorrate bei Rom. Er befand sich in Nord- und Mittelitalien. Daher konnte General Westphal, wie in dem Verfahren gegen Kesselring in Venedig behauptet wurde, seinen Oberbefehlshaber beim Aussteigen aus dem Wagen am 23. März 1944 gegen 19 Uhr n i c h t über das Attentat in Rom, die Zahl der bisherigen Opfer, das Ergebnis der Untersuchung, die übertriebenen Forderungen Hitlers und die Einsprüche des Chefs und des IA des OBSW sowie die Meldung der 14. Armee über das notwendig erachtete Verhältnis 1:10 und die Weitergabe der Meldung an das OKW unterrichten.

Generalfeldmarschall Kesselring berichtet, daß von Juni bis August 1944 hinter der Front 7000 Deutsche getötet und etwa 25 000 verwundet worden seien. In der zweiten Hälfte des August 1944 stieg die Zahl der Partisanen in Italien auf über 82 000 Mann an. Kleinere und größere Partisanenrepubliken bildeten sich in den Alpen und im Apennin.

Seit spätestens Ende 1943 standen die Special Operations Executive (für Italien zuständig Mac Caffery) und das Office of Strategic Service (O. S. S. – Alan Dulles) mit der italienischen Resistanza in Verbindung. Im September 1943 nahm das Commitato di Liberazione Nationale zum ersten Mal Fühlung mit den alliierten Geheimdiensten auf. Am 3. November 1943 trafen sich Ferruccio Parri und Leo Valioni als Vertreter der C. L. N. mit Mac Caffery und Dulles in Lugano. Parri, der mit Luigi Longo (P. C. I.) zusammenarbeitete, war im Jahre 1945 (vom 11. Juni bis 9. Dezember) Ministerpräsident in Rom.

Leo Valioni, häufig Kontaktmann des italienischen Widerstandes zu alliierten Dienststellen, saß 1945/46 in der italienischen Nationalversammlung.

In einem im August 1944 von Mac Caffery an Parri gerichteten Schreiben heißt es: ,,Ich habe oft gesagt, daß der größte militärische Beitrag für die alliierte Sache viele kontinuierliche Sabotageakte sind . . . Die Banden haben gut gearbeitet. Wir wissen es."

Die englische Konzeption des Sommers 1944 war, das auf über 80 000 Mann angewachsene ,,Partisanen-Heer" für die auf den 26. August 1944 festgesetzte Offensive gegen die Grünstellung zu mobilisieren.

Als militärischer Berater wurde den Partisanen General Raffaele Cadorna, Sohn des italienischen Generalstabschefs im Ersten Weltkrieg, zugeteilt, der von anglo-amerikanischer Seite seine Instruktionen erhielt.

Von 1945 bis 1947 bekleidete Cadorna das Amt des italienischen Generalstabschefs, später findet er sich als Mitglied im römischen Senat. Englischer Verbindungsoffizier zu den Partisanen war Oliver Churchill. Die Special Operations Executive (S. O. E.) war am Untergrund- und Partisanenkrieg maßgebend beteiligt.

Die englischen und amerikanischen Richtlinien setzte Luigi Longo, eine der stärksten Persönlichkeiten der kommunistischen Partei Italiens, in die Tat um.

Cadorna traf am 12. August 1944 in Oberitalien ein.

In einer Direktive in der zweiten Hälfte September 1944 wird festgelegt, die Bewegungen und Aufstellungen der deutschen Truppen zu hemmen.

Wörtlich heißt es: „. . . ist es nötig, die auf dem Rückzug befindlichen deutschen Kolonnen von der Seite her zu attackieren, Störaktionen gegen sie an Brücken sowie geeigneten Straßenstrecken zu unternehmen und ihre Aufstellung zum Kampf gegen die Alliierten zu verhindern."

Anfang Juni 1944 war über den Sender Bari zur Intensivierung des Partisanenkampfes ein von Badoglio verfaßter Aufruf mit der Unterschrift des britischen Feldmarschalls Alexander verlesen worden, aus dem eine Stelle zitiert werden darf: „. . . Greift die Kommandostellen und die kleinen militärischen Zentren an! Tötet die Deutschen von hinten, damit Ihr Euch der Gegenwehr entziehen und wieder andere töten könnt!"

In der Anlage zum Beitrag Ia des KTB der Heeresgruppe C vom 22. Juni 1944 wird ausgeführt: „Bezug: OB Südwest Ia T Nr. 0402/44 gKdos. v. 17. Juni 1944. Die Kämpfe der letzten Tage an der Front haben bewiesen, daß die männliche italienische Bevölkerung in großem Maße dem Feind Vorschub leistet und teilweise sich aktiv gegen die deutsche Truppe am Kampf beteiligt. Zur Sicherung der Front sind durch die Armeen in Rom zwischen der HKL und der allgemeinen Linie . . . die zivilen männlichen Landeseinwohner im Alter von 18 bis 45 Jahren einschließlich im Rahmen des Möglichen zu erfassen und sicherzustellen.

Die Erfaßten sind durch die Divisionen und die ihnen gleichgestellten Dienststellen in das Sammellager der Militärkommandantur Florenz . . . abzuliefern . . . Die Haltung der Soldaten bei der Durchführung der Aktion muß trotz der erforderlichen Härte dem Ansehen der deutschen Wehrmacht entsprechen . . . ."

Nach der Räumung der italienischen Hauptstadt bestand zu keinem Zeitpunkt die Absicht, die Arnolinie zu halten. Die alte Hauptstadt der Toscana, Florenz, die den Mittelpunkt der geistigen Entwicklung Italiens vom Mittelalter bis zur Neuzeit darstellt, wurde in der Nacht vom 2. auf 3. August 1944 aufgegeben. Allmählich folgte die Arnofront nach. Die Apenninstellung sollte bezogen werden.

Wichtige Übergänge in die Poebene stellen die Apenninpässe „Passo de Cerrato", „Abetone", „Futa" und „Radicosa" dar.

Der Apennin wurde dem SS-Sturmbannführer Reder zum Schicksal.

Im Apennin-Raum ereigneten sich starke Bandenüberfälle. Der Generalstabschef der 14. Armee weist Ende September 1944 auf die starke Bandentätigkeit hin, durch die im Gesamtbereich der Armee täglich 10–15 Soldaten ausfielen.

Wie in dem ganzen Buch habe ich mich auch hier bemüht, so nüchtern wie nur möglich die Zusammenhänge zu schildern. Zahlen waren zu nennen, um aufzeigen zu können, wie schwierig die Lage der Heeresgruppe C geworden war.

Ich glaube, daß die Zeit zwischen den damaligen Ereignissen und dem Heute es möglich macht, ohne Haß zurückzublicken. Wie die verflossenen Jahre Wunden heilen können, so schufen sie auch die Möglichkeit zu einer objektiven Betrachtung. Im Rahmen einer solchen ist der Einzelmensch im geschichtlichen Raum und seinen Verstrickungen zu sehen.

Ich bin mir der Schwierigkeiten bewußt, vor denen die Verteidigung in den Prozessen von Rom und Venedig stand.

Dokumente, die die Erinnerung hätten stärken können, fehlten. Aber die Frage sei erlaubt: Gab es keine offizielle Möglichkeit, schon zwischen den Jahren 1952 und 1960 nach klärenden Dokumenten zu forschen?

Westeuropa

Frankreich

Frankreich hatte stets eine starke kommunistische Partei. Paris stellte in Westeuropa den Mittelpunkt der Komitern dar.

In dem früheren Reichssicherheitshauptamt lag seit dem 4. Dezember 1937 mit Bezug auf Frankreichs Hauptstadt ein Bericht mit der Überschrift „Die getarnten Buchhandlungen der Komintern" vor.

Es lautete:

„Nachdem ich verschiedene Berichte über die Tätigkeit der Komintern in Zentraleuropa und auf dem Balkan erhalten hatte, beschloß ich, persönlich nach Paris zu fahren, um die Wahrhaftigkeit dieser Angaben zu kontrollieren.

Meine erste Feststellung ging dahin, daß die Komintern in den verschiedenen Stadtteilen von Paris unter einer geschäftlichen Maske Buchhandlungen eingerichtet hat, deren Aufgabe es ist, kommunistische aufrührerische Schriften in den totalitären Ländern sowie auf dem Balkan zu verbreiten.

Diese Buchhandlungen sind: Bureau d'édition (Verlagsbüro), Magenta-Boul. 31 (IXe); Editions sociales Internationales (Internationaler sozialer Verlag) 24, rue Racine (VIe); Editions de Culture Sociale (Verlag für soziale Kultur); 4; Rue St-Germain l'Auxerrois (Ier); Galeries St. Demis, 7 Boul. Bonne Nouvelle (IIe); Horizone, 12 rue de l' Echaude St-Germain (VIe); Librairie de la Maison de la Culture (Buchhandlung des Kulturhauses) 29, Rue de Anjou (VIII e); Librairie Mercure, (Buchhandlung Mercure), 69 Boul. St-Germain (Ve); Librairie Populaire Espagnole-Française (Spanisch-französische Volksbuchhandlung), 3 rue Valette (Ve); Librairie populaire franco-italienne (französisch-italienische Volksbuchhandlung) 128, Boul. de Charonne (XXe); Librairie syndicale, (Syndikatsbuchhandlung) 211, rue Lafayette (IXe); Libreria Italiana (italienische Buchhandlung), 24 rue du 4 septembre (II) Ouvert de nuit, („Nachts geöffnet") 1 rue Chaptal (IXe); Pont de l' Europe, („Brücke Europas") 17, rue Vignon (VIII e); Aux librairies du C. D. L. P., 120 rue Lafayette (Xe), 138, Rue Montmartre (IIe).

Ich habe verschiedene dieser Buchhandlungen besucht und fand dort tatsächlich ein reiches Material, welches zweifellos dazu bestimmt war, in anderen Ländern in versteckter Form verteilt zu werden. Es handelt sich um Broschüren, Flugblätter, Aufrufe usw.

Die Tätigkeit dieser Buchhandlungen baut sich auf einer sehr einfachen Grundlage auf, und man kann wohl behaupten, daß der Arbeit dieser Unternehmen gerade durch die besagte Einfachkeit ein großer Erfolg beschieden ist.

Die erwähnten Broschüren haben im allgemeinen ein kleines Format und wiegen recht wenig. Man schickt sie in kleinen Postpaketen, die das Gewicht von 0,5 Kilogramm nicht überschreiten. Auf diese Weise kommen sie ohne Zoll- und Polizei-Kontrolle zu den Bestimmungsländern. Durch die aufgeklebten Etiketten der Pariser Buchhandlungen wird außerdem die Aufmerksamkeit der mit der Kontrolle beauftragen Behörden abgelenkt.

Da ich hauptsächlich an der aufrührerischen Propaganda gegen Ungarn interessiert bin, suchte ich hauptsächlich nach Beweismaterial, welches sich mit diesem Lande befaßte. Im Laufe meiner Nachforschungen konnte ich aber auch feststellen, daß zur Verbreitung von verbotenem Material in Deutschland und Italien dieselben Methoden angewandt werden.

Das ganze Material, das ich auf Grund meiner Nachforschungen als für Ungarn bestimmt feststellte, existiert auch in deutscher und italienischer Sprache, und aus dem Text kann man entnehmen, daß es auch für diese Länder bestimmt ist.

Ich vermute, daß man zur Verbreitung dieselbe Technik anwendet, wie ich sie mit Bezug auf Ungarn kennengelernt habe.

Die in Frage kommenden Buchhandlungen müssen also in diesen Ländern Verbindungsleute an der Hand haben, die als ,,Empfänger" erscheinen. Sie empfangen die Postpakete und übermitteln dann den Inhalt anderen Agenten, welche mit der Verbreitung beauftragt sind.

Um die Tätigkeit genau zu illustrieren, füge ich folgende Broschüren bei:
1. Pjatnicki, Die faschistische Diktatur in Deutschland,
2. Die Beschlüsse des 8. Kongresses,
3. Béla Kun – Vereinte Tätigkeit, die wichtigste Tagesfrage,
4. Die 13. Plenarsitzung,
5. Imre Nagy – Die Lage des ungarischen Landes,
6. Dimitrov – Die Arbeiterklasse gegen den Faschismus,
7. Lajos Bebrits – Werte Kameraden!
8. Manuilsky – Die Ergebnisse der sozialistischen Arbeit in der UdSSR,
9. Klara Zetkin – Erinnerungen Lenins,
10. Aladar Komjat – Wir wollen alles!
11. Antal Hidas – Voller Sterne . . .!
12. Emil Madaras – Crozni, der Sieger!
13. Béla Kun – Marx,
14. Emil Madaras – Sowjetische Dampfschiffe,
15. Mate Zalka – Es ist nicht so leicht . . .!
Die erste Broschüre, die in ungarischer Sprache erschienen ist und sich auf

Deutschland bezieht, hat einen interessanten Text. Man will das ungarische Proletariat davon überzeugen, daß das augenblickliche Regime Deutschland nicht lange existieren kann. Ganz besonders muß ich hervorheben, daß diese Broschüre auf einem besonders dünnen Papier gedruckt ist, ihre 214 Seiten haben nur eine Dicke von 10 mm. Die Ausmaße sind 14 × 10 × 1 cm, und man konnte 35 000 Buchstaben drucken.

Die erste Ausgabe wurde im Jahre 1934 gedruckt; im Jahre 1936 erschien die Broschüre aber zum zweiten Male. Ich zog es aber vor, die Ausgabe von 1934 zu besitzen, denn sie hat einen dokumentarischeren Wert als die von 1936. Im allgemeinen habe ich mich immer darum gekümmert, die Erstauflagen zu bekommen.

Über das erste Jahr der Besetzung Frankreichs fand ich in dem Schweizer Informationsdienst unter dem 30. November 1940 nachstehende Beschreibung. Sie stammt aus Paris:

,,Noch kein ausgesprochener Haß gegen die Nazis, aber Neugier. Trotz dieser Neugier keine Unterhaltung mit den Soldaten. Man bleibt fern und beobachtet. Fast nur Prostituierte lassen sich mit ihnen ein . . .

Die Plakate gegen England werden schnell abgerissen. Fast jeder hört das englische Radio. Ebenso freut man sich allgemein, wenn die Royal Air Force am Himmel erscheint. Aber man zeigt die Freude nicht zu auffällig, ebensowenig die Abneigung gegen die Deutschen. Eine Ausnahme hiervor bildet das gelegentliche Auspfeifen der deutschen Wochenschau im Kino . . .

Parteien: Nur Kommunistische Partei äußerst tätig. Flugblätter, ,,Humanité" (gedruckt und abgezogen), Plakate und Klebezettel. Inhalt: Starke Propaganda für die Sowjetunion, für Lohnerhöhung, gegen Unternehmer, auch gegen englische Plutokratie . . .

Eine Partei führt De Gaulle: Gewährsmann hat Flugblätter gesehen, die das Erscheinen einer Zeitung ankündigen. Intelligent gemacht, besonders für Intellektuelle. Gegen deutschen Bluff, gegen Kommunisten . . .

Le jeune Front: Neue Partei, die von den Deutschen gefördert wird. Büros in allen Stadtteilen. ,Tritt ein für Regeneration de la France; für Juden ist der Beitritt verboten; Uniform und Programm zeigen deutsche Beeinflussung. Findet keinen Zuspruch.

Betriebe: Auf Citroen, Renault usw. weht die deutsche Fahne. Vier Tage pro Woche wird gearbeitet. Es gibt Fälle, wo Unternehmer sich weigerten, Arbeiter einzustellen. Sie wurden dazu gezwungen.

Die Deutschen: Im allgemeinen höflich, sogar zurückhaltend. Kino, Theater, Restaurant für sie reserviert. Fahren meist 1. Klasse in der Metro. Die Erlasse werden veröffentlicht durch die Deutschen, ihre Durchführung geschieht durch französische Behörden . . . "

Die Kommunistische Partei Frankreichs gibt heute eine Beschreibung des Widerstandes, in der behauptet wird, sie habe am meisten zur „Befreiung des Landes" beigetragen.

Nach Beendigung des Krieges kritisierte die Kommunistische Partei das Abwarten und die Untätigkeit der bürgerlichen Kreise nach dem Zusammenbruch Frankreichs im Jahre 1940. Die Kommunistische Partei Frankreichs stand auch im Gegensatz zu General de Gaulle. Von ihm behauptet die Kommunistische Partei, er habe den Widerstand in Frankreich auf den Sektor der Erkundung beschränkt. Unter dem von ihm vertretenen Gesichtspunkt, Frankreich könne nur von außen befreit werden, sei sein Ziel gewesen, die Ausbreitung der Kommunistischen Partei Frankreichs zu verhindern und das alte wirtschaftliche und soziale System in Frankreich zu erhalten.

Es wird von den Kommunisten auf die Memoiren des Generals hingewiesen, in welchen er ausführt, daß die Kommunistische Partei Frankreichs beabsichtigt habe, „sich mit der Gloriole des Retters des Volkes zu umgeben", um „an dem Tage, an dem Anarchie über das Land hereinbrechen würde, eine Art Ordnung sicherzustellen." Demgegenüber habe der General eine nationale Regierung gegenübergestellt, d. h. eine bürgerliche Regierung, die „den ersten Platz im Herzen der Franzosen einnimmt, wenn ihr Führer im Glanze des Sieges plötzlich in Paris erscheint."

Verübelt wird Charles de Gaulle der Satz in seinen „Memoiren 1942–1946", die auch in Gütersloh erschienen sind: „Wozu Risiken heraufbeschwören und vielleicht in ein neues Dünkirchen rennen, da sich ja der Feind an der russischen Front mit jedem Tag mehr abnutzt."

Die Kommunistische Partei weist darauf hin, daß General De Gaulle am 18. Juni 1940 die französischen Militärs auf englischem Boden zur Sammlung um ihn aufrief, während die Kommunistische Partei Frankreichs bereits im Juli 1940 mit dem Kampf gegen die deutsche Okkupationsmacht begann.

Herausgestellt wird, daß sie, während die „bürgerlich-imperialistischen Kreise Frankreichs" vor „Hitler zu Kreuze krochen", am 10. Juli 1940 an das französische Volk eine Proklamation richtete, in der es heißt: „Unser Land lernt jetzt die furchtbaren Folgen der verbrecherischen Politik jener unwürdigen Machthaber kennen, die für den Krieg, für die Niederlage und für die Okkupation verantwortlich sind ... Nichts aber kann verhindern, daß eines Tages Abrechnung gehalten wird und daß die Werktätigen mit der Forderung, Frankreich solle den Franzosen gehören, zugleich den Unabhängigkeitswillen eines ganzen Volkes und seine feste Entschlossenheit zum Ausdruck bringen, sich derjenigen, die es in die Katastrophe geführt haben, für immer zu entledigen ...

329

Nur im Bereich der so begeisterungsfähigen und hochherzigen Arbeiterklasse, die der Zukunft mutig und vertrauensvoll entgegensieht, weil die Zukunft ihr gehört, nur im Bereich der von der unantastbaren, ehrenhaften und heroischen Kommunistischen Partei geführten Arbeiterklasse kann die Front der Freiheit, der Unabhängigkeit und der Wiedergeburt Frankreichs erstehen."

Am 11. November 1940 seien die ersten Blutopfer gebracht worden, als anläßlich des Jahrestages des Waffenstillstandes von 1918 Studenten in Paris eine Demonstration zum Grabe des Unbekannten Soldaten durchführten und die Marseillaise sangen. Auf den Champs-Elysées hätten die Deutschen zwölf Personen erschossen und etwa 50 verwundet.

Die Kommunisten berichten weiter: In Paris hätten im Juli 1940 die ersten Kundgebungen gegen die Deutschen stattgefunden. Arbeitslosendemonstrationen habe es in Montreuil und anderen Städten gegeben. Streiks hätten in der Metallindustrie stattgefunden. Sabotageakte hätten sich in Betrieben und gegen Güter, die für die deutsche Wehrmacht bestimmt waren, ereignet. Die Motorenproduktion der Firma Gnomet-Rhone sei zeitweise eingestellt worden. 100 Motorräder aus den Renault-Werken seien im Dezember 1940 wegen Unbrauchbarkeit verschrottet worden.

Erste bewaffnete Gruppen des Widerstandes habe die Kommunistische Partei Frankreichs bereits im Herbst 1940 organisiert. Ende dieses Jahres, so lautet die Feststellung, seien bereits in den Bergbaugebieten Nordfrankreichs, im Bezirk von Paris und im Süden des Landes erste Partisanenabteilungen aufgetreten, als deren bekannteste Führer die Kommunisten Debarge, Hapiot, Lacazette sich hervortaten. In vielen Betrieben hätten sich Arbeiterkampfgruppen gebildet, die die Rüstungsproduktion sabotierten, Rohstoffe vernichteten, Ausschuß produzierten und durch Streiks die Produktion lahmlegten. Hervorgehoben wird schließlich, daß die erste bewaffnete Widerstandskampforganisation, der „Combat" (OS), als Vorläufer der 1941 entstandenen „Speciale de Francs-Tireurs et Partisans Français (FRTPE)" gewesen sei.

Die „L'Humanité d'Alsace et de Lorraine" in Straßburg gab am 16. Juli 1944 eine Feststellung des Präfekten der Provinz Aube wieder, in der festgestellt wird, daß nach der Kapitulation die Kommunistische Partei die Sammlung der durch die französische Armee hinterlassenen Waffen durchführe.

Die „L'Humanité" sei 1940 zum Sammlungsorgan des Widerstandes geworden. 1940 seien 10 950 000 Exemplare erschienen; jede Nummer habe eine Auflage von 150 000, eine sogar von 480 000 gehabt. Fast eine Million illegaler Flugblätter und 140 000 Broschüren seien bis Ende 1940 verbreitet worden.

1941 verhärtete sich das Bild. Die Kommunistische Partei Frankreichs zählt an Verhaftungen:

Am 24. Jan. 1941 Festnahme von 1250,
am 10. Febr. 1941 Festnahme von 1647,
am 7. März 1941 Festnahme von 1778 und
am 9. April 1941 Festnahme von 2098 „Genossen".

Ab Mitte Mai 1941 nahm der Widerstand organisierte Formen an. Der 15. Mai 1941 brachte die Bildung der „Nationalen Front", deren Hauptträger nach kommunistischen Angaben Arbeiter und Bauern waren. Weiter wird hervorgehoben: In dem gleichen Monat wurde unter Charles Tillon die FTPE gebildet.

Anfang Juli 1941 flog in Versailles ein Munitionslager in die Luft. Wenige Tage später überfielen Fischer ein Militärlager in Berk-sur-Meer, töteten die Bewachung und erbeuteten die dort lagernden Waffen. Im Departement Pas-de-Calais wurden unter Führung von Charles Debarge und Julien Hapiot Verkehrslinien zerstört und Sabotageakte in den Rüstungsbetrieben ausgeführt. In Henin-Lietard, Auchel und Harnes wurden deutsche Einheiten angegriffen. Selbst in Paris gab es Partisanenüberfälle. Von Mitte Juli bis Mitte September 1941 wurden 1800 Lastkraftwagen mit Militärgut zerstört und 194 Züge zum Entgleisen gebracht.

General Speidel zählt in einem Bericht vom 28. Febr. 1941 unter der Überschrift „Stimmung und innere Sicherheit" auf:

Sabotage November 1941: 83 Fälle
Dezember 1941: 80 Fälle
Januar 1942: 79 Fälle
Februar 1942: 60 Fälle.

Es ist nicht zu übersehen, daß General de Gaulle am 18. Juni 1940, dem Tage nach Pétains Bitte um Waffenstillstand, am Londoner Rundfunk seinen ersten Aufruf an die französische Bevölkerung richtete: „Was auch immer geschehen wird, die Flamme des französischen Widerstandes darf nicht erlöschen und wird nicht erlöschen."

De Gaulle wurde als „Chef der freien Franzosen" anerkannt. Churchill bringt dies auch in seinen Schreiben vom 7. August und 24. Dezember 1940 zum Ausdruck.

Eine unerhörte Wirkung übte die deutsche Niederlage vor Moskau aus.

Vor seinem Tod schrieb der Eisenbahnführer Pierre Semard im Gefängnis 1942 nieder, wie Maurice Thorez in seinem Werk „Ausgewählte Reden und Schriften" (1933–1960, Seite 292) berichtet: „In wenigen Augenblicken werde ich erschossen. Ich sehe dem Tode ruhig entgegen. Mein letzter Gedanke gilt Euch, meine Kampfgefährten, gilt allen Mitgliedern unserer Partei, allen französischen Patrioten und den heldenhaften Kämpfern der

Roten Armee. Ich sterbe in der Gewißheit, daß sie den Faschismus besiegen werden. Ich sterbe in der Gewißheit, daß Frankreich befreit wird. Sagt meinen Freunden, den Eisenbahnern, es sei mein letzter Wille, daß sie nichts tun, was den Nazis helfen könnte. Die Eisenbahner werden mich verstehen. Sie werden mich hören, und sie werden handeln! Davon bin ich überzeugt. Lebt wohl, liebe Freunde! Die Todesstunde naht. Aber ich weiß, daß die Nazis, die mich erschießen werden, schon besiegt sind. Es lebe die Sowjetunion mit ihren Verbündeten! Es lebe Frankreich!" „In ganz Frankreich häuften sich die Kundgebungen. In Paris, in der Rue de Seine stürmten Frauen ein deutsches Proviantlager und verteilten die Lebensmittel. Die Vichy-Polizei wurde von den Manifestanten in die Flucht geschlagen. Laval ließ zwei Frauen hinrichten, die dabeigewesen waren. In Südfrankreich kam es in Nîmes, Montpellier und Arles zu Hungerdemonstrationen. In Sète verteilten Hafenarbeiter und Frauen die aus Afrika eingetroffenen Waren, die für den Versand nach Deutschland in Eisenbahnwagen verladen wurden. In Onnaing an der französischen Grenze strömte die gesamte Bevölkerung zum Bahnhof und hielt einen für Deutschland bestimmte Getreidetransport an. Die Frauen kletterten in die Waggons und verteilten das Getreide. Auf dem Lande nahm der Widerstand gegen die Requisitionen lebhafte Formen an. Die Bauern verjagten die Requisitionsbeamten der Vichy-Regierung. In der Bretagne und in der Landschaft Beauce ließen sie die Requisitionskommandos der Hitler-Faschisten verschwinden. Wenn es den Bauern nicht gelang, den Raub zu verhindern, steckten sie die deutschen Korn-, Futter- und Strohlager in Brand.

In meinen folgenden Ausführungen, die dem Vergleich zur kommunistischen Darstellung dienen, stütze ich mich auf Angelo Rossi „Les Communistes français pendant la drôle de guerre" und „Physiologie du partie communiste français" (Paris 1951 und 1958). Die kommunistische Partei versuchte zunächst, die Unterstützung der deutschen Besatzung für ihre gegen die Vichy-Regierung gerichtete Agitation zu gewinnen, und zu freier Betätigung zugelassen zu werden.

Die Partei war am 26. August 1939, ihre Presse bereits am 25. August 1939 verboten worden. Im März 1940 wurde jede kommunistische Betätigung mit der Todesstrafe bedroht. Seit Januar 1940 baute die KPF illegale Organisationen auf. Das Ziel war es, im Augenblick des französischen Zusammenbruches einen bewaffneten Aufstand insbesondere in Südfrankreich durchzuführen, um an die Macht zu kommen.

Die am 1. Juli 1940 illegal erschienene „Humanité" brachte den „Wunsch nach freundschaftlichen Beziehungen zu Deutschland" zum Ausdruck.

In einem Lagebericht vom Oktober 1940 führt der Militärbefehlshaber aus: „Solange die Kommunisten die deutsche Besatzungsarmee nicht angreifen, auch der französischen Regierung keine ernsthaften Schwierigkeiten bereiten, ist für die deutsche Besatzungsmacht kein Anlaß zum Eingreifen gegeben; die Franzosen sollen ihre innenpolitischen Angelegenheiten selbst ordnen."

So der M. B. F.-Verwaltungsstab-Lagebericht Oktober 1940. Französischerseits beschwerte man sich, daß die Deutschen im Kampfe gegen den Bolschewismus nicht genügend Hilfe leisten würden.

Die französische Polizei verhaftete im Oktober 1940 ungefähr 200 kommunistische Funktionäre, vor allem in Paris, die in ein Konzentrationslager eingewiesen wurden. Aus einem leerstehenden Sanatorium im Département Seine et Oise war dieses gebildet worden.

Bis Dezember 1940 unterließen die kommunistische Presse und zahlreiche illegale Flugblätter jeden Angriff gegen die Besatzungsmacht. Gegen Pétain wurden dagegen „versteckte Angriffe, in Seidenpapier gepackt", gestartet.

Erst mit Beginn des Balkankrieges begann die Propaganda gegen Deutschland. Die „Humanité" sprach am 12. April 1941 von den „Berliner Brandstiftern."

Im Lagebericht des Militärbefehlshabers, Kommandostab, vom 31. Mai 1941, wird hervorgehoben, daß die Sabotagehandlungen (zumeist Kabelsabotagen) sprunghaft anstiegen.

Im September 1940 wurde das „Comité National Français (CNF)" gebildet. Es beanspruchte nicht nur die Souveränität über die überseeischen französischen Beziehungen, sondern vielmehr über ganz Frankreich. Als „Präsident" stand an der Spitze de Gaulle. Namens dieses „Freien Frankreichs" erklärte de Gaulle Deutschland den Krieg, obwohl seine Organisation von England und den USA nicht als „Regierung" anerkannt wurde. Die Note der englischen Regierung vom 13. Juli 1942 brachte auch keine Anerkennung.

Die Engländer erklärten sich mit folgenden Definitionen einverstanden: „France Combattante: Gesamtheit der frz. Staatsangehörigen, gleichgültig, wo sie sich aufhalten, und der frz. Gebiete, die sich zusammenschließen, um mit den Vereinten Nationen im Kriege gegen den gemeinsamen Frieden zusammenzuarbeiten; zugleich das Symbol aller frz. Staatsangehörigen, die die Kapitulation nicht anerkennen und welche durch die ihnen möglichen Mittel, gleichgültig an welchem Orte, zur Befreiung Frankreichs beitragen.
Comité National Français: Leitende Stelle des kämpfenden Frankreich, organisiert die Kriegsteilnahme der frz. Staatsangehörigen und Territorien, welche sich zusammenschließen, um mit den Vereinten Nationen

zusammenzuarbeiten und um ihre Interessen bei der Regierung des Vereinigten Königreiches zu vertreten."

In einem Rundschreiben vom 29. Juli 1942 ersetzte de Gaulle den Begriff „France libre" mit „France Combattante". In einem circulaire v. 29. Juli 42 erklärte er[118]): „Indem das CNF die Bezeichnung „Freies Frankreich" durch die des „Kämpfenden Frankreich" ersetzt, hat es im Hinblick darauf, daß alle im Inneren des Landes am Widerstand teilnehmenden Gruppen sich ihm angeschlossen haben, deutlich machen wollen, daß das Kämpfende Frankreich sowohl das durch die freifranzösischen Streitkräfte, die überseeischen Besitzungen und die im Auslande lebenden Franzosen gebildete Freie Frankreich wie auch das Gefangene Frankreich umfaßt, welches im Kampf gegen den Eindringling und gegen die Staatsführung („autorité") steht, welche von einer unter der Kontrolle des Feindes stehenden Pseudo-Regierung usurpiert worden ist."

Die französische Widerstandsbewegung war 1942 sehr stark gewachsen. Aus der Akte des Höheren SS- und Polizeiführers in Paris, Oberg, ergibt sich, daß Bousquet, „Secrétaire géneral à la Police", der Vichy-Regierung Unterlagen lieferte, aus denen sich das deutsch-französische Polizeiunternehmen „Donar" entwickelte. Dabei wurden zahlreiche Agentenfunker mit ihren Geräten festgenommen. Unter den Festgenommenen befanden sich auch englische Offiziere in Zivil und ein französischer Major, der gerade die Verbindung zwischen Giraud und den Alliierten zur Vorbereitung der Landung in Nordafrika herstellte. Der Offizier floh bei Einlieferung in das Gefängnis.

De Gaulle forderte am 26. Juni 1941 über BBC London die französische Bevölkerung für den Fall der alliierten Landung auf, die versteckten Waffen zu ergreifen, sämtliche Fernsprechkabel zu zerschneiden und den Straßenverkehr zu lähmen.

In seinem Aufruf findet sich der Satz, daß „jeder getötete Feind einen freien Mann" ergebe.

Im Lagebericht Oktober/November 1941 des MBF, Kommandostab, wird festgestellt: „Das Eintreten De Gaulles für die Mörder von Nantes und Bordeaux (Rundfunkrede und Verleihung des De Gaulle-Kreuzes an die Stadt Nantes) hat seinem Ansehen in weiten Kreisen geschadet." Am 23. Oktober 1941 schränkte de Gaulle im Zusammenhang mit den kommunistischen Terrorakten ein:

„Es ist durchaus richtig und völlig gerechtfertigt, daß die Deutschen von den Franzosen getötet werden. Wenn die Deutschen nicht den Tod von unseren Händen empfangen wollen, brauchten sie nur bei sich zu Hause zu bleiben . . . Im Kriege gibt es eine Taktik. Der Krieg muß von denen geleitet werden, die damit beauftragt sind, d. h. durch mich selbst und durch das

Nationalkomitee. Alle Kämpfer sowohl im Ausland wie daheim müssen sich genau an die vorgeschriebene Linie halten. Im Augenblick lautet der Befehl, den ich für das besetzte Gebiet gebe, keinen Deutschen offen zu töten (,,Actuellement, le consigne que je donne pour le territoire occupé, c'est de ne pas y tuer ouvertement d'Allemands"). Dies aus einem einzigen Grunde: es ist derzeit für den Feind zu einfach, sich durch ein Massaker an unseren augenblicklich entwaffneten Kämpfern zu rächen. Sobald wir in der Lage sein werden, zum Angriff überzugehen, werden die erforderlichen Befehle gegeben werden."

Der Keitel-Erlaß ist bekannt:

Die Quoten 1 : 100 und 1 : 50, die in ihm enthalten sind, sind rechtlich und militärisch problematisch. Richtig ist allerdings die Passage, die ausführt: ,,Seit Beginn des Feldzuges gegen Sowjetrußland sind in den von Deutschland besetzten Gebieten allenthalben kommunistische Aufstandsbewegungen ausgebrochen . . . Es ist festzustellen, daß es sich um eine von Moskau einheitlich gelenkte Massenbewegung handelt." In Frankreich wurde das Schlagwort der ,,Front National" in den Mittelpunkt der Propaganda gestellt. Ihr dienten Symbole und Gedenktage, so z. B. im Flugblatt zum Jahrestag der Schlacht von Valmy.

Im Herbst 1941 setzten die Kommunisten organisierte Anschläge an. Die illegale ,,Humanité" vom 2. Juli 1941 hatte bereits die Fehlleitung von Eisenbahnzügen gefordert. Am 7. Juli 1941 rief sie zur Verhinderung der Versendung von Waffen, am 17. Juli 1941 zur Zerstörung von Verbindungen und Sabotierung von Transporten auf. Geschulte Sabotagetrupps wurden eingesetzt.

Am 16. Januar 1942 und 1. Mai 1942 forderten zwei Anschläge gegen Urlauberzüge der deutschen U-Boot-Waffe durch Schienenlockerung 28 und 10 Tote. Am 21. August 1941 waren in Paris die ersten deutschen Soldaten durch kommunistische Terroristen getötet worden. Borkenau schreibt: ,,Die Kommunisten wiesen jede Verantwortung für dieses gemeine Verbrechen von sich und schrieben es der Unterwelt zu, zu der es seiner Art nach paßte. Nach dem Kriege jedoch brüstete sich ein kommunistischer Offizier, colonel Fabien, stolz der Tat. Von da an wurde die tückische Ermordung deutscher Soldaten ein regelmäßiger Bestandteil der kommunistischen Parteitätigkeit; eine ausgezeichnete Vorschule, zunächst für den Mord an franz. Kollaborateuren, dann an angeblichen Kollaborateuren und schließlich an Tausenden von Franzosen, darunter einer Anzahl von Helden der Résistance, deren einziges Verbrechen darin bestand, daß sie den Kommunisten mißfielen."

Paris und Umgebung blieben Mittelpunkt der Terroranschläge. Aber auch in anderen Bezirken treten sie auf, so z. B. im Industriebezirk Rouen–

Le Havre. Terrorgruppen wurden Anweisungen gegeben, den ersten ihnen begegnenden deutschen Offizier zu erschießen, um Repressalmaßnahmen auszulösen, durch die haßerfüllte Gefühle bei der Bevölkerung gegen die deutsche Besatzungsmacht erweckt werden sollten.

Abetz berichtet in seinem Buch, daß am 20. Oktober 1941 durch eine ,,ausgezeichnet organisierte jungkommunistische Terrorgruppe, . . . auf deren Konto noch verschiedene Mordanschläge und Sabotageakte im Pariser Stadtgebiet'' kamen, der Feldkommandant von Nantes ermordet wurde.

In einem deutschen Lagebericht vom Dezember 1942 wird hervorgehoben: ,,Nach den bisherigen Beobachtungen gehen alle Attentate und Sabotageanschläge auf die kommunistische Partei zurück.'' Die KPF hatte eine Organisation, die ,,Organisation spéciale (OS)'' gebildet.

Die KPF schuf sich gemäß den Internationalen Komintern-Richtlinien eine Guerilla-Streitmacht. In Frankreich waren auch englisch geleitete Organisationen eingesetzt. Die Bedeutendste war das ,,reseau Buckmaster'', die nach einem englischen Oberst von der ,,War office Secrete Operations Execution (SOE)'' benannt wurde. Vielfach tritt sie auch unter dem Namen ,,French Section'' in Erscheinung.

,,Die militärische Ausbildung der Chefs der einzelnen Netze ermöglichte es, Fallschirmabwürfe, geheime Flugzeuglandungen und Sabotagen, so die rationellste Zerstörung der für Rechnung des Feindes arbeitenden Fabriken, die Zerstörung von Kunstbauten, Brücken, Viadukten, Eisenbahnen, Angriffe auf Flugplätze, auf Treibstofflager, auf dtsch. Befestigungsanlagen usw. vorzubereiten und zum Erfolg zu führen.''

Der Militärbefehlshaber Frankreich meldet vom Juli 1941 bis Juni 1942 die Zahlen der Eisenbahnsabotagen, Brandstiftungen und Überfälle:

Juni	1941	54
Juli	1941	37
August	1941	82
September	1941	162
Oktober	1941	163
November	1941	83
Dezember	1941	80
Januar	1942	79

Landung der Alliierten in Nordafrika am 8. November 1942

Die Landung legte die Gegensätze zwischen den Generalen de Gaulle und Giraud offen. Am 31. Mai 1943 kamen es zur Begegnung zwischen beiden Generalen, die einen Führungsanspruch erhoben. Es kam zu einer vorläufigen Einigung und zur Bildung des ,,Comité Français de la Libération Nationale"

In der Vereinbarung von Algier vom 3. Juli 1943 wird festgestellt: ,,General Giraud, handelnd auf Grund der Erklärung und der Verordnung vom 14. März 1943, General de Gaulle, handelnd auf Grund des ihm vom Comité National Français am 27. Mai 1943 erteilten Auftrages, erwägend, daß durch die Besetzung des frz. Staatsgebietes durch den Feind die Ausübung der Souveränität des frz. Volkes, die Grundlage jeder legalen Staatsgewalt, suspendiert ist, . . . ordnen an:

Artikel 1: Es wird eine einzige frz. Zentralgewalt gebildet, welche den Namen eines Comité Français de la Libération Nationale annimmt.

Artikel 2: Das CFLN leitet die frz. Beteiligung am Kriege unter allen seinen Formen und an allen Orten.

Artikel 3: Das CFLN übt die frz. Souveränität über alle Gebiete aus, die sich nicht unter der Gewalt des Feindes befinden; . . .

Artikel 4: . . . Das CFLN übt seine Aufgaben bis zu dem Tage aus, an dem die fortschreitende Befreiung des Landes die Bildung . . . einer provisorischen Regierung erlaubt, an die es seine Machtbefugnisse abtreten wird. Dies wird spätestens am Tage der Befreiung des Landes der Fall sein. . . .

Die alliierte Landung in Afrika brachte große Probleme mit sich: Das unbesetzte französische Gebiet kam unter deutsche Kontrolle, Teile der französischen Waffenstillstandsverbände wurden in den Widerstand getrieben. Die deutschen Besatzungstruppen konnten die zur Bandenbildung geeigneten südfranzösischen Räume nicht unter Kontrolle halten.

Die wichtigsten südfranzösischen Bewegungen schlossen sich im Herbst 1943 zu den ,,Mouvements Unis de la Résistance (Mur)" zusammen. Als ihre paramilitärische Organisation ist die ,,Armée Secrète" zu nennen.

In vier Gruppen wurde diese organisiert: ,,AS" unter der Leitung von Berufsoffizieren, ,,Groupes Francs" unter dem später verhafteten Divisionsgeneral Dé Lestrain, ferner ,,Maquia" und ,,Parachutages".

In Nordfrankreich gelang ein solcher Zusammenschluß nicht. In beiden Gebieten traten die kommunistischen Organisationen (KPF, Front Nationale und FTP) der Armée Secrète nicht bei.

Die Vorkriegsparteien und Vorkriegsgewerkschaften schufen auf englische Initiative den ,,Conseil National de la Résistance (CNR)".

Ein einziges Mal trat er am 27. Mai 1941 in Paris zusammen. Der CNR und sein ,,bureau permanent", dessen Leitung der spätere französische Außenminister Bidault übernahm und das unter fünf Mitgliedern drei offene oder geheime Kommunisten hatte, wurde als potentielle Gegenregierung zur Algier-Regierung de Gaulles aufgebaut. Die Sowjets anerkannten die CFLN ,,als den Vertreter der Interessen des französischen Staates und als einzigen bevollmächtigten Vertreter aller den Hitlerismus bekämpfenden französischen Patrioten" an. Die Angloamerikaner verweigerten eine solche Anerkennung. Sie erklärten: ,,Die Regierungen verpflichten sich nicht, bis zur Befreiung des Staatsgebietes über alle Frankreich betreffenden Fragen ausschließlich mit dem CFLN zu verhandeln." Die USA betonten darüber hinaus: ,,Diese Note bedeutet nicht die Anerkennung einer Regierung Frankreichs oder des französischen Empires durch die Regierung der USA.

Die KPF bemühte sich, in das ,,bureau permanent" ihre Funktionäre hineinzubringen. Vorbild war die ,,leninistische Haltung des Jahres 1917".

Die CNR sollte gegen die Algier-Regierung ausgespielt werden. Die ,,Humanité" schrieb: ,,Das CNR verlangt auf dem gesamten Staatsgebiet die Rechte und die Verantwortlichkeit eines Treuhänders und provisorischen Organes der nationalen Souveränität."

Einer der größten Fehler war die Zwangseinziehung französischer Arbeitskräfte für den Einsatz durch den französischen ,,Service de Travail Obligatoire (Sto)" seit Oktober 1942.

Dadurch wurden junge Franzosen auf das Land und in unzugängliche Berggegenden getrieben. In Savoyen, im Zentralmassiv und in den Pyrenäen entstanden immer neue Partisanengruppen.

Die ,,Humanité" forderte am 19. März 1943: ,,Wir müssen das Vorbild der Savoyer nachahmen, die als Partisanen in ihren Bergen kämpfen."

Die deutsche Militärmacht war im Niedergang. Stalingrad hatte die endgültige Wende gebracht. So ging es noch um die Diktatur der kommunistischen Partei in Frankreich.

Mit Recht wird im Bericht des Reichsführers SS ausgeführt: ,,Das eigentliche Ziel der KPF und ihrer Organisationen ist die Vorbereitung des bewaffneten Aufstandes mit dem Ziele, in Frankreich die Macht zu übernehmen, sobald die Deutschen daraus verjagt sind. Die Lage ist in Frankreich ähnlich, wie sie es 1917 in Rußland war. Die UdSSR versucht zusammen mit der KPF den Befreiungsausschuß de Gaulles die Rolle Kerenskis spielen zu lassen, welchem Ausschuß neuerdings auch Kommunisten angehören, während Giraud daraus verdrängt wurde."

Es ist hervorzuheben, daß die Kommandeure der Sicherheitspolizei in einem schwierigen Abwehrkampf beachtliche Erfolge aufzuweisen hatten. Der Kommandeur Bordeaux übernahm im Austausch gegen die Freilassung von 300 verhafteten Widerstandskämpfern 45 000 kg Waffen, Spreng- und Sabotagemittel aus Lieferungen der ,,French Section", darunter 2000 MP mit einer Million Schuß.

Durch Funkspiele fielen der Sicherheitspolizei 30 000 MP in die Hände.

Bei den Abwürfen handelt es sich in der überwältigenden Masse nicht um Waffen im Sinne des Artikel 1 HLKO, sondern um ausgesprochene Guerilla-Waffen und um gezieltes Sabotagematerial englischer und amerikanischer Herkunft.

Folgende Zahlen von Sabotage, Bränden und Überfällen wurden von Januar bis August 1943 gemeldet:

Monat		1	2	3	4	5	6	7
Januar	43	68	90	42	37	12	54	34
Februar	43	56	98	35	18	46	46	30
März	43	96	153	68	69	10	38	85
April	43	82	142	66	57	19	29	35
Mai	43	108	178	118	48	20	17	47
Juni	43	65	123	120	54	22	19	43
Juli	43	97	202	166	57	39	33	46
August	43	114	378	326	154	30	17	42
		686	1364	941	494	198	253	362

Es bedeutet: 1 Kabel-, 2 Eisenbahn-, 3 sonstige Sabotagen, 4 Lager und Scheunenbrände, 5 sonstige Brände, 6 Überfälle auf Wehrmachtseinrichtungen, 7 Überfälle auf Wehrmachtsangehörige. Von Januar bis September 1943 fanden im Bereich des Militärbefehlshaber Frankreich 281 Mordanschläge gegen die deutsche Besatzungsmacht, 79 gegen französische Polizeibeamte und 174 gegen Kollaborateure statt.

Die Anzahl der Sabotageakte betrug das Dreifache der Zahl des Vorjahres. Rückblickend schreibt der Ia des Militärbefehlshabers Frankreich, Oberst Arends, in seiner eidesstattlichen Erklärung vom 27. Juni 1946: ,,Der Übergang von der reinen Terrororganisation zu einer geschlossenen Widerstandsbewegung war für die deutsche Wehrmacht nicht feststellbar, nicht zuletzt auch deshalb, weil beide Gruppen nebeneinander in Aktion traten. Etwa im Sommer 43 sind die ersten Meldungen erstattet worden, daß truppenähnlich organisierte, teils mit Uniformen aller Art, teils mit Armbinden kenntlich gemachte Widerstandsverbände aufträten. Zu gleicher Zeit und in den gleichen Gebieten wurden aber weiterhin Überfälle und Terrorakte aller Art durch nicht als ,,Soldaten'' kenntlich gemachte Personen festgestellt, die von der Zivilbevölkerung nicht unterschieden werden konnten.'' Vom Juni bis August 1943 konnten in Frankreich 24 englische Offiziere in Zivil außer Gefecht gesetzt werden.

Im Januar 1944 trafen sich in Lyon die Führer der französischen Maquis.

Sie beschlossen den sofortigen Beginn des Guerilla-Krieges. Am 6. Juni 1944 erklärt die ,,Humanité'':

,,Während die alliierten Soldaten auf dem Boden Frankreichs landen, muß sich das französische Volk . . . zum Aufstand vorbereiten.''

Am 11. Juni 1944 schrieb sie: ,,Geht überall entschlossen mit Generalstreik und bewaffnetem Aufstand voran!'' Das Ziel der Kommunistischen Partei war die Entfachung des Aufstandes gegen die Besatzungsmacht und zugleich gegen die Alliierten.

Es wird berichtet, daß die Zahl der Maquisards in Hochsavoyen 1200, in Savoyen 1000 und in der Ardèche 2000 betrug. Im Oktober 1943 ermittelte man bei einer Zusammenkunft der Regionalchefs der Maquis 22 000 gruppierte und 8000 ,,individuelle Maquisards''.

Mitte August 1944 sollen allein in der Bretagne 80 000 FFI gestanden haben. Die Endstärke der Bewaffneten wird in einigen Quellen mit 200 000 angegeben. Unter dem Dienstpersonal der Eisenbahnen und der Post in Frankreich sollen sich 100 000 Widerstandskämpfer befunden haben. In der Meldung der ,,Humanité'' vom 23. Juni 1944 wird geschrieben, daß fast das ganze Département Basses-Pyrénées, das ganze Alpengebiet nördlich Gap und große Teile der Départements Drôme Vaucluse und Ardèche unter französischer Kontrolle seien. Am 30. Juni 1944 gestand die ,,Humanité'', daß gewisse Teile des ,,befreiten Gebietes'' wieder geräumt werden mußten.

Donald B. Richardson schätzte im ,,American Mercury'' die Zahl der ermordeten Franzosen auf 50 000.

Aus den Unterlagen des Oberbefehlshabers West ergeben sich vom September 1943 bis März 1944 für durchgeführte Sabotage, Brände und Anschläge folgende Zahlen:

Monat:		1	2	3	4	5	6	7
September	43	150	534	345	246	19	18	67
Oktober	43	92	512	273	154	28	15	55
November	43	83	506	390	104	25	25	67
Dezember	43	55	538	332	64	20	16	68
Januar	44	45	625	325	85		125	
Februar	44	38	448	265	65		105	
März	44	10	456	95	38		75	
Insgesamt		473	3619	2025	848		636	

Im gleichen Zeitraum wurden getötet oder verletzt:

Oktober	43	312	19	77
November	43	64	45	122
Dezember	43	149	43	103

Insgesamt	525	107

Die Auswirkungen der Anschläge waren nicht leicht.

Am 6. Oktober 1943 verunglückte infolge Schienenlösung ein italienischer Transportzug. In seine Trümmer fuhr ein französischer D-Zug hinein: Italiener: 80 verbrannt, 5 verletzt, 36 vermißt. Franzosen: 10 tot, 60 verletzt. Deutsche: 5 verletzt. – Am 9. Okt. 43 entgleiste durch Sabotage ein Zug des RAD: Opfer: 3 Tote, 8 Schwerverletzte, 25 Mann noch unter den Trümmern. – Am 6. Nov. 43 geriet ein Güterzug mit einigen Munitionswagen der Kriegsmarine infolge Laschenlösung in Brand: Opfer: 30 Marineangehörige verbrannt, 19 Marineangehörige verletzt. Französische Quellen melden Erfolge der FFI:

Am 18. Juni 44 bei Malestroit im Morbihan verloren die Deutschen bei einem Gefecht 500, die FFI 200 Mann; am 27. Juni 44 bei einem Angriff auf ein maquis im Walde von Viorreau nördlich Nantes verloren die Deutschen 100 Tote, die FFI 27 Tote und 27 nachträglich erschossene Gefangene; zwischen 10. Juli und 4. Aug. 44 setzten die FFI im Dep. Côtes-du-Nord 2500 Deutsche (Tote und Verwundete) außer Gefecht; in den Dep. Vienne und Charente verloren die Deutschen in einem Monat über 2000 Tote und Verwundete; am 20. Sept. 44 nahmen die FFI bei Issoudun 25 000 Deutsche, ein Konglomerat aus kleinen und kleinsten Stäben, Depots und Wacheinheiten aus dem Raume südlich der Gironde gefangen; um 18. Aug. 44 eroberten FFI Annemasse und Cluses (Hoch-Savoyen): deutsche Verluste 400 Tote, 800 Verwundete, 1400 Gefangene; im Kampf gegen die 19. Armee wurden durch FFI allein über 8000 Deutsche getötet und 42 000 gefangengenommen.

Das alliierte Oberkommando setzte die FFI zu drei Großaktionen ein:
1. Befreiung der Bretagne und Einschließung der dort verbliebenen deutschen Kräfte,
2. Bindung deutscher Kräfte der I. Armee südlich der Loire und Erschwerung des Rückzuges,
3. Einsatz gegen die aus Südfrankreich auf den Rhone-Straßen auf Lyon zurückgehende 19. deutsche Armee.

General Ramke berichtete, daß die 2. deutsche Fallschirmjägerdivision in der Bretagne ein paar hundert Tote und Verwundete durch die Maquisards gehabt haben. Abetz telegraphierte am 25. Februar 1944 an Staatssekretär

Steengracht vom Auswärtigen Amt: „Es ist eindeutig, daß der Kommunismus durch verstärkte Aktivität die Herrschaft an sich zu reißen versucht. Bei den Sabotageakten ist zunehmende Planmäßigkeit festzustellen. Laufende Überfälle auf Bürgermeistereien (Lebensmittelkartendiebstähle), Lebensmittel- und Tabakhandlungen. Aus Einzelbezirken im Süden wird gemeldet, daß Überfälle auf Polizei- und Gendarmeriestationen zu den Alltäglichkeiten gehören. Gesamtzahl solcher Anschläge auf frz. Einrichtungen erreichte im Dezember 43 mit 1100 einen Höchststand."

Gemeldet wird am 6. März 1944:

„Belieferung der Widerstandsorganisationen mit Waffen in der ersten Februarhälfte besonders umfangreich. Gegner versucht, die zugefügten Verluste des Winters auszugleichen". „Seit Nacht v. 29. Febr. zum 1. Mrz. läßt alliierte Luftwaffe in bisher unbekanntem Umfange feindliche Agenten, Waffen, Munition und Sprengstoffe über dem besetzten frz. Gebiet abwerfen. Vom 1. bis 3. Mrz. 44 wurden hierbei 11 engl. Offiziere, 1205 Abwurftrommeln mit Waffen, Munition und Sprengstoffen und 61 Abwurftrommeln mit persönlichen Effekten der Agenten sowie Funkgeräten sichergestellt. Feind scheint bestrebt, die in letzter Zeit durch unsere Zugriffe verlorenen Waffenlager in kürzester Frist wieder aufzufüllen" (6. Mrz. 44). „Die Waffen- und Sprengstoffabwürfe der letzten Tage in Mittel- und Südfrankreich beweisen, welche Bedeutung der Feind der Mitwirkung der frz. Terrorgruppen im Falle einer Landung beimißt. Während der mondhellen Nächte ganz erheblich gesteigerte Agentenversorgungsflüge mit Abwurf von zahlreichen Sabotagematerial (bis zu 100 Flugzeuge nachts). Dabei neu Abwurf von leichten Granatwerfern. Z. T. Abwurf im freien Gelände ohne Zusammenwirken mit einer Bodenorganisation. Der Agentenfunkverkehr Frankreich-England ist plötzlich bis zur doppelten Höhe angeschwollen."

20. März 1944: „Anhaltende schwere Eisenbahnsabotage unter planmäßiger Berücksichtigung empfindlicher Stellen" (13. Mrz. 44). „Anhaltende planmäßige Sabotage mit schweren Folgen; Energieversorgung in Südwestfrankreich infolge Leitungssprengung im wesentlichen nur durch Dampfkraftwerke für wichtigen militärischen Bedarf. Gesamte Industrie vorläufig stillgelegt."

10. April 1944: „In Südfrankreich gehen einzelne regionale Führer zu selbständigen Aktionen vor, die im Gegensatz zu den Anweisungen von London stehen, sich im allgemeinen ruhig zu verhalten."

„Verstärkte Agentenversorgungsflüge beiderseits des frz. Zentralmassivs deuten auf Vorbereitung frz. Aufstandsgruppen hin" (1. Mai 44). „Die Versorgung von Agenten und Widerstandsbewegung aus der Luft ist sehr stark angestiegen" (8. Mai 44). „Versorgungsflüge bis zu 100 Maschinen nachts in die bekannten Räume" (4. Juni 44).

„Starke Zunahme der Aktivität der Widerstandsbewegung in Südfrankreich. Anscheinend einheitliches Vorgehen der Widerstandsgruppen im Kampf gegen Deutschland unter Zurückstellung innerpolitischer Gegensätze. Meldungen über umfangreiche ‚Aushebungen‘ zur ‚AS‘, teils durch Drohung und Zwang, teils durch Werbung gegen den Arbeitseinsatz in Deutschland. Zusammenziehung von Kräftegruppen bei Tulle und im Zentralmassiv. Starke terroristische Tätigkeit im Dep. Corrèze. Laufend Überfälle auf Eisenbahnzüge, ungesicherte Ortschaften, frz. Verwaltungsdienststellen, Plünderung frz. Arbeitsdienstlager, Diebstähle von Kraftfahrzeugen und Treibstoffen" (4. Juni 44).

„Rundfunküberwachung meldet Aufnahme von Sprüchen des Radio London um 21.15 Uhr, die ihrer Bedeutung nach bekannt eine bevorstehende Invasion anzeigen sollen; . . . beachtet, weil sie mindestens teilweise für ‚French Section‘ bestimmt sind" (5. Juni 44, 21.45 Uhr).

„Die immer deutlicher in Erscheinung tretende Bildung der ‚AS‘ in Innerfrankreich . . . verlangt durchgreifende Maßnahmen" (7. Juni 44).

„MBF meldet fortschreitende Mobilmachung der Widerstandsgruppen und wachsende Bedrohung vereinzelter Stäbe, Kommandos und Wachen in Innerfrankreich" (9. Juni 44). „In Südfrankreich starke Bandenansammlungen der ‚AS‘ in zahlreichen Räumen" (12. Juni 44). „Zunehmende Tätigkeit geschlossener feindlicher Aufstandsgruppen unter Führung engl. und gaullistischer Offiziere in der Bretagne" (18. Juni 44). „Erscheinungen im Straßenbild, die auf geheime Einberufung und Zusammenziehung jüngerer Jahrgänge schließen lassen" (19. Juni 44). „Auf den Landstraßen mehrten sich die Bilder, daß junge Leute auf Fahrrädern mit leichtem Gepäck den einsam gelegenen Sammelplätzen zueilten; ganze Dörfer leerten sich zusehends von der jungen waffenfähigen Bevölkerung". „Harte Kämpfe in Innerfrankreich, wo Lage zwar jeweils nach Erscheinen dtsch. Truppen rasch geklärt, Banden jedoch beweglich ausweichen" (19. Juni 44). „Erfahrung zeigt, daß Terroristen zwar vor Truppen ausweichen, nach deren Abzug aber alsbald zurückkehren" (22. Juni 44).

Die eingetretene äußere Beruhigung der Lage darf nicht darüber hinwegtäuschen, daß im Falle etwaiger Rückschläge auf dtsch. Seite der vorbereitete Aufstand erneut und besser vorbereitet zum Ausbruch kommen kann" (Junibericht 44).

„Deutlich zeichnete sich das Vordringen der Terroristen aus Südfrankreich nach Westen über die Demarkationslinie ab". „NW Rodez und in Arles Raubüberfälle stärkerer Terroristenbanden, Plünderung von Banken und Finanzamt, Raub von Betriebsstoff und Lebensmitteln, . . . Aufdeckung einer frz. Organisation in Dives . . . durch Rotes Kreuz getarnt" (7. Juli 44).

„In den letzten Tagen erstmalig bei drei Gruppen der Widerstandsbewegung engl. Offiziere festgestellt und ausgehoben; in Uniform, wahrscheinlich ‚French Section'" (30. Juni 44). „In der Bretagne planmäßige Terroristenüberfälle, dabei uniformierte Fallschirmjäger erkannt; in Südfrankreich, N Auriac, neue Bande unter engl. Instrukteuren" (7. Juli 44). „In der Region Limoges angegriffene Terroristenlager, größtenteils desertierte Gendarmen" (8. Juli 44). „Bewaffnete Zivilisten unter Führung von Kommandoangehörigen festgestellt in Verson" (10. Juli 44). „Dabei wurde in zunehmendem Maße die Absicht der feindlichen Führung erkannt, durch Absetzen von engl. und frz. Offizieren mit kleinen Trupps in Uniform mittels Fallschirm eine straffe und auf die Operationen abgestellte Organisation und Führung der Banden sicherzustellen" (13. Juli 44).

„Am 11. Juli 44 Überfall auf Geldtransport der Banque de France 14 km NW St. Germain-en Laye durch Terroristen". „Zunehmende Gefährdung auch kampfkräftiger Geleite im Dep. Hautes-Alpes; besonders schwerer Überfall auf 100 Mann starkes Geleit" (11. Juli 44). Unter dem 16. Juli 44 wird als Ergebnis eines Großunternehmens im Dep. Ain gemeldet: „1200 bis 1500 Mann zersprengt, 400 Feindtote".

„Am 17. Juli 44 hat Radio Algier einen Aufruf an die Offiziere und Unteroffiziere der frz. Armee erlassen, unverzüglich zu ihren auf nationalem Boden kämpfenden Einheiten zu stoßen; diejenigen, die dem Rufe nicht folgen, werden darauf hingewiesen, daß sie die Folgen zu tragen haben werden" (20. Juli 44).

„Die Kampfführung der Banden ist nachgiebig; sie weichen vor der Truppe aus und warten auf deren Abzug. Zu starkem Widerstand, harten Kämpfen und entscheidenden Schlägen kommt es im allgemeinen nur dort, wo die Banden über befestigte Stellungen und schwere Waffen verfügen" (13. Juli 44). Die militärischen Gegenunternehmungen „scheiterten an der elastischen Kampfführung der einzelnen Gruppen, die bei ihren Ausweichbewegungen von der Bevölkerung weitgehend unterstützt wurden".

„In den Niederlanden infolge der bekannten Abneigung des Volkes gegen terroristische Aktivität bisher keine Bandenbildung . . . In Belgien zwei voneinander unabhängige Widerstandsorganisationen: nationaler Widerstand („Armée Belge") und Kommunisten. Bisher kein offener Aufstand. Im Vergleich zur Bandenlage in Frankreich sind die Auswirkungen der Widerstandsbewegung in Belgien bis jetzt bedeutungslos . . . Frankreich: im altbesetzten Gebiet Bandenbildung in den Räumen Chartres, Orléans, Melun, Beauvais. Gesamtstärke der noch in der Entwicklung begriffenen Organisationen infolge dauernden Abganges und Zulaufes schwer zu schätzen; z. Zt. vermutlich 20–25 000 Mann. Bewaffnung noch uneinheitlich, Pistolen, MPi, MG, wird durch laufende Abwürfe verstärkt . . . Anhaltende Sabotage ... mit weiteren schweren und nachhaltigen Störungen Anschläge auf Eisenbahn- und Hochspannungsleitungen in Zusammenarbeit mit feindlicher Luftwaffe planmäßig von England gesteuert ... Feuerüberfälle auf einzelne Soldaten, kleine Abteilungen und Versorgungskolonnen bei Tag und Nacht ... Südfrankreich: Der bereits gemeldete, auf den Abzug der dtsch. Truppen zurückzuführende Wiederbeginn größerer Bandenansammlungen führte zur Bildung starker Widerstandszentren in den Räumen um Bourganeuf (40 km O Limoges), um Oyonnax (30 km W Genf) und im Vercors-Gebiet (SO Valence). Bewaffnung und Ausrüstung wesentlich besser: MPi, MG, Panzerbüchsen, Granatwerfer, vereinzelt Pak. Munitionsausstattung gut, große Bestände an Sprengmitteln, Bewaffnung und Munition werden durch anhaltende Luftabwürfe verstärkt. Nachrichten- und Meldewesen ausgezeichnet, z. T. mit neuestem engl. und amerik. Gerät ... Stärke großen Schwankungen unterworfen, z. Zt. nach grober Schätzung 60–70 000 Mann, von denen der größere Teil infolge des harten Zuschlagens der Truppe sich z. Zt. vom aktiven Widerstand fernhält" (21. Juli 44).

„Unterstützung der frz. Widerstandsbewegung durch Abwurf von Material sowie Absprung von Führungspersonal und Sabotagetrupps hält weiter erheblich an. Zunehmende Stärkung der Widerstandsbewegung äußert sich u. a. in besatzungsarmen Räumen durch selbstsicheres Auftreten der Banden unter scharfer Betonung der Disziplin innerhalb der einzelnen Gruppen und gegenüber der Bevölkerung. Im Pyrenäengebiet nimmt kommunistischer Einfluß auf die Führung der Bandengruppen zu. Es mehren sich die Fälle, in denen Sühnemaßnahmen an dtsch. Gefangenen als Vergeltung für die Erschießung gefangener Terroristen angekündigt werden. Haltung der Bevölkerung weiterhin abwartend, vom baldigen Zusammenbruch Deutschlands überzeugt" (24. Juli 44).

„Es beginnt sich ein Unterschied in der Haltung der nationalen und der kommunistischen Widerstandsgruppen abzuzeichnen. In den von frz. Offizieren stammenden Anlagen zeigt sich das Bestreben, die Regeln des Völkerrechtes und der militärischen Kriegführung einzuhalten. Bei den von frz. Offizieren geführten FFI wurde das mehrfach beobachtet; 72 dtsch. Soldaten, die in die Gefangenschaft der FFI geraten waren und wieder befreit wurden, sind wie Kriegsgefangene behandelt worden, und zwar im allgemeinen anständig, allerdings bei knapper Verpflegung, aber ohne Mißhandlungen. Repressalien gegen dtsch. Gefangene wurden zwar von frz. Offizieren in schriftlichen Botschaften an dtsch. Kommandeure mehrfach angedroht. Über Ausführung solcher Repressalien liegen aber bisher keine Meldungen vor. Dagegen verfährt das „Sicherheitskommissariat" der kommunistischen „FTPF" kurzerhand nach bolschewistischen Methoden. Außer den Fällen in Anlage 4 sind mehrere Fälle bekannt geworden, in denen gefangene dtsch. Soldaten durch Genickschuß getötet worden sind" (26. Juli 44).

„Die Banden sind eine straff von außen geführte und unter absolut sachkundiger Führung arbeitende Organisation" (9. Juli 44), „eine im Rücken der dtsch. Besatzung aktiv kämpfende Armee, die trotz ihrer uneinheitlichen Zusammensetzung und ihrer Teilung in nach terroristischen Gesichtspunkten und russischem Vorbild arbeitende Maquisgruppen und straffer militärisch aufgebaute und sich zunächst zurückhaltende Résistanceeinheiten offensichtlich je nach der zu lösenden Aufgabe von einer einheitlichen, zielbewußten Führung eingesetzt wurde". Für Südfrankreich urteilte der Chef des Stabes der Armeegruppe G am 7. Aug. 44: „Im großen kann nicht mehr von einer Widerstandsbewegung gesprochen werden, sondern es handelt sich bereits um eine organisierte Armee, die in unserem Rücken steht."

Oradour

Den Höhepunkt der Partisanen- und Untergrundbewegung in Frankreich stellt die Phase der Invasion dar. In den ersten Tagen der Invasion erhoben sich überall in Frankreich die Maquis. Sie gingen gegen die Deutschen als auch gegen Widerstandsgruppen anderer politischer Richtung, mutmaßliche Kollaborateure und sog. Verräter vor. Gleich brutal war die Reaktion der Deutschen.

In diese Zeit fällt auch das schreckliche Vorkommnis „Oradour". Die Division der Waffen-SS – eine Panzerdivision – lag im Periogord bei Montauban am Tarnefluß. Der Kommandeur dieser Division, SS-Brigadeführer und Generalmajor der Waffen-SS Heinz Lammerding, bekam den Befehl, in die Normandie zu verlegen, damit die Truppe dort am 9. Juni gegen die gelandeten Alliierten eingesetzt werden konnte. Die direkte Bahn- und Straßenroute führte durch Brive, Limoges, Poitiers, Tours, Le Mans und Caen. Es ist selbstverständlich, daß die Alliierten bestrebt waren, den Marsch zu verzögern. Die alliierten Luftstreitkräfte wurden eingesetzt. Sie zerstörten die Straßen und Eisenbahnbrücken über die Loire zwischen dem Atlantik und Orléans. Der Eisenbahntunnel unter der Loire auf der Strecke Saumur–Parthenay wurde zerstört. Eine Bombe explodierte im Tunnel; dieser stürzte ein. Ein großer Teil des Treibstofflagers der Division flog in die Luft.

Lammerding wollte wegen Treibstoffmangels seine Division zunächst mit der Bahn befördern. Jedoch Antony Brooks, der Angehöriger der Organisation SOE war, gelang es, mit seiner Abteilung den Bahnverkehr auf der Strecke Toulouse–Montauban zu unterbrechen und die Nachschub- und Munitionszüge sowie die Brückenbauzüge der Division, die zum Überqueren der Loire notwendig waren, zu stoppen. Daher konnte Lammerding den Umweg nach Osten nicht einschlagen, um dann nordwestlich in die Normandie vorzustoßen.

Die Marschroute führte die Divsion zunächst in die Gegend von Bergorac und Perigueux, in die Täler der Dordogne, der Vezère, der Auvezère, der Isle und der Dronne. Die Maquisards des Baron Philippe de Gunzbourg legten gefährliche Hinterhalte, verteilten Zyklonit-Minen, schossen auf stehende Panzerkommandanten und hielten die Marschkolonnen auf. Am 9. Juni 1944 erreichte die Division gegen 2 Uhr Limoges.

Limoges war seit zwei Tagen von der Außenwelt abgeschnitten. Die Maquisards verhinderten durch einen Sperring nach außen oder von außen den Verkehr in die Stadt. Das erste Bataillon, das nach einer anstrengenden Fahrt in den Vormittagsstunden in Limoges eintraf, hatte in der linken Flanke schwere Feuergefechte zu bestehen. Die ersten Verluste traten ein. Viele Baumsperren waren zu beseitigen.

Bei Limoges war von den Engländern eine SAS-Gruppe (Special Air Services) gelandet worden, die die Aufgabe hatte, gemeinsam mit den Maquisards die Deutschen auf dem Marsch vom Süden in die Normandie zu behindern. Auf dem Marsch gab es Tote und Verwundete. Auf den Bahndämmen entgleisten Waggons und Lokomtiven. Die Straßen waren von liegengebliebenen oder ausgebrannten deutschen Fahrzeugen verstopft.

Ein schwerer Zwischenfall ereignete sich bei Tulle an der Corrèze zwischen Limoges und Clermont-Ferrand. Dort ermordeten die Maquisards die gesamte deutsche Garnison in der Manufacture des Armes, der Ecole Normale und dem Hotel La Tremolière. Der Bürgermeister der Stadt erklärte sie für befreit und begann sie zu befestigen. Über die Ereignisse in Tulle wurde der Divisionsstab unterrichtet. Panzerwagen erkämpften sich den Weg in die Stadt. Von der Aufklärungsabteilung II wurden die Leichen von 40 deutschen Soldaten mit eingeschlagenem Schädel und ausgestochenen Augen aufgefunden.

An der Friedhofsmauer von Tulle waren außerdem 10–12 deutsche Soldaten erschossen worden. Wie SS-Standardenführer Otto Weidinger berichtet, befanden sich unter den Aufständischen Polen, Rotspanier und Russen. Über noch lebende deutsche Soldaten fuhren schwere Lastwagen der Aufständischen hinweg und verstümmelten sie bis zur Unkenntlichkeit. Bei einem Toten wurde festgestellt, daß ihm beide Fersen durchbohrt waren und durch die Löcher ein Strick gezogen war. Weidinger berichtet am 27. Nov. 1963 weiter:

,,Daraufhin wurden 99 Maquisards, die mit Unterstützung der Bevölkerung aus den festgenommenen Männern ausgesucht, als Maquisards erkannt und bezeichnet wurden – es handelte sich größtenteils um Ortsfremde –, nach einem Standgerichtsverfahren durch Erhängen hingerichtet. Ein französischer Geistlicher leistete ihnen letzten Beistand. Anschließend wurde die französische Arbeitsdienstabteilung zur Bestattung der Hingerichteten auf dem Friedhof in Tulle eingesetzt.

Wie später bekannt wurde, sind am 9. oder 10. Juni 1944 in einem Wäldchen bei Naves (10 km nördlich Tulle) 62 weitere deutsche Soldaten, die den Maquisards beim Angriff auf Tulle in die Hände gefallen waren, darunter Sanitäter und Eisenbahner, durch die Aufständischen erschossen worden. Allein im Raum Tulle betrugen die Verluste der deutschen Truppen durch die Maquisards 110–112 Tote."

Am 10. Juni vormittags meldet der Kommandeur des 1. Bataillons, Sturmbannführer Dickmann, beim Regiment, ihm sei berichtet worden, daß in der Ortschaft Oradour sur Glane ein höherer deutscher Offizier von den Maquisards gefangengehalten würde. Dieser solle am gleichen Abend im Rahmen einer Feier öffentlich hingerichtet und verbrannt werden. Die gesamte Bevölkerung von Oradour sur Glane arbeite mit den Maquis zusammen, und in der Ortschaft befinde sich ein höherer Maquis-Stab. Dickmann brachte zum Ausdruck, daß es sich nur um Sturmbannführer Kämpfe handeln könne.

Der Kommandant der Sicherheitspolizei im Limoges wurde gebeten, einen gefangenen Maquisführer, der sich im Gewahrsam der Sicherheitspolizei befand, zur Verfügung zu stellen.

Weidinger berichtet in diesem Zusammenhang weiter: „Obersturmbannführer Meier von der Sicherheitspolizei sichert dies sofort zu und verspricht außerdem, noch 15 weitere Maquisards freizugeben, falls Kämpfe zurückgegeben werde. Der zur Verfügung gestellte Maquisführer wird zum Regimentsgefechtsstand gebracht. Der O 3 als Dolmetscher teilt ihm mit, daß er seine Freiheit erhalte gegen das Versprechen, sofort mit seinem Stab Verbindung aufzunehmen und dort mitzuteilen, daß noch weitere 15 Maquisards freigelassen würden, sobald Kämpfe lebend zurückgegeben werde . . . Der Regimentskommandeur hat in diesen Tagen alles versucht, um Kämpfe wieder zurückzubekommen und dabei unnötiges Blutvergießen zu vermeiden. Der Maquisführer erklärt sich mit dem Angebot einverstanden und wird daher mit einem PKW an den Stadtrand von Limoges gebracht, wo er bei dem letzten deutschen Posten freigelassen wird. Am späten Abend ruft er noch einmal an und meldet, daß er seinen Stab nicht mehr gefunden habe. Dann hört man nichts mehr von ihm."

Hinzuzufügen ist, daß dem ebengenannten Maquisführer als zusätzliche Belohnung ein Betrag von RM 35 000 versprochen worden ist.

Der anglo-amerikanische Schriftsteller Anthony Cave Brown schreibt in seinem Buche „Bodyguard of lies": „Ein Bataillonskommandeur der Division „das Reich" wurde von den Maquisards des Dorfes Oradour-sur-Vay-res, ungefähr 30 km westlich von Limoges, in seinem Befehlswagen entwe-der von Heckenschützen beschossen oder getötet, oder er geriet in einen Hinterhalt, wurde gefangengenommen und dann erschossen. Am nächsten Morgen, den 10. Juni, umzingelte eine Abteilung der Division den Ort Oradour-sur-Glane, den falschen Ort, der aber annähernd in derselben Gegend lag, und trieb alle Bewohner auf dem Dorfplatz zusammen.

Der Regimentskommendeur teilte der Bevölkerung – hauptsächlich Landarbeiter – mit, es seien Waffen und Sprengstoff im Dorf versteckt und die Dorfbewohner hätten Terroristen geholfen. Er kündigte eine Personen-kontrolle an und befahl den Männern, dort zu bleiben, wo sie waren, wäh-rend sich Frauen und Kinder in die Kirche begeben sollten. So geschah es – unter SS-Aufsicht. Die Männer wurden auf der Stelle mit Maschinengeweh-ren niedergemacht. Die Kirchentür wurde verrammelt, und die SS-Männer steckten die Kirche in Brand. Von 652 Einwohnern kamen 642 um, 245 Frauen, 207 Kinder und 190 Männer. Das Massaker von Oradour sur Glane wurde später als „die grausamste und beschämendste Seite im Buch der deutschen Kriegsverbrechen bezeichnet."

Lassen wir Otto Weidinger in seinem Bericht sprechen: „Spät am Nach-mittag desselben Tages kommt Sturmbannführer Diekmann zum Regiment zurück und meldet dem Regimentskommandeur etwa folgendes: Die Kom-pagnie habe in Oradour Widerstand gefunden. Darauf habe sie die Ort-schaft besetzt und sofort eine genaue Durchsuchung der Häuser durchge-führt. Kämpfe sei dabei nicht gefunden worden, jedoch viele Waffen und Munition. Deshalb habe er alle Männer der Ortschaft, die mit Sicherheit Maquisards gewesen seien, erschießen lassen. Die Frauen und Kinder seien während dieser Zeit in der Kiche eingesperrt gewesen. Anschließend sei die Ortschaft in Brand gesetzt worden; dabei sei fast in allen Häusern noch versteckte Munition hochgegangen. Durch den Brand des Dorfes habe das Feuer auch auf die Kirche übergegriffen, in der ebenfalls im Dachstuhl Munition versteckt gelegen habe. Dadurch sei die Kirche sehr schnell abge-brannt, die Frauen und Kinder seien so ums Leben gekommen.

Standardenführer Stadler ist im höchsten Maße über diese Meldung er-schüttert und sagt, aufs höchste erregt, zu Sturmbannführer Diekmann: ‚Diekmann, das kann Ihnen teuer zu stehen kommen. Ich werde sofort beim Divisionsgericht eine kriegsgerichtliche Untersuchung gegen Sie beantra-gen. So etwas kann ich nicht auf dem Regiment sitzen lassen!'

. . . Sofort nach Ankunft des Divisionskommandeurs, Brigadeführer Lammerding, meldet der Standartenführer die Vorkommnisse in Oradour sur Glane und erbittet eine kriegsgerichtliche Untersuchung gegen Diek-mann. Sie wird zugesichert, sobald die Kampflage ihren Beginn erlaube."

Aus den Akten des ständigen höheren Militärgerichts Bordeaux (Untersuchungsrichter Lesieur) darf entnommen werden:

„In der Abenddämmerung riskierte es der Major Kämpfe, Kommandeur des III. Bataillons, der Marschkompanie allein in einem PKW vorauszufahren. In der Höhe des Ortes La Bussière der Gemeinde St. Leonard de Noblat wurde er durch einige Maquisards, darunter der Sergeant Canou, gefangengenommen. – Der Major Kämpfe wurde in die Nachbargemeinde Cheyssons gebracht. Seine Gefangennahme sollte als Vorwand für eine ganze Reihe von Repressalien dienen.

Das III. Bataillon folgte seinem Kommandeur mit ungefähr zehn Minuten Abstand. Nachdem der verlassene PKW gefunden wurde, durchsuchten die Deutschen, die von einigen Milizleuten begleitet waren, die Häuser der Ortschaft und ergriffen Repressalien. Im übrigen wurde der Major Kämpfe als Folge des Blutbades von Oradour sur Glane durch die Maquisards hingerichtet." Otto Weidinger nimmt auch zu den Behauptungen Stellung, daß Oradour sur Glane mit einem anderen Oradour verwechselt worden sei. Er erklärt, daß eine Verwechslung so gut wie ausgeschlossen sei.

Im Jahre 1963 wurde eine Erklärung bekannt, die in der „Deutschen Wochenzeitung" wiedergegeben wurde. Diese stammt von dem damaligen Ordonanzoffizier der Sturmgeschütz-Abteilung „Das Reich", dem früheren SS-Obersturmführer Gerlach. Durch seine Aussage wird die Ansicht von Otto Weidinger vollständig gedeckt.

Gerlach erklärt: „Das Regiment war, vom Süden Frankreichs kommend, in der Nacht vom 8. zum 9. Juni 1944 in Limoges eingetroffen. Am Morgen des 9. Juni erhielt ich in Limoges vom Regimentskommandeur Stadler den Auftrag, für die Sturmgeschützabteilung im Raum von Nieul Quartier zu nehmen. Er wies mich anhand der Karte ein und warnte mich vor den in diesem Raum tätigen Widerstandskämpfern. Ich fuhr daraufhin mit sechs Männern in drei PKW's nach Nieul. Wir machten dort Quartier. Da dies aber nicht ausreichte, fuhren wir anhand der Karte in die Nachbarorte. Mein Wagen war schneller als die beiden anderen Fahrzeuge; ich mußte daher bald halten, und da sie mir nicht gefolgt waren, kehrt machen, um sie wieder zu finden. Nach kurzer Zeit wurde ich auf offener Straße plötzlich von einem LKW gestoppt, in dem ich Militäruniformen sah . . . Bevor ich weiter nachdenken konnte, geschweige denn von meiner Maschinenpistole Gebrauch machen konnte, waren 7–8 uniformierte Männer aus dem Wagen gesprungen, hatten ihre Waffen auf uns gerichtet und waren, wild gestikulierend, schreiend und ‚Hände hoch' fordernd, auf meinen Wagen zugekommen. Sie zerrten meinen Fahrer und mich aus dem Wagen, rissen uns die Uniformstücke vom Körper, schlugen uns ins Gesicht und sagten unter unmißverständlichen Zeichen: ‚SS! Sofort kaputt!' . . . Ich sah nach einiger

Zeit Ortsschilder, so daß ich mich orientieren konnte; dann kam ein Schild am Eingang eines Dorfes, auf dem stand: Oradour sur Glane. In der Hauptstraße von Oradour sur Glane hielten wir an. Wir mußten aussteigen. Wir wurden von Maquis und vielen Neugierigen umringt. Ich sah viele Uniformierte, auch Frauen in gelber Lederjacke und mit Stahlhelm. Die Bevölkerung nahm von Minute zu Minute eine immer drohendere Haltung ein . . . Ich sah, wie aus einer Scheune neben einem Bäckerladen in der Hauptstraße von Oradour sur Glane Stricke herausgeholt wurden. Mein Fahrer und ich . . . wurden mit den Stricken gefesselt . . .‟

Die Erklärung schließt mit den Worten: ,,Ich meldete mich bei meinem Regimentskommandeur Stadler und schilderte den Vorgang. Er sagte mir, daß ich nicht der einzige gewesen sei, der tags zuvor aufgegriffen und gekidnappt worden sei. So erzählte er mir von dem Kommandeur des III. Bataillons des Regiments ,Der Führer' namens Kämpfe, der noch nicht zurückgekehrt und wahrscheinlich umgebracht worden sei. Mir befal der Regimentskommandeur, mich auszuschlafen, da noch schwierige Märsche bevorstünden. Als ich wieder auf war, ließ mich der Kommandeur des I. Bataillons ,Der Führer', Diekmann, auf der Karte den Ort meiner Gefangennahme und den Weg bis zur Erschießung meines Fahrers zeigen. Er ging bald darauf mit der 3. Kompanie (Führer Hauptmann Kahn) fort mit dem Ziel Oradour sur Glane.‟

Im Einsatzraum in der Normandie begannen sofort die Vernehmungen von Diekmann und verschiedenen Angehörigen der 3. Kompanie durch den Divisionsrichter. Als die Division in die dortigen Kämpfe eingesetzt war, wurden die Ermittlungen abgebrochen. Sturmbannführer Diekmann fiel bei den ersten Kämpfen. Weidinger erklärt: ,,Aus seinem Benehmen kann man schließen, daß ihm das Schreckliche seiner Tat bewußt geworden war und er den Tod suchte. Denn nach Augenzeugenberichten stand er ohne Deckung aufrecht mitten im ärgsten Feuer, ohne Stahlhelm, nur mit einer Feldmütze, bis ihn ein Granatsplitter tödlich verwundete.‟

In seinem Buch schreibt Anthony Cave Brown über die Bedeutung des Einsatzes der Maquis im Zusammenhang mit der Schlacht in der Normandie, indem er auf eine Stellungnahme der SOE verweist: ,,Diese vierzehntägige Verzögerung eines normalerweise drei Tage dauernden Marsches kann für die Befestigung des Brückenkopfes in der Normandie durchaus von entscheidender Bedeutung gewesen sein. Die Lage der Alliierten war dort während der ersten Tage so kritisch, daß der Einsatz einer weiteren erstklassigen und voll ausgerüsteten Panzerdivision mit mehr als normaler Kampfstärke einen Teil der ohnehin noch immer schwachen alliierten Front in einem Zug bis zum Strand hätte zurückdrängen und das gesamte Unternehmen ,,Neptune‟ zum Scheitern bringen müssen.‟

Belgien und Nordfrankreich

Ende 1940 wurde die belgische Partisanenarmee gegründet. Die geographischen Voraussetzungen waren andere als in Frankreich. Es entstand ein illegales System, das sich auf Dreiergruppen aufbaute, die zu Kompanien zusammengefaßt wurden. Aus je drei Kompanien wurde ein Bataillon gebildet. Drei Bataillone stellten ein Partisanenkorps dar, an dessen Spitze ein Kommandeur mit seinem Stab stand.

Belgien wurde in fünf Sektoren geteilt, in denen 16 Partisanenkorps operierten.

Die belgische Partisanenarmee wurde von Kommunisten geführt. Neben ihr gab es die Sabotageorganisation ,,Groupement général de Sabotage". 1942 entstand die ,,Geheime Armee". Sie wurde von London aus geleitet. Ihr gehörten vorwiegend Soldaten und Offiziere der ehemaligen regulären belgischen Armee an.

1941/42 führten die belgischen Partisanen 1657 Aktionen durch, darunter 246 Sprengungen und Entgleisungen. Im Winter 1941 wurden 125 Züge zum Entgleisen gebracht. 500 deutsche Soldaten und Offiziere wurden in Antwerpen von 1941 bis 1945 getötet.

Meldungen des Beauftragten des Chefs der Sicherheitspolizei und des SD für den Bereich des Militärbefehlshabers in Belgien und Nordfrankreich im Jahre 1944 im Auszug vom 15. Juni 1944 mögen das erste Wort haben.

Sie lauten:

Auf dem Gebiet von Terror und Sabotage war neuerdings wieder eine Verschärfung festzustellen, was aus Zahlen hervorgeht, die durch den Gendarmeriestab im belgischen Innenministerium erfaßt wurden. Hiernach ereigneten sich im Monat Mai 1944 (die Zahlen für den Monat April sind in Klammern beigefügt):

Anschläge auf Personen	94	(101)
Morde	74	(59)
Sabotagefälle an Ernteprodukten und sonstigen Lebensmitteln	33	(38)
Sabotage an Verkehrsanlagen, Kanälen, Eisenbahn, Telefon	139	(79)
Sabotage an Versorgungsbetrieben (Bergwerke, Fabriken, Molkereien)	11	(12)

Immer wieder wird festgestellt, daß besonders der Adel maßgeblich an der Schleusung und Beherbergung von Feindfliegern beteiligt ist. Als Beweggrund wird Patriotismus oder Deutschfeindlichkeit angegeben.

Bei Lees (Departement Nord) stürzte ein Feindflugzeug ab. Die fünfköpfige Besatzung konnte sich retten, ohne jedoch aufgefunden zu werden. Zwei französische Zollbeamte sahen die Flieger schweben, ohne daß sie sich um die Ergreifung bemüht hatten. Zehn Personen aus der Gemeinde Lees wurden in diesem Zusammenhang festgenommen.

Die Feindpropaganda der letzten Tage behandelt in ihren Flugblättern bereits die militärischen Ereignisse an der Kanalküste.

Der Beginn der Invasion hat eine erhöhte Aktivität der Terror- und Sabotagegruppen nach sich gezogen. Eine einheitliche Ausrichtung bei der Ausführung der Anschläge ist jedoch noch zu vermissen. Vermutlich sind die widersprechenden Anordnungen, die dieserhalb an die Widerstandsbewegungen ergangen sind, daran schuld. Während von alliierter Seite ein Kurztreten befohlen ist, besagen sämtliche Anweisungen, die die KPB und die Unabhängigkeitsfront für die Stunde herausgegeben hatten, ein sofortiges Aktivieren aller Sabotage- und Terrorhandlungen. Es muß angenommen werden, daß das Ansteigen der Anschläge zur Zeit noch im wesentlichen dem links organisierten Gegner zuzuschreiben ist. Die Rechtsopposition dürfte aus ihrer Reserve noch nicht herausgegangen sein. Wesentlich ist die Zunahme der Eisenbahnsabotagen. Die Schienensprengungen haben ein erhebliches Ausmaß angenommen. In einem Fall wurden in einer einzigen Nacht auf einer Strecke 22 Schienensprengungen bekannt. Auch Eisenbahnbrücken wurden durch Sprengstoffanschläge beschädigt. Schwerpunktgebiete sind die Bezirke um Lüttich, Dinant, Charleroi, Mons und Ath.

Auch die Überfälle auf Wehrmachtsangehörige haben eine Steigerung erfahren. In der Berichtszeit wurden im Befehlsbereich acht Wehrmachtsangehörige getötet und drei verletzt. Zugenommen haben weiter die Mordanschläge auf Landeseinwohner.

Eine Großaktion gegen Terroristen, Arbeitsdienstverweigerer und sonstige Mitglieder von Widerstandsbewegungen wurde durch den Abwehrtrupp 364 in Gent veranlaßt. Bisher wurden 40 festgenommene Personen der Terroristentätigkeit überführt. 16 Schleusensprengungen konnten dadurch bereits geklärt werden.

In weiteren Zugriffen gegen die Terror- und Sabotagegruppen in Ecaussinnes und Umgebung gelang es der Außendienststelle Charleroi, 41 Mitglieder von Widerstandsbewegungen aus der Unabhängigkeitsfront und nationalen Gruppen, die vor der Übernahme in diese standen, in Haft zu nehmen.

Im Bereich des Kommandeurs Lüttich wurden insgesamt 16 Personen aus dem Terrorapparat der Unabhängigkeitsfront in Haft genommen. Durch diese Festnahmen wurden verschiedene Anschläge, u. a. auch zwei Mordfälle zur Aufklärung gebracht.

Der Kommandeur von Lille meldet nach Beginn der Invasion eine intensive Tätigkeit der kommunistischen Terror- und Sabotagegruppen. Neben Anschlägen auf Anlagen des Eisenbahnnetzes wurden Kabel- und Fernsprechleitungen planmäßig zum Objekt von Sabotageanschlägen auserwählt. Es gelang dem Gegner dadurch, für einige Stunden den gesamten Überlandfernsprechverkehr lahmzulegen. Im Zuge der Bekämpfung der Terror- und Sabotagegruppen wurden in Roubaix sieben Terroristen erfaßt, die geständig und überführt sind, eine größere Anzahl von Anschlägen verübt zu haben.

Die Gesamtfestnahmen belaufen sich in der Berichtszeit auf:

Brüssel	113
Gent	17
Charleroi	66
Antwerpen	11
Lüttich	16
Lille	20
insgesamt:	243

Während in Lille die Festnahme von 56 Angehörigen der nationalen Widerstandsorganisationen gelang, konnten im Bereich der Außendienststelle Charleroi 17 Personen, die zum Teil der „Weißen Brigade" und zum Teil dem „Mouvement National Belge" angehörten, festgenommen werden.

In Brüssel gelang durch die Festnahme weiterer zwölf Mitglieder verschiedener nationaler Widerstandsorganisationen, die z. T. als Unterführer eingesetzt waren, wiederum ein Einbruch in verschiedene Gruppen.

Die Tätigkeit der Widerstands- und Terrorgruppen hat sich in der Berichtszeit verstärkt. Der Kampf gegen diese reichlich mit Waffen ausgerüsteten Banditen hat sich ganz erheblich verschärft. Auch auf seiten der Sicherheitspolizei entstanden Verluste. So wurden im Bereich der Außendienststelle Antwerpen bei der Aushebung einer derartigen Gruppe zwei Angehörige der Dienststelle beim Schußwechsel getötet. Diese Gruppe wurde mit Ausnahme eines Mitgliedes erfaßt, zwei Angehörige der Gruppe wurden im Feuergefecht erschossen, ein weiterer schwer verletzt. Durch die Vernehmungen gelang es, weitere vier Personen festzunehmen, wobei während des sich entwickelnden Feuergefechtes eine Kurierin erschossen und ein deutscher Deserteur schwer verletzt wurde.

Das Sonderkommando Dinant meldet die Festnahme von 36 Angehörigen der Widerstands- und Terrorgruppen, deren Vernehmungen es ermöglichten, in den frühen Morgenstunden des 25. Juni 1944 eine weitere Aktion auszulösen. Es handelte sich hier – wie erst später bekannt wurde –

um die Aushebung des Generalstabes der „Weißen Armee", der sich in einer Ferme in der Gegend von Ciney festgesetzt hatte. Bei dem sich ergebenden Feuerwechsel wurden drei Dienststellenangehörige, darunter der Führer des Sonderkommandos Dinant, und 1 Feldgendarm getötet, zwei weitere Dienststellenangehörige und 1 Feldgendarm verletzt. Von den Banditen wurden nach bisherigen Feststellungen 17 im Feuergefecht erschossen und zwei festgenommen. Die sich an das Feuergefecht anschließende Aktion ist noch nicht abgeschlossen. Weitere Veröffentlichung im nächsten Lagebericht.

Der Außendienststelle Charleroi gelang die Festnahme von 21 Angehörigen dieser Gruppen, während in den übrigen Bezirken weitere 8 Personen festgenommen werden konnten.

Am 15. Juli 44 heißt es: „Trotz Einsatzes aller zur Verfügung stehenden exekutiven Kräfte konnte ein erneutes, sprunghaftes Anwachsen der Mord- und Terrorwelle nicht verhindert werden. Ohne die Entwicklung für die erste Juli-Hälfte zu berücksichtigen, geht dies schon aus der Statistik des belg. Innenministeriums für den Monat Juni 1944 hervor. Danach ereigneten sich (die Zahlen für den Monat Mai sind in Klammern beigefügt):

Anschläge auf Personen	151	(94)
Morde	110	(74)
Sabotagefälle an Ernteprodukten und sonstigen Lebensmitteln		
	9	(33)
Sabotage an Verkehrsanlagen, Kanälen, Eisenbahnen, Telef.		
	331	(139)
Sabotage an Versorgungsbetrieben (Bergwerke, Fabriken, Molkereien)	24	(12)
Diebstähle mit Waffengewalt, Bandenüberfälle		
Lebensmittelmarken	122	(137)
Geld und Lebensmittel	613	(525)
Verwaltungsurkunden (Arbeitsämter)	34	(37)

„Das Problem von Terror und Sabotage beherrscht wachsend die innerpolitische Lage und ist unter Würdigung aller dafür in Frage kommenden Gesichtspunkte nicht ernst genug zu nehmen. Den Mordanschlägen, die sich zu allen Tageszeiten, in Wohnungen, auf offener Straße und häufig in Gegenwart von Zeugen abspielen, sind nicht nur als deutschfreundlich bekannte Landeseinwohner ausgesetzt, ganz gleich, ob sie sich in beamteten Stellungen befinden oder nicht."

Beteiligt sind nicht nur Männer, sondern neuerdings auch in erschreckendem Umfang Frauen und sogar Kinder aus den genannten Kreisen. Es liegt eine Menge von Fällen vor, in denen schon das geringste Anzeichen einer

Zusammenarbeit mit der Besatzungsmacht genügte, um dem brutalen Mordterror zum Opfer zu fallen. Die Beunruhigung unter den bedrohten Kreisen ist erneut um so mehr angewachsen, als man sich der Entwicklung schutzlos ausgesetzt fühlt. Die durch die Aufhebung der Verordnung des Militärbefehlshabers vom 8. Okt. 43, nach der die von der belgischen Gendarmerie und Polizei ergriffenen Täter der belgischen Justiz zur Verfolgung, Aburteilung und Strafvollstreckung auch bei Waffenbesitz überlassen wurden, erwirkte fast vollkommene Untätigkeit der landeseigenen Exekutive bei der Bekämpfung von Terror und Bandenunwesen. Das fällt dabei jetzt besonders fatal ins Gewicht. Die deutschen Exekutivkräfte reichen zu einer Verfolgung der täglichen Mordfälle bei weitem nicht aus, ihre Verstärkung mußte von zentraler Stelle infolge Personalmangels abgelehnt werden.

Aus neuordnungsbereiten Kreisen wird in diesem Zusammenhang berichtet, daß unter dem laufenden Druck der Mord- und Terrorwelle heute bereits absolut deutschfreundliche Landeseinwohner gezwungen seien, sich nach außen hin anglophil zu zeigen, um am Leben zu bleiben. Die vor einigen Tagen bekanntgegebene Erschießung von 25 ,,überführten Terroristen'' als Sühnemaßnahme für die Fortsetzung von Terroranschlägen auf Mitglieder der Erneuerungsbewegungen wird dabei als unzureichende Maßnahme bezeichnet. Man führt an, daß sich neuerdings eher noch eine Vermehrung der Mordfälle bemerkbar mache, und hält es für ungenügend, daß für unschuldige Opfer des Mordterrors überführte Terroristen, die ja sowieso doch dem Tode verfallen seien, erschossen werden. Der Ruf nach Inanspruchnahme von führenden Freimaurern, Marxisten und Vertretern der anglophilen Oberschicht wird dabei immer wieder laut. Man weist dabei darauf hin, daß diese Kreise auch heute noch den bestimmenden Einfluß hätten, um bei einigermaßen gutem Willen das drohende Chaos zu verhindern.

Bei Bekämpfung der oppositionellen Rechtsbewegung wurden in der ersten Juli-Hälfte in größeren Aktionen vor allen Dingen in Brüssel und Antwerpen zahlreiche Festnahmen getätigt. Als bemerkenswert aktive Gruppe trat dabei neuerdings die ,,Armée Belge Réorganisée'' hervor. Die bekannteste Hetzschrift der nationalen Widerstandsbewegung, die ,,Libre Belgique'', ist weder im Juni noch in der ersten Juli-Hälfte erschienen. Dies dürfte ein sichtbarer Beweis für die Wirksamkeit der exekutiven Maßnahmen gegen die oppositionelle Rechtsbewegung sein.

Während die kommunistische Flugblattpropaganda im allgemeinen etwas zurückhielt, hielt die seit Beginn der Invasion gestartete Sabotagewelle, vor allen Dingen gegen die Verkehrseinrichtungen, mit unverminderter Stärke an. Neuerdings liegen auch Anhaltspunkte dafür vor, daß Terrorakte gegen Angehörige der Besatzungsmacht nunmehr auf direkten Befehl der zentralen Leitung der Widerstandsorganisationen erfolgen. Bei allem kann die Absicht der kommunistischen Partei festgestellt werden, im Falle eines bewaffneten Aufstandes die Führung zu übernehmen . . .

Opposition – Rechtsbewegung

Die Aktivität der nationalen Widerstandsorganisationen, die bis zum Beginn der Invasion nicht festzustellen war, belebte sich auch in der Berichtszeit. Vor allen Dingen konnte dies in den kleineren Gruppen festgestellt werden.

Während im nordfranzösischen Raum die ,,O.C.M." (,,Organisation Civile et Militaire") als eine der stärksten Gruppen angesehen werden kann, ist in der letzten Zeit im belgischen Raum die ,,Armée Belge Réorganisée" mehr in den Vordergrund getreten. Durch die bereits im vorigen Lagebericht aufgeführte Zerschlagung eines Teils dieser Widerstandsgruppen im Bereich von Gent konnten wichtige Erkenntnisse gesammelt werden, die es ermöglichen, die Organisation in ihrem Aufbau klar zu erkennen. Dem Hauptquartier, das vermutlich von einem ehemaligen belgischen General – nur sein Deckname ist bekannt – geleitet wird, unterstehen fünf Zonen, die ihrerseits wieder in Sektionen und Gruppen unterteilt sind. Die Bewaffnung und einheitliche Bekleidung erfolgt nach den bisherigen Feststellungen durch Abwürfe von englischen Maschinen. Eine ausgesprochen aktive Betätigung ist jedoch auch bei dieser Widerstandsorganisation noch nicht festzustellen. Es muß jedoch damit gerechnet werden, daß sie durch eine zentrale belgische Führung, die angeblich auf dem Funkwege mit England in Verbindung steht, in der Lage ist, bei entsprechender Bewaffnung der Besatzungsmacht erheblichen Widerstand zu leisten. Die Ermittlungen zur Erfassung dieser Organisation werden weiter betrieben, so daß nach eingehender Vorbereitung ein Eingriff erfolgen kann . . .

Opposition – Linksbewegung

Die Hetzschriften- und Flugblattpropaganda der Kommunistischen Partei ist bis auf den nordfranzösischen Raum etwas zurückgegangen. Vermutlich sind die Widerstandsgruppen mit Organisationsaufgaben für die sogenannte Stunde ,,H" so belastet, daß sich daraus der Rückgang des illegalen Propagandamaterials erklärt. Im Bereich des Kommandeurs von Lille stehen die Hetzschriften der ,,Front National" an erster Stelle. Es konnten neben den bekannten Schriften eine Reihe von Neuerscheinungen erfaßt werden, so z. B. ,,Pour la Libération", Zeitschrift der FN für das Gebiet Lille – Roubaix – Tourcoing, ,,Le Metallo", Zeitschrift des illegalen komm.

Syndikats der Metallarbeiter für das Gebiet Lille – Roubaix – Tourcoing, „Le Nord Libre", Zeitschrift der FN aus dem Dep. Nord.

Der Inhalt der gesamten Presseerzeugnisse beschäftigt sich vorwiegend mit der Landung der Anglo-Amerikaner in der Normandie. Jetzt, nachdem die Festung Europa in so glänzender Weise durchbrochen worden sei, werde den Deutschen bis zu ihrer endgültigen Niederlage keine Ruhe mehr gegönnt werden. Was in Teheran zwischen den verantwortlichen Staatsmännern der alliierten Nationen vereinbart worden sei, werde sich jetzt folgerichtig abwickeln. Neben dem Invasionsverlauf wird auf die von Stalin angekündigte orkanartige Offensive der Sowjets besonders hingewiesen. Die kommunistische Presse betont, es werde diesmal nicht möglich sein, daß ein Deutscher am Brandenburger Tor deutsche Soldaten mit dem Worten empfängt: „Ich grüße Euch, die Ihr unbesiegt von den Schlachtfeldern zurückkehrt." Die Niederlage der Deutschen werde nach diesem Kriege vollkommen sein. Es wird in der kommunistischen Presse noch auf den 21. Juli, den Nationalfeiertag Belgiens, hingewiesen, der zum erstenmal seit 1940 angesichts der bevorstehenden Befreiung freudig verlebt werden könne.

Während der Berichtszeit hat die seit der Invasion eingesetzte Sabotagewelle mit unverminderter Stärke angehalten. Nach wie vor stehen die Eisenbahnanschläge an erster Stelle. Als Schwerpunktgebiete sind dafür im Bereich der Außendienststelle Charleroi die Bezirke Mons, Ath und Namur sowie Ostflandern im Bereich der Außendienststelle Gent erkennbar. In überwiegender Zahl wurden Schienen- und Weichensprengungen durchgeführt. Besondere Bedeutung haben die Reihensprengungen, die in letzter Zeit sehr häufig auftreten. Hierbei weist eine Bahnstrecke bis zu 30 oder mehr Sprengstellen auf. Die Kabelsabotagen sind in der Berichtszeit etwas zurückgegangen. Sie liegen vor allem in den Bereichen Gent und Lüttich. Die Anschläge und Überfälle auf Landeseinwohner haben gegenüber der vorigen Berichtszeit noch eine Steigerung erfahren. Nach hier vorliegenden Meldungen wurden 22 Personen getötet und sechs verletzt.

Aufstellung über Anschläge in der Berichtszeit

		(vorige Berichtszeit)
Eisenbahnsabotagen:	193	(218)
Kabelsabotagen:	31	(57)
Überfälle auf Wehrmachtsangehörige und Wehrmachtsgut:	15	(20)
Brände	4	(2)
Sabotage aller Art:	17	(29)
Überfälle auf Landeseinwohner:	76	(68)

Die Annahme, daß die Verübung von Terrorakten gegen Angehörige der Besatzungsmacht jetzt auf direkten Befehl der zentralen Leitung der Widerstandsorganisation erfolgt, fand ihre Bestätigung durch das Auffinden schriftlicher Anweisungen der FTP im Bereich des Kommandeurs von Lille. In dieser Anweisung, die an die Sektionen und Gruppen gerichtet ist, heißt es u. a.:

„Im Einverständnis mit allen Widerstandsorganisationen feindliche Lager überfallen und Waffen verteilen. Feindliche Transporte verhindern (Sabotagen an Straßen und Wegen). Umhacken von Bäumen, Anlage von Wegesperren. Polizeiliches Einschreiten verhindern. Gefangene befreien. Arbeit für die Deutschen verhindern (insbesondere diejenigen, die mit der Anlage von Schutzgräben und -löchern beschäftigt sind). Transporte verhindern. Die Anweisung in großen Mengen durch Flugblätter usw. verbreiten!"

Wenn in Betracht gezogen wird, daß die Träger des aktiven bewaffneten Widerstandes gegen die Besatzungsmacht mit wenigen Ausnahmen nur die kommunistischen Kampfgruppen sind, so ist die Absicht der kommunistischen Partei, beim allgemeinen bewaffneten Widerstand die Führung zu übernehmen, unverkennbar.

Bemerkenswert ist die Feststellung, daß die nach Beginn der Invasion einsetzende Abwanderung bewaffneter Trupps, insbesondere im nordfranzösischen Minengebiet, in der Richtung nach der Somme aufgehört hat. Dieser Umstand sei nach vertraulich erfaßten Nachrichten damit in Einklang zu bringen, daß von kommunistischer Seite aus ein zentraler Befehl ergangen ist, die Abwanderung in die Maquis zunächst einzustellen.

Die Bekämpfung des Terrors wurde sowohl in Brüssel als auch im gesamten Befehlsbereich mit guter Wirkung fortgesetzt. Nach gründlicher Vorarbeit gelang es, den National-Kommandanten der kommunistischen Terroristen in Belgien, den jüdischen Richter Henri B u c h, festzunehmen. B. ist bei der hiesigen Dienststelle bereits seit langer Zeit als führender Funktionär der KPB bekannt. Bereits im Juli vergangenen Jahres wurde bei der Zerschlagung der Landesleitung der illegalen KPB in Erfahrung gebracht, daß B u c h als Kadermann im Landesmaßstab für die Partei tätig war. Wie er selbst zugibt, hat er diese Funktion bis Anfang d. J. ausgeübt und wurde dann zum National-Kommandanten der kommunistisch gesteuerten „Armée Belge de Partisans"ernannt. Über seine Schwester Edith B u c h, eine seit langen Jahren für die kommunistische Partei arbeitende Funktionärin, hatte er regelmäßig Verbindung zu dem Vertreter der Komintern in Belgien. Die Festnahme des B u c h ermöglichte auch die sofortige Inhaftierung der kommunistischen Spitzenfunktionärin Andrée T e r f v e geb. Legros. Die T e r f v e lebte unter dem falschen Namen T i b o u mit B u c h zusammen und war als seine Sekretärin und Kurierin tätig. Sie ist die Ehefrau des belgischen Rechtsanwalts T e r f v e , der gegenwärtig der Leiter des Exekutivbüros der Unabhängigkeitsfront ist. Bemerkenswert ist die Tatsache, daß die belgische Intelligenz recht zahlreich in der kommunistischen Führungsschicht vertreten ist. Neben dem Nationalkommandanten B u c h , dem in der Landesleitung der Unabhängigkeitsfront tätigen Rechtsanwalt T e r f v e ist auch der in Lüttich festgenommene Rechtsanwalt und Korpskommandant der Terroristen L e j o u r als Beispiel dafür anzusehen. Bei der Festnahme des Nationalkommandanten konnte auch das Archiv sichergestellt werden. Es enthält eine Unmenge von Schriftmaterial, das nach Sichtung wesentliche Erkenntnisse über den Aufbau und die Arbeitsweise der Widerstandsbewegung vermitteln dürfte. Festgestellt wurde bereits, daß die Partisanenorganisation auch wesentliche Spionageaufgaben erfüllt und das Material über ihre Erkundungen englischen Agenten zuleitet.

Durch weitere exekutive Zugriffe wurde das Korps 75 der Partisanenorganisation in Brüssel seiner Führungsschicht beraubt. Der Korpskommandant wurde bei Widerstand erschossen. Nach Aussage des National-Kommandanten ist es vor allem diesen exekutiven Zugriffen zu verdanken, daß Anschläge auf Wehrmachtsangehörige in Brüssel kaum zur Ausführung gelangt sind. Auch die Militär-Organisation der Unabhängigkeitsfront wurde in laufenden Aktionen wesentlich geschwächt. In der Berichtszeit wurden allein in Brüssel 46 Funktionäre und Mitglieder dieser Organisation unschädlich gemacht. Bekanntlich ist die Militär-Organisation, die selbständig auch Überfälle und Anschläge ausführt, das Sammelbecken, aus dem die Partisanen-Organisation laufend Menschenmaterial herauszieht.

Im Bereich des Kommandeurs von Lille wurden in der Berichtszeit ebenfalls verschiedentlich gegen Terroristen Aktionen durchgeführt. Die Nebenstelle in Douai nahm in Orchies und Umgebung zehn Terroristen in Haft, deren Vernehmungen die Durchführung weiterer Festnahmen ermöglichen werden.

Der Kommandeur von Wallonien meldet die Festnahme einer abgesprengten Gruppe des Korps 79. Das Waffenlager der Gruppe wurde ebenfalls erreicht.

Von der Außendienststelle Gent wurde Anfang des Monats in Verbindung mit der GFP unter Beteiligung von Landesschützen und Feldgendarmen in West-Flandern eine größere Aktion gegen Terroristen durchgeführt. Hierbei wurden insgesamt 47 Personen festgenommen, von denen 30 aktive Banditen sein dürften. Verschiedene Sabotageanschläge sind bereits durch die Vernehmungen der dort Festgenommenen geklärt worden. Es handelt sich um Mitglieder der 5. Kompanie des dortigen Korps, deren Vernehmung weitere Festnahmen ergeben wird.

Die Gesamtfestnahmen aus Linksoppositionskreisen im Bereich betragen:

Brüssel	115
Lille	34
Lüttich	68
Antwerpen	20
Charleroi	50
Gent	66
Insgesamt	353.

Die umfangreichen Sabotageakte im belgischen Raum auf Verkehrseinrichtungen (insbesondere Schienensprengungen) hatten dagegen keinen nennenswerten Rückgang zu verzeichnen. Allein infolge der hierdurch aufgetretenen, wenn auch meist kurzfristigen Betriebsstörungen waren z. T. erhebliche Auswirkungen auf die Beförderungsleistungen (Personen- wie auch Güterverkehr) zu verzeichnen. Durch die Oberfeldkommandanturen wurden in bestimmten Bezirken alle wehrfähigen Männer im Alter von 17–60 Jahren aufgerufen, Wachdienste an den Eisenbahnstrecken abzuleisten. Wenn auch dieser Aufforderung, so wird hierzu berichtet, zum großen Teil nachgekommen wurde, „so scheinen manche der zum Wachdienst eingeteilten Landeseinwohner hierin nur ihren eigenen Vorteil zu erkennen, indem sie sich selbst an den Plünderungen der Güterwaggons beteiligen". So wurde beispielsweise am 1. Juli ein mit Koks beladener Güterzug in Marcheles-Ecausinnes geplündert. Es befanden sich unter den Beteiligten mehrere Angehörige aus dem Wachdienst. Abends wurde der gleiche Zug vor der Einfahrt in Familleurex nochmals von Plünderern, darunter Wachmänner, überfallen. Um diesen Mißbrauch abzustellen, müßten nach Meinung deutschfreundlicher Kreise die ausgestellten Zivilwachen durch Patrouillendienste wiederum einer strengen Beaufsichtigung unterliegen und vor allem bei Feststellung von Verstößen erheblich bestraft werden.

Weitere Berichte liegen vom 1. Aug 44 vor. Sie sagen:

In Kreisen der kommunistischen Bewegung wurden Äußerungen erfaßt, nach denen alle die Landeseinwohner, die sich irgendwie für die Verwirklichung des Programms des neuen Reichskommissars einsetzen werden oder mit ihm zusammenarbeiten, ohne Rücksicht zu liquidieren sind.

Aus Nordfrankreich wird berichtet, daß die Einsetzung des Reichskommissars zunächst nur durch Radio-Vichy bekannt wurde und die landeseigene Presse die Meldung erst am folgenden Tage kommentarlos veröffentlichte. Dies hatte zur Folge, daß die Kreise, die frühzeitig durch andere Quellen verständigt wurden, Unruhe in die bisher mangelhaft unterrichtete große Masse der Bevölkerung zu bringen vermochten; u. a. wurde verbreitet, die deutsche Regierung wolle Nordfrankreich abtrennen, und bei der ganzen Angelegenheit handle es sich nur um einen Schritt Degrelles.

Die durch den laufenden Mordterror wachsend gefährdete Sicherheitslage großer Gebiete des Landes stellt nach wie vor das wichtigste innerpolitische Problem dar. Die Verhältnisse haben sich im Laufe der letzten Wochen so verschärft, daß man in Kreisen der neuen Ordnung von einem latenten Bürgerkrieg spricht. Infolge der bekannten Untätigkeit der landeseigenen Exekutive und Justiz und der zahlenmäßigen Schwäche der deutschen Sicherheitsorgane sehen sich die Betroffenen, die meist den neuordnungsbereiten Organisationen angehören oder sonstwie mit der Besatzungsmacht zusammenarbeiten, dem Terror fast schutzlos ausgeliefert. Hinzu kommt, daß weite Kreise der Bevölkerung unter dem Einfluß des feindlichen Rundfunks die Terroristen, soweit sie angeblich nationale Ziele verfolgen und insbesondere Handstreiche gegen ,,Verräter" und die Besatzungsmacht unternehmen sowie sich auf Sabotage beschränken, als ,,Patrioten" ansehen, denen man zumindest keine Schwierigkeiten in den Weg zu legen habe. Die Opfer dieser Gruppen bemitleidet man nicht, man schreibt ihnen vielmehr wegen ihrer deutschfreundlichen Einstellung die Schuld selbst zu. Von den in den letzten Wochen besonders häufig vorgekommenen und mit äußerster Brutalität durchgeführten Mordtaten an Frauen behauptet man in diesem Zusammenhang, die Opfer seien der Rache von Landeseinwohnern anheimgefallen, weil sie Arbeitsverweigerer und sonstige ,,Patrioten" denunziert hätten.

Aber auch den zahlreichen Banditen gegenüber, die ohne irgendwelchen Anschluß an politische Organisationen in kleinen Gruppen rauben, plündern und morden, um aus rein kriminellen Instinkten heraus sich zu bereichern, verhält man sich passiv, selbst wenn man ihre Taten verurteilt. Man fürchtet ihre Rache und wagt nicht, ihren Opfern irgendwelche Hilfe angedeihen zu lassen, aus Angst, selbst von ihnen verfolgt zu werden.

Die Terror- und Sabotage-Anschläge haben insgesamt eine leichte Steigerung erfahren. Der Kommandeur in Lille meldet eine bedenkliche Zunahme der Anschläge. Im dortigen Bergbaugebiet treten immer häufiger bewaffnete Banden in Stärke bis zu 30 Mann auf, die in der Hauptsache bergwerkstechnische Einrichtungen angreifen und oft recht empfindlichen Schaden anrichten. Aus dem Gebiet um Maubeuge zeigen sich Ansätze zur Bildung starker Maquis-Lager.

Der Kommandeur in Lille meldet die Festnahme von zwei Regional-Chefs der ,,Front National" mit zahlreichem Schriftmaterial. In Aktionen wurden in der Nähe von Lille und bei Douai mehrere hundert Einwohner überprüft und viele wegen Verdachts der Verübung von Terror- und Sabotage-Anschlägen in Haft genommen.

Der Kommandeur Wallonien – Außendienststelle Charleroi – hat weitere Festnahmen aus der 3. Kompanie des Korps 72 im Centre-Gebiet vorgenommen. Auch bei La Louvière erfolgten Einzelfestnahmen von Terroristen. Bei einer Säuberungsaktion durch eine Einheit des Sicherungs-Regimentes 16 wurden in einem Schloß bei Henri-Pont weitere Mitglieder des Terroristen-Korps 72 erfaßt. Ein Waffendepot mit einer M-Pi, sieben Handfeuerwaffen, Sprengkapseln usw. konnte sichergestellt werden.

Die Sabotage- und Terrortätigkeit im Bereich der Außendienststelle Gent hielt unvermindert an. Auch jetzt wurden dort wieder insbesondere Schienenwege und Wehrmachtfernsprechleitungen total oder erheblich zerstört. Es hat den Anschein, daß die Anschläge auf Schienenwege und Fernsprechleitungen zentral gesteuert werden. Es wurde unter Heranziehung von Wehrmachtsdienststellen damit begonnen, größere Razzien durchzuführen. Hierbei wurde eine Ortschaft umstellt und durchsucht. 24 Personen wurden festgenommen, darunter acht Mitglieder der ,,Weißen Brigade'', 1 Unterpastor und 15 Dienstpflichtverweigerer. Waffen wurden hierbei nicht vorgefunden.

Die Außendienststelle Lüttich meldet eine gleichbleibende kommunistische Tätigkeit.

Sabotage-Abwehr

Aufstellung über Anschläge in der Zeit vom 17. Juli 44 bis heute. Zahlen des letzten Berichts in Klammern.

Eisenbahnsabotagen:	138	(193)
Kabelsabotagen:	71	(31)
Überfälle auf Wehrmachtsangehörige und Wehrmachtsgut:	18	(15)
Brände:	22	(4)
Sabotage aller Art:	33	(17)
Überfälle auf Landeseinwohner:	152	(76)

Schwerpunktgebiete sind nach wie vor die Industriebezirke der Außendienststelle Charleroi. In den übrigen Provinzen Belgiens und auch in Nordfrankreich wurden Eisenbahnsabotagen durchgeführt, jedoch reichen diese an Zahl und Dichte nicht an die Schwerpunktgebiete im Hennegau heran. Betroffene Objekte sind in überwiegender Zahl Schienen und Weichen. Weitere Sprengungen richteten sich gegen Lokomotiven, Brücken, Signaleinrichtungen und Stellwerke. Die Reihensprengungen treten auch in dieser Berichtszeit wieder auf. Besonders gefährdet in dieser Hinsicht ist der Hennegau. Von dort werden mehrere solcher Sprengstoffanschläge gemeldet, u. a. eine Reihensprengung mit 24 Sprengstellen auf der eingleisigen

Eisenbahnstrecke Renaix–Leuze zwischen den Bahnhöfen Renaix und Dergenai. Diese auf verhältnismäßig kurzer Strecke durchgeführten Sprengungen verursachen erhebliche Schwierigkeiten, zumal die Linie eingleisig ist. Terroristen verfügen über ein vorzügliches Nachrichtennetz. Darüber hinaus lebt die Bevölkerung allgemein in einer Angstpsychose vor den Terroristen und deckt aus dieser heraus teilweise deren Verbrechen. Die Angehörigen der mit bestialischer Grausamkeit ermordeten Opfer finden in der Regel bei ihren nächsten Nachbarn und in engster Umgebung des Tatortes nicht die geringste Hilfeleistung. Oft müssen sie die Toten eigenhändig auf Handkarren abtransportieren. Die Tätigkeit der belgischen Exekutivorgane beschränkt sich dabei offensichtlich auf die notwendigsten formalen Feststellungen und schließt von vornherein jede Aussicht auf Ermittlung von Tätern und Spuren aus. Ähnlich verhält es sich mit der Mithilfe der landeseigenen Bevölkerung bei der Aufdeckung dieser Verbrechen: Auch bei Attentaten, die am hellen Tage und in offensichtlicher Anwesenheit von zahlreichen Zeugen begangen wurden, meldet sich nie jemand, der irgendwie sachdienliche Angaben machen kann. Die Terroristen, die sehen, mit welcher Leichtigkeit sie infolge dieser Verhältnisse ihre Verbrechen begehen können, werden deswegen immer dreister; in einzelnen Orten quartieren sie sich kurzerhand bei den Bauern ein und lassen sich von ihnen verpflegen, wobei sie jeden, der ihnen nicht willfährig ist, mit dem Tode bedrohen. Typisch hierfür ist ein Fall aus der Gemeinde Werbomont (Bez. Brüssel), wo eine maskierte Bande eine ganze Bauernsippe, bestehend aus zwei unverheirateten Brüdern, einer Schwester und einem weiteren Bruder mit dessen Frau und vier Kinder in einem Gehöft zusammentrieben, knebelten und dann auf die scheußlichste Art ermordeten. In dem Anwesen, das die Attentäter nach Begehung der Tat in Brand steckten, fand man neben diesen neun Opfern noch weitere drei Leichen unbekannter Identität.

In fast allen Fällen kann beobachtet werden, daß bald nach Begehung der Tat, mag sie noch so grausam und brutal durchgeführt worden sein, dank der Propaganda deutschfeindlicher Elemente das Gerücht auftaucht, das Opfer habe „Patrioten" denunziert, Arbeitsverweigerer angezeigt oder sonstwie „Verrat" geübt und sei deswegen selbst schuld. Es wurden auch Fälle bekannt, in denen Banden von Terroristen bei Überfällen auf Wachen und sonstige Betriebe von der Bevölkerung mit Beifall begrüßt wurden, wobei man die belgische Nationalfahne zeigte. Vielfach wird auch behauptet, daß sich in den Terrorbanden Deserteure der deutschen Wehrmacht befänden oder dieselben sogar anführten.

Von Interesse sind Zahlen, die durch die belgische Polizei für den Monat Juli 1944 angegeben wurden (die Zahlen für den Monat Juni sind in Klammern beigefügt):

Anschläge auf Personen	286	(151)
Morde	217	(110)
Sabotagefälle an Ernteprodukten und sonstigen Lebensmitteln	126	(9)
Sabotagefälle an Verkehrsanlagen, Kanälen, Eisenbahnen, Telefon	508	(331)
Sabotage an Versorgungsbetrieben (Bergwerke, Fabriken, Molkereien)	45	(24)
Diebstähle mit Waffengewalt, Bandenüberfälle, Lebensmittelmarken	159	(122)
Geld und Lebensmittel	790	(613)
Verwaltungsurkunden (Arbeitsämter)	54	(34)

Opposition – Rechtsbewegung

Die Entwicklung der politischen und militärischen Ereignisse verfehlt nicht ihre Einwirkung auf die Bevölkerung und nicht zuletzt auf die nationalen Widerstandskreise. Wenn auch von einer ausgesprochenen Aktivität nicht gesprochen werden kann, so darf nicht übersehen werden, daß sie nach wie vor bestrebt sind, ihre Organisations- und Aufbauarbeit intensiv weiter zu betreiben.

Der von England aus geforderte Zusammenschluß aller nationalen Widerstandskreise im belgischen und nordfranzösischen Raum verläuft, wie die bisherigen Erkenntnisse gezeigt haben, nicht reibungslos. Die ,,Armée Belge Réorganisée", die – wie schon berichtet – als die einzige Widerstandsorganisation für Belgien von England aus anerkannt und gefördert wird, hat es bisher nicht vermocht, die nationalen Widerstandsgruppen in sich zu vereinigen. Nach wie vor sind einzelne Gruppen zu einer Einigung nicht bereit, weil ihre Führer sich nicht ohne weiteres unter- oder einordnen wollen. Neben der ,,A.B.R." bestehen im belgischen Raume noch kleinere Widerstandsorganisationen, die jedoch nicht unterschätzt werden dürfen, weil auch sie dahin streben, mit allen zur Verfügung stehenden Mitteln bei geeigneter Gelegenheit gegen die Besatzungsmacht vorzugehen. So haben sich im Bereich der Außendienststelle Antwerpen die ,,Kempsche Legion", die ,,Belgische National-Bewegung" und auch die die kleineren Gruppen umfassende ,,Weiße Brigade" nicht zu einer Unter- bzw. Einordnung bereit erklärt. Sie arbeiten nach wie vor selbständig. Die erfolgte Festnahme von Führern und Mitgliedern der ,,Kempschen Legion" und der ,,Belgischen National-Bewegung" in dem oben angegebenen Raum hat eine erhebliche Schwächung dieser Gruppen mit sich gebracht, jedoch noch nicht zu einer restlosen Zerschlagung geführt. Auch im Brüsseler Raum wurde die ,,Armée Belge Réorganisée" durch verschiedene Aktionen ganz erheblich an-geschlagen, jedoch nicht so geschwächt, daß man nicht mehr mit der Wider-standskraft dieser Organisation zu rechnen hat.

Im nordfranzösischen Raum kann von einer strengen Trennung der Rechts- oder Linksbewegung nicht mehr gesprochen werden. Vielmehr wurde dort die Feststellung getroffen, daß sich der Widerstand der gesam-ten Bevölkerung gegen die deutschen Bestrebungen und Ziele ganz erheb-lich verstärkt. Die nationalen Widerstandskreise in Nordfrankreich, zu de-nen vor allen Dingen Personen der französischen Intelligenz, des Bürger-tums sowie frühere Offiziere und höhere Beamte zählen, werden infolge des kommunistischen Führungsanspruchs bei der Organisation des bewaffneten Widerstandes immer mehr zurückgesetzt. So ist es zu erklären, daß seitens der nationalen Widerstandskreise im nordfranzösischen Raum derzeit fast keine aktiven Handlungen gegen die Deutschen durchgeführt werden.

Durch die mit äußerster Vorsicht betriebenen Aufbau- und Organisa-tionsarbeiten gestaltet sich die Bekämpfung der Widerstandsgruppen von Tag zu Tag schwieriger. Trotzdem gelang es, in einzelne Widerstandsgrup-pen erhebliche Einbrüche zu erzielen. Die Vernehmungen der Festgenom-menen werden weitere Aktionen ergeben.

In Brüssel konnte durch die Festnahme von 37 Angehörigen der ,,A.B.R." – darunter einige Führer und Kuriere – wiederum ein erheblicher Einbruch erzielt werden. Es gelang u. a., zwei Lager, in denen unter Füh-rung von früheren Offizieren und Unteroffizieren des belgischen Heeres Ausbildungsdienst betrieben wurde, zu erfassen und zu zerschlagen. Die bisherigen Festnahmen weisen klar darauf hin, daß diese Widerstandsgrup-pe Verbindung zu höheren belgischen Verwaltungsstellen hat, die im einzel-nen noch geklärt werden muß.

Durch die Festnahme von insgesamt 51 zum Teil führenden Mitgliedern der Widerstandsorganisationen ,,Kempsche Legion" und ,,Belgische Natio-nal-Bewegung" im Bereich der Außendienststelle Antwerpen gelang auch hier ein beträchtlicher Einbruch und die Zerschlagung einzelner Ortsgrup-pen. Es steht zu erwarten, daß die Vernehmung der Festgenommenen die Möglichkeit ergeben wird, vor allen Dingen die ,,Kempsche Legion" zu erfassen und zu zerschlagen. Bei Vernehmungen von Angehörigen der ,,Kempschen Legion" ergab sich, daß diese Widerstandsorganisation Ver-bindung zum Intelligence Service und zur ,,Unabhängigkeitsfront" hat. Einige der Festgenommenen gehörten auch der ,,Weißen Brigade" an. Ihre Vernehmung stellt erneut die Tatsache unter Beweis, daß die ,,Weiße Briga-de" keine zentral gesteuerte Organisation, sondern nur eine Sammlung von kleinen Gruppen ist, die unter dem Deckmantel der nationalen Wider-standsorganisation Überfälle und Sabotageakte durchführen.

Die Außendienststelle Gent meldet die Festnahme von insgesamt 35 Angehörigen nationaler Widerstandsgruppen, darunter einige Unterführer der ,,A.B.R.", deren Vernehmung Hinweise auf die Organisation und den Aufbau dieser Widerstandsgruppe erbracht hat. Unter den Festgenommenen befinden sich der Verbindungsoffizier zu dem Zonenchef in Flandern und den einzelnen Sektionen sowie zwei Gruppenchefs. Es handelt sich bei dem Verbindungsoffizier und einem Gruppenchef je um einen ehemaligen Leutnant des belgischen Heeres, während der zweite Gruppenchef Soldat der früheren belgischen Armee war.

Die im Bereich des Kommandeurs Lüttich durchgeführten Aktionen gegen nationale Widerstandskreise ergaben die Festnahme von 61 Angehörigen der ,,A.B.R.". Durch deren Vernehmung konnten einzelne Lager, deren Aushebung in Vorbereitung ist, festgestellt werden.

Der Kommandeur Lille meldet die Festnahme von 16 Personen aus nationalen Widerstandskreisen. Dabei wird besonders darauf hingewiesen, daß sich im nordfranzösischen Raum die Tätigkeit der nationalen Widerstandskreise nicht aktiviert, jedoch im Aufbau und der Organisation intensiviert hat. Hier wie auch im belgischen Raum tritt die Unzuverlässigkeit der Polizei, die in einzelnen Fällen mit den Widerstandsorganisationen direkte oder indirekte Verbindung hat, immer mehr in den Vordergrund.

Der ständig wachsende Einfluß der KPB hat die illegale Presse der sozialdemokratischen Partei Belgiens veranlaßt, die Gefahr aufzuzeigen, die Belgien drohen würde, wenn nach einem Rückzug der Deutschen die Staatsgewalt in die Hände der Partisanen fallen würde. Wenn auch nicht verkannt wird, daß die Erfolge der Roten Armee an der Ostfront auch die Befreiung Belgiens beschleunigen, so betont die SPB jedoch ganz eindeutig, daß sie ihre politische Macht einsetzen werde, der legalen belgischen Regierung, die sich zur Zeit in London aufhält, die Staatsführung wieder zu übertragen. In ihrer Angst vor einer Bolschewisierung Belgiens versucht die SPB mit allen Mitteln, ihre Leser zu bewegen, sich nie vom demokratischen System zu trennen und vor allem nie ein Einparteisystem zuzulassen.

Ascq

Der verstorbene Vizepräsident des Deutschen Bundestages, Carlo Schmid, Sohn einer französischen Mutter und eines deutschen Vaters, setzte sich bei McCloy, dem amerikanischen Hochkommissar für die Landsberg-Häftlinge ein. An seiner Lauterkeit besteht kein Zweifel. Während des Zweiten Weltkrieges machte er Dienst bei der Feldkommandantur in Lille.

Carlo Schmid schreibt auf Seite 190 seines Buches ,,Erinnerungen" (Scherz 1979): ,,Im Oktober 1940 wurde durch Führerbefehl auch beim Befehlshaber Belgien und Nordfrankreich ein Sonderbeauftragter der SS für Judenfragen eingesetzt, der dem Militärbefehlshaber unterstand, aber faktisch nur Weisungen aus dem Sicherheitshauptamt erhielt. Die Haltung der Militärbefehlshaber den Juden gegenüber änderte sich. Zwischen der kommunistischen Widerstandsbewegung und jüdischen Kreisen wurden Zusammenhänge vermutet. Französische Polizeistellen berichteten, Attentate auf Wehrmachtsangehörige seien von kommunistischen Freischärlern ,unter jüdischer Führung' verübt worden. Kommunismus und ,jüdischer Kapitalismus' galten manchen als gleichwertige Formen der Weltherrschaft des Judentums. Ortskommandanten, die so dachten, hielten es für richtig, für Sühnemaßnahmen ,bevorzugt' Juden festzunehmen. General Karl-Heinrich von Stülpnagel, der doch durch die Tat bewiesen hat, daß er nicht ein Mann Hitlers war, empfahl, besser als Massenerschießungen sei die Deportation ,größerer Massen von Kommunisten und Juden nach dem Osten'. Das werde auf die Bevölkerung abschreckender wirken als die Geiselpraxis . . .

Als am 6. Juni 1944 die Landung in der Normandie erfolgte, wunderten wir uns nicht über den Zeitpunkt, sondern nur darüber, daß sie gerade an dieser Stelle erfolgte. Stets war bei den Dienstbesprechungen zu hören gewesen, der Feind werde sicher an der schmalsten Stelle – also im Abschnitt Calais-Dünkirchen – angreifen. Und nun griff er in der Normandie an! Wie hatte unsere Aufklärung so versagen können? Aber man vertraute dem ,Wüstenfuchs', der schon mit schlimmeren Lagen fertig geworden sei und der es auch diesmal schaffen werde. Außerdem waren wir überzeugt, der Führer werde von überallher auf raschestem Wege für diesen Fall bereitgestellte Kampfdivisionen an die Einbruchstelle werfen.

Tatsächlich rollten immer mehr Transportzüge mit frischen Truppen durch unser Gebiet – und immer öfter traten Sabotagetrupps der Widerstandsgruppen in Erscheinung, sprengten Geleise und machten Lokomotiven unbrauchbar. An einem Sonntag im Juni, an dem ich Bereitschafts-

dienst hatte, wurde gemeldet, daß in dem Städtchen Ascq vor einem Transportzug eine Dynamitladung hochgegangen sei und den Zug zum Stehen
gebracht habe; daraufhin habe der Kommandant das Feuer auf die Stadt
eröffnet; es habe unter der Zivilbevölkerung viele Opfer gegeben. Ich fuhr
sofort nach Ascq und stellte fest: Der Transportzug einer Einheit der SS-
Division ‚Hitlerjugend‘ war nahe bei Ascq auf eine Mine gefahren. Der
Kommandant, ein SS-Sturmführer, ließ aus Vierlingskanonen das Feuer auf
die Häuser eröffnen, die Ortschaft ‚durchkämmen‘ und etwa achtzig Männer am Bahndamm zusammentreiben, die mit Maschinengewehrfeuer niedergemacht wurden. Das französische Rote Kreuz und Beamte der Präfektur waren zur Stelle. Ich setzte sofort einen Tatbericht auf, der vom Ober-
feldkommandanten an den Gerichtsherrn der SS-Einheit weitergeleitet
wurde. Der Gerichtsherr war SS-Obergruppenführer Sepp Dietrich . . . Aus
den Akten, die Oberfeldrichter Kiinkert mir zugänglich machte, war zu
entnehmen, daß Sepp Dietrich den Sturmführer zu seinem Vorgehen be-
glückwünschte. Wenn er weiter so entschlußfreudig sei, werde er es als
Offizier weit bringen . . . Ein Verfahren gegen den Sturmführer ist nicht
eröffnet worden. Ich nahm die Akten an mich, um sie eines Tages dort
vorzulegen, wo abgerechnet werden sollte."

Dazu ist zu sagen, daß der Vorgang Ascq sich am 1. Apr. 1944 abspielte
und der Botschafter der ,,Vichy-Regierung", de Brinon, am 4. Apr. 1944
bei dem Oberbefehlshaber West, Generalfeldmarschall von Rundstedt, im
Namen seiner Regierung protestierte.

In seiner Antwort führte der Oberbefehlshaber West aus: ,,Der Führer
des in Frage kommenden Truppentransports hatte mit Rücksicht auf die
zahlreichen Eisenbahnattentate der letzten Zeit schon vor Abfahrt befehls-
gemäß seinen Truppentransportzug besonders gesichert. Da er wußte, daß
der Schnellzug Brüssel–Lille seinem Transport um wenige Minuten voraus-
fuhr, mußte ihm im Augenblick der Entgleisung seines Zuges durch zwei
Sprengladungen klar werden, daß hier ein eigens gegen seinen Transportzug
gerichteter Überfall vorlag. Es war daher nicht nur die Folge einer begreifli-
chen Erregung der Truppe, sondern durchaus im Sinne der von mir gegebenen Befehle, wenn die Truppe auf einen Anschlag gegen ihre Sicherheit mit
sofortiger Gegenwehr antwortete. Die Höhe des erlittenen Schadens ist
dabei unerheblich. Die Ermittlungen haben darüber hinaus folgendes Ergebnis gehabt:

1. Nach mehreren Zeugenaussagen fielen aus einem unweit der Spreng-
stelle gelegenen Hause mehrere Pistolenschüsse. An zwei Fahrzeugen wurden entsprechende Einschüsse festgestellt.

2. Während der vom Transportführer befohlenen Sicherstellung aller
männlichen Personen der Ortschaft Ascq im Alter zwischen 17 und 50

Jahren wurde einer der Soldaten durch zwei Zivilpersonen angefallen und durch Schläge auf den Kopf verletzt. Eine Anzahl der bereits zum Bahndamm gebrachten Zivilpersonen versuchte, aus dem Waggon, in dem sie inhaftiert waren, zu entfliehen. Diese Vorgänge haben dazu geführt, daß eine Anzahl von männlichen Personen bei versuchter Gegenwehr bzw. beim Fluchtversuch erschossen wurden.

3. In den Händen der deutschen Polizei befinden sich Unterlagen, aus denen hervorgeht, daß die Täter in Ascq zu suchen sind.

4. Bereits am 27. und 30. 3. sind nahezu an der gleichen Stelle zwei weitere Sprengstoffattentate durchgeführt worden.

5. Die in der Nähe von Ascq untergebrachte Truppe meldet, daß die Bevölkerung von Ascq seit etwa einem Jahre ausgesprochen deutschfeindlich eingestellt ist.

6. Die von Ihnen geäußerte Auffassung, daß die Gegenmaßnahmen erst durch das Eintreten der Präfektur beendet worden seien und länger als drei Stunden gedauert hätten, trifft nicht zu. Die Aktion dauerte von 23.15 bis 0.40 Uhr. Der Feldkommandant wurde erst um 2.05 Uhr, also zu einer Zeit, als die Aktion längst beendet war, um Unterstützung gebeten.

Sosehr ich den Zwischenfall an sich bedaure, bin ich angesichts dieses Ermittlungsergebnisses nicht in der Lage, den Protest der Französischen Regierung anzuerkennen . . .''

Klarzustellen ist, daß von Rundstedt eine gewisse Zeit von Generalfeldmarschall Sperrle (Luftwaffe) vertreten wurde. Letzterer war der Auffassung, daß die Sorglosigkeit gegenüber der Zivilbevölkerung kaum noch zu übertreffen sei. Daher befahl er: ,,Wird eine Truppe in irgendeiner Form überfallen, so ist der Führer verpflichtet, sofort von sich aus selbständige Gegenmaßnahmen zu treffen. Dazu gehören:

a) Es wird sofort wieder geschossen! Wenn dabei Unschuldige mitgetroffen werden, so ist das bedauerlich, aber ausschließlich Schuld der Terroristen.

b) Sofortige Absperrung der Umgebung des Tatortes und Festsetzung sämtlicher in der Nähe befindlicher Zivilisten ohne Unterschied des Standes oder der Person.

c) Sofortiges Niederbrennen von Häusern, aus denen geschossen wurde.

Erst nach diesen oder ähnlichen Sofortmaßnahmen kommt die Meldung. Bei der Beurteilung des Eingreifens tatkräftiger Truppenführer ist die Entschlossenheit und Schnelligkeit ihres Handelns unter allen Umständen an die erste Stelle zu setzen. Schwer bestraft werden muß nur der schlappe und unentschlossene Truppenführer, weil er dadurch die Sicherheit seiner unterstellten Truppen und den Respekt vor der deutschen Wehrmacht gefährdet. Zu scharfe Maßnahmen können angesichts der derzeitigen Lage kein Grund zur Bestrafung sein.''

Nach der Invasion wurde am 16. Juni 1944 im Bereich der Oberfeldkommandantur Lille eine Anzahl von Partisanen verurteilt. In einer Bekanntmachung wurde die Verurteilung und die Vollstreckung des Urteils durch Erschießen veröffentlicht (Vgl. IMT Band XXXVII).

Ausgeführt wird: ,,Im Verlaufe der Verhandlungen des Kriegsgerichts ist zugleich der Anschlag restlos aufgeklärt worden, der in der Nacht vom 1. zum 2. April 1944 in Ascq gegen einen deutschen Wehrmachtstransportzug verübt wurde.

Die drei Sprengstoffanschläge gegen die Eisenbahnlinie in Ascq, insbesondere gegen den deutschen Wehrmachtstransport, stellen sich daher eindeutig als in Ascq ausgedachte und von Angehörigen der französischen Eisenbahn durchgeführte Sabotage- und Terrorakte dar . . .

Darüber hinaus haben die gerichtlichen Feststellungen ergeben, daß ein großer Teil der Einwohner der Gemeinde Ascq Widerstandsbewegungen angehört hat. Insbesondere haben die Verurteilten im Verfahren unabhängig voneinander mehr als 30 der bei den Ereignissen am 1. Apr. 1944 Erschossenen als Angehörige von Widerstandsbewegungen bezeichnet. Die illegalen Organisationen in Ascq sind . . . als verantwortlich für die durchgeführten Sabotage- und Terrorhandlungen anzusehen." Sechs Männer und eine Frau waren verurteilt worden.

Niederlande

Auch in den Niederlanden zeigte sich der Widerstand. Im Sommer 1940 bildeten sich die ersten Widerstandsgruppen.

Im Februar 1941 kam es zur ersten Massenkundgebung, die sich gegen die Einführung der Arbeitsdienstpflicht und gegen antijüdische Maßnahmen und Deportationen von Juden richtete. Am 17. Februar brach ein Streik der Werftarbeiter aus, der am 26. Februar 1941 zu einem Generalstreik wurde. Der zweite Massenstreik ereignete sich im Mai 1943. Es wurde die Nachricht verbreitet, es sei deutscherseits ein Erlaß veröffentlicht worden, daß sich sämtliche früheren niederländischen Kriegsgefangenen zur Internierung melden sollten. Hitler hatte im Sommer 1940 praktisch alle niederländischen Kriegsgefangenen aus der Kriegsgefangenschaft entlassen.

Am 20. Oktober 1942 schrieb der Höhere SS- und Polizeiführer der Niederlande an den Generalsekretär im Justizministerium in Den Haag, daß sich in der letzten Zeit die Aktionen der Widerstandskämpfer in auffallender Weise mehrten. In dem Schreiben wurde erwähnt, daß ,,Stroh- und Heuschober, Garagen-Einrichtungen, Verpflegungsmagazine und ähnliche Wehrmachtseinrichtungen" dauernd von Saboteuren heimgesucht würden.

10 Monate, bevor die Niederlande von den deutschen Streitkräften geräumt wurden, bildete sich die ,,Grote Adviescommissie der Illegaliteit".

Die ersten Geiselerschießungen fanden erst 27 Monate nach der Besetzung der Niederlande im August 1942 statt. Fünf Personen wurden erschossen.

Noch im gleichen Jahre brachte die Untergrundzeitung ,,Vrij Nederland" einen Artikel heraus, in dem zum Ausdruck gebracht wurde: ,,Wir wissen, daß wir die Stimme Tausender von Menschen sind, die heute noch schweigen, daß wir der geheime Herzschlag einer Nation sind, die weiß, daß ihr Herz in uns schlägt. Wenn wir heute den Ruf zum Widerstand hinausgehen lassen, so hört ihr nicht unsere Stimme, sondern die Stimme eures eigenen Volkes, eure eigene Stimme, unser gemeinsames Erbe, unsere gemeinsamen Überzeugungen, unser Sehnen und unser Hoffen. Wir existieren, weil ihr existiert."

Ein operatives Zusammenwirken mit den Alliierten begann am Ende der Kampfhandlungen in den Niederlanden wie auch in anderen Ländern. Neapel z. B. hielten vom 27.–30. September 1943 bewaffnete Gruppen von Italienern, bis die Alliierten eintrafen.

Ähnliches ereignete sich in norditalienischen Städten, wie z. B. in Turin. In Belgien und Holland zeigen sich vergleichbare Widerstandshandlungen.

Der belgische Hafen Antwerpen wurde am 4. September 1944 durch belgische Widerstandskämpfer gerettet. Als bei Arnheim alliierte Luftlandetruppen landeten, brach in den Niederlanden ein allgemeiner Eisenbahnerstreik aus.

Bericht aus den Niederlanden

Die optimistische Meinung der hiesigen deutschfeindlichen Kreise über den Endsieg der Alliierten und den Willen zum aktiven Widerstand waren in der Berichtswoche unverändert stark. Flugblätter besagen:
1. Wer sich meldet und in die Kriegsgefangenschaft geht, ist ein Landesverräter.
2. Jeder Beamte hat seine Mitarbeit zu verweigern.
3. Allgemeine Streiks bei den Eisenbahnen, in der Binnenschiffahrt, im privaten Frachtendienst und bei der PTT sind erforderlich.

Weiter wird aufgefordert, in jeder Beziehung Sabotage zu betreiben. Bei der Eisenbahn sollen Weichen, Brücken, Bremsen und Lokomotiven beschädigt oder vernichtet, in der Schiffahrt Schiffe und Schleusen vernichtet werden. Die Autobahnen sollen durch Drahtsperren, Stacheldrahtspannungen und Nagellatten blockiert werden. Der PTT sollen alle Telefonkabel zerschnitten bzw. in der Erde zerhackt werden. Deutschgesinnte Personen und insbesondere Beamte, die mit den deutschen Behörden zusammenarbeiten, sollen terrorisiert werden.

In Maastricht und Umgebung wurde am 26. Mai 43 eine Anzahl kleiner Streuzettel mit folgender Aufschrift vertreitet: ,,Landgenossen! Boykottiert die deutsche Lügenpropaganda! Sagt Euer Abonnement bei der Radio-Zentrale auf, bestellt den Limburger Koerier ab! Es geht um unser aller Freiheit.''

Führenden Persönlichkeiten der NSB in Maastricht und Heerlen wurden Flugblätter mit nachstehendem Text zugesandt:

,,Tunis, den 15. Mai 1943 – Kriegsrat zu Felde –
Kriegsrat: Französische Offiziere.
Angeklagte: Die Franzosen, die mitgekämpft haben an deutscher Seite, und die Personen, die den Deutschen Hilfe verliehen haben. Sie werden wegen Hochverrats angeklagt und zum Tode verurteilt. So straft man Landesverräter. So werden wir auch *Sie* bestrafen.''

Mit Gegnern aus allgemeinen nationalen Widerstandsbewegungen beschäftigt sich ein anderer Bericht vom 28. Mai 1943. Er sagt aus:
In Maastricht und Umgebung wurde am 26. Mai 43 eine Anzahl kleiner

Streuzettel mit folgender Aufschrift verbreitet: „Landgenossen! Boykottiert die deutsche Lügenpropaganda! Sagt Euer Abonnement bei der Radio-Zentrale auf, bestellt den Limburger Koerier ab! Es geht um unser aller Freiheit." Die Ermittlungen nach den Herstellern und Verbreitern wurden sofort aufgenommen, verliefen jedoch bisher ergebnislos. Man vermutete, daß diese Zettel von kirchlicher Seite herausgegeben worden sind.

Dem Niederländer L. P. M. Cremers, Hoensbrock, wurde durch die Post aus Den Haag – 15. Mai 43 – eine Flugschrift „Proklamation" zugesandt, die nachstehend in Übersetzung wiedergegeben wird:

„Proklamation:

Offiziere und Soldaten des niederländischen Heeres! Die niederländische Regierung nimmt mit tiefer Entrüstung Kenntnis von der letzten Maßnahme des Feindes, wobei er das niederländische Heer in die Kriegsgefangenschaft zurückruft! Mit teuflischer Überlegung will der Deutsche noch schnell unsere wehrfähigen Männer abführen, um sie in der Fremde nach Leib und Seele zu verseuchen. Ihr jungen Männer im Alter von 18–35 (vielleicht sogar bis 50) Jahren, meldet Euch nicht! Versteckt Euch!

Eine Million Niederländer versteckt sich, kommt jedoch wie ein Heer zum Vorschein – mit Waffen in der Hand –, wenn die Trompeten schmettern.

Vergeßt nicht: Eine Million Niederländer nach Deutschland, d. h., die Niederlande von morgen auslöschen, das will sagen: Keine wehrfähigen Männer mehr, aber das will auch sagen: eine Million neuer Geiseln!!!! Unsere Niederlande fordern sehr schwere Opfer, aber das Interesse unseres Vaterlandes steht gewiß über dem unserer Eltern oder anderen Angehörigen, selbst wenn sie erschossen würden. Es ist Krieg. Männer im Dienst bei Behörden, Eure teure Pflicht ist es, jede deutsche Verordnung zu sabotieren oder ungeschehen zu machen.

Versagt Ihr durch Feigheit oder Schlaffheit, treibt Ihr Landesverrat!

Zu Euch, Zweifler, sprechen wir nur diese Warnung aus: Wer sich meldet, treibt Landesverrat!!!!

Skandinavien

In Dänemark und Norwegen trug die Partisanen- und Untergrundkriegführung keine so ausgeprägten Züge wie in anderen Ländern Europas. Aber es ist nicht zu leugnen, daß es eine nicht geringe Anzahl von kleineren Aktionen und Sabotagehandlungen gegeben hat. Ende 1941 wurde eine breite Widerstandsorganisation unter dem Namen „Freies Dänemark" gebildet, die zum Ziele die Verbreitung illegaler Flugschriften, die Durchführung von Sabotageakten und schließlich auch vor dem Ende des Krieges die Aufstellung von bewaffneten Gruppen hatte.

Zeitgeschichtlich gesehen, muß der kommunistischen Sabotageorganisation „Bopa" die aus bürgerlichen Kreisen bestehende „Holger Danske" gegenübergestellt werden.

Im Februar 1942 beschloß die Kommunistische Partei Dänemarks die Bildung von Sabotagetrupps. In ihr waren zum großen Teil Teilnehmer des Spanischen Bürgerkrieges beteiligt.

Ab Dezember 1942 ging die Bildung von bewaffneten Gruppen in den Betrieben vonstatten. In diesen blieb jedoch die Hauptform des Kampfes die Sabotage.

In Skandinavien ereigneten sich wie in den anderen europäischen Ländern Störungen des Eisenbahnverkehrs durch Beschädigung und Vernichtung von Gleisanlagen, Weichen, Signalanlagen, Lokomotiven und Brükken. Es ist selbstverständlich, daß auch von dem Kampfmittel des Streiks Gebrauch gemacht wurde.

Um die Entwicklung der Widerstandsbewegung in Norwegen aufzuzeigen, möchte ich auszugsweise eine Anzahl von Unterlagen vorlegen.

Dänemark

Aus dem Tagebuch des Befehlshabers der Ordnungspolizei in Dänemark. [Fundstelle: ehemaliges RSHA]
22. Okt. 43: Auf Ersuchen der SD-Außendienststelle Kolding erfolgte am 18. Okt. 43 in der Zeit von 5.45 Uhr–13.15 Uhr auf Gut Olufskär, Luftlinie 5,5 km südostwärts Haderslev, zusammen mit SD ein polz. Einsatz der 3. Komp. des Wach-Btl. Dänemark in Stärke von 3/51 unter Führung des Komp.-Führers Hauptm. Höpfner. Das Gut wurde schlagartig umstellt und alle anwesenden Personen festgesetzt. Die planmäßige Durchsuchung aller Baulichkeiten förderte größere Mengen deutschfeindl. Hetz- und Propagandaschriften und Flugblätter engl. Ursprungs sowie streng vertraulichen deutschfeindl. Informationsmaterials zutage. Beweise für Anwesen-

heit eines engl. Fallschirmagenten wurden nicht gefunden. Der Gutsbesitzer Klausen wurde durch den SD festgenommen.

Verhängung des zivilen Ausnahmezustandes über Kopenhagen als Folge des am 27. Okt. 43 abends 22.20 Uhr im Restaurant „Mokka", Frederiksberggade 38, verübten Sprengstoffattentats mit Zeitzünderbomben, bei dem zwei Wehrmachtsangehörige getötet und 47 Personen verletzt wurden (darunter 9 Pol. Angehörige, von denen d. Rev. Obw. Heydhausen v. III./ SS-Pol. 15 inzwischen seinen Verletzungen erlegen ist). Es wurde die Schließung aller Gaststätten, Theater u. Kinos ab 19 Uhr und Ausgehverbot von 20–5 Uhr angeordnet. Einsatz von motorisierten Polizeistreifen.

8. Nov. 43: Die 5. Komp. d. Wachbatl. Dänemark meldet aus Odense, daß am 7. Nov. 43 abends 22.25 Uhr auf den Posten vor der Unterkunft geschossen u. vier Handgranaten gegen das Gebäude geworfen wurden. Während drei davon explodierten, aber nur geringen Schaden anrichteten (sieben Fensterscheiben), wurde die vierte unversehrt gefunden u. als Eierhandgranate englischen Ursprungs festgestellt. Der Posten, Rev. Obw. Hartmann, erlitt einen Durchschuß der linken Hüfte. Von den 60 festgenommenen Personen wurden sieben in Haft behalten. Weiterer Bericht u. Ergebnis d. Untersuchung durch den SD folgt.

11. Nov. 43: Am 11. Nov. erfolgte ein Einsatz des Verfügungsbatl. I/25 „Cholm" zum Zwecke d. Durchsuchung der am Finsensvej gelegenen Baracken. Es wurde vermutet, daß auf Grund des Überfalls am 10. Nov. um 6.30 Uhr, wobei dem Doppelposten auf der Transformatorenstation Finsensvej 86 durch fünf bewaffnete Männer die Waffen weggenommen wurden, die Täter daselbst wohnen würden und die Waffen gefunden werden könnten. Das Kommando setzte sich in Stärke von fünf Offizieren und 205 Mann, zu denen noch 25 Mann vom SD kommen, um 6.15 Uhr in Bewegung. Der Einsatz erfolgte schlagartig.

Norwegen

Berichte aus dem ehemaligen RSHA liegen auch von dort vor.

Abschrift
des Tagesberichtes Nr. 51 des Befehlshabers der Sicherheitspolizei und des SD in Oslo vom 2. September 1940.

Fortsetzung der Auswertung des sichergestellten komm. Materials und der Vernehmungen.

Um den Beschwerden des Sowjetrussen Wasili Karjakin in seiner Eigenschaft als Tass-Vertreter in Oslo den Boden zu entziehen, wurde der Leiter der Zeitschrift „Nytt-Land", der Redakteur Christian Gottlieb Hilt, geb.

29. Jan. 88 in Oslo, wohnhaft Olav Schou-Terrasse, sofort vernommen. Dabei ergab sich, daß Hilt wohl einer der wichtigsten kommunistischen Funktionäre in Norwegen ist. Er gehört seit 1923 als führendes Mitglied der KPN an und war bereits 1925 deren Org.-Sekretär. Im Jahre 1924 war er der Repräsentant für die Aktion Norwegen in der Komintern. Erst 1936 kehrte er nach Norwegen zurück und war als Sekretär des Bundes der ,,Freunde der Sowjet-Union" und Redakteur der Zeitschrift ,,Sowjetnytt" tätig. Diese Zeitschrift wurde später in die Anteilgesellschaft ,,Nytt-Land" umgewandelt. Seit 1939 ist Hilt Vorsitzender der Kontrollkommission der KPN. Außerdem gehört er der kommunistischen Bezirksleitung Oslo-Akershus an. Als Mitglied der Kommunistenvereinigung Oslo und Leiter des Verhandlungsausschusses der kommunistischen Mietervereinigung Oslo-Sinsen spielte er eine bedeutende Rolle.

Bei der Durchsuchung seiner Privatwohnung wurde ein 20 Seiten langer handschriftlicher Bericht, den er als Leiter der Kontrollkommission der KPN gemacht hatte, gefunden. In ihm ist auch die Stellungnahme der kommunistischen Partei zur deutschen Besetzung Norwegens niedergelegt.

Die in Bergen bis vor wenigen Jahren vorhandene parteieigene Zeitung ließ man merkwürdigerweise eingehen, obwohl die kommunistische Partei gerade im Festland, insbesondere in Bergen, verhältnismäßig viele Anhänger hat. Die Zeitungen in Narvik und Vardö dagegen blieben trotz der dünnbesiedelten Bezirke bestehen. Zweifellos kann man hierin die Absicht der kommunistischen Partei erkennen, den nördlichsten Teil Norwegens vordringlich für den Kommunismus zu gewinnen. Diese Annahme deckt sich mit einer weiteren Feststellung, die vor einigen Tagen gemacht wurde und das Interesse Sowjetrußlands für genau denselben Bezirk erkennen läßt. Der Tass-Vertreter Karjakin hat am 10. bzw. 12. Aug. mit Wirkung vom 15. Aug. sämtliche Lokalzeitungen des nördlichen Norwegens bis etwa zur Höhe von Mo-Rana bestellt. Es handelt sich um 18 Zeitungen, die sonst niemand in Oslo liest. Bisher bezog Karjakin lediglich die großen Tageszeitungen Norwegens.

Auszug
aus dem Bericht des Befehlshabers der Sipo und des SD Oslo vom 3. Juli
1941 – IV C 3 – B-Nr. 455/41 g
2. Kommunisten und Marxisten.

Am 1. Juli 1941 wurde ein norwegischer Staatsangehöriger von der Flughafenleitung V a e r n e s festgenommen und der Sicherheitspolizei in Drontheim übergeben. Nach Bekundungen der Flughafenleitung in Vaernes haben die Arbeitsleistungen der norwegischen Arbeiter in den letzten 14 Tagen um etwa 50 % nachgelassen. Besonders auffällig tritt dies seit dem Kriegsbeginn mit Rußland hervor.

Abschrift.

FS des BDS – Oslo, Nr. 8755 vom 17. Juli 41 – Geheim.

Betr.: Ultimatum der norwg. Gewerkschaften an das Reichskommissariat

Vorg.: Dort. FS Nr. 103 602 v. 3. Juli 41.

Auf das dortige FS vom 3. Juli 1941 wird mitgeteilt, daß nach den hiesigen Informationen die feindliche Haltung der Gewerkschaften weniger auf Einflüsse der Komintern als vielmehr auf den Einfluß der fanatisch englisch eingestellten Kreise zurückzuführen ist. Dies geht insbes. daraus hervor, daß die seit jeher englisch orientierten Gewerkschaftler einer guten Zusammenarbeit mit der NS und den Deutschen den stärksten Widerstand entgegenbringen. Auch sind bei den seit kurzer Zeit zu beobachtenden Ausmeldungen aus den Fachorganisationen, wozu unter anderem auch der Londoner Rundfunk des öfteren aufgefordert hat, vor allem die englisch eingestellten Kreise verantwortlich zu machen. Hiesige Gewährsmänner sind der Ansicht, daß, solange keine Sabotageakte auf Schiffswerften und in anderen für die deutsche Kriegswirtschaft arbeitenden Betrieben vorkommen, man von einem größeren Einfluß kommunistischer Kräfte nicht sprechen könne.

Auszug
aus dem Bericht des Befehlshabers der Sicherheitspolizei und des SD Oslo
– III Tgb. Nr. 31/42 g. vom 26. Apr. 42

Schon seit einiger Zeit waren Anzeichen vorhanden, daß sich aus der aufgelösten KPN heraus illegale Gruppen bildeten, die zunächst in den Gewerkschaften Boden zu gewinnen versuchten und die illegale Schrift „Fri Fagbevegelse" herstellten und verbreiteten. Nach eingehenden Erörterungen verstärkte sich der Verdacht, daß sich flüchtige kommunistische Führer in Oslo aufhielten und die illegale KPN organisierten.

Am 13. Apr. d. J. konnte einer dieser Führer, ein früherer Mitarbeiter eines kommunistischen Verlages und Leninschüler, nach dem bereits seit dem vorigen Jahr gefahndet wurde, in der Wohnung eines früheren Rotspanienkämpfers festgenommen werden. Bei ihm wurden ein Geheim-Code, verschiedene gefälschte Ausweise, eine Reihe kommunistischer Flugblätter, Berichte über die illegale kommunistische Parteiarbeit in Norwegen, eine erst in diesem Jahr herausgegebene Broschüre mit einer Rede Molotows über angebliche von den deutschen Truppen in der Sowjet-Union begangene Greueltaten und Zettelvermerke mit Angaben über die deutschen Truppen und Waffenstärke in Norwegen gefunden. Bei der Überwachung einer anderen Wohnung wurde ungefähr zur gleichen Zeit ein anderer Kommunist festgenommen, als er zwei Blätter mit verschlüsselten Angaben eines Feindsenders in den Briefschlitz einwerfen wollte. Die Vernehmung dieser beiden Festgenommenen ergab, daß sie zu einer kommunistischen Nachrichtengruppe gehörten, die politisch-militärische Nachrichten sammelte und bereits seit Anfang des Jahres 1940 nach Moskau, möglicherweise auch nach England weitergab. Die weiteren Ermittlungen führten zur Festnahme anderer wichtiger Mitarbeiter und zur Auffindung und Sicherstellung des für die Nachrichtenübermittlung benutzten Geheimsenders.

Bei der Durchsuchung der Wohnung eines im Zuge dieser Aktion Festgenommenen wurden neben illegalen Flugblättern und einem Trommelrevolver mit Munition in einer Schachtel eingepackt vorgefunden:

     56 Sprengkapseln,

     3 m isolierter Klingeldraht,

     1 Taschenlampenbatterie,

     2 Beutel mit Calium Chlorid, bzw. noch nicht festgestelltem Pulver,

     1 Niveadose, enthaltend ein Gemisch von chlorsaurem Kali und Zucker,

     1 Gummihülle mit einer hochempfindlichen Sprengstoffmasse sowie Putzwolle.

Da die Chemikalien von der gleichen Art waren wie die, welche bei den Sprengstoffattentaten auf den Osloer Bahnhöfen verwendet worden sein mußten, wurden die Erörterungen in dieser Richtung geführt. Sie führten schließlich zu dem Geständnis zunächst eines der Verhafteten, und im Anschluß an dieses Geständnis zu der weiteren Feststellung, daß zwei der in dieser Sache verhafteten Kommunisten teils allein, teils mit anderen folgende Sprengstoffattentate durchgeführt haben:

1. Den geglückten Eisenbahnanschlag bei Loenga und rechtzeitig entdeckte Anschläge auf dieselbe militärische Nachschubstrecke.
2. Die Sprengstoffanschläge auf den Osloer West- und Ostbahnhof in der Nacht zum 1. Februar 1942.
3. Den Anschlag auf die für deutsche Rüstungszwecke eingesetzte Waffenfabrik Norma in Oslo-Sinsen.
4. Den Sprengstoffanschlag auf ein Munitionslager im Osloer Westhafen am 13. Apr. 1942, d. h. insgesamt acht Sprengstoffanschläge.
5. Den Sprengstoffanschlag am Gartentor des Hauses eines Beamten der norwegischen Staatspolizei.

„Aftontidningen" vom 16. Sept. 1942.
Russische Partisanen weit hinein nach Nordnorwegen

Moskau (Exchange): Über die früher genannten russischen Partisanen-Operationen in Nordnorwegen meldet das Oberkommando der russischen Partisanen u. a. folgendes: In den letzten acht Wochen haben russische Kleinkriegsverbände gefährliche Expeditionen weit nach Nord-Norwegen

hinein unternommen. Die Partisanen wurden von Armeeoffizieren ange-
führt. Der Verband verließ Murmansk in Torpedobooten und landete an
der norwegischen Küste, von wo aus er nach mehrtägigen Märschen eine
wichtige Eisenbahnlinie erreichte. Gegen drei deutsche Militärzüge wurde
Sabotage verübt, eine große Brücke wurde in die Luft gesprengt, und alle
Versuche, sie zu reparieren, wurden verhindert. Den Partisanen glückte es
schließlich, mehrere deutsche Munitionslager zu zerstören. Über 100 deutsche Soldaten wurden im Kampf gegen die Freischärler getötet, die mit
verhältnismäßig geringen Verlusten nach Murmansk zurückkehrten.

Tromsö Nr. 6522, 15. 10. 42 2040 – PF – geheim an den B.D.S. – in Oslo
Betrifft: Bandentätigkeit im Raum Kirkenes.
Die Tätigkeit sowjetruss. Banditen läßt darauf schließen, daß besonderer
Wert auf Erkundungen im Raume der Festung Kirkenes gelegt wird. Aber
auch auf norwegischem Gebiet, vor allem im Pasvikdal, sind die Banditen
tätig. –
So wurden vor kurzer Zeit von der Wehrmacht an der Eismeerstraße
zwei Banditen festgenommen, die ein Funkgerät bei sich führten und den
gesamten Verkehr an dieser Stelle der Feindseite mitteilten. In der Nähe
von Nautsi wurde ein Wachtposten der Wehrmacht angeschossen. Einige
Tage später traten bei Petsamo und Parkkina stärkere Gruppen von Banditen auf, die neben ihrer Zerstörungstätigkeit auch Zivilpersonen um militärische Nachrichten erpreßten. Zwischen Heteoja und Nautsi versuchte man
die Hochspannungsmasten zu sprengen. Am 20. September wurden an der
Brücke bei Salmijärvi von einer größeren Gruppe drei Wehrmachtsposten
beschossen. –
Während sich diese Banditentätigkeit also hauptsächlich auf finnischen
Boden an der norwegischen Grenze von Nautsi bis zur Küste beschränkt,
werden nunmehr auch von russischen Flugzeugen auf norwegischem Gebiet
südlich Kirkenes in Gefangenschaft geratene deutsche Wehrmachtsangehörige mittels Fallschirm abgesetzt, mit dem Auftrag, nach genauen Skizzen
bezeichnete Brücken oder andere militärische Anlagen zu zerstören. Die
betreffenden sind mit Höllenmaschinen und anderen hochexplosiven
Sprengstoffen, Marschkompaß und Skizzen sowie mit größeren Geldbeträ-
gen ausgestattet und schwer bewaffnet. Wenn sich auch einige sofort nach
ihrer Landung meldeten, so ist doch mit der Möglichkeit zu rechnen, daß
von einzelnen die Aufträge ausgeführt werden.
Zum ersten Male in größerem Umfange wurden in der Berichtszeit Sabotageanschläge gegen Schiffe mit Erfolg durchgeführt. In den frühen Morgenstunden des 28. April 1943 wurden auf mehrere im Osloer Hafen liegende Schiffe Sabotageanschläge verübt, die teilweise beträchtlichen Scha-

den verursachten. Während ein deutscher Dampfer von 1380 BRT und ein norwegischer Leichter von 200 BRT nach starken Explosionen auf Grund sanken, erlitt ein im Dienst der Kriegsmarine fahrender norwegischer Dampfer von etwa 5500 BRT so schwere Beschädigungen, daß das Schiff mit dem Heck unter Wasser geriet. Die Explosionen sind in jedem Falle durch Magnetminen herbeigeführt worden, die an der Außenbordwand der Schiffe bis etwa 1 m unter Wasser angebracht waren. Beim systematischen Absuchen sämtlicher im Hafen liegender Schiffe wurden weitere vier Minen an zwei norwegischen Dampfern und einem noch in Bau befindlichen deutschen Vorpostenboot festgestellt und unschädlich gemacht. Die sichergestellten Minen in der Größe von etwa 35 × 20 cm sind mit zwei Magneten, Zusatzsprengladungen und Zeitzündern versehen. Nach den einwandfreien Feststellungen sind die Minen englischer Herkunft. Bei den bisher noch nicht ermittelten Tätern handelt es sich vermutlich um eine bestimmte Sabotagegruppe, die die Minen während der Nacht unbeobachtet von Booten aus an die Schiffe angebracht hat.

Ein weiterer Anschlag, der unter Umständen mit den Anschlägen im Osloer Hafen in Verbindung zu bringen ist, erfolgte am 2. Mai im Hafen von Kopervik bei Haugesund. Durch ihn wurde ein deutsches Minenräumboot schwer beschädigt. Die Ermittlungen gegen die Täter laufen.

Oslo FS 2437 11/2 2200 = FR. =
An RSHA –
1.) SS-Gruppenführer Müller . . .

Im Verlauf der weiterhin eingehend geführten Ermittlungen gegen die Flugblattorganisation ,,Radio Nytt" und die illegale kommunistische Militärorganisation wurden bisher 85 Personen festgenommen. Bei den Ermittlungen gegen die Flugblattgruppe wurde, wie ich bereits in meinen Tagesberichten berichtet habe, die Druckerei dieser Hetzschrift sichergestellt. Bei der Aufrollung der unter kommunistischer Leitung stehenden Militärgruppen wurde in den früheren Nachmittagsstunden des 10. Febr. (1943) in einer Hütte in der Nähe von Oslo ein Waffenlager gefunden . . .

Meldung
Allgemeine Widerstandsbewegung und Marxismus

Die Ermittlungen in den letzten Monaten haben ergeben, daß die Zentralleitung der Militärorganisation systematisch den Ausbau der örtlichen Gliederungen betrieben hat und nunmehr in Süd- und Mittelnorwegen über verhältnismäßig starke Verbände verfügt. Der Ausbildungsstand ist sehr verschieden und dort am besten fortgeschritten, wo in England geschulte Instrukteure die Übungen der Unterführer abgehalten haben. In einigen Bezirken steht offensichtlich nur ein unvollständiges Führungsgerippe, während die Mannschaft nur befragt worden ist, ob sie bereit ist mitzumachen. In einer Reihe von Fällen haben die starken sicherheitspolizeilichen Einbrüche in die Organisation nur ein vorübergehendes Ruhen der Arbeit im Gefolge gehabt. Es ist dem Gegner wiederholt möglich gewesen, nach ungefähr einem halben Jahr wesentliche Teile wieder aufzubauen. Die Zentralleitung hat es mehr und mehr verstanden, die örtlich aufgrund eigener Initiative entstandenen kleineren Widerstandsgruppen sich einzugliedern und ihren Befehlen dort Geltung zu verschaffen. Diesem Zentralisierungsbestreben wird von den einzelstehenden Gruppen im allgemeinen kein Widerstand entgegengesetzt, da die Militärorganisation in mancherlei Hinsicht für die illegale Arbeit Vorteile bietet, z. B. die Versorgung mit Nachrichten, Lehrmaterial, Waffen und Sprengstoffen . . .

Wegen der Besetzung wichtiger Posten der Militärorganisation durch kommunistische Vertrauensleute ist die kommunistische Landesleitung bestrebt, eigene ihr gefügige illegale Einheiten zu bilden. Es fiel auf, daß in der letzten Zeit mehr und mehr Namen wie ,,Nationalkomitee'', ,,Nationalgarde'' und ,,Betriebswehr'' bei illegalen Organisatinen auftauchten. Derartige Gruppen wurden in den meisten Fällen als kommunistische Gründungen erkannt. Entsprechend der alten kommunistischen Taktik werden hier unter nationalistischer Tarnung Personen erfaßt, die an sich nicht ohne weiteres bereit wären, unter einer kommunistischen Leitung tätig zu werden. Kennzeichnend ist ein in Oslo erfaßtes Flugblatt ,,Wegweiser für die Organisierung von Widerstandsgruppen'', das inhaltlich zunächst nicht seine kommunistische Tendenz erkennen läßt, von dem aber feststeht, daß es als Anleitung zur Aufstellung derartiger kommunistischer Gruppen dienen soll. Es ist nicht gesagt, daß diese kommunistischen Einheiten in einem Gegensatz zur Militärorganisation stehen. Es scheint auch so zu sein, daß sie sich mehr auf die Betriebe stützen, während die Militärorganisation örtlich gegliedert ist.

In Nordnorwegen sind in der letzten Zeit mehrere für die Sowjets arbeitende Nachrichtensender ausgehoben worden. Anfang August wurden an der Nordküste der Varanger-Halbinsel nach eingehenden, gemeinsam von Wehrmacht und Sicherheitspolizei durchgeführten Suchaktionen je ein Funkgerät im Porsangor- und Syltofjord und je zwei Funkgeräte im Kongsfjord und Porsfjord aufgefunden. Die Sender wurden von verschiedenen Norwegern und einem Sowjetrussen betrieben. Diese hatten seit November 1942 den gesamten Schiffsverkehr beobachtet und täglich nach Murmansk gefunkt. 30 Personen wurden festgenommen; drei Norweger wurden, als sie – in einer Höhle überrascht – sich zur Wehr setzten, erschossen. Zweien der Täter gelang es, von Kiberg zu fliehen. Die Vernehmung der Festgenommenen hat ergeben, daß drei von ihnen im Jahre 1941 von Kiberg nach Rußland geflohen und später von dort mit einem U-Boot wieder am Kongsfjord abgesetzt worden waren. Am 16. Aug. 43 sind bereits elf der festgenommenen Norweger zum Tode verurteilt und später erschossen worden.

Eine andere Feindagentengruppe mit russischen Geräten wurde auf der Insel Arnöy in Nordnorwegen ausgehoben. Sie war aufgrund von Nachrichten und Ermittlungen erkannt worden und wurde nach einer gemeinsam mit der Wehrmacht durchgeführten systematischen Durchsuchung der Insel in einer Felshöhle gestellt. Es kam zu einem Feuergefecht, in dessen Verlauf ein Angehöriger der Sicherheitspolizei getötet und ein Wehrmachtsangehöriger verletzt wurde. Nach Hinzuziehung von Pionieren wurde die Agentengruppe vernichtet. Eine Anzahl Helfer und Mitwisser der Agenten sind festgenommen worden. In Südnorwegen bei Kristiansand wurde ein Sender der Mil. Org. nach Anpeilung durch Peiltrupps der Ordnungspolizei ausgehoben. Er wurde von zwei Norwegern betrieben, von denen der eine entfliehen konnte, der andere sich selbst erstach . . .

Im Nebel der Nachrichtendienste

Blicken wir auf die Ereignisse des Zweiten Weltkrieges zurück, so könnte mit Recht ein Buch mit dem Titel „Die Tragödie des militärischen Befehlsempfängers" geschrieben werden. Es besteht kein Zweifel, daß zur Niederlage des deutschen Volkes auch die Tätigkeit der Nachrichtendienste beitrug, durch die der Gegner wertvolle Erkenntnisse erhielt. Darüber ist viel geschrieben worden. Im folgenden möchte ich dazu nur Probleme aufreißen und Fragen stellen.

Dr. Sorge

Man ist heute geneigt, die Bedeutung von Dr. Richard Sorge herunterzuspielen; er erhielt seine ersten Gelder über eine niederländische Bank und unter Mitwirkung des Chefs der „Roten Kapelle", Leopold Trepper.

Seit Anfang Juli 1941 setzte Dr. Sorge eine Reihe von Nachrichten nach Moskau ab, in denen er über die Haltung der japanischen Regierung berichtete. Dadurch wurde den Sowjets in einem viel größeren Ausmaß, als ursprünglich angenommen, ermöglicht, Streitkräfte vom asiatischen Teil der Sowjetunion an die sowjetische Westfront zu werfen. Zur Stabilisierung der Front vor Moskau trugen 13 Schützendivisionen und fünf Panzerbrigaden bei, die bis Ende Oktober 1941 aus Fernost, Mittelasien und Sibirien kamen. In den Frontabschnitten West, Kalinin und Brjansk wurden festgestellt: die 32., 77., 78., 82., 88., 91., 134., 178., 238., 312., 313. und 316. Schützendivision sowie die 4., 8., 11. und 42. Panzerbrigade. Stalin ernannte General Golikow am 21. Okt. 1941 zum Oberbefehlshaber der im Raum von Pensa neu aufzustellenden 10. Armee, die aus sibirischen und in den Gebieten von Moskau–Orel liegenden Verbänden aufgebaut wurde.

Die obengenannten Zahlen sind Mindestwerte. Noch heute sind die Nachrichten aus Moskau zu ungenügend, um ein vollständiges Bild zu geben. Die Frage lautet: Wie groß ist tatsächlich die Stärke der Verbände, die aufgrund der Meldungen Dr. Sorges der sowjetischen Westfront zugeführt werden konnten? In welchem Umfange konnten die Sowjets ihre ungeheuren Verluste, die sie in der Panzerschlacht um Kiew erlitten hatten, ausgleichen?

Rößler und seine Verbindungen

Tatsache ist, daß Meldungen, die von der Schweiz ausgingen, für „Stalingrad" und „Kursk" mitentscheidend waren. Dieses Nachrichtenthema ist von vielen Seiten erörtert worden. Doch liegt weder in materieller noch in personeller Hinsicht ein vollständiges Ergebnis vor. Es fehlen viele Einzelheiten. Klarheit jedoch dürfte darüber bestehen, daß die Folgen der Nachrichtenarbeit der „Roten Drei" verhängnisvoll für die deutsche Kriegführung waren.

Leopold Trepper schreibt in seinem Buche „Die Wahrheit" auf Seite 126: „. . . Derselbe Stenograph warnte neun Monate im voraus vor der Offensive im Kaukasus. Ende des Jahres 1941 erhält die Zentrale folgenden Funkspruch: ‚Plan III mit Ziel Kaukasus, ursprünglich für November vorgesehen, tritt im Frühjahr 1942 in Kraft. Aufmarsch soll bis 1. Mai beendet sein. Aller Nachschub geht ab 1. Februar auf dieses Ziel. Aufmarschraum für Kaukasus-Offensive: Losowja–Balakleja–Tschugujew–Belgorod–Achtyrka–Krasnograd–Oberkommando in Charkow – Einzelheiten folgen.'"

Leopold Trepper berichtet, daß in diesem Zusammenhang am 12. Mai 1942 ein Spezialkurier eingesetzt wurde. Am 12. Juli 1942 wird ein Generalstab für die Front bei Stalingrad unter Führung von General Timoschenko aufgestellt. Die Falle wird vorbereitet.

Zum Teil beachtenswert sind die Bücher „Moskau wußte alles" von P. Accoce und Pierre Quet sowie Bernd Rulands „Die Augen Moskaus – zwei Mädchen gegen Hitler – Fernschreibzentrale der Wehrmacht in Berlin". Beide Bücher erschienen im Schweizer Verlagshaus Zürich. Ruland berichtet, daß Rudolf Rößler das Geheimnis über seine wichtigsten Informanten nicht mit ins Grab genommen hat. Im Mai 1947 aber hätten den Meisterspion die beiden Nachrichtenhelferinnen, die ihm drei Jahre lang eine wahre Flut geheimster Nachrichten lieferten, in der Schweiz – in Zürich – getroffen. Diese Begegnung habe ein amerikanischer Offizier ermöglicht, der ihnen Pässe und Einreisevisa besorgte. Wortwörtlich schreibt Bernd Ruland in seinem Buch „Die Augen Moskaus": „Rößler hat den beiden unter dem Siegel strengster Verschwiegenheit alles das enthüllt, was bis heute ein Rätsel und Spekulationsthema geblieben ist . . . Wenige Wochen nach ihrem Besuch in der Schweiz habe ich . . . lange Gespräche mit den beiden geführt. Ich kannte sie aus Kriegszeiten sehr gut, aber nur von einer wußte ich seit dem 14. Juni 1941, daß sie das tat, was landläufig ‚spionieren' genannt wird. Über alles, was ihnen Rößler in Zürich berichtet, wurde von mir ein Memorandum verfaßt, beide haben es unterschrieben mit der ausdrücklichen Versicherung, daß alles ‚nach bestem Wissen und Gewissen' so wiedergegeben ist, wie sie es von Rößler erfahren haben. Ein Notar hat ihre Unterschriften beglaubigt."

Das Buch ist 1973 erschienen. An einer weiteren Stelle weist Ruland darauf hin, daß die beiden Nachrichtenhelferinnen noch leben. Es sei aber sichergestellt, daß sie und andere Rößlerhelfer im damaligen „Großdeutschland" nach ihrem Tode nicht mehr anonym bleiben. Wortwörtlich heißt es weiter: „Das gilt auch für ehemalige Offiziere der Wehrmacht, die bei der Weiterleitung aller von den beiden Mädchen beschafften Nachrichten in der Schweiz behilflich waren. Es gilt außerdem für einige andere Offiziere der Wehrmacht und für hohe Beamte von Ministerien, die Informationen aus ihren Dienstbereichen lieferten. Und es gilt schließlich und vor allem für jenen Offizier aus einer Abteilung des Befehlshabers des Ersatzheeres, bei dem alle für Rößler bestimmten Nachrichten zusammenliefen. Er sorgte auch dafür, daß die Informationen schnellstens und sicher auf verschiedenen Wegen . . . in die Schweiz und nach Luzern gelangten."

An diese Schilderung im Buche schließe ich die Frage an: Wer sind die amerikanischen Offiziere? Nach diesen Angaben deckte ein hoher Offizier der Wehrmacht die Mädchen, nach meiner Ansicht leitete er sie. Diese Mädchen sind nach dem Buche seit April/Mai 1941 für die Sache der Sowjetunion tätig gewesen. Wie Ruland sagt, wußte Moskau von Anfang Mai 1941 bis zum 13. Oktober 1943 alles, was es wissen wollte.

Franz Halder erklärte nach dem Zweiten Weltkrieg: „Nahezu alle Angriffshandlungen wurde nach ihrer Planung im Oberkommando der Wehrmacht, noch ehe sie auf meinen Schreibtisch landeten, dem Feinde durch Verrat eines Angehörigen des OKW bekannt. Die Quelle zu verstopfen, ist während des Krieges nicht gelungen."

Allan W. Dulles, von 1953 bis 1961 Chef der CIA und von 1942 bis 1945 im Dienste des amerikanischen Nachrichtendienstes OSS (Office of Strategic Service) in der Schweiz, erklärte in seinem Buche „Im Geheimdienst": „Nie in der Geschichte der Kriegführung hat die Spionage eine so entscheidende Rolle gespielt wie für die Sowjetunion in den Jahren 1941 bis 1944."

Rößler, der am 22. November 1897 in Kaufbeuren geboren wurde, am 17. April 1937 die deutsche Staatsangehörigkeit verlor und nach seiner Emigration in die Schweiz den Vita nova-Verlag in Luzern leitete, war Kommunist. Allan W. Dulles stellt in seinen Memoiren über Rößler sinngemäß fest: Es gelang den Sowjets, in der Schweiz eine phantastische Quelle aufzutun, einen Mann namens Rudolf Rößler. Über Verbindungen, die bis heute ein ungelöstes Rätsel geblieben sind, verschaffte Rößler sich von der Schweiz aus ständig Nachrichtenmaterial aus der Obersten Heeresleitung in Berlin; er kannte ihre Tagesbefehle oft 24 Stunden, nachdem sie gegeben waren. Rößler war im übrigen ein weißer Rabe, ein prokommunistischer Katholik.

Ruland hebt hervor: „Als Hitler am 18. Juni 1941 den Angriff endgültig auf den 22. Juni 1941 3.05 Uhr festlegte, hatte ‚Lucy' das Datum genau 12 Stunden später."

Im allgemeinen ist zu sagen, daß die Nachrichten, die Rößler bekam, 2–4 Tage nach getroffenen Entscheidungen eintrafen.

Rößler war seit 1939/Mai 1941 ausschließlich für Nachrichtendienste (N. D. der Schweiz) tätig. In enger Beziehung stand er zu dem Büro Ha (Deckname „Pilatus" unter Hans Hausamann), wie gesagt zum N. D. (Nachrichten- und Sicherungsdienst der Schweizer Armee unter Oberstbrigadier Roger Mason und NS 1, Deckname „Rigi", Chef Dr. Max Waibel). Kontaktmann Rößlers zu NS 1 ist der Stellvertreter von Dr. Waibel, Hauptmann Berhard Meyer von Baldegg.

Ungefähr vier Wochen vor Beginn des Rußlandfeldzuges gelangten Meldungen, die Rößler an westliche Geheimdienste geliefert hatte, zum Teil an den sowjetischen Nachrichtendienst.

Als Mitarbeiter von Rößler ist Dr. Schneider zu nennen. Rößler arbeitete auch mit der polnischen Kommunistin Rahel Dübenhof und ihrem Lebensgefährten Paul Böttcher zusammen. Letzterer war 1923 in der Sozialdemokratischen Regierung Sachsens mit dem Ministerpräsidenten Erich Zeigner vier Wochen lang Finanzminister.

Böttcher – Dübenhof (Sissy) übermittelten die Nachrichten Rößlers (Lucy), die sie von „Taylor" (Deckname für Schneider) erhielten, an Alexander Rado („Dora") weiter. Die Endstation war „Direktor" in Moskau. Unter diesem Begriff verbirgt sich die Zentrale der GRU, der 4. Abteilung des Generalstabes der Roten Armee. Der Leiter dieser Dienststelle war damals Generaloberst Ivan Terentjewitsch Peresypkin.

Rados Geburtsland war Ungarn. Er wurde Oberst der Roten Armee. Seine Nachrichtenzentrale kannte er unter einem wissenschaftlichen Dienst, der „Geopress".

Erst im November 1942 trat Rößler offiziell in den sowjetischen Nachrichtendienst. Von März 1940 bis Anfang 1941 händigte er seine Informationen dem ND unter dem „Büro Ha" sowie teilweise an Schneider aus. „Dora" standen drei Sender zur Vergügung. Zwei befanden sich in Genf, einer in Lausanne.

Als weiterer Vertrauter Rößlers ist ein linkskatholischer Schweizer Journalist namens Dr. Xaver Schnieper zu nennen. – Endlich sei auch die Tätigkeit des Journalisten Otto Pänter (Pabko) erwähnt. Der Deckname Pabko entstand aus Absendeorten von Nachrichten: P (Pontresina), A (Arth), B (Bern/Basel), K (Kreuzlingen) O (Orselina).

Eine vollständige Aufklärung des Nachrichtenkomplexes „Dora" ist von fundamentaler Bedeutung. Nachstehende Funksprüche beweisen dies: Am 26. November 1942 funkte „Direktor" an „Dora": „Senden Sie Angaben über konkrete Maßnahmen, die das OKW in Verbindung mit Vorstoß Rote Armee bei Stalingrad zu treffen beabsichtigt." Am 16. Januar 1943 fällt zum ersten Mal der Name „Werther" in einem Funkspruch: „An Dora – Lucy und Werther. Informationen über kaukasische Front und das Wichtigste über Ostfront sowie Entsendung neuer Divisionen an Ostfront senden Sie uns ohne Aufschub vor jeder anderen Information. Letzte Informationen Werthers waren sehr wichtig – Direktor."

Am 31. Jan. 1943 kapitulierte Generalfeldmarschall Paulus in Stalingrad. Bemerkenswert ist, daß im Sommer 1942 in Warschau-Otwock die ehemaligen polnischen Offiziere Arzyszewski und Meyer als Agenten verhaftet wurden; sie hatten durch Funksprüche die Schwerpunkte der geplanten Frühjahrsoffensive 1942 durchgegeben. Ein Bericht über diese Tatsache wurde erstellt. Weder wörtlich noch verkürzt kam er in das Führerhauptquartier.

Am 17. April 1943 erhielt Moskau über neu aufgestellte deutsche Einheiten einen Bericht, der lautet:

,,Neu aufgestellte deutsche Einheiten:

1. Das eine Panzerregiment der 14. Panzerdivision wird im Lager Zeithain, ein anderes Panzerregiment derselben Division in Bautzen neu formiert.
2. Die 11. Grenadierdivision traf zwecks Neuformierung kürzlich im hessischen Lager Wieber ein.
3. Die 94. Grenadierdivision wird im Lager Königsbrück neu aufgestellt.
4. Die 294. Grenadierdivision steht in Nieder-Österreich ab 31. März zum Abtransport an die Front bereit.
5. Die 29. motorisierte Division steht am 20. April bereit, um an die Front zu gehen.
6. Die neugebildete 305. Grenadierdivision wird ebenfalls am 20. April zum Abtransport an die Front bereitstehen.
7. Bis 10. Mai stehen die folgenden Divisionen in Bereitschaft zum Abtransport an die Front: Die Waffen-SS-Division ,,Deutschland", die 41., die 295., die 371. Grenadierdivision sowie die 60. motorisierte Division.
8. Bis Ende Mai stehen zwei neuaufgestellte Panzerdivisionen marschbereit, mindestens eine motorisierte und noch acht Infanteriedivisionen, möglicherweise auch eine Gebirgsjäger-Division.

Am 29. April 1943 meldete ,,Dora" den Termin der Operation ,,Zitadelle": ,,Neuer Stichtag für deutsche Offensive 12. Juni 1943." 13. Mai 1943: ,,Von Werther – deutsche Aufklärung hat russische Kräftekonzentration bei Kursk, Wjasma, Welikije Luki erkannt."

Wann geschieht etwas zur endgültigen Aufklärung dieses Komplexes?

Canaris

Vorgänger von Canaris in der Abteilung Abwehr war der Kapitän zur See Conrad Patzig. Am 31. Dezember 1934 veranlaßte von Blomberg, der damalige Reichswehrminister, daß Patzig wegen seiner offenen Gegnerschaft zu Heydrich, dem Chef des Sicherheitsdienstes des Reichsführers SS, abgelöst wurde. An seine Stelle trat am 1. Januar 1935 der Kapitän zur See Wilhelm Canaris, der bis zum Vizeadmiral aufstieg. Canaris war vor dem Jahre 1930 auf einem Schulschiff der Marine Vorgesetzter des damaligen Leutnants Reinhard Heydrich.

Canaris' Charakter ist schwer zu deuten. Hans Rudolf Fuhrer schreibt in seinem Buch ,,Spionage gegen die Schweiz", das im Jahre 1982 erschienen ist: ,,Gegen eine ,Aktion Schweiz' sprachen sich in allen Phasen des Krieges einflußreiche Persönlichkeiten aus und konnten auf Führerentscheidungen einen beschränkten Einfluß nehmen." Fuhrer zitiert eine angebliche Canaris-Eintragung vom 17. Januar 1940: ,,Jetzt will dieser Narr auch noch die Schweiz hereinziehen. Es wäre der letzte und tödliche Schlag für die deutsche Ehre, wenn der ,Weltlump', nicht genug, daß er schon einen Anschlag auf Holland und Belgien plant, nun auch noch über die Schweiz mit ihrer von jeher respektierten Neutralität herfallen will. Dann würde in Zukunft niemand von einem Deutschen noch ein Stück Brot annehmen." U. a. zählt Fuhrer als ,,Retter" der Schweiz auch die Schweizer Nachrichtenlinie ,,Wiking" auf, zu der angeblich Generalmajor Oster Verbindung gehabt haben soll.

Auszuschließen ist diese Verbindung nicht. Es ist ja bekannt, daß Oster mit seinem Freund, dem niederländischen Oberst Gigsbertus Jacob Sas, vor dem deutschen Einmarsch in die Niederlande ein Gespräch führte, in welchem er aufforderte: ,,Sprengt mir die Maasbrücken."

Über das Unternehmen ,,Seelöwe" liegen zwei Studien aus dem Jahre 1939 (15. Nov. 1939 und 13. Dez. 1939) vor.

Erstere stammt vom Oberkommando der Marine. Die Führerweisung Nr. 16 vom 16. 7. 1940 befahl, die Vorbereitungen für die Landung aufzunehmen.

Als Landungstermin wird der 21. Sept. 1940 vorgesehen. Neue Weisung wurde am 3. Sept. 1940 erlassen. Am 17. Sept. 1940 befiehlt Hitler die Verschiebung des Unternehmens auf unbestimmte Zeit.

Canaris erhielt im Zusammenhang mit der Vorbereitung des Unternehmens ,,Seelöwe" am 21. Juli 1940 den Auftrag von Keitel, in England die Aufklärungsoperation zu starten (Aktion ,,Hummer"). Der Admiral gab an Hauptmann Wichmann in Hamburg den Auftrag Keitels weiter. Anthony Cave Brown, der Verfasser des Buches ,,Bodyguard of Lies", interviewte Oberst Ulrich Ließ, der während des Zweiten Weltkrieges in der Abteilung ,,Fremde Heere West" tätig war. Ließ erklärte: ,,Während des Falles ,,Gelb" kam ich zu dem Schluß, daß seine (= des Admiral Canaris) offensiven geheimdienstlichen Operationen gegen Frankreich, Norwegen, Belgien und die Niederlande vorbildlich waren. Von dem, was er im Zusammenhang mit „Seelöwe" tat, konnte man das nicht behaupten. Damals glaubte ich, daß er zwar nach außen hin so tat, als gäbe er sich alle Mühe, während er nicht mit voller Überzeugung gegen England vorging. Wir bekamen nie die Nachrichten aus England, die wir brauchten, um die Stärke der Briten und ihren Aufmarsch richtig einzuschätzen."

Am 2. September 1940 meldete Canaris an Hitler, . . . die Briten würden über 37 voll ausgebildete, kampfbereite und ausgebildete Divisionen verfügen. In Wirklichkeit waren es papierstärkemäßig 29 Divisionen. Hitler wurde unschlüssig; zudem sah er im Osten eine Gefahr. Er verschob die Operation „Seelöwe" auf unbestimmte Zeit. Der Admiral konnte mit seinen Warnungen bei Hitler um so mehr durchkommen, als es der deutschen Luftwaffe nicht gelungen war, die Luftüberlegenheit über dem Ärmelkanal zu erkämpfen.

Felix

Zum Zeitpunkt der Invasionsplanung in England hatte Jodl auch die Bedeutung von Gibraltar vom strategischen Standpunkt herausgestellt.

Ende Juli 1940 riet Canaris einerseits Hitler von einem Überraschungsangriff auf Gibraltar ab. Andererseits übermittelte er Franco, er solle sich aus dem Unternehmen „Felix" (Angriff auf Gibraltar) heraushalten und von Hitler zehn 38 cm Geschütze als Voraussetzung fordern, die dieser nicht liefern könne.

So wurde die Begegnung Hitlers mit Franco am 23. Oktober 1940 in Hendaye am Fuß der Pyrenäen für das deutsche Staatsoberhaupt zum Fehlschlag. Der damalige spanische Außenminister Serrano Suñer hatte Franco vorher, wie Jan Colvin in „Master Spy" schreibt, dahingehend unterrichtet, er habe in Berlin den Eindruck gehabt, daß alles, was mit spanischen Belangen zu tun hat, völlig durcheinandergeraten sei. Er fügte hinzu: „Einer der Gründe für diese Verwirrung ist die eigenartige Rolle, die Admiral Canaris spielt."

Nordafrika

Mitte Februar 1941 kam Rommel nach Afrika. Er sollte mit dem Afrika-Korps den rechten Flügel einer Zangenbewegung bilden, durch die der Nahe Osten aus dem englischen Herrschaftsbereich herausgelöst werden sollte. Über den Kaukasus als rechten Flügel der Zange sollten deutsche Truppen in den Orient einmarschieren.

Rommel hatte Erfolg vom 31. März 1941 bis zum 3. September 1942, an dem die Niederlage von Alam Halfa besiegelt war. Im August 1942 versanken 30 % von Rommels Nachschub auf den Grund des Meeres. Im Oktober waren es bereits 40 %. Am 19. Okt. 1942 – vier Tage vor der Schlacht von El Alamein – fingen die Engländer die Meldung auf, daß die Panzerverbände nur noch Treibstoff für eine Woche und die Einheiten Brot bei einem Pfund je Tag und Mann nur für drei Wochen hatten. Die Kampfstärke Montgomerys betrug 150 000 Mann, Rommel verfügte über 90 000 Deutsche und Italiener. Der deutsche Munitionsbedarf war für neun Tage gedeckt.

Rommel war verzweifelt: er wollte die katastrophale Versorgungslage Hitler vortragen und sich dann einer dringenden ärztlichen Behandlung unterziehen. Bereits einmal war er bei Beginn einer größeren Operation nicht in seinem Gefechtsstand. Als der damalige englische Oberbefehlshaber in Nordafrika, General Sir Claude Auchinleck, seine Offensive am 17. Nov. 1941 begann, durch die das deutsche Afrika-Korps bis El Agheila am Golf von Sidra zurückgedrängt wurde, hielt sich Rommel im Rom auf.

Rommel forderte vom deutschen Nachrichtendienst Lageberichte an. Zuständig war die Abteilung ,,Fremde Heere West'', in der Oberst Alexis Frhr. von Roenne mit Ausnahme der Zeit zu Beginn des Feldzuges gegen die Sowjetunion arbeitete. In Tukkum wurde er verwundet, was zu einem monatelangen Lazarettaufenthalt führte. Roenne war Canaris sehr ergeben und ein enger Freund Osters. Der deutsche Oberbefehlshaber in Nordafrika wurde von der Abteilung ,,Fremde Heere West'' dahingehend unterrichtet, daß die 8. britische Armee vor Ablauf mehrerer Wochen keinen größeren Angriff durchführen werde. Die Briten würden bis November und Dezember nur fähig sein, in der Libyschen Wüste defensiv zu operieren. Die Regenfälle würden dann eine Pause bis zum Frühjahr 1943 hervorrufen.

Am 23. September 1942 verließ Rommel nach längerem Zögern Afrika. Der herzleidende Panzergeneral, General Stumme, übernahm das Kommando. Nach einer Besprechung mit Mussolini traf er Hitler in Winniza, der ihm eine Nebelwerferbrigade mit 500 Rohren und 40 Tiger-Panzer mit Sturmgeschütz-Einheiten zusagte. Am 6. Oktober 1941 flog Rommel dann nach Wiener Neustadt, von wo er sich – gealtert und krank – in ein Sanatorium auf dem Semmering begab.

Am 23. Oktober 1942 beginnt Montgomery seinen Angriff. Die Deutschen waren, systematisch getäuscht, überrascht worden. General Stumme erliegt einem Herzanfall. Das Afrika-Korps ist führerlos. Rommel, zurückgekehrt, kann nichts mehr retten. Nur einen Teil seiner Panzerverbände kann er vor der völligen Vernichtung bewahren. 59 000 Soldaten, darunter 34 000 Deutsche, fielen. Von 500 Panzern blieben Rommel 100. Seine Bedenken, Nordafrika Ende September 1942 zu verlassen, kamen nicht von ungefähr. Es lagen Meldungen vor, daß die Briten nach Westen durchstoßen wollten, während die Amerikaner in Nordwestafrika eine Landung beabsichtigten. Am 2. Oktober 1942 hörte eine deutsche Auffangstation ein unverschlüsseltes Telefongespräch zwischen einem gaullistischen Nachrichtenoffizier und einem Diplomaten des „Freien Frankreich" ab, wie Anthony Cave Brown in „Bodyguard of Lies" berichtet.

Nach der Landung würden die Alliierten in Algier ein Hauptquartier errichten. Am 8. Nov. 1942 wußte Hitler, wo die Alliierten landeten: in Französisch-Nordafrika, und zwar in einem weiten Bogen zwischen Casablanca und Bougie, zunächst 90 000 Mann, später weitere 200 000 mit der gesamten Versorgung und Bewaffnung, von Großbritannien 1500 Meilen, von den USA 3000 Meilen entfernt.

Das Oberkommando der Wehrmacht hatte 40 U-Boote zwischen Gibraltar und Dakar stationiert. Diese U-Boot-Rudel, die die Gewässer an der Einfahrt zum Mittelmeer kontrollierten, wurden plötzlich abgezogen, um einen leeren Geleitzug anzugreifen, der sich auf der Fahrt von Sierra Leone nach England befand.

Festzustellen ist, daß sich Canaris während des Unternehmens Torch (= Landungsunternehmen in Französisch-Nordafrika) in Algeciras, einer in unmittelbarer Nähe von Gibraltar gelegenen spanischen Stadt aufhielt. Dort befand sich eine wichtige Zweigniederlassung der Abwehr. Bezeichnend ist die Episode: Mit Zustimmung des Gouverneurs von Gibraltar, General Mason Mac Farlane, sollte der deutsche Abwehrchef nach London entführt werden. Jan Colvin schreibt in „Master Spy", Seite 149: „Gibraltar erhielt einen Funkspruch aus London, mit dem die Aktion abgesagt wurde . . . Er (Canaris) ist viel wertvoller dort, wo er sich zur Zeit befindet."

Kapitän Herbert Wichmann, der Sektions-Chef von Canaris in Hamburg, der die Aufklärung gegen Großbritannien und die Vereinigten Staaten leitete, hat nach seinen Angaben, wie Anthony Cave Brown feststellt, einen hervorragenden Bericht erhalten, aus dem zu entnehmen war, daß Französisch-Nordafrika das Operationsziel „Torch" war. Wichmann schickte ihn über seine Zentrale an das OKW. Die Meldung kam nie an.

Als Ergebnis darf festgehalten werden: Die Achsentruppen hatten Afrika verloren. Eine neue Front an der Mittelmeerküste war entstanden. Gegen die Südflanke Europas waren neue Operationen möglich.

Wann wird dieser Komplex in nachrichtendienstlicher Hinsicht geklärt?

Nach der Räumung Siziliens und während der Kämpfe in Süditalien kam Admiral Canaris am 21. Jan. 1944 nach Italien. Obwohl im Hafen von Neapel italienische Jugendliche bereits an die sich für das obengenannte Unternehmen einschiffenden amerikanischen Soldaten Karten der kleinen Küstenstädte Anzio und Nettuno (48 km südlich Roms) verkauften, in denen Römer ihre Ferien zu verbringen pflegten, sagte der Admiral dem Chef des Stabes Kesselring, General Siegfried Westphal, mit einer weiteren alliierten Landung sei nicht zu rechnen. Einige Stunden später landeten die Amerikaner bei Anzio und Nettuno.

Peenemünde

Im Gegensatz zu dem deutschen Staatsoberhaupt ahnten die Engländer die entscheidende Rolle des „Aggregatprogramms" oder „Raketenprogramms". Der späteste Zeitpunkt ihrer Erkenntnisse ist 1941/1942. Die Mitteilung des Raketenprogramms dürfte nach Anthony Cave Brown auf Canaris zurückgehen. Die Vermutung liegt nahe, daß ein weiterer Bericht, der Lisbon-Report, von einem Mitglied des deutschen Nachrichtendienstes, Ludwig Gehre, an den westlichen Gegner gegeben wurde. In ihm heißt es, daß Hitler und die Mitglieder seines Kabinetts kürzlich beide Waffen, die V 1 und die V 2, in Peenemünde besichtigt hätten. Etwa am 10. Juni habe Hitler vor einer Versammlung militärischer Führer gesagt, die Deutschen brauchten nur durchzuhalten, denn Ende 1943 werde London dem Erdboden gleichgemacht, und Großbritannien werde zur Kapitulation gezwungen. Hitler habe den Bau von 30 000 A-4 (die ursprüngliche Bezeichnung der V 2) bis zum 20. Oktober befohlen, dem Tag, an dem die V-Waffen-Offensive beginnen sollte. Die Herstellung beider Waffen genieße die erste Priorität, und 1500 Facharbeiter seien aus der Fabrikation, in denen die Fliegerabwehrwaffen und Geschütze gebaut würden, zu dieser Produktion abgestellt worden. Die Reaktion auf der Seite des Gegners ist bekannt: Alle mit dem V-Waffen-Programm im Zusammenhang stehenden Ziele wurden mit starken Kräften angegriffen.

Den entscheidenden Angriff auf Peenemünde in der Nacht vom 17. auf 18. Aug. 1943 beschreibt Walter Dornberger: „Kurz nach 24 Uhr ist die erste Welle über Peenemünde ohne Bombenabwurf nach Süden geflogen. Richtung Berlin. Der Flaksender gab daraufhin als vermutliches Angriffsziel die Reichshauptstadt an. Seit 0.15 Uhr fliegt dann Welle auf Welle, von Rügen kommend, Peenemünde an . . . Großfeuer färbten den alles einhüllenden, durch beißenden Rauch verstärkten Nebel dunkelrot. Aus dem Dach des Konstruktionsgebäudes schlagen an vielen Stellen helle Flammen . . . Nach Londoner Radiomeldungen sind 1,5 Millionen kg Sprengbomben abgeworfen worden . . . 735 Tote hat der Angriff gefordert, davon 178 Bewohner der von 4000 Menschen bewohnten Siedlung."

Hitler und Göring machten für die schwarze Nacht von Peenemünde den Chef des Generalstabes der Luftwaffe, Generaloberst Jeschonnek, verantwortlich. Jeschonnek erschoß sich am Morgen nach dem Angriff in seinem Büro.

Verblüffend ist die Parallele zwischen dem geplanten Unternehmen „Seelöwe" und der Invasion der angloamerikanischen Streitkräfte in Nordfrankreich. Damals – 1940 – erhielt das deutsche Oberkommando Meldungen, die die Kampfstärke der englischen Truppen auf der Insel weit übertrieben. Durch die Abteilung „Fremde Heere West" – Oberst Alexis Frhr. von Roenne und Oberstleutnant Roger Michel, letzterer setzte sich 1945 in die Sowjetzone ab – geschah nach der Landung der Alliierten in der Normandie ähnliches. Die Zahl der in England befindlichen anglo-amerikanischen Divisionen wurde verdoppelt, so daß die deutsche Führung an der Nordküste Frankreichs und in Belgien mit einer zweiten Landung rechnete.

Im Bundesarchiv, Militärarchiv Freiburg, befindet sich eine Mitteilung des Generals Blumentritt, Stabschef des Oberbefehlshabers West, in der mitgeteilt wird, daß Hitler als erster die Auffassung vertrat, die Alliierten würden an der Küste der Normandie landen. Heute wissen wir, daß der Zeitpunkt der geplanten Landung an der normannischen Küste bekannt war. Es gab genügend Anzeichen dafür, daß die Großlandung der Alliierten auf der Halbinsel Cotentin stattfinden werde.

Am 6. Juni 1944 trägt das AOK 7 in das Kriegstagebuch ein: „Der Feind ist in den ersten Morgenstunden zu einem Großangriff zwischen Seinemündung und Cotentin angetreten. Nachdem ab Mitternacht starke Bomberverbände insbesondere die Küstenbatterie angegriffen hatten, sind ab 0.30 Uhr größere Fallschirm- und Luftlandeeinheiten in den Räumen beiderseits Ornemündung, Caen–Bayeux, beiderseits Vire sowie um Carentan und St. Malo Église abgesprungen. AOK befiehlt 1.15 Uhr sofort Alarmstufe II für Bereich LXXXIV.AK und Alarmstufe I für übrige Korpsbereiche und II. Fallschirmkorps. Stab AOK 7 wird gleichfalls alarmiert.

In der Eintragung heißt es weiter: „Abweichend von Ansicht der Heeresgruppe B und OB West hält Chef des Generalstabes der 7. Armee (Generalleutnant Pemsel) die Luftlandungen für Auftakt zu größerer Feindaktion. Durch laufende starke Nachlandungen aus der Luft verstärkt sich Gegner vor allem im Raum Ornemündung (Caen) und St. Mère Église. Nach Ansicht Chef des Stabes scheint Gegner Abschnürung der Halbinsel Cotentin an engster Stelle zu beabsichtigen. Chef des Stabes schließt auf feindlichen Großangriff gegen die Normandie."

In dem Tätigkeitsbericht des Ic des Oberbefehlshabers der Heeresgruppe D, d. h. des Oberbefehlshabers West vom 1. Apr.–30. Juni 1944, wird auf Seite 19 festgestellt: „Von Anfang des Jahres 1944 bis Ende Mai wurden vom Radio London über 20 Sprüche durchgegeben, von denen nach den gewonnenen Erkenntnissen anzunehmen war, daß sie die für die

Invasion vorbereiteten Sabotagehandlungen auslösen oder die Invasion selbst ankündigen sollten . . . Alle diese Ankündigungen, die sich von Woche zu Woche änderten, waren falsch. Sie waren das beliebteste Täuschungsmittel des Feindes, um Führung und Truppe nervös zu machen.

Am Vorabend der Invasion, dem 5. Juni um 21.15 Uhr, wurden vom Radio London wiederum mehrere verschlüsselte Sprüche durchgegeben, die die Weisung zur Ausführung von Sabotagehandlungen im Zusammenhang mit bevorstehender Invasion enthalten sollten. Von einem dieser Sprüche („Les Sanglots longs des violons de l'automne – blessent mon coeur d'une longueur monotone" – aus einem Sonett von Verlaine) war mit Sicherheit bekannt, daß er sich an die unter scharfer englischer Steuerung stehende Sabotage-Organisation ‚french section' richtete.

Aus diesem Grunde wurden die Sprüche vom 5. Juni abends trotz der vorhergegangenen monatelangen Täuschung vom Oberbefehlshaber West besonders beachtet. Die unterstellten Verbände, die Kommandostellen der anderen Wehrmachtsteile und die Militärbefehlshaber, wurden über Durchgabe und Bedeutung der Sprüche unterrichtet und gewarnt, OKW/WFSt/ Op (H) West und OKH/Gen.St. dH/Fremde Heere West benachrichtigt."

Die Bedeutung der Sprüche, die den Beginn der Invasion ankündigen sollten, war seit 1943 bekannt. Die Meldung von einer bevorstehenden Invasion sollte von der Heeresgruppe B an die 7. Armee weitergegeben werden. Es spricht nichts dafür, daß dies geschehen ist, während dies bei der 15. Armee der Fall war. Die 7. Armee an der Invasionsküste wurde nicht rechtzeitig in Alarmbereitschaft versetzt und damit natürlich auch nicht das LXXXIX. Korps, das die Verantwortung für Utah und Omaha und den größten Teil des britischen Sektors trug. Erst um 2.15 Uhr, als der Angriff aus der Luft bereits anrollte, ordnete die 7. Armee für ihre Divisionen höchste Alarmstufe an.

Eine interessante Passage aus Browns Buch ist erwähnenswert: „Es wird häufig gesagt, daß Hitler und das Oberkommando der Wehrmacht in ihrer Einfalt die Auffassung vertraten, die Landung in der Normandie sei nur ein Ablenkungsmanöver und die Hauptlandung werde zwischen Seine und Somme erfolgen, vor allem im Raum von Calais."

Dem ist nicht so. Am 17. Juni weilten Oberbefehlshaber West – Generalfeldmarschall v. Rundstedt – und der Oberbefehlshaber der Heeresgruppe B – Generalfeldmarschall Rommel – mit ihren Chefs im Führerhauptquartier. Darüber gibt es eine Niederschrift, in der ausgeführt wird: „Der Führer ist der Ansicht, daß der Feind nicht seine letzten Kräfte einsetzen wird. Die Tatsache, daß er bereits alle kriegserfahrenen Verbände in der Normandie eingesetzt hat, zeigt, daß er sich dort bereits weitgehend gebunden hat. Es ist möglich, daß der Feind durch den jetzt begonnenen Fernkampf (V-Waffen) gezwungen wird, bei AOK 15 ebenfalls zu landen."

Ich habe die festgehaltenen Ferngespräche des Oberbefehlshabers West geprüft. Aus ihnen ergibt sich, daß Oberst Alexis v. Roenne die falsche Lagebeurteilung verursacht hat. Unter dem 2. Juli 1944 heißt es: ,,Major v. Graevenitz: Rückfrage wegen Anzeichen für bevorstehende zweite Landung. Sämtliche Erkenntnisse an Jodl." Nach der Eintragung vom 4. 7. 1944 führte Oberst v. Roenne aus, daß das entscheidende Problem ist, ob der Gegner alles in das Normandie-Unternehmen hereingesteckt hat. Wörtlich heißt es: ,,Wir müssen mit einer weiteren Landung rechnen."

Bemerkenswert ist, daß Oberstleutnant Michel, der bei v. Roenne die Abteilung der Gruppe England leitete, im Frühjahr 1944 mit der Bitte zu Roenne kam, er möge unterbinden, daß der SD andere Schätzungen über die Stärke der feindlichen Streitkräfte abgab. Roenne erklärte angeblich, er könne nichts machen. Michel schlug daraufhin als Lösung vor, die Abteilung Fremde Heere West solle die geschätzte Zahl der in Großbritannien versammelten Divisionen verdoppeln. Nach anfänglicher Ablehnung stimmte v. Roenne dann später zu.

Die Schätzungen Roennes wurden beim OKW in die Lagekarten eingetragen. Die Alliierten, die täuschen wollten, hatten einen Verbündeten gefunden; Oberst v. Roenne mußte diese Intrige mit dem Leben bezahlen. Er wurde in Flossenbürg hingerichtet.

*

Zuweilen hört man heute das Wort ,,Dolchstoß", der aus der Nachrichtenebene heraus gegen die damalige Reichsführung geführt worden sei. Der angesehene Schweizer Hans Rudolf Kurz schreibt im ,,Nachrichtenzentrum", daß Behauptungen, wonach der Krieg an der Nachrichtenfront oder konkret in der Schweiz gewonnen worden sei, reinen Unsinn darstellen würden.

Dr. jur. Hans Rudolf Kurz bekleidete den Rang eines Oberst im Generalstab und war Chef der Unterabteilung im Eidgenössischen Militärdepartement.

Das Thema ,,Dolchstoßlegende" gehört nicht zu den Fragen, die dieses Buch mehr als aufwirft. Es steht fest, daß wichtigste Informationen von den Nachrichtendiensten geliefert worden sind. Sie hatten für manche Operation entscheidenden Charakter. Es ist noch zu früh, um ein abschließendes Urteil zu fällen. Berücksichtigt muß ebenfalls werden, daß 140 Sender den sowjetischen Frontaufklärungstrupps unter den Partisanen zur Verfügung standen.

Viel ist noch zu klären. Die Öffentlichkeit hat ein Interesse an der Aufklärung des grauen Nachrichtenhintergrundes. Vergessen wir jedoch nicht, daß von maßgebendster Stelle die deutsche Kraft überschätzt und die der Gegner unterschätzt wurde.

Nachwort

Ich habe mich bemüht, sehr nüchtern die Zusammenhänge und Tatbestände zu schildern. Dabei bin ich mir bewußt, daß die geschichtliche Entwicklung einem reißendem Strom gleicht, in welchem wie Baumstämme einzelne Menschen mitgerissen werden.

Für das Weltgeschehen dürfte das Grundsätzliche in der Evolution liegen. Geschehnisse im Zweiten Weltkrieg können nur aus der Vorgeschichte erklärt werden.

Ich versuchte nichts zu beschönigen. Herausgestellt aber muß werden, daß auch die Siegermächte dem deutschen Volke nichts vorzuwerfen haben. Fern liegt mir der Gedanke der Aufrechnung. Ich kann mir aber auch einen ,,häßlichen Nichtdeutschen" vorstellen.

Klar dürfte sein, daß der Totalitarismus keine geeignete Regierungsform darstellt. Ebenfalls, daß die Regeln des Kriegsvölkerrechtes auch auf alliierter Seite nicht eingehalten wurden. Fast kann man von einem illusionären Recht sprechen. Wenn wir die gegenwärtigen politischen Ereignisse betrachten, so bestätigen sie das Gesagte.

Heute beschäftigen sich immer wieder insbesonders Kräfte im Ausland mit den Vorkommnissen des Zweiten Weltkrieges im deutschen Bereich. Sie sprechen von Ordnung und geben der geschichtlichen Wahrheit unzureichend Raum. Sie sollten sich an die Sätze in Ljesskow's ,,Der verzauberte Wanderer" erinnern:

,,Da stand nun geschrieben, der heilige Tychon habe gebeten, es möge noch lange Friede auf Erden sein, und da habe der Apostel Paulus ihm mit lauter Stimme ein Zeichen genannt, wann der Frieden aufhören würde. Er habe also gesprochen: Wenn alle von Frieden und Ordnung reden werden, dann wird die allgemeine Vernichtung plötzlich über sie hereinbrechen."

Quellenverzeichnis

Generalstab des Heeres. Fremde Heere Ost, Militärarchiv Freiburg

Meldungen Ast. Unterlagen der Heeresgruppen und Armee-Kommandos, Militärarchiv Freiburg

Ic Bericht und Meldungen der Leitenden Feldpostdirektoren, Militärarchiv Freiburg

Berichte Korrück, Militärarchiv Freiburg

Berichte der Einsatzgruppen, Militärarchiv Freiburg

Die Berichte der Einsatzgruppen der Sicherheitspolizei im Polenfeldzug, 1939, Militärarchiv Freiburg

Reichssicherheitshauptamt. Bericht über das Attentat auf Heydrich, Bundesarchiv Koblenz

Dokumentation der Vertreibung der Deutschen in Mitteleuropa

Aufzeichnung Bormans über die Besprechung Hitlers mit Göring, Rosenberg, Lammers, Keitel, Bormann vom 16. Juli 1941, Militärarchiv Freiburg

Der Prozeß gegen die Haupt-Kriegsverbrecher vor dem Internationalen Militärgerichtshof in Nürnberg – 14. November 1945 bis 1. Oktober 1946 (Blaue Serie 42 Bände), Nürnberg 1949

Akten des Prozesses gegen die Südostgenerale vor dem Amerikanischen Militärgerichtshof, Bayerisches Staatsarchiv Nürnberg

Trials of War Criminals before the Nürnberg Military. Tribunals – Grüne Serie 15 Bände, Washington Government Printing Office 1949–1953

,,Das Jahr des Grauens". Lettland unter der Herrschaft des Bolschewismus. Dokumentation, Riga 1943

,,Das Leidensjahr des estnischen Volkes", Reval 1943

Ausrottung und Widerstand der Juden in Polen während des Zweiten Weltkrieges, Frankfurt 1972

Schweizer Informationsdienst Hausamann – St. Gallen

,,Neuer Vorwärts" 26. Sept. 1937, Prag

,,Deutsche Wochenzeitung" Oktober 1963, Hannover

Literaturhinweise

Accore P. und Pierre Guet: Moskau wußte alles

Ainzstein Reuben: Jewish Resistance in Nazi Occupiet Eastem Europe, London 1974

Aschenauer Rudolf: Kriegsbefehle

Aschenauer Rudolf: Der Fall Kappler

Aschenauer Rudolf: Der Fall Reder

Von Bock Fjedor: Aufzeichnungen, Militärarchiv Freiburg

Borkenau Fanz: Der europäische Kommunismus, Bern 1952

Brown Anthony Cave: Bodyguards of Lies, München 1976

Bulitt William: Approach to the Sowjetunion

Burkhardt: Meine Danziger Mission, 1960

Colvin Jan: Admiral Canaris, 1953

Craig William E.: Die Schlacht um Stalingrad, München 1977

Czesany Maximilian: Nie wieder Krieg gegen die Zivilbevölkerung. Eine völker-rechtliche Untersuchung des Luftkrieges 1939–1945, Graz 1961

Dixon-Heilbrunn: Partisanen, Frankfurt 1956

Dulles Allan W.: Im Geheimdienst, Düsseldorf 1963

Dragolow Fedor: Art u. Organisation des Partisanenkrieges 1941–1945 auf dem Gebiet des „Unabhängigen Staates Kroatien". In Allgem. Schweizer Militärzeit-schrift 1956

Ermitage S.: The Desert and the Stars – A biographie of Lawrence of Arabia (Die Wüste und die Sterne – eine Biographie von Lawrence von Arabien)

Fleming Peter: Operation Sea Lion, New York 1957

Fredborg Arvid: Behind steel wall, 1944

Fehst: Bolschewismus und Judentum, 1934

Frank Hans: Das Dienst-Tagebuch des Deutschen Generalgouverneurs in Polen, 1975

Führer Hans Rudolf: Spionage gegen die Schweiz, Frauenfeld 1982

Comerski: Die Bedeutung des bewaffneten Kampfes der bulgarischen Partei zur Vereitelung des deutschen Imperialismus, Ost-Berlin 1961

Grotius Hugo: De jure belliac paris, Paris 1965

Hahlwege Werner: Lenin und Clausewitz, in Archiv f. Kulturgeschichte 1950

Haupt Werner: Kriegsschauplatz Italien, Stuttgart 1970

Hecimovic Joseph: In Titos Death Marches and Extermination Camps, New York 1963

Hedin Sven: Bagdad, Babylon, Ninive, Leipzig 1917

Hedin Sven: Jerusalem

Henderson Sir Nevile: Failure of a mission. Fehlschlag einer Mission, London 1945

Hesse Erich: Der sowjetische Partisanenkrieg 1941–1945, Göttingen 1969

Himmler Heinrich: Oktober Rede 1943 in Bad Schachen

Hnilicka Karl: Das Ende auf dem Balkan, Göttingen 1970

Hobbes Thomas: De Homine

Hubatsch Walther: Hitlers Weisungen für die Kriegsführung 1939–1945, Frankfurt 1963

Jacobs Walter D.: Mao Tse-tung als Guerilla-Kämpfer

Katz Robert: The Death of Roma, München 1962 (Übersetzung)

Klink Dr. Ernst: Das Gesetz des Handelns. Die Operation Zitadelle, Stuttgart 1966

Kordt: Die Außenpolitik des Dritten Reichs – Wahn u. Wirklichkeit, Stuttgart 1948

Korowin: Völkerrecht der Übergangszeit

Krannhals Hans von: Der Warschauer Aufstand, Frankfurt 19

Kühnrich Heinz: Der Partisanenkrieg in Europa, Ost-Berlin 1965

Kurowski Franz: Der Luftkrieg über Deutschland, Econ Verlag 1972

Lawrence T. E.: Sieben Säulen der Wahrheit

Lawrence T. E.: Revolt in the Desert

Lenin W. I.: Ausgewählte Werke, Institut für Marxismus–Leninismus in Berlin 1966

Liddell Hart Basil Henry: The revolution in warfare, New Haven Yale University 1942

Mackiewicz Josef: Katyn, ungesühntes Verbrechen, Zürich 1949

Mao Tse-tung: Ausgewählte Werke, Ost-Berlin 1958/1960

Messe Giovanni: Der Krieg im Osten, Zürich 1958

Morača Pero: Die Völker Jugoslawiens im Zweiten Weltkrieg. In: Der deutsche Imperialismus und der Zweite Weltkrieg Band 4, Ost-Berlin 1961

Oberländer Dr. Theodor: Denkschrift, Herbst 1942

Redelis Valdis: Partisanenkrieg, Heidelberg 1958

Ringelblum Emanuel: Notatki a Getta. Notes from the Ghetto, Warschau 1954 und 1955

Rosenberg Alfred: Der Zukunftsweg einer deutschen Außenpolitik, 1927

Rossi Angelo: Les Communist français pendant la drôle de guerre, Paris 1955

Rossi Angelo: Physiologie du parti Communiste français, Paris 1958

Ruland Bernd: Die Augen Moskaus – zwei Mädchen gegen Hitler – Fernsprechzentrale der Wehrmacht in Berlin, 1973

Rumpf Hans: Das war der Bombenkrieg, Oldenburg 1961

Schagatin N. I./Prussanow: Die Sowjetarmee. Armee neuen Typs, Ost-Berlin 1959

Schmitt Carl: Die Partisanen, Berlin 1963

Schmitt Carl: Das Raumbild von nach Land und Meer getrennten Kriegsschauplätzen

Schmitt Carl: Wandel der Kriegsschauplätze, Dunker und Humblot Verlag

Schmitt Carl: Der Nomos der Erde

Schwarz Salomon: The Jews in the Sowjetunion, Syracuse 1951

Snow: Red Star over China, übersetzt 1975

Soschalsaski: Rede Frühjahr 1943 vor Angehörigen von Propaganda-Kompanien, Militärarchiv Freiburg

Telpuchowski Boris Seminowitsch: Die sowjetische Geschichte des Großen Vaterländischen Krieges, Frankfurt/M. Übersetzung

Tennenbaum: Underground, The Story of a people, New York 1952

Teske Hermann: Die Silbernen Spiegel, Heidelberg 1959

Teske Hermann: Partisanen gegen die Eisenbahn, Wehrwissenschaftliche Rundschau 1953

Thorez Maurice: Ausgewählte Schriften, Ost-Berlin 1962

Trepper Leopold: Die Wahrheit, München 1975

Verrier Anthony: Bombenoffensive gegen Deutschland 1939–1945, Frankfurt 1970

Weidinger Otto: Division Das Reich, 1977

Krieg ohne Grenzen

In den letzten drei Jahrzehnten konnte Dr. Rudolf Aschenauer, ein über die Grenzen Europas hinaus bekannter Strafverteidiger, Einblick und Einsicht in eine Vielzahl von zeitgeschichtlich brisanten Dokumenten nehmen. In seinen Verteidigungen vor alliierten Gerichten und deutschen Schwurgerichten, in den sog. NS-Verfahren, aus seinen Vertretungen vor dem Clemency- und Modification-Board sowie in vielen Gnadenverfahren sah er bedeutende Unterlagen, die den Historikern und auch der Öffentlichkeit weitgehend unbekannt waren. Gestützt sowohl auf diese Quellen als auch auf andere zahlreiche unbenutzte, z. T. noch umstrittene Dokumente, konnte der Verfasser ein Buch über den Partisanenkrieg gegen Deutschland schreiben, das einzig und allein der Wahrheit dienen will.

So ist ein Werk entstanden, wie es zur Kriegsgeschichte des Zweiten Weltkrieges noch nicht erschienen ist. Wurden bislang in der Geschichtsschreibung strategische Planungen und taktische Überlegungen von beiden Seiten berücksichtigt, so trifft dies auf den Partisanenkrieg nicht im nötigen Umfang zu. Die Bedeutung des Kampfes aus dem Dunkeln gegen die deutsche Wehrmacht von 1939 bis 1945 hat bislang noch viel zu wenig Beachtung gefunden.

Diese Dokumentation schließt eine empfindliche Lücke. Jetzt wird dem interessierten Leser klar vor Augen geführt, welche deutschen Kräfte die Untergrundbewegungen banden, welche deutschen Aktionen vereitelt und damit der Kriegsausgang festgelegt wurden.

Der Untergrundkampf gegen die deutsche Wehrmacht an allen Fronten ist keineswegs eine Zufallserscheinung gewesen. Gegründet auf marxistisch-leninistischen Thesen vom bedingungslosen Krieg, der die Regeln des Kriegsvölkerrechts verließ, hat Stalin schon frühzeitig eine Untergrundbewegung über ganz Europa aufgebaut, die seinem Kommando gehorchte. Die deutsche Wehrmacht hatte damit nicht nur einen Zweifrontenkrieg sondern auch den Kampf gegen eine Dritte Front zu bestehen.

Dieses Buch, für den interessierten Laien ebenso unentbehrlich wie für den Fachhistoriker, zeichnet sich darüber hinaus durch kühle Sachlichkeit aus, und wird damit zu einem wesentlichen Werk zur Geschichtsschreibung des Zweiten Weltkrieges.